# PESSOA

# PESSOA

*A Biography*

## Richard Zenith

LIVERIGHT PUBLISHING CORPORATION

A Division of W. W. Norton & Company

*Independent Publishers Since 1923*

Frontispiece: Courtesy Manuela Nogueira

Maps by David Lindroth Inc.

For information about permission to reproduce selections from this book,
write to Permissions, Liveright Publishing Corporation, a division of
W. W. Norton & Company, Inc., 500 Fifth Avenue, New York, NY 10110

For information about special discounts for bulk purchases, please contact
W. W. Norton Special Sales at specialsales@wwnorton.com or 800-233-4830

Manufacturing by LSC Communications, Harrisonburg
Book design by Lovedog Studio
Production manager: Anna Oler

Library of Congress Cataloging-in-Publication Data

Names: Zenith, Richard, author.
Title: Pessoa : a biography / Richard Zenith.
Description: First edition. | New York, N.Y. : Liveright Publishing
    Corporation, [2021] | Includes bibliographical references and index.
Identifiers: LCCN 2021005140 | ISBN 9780871404718 (hardcover) |
    ISBN 9781324090779 (epub)
Subjects: LCSH: Pessoa, Fernando, 1888–1935. | Poets, Portuguese—20th
    century—Biography.
Classification: LCC PQ9261.P417 Z955 2021 | DDC 869.1/41 [B]—dc23
LC record available at https://lccn.loc.gov/2021005140

Liveright Publishing Corporation, 500 Fifth Avenue, New York, N.Y. 10110
www.wwnorton.com

W. W. Norton & Company Ltd., 15 Carlisle Street, London W1D 3BS

1 2 3 4 5 6 7 8 9 0

# Contents

# Dramatis Personae

*Pessoa created dozens of fictional authors who peopled his written world and even, in a certain way, his very life. Some of them were enduring presences and dubbed "heteronyms," while others quickly faded from the scene. This list—which the reader can consult as needed—includes most of the fictional authors mentioned in the following pages, where their roles and writings are described more fully. A heteronym mentioned in another author's entry is in small caps.*

### A. L. R.

Known only by his initials, A. L. R. was listed as the translator and commentator of a Portuguese edition of *The Protocols of the Elders of Zion*, a fraudulent document that purported to show how prominent Jews were plotting to destabilize and dominate the world. *The Protocols* was one of many books Pessoa hoped to publish at Olisipo, a small publishing house founded in 1921.

### Giovanni B. Angioletti

This anti-Fascist Italian critic stole the identity of a real Milan-based literary critic named Giovanni Battista Angioletti (1896–1961) and exiled himself to Portugal. In an interview published by a Lisbon newspaper in the fall of 1926, he declared that Mussolini was a madman and described some of the deplorable aspects of his regime.

### Charles Robert Anon

Active between late 1903 and 1906, this was the first fictional author with an extensive literary output, both in poetry and prose, all in English. *The Natal Mercury* (Durban) published one of his poems in July 1904 but rejected three sonnets submitted to the newspaper a year later. He accompanied Pessoa back to Lisbon in the fall of 1905.

### Dr. Faustino Antunes

This psychiatrist wrote letters in 1907 to at least three people Pessoa had known in Durban, requesting confidential information about the character and behavior of his client (Pessoa), who had developed serious mental problems after leaving South Africa.

### W. W. Austin

Austin lived for a time in Australia, where he met KARL P. EFFIELD, who was working as a miner. Austin sent Effield's "The Miner's Song," along with a cover letter, to *The Natal Mercury* (Durban).

### Raphael Baldaya

Endowed with a long beard and fluent in English as well as Portuguese, this student of astrology and the occult received his first writing assignments toward the end of 1914 or in the beginning of 1915. Pessoa later drew up plans (never realized) to sell Baldaya horoscopes by mail.

### Pero Botelho

An author of short stories and letters dating from around 1913.

### Alberto Caeiro

Born in Lisbon on April 16, 1889, Alberto Caeiro da Silva lived with a great-aunt in a white house in the country, northeast of Lisbon, and died from tuberculosis in 1915. A poet with little formal education who believed that things are exactly what they seem to be, Caeiro loomed into existence in March 1914 and was immediately recognized by Pessoa as his "master." He was also the master of ÁLVARO DE CAMPOS and RICARDO REIS. Besides *The Keeper of Sheep*, which contains forty-nine poems, Caeiro authored a smaller collection, *The Shepherd in Love*, as well as dozens of miscellaneous poems.

### Álvaro de Campos

The liveliest, most opinionated, and most prolific of the heteronyms, Álvaro de Campos emerged in 1914 some three months after ALBERTO CAEIRO. Born on October 15, 1890, in Tavira, the town in the Algarve where Pessoa's paternal relatives were concentrated, Campos studied engineering in Scotland, journeyed to the Far East, lived for a time in London, worked as a naval engineer in northern England, and eventually settled in Lisbon. He was sexually attracted to men as well as women, and complained that no matter how much he saw, felt, and tasted, he needed to see, feel, and taste still more. Besides poetry, he wrote and published provocative prose texts in which he sometimes took issue with the views of Fernando Pessoa.

## J. G. Henderson Carr

Carr colluded with TAGUS to help him win the Puzzle Prize. He was slated to author some "Essays on Reason," but these never materialized.

## João Craveiro

An author of political commentary intended for a magazine that Pessoa vaguely thought of launching in 1918.

## A. A. Crosse

A competitor in the word games published by various English newspapers.

## I. I. Crosse

This English critic wrote favorably about the poetry of ALBERTO CAEIRO and ÁLVARO DE CAMPOS.

## Thomas Crosse

Created around 1916, Thomas Crosse wrote essays on Portuguese history, Portuguese literature, and other topics for the English-speaking world. He was also scheduled to translate the *Complete Poems of Alberto Caeiro*; although he failed at this task, he did write a few pages for the "Translator's Preface."

## Karl P. Effield

Pessoa's first fictional author to write in English and the first to sign a poem published in a real newspaper, *The Natal Mercury* (Durban), in July 1903. Born in Boston, Massachusetts, Effield traveled to east Asia and Australia.

## Horace James Faber

An author of detective stories and an occasional co-author with CHARLES ROBERT ANON in Durban.

## Gaveston

Pessoa's papers from 1904 to 1910 contain dozens of signatures for this mysterious personage—linked by his creator to Piers Gaveston (1284–1312), the favorite of Britain's King Edward II—but he signed no literary works.

## Vicente Guedes

Conceived in 1909, around the same time as JOAQUIM MOURA-COSTA and CARLOS OTTO, Guedes was a poet, short story writer, and translator for the unsuccessful Ibis press, which folded in the summer of 1910. In 1914 Guedes would be designated the author of *The Book of Disquiet*, a job he held until 1920, when he dropped out of circulation.

### Sher Henay

Henay's task was to compile and introduce an English-language *Sensationist Anthology*, conceived in 1916. It was to include work by Pessoa and his sensationist compeers.

### William Jinks

A friend of CHARLES ROBERT ANON and a quack promoter of healthy living, he somehow ended up in a London jail, where in April 1905 he wrote a letter in English full of comical misspellings.

### Eduardo Lança

Supposedly born in Brazil, in 1875, Lança moved as an adult to Portugal, where he began publishing poetry and prose. A couple of his poems were included in Pessoa's homemade newspaper *The Tattler* in 1902.

### Maria José

A nineteen-year-old hunchback who suffered from tuberculosis and crippling arthritis, Maria José spent her days next to a second-floor window and felt her heart flutter each time Senhor António, a handsome metalworker, passed by on his way to or from work. While she had no intention of sending it, she wrote him a long and poignant letter, dating from 1929 or 1930, in which she described her pathetic existence and her ardent feeling of love.

### Friar Maurice

Beset by doubts as to whether God actually exists, this monk—who wrote prose passages for *The Book of Friar Maurice*—was a disquieting presence in the real-world life of Pessoa, according to an autobiographical text dating from 1907.

### David Merrick

Invented in 1903, he was tasked with writing a novel, two volumes of short stories, a book of plays, and a poetry collection. His writing tasks floundered or were transferred to others.

### Lucas Merrick

Presumably the brother of DAVID MERRICK, Lucas was supposed to write a number of short stories, but their authorship was passed on to SIDNEY PARKINSON STOOL and CHARLES ROBERT ANON.

## António Mora

In a short story Pessoa began writing in 1909, Mora was a Greece-obsessed lunatic who wore a toga and lived in an asylum. The story languished, but six years later Mora was revived and became a heteronym who, together with RICARDO REIS, promoted a renewal of paganism in the modern world. He was also the author of a dissertation that favored Germany in the Great War.

## Henry More

This astral spirit, whose earthly incarnation was Henry More the Cambridge Platonist (1614–1687), began communicating with Pessoa through automatic writing in 1916.

## Joaquim Moura-Costa

Moura-Costa wrote satirical poems against the monarchy and the Catholic Church for two newspapers that Pessoa hoped, but failed, to launch in 1910.

## Dr. Gaudêncio Nabos

A jokester and the author of humorous poems and sketches, Nabos ("Turnips") wrote in English when he first emerged in Durban in 1904, but later wrote in Portuguese as well. He practiced medicine for several years in London, and it was from that city that he sent a long letter to Pessoa in 1906. Nabos remained active until around 1914.

## Carlos Otto

Created in 1909 to be a contributor to the newspapers Pessoa planned to launch the following year, Otto, besides poetizing and translating, wrote a treatise on wrestling.

## Dr. Pancrácio

The author of six poems and two epigrams appearing in Pessoa's make-believe newspapers, between 1902 and 1905.

## Pantaleão

Pantaleão was created in 1908 as a Portuguese author of political essays, fictional letters, maxims, and reflections.

## Chevalier de Pas

Pessoa, when just five or six years old, wrote letters to himself in the name of this French knight, one of his imaginary childhood companions.

### Fernando Pessoa

The persona bearing Pessoa's own name had various "subpersonalities," according to the poet, and was just as much a *fingidor* (feigner, forger, pretender) as the heteronyms.

### Pip

The author of a poem "published" in the homemade newspaper *The Tattler* when Pessoa was thirteen years old.

### Frederico Reis

The author of a critical appreciation of his brother Ricardo's poetry, Frederico also drafted a pamphlet on the so-called Lisbon School of writers, which consisted of the three major heteronyms: ALBERTO CAEIRO, ÁLVARO DE CAMPOS, and RICARDO REIS.

### Ricardo Reis

A writer of classical odes in the style of Horace, Ricardo Reis appeared in Pessoa in June 1914, a few days or weeks after ÁLVARO DE CAMPOS. Born in Porto on September 19, 1887, he studied medicine but became a high school Latin teacher, immigrated to Brazil in 1919, and was still living in the Americas, perhaps in Peru, when Pessoa died in 1935. In addition to his strictly metered odes, which counseled peaceful acceptance of whatever the gods ordain, he wrote essays defending a modern revival of paganism. He expounded at length on the genius of ALBERTO CAEIRO, his much admired master, but sparred with ÁLVARO DE CAMPOS on various literary matters.

### Alexander Search

Born in Lisbon on the same day as Fernando Pessoa, Search emerged in 1906 and soon supplanted CHARLES ROBERT ANON as Pessoa's major English-language heteronym. Active until 1910, he would sign well over a hundred poems, including many that were written between 1903 and 1905 and originally credited to Anon. Search also authored a short story, "A Very Original Dinner," as well as various essays.

### Charles James Search

The older brother of ALEXANDER SEARCH, Charles was born on April 18, 1886. He emerged in 1908 as a translator of (mostly) Portuguese literature into English.

## Jean Seul de Méluret

Pessoa's only French heteronym was born on August 1, 1885. He emerged in 1908 as the author of three somewhat satirical, somewhat serious essays about sexual depravity in France.

## Bernardo Soares

Fleetingly mentioned in 1920 as a short story writer, the name of Bernardo Soares disappeared forthwith but would resurface in 1929 as the author of *The Book of Disquiet*. Pessoa's notes indicate that passages from *The Book* written in the 1910s and originally credited to VICENTE GUEDES now became the literary property of Soares, who worked as an assistant bookkeeper in downtown Lisbon, on Rua dos Douradores. A man of solitary habits, he lived in a fourth-floor rented room on the same street.

## Sidney Parkinson Stool

A failed writer, invented in Durban in 1903, he participated in Pessoa's virtual sporting activities and would eventually immigrate to Washington, D.C.

## Tagus

An inventor and solver of riddles, he won the Puzzle Column Prize, awarded by *The Natal Mercury* (Durban) in December 1903.

## Baron of Teive

The 14th Baron of Teive, who came into existence in a notebook used by Pessoa in 1928, lived on a country estate in Portugal but had spent time in Paris, where he fought a duel with a French marquis. Frustrated by his timidity with women and even more so by his shortcomings as a writer, he set fire to all his literary works and committed suicide, but not before writing one final, rambling work in which he explained his motives.

## Voodooist

HENRY MORE and WARDOUR struggled to protect Pessoa from this malefic spirit, lest his communications lead their disciple astray.

## Wardour

Like HENRY MORE, this astral communicator sent messages predicting that Pessoa would meet and mate with one or another woman. On at least one occasion he also acted as a poetry coach.

## *Frederick Wyatt*

An Englishman who resided in Lisbon and whose eccentric manner of dress-
ing elicited smiles from passersby, Wyatt emerged in 1913. By the following
year he was credited as the author of twenty-one English poems previously
signed by ALEXANDER SEARCH.

# Notes to
# the Reader

THE PORTUGUESE COUNT FLOORS IN BUILDINGS IN THE TRADITIONAL European manner: "first floor" corresponds to what is called the second floor in the United States, Canada, and some other countries, "second floor" corresponds to the third floor, and so forth.

Quotations from Pessoa's writings in English retain his British spelling.

Generally, Portuguese proper names are spelled according to current national usage. One notable exception is the first name of Pessoa's only sweetheart. Born Ophelia Queiroz, she began to sign herself Ofelia after Portugal introduced a phonetic spelling reform, in 1911. Nowadays her name is written with an accent: Ofélia. Pessoa rejected the spelling reform and wrote his love letters to "Ophelia," which is how her name appears in this book.

Some Portuguese people use a compound surname, typically formed by one surname from each parent (Eça de Queiroz) or else by two surnames inherited from the father (Almada Negreiros). While the text that follows respects these compounds, the index and bibliography list people by the very last of the names they used, except where there is a hyphen (Sá-Carneiro).

In prose quotations, bracketed ellipses indicate my abridgement; any unbracketed ellipses are in the original.

Except where indicated, all translations are my own.

# PROLOGUE

W HEN THE EVER ELUSIVE FERNANDO PESSOA died in Lisbon, in the fall of 1935, few people in Portugal realized what a great writer they had lost. None of them had any idea what the world was going to gain: one of the richest and strangest bodies of literature produced in the twentieth century. Although Pessoa lived to write and aspired, like poets from Ovid to Walt Whitman, to literary immortality, he kept his ambitions in the closet, along with the larger part of his literary universe. He had published only one book of his Portuguese poetry, *Mensagem* (*Message*), with forty-four poems, in 1934. It won a dubious prize from António Salazar's autocratic regime, for poetic works denoting "a lofty sense of nationalist exaltation," and dominated his literary résumé at the time of his death.

Some of Pessoa's admirers—other poets, mostly—were baffled by the publication of *Message*, whose mystical vision of Portugal's history and destiny seemed to rise up out of nowhere. In periodicals he had published other, very different kinds of poems, over half of which were signed by one of three alter egos, all of whom came into being in 1914, shortly before the outbreak of World War I. The first to emerge was Alberto Caeiro, an unlettered but philosophically minded man who lived in a simple white house in the country, where he wrote free-verse poems proclaiming that things must be seen for what they are, without interpretation. Ricardo Reis, a trained medical doctor and an ardent classicist, composed Horace-inspired odes recommending stoical acceptance of whatever the gods give us. A third bundle of force and feeling took shape as Álvaro de Campos, a dandyish naval engineer who traveled around the world, was charmed by young men as easily as by women, aspired to live to the extreme, and signed unbridled poems that vented his exalted sensations but betrayed, at the same time, his melancholy awareness that life, no matter how intensely he lived it, was never enough. Campos, the most restless of the three alter egos, could not be contained by the poetry section of magazines and newspapers. In interviews, articles, manifestos, and letters to the editor, he commented on politics and culture with caustic brio and took special delight in contradicting the logically laid out opinions of Fernando Pessoa, whom he mocked for his "mania of supposing that things can be proven."[1]

Despite his assertive personality, Campos deferentially acknowledged Alberto Caeiro, the sublimely serene poet of nature, as his master. So did Dr. Reis. And so did Fernando Pessoa, who invented the prodigious trio, providing them all with biographies, individualized psychologies, religious and political points of view, and distinctive literary styles. Too radically different from him to be considered simple pseudonyms, as if only their names had changed, Pessoa called them "heteronyms," and in a "Bibliographical Summary" of his works published in 1928 he explained the conceptual distinction: "Pseudonymous works are by the author in his own person, except in the name he signs; heteronymous works are by the author outside his own person. They proceed from a full-fledged individual created by him, like the lines spoken by a character in a drama he might write."

Apart from his writer friends, hardly anyone had noticed the extraordinary diversity of Pessoa's published poetry in Portuguese, most of which had appeared in literary journals with small print runs. And not even his friends, with one or two exceptions, had read his self-published chapbooks of poetry written in English. Pessoa, who was born in Lisbon in 1888 but spent nine years of his childhood and received most of his schooling in the British-governed town of Durban, South Africa, originally aspired to be an English poet, and his *35 Sonnets* and *Antinous: A Poem*, both issued in 1918, garnered a favorable review in *The Times Literary Supplement*. The reviewer warned, however, that most English readers would deplore the subject matter of "Antinous," in which the Emperor Hadrian fondly recalls the sensual love of his young male companion, who drowned in the Nile. The warning was unnecessary, since neither of the chapbooks was distributed in the United Kingdom, and they were ignored in Portugal, where the cultural elite read French, not English, as a second language.

Pessoa was also an occasional writer of literary criticism and opinion pieces on political and social issues. Quite a few people, at the time of his death, had never read any of his poems but knew his name very well, since he had caused a stir earlier that year with an audacious front-page article opposing a bill to ban Freemasonry, which Salazar's puppet assembly would unanimously pass into law. And yet Pessoa, just one month before publishing his article, had won a government-sponsored prize for his book of "nationalist" poems. Whose side was he on? Nobody seemed to know for sure.

Even among his friends, whom he habitually met in Lisbon's cafés, Pessoa, a resolute bachelor, was a bit of a mystery. He loved talking about literature, philosophy, politics, and religion, but about his personal life he was not forthcoming. Rarely did he invite anyone to his apartment, where he was rumored to have a large wooden trunk full of hundreds, maybe thousands, of unpublished poems and prose pieces.

◆

THE TRUNK INDEED EXISTED, and some ten years after Pessoa's death more than three hundred of the poems it contained found their way into a handsome edition of his poetry, with separate volumes for Alberto Caeiro, Ricardo Reis, Álvaro de Campos, and Fernando Pessoa himself. Since each of the three heteronyms boasted a large and exquisite body of work stylistically unlike the poetry of his fellow heteronyms or of Pessoa himself, one could say that Portugal's four greatest poets from the twentieth century were Fernando Pessoa. But while some people were duly impressed by Pessoa's feat of poetic self-division, or self-multiplication, his work was still not widely read. And the superabundant poet was a more mysterious figure than ever. Pessoa's last name happens to be the Portuguese word for "person," but there seemed to be no person there, just poems and personae.

A vivid picture of Pessoa the man finally materialized in 1950, in Portuguese, with the publication of a seven-hundred-page biography by João Gaspar Simões, a critic and former co-editor of the magazine *Presença*, where Pessoa had published several of his greatest poems, including "The Tobacco Shop" and "Autopsychography." Gaspar Simões's undertaking took readers by surprise, for it was still not clear to most of them that the poet merited such attention. In the book they learned for the first time about Pessoa's turbulent childhood, marked by the deaths of his father and little brother, his mother's second marriage, and the years he spent in South Africa; about his aborted career as a college student in Lisbon, his failed attempt to start a publishing house, and his freelance work drafting business correspondence in English and French; about his only sweetheart, Ophelia Queiroz, a secretary at one of the offices where he worked; about his interest in the occult and his meeting with Aleister Crowley, an English magus reviled in his home country as a minister of Satan; and about his literary life and friends.

Gaspar Simões also discussed Pessoa's literary work, viewing it through a Freudian lens, and devoted separate chapters to each of the three heteronyms. Despite admiring their poetry, he deemed them symptomatic of the author's inability or unwillingness to concentrate his entire self in the act of writing. The heteronyms, in his view, were a kind of subterfuge, or a gimmick. Ingenious instruments for producing some undeniably seductive literature, they were ultimately a sign of the author's limitations. Perhaps this is a defensible thesis, but if the heteronyms were a gimmick, then Pessoa's very personality was defined by gimmickry. What the poet lacked was not concentration but any notion of a cohesive, unified self. This was the "problem," of which his heteronyms were the most glaring evidence.

After Rimbaud famously and ungrammatically announced *"Je est un autre"* ("I is another"), he went on to compare himself, a still emerging poet, to a piece of wood transformed by destiny into a violin.[2] Fernando Pessoa, who might have said "I are many others," described himself as a "secret orchestra" made up of numerous instruments—strings, harps, cymbals, drums.[3] The history of literature contains some faint parallels to his performance of multiple authorship. William Butler Yeats created Michael Robartes and Owen Hearne, a duo of "collaborators" with contrasting personalities. The Spanish poet Antonio Machado (1875–1939) also signed some of his poems and prose pieces with the names of two alter egos: Juan de Mairena and Abel Martín, who was Mairena's "master." But no writer can rival Pessoa's achievement of configuring, through his heteronyms, radically different poetic and philosophical attitudes that formed a glorious if not always harmonious musical ensemble.

Pessoa's first biographer had not dug deeply or thoroughly into the famous trunk, which is understandable, since to do so would have taken him the rest of his life, and he wasn't wealthy, he needed to earn a living. Some of the more than 25,000 papers left by Pessoa—most of which are now at the National Library of Portugal—were well organized and neatly written or typed, but many others were taken up by half-formed, fragmentary, or hard-to-decipher texts. Pessoa was a volcanic writer, and when the words started flowing, he used whatever sort of paper was close to hand—loose sheets, notebook paper, stationery from the cafés he frequented, pages ripped from agendas or calendars, the backs of comic strips and flyers, book jackets, calling cards, envelopes, and the margins of manuscripts drafted a few days or a few years earlier. All of which he deposited in the large wooden trunk, his legacy to the world. It would take decades of dedicated labor by scholars and librarians for that textual trove to be inventoried and extensively published, astonishing us with its quantity, quality, and heterogeneity. Besides his many poems, his plays, short stories, and detective fiction, Pessoa produced translations, political commentary, history texts, sociological treatises, philosophical studies, linguistic theory, economic theory, essays on religion and on psychology, self-analyses, automatic writing, and hundreds of astrological charts.

Even more startling than the copious writings exhumed from the trunk were the dozens of unknown alter egos who, after lurking there for years, suddenly stepped into the world as if awakened from an enchanted sleep. Some of them, such as the long-bearded astrologer and esoteric philosopher named Raphael Baldaya, were only hazily defined. Others, like the ultrarational Baron of Teive, whose insistence on living solely according to reason led him to commit suicide, were endowed with complex psychologies. Baldaya wrote a number of pages for pamphlets and treatises on astrology. The Baron of Teive left a long, diarylike meditation on why he had decided to take his own life. And António Mora, a philosopher and apologist of neo-paganism, left hundreds of pages for several book-length but unfinished works. The writing projects of numerous other personae failed to move forward, or the personae were simply not created to be ambitious writers. Maria José, a pathetic hunchback dying of tuberculosis and the only female alias generated by Pessoa, was the author of a single impassioned love letter addressed to a handsome metalworker who passed by her window on his way to work each day. Most of the literary personalities wrote in Portuguese; some wrote in English; lonely Jean Seul de Méluret wrote in French. All of them were projections, spin-offs, or metamorphoses of Fernando Pessoa himself.

Or did they control and define him? Should we take seriously his claim that he had no personality of his own, that he was just a "medium" for the many writers who welled up in him and whom he served as "literary executor"? Was he indeed "less real" than his alter egos, "less substantial, less personal, and easily influenced by them all"?[4] The short and apparently obvious answer to these questions is no. But while it no doubt made Pessoa giggle a little to imagine how we, his future readers, would react to his provocative assertions about who he was or wasn't, we cannot dismiss his self-partitioning into subsidiary personalities as a mere literary hoax. It was a game, yes, but one that began in early childhood—as soon as he began writing—and persisted with increased vigor into adolescence and adulthood.

And the game was not only about literature. Pessoa staked his very identity on the heteronymous system. In so doing, he not only acknowledged the unsteady nature of who he was; he embraced and embodied, through language, that unsteadiness. He was able to give verbal substance and contours to his sense of self without falsifying its inherent uncertainty, since the heteronyms—like particles in a quantum field—existed in dynamic tension with one another. Running sometimes in parallel though more often than not in different directions, they complemented and contradicted and competed with each other. Through their contrasting poetries and occasionally heated prose exchanges, the heteronyms were in continual dialogue—with one another and with their maker.

If we include his childhood riddlers and humorists, Pessoa created more than one hundred fictitious authors in whose name he wrote or at least planned to write *something*. About thirty of these pseudo-authors signed at least one significant literary work, but there were only three full-fledged heteronyms: Alberto Caeiro, Ricardo Reis, and Álvaro de Campos. This is an important distinction, and yet Pessoa, in a letter to a poet and magazine editor, stated that his "first heteronym" was the Chevalier de Pas, an imaginary knight in whose name he wrote letters to himself when he was just six years old. Authorized by Pessoa's example, I will also use the word "heteronym" rather loosely in the pages that follow.

More important than the terminology used to designate Pessoa's coterie of invented writers is the *phenomenon* of splintered authorship, which we find reflected in the jagged and disjointed nature of his writing. Before he could finish one thing, he was already on to something else, and in the trail of his restless pen he left thousands of alternate wordings, which scholars call "variants," and they debate among themselves about how these should be handled in published editions. In defiance of his undisciplined personality and writing habits, Pessoa managed to produce a substantial number of perfect poems and prose pieces, but this biography will just as often be quoting from the rubble of his fragmentary and half-finished works, which in their ensemble form a kind of literary Pompeii, concealing an untold number of curious ideas, luminous observations, and unexpected confessions waiting to be discovered. Much of Pessoa's prose and a number of his unfinished poems, eighty-five years after his human life ceased, have yet to be transcribed and published.

Pessoa lamented the hesitation and incompletion that plagued so much of what he wrote, especially in his larger literary projects, but all he could do was keep writing. In notes recorded in English when he was twenty-one years old, he remarks on his instinctive hatred "for decisive acts, for definite thoughts." As soon as anything crosses his mind, "ten thousand thoughts and ten thousand interassociations of those ten thousand thoughts arise, and I have no will to eliminate or to arrest them, nor to gather them into one central thought, where their unimportant but associated details might be lost."[5]

Pessoa's most important prose work, *The Book of Disquiet*, magnificently illustrates the uncertainty principle that runs throughout his written universe. It is also the best example of the author's ability to expand and surprise us in his afterlife. A semifictional diary consisting of some five hundred passages on diversified subjects and employing various stylistic and tonal registers, the inaugural edition in Portuguese was not published until 1982, forty-seven years after Pessoa's death. It was based on about three hundred passages—typed, written, or quasi-illegibly scrawled on the most varied kinds of paper imaginable—that Pessoa himself had collected in a large envelope, as well as on dozens of additional passages that researchers ferreted out from his notoriously labyrinthine archives. Subsequent editions, including my own, have added new material, but since the author did not always label his texts, editors disagree about what really belongs in *The Book of Disquiet*. Moreover, Pessoa left only vague and contradictory indications of how he might have ordered its contents, and the competing editions have arranged the passages in completely different ways. To say that this is a book for which no definitive edition is possible would be a flagrant understatement were it not a conceptually erroneous statement, since there is no ur-book begging for definition. What the author actually produced is a quintessential non-book: a large but uncertain quantity of discrete, mostly undated texts left in no sequential order, such that every published edition—inevitably depending on massive editorial intervention—is necessarily untrue to the nonexistent "original."

No other posthumous publication bearing the name of Fernando Pessoa has caused more of a sensation, radically altering our critical perception of this author and his place in the literary and cultural landscape of the twentieth century. Like much of his poetry but more directly so, *The Book of Disquiet* speaks to us with disarming candor about the most secret human thoughts and feelings. The courageous speaker is Bernardo Soares, the book's purported author, whom Pessoa dubbed a "semiheteronym"—a variation on his own personality. But as we read the work, it almost seems that Fernando Pessoa, and even we ourselves, are variations on this invented self, who expresses with uncanny precision our unuttered feelings of disquiet and existential unsettledness, speaking not only *to* us but also *for* us. "The only way to be in agreement with life is to disagree with ourselves," observes Bernardo Soares, who refuses to adapt to the world. He also, thankfully, refuses to indulge in self-pity, and he even jokes, a little grimly, about his condition: "I'm suffering from a headache and the universe."[6]

*The Book of Disquiet* bears comparison with another weirdly wonderful book of the twentieth century: Robert Musil's *The Man Without Qualities*, an unfinished novel whose first volume was published in 1930. Both of these unlikely masterpieces are powered by ideas rather than plot, and both of their respective protagonists are meticulous observers who lack the requisite willpower to be men of action. The nature of their passivity differs, however. "The active life has always struck me as the least comfortable of suicides," quips Bernardo Soares,[7] and it is the sort of comment that quality-deficient Ulrich might also make, but Musil's antihero wants to be a great man, if he could only decide what a great man is, and his passivity is a function of his dithering. It is as if he and his many thoughts were forever waiting, in an antechamber whose name is Hesitation, for real and decisive life to begin. His reveries are a stumbling block. Soares, though a more solitary and melancholy figure, is self-satisfied and experiences moments of considerable euphoria. He is actively, militantly passive. Dreaming is not a vice that hinders him from accomplishing his goals; dreaming is what he lives for, and he organizes his existence accordingly. "Dreaming" includes the imaginative world of writing and also the spiritual imagination.

Ulrich and Bernardo Soares are equally ill suited to the task of living in modern society, but the Austrian mathematician makes some attempt to connect and to be someone in the real world. For Soares, an assistant bookkeeper by trade, not only would any such attempt be futile, it would be misguided. Reality, to his way of thinking, is what we *imaginatively* make of it. If external circumstances shape and determine Ulrich, they are mere fuel for the real life—the thinking and dreaming life—of Bernardo Soares and his progenitor, Fernando Pessoa. Far from being a lost soul in search of qualities that would define him, Pessoa, like his semi-heteronym, was an abundance of qualities that did not cohere and would not settle into just one soul.

✦

PESSOA BEGAN TO MAKE plans for publishing *The Book of Disquiet* as early as 1913, the year he started working on the book, and the hundreds of publication projects he drew up for his myriad poetic and prose works would on their own fill up a hefty volume. But the writer, paradoxically, was in no hurry to publish, and only slowly, after his death, did his editorial fortunes change. The chaotic state of the trunk, Pessoa's difficult handwriting, and the vagaries of publishing all conspired to make him, editorially speaking, an author of the second half of the twentieth century, since it was only then that his enormous output of unpublished prose, including *The Book of Disquiet*, began to see print. While it is true that a large nucleus of his poetry had been published in the 1940s, Pessoa's first editors excluded not only fragmentary and unfinished poems, which was reasonable enough, but also poems that did not coincide with their own rather conservative aesthetics. A number of fascinating poems, including some that reveal the author's more intimate side, have come to light only in recent decades, reconfiguring the poetic panorama of his oeuvre in important ways.

One might regret that it took so long for some of Pessoa's finest work to become available to readers, but I am inclined to consider this delay serendipitous. The fact is that his contemporaries were not ready for a poetics of fragmented selfhood, as Pessoa knew and prophetically explained to us, his posthumous readers. In "Erostratus," a long but unfinished essay written in English around 1930, he cogently argued that literary genius, because it is an advance over the status quo, is never recognized in its own time. Only future generations can properly see and appreciate it. Shakespeare, the essay maintains, was esteemed by theatergoers of the day for his wit; they could only dimly perceive the psychological and linguistic genius that would become the subject of thousands of books and doctoral dissertations in succeeding centuries. Pessoa's rationale is by no means universally valid. There are writers—such as James Joyce, born six years before Pessoa and deceased six years after him—whose genius is recognized and even studied, analyzed, in their lifetimes.

Pessoa's genius, on the other hand, was ahead of its time in such a way that not even he could grasp it completely. He knew he had achieved something marvelous and unprecedented with the creation of his three major heteronyms, but he does not seem to have understood the importance of all the lesser fictitious personalities he spawned. He considered "Nature is parts without a whole" to be the crucial insight of Alberto Caeiro, the master poet and his most clear-minded heteronym, yet he often berated himself for being unable to create whole works of literature. His Goethe-inspired *Fausto* (left as several hundred fragments), the poem "Salutation to Walt Whitman" (over twenty disconnected pieces), and the essay "Erostratus" (five or six dozen unarticulated passages) are typical. And they burst with genius. His most widely read work, *The Book of Disquiet*, was the most fragmentary of all.

Pessoa could not imagine that his literary dispersion, which faithfully mirrors our ontological instability and the absence of intrinsic unity in the world we inhabit, would make him required reading by the time the next century arrived. Without quite knowing what he was doing, he pre-diagnosed us, insofar as his writings speak to our contemporary sense of self-estrangement (when we stop and think about self). His universe of disconnected parts prefigured our own worldview, with developments in history, science, and philosophy having disabused us of whatever harmonious wholes we once cherished. Of course, everything that exists must ultimately connect, since it is part of the existent, and today's cosmologists and philosophers of the world's origin have developed some elegant theories of the total picture, in which the Big Bang may be just a local event. In an analogous fashion, Fernando Pessoa took an astonishingly broad view of what constitutes a self, life, meaning.

✦

PESSOA, EVEN SO, WAS very much a product of his time and geography. However scattered or hazy or uncertain the self, he knew that it only had meaning in relation to other selves and to the rest of the world. Although he abhorred the very idea of collaborating with others to reform the world, he closely observed its political and social dramas, writing about them in dozens of unfinished essays as well as in the articles he actually published. Since his life transpired in volatile times, the dramas he witnessed tended to be ideologically and/or physically violent, beginning in racially segregated Durban, his home during the Anglo-Boer War, which broke out in 1899. Thousands of soldiers, including many wounded men and prisoners of war, passed through the streets of the town, and thousands of refugees took shelter there. Back in Lisbon, where Pessoa arrived in 1905, a dictator soon came to power, the king was assassinated, and in 1910 a republican revolution toppled the monarchy. Then came the Great War, in which Portugal imprudently participated, with disastrous human and economic consequences, making the country ripe terrain for the authoritarian ideas being embraced elsewhere in Europe. A military dictatorship assumed control of the country in 1926, morphing into the Salazar regime and the so-called Estado Novo, or New State, which was proclaimed in March 1933, the same month that the Enabling Act effectively made Adolf Hitler the dictator of Germany.

In his own name and as Álvaro de Campos, Pessoa declared his yearning to feel everything in every way possible. He also wanted to see everything from all possible points of view, which is why his opinions on politics, social issues, and the events of the day were not always consistent. In the hundreds of pages he wrote about the First World War, for instance, we find the heteronym António Mora defending the German cause, while texts signed by Pessoa himself usually sided with the Allies, albeit without enthusiasm. But through all his variable ideas on politics, which included some frankly reactionary theories as well as idealized, semimystical forms of government, we can trace an evolution that shows him, ultimately, in virtual solidarity with the human race, notwithstanding his preference for treading a solitary path.

Interested as he was in the visible world he inhabited, Pessoa was even more attracted to invisible reality. Already as a child he meditated on the unknown, which he sometimes tentatively referred to as Truth, and this became the object of a focused quest in the youthful poetry and prose signed by Alexander Search, his most prolific English heteronym. The quest was subsequently taken up by Pessoa's other literary personalities, or they were responses to it (Caeiro, for example, denied there was any reality or "truth" beyond what we see), and metaphysical concerns pervade the vast body of work he signed with his own name. Pessoa's reflections were informed by his extensive readings in philosophy and religion in many of its varieties—from the great traditions of paganism, Judaism, Christianity, and Buddhism to esoteric systems such as Gnosticism, Kabbalah, Rosicrucianism, Freemasonry, Theosophy, and magic.

Pessoa's interest in the occult graduated to an obsession in his later years, when he wrote a number of patently esoteric poems, and allusions to hidden realities are frequent even in his early work. Indeed, his dogged pursuit of literature was also, at heart, a spiritual pursuit—a means to strive after truth, and even to create it. His fashioning of the heteronyms may be construed as a religious act, as his way of paying homage to God, by realizing his divine potential as a co-creator, made in God's likeness and image. Not only that, Pessoa strongly implied that the heteronyms were a means for alchemically transforming the self, enabling it to progress on its spiritual journey.

And his sexual self? Pessoa claimed not to be very interested in sex, and we know, from his personal notes, that he almost certainly died a virgin. All the more remarkable, then, that he wrote and published not only the aforementioned "Antinous" but also a lascivious "Epithalamium," in which a bride looks forward to being ravished by the groom on her wedding night. These were not short poems; each one ran to more than three hundred lines of verse. Pessoa wrote other poems about love and sexual attraction, in Portuguese, English, and French, and sexual references repeatedly crop up in his fiction, his essays, and his autobiographical notes. In his desultory affair with Ophelia Queiroz, there had been some kissing and petting, and two of Pessoa's close friends were open homosexuals, whom he defended against scurrilous attacks in the press, but it was mainly through his writings that he slowly came to grips with his own sexuality. I don't mean that he symbolically "lost" his virginity but that he lost his shame, his preconceptions, and came to accept his chastity with equanimity.

The stories of how Pessoa evolved as a sexual being, as a spiritual seeker, and as a political and social thinker are like the weft interlaced with the warp of his literature, with all the strands forming a variegated tapestry, but even this capacious and inclusive fabric is overwhelmingly literary, since his sexuality, spirituality, and politics were primarily expressed and experienced through words. Pessoa copulated with no man or woman, prayed to no god, and joined no political party. And after returning from South Africa to Lisbon, he rarely strayed far from this city. He wrote, and wrote, in multiple genres about countless subjects. But what about the Fernando Pessoa made of flesh and blood who had appetites, fears, sorrows, headaches, haircuts, memories, dashed hopes? What is the connection between this quotidian man and the compulsive writer?

In the first half of the nineteenth century and in a country at the opposite end of Europe, Søren Kierkegaard (1813–1855) experienced a similar dichotomy. His worldly existence was even more circumscribed than Pessoa's, with his travels out of Copenhagen taking him no farther than Berlin. Like Pessoa, he ended up renouncing romantic love, had solitary habits, and led an outwardly uneventful life. His writing life, meanwhile, was in a perpetual ferment. More adept than Pessoa at channeling his restive genius, the Danish philosopher completed and published book after book of provocative thinking conveyed in sparkling prose and as often as not signed by a pseudonym: Victor Eremita, Constantin Constantius, Johannes Climacus. . . . There were more than a dozen of these fictitious collaborators, who had individuated points of view and sometimes critiqued one another. Since Pessoa did not know Kierkegaard's work (translated initially into German, which Pessoa could not read, and not into English and French until the 1930s), the resemblance between their creative universes is all the more striking.

Self-multiplication was, for both men, a means toward self-realization, and selfhood was a topic they both took up in their writings. Kierkegaard, however, was a praying man and a theologian, deeply religious and specifically Christian. He saw suffering as a necessary condition of spiritual progress and defended martyrdom—the laying down of one's life for others, or for God—as the highest good. Pessoa, who rejected his Catholic upbringing, never held suffering to be a virtue. But he knew all about it from experience and was a kind of accidental, or perhaps even willing and deliberate, martyr. One day he copied out, on a sheet of paper tossed into the trunk and not discovered by researchers until the present millennium, a single verse from the ninth chapter of St. Paul's First Epistle to the Corinthians: "I became all things to all men, that I might save all."[8] This inscription, which can serve as one among other explanations for Pessoa's creation of the heteronyms, suggests he was convinced that he and his work were nothing if they were not for others. One way or another, Pessoa's protean literary project had something profoundly in common with Kierkegaard's existentially religious one.

◆

PORTUGAL DOES NOT HAVE a strong tradition of biographies, and
João Gaspar Simões has to be commended for endeavoring to write one
on Pessoa, whose unusual literary enterprise he helped to illuminate for
several generations of Portuguese-speaking readers. He has been criticized for drawing a somewhat fanciful portrait of his subject as a hard-
drinking and penniless *poète maudit*, accursed poet, and for interviewing
only a few of Pessoa's friends and relatives, many of whom were still living at the time he wrote. With more thorough and rigorous research, he
could have avoided many of his book's factual errors, which have unfortunately been repeated by others. But I am not absolutely certain that
additional interviews with those who knew Pessoa would have brought
the biographer much closer to his subject. Perusing the interviews with
Pessoa's friends published in old newspapers or aired on television, I have
been struck by how little they had to say. Shy and soft-spoken—they all
agreed—but with a good sense of humor, and extremely polite, impeccably dressed, a perfect gentleman. More helpful are the interviews with
Pessoa's half sister, who had lived with him as a little girl in Durban and
again as an adult in Lisbon. He never told her, however, about his onetime girlfriend, Ophelia, whose existence she learned about only after
his death. He was fanatically private. The dozens of letters he wrote to
his closest friend, Mário de Sá-Carneiro, a poet who committed suicide,
might have been a gold mine but have almost all been lost. His surviving
letters to other friends and to family are relatively few in number. Pessoa
commenced three diaries, consisting of succinctly factual entries that
divulge very little about his emotional state, and he abandoned them all
within three months' time.

   The biographer's most valuable source of information is the trunk,
now known as the Pessoa Archive, which encompasses notebooks and
papers going all the way back to the writer's childhood in Durban. Some
of the manuscripts contain extraneous, biographically useful scribblings:
lists of things to do or to buy, the dates and times of appointments, and
reminders to write so-and-so or to purchase a certain book or to pay off
an outstanding debt. Pessoa cast many astrological charts for himself,
with interpretive notes that shed light on significant moments in his life.
And there are revealing letters he drafted but did not send.

More revealing than any letters, scribblings, or his short-lived diaries are Pessoa's poetry and literary prose, much of which is autobiographical, though usually only partially or distortedly so. This most crucial of resources for getting at the heart of the man is also, therefore, the most treacherous. In "The Tobacco Shop," the heteronym Álvaro de Campos, amid poetic ramblings on the meaning of his life on Earth and in the universe, ironically remarks: "If I married my washwoman's daughter, perhaps I would be happy." I would not dare to infer from these words that the poem's ultimate author, Fernando Pessoa, had a weakness for the daughter of *his* washwoman and perhaps even flirted with her and fantasized marriage, but others have assumed this was the case, and to justify their interpretation they can point to the fact that, at the end of the same poem, Campos looks out the window and waves at a friend called Esteves, the very real last name of a man Pessoa knew.

I have tried to construct, with as much credible detail as I could muster, a "cinematographic" life: what Pessoa looked like and how he behaved, where his steps took him, the people he interacted with, and the lively settings where his life unfolded. But this film, on its own, would tell us little about Pessoa the writer, whose essential life took place in the imagination. And so my larger ambition has been to chart, as far as possible, his imaginative life.

"A Man's life of any worth is a continual allegory," affirmed John Keats in a letter to his brother and sister-in-law. "Lord Byron cuts a figure, but he is not figurative—Shakespeare led a life of Allegory; his works are the comments on it." Shakespeare, unlike Byron, not only failed to cut a dashing figure; he left, for posterity, almost no figure at all. We know almost nothing about the man. Therein lies the allegory. He left, instead, a plethora of dramatic characters far more vivid than most human personalities. Pessoa's legacy is not comparable to Shakespeare's, at least not in terms of what he actually realized. But what he imagined, envisioned, and projected was uniquely vast and varied. "Be plural like the universe!" he imperatively wrote on a slip of paper found in the trunk in the 1960s.

His life, no less than Shakespeare's, was an allegory.

# Part I

# THE BORN FOREIGNER
## *(1888–1905)*

> I was a foreigner in their midst, but no one realized it. I lived among them as a spy and no one, not even I, suspected it. They all took me for a relative; no one knew I'd been swapped at birth. And so I was one of their equals without anything in common, a brother to all without belonging to the family.
>
> —*The Book of Disquiet* (text 433)

Fernando Pessoa wearing a sailor suit, which was the
de rigueur outfit for studio portraits of seven-year-old
Portuguese boys.
*(Courtesy Casa Fernando Pessoa)*

# CHAPTER 1

O N A PLEASANTLY WARM BUT BLUSTERY AFTER-
noon, as gusts of wind blew the hats off pedestrians down
below, Fernando António Nogueira Pessôa was born to an
excited young mother—her first child—in a fourth-floor apartment in
the city of Lisbon. It was June 13, 1888, the feast day of St. Anthony of
Lisbon, and the feasting was not only religious. There were years when
the merrymaking that filled the streets, particularly around Praça da
Figueira, got too boisterous, even violent, with fighting and crime spoiling the fun, but not in 1888. The newspaper reported that "the eve of
St. Anthony's passed by calmly, without giving the police much work to
do"—just a few scuffles, two or three drunks who had to be locked up
for the night, and a pair of petty thieves who were arrested for trying to
steal a gold ring.[1]

Nowadays the saint's birthday is celebrated with more pomp and
variety. Things kick off on the evening of June 12 with a huge parade
formed by groups of costumed dancers from each of Lisbon's twenty or
so neighborhoods. The streets and squares of the older quarters, decked
out with colorful streamers and paper flowers, are packed with people moving their hips or just listening to traditional Portuguese music
played by professional and amateur bands. Makeshift stalls sell sar-
dines and pork, beer and sangria. In the wee hours a few drunken par-
tiers sometimes get out of hand, and more than a few get sick from
having drunk too much. On the morning of the thirteenth, after the
last revelers have staggered home, the first Masses are held in honor
of St. Anthony—Santo António, in Portuguese—and they continue
throughout the day, with a procession of the faithful capping off the
religious homage in the late afternoon. And in recent years a new tradition has developed: there are lectures, readings, and dramatic performances to commemorate the birth of Fernando Pessoa. It would have

pleased him to know that he, or our remembrance of him, is mixed up in so much reverent and rowdy company.

Pessoa (he dropped the circumflex from his surname in 1916) had the same second name as both his grandfathers, but his mother was probably more concerned to honor Lisbon's favorite saint, so that he would smile upon and bless her son. She was mildly religious, in a superstitious sort of way. Pessoa's first name may also have been a homage to St. Anthony, who was called Fernando for more than half his life. Born in the twilight of the twelfth century into a wealthy family, the future saint forsook his birthright of ease and comfort to become a friar, changing his name from Fernando to António when he joined the Franciscans. He left Lisbon for Morocco at age twenty-five, eventually ended up in Italy, and died near Padua, where he spent his last years. Outside Portugal he is mostly known as St. Anthony of Padua. Fernando Pessoa, who grew up in economically comfortable circumstances, likewise cared little for worldly riches, but he was viscerally attached to Lisbon. His geographical path was somewhat the opposite of St. Anthony's, for at age seventeen he returned to Lisbon after nine years abroad, and during the rest of his life he rarely ventured out of the city and its environs.

◆

LISBON WAS AN IMPERIAL city in seemingly perpetual decline. Although it was hard to picture, historians affirmed that it had once been a thriving and even luxurious capital. Back in the mid-sixteenth century, it had ranked as one of the world's leading centers of international commerce, thanks to the network of trading posts and alliances the Portuguese had established in Africa, Asia, and Brazil. Portugal's sprawling empire was more mercantile than political, and Lisbon became a unique emporium for pepper, cinnamon, and other spices, myrrh, ebony and brazilwood, parrots, monkeys and animal hides, silks and porcelain from China, textiles and manufactured goods from Europe, and ivory and slaves from Africa. Slave auctions began in Lisbon in the fifteenth century, and Portuguese traders—pioneers of the Atlantic slave trade—shipped between five and six million slaves from Africa to the New World, mostly to Brazil. The considerable revenue from the nation's diversified trade activities did not trickle down, nor was it invested at home. Spread far and thin, the empire started to crack, enabling the Spanish crown to rule a weakened Portugal from 1580 to 1640.

In the first half of the eighteenth century, gold and diamonds from the colony of Brazil could not reverse the fortunes of the much diminished empire, but they brought new wealth to the home country. It was a wealth that flowed in and then out, stimulating economies around the rest of Europe. England, a huge exporter of wool to Portugal, was the largest end recipient of Brazilian gold. This mineral also paid for increased shipments of cereal grains from northern Europe, while domestic agriculture continued to languish. Lisbon's small but pampered upper class bought linens from Flanders, velvets from Venice, silverware, brassware, and clocks from Germany, and tapestries and fine apparel from France. King João V, who reigned from 1706 to 1750, spent massive sums to build lavish churches and monasteries, most notably the convent complex at Mafra, which was decorated with ecclesiastical art imported from Italy.* Virtually no money was spent on improving infrastructure or on developing local industry. Lisbon's streets were narrow and dirty, and crime was rife.

In his *Journal of a Voyage to Lisbon*, written in 1754, Henry Fielding called the endpoint of his six-week ocean journey "the nastiest city in the world." It was a hasty judgment, and without worldwide travel experience to back it up, but almost all foreign visitors rated Lisbon badly in comparison with other European capitals. Fielding, it must be remembered, was in wretched health, having sailed from England to Lisbon in hopes the milder climate might alleviate his excruciating gout. Two months after landing he died, in October, and was buried in the city's English cemetery.

One year later, the calamitous 1755 earthquake, with its attendant tsunami and rampant fires, leveled most of Lisbon and killed more than ten thousand of its residents, prompting Voltaire—in *Candide* and in his "Poem on the Lisbon Disaster"—to loudly mock the notion that all was for the best in what Leibniz and other optimists assumed was the best of all possible worlds. And yet the catastrophe probably *was* an urban blessing in the long run. The future Marquis of Pombal, chief minister to King José I, who reigned from 1750 to 1777, relied on Enlightenment ideals and innovative, antiseismic construction methods to despotically

---

* The construction of the sumptuously monstrous convent is the backdrop of José Saramago's *Baltasar and Blimunda*.

but energetically rebuild the city. Pombal encouraged manufacturing and founded several state-sponsored industries. He also bridled the aristocracy, expelled the Jesuits, enfeebled the Inquisition (which had been established in Portugal in 1536), and abolished the "blood purity" laws that prevented New Christians—as coercively converted Jews and their descendants were called—from holding government posts and exercising certain professions.

Pombal could inhibit but not eliminate the old guard, old money, and old habits. While a revolution was getting under way in America, Portugal turned its back on change. As soon as King José died, in 1777, Pombal was stripped of his powers, and many of his reformist policies were attenuated or reversed. Conservative Catholic clergy and the indolent aristocracy regained their standing, and Portugal limped ahead, slowly and unsurely, through the Napoleonic invasions (1807–1810) and a civil war (1828–1834), lagging behind the rest of Europe by almost every measure of progress. That very disparity at least prodded the nation's leaders to keep trying to catch up, and by the time Pessoa was born the capital city had a serviceable sewage system, gas lighting on the main streets and in wealthier neighborhoods, and a broad and forward-looking Avenida da Liberdade (Liberty Avenue; built 1886), inspired by the Champs-Élysées.

So Portugal had a modern edge, or veneer, and the ruling class and cultural elite longingly envisioned full-tilt modernity, but the vision was clouded by a nagging suspicion that the country was destined to forever play copycat, following the lead of countries like France and doing the political bidding of Great Britain, Portugal's oldest ally and protector. In 1887 a group of notable intellectuals, who would later be joined by the poet Guerra Junqueiro (1850–1923) and the novelist Eça de Queiroz (1845–1900), began to call themselves the Vencidos da Vida, or "Life's Defeated." What united them, besides the succulent food in the fine restaurants where they met, was not a feeling of failure in their personal careers as writers and artists but the conviction that, despite their best efforts to encourage reform, Portugal had failed and would continue to fail to be *organically* progressive, original, and self-determining.

This larger failure was both the cause and consequence of *saudade*, a word that signifies intense longing, yearning, nostalgia, both as a temporary mood or state of mind and as an existential condition. Its meaning is akin to *Sehnsucht*, but the German word never served, on its own, as the basis for a collective identity. *Saudade*, promoted as a uniquely Portuguese feeling, became a national obsession in the late nineteenth and early twentieth centuries. The specific historical object of that obsession was the Age of Discoveries, when Portugal controlled vast tracts of ocean and numerous seaports around the world. Accomplished against great odds, this maritime supremacy might have transformed life in the home country, were half of the resulting wealth not grossly mismanaged and the other half squandered, leaving future generations to pine after glory days that had never existed, except for an exiguous group of profiteers, investors, and aristocrats. Pessoa was born into a world in which ghostly shades of former splendors hovered amid palpable poverty and decay.

◆

BUT LISBON WAS AND remains, even in the twenty-first century, majestic. Built, like Rome, on seven hills—or six, or eight, depending on what you call a hill—and stretching along the wide estuary of the Tagus River, which is sometimes called the Mar da Palha, or Straw Sea, because of how it goldenly reflects the sun at dusk, the city offers an ever-changing spectacle of light glinting off the pastel-colored buildings of its slopes. And the sky in Lisbon is more dynamic than in other European capitals, with sun and clouds and rain often entering and exiting in rapid succession, as if the pagan gods were still alive, vying for control of the weather. The city is a natural feast for the eyes, and Pessoa immortalized his visual pleasure by recording his particularized impressions in *The Book of Disquiet*, using words like so much paint. For instance: "Against the blue made pale by the green of night, the cold unevenness of the buildings on the summer horizon formed a jagged, brownish-black silhouette, vaguely haloed by a yellowed gray."[2]

Fernando Pessoa is one of those writers, like James Joyce, whom we automatically associate with the city of their birth, as if one were the reconfigured equivalent of the other. Perhaps because the identification was so strong, Dublin so inevitably present in everything he wrote, Joyce could not stand to live there as an adult. Pessoa, on the other hand, carried his exile with him. He lived in Lisbon, but at a certain remove, and not only because he wafted in the heights of literature. His Lisbon was a vivid, living symbol for the world at large. A streetcar ride from the city's center to its outskirts could, he claimed, afford a greater sensation of freedom than a trip to China, provided the passenger knew, as he did, how to feel with intricate intensity.[3]

Pessoa's capacity for being intimately yet detachedly Portuguese— hence universal—is partly due to the English language, which he continued to use in literary works and in private notes long after his childhood years in South Africa were behind him. In his most revealing diary, kept for just two months in 1915, and in his most sexually charged poems, Pessoa significantly chose English as his medium of expression. But any language, no matter where he happened to be, could serve him as a haven or a hiding place, reinforcing his feeling of otherness. "My nation is the Portuguese language," he famously wrote in 1931, affirming a patriotism that was in the first place linguistic, rather than geographical. Far less quoted, since it is politically or socially incorrect, is this admission: "An adjective matters more to me than the real weeping of a human soul."[4] Which is not to say that Pessoa was insensitive to human tears. He shed many of his own. But words—and what words could represent—were what he lived for.

✦

PESSOA'S LOVE AFFAIR WITH language began as a young boy, but first there was the love he felt in his family. The two loves were related, since both his parents were writers of a sort—without great ambitions or superior talent—and encouraged their son, who followed their lead with unusual fervor, the way certain people follow a religious vocation.

His mother, Maria Madalena Pinheiro Nogueira, was born on the Azorean island of Terceira on December 30, 1861, but moved to the mainland when she was a little over three years old. Her father, Luís António Nogueira, who earned his law degree at the university in Coimbra, had been appointed to a government post in Porto, and a few years later he was named the kingdom's head of the Home Civil Service, whereupon he took his family to Lisbon. Maria, who grew up between these two cities, never went back to the Azores to live. According to family accounts, she was a bright and spunky, not entirely conventional young woman. She learned French early on, which was typical of Portugal's educated class, and she was proficient at the piano, typical for her sex; but she became fluent in English as well, thanks to her studies at the British School in Lisbon, run by a woman named Miss Calf, and from her father she learned some Latin. His high-placed friends were impressed with her intelligence and regretted that she had not been born a boy, in which case she could have aspired to a brilliant career.[5]

Luís António Nogueira's concern to provide a first-class education for his children, including "even" his daughters (one of his obituaries described the two young women as "exquisitely educated"), stemmed from the importance he gave to erudition in his own career. Besides devotedly performing his duties as a government official, he was a scholar and writer—not of literary but legal matters. From the date of its founding, in late 1868, he wrote prolifically on administrative law for *O Direito* (*The Law*), which to this day is Portugal's premier journal of jurisprudence. His name soon featured on its masthead, remaining there until he died, devastated by diabetes and by the death, two years earlier, of his nineteen-year-old son. He had not been a lucky father, having already lost his oldest son, likewise a teenager, a dozen years earlier.[6]

Maria Madalena was twenty-two when her father died. She still had her mother and her sister, Ana Luísa, or Anica, who was almost two years older. It was a tight-knit family, and the death of their two brothers, then their father, brought the two sisters even closer together. Both were attractive, but Maria, more self-assured, was the one who stood out. She was a romantic who read novels and poetry, and she wrote her own poetry, mostly autobiographical; the surviving examples of her work employ a considerable variety of verse forms, though without much originality or technical bravura. She freely spoke her mind and had a rebellious streak. When it was the fashion for young women to put up their hair, a coming-of-age sort of ritual, she had her hair cut short.[7] Her transgressions were of this capricious, nonthreatening kind. She might rock the boat; she would never tip it over. Unless perhaps for a great love. Love and family defined the limits of her and almost every Portuguese woman's horizons.

◆

IF WE KNEW IN what circumstances this intelligent, talented, and handsome young woman met her first husband, Pessoa's father, it might help explain why she chose him rather than another suitor. Joaquim de Seabra Pessoa was eleven years her senior, but without the brilliant career that someone his age might already have achieved. By day he worked at the Ministry of Justice, where he had climbed up the civil service ladders to a dull and respectable post: section chief in the accounting department.

By night he had a diametrically different occupation: music and theater critic for the *Diário de Notícias* (*Daily News*), one of Lisbon's major newspapers, then as now. There too he had worked his way up, having started out when he was just eighteen, probably as a junior reporter. Whether he had aspired to write about music or the needs of the newspaper led him in that direction, it was a job he loved, even if the pay was slight. He was passionate about music and especially the opera. Between 1876 and 1892, he published more than eight hundred long and short pieces about musical and theatrical performances in Lisbon. So great was his passion for Wagner that he wrote a booklet about the German composer's first mature opera, *The Flying Dutchman*, whose story is based on the legend of the eponymous ghost ship. The booklet, like everything Joaquim wrote, was published anonymously.[8] He also collected autographed photos of famous singers. And when Sarah Bernhardt, then the most celebrated actress in Europe, came to Lisbon in April 1888, he took his wife—seven months pregnant—to see her perform.[9]

Joaquim de Seabra Pessoa was born in Lisbon, on May 28, 1850, but his paternal roots were from the southern town of Tavira, in the Algarve. One of his great-grandfathers, an army captain descended from an illustrious family of military men, was granted a title of nobility in 1799. The soldierly tradition continued down to his father, Joaquim António de Araújo Pessoa (1813–1885), a highly decorated general who made a name for himself when still young, in the civil war that broke out in 1828. Blessed with the good fortune of having fought on the winning side, he moved from the Algarve to Lisbon and married Dionísia Rosa Estrela de Seabra (1823–1907), who came from a less illustrious but equally prosperous family, Algarvian on her father's side. The couple had a daughter who died in infancy and two sons, one of whom also died young. The surviving child, Pessoa's father, had neither the inclination nor the physical stamina for the armed forces. Joaquim was consumptive, to use an outmoded word that has the virtue of graphically evoking the effect of pulmonary tuberculosis. The disease had destroyed his brother early on and was wasting him away more slowly, but surely.[10] A Portuguese editor and bibliographer, writing about his work as a collaborator on a Portuguese dictionary in the late 1870s, recalled in his memoirs that the editorial team included "a certain Pessoa [. . .] a reporter for the *Diário de Notícias*, a skinny fellow, gaunt and consumptive looking, whom I never heard of again." Although he never attended university,

Joaquim was a studious type, fluent in both French and Italian.[11] He loved books, and there were many of them in the spacious apartment he occupied with his widowed mother in Lisbon's fashionable, centrally located neighborhood of Chiado.[12]

In a sympathetic obituary after Joaquim's death in 1893, at the age of forty-three, the *Diário de Notícias* would note that their longtime music and theater critic was "appreciated for his modesty, his right-mindedness and his candor, and for his dispassionate and impartial criticism. His analyses were always sensitive and correct." Indeed his reviews of recitals, concerts, operas, and plays were not daring or stylistically noteworthy but they did offer intelligent, balanced, and heartfelt criticism. They were his greatest source of professional satisfaction. He clipped and pasted them into sixteen large scrapbooks.[13]

◆

IT COULD BE THAT Joaquim's modesty and rectitude, his lack of interest in making a splash, favorably impressed Maria, Pessoa's mother. But what really charmed her, I suspect, was his aesthetic sensibility, apparent not only in his passion for music: her fiancé cultivated a lifestyle full of beautiful things. The marriage, celebrated on September 5, 1887, at Santos-o-Velho, the parish church of the bride's family, got off to an auspicious start. Maria moved in with Joaquim and his mother, and before the month was over she was pregnant. The Pessoas' apartment, on the top floor of an elegant building that fronted a small square, was comfortable and even a little posh, as Joaquim insisted on fine furnishings, being especially partial to his set of Chinese porcelain.[14] There was a piano, which Maria enjoyed playing. The balcony afforded an exceptional view of the Tagus, and directly across the square stood the externally sober, inwardly luxurious São Carlos Theater, Lisbon's opera house, modeled after Milan's La Scala and the San Carlo Theater of Naples. Joaquim needed to walk only a hundred feet to reach what may justifiably be called his temple of devotion. The music aficionado and critic was a nominal but nonpracticing Catholic; music was the closest thing he had to a religion.

Part of Joaquim's tepidness toward the Roman Catholic Church was genealogically determined. His ancestors from the seventeenth and eighteenth centuries included a number of New Christians surnamed da Cunha and hailing from the center of the country, particularly the town of Fundão, where there had been a large Jewish community. Doubting the sincerity of their conversions, the Inquisition arrested and tried successive generations of da Cunha family members for continuing to secretly practice Judaism. Sancho Pessoa da Cunha, arrested circa 1705, was the first male ancestor to use the name Pessoa, which he got from his mother, Madalena Pessoa, whose New Christian husband (from the da Cunha clan) had been imprisoned by the Inquisition in 1669. Fernando Pessoa, in autobiographical notes written toward the end of his life, defined his ancestry as "a mixture of aristocrats and Jews."[15] The majority of his ancestors, however, were neither Jews nor aristocrats.

Any crypto-Judaism that the Inquisition may have correctly sniffed out among Joaquim Pessoa's ancestors had long ago dissipated, but very little Christianity had filtered in to take its place. Most of Joaquim's paternal ancestors were not even baptized, and one of his uncles, Jacques Cesário de Araújo Pessoa (1816–1885), was a self-professed atheist.[16] Joaquim, if not himself an atheist or agnostic, was thoroughly secular. In the many letters he would write when dying of tuberculosis, there is not a single entreaty to God or expression of religious sentiment. His wife, Maria, did pray to God, at least rhetorically, in her poems and in some of her letters to relatives, and she raised all her children as Roman Catholics—because that's how she had been raised, not because she was a fervent believer. It was not from his parents that Fernando derived his restless religious curiosity.

◆

FERNANDO PESSOA'S BIRTH WAS front-page news in the June 14, 1888, issue of *Correio da Noite* (*Evening Mail*). In those days a lot of small news items were crammed onto the front page, but for the event to make it into the newspaper at all was proof of the editors' esteem for their "friend and colleague from the *Diário de Notícias*, Joaquim Pessoa," and suggestive of a certain social status enjoyed by the young couple. Their child had been born the previous day at "around" 3:20 p.m., according to his birth record. The inexactitude of the reported time was a source of some anxiety for Fernando Pessoa the adult, who was a dedicated astrologer and regularly cast charts mapping his character and destiny. Had he been born several minutes earlier, or several minutes later, the whole course of his life might, according to the stars, have been different. This hypothesis will strike most readers as preposterous, but it might seem slightly less so if we consider that other minuscule events occurring at key moments of infantile impressionability—an image fleetingly seen, a frightening or soothing sound, a feeling of warmth, a smell, even pressures on the womb before the child emerges—can decisively shape an individual. If these events are mere chance at work, that itself is a mystery, and mystery is a door to the possibility of other forces, such as the stars, operating at other levels.

Like most advocates of astrology, Pessoa claimed it did not depend on faith, but he did not suppose, as some do, that the stars rule our lives by virtue of magnetic or other physical laws. When he was already past the age of forty he explained, in English, his point of view: "Astrology is verifiable, if anyone will take the trouble to verify it. Why the stars influence us is a difficult question to answer, but it is not a scientific question. The scientific question is: do they or do they not? The reason why is metaphysical and need not trouble the fact, once we find that it is a fact."[17] This was an elegant way of admitting that astrology has absolutely no scientific basis; it depends on metaphysics. As for when exactly he was born, Pessoa came to suspect that it happened a little before 3:15 p.m., according to a 1918 letter he sent the *British Journal of Astrology*, along with a postal order for two shillings and six pence, the fee for having his birth time rectified and his "prenatal epoch," or date of conception, calculated.[18]

Pessoa's baptism took place on July 21 at Our Lady of the Martyrs Church, a short block away from where the family lived. One of Lisbon's oldest churches—relocated and rebuilt, however, after the 1755 earthquake—Our Lady of the Martyrs was founded in 1147, the same year Lisbon was reconquered from the Moors. The "martyrs" were the Christian soldiers who died in the four-month-long battle. The website for the venerable church points out that many illustrious people have been baptized there over the centuries, not least of all Fernando Pessoa. The irony of this little boast would merit a chuckle from the famous writer, who, one month before his eighteenth birthday, drafted an open letter to the prior of the church expressing indignation for having been baptized there with no say in the matter.

Baptism, states the letter without pussyfooting, implies "the integration of the victim into the Catholic Church; it obliges the individual, when still an irrational creature, to become part of an all too human association whose theories his more manly reason may not wish to subscribe to." Leaving no doubt as to what his own "manly reason" had concluded, the letter writer describes the Church as "powerful and stupid, irrational and decrepit."[19] By the time he wrote his letter, which he planned to publish as a pamphlet but failed to complete, Pessoa must have known about his Jewish ancestry; however, the rejection of his Catholic baptism had little to do with his religious beliefs, which at that point in his life were ill defined. He blamed the Church, closely partnered with the monarchy, for helping to nurture the conservative, provincial mentality that was inhibiting Portugal from prospering intellectually, politically, and economically.

In elementary school Fernando learned the Catholic catechism as well as the multiplication table. Although the warm feelings he felt for Jesus, the Virgin Mary, and certain saints whose life stories he admired did not stay with him into adolescence, he did hold on to several holy cards, as mementos of a time in his life when wholehearted, uncritical belief was still possible. One of the cards depicted a haloed St. Anthony. Another was from his first communion, and on the back of the card a nun from St. Joseph's Convent School wrote, "To my good boy Fernando a little souvenir of the happiest day." That day occurred in Durban, South Africa, when he was eight or nine years old.[20]

His fondest memory of the Church of the Martyrs was its tolling bell, which he and the rest of the family heard with resounding clarity even when the windows of their apartment were closed. That memory inspired one of the first two poems he published as an adult, in February 1914:

> O church bell of my village,
> Each of your plangent tolls
> Filling the calm evening
> Rings inside my soul.

In a December 1931 letter to João Gaspar Simões, his future biographer, Pessoa identified the poetically invoked bell as the one that tolled at the Church of the Martyrs, and the "village" as the Largo de São Carlos, the square where he was born. The bell seems to haunt the poem's narrator:

> However closely you touch me
> When I pass by, always drifting,

worked two jobs to be able to provide sustenance and a little luxury for himself and his family; he was attentive to those who depended on him; he had a couple of close friends. But he was at the same time abstracted, easily and delightedly lost in the world of music, the world of books, the world of his fine china and other beautiful objects.

Something of that abstraction—perhaps not unrelated to Dionísia's "alienation"—was passed on to Fernando, if not genetically, then by way of example. With his vivid imagination the little boy, short on playmates, inhabited strange scenarios peopled by unreal characters. It was a practice he would replicate in his writing. Pessoa's first published piece of creative prose, from 1913, is fittingly titled "In the Forest of Estrangement." Nothing for its somnambulant narrator is quite real, including the voiceless woman who accompanies him in the weirdly lush woods. One year later he published his next piece of creative prose, in which the first-person narrator tells of meeting a "scandalously human" professor from the University of Tokyo who lectures him on industrialization and the socialist workers' movement in Japan. Explaining to the reader that his own ideas and impressions of Japan "derive from a careful study of various teapots and teacups," the narrator refuses to believe in the real country described by the Japanese professor, whom he suspects may be an impostor, or a mere illusion. He prefers the two-dimensional Japan of his porcelain tea service, with its blue figures "eternally sitting" next to "absurd lakes," with "totally unreal mountains" in the background.

We cannot know how much Fernando's eyes lingered over the figures depicted in his father's porcelain, peering with imagination into their private lives and traveling to a blue-tinted Far East, but we know that he became precociously adept at envisioning realities in spatial dimensions unlike those in which our human bodies move. As an adult he defended the idea that other universes might coexist with our own.[25]

◆

PESSOA'S PARENTS WERE SOLID members of Portugal's semienlightened bourgeoisie, a class that embraced new ideas and the ideology of progress as long as its own interests were not adversely affected. The couple shared, with their economic and social peers, a cautious optimism that their country was going mainstream, becoming as European in spirit as it was in geography. They got married in the middle of the Belle Époque[26]—a sustained period of prosperity for much of the world, still with great disparities in wealth and glaring class discrimination but also with real wage growth and improved standards of living for many workers. The use of electricity and telephones was spreading, and the first automobiles, phonographs, and motion picture cameras were already being produced.

Many of the new inventions were coming out of the United States, whose dynamic economy and higher-paying jobs, both for skilled and unskilled labor, attracted millions of European immigrants. But Europe also felt vigorous and looked toward the future with optimism. The British Empire was at its apogee, and the United Kingdom, with its so-called Pax Britannica, assumed the role of global policeman, providing protection in exchange for subservience. Portugal, like other small and dependent countries, was brought to heel when it ran afoul of the international rules laid down by Britain. In neighboring Spain, which had been a short-lived republic in 1873–1874, liberal reforms and a growing economy assured, for now, wide support for the constitutional monarchy. To the north, France had experienced an existential crisis of confidence when it lost Alsace-Lorraine after the Franco-Prussian War, but it rebounded to set the tone for the audacious and enterprising spirit of the age. The Eiffel Tower, halfway completed by the time Pessoa was born, would be inaugurated for the Paris world's fair of 1889. This wrought-iron marvel of engineering, though it had its detractors among the French elite, became the European symbol of industrial, technological, and artistic modernity.

In Portugal foreign investment and government spending had enabled railroads to be built and infrastructures to be considerably improved, creating the conditions for modernizing agriculture and developing industry. The hoped-for results were slow in coming, but expectations ran high, and the nation prided itself on the course it was taking. On June 7, 1888, six days before Pessoa's birth, an ambitious Portuguese Industrial Exposition opened on Lisbon's Avenida da Liberdade in buildings erected especially for the occasion. This was far larger than previous expositions held in the capital, in 1838 and 1849, and it was the first "with a well-defined and scientific program," according to a leading newspaper.[27] It showcased manufactured goods from around the country, including dishware, hardware, distillery equipment, faucets, pumps, lanterns, textiles, shoes, paper, liquors, canned goods, electrical devices, and pharmaceutical products—nothing that might be classified as cutting-edge. There was also a hall dedicated to the fine arts, with a display of paintings and musical instruments, as well as a concert program. The gala event was promoted with fanfare—King Luís kicked things off with a speech—but its practical import was negligible. Some awards were given, and a few manufacturers found domestic outlets for their goods. Although there was no international presence at or interest in the fair, its organizers clearly wanted participants, who came from as far away as the Azores, to realize they formed part of a self-respecting national project, which had its place on the European playing board.

Its place, however, was on the board's periphery. There was a very gradual development of industry but no industrial "revolution" in Portugal, whose economy was still fundamentally agricultural. Seventy-five percent of its people over the age of seven were illiterate, and per capita domestic production was half of what it was in France, only a third of what it was in Great Britain. And while Spain was also slow to industrialize, its per capita output was still 50 percent greater than Portugal's.

Portugal's economy skidded in the early 1890s, but Joaquim Pessoa was secure in his government job, and his evening work as a music critic continued, with the moneyed class still filling up the São Carlos Theater to hear opera singers from Italy, Spain, and France. Operas were also performed in the much larger Coliseum, inaugurated in 1890, for a diversified audience and at more affordable prices. Life went on much the same for the Pessoas, focused on the family they were building.

Since both parents were literary in their different ways, they did not find it strange that Fernando chose words as his favorite playthings. As the small boy rode on the streetcar with his mother, it tickled him to call out each letter of the signs they passed. This caused a fellow passenger to remark on his unusual ability to recite from memory what he had previously heard his mother spell out. No, she corrected, he already recognized all the letters of the alphabet.[28] By age four he was reading whole sentences.[29] Like most infant readers, Fernando loved comics—a tradition initiated in Portugal by the talented caricaturist and ceramics designer Rafael Bordalo Pinheiro—as well as adventure stories, and his taste for fictionalized adventure never waned. He would develop an insatiable appetite for British and American detective novels, gobbling them up like mental snack food in between weightier fare such as poetry, criticism, and books on religion, history, or philosophy. His fondness for the comical and the playful likewise carried into adulthood, coming out strongly in his letters, in his occasionally impish behavior among family members, and in his private "family" of make-believe literary collaborators.

While Pessoa the adult would retain certain childlike traits, the young boy named Fernando already possessed a grown-up sense of his own dignity. Shy but not easily intimidated, he despised being treated with condescension, no matter how innocent or good-humored. When a family friend from the Azores finally laid eyes on the bright five-year-old he had heard so much about, he hoisted the boy up in his arms, saying, "Pleased to meet you! I've been very curious to make your acquaintance." Fernando, with his feet back on the ground, smoothed the ruffles out of his suit and commented with a dash of pique in his voice, "So now your curiosity has been satisfied."[30] Proud and independent, occasionally even insolent, Fernando was at the same time mild-mannered, timorous, preferring indoor games to rough outdoor play. He could be violent in his words, never in actions. He was also, already, a very private individual.

# CHAPTER 2

AMID A PREDICTABLE CHORUS OF FAMILY CHEERS and congratulations, Fernando's only full brother, Jorge Nogueira Pessoa, was born on January 21, 1893. No one could have imagined that it was the beginning of the end of the Pessoa household. We see Jorge giggling in a baby photo, looking more robust than Fernando at the same age, but he was soon diagnosed with TB, contracted from his father, whose condition had taken a sharp downward turn from which he would not recover. With no truly effective cure for it until the discovery of antibiotics, tuberculosis was woefully common around most of the globe. Joaquim's worsening symptoms included an obstinate cough that thwarted his sleep, and no doubt his wife's.

It was a harrowing year for her and Fernando, surrounded as they were by sickness, dementia, and impending death. While Maria cared for her baby, her mother-in-law, and her husband, Fernando retreated a little more into himself. By May it was obvious that Joaquim, who had quit working altogether, would not hold on much longer. One of his cousins, Lisbela Pessoa Machado (1845–1929), came up from the Algarve to stay with the family and help out. She could sympathize with everyone, since she herself had married a man with TB—a twenty-two-year-old soldier who died in 1873, fourteen months after the wedding. The baby girl she had by the soldier also died, after just a few weeks. Lisbela, well-to-do but unattractive, with a jowlish face, remained a widow and childless. She was delighted to be godmother to Jorge, and she cultivated her relationship with the first-born son, Fernando. When he was two going on three, he and his parents had visited her in Tavira, where she split her time between a house in the town and a farmhouse outside it, perched on top of a hill. Lisbela was the only paternal relative Pessoa would remain close to as an adult—their closeness being ensured, as we shall see, by her financial patronage.[1]

Joaquim Pessoa calmly played out his part as a man condemned to fight a doomed battle, resorting to alternative treatments as well as some of the usual remedies then in vogue for combating tuberculosis, such as quinine, arsenic, and salubrious country air. It was for a change of air that his physician, João Korth, sent him to Caneças, a village just outside Lisbon that was like a humble version, without the mountains or the magic, of the Swiss town whose sanatorium was immortalized by Thomas Mann. Its mineral waters—sold in clay jugs throughout the capital—were reputed to alleviate all kinds of ailments, and its pure, invigorating air was recommended for diseased lungs.

Caneças was a poor village, with nothing like a sanatorium, but those doing a cure could stay at the Hotel Progresso, which got high marks for its cleanliness, good food, and friendly staff.[2] Joaquim checked into the hotel on May 19, 1893, accompanied by Fernando and by the boy's maternal grandmother, Madalena, who usually lived with the family of her older daughter, Anica. A year after Fernando's birth, his aunt Anica had married a cousin from the island of Terceira, João Nogueira de Freitas. They'd been living on the mainland for the last eighteen months but were now getting ready to return to the Azores with Grandma Madalena and their two children: Mário, who was two years old, and Maria, less than two months old. These were Fernando's only first cousins. When they grew up, he and Mário would be almost like brothers, albeit brothers who had few interests in common.

Joaquim Pessoa wrote a daily letter from Caneças to his wife, reporting on his health, on Fernando, and on his mother-in-law. Maria kept him updated on tiny Jorge and on *her* mother-in-law, Dionísia, who was in one of her bad periods, self-absorbed but at the same time given to nervous outbursts. These were more apt to occur if she was left alone with the housekeepers, and Maria, understandably, became somewhat exasperated. She had preferred, initially, to say little about Dionísia in the letters she sent her husband, who chided her on that account. "My mother *knows* that I've *come* here, and you've told me nothing," he wrote on May 23, to which she replied by questioning whether his mother had even that much mental awareness. Joaquim's letter to her of May 26 begins:

> I received your note a short while ago and am very worried about my mother. You say she's demented and feeble-minded, but the fact is she keeps having these agitated fits, which are what I most

fear and which leave her prostrate. If she just remained calm, that would at least be a sad consolation. As it is, she suffers from both troubles.

Dionísia was bound to get short shrift from her daughter-in-law, who was preoccupied with her husband, attending to his almost daily requests to send one thing or another to Caneças.

On May 28 Maria and the baby, Jorge, took a horse-drawn carriage to Caneças, returning to Lisbon that evening with Fernando. Joaquim began to get impatient with his cure. Now he had only his mother-in-law to talk to or play cards with, the weather had turned too cool and damp for him to take walks, and his physical condition was not improving. Dr. Korth, like Joaquim's previous physician, was a homeopath, but the things he prescribed were upsetting the patient's stomach and made no dent in his fever, which stubbornly remained above 100 degrees, leaving him weak and listless. Against the doctor's orders, Joaquim medicated himself with solutions of quinine and arsenic. His fever went down a little, then shot back up. He finally decided to return to Lisbon, arriving there on Saturday, June 3. He had instructed his wife to buy fresh fish or else cook the traditional Portuguese salt cod for lunch, but she wasn't to worry about dessert, since he could buy excellent cakes and cookies near Caneças. Everyone did their best to ignore his growing pallor, his spectral gaze, the cough now soft and intermittent, now uncontrollable.[3]

June 13 was Fernando's fifth birthday. It was celebrated in style, with lots of food, lots of desserts, and more people than he had ever seen the dining room accommodate. All his close relatives were there: his parents, his baby brother, both grandmothers, Aunt Anica and Uncle João, and his cousins, Mário and Maria. There was his favorite great-aunt— named Maria, like his mother—and her husband, Manuel Gualdino da Cunha. The childless couple lived in Pedrouços, an outlying neighborhood, and doted on Fernando. There were other great-aunts, plus their husbands and children. And "Aunt" Lisbela, as she was called by her young cousin once removed, was surely still in Lisbon to help commemorate the special day. It became more special as the years went by. In 1930, on his forty-second birthday, Pessoa would write a poem dramatically depicting the birthdays of his childhood, when he still "enjoyed the good health of understanding nothing." The sixth stanza is particularly evocative:

I see it all again, so vivid it blinds me to what's here . . .
The table with extra place settings, fancier china, more glasses,
The sideboard full of sweets and fruits, and other things in the
　　shadow of the lower shelf.
Elderly aunts, different cousins, and all for my sake,
Back when they used to celebrate my birthday.

The poem's first two lines—the second of which reads like a statement
of logic, as if the boy's happiness were a corollary of no one yet having
died—make it clear that the author had his fifth birthday in mind:

Back when they used to celebrate my birthday
I was happy and no one was dead.

Two days later, on June 15, Joaquim sought healthier air in another
village, Telheiras, just north of Lisbon, where he stayed at the house of
his friend Dr. Korth, who was there with him to monitor his condition.
On June 17 he remarked in a brief letter to his wife: "Today is my mother's birthday. How sad! What if she should remember?" Chances are that
she did not. A week or so later he went to Lisbon for the day, and at the
beginning of July he spent the weekend there so as to bid farewell to
Anica and her family, including his mother-in-law, before they set sail
for Terceira, on July 5. On the tenth, Maria Nogueira Pessoa took the
two boys to visit their father in Telheiras. The next day he wrote her of
a splitting headache that had kept him from sleeping for the past four
nights. His letter of July 12, 1893, complained of the same headache, and
of chills. "I feel feverish and don't know what this might be," he added,
telling Maria of his intention to go home the next day, though he wished
he could go that same day. "I don't know what this might be," he reiterated, "I know that I'm greatly out of sorts and feel very feverish."

He got his wish, returning not the next day but that very same day to
Lisbon and to his family on Largo de São Carlos. To drag his enervated
body up the four flights of stairs, even with assistance, was like climbing
four steep hills. However much he wanted to hold his loved ones, he was
coughing and would have avoided getting too close to Fernando. By then,
TB was known to be an infectious rather than inherited disease. Joaquim
naturally gazed around at the familiar surroundings, already feeling far
away from the solid, well-made furniture, the piano, the shelves full of

books, his blue and white porcelain, his wife and two sons. His normally slender frame now looked even thinner, emaciated, and his face—also slender, with a prominent nose, dark eyes, well-shaped lips, and a sparse moustache—looked decisively haggard. Perhaps it was in that moment that Fernando, gazing at his father sitting there, just a few feet away and yet irrevocably distant, lost the "good health of understanding nothing." Joaquim lay down but surely did not expect to sleep—afflicted by the same headache he had endured on previous nights, along with chills, sweating and a hacking, wet cough. Maria Madalena asked whether she should send for a priest. Joaquim shook his head. Like his freethinking father, he refused the Church's last rites. The coughing subsided, liquid filled his tattered lungs, and at 5:15 a.m. he expired.[4]

◆

ALTHOUGH IT WAS A small consolation, Pessoa's mother was pleased to see her husband's obituary prominently displayed on the front page of the *Diário de Notícias*. The same edition of the paper announced the imminent arrival from Spain of the queen dowager, who would be met by her son, King Carlos I, and published an article on the previous day's *corrida* at Lisbon's new bullring, in Campo Pequeno. There was the usual assortment of political news, none of which was interesting, as well as a notice about a performance that evening by Ida Fuller, an American based in Paris famous for her "serpentine" dancing, which involved waving a profusion of long gossamer skirts high up in the air as colored lights shone through the flutter, creating impressive visual effects.[5] Maria Madalena might have liked to attend that show, held at the Coliseum, had her married life with Joaquim turned out differently. The funeral was that same morning, no doubt followed by lunch with aunts, uncles, and cousins, who wanted to know about Joaquim's last days. They probably discussed how she would manage with her two children, crazed mother-in-law, and the considerable expenses of maintaining such a large apartment. There were many things about his father, his grandmother, and his family's finances that Fernando must have heard, or overheard, for the first time.

The apartment, with its enviable views of the Tagus, was suddenly much emptier, and Pessoa's father was not the only thing missing. All the to-and-fro between Lisbon and Caneças, then Telheiras, all his mother's chasing after this item of clothing and that medication requested by

Joaquim in his letters, her anxious looks as she opened and read those letters, the comforting presence of Lisbela in May and June, and the regular visits of Grandma Madalena, Aunt Anica, and his cousins, who had been living nearby as recently as ten days ago—it had all ceased. With Grandma Dionísia either mum or uttering nonsense, the young widow reeling between grief and a scary feeling of freedom, and tiny Jorge unable to do more than laugh or whine, Fernando absently wandered through the rooms or took refuge in his toys, games, imagination. His emotional behavior in the new circumstances is suggested by a passage from *The Book of Disquiet* in which the narrator, Bernardo Soares, describes his reaction as a three-year-old to the news that his father had died:

> I remember his death as a grave silence during the first meals we ate after learning about it. I remember that the others would occasionally look at me. And I would look back, dumbly comprehending. Then I'd eat with more concentration, since they might, when I wasn't looking, still be looking at me.[6]

The circumstances are not quite the same, since Soares's father died by suicide and lived far away from his son, but Fernando was self-guarded like the child described, and he probably showed little outward emotion, despite his mother's efforts to draw him out and dispel the gloom. Perhaps he was already using words—silently, in his head—to construct fictional worlds that were more to his liking than reality.

And what did he make of his half-mad grandmother? Unmitigated madness is easier to dismiss, to relegate to the realm of all those things that can't touch us since we can't identify with them. But someone who is half sane, half like us, challenges us to pause and wonder about the crazy half, and about the fact there can be two such different halves, like two persons in one. And Dionísia's mental condition was not a simple dichotomy. She had more than two faces, since even in her "bad" periods she alternated between sullen withdrawal and exalted verbal eruptions. Who or where, in all of this, was the real Dionísia? Or were there various Dionísias, all different from one another yet all valid? For the people who lived with her, including Fernando, she was an unsettling, compelling demonstration that multiple personalities can dwell in one and the same human body.

✦

WHILE THEY HAD NOT spent beyond their means, the Pessoas had lived expansively on the income Joaquim pulled in from his two jobs, supplemented by a monthly contribution from his mother, who had income from savings and a widow's pension. Now, with less money coming in, Maria was forced to downsize. In mid-November she moved with her two children, the two housekeepers, and her ailing mother-in-law into a smaller apartment at Rua de São Marçal, 104, a decent enough building but in a less prestigious neighborhood and without a good view of the Tagus. She took the piano, the table and matching chairs that had belonged to her parents, and enough of the remaining furnishings to comfortably outfit their new quarters. Everything else— including her late husband's books and the fine Chinese porcelain—was sold at auction.[7]

The young widow liked her new home, which was less stately and cozier, and the move helped lighten her spirits. Her mother-in-law, unfortunately, started acting up again in December, shouting incoherently in the middle of the night, but the two boys were both doing well. Jorge, who had reacted badly to a smallpox vaccine in June, now looked strong and happy. He was a cute baby, according to all the relatives. "Jorge is almost eleven months old, and everyone tells me he's very handsome," commented Anica to her sister in a letter written that month from Terceira.

But no sooner had the baby's mother read those words than he fell suddenly and seriously ill—it wasn't clear whether from meningitis or something else.[8] Instead of being able to just relax at all the lunches and dinners organized by her extended family between Christmas and New Year's, Maria Madalena desperately tried to comfort and cure Jorge, closely following the doctor's instructions and wondering how it was possible that so many things could go wrong in her life. At least Fernando was healthy and clever, and knew how to amuse himself when she couldn't give him her full attention. All her effort, however, could do nothing to save Jorge, who died on January 2, 1894. The obituary in the loyal *Diário de Notícias* remarked the obvious: that this would redouble the grief of the family still in mourning over the death, six months earlier, of the paper's longtime music critic.[9]

Maria Nogueira Pessoa, who was pragmatic as well as romantic, had managed to rise above the sorrow of losing her husband, but the fresh loss, this time of her own child, did indeed have a compounding effect, making misfortune loom like a destiny she would never escape from. And there was something besides death that was stalking her. She had left the old apartment and the old neighborhood, but she still had to deal with that weighty, absurd inheritance: old and demented Dionísia, whose only close relatives were her grandson and daughter-in-law. The truth of Maria's situation was even worse, since she depended on her mother-in-law's income to make ends meet.[10]

◆

THEN—AS HAPPENS IN FAIRY tales and also, less often, in real life— her fortune abruptly changed. In that same month of January, while running errands, she boarded one of the open-air, horse-drawn *americanos* that crisscrossed Lisbon. Imported from the United States, these streetcars traveled faster and more smoothly than carriages pulled over uneven, stone-paved roads. (Motorized streetcars, also imported from America, would not begin circulating until 1901.) Seated on one of the car's wooden benches, Maria Madalena watched the storefronts and motley pedestrians slowly slip past. The genteel classes—whose gloves and stylish hats, including plumes for women, were indicators of social status—mixed freely on the streets with the plainly dressed, occasionally barefoot poor. At a certain point she realized that a man sitting across from her on the *americano* was watching her, discreetly but not too: he wanted her to notice that she was being noticed. She eyed him quickly, veered her gaze, then eyed him again. He had a broad forehead and full cheeks, a ruddy complexion, blue eyes, and an English-style moustache, with long whiskers pulled to each side. He must have made a casual remark to start a conversation, soon revealing that he was a ship's captain who had sailed all over the world for the Portuguese navy. How unlike her late husband! She no doubt explained why she was dressed in black, and he responded with the usual condolences. She liked the sound of his voice and his polite yet self-confident manners. His name was João Miguel Rosa.[11] She agreed to meet with him again, probably on the same streetcar—an expedient that Fernando Pessoa would also use, many years later, to rendezvous with a young woman.

The decorum of the day did not allow unaccompanied women to meet with men, and Maria Madalena was a widow still in mourning, which made everything even more complicated. The problem was not only how society might judge her but how *he*, this unexpected suitor, would interpret her every move. According to an old stereotype, widows were likely to be sexually rapacious and quite capable of dominating any man off his guard. So she and the captain proceeded slowly; nonetheless, the attraction was magnetic, and before long they declared to each other their love. Maria's new sweetheart was many things that her first husband was not: close to her in age (four years older instead of eleven), strong and a little husky, outgoing, jovial, and serene. In her mind his whole being radiated serenity and safety. Though not himself an intellectual or a writer, he inspired Maria to write a number of adoring poems, one of which provides the basis for my description of his physical appearance.

Any poems Maria Madalena may have written to her first husband, or to his memory, have not survived.[12] She had been a faithful companion to Joaquim Pessoa and much enamored of him in the beginning, but João Miguel Rosa, the man who would become her second husband, was the great love of her life. How could she justify to the world and to herself such a sudden and passionate attachment? Conventional morality would construe it as a kind of spiritual adultery, since Joaquim had been dead for less than a year. And to marry this gentleman without letting one or two years go by would, according to the same moral logic, count as spiritual bigamy. How, above all, could she tell her mother?

She didn't tell her. The Lisbon relatives, however, quickly learned that Maria had a new romantic interest and encouraged her. Between a first husband whose body had wasted away, a mother-in-law whose mind was disintegrating, and a baby who had been snatched away from her by an uncertain illness, she had suffered more than enough. João Rosa was a solid, likable, and professionally successful individual who stood a good chance of making her happy. His only drawback was the itinerant nature of his work. Where in the far-flung Portuguese empire would he be sent to next? Certain posts in Africa and Asia were considered inhospitable for women, no doubt with good reason. For Fernando they would be even less advisable. He had his father's physique—a little frail, ill suited for strenuous exertions or harsh environments.

◆

BORN IN LISBON IN 1857, João Miguel Rosa joined the Portuguese navy at age fourteen and began his life at sea two years later. After numerous commissions that took him all over the world—to Macau, Angola, Portuguese Guinea, England, South America, and, lastly, Mozambique, where he was part of the Portuguese East Africa fleet— Captain Rosa and his current ship, the *Liberal*, returned for a year to the home country, docking at Lisbon on December 24, 1893. One month later he met Pessoa's mother. He had four or five weeks to woo her before sailing with the *Liberal* up to Porto, where it participated in festivities commemorating the great patron and promoter of Portugal's maritime explorations, Prince Henry the Navigator, born in that city on March 4, 1394, exactly five hundred years earlier. Built in ancient times on the shores of the Douro River, at the point where it empties into the sea, Porto was an important shipping center, like Lisbon, and Rosa's ship, in need of repairs and general maintenance, remained there for six months. This gave the captain plenty of time to continue courting his new darling.

The courtship was a formality, a piece of theater with a foregone conclusion, since they were already sure of each other's love. Maria's mother could sense that romance was in the air, and on March 5, 1894, she wrote her daughter from the Azores that, as a young and attractive widow, she should watch out for her reputation, being careful not to do anything that might raise eyebrows. In April, Maria finally let on that she had a serious boyfriend in a letter to her sister, Anica. Their mother, who was living under the same roof with Anica in Angra do Heroísmo, the capital of Terceira, read the letter and immediately shot off a missive once again warning her widowed daughter to proceed with caution: people would talk if they knew that, a mere nine months after laying her first husband to rest, she already had her eyes on another one. In the mother's opinion, it was too soon for her daughter to take up with another man, but all the relatives in Lisbon had sterling things to say about João Miguel Rosa, whose only obvious character fault—fierce jealousy when another man so much as glanced at Maria—they easily pardoned.[13]

By June it emerged that João Rosa was due for a promotion, from ship's captain to port captain, and Maria's mother and sister suggested he try getting posted at the port of Angra do Heroísmo, a beautiful, well-preserved town that had once been a major port of call for trading vessels sailing between Europe, Africa, and the Americas. Uninhabited when the Portuguese explored and colonized them in the fifteenth century, the Azores were an early success story in Portugal's program of overseas expansion, and Angra was the first settlement in the archipelago elevated to the status of a city. Various Portuguese royals had sojourned or taken refuge there, and the architecture of its historical center reflected the mercantile prosperity of former times. With its temperate climate and with close family members among its residents, Angra would make an ideal home for Fernando. The future groom and bride seemed to be receptive to the idea of moving there. Rosa made some inquiries at the navy's placement office, and Maria asked her mother and Anica about the rental market for houses, but the idea soon faded, at least from the Lisbon side of the epistolary exchange with Terceira. Maria Madalena's mother and sister held out hope.

By mid-September the *Liberal* was once more fit to sail, and for several months it was placed at the service of King Carlos, plying back and forth between Lisbon and the royal palace in nearby Cascais. In November the king issued an official note of commendation for the exemplary performance of Rosa and his crew. Finally, on December 14, 1894, João Rosa received his new title and commission: captain of the Mozambican port of Lourenço Marques (now Maputo).[14] This qualified as one of the "unhealthy posts" that Maria's mother considered unsuitable for ladies,[15] but that did not deter the fiancée, who would probably have followed her captain anywhere in the world—even if it meant leaving her son behind.

Maria sent a telegram to Terceira to announce her imminent marriage and departure overseas, without revealing exactly where she and her husband would be going to live. Madalena Pinheiro Nogueira, who was not yet sixty but had health problems, boarded the next steamer for the mainland, anxious to bid her daughter and grandson farewell. Although the ship was reasonably comfortable, the voyage took five days. Lisbon's port facilities were not yet well developed, so that large vessels usually had to anchor in the Tagus, with passengers and freight being taken to shore in small boats. After her ship had dropped anchor, on the morning of December 28, Maria's mother was surprised to be met by her future son-in-law—like a Portuguese Captain Nemo come to the rescue. Mustering all his considerable charm for the occasion, he introduced himself with a bow, had a sailor from his crew take her luggage, and helped her onto the tender from the *Liberal*. Soon they reached Lisbon's downtown wharf. With such a grand display of gallantry he easily won her over, as he had won over all the Lisbon relatives, some of whom were waiting for her at the wharf, but not Maria, who was sick with the flu. They all went to her apartment, where Fernando was excitedly waiting for his grandmother.[16]

The engaged couple wanted to get married the following month, January 1895, and sail together for Lourenço Marques, but unrest among indigenous peoples from the surrounding areas caused those plans to fizzle. Still without proper sanitation, and with most of its buildings huddled around the port, Lourenço Marques—which had fewer than three thousand inhabitants, about half of whom were Portuguese—was like a frontier town next to the sea, isolated and vulnerable. Portugal had never completely and securely controlled Angola, Portuguese Guinea (now Guinea-Bissau), or Mozambique, its three colonies on the African mainland. For several centuries it had only been interested in controlling trade—of slaves, ivory, and other profitable commodities.

With the end of the slave trade, and given its shrinking position in worldwide trade generally, Portugal slowly changed its African strategy to one of using native labor to extract minerals and grow crops for export. This same model had already been successfully used in Brazil and on the islands of São Tomé and Príncipe, where African slaves mined gold or else cultivated sugar, cocoa, and coffee. (São Tomé and Príncipe, like the Cape Verde Islands, were uninhabited when discovered by the Portuguese, who peopled them with Africans from the mainland and exiled Jews from Portugal.) Although slavery had finally been abolished in Brazil in 1888, exactly one month before Pessoa was born, the use of African labor in conditions sometimes reminiscent of slavery would continue.

In addition to economic considerations, the increasing threat of encroachment by other colonial powers induced the Portuguese to assert more forcefully and visibly their authority over native Africans. This policy met with armed resistance in southern Mozambique, much of which was occupied by the powerful Gaza empire, ruled by King Ngungunhane. A revolt among several Mozambican tribes seemed to have been quelled toward the end of 1894, but on January 7, 1895, three thousand rebels attacked. The rebels killed two white overseers and a number of laborers working on the rail line that led out of Lourenço Marques, connecting it to Pretoria and the Transvaal mines.[17] Surprised by this unexpected show of strength, the Portuguese decided to mobilize more troops and mount a full-scale combat mission against the native insurgents. With Lourenço Marques gearing up for war, it was not by anyone's reckoning a good place for a young European wife to be. On January 17, Maria Madalena aired her disappointment in a letter to her cousin Jaime de Andrade Neves, who was studying medicine in Paris and would eventually become Fernando Pessoa's doctor:

> Mother is here in Lisbon, she came for my wedding, which was supposed to take place this month, but as you've probably heard, I was planning to go to Lourenço Marques, and these recent events, the uprisings of the blacks, have made that impossible, at least for now. I'm devastated, since my fiancé will have to go without me, and the pain of separation is almost too much for my heart to bear. Such is my fate—how can I escape it?[18]

Like virtually everyone else in Portugal and the rest of Europe, Maria Madalena never stopped to wonder about the moral propriety of using whatever means were necessary to impose foreign control over black people's ancestral homelands. Her son would eventually become a critic of Portuguese colonialism, saying it was a symptom of national decadence, but only rarely would he show any concern for the rights and welfare of the colonized.

Captain Rosa departed from Lisbon in mid-February 1895, and eventually he would receive a gold medal for his participation in the campaign to subdue the Mozambican rebels—though he himself bore no arms; his role was logistical. When he assumed his duties as port captain in Lourenço Marques on March 16, his first order of business was to boost the port's capacity to handle the increased traffic of troops and equipment arriving from Europe. This he did by purchasing and transporting barges from the South African ports of Durban and Port Elizabeth, both of which served British colonies. Rosa was expected to remain in Mozambique for at least six months, after which he hoped to obtain a transfer and return to Lisbon between assignments to marry his fiancée. The bride-in-waiting's mother, entrenched in Lisbon, was determined to see her daughter wedded before returning home to the Azores.[19] Good news came in September, when the port captain was tapped to become the next Portuguese consul in Durban, the largest city in the British colony of Natal. Rosa sailed southward from Lourenço Marques on October 3, reaching Durban two days later, and soon thereafter a wedding date was set: December 30, 1895, Maria's thirty-fourth birthday.[20]

Meanwhile the Portuguese forces in Mozambique, tasked with solving the problem of indigenous resistance once and for all, continued to do battle until, in December, they finally captured King Ngungunhane, who was dispatched to the mother country, to be shown off in Lisbon like a trophy, along with his cook, several other men, and seven of his favorite wives. In a reversal of fortunes that must have startled Pessoa's mother, whose plans to go with her beloved to Mozambique had been foiled by the "uprisings of the blacks," the defeated African king was exiled to her hometown, Angra do Heroísmo, where he lived from 1896 until his death ten years later—without any of his wives, since Catholic morality was unwilling to countenance polygamy. He learned to speak, read and write Portuguese, adopted European-style clothing, was baptized by the local bishop, and drank heavily. The seven wives were exiled to São Tomé.[*]

---

[*] Ngungunhane actually had more than two hundred wives, forty of whom lived in his court. When captured, he was allowed to choose seven to go with him into exile, not expecting that they would later be separated from him. Three of the wives died in São Tomé, and the other four were eventually repatriated to Mozambique. See Maria da Conceição Vilhena, "As mulheres do Gungunhana," *Arquipélago-História* (Ponta Delgada), 2nd ser., vol. 3 (1999): 407–16.

# CHAPTER 3

S EEING HIS MOTHER FALL SO PASSIONATELY IN
love was a deeply unsettling experience for Fernando. In late January 1894, six months after his father had died and just a few
weeks after his baby brother's death, there she was lilting about their
home on Rua de São Marçal in a state of at least mild euphoria, which
someone in love cannot help feeling, no matter how many widow's weeds
she may be wearing. It was a strange sight, the more so since he was
initially in the dark about whom she had met and what that man meant
to her. If she mentioned the navy officer at all, it was with feigned nonchalance. The boy may have heard her whispering excitedly to Joana, the
head housekeeper, with whom she had a close rapport, but he had no idea
what it was about. Only after seeing them together a few times would
he realize how special the captain was to his mother, and that did not
happen for a few months. Unless chaperoned, reputable single women
did not receive male visitors, and Maria Madalena, even with a duenna,
did not admit João Rosa into her home until the end of 1894, when
her mother arrived.[1] Budding sweethearts arranged to meet in public
places, or at family gatherings. It was undoubtedly at such a gathering
that Fernando first met the athletic, affable man who would become his
stepfather, but he did not fully understand that his mother was in love
with him until shortly after his sixth birthday, in June. Fernando made
a written note of that momentous, possibly shattering awareness more
than thirty years later, on a sheet of paper correlating planetary conjunc-
tions from his astrological chart with key events in his life.[2]

Pessoa's first biographer, João Gaspar Simões, has been criticized for
molding his subject into a too rigidly Freudian tale of personal development. An early chapter of that tale has young Fernando competing with
João Miguel Rosa for his mother's affection, which was surely the case.[3]
He could not have acted any differently. Now that he had lost his father
and only sibling, his mother had gone from being the privileged to the

almost exclusive object of his own tender love. The elderly housekeepers kept the boy company when she was absent, but their attention was a poor substitute for hers. Indeed he might have preferred to play on his own, to read, which he could already do quite well, to go places in his imagination, and to brood. Any normal child in Fernando's situation would react with jealousy to this newcomer who had the capacity to alter his mother's mood in ways he himself never could. And Fernando Pessoa, despite his sometimes idiosyncratic social behavior, had perfectly normal emotional reactions.

The only problem with Gaspar Simões's reading on this particular point was that he overemphasized it—as if Fernando's jealousy were somehow out of the ordinary, or as if he nurtured actively homicidal thoughts toward his rival. A vague thought of slipping some rat poison into the captain's coffee may have sprung up in the boy's effervescent imagination, but João Rosa went out of his way to win over Fernando, and before long they were friends, getting on well together. So wrote Maria to her relations in Terceira, no doubt with exaggerated optimism, seeing problem-free harmony where there was strategic accommodation and reluctant acceptance—the normal stuff of human relations operating under strain.[4]

Less normal was Fernando's intellectual response to all that had happened in recent months—the two family deaths, the change of address, and the changes in his mother, from listless and dejected to lively and cheerful, full of restless energy. While it is odd, and perhaps not strictly correct, to use the word "intellectual" with respect to a five- or six-year-old boy, Fernando, besides reacting to events on an emotional level, was already responding to them as a thinker, contemplating them from a distance, observing specific behaviors—his and other people's—and extrapolating to arrive at more general rules of human conduct. And underlying all human behavior, he learned very early, was an instinctive drive to survive, to keep going—what Schopenhauer, a philosopher he would come to admire years later, characterized as blind will, blind striving. No less strange for Fernando than the fact that things end, including things as enormous and profound as his father's soul, was the fact that life continues, inexorably. His mother had already found another husband to replace the one she had lost. As for little Jorge, Aunt Anica pointed out in a letter sent to her sister several weeks after the baby's death that the poor creature was consumptive, and had God allowed him to survive it would have meant a "perpetual torment" for both child and mother until the inescapable end arrived, so just as well he died now. And Anica went on, naturally enough, to tell about her own two children—Mário with his new boots and Maria with her new baby shoes.[5]

Pessoa's writings refer repeatedly to the unique suffering of a mother who loses a son. They also mention how quickly that suffering is bound to pass and the son's memory fade into the dull background of conscious thought. A tragicomic, undated poem signed by the heteronym Álvaro de Campos tells of a family that, thanks to a tidy sum of insurance money, laughs and celebrates after the mother's baby is run over by a car and killed.

> Thus an entire house was wallpapered.
> Thus the last installment on the furniture was paid.
> Poor baby.
> But if it hadn't been run over, who would pay the bills?[6]

Even without insurance money, humanity, according to *The Book of Disquiet*, "keeps on eating and loving, weeping over only what it must weep, and for as short a time as possible—over the death of a son, for instance, who is soon forgotten except on his birthday." Another passage in the same book notes how easily a mother who loses her son "laughs and is back to normal in a few months' time."[7] And a Campos poem from 1929 turns that theoretical mother into a specific one:

> The lady who lives at #14 was laughing today at the door
> Where a month ago her little boy was carried out in a coffin.
> She laughed naturally, wholeheartedly,
> And she's right: life goes on.
> Grief doesn't last because grief doesn't last.[8]

The building number, 14, is suspiciously similar to the 104 of the street address where Fernando lived with his widowed mother. She was the lady who laughed while still mourning. Within a month after tiny Jorge's death, Maria was too filled with bliss over her love for the captain to have any heart left for grief.

Despite the sarcasm of the Campos poem about the lucratively dead baby, Pessoa never reproached his mother for not remaining a widow and bereaved mother, mournfully "faithful" to the memories of her husband and her second son. At the age of five or six, it would not yet have occurred to Pessoa that his mother was fallible; once he had grown up, he judged her behavior to be typically human, and healthy: "And she's right: life goes on." Nor was his own behavior essentially different. He was not a mourner. He moved on, albeit more slowly and reluctantly. It bothered him that he moved, that everyone moved, and nothing stayed in one place or one state for long.

A year or so after the losses of his father and brother, what Fernando felt was probably not classifiable as grief. It was more like bewilderment, as if, obscurely, the rapid turn of events and feelings, particularly those he noted in his mother after she met Captain João Rosa, had led him to wonder: "Is there anything sacred? Is anything permanent?" These were questions he would ask outright as he got older. The first one, which was harder to decide on, motivated his spiritual search. The answer to the second question, which was a definite no, would prompt several sets of additional questions. On the one hand: "How can something be and then stop being? If something stops being, did it ever have true being to begin with?" And conversely: "How can something not be and then suddenly be? Did it have some sort of pre-being? Is the potential to exist already a form of existence?" In 1894 all of this questioning was still inchoate, of course, but the urge to question was strong, goading him to learn more words, more grammar, and more concepts, along with the art of combining them into precision tools for exploring and expressing.

✦

TWO STUDIO PORTRAITS OF Fernando at around age six show a boy who looks misplaced, as if he no longer belonged to childhood. In a photograph of him posing on a tricycle, he looks at the camera with an air of befuddlement, as if he doesn't understand where he is, or why. In a head shot from the same session, his expression is disturbingly serious—not exactly sad, but sullen, preoccupied.[9] Yet in spite of his adultishly pensive manner, Fernando was still a child, and he enjoyed being one. He was fond of reading but also of playing: with balls, tin soldiers, and other toys. He especially liked board games—and he would invent some of his own as a teenager and adult. In the fall of 1894, his mother mentioned in a letter to her family that he was doing "very well in his lessons,"[10] which he may have received in a schoolroom, but it is more likely that she or a private teacher gave him lessons at home. And she had probably helped him learn how to read, though he claimed to have taught himself.[11]

Pessoa's great-aunt Maria also contributed to his early education. Fernando often stayed with her and her husband—known in the family as Uncle Cunha—at their house in Pedrouços on the western edge of Lisbon, where he had his own bedroom, full of toys, and a backyard to play in. He would later describe this great-aunt as a cultivated woman in the style of the eighteenth century—"skeptical about religion, aristocratic and a royalist, and not admitting skepticism in the masses"—and he left a copy of one of her sonnets that he knew by heart.[12] The final tercet reads:

> Know that in my soul, for many years now,
> A true and intimate disbelief
> Has made the whole world a desert for me.

This aridity seems to confirm Pessoa's assertion that she had little "female tenderness," but he also noted that he was the privileged recipient of her affections. In fact both she and Uncle Cunha treated Fernando like a prince.

Whereas his wife fostered the boy's intellectual development, Uncle Cunha, a gregarious fellow, liked to take Fernando along when running errands or making the rounds to visit friends. One of their regular stopping places was the newsroom of the *Correio da Noite*, the official paper of the Progressive Party, which Cunha fervently supported. As the staff of journalists drafted the stories that would be published late that afternoon, he talked with them about the day's events and showed off his grandnephew, whom they adopted as a kind of mascot. They showed him how copy was produced in columns and how pages were laid out for printing. Completely fascinated, Fernando stored away what he learned for future use.

Uncle Cunha, who spent long hours playing games with Fernando at Pedrouços, also introduced him to a more visceral entertainment: bullfights at Campo Pequeno. The *corrida* in Portugal had by then developed into the spectacle it is today, rather different from the one practiced in Spain. After first being stabbed in the back by a set of *bandarilhas*, which are like the Spanish *banderillas*, the weakened bull faces eight unarmed, unprotected men known as *forcados*, one of whom will grab the head of the charging animal, holding on tight while the others bring it down. The bull is not killed in the ring, making the spectacle less gruesome to watch but no less painful for the wounded creature, which is taken to a slaughterhouse, where it will endure, in all likelihood, more suffering than if it had been killed quickly. In Portugal as in Spain, the *corrida* is associated with a subculture that prizes national traditions, family pedigree, bravery, honor, the noble gesture, and manliness. Though they didn't necessarily belong to the subculture, a number of Pessoa's maternal relatives were aficionados of the *corrida*, a popular pastime on the island of Terceira. Pessoa did not become a fan.

Music was more to Fernando's liking. With Uncle Cunha, and sometimes Aunt Maria, he attended concerts and the opera, which might seem a bit much for a small boy, but in those days opera was a form of popular entertainment, and even adult spectators were not always well behaved. They might have ongoing conversations or even play cards while a diva was reaching the high notes of an aria. If she was good, they might also roar with applause. When he was six and a half, Pessoa's uncle took him to an Italian opera that a reviewer for a Lisbon paper declared to be virtually inaudible. "So loud was the hubbub and the shouting of the audience that no one could tell what was being sung, except vaguely."[13]

Thanks to Aunt Maria and Uncle Cunha, no less than to his own parents, Fernando was raised with an unusually large amount of culture—literature and music but also bullfighting, journalism, and politics. More important, for his future development, was this great-uncle's talent and fondness for making up elaborate stories that imitated and ran parallel to real life, like serial dramas that keep on going, with no end in sight. One of the stories involved Fernando running for office to become the representative of an imaginary town. It was a story that for Pessoa would continue, astonishingly, into young adulthood, when he used a mimeograph to produce a couple of "newspapers" linked to make-believe political parties and filled with facetious reportage on the activities of "Congressman" Pessoa and various cousins and family friends converted into pseudo-politicians.[14]

◆

**BY THE TIME THEY** reach puberty, most children lose the ability to believe, or to passionately act *as if* they believed, in things they know are unreal. That was not the case for the future inventor of heteronyms, descendants from a long line of literary alter egos that he traced back to his early childhood. Pessoa wrote two accounts of how the heteronyms evolved. The first dates from the late 1920s:

> Ever since I was a child, I've felt the need to enlarge the world with fictitious personalities—dreams of mine that were carefully crafted, envisaged with photographic clarity, and fathomed to the depths of their souls. When I was just five years old, an isolated child and quite content to be isolated, I already enjoyed the company of certain characters from my dreams, including a Captain Thibeaut, the Chevalier de Pas, and various others whom I've forgotten, and whose forgetting—like my imperfect memory of the two I just named—is one of my life's great regrets.
>
> This may seem merely like a child's imagination that gives life to dolls. But it was more than that. I intensely conceived those characters with no need of dolls. Distinctly visible in my ongoing dream, they were utterly human realities for me, which any doll—because unreal—would have spoiled. They were people.[15]

These "carefully crafted" dreams featuring two Frenchmen were, of course, daydreams, which together formed an "ongoing dream" as vivid and satisfying as life itself, which is why the boy could feel "quite content" being "an isolated child." Or was it Pessoa's retrospective explanation of his daydreaming that was carefully crafted, and injected with hyperbole? The people and situations of our *sleeping* dreams can make our heart race, strike us with terror, excite us sexually, or instill in us a religious peace. Pessoa would have us believe that his waking dreams were similarly realistic and emotionally powerful. Maybe they were. Harder to believe is that their power to compete with reality not only continued, it increased to the point of redefining his reality:

> And instead of ending with my childhood, this tendency expanded in my adolescence, taking firmer root with each passing year, until it became my natural way of being. Today I have no personality: I have divided all my humanness among the various authors whom I've served as literary executor. Today I am the meeting-place of a small humanity that belongs only to me.

Pessoa's second explanation of the genesis of the heteronyms is from 1935. It states that the Chevalier de Pas emerged when he was six years old, rather than five, and that the knight had a kind of rival whose similarly foreign name he could no longer remember—presumably Captain Thibeaut, mentioned in the earlier account. Inspired by adventure stories, and with the collaboration of his playful uncle Cunha, Fernando apparently pitted the knight against the captain in fantastic combat. More significantly, the six-year-old reportedly wrote letters to himself in the name of the knight, thus initiating a lifelong practice of writing *as someone else*. The French *pas* can mean either "not" or "footstep," and scholars have speculated about exactly what young Fernando had in mind for the Chevalier de Pas—whether he was a knight on the go or the Knight of No. Probably nothing so consciously elaborated. Like Thibeaut, de Pas is a surname that he might have come across in one of his father's books, many of which were in French. But the most likely origin of the Chevalier was Uncle Cunha's fertile imagination.

No letters from the imaginary French knight have survived, but Fernando inscribed his name in *The Floral Birthday Book*, a Victorian creation that belonged to his mother and now belongs to the Casa Fernando Pessoa.* For each day of the year there is an engraved flower, a short poem, and space for entering the names of friends and relatives born on that day. Among the many names in the book neatly recorded by Maria Madalena are two registers, for July 1 and again for July 11, in the childish script of her small son: "Cavalier de pá" and "le Chavalier de pá." These are the oldest surviving examples of Pessoa's handwriting, dating from 1894 or 1895.

Pessoa did not make extravagant, mystical claims for his incipient heteronymy. His invented companions were imagined and experienced with an intensity unusual even for a child ("they were utterly human realities for me"), and to write letters to oneself in someone else's name is an unusual activity at any age. But many children before and after Fernando Pessoa have conversed and spent time with friends who are purely mental fabrications, without any accompanying doll or other physical prop, and it's unusual but perhaps not extraordinary for a boy who sees

* A museum, library, and cultural center, the Casa occupies the building where Pessoa lived during the last fifteen years of his life.

his mother constantly writing and receiving letters—a steady stream of them flowed between Maria Madalena Pessoa and her family in the Azores—to imitatively write and receive his own. It was the irrepressible Uncle Cunha, however, who directly inspired and fostered Fernando's imaginary universe. Besides inventing make-believe politicians, aristocrats, and military men, this elderly relative regaled his great-nephew with tales of international wars between humanized crickets, beetles, ants, and monkeys. Fernando did not just sit and listen; he helped invent the characters and their deeds.

Posterity was unkind to the memory of Manuel Gualdino da Cunha. João Gaspar Simões, in his biography from 1950, reported that this jovial fellow was well liked among all the relatives but practically illiterate, to the point of almost having to sign documents with an X. This thumbnail portrayal, the second half of which was completely erroneous, was offered to the biographer by Pessoa's half sister, who never met Uncle Cunha but who heard all about him from Fernando. Perhaps Pessoa was responsible for leading her into error. He owed a lot to this great-uncle and may have wanted to conceal his debt. In 1914 Pessoa explained to a friend interested in his early literary influences that Aunt Maria, Cunha's wife, was an intellectual and wrote poetry, but he never told anyone about how Uncle Cunha took him to the opera and introduced him to the behind-the-scenes world of journalism. When he later revealed that a Captain Thibeaut and a Chevalier de Pas had enlivened his solitary childhood, he neglected to mention that they were part of a world of let's pretend constructed with the help of his uncle. The crucial role of this man for the development of Pessoa and his para-universe of fictional personalities came to light only in the twenty-first century, when the poet's niece, Manuela Nogueira, found and published some of Uncle Cunha's letters to Fernando.[16]

◆

**ALONGSIDE THE INVISIBLE WORLD** of his made-up characters, Fernando had tangible dolls and tin soldiers that he talked to and put into action, christening some of them with names. And during Carnival he himself, like other Portuguese children, would dress up and become someone exotic. When he was five going on six he was a Spanish lady, and the next year a Zouave—complete with breeches, sword, knapsack, musket, and moustache. It was his mother who sewed his costumes and decked him out. Being in love with the captain did not make her less dedicated to her son. Although she did not give him formal piano lessons, she taught him to tap out some simple melodies and let him make whatever music he could. In the summer months she took him to the countryside and to the beach, so that he could breathe fresh air and bathe in seawater, which was supposed to stimulate bodily functions and help stave off diseases. When, at the age of seven, he started to collect postage stamps, she relayed his request for old and rare issues to the relatives on Terceira.

Fernando's mother and her sister, Anica, sent each other parcels as well as letters by the twice-monthly steamers connecting the Azores with the mainland. Maria Madalena posted clothing, shoes, and hats. From Terceira she received shipments of butter, various kinds of sausage, oranges, and other foods. Fernando specifically asked for, and received, sweet potatoes.[17]

While Fernando was particularly fond of board games, playing cards, and reading, he had nothing against playing outside. In the partly autobiographical poem that concludes "Chuva oblíqua" ("Slanting Rain"), a sequence dating from 1914, the reminiscing narrator recalls tossing a ball against a garden wall. This would have been at the house of his great-aunt Maria and great-uncle Cunha, in Pedrouços. There are family photos of the boy, his mother, and assorted female relatives—no other children—posing on the house's back porch, with the garden behind them. Uncle Cunha was the likely photographer.

Fernando had three other great-aunts besides Maria.* All were born and raised in the Azores but ended up in Lisbon. There was a by then old tradition of people leaving those remote islands to try for a better life elsewhere. Large numbers of Azoreans had resettled in Brazil, responding to the demand for colonists in the seventeenth and eighteenth centuries. Smaller numbers immigrated to New England, where the first Azoreans to put down roots worked on whaling ships from New Bedford and Nantucket. Melville, in *Moby-Dick*, remarked that whalers often stopped at the Azores to fill out their crews with "the hardy peasants of those rocky shores." Poverty, stemming from the islands' isolation

---

* The four great-aunts—Rita, Maria, Carolina, and Adelaide—were sisters to Madalena, Pessoa's maternal grandmother. The sisters had one brother, who had immigrated to Brazil.

and the periodic blights that ravaged crops, was the main driver behind migratory waves, which also took the islanders to California, Bermuda, and Hawaii. Better-off Azoreans such as Pessoa's maternal forebears had little incentive to join these mass movements, but they often left home to pursue university studies in Coimbra or Paris and to forge their careers in places with more opportunities. A few went to Brazil, but a more frequent destination was the Portuguese mainland.

The majority of Fernando's maternal relatives—his great-aunts, the men they married, and their children—were living in Lisbon, and he saw nearly all of them on a regular basis, but his cousins Mário and Maria, who were the only relatives close to him in age, grew up in the Azores. And so his companions in Lisbon were mostly adults, and not just any adults. The men all stood out in their chosen professions, and the women were unusually well-educated homemakers. The boy had to be on his toes to keep up with the conversation. Almost as a matter of social survival, he developed the capacity for processing and responding to other people's ideas at an age when other children are still learning how to verbally exchange basic information and immediate feelings. What he did not learn was to interact with people his own age, which would have meant relying on instinct rather than intelligence. It's as if his ability to consider, reflect, and reason were acquired at the expense of spontaneous expression.

# CHAPTER 4

○☒○☒○☒○☒○☒○☒○☒○☒○☒○☒○☒○☒○

T
HE GATHERING SCANDAL KNOWN AS THE DREYFUS
affair became a cause célèbre in December 1894, when Alfred
Dreyfus, a Jewish captain in the French army, was convicted
on flimsy evidence of treason. For the next twelve years, until he was
exonerated, defenders of the captain's innocence—and of secular republican values such as religious tolerance—pitted themselves against right-
wing Catholics whose passions were stirred up by blatantly antisemitic
rhetoric. In its ongoing coverage of the acrimonious war of words in
France, the Portuguese press, particularly republican newspapers, consistently took the side of Dreyfus and denounced French antisemitism.
But despite the absence of an anti-Jewish movement in fin de siècle Portugal, a sharp divide was growing, there as in France, between anticlerical republicans and Catholic traditionalists.[1]

Pessoa's mother, an apathetic traditionalist, lately paid even less attention to politics than usual. That same December when Dreyfus was
wrongly convicted, she was busy making plans for her imminent wedding and new life in Mozambique, looking through her wardrobe to
decide what clothes she would pack for the warmer climate and pondering whether she should sell her furniture or put it in storage. The thought
of starting all over again, in a different country with a different sort of
husband, must have been a little intoxicating, but the dreamy prospect
was intermittently interrupted by a dark consideration: she felt she could
not risk taking her adored son to Africa, and she hated the thought of
going without him. Fernando had been lucky not to contract tuberculosis, and his health was generally good, but his spindly frame made him
more susceptible than most to flus and colds. How would he react to
tropical fevers? She was too afraid to find out. In a letter sent to her sister, Anica, on January 4, 1895, one week after their mother had arrived
at Lisbon from Terceira and three weeks after João Miguel Rosa was

named captain of the port of Lourenço Marques, she was decided about what had to be done:

> Fernando will go to the island with Mom. Mindful of the fact that this poor innocent has no father and will live far away from his mother for a long time, treat him like another son, and I'm sure he'll be as affectionate as if he really were yours. You can't imagine how hard it is for me to be separated from the boy. The pain is so strong and so deep that I don't know how I'll bear it. I suppose that God, who has given me courage for everything, will give me courage to endure this new blow, which will surely subtract years from my life. For me things never go completely right.

Grandma Madalena, in her own, contemporaneous letter to Anica, claimed that Fernando was excited about going back with her to the Azores, which strains credulity. If he showed a little excitement, it was because they didn't tell him that the separation from his mother was likely to last for years. Aunt Maria and Uncle Cunha were pushing for the boy to live with them, which Grandma Madalena thought was a terrible idea. She felt they spoiled him too much, and they probably did. When Fernando visited the aging couple in Pedrouços, his indulgent great-aunt was known to say, "Everything in this house is yours, you can play and break what you like."[2] Growing up in Anica's family, Fernando would receive loving care but also some needed discipline, as Madalena explained to her older daughter.

If indigenous Mozambicans had not chosen that moment to take up arms against the Portuguese colonizers, obliging Pessoa's mother to postpone her marriage and departure to Africa, then Fernando Pessoa might have spent the rest of his childhood on the island of Terceira, in which case the rest of this story would be very different, or, more likely, there would be no story to merit a biography. Not only genes but also myriad contributions from one's surroundings all combine to shape one of those rarely occurring specimens known as a genius. But behind a genius's genetic endowments and the accidents of time and place, might there be higher forces at work? Might genius, after all, be a matter of destiny? This was a question that pestered Pessoa when he got older, like a housefly he could neither catch nor shoo away. It famously comes up in the sixth stanza of what many consider to be his greatest poem, "The Tobacco Shop":

> Genius? At this moment
> A hundred thousand brains are dreaming they're geniuses
>     like me,
> And it may be that history won't remember even one,
> All of their imagined conquests amounting to so much dung.
> No, I don't believe in me.
> Insane asylums are full of lunatics with certainties!
> Am I, who have no certainties, more right or less right?
> No, not even in me . . .
> In how many garrets and non-garrets of the world
> Are self-convinced geniuses at this moment dreaming?

The poem was signed by never inhibited Álvaro de Campos, the heteronym Pessoa resorted to when he had something shocking to say or embarrassing to talk about—in this case, his own feeling of genius. I wonder, however, whether this professed self-doubt applies to anyone but Campos himself. Elsewhere Pessoa, writing under his own name and in English, called genius "the greatest curse that the Gods bless us with," and he obviously considered himself to be one of the blessed. The blessing was a curse because of the responsibility it entailed. "What man of genius is one who is not haunted by a sense of a mission?" the poet rhetorically scribbled, again in English, on the back of an envelope dating from 1910.[3] A man of genius who believes his gift comes from God, or from the gods, might naturally feel himself morally obliged to use it on behalf of others, but it is also possible that Pessoa's missionary zeal contributed to the formation of his genius, without which his mission could not be carried out. In fact, the zeal was already firmly in place in his late teens, when the genius was still maturing. Pessoa's genius, according to this line of thought, might have resulted from an ardent necessity, from a *will* to genius.

✦

FERNANDO PESSOA'S FIRST LITERARY composition was not an obvious indicator of future genius, but it did show how *ingenious* he was for a boy who had just turned seven. Although his mother's Africa plans had been postponed, she was still committed to going there—or to wherever else her fiancé might be posted—and she still had in mind sending her son to the Azores to live with Aunt Anica and his cousins Mário and Maria. Wouldn't that be better than subjecting him to a completely unfamiliar place, possibly rife with tropical diseases? This was a matter she occasionally discussed with her mother, who would continue to live with her until the end of 1895, and probably with her son as well, explaining to him the difficulties of life overseas, especially for a little boy. Fernando was not convinced. On July 26 he walked up to his mother, hands behind his back. She was fond of French novels and might have been reading one when, interrupted by her son, she looked up and smiled. "Yes, dear?" Just a few strands of white hair were faintly visible in her somewhat unruly curls, but her skin was still perfectly smooth, her gaze as soulful as ever.[4] Looking bashfully at the floor, then at her, he recited:

### *To My Dear Mother*

Here I am in Portugal,
The land where I was born.
However much I love it,
I love you even more.

As any normal mother would do, she hugged her brilliant little boy and told him not to worry, she loved him so much. She copied down the quatrain on a slip of paper and dated it, converting her son's words into a written entreaty, which she could not ignore. Though part of her still wavered, the boy's will prevailed. Together they would set sail (as they learned several months later) for the town of Durban, on the eastern seaboard of South Africa, where Fernando would always feel a little out of place, there but not all there, irremediably foreign. Strange soil, it turned out, was exactly what he needed for his kind of genius to flower.

João Miguel Rosa assumed his duties as Portugal's consul in Durban on October 5, 1895. His new home lay only 350 miles south of Lourenço Marques, but how different! Durban had ten times more people, excellent port facilities, attractively laid out streets, English efficiency, and an assured air of prosperity. The town was not entirely new to Rosa, for in July 1893, when still a captain in the Portuguese East African fleet, he had sailed there with the *Liberal* and stayed for a whole month, rather longer than he was supposed to. The delay was due to the failure of the then Portuguese consul to promptly issue the bill of health needed for his vessel to return to Lourenço Marques. In fact, one of the major duties of the consulate in Durban was to provide ships bound for Portuguese ports with all the necessary paperwork. Besides issuing bills of health, which certified that the port of departure was free of contagious diseases and that no crew member had visible signs of disease, the consulate had to authenticate bills of lading and passenger lists. Delayed departures could be very costly, and after a string of short-lived consuls who did not excel at this part of their job, the Foreign Ministry decided to try out a ship's captain and port administrator with enormous practical experience in maritime matters.[5]

◆

ON DECEMBER 30, 1895, the long-desired, long-delayed wedding between Pessoa's mother and João Miguel Rosa finally took place in Lisbon at the baroque Church of Our Lady of Mercy—without the groom. It was yet another blow to the weary bride, who had dreamed of wearing a fancy dress made of black velvet for the occasion, but since the captain-turned-consul could not make a trip home so soon after taking up his new post, she had to settle for a wedding ceremony with his older brother, a gentleman with wild eyes and a walrus moustache whom she hardly knew, serving as proxy.[6] This older brother, in other words, legally represented the groom, taking all the romance out of the occasion. A military officer himself, but an army man, Henrique was also a poet and intellectual, full of curiosity about philosophical questions, life's origins and meaning, evolutionary theory, and new political movements such as socialism, anarchism, and republicanism. He would become an important influence on Fernando, who at this point knew nothing about the man, though he must have been impressed by the piercing intensity of the officer's eyes.

Satisfied to see her daughter remarried to a man of good standing, Madalena Pinheiro Nogueira sailed home to Terceira on January 5. Her sojourn in Lisbon had lasted a full year, drawing her much closer to Fernando, her oldest grandchild, now seven and a half. She could not disagree that it was better, after all, for him to go with his mother to Africa rather than return with her to the Azores, but would she ever see him again? It would depend on her precarious health. The parting was probably even sadder for Fernando. Whereas Madalena had other grandchildren, Mário and Maria, waiting for her in Terceira, his other grandmother, Dionísia, inhabited a world all her own, accessible to no one else. At this point she was not even in the apartment on Rua de São Marçal. She had been admitted to Rilhafoles, Lisbon's mental hospital, on May 3, 1895, after the neighbors warned that something had to be done or they would take matters into their own hands. The ranting had become so loud that, one night in April, Fernando's mother and the two housekeepers had to take Dionísia from her bedroom and tie her down to a chair in the living room. His mother was kicked and bruised in the process.

After two months in the hospital, Dionísia was released, but the fits of uncontrollable screaming resumed, and she was readmitted on September 3. This time she would stay for over a year, with Pessoa's great-aunt Maria looking after her needs and managing her finances. While Dionísia received more than enough money from her widow's pension and investment income to cover her hospital bills and other expenses, Aunt Maria was an especially careful administrator, doing all she could to make the modest estate grow for the benefit of the only heir who would be entitled to it: Fernando Pessoa. In November 1896 Aunt Maria would bring Grandma Dionísia to live with her and Uncle Cunha at their home in Pedrouços, where Aunt Rita—the only great-aunt who never married—was by then also living.[7]

Maria Madalena Nogueira Rosa, as she now signed herself, put her piano and other furniture in storage, gave some things away, sold others, and on January 20, 1896, she and Fernando and Uncle Cunha—who accompanied them on the long voyage—were ready to depart on the SS *Funchal*, bound for Madeira, where they would continue their southward journey on a steamer originating from England. It was cool but not cold, a good day for setting sail. A number of Lisbon relatives—Great-aunts Rita, Maria, Carolina, and Adelaide, assorted cousins and spouses—came aboard to say their goodbyes to the three voyagers. Uncle Cunha was coming back soon enough, but it might be years before Fernando and his mother returned to Portugal. They would keep in touch through letters, being sure to inscribe "via London" on the envelope (otherwise, the missives could go astray), and it was important to send photos, especially of Fernando, since children at that age change so quickly. No doubt it

would be a wonderful learning experience for the boy. But as the relatives chattered, someone suddenly noticed that Fernando was nowhere
in sight, and a brief moment of panic ensued. They glanced up and down
the decks, then searched inside the ship and, to their great relief, found
him sprawled out on his berth in the cabin, concentratedly trying to
work out a word game from a newspaper or a puzzle book.[8] They might
have guessed. Since there was no one to play with, he had snuck off to
entertain himself with words—his ever dependable companions. More
than any of the people he would meet or the things he would see during
his South African experience, Fernando would treasure the new world of
words opened up to him by the English language.

◆

FERNANDO PESSOA'S VERY FIRST lines of poetry, in the quatrain
to his "Dear Mother," don't stand out for their poetic quality, even taking into account the tender age of their author, but they are remarkable
for the patriotic sentiment they embody. Even if some seven-year-olds
already have a clear idea of what constitutes a country, very few feel an
affective attachment to one. True, those four lines were born out of an
agenda, with Fernando's declared love of Portugal serving to accentuate
the much greater love he felt for his mother. But love of country was
a concept he fully understood and a feeling he had already embraced,
thanks to his politically passionate uncle Cunha. Neither of Pessoa's parents was especially interested in politics, even if they read the newspaper
and kept up with national and world affairs. As an adult, Pessoa was far
better informed than they had ever been, often digesting three or four
newspapers in a day. Yet he was apt to be indifferent to the world events
that filled the front page—unless they impinged directly on Portugal.
He would write, in *The Book of Disquiet*: "I've never thought twice about
anything tragic that has happened in China. It's just scenery in the distance, even if painted with blood and disease."[9]

Pessoa felt a deeply emotional connection to Portugal, making it fair
to call him a nationalist. But his nationalism was more about amelio-
rating than celebrating. His political writings—including a number of
articles published in newspapers and magazines—criticized Portugal's
governing class, its provincialism, and its tendency to rely on foreign
ideas instead of native ingenuity to find a way forward. The one book of
poems in Portuguese he published, *Mensagem* (*Message*), was a plea to the

nation to search its own history for the virtues and lessons that could help it emerge from its chronic state of anemia, which persisted even in periods of political and economic upheaval. Pessoa's was not a lonely voice in the desert. Most writers of his generation felt duty bound to address the "problem" of Portugal and to take some sort of political stand. Pessoa lived during the most politicized and turbulent period of modern Portuguese history, marked by traumatic transitions from monarchy to republic and from republic to dictatorship, which inevitably shaped both his writing and his personal trajectory. When he was an infant still learning how to talk, such thoroughgoing changes in Portugal's governing system were almost unimaginable, but then suddenly seemed possible and even likely, thanks to a diplomatic disaster that rocked the monarchy like a new, virtual earthquake: the British Ultimatum of 1890.

Pessoa was born at the end of a decades-long stretch of unusual political stability in Portugal. The constitutional monarchy—in place since 1822, but interrupted in 1828–1834 by a civil war—had settled into a system known as "rotativism," with power seesawing between two major political formations. In the late nineteenth century it was the Progressive Party and the Regenerator Party that alternately controlled parliament, while the House of Braganza continued to fill the throne, as it had been doing since 1640. King Luís I, a man of science—he used part of his fortune to promote oceanographic research—and a translator of Shakespeare into Portuguese, died in October 1889, after a mostly calm and uneventful reign. He was succeeded by his twenty-six-year-old son, crowned King Carlos I. That was when everything began to fall apart, although through no particular fault of the new monarch. Along with the crown, he had inherited the problems and challenges of the Portuguese colonies. Poorly secured and administered, they were not a very profitable source of revenue, and soon they would become a source of deep mortification, about which King Carlos could do nothing except try to limit the damage.

The legally sanctioned enslavement of Africans, once promoted or at least condoned by most of Europe as well as the United States, was now sanctimoniously condemned by all, but foreign control of African lands and resources was acceptable and even commendable, insofar as it meant "developing" and "civilizing." Germany was a relative newcomer to Africa, and it was at the invitation of its chancellor, Otto von Bismarck, that Europe's colonial powers had recently met in Berlin to divvy up the south-lying continent or, more exactly, to draw up a joint certificate of approval and agreement as to who actually controlled what, or had the legitimate right to control it. Delegates from thirteen European nations and the United States attended the Berlin Conference, which opened in November 1884 at Bismarck's official residence. After three months of haggling, the participating nations signed the Berlin Act, which defined European spheres of influence and recognized only a small handful of African nations—including, with notable irony, Liberia, a country colonized by ex-slaves from America—as safely independent.

The Portuguese, who boasted five of the oldest colonial possessions in Africa, also claimed commercial rights over the Congo River basin, based on the fact that they were the first Europeans to explore it, in the fifteenth century; but since they did not effectively occupy it, the conference balked. The requirement of effective, physical occupation to achieve international recognition of colonial claims also cast a menacing shadow over the so-called Pink Map, which featured a roughly horizontal band of pink stretching from Portuguese West Africa (Angola) to Portuguese East Africa (Mozambique) and including the land in between, equivalent to most of modern-day Zambia, Zimbabwe, and Malawi. In these parts, too, the Portuguese had arrived first but had no fixed settlements. Their pretension to a vast colony running from the Atlantic to the Indian Ocean was rejected by the United Kingdom, which had its own interests to defend. Nevertheless, a year after the conference ended, in 1886, Portugal managed to get France and Germany to sign individual treaties that recognized its claim to the impressive swath of territory delimited by the Pink Map, which was officially published that same year.

The word for "pink" in Portuguese is *cor-de-rosa*, literally rose-colored, and it was as if the nation's entire political culture were viewing southern Africa through rose-colored glasses. There were a few dissenters, who noted the unlikelihood of Britain's coming around on the issue, as well as the practical difficulty of small and poorish Portugal trying to administer so much territory and to extract material advantages from it. But the majority accepted the argument that Portuguese Africa—in this new, enlarged pink version—could become another Brazil, which had been a great boon to the nation's coffers. Besides material considerations, there was the matter of prestige. Here was pint-sized Portugal playing in the same league as Britain and France, far outpacing Spain in what came to be known, all too aptly, as the "scramble for Africa."[10] Without the slightest compunction—as if indigenous Africans were just part of the landscape, local prey to be slaughtered or subdued—colonial powers now rushed in to secure their claims and grab whatever chunks of unclaimed territory could still be found.

Seeking to comply with the criterion of physical occupation established at the Berlin Conference, Portugal sent military expeditions into the region between Angola and Mozambique. One such expedition ventured into the lands along the Shire River, in what is now Malawi, making treaties and offering Portuguese flags to a number of local chiefs. It was an area where David Livingstone (1813–1873) and other Scottish missionaries had spread Christianity and where British businessmen, linked to the missionaries, actively negotiated with African ivory hunters. Although Britain had not yet annexed this area, it opposed any attempt by Portugal to assert its sovereignty there. In August 1889 the British consul-general for the region warned the Portuguese expeditioners not to penetrate farther, but soon they did, clashing in November with the Makololo tribe, which was under nominal British protection. The indigenous forces were defeated, allowing the expedition to proceed northward on the Shire, and Portugal celebrated the victory.

Great Britain, embroiled in a fierce competition with France and Germany to expand its control in the southern continent, both for strategic as well as economic reasons, did not take kindly to the impudent behavior of politically insignificant Portugal. English newspapers called for retaliatory action, and on January 11, 1890, after concentrating some of its powerful navy near key ports along the African coast, the British government issued an ultimatum: Portugal had to immediately withdraw all its forces from the Shire region and two other disputed territories. If it did not accede to the demand that very day, diplomatic ties between the two countries would be severed. The unstated, concomitant consequence of a refusal would be a British military response in Africa—the invasion and occupation of territories in Angola or Mozambique, for instance. And there might be yet other reprisals. Portugal could not afford to see what form the British retaliation would take, for it was certain to be devastating, nor could it dream of going it alone in Europe and the world at large. Mighty Britain, Portugal's ally since the fourteenth century,[*]

---

[*] The 1386 Treaty of Windsor, still in force, commits England and Portugal to helping each other guarantee their mutual security. Commercial treaties have existed between the two nations since 1294.

had helped defend it against the Spanish and more recently against the French, during the Napoleonic Wars. Unless King Carlos were willing to risk a much more serious debacle in Africa and jeopardize his nation's long-term survival, he had no choice but to accept its short-term humiliation, acquiescing to the British demand.

Although it did not rock Portugal's economy or change its standing in the world as a weak power that happened to have colonies, acquiescing to the Ultimatum had cataclysmic effects. It shattered all illusions, reifying for the Portuguese the feebleness and decadence into which their nation had long ago descended. The immediate reaction of the shocked public was extraordinarily virulent and seemingly unanimous: as soon as news of the king's "betrayal" of the nation was out, people poured into Lisbon's streets to protest. There were shouts of "Death to England!" and "Down with the Braganzas!"; the British consulate was stoned; and Portuguese flags were displayed at half-mast. The following weeks saw a massive boycott of all things British. Shops stopped selling British goods. Tailors quit using British patterns. Longshoremen refused to load or unload British ships. Capitalists withdrew their funds from British banks. Workers' associations, municipalities, members of the Catholic episcopate, chambers of commerce, theater companies, farming cooperatives, student groups, even the Lisbon Zoo—all expressed solidarity with the protest movement. As for British subjects unlucky enough to be living in Lisbon, they had a hard time finding a barber who would cut their hair or a newsboy who would sell them a paper.[11]

The chief fomenter and beneficiary of so much public wrath was the Portuguese Republican Party, founded in 1876 but up until then not taken very seriously, even by those in the party, which had only a couple of deputies in parliament. Many early Republicans did not dream of overthrowing the constitutional monarchy, which was firmly in place and had lately not been doing such a bad job. They simply wanted to "republicanize" it. The Ultimatum and its political fallout completely changed the game. Seeing their opening, the Portuguese Republicans rushed in, rallying people to the cause of national honor and systematically bashing the two parties that held sway in the monarchical system. On January 31, 1891, the Republicans staged a revolt in Porto that was quickly crushed, but their ranks continued to swell—helped by the international recession of the early 1890s, which brought Portugal to the brink of bankruptcy—and regime change was now at the top of their agenda. It would take many years of chipping away at the monarchical establishment before they would finally prevail, and with a young poet named Fernando Pessoa on their side.

The British Ultimatum of 1890 not only kindled an enduring and eventually fatal disenchantment with the Portuguese monarchy, it also sparked an intense national reflection on the country's Destiny, with all the historical and philosophical weightiness that capitalized word can bear. Was Portugal not a chosen country? Had its maritime enterprise of old not miraculously prevailed against all logical odds, thereby giving "new worlds to the World"? (This phrase is from Portugal's national anthem, written in 1890 as a protest against the Ultimatum.) Might the insult Portugal had suffered from the British, serving as a tocsin, actually be a "sign of its resurgence" (quoting the anthem once more)?

While the present state of national stagnation had become an incontrovertible reality, the myth of a former age of grandeur grew new wings. Deploring the decadence in which the country floundered, the new nationalists looked ahead by looking backwards, to that distant past when diminutive Portugal grandly succeeded in spreading its influence around the world. To recapture some of that glorious past, they proposed reimagining and reinvesting in the Portuguese empire, which, despite having shrunk, still stretched not only as far as Cape Verde, São Tomé, western Africa, and southeast Africa, but also to the Asian lands of Goa, Macau, and East Timor. By a curious twist of history, the left-wing Republicans, besides being zealous advocates of freedom, equality, and justice for all men—women's suffrage was not part of their program— were also the most vociferous defenders of Portuguese colonialism, which became a synonym of patriotism after the British affront of 1890.

Six years later, while Portugal was still smarting from its collective humiliation, Fernando Pessoa was taken to live in the British colony of Natal, South Africa, some fifteen hundred miles south and a little east of the Shire region that Portugal had claimed and that Britain forced it to unclaim. In Durban the future poet would receive not only a thoroughly English education but also an indoctrination into the social mores, political precepts, and imperialist attitudes of Great Britain. Except for British imperialism, Fernando Pessoa seemed to take it all on board, becoming Anglicized in many ways, yet claiming loyalty to Portugal in his adolescent writings. The obvious conclusion is that he felt divided between two cultures. It is possible, however, that he was merely and always pretending, changing color like a chameleon committed only to its own survival. This much is certain: he was a quick and intuitive learner, and one of the things he learned early on, even before going to Durban, is that truth is in the mind of the believer, just as beauty is in the eye of the beholder. His demented Grandma Dionísia, from her forever shifting point of view, had perfectly good reasons to rant on about whatever she ranted. It was at least partly her example that inspired an observation, written years later in the language Fernando was about to start learning. "When I consider how real and how true the things of his madness are to the madman, I cannot but agree with the essence of Protagoras' statement: that man is the measure of all things."[12]

# CHAPTER 5

○◕◗○◕◗○◕◗○◕◗○◕◗○◕◗○◕◗○◕◗○◕◗○◕◗○◕◗○◕◗○

**I** T WAS A TWO-DAY VOYAGE FROM LISBON TO MADEIRA, where Fernando, his mother, and his uncle Cunha arrived on January 22, 1896. Sloping upward from the wide sweeping bay of Funchal, the capital and main port, was a hilly island whose verdant, subtropical landscape and mild year-round climate had made it a favored destination for "invalids" from Great Britain and the European continent, in particular those seeking to cure tuberculosis or alleviate its symptoms. Besides several sanatoria there were a number of hotels for regular tourists, one of which accommodated the three travelers, whose next steamer would depart in a week's time. They spent their days seeing the sights and doing what tourists on the island did. This included taking a ride on one of the wicker toboggans that whizzed down from a hilltop neighborhood to the center of Funchal—an especially fun activity for a seven-year-old boy. But it became frightening when a piece of wood somehow flew into the toboggan and landed on Maria Madalena's thigh, bruising it enough to lay her up for a couple of days.[1] Fernando and Uncle Cunha continued to see sights on their own until the twenty-ninth, when they all boarded the *Hawarden Castle*, which had sailed out of London and would take them on a three-week voyage around the southern tip of Africa to Durban.[2]

The *Hawarden* was one of various midsized steamers (between four and five thousand tons) that transported mail, cargo, and passengers between Britain and South Africa. Since two competing shipping lines plied this route, they vied to make life on board as enjoyable as possible. There were stately lounges, recreational activities that included deck cricket and quoits, and evening entertainments such as dances and dress competitions. Fernando had brought along reading material, and his great-uncle was an endless source of invented adventure. "See those two suspicious-looking characters on the far end of the deck?" he said to his nephew. "English spies!" During the rest of the voyage he offered wild speculations about the nature of their covert activities.³ Fernando's mother no doubt spent a part of each day teaching him some of the English she had learned as a girl.

Sailing through the Canaries, Fernando could see in the distance, rising up from the island of Tenerife, the lofty peak of Mount Teide, the world's third largest volcano. He saw land again when the ship passed between the Cape Verde Islands and Senegal, but it did not stop there or anywhere else on the west African coast. The voyage southward was nearly always smooth, until the last several days before reaching Cape Town, when strong headwinds made even a steamer like the *Hawarden* pitch a little. A couple of hours before reaching dry land, the passengers could begin to make out broad and flat-topped Table Mountain, majestically hulking behind and above the still invisible city. A member of the crew, or a fellow passenger returning home, would have explained that to the left of the massive plateau is Devil's Peak, while the peak on the right side is known as Lion's Head. Slowly the city, with its grid of mostly narrow streets lined by low buildings, hove into view.⁴

The three voyagers from Lisbon had a whole day in which to tour the town, with its gabled houses and a few municipal buildings in the older, Cape Dutch style, although two of the most imposing structures—the Houses of Parliament and the Standard Bank—were British neoclassical. The best tourist attraction for Fernando was the Castle of Good Hope, a pentagonal fort built in the 1600s by the Dutch East India Company, which settled the area to serve as a refueling station for ships sailing between the Netherlands and the Dutch East Indies (present-day Indonesia). More intriguing than any of the architecture was the city's human diversity, observable even without leaving the port zone: Britons, Dutch descendants, native Africans including Xhosa, Mfengu, and Mozambicans, some Indians, and a diversified ethnic group known as Cape Coloureds. The Cape Coloureds (as they are still called today) resulted from more than two hundred years of intermarriage between European settlers, indigenous peoples, and slaves brought to the Cape Colony from India and the Malay Archipelago as well as from other parts of Africa.

After dropping off some passengers and taking new ones aboard, the *Hawarden* continued southward and then east around the Cape of Good Hope, a commanding headland of jagged gray stone rising straight out of the sea. The site of treacherous gales in winter, and battered in all seasons by surging waves, it was initially christened the Cape of Storms by Portugal's Bartolomeu Dias, the first European since ancient times to sail around it, in 1488. If Fernando was not already familiar with this piece of national history, Uncle Cunha enlightened him. Years later, Pessoa would write a poem in homage to the navigator.

The ship passed other rocky promontories before reaching the southernmost Cape Agulhas, where the Atlantic officially ends and the Indian Ocean begins. At that point the scenery changes, with the rugged shores gradually giving way to long stretches of sandy dunes as the coastline curves northeast, toward Port Elizabeth, where the *Hawarden* called two days after leaving Cape Town. It took another day to make East London, where the ship anchored off the Buffalo River, and a day and a half more to reach Durban, the largest city of the colony of Natal and the final port of call.

As the ship entered Natal Bay, the passengers saw on their left side the towering green headland called the Bluff, surmounted by a white lighthouse and a signal mast that communicated with incoming vessels through a system of raised flags. On their immediate right were the docks, where friends, relatives, and baggage handlers patiently waited. If they looked straight across the pear-shaped bay the passengers could see, along its indented shore, not only shipping-related warehouses and industries but also leisure boats moored to small piers, points for fishing and swimming, and wavy green slopes dotted by houses in the background. It was Friday, February 21, 1896.[5] They debarked onto one of the docks at the Point, a long spit of land that bustled with cranes moving cargo up, over, and down, railway cars pulling in and out, dozens of dockworkers, sailors of various nationalities, native Africans shoveling coal, policemen, harbor officials, shipping agents, businessmen, chandlers, passengers—Victorian colonialism efficiently at work. What Fernando did not see were the squalid barracks and the shacks of nearby Bamboo Square, which housed the low-wage African and Indian laborers on whom the port economy depended.

To get to the town proper there were trains, horse-drawn streetcars, horse-drawn carriages, and human-drawn rickshaws, a conveyance that Fernando had never seen before. Introduced four years earlier by the sugar industrialist Marshall Campbell, these two-wheeled carts quickly became the European population's favorite way of traveling a short distance quickly. They were pulled by barefoot Zulus, who had developed a distinctive costume consisting of colorful chest coverings, whitewashed designs on their lower legs, and a flamboyant headdress that usually included quills and a pair of cow horns. The work was well paid but terribly taxing, and most rickshaw pullers could not endure it for long. João Miguel Rosa, the Portuguese consul, almost certainly hired a carriage to take the family and all their luggage from the port to downtown Durban and then up Smith Street or West Street to Berea Road. From there it was an uphill climb, with houses poking out of the lush landscape of tulip trees, crimson flamboyants, coral trees, and flowering shrubs. At the top they turned left and then kept straight until, on their right-hand side, they came to a wooded, one-acre lot with a house named Tresilian, on Ridge Road. There was a driveway leading up to the dwelling, which lay just outside the town limits. It was a large, one-story house with verandas on three sides. Durban houses at that time were usually timber framed and had corrugated metal roofs. Their layout followed a typical Victorian plan, with a front hall giving access to the living room on one side, the main bedroom on the other, and with the kitchen and other rooms located at the rear.[6]

Fernando had played in a yard with a few trees at Uncle Cunha and Aunt Maria's house in Lisbon, but now he was surrounded by exuberant subtropical vegetation. He must have found it enchanting, and maybe a little unnerving. The first Europeans to explore the region reported seeing herds of fifty or more elephants, and hippos once grazed among mangroves on the shores of the bay. Although the big game had long ago been hunted to extinction, vervet monkeys and tropical birds were still abundant in the suburban part of town known as the Berea, which was Pessoa's first neighborhood in Africa and the fashionable place for Durban's white people to live. Perched above the city center, there the summer heat was less sultry, and malaria from outlying marshy areas never ascended. The Berea also afforded splendorous views of the bay, the Bluff, and the Indian Ocean.

The Portuguese Consulate was located downtown, on Gardiner Street, close to the post office and the Central Railway Station and close as well to the St. Joseph's Convent School, where Fernando was promptly enrolled. Managed and staffed by the Holy Family Sisters, a congregation founded in Bordeaux and dedicated to education, the convent school was already three weeks into the new term. It was a girls' school in the higher grades but welcomed children of both sexes for its "Jardin d'Enfants." The academic standards were high, and since the school received some government aid, it was obliged to admit students of other faiths, not just Catholics. For Pessoa, a Roman Catholic, St. Joseph's was the natural choice. He and his stepfather probably set out each morning from the Berea together, with the consul heading to work and Fernando to school.[7] They had hardly if ever been alone together, just the two of them, and it took time for a comfortable rapport to develop. João Rosa was easygoing, dedicated, and generous, while Fernando was by nature reserved and reticent; still, he would soon learn to address this new parent and guardian as "Papá."

✦

UNCLE CUNHA STAYED IN Durban for three weeks, then boarded a steamer to go back home, taking along some precious memories of Fernando in his new surroundings. A few weeks after Cunha arrived back in Portugal, his wife wrote a letter to the boy signed by both of them. After declaring how much Fernando is loved and missed, the missive continues:

> And tell me, Fernando, do you still remember your house in Pedrouços? Here you have your bedroom waiting for you, if God lets your aunt and uncle live long enough to see you come back to your country. Uncle Cunha asked me to tell you that all his friends who were used to seeing you with him are always asking about you, because they were all very fond of you. Uncle Cunha never stops talking about you, his conversations with your Aunt Maria always have to do with you. He tells me about your life in Natal during the time he was there, what you said, what you did, because you, my dear Fernando, are our one and only thought.[8]

Uncle Cunha's letters to Fernando contained even stronger expressions of affection. On June 22 he wrote that "no one in this life loves you more than your aunt and uncle." The boy's mother, livid with indignation, wrote back saying that in fact she loved him more than they did, and to emphasize the point to all concerned, she made Fernando copy her letter in his own hand. She posted the copy on July 22. Undaunted, Uncle Cunha replied on August 31: "I never doubted that your mother is very fond of you. What I said and can assure you is that, after your dear

Mother, no one in the world loves you as much as me and your Aunt Maria, for our hearts are the only ones in which you have first place." He was apparently suggesting that Fernando had only second place in his mother's heart, with first place going to her new husband.

Uncle Cunha kept Fernando informed about battalions of crickets marching off to war, about a ship setting out for the Amazon to help bands of beetles fend off mosquitoes, and about other battling arthropods. Fernando, in his letters to Uncle Cunha, reported on his studies at school and his progress learning English. After only six months, he could read better than most of his classmates. The creative bent of his intelligence was already evident in his droll humor. In June, after several baby teeth fell out, he wrote a letter saying that he was now older than his uncle since, although only four feet tall, he was already losing his teeth.

It would be hard to overestimate the influence of Manuel Gualdino da Cunha on the boyish imagination of the poet renowned for consorting with invented personalities. Uncle Cunha's letters shifted abruptly between fiction and reality, or rather, there was no shifting—it was as if fact and fiction were all of a piece. Not only that, he adjusted the fictions to his nephew's new circumstances. Along with insect warfare, he began to describe the travels of make-believe Portuguese consuls. In a letter dated September 13, 1897, he wrote that their friend "Tibô"—a phonetic spelling of Thibeaut, the onetime captain and rival of the Chevalier de Pas—had been relieved of his consular duties in France and would soon, after making a voyage to Mexico, visit Fernando in Durban. In that same letter Uncle Cunha reported that Grandma Dionísia was crazier than ever, and he was afraid she would make Aunt Maria go mad. Dionísia had been living with them for almost a year. His own health was slipping, and he ended his letter with these words: "Listen, my dear Fernando, I'm never going to see you again. Excuse my nonsense, but dealing with nutty people makes one a little nuttier. Your friend, M. G. da Cunha." Uncle Cunha became too ill to write any more letters and died on January 25, 1898, just two years after accompanying Fernando and his mother to Durban.[9]

◆

ALTHOUGH HE NEVER STUDIED geography at any of the schools he attended in South Africa, Fernando Pessoa learned a great deal about human communities in relationship to their environment just by living in a new and unfamiliar place where various cultures uneasily coexisted, each with its own customs and social behaviors. Young and small, unsophisticated but energetic, Durban was the antithesis of ancient Lisbon with its ornate churches, stately squares, and tired monuments, its remembered grandeur. The layout and management of this town alongside the Indian Ocean, the brisk pace of life eager to go forward, the cool but dry winters, the hot and stormy summers—none of this had much in common with Portugal's capital, as seen and experienced by Fernando on his frequent outings with Uncle Cunha. But the most flagrant difference was the heterogeneous population. In 1896, the colony of Natal had about 50,000 people of European descent, a slightly larger number of Indians, and almost ten times as many native Zulus. The Europeans were concentrated in the cities, where they were the largest of the three population groups. There were close to 16,000 Europeans in Durban, some 10,000 Indians, and over 8000 mostly male natives. (Today, the city's metropolitan area has 3.5 million people, of whom black Africans are a majority, with people of Indian descent still making up a quarter of the population.)

Natalian Zulus were hired to do manual labor in towns and in the fields, but since they had their villages to return to whenever they wished, they could quit at a moment's notice and were hence less easy to exploit. So the Europeans lured Mozambicans and other foreign Africans with higher wages than they received at home, organized them into labor camps, and turned them into migrant workers. Some of the Mozambicans came by ship and disembarked at Durban, where their passports were handled by Pessoa's stepfather.[10] Imported Africans began working on Natal's sugar plantations in the 1860s and '70s, but in the 1890s the vast majority worked at the gold mines around Johannesburg, in the Transvaal Republic. Before the Anglo-Boer War, as many as 25,000 Mozambican natives were employed each year in the Transvaal mines, which they reached by train from Lourenço Marques.[11]

Indians initially came to Natal as indentured laborers in 1860, with the first two shiploads arriving from Madras and Calcutta. They were given five-year, renewable contracts to work, in most cases, on the sugar plantations stretching north of Durban along the coast. After ten years of service (this period was later reduced), they were entitled to free passage back to India, but the majority chose to stay, working in agriculture or in the coal mines, or they settled in Durban, where they were employed as domestics, dockhands, and in other capacities. A new wave of indentured Indians was recruited in the 1870s, mainly to lay track for the expanding railroad, but also to replenish the labor force of the sugar industry and to work the tea and coffee estates. After completing the terms of their service, many of these laborers, like their predecessors, made their way to Durban. As the resident Indian population increased, so did the uneasiness of whites. Because of their lighter complexion, Indians had a higher standing in the social hierarchy than black Africans. That made them potentially more threatening to European hegemony. The colonial government levied a poll tax on unindentured Indians to discourage them from staying. Most of them stayed anyway. Lighter- or darker-skinned, they were classified as members of an "uncivilized race" and had to carry a pass at all times, to prove they were duly registered with the authorities.[12]

While thousands of Indians came as guest workers under contract, a small number—many of whom were merchants from the western state of Gujarat—simply exercised their legal right, as British subjects, to immigrate to Natal on their own initiative. In Durban and other towns they opened shops that catered to fellow Indians, to the native Zulu community, and soon enough to Europeans as well. Since they had paid their own passage on ships departing from Bombay, these better-off and better-educated immigrants were called "passenger" Indians. And since most of them were Muslims, it also became common to refer to them as Arabs. It happens that the historically most important of these so-called Arabs was a Hindu, not a Muslim. Born in the Gujarat town of Porbandar and trained as a lawyer in London, Mohandas Karamchand Gandhi was the secretary of the Natal Indian Congress and lived in central Durban in a two-story house on Beach Grove. Slight in stature, and only twenty-six years old when Pessoa arrived there, Gandhi was already making a name for himself as an impassioned and capable defender of the Indians' civil rights.

◆

WHILE MUCH SMALLER THAN Lisbon, Durban was in a certain sense more cosmopolitan, thanks to its international ethnic composition, with people of various colors from four different continents. Founded in 1835, the town was named after Sir Benjamin D'Urban, then governor of the

Cape Colony, from where the first settlers arrived, in 1824. Once Natal had come firmly under British control, in the 1840s, new settlers started to pour in from Britain, the Cape, and elsewhere. Durban grew rapidly and prepared for its growth, becoming a model of good planning and enlightened government—for the white population, that is, although Indians and native Africans could at least benefit from some of the urban amenities. By the time of Pessoa's arrival in 1896, the town and suburbs were spread out over more than two hundred streets, connected by an efficient network of public transportation, and Durbanites had most of the things a city dweller could want: a public library, parks, public gardens where bands sometimes played in the evening, a well-stocked botanical garden, a sports field, two daily newspapers, a museum, plays and concerts, several literary societies, religious groups, social clubs, and associations for special interests.

In a 1928 article titled "Portuguese Provincialism," Pessoa noted with dismay how easily his compatriots were enthralled by foreign cities such as Paris, and he credited his own exemption from the syndrome to the fact he had been educated abroad, "under the influence of a great European culture." This was an odd claim to make, since the Durban that Pessoa knew, with 35,000 inhabitants in 1896, had a distinctly provincial mentality, proven by the fact that it went out of its way to be as English as possible, as if to compensate for being an imperial outpost. For Pessoa, however, this circumstance had the great advantage of providing him with a concentrated dose of British culture, even if it was a somewhat ready-made, caricatural variety. As a foreigner, he might not have done any better living in London, which could be overwhelming and sometimes hard to penetrate for outsiders. Despite having a far smaller array of cultural offerings at their disposal, Durban's colonists were more likely to be culturally or politically engaged than the average Londoner. They invested heavily in British-style education, celebrated British customs, and felt eminently British. Most of them, after all, were British subjects, and Queen Victoria was their queen.

It was not only his early exposure to "a great European culture" that immunized Pessoa against Portuguese provincialism; it was also his contact with Durban's Indians and native Africans. It must have fascinated Fernando to overhear Zulus in conversation, since their language, besides being tonal, has highly distinctive click sounds. Or did their way of speaking merely mark them as irrevocably "exotic," never to be taken seriously as persons mentally and emotionally comparable with European whites? They worked in Durban as laborers, policemen, and domestics. The Portuguese consul usually employed four or five of them to clean, cook, and garden.[13] Indians, on the other hand, would have been encountered by Fernando behind shop counters and around the public market on Gardiner Street, near the consulate, where they hawked fruits and vegetables brought in from Indian-run truck farms.

Fernando's life in Durban was privileged but not exactly sheltered. Like the rest of the town's residents, whatever their national origin or social standing, he was never far from people who looked and dressed very differently, spoke other languages, and had other ways of conducting themselves. On the wide downtown thoroughfares, people of all ethnicities freely walked, though without much intermingling, and the civil liberties of non-Europeans were limited. The racially defined class system ensured that white colonists would maintain their superior economic and social status, but the safeguarding of privileges was not their only concern. They clung to their British identity as to a security blanket, since every day they were confronted by cultures—"native," "Indian," and the many distinct subcultures within these two general categories—that felt vaguely menacing simply for having little or nothing to do with their own. However much they resisted mixing with and being influenced by other groups, and however superior they deemed their own culture to be, they were forced to recognize that it was not the only one. Even Durban's white population was not culturally homogeneous, because there were a sizable number of immigrants from continental Europe and Australia.

Late-nineteenth-century Durban was, at least for some people, an appealing land of opportunity—a little raw, but no longer rough and not in the least backward. The Irish historian and politician James Bryce, who traveled extensively in South Africa in 1895 and published a book with his detailed observations two years later, made this extraordinary appraisal of Pessoa's new home: "Durban has been a pioneer of what is called, in its extremer forms, municipal socialism, and enjoys the reputation of being the best managed and most progressive town in all South Africa."[14] Durban was indeed well managed, for the comfort of white people, and if life there impressed the writer as a quasi-socialist paradise, it was because even strictly middle-class whites could live like kings and queens, thanks to the racist division of labor.

In a memoir called *Dear Old Durban* published during the apartheid era, an elderly woman descended from an English colonial family would recall how in the "halcyon" days of her childhood "even people with very modest incomes could still have at least two African servants, and the 'garden boy' was quite happy to act as rickshaw puller in the afternoon." (Some European families had their own rickshaws.) She also recalled how much easier life was for housewives, since "Indian hawkers brought vegetables every day in two large baskets hanging from a bamboo pole across one shoulder."[15] She made no mention of the fact that African servants lived in a shed at the back of the yard or else in shantytowns on the city's outer edges. Indians lived in cramped quarters with poor sanitation around Grey Street, their main commercial area, and in other pockets around Durban. Overcrowded and poorly ventilated barracks built near the harbor, north of the business district, and at other locations housed several thousand African and Indian laborers. Many of the latter worked for the municipality and the rail service. The small number of prosperous Indians who lived in European neighborhoods kept a low profile.

No one ever discussed with Fernando the living conditions of Durban's non-European population, and his only firsthand knowledge of those conditions was afforded by the Rosa family's domestic servants. Although they were probably treated better than many others, their living quarters in the backyard were most likely ramshackle, without proper sanitation and poorly protecting them against the cold. Chances are that Fernando, despite being a naturally curious child, never bothered to investigate exactly how the family servants lived. Like virtually all the city's white residents, he would have instinctively preferred to remain as ignorant as possible. For him as for others, Africans and Indians effectively existed only in their daytime capacity as cheap labor.

✦

TURN-OF-THE-CENTURY DURBAN MADE A favorable impression not only on James Bryce but on many other visitors from abroad, including Olivia and Clara Clemens, wife and daughter of Mark Twain. The American writer and humorist was on a yearlong worldwide speaking tour that took him to Canada, Australia, New Zealand, India, and lastly South Africa, where Durban was his first stop. He and his party landed there on May 6, 1896, just two and a half months after Fernando Pessoa, and were delighted by the town and by the people they met, in particular the social set revolving around Samuel George Campbell, a physician and younger brother to sugar baron Marshall

Campbell.* Twain and his family were surely not blind to the racial hierarchy that defined Durban, but they did not let it ruin their fun. Being Americans, they were quite used to living with and benefiting from racism, even if they recognized its injustice. Olivia and Clara were so enchanted with Durban that they stayed on for three extra weeks, from May 14 to June 6, while Twain proceeded inland to do shows in Johannesburg and other towns.[16]

Twain's tour helped boost local interest in his books, a couple of which Pessoa acquired as an adolescent. One of the books, *Information Wanted, and Other Sketches*,[17] is dated 1903 and bears the signature not only of "F. A. N. Pessoa" but also of "David Merrick," an English-language heteronym who was supposed to write poems, stories, plays, and a novel, though none of the projects got very far, or they were passed on to other fictional authors. It's quite possible that Pessoa's habit of signing his youthful literary texts with other names was spurred on, if not actually inspired, by Samuel Clemens. It's also possible that the boy, when not quite eight years old, attended one of the "At Home" lectures given by Twain at Durban's Theatre Royal on May 12 and 13, 1896. Part of the Portuguese consul's job was to be sociable, and such an event would have appealed to both his stepson and his wife.

João Rosa was a diligent diplomat, excelling at all aspects of his job. Besides defending Portugal's interests and public image in Natal, he regularly reported on local news to the home country and to Portuguese officials in Mozambique. Worrisome news included the periodic outbreaks of tropical and global diseases, including dengue fever, cholera, smallpox, and bubonic plague. Hardest hit were the native and Indian populations, due to their substandard housing, much of which was located on marshland that had not yet been properly drained. Like other port towns, Durban was forever on the lookout for contagious diseases, which could spread all too swiftly among sailors and harbor personnel, devastating maritime commerce, since foreign-bound ships needed signed and sealed bills of health before they could sail. No consul in Durban processed more of these than João Rosa, for the simple reason that Lourenço Marques, controlled by the Portuguese, was the closest foreign port.

---

* Sam Campbell founded Durban's Technical College in 1907; his son, the poet Roy Campbell (1901–1957), was one of the first translators of Pessoa into English.

✦

A CONSCIENTIOUS PROFESSIONAL, PESSOA'S stepfather was
equally dedicated to his family. He had purchased a piano for his wife,
he himself played the flute, and together they played duets after dinner. Fernando wrote his grandma Madalena about their small evening
concerts, which he quite enjoyed.[18] He was learning to share his mother
with the consul and would soon have to learn to share her with other offspring. On November 27, 1896, scarcely nine months after their arrival
in Africa, his mother gave birth to a girl, Henriqueta Madalena. Two
more girls and two boys would follow, but the two younger girls died in
infancy. Henriqueta was the sibling Pessoa would feel closest to. Besides
being nearer in age to him than his two half brothers (born in 1901 and
1903), she would live with him on and off during the last fifteen years of
his life, taking care of him and becoming like a second mother. Another
bond they shared was linguistic. João Miguel Rosa and Maria Madalena
taught all their children to read and write in Portuguese, which was the
only language spoken at the dinner table, but as the years wore on and
South Africa felt more and more like home, the couple got lax about
restricting the use of English in the family. Whereas Henriqueta grew
up perfectly bilingual, both in speech and in writing, her younger brothers, who as adults would live in England, wrote Portuguese with frequent errors and were not entirely comfortable speaking it.

Contrary to what we might expect, Fernando's Portuguese, instead of
deteriorating, became more proficient. Despite the considerable demands
that St. Joseph's Convent School placed on its young pupils, who began
studying Latin and French in the fourth or fifth grade, he found time
to read books in his mother tongue. And from early on his leisure reading, in whatever language, included poetry.[19] But nothing better illustrates the boy's intellectual precocity than his astonishing performance at
school. A foreigner who arrived at Durban with practically no English,
he was soon at the top of his class—and not because of his skill in mathematics. In fact, "top of his class" states only half the case, since he left his
class behind and jumped ahead. Although he had had a year and a half
of (probably at-home) schooling in Lisbon, his lack of English meant he
had to start all over in Durban, where he completed the five-year primary school program in just three years. At a graduation ceremony on
December 20, 1898, the school would award Fernando the Examination

Prize for all-around academic excellence, the First Prize in Latin, and, most remarkably, the First Prize in English.[20]

In addition to Latin, English, and arithmetic, Fernando's class schedule during his last year of primary school included geometry, history, science, and French. Some subjects were taught on alternate days; Latin was taught every day, Monday through Friday. So was English, but the Tuesday and Thursday classes were devoted specifically to poetry. Two hours of weekly poetry instruction seems to have been a peculiarity of the convent school rather than a standard feature of the fifth-grade curriculum in South Africa. Black-robed and white-bibbed Catholic nuns, while they may not have served as inspiring muses, were the ones who instilled an early love of poetry in Fernando. It was in the form of a poem that he scrawled a warning to would-be thieves in the front of *Principia Latina*, his Latin primer, opposite the flyleaf where his class schedule was affixed:

Don't steal this book
For fear of shame
For in it is
The owner's name.

And if I catch
Him by the tail
He'll run off
To Durban gaol.[*]

At the back of the textbook he wrote a bilingual message, in English and French, instructing whoever might find the book to return it to him at his home address. In February 1898 Fernando, four months away from his tenth birthday, was flaunting his still rudimentary skills as a linguist and poet.

It might seem that books and schoolwork were a cozy refuge for a boy who felt a little out of place not only in his new environment but also in his new family, at least in the beginning, since he could not help being an outsider to the amorous passion that tightly bound his mother to her

---

[*] Dissatisfied with the fifth and sixth lines, Fernando crossed them out.

second husband. In Lisbon, however, he had already taken shelter in the printed word and in his mental life; even there he had been a bit of an outsider. While he knew how much his aunts and uncles and various cousins loved him, he used to sometimes flare up for no apparent reason or, on the contrary, he would suddenly clam up.

Recalling this capricious, infantile behavior when he was nineteen, Pessoa would retrospectively diagnose himself as a seven-year-old with a predisposition to neurasthenia, a then popular designation for a poorly defined disorder whose symptoms ranged from anxiety and nervous exhaustion to depression and listlessness. It was a strange diagnosis to make for a child. The same pages of self-analysis state that this vague trouble was "inhibited" during his early years in Durban, thanks in part to his time-consuming studies, but that it would return with a vengeance when he reached puberty. Although the nineteen-year-old may not have been ready to call it by its real name, he strongly implies that his childhood anxiety derived from a hazy but uncomfortable awareness of sex and sexuality. Yet as a youngster in Durban, before he had experienced any "mental deflowering" and was hence still blessed with a "perfect virginity of the imagination" (curious expressions!), he was to all appearances quite normal—more normal and more tranquil, according to the self-analyst, than when he left Lisbon for South Africa in 1896.[21]

Except for the exaggerated amount of time he spent studying and reading, Fernando in Durban seemed, indeed, like other children his age. He liked to play after school and was an eager participant in family activities, which included outings to the countryside, especially during the school holidays in January and July. His vague sexual trouble remained, for the time being, dormant.

# CHAPTER 6

**I**N JANUARY 1897, BETWEEN PESSOA'S FIRST AND second year at St. Joseph's Convent School, Durban was gripped by a commotion that opened his eyes to the racial hostility simmering under the town's peaceful veneer. If he did not read about the news in the local papers, he heard his mother and stepfather discussing the matter, and on a trip downtown with one or another parent he might have seen the irate white men gathered around the Central Hotel on West Street. They had formed a committee to oppose the landing of two ships from India, one of which was bringing back Mohandas K. Gandhi. Word had spread that the small but eloquent young man with large ears was accompanied by six hundred new, unwanted Indians to Natal. And Gandhi himself had become persona non grata.[1]

Gandhi had first come to Natal in May 1893, three years before Fernando Pessoa. A twenty-three-year-old lawyer with a surfeit of energy but almost no experience, he had been hired by Dada Abdulla, an Indian businessman in Durban, to help settle a legal dispute with a rival firm based in Pretoria, capital of the Transvaal. In early June, after learning the particulars of the case, Gandhi set out inland from Durban in a first-class train compartment. It would be an exhausting journey, and not only because he had to use various conveyances—coaches as well as trains—to reach Pretoria. His troubles began in Pietermaritzburg, Natal's capital and second largest town, where he was instructed by railway officials to move to the van compartment, where baggage was kept, after a European passenger complained about having to share first-class space with an Indian. When Gandhi refused to leave voluntarily, a policeman came and forcibly removed him and his luggage. It was nine o'clock on a chilly winter evening, and he had to wait until morning to continue his journey, which would be further marred by similar incidents. But Gandhi had already made a decision of sorts. It was the night he spent shivering in the Pietermaritzburg station that would stand out for him as the transformative moment of his life, committing him to what he would later call "satyagraha," the struggle for political reform through passive resistance.[2]

Gandhi stayed for a year in Pretoria and eventually persuaded the two disputants in the intricate case to come to an out-of-court settlement. In May 1894, back in Durban and getting ready to sail home, he learned of a bill before the Natal Legislative Assembly that would disenfranchise Indians. It would have little practical effect in the short run, since only a tiny number of Indians met the property requirement to be able to vote, and fewer still exercised the privilege, but Gandhi saw it as a humiliating first step toward ensuring that they would forever remain a subservient class. Sharing his indignation, Dada Abdulla and other prominent Indians convinced the vivacious young lawyer that he should stay in Durban to organize Indians to campaign against the bill. On August 22 the Natal Indian Congress was founded, with Gandhi at the helm as its honorary secretary.[3] He was a skillful organizer, uniting Indians of different religions (Muslims, Hindus, Parsis, Christians) and social categories (merchants, indentured laborers, and the ex-indentured) into a coherent movement of protest against their treatment as second-class citizens. In Natal they were subject to a nine o'clock curfew, were not welcome in most hotels or at Durban's public baths, had to stand on the streetcar or else sit on the upper level, and were frequent victims of arbitrary discrimination. All of which no doubt seemed to Fernando, the stepson of a European diplomat, like the natural order of things.

At this early stage, Gandhi's perspective on human rights was not wide in scope. He was specifically defending the Indian cause, and in the most pragmatic way possible. More than once in his pleas to officials and in published pamphlets or letters to the editor, he made a point of racially and culturally distinguishing the Indian from the native African, so as to justify better treatment and full civil rights for the former. For that matter, he also distinguished the poor and uneducated indentured Indians from their more genteel and prosperous compatriots, admitting that only the latter could rightfully demand to be on an equal footing with the Europeans. Gandhi denounced the mistreatment of the indentured, but his social and political views still bore the imprint of his upbringing in the caste system. Those views would change, however, as his spiritual vision expanded, looking past outward distinctions between people and their creeds.

Gandhi the passive resister developed in tandem with the religious seeker and thinker. Besides the sacred texts of Hinduism, he read the Qur'an and the Bible. He was profoundly affected by Tolstoy's *The Kingdom of God Is Within You*—a passionate apology for nonviolence and nonmaterialism, as preached by Jesus in the Sermon on the Mount. But he felt an enduring affinity for the religion he was born into. Though he would never completely reject the caste system, he would strongly oppose caste discrimination and the doctrine of untouchability, arguing for the equal dignity of all types of work.

✦

ON JUNE 5, 1896, while Fernando was finishing his first semester at the convent school, Gandhi boarded a ship in Durban harbor. He was sailing for India to spend six months and to fetch his family, from which he had been separated for three full years. A week before Christmas he was back at the same harbor, with his wife, Kasturba, their two sons and an orphaned nephew, but disembarking proved to be difficult and dangerous. They were on board the *Courland*, which had sailed from Bombay together with the *Naderi*. Many of Durban's white citizens, particularly wage earners and small businessmen, had joined a so-called Demonstration Committee to protest the arrival of more Indians, who were now as numerous in Natal as the Europeans. They especially resented the Indian shopkeepers, who worked long hours and at lower margins, making it hard for European merchants to compete. Their contempt was concentrated on the figure of Gandhi, for having incited the Indians to clamor for their civil rights.

The *Courland* and the *Naderi* sat at Durban's outer anchorage for twenty-four days. Owing to a recent outbreak of bubonic plague in Bombay, the Natal Medical Board had ordered a twenty-one-day quarantine, but this had expired on January 10 and still the ships could not land. The Demonstration Committee held daily rallies on West Street, with hundreds of men in attendance, and it was feared they might resort to violence: the anger and ill will possessing the protesters is evident in the newspapers of the period. Day after day *The Natal Mercury* ran the same headline, "The Asiatic Invasion," and reported on the committee's latest declarations, on the status of its negotiations with government dignitaries, on the expressions of solidarity it was receiving from towns throughout Natal, and on the prospects for a resolution to the standoff.

Finally, on January 13, the ships steamed nervously into the tense harbor, where about four thousand demonstrators had gathered at the wharf to "greet" them. The Demonstration Committee hoped that the government, impressed by this show of numbers and dreading a riot, would intervene and concede to some of its demands—guaranteeing, for instance, that only returning Indians would be allowed to stay, with newcomers being sent back home. "Gandhi, Gandhi, you come here, for all the tar and feathers!" shouted a voice in the crowd. The attorney general, who lived down the block from Gandhi on Beach Grove, delivered an adroit speech, explaining that the two shiploads of Indians were innocent and promising legislative action during the next parliamentary session to stem the flow of new arrivals. (He would make good on this promise.)

The crowd finally dispersed, and several hours later the weary passengers, including Mrs. Gandhi and her children, began to debark. Gandhi himself stayed behind, heeding a message from the attorney general that his own safety was in peril and that he should not come ashore until dusk. A little while later, however, a professional colleague and good friend, one Mr. Laughton, boarded the *Courland* and convinced him that no harm would come to them if they disembarked together. No sooner were they on dry land than Gandhi was sighted, and a few people began following. He and his British companion tried to take a rickshaw, but some youngsters grabbed hold of the wheels, so the two men had no choice but to walk briskly while more and more people followed, hooting and crying, "Gandhi, Gandhi!"

Given that Pessoa the adult was a great admirer of Gandhi, I can't help but wonder if precocious Fernando, who had learned English quickly, read the article in *The Natal Mercury* describing how the hostile crowd of pursuers "began to assert itself, and Mr. Gandhi became the object of kicks and cuffs, while mud and stale fish were thrown at him. One person also produced a riding whip, and gave him a stroke, while another plucked away his peculiar hat. As the result of the attack, he was very much bespattered, and blood was flowing from the neck."[4]

The day was saved by Sarah Jane Alexander, the wife of the police superintendent. She happened to be walking by and, seeing the brouhaha, opened up her parasol and stood between the assailants and the injured man, whom she recognized. Gandhi pressed no charges against his aggressors, things calmed down in a few days, and he got on with his work for the Natal Indian Congress. The newspapers criticized the harassment he had received.

◆

GANDHI'S REMAINING YEARS SPENT in Durban would partly coincide with those of the young pupil and future great poet from Portugal. The Portuguese consular office moved in 1897 from Gardiner Street to Field Street, one block down from where Gandhi had his own office. How often Pessoa may have seen the Indian lawyer or how many of his circulars and letters to the editor he may have read, if any, we can never know. He made no mention of Gandhi in his youthful writings. Thirty years later, however, in the mid-1920s, he began to draft an essay on the man from Porbandar, whose bony face and penetrating eyes would soon grace the cover of *Time* magazine.[5] Like the majority of Pessoa's hundreds of writing projects, this one did not get very far, but the two brief passages he produced make extraordinary reading when we consider that their author rarely heaped praise on celebrated living figures, was himself staunchly Western in his models and his worldview, and tended to mock the very notion of political and social reform.

One of these passages consists of two sentences so succinctly complete that their author did not know how to continue: "Mahatma Gandhi is the only truly great figure that exists in the world today. And this is true because, in a certain sense, he does not belong to the world and he denies it." The other passage describes the Indian leader's humility, austerity, and asceticism, noting that "his lofty example, of no benefit to our weakness of will, puts our ambiguity to shame." It also mentions, and rejects, several other models of personal greatness: the American carmaker Henry Ford and the French statesman Georges Clemenceau, who led his country to victory in World War I. Without bothering to offer any critique or justification, Pessoa summarily wrote the two men off: "Toss them into the trash, which is what they are." Whatever virtues they may have had, next to Gandhi they were worthless. But what was the Mahatma's worth to Pessoa? What exactly was the attraction?[6]

Only in a subliminal way might Gandhi's "lofty example" have influenced Pessoa's life and work, as one among many other examples he read about or heard about while growing up in Durban. And yet the admiration he expressed for him in the later years of his life suggests that Pessoa—who was not a vegetarian, a teetotaler, or a nonsmoker, let alone an active defender of humanitarian causes—somehow identified with Gandhi, almost in an atavistic way. There were good grounds for that identification.

For one thing, Pessoa was just as much of an ascetic. Not only was his disinterest in material things extreme, he remained celibate, and chastity, according to Gandhi, was one of the highest manifestations of worldly detachment. Pessoa became a heavy drinker, true, but alcohol for him was a kind of medicine, or antidote, as well as a necessary stimulus for his writing. "If a man writes well only when he's drunk," he would write in *The Book of Disquiet*, "then I'll tell him: Get drunk."[7]

For another thing, Pessoa's spiritual searching, which traces back to Durban, was as dogged and as eclectic as Gandhi's. He received religious instruction at St. Joseph's Convent School and his first communion at the church next door, but from early on he felt that Catholicism was too confining. Although there were Catholics and other Christians he admired for their faith, he repudiated—like Gandhi—the theology of the saved and the damned. For both thinkers, it was absurd to suppose that transcendent truth could be the hostage of any one creed. They conceived salvation as a private matter, insofar as each person has to find and follow their own path toward self-realization, and at the same time as a joint concern, with all individual efforts contributing toward human betterment. Their asceticism, taking different forms, implied in both cases a rejection of conventional notions of well-being and progress. But while Gandhi adopted Hinduism as a useful vehicle for his spiritual journey, Pessoa could not practice any religion, since rites and rituals were not a language he felt comfortable using, though he was fascinated by their symbolic significance. Nor could he be an effective agent for political or social change, since he was inwardly too disconnected from the world, mentally too bound up in literature. We shall see how his political ideas, tinged with poetry, were as marvelous as they were impractical. Gandhi may not have belonged to the world, but he understood very well how it worked. The onetime lawyer's focused, persistent dedication to causes seems to have been envied by the Portuguese eulogist, who upbraided himself for not having a strong will, for not being able to commit and to follow through. Gandhi, on the other hand, had he known and read Pessoa's writings, might have envied the freedom their author achieved in them.

Since these two men pursued their life's work in entirely different fields—one of them as a social reformer and the other as a poet beyond reform—they seem at first glance to have almost nothing in common. Looking more closely, at their underlying motivations and attitudes, at the detachment they cultivated, and at the missionary spirit that impelled them, we discover similarities that go beyond the mere circumstance of their walking down the same streets in the same city during the same years. And that "mere" coincidence in time and place may be partly responsible for at least one other distinctive similarity. Racially tripartite Durban, with its imbricated subdivisions along religious, economic, and class lines, may have been just the right breeding ground for the spirit of tolerance that marked the thinking of Pessoa as well as of Gandhi, both of whom deemed truth to be as variable as the people who live by truth.[8]

# CHAPTER 7

OWARD THE END OF 1897, FERNANDO, HIS MOTHER,
stepfather, and half sister lodged for a time at the Ocean View
Hotel, which was also in the Berea, less than two miles from
the Tresilian House. A charming, three-floor brick building with shaded
verandas and an elegant dining room, the recently opened hotel provided
stunning vistas of Natal Bay and the Indian Ocean. But with forty-seven
bedrooms and only four bathrooms, it was not a place where João Miguel
Rosa and his family would have wanted to stay any longer than they had
to—perhaps a couple of months. They were waiting to move into their
new home at 157 West Street, next door to the Central Baptist Church.
It was a squarish, one-story dwelling, about 1500 square feet in area,
with a large front porch, but part of the building was taken up by the
consular office, for which there was a separate entrance. Both the consulate and the consul's family moved there together, in December 1897 or
January 1898.[1] Fernando now had only a small yard to play in, and none
of the luxuriant, colorful vegetation of the Berea. These losses, however,
were more than offset by the advantages of West Street, the main artery
of downtown Durban, with dozens of businesses and shops, including a
bookstore, city hall, the post office, and other municipal buildings. And
since the Rosa family lived on the eastern end of West Street, they were
within walking distance of the ocean and just two blocks away from
Natal Bay, where they sometimes went for a swim or to lie in the sand.
Durbanites, in those days, rarely frequented the ocean beach.[2]

On October 22, 1898, when Fernando was ten years old, his mother
gave birth to her second daughter, Madalena Henriqueta, whose given
names were an inversion of the first daughter's, Henriqueta Madalena.
The names honored the two grandmothers, one of whom, Grandma
Madalena, had died at the beginning of that same month, though the
news might not have reached Durban until after the new baby was born.
The arrival of another member of the family was in any case a joyous

occasion—except for Fernando, who already had to put up with the attention lavished on his first half sister. He sulked. Three days before giving birth, his mother responded to his jealousy with a poem titled "Escuta!" ("Listen!"). In it she explains that:

> We greatly love our children.
> They all have equal right.
> Our heart beats in our chest
> For all of them, alike.
>
> Since all have their place
> And all of them are equal
> Inside their mother's heart,
> All of them are rivals.

In the poem's succeeding stanzas, she declares her affection for her son but also admonishes him for resenting the equal amount of affection she feels for her infant daughter and the baby she is about to deliver. Actually, there was no equality in the matter. Fernando, her first and most brilliant child by far, always had a special place in her heart; none of his half siblings could compete for that spot. He knew that. But this flourishing new family, to which he belonged only because of his mother, encroached on the memory of the family he was born into, and while part of him adapted, another part withdrew into the world of his imagination, becoming a family unto himself. Maybe he took comfort in his scholastic success, and maybe he became the top student at school to remind his mother—and himself—how special he was.

During her pregnancy and in the months following childbirth, Maria Madalena wrote other poems addressed to family members: to her husband, to their first daughter, to her deceased mother, and to her sister, Anica. She collected some of her poetry into a small handwritten collection titled *Flores singelas* (*Simple Flowers*) and dedicated "to the husband I adore" on December 30, 1898, the couple's third anniversary. Now and then, during teatime or after dinner, she probably read some of her poems out loud—in those pre-radio days, recitation was a form of home entertainment—and she may have let Fernando read the whole lot on his own. Although they lack punch, rarely expressing more than thematic and emotional generalities, the mere fact she wrote poems and assembled them into a modest little book no doubt inspired him. It would be two more years, however, before he composed his first serious poem.[3]

◆

THE YEAR 1898 SAW the "scramble for Africa" advance still further toward its execrable terminus, with France consolidating its possessions in west Africa; Germany fortifying its hold over territories corresponding to modern-day Burundi, Rwanda, Tanzania, Togo, Cameroon, and Namibia; and the United Kingdom securing its control of the Sudan through the horrifically deadly Battle of Omdurman. Imperialist expansion was not limited to Africa. In 1898 the Chinese coastal enclave of Guangzhouwan was added to French Indochina; Great Britain negotiated a ninety-nine-year lease of Hong Kong, which it had been governing since 1842; the United States annexed Hawaii; and the Spanish-American War, while it liberated Cuba, made the States the new foreign ruler of the Philippines, Puerto Rico, Guam, and Guantánamo Bay.

In South Africa all was peaceful for now, and nowhere more peaceful than in Natal's largest city. Between the two ruling white groups—the Boers and the British—there was an old and stubborn animosity, like a personality clash, but virtually no Boers (or Afrikaners) lived in Durban. For the Rosa family the end of 1898 brought only blessings to be thankful for. The new baby, Madalena Henriqueta, beamed with good health; the couple's first daughter turned two years old on November 27; and Fernando, five days before Christmas, came away from his school's graduation ceremony as the great foreign conqueror, winning three out of the five prizes awarded for his class.*

Three days later, the consul also had a moment of glory. On December 23 he helped inaugurate an ornately decorated cast-iron water fountain, covered by a likewise cast-iron canopy surmounted by a public clock, to commemorate the 400th anniversary of the discovery of Natal by Portugal's Vasco da Gama. The navigator sighted the territory on December 25, 1497, during his voyage to India and named it after Christmas Day—*Natal*, in Portuguese.† Almost exactly 401 years later, the Portuguese

---

* He failed to win the prizes in calisthenics and arithmetic.
† The indications in Vasco da Gama's logbook suggest that what he actually sighted was Pondoland, south of the area that became known as Natal.

consul, instead of having to defend his country against the occasional charges of "insignificance" and colonial incompetence that appeared in the local newspapers, was invited to speak at a ceremony honoring one of its illustrious maritime heroes. In his remarks, he pointed out that Natal's very name was a permanent, constantly pronounced memorial to the Portuguese discovery of the colony.[4] As for the memorial clock, an arguably hideous but rare surviving specimen of its kind, manufactured by a foundry in Glasgow, it still stands in Durban, though not at its original location.

✦

THE HISTORY TAUGHT IN Durban schools was largely English history,[5] but Fernando, whether through formal instruction or incidental discussions and his own readings, acquired enough of a knowledge of South African history to understand why the Boers (boer is the Dutch word for "farmer") and the more recently arrived settlers from Britain had a hard time getting along. During the Napoleonic occupation of the Netherlands (1795–1813), the British succeeded in wresting control of the Cape Colony from the Dutch. Immigrants were recruited from the United Kingdom, and the use of English quickly spread, along with English customs and a more secular, materialistic lifestyle. The British were concentrated in the towns, and for them to be in political control of the colony rather than the Dutch East India Company, which had founded Cape Town back in 1652, was a matter of indifference to the Boers, as long as their rural way of life was not affected.

This grace period did not last long, however, due to diverging opinions about the status and treatment of native Africans. Since Britain dominated the playing field of overseas imperialism, it could afford to show at least some respect for indigenous rights in the foreign lands it ruled, and the abolitionist movement had succeeded in making slavery unpalatable to the collective conscience of the British public. Free Africans in the Cape Colony were eventually granted the same rights as Europeans, at least on paper, and in 1834 all slaves in the British Empire were declared emancipated. This was the last straw for the Boers, who depended on slave labor for their farms and whose Calvinist theology easily accommodated the notion that certain races were divinely predestined to be subjugated. Their indignation was compounded by the tangle of red tape that rendered Britain's promise to compensate the slave owners practically worthless.[6]

No doubt for Fernando, as for virtually all Europeans in South Africa, whatever their views on slavery, the African natives—who hailed from a number of genetically and culturally distinct ethnicities—were all kaffirs and best ruled by members of the "superior" white race.* About the Boers he would later comment: "They're wonderful farmers and read the Bible every Sunday."[7] In spite of his sarcasm, he admired the Boers' tenacity. Eager to do things their way, without outside interference, more than ten thousand of them had migrated north and east from the Cape Colony in the so-called Great Trek, which lasted from around 1835 to 1845. Overpowering indigenous Africans, they occupied vast tracts of land that would soon become two agrarian, landlocked countries, the Orange Free State and the Transvaal Republic, which bordered Natal on its western and northwestern perimeter. Britain's ill-conceived annexation of the Transvaal Republic, in 1877, resulted in a humiliating defeat for the British army at the hands of the Boers, who rose up in arms in December 1880 and regained the right to self-government after three months of fighting.†

One and a half years before this temporary setback, Great Britain had successfully fought a brief but gruesome war against the Zulus, whose once powerful kingdom, which included a long stretch of coastline reaching as far as Mozambique, was eventually incorporated into Natal. Meanwhile the Cape Colony, after a series of wars against the Xhosa people, had solidified its control in the southeast, so that the British now controlled all of western and southern South Africa as well as the eastern coast. Goaded on by the logic of imperialism to fill in the north-central section of its ideal map of South Africa, Great Britain was practically predestined to revisit the problem of the tenacious, intractable Boers, making war on their two republics. Durban, which had become the largest town of South Africa founded by Britons, would be a major launching platform for waging the conflict.

---

* The word "kaffir," which is today highly offensive, was not at that time considered derogatory, though it was of course reductive.
† This armed conflict is sometimes known as the First Anglo-Boer War.

✦

As THEY BID FAREWELL to the outgoing year and made their reso-
lutions for 1899, few people in Durban could have imagined that war
would break out just ten months later, and even those who foresaw that
the mounting tension in the Transvaal was apt to end in bloodshed did
not suppose it would especially affect them. In a way they were right,
since most people's lives would not be much altered, but the face of the
city would change dramatically. With the onset of war, Durban became
a turnstile for thousands of troops from around the British Empire making their way to the lines of battle, and it was to Durban that most of
those same soldiers returned, wounded or dead or else or on their way to
some other imperial outpost. The port city, located at a safe remove from
the fighting, was also where many civilians from the war zones came to
seek refuge, causing its population—and urban problems—to swell. It
would have been difficult to remain oblivious to the effects of war, but
Fernando Pessoa may have almost succeeded in doing so. Being neither
South African nor English, and only eleven years old come June, he was
at any rate more preoccupied by the Gallic Wars, particularly since the
headmaster of his new school was a fanatical Latinist.

All schools opened for classes on or shortly after February 1, but Pessoa did not enroll in Durban High School until April 7. Chances are that
he spent the first two months of the term at St. Joseph's Convent School.
Its high school division was for girls, but perhaps, since he was still quite
young, he continued in the primary school, where at this point he must
have been an academic light-year ahead of the other students. The nuns
themselves no doubt recommended that he transfer to Durban's premier
school for boys. The high school was in the Berea, far from the downtown area where Pessoa and his family were now living, which might
have made his mother hesitate to send him there in February. And she
may have had other qualms. Her gifted son was bashful and slight of
build. How would he get on at an English-style boys' school?

Durban High School, founded in 1866 and flourishing even today,
has long been renowned for its academics as well as its sports teams, particularly rugby and cricket. Luckily for Fernando, who had no aptitude
for athletics, team sports were still getting off the ground when he began
studying there. The school had moved into new, impressive buildings in
1895, but the playing fields were not yet properly laid out and leveled, and

the students ran around and played ball in their ordinary school clothes.[8] Although Durban High School was on its way to becoming a South African version of an English public school (called "public" for being accessible to whoever could pay the tuition), contemporary accounts suggest there was not yet any serious bullying. Fernando Pessoa went unnoticed, except by his impressed teachers—most of whom were Oxford or Cambridge graduates—and by the few other students who competed for academic honors.

There were about 150 students at Durban High School in 1899, all of them white and a quarter of whom were boarders. The school had a preparatory section for younger boys, but ten-year-old Fernando entered directly into the high school proper, in the class designated as Form II-B, where most of the students were at least thirteen. D.H.S., as the school was popularly known, offered four years of basic high school instruction, Form I to Form IV, typically lasting from age twelve to fifteen or sixteen. Form V was a college prep year, and Form VI was college level. In June 1899, the same month he turned eleven, Fernando was promoted to Form II-A. The fact he was two years younger than the rest of the class and had enrolled two months late in the school year did not stop him from winning the Form II-A prize for general excellence in December. The prize book, signed and probably selected by the headmaster, was *Rome: From Earliest Times to the End of the Republic*, by Arthur Gilman.

Wilfrid Harry Nicholas, the headmaster of D.H.S. from 1886 to 1909, was already a legendary figure when Fernando Pessoa first walked through its gates. A little swarthy owing to some Spanish blood, with striking features and a dashing manner, Nicholas was self-confidence personified, generous and authoritarian, quick to assist, quick to criticize, passionate about literature and especially the classics, intolerant of stupidity, and never at a loss for words. He was usually accompanied by Jack, a white hunting dog that looked a little like his white-haired and white-moustached owner. The power of this English scholar's personality was difficult to resist, but not all the students appreciated his uncompromising rigor and methodology. A boy who graduated from the school in 1899 and went on to become a judge said about Nicholas: "His knowledge was massive, comprehensive. He was as near to being the complete man as anyone I have ever met." But another classmate of Pessoa reported: "I remember him as a very handsome man who had the happy knack of making everyone look a perfect idiot when he was taking a

Latin Class."[9] Pessoa, fortunately, was an excellent student of Latin, and
he seems to have received nothing but admiring encouragement from the
headmaster. Nicholas was known to demand a lot from his students, but
Fernando did not need much prodding.

Except for the absence of science, Pessoa's initial course load at D.H.S.
included basically the same subjects he had studied in his last year at the
St. Joseph's Convent School. His school day was a little longer, ending at
four o'clock, when he and the other students who lived downtown would
crowd into a pair of horse-drawn streetcars and head home.[10] Back on
West Street, in the privacy of his own bedroom, Fernando, with the aid
of his febrile imagination, would spend time with a different set of classmates. So we can glean from a passage written by Pessoa years later, for
*The Book of Disquiet*.[11] In it he recalls how, as a child, he used to collect old
cotton spools and stray chessmen, giving them names and personalities.

> One of them, who I had decided was rowdy and liked sports, lived
> inside a box on top of my dresser, where a streetcar would pass by
> each afternoon, when I—and then he—came home from school.
> The streetcar was made of the interiors of matchboxes, strung
> together somehow by wire. He'd bounce up and down when the
> car was in motion.

Pessoa goes on to describe how the "primitive streetcar" went from his
dresser to the nightstand, and from the nightstand to his bed, dutifully
taking all of his "ridiculous wooden schoolmates" home. He reports that
some of these schoolmates liked to peek at girls' legs, while he endowed
others with "bad habits" such as smoking or stealing. Sometimes he
would make one of the wooden spools or chessmen smoke rolled paper
behind a large box on top of a suitcase, and when a make-believe schoolteacher (held by his other hand) would suddenly come around, the smoker would hide the cigarette behind his back and act nonchalant, while
Fernando himself was on pins and needles, lest the smoker be caught.

Proud as he was of rising to the top of his class, having perfectly mas-
tered the ablative and dative cases of Latin, the young scholar was a
little sorry that he could not, at the same time, be a prankster, smoke
in the bathroom, steal, and act fresh with girls after school, so he constructed an alternate, imaginary school life in which he played out all
those naughty behaviors. He also played the part of the scolding teacher.

He played everything, and directed everything. He was the whole show. "What I am essentially [. . .] is a dramatist," Pessoa would write in his final year of life,[12] and so he was—but he was also the stage and everyone who walked on it, as well as the lone spectator in the audience.

Toward the end of the passage, the narrator regrets having lost his childhood capacity for invention:

> Why didn't I remain a child forever? Why didn't I die there, in one of those moments, preoccupied with the wiles of my school-mates and the as-if-unexpected arrival of my schoolteachers? Today I can't do this. . . . Today I have only reality, which I can't play with. . . . Poor little boy exiled in his manliness! Why did I have to grow up?

Actually, Pessoa did not grow up, at least not in the way most people do. He continued to indulge and delight in the pretended life. The wiles of his heteronyms are notorious, and the writer was wily with us, his posthumous readers. We don't know, after all, whether the passage I have been lingering over is true to his boyhood experience, nor if his alleged nostalgia of that experience was real. Even if this was a genuine recollection, but Pessoa may have greatly changed the details, and it is even possible that he made the whole thing up, which would not make it any less true from his point of view, accustomed to blending imagination into reality.

◆

By August 1899, as Pessoa embarked on his second semester at Durban High School, there was already more than a whiff of war in the air. Like most incipient wars, it was supposed to be a quick and tidy affair, with Britain's military machine easily trouncing the Boers, who had almost no professional army, relying instead on militiamen ready to lay down their hoes and take up rifles at a moment's notice. It had been shortsighted of the British to capitulate after just three months in the first clash with the Boers over the Transvaal, eighteen years earlier, and they needed to redress that error of judgment. So one could argue in 1899, only because the landscape had very lucratively changed in the meantime.

In 1880–1881, Britain had been loath to get bogged down in a war whose payoff, if won, would amount to political control over land that was good for little besides growing corn and herding sheep. A few years later, in 1886, vast gold deposits were discovered on the Witwatersrand, a long ridge south of Pretoria, the capital of the Transvaal, and almost overnight a new city was born—Johannesburg—populated not by Boers but by droves of Britons and other foreigners who came to extract, process, buy, and sell the yellow mineral. Within five years after the rush began, the Uitlanders (foreigners) in the Transvaal outnumbered the Boers, who feared they would lose control over the land they had fought so hard for.

The Uitlanders, in 1899, did not consist only of adventurers and profiteers. Many who had come looking for gold ended up in more conventional lines of work, settled down, married, and had children. They identified as South Africans and had every reason to complain about discriminatory Boer policies, such as lengthy residence requirements for voter eligibility. But their list of grievances did not remotely resemble a manifesto calling for war. It was certain British generals and politicians who had visions of charging cavalry and booming cannons deftly crushing the enemy as the tune of "Rule, Britannia!" reverberated in their ears. The generals yearned to avenge the Battle of Majuba Hill, in which weathered Boers and their teenage sons, back in 1881, overwhelmingly defeated two regiments of trained British soldiers, leading to imperialistic retreat and the restoration of Transvaal independence. The politicians, for their part, yearned to bring the entire South African house under British management.

The Boers had no desire to go to war, and the government leaders of Natal were also anxious to avoid it. On June 17, 1899, they sent a letter to Joseph Chamberlain, Britain's secretary of state for the colonies, stating that "war between the two principal white races in South Africa would be a terrible calamity, and should not be resorted to until all possible means of bringing about a peaceful solution of the difficulties had been tried and had failed."[13]

South Africa's richest and most ardent colonialist, Cecil Rhodes (1853–1902), contended that the United Kingdom, on the contrary, should use any means necessary to make the Boer nations submit to its authority. After amassing an enormous fortune in South African diamonds, augmented by gold from Johannesburg, Rhodes had obtained a royal charter from Queen Victoria that granted his British South Africa Company jurisdiction over a vast territory corresponding to present-day Zimbabwe and Zambia. Christened Rhodesia in 1895, it covered much of the same area that the Portuguese had been trying to annex until the British Ultimatum of 1890 punctured that improvident dream. Rhodes firmly believed that the world would be a better place to the extent that Britain succeeded in expanding its empire. Fernando Pessoa would later cite him and his colonial activity as the paradigmatic example of Great Britain's "administrative" and "material" style of imperialism, entirely opposed to the cultural, "spiritual" imperialism he envisioned for Portugal.[14]

In 1895 Rhodes, then the prime minister of the Cape Colony, had helped to mastermind a raid in which close to six hundred armed men on horseback, led by Leander Starr Jameson, the administrator of his South Africa Company, bounded toward Johannesburg, where the Uitlanders were supposed to rise up in arms so that together they could pull off a coup. Although the half-baked scheme resulted only in the capture of the raiders, the Jameson Raid may be considered the first salvo of the Anglo-Boer War, which would officially begin four years later, in October 1899.

# CHAPTER 8

TRUE TO THE USUAL PREWAR PATTERN, BOTH sides prepared for armed struggle—the Boers by spending lavishly on weapons for their militias, the British by dispatching ten thousand soldiers from around the empire to Natal—as each avowed that these merely "defensive" measures were intended to preserve peace, by discouraging the other side from attacking. Neither side had legitimate grounds for starting a war, but the Boers, convinced that the British were about to strike, fell into the trap of striking first—at which point Joseph Chamberlain and his appointee to the post of high commissioner for southern Africa, Alfred Milner, had all the motive they needed for war. They could claim it was their political and moral duty to defend the aggressed British colonies.

Looking back on the war when he was sixteen, it was obvious to Fernando Pessoa that England had been the aggressor, and particularly in the person of Joseph Chamberlain, whom he vilified in a sonnet, predicting that the spilled blood of all the Boer "sons and husbands" needlessly killed in the conflict would crush the "dark soul" of the British colonial secretary.[1] When the war first broke out, it's hard to say whether eleven-year-old Fernando remained impervious to the pro-British sentiment that entranced the town of Durban and completely dominated the local press. However, many people in Europe, especially in Ireland, which was still struggling for Home Rule, spontaneously sided with the underdog. No country, however, dared to lend aid to Britain's enemy. Public opinion also favored the Boers in the United States, where several declarations of solidarity were introduced in the Senate, albeit with no impact on the government's decision to remain neutral. How could the United States, which was at that moment gunning down thousands of Filipinos who were valiantly fighting to become independent, coherently support the Boers in their bid to remain independent? There were uncomfortable parallels between the

Philippine-American War and the Anglo-Boer War, both of which lasted from 1899 to 1902.[2]

Galloping through passes in the Drakensberg Mountains and across the hilly grasslands of the veld into Natal and the Cape Colony, the Boers, who were excellent marksmen and could keep well hidden since they knew the lay of the land, initially defeated the better-armed British troops. They laid siege to several garrison towns in both the English colonies, stunning their adversaries. Many tens of thousands of additional British soldiers were mobilized, and it soon became apparent that what was supposed to be a quick war would be a protracted conflict.

During the buildup to war, it occurred to military strategists and local politicians that the Transvaal Boers might make a rush for Durban before sufficient British troops could arrive to repel them. To prepare for that contingency, volunteer reserve troops had been organized into the Durban Light Infantry and three smaller militia units. Because the Boer commandos entrenched themselves in the interior, aspiring only to defend their national territories, the militias drawn up in Durban were deployed to the battle lines in western Natal. Called into active duty on September 30, 1899, a Saturday, the soldiers started out from the Drill Hall—about three blocks from where Pessoa's family was living—and marched up West Street to the train station while townspeople cheered amid intermittent drizzle and a biting wind. Roughly a thousand in number, they boarded open trains that took them to the war zone, where in two weeks' time they would trade fire with the Boers.

Between December 10 and 15, in what was quickly dubbed Black Week, the British suffered heavy losses on the three main fronts, with the third and most rattling defeat occurring in Natal, at Colenso, where five thousand Boer soldiers pushed back twenty thousand British troops. Like the Battle of Majuba Hill in the Anglo-Boer conflict of 1881, the Battle of Colenso was the great British embarrassment of the Anglo-Boer War—as Pessoa would recall with mirth years later, while at the same time excoriating Rudyard Kipling, whom he styled a "poetry pragmatist and scrap-metal imperialist, England's epic to answer Majuba and Colenso."[3] At the start of the Philippine-American War, in February 1899, Kipling had published "The White Man's Burden," a poem urging the United States to do its imperialistic duty by conquering and civilizing the "sullen peoples" of the Philippines.

The Boers did not capture the towns they had surrounded, and they made no attempt to penetrate farther into the English colonies. To gain more territory was not their objective; all they wanted was to keep their independence. The British, provided they were willing to pour enough resources into the war, could not lose it, and this time around they were willing. By early 1900, close to two hundred thousand British troops had been committed to the fight, and within two months they had gained the upper hand, sweeping into the two Boer republics, both of whose capitals fell in June. The war was thought to be almost over, but it ground on as a guerrilla conflict for another two years, until the Boers finally surrendered on May 31, 1902.[4]

◆

**DURBAN WAS THE SECOND** largest base for British military operations, after Cape Town, but while the war noticeably affected the local economy and the town's social fabric, it all happened as if in a film. The townspeople were like walk-ons in an epic tragedy whose central action they could not influence, though they passively participated in its development and witnessed some of its devastating consequences. The proclamation of martial law on October 22, 1899, eleven days after the war began, and the imposition of an 11:00 p.m. curfew two days later, had no practical effect on Pessoa or his family. Nor did they—or anyone else—have to contend with shortages of food, clothing, or household goods. The British controlled the seas, their ships kept the town well stocked, and many Durbanites grew more prosperous thanks to the war. The thousands of military personnel and other transients who passed through the town boosted the sales of local merchants. Shipping at the port shot up by more than 50 percent, with war-related ships transporting not just soldiers but also horses, mules, guns, and ammunition. The native African stevedores and coal heavers, finding themselves in high demand, were able to bid up their wages. And the businesses serving the port saw their revenues jump. The harbor—always an important hub of the Durban economy, with its traffic of ships dotting the seascape in all seasons—now ruled the town.

Ships arriving, ships departing, and ships on the high sea would provide the setting or be the subject matter for some of the finest poems signed by Pessoa's heteronym Álvaro de Campos, a naval engineer who had traveled widely and sometimes got inspiration by milling around the docks of Lisbon and recalling his long ocean voyages. But it was in

Durban, not in Portugal's capital, that the real-life Pessoa continually saw steamships with their distinctively colored funnels and flag-bearing masts sailing in and out of the busy yet somehow timeless harbor or else lingering at the outer anchorage, beyond the bar. In Durban he saw navy men, sailors, deckhands, dockworkers, and harbor officials.

The young boy's notions of maritime life also owed a lot to his stepfather, who had navigated in all the oceans during more than twenty years in the Portuguese navy. João Miguel Rosa, still a captain at heart, closely followed all matters of the sea. The consular archives from his time in Durban suggest it was more pleasure than work for him to attend to ships' officers in need of documents before continuing to their next destination, and some officers stopped by just to visit an old friend. A classmate at Durban High School reported that Pessoa, when he was fifteen years old, wrote him a long letter "in brilliant style and mostly about the seafaring characters he had met in his father's office."[5]

Although the increased shipping activity in Durban's harbor was mostly for transporting soldiers, animals, and weapons for war, as the conflict deepened, a few ships were fitted out as hospitals or as temporary jails for Boer prisoners of war. Still other ships brought hundreds of refugees to Durban. A majority of the European Uitlanders fled to Cape Town, but many others preferred Durban, and they were not the only ones pouring into Natal's port. On October 14, 1899, three days after the start of war, Gandhi wrote the Natal government to ask that Transvaal Indians be allowed to come to Durban by ship from Lourenço Marques. His request was granted.[6] Africans employed in the Transvaal goldfields also fled. On October 6, when passenger trains to Natal were no longer in service, over seven thousand Zulus had set out on a nine-day march, singing traditional songs as they went, from Johannesburg to the border and then on to the Natalian town of Dundee, where most of them boarded trains. Durban was one of their main destinations.[7]

The mounting human spectacle was in plain view for all to see, including Fernando. By early November, some four thousand white refugees were accommodated in the Drill Hall on West Street, another eleven hundred were camped at the grounds of the Durban and Coast Agricultural Society, a tent community for five hundred more sprang up close to the beach, in Victoria Park, and various public and private buildings provided shelter for smaller numbers of men, women, and children. Many refugees found some kind of work, and the town council coordinated efforts with several benevolent societies to distribute food and clothing. Some of the displaced Europeans were relatively well off and could afford to rent rooms or take lodging in hotels.

Durban also received about four thousand Indian refugees, for whom the town council did nothing, counting on the local Indian community to house and feed them. About fifteen hundred native African refugees were camped in the backyards of Durban, according to police estimates; several hundred others were allowed to set up camp on a section of the Agricultural Society fairgrounds, and many others were not accounted for.[8] (Colonial governments of the time kept only sketchy records on the black population.)

Hundreds of the refugees were penniless, and while most were law-abiding, the Transvaal gold rush had attracted its share of gruff characters reminiscent of the American Wild West. Behind the many Uitlanders who were single men came the prostitutes they had been patronizing in Johannesburg. They competed for clients by riding around in rickshaws to advertise their charms, sometimes relying on the Zulu rickshaw pullers to act as their pimps.[9] Other female refugees arrived at Durban with children but without husbands, not knowing how they would provide for their dependents. The potential for social tension and troublemaking was exacerbated by the fact that officials in the Transvaal, seeing an opportunity, had unlocked a few jails, letting the convicts join the Uitlander exodus.[10] If Fernando did not see them with his own eyes, he heard about the assorted kinds of crime that had spiked in Durban, along with begging, gambling, and prostitution—predictable local by-products of the deadly contest playing out in the hinterland.

Durban, despite everything, remained solidly Durban. The war caused no seismic shifts, but the motley influx of refugees noticeably enriched the social landscape. The already ethnically and racially variegated town became, as well, a vivid catalogue of assorted character types and unique life stories. Fernando Pessoa often had his nose in a book but, like most other writers or writers-to-be, he had a keen eye, and the house where he lived on West Street was practically at the epicenter of the town's heightened activity and community metamorphosis, with the harbor on one side, the municipal buildings on another, and refugee enclaves all around. The high school student from Portugal—himself split between two different languages and cultures, surrounded by all that human diversity, and standing in a gateway through which the men, the materials, and the mixed fortunes of war entered and exited or else lingered on—took everything in and acquired, inevitably, a nascent social and political awareness. And yet the net result of so many impressions was to reinforce his preference for the literary imagination.

Several decades later, in *The Book of Disquiet*, Pessoa—writing as Bernardo Soares—would allude to the world's "colorful parade of customs and fashions, the complex path of civilizations and progress, the grandiose commotion of empires and cultures." Two other passages from the same book contain similar phrasing, plus an added reference to "the vast variety of nations."[11] The colorful parade mentioned in all three passages is a global phenomenon, but it was specifically in Durban that Pessoa observed cultural diversity in high concentrations. In the first of these passages, the *Disquiet* narrator calls this parade "a myth and a fiction," while in the other two he argues that Earth's multifariousness can be seen and felt in a good imagination, making it unnecessary, even superfluous, to travel abroad. "Travel," he decrees, "is for those who cannot feel."

The *idea* of travel and especially of the seafaring life enchanted Pessoa—who relished, as an adult, the sailor and sea stories of British writer W. W. Jacobs—but he rarely referred to his own youthful voyages, and not even his adolescent writings reveal any particular enthusiasm for *actual* travel, whether by land or sea. Nor was he especially fascinated by the colorful mix of humanity on permanent display in Durban. Conceptually it was interesting, and it made him more open-minded, more world-aware, but he vastly preferred literature to anthropology. How to see and describe what he saw, the imaginative use and transformation of what he saw and felt—this was what mattered to Fernando, in thrall to an irresistible literary calling. Not even war, its massive repercussions, and the human suffering it causes were able to distract him. The historical commotion he witnessed seems merely to have inured him, if he was not somehow pre-inured, to the large and small troubles afflicting the world. He would address those troubles in his poetry, but he was more concerned with getting his rhyme and meter right than with trying to correct social evils and injustice.

Pessoa's first year at Durban High School ended on December 20, 1899, a few days after Black Week, when the heavy casualties inflicted by the Boers threw Natal into a state of jittery trepidation. Meanwhile a young war correspondent named Winston Churchill, who had been captured by the Boers on his way to the fighting front in November, managed to escape from a Pretoria jail and, after jumping several coal trains and enduring other adventures that are the stuff of charmed lives, turned up in Durban two days before Christmas. Received as a hero by cheering crowds, he gave a couple of impromptu speeches, declaring in the first one that "our cause is a just and right one, because we strike for equal rights for every white man in South Africa, and because we are representing the forces of civilization and progress." (It was most assuredly not to defend black or Indian equality that the British had gone to war.) Churchill delivered his second speech on the steps of city hall, three blocks up from the Portuguese consulate and consul's residence at 157 West Street. The local papers remarked on the speaker's "splendid dash and fire."[12] A member of England's upper class and an impassioned defender of the British Empire, the intrepid reporter soon returned to the front as a soldier. The following year he would be elected to the British Parliament.

◆

THE EMPHATIC BOER VICTORIES of December were followed by several less spectacular wins in January 1900, causing the flow of refugees into Durban to continue, with some twenty thousand having descended on the town by the month of March.[13] Then the tide of war turned and the refugee population began to ebb, at the same time that a new sort of war victim showed up. As the British army closed in on Boer strongholds, large numbers of bedraggled POWs began passing through Durban's port on their way to overseas prisons. If Fernando saw some of them file by, he must have marveled at the strange sight. Without uniforms, clad only in their raggedy farmer clothes, they looked anything but soldierly. And yet in the early fighting, blending in with the bush, they had devastated the smartly outfitted British troops, picking them off like rabbits. By mid-1900 the colonists no longer had anything to fear, but the Boers would not give up. They had become the rabbits—armed rabbits that were not easy to catch. Driven into the western and northern reaches of their former republics (annexed by the British), they kept on sniping, albeit with no chance of mounting a productive offensive against hundreds of thousands of imperial soldiers.

Like other modern wars, the one between the British and the Boers quickly spawned an industry of memorabilia, with war heroes pictured on badges, printed on teacups, and etched into silver spoon handles. Visual representations of war heroes and other aspects of the armed conflict reached Fernando through the medium of cigarette cards. British cigarette companies had for some time been including a collectible card in each pack sold, and military themes were especially popular.* Fernando began to collect two Boer War series of cigarette cards—depicting key statesmen, generals, battle scenes, maps—in late 1900 or early 1901. His main supplier of cards was his stepfather, an avid smoker, and the markings in a memo book where Fernando kept track of his collection suggests he did some swapping with classmates.[14]

The same memo book contains the record of another sort of collection, consisting of a few precious items he kept in a safe place. One of the listed items, "2 Portuguese Naval Officer's buttons come off Mr. J. M. Rosa's Uniform Coat," speaks to the boy's interest in things nautical and to the amiable but slightly formal nature of his relationship with "Mr." João Miguel Rosa, his ruddy and broad-chested stepfather. Another item, a couple of buttons "reported to have been taken off a pro-Boer German officer in some encounter with the English," shows us that the juvenile collector, despite being focused on his intellectual and imaginary life, was rather in awe of the war being waged in South Africa, or of war generally, the two buttons being like relics of a dead unknown soldier. Germans were especially sympathetic to the desperately fighting Boers, and some took up arms on their behalf.

People in Portugal also sympathized with the Boers, notwithstanding the government's policy of collaborating with the British, allowing them to use Lourenço Marques—officially neutral—as a port of entry to reach the Transvaal. In return for its cooperation, Portugal secured British recognition of its sovereignty over both Mozambique and Angola, territories that Germany had recently proposed divvying up with the United Kingdom. The odium stirred up by the British Ultimatum of 1890 still smoldered in the hearts and minds of the Portuguese, however, and the antiroyalist faction, spearheaded by the republicans, was not about to let it die out. The unsurrendering Boers were exalted for standing up to the imperial and imperious power of Britain: when over a thousand of them

---

* Cigarette cards originated in the United States, where baseball players were a favorite theme. Makers of chewing gum would eventually replace tobacco companies as the main distributor of baseball cards.

arrived as refugees at the port of Lisbon in late March 1901, they were greeted by a cheering crowd.[15] Nobody in Durban openly supported the Boers—to do so would have been treason—and the patriotic fervor of his teachers and classmates may have induced Fernando to side with the British while the war was in progress. But I think it more likely that he took no side until, at the age of fifteen or sixteen, a couple of years after the bloody conflict was over, he reflected on the costly human and material damages and found no reasonable justification, just hubris, for Britain's insistence on making the Boers submit. He sympathized with the losers.

In the same memo book where twelve-year-old Fernando recorded the objects that belonged to his several collections, he drew a chart that listed his marks at Durban High for the second semester of 1899 and the two semesters of 1900.[16] He also made a point of noting his class rank: first place in each of the three semesters. The only other student who, through diligent study, would eventually give him a run for his money—rather literally, as we shall see—was Clifford Geerdts, who was two years older than Pessoa. It was in 1901 that the two boys became classmates, and Geerdts would report many years later that the "little fellow with a big head" had introduced himself as Fernando António Luís Nogueira Pessoa, explaining to him that *nogueira* means "walnut tree." Geerdts's remembrance is confirmed by Pessoa's signature—F. A. L. N. Pessoa—in one of the opening pages of *La Mare au diable*, a novel by George Sand assigned to his French class in 1901.[17] The birth of his half brother Luís that January aroused yet another bout of sibling jealousy, aggravated by the fact that the newest addition to the Rosa family was a boy. It meant that Fernando's maleness had ceased to be unique. With a son and two daughters by her second marriage, his mother no longer needed him; her new family was enough; he had become dispensable. So he may have feared, which would be normal enough, but he had a highly original way of dealing with his insecurity. By inserting "Luís" into his own name, he linguistically grafted a piece of the Rosa family onto himself, and made himself into a bit of a Rosa. Like the God of the Book of Genesis, who said "Let there be light," and there was light, Pessoa used words and names to alter his world.

◆

REFUGEES COULD BE SEEN all over downtown Durban, where they did their shopping and ran errands like everybody else, and Pessoa probably saw wounded soldiers returned from the front, but he had no contact with a particularly tragic class of war victims, namely the several hundred thousand people placed in concentration camps. These detainment centers were necessitated by the British army's "scorched earth" response to the tooth-and-nail guerrilla war waged by the Boers once the capitals of their two republics had fallen. British forces ranged through the countryside, setting fire to farms, farmhouses, and even entire villages so as to remove all sources of sustenance for the guerrillas, who were forced to flee or lay down their arms. The Boer women and children, along with a few Boer men too old to fight, were relocated to several dozen hastily built camps. An even larger number of camps accommodated the black families who had worked the Boer farms or made a living on their own in the villages and the fields that were incinerated.

The conditions in the camps were appalling, due mostly to ineptitude and indifference, but British policy was deliberately inhumane on one shameful point: while the rations for Boer women and children were minimal and included little meat and no vegetables, even smaller allotments were given to those whose husbands and fathers were still in the field fighting. By half starving their wives and children, the British hoped to break the Boer guerrillas' obstinate will.

In 1901 Emily Hobhouse, who had set up the South African Women and Children's Distress Fund in Britain, visited camps in the Orange River Colony, as the defeated Orange Free State was now called, and wrote a damning report whose particulars were corroborated by a Ladies' Commission to South Africa, organized by the British government and led by British feminist Millicent Fawcett. Conditions in the camps improved, but medical attention was still wanting, and some 28,000 Boer women and (above all) children died, mostly from measles and other communicable diseases. This was about a quarter of the total white population in camps. The even worse conditions in the camps for native Africans were largely ignored, along with the number of fatalities they suffered, but it is estimated that 15,000–20,000 of the more than 115,000 black internees perished. Many able-bodied men in the black camps were put to work for the British military campaign as scouts, manual laborers, and miners. The Transvaal gold mines, shut down when the war started, reopened in 1901.[18]

The term "concentration camp" originated, in fact, with these camps created by the British during the Anglo-Boer War, and while it would be grossly unfair to compare their intent or their conditions with the Nazi camps, many of them were also sites of infamous horror—unintended but preventable. Inquisitive boy that he was, and by then a regular reader of newspapers, Fernando Pessoa was well informed about the camps, after the fact if not during, and their grim irony was not lost on him. In an article published in 1919, he would point out how British actions frequently belied their vaunted policy of respecting and defending basic human rights. It was on behalf of those rights that British politicians justified the war against the Boers and yet, he wrote, "they let the Boer women die in the Transvaal concentration camps."[19] Although most camps were located in the two conquered Boer republics, the largest camp of all—Merebank, which held as many as 9000 inmates—was built just south of Durban. That was in September 1901, however, one month after Pessoa and his family had departed for a yearlong holiday in Portugal. When they got back, the war was over.

◆

TWO AND A HALF months before setting sail with his family for Lisbon, Fernando the exceptional student suddenly gave birth to Pessoa the poet—in English. On May 12, 1901, he wrote his first serious poem:[20]

> Separated from thee, treasure of my heart,
> By earth despised, from sympathy free,
> Yet winds may quaver and hearts may waver,
> But I'll never forget thee.
>
> Soft seem the chimes of boyhood sweet
> To one who is no more free,
> But let winds quaver and men's hearts waver,
> I'll never forget thee.
>
> In a dim vision, from school hailing
> Myself, a boyish form, I see,
> And winds have quavered and men's hearts wavered,
> But I've not forgotten thee.

The poem continues in the same vein for four more stanzas, which are poetically no better than the first three. The rhymes are poor, the meter is inconsistent, and the story told by the poem's twenty-eight lines is unconvincing. There is no real beloved here, just a weakly imagined one, wrapped in a "dim vision" belonging to the distant future, as if the poet were already a full-grown adult looking back. This last point is what makes the poem biographically noteworthy. Though unsatisfying as a literary composition, it is a foretaste of what Pessoa's poetry would be most famous for: *fingimento*, which means "feigning," "faking," "pretending." This method, which most poets resort to at least some of the time, was Pessoa's almost exclusive basis for writing poetry. In 1901, posing as a mature man who has not forgotten the "treasure" of his heart from long, long ago, he feigned a love he did not feel as well as years of experience he did not have. So it was already a double act of *fingimento*.

"The poet is a feigner" (*fingidor*, in Portuguese) is the first line of Pessoa's most translated poem, "Autopsychography," written on April 1, 1931. The "foolish" date of its composition might make us suspect that he was pulling our leg, by resorting to the liar's paradox. According to the rules of logical syntax, if the poet is a feigner, then his statement "The poet is a feigner" must be feigned, and therefore not true. But Pessoa was not trying to be sly with us; the conundrum was his own. He didn't know how *not* to feign, and so the closest he could come to being sincere was to accept himself as a feigner. Already as a child, Fernando was determined to change himself and his world. He was interested not just in make-believe but in making, and remaking, reality.

One month before he wrote his first poem, Fernando produced a homemade newspaper dedicated to humor. "The following jokes were received on 2nd April 1901," announced the young editor at the top of the first page. This was the kind of announcement that might appear in a legitimate newspaper at the head of a section reserved for jokes, riddles, and witty poems sent in by readers. In Fernando's paper, the announced "jokes" consisted of eleven pages of anecdotes, a funny poem, comic dialogues, and the like—half in English, half in French. A few of the items were serious rather than humorous in tone. Not one was his own work. All were copied, in Fernando's neatest schoolboy penmanship, from real newspapers or from books.

The twelfth and last page of the newspaper introduced a sports section listing the results of cricket matches between fictitious clubs made up of fictitious players. The contents for this section did come out of Fernando's own head, and I will soon be returning to his wide world of virtual sports.[21] What I want to point out now is that the boy's reading, writing, publishing aspirations, and private world of fictional characters, including athletes, all evolved together. And newspapers were the place where all these interests converged. It would have warmed the heart of his late uncle Cunha to know that the boy had combined their old game of inventing imaginary people with a new game, journalism, inspired by their frequent visits to the newsroom of the *Correio da Noite* when he was younger. Uncle Cunha had also supplied his nephew with newspapers or sections of newspaper, such as the humor pages, that a small boy fond of reading could appreciate, and, up until his death, he continued this practice—sending them by mail—once Fernando moved to Durban.

◆

FERNANDO PESSOA'S FAVORITE BOOK was *The Posthumous Papers of the Pickwick Club*, which he kept returning to throughout his life.[22] He read it for the first time in 1900 or 1901, and it inspired one of his first large-scale (but unrealized) literary projects, *Papers of the Nonsense Club*, which was to include essays with titles such as "On the Runaway Hat" and "On the Sublimeness of the Obscure."[23] *The Pickwick Papers* is not a typical book for children, who are more likely to be drawn to the growing-up dramas of Oliver Twist or David Copperfield. Mr. Pickwick and his three traveling companions are adult men with adult interests. Their antics, it is true, are good for laughs at any age, and comic writing greatly appealed to Pessoa as a child, but it was not on the strength of gags and funny scenes hanging on to no real plot that he fell in love with the novel. He was charmed by its colorful characters and by their *liveliness*, which existed on its own, without the need for plot. In a passage from *The Book of Disquiet*, Pessoa would describe the Pickwickians as "extrahuman figures" who, in a different way from us, are every bit as real.[24] Expanding on this idea, an unfinished essay he drafted in English would claim that Dickens's first novel, which appeared in 1836–1837, confers on its readers a "mystic vision" that involves a "recasting of the old pagan noise, the old Bacchic joy at the world being ours, though transiently, at the coexistence and fullness of men, at the meeting and sad parting of perennial mankind." The words "men" and "mankind" are gender-specific, as the next paragraph in the essay makes clear:

It is a human world, and so women are of no importance in it, as the old pagan criterion has it, and has it truly. The women of Dickens are cardboard and sawdust to pack his men to us on the voyage from the spaces of dream. The joy and zest of life does not include woman, and the old Greeks, who created paederasty as an institution of social joy, knew this to the final end.[25]

The middle sentence of this passage is an objective, true enough observation: women are indeed like scenery or furniture in this novel about men relating to men. The first and third sentences, on the other hand, tell us little about the novel but a great deal about Pessoa, who excluded women from any "human world" of lively joy. Taken together, the three sentences seem to be a confession of his own preference for keeping company with men. He would celebrate male camaraderie in his literary criticism and in comments sprinkled throughout *The Book of Disquiet*. And the society of his heteronyms was a virtually all-male club, where women are not even conversationally appreciated as sexual objects. In his private reflections, the narrator of *The Book of Disquiet*, Bernardo Soares, does spend some time exalting a "Lady of Dreams," whom he says he can adore only because she was "never defiled by the horror of being fertilized or the horror of giving birth."[26] But in the world of downtown Lisbon, where he lives and works as an assistant bookkeeper, he prefers the congenial, undemanding company of his co-workers, all of them male.

Pessoa in his real life, like Soares in his invented one, was a little afraid of women, but he interacted with just about everybody—men as well as women—from a slight yet unbridgeable distance. There is no evidence that he engaged in pederasty or any kind of sex with men, nor is there much evidence of emotional intensity or reciprocal passion in his male friendships. He would spend hundreds of hours with men in cafés and had friendships that endured for many years, but as if by accident, as if he and the friends just happened to belong to the same club. He rarely opened up his heart to anyone.

The men's club formed by Samuel Pickwick and his friends would serve Pessoa as a model of social amiability, but Dickens's book had another, more important impact on the budding writer. As the first novel he read that managed to transport him into its own, fictionally vast and vivid realm, *The Pickwick Papers* was the initiatory, incantatory book that revealed to Pessoa the full potential of literature as an alternate, large-as-life reality.

✦

FERNANDO'S FIRST HOMEMADE NEWSPAPER and the composition of his first juvenile poem added another dimension to literature's practical significance. It went from being a reality he could inhabit, through reading, to one he could also create—for himself, for others, and for posterity. In the short run, however, he had little time for creating, since his mental energy was focused on preparing for the School Higher Examination, held in June 1901. This was actually a grueling battery of exams, which Form IV students needed to pass to earn their diploma. Not even a genius can absorb Latin without disciplined, concentrated study, and Fernando—who would be notoriously undisciplined as a writer and in his daily life—still had the patience to methodically memorize declensions, conjugations, and new vocabulary. Of the subjects tested—English, Latin, French, arithmetic, algebra, and geometry—his best result was in Latin, his worst in arithmetic. His combined score was the highest for his school, and he ranked in 48th place among the 673 South Africans who took the exam.[27] Pessoa had finished high school, eclipsing all his classmates, and he was barely thirteen years old.

He could relax on his thirteenth birthday, which fell one week after he sat for the five-day examination, but then a sad thing happened: the younger of his two sisters, Madalena Henriqueta, contracted a fatal case of meningitis. Fernando missed the last week of classes for the term, which ended on June 26, the day after she died.[28]

On July 7, 1901, João Miguel Rosa sent a telegram to the minister of foreign affairs, requesting leave to travel to Portugal for health reasons. In a follow-up letter, he explained that his doctor had advised a respite from the African climate and that the Belgian consulate would handle Portuguese affairs in his absence.[29] João Rosa did not suffer from any ailment in particular, but after six straight years in South Africa he was entitled to a holiday with his family in the home country, and he timed the trip to allow Fernando to finish high school. The consul's request was granted, and on August 1, the Rosa family and their head housekeeper, a native Mozambican named Paciência, boarded the SS *König*, a German steamer that would take them all the way to Lisbon. Their luggage included a small coffin with the remains of two-and-a-half-year-old Madalena Henriqueta, who would be buried on Portuguese soil.[30]

The usual passenger route from Durban to Lisbon was around the impassive crags of the Cape of Good Hope and up the western side of Africa, a voyage lasting about twenty-five days, but the *König* went up the eastern seaboard and through the Suez Canal, calling at Lourenço Marques, Beira, Zanzibar, Dar es Salaam, Tanga, Aden, Port Said, and Naples, before reaching Portugal's capital—a forty-three-day voyage.

This journey would bear poetic fruit through one of Pessoa's future heteronyms, Álvaro de Campos, the world traveler and naval engineer. In his poem "Time's Passage," written in 1916, the engineer would make a cryptic reference to the "almost North African stature of Zanzibar in the sun" and remark that Dar es Salaam was a tricky port to sail out of. Another Campos poem, titled "Opiary" and dating from 1915, was supposedly written in the Suez Canal on his return voyage from the Far East. The characters on his ship included a "swindling French count who lingers at funerals" and a cabin boy with the "lofty bearing of a Scottish laird who's been fasting." Perhaps these colorful descriptions were founded on fact. Perhaps the *König* had a rough time negotiating the port of Dar es Salaam, and perhaps it carried passengers who would travel again, years later, on Álvaro de Campos's steamer. Or perhaps not. But one way or another, directly or indirectly, the young man's real voyages were an inspiration for his imaginary ones.

# CHAPTER 9

O N SEPTEMBER 13, 1901, THE SS *KÖNIG* FINALLY
sailed into the harbor of sedate, softly hilly, and pleasantly
familiar Lisbon. Except for the novelty of electric-powered
streetcars, which had begun operating in August, the face of the city had
changed very little in the five and a half years since Fernando and his
mother had immigrated to South Africa. The *Jornal do Comércio*, a paper
specializing in news of shipping and commerce, duly reported the arrival
of the *König* and dedicated a separate notice to one of its passengers, João
Miguel Rosa, praising the diplomat for all his good work and in particular for keeping the Portuguese authorities in Lourenço Marques well
informed of the latest developments in South Africa. "Moreover, any
Portuguese passing through Durban has been so warmly received at the
residence of Sr. Rosa on West Street that the memory will remain forever
engraved in their heart." The paper extended a cordial welcome to him
and his family.[1]

The family rented an apartment on Rua de Pedrouços, just a block
away from the house where Pessoa's great-aunts Maria and Rita lived,
along with Grandma Dionísia, and where Fernando occasionally stayed
as a small boy. His doting aunt Maria had left his bedroom intact, with
the collection of old toys he'd outgrown, though perhaps not completely.
And besides the toys, there was the ghost of his mischievous uncle Cunha,
reminding him of how they used to make up stories in which invented
knights, captains, and politicians were protagonists. Soon enough the
boy on holiday would invent a new cast of imaginary characters to help
him while away the days.[2]

At some point Fernando, alone or accompanied by his family, made a
trip to Tavira, in the Algarve. His mother encouraged him to maintain
a good rapport with his paternal relatives, especially his "aunt" Lisbela,
who had grown close to him during the several months she spent in
Lisbon in 1893, when his father (her cousin) was dying of tuberculo-

sis. She had returned to Lisbon the following year, for Fernando's sixth birthday, and continued to stay in touch with him through letters.[3] Since demented Grandma Dionísia could no longer hold a proper conversation with Fernando, let alone keep up with and appreciate his development as an unusually talented adolescent, Lisbela was a kind of surrogate grandmother, and the only relative on his father's side with whom he felt a lively emotional connection.

In Lisbon Fernando was instantly reimmersed in the sprawling web of relatives from his mother's side. Maria Madalena's various aunts and cousins continually invited the Rosa family for lunch, tea, or dinner. João Rosa was happy to let his wife's relations be the center around which he and their children revolved during their Portuguese holiday, but he also wanted to show off his family to his two older brothers, Júlio Leopoldo[4] and Henrique, who had represented him in his proxy marriage with Maria Madalena. Unfortunately for Fernando and his sister Henriqueta, neither brother had children for them to play with. Fernando, however, was understandably intrigued by the oldest brother, Henrique Rosa, the army officer who *wrote poetry*, read books on many different subjects, and periodically sequestered himself in his apartment. This stepuncle, Fernando quickly realized, was a classic example of the quirky sort of individual known as an "eccentric." Fernando may have wondered if he himself might be an eccentric, and if this was a quality that predisposed one to being a poet.

Informed of Fernando's scholastic accomplishments and his interest in literature, Henrique Rosa took a shining to him, and he would eventually become an important friend. At this point, however, their social contact was limited to family visits, in which Pessoa observed him with more than usual curiosity.

Liberated from classes and from upcoming exams, Fernando spent a lot of time reading, now mostly in Portuguese: literary classics, books of general knowledge, modern poetry, and humorous writing. He was on holiday, he read for pleasure, and one of his favorite publications was *O Pimpão* (*The Fop*), a twice-weekly newspaper featuring sketches, light verse, anecdotes, riddles, and satirical cartoons, though it also published poems about serious subjects written in an elevated style. Fernando learned about *O Pimpão* from his stepuncle Henrique Rosa, who regularly contributed poems to the paper between December 1901 and September 1902. He signed them all with a pseudonym, Azor, which was his last name (originally "Roza") spelled backwards.[5]

IN 1902 FERNANDO DECIDED to start his own newspaper, *O Palrador* (*The Tattler*), which he filled with fictional news and real news, jokes and riddles, science topics, short fictions, and poems—all in excellent Portuguese. Unlike the periodical of humor he had attempted a year earlier, in Durban, *The Tattler* contained only his own, original work. But the articles, poems, and other pieces were all attributed to fictitious writers and journalists. The first surviving issue is the fifth, dated March 22, 1902. It was neatly handwritten on a large, single sheet of paper folded into four pages with three columns on each. The lead article, "Monsters of Antiquity," tells about dinosaurs but also provides a summary account of Darwinian evolution. At a certain point, the essayist soberly reminds us that "[m]an himself, who proudly deems himself the king of creation, is no more than a link in the vast chain of organisms that live on earth." Although there was endless debate about the details, evolutionary theory was beginning to be widely accepted in Europe by the early twentieth century.[6]

Signed by Francisco Angard, whose last name seems to be a play on "On guard!," this article about dinosaurs is followed by part 2 of a factual essay on pearl diving, signed by Dr. Caloiro (Dr. Freshman) and continuing from the previous issue. Both articles, written in an engaging style and showing off the writer's learning, are entirely serious. The rest of the issue is fun and games, consisting of anecdotes, various types of riddles, answers to the previous issue's riddles, and a humorous poem titled "The Mice," which tells how three mice in a grocery shop all die from eating artificially colored sausage or adulterated flour and milk. The fourth mouse in the family, left all alone and disconsolate, decides to commit suicide, but the rat poison he finds on one of the shelves and gobbles up to achieve his purpose is also adulterated, so that instead of dying he just gets fat.

"The Mice" was signed by Pip, a name borrowed from the upwardly mobile hero of *Great Expectations*, one of Dickens's most memorable characters. Fernando's Pip, besides authoring poetry, was an inventor of riddles for *The Tattler*. His name would resurface in Durban as a signature in a Latin primer used by Pessoa in 1904.[7] *The Tattler*'s most prominent poet and riddle maker was Dr. Pancrácio (Dr. Know-Nothing). Another contributor of riddles, Diabo Azul (Blue Devil), took his name from the Diabo Azul who signed short stories and sketches published in Fernando's recent discovery, *O Pimpão*.[8] Since Blue Devil was not a legal name, Fernando could use it with impunity, thereby conferring a borrowed prestige on his modest journalistic endeavor. This may have been a marketing strategy. *The Tattler* sold for twenty reis, the going rate for a few Portuguese newspapers; others sold for half that amount. The first four issues, missing from the Pessoa Archive, were probably purchased by amused relatives.

Pessoa's make-believe newspapers were the catalyst for his first sustained run of creative writing, and although the poems and prose pieces he produced for them are not great literature, they prefigure, in miniature, some salient traits of Portugal's most fascinating author of modern times. What immediately stands out is the dizzying number of writer-characters who signed what thirteen- or fourteen-year-old Fernando wrote. Whatever scholars may conclude about the real nature and significance of Pessoa's self-dispersion into a cadre of invented authors, it was a practice that originated with his earliest attempts at serious writing. Indeed, so intrinsic was it to his creative process that the pseudo-authors from *The Tattler* sometimes had their own pseudonyms—as if self-othering were a necessary condition for the act of writing, even when the writer was himself already a fiction. The juvenile newspapers, besides foreshadowing Pessoa's complex family of heteronyms, also functioned as a one-man writing workshop, in which the young author tried out various styles and set forth several of the major themes that would recur in his mature work.

The second surviving issue of *The Tattler*, "published" on May 24, 1902, led off with the conclusion of the article on dinosaurs, and there was the usual assortment of riddles, but the heart of the paper was devoted to three poems, two of which were signed by Dr. Pancrácio. One was a satire against a lexicologist's proposal to modernize Portuguese spelling based on phonetic principles. These principles would be adopted a few years later, in 1911, when the government—as part of a campaign to increase literacy—mandated sweeping changes to simplify spelling. The new orthography did make it easier for beginners to learn how to write, but it also obscured the Greek and Latin origins of many words. Rejecting the 1911 spelling reform, Pessoa would continue to write in the old manner—*rhythmo, prompto,* and *philosophia* instead of *ritmo, pronto,* and *filosofia*. He justified his recalcitrance by arguing, in

*The Book of Disquiet*, that "the pageantry of Greco-Roman transliteration" dresses the word "in its authentic royal robe, making it a lady and queen."

Dr. Pancrácio's other, very different poem was a sonnet—the first known sonnet produced by Pessoa. Titled "Sonho" ("Dream"), its theme is reminiscent of the most famous play by the Spanish Golden Age playwright Calderón de la Barca (1600–1681), *La vida es sueño*, usually translated as *Life Is a Dream*. The sonnet concludes with the following tercet:

> Caught up in dreaming, I never dreamed
> That in this life we dream while awake,
> That in this world we live by dreaming!

These were deep thoughts for a boy his age. "Life is but a dream" is the last line of a much recited nursery rhyme, true, but how many children ever think about what they're singing? The dreaminess of reality, and the possibility of creating and augmenting reality through dreams, would be a central theme of *The Book of Disquiet* as well as of Pessoa's only complete play, *O Marinheiro* (*The Mariner*), which he would publish in 1915.

The two Dr. Pancrácio poems—one a humorous invective against simplified spelling and the other a solemn meditation on the wispy, dreamy nature of life—are as different as night and day; like night and day, they form a complete circle. In a world of dreams where nothing is solid, words are crucial, since they give shape and weight to the things we see, or imagine we see. When, upon waking, we recall a nighttime dream, it is our words that give it substance and a kind of reality, a linguistic reality. To Pessoa's way of thinking, words were objective, objectifying; they endowed the dream-stuff of life with clear contours. Because his language world was a written world, it mattered to him how words were spelled.

The third poem included in the May 24 issue of *The Tattler*, "Estátuas" ("Statues"), is poetically less interesting but marks a new stage in Pessoa's career of self-othering, since its fictional author, Eduardo Lança, has a life quite independent of the poems he supposedly writes and the newspaper where they appear. A biographical note signed by Luís António Congo, the *Tattler*'s "assistant editor," informs us that Lança was born on September 15, 1875, in the state of Bahia, Brazil, where he went to business school and landed a job in a large firm, by which time his parents had both died. The firm sent him on a business trip to Lisbon, where he settled down. After publishing *Impressions of a Traveler to Portugal*, written in "a beautiful and truly Portuguese style," Lança went on to publish three collections of poetry. He has another book forthcoming and is a frequent contributor to magazines both in Portugal and in Brazil.

The thumbnail life of Eduardo Lança becomes more interesting once we realize its true significance: it was a prophetic emblem of Fernando's immediate future back in South Africa and his long-range future in Portugal. Indeed, no sooner did he return to Durban, in that same year of 1902, than he started studying business, the same subject Lança had reportedly studied in Brazil. Fernando evidently knew, by May 1902, that he would soon be enrolling in business school. Whether the idea came from his stepfather or from his sensible-minded maternal relatives, it would have been fully endorsed by his mother, and Fernando went along, animated at least by the thought of a livelihood that promised him autonomy. It was Eduardo Lança's job at a business firm, after all, that enabled him to move from Bahia to Portugal, where he went on to become a successful poet. This Brazilian poet, whose last name can mean (as a noun) "lance" or "javelin" but also (as a verb) "launches" or "hurls," personified Fernando's hope of hurling himself back to Lisbon for good and then launching himself as a writer.

The fact that Lança's parents die before he takes his degree, thereby freeing him to do exactly what he wants with his life, is too odd a detail not to be meaningful. Although Fernando never remotely wished for the death of his parents, he was looking forward to escaping from their control, to being on his own. And he seems to have felt that he was mentally and emotionally already his own man—inwardly independent, and essentially alone. So he would remain. Not a single one of his alter egos—beginning with Eduardo Lança, the first to be endowed with a biography—was ever married, and not one of them had a mother or father, either because they had already died or simply because they are never mentioned.

✦

THE CAPACITY FOR POWERFUL emotions, including love, develops early on; the ability to conceptualize them comes later. Fernando Pessoa was a strange case, however. He was emotionally on par with other fourteen-year-olds but was intellectually advanced for his age, and this imbalance had consequences for his personality, his social relationships, and his literary work. He had by now reached puberty, and the stirrings of his adolescent libido coincided with his first outpouring as a creative artist, but the relationship of those stirrings to that outpouring is at best implicit; it doesn't jump off the page. Young boys in love, if inspired to write poems, are apt to express their ardent feelings in a candidly lyrical style bordering on sentimentality, if not actually swimming in it. Far removed from all that, Fernando's youthful poems about love exhibited a conceptual and aesthetic sophistication acquired from his extensive readings of mature poets.

One of Fernando's first literary masters was Luís Vaz de Camões (c. 1524–1580), whose exquisite and varied poetic output makes him comparable to poets as diverse as Virgil, Petrarch, Dante, and Shakespeare. Camões, who spent his earliest and last years in Lisbon, is best remembered for *The Lusiads*, his epic poem about Vasco da Gama's inaugural voyage to India, but he authored a no less stunning body of lyric poetry, much of it inspired by his many loves and bohemian adventures on three continents. Pessoa mimicked his style more than once in his adolescent poetry. The sonnet "Metempsychosis," included in the third surviving issue of *The Tattler*,[9] describes how the "pure soul" of a woman admired from afar arouses "pure impulses" in the narrator, whose soul she comes to inhabit. This is an amorous scenario taken straight out of Camões, but whereas the spiritualized presence of an unattainable woman brings real elation and real suffering to the great Renaissance poet, who naturally desired physical consummation, the narrator of "Metempsychosis" feels no such tension. His talk of a pure lady who inspires a pure love is purely abstract poetry, with little or no connection to his experience. The young poet reworks old models in the manner of an apprentice sculptor, handling literary conceits like so much clay.

"Ave Maria," a poem written on April 7 and not included in *The Tattler*, embeds in its nine quatrains, one small phrase at a time, the whole of the popular Catholic prayer alluded to in the title—"Hail Mary, full of grace, the Lord is with thee," and so on. Pessoa dedicated the poem to his mother, Maria. While this sanctifying homage was no doubt sincere and must have deeply touched his mother, neither she nor the Holy Mother of God was the poem's real inspiration. The poet was copying yet another trick he learned from Camões, whose most famous religious poem, "Sôbolos rios que vão," is an expansion of Psalm 137 ("By the rivers that flow"), the whole of which it likewise, gradually quotes through the course of its 365 lines.

Some of Pessoa's poems enabled him to identify, confront, and come to terms with certain feelings, but this was usually an incidental benefit rather than his motivation for writing. From the beginning, he wrote under the shadow of a monumental literary tradition that he devoutly admired and longed to become part of. Perhaps most aspiring young writers have a similar ambition. Unlike most young writers, Fernando was already familiar with many of the works that make up that tradition. Much of his writing was rewriting, disconnected from his emotional or psychological life, except insofar as that life was dominated by art. His models were often from English poetry, even when he was writing in Portuguese. A sonnet from June 1902 titled "Antígona" ("Antigone"), for instance, partly paraphrases and partly reinvents Elizabeth Barrett Browning's most famous sonnet, in which she counted all the ways she loved her soon-to-be husband, Robert Browning. Fernando's sonnet, on the other hand, addresses a character of Greek mythology infinitely remote from his own experience.[10]

About half of the fifteen or so poems that Pessoa wrote between March and August of 1902 invoke a beloved lady or feature women as objects of desire. Without feeling any love himself, the novice poet freely pilfered the amorous discourse of poets such as Camões and Elizabeth Barrett Browning. Either that, or he used their mature poetic examples to embody his still immature feelings of amorous attraction. The latter is a far less likely hypothesis. If true, then Pessoa left his amorous feelings there—poetically resolved, at least for the time being. It would be a few more years before he would write another, likewise not very convincing love poem.*

Doubts about his attractiveness to others, an affective fixation on his mother, insecurity about his sexual orientation—these are all possible reasons for why Fernando Pessoa only read and wrote about love. Actual

---

* That next love poem is "Sonnet," which begins "Lady, believe me ever at your feet" and is dated March 1907. As in his poems from 1902, the beloved lady seems to be merely hypothetical. Never, in all his poetry, do we find a concentrated bunch of love poems directed to a specific person.

love was a complicated undertaking, which he avoided. Or perhaps it was a gift, bestowed on others but not on him. As a young man, absorbed as he was by his literary pleasures, he did not seem to especially miss it, but in his twenties he would begin to wonder if maybe he wanted it after all, whatever "it" was. His writing, which had always been a safe, unworldly haven, would become a secret vehicle for sexual exploration and self-discovery. Not so secret, actually, since Pessoa not only wrote but also published poems depicting heterosexual and homosexual passions and even some graphic sadomasochistic fantasies.

But he was never comfortable with the idea of real live sex. He preferred the jovial bonhomie that he had remarked among the members of the Pickwick Club and that he fostered, if possible, among his imaginary friends and literary collaborators, beginning with the journalistic team of *The Tattler*. If we turn to this newspaper's jokes and riddles section, we find the Blue Devil dedicating a riddle to Dr. Pancrácio, who offers a logogriph (a kind of word puzzle) to Gee, who addresses a metagram (a word game relying on letter substitution) to Pip, who dedicates a riddle to Parry, and so on. Other riddlers had names from the garden: Pimenta (Pepper), Rabanete (Radish), and Zé Nabos (Joe Turnips). And there were three women who joined in the fun: Cecília, the Nymph, and the Black Nymph. All were solvers as well as inventors of riddles, and a column regularly listed the number of correct solutions from the previous issue for each of the participants. They were in friendly competition.

If we are to believe Pessoa, his interacting journalists and invented poets were important not only for his writing. In a letter dated January 13, 1935, he would claim that, since childhood,

it has been my tendency to create around me a fictitious world, to surround myself with friends and acquaintances who never existed. (I cannot be sure, of course, if they really never existed, or if it is me who does not exist. In this matter, as in any other, we should not be dogmatic.) Ever since I have known myself as "me," I can remember envisioning the shape, motions, character and life story of various unreal figures who were as visible and as close to me as the manifestations of what we call, perhaps too hastily, real life. [. . .] This tendency to create around me another world, just like this one but with other people, has never left my imagination.

As mentioned earlier, Pessoa wrote elsewhere of the compelling need he felt, when still a small child, "to enlarge the world with fictitious personalities" such as the Chevalier de Pas—a need that grew even stronger in his adolescence, "taking firmer root with each passing year." Pip, Pancrácio, and other contributors to *The Tattler* were merely the first wave of "fictitious personalities" to emerge in Pessoa's adolescence. They would be followed up, in Durban, by pseudo-selves who wrote in English.

There is an essential difference in these two accounts of the heteronyms' origins. One of them is predicated on Pessoa's natural impulse to create *"another world"* populated by "other people," while the second account hinges on his tendency to *"enlarge the world"* with invented personalities. The two explanations are complementary. Pessoa generated an alternate reality into which he could and did retreat, but he also tried to insinuate parts of it into the reality he shared with the people around him. We saw this already with the Chevalier de Pas, whose awkwardly scrawled signature infiltrated *The Floral Birthday Book* of Pessoa's mother, taking its place among the neatly inscribed names of various family members and friends. Pessoa's mixing of imaginary and real worlds is also apparent in *The Tattler*, where factual articles and the pen names of real journalists intruded into a newspaper that was mostly sheer invention.[11] Throughout the rest of his life, the world in which Pessoa moved and the world of which he dreamed would promiscuously intermingle.

◆

IF, DURING HIS YEARLONG sojourn in Portugal, Fernando needed to invent "friends and acquaintances who never existed" as well as make-believe newspapers in which they kept busy as journalists and poets, it was partly just to keep himself from getting bored, since most of his Lisbon relatives were all much older. Only in the ninth month of his sojourn did he finally get to visit with his first cousins, Mário and Maria. On May 2, 1902, João Miguel Rosa and his family, including Paciência, their Mozambican housekeeper, departed from Lisbon for the island of Terceira, arriving at their destination on the seventh, a day late. Unexpected gales and heavy rains across the Azores had hindered their ship's progress, but even under a leaden sky the approach to Terceira's capital, Angra do Heroísmo, was an impressive sight, dominated by the extinct volcano known as Monte Brasil, which rises from a peninsula to the left of the open harbor and overlooks the town like a faithful guard.

Waiting at the dock for the Rosas and Fernando Pessoa were Aunt Anica, her husband, João Nogueira de Freitas, and their two children, Mário and Maria. Almost nine years had passed since Maria Madalena had seen her sister, brother-in-law, nephew, and niece, and she was excited to introduce them all to her new husband and new children: five-year-old Henriqueta, whom everyone called Teca, and one-year-old Luís. She was no less proud of her elder son, elegantly dressed in black breeches and a white shirt with an impeccably starched collar, now well on his way to becoming a man, though with strangers he still had the meek manner of a child not sure of himself.[12] Aunt Anica looked more or less as Fernando remembered her, with more white in her hair, but Mário had been a toddler and Maria just a baby when they moved from Lisbon back to the Azores in the summer of 1893, so the cousins were meeting as if for the first time.

Fernando's enterprising uncle João, who had studied agronomy and worked for a few years in agriculture, was now an agent for a shipping firm, sat on the board of a bank, and served as a vice-consul of France. He was also the co-owner of a soap factory and took everyone on a tour, explaining how it was manufactured.[13] Fernando, meanwhile, enticed his cousin Mário to participate in his own, imaginary enterprises. Three years younger, Mário naturally looked up to Fernando and followed his lead. On May 14, one week after arriving at Terceira, Fernando brought out the inaugural issue of *A Palavra* (*The Word*), a daily paper that lasted for three days. The first issue has not survived, but its format was presumably similar to the next day's, consisting of just two pages and with a masthead listing "F. Pessoa" as the editor in chief and "M. N. Freitas" (his cousin Mário) as the chief reporter.

Pessoa's best-known adolescent poem, "Quando ela passa" ("When She Passes"), takes up fully half of the May 15 issue of *The Word*. Signed by Dr. Pancrácio, who at this point was Pessoa's most prolific alter ego, the poem tells of a luminously pale young woman with a melancholy air who passes by the narrator's window every day, looking ever paler and more melancholy, until one day she fails to appear. Two days later it is her coffin that passes by. She was a victim, clearly, of the "white plague," TB, which was rampant on both sides of Pessoa's family, especially among the men. Coughing and other symptoms may not yet have been very noticeable in his uncle João, who would die of it in less than two years' time, but Fernando was haunted by the memory of his own father's long struggle with the disease.

It is possible that "When She Passes" was a subconscious homage to Pessoa's father, but the direct source of the poem's inspiration was the Portuguese poet António Nobre (1867–1900), whose "Pobre tísica" ("The Poor Consumptive") uses similar language to tell essentially the same story. The final stanzas of "When She Passes," however, owe their existence to the English poet Thomas Gray (1716–1771). The way Pessoa's narrator learns of the young woman's death—by seeing her funeral pass by—as well as the idea of incorporating an epitaph into the body of his poem were imported from Gray's masterpiece, "Elegy Written in a Country Churchyard." This justly famous work was at the front of Pessoa's mind, for in that same year, 1902, he translated its first nine stanzas into Portuguese.[14] At this stage in his literary development, many of Pessoa's own poems might loosely be called "translations," or transpositions, of works he aspired to equal or surpass.

While "When She Passes" springs almost entirely from the literary realm, the rest of Fernando's Azorean newspaper is based on events close to home, recounted with panache and hyperbole. The news section of *The Word* offers witty reports about the "toilet fever" (diarrhea?) that afflicted his sister, Teca, and about his cousin Maria's "appalling habit" of waking up late. The "Supplement" from the next day's paper consists of a feature story about a cyclone that wreaked disaster at "Vegetable Wharf," hurling a number of anchored ships against tall rocks or into the docks, so that valuable cargo and even a few lives were lost. The story—complete with illustrations—is an exaggerated account of the actual storms that had been intermittently pounding Terceira during the previous week.

Although Mário, *The Word*'s nominal chief reporter, no doubt offered some ideas for its stories, the actual writing all came from the hand of Fernando, who adapted his new paper's style to his new circumstances. Since the inclement weather forced the two families to spend a lot of time indoors, he had a captive readership, and he opted for news and for newsmen they could identify with easily. The large cast of fictional journalists from *The Tattler*, on whose crowded masthead Pessoa's own name never appears, gave way to the simple partnership of "F. Pessoa" and "M. N. Freitas," making *The Word* an expressly family enterprise. On the other hand, it was a *Tattler* journalist and poet, Dr. Pancrácio, who supposedly authored the poem "When She Passes." At the same time that he brought family names and news into his Azorean paper, Pessoa offered his family a glimpse into his mostly private community of imaginary others—as if he wanted them all to be one big family.

◆

THE MAY 16 ISSUE of *The Word* was necessarily Fernando's last, since he and his family set out for the mainland that same day. Their trip to Terceira was cut short due to a local outbreak of meningitis, which had claimed its first victims—three children—on May 10. Having lost a child to this disease eleven months earlier, João Miguel Rosa and his wife did not want to put Teca and Luís at risk. Pessoa's mother, pregnant again, also needed to look after her own health.

Back in Lisbon, or else during the four-day voyage to get there, Fernando invented two ocean vessels, the *Tejo* (*Tagus*) and the *Etna*, scribbling their names and specifications in a memo book he had brought from Durban. The *Tejo* was a longboat whose captain was initially designated "F. Pessoa," but then, reconsidering, Fernando crossed out his own name. The *Etna*, a sloop or yacht, weighed twenty tons, had a crew of ten sailors, and was commanded by "Lieutenant H. Rosa," with the H obviously standing for Henriqueta (Teca). In this case, too, he reconsidered and decided against using his sister's real last name, altering it from "Rosa" to "Ross."[15] Thus began a vivid and constantly evolving tale.

In an interview given in 1985, fifty years after her brother's death, Henriqueta Rosa Dias reported that he had been a solitary child in the habit of entertaining himself, but she remembered a game he used to play with her and her little brother Luís:

> We were the characters of a story that he kept on spinning. I played the part of a French lieutenant, and my brother played another role, I can't remember what. . . . Fernando took the game so seriously that sometimes, even outside the fiction, I kept right on being a French lieutenant. In fact, I continued to be one for many years. Reality was constantly being transformed, and we were the protagonists of his reverie.[16]

Her earliest memory of the game went back to Durban in late 1902 or the following year, but it was a little before that, in Portugal, that Fernando had made his sister Teca into a lieutenant, whose nationality was initially Portuguese, then English or Scottish ("Ross"). When at last she became a French lieutenant, perhaps he mentally placed her in the company of his two other military playmates from France, the Chevalier de Pas and Capitaine Thibeaut, both of whom he had invented, with the help of his uncle Cunha, before she was even born.

Everything was fair game for Pessoa's creative attempts to tamper with reality. At the same time that he tried to confer quasi-concrete substance onto abstractly imagined characters—by giving them biographies, for instance, or by making them the putative authors of real poems—he turned real people, such as his siblings, into fictions. Considered separately, the only unusual thing about Fernando Pessoa's antics from this period of his life is that, in some cases, they strike us as a bit childish. Considered in their ensemble, they constitute a quiet assault on the world as it is.

Arriving safely in Lisbon on Tuesday afternoon, May 20, after a voyage once more hampered by contrary winds, Pessoa and his family occupied an apartment on Avenida Dom Carlos I, just one block away from the Portuguese parliament. The broad avenue was lined with flowering trees now in their late-spring glory, and close by there was a small park, the Jardim de São Bento, but the vacationers made little effort to explore the neighborhood. They continued to spend their days with relatives, and especially with Aunt Maria and Aunt Rita in Pedrouços. It was at their home that they celebrated Fernando's fourteenth birthday on June 13.[17] He had let on to his parents that he wanted a certain stamp album made in France, and that was the present he received from them.[18]

Summer was just beginning, but the family vacation was coming to an end. On June 26 the Rosas and their housekeeper boarded a German steamer, the SS *Kurfürst*, which would take them back to Durban, where the consul was scheduled to resume his duties on August 1. Saying her goodbyes to all the relatives assembled on the wharf, Maria Madalena must have reserved her last hugs and kisses for her son, Fernando, who was staying behind in Lisbon for the summer. He was fourteen, not four, a proud young man and guarded with his emotions, but he was still fiercely attached to his mother. Never before had they lived apart—except for a few days at a time, when he was staying with his aunt Maria and uncle Cunha. Now they would be separated for more than three months and by the whole of the African continent.

We might have expected Fernando to spend the summer of 1902

in Pedrouços with his beloved Aunt Maria, Aunt Rita, and Grandma Dionísia, but he remained in the apartment on the Avenida Dom Carlos I, in central Lisbon. His mother sent a postcard to this address from Las Palmas, capital of the Canary Islands, the family's first port of call on their voyage home.[19] It's not clear who was living with the teenage boy. Aunt Maria or Aunt Rita might have moved there temporarily, to cook and clean and to keep him company, or he may have been staying with relatives who were the apartment's full-time tenants—his great-aunt Carolina's family, for instance. Fernando's vacation, in any case, had also ended. He was staying on in Lisbon in order to sit for the national elementary education exam, which he needed to pass if he wanted to pursue advanced studies or apply for certain kinds of jobs in Portugal.[20] Although far beyond his peers academically, he still had to prepare, since the body of knowledge he was expected to have at his fingertips was not the same as in Natal, and virtually all his previous education had been in English. Attending preparatory classes or receiving lessons from a tutor, he now studied arithmetic and other subjects in Portuguese.[21]

Fernando's studies did not compromise his literary and journalistic activities. On July 5 he brought out issue 7 of his mock newspaper *The Tattler*, and July 18 saw the publication of his first poem in a genuine newspaper, *O Imparcial* (*The Independent*). It was a clever, acrobatic sort of poem known in Portuguese and Spanish as a *glosa*, or gloss, which quotes and expands on lines from a preexisting poem, usually by someone else. A brief biographical note described the young author as an "amiable and restless" boy, "quick-witted and intelligent." The newspaper did not usually publish poetry, and how Pessoa's poem made it onto its first page remains a mystery. One possible intermediary was Henrique Rosa, a frequent contributor of poems to newspapers, though not to that paper.

*O Pimpão* (*The Fop*) remained the main outlet for Henrique Rosa's poetry in 1902, and Fernando Pessoa—or rather, Dr. Pancrácio—also became a contributor to the humorous biweekly, participating in its puzzle section. The doctor's name was regularly listed as a solver of riddles and word games, and in late summer and fall the newspaper published some original riddles signed by Dr. Pancrácio.[22]

In August and under his own name, Fernando wrote two sonnets, one of them for the fourth birthday of Miguel, a grandson of his great-aunt Carolina. The "amiable and restless boy" had already established himself as the family bard.

A survey of Pessoa's first large swath of creative production—the make-believe newspapers from 1902 plus half a dozen poems not included in the papers—reveals that significant portions of his lifetime literary project were in place almost before he had written anything down. From the outset he was unfolding himself into a network of collaborating pseudo-authors, one of whom, Eduardo Lança, already boasted a rather detailed biography. The seemingly most natural thing in the world for the fledgling author was to forge when he wrote, both in the sense of to *form* or to *fashion* and in the sense of to *imitate* or to *counterfeit*, and in him the two senses coincided. Love in his first poems was instantly sonnetized, or sanitized—spirited away from everyday existence and placed at a literary remove. But it was not only his Pickwickian coterie of imaginary companions and the larger world of literature that engrossed his attention and affections. Fernando was enchanted by language itself—how words are used and fitted together, how they look on a page, how they sound, how they are spelled, what they weigh, where they come from.

# CHAPTER 10

**T**HE PORTUGUESE ELEMENTARY EDUCATION EXAM proved to be far simpler than the exams Pessoa was used to in Durban, but before he could set sail to rejoin his mother, stepfather, and siblings, he had to attend to one more practical matter. On September 5, 1902, he presented himself at a Lisbon army post to request exemption from military service. Available to young men over the age of fourteen who were going abroad, the exemption was automatically granted for a fee that not everyone could afford: 150,000 reis, equivalent to three months' rent at the apartment in Pedrouços where Pessoa's family had stayed earlier in the year.[1] Ready at last to embark, on the nineteenth he boarded the *Herzog*, a German steamer that would take him back to Durban. Pessoa left no written memoir of any of his voyages, but this one must have especially impressed him: fourteen years old and alone on the high seas for nearly a month.

When he was more than twice his current age, Pessoa would write an untitled poem that begins:

It was on one of my voyages . . .
High sea, and the moon was out . . .
The evening hubbub aboard ship had quieted.
One by one, group by group, the passengers retired.
The band was just furniture that for some reason had remained
    in a corner.
Alone in the smoking lounge I played chess in silence.
Life droned through the open door of the engine room.
Alone . . . A naked soul face to face with the Universe!
(O town of my birth in faraway Portugal!
Why didn't I die as a child, when all I knew was you?)

This poem is signed by the heteronym Álvaro de Campos, who during his frequent travels was occasionally seized by nostalgia for his native country—or, rather, for the simplicity and smallness of his life there as a child. I suspect that Fernando, during his yearlong stay in Portugal, missed Durban about as much as he missed Lisbon when he was living in southern Africa. He was too engaged in growing up to miss either place very much, and what he probably felt when sailing between the two was a slight confusion about where he belonged. And in the grand scheme of things? "Alone . . . A naked soul face to face with the Universe!" The solitary traveler could never have felt so strongly the mystery of existence as he did there in midocean, wrapped in dark silence, beneath the countless and impossibly distant stars.

Reaching his destination after twenty-eight days at sea, on October 17,[2] Pessoa found a Durban not quite like the one he had left. The Anglo-Boer War had officially ended on May 31, and while a number of refugees had settled in Durban for good, the majority had returned to Transvaal and the other embattled areas from which they had fled. But what made the town especially different for Pessoa were personal circumstances, the most obvious one being residential: his family had moved back to the suburban area on the Berea ridge. And just in time, Pessoa's parents must have thought with relief, after bubonic plague broke out. It flared up among dockworkers at the Point in late November 1902 and soon spread to Durban's downtown area, where the family had recently been living on West Street. As part of the containment effort, the fire department burned down several produce shops thought to be focal points of the disease, which claimed at least 124 lives before it was eradicated, in July 1903. The victims were mostly native Africans and Indian immigrants, and the town authorities took advantage of the crisis to justify the demolition of Bamboo Square, the conglomerate of barracks at the Point that housed marginalized African and Asian laborers, who were thus forced to seek housing in shantytowns on Durban's periphery.[3] The plague hardly affected the predominantly white Berea, where the consul and his family now lived in a spacious house with a yard on Tenth Avenue.

◆

THE MOST SIGNIFICANT CHANGE in Pessoa's day-to-day life was the radically different academic environment, in which subjects like shorthand took precedence over Latin. He probably entered the Commercial School in late October, as soon as he got back to Durban. The school, which had opened its doors to twenty-two students in February and by October had more than eighty on its rolls, catered to individual needs and accepted new enrollments at any time of the year. Some of the students were refugees from Transvaal, and a few were foreigners who studied English as a second language. Although subjects such as shorthand, typing, bookkeeping, and commercial letter writing were at the heart of the curriculum, classes were also offered in practical chemistry, modern languages, and even Latin. Fernando's Latin was far beyond the rudimentary variety taught at his new school, and he focused on courses that would prepare him to be a businessman—or an office secretary. In fact, many of his classmates were young women learning secretarial skills.[4]

It was surely Pessoa's parents who thought that business school was a good idea, but if the boy had strenuously objected, they would just as surely have let him return to Durban High School, where he had excelled. He tried the Commercial School for a few months and apparently decided that it suited him. Classes were held in the evening, leaving him the whole day to do as he pleased. The new school—with no sports program and with its heterogeneous student population, which included foreigners—also proved a boon for his social life. He no longer stuck out for being incorrigibly unathletic or for having a funny-sounding name. Though still basically a loner, he opened up a bit and struck up at least one friendship, with a classmate named Augustine Ormond, who would remember Pessoa as being "a bashful and likable boy" as well as "extremely intelligent." And Ormond recalled how his mother, who also got to know Fernando, was amazed at how much common sense he had for a boy his age. (If indeed he had this quality in abundance, he lost it all by the time he was an adult.) When informed that his former friend and classmate had become a great poet in Portugal, Ormond said that he could feel, back in 1903, that Fernando was some kind of a genius.[5]

Ormond's daughter, interviewed in 1972, would remember her father's stating that he and Pessoa had been "great friends and both had the ambition of becoming great writers. They wrote letters to one another for years with the frank object of practicing their skill upon one another."[6] Her father probably exaggerated the extent of their correspondence, but Pessoa's only extant letter to Ormond, which survives in a draft copy, confirms that the missives they exchanged were consciously literary, or even linguistic, exercises. Pessoa, according to his friend, endeavored "to speak and write English in the most academic way possible."[7] Actually, he did his best to make fun of how ostentatiously erudite people write.

November 27th, 1903

My dear Ormond,

Having fortunately attained the conclusion of your petulant composition, the main intention of which is to disprove that which has been proved disproved, I have thence drawn the felicitous inference that the sooner a termination is put to this asinine discussion, the better it will be for the stability of our intellects.[8]

The letter goes on in the same mock-pretentious tone. This was parody, the writer was deliberately overwriting, and if he ever used this sort of vocabulary and syntax in conversation, it was only with Augustine Ormond. But Pessoa's caricature of pretentious language was itself a form of pretentiousness, an opportunity to show off.

At the same time he developed his writing skills, Pessoa cultivated a unique personal style. Rather than conform to a received notion of the well-rounded adolescent, he flaunted idiosyncratic qualities, such as his talent for using words to mimic, impress, and confound. He was naturally timid, but the curious observer could readily detect, beneath his docile exterior, an aristocratic attitude of superiority, as if to compensate for his social insecurity, and a quietly domineering personality. Although remembering him as a shy type, Ormond also described the fifteen-year-old Pessoa as "a spirited, cheerful, humorous lad," and he admitted feeling attracted to him like "steel to a magnet." It was a power of attraction that Fernando exerted over the few, not the many, and those few had to be willing to play by his rules. Throughout his life it was Pessoa who, in his more intimate relationships, generally called the shots.

The ability of the Commercial School to accommodate an unusually diverse student population with widely varying professional goals depended on its colorful founder and principal, Charles Henry Haggar, a short man with a long beard and round glasses who thrived on reinventing himself. Born in England in 1854, he studied philosophy and divinity to become a priest; lived for about fifteen years in Australia, where he worked first as a Congregational minister and then as a professor of languages and chemistry; and finally moved to Durban in 1898, just as the Anglo-Boer War was about to erupt. He became secretary of the local YMCA, devoted himself to caring for wounded soldiers and helping war refugees, ran for political office, and—on top of everything else—was a writer.[9]

Like Wilfrid Nicholas, the headmaster at Durban High, Haggar was a kind of mentor for Pessoa, but a mentor whose intellectual stimulation was indirect and unintentional. Nicholas was the far better scholar, careful and concentrated, but Haggar, besides nurturing a sincere interest in literature, actually wrote and published poetry. Unfortunately, C. H. Haggar, as he invariably signed himself, was a lousy poet, useful to Pessoa only as a negative model—an example of how *not* to write. Haggar made an easy target for literary ridicule and one-upmanship, since most of what he published was doggerel, and when a good opportunity came along, in 1904, Fernando used it to deride the poor man's singsong verses. At that point he was no longer under Haggar's tutelage, though it would not have mattered, since his identity was concealed behind the name of a literary man that nobody in Durban had ever heard of: Mr. Charles Robert Anon.

✦

ANON WAS PESSOA'S FIRST alter ego with a large literary output, which included both poetry and prose. Like his maker, he had a high opinion of his own talent and critical discernment. Unlike his maker, there was nothing shy about him, unless not actually existing is a form of shyness. Charles Robert Anon was fond of airing his opinions, and a literary minidebate in the pages of *The Natal Mercury* was a perfect occasion for him to do just that. It all began in June 1904, when a former Durban mayor named Hillier published a mediocre English rendering of an ode by Horace. C. H. Haggar, in a long and plodding poem titled "Poetic License," took the translator to task for a job badly done. Then someone who signed himself "Fairplay" published twenty-four limp verses marred by grammatical errors to criticize Haggar for being critical of Hillier. Finally, on July 9, C. R. Anon liquidated all three would-be poets in eight devastating lines:

Hillier did first usurp the realms of rhyme
To parody the bard of olden time;

Haggar then follows, and, in shallow verse,
Proves that to ev'ry bad there is a worse;
Some nameless critic next, in furious strain,
Causes the harmless reader cruel pain
While after metre pure he seems to thirst,
But shows how ev'ry worse can have a worst.

This was the public debut of Charles Robert Anon, but Pessoa's first published poem in English had appeared almost exactly one year earlier, under the name of another alter ego: Effield. The July 11, 1903, issue of *The Natal Mercury* published Effield's poem and also the accompanying cover letter, which was signed by yet another alias, W. W. Austin, who explained that he had been to Australia, where he "fell in with some miners" and copied down some of their stories and songs, including the song, or poem, he was submitting to the newspaper. It was written, he pointed out, in perfect alexandrines.

## The Miner's Song

We left the grassy paths where oft we used to roam,
    We left the mournful lake where oft we used to sail,
We left the mother dear in our far away home,
    We came out here with hope, we came perhaps to fail.

For in our eyes then shone th'unholy lust of gold,
    We longed to go back rich, back to our home again,
Back to the lone farm-yard, back to the lowing fold,
    And back to her we love who waits perhaps in vain.

And the poem continues for seven more stanzas of twelve-syllable lines in which the narrator admits it was folly for him and his fellow gold miners to leave their homeland in the hope of striking it rich. Pessoa knew that it was financiers and middlemen, rarely the miners themselves, who reaped big profits from the gold found near Johannesburg, and he assumed that gold mining in Australia was no different. Perhaps C. H. Haggar, who had lived there for many years, told him as much.

Fond of a challenge, Pessoa used alexandrines in a number of his early poems in English, but the narrative style and conventional morality of

"The Miner's Song" make it otherwise atypical. He must have shown the published poem to his parents and sister, but the newspaper or clipping got lost, and with it the poem, which languished in the underworld of newspaper archives for over a hundred years, its true authorship hidden behind a double veil of false names. I came across the poem in 2010, while searching old issues of *The Natal Mercury* at the Killie Campbell Africana Library, in Durban, but only upon my return to Lisbon could I be absolutely certain it was by Pessoa. Consulting one of his adolescent notebooks, I found a draft version of the poem's first two stanzas in a section labeled "Trifles." The young poet evidently did not think that "The Miner's Song" was anything special, and indeed it was not, if judged strictly as a piece of poetry. But its complicated framing and the imaginary geographical circumstances make the work an illuminating preview of what the future literary fabricator would do. A few pages earlier in the same notebook, Fernando wrote down Effield's full name and place of birth: "Karl P. Effield (of Boston, U.S.A.)." He was listed as the author of a travel book to be titled *From Hong-Kong to Kudat* (a rural outpost in present-day Malaysia) but never written, and he was also supposed to write a play.

Although this potentially versatile alter ego produced almost nothing except for his one published poem, he could boast of having a kind of extraliterary reality. Among Pessoa's papers I found an intriguing, neatly handwritten request: "Please give bearer any letters or parcels for K. P. Effield." It is the sort of document that would have allowed a friend in Boston to pick up Effield's mail while he was gallivanting in the Eastern Hemisphere. But since Pessoa was in Durban, this was probably an artifice enabling him to receive mail addressed to K. P. Effield care of the local post office, general delivery. In fact, an envelope for one such piece of mail, sent from England, survives in the Pessoa Archive.[10] It's a large brown envelope, which suggests that Pessoa, posing as Effield, had requested a catalogue, a sample copy, or general information from a publishing house, a magazine, or a literary organization.

Putting together the assorted bits of information left by Pessoa, we can deduce that Karl P. Effield was an American-born poet, travel writer, and frustrated playwright who wandered around Asia and at some point went to Australia to mine for gold. Might the miner's nostalgia for his homeland betoken Fernando's own nostalgia for his native Portugal? Not likely. "The Miner's Song," on the contrary, enabled him to go still farther afield. A boy from Europe, residing in South Africa, invents a man (W. W. Austin) who travels to Australia, where he discovers a poem attributed to an American alter ego (Effield) who had lately been in Asia or else was about to go there—it gives one vertigo. At age fifteen, Fernando Pessoa was already a master in the art of traveling without any need for a suitcase.

As for Australia, years later it would make several appearances in the poetry of Álvaro de Campos, who ends a poem written on June 4, 1931, with the line "You can be happy in Australia, as long as you don't go there." If we give credit to this principle and expand its geographical reach, we may conclude that Pessoa—by *not* going to Boston, to Australia, and to so many other places he imaginatively inhabited—must have been uncommonly happy.

◆

WHETHER IT WAS HAPPINESS or sadness, exhilaration or anxiety, Pessoa felt what he felt uncommonly, from the remove or through the microscope or in the echo chamber of literature (all three metaphors are apt). His experiences, whether real or imaginary, were literary episodes. And while some of his writing is obviously autobiographical, the point of nearly all his works is the works themselves, by which I mean the finished artifacts as well as the experience of producing them. There is nothing autobiographical about "The Miner's Song," but when, at the end of the poem, the narrator invokes "the great merciful God," this was undoubtedly a God that Pessoa—as Effield, disillusioned with mining—truly felt, at least while he was writing the poem. The poem he seems to have written immediately before "The Miner's Song" was titled "The Atheist," and the writer was a convinced atheist while composing the first thirty lines of what was intended to be a large work, divided into cantos. The fact he wrote no more than thirty lines may mean that his momentary atheism was not very convincing or interesting to him.[11]

To lose oneself and become somebody else in the act of writing is normal enough for an experienced creative writer. Unusual was the already dizzying rate at which Pessoa could shift between personae and genres. At the same time he began to turn out poems in English, he started writing stories, and he planned to produce a full-length novel, whose working title was *Martin Kéravas*. The novel's ostensible author, David Merrick, was a poet and playwright as well as a fiction writer, according to a list of his "Books to Come." The list contains pithy descriptions of all his forthcoming books, with word lengths and due dates, as if Merrick were under contract to a publisher, or under obligation to Fernando Pessoa. Clearly aware of how publishing contracts stipulate "deliverables," Pessoa noted that *Simple Tales* was to consist of at least twenty "short and pathetic" stories containing from 5000 to 7000 words each. The deadline was July 31, 1904. Pessoa's English-language alter egos, besides being commissioned to write books, also allegedly read and owned books, which explains the signature "David Merrick, 1903" on the inside of Pessoa's copy of Mark Twain's *Information Wanted, and Other Sketches.* Whether inspired or not by the American author, David Merrick had until June 30, 1905, to finish *Martin Kéravas*, a novel that was to "plead for peace" in 120,000 to 150,000 words. If Merrick's creator believed that the existence of a "contract" would coerce him to deliver the work on said date, he was disappointed. None of it got written except for a brief opening paragraph.[12]

David Merrick's *Longer Tales*, a work scheduled for completion by December 31, 1904, was to include a story titled "The Atheist" (Pessoa was evidently undecided whether his unbeliever would be better served by poetry or prose) and another called "The Philanthropist." The same two titles are found in a second list of "Tales" to be written by David Merrick, whose name, however, was subsequently crossed out and replaced by C. R. Anon's. A similarly peremptory dismissal befell Lucas Merrick, David's presumed brother. After being entrusted to produce a group of stories that included "yachting yarns," Lucas's name was obliterated and his writing assignment passed on to one Sidney Parkinson Stool.[13] Stool suffered his own reverses. He was initially made the owner of a copy of Henry Fielding's *Joseph Andrews*, only to have his signature crossed out and replaced by Lucas Merrick's, which was crossed out in its own turn, the book being ultimately signed by F. A. N. Pessoa. Fernando apparently decided that the picaresque style of Fielding's novel was not in keeping with the kind of prose fiction he expected from Lucas Merrick and the painfully named Sidney Parkinson Stool.

There was a practical reason for Pessoa's sudden interest in writing fiction: he hoped it could make him some money. In the same notebook where he jotted down notes and titles for stories by K. P. Effield, S. P. Stool, the Merrick brothers, and C. R. Anon, he reserved a page for the addresses and submission requirements of periodicals publishing fiction.

Under the subheading "Sources of Income," he copied down the relevant information for two cash-paying publications from England: *Tit-Bits*, an enormously popular weekly newspaper of light news, anecdotes, and literature that ran an "Original Complete Story" competition, and *Answers*, which was modeled after *Tit-Bits* and offered prizes for the best "storyettes" submitted (the stories had to be funny as well as short).[14] Fernando had already decided that he would earn his living from literature. The business skills he was acquiring at the Commercial School would be a useful backup, a means for making a quick buck when necessary. It was not a bad strategy. As things turned out, he earned very little money from his writing, but he would make a modest, dependable income as a freelance letter writer for business firms in Lisbon. The backup also backfired, however, since Pessoa repeatedly tried to be an actual businessman, for which he had no flair.

# CHAPTER 11

○ ⬛ ○ ⬛ ○ ⬛ ○ ⬛ ○ ⬛ ○ ⬛ ○ ⬛ ○ ⬛ ○ ⬛ ○ ⬛ ○ ⬛ ○ ⬛ ○

T HE BRONTË SISTERS, TOGETHER WITH THEIR brother Branwell, produced what must be the most exuberant, most fascinating output of juvenilia in the English language. Raised in a parsonage in northern England, the four siblings—close to one another in age—amused themselves by inventing countries inhabited by historical and invented characters in whose voices they wrote stories and poems. They "published" their work in handmade manuscript books and in a monthly, make-believe magazine founded by Branwell but later edited by Charlotte, after he started up a newspaper. The siblings assumed different masks and reviewed each other's works in the mock periodicals that circulated only among themselves. Literary classics such as Milton's poems, Shakespeare's plays, and *The Arabian Nights*, actual periodicals such as *Blackwood's Magazine*, and current events of the 1820s and 1830s were important sources of inspiration for what Charlotte dubbed their "scriblomania," through which they constructed new worlds and modified the world they were born into. In a geography book that belonged to the family library Anne Brontë inscribed, in pencil, a list of place-names from Gondal, an island in the north Pacific invented by her and Emily, whose *Wuthering Heights* would draw on material written by the two sisters for the Gondal saga.[1]

This blending of invention and reality, the creation of an ersatz publishing industry and the ongoing metamorphosis of fictional characters, geographies, and literary projects also characterized Pessoa's juvenilia, less prolific than the Brontës but in some ways even more remarkable, particularly when we consider that his was a one-man enterprise. Instead of collaborating and competing with siblings, he transferred a portion of his own "scriblomania" to imaginary collaborators who competed with him, with one another and with established authors. He also channeled his passion for writing into two different languages.

Since late 1902, when he returned to South Africa, Pessoa had been writing all his poetry and prose in English. But in July 1903, the same month he published "The Miner's Song," he revived *The Tattler* (*O Palrador*), which continued to be a strictly Portuguese production, though it now resembled a magazine more than a newspaper.[2] One year had passed since the last issue was assembled, in Lisbon, and almost everything about the new series was different. Some of the names on the masthead remained, but their titles and duties had changed. Dr. Pancrácio, literary editor of the last 1902 issue, was now entrusted with the humor section. There were ten other editors and subeditors, one of whom handled a sports section and another a short story section. This elaborate editorial scaffold was clearly conceived with future issues in mind, but these never materialized.

Volume 1, issue 1 of the new *Tattler*, billed as a "monthly periodical," was the only issue. An introductory editorial announced the first installments of "four fascinating novels," along with some "military short stories" and other articles. The army tales did not get written, and the journal commenced "publication" of only two of the promised serial novels. The most interesting one, *Os rapazes de Barrowby* (*The Boys of Barrowby*), is signed by Adolph Moscow and set in rural England, as the narrator eventually discloses, but only after taking up the first several pages explaining how much time and eyesight he has lost poring over atlases, maps, and books in a fruitless effort to discover the exact whereabouts of "the celebrated village of Barrowby." Not that it really matters, finally, since it makes no difference to Moscow "whether the village of Barrowby is located in Europe, in Asia, in Africa, in America, in Oceania, or in the chaotic depths of Dante's inferno." For the sake of the story, he arbitrarily supposes that Barrowby is an English village not far from Brighton.

The narrator's disdain of geographical detail is not surprising, given the scant attention paid by Pessoa to the factual particulars of the many destinations he imaginatively visited, but he must have undertaken at least some of the humorously described research to try to locate Barrowby. Without a good gazetteer at his disposal, he failed to find the village, which is in Lincolnshire county, near Nottingham. So much fuss over a place-name led me to suspect—and to quickly confirm, through online research—that the young author, without making the slightest acknowledgment of his debt, had been inspired by a story in English whose title he had translated directly into Portuguese. The original *The*

*Boys of Barrowby*, by a certain Sidney Drew, was serialized in forty-seven issues of *The Boys' Friend* magazine, beginning in April 1903. Since it took a month for British publications to reach Durban, Pessoa would have read no more than ten installments (the eleventh was published on June 20) when he began writing his own, Portuguese version for *The Tattler*. He conserved the story's shell—its title, the division of Barrowby School into two rival houses, the names of various characters and some of their personality traits—while drastically altering the story line and literary style.[3]

Sidney Drew's *The Boys of Barrowby* is a lighthearted tale of student pranks and scuffles. In Pessoa's *Barrowby*, three older students verbally and physically harass two new arrivals to the school: a skinny fellow named Ralph Tig and a large-nosed Jewish boy named Zacharias. Fernando, who was probably teased if not actually roughed up by other students at Durban High School because of his slight build, seems to have gotten revenge through Ralph, who puts up a fight against one of his tormentors and gets the better of him. But Fernando clearly did not identify with Zacharias, portrayed as a ridiculous-looking Jew bedecked with phony jewelry: fake diamond and gold rings, a gold-painted tie clasp decorated with a fake emerald, and a fake silver pocket watch. If autobiography was at work here, it worked by way of denial, with the teenage author establishing a distance between his own, considerably diluted Jewishness and the unflattering caricature he drew of a "real" Jew. Despite having New Christian ancestors on his father's side, Fernando was at least superficially infected by the antisemitism then rampant in much of the Western world, including South Africa, where a few thousand Jews had emigrated from eastern Europe. We shall see Pessoa, years later, devoting a considerable number of written pages to the question of Jewish influence and the purported machinations of certain Jews intent on destabilizing the world order.

The other novel presented in *The Tattler*, signed by one Marvell Kisch and titled *Os milhões dum doido* (*A Madman's Millions*), describes a snowy night in a posh neighborhood of London, where two wealthy women—one older, one younger—exit their mansion to enter a fancy coach, at which point they are accosted by a beggar with a baby in her arms, whom they haughtily rebuff. It is the sort of scenario that Dickens could have sketched for a novel such as *Bleak House* or *Hard Times*, but the actual prose of this story reads suspiciously like a Portuguese translation of the first installment of yet another boys' book, or possibly a girls' book. In *Os rapazes de Barrowby*, Pessoa's Portuguese is occasionally contaminated by English syntax; in *Os milhões dum doido*, we find entire sentences directly imported from English. Whatever its origins, the embryonic story was quickly abandoned. Pessoa had no interest in or talent for writing effective descriptions of rich nobles in their well-cushioned coaches and poor people shivering in the cold on snowy winter nights. His inclination, conspicuous in his remake of *The Barrowby Boys*, was to transgress the traditional rules and expectations of storytelling.

Fernando had no qualms about filching ideas, characters, and even complete sentences from British serial novels, but some sort of scruple constrained him to attribute his partly borrowed stories to fictional English authors, even though they were written in Portuguese. Perhaps this was his way of covertly admitting the foreign influence behind the works they signed. Adolph Moscow and Marvell Kisch are atypical of Pessoa's pseudo-authors. Although Moscow has a definite narrative posture that affects the tone and framing of his story, it is probably better not to count him or Kisch as heteronyms. They were one-offs, whose ephemeral existence began and ended with their respective stories.

✦

THE LEGITIMATE HETERONYMS, THOUGH inseparable from their writings, in a certain way transcended them. They were not names tacked on to a poem or prose text as an afterthought. Pessoa nurtured them in his mind and affections, imagining their personalities and, in some cases, their biographies. He often practiced their signatures, and sometimes a signature was the first visible manifestation of a heteronym. Signatures, for Pessoa, were like magical formulas with conjuring powers, but certain formulas conjured up nothing at all. There are signatures, in fact, for a number of inchoate, potential personae that never amounted to more than their names —António Caldas, Augustus West, Aurélio Pereira Quintanilha, Dalton, G. M. Dent, and many others.

Signatures are markers of personality, and an evolving or unstable heteronym might have various signature styles. In 1903, before actually making him the author of any poem or prose piece, Pessoa was already scribbling signatures for Charles Robert Anon in one of his notebooks.[4] Dozens of additional signatures date from 1904 to 1906 and take half a dozen different forms: the full name, C. R. Anon, Ch. Robert Anon,

Ch. R. Anon, C. Robert Anon, etc. The inside cover of a notebook used
by Pessoa in 1904 contains ten signatures for this heteronym as well
as half a dozen instances of "Stratton Street." This was apparently the
street where the heteronym lived—in London, near Piccadilly Circus,
given that there was no Stratton Street in Durban. On the other hand,
there is a signature of an L. R. Anon with Boston written four times
above the name, as if this were his hometown. Perhaps L. R. Anon was
a Boston "friend" of Karl P. Effield before morphing into C. R. Anon,
who was from London. Or perhaps C. R. had a brother or cousin based
in Boston.[5]

Turning over the scrap of paper with L. R. Anon's signature, we find
three signatures for Gaveston, the most enigmatic of all the fictional
selves dreamed up by Pessoa. Gaveston's signature—last name only—
appears in a Latin primer used by Pessoa in 1904, and it repeatedly
pops up in his notebooks and literary papers between 1904 and 1910.
Guarded or undecided about Gaveston's first name, Pessoa nearly always
suppressed it, but on a paper scrap from 1904 he wrote out his full name
as Jerome Gaveston and, below it, jotted down the name of a possible
spiritual ancestor: Piers Gaveston (c. 1284–1312), the favorite of King
Edward II and widely rumored to be his lover. The connection of Pessoa's Gaveston to the historical figure—and to this figure's relationship
with the English king—is reinforced by another signature dating from
around 1904, "Ed. Gaveston," that effectively marries the two names,
assuming that "Ed." stands for Edward.[6]

Elsewhere among Pessoa's papers we find five signatures of "Gaveston"
next to three playful lines of verse:

(Oh, how shocking!),
This very holy man would (hard to relate)
Rather unfrock a woman than a prelate.[7]

The joke depends on the ambiguous meaning of "unfrock." Either the
speaker (Gaveston?) feigns shock that the holy man would rather strip
off a woman's clothes than strip a prelate of his priestly functions, or he
is surprised that the holy man would prefer to remove a woman's frock
rather than a prelate's frock. The latter attitude would make sense for a
writer with Piers Gaveston's putative sexual proclivities. Equally suggestive is the parenthetical "hard to relate." If Pessoa's Gaveston is an

early example of an alter ego whose sexual orientation is ambiguous, he is certainly not the last.

The name Gaveston also appears at the top of a passage for a satirical "Essay on Poetry," which advises aspiring poets to eschew correct grammar, since "the darker and more uncertain the parts of your sentence (if you be so unpoetical as to write in sentences or periods), the more impressive will be your verse, the more evident your philosophic depth." Gaveston's signature, however, may have been scrawled there at random. The essay as a whole was attributed first to Dr. Pancratium (a Latinization of Pancrácio), then to Professor Trochee, and ultimately to Professor Jones.[8]

Despite dozens of Gaveston signatures sprinkled across Pessoa's writings over a seven-year period, this shadowy character was not specifically, unequivocally credited with a single poem or prose piece. His case is unique. While various could-have-been heteronyms hesitantly surfaced into view through one or another signature jotted down in a notebook before sinking back into nameless nonexistence, Gaveston hesitantly endured, with his signatures becoming more frequent after Pessoa returned to Lisbon in 1905. This ghostly entity represented something important for the master author, who could not decide what kinds of works were appropriate for him. Either that, or he was not ready to have Gaveston write what he had been created for. He kept waiting, putting it off . . . and nothing. But Gaveston served at least a psychological function. Though he failed to become a subauthor, he existed as a hazy member of the family of alter egos whom Pessoa, part artist and part analyst, extracted from his own self and closely observed, like a gallery of portraits or of clinical cases. The heteronyms, ingenious vehicles for producing literature, were also paths to self-knowledge.[9]

✦

FERNANDO'S PASTIMES WERE NOT all literary, and the literature he produced was not only for his own amusement and writerly development. The Durban issue of *The Tattler* was probably undertaken for his family's benefit. After "The Miner's Song" saw print in early July 1903, Pessoa's parents, while proudly congratulating him, no doubt encouraged him to keep up his creative writing in Portuguese, reminding him of the newspapers he had created in Lisbon and the Azores. We know he showed them the new issue of *The Tattler*, for he used several blank pages in the middle of the in-progress periodical to keep score for a parlor game in which the whole family participated. Called Derby, it mimicked the Durban July Handicap, held on the first Saturday of that month. The July Handicap was and still is South Africa's premier horse race. Derby, played with dice, was Fernando's invention. The family members were assigned differently colored horses, mounted by imaginary jockeys with names such as Clumsy Dick, Yreka Jim, and Tom Wallis. (The last two names were protagonists of boys' adventure books popular at the time.)[10] Even Pessoa's younger brother, João Maria, born just six months earlier, on January 17, had his own horse, colored gray and yellow.

Shorter runs were possible, but a full Derby race was one mile long, just as in the July Handicap of the time (today's race is 2200 meters, about 1.4 miles), and betting was also part of Fernando's game. Some of the names of the make-believe bettors—Gould, Gower, and Saville—belonged to actual Durban families, but a fourth bettor, Nabos, was related to or was himself Zé Nabos, an inventor of riddles for the Lisbon edition of *The Tattler*.[11] Fernando's parents may or may not have taken him to the July Handicap races, but no matter: his Derby game allowed everyone in the family to enjoy horse races in the comfort of their own living room. The equestrian enthusiast had another method for playing out his fondness for horse racing: he dressed up like a horseman, complete with high boots, hat, and a riding whip. There is a photo of him in such a getup, taken when he was about twelve.

Fernando enjoyed other games, including soccer and cricket, which he likewise played at home and on paper, with his imagination and a pair of dice. The Cato Lodge Cricket Club, which he invented in 1901, played against the Anchor Club, Pennyghast, Dives County, and other rival clubs. Fernando drew up rosters of athletes and their respective positions, and he tallied the goals and runs made by each player during the matches that took place in his bedroom. Nathaniel Rattan Gould, supposed captain of the Anchor soccer and cricket club, was probably the same Gould who was a bettor in Fernando's horse racing game. He was also listed on the masthead of the July 1903 issue of *The Tattler* as "Nat Gould, Short Story Editor."*

Pessoa's interest in horse racing waned, but he continued to organize

---

* This name was borrowed from a real writer. British-born Nat Gould (1857–1919), now little remembered, was one of the world's best-selling authors, and horse racing was the main theme of his novels and short stories.

virtual cricket and soccer matches over the next two years. One of the regular players was Sidney Parkinson Stool, mistakenly listed on one score sheet as "S. R. Stool"—unless S. R. was S. P.'s brother, in which case they could commiserate with each other over their unfortunate last name. Although most of the players' names were fictional, three or four names on score sheets from 1904 and 1905 belonged to classmates from Durban High. In Pessoa's pretend sporting events, as in his do-it-yourself newspapers, reality could freely coexist with fantasy. According to a score sheet for a cricket match from 1904, the Anchor Club won by thirty-five runs in "extremely bad weather." There is no way for us to know whether it was raining over all Durban or just over the imaginary cricket field. For the organizer of the match, it made no difference.[12]

Fernando's enjoyment of sports was not limited to the confines of his home on Tenth Avenue. To be so familiar with the rules of cricket and soccer, either he had some experience playing each sport on an actual field or he was a very attentive spectator. Not to be outdone just because he lacked physical strength and stamina, he even invented a field sport he called Racket Goal, which was basically a cross between tennis and rugby. On a large field, two teams of fifteen players use standard tennis rackets to advance the ball—a tennis ball—with points being scored when it passes through the goalposts and beneath the crossbar. At the end of a set of detailed playing instructions left by Pessoa in neat schoolboy cursive, someone else who was also Pessoa came along and wrote, several years later and in a more assertive calligraphy, "Very beautiful game."

No one, as far as I know, has ever played it.[13]

◆

PESSOA'S FAVORITE GAMES, PLAYED throughout his life, were word games—particularly the ones published in English-language newspapers, including *The Natal Mercury*. In July 1903, exactly one week after it brought out Karl P. Effield's "The Miner's Song," the newspaper announced a puzzle contest based on a weekly batch of from four to six puzzles. These included various kinds of riddles, word squares or word diamonds (in which the words going across are the same as the words going down), transpositions, and reversions. The puzzle master asked interested readers to send in not only their solutions but also some puzzles that he might use in the column. Fernando complied on both counts, competing as a solver and providing puzzles of his own making.

Like the majority of participants, he used a pen name, signing himself as J.G.H.C.

On August 22, the *Mercury* announced that the warm-up period was over and that the competition was beginning in earnest with the set of puzzles published that day. At this point J.G.H.C. abruptly retired to the sidelines, while a new solver, Tagus, entered the field. (The names of solvers and the number of correct answers submitted by each were duly listed in the paper.) "Tagus" was an obvious homage to the ancient and dependable river of Pessoa's childhood in Lisbon, while J.G.H.C. was a more complex entity, full of unrealized literary promise. There are two signatures of J. G. Henderson Carr at the back of the *Pitman's Shorthand Instructor* used by Pessoa at the Commercial School, and his name also appears in the teenager's writing projects. A contemporary of Karl P. Effield, David Merrick and Sidney Parkinson Stool, Mr. Carr was created to be both an essayist and a poet. Pessoa changed his mind about the poetry but continued to entrust the heteronym with a book project titled *Essays on Reason*—all in vain. J. G. Henderson Carr, disinclined to such a weighty endeavor, limited himself to being a riddler.

In October, more than a month into the puzzle contest, J.G.H.C. was suddenly back in the game. It was too late for him to possibly win, but like any other participant he could—and he did—contribute puzzles, which Tagus, his ostensible adversary, managed to solve every time. No riddle there. In addition to having a genius IQ, Fernando was a shrewd operator. When submitting riddles and solutions as Tagus, he wrote his real name and home address on the envelope; J.G.H.C. identified himself only as J. G. Henderson Carr and had a different home address, probably 157 West Street, where the Portuguese consulate was still located.[14]

In the same notebook where he recorded the racing results for Derby and drew up rosters of imaginary cricket and soccer teams, Pessoa kept track of who was ahead in the puzzle contest, which was ultimately won by Tagus. On December 12, the puzzle master wrote in his column: "The book prize therefore goes to 'Tagus.' Mr. F.A.N. Pessoa, Tenth Avenue, Durban ('Tagus'), please call upon the editor for his prize." The editor was surprised when the "Mr." Pessoa who dropped by the office to claim his book (*Oeuvres de Molière*) turned out to be a fifteen-year-old. This prompted the puzzle master to publish a correction the following week: "Master 'Tagus'—The editor has just informed me of my mistake in the prefix to your name, but, judging by your ability as a solver, I can be excused in my conjecture. I heartily congratulate you, my lad, and hope you will long continue a bright light in our puzzle column."

Fernando continued to send in solutions and riddles, both as Tagus and as J.G.H.C., but his light quickly dimmed. He had proven his skill and needed a bigger challenge. Ignoring the occasional published pleas of the puzzle master ("And Tagus, where art thou this week?" or "By the way, Tagus, I hope to see your neat, precisely written sheet turn up weekly again"), he let his participation dwindle, and it ceased altogether after May 1904. He would recover his appetite for puzzles as an adult living in Lisbon, where he regularly bought English papers to compete for puzzle awards that could, in the case of first prizes, amount to small fortunes.[15]

✦

FREE, UNSTRUCTURED TIME WAS an aphrodisiac for Pessoa's creative powers. The year 1902, when the family was on holiday in Lisbon, saw Fernando blossom as a Portuguese poet. The relatively relaxed year of 1903—without the rigors of Durban High School—saw him expand in all sorts of literary directions. In poetry he tried out various kinds of rhyme, experimented with blank verse, studied and applied metrical devices such as the caesura, and produced fragments for a verse drama. He wrote fiction, conceived several essay projects, and penned short humorous sketches. More significant, for the great writer he would become, was the triumph of his existential multiplicity, by way of the mysteriously emerging heteronyms. There is a long and illustrious tradition of literary alter egos. But whereas Kierkegaard, Yeats, Machado, Valéry, and others created their personae as adults, after they had become established authors, the still immature Pessoa invented fictional co-authors, or collaborators, to aid him in developing his gift for writing.

If it is true that words, for many writers, have quasi-supernatural properties, it was a truth with extreme consequences for Pessoa. Not only did words open up alternate worlds, they could transform the given world and even his own person. Or so he thought and so he proceeded. Why be this person, or why be only this person? Pessoa's experiments were in literature but also on himself. The heteronyms are the most spectacular manifestation of his experimental research in personal identity, but that research did not depend only on the use of alter egos. In a passage from *The Book of Disquiet* called "Aesthetics of Artificiality," Pessoa would write:

I live aesthetically as someone else. I've sculpted my life like a statue made of matter that's foreign to my being. Having employed my self-awareness in such a purely artistic way, and having become so completely external to myself, I sometimes no longer recognize myself. Who am I behind this unreality? I don't know. I must be someone.[16]

Self-questioning and self-inventing are conspicuous in Pessoa's adolescent writing even when there is no assumed name. In a still unpublished prose piece from 1903, the first-person narrator tells how he feels pressured by his parents and other relatives to accept the sea as his "natural vocation" and to orient his professional goals accordingly—all because one of his ancestors was a renowned sea captain. Further on in the piece he reveals that, "far from having any natural leaning towards the sea, my feelings towards this powerful element are decidedly inimical." The unfinished sketch, written in English and just a page long, reads like autobiography, but the wry humor—we're told that the renowned captain once attempted to "hustle Cape St. Vincent out of Portugal with his glorious frigate"— gives it away as a fiction.[17] It was what would come to be known late in the twentieth century as "autofiction," mixing up and turning around the real facts of Pessoa's life and background. His ancestral lineage included several illustrious army generals but no sea captain—which of course had been his stepfather's profession before he became a consul.

Neither of Fernando's parents, nor anyone else in the family, would ever have encouraged him to pursue an army or a seafaring career, for the simple reason that he lacked the right constitution, but the boy— contrary to the narrator of his sketch—did feel strongly attracted to the ocean, as has already been observed. In 1904 he would write, and rewrite, dozens of lines for an unfinished "Ode to the Sea":

Hail, thou sea!
How thy fury taketh me,
Let it thunder, let it roar
O'er the panic-stricken shore

and so forth.[18] Of course, Pessoa's love of the sea was itself partly a creation of his fancy. Personal observations and experiences, isolated from their original contexts and broken up into useful bits, become precious raw materials that writers reassemble and rework to produce fiction. Pessoa followed this recipe, and he also inverted it. Many of his fictions, at the same time that they existed as autonomous artistic productions, were a means for him to recast, in words, his forever restless sense of self.

Pessoa never quit reconfiguring his identity, and we should take care not to stop too long at any one of his existential resting points. Even the persona of the self-doubter is just that: one more persona, an assumed character, a construct. More than a self-doubter, Pessoa was an unrelenting self-transformer. When still at the Commercial School, he began writing a verse play tentatively titled *Marino*, or *Marino, the Epicure*. In one of the passages the protagonist's interlocutor asks "Who art thou?," to which Marino echoingly replies:

Who am I?
Indeed thou askest well. Full many a time
I asked myself that question, and no answer
Could my mind give to what my tongue did speak.

The "Who am I?" question is a classic for thoughtful adolescents, and Fernando, more thoughtful than most, was obsessed by it. Marino asked the question, according to other lines from the quoted passage, because of an incipient mental illness, possibly inspired by the teenage author's fear of inheriting his grandmother's insanity, but Marino's story evolved and ramified. In several fragments written the next year, 1904, the protagonist voices his metaphysical speculations to a bosom friend named Vincenzo. Still later, in 1905 or 1906, a sketch for a dialogue places Marino opposite a character named António, who warns him that his mistresses have been unfaithful. Marino also learns the devastating news that he has contracted leprosy and is doomed to die. Pessoa, meanwhile, had moved backed to Lisbon, where he was attending college without enthusiasm and feeling somewhat out of place in the country where he was born.

By late 1907, Pessoa's dramatic work in progress had split into two works: a poem in blank verse called "Vincenzo" and a five-act play, *Marino (A Tragedy)*, whose characters sometimes speak in metered verse, sometimes in plain English. In the poem, Vincenzo is a high-minded soul who, after befriending a man struck with leprosy, also catches the disease and similarly becomes an outcast, despised by all. In the play,

which Pessoa continued to work on until at least 1910, Marino is a cuck-
olded nobleman driven to insanity after his wife runs off with a lover at
the same time that his daughter (by said wife) dies. At this late stage,
whether in the poem or in the play, there are no obviously autobiographical points of contact, although a psychoanalytical reading might propose
a connection between Marino's cuckoldry and a rancorous feeling, in
Pessoa, that his mother betrayed him by remarrying.

The mutating nature of *Marino* is typical of the writer's larger works,
and the same unsettledness characterizes his heteronymous project. The
heteronyms sometimes switch their literary specialties, going from writing poems to writing stories to authoring *The Book of Disquiet*, for instance
(the case of Vicente Guedes); several of them oscillate between English
and Portuguese as their language of expression (Dr. Gaudêncio Nabos,
Raphael Baldaya); and literary property as well as biographical attributes
can pass from one name to another (Vicente Guedes's authorship of *Disquiet* passed on to Bernardo Soares, who was an assistant bookkeeper
and lived in Lisbon's Baixa district, exactly like his predecessor). Characters from short stories can later be promoted to the status of free-ranging
heteronyms (António Mora), and one of the heteronyms—Álvaro de
Campos—would play a role in Pessoa's real-world life.

There are numerous levels of fiction in Pessoa but no clear lines of
demarcation between them, or between fiction and reality. The whole lot
is Fernando Pessoa, in continual motion and expansion, susceptible to
dozens of psychological readings that can never pin him down, since his
imagination is forever hijacking him elsewhere. If he was in some sense
the Marino of 1903 who questions his own identity and the reality of the
surrounding world, he was also the later Marino who sinks into delirium
after being abandoned by an unfaithful woman he dearly loves, and he
was in some sense the good-hearted Vincenzo who becomes a lonely,
leprous outcast. It is inconceivable that the real-life Pessoa would ever
have suffered such drastic fates, but in literature there was no practical
limit to what he could do and be.

Literature beckoned, because it represented freedom, and he used it to
make more literature, and to keep on remaking himself. But while *Marino,
the Epicure* and its several offshoots were creative journeys of personal
self-discovery and self-expansion, they did not spring directly out of Pessoa's own imagination. Their likely inspiration was Lord Byron's *Marino
Faliero*, a blank-verse play whose tragic hero, a fourteenth-century Vene-

tian doge, dies as an indirect consequence of being slanderously branded a cuckold. The play's cast of characters includes a Vincenzo and an Antó- nio. Another possible influence was Walter Pater's *Marius the Epicurean*, whose protagonist, when still a young man, discusses literature and phi- losophy with Flavianus, a close friend who is dying.[19] Pater (1839–1894), an English essayist whose emphasis on living life and feeling beauty with intensity made him a foundational writer for the aesthetic movement, is best remembered for his *Studies in the History of the Renaissance*, which Pessoa would read in his late twenties.

◆

I FAST-FORWARDED TO LISBON to show how Pessoa's literary works were capable of successive, unpredictable mutations. Returning now to Durban, in the second half of 1903, we find Fernando not only pursuing literature, with time off for imaginary cricket games, but also engag- ing in serious academic study. Shorthand and the principles of business management were not especially demanding subjects, but he was also prepping for the matriculation exam administered by the University of the Cape of Good Hope. Since there were subjects he had not studied since June 1901, Pessoa needed help getting ready for this important test, known commonly as the matric, and he got help. In its second year of operation, the Commercial School had widened its scope to include prepping students for matriculation, law, civil service, and other public examinations. The school's director, C. H. Haggar, was not especially well qualified to prepare Pessoa, the school's only pupil to sit for the matric in 1903, but he did what he could.[20]

As Pessoa himself must have expected, his exam results were less than brilliant. He did reasonably well in English and French, so-so in Latin, which had previously been his best subject, quite well in arith- metic yet poorly in algebra and geometry, and abominably in physics. To pass even with a mediocre score was still an accomplishment, espe- cially for a fifteen-year-old, but his truly astonishing feat was besting his mostly older, native-English-speaking peers to claim the Queen Victoria Memorial Prize, awarded for the best English essay submitted as part of the exam. There were 899 examinees. The prize consisted of seven pounds sterling toward the purchase of books that were specially bound and stamped. Pessoa requested and received Samuel Johnson's *Lives of the Poets* (3 volumes), *The Poetical Works of John Keats*, *The Choice Works of*

*Edgar Allan Poe, The Works of Alfred Tennyson,* and *The Works of Ben Jonson*
(3 volumes). Keats and Poe, who was more highly esteemed in Europe
than America, would become two of his favorite authors.[21]

Winning the Queen Victoria Prize was a lifelong source of pride for
Pessoa. In 1928, at the request of the Coimbra magazine *Presença,* he
would draw up a bibliographical overview of his works, which he prefaced with two or three snippets of biographical information, including
a mention of the obscure prize he had won as a fifteen-year-old student.
In 1932, as part of his application for the post of curator of a museum-
library in the town of Cascais, he would append the prize notification
sent to him care of the Commercial School on February 20, 1904.[22] And
in 1935, eight months before his death, he would draft a résumé that
mentions the award. Pessoa's pride was entirely justified, since he had
begun learning English only at age seven and a half, and he was one of
the youngest candidates to sit for the matriculation exam.

One of the consequences of the prize was to steel the young man in
his ambition to become an English writer. If his English was better than
that of the other 898 examinees, surely it made sense for him to pursue
his writing career in that language, with its growing international preva-
lence and its incomparable literary tradition. So Fernando must have reasoned, to judge by his obstinate struggle to become part of that tradition,
but his mastery of the English language was not quite what he thought
it was. While his talent for "academic" English, reported by his friend
Augustine Ormond and plainly evident in his writing from the period,
served Pessoa well for school essays and for prose pieces employing irony,
it yielded less felicitous results in other genres, such as poetry, unless the
tone was humorous. When writing lyric poems in English, Pessoa relied
on models such as Milton, Shelley, Keats, and other Romantics, whose
examples guaranteed a high degree of technical proficiency. But the Portuguese poet did not know how to intensely *feel* in English; his poetic
diction in this language was, oddly enough, too "poetical," too disconnected from his personal experience, too far removed from his heartfelt
emotions. Pessoa's English lacked the primitive, carnal, sensorial naturalness suggested by the term "mother tongue."

Having passed the matric, Fernando was ready to attend university,
but there was no such institution in Natal. The only two schools of higher
learning in South Africa that turned out a large number of successful
B.A. candidates were in the Cape Colony: South African College and

Victoria College (now the University of Cape Town and Stellenbosch University, respectively). Degrees were earned by testing through the University of the Cape of Good Hope—which did not offer classes—and candidates could study anywhere, including in the privacy of their own homes, but without some scholarly guidance they were not likely to pass higher-level exams. Like other schools of similar caliber, Durban High School offered post-matric instruction, and Fernando, who had left the school two and a half years before, returned there in February 1904, enrolling in Form VI—equivalent to the first year of university.

So it was back to full days of classes and evenings dominated by homework. The intensive course of study for Form VI was tailored to prepare students for the next evaluative hurdle: the Intermediate Examination in Arts. Pessoa's tall stack of study materials included textbooks for subjects such as trigonometry, British history, and French, and no less than four Latin books. In English the examinees would be specifically tested on the seventeenth-century poetry in *Palgrave's Golden Treasury of English Songs and Lyrics*. Pessoa, practically from the moment he reentered his old school and sat down at a desk, began prepping for this marathon exam, which he would take in late November and early December—nine test papers, with three hours allotted for each section.[23]

Sitting next to Fernando in class was the familiar face of Clifford Geerdts, who had studied at Durban High School for five and a half straight years, more than twice as long as the "little fellow with a big head" from Portugal. There were several other students in Form VI, but these were the only two who would take the intermediate exam, on which Pessoa scored a total of 1098 marks, a showing that was almost 20 percent better than Geerdts's 930. This time around, Fernando tested remarkably well in physics, but his best result was in English. He was the obvious winner of the Form VI prize, which, as usual, consisted of a book.[24]

Pessoa's only extracurricular activity at D.H.S. was the most literary one possible: he was an assistant editor of the school magazine, where he published an article on the historian Thomas Babington Macaulay with insights that even a professional critic could be proud of.[25] It stood out in a student quarterly where news about cricket and soccer prevailed. Team sports had grown in importance during Pessoa's long absence. Geerdts, although not an athlete, was an officer in the cadet corps and represented the school in shooting competitions. He and other students, while in awe of Pessoa's academic performance, thought that he "worked far too much and that he would ruin his health by so doing." These were Geerdts's own words, in a letter he sent a few years later to Pessoa himself—or rather, to Pessoa masquerading as a psychiatrist. It was a stratagem devised by the timid poet to find out what other people really thought of him.

◆

IN SEPTEMBER 1907, TWO years after Pessoa's return to Lisbon, Geerdts received a letter from a Dr. Faustino Antunes, who claimed to be treating his former classmate for a serious mental disorder. (Pessoa must have typed the letter or else disguised his handwriting.) Would Geerdts be so kind as to answer a few questions about the patient's character and behavior while a student at Durban High School? Geerdts obliged, and although he would later say that he suspected a hoax, his answers did not spare the hapless young man who used to sit next to him in class. They painted the sixteen-year-old Pessoa as "pale and thin," with "some defect in his eyes," a "narrow and contracted chest," a "peculiar walk," and a tendency to stoop. Socially Fernando had scarcely existed, since he took "no part in the sports or other school life outside of the class room" and was "inclined to avoid association with his schoolfellows."

Asked about the patient's love life and whether he had been prone to "sexual excesses," Geerdts replied that he had no inkling of any "love affair" of Pessoa, nor were his schoolmates "of such a class as to raise a suspicion that he had indulged in sexual excesses." The student from Portugal did, however, possess "certain indecent French and Portuguese comic papers." This taste for European smut was the only spicy particular about a boy otherwise described by the informant as "meek and inoffensive."[26]

Dr. Antunes, upon reading these last three words, might have winced on behalf of his mentally ill client. Or perhaps he was able to maintain perfect clinical detachment from the case. Pessoa could be a brutal self-analyst, particularly when carrying out his scrutiny from behind a medical mask. Writing to Hardress O'Grady, Fernando's former French teacher at D.H.S., Dr. Antunes explained (in French) that the patient under his care had been a disconcertingly serious child who liked to be alone and play alone, or just read and write. Unusually intelligent and highly imaginative, the small boy was beset by fears and subject to fits of rage, making him "a budding psychopath" at the age of seven. Then

Fernando went to Durban, where the climate and the discipline of being at school had a calming effect on the patient, or so the doctor surmised, and the boy outwardly appeared to be normal. But the year he spent back in Lisbon, when he was thirteen, brought out the beast, so to speak, for it exposed him to the "corrupting" influence of "urban sensuality." Here ends the draft of the presumably unsent letter.[27]

Like most cities in Europe, Lisbon had no shortage of prostitutes—more than twelve hundred officially registered ones in 1902, and perhaps twice that number who worked without a license—but sex workers also abounded in Durban, where prostitution was illegal but tolerated.[28] It is unclear what exactly the pseudo-doctor meant by "urban sensuality," but his theory that this somehow corrupted Pessoa, taken together with the effort to find out Geerdts's impressions of the boy's sexual habits once he returned to Durban, raises questions. Did Fernando, while in Lisbon, have some kind of possibly traumatizing sexual experience, or was it simply that the onset of puberty, occurring in Lisbon and arousing in him a vastly heightened interest in sex, had confused and alarmed him? What sort of "sexual excesses" could Geerdts have possibly known or suspected in Pessoa, whom he saw only within the confines of the all-boys school? Was the doctor hinting at masturbation, or at some sort of sexual activity with other boys? Although we can only guess at the answers to these questions, it is clear that the timid teenager had the feverish sexual stirrings typical for his age. He perused his pornographic comics just as often as any favorite story or poem. But the whole business of sex troubled him, as it does many adolescents when they discover that new and still mysterious terrain.

William Storm, the owner of a Durban shipping company and a good friend of Pessoa's parents, was also contacted by the pertinacious Dr. Antunes. Storm's reply has unfortunately gone astray, but we know that he had very complimentary things to say about Fernando.[29] Yet another respondent was Mr. Belcher, who taught English at Durban High School and was editor of the school magazine. He received a letter signed by Faustino Antunes in July 1907, two months before Geerdts. Belcher, in fact, suggested that the good doctor contact Geerdts in order to get "some useful information from the schoolboys' point of view." The suggestion was unnecessary, since Pessoa had already intended to contact Geerdts. His archives, in fact, contain the draft of a letter informing the D.H.S. alumnus that his old classmate from Portugal had apparently committed suicide by blowing up a house in the country with himself and several other people inside it. In the end, realizing that Belcher and Geerdts might well be in touch, since Geerdts was now studying at Lincoln College, Oxford, which was Belcher's alma mater, Pessoa used the same story for both men, as well as for William Storm, reporting himself to be gravely mentally ill.

Dr. Antunes posed rather general sorts of questions to Belcher, who wrote back saying that Pessoa was an original thinker, "loyal and public spirited," open-minded in religious matters, and, although not himself an athlete, he was "easily excited after watching a game of football." Belcher's most revealing comments concerned his former pupil's literary talent, taste, and method:

> His English composition was generally remarkably good and sometimes approached to genius. He was a great admirer of Carlyle and I had some difficulty in checking a disposition on his part to imitate very closely Carlyle's style.
>
> I gather from your letter that you are a student of English Literature and you will understand that Carlyle is the last man to be *imitated* by a boy whose composition is still immature.[30]

The schoolmaster may have exaggerated the danger, for an aspiring writer, of closely following Thomas Carlyle's style, but young Pessoa was indeed prone to imitate, and in 1904 his new literary fetish was Carlyle—taught to him by the selfsame Mr. Belcher. "The Ancient Monk," a long essay from Carlyle's *Past and Present* (1843), was required reading for the intermediate exam, but Belcher also had his students read *Sartor Resartus: The Life and Opinions of Herr Teufelsdröckh* and *On Heroes, Hero-Worship and the Heroic in History*. Both works deeply impressed Pessoa, particularly the first one.

✦

THE MOST ORIGINAL PROSE work to appear in English since Laurence Sterne's *Tristram Shandy*, issued in nine installments between 1759 and 1767, *Sartor Resartus* (*The Tailor Retailored*) was also published serially—in *Fraser's Magazine*, in 1833–1834—and as a book several years later. Ostensibly about Herr Teufelsdröckh (Mr. Devil's Dung) and his Philosophy of Clothes, it is a wildly meandering compendium of reflections about society, religion, the march of history, and the search for individual and universal meaning. It takes us on a bumpy, discombobulating journey that aspires to make written philosophical sense out of life. Much admired by Ralph Waldo Emerson and other transcendentalists, Carlyle's densely whimsical masterpiece was never an easy sell, but it had and still has a cultish following. One of the book's main topics of reflection is itself, its pretension and endeavor to be a book, and *how* it expresses is at least as important as *what* it expresses. Fernando, who noticed this immediately, described the entrancing power of Carlyle's luxuriant style: "We feel an immense commotion in reading him, in his electrical attraction for us, and in his majestic sky-disturbance: we now are astonished by a period of breathless calm, and now are dazzled and bewildered by a lurid outburst of chaotic force."

These words—themselves floridly reminiscent of Carlyle's style—were written in 1904, as part of the article on Macaulay that Pessoa published in the school magazine. Mr. Belcher revered this British politician, poet, and historian as the greatest nineteenth-century prose stylist in the English language and included his essays in the class syllabus. But Pessoa adroitly used his published article, which no doubt began as a homework assignment, to heap praise on Carlyle, whom he repeatedly compared with Macaulay, always to the detriment of the latter.

In April 1904 Pessoa acquired a biography of Carlyle that he in short order devoured, making pencil markings on dozens of its pages. Although outwardly their lives had little in common, he found himself closely identifying with certain core attitudes of the Scottish writer. Carlyle, who had lost his faith in Christianity as a young man, retained the work ethic and strong sense of mission inherited from his father, a Calvinist preacher who never doubted. The preacher's son thrived on doubt, but like the similarly skeptical Shelley of *Queen Mab*, he was vividly aware of a spiritual dimension. In spite of not subscribing to any religious creed, Carlyle wrote—and Pessoa underlined—"Belief I define to be the healthy act of a man's mind" (from "The Hero as Man of Letters"). He believed in believing, which is why Herr Teufelsdröckh moves away from the "Everlasting No" to ultimately embrace the "Everlasting Yea"—a notion that anticipates Nietzsche's "Eternal yes." Pessoa, like Carlyle, was averse to anything resembling a doctrinal statement of faith, yet even more averse to a materialist or utilitarian view of the world.

What Carlyle brought to literature, according to a note written by Pessoa in English years later, was "the sense of mystery girding around all human action, the metaphysical sense of history." In another note—this one from his Durban days—he wrote that Carlyle's "frantic" prose style, with its "frequent extravagance of diction," however exasperating it may prove for readers, was the perfect style for expressing the tremendous "force" and "earnestness" of his untrammeled thought.[31] The wide and wild sweep of Carlyle's language exquisitely mirrored the chiaroscuro world of luminous heights and dark depths that his words conveyed. It was this quality in his writing that thrilled his young imitator. Here is a sentence from a short essay, both thematically and stylistically Carlylean, drafted by Pessoa in 1904:

There is in the world [. . .] a horrible enigma—a dreadful depth, dreadful even to the mind, that cannot scan it; everywhere in the world, everywhere in nature a deep and fearful hint at the great secret; in the great records half-lost of the earth's existence, in the long, dreary line of men and women that have enlightened or darkened the daylight of their times, there is evident something horribly strange and constant, some grim, prosaic truth amid all the ideals and the poetry of the eternal loves.[32]

The dizzying sensation that life is imbued by a wondrous and terrifying mystery came to Pessoa quite on his own. Carlyle also felt it, which is what drew Pessoa to him, and Carlyle helped him articulate it.

Pessoa would reread *Sartor Resartus* in 1907 and make allusions to it and its author's other writings throughout the rest of his life—most emphatically in *The Book of Disquiet*, which contains explicit references to Carlyle, some kindred premises and guiding concepts (the world as a world of appearances, for instance), and one entire passage directly inspired by Teufelsdröckh's Philosophy of Clothes.[33] It is not by chance that the *Disquiet* narrator—whose reflections frequently allude to both real and metaphorical clothes—works as an assistant bookkeeper for a wholesale fabric supplier. Turning out well-written pages was the real work of Bernardo Soares, however. If acuity of expression was highly valued in *Sartor Resartus*, it became the almost exclusive ambition of *The Book of Disquiet*, at the expense of thematic continuity and structural unity, so that the book fails to form a coherent whole. It remains a heap of beautiful fragments, forever unstitched.

## CHAPTER 12

W HILE HIS CLASSMATES SPENT THEIR AFTER-
school hours doing required homework but also playing
sports, boating or swimming in the bay, flirting with girls
from other schools, or just goofing off, Fernando mostly read, studied,
and wrote, driven by an almost monomaniacal obsession with literature. His intellectual enthusiasm for Carlyle's prose far exceeded what
his mystified teacher expected from the students in Form VI. With
equal passion he dissected, ingested, and assimilated the poetry from
*Palgrave's Golden Treasury* that had been flagged for the intermediate
exam. The selection ranged from Ben Jonson and George Herbert to
Andrew Marvell and John Dryden, but the poetry of John Milton pre-
dominated. "Lycidas," "L'Allegro," and "Il Penseroso" were all there—
all of them abundantly annotated by Fernando—along with seven of his
other poems.

The first of the flagged poems, also richly annotated by Pessoa, was
Milton's ode "On the Morning of Christ's Nativity." It set the tone, or
genre, since a number of the prescribed poems were either odes or ode-
like. Fernando learned his lessons well, and not only for the sake of the
examination. First he diagrammed the verse patterns for various odes in
a notebook, beginning with the complex eight-line stanza of the "Nativity" ode: two trimeter lines (three stresses) followed by a pentameter
(five stresses), two more trimeters, and a pentameter, then a tetrameter
(four stresses) and a closing hexameter (six), obeying an *aabccbdd* rhyme
scheme. Next he set out to compose not just one but four English odes
of his own. Two of them emulated the eight-line Miltonic stanza just
described. Here is the first stanza of Pessoa's "Ode to the Storm":

> Too early day has fled,
> With soilèd rays of red
> The sun hath sunk beneath its dismal shroud,

Ingathering stern array.
On the steps of day
The storm-fiend heaps a cloud upon a cloud,
As in some dreary poet's tale
The horrid hordes hell-torn of flocking phantoms pale.

As well as perfectly replicating the metrical pattern and rhyme scheme of the "Nativity" ode, the apprentice poached several images from Milton's twenty-sixth stanza, in which the sun is "curtained with cloudy red" and "flocking shadows pale / Troop to th'infernal jail."[1]

Fernando, however, did not steal the conceit for his poem from Milton. He stole it from his French teacher. Hardress O'Grady, like C. H. Haggar of the Commercial School, was an amateur poet who occasionally published verses in *The Natal Mercury*. In the same issue of the paper where Pessoa—alias Tagus—was congratulated in December 1903 for winning the puzzle contest, there is a long poem by O'Grady titled none other than "Ode to the Storm." Its formal structure has nothing in common with the Miltonic template of Pessoa's homonymous composition. But the teenager's "Ode to the Storm" owed more than just its title to the poem he read in the paper. O'Grady's ode begins in the same way, with a description of the sun disappearing at the "stern behest" of the approaching storm. Clouds "pile / Their mighty masses," and "Ghost armies hurry in a close array." Other images and words in Pessoa's ode, including the rather unusual "storm-fiend," were directly lifted from O'Grady's poem. Although he tried to cover his tracks by using synonyms and by rearranging the order of borrowed vocabulary, it is easy to see that Fernando crunched the first two stanzas of his French teacher's ode into one stanza and shaped it after the model of Milton's ode, from whose twenty-sixth stanza he took an image or two and tossed them into the mix, as if adding thyme and oregano.

Pessoa would have gladly acknowledged his poetic debt to Milton, whom he praised to the heights of paradise as an adult—even if he admitted that the English poet's masterwork, for all its gorgeous craftsmanship, was dull reading.[2] By contrast, not only did O'Grady receive no credit for his contribution to Pessoa's "Ode to the Storm," the ungrateful youngster wrote a poem in French that made fun of his teacher for being a facile poet. Typed on the back of a program for Gilbert and Sullivan's

*The Mikado*, performed by the D.H.S. Old Boys' Club in July 1904, the lampoon was narrated by Hardress O'Grady himself, whose signature was spelled in mock French as "Ardrèce Augradi."[3]

With some self-justification, and a great deal of truth as well, Pessoa would later argue (in his essay "Erostratus," for instance) that great artists are rarely precursors and never wholly original; they capitalize and improve on what came before. Like a Portuguese Picasso of literature, he would prodigiously shift from style to style, and language to language, boldly stealing topics and formal devices and even verbatim phrases from other writers, which he transformed either directly or by placing them in transforming contexts. Perhaps the suggestion, two paragraphs up, that he wanted to "cover his tracks" should be withdrawn. Fernando, in 1904, was busy experimenting in his literary laboratory, not yet with well-defined objectives but as someone getting familiarized with equipment and procedures. He was not too concerned about completing his "Ode to the Storm," for which he wrote a few more fragments before abandoning the poem.[4] But if, instead, he had joined up the fragments and fleshed them out into a finished work, he might well have published it in *The Natal Mercury*, for the express purpose of flaunting his superior poetic technique when applied to the thematic raw material provided by his French teacher. Socially "meek and inoffensive" Fernando was already poetically self-confident and combative.

✦

PESSOA ALSO SET OUT to write an "Ode to Music" and an "Ode to the Poor," in addition to the aforementioned "Ode to the Sea." They all demonstrate remarkable skill and versatility with meter and rhyme, but these ambitious works were just one facet of the teenager's literary activity during his last two semesters at Durban High School. In that same year, 1904, he tried out a number of other poetic forms and subjects, all of them gleaned from his extensive readings. Although Fernando could appropriate ideas and phrasings from any source, including a mediocre poem by his French teacher, his usual method of self-instruction was to produce works in the style of an acknowledged master. His literary masters are not hard to identify. From each of his poetic undertakings from this period, we can usually draw a straight line to an English poet, more often than not one of the Romantics, such as Byron, Keats, or Wordsworth.

The English Romantics were a motley group, each with an unmistakably individual voice. As suggested by the word "romantic," they exalted in emotion, imagination, visions, dreams, albeit in very different ways. Pessoa exalted with and through them. In a mature poem that dialogues with William Wordsworth, he would famously write, "The one who feels in me is thinking."[5] Meaning not that he used his intellect to bridle or repress his feelings but simply that he thought deeply, unceasingly, about all that he felt, so as to express it as well as he could in words. Like the Romantics, he wanted to be a medium of the most powerful human feelings, translating them into thought, language, poetry.

Pessoa acknowledged Lord Byron as the earliest English influence on his poetry,[6] and we can feel a distinctly Byronic pulse and panache in the hundred or so lines he wrote for "The Woman in Black," an adolescent poem whose unhappy narrator complains that his rational mind is hopelessly at odds with the world's absurdity: "Too young I learnt to reason coldly / And draw conclusions firmly, boldly."[7] What Pessoa adopted from Byron, who exuberantly commented on events of the day that he witnessed firsthand, was limited to matters of poetic tone and versification. The influence soon faded, however, or it was assimilated into Pessoa's poetry beyond easy recognition. And Byron's flamboyant life of worldly battles and illicit loves was not one that could ever have served the young poet as a model.

Pessoa was more deeply influenced by John Keats, a self-conscious visionary who pointedly drew a distinction between his poetic ambition and Byron's, saying: "He describes what he sees—I describe what I imagine." From an early age Pessoa, too, wrote out of his imagination, or out of what he read and reimagined. His youthful "Gahu the Titan," a fragmentary composition written in blank verse and epic style, was a variation on Keats's pivotal *Hyperion*, an unfinished epic poem whose protagonist is the ruler of the sun and the only Titan deity not yet defeated by the new, Olympian race of gods. While sympathizing with Hyperion, whose days are numbered, Keats's poem also looks forward to what lies ahead. Behind the doomed Titan lurks a young hero still finding his wings: Apollo, the new sun god, who can feel his divinity but needs to gain confidence before he can embrace his immortal destiny. Apollo has to "die into life," according to the last lines of *Hyperion*, just as Keats knew he must do as a poet, to realize his full potential and become a literary immortal.*

Pessoa's Gahu—whose name seems to be a fusion of **Ga**ia (Earth) and **U**ranus, mother and father of the Titan gods—miserably lingers on as the very last Titan and represents, like Hyperion, an old order that must be overcome. "Gahu the Titan" laments the passing of that order but also pleads for it to be definitively put to rest. No less than Keats's *Hyperion*, Pessoa's poem described a rite of passage.[8]

Fernando, it seems, obscurely understood that all of his classical education, all the Latin drilled into him by his teachers at D.H.S., and all the intricate verse patterns he learned from Milton and other poets, advantageous as they were for his literary ambitions, also constrained him, weighed him down, prevented him from soaring as himself, Fernando Pessoa. He needed to throw off that old order and "die into life," like Keats, but it was hard for him to let go. Although he was beginning to acquire spontaneity in his writing, it would be many years before he would completely break out of the chrysalis formed by so much learning and come into his own as an astonishingly original poet—a status, of course, that he would never have attained without that chrysalis.

Gahu had to die. "Kill me, kill me!" implores the desolate hero of "Gahu the Titan." His request was granted in "The Fall of the Titan," the very first sonnet written by Pessoa in English, in April 1904.[9] The Titan's demise, felt throughout the world as a cataclysmic shock, is recounted by the sonnet's narrator with solemn respect and a hint of compassion. Pessoa, who would soon turn sixteen, accepted that death is a normal, necessary stage in the regenerative process, but it troubled him both philosophically and emotionally that all things must end to make way for the new. In May he wrote his second sonnet in English, a soliloquy about death that concludes with:

I know not death and think it no release—
The bad indeed is better than the unknown.

---

* This idea was further developed by Keats in *The Fall of Hyperion*, which revisits his earlier poem.

There was no Drydenesque "Death be not proud" for Fernando Pessoa, no belief in a redemptive postmortem reawakening, nothing that could possibly neutralize the sting of losing all that we love and dream. Nor did Pessoa fear eternal condemnation, despite the religious indoctrination he received from the nuns at St. Joseph's Convent School. His was not the fear of anything specific; it was an instinctive gut horror, because death represents Mystery, the Unknown. Unlike most young people, Pessoa was aware not in the back of his mind but at the forefront of his thoughts and with the full force of his feelings that he would one day cease as an earthly being. That awareness—indelibly engraved in him by his father's slow death from disease, followed by his infant brother's sudden decease months later—may account for his lack of interest in pursuits typical of the human species. Accumulation of wealth and power, the formation of a family, and fame in this life held no attraction for him. Fame *after* he was dead, on the other hand, was extremely appealing, since it could confer at least a contingent immortality, able to last for as long as humanity lasts. In 1904 Pessoa was already athletically training himself—using the techniques of Milton, Carlyle, and the English Romantic poets—to become a literary Olympian.

◆

IF **"THE WOMAN IN BLACK"** reminds us of Byron, and "Gahu the Titan" of Keats, yet another unfinished poem with epic aspirations— "The Old Castle," written in blank verse—recalls Wordsworth. The castle, which lies in ruins, is situated in the Spanish countryside, where the poem's speaker happened to be hiking. He meets an old man who tells him the story of how in a former age the castle, when only half ruined, was inhabited by a knight and the knight's fair cousin, Dolores. They lived happily together in love, until the knight joined a military expedition launched by Portugal's King Sebastian against "the hated Moor." This was the disastrous campaign of 1578 to regain territories in north Africa that the Portuguese had previously controlled. (Two thousand Spanish soldiers, and even more Germans, fought alongside a much larger number of Portuguese troops.) Since the knight's body was not found among the carnage on the battlefield, Dolores nourishes the hope that he is still living and will come home. The knight is emblematic of King Sebastian himself, whose body was also said to have gone missing, giving rise to the enduring myth that he would return to rescue Portugal, which fell under Spanish domination in 1580. "The Old Castle" contains Pessoa's first literary use of the Sebastianist myth, which will become a major motif in his mature work. Just as the Portuguese people kept waiting in vain for the return of King Sebastian, Dolores waits and waits for her cousin, sinks quietly into madness, grows old, keeps waiting, and finally dies. As her coffin is being lowered into the ground, an old man comes running. It is the long lost knight, her cousin and lover.

Against the background of the variously interpretable tale of the castle and its last inhabitants, the poem's narrator offers his meditations on humanity's place in the world, on mortality, and on the nature of Nature. He is as pantheistic as any Romantic, having one day been startled by the vision of "a Being that pervades / All things that are," such that outward forms are but "embodiments / Of this great soul that thrills the universe." Although his descriptions of Nature's power to uplift a human sensibility cannot begin to rival, in poetic intensity, the lines that Wordsworth composed near Tintern Abbey and at other places where he toured on foot with his sister, Dorothy, they rank among the best verses Pessoa produced as an adolescent. About a stupendous "something in Nature" that transcends human thought, he writes:

I know not what it is, but I can feel
Its power and hear its voice in everything.
Thus when I walk the fields at early morn
It finds expression in the meanest sight—
The blades of grass, the flowers that varied glow
Upon the sward, the gentle plants, the trees,
The housewife ants and working bees, the birds,
The simple flocks and grazing herds disperst.

But despite what these lines of verse suggest, I doubt that Pessoa was acutely attentive to the sights and sounds in the world of nature. He was interested, rather, in the descriptive and rhythmic power of words.

William and Dorothy Wordsworth were assiduous observers of fields and woods, with Samuel Taylor Coleridge sometimes joining them on their excursions in the Lake District. The ruined cottages and rustic characters of Wordsworth's poems were known to him through direct contact, or they were composites based on what he had seen and heard.

Byron and Shelley, in their travels to the continent, roamed the countryside as well as cities, and the impressions they gathered in both environments—rural and urban—inspired many of their poems. Fernando, in Durban, had the possibility of hiking in semitropical bush not far from the Berea, where he lived with his family. And even without stepping out of his woodsy neighborhood, he could have enjoyed many a literal field day rambling amid its lush vegetation and beholding the colorful bird and other wild life that abounded on all sides. As far as we can tell, he scarcely availed himself of these opportunities. His local surroundings certainly did not make it into his writings. He wrote about miners in Australia and a ruined castle in Spain. And he also wrote about nature—the nature described in poems by Gray, Wordsworth, and Shelley.

Throughout the summer Durban has frequent thunderstorms, usually in late afternoon, and Fernando, when still a small boy, once saw lightning split open a tree, filling him with awe and an exaggerated fear of storms that stayed with him his entire life.[10] But his "Ode to the Storm," as I have shown, was inspired by his French teacher's identically titled poem. In all of the poetry composed by Pessoa while in Durban, he made only one unequivocal reference to his own local setting:

> It was the glory of a peaceful night
> In Afric autumn, when the light sweet breeze
> Wakes from the calmness but awhile to stir
> The crowning leaves of trees, that seem to caper
> Grotesquely nodding to the silent moon.

These lines are from yet another large-scale poem, "The Palace of Thought," that was soon abandoned, like all the others.[11] On the manuscript containing the poem's longest fragment, Pessoa indicated next to each verse the number of the syllable where the natural pause, or caesura, occurred ("0," if there was none). Notations such as these were part of his self-directed lessons in how to write poetry. He vaguely hoped to finish "The Palace of Thought," as he would have liked to finish "The Woman in Black," "Gahu the Titan," and the quartet of odes from 1904, but these were all exercise pieces, études, which had served their purpose well enough: Fernando Pessoa was ready to be a poet.

✦

FERNANDO PESSOA, OR CHARLES ROBERT ANON? In 1904 this name emerged as Pessoa's predominant alter ego, credited with most of the poetry he was writing as well as a good portion of his prose. Anon was brash and bumptious, to judge by the cover letter sent in July to *The Natal Mercury*, along with his already cited poem that poked fun at Durban's former mayor, Mr. Hillier, and at Fernando's former schoolmaster, C. H. Haggar, as rhymesters of small worth. The paper prefaced its publication of the poem with the letter, whose author took condescending delight at the "magnificent crescendo of absurdity" resulting from the literary fray apropos of a poorly translated ode by Horace. The participants in the fray were lambasted for their "pseudo-poetical effusions" in a follow-up letter to the *Mercury* that Pessoa-Anon began writing on July 14.[12] In 1905 Mr. Anon would try to return to the columns of the newspaper with some unwelcome political opinions.

It might seem that Charles Robert Anon, since he was signing not only Pessoa's poetical works but also his letters to the editor, was no more than a pen name, as George Eliot was for Mary Ann Evans, or George Orwell for Eric Blair. This would make sense if, behind the poems and letters, we could identify a cohesive personality whose writing conveyed a set of preexisting feelings and opinions. No such personality existed. For Fernando Pessoa, writing was not a matter of conveying but of constructing, and C. R. Anon was one component—indeed, a key component—in his poetic edifice. Anon was not a mere cover for the "real" poet, even as the poems were not expressions of "real" feelings. Pessoa's real feelings informed his work, but they were recast, and C. R. Anon was a literary, specifically English remake of his Portuguese creator.

Although Anon took center stage, other heteronyms continued to play lesser roles. Karl P. Effield, who in 1903 was a travel writer and published poet ("The Miner's Song"), was given a rather different assignment the following year: a historical essay titled "The Sea Way to India," describing in detail how Portuguese navigators opened up that crucial maritime route.[13] Sidney Parkinson Stool, initially entrusted with writing "yachting yarns" and other stories, became associated with a work called "Atlantis," probably an essay.[14] And signatures of Gaveston continued to proliferate, as if he were anxiously waiting for an assignment that never materialized.

New heteronyms also emerged. Horace James Faber was the purported author of Pessoa's first sustained detective story, "The Case of the
Science Master." A murder mystery set in a school similar to Durban
High, it was more ambitious than the mystery tales published in the
boys' books of Fernando's early teen years. In 1904 Pessoa continued to
read the short stories of Edgar Allan Poe, and psychological deduction,
in the manner of C. Auguste Dupin, was the preferred method of his
own investigating detective, Ex-Sgt. William Byng, who was brought
in to solve the homicide of the science teacher. The onetime sergeant—
whose name may have been inspired by fictional detective Sergeant Byng
of the New York Police Department, invented by mystery writer Herbert
Flowerdew in or before the year 1900—would be put to work in several
other crime stories written in English.[15]

According to a list of his literary duties, Horace James Faber was
first and foremost an author of detective stories but also an essayist and
satiric poet. C. R. Anon, whose curriculum vitae follows Faber's on the
same sheet of paper, was first of all a poet, though responsible as well
for authoring "stories of imagination" and critical essays on great writers
such as Carlyle, Byron, and Shelley. It was no accident that the two CVs
occupied the same page. Their names appeared as co-authors on various sheets for "The Case of the Science Master," written intermittently
between 1904 and 1907.[16]

The two heteronyms also jointly authored an unfinished essay titled
"Plausibility of All Philosophies," which disputed a philosophical theory
much admired by their friend Dr. Nabos. This Nabos, whose first name
was Gaudêncio, was presumably a brother or cousin of Zé Nabos, who
wrote riddles for *The Tattler* newspaper in 1902. The theory he admired,
traceable to Aristotle and the Stoics but more recently set forth by the
philosophers John Locke (1632–1704) and Claude-Adrien Helvétius
(1715–1771), holds that a human mind starts out as a blank slate, to be
written on by one's particular education and environment. Faber and
Anon argued, on the contrary, "that the mind of man, instead of taking
colour from its surroundings and natural encompassments, does rather
impart to them its thoughts." According to this view, the validity of a
thought depends only on the thinker; hence all philosophies are plausible.[17] Fernando Pessoa may not have wholly agreed with Faber and
Anon's reasoning, but he agreed with their conclusion, and even more so
with its corollary: no one philosophy can claim to be truer than the rest.

Pessoa's family of heteronyms was growing larger, and their relationship involved more than the common circumstance of deriving from the same creative intelligence. They sat down, as it were, to have serious discussions, in which their opinions sometimes clashed. In a passage for an unfinished preface that attempted to explain how and why the heteronyms came into being, Pessoa would write, many years later: "Given the dearth of people he can get along with, what can a man of sensibility do but invent his own friends, or at least his intellectual companions?"[18] The writer was not being facetious; he was recalling what he himself began doing as a teenager.

# CHAPTER 13

"**G**O OUT AND GET SOME FRESH AIR!" HIS MOTHER must have repeatedly suggested, each time in vain. To unwind from literature and deep thinking, Fernando played ball without any ball, indoors. In July 1904 he organized a major soccer match between the Anchor Club and the Marine Football Club. The respective club managers (Nat Gould, for the Anchor Club) issued separate notices announcing the names of the team members who were scheduled to play on Tuesday, July 5, "at 2:30 p.m. sharp," but the score sheet for the imaginary match was not preserved.[1] Our knowledge of Pessoa's virtual sporting events is spotty, since he saved only the information about game times, team rosters, and final scores that happened to be recorded in his notebooks or on pieces of paper that also contained literary notes and compositions. There may have been many soccer and cricket matches for which no record has survived, but they seem to have ceased by the summer of 1905, when references to matches disappear from his papers.

Pessoa loved other games of imagination, and he did not mind playing with his much younger siblings, who retained vivid memories of their older brother as a game master and prankster. The prank they most remembered involved the use of blackface, which became popular in the British-ruled towns of South Africa after American and British minstrel shows began to tour there in the 1860s.[2] Promoted as an innocuous form of mass entertainment, minstrel shows—in which white actors and singers portrayed blacks as comical and happy-go-lucky simpletons—reinforced myths of black inferiority at a time when the colonists, while rejecting actual slavery, were passing laws and using coercion to establish native Africans as a subservient class.*

---

* Blackface is still an annual tradition in the Cape Town Minstrel Carnival (formerly known as the Coon Carnival), whose participants—mostly mixed-race Cape Coloureds—use the occasion to celebrate Creole as well as African American culture, but some critics argue that the festival perpetuates racist stereotypes.

Even if Fernando never attended a minstrel show, he had seen pictures of blackface or seen fellow students in blackface and knew very well how it was done. One afternoon, when his parents had gone calling on friends, he wrapped himself in a white sheet, blackened his face with burnt cork, and donned a black hat, while his little sister and brothers looked on. Then he climbed on a stool and peered through the fan window over the door to the service area, where the native African domestics were taking a break from their chores. So frightened were they by the apparition that they ran out of the house, at which point Fernando shed his costume and ran after them, shouting, "It's me, it's me!"

Or did they march out of the house in indignation? The details of how the domestics reacted, as if they had seen a ghost, were embellished over the years as the story was retold, with different versions of events circulating among family members.[3] The incident, in any case, confirms that Fernando was no more sensitive than the rest of Durban's white residents to the inherent offensiveness of blackface. Looking beyond the casual racism it reveals, the prank may be seen as yet another experiment in self-transformation. According to Pessoa's sister, on the day he wore blackface he was playing the part of Quebranto Oessos (I Break Bones), a character invented by him to playfully frighten her and her little brothers.[4]

It was during the school holidays that Pessoa staged the big soccer match between the Anchor and Marine clubs, took on the local literati in the pages of *The Natal Mercury*, and doubtless spent more time entertaining his siblings. In the evenings, after dinner, he liked to read while listening to his mother play piano, sometimes accompanied by his stepfather on the flute.[5]

Fernando was sixteen when he began his last semester at Durban High, in August 1904, and soon he and all the other students were studying in earnest for the year-end exams. Their attention was distracted, however, by the sudden death of the most popular student, Wilfred Hobley, on October 3. Captain of the school and senior prefect, Hobley was a star athlete, he radiated charisma, and his good-heartedness endeared him to nearly everyone. Just a few days after his magnificent performance brought victory to the soccer team in an important match, he caught rheumatic fever and died within a week, shaking up the whole school,[6] though probably less so Fernando Pessoa, his classmate in Form VI. Pessoa was all too familiar with death, and rather than mourning Hobley's

demise with the rest of the school, it's more likely that he recalled the
relatives he had lost: his father, his brother, Uncle Cunha, his maternal
grandmother, one of his half sisters, and, most recently, Uncle João (Aunt
Anica's husband), who in February had finally succumbed to tuberculosis.[7] He could not, in truth, have greatly missed his brother, sickly Jorge,
who did not make it to his first birthday, but he missed the *idea* of a
brother, he missed what Jorge might have meant to him had he lived.

Pessoa's archives include a scrap of paper from Durban with five slightly
awkward but telling lines of verse that evoke his "unhappy brother."[8]
They might have been written in January 1904, upon the tenth anniversary of Jorge's death, or in October of that same year, when Durban
High School was grieving the loss of its most popular student, or perhaps they date from 1905. "In thee are buried all our family's hopes,"
laments Pessoa in one of the lines he addressed to Jorge, who died before
learning how to talk. Fernando got on well with his stepfather and his
half siblings, but *"our* family" meant for him the one he had lost. He
wishfully supposed that Jorge would have understood him in a way his
mother's second family could not. His words of lament also suggest that,
without Jorge to prolong it, the Pessoa family line was doomed to extinction. Because of his calling to be a poet and his inclination to live life in
a different way from most, and perhaps also because he slightly dreaded
the thought of physical contact with women, Fernando was not expecting to have a wife and children. "Common things are disagreeable to me.
I long for much not material," the poet wrote on p. 390 of his algebra
textbook for Form VI.[9]

In December he successfully passed the Intermediate Examination
in Arts with a second class placement, having missed the cutoff for first
class by a few points. His score, nonetheless, was the highest in the Natal
colony, which should have entitled him to a coveted Natal Exhibition
scholarship, providing for all his expenses while he pursued a college
degree in Great Britain. Here was something material that Fernando
surely longed for, notwithstanding what he wrote in his algebra book,
but there was a catch: only students enrolled in a Natal school during the
preceding four years were eligible for the scholarship. The trip to Portugal in 1901–1902 had disqualified him, and so the award went to Clifford Geerdts, who used it to study at Oxford, where in 1907 he would
receive Dr. Faustino Antunes's letter.[10]

That providential four-year rule established by Natalian lawmakers saved Fernando Pessoa for Portuguese letters as well as for world poetry generally. He would not have soared as a poet writing in English. His self-education in poetic technique—taking Milton and the English Romantics as his major models—was bearing fruit. His English poetry from 1904 was considerably more sophisticated than his Portuguese output from 1902. He naturally had more interesting things to say, given his intellectual and emotional development in the intervening two years. But we read those earlier Portuguese poems without a hitch; in his English poetry we occasionally stumble. In the poetic fragment addressed to his dead brother, for instance, Pessoa wrote: "In thee is gone for ever the content / That love of having thee did ever raise." Jorge's death, in other words, deprived him of the pleasure of having a brother. The poetic formulation sounds merely odd, not interestingly odd. Most of Pessoa's English verse reads much better than the five lines to his brother, but in poetry even a slight linguistic misstep can spell disaster. If Pessoa had spent his early years in Durban playing with other children rather than studying and reading books, his English would have been a fitter instrument for singing, for shouting, for whispering, for declaring out loud—all of which his Portuguese poetry would do extraordinarily well. It is possible that in Britain, given a few more years, Pessoa's English would have become rough-and-tumble, suitable for playing poetic ball. But a more likely outcome, had he gone to study at Oxford, is that he would have become a brilliant professor and an outstanding critic, who also published some moderately good, forgettable poetry.

✦

DURBAN HIGH SCHOOL HAD taught Pessoa what it could teach him—and now what? There was no point in his studying at a college in the Cape Colony unless he were planning to remain in South Africa for good. To send him to study in England would have been financially challenging if not ruinous for his parents, who had four young children to raise. Besides Henriqueta, Luís, and João, there was a new baby, Maria Clara, born in August 1904. And since Fernando was not very outgoing and had a delicate constitution, his mother would have worried about him being so far away, without a single relative nearby. The only sensible, feasible option was for him to continue his studies in Lisbon, where the school year began in October 1905. He would sail for Portugal in mid-August.

In the first eight months of 1905, his last eight months in Durban, Fernando Pessoa had no classes or exams to prepare for, yet he kept right on studying. It was what he enjoyed doing, and an ill-defined ambition—as if for some future exam—spurred him on. He routinely drew up lists of books to read and set himself goals, like a runner in training, to help him keep up his pace.

Actual running never appealed to Pessoa, but now that he had time to spare and had already proven himself intellectually, he decided to devote some attention to his body. In late January he ordered the book *Strength and How to Obtain It*, by the pioneer of modern bodybuilding, Eugen Sandow (1867–1925). Born in Prussia, this precursor of Charles Atlas gained his fame in London, where he founded the Institute of Physical Culture. He published a magazine and traveled widely to show off his physique and to sell his muscle-building method. Sandow had been an icon for some of the soldiers of the Anglo-Boer War, and in 1904 he toured South Africa, appearing mainly in Cape Town and Johannesburg and making shorter stops in other towns, including Durban.[11] Even if Fernando did not see the he-man in action, he noticed the publicity promoting Sandow's performances. Tantalized by the prospect of a body he could be proud of or at least not embarrassed by, Fernando ordered the same Sandow book that James Joyce would place on Leopold Bloom's bookshelf. A form letter from Sandow addressed to F. Pessoa, Esq., and dated February 27, 1905, recommended that the sixteen-year-old fill in and send back the measurement chart at the back of the book, as a first step toward receiving instruction from the muscle master.[12] We don't know whether he complied with the recommendation, but he at least tried out, like Bloom, some of the exercises described in the book. So did Yeats in Dublin, Kafka in Prague, and T. S. Eliot while an undergraduate at Harvard College.[13]

In the same week he sent off for Sandow's book, Pessoa wrote to Liverpool to inquire about a product called Venustro Bust Developer. Unhappy with his slightly sunken chest, he was willing to consider multiple approaches to remedying the problem. A note in his archives reveals that a few years later, as a young adult in Lisbon, he planned to order some "chest-expanding braces" from England. He may have imagined that Venustro Bust Developer was something along the same lines. Or did he actually think of trying out a therapy that, for a man especially, would have been highly unconventional? Whatever the case, the Dourais Medicine Co. of Liverpool sent him their booklet *Beauty, Health, Happiness and Development of the Bust, with Testimonials* and a letter dated March 2, 1905. Addressed to "Dear Madame," the form letter explained that the Developer consisted of an orally administered elixir and a topically applied ointment whose active ingredient was "a rare tropical oil." Their combined effect would soon cause the user's bust "to fill out and form to become well developed to the full proportions of nature, beautifully rounded and symmetrical." Despite assurances that the product would be sent "safely packed and securely sealed from observation," there is little likelihood that the inquirer placed an order.[14]

Pessoa also looked into William Macdonald Smith's "System of Physical Culture." Akin to Sandow's method, it advocated full muscular contractions for building up one's physique and improving overall body health.[15] The adolescent's interest in physical culture, and specifically in expanding his chest, was health related but also aesthetic. He dreamed of having a visually pleasing, manly torso.

Fernando Pessoa was too systematically skeptical to put heart and soul into any self-help program, whether it aimed at bettering his body, his mind or his morals. He lent an ear and sent some money to Eugen Sandow, for his book, and perhaps to Macdonald Smith, but he also parodied these and other champions of good health through his creation of Dr. William K. Jinks, a heteronymous crusader dedicated to the "physical, moral, and mental elevation of man, woman and child." Like Sandow, Jinks was the editor of a magazine that promoted "physical culture" and other disciplines conducive to healthy living, all of which contributed to the ultimate goal—more ambitious than Sandow's—of "correcting vice and overthrowing society." An unnamed narrator, who might be Fernando Pessoa himself, recounts how he was accosted by the effusive Mr. Jinks in a cheap café, where the health advocate lost no time in trying to win over a new convert:

"You stoop," he suddenly remarked.
I was slightly confused but, being deflected by about 45 degrees, I admitted the imputation.
"I don't," remarked Mr. Jinks. "Moreover you are tired."
I said that I *was* tired.

"I am never tired," Mr. Jinks went on, regarding the lemonade I was drinking as something poisonous, while he ordered a concentrated essence of something particularly healthy and pure.

Soon the stooping and tired-looking narrator was shown a book that would "regenerate the world and could be obtained from Professor William K. Jinks, 23 and 24 Crank Buildings, 2306, Bandit Street, New York."[16]

Pessoa's creation of William K. Jinks, though an obvious takeoff on Sandow and his ilk, did not mean he was renouncing his good intentions to strengthen his body and adopt a healthy lifestyle. In him skepticism and enthusiasm could flourish together, and it was with both these attitudes that he extended his interest in the human body to the possibility of discovering, through physical attributes, his own and other people's essential personality and future destiny. He probably did not believe too much in chiromancy, but palm reading was a fun family activity, and he owned a manual on the subject. Physiognomy and phrenology exerted a more powerful and enduring attraction. The former proposes to reveal character through an analysis of facial features, while the latter aspires to unveil one's personality through precise measurements of the skull, with each small area of the brain being responsible for a particular behavioral tendency. (Phrenology also provided racists with pseudoscientific grounds for defending, based on skull shape, the superiority of Europeans.) Both disciplines had been widely debunked by the late nineteenth century, but phrenology enjoyed a slight comeback in the early twentieth century thanks to the British psychiatrist Bernard Hollander. Fernando received a copy of Hollander's *Scientific Phrenology* (1902) for his seventeenth birthday, in June 1905, at which point he began to record and analyze cranial measurements for himself and other members of the family.

✦

BEYOND POETRY, IMAGINARY SPORTS, and his interest in things like bodybuilding, palm reading, and phrenology, which focus almost exclusively on the individual, there was a vast and conflict-ridden world that demanded Pessoa's attention. In 1905, unburdened by classwork, he began to be politically aware and involved, at least "Anon-ymously." It was Charles Robert Anon who on July 7 signed an indignant letter to

*The Natal Mercury*, criticizing the paper for the mean and "slavish way" in which "sarcasm and irony are heaped on the Russians, on their army, and on their Emperor." The Japanese were winning the Russo-Japanese War, which had broken out a year and a half earlier, and since Britain sided with Japan, so did Durban's newspapers, gloating over how the larger country was being trounced by the smaller one. "Every reverse and disaster of the Russian army or navy is in such a way made the subject of a jest among us that we seem to have nothing more amusing," observed Mr. Anon, who, to counter the barrage of mockery, submitted three sonnets for which he requested "such publicity as has been extended to writers on the other side." The editor of *The Natal Mercury*'s literary and opinion page printed a curt response on July 15: "C. R. Anon—In your sensitiveness (for which I beg to express all respect) you have exaggerated the offense." Neither Anon's letter nor his poems were published.

The three rejected sonnets, besides chastising British subjects for rejoicing in Russia's humiliating setbacks, also excoriated the stewards of British imperialism for having made war on the Boers and for keeping Ireland under subjection.* Just as interesting as the sonnets, from a biographical point of view, is the unpublished letter to the editor, in which Charles Robert Anon, even as he reviled the English for being unfair and unfeeling, clearly identified himself as an Englishman. Anon's stance accurately mirrors Pessoa's ambivalent relationship with England and all things English. He boasted of his mastery of the English language, he longed to be part of its literary tradition, and he endorsed key aspects of Britain's political tradition, such as its emphasis on individual rights and free speech; he loathed its foreign policy, however, particularly with respect to Portugal. Britain's high-handed manner with its Iberian ally was a hidden though not exclusive motive for C. R. Anon's condemnation of British imperialism elsewhere around the globe. Like other Europeans, particularly those who were privileged colonists, Pessoa had been educated to view the world through the prism of imperialism,[17] but he could see nothing grand or glorious in the gray, administrative, impersonal British Empire, which never, he observed, had a leader in

---

* The three submitted sonnets included a diptych, "To England," preceded by the epigraph "When English journalists joked on Russia's disasters," and "Liberty," which contains the lines "Ireland and Transvaal, ye are a shame / On England and a blot!"

the mold of Alexander the Great, Caesar, or Napoleon—empire builders whose achievements he admired.

It was in the written word, in literature, that Pessoa felt himself to be partly and even profoundly English, and he was confident enough with the language to parody its nonstandard varieties. William K. Jinks, the crank doctor and health guru from New York, somehow landed in a London jail, where in April 1905 he wrote a hilariously misspelled letter, signing himself "Willyum Jinks Esk." The draft of the letter in Pessoa's archives is marked "copy," suggesting that he sent another, neatly written copy to a newspaper or magazine he hoped would publish it.[18] American English was also a butt of Pessoa's linguistic humor, in this case reflecting more keenly the attitudes of the British, who even in the early twentieth century seemed to have forgotten that they lost the Revolutionary War. In 1904 he wrote an absurd sketch about a British seller of "portable houses and shanties" based in rural America, where he tries to sell a shanty to a "feller" named "Jem" (for Jim) whose vocabulary and accent mimic those of a yokel from a Twain novel.[19]

✦

SINCE HIS EYES WERE ineluctably drawn to almost any form of the printed word, we can safely assume that Pessoa browsed through one or more issues of *Indian Opinion*, a weekly paper founded in Durban in June 1903. He would have been intrigued by its quadrilingual format: English, Gujarati, Hindi, and Tamil. This proved too cumbersome and costly, so that the latter two languages were soon dropped. As well as offering general news of interest to South African Indians, the paper called attention to discrimination in the towns and to the abysmal conditions on Natal's plantations, where the suicide rate among indentured Indians was disturbingly high.

Although he never served as its editor, Mohandas Gandhi was the *Indian Opinion*'s founder and most important contributor in the early years. In 1903 he had opened a law practice in Johannesburg, but he occasionally visited Durban to deal with Indian issues and problems at the newspaper. The publication's main problem was chronic indebtedness, and in September 1904 Gandhi traveled to Durban in hopes he could put it on a sounder financial footing. On the train he read John Ruskin's *Unto This Last*, a critique of capitalism and classical economics. This book, along with the nonfiction writings and practical example of

Leo Tolstoy, persuaded Gandhi that a radical change in human lifestyle was necessary. He was as persuasive as any of the writers he read, and he soon convinced his friends at the *Indian Opinion* that the newspaper and its associated book press should be relocated to a rural setting, where workers would live in a communal fashion and all receive the same wage. By December they had relocated to Phoenix, a hilltop farm fifteen miles outside of Durban. In an editorial published in the December 24, 1904, issue of *Indian Opinion*, Gandhi described his vision of the Phoenix Settlement as a place where "the workers could live a more simple and natural life, and the ideas of Ruskin and Tolstoy [be] combined with strict business principles," thereby making the newspaper self-sustaining.

Fernando Pessoa may never have read *Unto This Last*, but he read enough of Ruskin (1819–1900), a prominent social thinker as well as the most important art critic of the Victorian era, to remark that his prose contained "fine passages of poetry."[20] One passage that especially impressed Pessoa, who emphatically underlined it, was from *Fors Clavigera*, a collection of open letters addressed to Great Britain's working class. In the seventy-sixth letter Ruskin, a former evangelical Protestant, tells how, after studying the great masters of Venetian painting and finding "no religion whatever" in the sublime art of Titian, he soberly concluded "that human work must be done honorably and thoroughly because we are now Men," independent of any spiritual afterlife. Furthermore, "resolving to do our work well" is "the only sound foundation of any religion whatever."[21] Similar words could have been written by Pessoa, or by Mahatma Gandhi. Whether the ambition was to write great poetry or to campaign for social justice, they both brought the whole of their human selves to the task.

On April 4, 1905, a massive earthquake struck the Kangra Valley of northern India, killing more than twenty thousand people. The *Indian Opinion* naturally gave more coverage to the tragedy than did other South African newspapers, and Gandhi mounted a relief campaign on behalf of the survivors. Pessoa's reaction to the news was, predictably, literary rather than humanitarian. He invented a story about an earthquake that plays havoc with the lives of several respectable citizens in a normally quiet town.[22] It was a humorous tale featuring Dr. Gaudêncio Nabos ("Turnips"). A colleague of Dr. Nabos from another corner of the vegetable patch, a professor named Dr. Cenouras ("Carrots"), was ridiculed for his academic pedantry in yet another humorous short story written around the same time.[23]

The strangest work conceived by Pessoa while still in Durban had a Latin title, *Ultimus Joculatorum*, translatable as *The Last of the Jokers* (or *Jesters*). This was not a literary work in any traditional sense but an ongoing mise en scène of Fernando Pessoa's various alter egos playing opposite one another and even opposite him, their creator. Or so it would eventually unfold, after his return to Lisbon. In Durban perhaps only his heteronyms took the stage, with Fernando directing. From a few surviving notes we know that this hard-to-define work began as a series of "anecdotes" and "incidents" involving such heteronyms as Gaudêncio Nabos and Sidney Parkinson Stool. More than a literary project, *Ultimus Joculatorum* was a forum where Fernando's fictional friends met, told jokes, and played jokes on each other, like so many Pickwickians.[24] There was an esprit de corps, even if only one member of the group—its author—existed in flesh and blood. The personal dedication of the group members to one another, notwithstanding their unreality, is confirmed by the literary dedication, "To G. N." (Gaudêncio Nabos), that precedes "Liberty," one of the three sonnets signed by Charles Robert Anon and sent to *The Natal Mercury* in July 1905.

✦

IN *THE BOOK OF DISQUIET* Pessoa would write, "I'm the naked stage where various actors act out various plays."[25] Some of these "plays," having commenced in Durban, would be continued in Lisbon, with changes in the stage sets and the cast of characters. The Merrick brothers, Karl P. Effield, and J. G. Henderson Carr—variously tasked with writing fiction, poetry, travel literature, and essays—had vanished for good, to be replaced soon enough by new characters. But other invented friends, such as Charles Robert Anon, accompanied Pessoa as he once again stepped aboard the *Herzog*, the same German steamer that had brought him to Durban from Lisbon in 1902.

Now it would make that voyage in reverse, returning him to a Europe where ongoing innovations promised a bright future for the arts and sciences even as social and political tensions were exposing rifts that would eventually tear the continent apart. In Paris a young Spanish painter, Pablo Picasso, had entered his so-called Rose Period and was about to paint a portrait of Gertrude Stein, the exiled American writer and art collector who would become his main patron. In that same year, 1905, an unknown employee of the Swiss Patent Office, Albert Einstein, published four groundbreaking papers, including one on the theory of relativity, which would revolutionize physics. In politics it was Russia that dominated the international headlines, and not only because of the war it was unexpectedly losing to Japan. The Russian Revolution of 1905 began in January and continued throughout the year, stirring up powerful waves of protest across the country and setting the stage for the more radical revolution that would end tsarism and usher in communism twelve years later. The inspiring drama of Russia's rebellious proletariat helped galvanize labor movements in central and western Europe, especially Germany and France, where Marxism and socialism were steadily attracting adherents. These movements were countered by nationalist parties that promoted traditional values, more assertive foreign policies, and, often enough, xenophobia.

Portugal, in the arts and sciences, continued to trail behind other European countries, while politically it followed a somewhat different path. There was a Portuguese Socialist Party, founded in 1875, but the majority of the urban working class, along with many other dissatisfied citizens, placed their hopes in republicanism to transform society by firstly overthrowing the monarchy. Although a rigged electoral system prevented the republicans from winning more than token representation in the parliament, public opinion in the larger cities was increasingly on their side.

Fernando Pessoa still supported the monarchy, simply because it had never occurred to him to question its legitimacy. But his political consciousness had lately been kindled, preparing him to call all the reigning systems of power into question. An instinctive patriot from a young age, he was about to become a passionate student of Portuguese politics, though he would often view them through a poetic lens, seeing his nation's social and governmental crises as the chapters of a moral or exemplary tale, one whose resolution he sought in literary and historical myths. Strange as it may sound, it is fair to say that Pessoa's growing self-assurance as a poet helped make him ready to take on politics.

Taking leave of his mother, his stepfather, and his four much younger siblings—Maria Clara, the youngest, had just turned one year old—Pessoa departed from Durban on Sunday, August 20, 1905. Perhaps they were all there at the Point, waving their hands or handkerchiefs as his ship pulled out of Natal Bay, where his mother used to take him to swim when he was still a little boy. During the nine years he had lived there, the town's population had almost doubled, but its character had not changed. With the Anglo-Boer War having brought all of South Africa firmly under British control, Durban's white residents were more secure than ever in their position as privileged overlords.

Rounding the verdant Bluff, the *Herzog* called at southern ports as far as Cape Town, where Pessoa gazed for the third time in his life at Table Mountain, looming over the city like an enormous stone altar to unknown gods. This was the young man's last point of physical contact with Africa. From there he headed north to Portugal, before continuing on—through his heteronyms—to England, America, Scotland, Ireland, east Asia, France, Brazil, and Peru. But even those heteronyms who remained in Portugal would be vehicles for great existential journeys. Years later, in a poem dated September 20, 1933, Pessoa would describe the method of travel he used throughout his life:

To travel! To change countries!
To be forever someone else,
With a soul that has no roots,
Living only off what it sees!

To belong not even to me!
To go forward, to follow after
The absence of any goal
And any desire to achieve it!

This is what I call travel.

In his imagination Pessoa took to Lisbon his private theater of changing personae and literary collaborators, while in his luggage he took the beginnings of an impressive personal library. The last book he had acquired in Durban, *The Complete Works of William Shakespeare*, was the one that aroused in him the most awe, respect, fondness, and envy. The massive volume was a going-away present, given to him on August 16, four days before his departure. The gracious donor was the family friend William Storm, an Englishman who served as Denmark's consul in

Durban and who, like the Portuguese consul, had for many years been a ship's captain.

And so it was with the blessing of two captains—the one Portuguese, the other English—and with Shakespeare as a pilot's manual that Fernando Pessoa set off on his voyage to Portugal, to adulthood, and to literary maturity. Given his growing attentiveness to signs and symbols, perhaps it struck him as more than a coincidence that Mr. Storm's Danish wife was from Elsinore.[26]

# Part II

# THE POET AS TRANSFORMER

## *(1905–1914)*

> I've created in myself various personalities. I constantly create personalities. Each of my dreams, as soon as I start dreaming it, is immediately incarnated in another person, who is then the one dreaming it, and not I.
>
> —*The Book of Disquiet* (text 299)

Pessoa at age twenty, scrupulously dressed in a three-piece suit—his standard attire during the rest of his life.
*(Courtesy Casa Fernando Pessoa)*

# CHAPTER 14

**A** LTHOUGH PESSOA, IN 1905, WAS RETURNING TO a reality he knew well enough—only three years had elapsed since he'd last been in Lisbon—it seemed much further away in time. His homecoming accentuated his chronic feeling of estrangement and aroused in him a new form of anxiety, perhaps the same anxiety expressed years later in a poem by Álvaro de Campos, who returns to Lisbon after having lived abroad and realizes that he's

> A foreigner here like everywhere else,
> Incidental in life as in my soul,
> A ghost wandering through halls of remembrances
> To the sound of rats and creaking floorboards
> In the accursed castle of having to live . . . [1]

Not only did Pessoa, after spending almost a decade abroad, feel a little foreign, incidental to the city of his birth and early childhood; he suddenly found himself in the position of "having to live." He had just turned thirteen when he returned to Lisbon on vacation in 1901–1902; now he was a college student who had to start thinking about his future. What sort of professional path would he follow? And how would he fit in socially? He had reached that age when people start to fall in love and become sexually active, which he didn't feel ready for. On the cusp of adulthood and deprived of the shelter of his immediate family, Pessoa saw a rather different city from the one etched in his memory.

Pessoa's perspective had changed, and Lisbon itself had objectively, physically changed. Five years into the new century, it was in the throes of a building boom. Thousands of people from northern Portugal were drawn by the prospect of a better life to the nation's capital, which expanded along several avenues radiating out from the downtown area. But the new neighborhoods, with art nouveau flourishes on some of the houses and apartment buildings, were for the middle and prosperous classes. Proletarians had to squeeze into older neighborhoods, where sanitation facilities were often jerry-built or nonexistent. Their housing included traditional "patios," in which several rows of cramped dwellings huddled around a small courtyard, and more recent *vilas operárias*, worker villas, which, like the patios, were self-contained developments that sequestered from public view the lives of people at the bottom of the income ladder. Certain neighborhoods, such as Alfama and Mouraria, had been practically abandoned to underpaid workers living in dilapidated buildings.

Despite their contrasting fortunes and lifestyles, the city's different social classes often came together in the same public spaces. In that summer of 1905, people of all sorts flocked to the park of Campo Grande, where on Sunday afternoons bourgeois couples and families, in scenes vaguely reminiscent of an impressionist painting, rowed rented boats around the pond, while common laborers, seamstresses, and housekeepers enjoyed (at no cost) a stroll in the shade, or they browsed the bric-a-brac for sale in the bazaar and perhaps tried their luck in a raffle. In the evening a band played, the crowd swelled, and groups of men in stylish suits and ladies wearing flamboyant hats almost—but only almost—rubbed shoulders with groups of drably dressed workmen and women wearing simple scarves on their heads.[2] It was a delicate dance that reflected and indeed preserved a complex social hierarchy.

Automobiles were still a luxury item—there were fewer than two hundred in the whole city—but the recently arrived disc-playing phonograph was in high demand. It was more practical and produced a clearer, richer sound than the cylinder-playing machine invented by Thomas Edison, and the cheaper models cost as little as twelve thousand reis, about the same price as a three-piece suit or a lady's outfit. Waltzes, polkas, mazurkas, and arias—especially in the recordings of Enrico Caruso (1873–1921), the already legendary tenor from Naples—were all popular listening music. Caruso had caused a sensation when he performed at the São Carlos Theater in 1903. Another cultural and technological novelty, moving pictures, had lately been introduced by the Salão Ideal, which opened in 1904 on Rua do Loreto, several blocks from where Pessoa was born.[3] (The Salão lives on as the Cinema Ideal, though the interior has been completely remodeled.) Other movie houses would open soon enough, but it would take many years for cinema to overtake theater,

which was hugely popular—especially the satirical and bawdy revues—
and accessible even to those on a tight budget.

A less edifying but no less dramatic or less comic entertainment was
provided by the Portuguese parliament, many of whose members were
crying "Scandal!" over a new monopoly contract for importing and con-
fecting tobacco that the government was negotiating with Henry Bur-
nay, one of the country's most adroit capitalists. On September 9, 1905,
after many days of fierce debate, some irate statesmen rocked the legislative chamber with their screaming and smashed a dozen desks to pieces.[4]
They were incensed, above all, because the aging and timorous prime
minister had skipped the session without explanation. His government
was quickly becoming untenable. The next day Lisbon republicans held
a rally, attended by several thousand people, to protest the machinations
of politicians and businessmen involved in the so-called *questão dos tabacos*, or tobacco question. (Many years later, Pessoa himself, in his little-
known role as a not entirely scrupulous commercial agent, would try to
get involved in the opaque business of securing government contracts for
suppliers of tobacco in America.)

On September 14, four days after the republican rally, Pessoa disembarked from the SS *Herzog*. Seventeen years old, he had reached his full
height of five feet, eight inches, which was tall for a Portuguese man of
the time. Slender in build, he had a small mouth, a slightly large but
well-shaped nose, and dark, wavy hair. Some people thought he looked
Jewish. He was doubtless met on the dock by relatives, who took him to
the still peaceful, riverside neighborhood of Pedrouços, where he stayed
for a week or two with his great-aunts Maria and Rita and Grandma
Dionísia. Now eighty-two, his paternal grandmother had settled, it
seems, into a more tractable state of dementia. There are almost no family references to her from this period, but in a photo taken soon after
Pessoa's return she looks fiercely unapologetic. She had a German maid
who took care of her personal needs. Fernando seems to have basically
ignored her.[5]

Fernando must have made the rounds catching up with his great-
aunts Adelaide and Carolina and their families, or perhaps they came to
Pedrouços, where Aunt Maria was used to receiving visitors, but in his
first two days back he also spent at least several hours all alone, writing.
It was not that he had a poem in his head or some original idea that
urgently needed to be committed to paper; he was inspired, rather, to

produce something completely futile. On September 17, the third day after he docked, he brought out issue no. 1 of a new series of his make-believe newspaper *O Palrador* (*The Tattler*). More than two years had passed since the last, Durban issue of *The Tattler*, which had more closely resembled a magazine. Now, as in the original Lisbon series from 1902, Pessoa divided the pages of his paper into narrow columns that he filled with news, riddles, and poetry. It was shorter than previous issues, just two pages long, and totally humorous in content. Its only poem, signed by Dr. Pancrácio, was a scatological epigram. More than half the paper was taken up by an update on the Russo-Japanese War that ridiculed the imaginary commanders of both sides, particularly a self-important Russian general named "Pimpampunski," whose contempt for conven-tion had led him to shun taking baths. The reporter also tells of a short-lived but "very serious revolution in Russia," staged by "a baker and three shoemakers."

This jeering surprises us given that, three months earlier in Durban, Charles Robert Anon had blasted *The Natal Mercury* for siding squarely with the Japanese and heaping scorn on the Russians. That was Charles Robert Anon, however. *The Tattler*'s new literary editor was Pessoa's humoristic heteronym, Gaudêncio Nabos, for whom the Japanese and the Russians were equally legitimate targets of his wit: he cared little who won. In fact, a peace treaty ending the war had just been signed, yet the conflict carried on in *The Tattler*. Perhaps Pessoa, or Gaudêncio Nabos, had not heard the news.

How is it possible that a university-level student as sophisticated as Pessoa would devote time to inventing the comic figures and content of *The Tattler*? While he undoubtedly showed some of the newspaper's issues from 1902 and 1903 to his family, the 1905 "edition" does not seem like the sort of thing he would have shared with Aunt Maria, much less with his no-nonsense aunt Rita. His writing hand was guided, it seems, by a sentimental force of habit. Returning to Lisbon, where in 1902 he had created seven issues of *The Tattler*, most of them in Pedrouços, he spontaneously brought out another one, as if the three intervening years had not transpired. Part of him clearly wished they had not. In certain ways Pessoa was still astonishingly childish. The latest *Tattler* did have at least one reader: his cousin Mário, who was fourteen years old, young enough to still appreciate its puerile humor.

✦

AUNT ANICA, MÁRIO, AND Maria had also moved to Lisbon, having just arrived from the Azores on September 5, the very day that Japan and Russia made peace and nine days before Fernando landed. The widowed Anica had decided it made more sense to be on the mainland, where virtually all her close relatives were now living and where her two children would have more options and opportunities as they grew up. The fact that her nephew (and godson) was returning to the capital made the move even more advantageous, since they could all live together. Financially secure, she was able to lease a spacious second-floor apartment on Rua de São Bento, where Fernando joined her and his cousins toward the end of September.

Pessoa's new address was near where he had lived in the summer of 1902, before going back to Durban, and close to the Portuguese parliament. It was also easy walking distance from the Curso Superior de Letras (School of Arts and Letters), where classes began on Monday, October 2. The college-level school occupied a building contiguous to the Lisbon Royal Academy of Sciences, and some of the classrooms were in the academy itself. This was an already august institution, created in the eighteenth century and housed in a former convent. With its sumptuously decorated library full of rare books and manuscripts, the academy emanated classical order and erudition but made little impression on Pessoa, who loved books only for what they contained. He would make good use of the library, consulting especially the philosophy section, but he was not a bibliophile and had no taste for pomp and lavish décor.

Enrollees in the School of Arts and Letters could pursue general studies or elect a course tailored to one of three professional areas: library and archival science, education, or the foreign service. Pessoa chose this last variant of the course. Like most of his classmates, he was a "voluntary" student, a category created by the school's founder, King Pedro V (reigned 1853–1861), who wanted to give everyone the opportunity to study, free of charge and without having to meet formal entrance requirements. Pessoa was better prepared than most, which no doubt accounts for some of his frustration with the school, but he regularly attended his classes—in English, French, Romance philology, world history, and geography.[6]

Two days into the term, Pessoa had his vision checked. Moderately nearsighted in both eyes, he had probably already been using corrective lenses, although they're not in any of the photos of him taken in Durban. Now, as if wanting to look the part of a young European intellectual, he got a prescription for pince-nez glasses, then very much in fashion.

Sartorially, Pessoa also followed fashion. He opted for discreet elegance, sparing no expense to maintain a small wardrobe of high-quality apparel, whether or not his budget could afford it. Having been raised in handsome breeches and starched collars, he now clad himself in well-pressed trousers, white shirts, and perfectly fitting jackets, which in 1905 were still long, with four buttons rather than three. It would not have occurred to him to dress any other way than with classical refinement. Despite his tendency to get lost in imaginary realities, far removed from the world of human affairs, he cared about how others saw him, and about how he saw himself.

While he would always feel a little like an outsider, Pessoa was gradually becoming more sociable and made three or four friends among his classmates, most of whom were a few years older. He cultivated one-on-one relationships, without becoming part of any clique. Sometimes after classes, or later in the evening, he and one of his new friends—Carlos or José or Armando—would walk about town discussing literature, philosophy, and other, less lofty matters. Carlos Celestino Corado was one of the brainier students, fond of philosophy, and he and Pessoa would remain vaguely in touch, seeing each other in cafés, long after they had left the School of Arts and Letters.

Two of the school's students, Armando Teixeira Rebelo and Beatriz Osório de Albuquerque, Rebelo's girlfriend and future wife, would become Pessoa's lifelong friends. Armando, like Fernando, had sailed for South Africa when he was seven, and his father, like Fernando's stepfather, was a Portuguese consul, but in Pretoria. Although the Teixeira Rebelos did not stay for long—just a little over a year, in 1891 and 1892—it was enough time for Armando to learn excellent English, which he continued to practice back in Portugal. English, rather than Portuguese, was the language he spoke with Fernando, creating a special bond that was reinforced by their shared African cultural experience. Beatriz Osório de Albuquerque, whose parents were both part British or Irish, was even more fluent in English than Armando.[7]

◆

IN HIS SECOND SEMESTER Pessoa began keeping a diary with succinct accounts of each day's activities, which often included a trip to
the National Library, where he went to read and study after school. The
diary mentions the classmates Pessoa was friendly with and also a number of other, unnamed students who aroused in him nothing but disdain.
Convention, according to one of his recent poems, was the "Mother of
slaves and fools," and he had decided, with more than a little arrogance,
that most of his classmates were hopelessly conventional. The kindred
understanding he felt with Armando Teixeira Rebelo was not enough
of a balm to keep Pessoa from bristling in an environment hostile to his
own sensibility.

But there was more to Pessoa's disgruntlement than what he revealed in
his diary. He was still learning to cope, at age seventeen, with the "urban
sensuality" that in the opinion of his heteronymous psychiatrist, Dr.
Faustino Antunes, had profoundly troubled him the last time he was in
Lisbon, three years earlier. Now that sensuality confronted him directly,
aggressively. Each time he walked from the School of Arts and Letters to
the National Library, which was located in Chiado, he inevitably passed
through the Bairro Alto, an old and poor but lively neighborhood. Even
today it is full of bars and restaurants; back then it had the city's highest concentration of prostitutes. Since they were numerous and in competition, and Pessoa was a young single male, they tried to entice him
with salacious gestures, whistles, and comments, stepping up their efforts
when ignored, or else laughing at the lanky, embarrassed boy who walked
quickly past, holding on to his briefcase like a shield. Early in 1906 Pessoa
wrote a few vengeful lines in English for an unfinished poem:

### To a Prostitute

How good to think that
Thou shalt one day be rotten
And worms shall crawl within thy womb
In the darkness of the tomb.[8]

It was quite usual for men of the time to thoroughly despise prostitutes, even if they patronized them, but there is a shocking viciousness

in these four lines by Pessoa, who knew perfectly well that poverty and necessity were what drove women to make their living as sex workers. (Four years later, in fact, he would write another unfinished poem in which he sympathizes with the unhappy lot of the Bairro Alto prostitutes.)[9] The vitriol of imagining, with satisfaction, a prostitute's womb crawling with worms can be explained only by his extreme uneasiness in relation to the female anatomy. Because he was inexperienced and unsure of himself? Or because he felt an instinctive repulsion? Softening his tone and changing his perspective, he apparently tried to imagine himself yielding to the advances of a woman. Turning over the sheet of paper with the cited lines of verse, he wrote this isolated bit of prose: "Thou art not a woman to me: thou art a problem. I do not so much love the pleasure I find in thee, but the *analysis* of that pleasure." This suggests that he may have found at least a little pleasure in the idea of sex with a woman, but it seems to have been a purely hypothetical idea, disconnected from any real desire.

Unhappy with his course of study, ill at ease socially and sexually, dogged by an awareness that he wasn't quite "normal," the seventeen-year-old announced in his diary entry for March 28 that he intended to go to England. But there was an impediment to this vague plan: "No money; must get it." And were money not an issue, Pessoa would have found other reasons to postpone the voyage he avowedly longed to make. He hated being thrust into new situations, surrounded by unfamiliar people, and in England he knew virtually nobody. There was Geerdts, who had gone to study at Oxford, but this former classmate had been more of an academic rival than a friend. And Pessoa no doubt had in mind going to London.

Imagine my surprise when, rummaging through papers still in the possession of Pessoa's heirs, I came across a chatty letter dated "London, 26th February 1906," addressed to "My dear P.," and sent to Pessoa by a friend he had known in Durban. Perhaps (I thought) Pessoa counted on staying with him if he managed to get to London. The letter was not easy to decipher, but soon enough I was astonished to discover that Pessoa had a rather larger circle of friends in Durban than I had realized. The letter writer mentioned a certain Saville, another young man whose last name was Nevers, a fellow called Biff, who had lately moved to Pietermaritzburg, the capital of Natal, and a fellow known as Esbara, who was always running into things. Esbara evidently got his nickname from

Pessoa, since *esbarra* in Portuguese means "bumps into." I gathered that Pessoa, besides having a solid group of friends in Durban, was a waggish and assertive member of this group. This completely contradicted the portrait of him as an adolescent established by all my other research.

But I began to wonder about the identity of the letter writer when I came across the following, humorous observation concerning yet another friend in the group: "Stool is in America, in Washington—and it's a ton of washing it will need with Stool there." At last I managed to decipher the scrawled signature at the end of the missive, "G. Nabos," which confirmed my doubts—and heightened my astonishment. The letter that offered extraordinary new information about Pessoa's set of friends in Durban became even more extraordinary once I understood that the friends were pure fiction. Stool was the same Sidney Parkinson Stool whom we have seen playing imaginary cricket and whose name began to sign literary projects in 1903. Saville also played cricket, but for an opposing team. Gaudêncio Nabos was referred to as "Dr. Nabos" as early as 1904, and his wry letter from London, in which he mentions "doctoring a little" as well as playing tricks on people, corroborates his status as the medical heteronym fond of jokes and prankish behavior. Although I could find no further references to Esbara or Biff, there is an isolated signature of the friend named Nevers among Pessoa's Durban papers.[10]

If originality and freedom from convention were what mattered, Pessoa's classmates at the Lisbon School of Arts and Letters could not begin to compete with the likes of Gaudêncio Nabos and Sidney Parkinson Stool, whose unconventionality reached the supreme extent of their not even existing. The name of their compeer Nevers sums up how often any of them obeyed the rules and conventions of the real world. Although Stool made no further appearances in Pessoa's written universe, Dr. Gaudêncio Nabos would produce humorous poems and prose texts for years to come. And in 1907 he would sign yet another, much shorter letter to Fernando Pessoa, which begins: "I am in receipt of your letter of the 10th instant and am sorry to say I am ill, and therefore unable to carry out personally your instructions." After assuring the addressee that he will attend to his request as soon as possible, Nabos closes the brief missive with a "yours very truly."[11] Even Pessoa's imaginary friends maintained a respectful distance.

We can relinquish whatever doubts we had about the letters Pessoa claimed to write to himself in the name of the Chevalier de Pas, when he was just six years old. Far less believable is that he would write letters to himself in the name of Dr. "Turnips" (Nabos) as a young adult, but the evidence is incontrovertible: two such letters exist. The second one purportedly responds to a letter Nabos received from Pessoa. Besides wondering whether Pessoa actually or imaginarily wrote this and perhaps other letters to Nabos, we may at this point wonder whether he spent time thinking about his good-humored doctor friend in London. Did he worry about his health and wonder when they would meet again? Suddenly anything seems possible.

One possibility is that Pessoa, now eighteen and already thinking of his postmortem reputation, wrote the two Nabos letters for the benefit of his future biographers, to convince them that he really did, as claimed, foster a social circle of fictitious friends and acquaintances. He would make this claim only many years later, however. Another possibility is that he mischievously hoped to fool posterity into thinking that Gaudêncio Nabos and his other made-up writer friends really existed. But if that was the case, why did he carelessly leave behind evidence to the contrary?

Except when playing a joke on an unsuspecting friend or acquaintance, Pessoa did not usually hide the fact that his alter egos were just that—alternative selves that derived from and depended on him. If some of them supposedly played sports and addressed letters to their inventor, those activities were literary phenomena, no less than the poems or prose pieces signed with their names. What dumbfounds us, finally, is Pessoa's capacity to live so much of his mental and emotional life on an imagined, literary plane. He repeatedly made the point, in *The Book of Disquiet* and elsewhere, that certain characters from novels (Mr. Pickwick and his friend Mr. Wardle are two examples he cites) were more vividly real for him than many people made of flesh and blood.[12] The same was true of his heteronyms, with an important advantage: they could exist without the need for structured, plotted novels. Pessoa's life was the ongoing story they all inhabited. But perhaps it would be more accurate to say that Pessoa, often enough, daunted by the expectations of the world all around him, preferred to inhabit the story of his heteronyms.

✦

AT THE SAME TIME that he was making his life into literature, Pessoa tried to put his literature into the world. On February 21, 1906, five days before he wrote the G. Nabos letter that was supposedly sent from London, he wrote a real letter to the London editorial office of *Punch*, the hugely popular English magazine of humor and satire:

Sir,

I submit the poem enclosed to your appreciation. In it I have tried merely to attain the ridiculous by the union of the serious and of the grotesque. I have attempted, moreover, to link the ridiculousness of expression thus produced to a lofty, elegiac verse-movement. You will judge how far I have succeeded.

I am aware that my manuscript should have been typewritten, but my means do not allow it. I am further conscious that I have no literary experience (none can be expected from a boy of sixteen); and that, for this reason, in the writing of my manuscript I may have injured Convention rudely: all this I hope will be excused.

I have signed my manuscript with a pseudonym; but when a foreigner writes anything—especially a poem—it is better not to father it directly.

If my poem be refused, I am afraid you must put it in the waste-paper basket, inasmuch as English stamps are here unobtainable. In hope of success, however, I enclose what I can—an addressed envelope.

Awaiting your decision,
I am,
Sir,
Yours faithfully,
F. A. N. Pessoa

The poem alluded to in the letter was "Elegy on the Marriage of My Dear Friend Mr. Jinks," a satire that tauntingly describes the gloomy outlook for Jinks's new life as a married man by borrowing language from one of Lord Byron's most quoted poems, written when he was recovering from too much carousing at the Venice carnival. Here is that poem's first stanza:

So we'll go no more a roving
    So late into the night,
Though the heart be still as loving,
    And the moon be still as bright.

And now a passage from Pessoa's "Elegy":

Ah, wilt thou be content to rove
From shop to shop with her, thy mother-in-law,
Or tremble full to hear at night,
With horror deep and deep affright,
The wordy torrent from thy spouse's jaw?

The Mr. Jinks who has just tied the knot is presumably William K. Jinks, the crank doctor and heteronymous promoter of healthy living invented by Pessoa in South Africa. Perhaps the poem—written in April 1905, when its author was still in Durban—marks the point when Jinks stopped sowing wild oats and settled down to a life of sobriety, regular exercise, and conjugal tranquility, which was certain to end in tedium, according to the "Elegy." But if Pessoa abhorred the idea of getting married, much less could he imagine himself as a Portuguese version of Byron, who was as famous for his philandering as he was for his poetry.

According to Pessoa's letter to *Punch*, he signed his poem with a pseudonym to hide his foreign identity. That disingenuous affirmation was, of course, a way to *reveal* his foreignness to the magazine's editor. Pessoa clearly hoped that this personal detail, along with his tender age ("a boy of sixteen," although he was actually seventeen and a half) and proud disregard of Convention, would be selling points for his poem, which was nonetheless turned down, if indeed it and the cover letter were actually sent.[13]

The pseudonymous author of the poem was Charles Robert Anon, who signed most of Pessoa's poetry between 1904 and 1906, and also much of his prose. He was even the nominal author of Pessoa's private diary, whose pages were nearly all rubber-stamped in the upper-right-hand corner with the name "C. R. Anon." It is hard to understand why. Begun on March 15, 1906, and discontinued on June 3, the diary was exclusively concerned with the quotidian particulars of Pessoa's life: his classes at the School of Arts and Letters, his readings, his family commitments. . . . By making Mr. Anon serve as the faithful scribe or make-believe author of these and other activities, it's as if Pessoa, their protagonist, wanted to convert his life into a novel. If his intention, on the contrary, was to invest his alter ego with the biographical details recorded in his diary, if he wrote it in English and rubber-stamped its pages so as to say, in effect, "This isn't me, this is Charles Robert Anon," then the net result was the same. Either way, he was turning his life into a literary reality. In either scenario, Mr. Anon was no ordinary pseudonym, and Pessoa was no ordinary man.

✦

PESSOA'S CONTEMPT FOR CONVENTION and his fear of being ordinary might seem like self-defensive attitudes, given that he felt socially awkward, but there is little evidence of his particularly wanting to fit in socially. He was committed, rather, to doing things his own way, usually as a lone operator. The burgeoning republican movement in Portugal enjoyed wide support among college students, including Pessoa, who could have asserted his solidarity with politically like-minded classmates, but even when in agreement he preferred to act alone, to fight battles single-handedly.

Pessoa's mother and stepfather were born and bred royalists, and Fernando himself, when he returned to Lisbon in September 1905, was at least a passive supporter of the monarchy. Not long after landing, he sent his sister a quartet of postcards depicting members of the royal family.[14] But within a few months, swayed by newspaper accounts of monarchical corruption and no doubt by the arguments of certain classmates, he embraced republicanism. Events in the spring of 1906 only confirmed for him that the monarchy was rotten at its core. A series of scandals had forced José Luciano de Castro, head of the Progressive Party that Pessoa's Uncle Cunha had so ardently supported, to resign as prime minister on March 19, whereupon the reins of government shifted automatically to the Regenerator Party, which was equally incapable of conciliating factions and efficiently running the country. The decades-old political system, alternately dominated by two parties whose ideology was essentially the same, had lost all credibility. Even certain Progressives and Regenerators were beginning to admit that the system had to be overhauled if not scrapped, while more and more people outside the system felt that the monarchy itself should be scuttled.

The republicans' program—cleaning up government, secularizing society, and promoting civil and political rights—had decisively won Pessoa over to their cause. Instead of attending meetings and working directly with other republicans to attract new converts, however, he hoped to stir people up through the power of his written words. In early

1906, although English was still his main literary language, he began writing antigovernment poems in Portuguese for a collection to be called *Revolta* (*Revolt*), and in April he drew up plans for a pamphlet titled *Pela República* (*For the Republic*), a "revolutionary treatise" that was "to be couched in simple language" and distributed free of charge.[15] Pessoa clearly dreamed of reaching the masses but wrote only a small number of protest poems and failed to follow through on the pamphlet. Later in the year and early in 1907, he came up with titles for other political essays he was planning to write, including "On the Necessity and the Method of Revolution."[16]

Few of the students at the School of Arts and Letters could have imagined that the bright but innocuous-looking boy who had lived in South Africa and spoke unaccented English was a radical Portuguese revolutionary.

# CHAPTER 15

F AR MORE IMPORTANT FOR PESSOA'S INTELLECTUAL development than his classes at the School of Arts and Letters was the increasingly important role in his life played by General Henrique Rosa, his stepfather's older brother. The eyes of both brothers were blue, but Henrique's shone with a fierce and restless glow. For Pessoa this general, born in 1850, the same year as his father, was a kind of beacon, an enlightened autodidact whose unorthodox ideas and lifestyle assured him that he, too, could dare to think and act differently from others.

A couple of Pessoa's teachers in Durban had served as academic mentors, encouraging the studious adolescent in his readings of Latin and English literature, but Henrique Rosa, an amateur scholar with a wideranging curiosity, incited his stepnephew to explore realms such as political theory, philosophy, psychology, and sociology. What the general lacked in intellectual depth was more than compensated by his infectious enthusiasm for the subjects of his research. Pessoa, who would turn eighteen in June 1906, was hungry for new and stimulating ideas. He lusted after knowledge—not the settled knowledge found in encyclopedias but the speculative knowledge derived from scientific or philosophical inquiry as well as from poetic reflection. The fact that Henrique Rosa was a serious poet, who embedded many of the ideas he espoused in lines of verse, made Pessoa all the more susceptible to his influence. His own poetry from this period was also built around ideas.

We noted a vague literary link between the two men in 1902, when four of Pessoa's riddles and dozens of Henrique Rosa's poems were published in the same humoristic newspaper, and they had no doubt seen each other once or twice since Fernando's return to Lisbon in the fall of 1905. But the real beginning of their intellectual intimacy dates from a meeting that took place on May 16, 1906. Pessoa came away from Rosa's apartment with a couple of borrowed books, including one that was a frontal assault on conventional morality and religion, and a very positive impression of the man whose conversation had enthralled him for several hours. That evening in his diary he made this assessment: "An enormous and wonderful mind; a philosophic pessimist of a very high order. His scientific knowledge is enormous."[1]

Forcibly retired from the army in 1903, when he was only fifty-two, Henrique Rosa could devote himself full-time to reading and writing. Even before retirement, he had for many years been on more or less permanent sick leave because of severe depression coupled with a mysterious, intermittent nervous disorder that caused partial paralysis of his limbs. During his good periods he was sociable and loved nothing better than to debate issues and talk literature in cafés, but for months at a time he remained practically confined to his bedroom, being waited on by Augusta, a woman of humble birth who lived with him as his common-law wife.[2]

Rosa published his poetry to small acclaim in newspapers and magazines, but Pessoa held it in rather high regard, partly because he sympathized with its "philosophic pessimism." He was more directly influenced by Rosa's ideas and opinions, beginning with his fervent defense of republicanism. Like virtually all republicans, Henrique Rosa was also an anticlericalist, opposed to the powerful role of the Catholic Church in Portugal's political and social life. A de facto branch of the Portuguese state bureaucracy, it was the Church, not the government, that recorded all births, weddings, and deaths, and the Church ran the majority of Portugal's schools. Its relationship to the monarchy was symbiotic and its influence in Portuguese society pervasive, especially in rural areas, where close to two-thirds of the people lived. But Rosa, besides objecting to the Church's presence and influence in matters of the state, also rejected Roman Catholic theology.

Such thorough and vehement opposition to the Church, delineated eloquently by his stepuncle, naturally stoked Pessoa's own anti-Catholic sentiments. It was ten days after the two men had their first real exchange of ideas that he began drafting the letter, mentioned earlier, to the prior of Our Lady of the Martyrs (see chapter 1), protesting his baptism there when he was but six weeks old, since it made him an involuntary member of a religion he had come to consider "stupid" and "irrational." And since the Church might not take the trouble to excommunicate him, he decided, in the name of Charles Robert Anon, to excommunicate the Church, or rather, all churches. Around the time of his eighteenth birthday, he used black ink and emphatic pen strokes to inscribe an "Excommunication" in a notebook:

I, Charles Robert Anon, *being*, animal, mammal, tetrapod, primate, placental, ape, catarrhina, man; eighteen years of age, not married (except at odd moments), megalomaniac, with touches of dipsomania, dégénéré supérieur, poet, with pretensions to written humour, citizen of the world, idealistic philosopher, etc. etc. (to spare the reader further pains),

In the name of TRUTH, SCIENCE and PHILOSOPHIA, not with bell, book and candle, but with pen, ink and paper,

Pass sentence of excommunication on all priests and all sectarians of all religions in the world.

Excommunicabo vos.

Be damned to you all.

Ainsi-soit-il.

Reason, Truth, Virtue per C. R. A.

*Ainsi-soit-il* is French for "So be it," or "Amen." Notice how Anon first of all declares himself to be a product of biological evolution. This is followed by a self-description that can also apply to Pessoa himself, who was eighteen years old, single, and already displayed signs of megalomania. Though he was not yet much of a drinker, let alone a dipsomaniac, he seems to have foreseen that alcohol would become his favorite vice.

Elsewhere, among his unpublished notes, Pessoa wrote that God struck him "only as the idea a simple and immature mind makes for itself of the Absolute." People must believe in something, he admitted, but he thought it "better to believe that science *will* than that God *has*."[3] Although he rejected the idea of a God with definable characteristics, particularly anthropomorphic ones, Pessoa was not an atheist, for the same reason that he never signed on the dotted line of any profession of faith in entities lying beyond the ken of human understanding. On the other hand, he placed considerable faith in science during his first several years back in Lisbon. He even began to write an "Ode to Science" in

February or March 1906.[4] Henrique Rosa vigorously fostered the young man's interest in science, especially in evolution, lending him books on the subject.

◆

EVOLUTIONARY THEORY APPEALED TO European intellectuals not only for its exciting new perspective on the world's biological panorama and the origins of humanity but also for its applications to psychology, sociology, and human governance. Pessoa shared in the general enthusiasm for a model that could explain so much without having to resort to God, but he was not too concerned about the model's precise details. Since he made not a single mark in his copy of *On the Origin of Species by Means of Natural Selection*, published by Charles Darwin in 1859, we can be reasonably sure he only skimmed it,[5] and he seems to have ignored the debate that carried on—in Portugal as elsewhere—over whether natural selection was indeed the chief mechanism governing the evolution of plant and animal life.[6] He was in any case far more interested in social, cultural, political, and psychological evolution, for which the Darwinian model was not the most useful. In fact the French naturalist Jean-Baptiste Lamarck (1744–1829), with his notions of environmental adaptation, a complexifying impulse in nature, and the inheritability of acquired characteristics, was bedrock for the sociocultural evolutionists, two of whom made a particularly strong impression on Pessoa: Ernst Haeckel and Herbert Spencer.

In late May 1906 Pessoa began reading Haeckel's most famous work, *Die Welträtsel* (1899), in its English translation, *The Riddle of the Universe*. Initially a physician, Haeckel (1834–1919) made a radical career change after reading Darwin's *Origin of Species*. He took up zoology and became one of Europe's most zealous defenders and propagators of evolution. But his ideas on this subject were more Lamarckian than Darwinian, and while he did important fieldwork (identifying and naming hundreds of new species, for instance), some of his science was sloppy and based on wishful speculation. He believed that the human races had evolved independently, with the white European race being superior and destined to prevail. The faith he placed in eugenics was encapsulated in the Nazi slogan that "politics is applied biology," which was used to justify their program of racial purification.[7]

Pessoa was not interested in Haeckel's racial theories, much less eugenics, but in his tidy explanation of life and the cosmos, as formulated in *The Riddle of the Universe*. The German scientist and thinker propounded a monistic worldview à la Spinoza, not allowing for a spiritual reality discrete from the natural world. In his rigorously deterministic system, there was no room for immortality, free will, or God, unless God meant something like "force of nature" or was pantheistically understood as the universe itself.

Pessoa's edition of *Riddle*, which has not survived, was undoubtedly the cheap reprint published by the Rationalist Press Association in 1903. Over the years he would acquire over forty titles issued by the secularist group's publishing arm, Watts & Co. These included his edition of Darwin's *Origin of Species* and once popular titles such as John M. Robertson's *Christianity and Mythology* and Samuel Laing's *Modern Science and Modern Thought*. He began reading this last work, which discussed everything from time and matter to evolution and agnosticism, on June 1, 1906, one week after launching into Haeckel's book.

Toward the end of June Pessoa began reading yet another Rationalist Press reprint, *An Introduction to the Philosophy of Herbert Spencer*, by William Henry Hudson; and in the coming years he would read no less than three books by Spencer (1820–1903) himself, as well as a biography of the philosopher, who was in some respects a British counterpart to Haeckel. Spencer's *System of Synthetic Philosophy*, which took up ten volumes published over the course of three decades, subsumed all natural laws under a single, master law of irresistible, evolutionary progress whereby the universe, from an initially amorphous mass, was flowering into an ever more intricate ensemble of individuated but harmoniously interconnected parts.

Enormously popular in their lifetimes, Haeckel and Spencer fell precipitously into posthumous disrepute, since their science was considered half baked and their approach to philosophy amateurish. They had attempted to conjoin the two fields—to produce philosophies that, in addition to being logical, coherent systems of thought, would also be attentive to and congruent with scientific truth. Neither thinker had really wrestled with basic epistemological issues, let alone tried to tackle the age-old question (that eternally nagged Pessoa) of why anything at all exists. Pessoa gave more credence to the ideas of Spencer, who admitted an independent "First Cause" impervious to human understanding and persisting as the driving force in the cosmos, and in 1913 he considered translating the Englishman's *First Principles* (1862) into Portuguese.[8] But his enthusiasm for Haeckel, who posited an ultimate substance that could account for spiritual as well as physical phenomena, quickly faded. Science, he would write in 1909, could have nothing to say about metaphysics, and Haeckel was an "idiot" for supposing he could prove that the soul was mortal.[9]

◆

SCIENCE-ILLUMINATED AVENUES OF RATIONAL inquiry were not the only paths explored by Pessoa while a student at the School of Arts and Letters. During his first semester, before discovering the evolutionists, he whiled away his spare time in the somber lanes and byways of Edgar Allan Poe and the French writers known even to themselves as "decadents." Poe's fiction inspired him to write "The Door" and "The Stolen Document," two stories begun in March and April 1906, in English. The latter story, according to his diary, was conceived as a "correction" of "The Purloined Letter," while the former is a tale of obsession in the style of "The Black Cat." Neither was ever finished.

Pessoa was also a close reader of Poe's poetry, whose aura of mystery, driving rhythms, and fondness for repeated sounds can be felt in some of his own poems written between late 1905 and 1908. He was no less influenced by the poetry of Charles Baudelaire (1821–1867), whose *Les Fleurs du mal* (*The Flowers of Evil*), with its scenes of urban alienation, sex, death, and corruption couched in exquisitely sculpted lines of verse, scandalized the bourgeoisie and marked several generations of writers and artists. Fittingly enough, Pessoa would later produce—and publish, in 1924—a superb rendering into Portuguese of "The Raven," just as Baudelaire, a great admirer of Poe, had done in French. One of his much younger half brothers would recall that Pessoa, as a teenager in Durban, used to make him and his other siblings giggle with fright by reciting lines such as "Quoth the raven *Nevermore!*" in a deep and cavernous voice.[10]

Though he was living again on his native soil and immersed every day in the sounds and cadences of Portuguese, Pessoa continued to write virtually all his poetry in English, the language he deemed most conducive to literary immortality. Posthumous fame would be very hard to achieve, and if he achieved it he would not even be around to enjoy it, but it was at least a definite, conceivable goal. Far more slippery and uncertain, if he thought about it, and he thought about it constantly,

was the idea of his present self. "My soul—what is my soul?" begins a
poem he wrote in February 1906. Resonating with echoes of both Poe
and Baudelaire, it tries to apprehend the human soul through a series of
symbols, such as this one:

It is an olden inn with corridors
Woven in a labyrinth and scarce of light,
Where through the night the sound of shutting doors,
Vague in its cause and place, fills us with fright.

The notion that a single life is an endlessly unfolding world shrouded
in mystery at times unsettling and even frightening was not new to Pessoa, but he learned to give it poetic shape thanks to Poe, Baudelaire,
and several other decadents: Maurice Rollinat (1846–1903), for instance,
who was appreciated mainly as a poet, and Joris-Karl Huysmans (1848–
1907), whose novel *À rebours* (1884), translated into English as *Against
the Grain*, or *Against Nature*, became something of a handbook for
apprentice decadents. Pessoa read many other French poets during his
first years back in Lisbon, including Stéphane Mallarmé, Paul Verlaine,
and Arthur Rimbaud, who are usually classified as symbolists but also,
occasionally, as decadents (especially Verlaine).

Decadents cultivated artifice and ultrarefinement in the arts, extravagant language, tortured forms of beauty, and heightened sensations,
remaining perversely indifferent to moral and civilizational decline.
Symbolism retained the aesthetics of decadence, its disillusionment with
society and its indifference to the given world, but aspired to evoke a
supernal world, a transcendent reality. The decadents dedicated themselves to art and voluptuosity for their own sake, not believing in any
truth beyond what they could see or create. The symbolists were equally
voluptuous but spiritually inclined. Despite the differences between the
two artistic camps, the boundary line between them can be hazy, since
all of the campers were at least distantly related, descending directly or
indirectly from Baudelaire. Morbid and melancholy, his *Les Fleurs du
mal* precociously announced the spirit of decadence but also the doctrine of *correspondances*, whereby we who walk the world are said to pass
through "forests of symbols" that give us "knowing looks." This doctrine
provided a theoretical underpinning for the symbolist movement in literature and other arts.

Symbolism would be responsible for some of the first and finest poems and prose pieces published by the adult Pessoa in Portuguese, between 1913 and 1916. His attraction to the movement, like his affinity for Shelley, was connected to his religious sensibility. Baudelaire's *correspondances* derived from Swedenborg (1688–1772), who held that the natural world is a complex system of symbols corresponding to spiritual realities that cannot be directly apprehended. The symbolist aesthetic—with its taste for the ethereal and the suggestive—largely faded from Pessoa's work after 1916 but the concept of multiple levels or dimensions of reality would permeate his thinking throughout the rest of his life.

✦

PESSOA'S INTEREST IN THE rationalist depictions of the universe proposed by Haeckel and Spencer acted as a counterweight to his enthusiasm for the shadowy world of mystery and symbols he found in Poe, Baudelaire, and the succeeding generation of French decadents and symbolists. Given that Haeckel was a scientist and Poe a fiction writer, this may seem like a fatuous correlation, but Pessoa used literature as well as science-based systems of thought as investigative tools in his search for truth. Traditional philosophy was yet a third route of intellectual inquiry followed by the poet and scholar after returning to Portugal. In the spring of 1906, he drew up a list of "Books for Study" that included several aforementioned titles as well as the names of four German and two English philosophers: Immanuel Kant, Arthur Schopenhauer, Johann Gottlieb Fichte, Georg W. F. Hegel, John Locke, and Thomas Hobbes. They were components of his self-directed crash course in Western philosophy. Pessoa had already spent many winter afternoons at the National Library plowing through two general histories of European philosophy—one in English, the other in French—as well as Aristotle's works on logic. Toward the end of that April he undertook Kant's *Critique of Pure Reason*, in a French translation, and in the summer he read a French rendering of Schopenhauer's *On the Freedom of the Will*, along with a book on Plato's philosophy.[11]

Given his infatuation with philosophy, Pessoa decided it would be useful to learn German. In a small notebook dedicated to this purpose, he copied down some rules of pronunciation, probably from a textbook he found at the National Library. That was in late April, and by mid-May he had succeeded in reading, with considerable toil, a small poem of Schiller's in the original. There his efforts to master yet another language ended. He would read Schiller, Goethe, Heine, and other German authors, along with German philosophers, either in English or French.

Pessoa's forays into French literature were not limited to Baudelaire and his heirs. For his French class he studied Molière and various eighteenth-century authors, including Voltaire. On his own initiative he began reading François-René de Chateaubriand, founder of French Romanticism, and his Swiss precursor, the philosopher Jean-Jacques Rousseau. Both writers are repeatedly referred to in *The Book of Disquiet*, whose style owes something to their uninhibited penchant for indulging in autobiography and the meticulous analysis of personal feelings. Pessoa's other readings during his first year back in Lisbon included Portuguese poetry, two Spanish poets still popular at the turn of the century—José de Espronceda (1808–1842) and Ramón de Campoamor (1817–1901)—and the English Romantic poets, whose verse had already enchanted him in Durban. For lighter reading, he enjoyed the science fiction of the recently deceased Jules Verne (1828–1905).[12]

Pessoa was not an aficionado of Russian literature, but in the summer of 1906 he picked up a French translation of *The Kreutzer Sonata*, possibly the only work of fiction by Tolstoy that he would ever read. Banned upon its publication, in 1889, the novella was catapulted to international fame, becoming the author's most widely read work. The story is told in the first person by an aristocrat named Pozdnyshev, who describes his unhappy and ultimately tragic relationship with his wife, questions the institution of marriage, and extols the virtues of sexual abstinence. Shortly after reading Tolstoy's novella, in which Pozdnyshev confesses to having killed his wife, Pessoa wrote a sketch for a more grisly tale, "Jack Wilde's Marriage," in English.[13] Jack Wilde, who has "a propensity to mad acts" and whose last name was surely inspired by the Irish writer who died in disgrace in 1900, announces to a friend that he is getting married on Friday the thirteenth of July, 1906. On that inauspicious date the marriage duly takes place, but it ends in a scene of horror, with thirteen wedding guests being hanged according to an elaborate plan executed by the unhappy groom, who also hangs himself.

That same year, Pessoa began writing a pamphlet attacking the institution of marriage, ostensibly as part of his campaign against convention—in this case a convention that in monarchical Portugal was nearly always performed under the auspices of the Catholic Church. "To be married ecclesiastically," asserted Pessoa in English, "is a stupidity." But it was not only the institutional and religious trappings of marriage that bothered him. In an isolated note from around this same time he asked, again in English: "What is, for the man, all married life? A stepping from the brothel to the nuptial bed and thence back to the brothel—not literally but metaphorically, yet truly by making a brothel of that marriage bed."[14]

Before he ever aspired to chastity, Tolstoy had fathered thirteen children with his wife, Sophia. For eighteen-year-old Pessoa, the very idea of sex in marriage, no less than sex with a prostitute, seems to have been a terrifying prospect.

# CHAPTER 16

**P**ESSOA'S HESITANT MARCH TOWARD AUTONOMY and manhood—a transition he was doing his best to embrace—was temporarily disrupted by the arrival of his family from Durban on July 1, 1906.[1] Once more he would be his mother's little boy, and now more than ever in need of her care. She was surprised, in fact, to find her son in bed, convalescing from an illness that had forced him to abandon his classes in June. Fever permitting, he read.

Pessoa often got sick, and it took him longer than other people to recover from whatever flu or cold happened to be going around. In *The Book of Disquiet* he would comment on "the vague bliss of a profoundly felt convalescence,"[2] and one suspects that he rather enjoyed being laid up in bed, obliged to do nothing at all. He never stopped thinking, however, and during his present illness, exalted by fever, one of the objects of his excited ruminations was Alexander Search, a name that had popped into his mind several months earlier. Not just another name, Search would emerge from this period of gestation as Pessoa's most substantial and prolific heteronym to date.

Entitled again to a long holiday in the home country, Consul João Miguel Rosa had come with his wife and their children to spend ten months in Lisbon. It was almost the height of summer, when some days would be sultry, but Lisbon nights almost always cool down to a pleasant temperature. They rented an apartment on Calçada da Estrela, close to the Estrela Basilica, whose cold, white neoclassical façade conceals a baroque interior covered by richly colored marbles. The address was conveniently situated on a streetcar line that descended a short steep hill to the vicinity of the parliament building and Aunt Anica's apartment, before continuing up a long incline to the Praça de Camões, where in the middle of the square a bronze statue of the national bard, erected in 1867, casts its prescient gaze toward the neighborhood of Chiado, where Pessoa was born.

The holiday apartment was also a scant two-minute walk from the Jardim da Estrela, or Estrela Garden. Though Portugal was one of Europe's poorest countries and going through politically agitated times, the Baedekers and other guidebooks from the period all agreed that Lisbon, notwithstanding its past reputation for filth and disorder, was now one of the continent's cleanest capitals and boasted some of its most luxuriant gardens. Laid out over more than ten acres, the Estrela Garden—with its cedars, palms, dragon trees, and ginkgoes, its exotic flowers, its small ponds with ducks, and a knoll that affords a good view of the Tagus—was a perfect playground for Fernando's siblings and a calm place of retreat for him and his parents. On Sunday afternoons a few couples and families, keeping up a nineteenth-century tradition, still promenaded through the park in fashionable attire to be seen and to see others. Pessoa's imagination took him even further back in time. In *The Book of Disquiet*, whose meditative prose is dotted with occasional parks and gardens, mythic and melancholy, he would write: "Estrela Garden, in late afternoon, suggests to me a park from olden times, in the centuries before the soul became disenchanted."[3]

It was probably in that same summer that Aunt Rita and Aunt Maria, now in their late seventies, moved with Grandma Dionísia, who had just turned eighty-three, to an apartment located half a block away from the Calçada da Estrela. Since Aunt Anica lived just down the hill, it was easy for them all to visit one another. Although he moved in with his own family, Fernando, an eighteen-year-old as of June 13, wanted his independence to be respected, and he was somewhat secretly aspiring to become financially independent. He had developed a close rapport with his cousin Mário, three years younger and not an intellectual but endowed with an entrepreneurial spirit (inherited from his father, along with some assets) that Pessoa admired and emulated. The two boys were already sending letters to foreign business firms, concocting schemes for making money, even though Mário was still a minor. The front cover of one of Pessoa's notebooks reads (in Portuguese) "1906 / Translations / M. N. de Freitas." Pessoa ended up filling the notebook with his own writings, but the initial idea had been to use it for making copies of letters translated by him into English or French, signed by his cousin, Mário Nogueira de Freitas, and posted to France, Britain, or America. One such letter—written by Fernando in French but signed by Mário—requested information from a wholesaler of typewriters and duplicators located in Paris.[4] That was in 1907, and two or three years later Mário, among his other early business ventures, would act as a Portuguese representative for the "American" brand typewriter.[5]

It was undoubtedly Fernando who, dreaming of getting published and also of becoming a publisher, encouraged Mário to try importing things like typewriters. He himself had signed and sent a letter of inquiry to Ellams Duplicator Co., a London-based manufacturer, on December 23, 1905[6]—apparently with an eye toward publishing, desktop style, some of his literary works. Around that same time, he created a neatly drawn masthead for *The Tattler*, listing "F. Pessoa" and "M. N. de Freitas" as the owners, with editorial offices located at the Rua de São Bento, 98, Aunt Anica's address. Pessoa entertained a vague hope that the homemade newspaper he had founded in 1902 could go commercial, and he drafted an editorial note explaining that the new *Tattler*, a bimonthly aiming at a wider audience, would contain "articles of general interest" as well as poetry. But the boys decided not to acquire a duplicator just yet, and *The Tattler* was definitively relegated to silence.[7]

Exams were held in July and Fernando, because of his illness, missed them all. He had grown too sick even to read in bed, according to the reading diary he began keeping in June. Nothing is recorded for the next month except "Illness and convalescence." In August, although still not entirely recovered, he resumed his independent study program: philosophy, science, a passage from Virgil's *Aeneid*, poetry by Shelley, and seven plays by Shakespeare. And he was writing: fiction, poetry, and the satirical "Essay on Poetry," which he had begun in Durban.[8]

By September Fernando's health was fully restored, and since classes for the next term would not begin until October, all the hours of each day were his to fill. He spent many of them at the National Library, concentrating on his readings in philosophy, sociology, and literature, but also allotted time to his family. And he astutely managed to combine work and play, integrating some of his research and creative interests into recreational activities with his siblings. With their willing cooperation he got practical training in phrenology, measuring their heads in as many as sixteen different ways: circumference, occipito-frontal arch, lower frontal arch, posterior temporal diameter, and so forth. Fernando carefully recorded, and presumably analyzed, cranial measurements for his sister Teca, his two brothers, and his cousin Mário. The head of his sister Maria Clara, who had turned two in mid-August, was spared the ordeal.[9]

João, the younger brother, who was three going on four, would report many years later that his earliest memories of the future poet famous for creating heteronyms were from the months they lived together on the Calçada da Estrela, and what most vividly stuck in the little boy's mind was not anything they did together by day but what he heard in the evening, after dinner, when Fernando would hold him and the others spellbound with the stories he told. It was actually one ongoing story, made of up numerous, almost daily episodes in which protagonists with names such as Mr. Turnip and Mr. Carrot found themselves in improbable situations. But these were described in such graphic detail, and the characters themselves defined with such vivid clarity, that the young listener almost wondered whether they might be real. Since Pessoa usually spoke with his brothers in English, it was probably in that language that he regaled them and his sister Teca with the adventures of Mr. Turnip and Mr. Carrot. What João, Luís, and Teca did not know is that he had already written about these characters in Durban, but with their names pluralized and translated into Portuguese: Dr. Nabos and Dr. Cenouras.

✦

ON OCTOBER 3, 1906, the academic committee of the School of Arts and Letters met in a special session to consider Fernando Pessoa's request to take the first-year exams three months late, in view of his illness. His request was denied, since it should have been submitted much earlier, along with a medical certificate. And so Pessoa, on October 10, re-enrolled as a first-year student, adding philosophy to his course load. He had tentatively signed up for Ancient Greek as well but decided, in the end, that it would be too much.[10] He dabbled, however, in this language on his own, to judge by the markings in his copy of *Prometheus Bound* (in Greek), which he acquired in December and signed, on a flyleaf, as Alexander Search, Pessoa's newest heteronym, whose first name seems to have been inspired by the greatest military commander of ancient Greece, would take over and enlarge the role played up until then by C. R. Anon. While the substitution and obliteration of one heteronym by another does not seem to have been Pessoa's original intention, he was often a pawn of his own games, or a bemused bystander.

Signatures of Alexander Search began to encroach on Anon's literary territory in the first half of 1906. Several of them appear on the backs of pages from the diary entrusted to Mr. Anon, and they show up in notebooks where texts or signatures of Anon can also be found.[11] By autumn Alexander Search had his own notebook, clearly signed, dated "September, 1906," and dedicated to "Philosophy, etc.," according to the front flyleaf. The "etc." included religion, science, political theory, sociology, and psychology, but this was not a notebook of Search's own reflections; it was an extensive bibliography, organized alphabetically by author. Pessoa was reading or had already read some of the listed books (such as Aristotle's *Organon*, Haeckel's *Riddle of the Universe*, Kant's *Critique of Pure Reason*), others he would read in the coming months, and there were hundreds more on the seemingly interminable list that he would never read.[12]

Such a monumental reading program, half a thousand books in all, suggests that Search was predestined to be the most intellectually curious heteronym, even if Pessoa had initially been grooming Charles Robert Anon for this role. In fact Anon had a notebook of his own with a somewhat smaller list of books to read, including a number of titles that would reappear on Search's list.[13] Search, however, was the only heteronym to have his own library, consisting of over twenty very real books, all bearing his signature and/or his monogram, "AS," imprinted in rococo majuscules. The books range across many topics—positivism, mental health, religion, the occult, politics, sociology, and especially poetry, mostly in English but also in French and Portuguese—perfectly mirroring Pessoa's own reading interests at the time. Search, in other words, seems to represent *all* of his inventor's intellectual self rather than a particular facet of it. Pessoa did not pretend otherwise. He wrote in his notes that this heteronym was born in Lisbon on June 13, 1888, the same place and date of his own birth. So was Alexander Search a mere pseudonym—in all respects exactly like Fernando Pessoa but with a different name? In a previous chapter I posed this same question with respect to Charles Robert Anon. Now, as then, the answer is no, but for different reasons.

We can think of Search as a Platonic or transcendent version of Pessoa—his mental and spiritual essence, without the flesh. The practical result of distilling his intellectual self in Alexander Search was to intensify that same self, thereby enabling him to nurture and shape it more effectively. Literally self-removed, Pessoa was free to handle himself like a work of art, or like the subject of a scientific experiment. Charles Robert Anon was a persona, a mask behind which his creator expressed lit-

erary attitudes and emitted opinions that were, for the most part, his
own. Alexander Search was not a conduit of opinions but a projection
of Pessoa himself. He had the same anticlerical views and iconoclastic
spirit as Anon, but this predecessor sometimes comes across as a poseur.
Search, in his professed love of country and desire to serve humanity,
is sincere to the point of naïveté. In October 1907 he solemnly vows,
in writing: "Never to fall off or shrink from the purpose of doing good
to mankind."[14] A year later, a prose text signed by the same heteronym
speaks of "my intense patriotic suffering, my intense desire of bettering
the condition of Portugal."

It was inevitable that Anon give way to someone like Search after
Pessoa moved back to his home country, where his political preoccupations changed and his interest in philosophy and sociology blossomed.
Anon was an Englishman whose political mission had been to open
the eyes of Anglo-Durbanites to the injustices of British imperialism.
Search, although English speaking, was Portuguese by affinity if not
by blood, and he would soon take a stand as a militant republican committed to bringing down the monarchy, which was an irreparably decadent institution, according to more than one historical essay written
in his name. Pessoa, through Search, wished to shake the Portuguese
out of their complacency and incite them to question all received wisdom. And Search, in contrast to the more earthbound C. R. Anon,
wanted to reach higher, into realms of knowledge that rational thought
cannot attain.

✦

ALTHOUGH SEARCH WAS TECHNICALLY trilingual, with a couple of
Portuguese and French poems to his credit, virtually all of his abundant
output in prose and poetry was in English. One of his first complete
poems was a sonnet, "Blind Eagle," dating from November 1906 and
ending with these four lines:

What is the thing thou seekest within things?
    What is that thought thy thinking cannot find?
For what high air has thy strong spirit wings?
To what high vision aches it to be blind?

Originally titled "The Poet," the sonnet embodies the inquisitive urgency of this intellectual and psychological projection of Pessoa, Alexander Search. In addition, Search can be thought of as an Anglo-Portuguese disciple of Percy Bysshe Shelley (1792–1822), who sought the spiritual dimension in things while simultaneously writing apologies for atheism. A political radical as well as a freethinker, Shelley wanted to reform English government and the world generally, and he believed that poetry could be a contributing force to the great changes he championed. More than any other writer, he was the immediate model for Pessoa at this stage in his career.

Shelley was not widely appreciated in his lifetime, and while he now holds rank with Wordsworth, Coleridge, Byron, and Keats, he is sometimes regarded as a Romantic for dreamy and idealistic young people, before they move on to more thoughtful, careful poets such as Keats or Wordsworth. T. S. Eliot considered "an enthusiasm for Shelley" to be an "affair of adolescence."[15] But Pessoa, though exposed to Shelley early on, in Durban, became a great enthusiast of his poetry only after returning to Lisbon. And he read not one but two Shelley biographies, eager to learn about his life as well as his poetry.

It was the tireless searcher in Shelley—a die-hard skeptic who nevertheless had unshakable faith in poetry—that enchanted Pessoa, who strongly identified with his first major poem, *Alastor; or, The Spirit of Solitude*. Its more than seven hundred lines tell of a young Poet, "led forth by an imagination inflamed," who wanders the world without finding satisfaction in the contemplation of nature or in the affections of a simple "Arab maiden" he meets during his journey. Pursuing an idealized beauty and ideal love, the solitary Poet is compared to an eagle hurtling forward in "blind flight / O'er the wide aëry wilderness." His peregrination becomes a conscious, almost willful journey toward death, where he hopes to be joined to his "Vision and Love."

Shelley's preface to *Alastor*, though sympathetic toward the Poet, also reproaches him for his "self-centered seclusion." The poet-protagonist of Pessoa-Search's "Blind Eagle" likewise has mainly himself to blame for his solitary condition, since he snubs the world around him in favor of his "high vision." The nameless poet addressed in the sonnet seems to be Alexander Search, but Search is also the questioning narrator, and in both these roles he stands for Pessoa.

In Pessoa-Search, no less than in Shelley, an attraction to rapturous poetic exaltation and higher truth was counterbalanced by a determination to use writing for the betterment of human society and government. Shelley castigated Wordsworth for having abandoned his passionate interest—prominently displayed in his earliest poems—in political reform and the plight of the poor. The older poet had come to accept that poetry would not change anything but was its own reward.

Had he not drowned in a storm off the coast of Italy one month before his thirtieth birthday, it's possible that Shelley, too, would have eventually backed down from his strident humanitarianism and belief in poetry's power to make things happen. Although the youthful Pessoa already had his doubts about the ability of poetry to do any practical good, he was certainly enamored of the idea that a writer could be an agent for change, and he shared Shelley's human brand of spirituality. By investing Alexander Search with all his Shelleyan idealism, Pessoa may have been concentrating his energies for more effective action. He may, at the same time, have vaguely suspected that this was all a game, a literary enactment of youth's implausible aspiration to improve society. But even if attempts to change human nature were folly, humans could at least become more educated, civilized, and considerate, and one of Pessoa's lifelong ambitions was to exert a civilizing influence on Portugal and the larger world.

✦

ALEXANDER SEARCH'S FIRST NAME means "the people's defender," so it was only natural that he sign Pessoa's copy of *Prometheus Bound*, about the Titan hero who brought fire and civilization to humankind, in defiance of Zeus. Prometheus further incensed the chief god by refusing to disclose a dire prophecy about his future. Pessoa planned to render this Greek tragedy into Portuguese (necessarily with the help of a French or English version of the play), but among his papers I found only a handful of translated lines.[16] Of far greater interest to the poet was his own handling of the ancient myth.

Pessoa's interest in *Prometheus Bound*, traditionally attributed to Aeschylus, was sparked by Shelley's *Prometheus Unbound*, which he read in the summer of 1906.* According to this sequel, the tyrant Zeus—

---

* There was also a *Prometheus Unbound* from antiquity, of which only a few fragments survive.

or Jupiter—is overthrown by a collective moral effort, whereupon Prometheus is released from his cruel punishment. It is a play about the triumph of human will, both individual and collective, over oppression and obscure forces of destiny.

Enter Fernando Pessoa, the spoiler. The poet and scholar shared in the "passion for reforming the world" affirmed by Shelley in his preface to *Prometheus Unbound*, but passion to reform is one thing, belief that it can be accomplished is another, and Pessoa was far less optimistic about what the world could become. He believed that Portugal, if it adopted a republican form of government, might overcome its stagnation, but the idea that oppression, war, and social classes could be eliminated struck him as sheer fantasy. Shelley's play ends in blissful anarchy, with people spontaneously getting along in a world ruled by no one. Wouldn't it be nice! Pessoa's less sanguine twist on the fate of the Titan and great benefactor of humanity was titled *Prometheus Rebound* or, in Latin, *Prometheus Revinctus*.

Pessoa would work on this English-language play in fits and starts throughout the rest of his life, but he conceived its gist and wrote the first scenes for it in 1907 or possibly already in late 1906, shortly after reading Shelley's *Prometheus Unbound*. In Pessoa's treatment of the myth, far more in keeping with the spirit of Greek tragedy, Jupiter enlists the aid of Asia—a sea nymph and major character in Shelley's play—to create the *illusion* that he has fallen from power. Hercules, fooled just like everyone else, liberates Prometheus, who marries Asia and eventually tells her the long-guarded secret of Jupiter's future. Asia immediately relays the information to the (supposedly fallen) king of the gods, who, having gotten what he wanted, vengefully rechains Prometheus to a bleak summit of the Caucasus Mountains, where a vulture will once more eat out, day after day, his nightly regenerated liver.[17]

✦

THERE WAS NEARLY ALWAYS a philosophical bent to Search's searching, even when the heteronym was occupied with literature, politics, or the social sciences, and philosophy was Pessoa's favorite subject during his second year at the School of Arts and Letters. He took especially copious notes on the Pre-Socratics, whom he had already read on his own in the spring of 1906. The kinds of questions first posed by these pioneers of rational thought in the West were fodder for Pessoa's poetry

and prose. What is the relationship of being to nonbeing? Can the former arise out of the latter? Is nonbeing something? How to reconcile
the notions of essential being and change? If things change, what essen-
tiality do they have? If there is *one* reality, how can there be plurality?
The most basic of mysteries that vexed the early philosophers—the existence of existence—haunted Pessoa for as long as he himself existed. In a
metaphysically anguished poem written more than twenty years later, for
instance, Pessoa would have Álvaro de Campos utter these lines:

> Ah, that there exists a way for beings to exist,
> For existence to exist,
> For the existence of "to exist" to exist,
> For anything to exist . . .[18]

Pessoa was particularly impressed by the ontological considerations
of Gorgias, a Pre-Socratic sophist who has been called the first philosophical nihilist. Some of the main points of his argument on behalf of
nonexistence were summarized by the Portuguese student of philosophy
in some notes written in English. Abridging them slightly, we have:

> Nothing exists.
> If anything existed, we could not know it.
> And if we could know it, we could not communicate this knowl-
> edge to others.[19]

Gorgias offered additional, skillful arguments for his thesis that we
can neither obtain nor convey any knowledge of objective reality, all
of which Plato wrote off as verbal sleight of hand, but present-day philosophy tends to see this Greek thinker from Sicily as a foil to the "es-
sentialism" of other Pre-Socratics and as a kind of analytic philosopher
*avant la lettre*.

Pessoa, who classified Gorgias as either a "very deep philosopher" or "a
happy blunderer," maintained that he was not at all a nihilist but a (possibly inadvertent) idealist, since he considered Being to be nonexistent
at the level of appearance and yet, simultaneously, "the only thing existing."[20] This interpretation would probably have prompted more grum-
bling from Plato, but the notion of a plane of true being that cannot be
apprehended by the senses had enormous repercussions in Pessoa's work

and thought. In 1910 he sketched an incomplete sonnet, "Sonho de Gorgias" ("Gorgias's Dream"), based on the idealism he had deduced from the philosopher's system. Pessoa's Gorgias dreams of a "colossal and eternal city" completely "alien to what we call *reality*" (Pessoa's emphasis).[21]

The real dreamer of such a city was Fernando Pessoa, with poetry as his magic carpet for getting there. He was an escapist, yes, but only because at least a part of him felt that what we usually call reality is as good as nothing, nonbeing. It was a feeling that persisted. His notes on Gorgias's theory ("Nothing exists. If anything existed, we could not know it.") and what he imagined to be Gorgias's dream would be transposed by him into the first person more than twenty years later:

I'm nothing.
I'll always be nothing.
I can't want to be something.
But I have in me all the dreams of the world.

These opening lines from "The Tobacco Shop," written in 1928, establish a radical dichotomy between "outward" reality—where the speaker and whatever he might achieve or become are ultimately nothing—and his "inward" reality of dreaming. In the poem's concluding line, the universe "falls back into place without ideals or hopes," an event that implies the speaker's reconciliation with the "real" world and also the defeat of his ideal, dreamed existence. It was only a temporary reconciliation, and a temporary defeat. Pessoa continually oscillated between a Promethean impulse to help humanity, to be involved in the world, and a contrary inclination to retreat and seek perfection in the artistic space of a poem or in the realms of spirit and of abstract thought. One can do nothing for the world without engaging with the world, as Gandhi well knew, but Pessoa was addicted to the dreamed life.

It goes without saying that the dreams Pessoa most appreciated were literary in nature. As much as actually writing them, he loved the imaginative act of planning poems and fictions, like an architect designing buildings, and he loved entering the imaginary worlds created by other writers. Because of the ideal constructions and verbal scaffolding they entail, he was similarly attracted to a number of philosophical systems, as if they were so many "stories" offering more or less ingenious explanations of life and the universe. And as he read the stories, he felt the

irresistible urge to write his own, or to refashion what others had formulated. In the same way that he "corrected" Shelley's version (which
was itself a correction) of the Prometheus myth, he presumed to correct philosophers who had spent their entire lives working out carefully
calibrated schemes of thought. Schopenhauer, for instance. Pessoa may
have perused but probably never read straight through *The World as Will
and Representation*, but that did not stop him from planning his own,
improved treatise in English, to be titled *The World as Power and as Not-
Being*. Pessoa quibbled with Schopenhauer's use of the word "will," writing in his notes that it made no sense to attribute this quality to a bar of
iron that expands when heated. He proposed, instead, the word "power"
as the irrational, driving force of existence.[22]

Pessoa had similar plans to rework other philosophies and to create
his own philosophical syntheses, but these never advanced beyond mere
outlines and preliminaries. Rather than rewrite philosophy as philosophy, he was more interested in exploiting it for literary ends. In 1907
or 1908 he wrote a prose piece in English whose opening sentence—"I
was a poet animated by philosophy, not a philosopher with poetic faculties"—has been frequently cited as evidence that philosophy was a crucial influence on his poetry. Interestingly, the rest of the five-paragraph
text talks about what poetry means and how it occurs to the narrator,
who never again mentions philosophy, not even obliquely. He finds that
"there is poetry in this table, in this paper, in this inkstand," and in
everything he sees and hears outside, even "in a fowl with its chickens
strutting across the road." The essence of poetry, according to the final
paragraph, "is astonishment, admiration, as of a being fallen from the
skies taking full consciousness of his fall, astonished at things."[23]

What most astonished Pessoa, as already noted, was that anything at
all existed. That astonishment stimulated his interest in philosophy, and
philosophy—in the primordial sense of the word: love of knowledge—
animated his poetry, which was itself an inquiry, an attempt to obtain
or to create knowledge. But although Pessoa greatly admired and even
envied Kant and Hegel, his poetry was not obviously influenced by the
former's *Critique of Pure Reason* or by the latter's doctrine of absolute idealism. He did, however, use certain philosophies as staging platforms,
or scenery. We can construe a radical nominalism from the poetry of
heteronym Alberto Caeiro, for whom each thing is singularly what it is,
without participating in a universal concept, and Álvaro de Campos at

one point promulgates and exemplifies the doctrine of the Übermensch (Overman), who creates his own values and overcomes his own humanity, but these and other philosophical notions were placed at the service of poetry. They were no more likely than chickens strutting across the road to be the immediate inspiration for individual poems.

Pessoa was a cerebral poet, and philosophy had a considerable, indirect influence on his creative work insofar as it stimulated and honed his thought processes. Philosophy for him was like mental gymnastics. He delighted in argument for argument's sake, and was particularly fond of logical absurdities. He took detailed notes on Achilles' unwinnable race against the turtle, according to the *reductio ad absurdum* proposed by Zeno, whose method of reasoning he defended against its detractors,[24] and he became a lifelong cultivator of paradoxes—partly to show off his skill as a logician but mostly to remind others and himself of the ur-absurdity of existence, any existence, and hence of any "true" statements made about this or that aspect of existence.

◆

DESPITE HIS DOUBTS ABOUT what the world was or if, philosophically, it even existed, Pessoa closely followed the messy unfolding of Portugal's political melodrama, in which a far from flawless but by no means despotic king had become the object of growing national discontent. Pessoa wrote about what was happening and why, in English, for a book aimed at the curious foreigner but unfortunately left unfinished, *Extent and Causes of Portuguese Decay.* According to his analysis, "the wave of anger and of hatred" that would eventually lead to the assassination of King Carlos began on November 20, 1906, when a republican congressman named Afonso Costa delivered a speech in parliament that attributed the disastrous state of the nation's finances to fiscal mismanagement and exorbitant expenditures by the monarch and his clan.[25] After more than an hour of haranguing, Costa was asked by the president of the assembly to make no further reference to the king, at which point the orator declared: "For far fewer crimes than those committed by King Carlos I, the head of Louis XVI rolled on the scaffold in France!" Costa, along with another republican, was expelled from parliament for thirty days. If his fiery words were not exactly a threat, they were indeed a prophecy: the king, whose expenditures were not even remotely comparable to those of Louis XVI, would be dead within fifteen months.

The royal expenditures were a sideshow shrewdly exploited by the republicans. The graver threat to the monarchy was the breakdown of the traditional parties that supported it. Prime Minister João Franco had been at his post for just six months but was already under attack from virtually all sides. It was Franco (no relation to the Spanish Franco) who had coined the term "rotativism" to characterize the ineffectual system whereby power passed back and forth between look-alike political parties—the Progressives and the Regenerators—that were taking the country nowhere, and in 1903 he formed a splinter group: the Liberal Regenerator Party. This was followed, two years later, by a split in the Progressive Party. The republicans, who were adding many intellectuals, young people, and city dwellers to their ranks, began to be courted by the dissidents of both traditional parties. The two houses of parliament, increasingly fractured, met for shorter and shorter sessions, since these often devolved into shouting matches in which no coherent legislative programs could be enacted.

Elsewhere in Europe, political parties likewise proliferated, with the difference that they often embodied sharp ideological differences. Germany was ruled by a center-right coalition, but the Social Democrats, who at that stage were doctrinaire Marxists, had become the nation's largest party, garnering around 30 percent of the vote in the 1907 election. French socialists were also a force that now had to be reckoned with. In Portugal, owing in part to the lagging pace of industrialization, support for far-left parties was minuscule, and the platforms of the traditional, alternately ruling parties were hard to tell apart. The nation's political center, rather than being caught in a tug-of-war between ideological extremes, was caving in on itself.

As might be expected, Portugal's seesaw method for distributing power had an exact analogue in its Iberian neighbor, Spain, where for several decades power had been regularly shifting, by mutual consent, between Liberals and Conservatives. There too the system, known as *turnismo* and relying, as in Portugal, on rigged elections, was threatening to break down as the established parties splintered—a process aggravated by regionalist movements, especially in Catalonia. The Spanish republicans were also divided into a number of parties and failed, for the time being, to muster significant popular support. Portuguese republicans, by contrast, maintained a remarkably united front for as long as they were the opposition. They jointly, relentlessly criticized the parties in power for perpetuating a cabal of vested interests that was holding back the nation from social and economic progress.

Hoping to avert a bloody insurrection by rolling out a modest "revolution" of his own, King Carlos had tapped João Franco, a tireless denouncer of political corruption and administrative inefficiency, to head up a reformist government. It was founded on an improbable coalition of Franco's Liberal Regenerators with the far more numerous Progressives, led by the aging and ailing José Luciano de Castro. On May 25, 1906, the new prime minister announced his intention to rule according to the British model, bringing all tendencies into the political process, including the republicans. His program contained specific proposals for achieving cleaner elections, transparency in government finances, greater independence of the judiciary, administrative decentralization, increased productivity in the private sector, social protections for workers, and more freedom of the press.[26]

Elections were held in August, the legislature convened in September, and at first everything seemed to bode well for the new government. Franco, however, overestimated his ability to change the long-standing rules of Portugal's political game, which was all about scoring points for one's own political party. Now that the system of rotating power was collapsing, cooperation between parties had become even more difficult. Sitting down to calmly discuss and enact progressive legislation was not on the republican agenda, since they had nothing to gain from a reform that might, as King Carlos was hoping, eliminate the motives that justified their crusade against the constitutional monarchy. Politicians of other stripes were in scramble mode, jockeying for position, skeptical that real reform was possible, as if it were too late for that.

Newspapers were the most powerful agents for shaping public opinion, and here the antiroyalists had the advantage, since it is easier to make news by being against than by being for. Reports of a royal family living proverbially high off the hog, by virtue of technically illegal loans from public coffers, kindled public indignation. In an attempt to bridle journalists, Franco pushed through a duplicitous Press Law whose first article guaranteed the right of free journalistic expression, without censorship, but whose subsequent articles established harsh penalties for slandering the king or government leaders. The bill, which took effect on April 11, 1907, is given only passing mention by most historians, but it warranted a full chapter in Pessoa's *Extent and Causes of Portuguese Decay*.

Almost three decades later, controls on free speech in writing would prompt Pessoa to repudiate the Salazar regime. To his way of thinking, words themselves—not just the people who speak or write them—had an inviolable right to be heard and read.

The next chapter in Pessoa's *Extent and Causes*,[27] which he wrote in late 1909 or early 1910, focused on the student strike that began at the University of Coimbra in March 1907, after a law student's thesis was unanimously rejected for political reasons. The degree candidate, the son of a former prime minister with republican sympathies, was himself an outspoken republican and had dedicated his thesis to Teófilo Braga (1843–1924), a liberal-minded writer and republican politician who was anathema to the conservative administrators of Portugal's oldest, and at that time only, university. Students from all faculties boycotted their classes in protest, forcing the rector to close the school. On March 4 more than three hundred Coimbra students took the train to Lisbon, where they aired their grievances to the government and easily won the solidarity of local students and the general population. University officials in Coimbra announced the expulsion of seven striking students, six of whom were republicans, for allegedly yelling insults at professors and pelting their homes with stones. The university reopened one month later, but the students balked, at which point the strike spread to nearly all Portuguese institutions of higher learning, including the School of Arts and Letters, where Pessoa was studying.

On April 15, Prime Minister Franco ordered all schools affected by the strike to shut down until further notice. The legislative session, meanwhile, had ended several days earlier, with virtually none of the government's reform program having been implemented. Abandoned by the Progressives, his coalition party, Franco was supposed to step down, but neither a newly formed government nor fresh elections were likely to resolve the political deadlock. The two traditional, rotative parties were too weak and discredited to be effective governing forces, even if they were still strong enough to sabotage anyone else's attempt to rule by due process. And so King Carlos invited João Franco to rule without due process. On May 10 the parliament was dissolved, inaugurating a dictatorial regime.

◆

IN THE MIDST OF all the student agitation, gleefully publicized by republican newspapers as proof of monarchical tyranny, the ten-month holiday of Pessoa's immediate family came to an end. Pessoa, in his notes, never referred to their sojourn, which we know was not all bliss. His youngest sister, two-year-old Maria Clara, had died of septicemia in December—the third child taken away from his mother by a sudden illness. Maria Madalena, who was five months pregnant, may have found some temporary solace in the thought of her new baby on the way, but in January she miscarried. They told her it would have been a boy.[28]

Fernando was not naturally talkative, and with his parents he probably avoided talking about what most interested him at the moment. They could have little to say about philosophy, his latest intellectual obsession, nor could they sympathize with his political convictions. They knew, of course, that their son was a republican, and they themselves were by no means fanatical supporters of monarchy, but from Maria Madalena's diplomatic letter to her son after the republican revolution prevailed— she said only that she regretted the loss of life on both sides—it seems clear that politics was not a topic of their conversations.[29] An overabundance of mutual respect inhibited Fernando and his parents from debating issues head-on, as if they were afraid of offending each other, or of upsetting the equilibrium of their relationship.

On April 25, 1907, Fernando and a number of relatives gathered at the dock to see off his mother, stepfather, Teca, Luís, and João, who boarded the SS *Ardeola*, bound for the Canaries, where they would transfer to another steamer and continue, once again, to Durban.[30] João Miguel Rosa had served as a consul for more than eleven years and expected to bring his family back to Portugal for good within another three or four. "Before you know it, we'll all be together again," we can imagine Pessoa's mother saying, reassuringly, to everyone who was there to say goodbye, and especially to her oldest son. But thirteen years would pass before she returned, along with her by then grown children, and herself a widow who could walk only with assistance, prematurely aged and frail.

Fernando, whose classes were still suspended because of the student strike, moved in with his grandmother and his great-aunts Maria and Rita, on Rua da Bela Vista à Lapa, a quiet street that ran perpendicular to the Calçada da Estrela, where he had been staying with his parents. Almost nineteen years old, he was relieved to no longer be under their watchful eye. He would miss his mother, but he yearned to be his own master, to do what he wanted exactly when he wanted, and to that end his new living arrangements were a distinct advantage. The authority of his elderly aunts would be easy to flaunt.

In May the academic committee of the School of Arts and Letters announced that exams would be held in October, with professors giving classes in June and July to make up for lessons lost during the strike. Pessoa attended no more classes and would sit for no exams. His waning interest in the school's program of study had soured, finally, into an outright aversion.[31] The philosophy class had kept him going during the second year—that, and the fact his parents were in Lisbon, minding his every move. But now they were back in Africa, where whatever advice and reprimands they cared to convey in letters would take a whole month to reach him. As for philosophy, he preferred to read it on his own.

João Maria Rosa, who was four years old at the time of the student strike, would claim sixty years later that his half brother was one of its instigators, and that the strike was what prompted him to quit the School of Arts and Letters.[32] There is no evidence to support the first assertion, nor was it corroborated by other family members. Only in writing did Pessoa know how to take a stand or raise a fist, and if, nevertheless, he had managed to overcome his antipathy toward the active life and help organize the strike, he would have mentioned the fact in the relevant chapter of his *Extent and Causes of Portuguese Decay*. On the other hand, it is possible that the strike and the way it ultimately played out, or petered out, contributed to his decision to terminate his studies.

Toward the end of May, the government issued a decree reopening the University of Coimbra and making it possible for students to take their exams late and avoid losing a full year. A few students, known as the *instransigentes*, stubbornly refused, since the unjustly rejected thesis that had inspired the strike continued to be rejected, but the vast majority forgot about justice and got on with their studies. Pessoa, in the pages he wrote about the strike, considered this denouement to be nothing less than "moral corruption," responsible for "distort[ing] the meaning of the strike" and for "break[ing] its power."[33] As a matter of principle, he may have quietly cast his lot with the "intransigents."

# CHAPTER 17

L IBERATED FROM HIS COURSE OF STUDY, PESSOA had no clear idea of what he would do next or of how he would earn money. He was incapable of being pragmatic, of taking practical steps to achieve realistic goals, but he did at least reorient his thought life so as to gain, he hoped, a better understanding of himself and the role he might play in the world. Instead of meditating on the nature of reality and the origins of the universe, he became more preoccupied with his own nature, how it came to be, and what it was suited to do. Reflecting this shift in focus, his ardent readings in philosophy gave way to the study of psychology.

Even before leaving Durban, Pessoa had become fascinated by the possibility of deciphering human character through phrenology, and he had delighted in Poe's pioneering use of psychological deduction in his short stories, but in 1907 he delved directly and deeply into psychological science. His choice of readings in this rapidly expanding field was largely inspired by his paternal grandmother's mental state, which had been progressively deteriorating since as far back as he could remember, though he knew that in her younger years she was, to all appearances, of perfectly sound mind. This gave him pause, as her direct descendant, since it meant that his future mental health might be at risk. But his readings also suggested that the same mental disturbance that had afflicted her with degenerative madness might, in him, have assumed a superior form: namely, genius. As usual in Pessoa, one idea led to another, entangling him in a web of theories about degeneration, genius, madness, and related matters connected to psychology. And these ideas, as usual, invaded his poetry and prose.

Far from ever regretting his decision to quit the School of Arts and Letters, Pessoa, if anything, seems only to have rued the two years he spent there without earning a single credit. Although several classmates became his friends, he had peremptorily judged most of them to be what he called "conventionals," not worth his time or consideration. He was equally unimpressed by his teachers, some of whom he would lampoon years later in epigrammatic poems signed by António Gomes, a "graduate in Philosophy from the University of the Useless," whose first name, not by accident, was one of Pessoa's given names. Pessoa hoped to bring out Gomes's stinging satires in a pamphlet titled *The University of Lisbon.* (The School of Arts and Letters would be incorporated into this university upon its founding, in 1911.)

Pessoa's parents were predictably disappointed to learn that he had dropped out of school, and miffed that he'd done so without consulting them. They suddenly realized that Fernando, despite his outwardly docile manner, was determined to do only and absolutely what he pleased. His stepfather, whose hard-earned money was supporting the young man while he pursued his studies, lost his temper, giving rise to a heated exchange of letters between Durban and Lisbon.[1] Pessoa's mother, who was naturally worried about his future, tried to reason with her son, though without great tact. "So much proven intelligence going to waste!" was the judgment, if not the actual words, expressed in her letters. Surely he could not make a living writing poetry.

Pessoa, however, thought that maybe he could—he, or Alexander Search. He had a batch of calling cards printed for this English-language heteronym who lived, like himself, at the Rua da Bela Vista à Lapa, 17, first floor, with his grandmother and two elderly aunts. During the next several years he posted letters signed by Alexander Search, Esq., to booksellers, publishers, and literary agents. The method back then for young poets writing in English to make themselves and their work known was the same as it is today: magazine submissions. In May 1907 Pessoa sent a copy of his humorous "Elegy on the Marriage of My Dear Friend Mr. Jinks" to *The Smart Set,* which labeled itself "A Magazine of Cleverness." Published in New York, it was one of the major literary periodicals in America at the time. In that same month the young poet planned to submit sonnets to *The Athenaeum,* a London-based magazine, and to "some other paper." A list of letters to write, dating from late August, includes one to the editor of *Harper's Magazine,* and a list of things to do for September 3 ends with "Send off poem"—if not to *Harper's,* then to some other magazine.[2] The National Library did not subscribe to any of these magazines, and it seems unlikely that Lisbon's English bookstore imported periodicals from the United States, but Pessoa, one way or another, managed to be well informed about the literary marketplace.

The poems that Pessoa actually submitted or thought of submitting for publication were signed by Alexander Search, the putative author of all the poetry he wrote in 1907, with the exception of some fragmentary political verses in Portuguese. Search was also retroactively credited with a trove of poems produced before he ever came into (imaginary) existence. In May 1907 Pessoa began making fair copies of his English poems, signing them all as Alexander Search, regardless of when they were written. In this way, Search expropriated virtually all the poetry attributed to Charles Robert Anon between 1903 and 1906. The clearest sign that Mr. Anon was dead, or reincarnated as another, appears in Latin at the end of a copy of the poem "Elegy on the Marriage of My Dear Friend Mr. Jinks," which was originally signed "C. R. Anon." Directly below this signature, Pessoa later added: "id est Alexander Search."[3] Anon had been reduced to a former alias of Search.

◆

ONE OF THE MOST memorable works of literature signed by Alexander Search was not a poem but a short story, "A Very Original Dinner," written in June 1907, in English. The story's setting is a Berlin gastronomical society whose president, Herr Prosit, promises his hard-to-impress fellow gourmands a truly original dinner at his house, to be held in ten days' time. The incentive for the dinner is the rivalry between Herr Prosit and five young men—likewise gastronomes—who are visiting from the city of Frankfurt. The five men say they have no interest in attending the dinner, but the president guarantees that they will "be there in body."

The day arrives for the much anticipated dinner, which is served to fifty-two guests by five dark-skinned men wearing turbans. It occurs to the narrator, who is a society member and one of the dinner guests, that Herr Prosit must have somehow coerced the five men from Frankfurt into blackening their faces and playing the part of waiters. Had he not sworn that they would be present at the dinner? Once the guests have all eaten heartily, Prosit reveals the "original" nature of the repast by making a toast "to the memory of the five young gentlemen of Frankfurt *who have been present in body* at this dinner" while he simultaneously points at a platter with some leftover meat—human meat. After a moment of catatonic shock, the "well-bred, well-dressed, refined semi-artistic men" are overwhelmed "by a fury of more than beasts." They lay their "animal hands" on Prosit and hurl him out the window. It turns out that the five servers were "old Asiatic pirates, of a murderous and abominable tribe." One of them escapes, but the other four are caught and punished.

Like some other Pessoa stories from this period, "A Very Original Dinner" is a tale of perverseness and ratiocination in the style of Edgar Allan Poe, although its cannibalism was no doubt inspired by Shakespeare's *Titus Andronicus*. Pessoa also brought sociology and heredity to bear on his story, which contains a number of pages about the character of Prosit, whose family background—son of an epileptic and with "several unmistakeable neurotics" among his ancestors—had produced in him an underlying "morbidness," which secretly flourished in his worldly milieu of excessive eating, drinking, and sexual indulgence.[4]

The pathological depiction of Herr Prosit's degenerate personality, based on environment as well as heredity, owes something to the naturalist school of writing, best represented in France by Émile Zola and in Portugal by Abel Botelho (1855–1917), author of five novels published under the general title of "Social Pathology,"* but it was Max Nordau who quickened Pessoa's interest in the general theme of degeneration. His book *Entartung*, published in 1892 and translated into English as *Degeneration* three years later, was a diatribe against modern art, literature, music, and philosophy, deemed to be the diseased fruit of pernicious social forces that came to a head in decadent, fin de siècle Europe. Pessoa read a French edition of the book at the same time he was writing "A Very Original Dinner."

Nordau (1849–1923)—a Hungarian-born Jew who trained as a physician, worked as a journalist and became an early leader of the Zionist movement—wrote in German and strongly identified with traditional German culture and values. He railed against the Pre-Raphaelites, the French symbolists, Tolstoy, Wilde, Ibsen, Wagner, and Nietzsche for being vague, subjective, irrational, mystical—the products of weakened brains and flaccid wills. His medically couched observations and diagno-

---

* In May 1907, less than one month before he wrote "A Very Original Dinner," Pessoa read Botelho's *The Baron of Lavos* (1891), which tells the story of an aristocratic homosexual whose "disease" is shown to be the scientifically logical result of several centuries of familial degeneration, exacerbated by the corrupting atmosphere of urban life.

sis of Paul Verlaine in *Degeneration* are typical. After spending ten pages analyzing the signs of degeneration in the Frenchman's poetry (impulsiveness, bestial lust alternating with exaggerated piety, abrupt shifting between excitement and depressiveness, etc.), Nordau concludes that "this most famous leader of the Symbolists" is "a repulsive degenerate subject with asymmetric skull and Mongolian face," who "manifests the absence of any definite thought in his mind by incoherent speech, meaningless expressions and motley images."[5] Nordau insisted that intellectual and artistic expressions should be positive, clear minded, and uplifting, in accord (as he saw it) with the evolutionary trend of humanity. If they were in disaccord, it was due to the deleterious influence of industrialized society, which bred nervous degeneration that then propagated on its own, like a contagious disease.

The central thesis and supporting arguments of *Degeneration* were premised on a mechanistic model of science, a physiological conception of psychology, and a materialist notion of progress—all of which were being seriously challenged at the turn of the century. Nordau's book, which had been an instant and resplendent success, would fall into obscurity by the First World War. Pessoa read the work with rapt attention and took detailed notes. Its impact on him can be gauged by his response to a survey, made in 1932, about the most important books in his life:

> In my childhood and first adolescence, when I lived and was educated in British territory, *The Pickwick Papers* of Dickens engrossed me and stood out above all other books. I still read and reread it today, therefore, as if I were merely remembering.
>
> In my second adolescence, my spirit was dominated by Shakespeare and Milton and, to a lesser extent, by the English Romantic poets who are their hazy shadows. Among the latter, Shelley was perhaps the one whose inspiration was most present.
>
> In what I may call my third adolescence, spent here in Lisbon, I lived in the atmosphere of the Greek and German philosophers and in that of the French decadents, whose influence was summarily swept from my spirit by Swedish gymnastics and by reading Nordau's *Dégénérescence*.[6]

It surprises us that Pessoa could have been so enthralled by Nordau—a fluent, effectual writer who was well read but intellectually rigid, priggishly moralistic, and aesthetically reactionary. Pessoa's fascination, it turns out, was restricted to the relationship that the writer posited between exceptional intellectual or creative activity and psychological deviation from the norm. He ignored Nordau's moral judgments and did not take him seriously as a literary and artistic critic. The link drawn between Verlaine's alleged degeneracy and his style of poetry seemed valid enough to Pessoa, but that did not diminish his admiration for the poetry. Nordau himself, for that matter, acknowledged that Verlaine's poetic method "often yields extraordinarily beautiful results."[7]

◆

TRUE TO HABIT, PESSOA gutted *Degeneration* for his own literary purposes. Percy Bysshe Shelley is mentioned only once in Nordau's book, as an example of a healthy, *non*degenerate artist,[8] yet Pessoa planned an essay, in English, on the "moral stigmas of Degeneration" present in his favorite Romantic poet. Not surprisingly, these so-called stigmas—which included a more than ordinary interest in mystery, a hatred of convention, and a hyperexcited brain—also existed in Pessoa himself.[9] He clearly took them to be probable indicators of his own Shelley-like genius as a writer.

Of all the degenerative manifestations mentioned by Nordau in his densely packed opus, the one that generated the most interest in Pessoa was "mania of doubt." Consulting a French dictionary of medical science, he found an entry on the "*folie du doute*"[10] and took detailed notes, but he also invested the term with his own ideas—or with the ideas of Alexander Search. It was supposedly this alter ego who defined mania of doubt as "a hallucinatory intensity of intellectual perception."[11] If this sounds more like a talent to be envied than the symptom of a mental disease, it is because the potential maniacal doubter was Fernando Pessoa, in whom the malady, according to his interpretation, had been diverted into genius.

There is, of course, no shortage of maniacs who hallucinate and perceive things that most people do not. So what distinguishes genius from mere mania? Both conditions, Pessoa observed, are marked by constant questioning, by "anxiety" to discover answers, and by "intellectual egotism," which results from an "abuse of the reasoning powers." But "mania of doubt does not attempt to solve the problems; the man of genius does."[12] With this line of argument, not only was Pessoa trying to prove that he had the qualities of a man of genius, he was tracing a pathway for affirming those qualities. To secure his place as a genius writer, he would "attempt to solve the problems" insistently posed by his questioning mind. Here again his model was Shelley, who never stopped addressing the philosophical, social, and political issues that relentlessly troubled his thoughts. Wordsworth may have been a greater writer than Shelley (whose life, it must be remembered, was fifty years shorter than Wordsworth's), but it was Shelley's restless sort of genius that the young Pessoa appreciated and emulated.

Genius and mania of doubt, according to Pessoa's notes from 1907, were "plainly degenerative" conditions and hence more likely to show up in families with a history of nervous disorders and insanity. A couple of years later, he would summarize his own family's medical history in a schematic family tree that highlights Grandma Dionísia's insanity and Aunt Anica's "nervous temperament" as well as his mother's "superior equilibrium." The implicit hope was that the madness and nervousness present on both sides of Pessoa's family had sprouted in him as genius, thanks to the mental stability he inherited from his mother.[13]

What was the use of proving, through dubious theories and arguments, that he was born to be a genius? Would it make him a better poet? It might. The status of "genius" was a challenge, an identity to live up to. And perhaps, as a secondary benefit, it reconciled him to the figure of his grandma Dionísia. She had been an often distressing presence in his early childhood and a general nuisance to the family thereafter, but according to the hereditary theories embraced by Pessoa, he had this mad relative to thank for the germ of his genius.

◆

LIKE A MAN WHO, after being diagnosed with a rare disease, goes to great lengths to learn about its causes, symptoms, and possible outcomes, so Pessoa tried to find out everything he could about the "disease" of genius. As soon as he had devoured Nordau's *Degeneration*, he pounced on a French translation of *L'uomo di genio* (*The Man of Genius*), by Nordau's Italian precursor, Cesare Lombroso (1835–1909), a physician who for a long time had been exploring the links between genius, madness, and degeneration.[14] Lombroso, best remembered as a criminologist, maintained that crime was also an inherited disposition, resulting from mental degeneration, and he proposed that prisons be converted into insane asylums.[15]

It was in July 1907 and at the National Library—where he probably arrived each day after having lunch with Aunt Maria and Aunt Rita—that Pessoa read Lombroso's treatise on genius and madness as well as books by French, German, and English authors dealing with psychiatry, mental illness, and physiology. Toward the end of the year or in 1908, he purchased and read John Ferguson Nisbet's *The Insanity of Genius* (1891) and William Hirsch's *Genius and Degeneration* (1896),[16] feverishly marking up the margins of nearly every page. But Pessoa's rapacious hunger for psychiatric insights into human character and behavior, particularly with respect to artists, did not yet lead him to Sigmund Freud. Though Freud had already published some of his important works, including *The Interpretation of Dreams* (1899), they were not widely translated until after 1910.

Comparing, synthesizing, and building on his readings, Pessoa filled several small notebooks and many loose pages with material for assorted, never completed essays on genius, degeneration, madness, and specific psychological pathologies. He drew occasional charts in an attempt to systematize genius in all its varieties as well as the neuroses or psychoses that each variety was likely to exhibit. In one of his earliest schemata, from a notebook he used in 1907, Pessoa divided geniuses into three basic types—those of thought, of feeling, and of will—and three hybrid types: thought-feeling, thought-will, and feeling-will. He noted that geniuses of thought are apt to be philosophers or thinkers, geniuses of feeling tend to be mystics, geniuses of thought-feeling will usually be poets, and so forth. Another schema, using the psychiatric jargon typical of that era, categorized geniuses according to their psychopathologies—as neurasthenics, hysterics, epileptics, or some combination thereof. A handful of celebrated geniuses served as illustrative examples, with Napoleon and Caesar being classed as epileptics, and Poe and Flaubert as hystero-epileptics. Shakespeare was labeled a hysterical neurasthenic, which is how Pessoa would occasionally refer to himself throughout the rest of his life.[17] In a letter from 1931 he would explain, "I'm a hysterical neurasthenic, with the hysterical element predominating in my emotions and the neurasthenic element in my intellect and will."[18]

"Hysteria," a term that originates from the Greek word for "uterus," was a medical diagnosis usually applied to women, with symptoms that ranged from irritability and inordinate sexual desire to hallucinations and psychosomatic disorders. Doctors in the nineteenth century had treated the condition by massaging women's genitals to provoke orgasms, a therapy that helped popularize the vibrator, invented in the 1880s to relieve muscle pain. Pessoa, who was perfectly well aware of the traditional understanding of hysteria, formulated his own, custom-tailored description of the syndrome. Hysteria, he wrote in English, manifested itself in sharp mood swings, a tendency to daydream, and "simulation and depersonalization, whether in the form of common lying [. . .] or of auto-suggestion of false emotions." Not by coincidence, depersonalization was for Pessoa the hallmark of great poets, who are able to feel intensely what they don't naturally feel. Neurasthenia, on the other hand, resulted from the mental strain "of overactive thinking" and typically manifested itself as "a dull anxiety" and "a weakening and abeyance of the will, a power-lessness to act and to decide."[19] This definition also fit Pessoa's own case. By the mid-twentieth century, both diagnoses would virtually disappear from the psychiatric lexicon.

Pessoa did not wear hysterical neurasthenia like a badge on his lapel, but in his notes and among his literary friends it pleased him to be able to interpret any eccentric or troubling aspects of his psychology as symptoms of the same malady that afflicted Shakespeare, who would not have been Shakespeare without that malady. According to Pessoa's analysis of their mutual "case," the depersonalization that gave rise to the heteronyms as well as to Hamlet, Lady Macbeth, King Lear, and Falstaff was an outgrowth, or diversion, of the two writers' feminine ("hysterical") impulses. And their "overactive thinking," which led to "neurasthenic" passivity, was a likely factor contributing to their literary dispersion in numerous character types.

✦

ALEXANDER SEARCH, WHEN HE first emerged, was no more psychologically troubled than Pessoa, but within a year's time the creator inflicted some serious mental disturbances on his helpless creature, who could thus serve as a "live" subject for his studies in madness and also, perhaps, as a prophylactic exorcism. No sooner had Pessoa happened on the concept of mania of doubt in Nordau's book than he wrote a poem, signed by Search, whose title was "Mania of Doubt." Dated June 19, 1907, the first of its three stanzas describes the syndrome:

All things unto me are queries
That from normalness depart,

And their ceaseless asking wearies
     My heart.
Things are and seem, and nothing bears
The secret of the life it wears.

The stanza's last two lines remind us that Search was created as a philo-sophical poet with a vocation for inquiring into the mystery underlying all that we see. The ardor of that inquiry had, in the meantime, become mania of doubt, an *obsessive* urge to question.

"Mania of Doubt" and a kindred poem written the same day, titled simply "Doubt," were both to be included in *Documents of Mental Dec-adence*, a poetry grouping probably conceived by Pessoa around that time. Other organizing titles for Search's poems included *Delirium*, *Before Sense*, and *Mens Insana*. These titles may have been intended for separate collections or for distinct sections within a single col-lection. Pessoa himself may not have been sure of his intentions, and he distributed and redistributed the Search poems among the differ-ent groupings. However they were organized, madness hovered like a storm cloud over the ensemble. In a poetic "Prayer" from 1908, Search, realizing that he is already "half-mad," spends seventy-three lines imploring God not to let him descend into "madness absolute." And in a sonnet written six months later and titled "Towards the End," the narrator announces, with resignation, the final snuffing out of his san-ity: "All grows dark. I feel / My reason leave me like a last sunbeam."

The anxieties expressed in these poems are patently autobiographi-cal, and the subject of the autobiography is Alexander Search, who even wrote his own poetic epitaph, which begins:

Here lieth Alexander Search
Whom God and man left in the lurch
And nature mocked with pain and woe.
He believed not in state or church
Nor in God, woman, man or love,
In earth below, nor heav'n above.

Search was a compulsive, maniacal doubter until the end, which would occur at the age of "twenty odd" years according to the same epitaph—like Shelley, who died at the age of twenty-nine, or Keats, who only lived to be twenty-five. The prophecy was correct: Search effectively ceased to exist in 1910, which would have made him twenty-two years old, since he was born, like Pessoa, on June 13, 1888.

Despite the visceral connection suggested by their coincidental birth date, as if they were identical twins, Search's semi-insanity and fear of completely losing his mind were not shared by his maker. Fernando Pessoa was the diligent student of psychiatry and of the theories linking genius to mental decadence. Alexander Search, himself a studious type, as well as a captive collaborator, became the experimental subject who played out madness itself, or near madness. When Pessoa's intellectual interest in the subject began to dwindle at the end of the decade, Alexander Search lost his raison d'être, and he signed no more poems. Throughout the following decade, Pessoa continued to write English poetry prolifically—all of it credited to his own name, with one exception. In July 1916 he would compose a poem that begins with

There is no peace save where I am not

and ends with

Oh, Mother of Shadows, whose ice-dead kiss
Is madness, hasten towards my brain!

Below the poem, he indicated the collection it belonged to: *Documents of Mental Decadence*. Although not actually signed, it was by association a Search poem. Even after disappearing from the coterie of active heteronyms, Search seems to have quietly lived on in Pessoa. But during the first several years after Pessoa left the School of Arts and Letters, Alexander Search was neither quiet nor composed.

◆

SEARCH BEARS SOME RESEMBLANCE to Edvard Munch (1863–1944), who lived in fear of going mad, painted works with titles such as *Melancholy, Anxiety, Despair*, and his world-famous *The Scream*, and who actually suffered a mental breakdown in 1908. The Norwegian's paintings would be included in the 1937 exhibition of so-called Degenerate Art in Munich. While the Nazis could not acknowledge Nordau's influence on their own thinking, given that he was Jewish, they co-opted and updated his narrative of how a degenerate society had corrupted modern art, which in turn had a corrupting effect on people exposed to it. The exhibition in Munich owed its existence to the unmentionable Nordau.*

Despite criticizing Nordau for evaluating art based on the mental state of the artist rather than on strictly artistic criteria,[20] Pessoa continued to read the polemical author's work. Of the six books by Nordau in his possession, a French translation of *The Psychophysiology of Genius and Talent* seems to be the last one he read, in 1914 or 1915.[21] At that point Pessoa quit buying and reading books on the psychology of genius, with one notable exception, which we will examine later: Freud's slender volume on Leonardo da Vinci.

Responding in 1916 to one of the literary surveys that were a frequent feature in Portuguese newspapers, Pessoa would affirm that all "superior artistic production is, by its nature, a product of decadence and of degeneration." And for a disarmingly simple reason: "it is original, and originality, biologically considered, amounts to a departure from the normal type, being therefore a deviation."[22] Pessoa was happy to agree with Max Nordau that Pre-Raphaelitism, symbolism, Tolstoyism, and a few other fin de siècle isms thrived in the soil of degeneration. Far from this circumstance leading him to question the worth of these movements and the works they produced, however, it merely stimulated his interest in the curious origins of creative genius. If degeneration was favorable to the production of good poetry, music, art, and philosophy, then there was no artistic reason to fear or discourage it.

Degeneration in the broadest sense—including physical, mental, and societal decadence, personal and collective ruin, and death in all its forms—was foundational to Pessoa's view of how the world and everything in it worked. New life in nature, innovative forms of literature, changed social orders, new systems of government (such as the imminent Portuguese republic), and spiritual transformations all implied the decay and death of what preceded them. "Death lurks in our every living motion," wrote Pessoa in a passage for *The Book of Disquiet* that I discovered among his unpublished papers. "Dead we're born, dead we live, and

---

* Nordau, moreover, had classed as degenerates both Nietzsche and Wagner, who were central figures of the Nazis' Aryan mythology.

already dead we enter death. Composed of cells living off their disintegration, we're made of death."[23]

◆

ON JULY 30, 1907, Alexander Search signed a poem, "The Circle," that seemed to emerge out of nowhere, without any relation to his previous work. Not quite, since this geometrical figure is suggestive of the mad train of his endlessly spinning thoughts. But Search's questioning mind had veered into a new field of exploration. "I traced a circle on the ground," he announces at the poem's outset, calling it a "mystic figure" that would encompass, he hoped, "mute symbols" of change and "complex formulas of Law." He explains his motivation in the second stanza:

> My simpler thoughts in vain had stemmed
> The current of this madness free,
> But that my thinking is condemned
> To symbol and analogy:
> I deemed a circle might condense
> With calm all mystery's violence.

Poor Mr. Search, by his own reckoning, is at the end of his wits, since the faculty of reasoning is "condemned to symbol and analogy," leading him to no conclusions. It goes around in circles. Accepting that this is so, he conceives a mystic circle as a symbol, or a container of symbols, capable of representing nature's inscrutable laws and life's mysterious processes and transformations. Search, in other words, hopes to calm his rampant speculations on existence and the workings of the world by admitting the possibility of a mystical, nonrational resolution of his doubts. The hope is frustrated, according to the poem's third and final stanza:

> And so in cabalistic mood
> A circle traced I curious there;
> Imperfect the made circle stood
> Though formèd with minutest care.
> From Magic's failure deeply I
> A lesson took to make me sigh.

No matter how carefully he traces it, Search's circle is doomed to imperfection—and the stanza's contorted syntax mimics that inevitable failure. Reason and philosophy, dependent on human words, cannot fathom the mystery of existence. But neither can mysticism or magic, which likewise depend on human conceptualizing and involve human effort.

Magic and Kabbalah were new entries in Pessoa's poetic vocabulary, and "The Circle" marked the beginning of a major shift in his standpoint for observing and investigating the universe. He did not repudiate the ultra-evolutionary world delineated by Herbert Spencer and darkly shaded in by Max Nordau and other theoreticians of degeneracy, but his intellectual inquiry modulated into a metaphysical quest. Search's latest poem was a warning that magical and Kabbalistic investigations, like philosophical or psychological ones, were liable to lead nowhere. That did not mean they were useless. Repeated trying and repeated failing are apt to be part of any transformational process. Fernando Pessoa, whether through spiritual or earthly means, was suddenly anxious to stir things up. Amid the cerebral pursuits that took up the better part of his days he felt that something was missing. In the summer of 1907, he was seized by an imperative that visits many a great artist and that Rainer Maria Rilke, in his "Archaic Torso of Apollo," would poetically immortalize in the summer of 1908: "You must change your life."

Rilke's poem, written when he was thirty-two years old, seems to have signaled a change in how he viewed his role as a poet. Several years later he would begin writing the *Duino Elegies*, whose narrator becomes a spokesman for humanity, conversing with angels that stand for the wondrous and terrifying mysteries of life, love, beauty, and death. Like few poets before or after him, Rilke was able to visualize in words a marvelously uplifting, mystical relationship between humankind and the unknown. Pessoa, who apparently never read Rilke, engaged with the unknown through myths. Instead of appealing to mystical, symbolic angels, he would entertain a belief in a host of superhuman entities that included actual angels and astral spirits. He would invent religions, foster the myth of a "spiritual" Portuguese empire, and forge a mythic drama about the origins and interrelationships of his major heteronyms, who would emerge in 1914.

But in 1907, not yet twenty years old, Pessoa was still trying to find his feet as a poet and as a man in an ever more uncertain world.

# CHAPTER 18

**P**ESSOA WAS KEENLY AWARE OF HIS FEMININE, "hysterical" side, to which he attributed his intense and swiftly fluctuating emotions as well as his propensity for pretending, for depersonalization. What he lacked was a boldly assertive masculine side. Although he was endowed with a powerful intelligence, his self-diagnosed "neurasthenia" had saddled him with a chronically weak will, which hampered him from putting his ideas into action. Moreover, his physical appearance was unimposing, so that he easily went unnoticed, and, being naturally shy, easily found himself all alone. If imaginary companions such as Alexander Search could to a certain extent fill the void, as some of Pessoa's writings suggest, they were also vivid evidence of the distance separating him from real people.

As we have seen, the effect of Nordau's *Degeneration* on Pessoa was hygienic, sweeping from his spirit the atmosphere and influence of Greek and German philosophy and French decadent literature. Although he would still read philosophy and the French decadents, he was no longer under their spell. But *Degeneration* was just one of the two agents responsible for freeing Pessoa's mind. The other one he mentioned, in his response to the survey about the books that changed his life, was not a book at all but a course in Swedish gymnastics, which he also credited with strengthening his body. While not life threatening, his long illness of the summer of 1906 was a disquieting reminder of his physical fragility. "To be a cadaver, the only thing missing was for me to die," he would jokingly remark in the 1930s, when looking back to 1907, and he thanked Swedish gymnastics for saving him. It was a psychological malaise, however, that led him to seek out professional help.[1]

Pessoa's stepuncle, Henrique Rosa, was doubtless the one who recommended that he see a friend, Dr. António Egas Moniz (1874–1955). This psychiatrist and neurologist would later become famous for his invention of lobotomy, which earned him a Nobel Prize in 1949—a distinction that devolved into a source of national embarrassment after this psychosurgery fell into disrepute. In 1907 Pessoa made an appointment to see Egas Moniz, who had just opened an office in Lisbon to treat nervous disorders.[2] The doctor decided that his patient needed exercise and sent him off to Luís Furtado Coelho, the apostle of Swedish gymnastics in Portugal.

The method of light gymnastics developed in Sweden by Pehr Henrik Ling (1776–1839) required little equipment and stressed careful posture, stretching, correct breathing, and freestanding movements under the supervision of a trainer. Pessoa received lessons three times a week for close to three months.

Enthusiastic about getting into shape, an ambition he had first acted on in Durban by ordering Eugen Sandow's *Strength and How to Obtain It*, Pessoa considered giving this more strenuous kind of "physical culture" another chance. In August he sent a letter to Bernarr Macfadden, America's answer to Sandow, requesting information about *his* system for achieving a healthy and handsome physique.[3] But Pessoa was not cut out for bodybuilding. Swedish gymnastics were more suited to his temperament, though he does not seem to have kept up with them after his lessons were over.

Pessoa did keep in touch with his instructor, Furtado Coelho, who many years later, in 1932, would give him a copy of a manual he published on "respiratory gymnastics," inscribing it to his "former disciple and good friend Fernando Pessoa." By that time the ex-disciple was no picture of health, as he smoked and drank far too much, but there was one reputedly healthy practice that he observed until the end of his days: cold-water baths. These may have commenced in the fall of 1907, when he read, or at least planned to read, Louis Kuhne's popular *The Natural Science of Healing*. Kuhne, a German naturopath, recommended cold-water bathing to stimulate the nerves, increase blood flow, and eliminate toxins.[4] Pessoa was also attracted to health-promoting contraptions that required no physical exertion, just money to buy them and the patience to wear them. Besides showing an interest in acquiring "chest-expanding braces," he also saved an advertisement for the Imperial Shoulder Brace, recommended for people with "narrow and weak chests" or "round shoulders." For energizing the body generally, many people were still wearing Pulvermacher electrical belts, either in bed or while going about their daily routines, and Pessoa apparently purchased one of these in 1908.[5]

Pessoa did not lose much time, just a little money, on quack gadgets such as braces and electrical belts, but gymnastics, by his own account, did his body a world of good. He does not report on the progress he made with his psychological health, nor is it clear what exactly he suffered from. We do not know if he had any follow-up appointments with Egas Moniz, but some notes on psychiatry made by Pessoa in 1915 indicate that he was not much impressed by this or by any other Portuguese psychiatrist, which may partly explain why he became his own shrink.[6] In June 1907 he invented Dr. Faustino Antunes, in whose name he wrote letters to at least three people he had known in Durban, as we have seen. At this point, it's worth recalling that the make-believe psychiatrist asked a former classmate about Pessoa's moral character, about his love life, and about any "sexual excesses" he might have noticed.

Pessoa, now nineteen years old, had never seriously flirted with anyone, let alone carried on any kind of romantic relationship. Perhaps it was anxiety about his stunted sexual and amatory life that had initially prodded him to consult Egas Moniz, who began his career as a sexologist, having published *A vida sexual: fisiologia e patologia* (*Physiology and Pathology of Sexual Life*; 1901), the first comprehensive study of the subject in Portugal. It's unlikely that Pessoa would have discussed his possibly unresolved sexual orientation with the doctor-author, whose book treated homosexuality as a disease, but he may have touched, more vaguely, on his sexual inhibitions and insecurity.

In the midst of his physical training, soul-searching, and self-analysis Pessoa wrote two pages of autobiographical confessions in English, both dated July 25, 1907. The first page begins:

> I am tired of confiding in myself, of lamenting over myself, of pitying mine own self with tears. I have just had a kind of scene with Tia Rita over F. Coelho. At the end of it I felt again one of those symptoms which grow clearer and ever more horrible in me: a moral vertigo. In physical vertigo there is a whirling of the external world about us; in moral vertigo of the interior world. I seemed for a moment to lose the sense of the true relations of things, to lose comprehension, to fall into an abyss of mental abeyance. It is a horrible sensation, one to strike with inordinate fear. These feelings are becoming common, they seem to pave my way to a new mental life, which shall of course be madness.
>
> In my family there is no comprehension of my mental state—

no, none. They laugh at me, sneer at me, disbelieve me; they say I wish to be extraordinary. They neglect to analyse the *wish to be* extraordinary. They cannot comprehend that between being and wishing to be extraordinary there is but the difference of consciousness being added to the second.

It seems that Pessoa's aunt Rita had chided her great-nephew about the cost of his lessons in Swedish gymnastics, which were surely not cheap. Furtado Coelho, a former director of the Royal Gymnasium Club and founder of the National Fencing Association, was tops in his field. Fernando could have done jumping jacks on his own and saved a lot of money. His insistence on a trainer-monitored program of gymnastics from Scandinavia only confirmed Aunt Rita's judgment of the young man as one who deemed himself a rare specimen of humanity, deserving of special treatment and predestined to do special things. Had she known he was predicting for himself "a new mental life, which shall of course be madness," she would have derisively raised her eyebrows. Indeed, it is hard to take such an assertion seriously, unless we understand "madness" as a literary conceit.

Pessoa formulated an odd distinction between *being* extraordinary and *wishing to be* extraordinary, based on the presence or absence of consciousness. According to his way of thinking, being extraordinary depends not on outward achievements but on the *impulse* to be extraordinary. And so he knew that, at heart, he was already extraordinary. But his relatives laughed.

The second page of Pessoa's confessional outpouring addresses his state of loneliness:

I have no one in whom to confide. My family understands nothing. My friends I cannot trouble with these things; I have no really intimate friends, and even were there one intimate, in world's ways, yet he were not intimate in the way I understand intimacy. I am shy and unwilling to make known my woes. An intimate friend is one of my ideal things, one of my day-dreams, yet an intimate friend is a thing I never shall have. No temperament fits me; there is no character in this world which shows a chance of approaching to that I dream in an intimate friend. No more of this.

But he went on, deploring his solitude and finding company only in a long dead poet:

> Mistress or sweetheart I have none; it is another of my ideals and one fraught, unto the soul of it, with a real nothingness. It cannot be as I dream. Alas! poor Alastor! Shelley, how I understand thee! Can I confide in Mother? Would that I had her here. I cannot confide to her also, but her presence would abate much of my pain. I feel as lonely as a wreck in sea.

Without a sweetheart or any truly intimate friends, or even the hope that he will ever have such relationships, Pessoa compares himself to the solitary traveler of Shelley's poem.* Not even to his mother, the person in the world he loves most, can he open his heart—particularly not after her hostile reaction to his dropping out of the School of Arts and Letters earlier in the summer. In the draft copy of a letter, probably rather different from the one he actually sent, he accused her of not sympathizing with him, of not treating him as an equal, and of responding to him with irony.[7]

✦

THE YOUNG POET WAS not altogether friendless. Besides a couple of classmates from school whom he still frequented, there was his stepuncle Henrique Rosa, his cousin and occasional business partner Mário, and other relatives from his mother's side of the family. It is true, however, that intimacy of whatever kind did not come easily to Pessoa.

"I'm a fellow most people like," remarks the narrator of *The Book of Disquiet*, "and they even have a vague and curious respect for me. But I don't arouse ardent emotions. No one will ever passionately be my friend."[8] This was not exactly the case for Fernando Pessoa, who did have one passionate friend: the poet Mário de Sá-Carneiro, an exuberant but troubled soul Pessoa would meet in 1912. And he made other good friends over the years who admired his talent and found him witty

---

* Like many other readers, Pessoa wrongly understood Alastor to be the name of the poem's protagonist. Alastor, from Roman mythology, is the name Shelley gave to the spirit of solitude that haunts the poem's unnamed hero.

and good company, even if they did not feel a deep emotional bond. How could they feel one? Bonds run in two directions, and Pessoa was not emotionally forthcoming in relationships. He felt intensely; it was hard for him to touch people directly. Nevertheless, he always had a few friends and acquaintances he saw on a regular basis.

It was his love life that was a desert—even internally, in his imagination. If his ideal of a "mistress or sweetheart" was "fraught, unto the soul of it, with a real nothingness," it was because he gave it no room, no water, no serious thought. Did he find it hard to imagine himself with a woman because he was in fact more attracted to men? If so, his love life was indeed condemned to be arid, since this was a kind of attraction he could not accept. In late August 1907, one month after his lament about being misunderstood and terribly lonely, Pessoa wrote about homosexuality in some notes for an essay in English called "The Process of Human Degeneracy." In support of his thesis that degeneracy is a "retrocession of a faculty in its advanced state," the essayist considers the phenomenon of "pederasty," a word he often uses—as the French use *pédérastie*—to mean homosexuality between males irrespective of age. He argues that sexual attraction and the feeling of beauty were indivisible for primitive humans but became separated as humanity evolved, with beauty coming to be appreciated in its own right, independent of any physical consummation. Indeed, its association with utilitarian sex is in a certain way debasing. "Pederasts," he allows, may be right to consider male beauty superior; their error is to act on that consideration by desiring physical union with a man, thereby reverting to the primitive association of beauty with sex. The essay's logic relied on an unexamined assumption that sex must be useful, aiming at procreation; otherwise, it is unnatural.

At the end of these notes, Pessoa jotted down the title for a related essay that he hoped to write, "Concerning Paederasty," along with this observation: "Though he may often think a beautiful landscape more beautiful than a woman, [. . .] a man does not for that desire sexual relations with a landscape. This example shows well the absurdity of which paederasty is a form."[9] Actually, the example shows Pessoa's logic at its most absurd. It is as if he were comparing the taste of lobster with a taste for the opera. Pessoa, at any rate, admitted the possibility of his favoring men over women, but only if the attraction was purely aesthetic.

✦

As soon as he quit school, Pessoa was under pressure from his parents and from his extended family in Lisbon to develop a remunerative profession, and in late July 1907 he began work at his first job, as an intern for R. G. Dun & Company. Like Dun & Bradstreet, the firm that succeeded it in 1933, R. G. Dun gathered and sold information on business firms and corporations around the world. Its Lisbon office opened in 1906, and Pessoa's task was to contact local businessmen, persuading and helping them to complete a one-page questionnaire as accurately as possible. It was dull work, for which his course of study at the Commercial School in Durban was far more preparation than he needed. For his own amusement, he filled in a blank questionnaire with credit information on the "businessman" Fernando Pessoa, who lived at the Rua da Bela Vista à Lapa, was single, "about 18 years old" (in fact he was nineteen), and self-employed as a "thief and rogue." The supposed businessman had a considerable amount of invested capital "obtained by stealing," was over his head in debt, had the worst possible "moral reputation," and could not be relied on to keep commitments.[10]

Like many a young man from the Portuguese bourgeoisie, Pessoa landed his first job through a relative. Laurinda, his mother's cousin, had married a well-connected Spanish businessman, Aniceto Mascaró, who managed to secure the position at R. G. Dun for Fernando. Mascaró soon regretted trying to be helpful, however, since in late September Pessoa sent a huffy, slightly insulting letter of resignation to the agency's director, complaining about the meager pay. Mascaró, who would himself become the director of R. G. Dun in Lisbon some years later, wrote Pessoa on October 2 to remind him that he had been hired as an intern whose pay—five thousand reis per month—was not supposed to be commensurate with the services he rendered. In the event of his becoming a regular employee, he would receive a normal salary.[11]

Pessoa might have felt compelled to consider full-time employment, with a normal salary, were it not for Grandma Dionísia, who on September 6 permanently closed her eyes to the world from which she had long ago withdrawn. Since the days were still scorching hot, with temperatures rising into the nineties, the few attendees at her funeral must have been glad it was held early the next day, at 7:00 a.m. Fernando placed a death notice in the newspaper, but it listed no surviving relatives except himself, and not even he mourned her passing. Though he never would have dreamed, like Dostoevsky's Raskolnikov, of hastening along the old woman's demise, the grandson could not have felt any real grief, since dementia had long ago rendered her completely detached from the people she'd once known and loved. He must have experienced, on the contrary, something like giddiness, since she left him an estate worth five million reis (the equivalent of $140,000 U.S. today). With that kind of a windfall, it was easy to turn up his nose at R. G. Dun. He had not become rich, but he was suddenly a man of means. There was only one hitch: his means were tied up until he reached the age of twenty-one. António Maria Silvano, the husband of his great-aunt Carolina and a retired general, was the estate trustee. Most of the estate funds were invested in bank shares; these paid enough interest to cover Pessoa's room and board (set at twenty thousand reis per month and paid directly to Aunts Rita and Maria), as well as clothes, birthday presents for his family, medicines, and incidentals such as cigarettes.

Throughout most of his adult life, Pessoa would work as an occasional translator and a writer of business letters in English and French for Portuguese import-export firms—setting his own hours, never adhering to a fixed schedule. It is often assumed that he embarked on his freelance activities shortly after leaving the School of Arts and Letters, but the evidence suggests this wasn't so: a list of accumulated personal debts that he charged to his inherited estate in March 1908 and a balance sheet of debits and credits drawn up by his uncle in May 1909 indicate that he relied heavily if not entirely on the estate for his sustenance.[12] Pessoa probably did a little translating here and there, at the request of friends and relatives, but with so much capital at his imminent disposal, he was not inclined to fritter his energy on piddly jobs. He had big plans and bided his time.

His plans were not just literary. Although he was loath to work for R. G. Dun as an information gatherer, he looked forward to using his knowledge of commerce and finance in more creative ways. In the same notebook where he made an inventory of his late grandmother's chattels (1 wooden bed, 1 dresser, 1 iron washbasin, etc.) he drew up a list of things to do, which included writing projects but also inventions to be developed and marketed, once he had full access to his inheritance. He was especially keen on an innovative system of shorthand, for which he filled up page after page with stenographic symbols and explanations. He would keep working on his new system, which he eventually dubbed Aristography (*aristo* = best, *graphy* = writing), during the next decade and into the 1920s. Other ideas on Pessoa's list of projects from the fall of 1907 included a "typewriter shifter," for which he left no details, and the elaboration of his own "commercial code," for condensing messages and saving on telegraph costs. He also planned to invent a cipher for use in business negotiations requiring strict confidentiality.[13]

Note that all of Pessoa's ideas for inventions involved the production or transmission of words. Compared to the words that make up literary compositions, those used in journalism and in the world of business ranked much lower in his estimation, but he treasured them nevertheless, for they still shared in the aura and mystique of language.

◆

AMID ALL THE LIFE changes he experienced in 1907—dropping out of school, moving in with his great-aunts, holding and quitting his first job, and becoming an heir—Pessoa kept trying to publish in magazines, an ambition he hoped would be facilitated by his purchase of a typewriter in August. This may have been a joint acquisition with his cousin Mário, on whose behalf Pessoa, as previously mentioned, had written to a French wholesaler of typewriting machines. For his part in the typewriter purchase, Pessoa may have borrowed money from one of his great-aunts. He shopped around for the best price. Using the name of Mr. Faustino Antunes, he sent a letter of inquiry to the Sun Type Writer Company of New York, whose machine sold for forty dollars, as compared to eighty and up for other American typewriters. He finally decided—or perhaps he and Mário decided—on a Moya typewriter, manufactured in England. It cost only five guineas, or about twenty-five dollars, but was not a very sturdy machine. Pessoa's notes suggest that, after fixing a broken spring, he managed to type up Alexander Search's "A Very Original Dinner," which he submitted in November to *Cassell's Magazine*, a British publication specializing in fiction. Typed or handwritten, the story was rejected.[14]

On October 25 Pessoa wrote a letter to the City Rubber Stamp Company of London, requesting a sample "Box of Type." It is uncertain who signed the missive, but the return address was Rua da Imprensa Nacional, 77, third floor, where Aunt Anica and her two children had moved from their previous apartment on Rua de São Bento.[15] Mário would need a few rubber stamps for the business ventures he was contemplating, and perhaps he thought of becoming a Portuguese distributor of the British-manufactured stamps, which used interchangeable type. Pessoa, on the other hand, was magnetically attracted to typewriters, duplicators, rubber stamps, and any other mechanical means for producing printed words. It was an attraction that would ultimately lead him to purchase a printing press and, if all went as planned, to start up a publishing house. But he would have to wait until he turned twenty-one.

When that time came, he hoped to have a cache of creative work ready to roll through the press. Poetry in English would not be lacking, with Pessoa writing more than fifty Alexander Search poems just between June 1907 and January 1908. Besides regularly referring to his incipient madness, Search's poetry from this period harps on two inter-related themes. Poems such as "The Sepulchre," "The Last of Things," "Endings," "Was . . . ," and "Sunset Song," as their very titles suggest, are meditations on how nothing is permanent, everything ends in dissolution and oblivion. In other poems—"The Curtain," "The Picture," "Horror," "Aspiration"—the narrator strives after knowledge hidden by the veil of space and time.

Missing from Search's poetical outpour are poems of love. One of his poems is titled "The Maiden," but the young woman turns out to be a virtual entity, a personification of beauty that cannot be found, since she "reigns eternally alone," in a region "beyond all love." And the poet, too, reigns in a vacuum, far from human warmth and with abstract conceptions as his dubious solace and compensation. There is one additional, essential compensation: poetry itself. In "A Question," a Search poem written in January 1908, a poet is asked whether, if forced to choose, he would rather suffer the death of his much beloved wife or the irreparable loss of all his poems. His silent, sad smile answers for him. Fernando Pessoa, age nineteen, seemed to be wanly accepting that poetry might be his only lifelong companion. But why did it have to be either/or? The work of many great poets is profoundly indebted to their beloved partners.

Even more self-revealing is the poem "In the Street," which is where Alexander Search happens to be walking, past rows of houses with lit windows. He muses on the family life inside the homes, laments his loneliness as the "eternally excluded / From socialness and mirth," and admits that he sometimes dreams of sitting by his own fire, next to a wife and with children scampering about. It is a dream that lasts but several stanzas before it triggers an allergic reaction, making him "shiver" and "tremble" to think that his "life might pass / Like that of men." He dreads the prospect "of a life sweet," full of "family and friends," and abhors "the houses and the street" because they are "finite." The world he inhabits and his "brother men / Are prisons, chains that bind and pen." These lines recall the aversion Pessoa felt for his "conventional" classmates at the School of Arts and Letters.

Search's madness, finally, is to repudiate the human collective and, with it, his own humanity. This rejection is announced in the epigraph to "In the Street," taken from one of Pessoa's favorite books, Carlyle's *Sartor Resartus*: "But I, *mein Werther*, sit above it all; I am alone with the stars." These words were uttered by Herr Teufelsdröckh, who, ensconced in his garret, invokes sorrowful young Werther—from Goethe's novel about an impossible love—to declare his aristocratic disdain for all the ordinary people living on the streets down below, "heaped and huddled together, with nothing but a little carpentry and masonry between them." Philosophizing Teufelsdröckh sits above them all, and also above the anxieties of love that afflicted Werther. Whether out of a similarly aristocratic disdain or owing, more simply, to social and sexual difficulties or uncertainties, Fernando Pessoa, in imitation of Carlyle's protagonist and with the help of Alexander Search, tried to place himself "above it all," with only partial success. The stars would become increasingly important for him—literally so when he took up astrology—but however high he rose, he never succeeded in completely shaking off his human longing for love. The compensations afforded him by his poetry, his ideal contemplations, and his spiritual discoveries could not make him forget his solitude.

◆

STRIKINGLY DIFFERENT FROM TORTURED and introverted Alexander Search was the vigorous and open-hearted figure of Walt Whitman, whom Pessoa had recently encountered for the first time. The clash of their sensibilities would have profound consequences for Pessoa's way of seeing and writing, though the effect of the American's influence would not be immediate. In 1907, stunned by his new discovery, the Portuguese poet hardly knew how to react.

The book that introduced Pessoa to Whitman's poetry was a small selection in *The Penny Poets* series, a cheap edition printed in London and surviving in his library. Its title page was signed with the name "A. Search" and stamped with the heteronym's florid monogram. Pessoa would return to the volume in 1914, underlining many lines of verse and making occasional comments in the margins, but even on his first reading he realized that Whitman's poetry was unlike any other he had read, in any language. Nor was there anything in his own poetry that remotely resembled lines like these:

All this I swallow, it tastes good, I like it well, it becomes mine,
I am the man, I suffer'd, I was there.

Pessoa drew an emphatic vertical line next to this declaration from "Song of Myself," the opening poem in the first edition of *Leaves of Grass* (1855), where it takes up no less than forty pages, all of them teeming with quotidian details of *real* life, whose splendor and squalor are lovingly embraced by the self who narrates them. What impressed Pessoa just as much as the headiness of the American poet's bold assertions was his poetic technique—the large and confident voice, the expansive rhythm, the concrete simplicity and directness of the language—in lines such as the following, which he underscored:

Agonies are one of my changes of garments,
I do not ask the wounded person how he feels, I myself become
    the wounded person.

The poetic technique of Whitman's narrator is all of a piece with the sentiments his words convey. Pessoa saw that, but he was still incapable of writing like that. The poem "In the Street" is Alexander Search's confession that he is not really in the street, not close to what he observes, not able to be—however fleetingly—the people mentioned in his verses, and we feel this distance whenever he speaks, no matter what the speech is about. Search talks, questions, ponders, and even exclaims, but his discourse lacks body, drama, *being*.

In a curious set of notes dating from December 1907, Pessoa classified himself, Alexander Search, and his stepuncle Henrique Rosa as *pessimistic* materialists, in contrast to Walt Whitman, an *optimistic* materialist. Whitman, he observed, united "mania of doubt, exaltation of personal-

ity, and euphory of physical 'ego.'" Pessoa, Search, and Rosa had just as
much mania of doubt (a quality, let me recall, that implied a keen power
of perception) and were exalted personalities to a lesser degree, but
Whitman alone had a euphoric "physical ego."[16] This seems to mean that
only Whitman, who describes himself as "turbulent, fleshy, sensual, eating, drinking and breeding," knew how to take rapturous delight in his
*physical* self. The *Penny Poets* selection of Whitman's poetry contained
a minuscule section titled "Songs of Sex," in which the editor regretted that questions of propriety prevented him from including important
poems such as "I Sing the Body Electric," and he made no mention at
all of "the manly love of comrades" celebrated in the collection *Calamus*,
but he noted that Whitman, in the "mere physical delight of being surrounded by human bodies [. . .] swims as in a sea."[17]

Whitman's genius was a revelation that remained, for the time
being, inaccessible to Pessoa. Though he had a remarkable talent for
imitating and appropriating, having produced admirable poems in the
style of Milton, Byron, Wordsworth, and others, he could not apply it
to a poet who encompasses all of life in a sprawling, immodestly titled
"Song of Myself." Whitman's exuberance and sexual freedom were not
in his character. And to incorporate the whole world perceived by one's
senses into an overarching poetic "I" was in a certain way contrary to
Pessoa's own project of dividing himself into many different "I"s. He
needed Alexander Search and his other youthful alter egos because he
did not know—not yet—how to be himself, nor did he know how to
be with others.

✦

WHILE WHITMAN REVELED IN the thought of being surrounded by
human bodies and immersed in everyday life, Pessoa inhabited an air-
less world of virtual companions. We saw him, when still in Durban,
embark on a literary adventure called *Ultimus Joculatorum*, or *The Last of
the Jokers*, a collection of humorous sketches that included playful interactions between some of his invented characters, who formed a kind of
club, or private society. After Pessoa left Durban, the club languished
for a couple of years, its membership having dispersed. From the letter
of heteronym Gaudêncio Nabos addressed to Pessoa and dated February 26, 1906, we can deduce that this founding member of the society
had moved to London, while another of the original Jokers, heteronym

Sidney Parkinson Stool, had immigrated to America. Stool would never be heard from again, but in 1907 Dr. Nabos, although still based in England, was summoned by Pessoa to participate once more in *Ultimus Joculatorum*, which resurfaced as a club with theatrical aspirations and with several new members, including Alexander Search, whose nickname in the club was Caesar Seek. According to Pessoa's terse descriptions on a membership list, or cast of characters, which he drew up in English, Seek's personality was "without laughter, running from deep thought and torturing to bitterness." Dr. Nabos's character ran "from bitterness to open mirth."

Originally a comic enterprise dreamed up by a high school student, *Ultimus Joculatorum* was resurrected as a Faustian performance in which the forces of light and darkness clashed. Other member-characters included a certain Erasmus Dare, who was a philanthropist, as well as a "spirit of ill" named Jacob Satan. This last character was not, however, a very evil demon. Pessoa's papers from 1907 include a curious "life-bond" entered into by Alexander Search and Jacob Satan and duly signed by both parties on October 2. The agreement obliged Search to work on behalf of humanity with the backing of Satan, who was evidently more charitable than diabolical in spirit.

Pessoa's vast drama was reminiscent not only of Goethe's *Faust* but also of medieval morality plays, with Jacob Satan and Erasmus Dare personifying evil and good, and Gaudêncio Nabos, ever a jokester, laughing at them both. The name of the only female character—before Pessoa crossed it out—was Magdalen, inspired perhaps by his mother's name, Maria Madalena, or by the biblical Mary Magdalene. Pessoa himself was a person in the drama but used, like Alexander Search, a nickname: Ferdinand Sumwan, a "someone" rather harshly characterized as a "useless, lazy, careless, weak individual."

It is hard to envision what sort of written work could have accommodated all these characters and the things they represented, and Pessoa did not seriously try to plot such a work. *Ultimus Joculatorum*—alternatively called *The Nothing Club*, or *The Zero Club*—was ultimately a "lively," performative literature, enacted by literary personae who met, according to the club notes, in a place called "Moment House," which apparently meant just that: the actual moment when the virtual meetings took place, in no physical location. Nowhere, in other words, except in Pessoa's own mind.[18]

We don't know to what extent Fernando Pessoa (alias Ferdinand Sumwan) imaginatively coexisted with Dr. Nabos, Alexander Search (alias Caesar Seek), and Jacob Satan, but he left some curious details about his relationship with yet another personality from his heteronymous circle of 1907. Around the same time that he invented the psychiatrist Dr. Faustino Antunes to help him explore and evaluate his psychological demons, he also invented a loopy English monk, Friar Maurice, with whom to wrestle over spiritual and moral issues. Defined as "a mystic without God, a Christian without a creed," Friar Maurice was experiencing a crisis of faith and suffered from mental instability. It is no wonder why. Infused with Pessoa's own religious doubts and perversely given a religious vocation, he was bound to be desperately confused. In one of the passages written for *The Book of Friar Maurice*, the godless mystic argues both for and against the idea of the soul's immortality, dividing his opinion down the middle.[19] He was similarly divided about how he viewed himself: "Half of me is noble and great, and half of me is little and vile. Both of them are me."[20]

This sounds suspiciously like Fernando Pessoa talking to himself, but the monk was not a passive mouthpiece. The game of reflection and self-division was more complex than that. An autobiographical note in English, from the fall of 1907, reads, "How gay was the dinner yesterday! How Aunts and Uncles and cousins male and female were joyous, how all was merry. All was wit, charm, warmth. Poor Friar Maurice, thou wert present, and thou wert cold, cold, cold. Poor Friar Maurice. Friar Maurice is mad. Do not laugh at Friar Maurice." When not working on *The Book of Friar Maurice*, Pessoa's religious alter ego—perhaps it would be more correct to call the friar an "alter conscience"—interfered in his daily life, in this case spoiling what could have been a perfectly enjoyable evening. The heteronyms compensated for Pessoa's lack of a vibrant social life even as they hindered the poet's relationships with real people.

◆

PORTUGAL, IN THE FRAUGHT years leading up to the Great War, was engrossed in its own internal drama, with its citizens wavering between dread and expectation. Life went on normally enough, but rumors of conspiracy against the increasingly unpopular regime abounded. Europe, meanwhile, was splitting into two adversarial camps. By the fall of 1907, the United Kingdom, Russia, and France had formed the Triple Entente, in opposition to the Triple Alliance of Germany, Austria-Hungary, and Italy. Though no one was yet talking very openly about war, the continent's most powerful nations were already drawing up sides, building up their military arsenals, and enlisting smaller countries as their proxies. In the United States the year had been marked by economic turmoil, with industrial output declining, unemployment rising, the stock market panicking, and an almost record number of businesses going bankrupt, but massive infusions of capital from J. P. Morgan and other investment bankers succeeded in restoring confidence by the end of the year, and on December 31 tens of thousands of New Yorkers stormed the hotels and restaurants to eat, drink, and sing "Auld Lang Syne." At Times Square, for the first time ever, an electric ball slowly slid down a pole during the sixty-second countdown to midnight.

On that same evening, Lisbon's theaters and restaurants filled up to capacity, but the general mood was not jubilant. It had been a cold and rainy December, turning the many unpaved streets to mud, which exacerbated the annual congestion of hired wagons freighted with furniture making their way from one domicile to another, in a city where automobiles were still few in number. The majority of apartment leases coincided with the calendar year, so that many vacating tenants were still clearing out their belongings as midnight approached, while new tenants were on the street clamoring to move in. A Vanguarda (The Vanguard), a republican newspaper, commented in a January 1 editorial that 1907 had for Portugal been a year to forget, sullied by government oppression and financial corruption.[21] João Franco, the prime minister and de facto dictator, was ensconced in his home on the northern edge of Lisbon, duly protected by policemen.

Pessoa's maternal relatives met for dinner on New Year's Day 1908, at the home of his cousin Laurinda and her husband, Aniceto Mascaró. The couple lived downtown and close to the river, on Rua do Alecrim. Fernando, who had originally agreed to accompany his great-aunts Maria and Rita to the family gathering, feigned sickness at the last minute. So we learn from a passage written in English for a personal essay, in which he grandiosely referred to his weaseling out of the dinner as his "first act of genuine revolt from the established, from the normal." He had a good rapport with his cousin and liked her husband "very much indeed." It was the large concentration of family members and his "growing distaste for society" that prompted his "first open showing of revolt." Open?

That was an odd word to describe his "revolt," given that he faked being ill. Even if his great-aunts and other relatives at the dinner suspected a ruse, surely no one had any idea that the quiet but independent-minded nineteen-year-old was staging a revolt. From an outsider's perspective, Pessoa's dropping out of the School of Arts and Letters, which caused a major rift between him and his parents, was a far more significant act of rebellion.

Pessoa was prone to convert even ordinary events into literary incidents, and the hyperbolic characterization of his no-show at the dinner naturally made for a more interesting tale. But while his incipient essay was manifestly autobiographical, since it alluded to his relatives by their proper names, the story he wanted to tell was of his *future* life. The passage he wrote was a preamble to what lay ahead and amounted to a New Year's resolution. His not going to the dinner defined, in his mind, a new stage of personal development. He had resolved, once and for all, not to court society or make concessions to his family.

So as his Aunt Maria and Aunt Rita spent a festive evening with other aunts, uncles, and cousins, the young man enjoyed having the apartment on Rua da Bela Vista à Lapa all to himself. Yet he did not spend this New Year's Day entirely alone. To keep him company there was a modest assemblage of curious "friends": Alexander Search, whose unreasonable fear of madness perhaps made Fernando feel quite sane by comparison; Dr. Faustino Antunes, who could offer him any insight he might need into his psychological state; Friar Maurice, ready and willing to debate the existence of God; the high-minded Erasmus Dare; the darkly appealing Jacob Satan; and a woman with a mother's tenderness whom he'd thought of calling Magdalen. Rounding out the group was Dr. Gaudêncio Nabos, Pessoa's good old friend from Durban, who could always be counted on to lighten things up with a funny story.

# CHAPTER 19

OKOKOKOKOKOKOKOKOKOKOKOKOKOKOKOKOK

FOR THE PORTUGUESE ROYAL FAMILY, 1908 BEGAN, like every year, with a monthlong holiday in the town of Vila Viçosa, where King Carlos and the other men staying at his country estate spent each day hunting wild game, while in the evening everyone played bridge. On February 1 the king, Queen Amélia, and Prince Luís Filipe, heir to the throne, returned to Lisbon via train, arriving at the station on the south shore of the Tagus, whose waters shimmered with the sun's reflection, for it was a perfectly clear day. A ferryboat took the royals and their attendants across the river to the Praça do Comércio, a huge open square, where they were met by the king and queen's younger son, Prince Manuel, and some government dignitaries, including João Franco, the prime minister. A small cavalcade of coaches left the dock area to set out for the royal palace on the western side of town. Despite the almost palpable tension in the air—just three days earlier, the government had put down a poorly organized coup attempt—the royal family rode as usual in an open carriage. The king wanted to project an air of confidence and normality.

But it was not just another clear and crisp winter day. As the royal coach was about to turn out of the square, conspirators who had been mixed in with the innocent bystanders emerged and opened fire on the four royals, instantly killing the king and soon afterward the crown prince. One of the assassins rushed at the carriage wielding a semiautomatic pistol, whereupon the queen struck back at him with the only weapon she had, a bouquet of flowers, and cried, "Scoundrels! Scoundrels!" The two conspirators who fired the lethal shots were killed on the spot by soldiers and policemen, while at least two others blended in with the fleeing crowd and escaped.[1]

Thus Carlos I joined the unlucky list of monarchs brutally murdered in an increasingly anxious and agitated Europe. He had been preceded by Italy's Umberto I and Serbia's Alexander I, killed in 1900 and 1903, respectively, and would be followed by King George I of Greece, shot dead in 1913. One year later the assassination of Archduke Franz Ferdinand, heir presumptive to the throne of Austria-Hungary, would precipitate the First World War.

Portugal's surviving prince, just eighteen years old and a student at the naval academy, was crowned King Manuel II. One of his first acts was to dismiss João Franco, whose mandate was blamed for breeding hostility against the monarchy. The inception of Franco's dictatorship, in May 1907, had alienated the political class, prompting some politicians from the traditional parties to consort and even conspire with republicans. Pessoa, whose antipathy for Franco was boundless, wrote a couple of hundred pages in English for an unfinished book, *History of a Dictatorship*, which proposed to analyze the prime minister's character according to "the principles of psychiatric science." Resorting to the paradigms of degeneracy, madness, and criminality developed by Nordau, Lombroso, and others, Pessoa concluded that Franco was a sophisticated type of "born criminal" who verged on insanity without actually falling into that category.[2] This fanciful diagnosis offers no real insight into Franco's behavior. An accidental autocrat thrust into that role by circumstances, he suffered from banal failings, such as poor discernment, and from the intoxicating, addictive effect of power.

Franco also merited a lot of attention—all of it negative—in Pessoa's *Extent and Causes of Portuguese Decay*, which reads more like a traditional history. In a passage for this book, Pessoa contended that Franco never had the slightest intention of carrying out the liberal reforms announced when he came to power in 1906.[3] Most historians disagree with that judgment: they acknowledge that the prime minister made some attempt at reform, but nobody wanted to cooperate, and once he became a dictator he was on his own, opposed by almost everyone except the king, who could withdraw his support at a moment's notice. Franco, on the other hand, could and occasionally did put the king in check—particularly when it came to his handling of the royal family's debts to the national Treasury. He had stirred up public wrath by revealing the extent of that indebtedness in November 1906. On August 30, 1907, he issued a decree that canceled the debts and increased the royal family's annual stipend— a measure that made King Carlos as beholden to Franco as Franco was to him. This may have guaranteed Franco's continuance as prime minister in the short run, but it exacerbated public ire toward both men, who might as well have drawn up a joint suicide pact. Franco, who had also been marked for assassination, had the good fortune to lose only his job.

✦

THE REGICIDE PROMPTED FEW expressions of outrage in Portuguese newspapers, and the public mourning for the royal victims was luke-warm. The majority did not remove their hats when the funeral proces-sion passed by. The two assassins, meanwhile, were treated as martyrs, and their mourners were more demonstrative, at least in the capital, where thousands of Lisboners descended on their graves. The rest of Europe, still largely ruled by royal dynasties, was shocked by Portugal's indifference to the loss of its murdered king, who was highly regarded by other monarchs, and particularly by Britain's King Edward VII, a personal friend. "Lisbon's Shame" read a headline in the London weekly *The Graphic*, which published a photograph of republicans placing flower wreaths on the murderers' graves.[4] How was it possible? Thanks to Car-los I's abilities as a diplomat, his country's prestige in the international arena had risen considerably since the ebb of 1890, when the British Ultimatum forced a submissive Portugal to abandon the Shire region of Africa. Unfortunately for the king, his diplomatic successes did not help his reputation at home, where he was perceived as a frivolous, spendthrift socialite who traveled too much.

Pessoa, too, swept up in the antiroyalist fervor, saw only the king's defects, remaining blind to his accomplishments. As a proud republican, it bothered him to learn, in the English periodicals he regularly pur-chased, how the Portuguese were being reviled abroad for their callous reaction to the regicide, and he decided to address the issue. He wrote some copy in English for articles he hoped to publish in Britain and the United States, explaining to his prospective readers that the king "had stolen his people's money, he had never loved nor honoured his country, he had cared for nothing save his own comfort, his own convenience." On the back of an advertising flyer dating from February 1908, the same month the king was killed, Pessoa jotted down, in English, some logical justifications for the crime: "Absolutism and regicide are complements. Each is as abnormal as the other. The best way to avoid regicide and lèse majesté is to have no king."[5]

In English and under the name of Alexander Search, Pessoa began to write a book titled *The Portuguese Regicide and the Political Situation in Portugal*. It opened with a long, theoretical discussion of the origins and symptoms of national decline. In 1909 the work in progress would give way to *The Extent and Causes of Portuguese Decay*, whose contemporary vantage point makes it an especially illuminating record. Though he wrote his history before the monarchy fell, there was no doubt in Pessoa's mind that it would and should fall. He did not side with the most radical republicans, however, nor did he condone violence as a legitimate tool for achieving commendable goals. The assassination of King Carlos and the heir to the throne was an exceptional occurrence, brought on by the monarch himself, and Pessoa defended the assassins as dedicated men who performed a noble act of self-sacrifice, but he recognized the royal deaths as a human tragedy and deplored the celebratory glee they aroused in certain quarters.

Pessoa happened to read about a particularly macabre celebration of the regicide—in the form of a Carnival-time reenactment—that took place in Salsas, a village with whitewashed, red-tiled houses in the northeast corner of Portugal. In 1908, Carnival fell at the beginning of March. As part of the local festivities, a family man from Salsas dressed up as João Franco and rode around town on a horse, while one of his sons and several other townspeople pretended to be the royal family, riding close by in a carriage. A second son, made to look like one of the assassins, suddenly ran out of the festive crowd and aimed a gun at the mock-royal carriage. Contrary to what the young man thought, the gun was loaded, and he mistakenly shot his brother dead, thus replicating a scene from Puccini's *Tosca*, whose heroine cries, "What an actor!" as her lover falls to the ground, truly dead, in what was supposed to be a sham execution. Under the title "Tragic Bad-Taste," Pessoa wrote an account of the fatal incident in English and submitted it, on March 15, to *Lloyd's Weekly News*, a mass-market newspaper published in London.

One could argue that it was in bad taste for Pessoa to publicize the story abroad. It was certainly inconsistent of him, since in other writings he complained that the British press had wrongly portrayed the Portuguese as a heartless people for not adequately grieving over the loss of their king. The card he included with his submission to *Lloyd's Weekly* clarifies his motives. It read: "Fernando Pessoa would not be above accepting remuneration for the news item enclosed, which is *absolutely true!*" With or without immediate remuneration, the author was grooming himself to be a freelance reporter and commentator. His morbidly amusing but politically inconsequential article was merely an attempt to get his foot in the door and to earn a few shillings.[6] But he submitted his article too late. Another London newspaper, *The Daily Telegraph*, had already reported on the disastrous Carnival of Salsas.[7]

Pessoa the journalist did not have any better luck in America. In May 1908 he submitted an article titled "Growth of Republicanism in Portugal," together with three photographs, to the Article Syndicate, an agency for freelancers based in New York City. The agency must have expressed tentative interest in the submission for him to go to the trouble and expense of obtaining the photos. A two-page typed original of the article, found among Pessoa's papers, was rubber-stamped with the agency's address in the upper-right-hand corner. It seems they tried to sell it and, not finding any takers, returned it to the author. "The Portuguese Monarchy is in rapid decay," began the article, which noted that the regicide aroused "little indignation and little pity," whereas a rally organized by Lisbon republicans on March 29 supposedly attracted as many as sixty thousand people—one-tenth of the city's population—who saluted the speakers with tumultuous rounds of applause. Two of the photos for the article depicted the rally.[8]

Supportive of regime change in his own country, Pessoa was sympathetic to political reform movements elsewhere, such as tsarist Russia, already in its twilight years. The Russian Revolution of 1905 had led to the creation of the Duma and some expansion of civil liberties, but the peasantry was still desperately poor and discontented—as Pessoa learned from an article published by one of Lisbon's republican newspapers in late February 1908. This inspired him to write an opinion piece evidently intended for an English newspaper, since it challenged Britain to "open the campaign" against oppression in the sprawling Eurasian nation. "In the name of liberty, in the name of Christ, in the name of all that is sacred, let us move against Russian absolutism."[9] This earnest plea stands in complete contrast to his mockery of the Russian Revolution in the last issue of *The Tattler*, from September 1905, before Pessoa's conversion to republicanism. But while he would not regret the downfall of the tsarist autocracy in 1917, he would despise Bolshevism even more. Marxism, in any of its incarnations, never appealed to Pessoa, for whom a dictatorship of the proletariat could only be a worse form of absolutism.

◆

DESPITE GLOATING OVER THE huge turnout of Lisboners for the
republican rally held in late March, Pessoa may well have stayed at home
and merely read about it in the next day's newspapers. However infected
he was by the spirit of revolution, he continued to play out his political and social enthusiasms almost entirely on paper—in his reading and
writing. English was still his preferred literary language, but he was writing more and more nonfiction in Portuguese, since he wanted to reach
out to his compatriots, and he also began writing in French, for reasons
that are harder to understand. He invented new heteronyms for expressing himself in these last two languages. And in the second half of 1908,
after his twentieth birthday, he drew up a master plan called *The Transformation Book, or The Book of Tasks*, which was designed to accommodate
his multilingual writing habits, his predilection for alter egos, and the
sundry areas of intellectual and humanistic endeavor that competed for
his attention, including literature, politics, religion, and sociology.

In its physical appearance *The Transformation Book*, a thin and crudely
handmade notebook, could not have been more unassuming, but its
contents confirmed the ambitious program announced in the title. The
neatly handwritten pages consisted of a brief curriculum vitae and a list
of writing assignments for four different heteronyms: Alexander Search,
Pantaleão, Jean Seul de Méluret, and Charles James Search. Pessoa's
intention, which he did not stick to for long, was to sign virtually all his
future literary and critical texts with one of these names. In this way he
could efficiently manage his writing projects and his heteronyms. The
transformation process was twofold, with Pessoa being metamorphosed
into four heteronyms, and these four potentialities being materialized in
the written productions set out in their "tasks." Heteronymy and writing,
according to this scheme, were practically the same thing.

The tasks assigned to Alexander Search included two collections
of poetry—*Delirium* and *Agony*—and three nonfiction works: his in-
progress book about the Portuguese regicide, an essay on rationalist philosophy, and a pamphlet titled *The Mental Disorder of Jesus*. The dozen or
so passages written for the pamphlet critiqued the recently published *La
Folie de Jésus* (*The Madness of Jesus*), by the French doctor and psycholo-
gist Charles Binet-Sanglé. Search questioned, among other things, the

author's assumption that claims of supernatural revelation were tantamount to insanity. He also pointed out that Binet-Sanglé, to argue his case for Jesus's madness, had to have faith, just like a believing Christian, in the authenticity of the four gospels that record the religious leader's life and sayings.[10] With each passing year Pessoa, though he did not believe in Christ's divinity, more willingly admitted the existence of supernatural powers.

Pantaleão—which is Portuguese for Pantalone, a stock commedia dell'arte character—was tasked with attacking the monarchy in essays such as "The Loaning Psychosis," which ironically attributed the royal family's habit of living off borrowed state money to a form of mental illness whose most salient symptom was kleptomania. Another essay, "Our Colonial Administration," argued that the Portuguese colonies, as currently administered, benefited nobody but the king and his entourage. The list of tasks for Pantaleão, who wrote exclusively in Portuguese, also includes poetry, and it was in this period—the fall of 1908—that Pessoa began writing Portuguese poems in earnest. He signed them with his own name, however. As if to compensate for not producing any poetry, Pantaleão took up several other writing "tasks" not mentioned in *The Transformation Book*. These included a group of fictional, morally instructive letters and some random reflections and aphorisms.

Just as Pantaleão was supposed to handle most of Pessoa's writing in Portuguese, Jean Seul was to take care of just about everything he wrote in French. That included poetry, and although only one poem was actually signed by Seul, Pessoa apparently intended for his only French heteronym to be the nominal author of all the verses he produced in that language. Jean Seul, however, would soon vanish from the stage, and so it was in his own name that Pessoa, throughout the rest of his life, wrote occasional poems in French, three of which he would publish in a Portuguese magazine.[11] Since he never set foot in a French-speaking country, not even for a brief visit, the poems he wrote in that language are in a certain way even more remarkable than his English poems. They're also marred by some of the same problems—stilted diction, tonal disparities—and even by outright grammatical errors.

Jean Seul, according to his CV in *The Transformation Book*, was born on August 1, 1885, and his main task was to write "satire or scientific works with a satirical or moral purpose." The CV lists three titles of such works, all of which were left as an assortment of disconnected fragments. The most startling work, *La France en 1950* (*France in 1950*), graphically imagines the future of a country where sensuality, sex, and sexual perversion dictate every facet of society and daily life. In fact we can read it as a kind of precursor to Orwell's *Nineteen Eighty-Four*, with the Sexual Imperative taking the place of Big Brother. We can also think of it as a sequel to Sade's *120 Days of Sodom*. People wash dishes with the blood of raped and murdered children. Animal sperm, after a run as a favorite beverage, has fallen out of fashion. Instead of technical schools, there is an École de Masturbation and an École de Sadisme, staffed by Professors of Abortion and Infanticide. A girls' school called the Institut Sans Hymen teaches students to be as lascivious and perverted as possible, with severe punishment meted out to anyone who betrays a hint of shame or modesty. French newspapers report that four-year-olds have been committing suicide when jilted by their adult lovers. And so forth.

Pessoa began writing *La France en 1950* and another satire, *Messieurs les souteneurs* (*Messieurs Pimps*), in late 1907, even before he invented Jean Seul, who became their fictitious author retroactively. The third essay on his list of tasks, *Des Cas d'exhibitionnisme* (*Cases of Exhibitionism*), was conceived in 1908, around the same time as Seul, who informs us in his introduction that exhibitionism is but one nefarious result of the "*forces de décadence*" affecting modern society, most especially in France. Couched as a scientific study, the essay focuses not on dirty old men who open their trousers to exhibit their genitalia to unsuspecting passersby but on the "*perversion sexuelle*" of scantily clad women in Paris's music halls. The essay also mentions Maud Allan, a Canadian dancer who had become famous in Europe for her sensuous interpretation of Salomé in a play loosely based on Oscar Wilde's *Salomé*. (Pessoa would write his own version of *Salomé*, around 1916 or 1917.) The upshot of Seul's analysis was that French girlie shows and performers such as Allan heralded the decline of Western civilization.[12]

Licentiousness in literature and the performing arts was by no means the exclusive province of Paris. Germany's Frank Wedekind (1864–1918) and Austria's Arthur Schnitzler (1862–1931) had boldly dealt with human sexuality—including (in the case of Wedekind) homosexuality, masturbation, and sadomasochism—in plays that incited bourgeois indignation and were banned as pornographic.* Information about the two playwrights was hard to come by in Portugal, and Pessoa knew little or nothing about them. He was familiar, on the other hand, with French authors in the same generation, including Victorien du Saussay and Jane de la Vaudère, whose decadent novels about adultery, incest, drug addiction, and other behaviors classifiable as vices (one of Saussay's novels was titled *The School of Vice*) were much translated and read in Portugal. Jean Seul disparagingly alludes to them in his introduction to *Messieurs Pimps*, in which the "pimps" are in fact racy novelists. Although Berlin—home to the first gay journal, *Der Eigene*, founded in 1896—was in certain respects just as sexually liberal as Paris, the Portuguese depended on France to supply them with titillating literature and traveled to the French capital if they wished to see half-naked girls on stage. Hence Pessoa-Seul's association of sexual prurience with France.

While it obviously delighted Pessoa to describe outlandish sexual and social behaviors in French, less clear is the exact object of his Jean Seul satires. Was he heaping ridicule on a decadent society and a degenerate literature obsessed with sex and sensuality? Or was he, more subtly, ridiculing the moralists preoccupied with nudity on stage, sexual permissiveness, and decadent writing? Even when it isn't waving or winking at the reader, satire often lurks under the surface in Pessoa, who took almost nothing very seriously except for his vocation to question, to rethink, and to reword. At the end of *Degeneration*, Max Nordau imagined a future in which every city in Europe would have clubs for mutual assassination by strangulation, taverns for drinking all manner of filth, professional injectors of morphine and cocaine, male citizens mostly dressed up as women and female citizens dressed up as men, and theaters where erotic and bloody homicides would be regularly staged, with flocks of volunteers waiting in line to voluptuously die while spectators deliriously cheer.[13] Jean Seul's even more lurid vision of France's decadently concupiscent future was a spoof on Nordau, whose dire prognosis on the state of culture and the world at large did not persuade Pessoa. At any rate, there was no reason to fret. If French civilization is moribund because

---

* Wedekind's sexually themed plays, it must be said, were largely inspired by his experience as a bohemian in Paris between 1892 and 1895.

decadent, then some other civilization will replace it—so Seul placidly remarks in his conclusion to *Des Cas d'exhibitionnisme*.

The Jean Seul enterprise was not entirely tongue-in-cheek, however. Pessoa really was worried about the effect of liberalized sexual mores on society. In unpublished notes dating from around 1908 and containing not a trace of irony, he wrote (in English) of the need to create "a moral sense" in Portugal, where the "degeneration of modern times" had led to "coarseness and dirtiness" in people's speech. Not only that, lewd postcards and "books of the obscenest kind" were shamelessly displayed in shopwindows. (Now we know how the pubescent poet, during his trip to Portugal in 1901–1902, managed to acquire the "indecent French and Portuguese comic papers" that he showed his classmate Geerdts back in Durban.) Pessoa, who counted on the republicans to overthrow a corrupt monarchy and sanitize Portugal's political system, also hoped that the nation's citizens would become purer in speech and thought. It dismayed him that the editor of *A Luta* (*The Struggle*), one of the republican papers he read regularly, thought it perfectly "natural and pure that naked women should be exposed in music-halls (as in Paris)." In defense of his position, the newspaper editor quoted St. Paul's dictum that "to the pure all things are pure." True enough, conceded Pessoa in his notes, "but where are the pure? They are very few."[14]

Pessoa was prudish, paternalistic, and elitist. The Pauline wisdom on purity was fine for a rarefied segment of society, but most people could not be trusted to live without rules. They needed to be continually moralized and their sexual instincts controlled. Not even Pessoa, in this case, formed part of the elite. He was worried about *his own* sexual instincts as much as about anyone else's. Sex for him was something dirty, not pure. He had acquired considerable knowledge on the subject, as we know from his writings, including those of Jean Seul, but actual sex? actual naked women? He cringed at the thought. The host of salacious characters he invented for Seul to write about with horrifying exaggeration may have been partly for his own benefit, to confirm him in his preference for chastity.

Rounding out Pessoa's transformative quartet of heteronyms was self-effacing Charles James Search, born on April 18, 1886, which made him two years older than Alexander, his brother, and half a year younger than Jean Seul. (Pantaleão's date of birth was not revealed.) Too modest to write anything of his own, Charles's task was to render literary works from Portuguese into English.[15] His translation projects included a novel by Eça de Queiroz, *The Mandarin*, a selection of sonnets by Luís de Camões, and poetry by Henrique Rosa, who had by now become a close friend as well as a mentor. The older intellectual showed his poems to his stepnephew, lent him books, and met with him in cafés—unless, of course, the retired general was in one of those periods when, unable to bear the outside world, he remained contentedly shut up in his apartment among his books like Jean Des Esseintes, the misanthropic protagonist of Huysman's *Against Nature*.

Besides identifying with his stepuncle as a poet, republican, and skeptic, Pessoa shared with him an inclination to spend long hours all alone, far from the madding crowd. Persuaded, however, that it was unhealthy to be too wrapped up in himself and in his books, he was trying to be more sociable and more socially involved. *The Transformation Book, or The Book of Tasks* was meant to be a turning point. It replaced *Ultimus Joculatorum*, which had played out Pessoa's inner world though symbolic figures such as the "good" Erasmus Dare and the "bad" Jacob Satan, without a larger focus than himself. Dr. Faustino Antunes and Friar Maurice, heteronyms that had lately attended to the poet's psychological and spiritual needs, also fell into oblivion. In 1908 *The Transformation Book* radically reconfigured Pessoa's heteronymous energies for the sake of two extroverted goals: the revitalization of his country and the civilizing of humanity at large. Pantaleão would work toward mobilizing the Portuguese to bring down their moribund monarchy and make way for a republic; Jean Seul would address the problem of Europe's decaying morals; Charles Search would burnish Portugal's international image by translating some of its fine literature into English; and Alexander Search would explain to Britain and the rest of the world, in English, why the regicide had been unavoidable and the Portuguese monarchy was doomed to fall. Alexander, ever since his emergence in 1906, was the most dynamic of Pessoa's alter egos and naturally stood out as the central ego in the system. His CV in *The Transformation Book*, besides listing specific writing projects, mentions one vastly general task: "all not the province of the other three."

Alexander Search's psychological proximity to his creator gave rise to some confusion about who was who. On October 30, 1908, he signed a long diaristic text that begins: "No soul more loving or tender than mine has ever existed, no soul so full of kindness, of pity, of all the things of tenderness and of love." Endowed with such a bountiful well of human love and kindness, Pessoa's heteronym was the fittest agent possible to work on behalf of the humanitarian and patriotic impulses outlined further on in the same text. An "intense desire of bettering the condition of Portugal" arouses in Mr. Search "a thousand plans," including his "writing of Portuguese pamphlets" to help spark a revolution, "the editing of older national, literary works," the "creation of a magazine" and of a "scientific review," and his "Jean Seul projects." But so many writing and publication plans, combined with an overwhelming urgency to carry them out quickly, paralyzes his will, so that he can accomplish little of what he wants to do and suffers, as a result, "on the very brink of madness."

While the real architect of all those plans was clearly Pessoa, the exaggerated fear of looming insanity belonged only to Alexander Search. And yet Dr. Faustino Antunes's diagnosis of mental illness in his "patient" named Fernando Pessoa, however clever a ruse it was to elicit opinions about his character from people he had known in Durban, contained a grain of truth. Although not mad, he sincerely feared that he might inherit, along with her money, his grandmother's madness, and he suffered from the vertigo of "a thousand plans" that he could not begin to keep straight, much less execute, his head forever bursting with new interests, new ideas, new ambitions. . . . This surfeit of mental divagations pulling him in myriad directions felt to Pessoa, no doubt, like the possible beginnings of a mental breakdown.

A weak, sometimes paralyzed will that prevented him from carrying out the torrent of ideas his mind kept on generating was one of his ongoing complaints—he would purchase a self-help book titled *Have You a Strong Will?* sometime after 1912—but no amount of will could adequately tame such a chaotic effusion. Besides the proliferating streams of new ideas and new interests, there was a continual welling up of new voices, the heteronyms, which Pessoa resourcefully put to work as vehicles for converting his impulses into doable writing projects. These heteronyms served another, related purpose. Pessoa relied on their mediation to avoid, or at least disguise, the contradiction inherent in his individualist ambition to be an altruist through his writing. He solved the problem of self-centeredness, at least at the formal level, by transferring his aspirations to subsidiary personalities.

*The Transformation Book* was his exemplary test case for regulating and methodically implementing his ambitions by way of his alter egos, but it was very soon abandoned. Unable to follow any kind of method, no matter how sui generis, Pessoa wrote a fair number of pages for most of the works listed as "tasks" in *The Transformation Book*, without finishing any of them. He was distracted, as usual, by the emergence of new writing projects and also by the exhilarating awareness that everything he wrote would soon have a sure outlet: his own publishing house, for which he was already laying plans, as the cited diaristic text makes clear. From those plans—the publication of Portuguese classics, a magazine, a science journal—it is also clear that he did not waver in his commitment to be a transformer of society, particularly of Portuguese society.

✦

EAGER TO CONNECT DIRECTLY with his people, King Manuel II, who was one year younger than Pessoa, traveled extensively around Portugal in 1908 and was warmly received wherever he went. But republicanism had already won over the citizens of Lisbon, who felt cautiously excited, and a little nervous, uncertain how such a novel political system, if it prevailed, would affect them. As revealed in his personal notes, and as demonstrated by his publication plans, Pessoa yearned to do his part to make sure that the new system was victorious and to help shape his country's future. Paradoxically, he was at the same time making plans to leave Portugal. That summer he drew up a "List of Things for Voyage" in a small notebook. A second list of "Necessary Things," found among some of his political writings produced the same year, includes many of the same items: a valise, a serviette, assorted clothes and accessories, a camera, and a folding bed.[16] The destination for his anticipated journey could only be royalist, Edwardian England, where Pessoa had been vaguely planning to go ever since 1906, a few months after having returned from South Africa. Pessoa's plans continued to be hazy, despite what his checklists of travel items might suggest, but soon he would have the wherewithal to finance a voyage. In 1909, on the day he turned twenty-one, he would come into his inheritance.

Like his dreamed-of publishing house, Pessoa's proposed trip was part of a strategy to further his writing career, which would—he believed— advance more quickly and more enduringly in the English language. He prepared for his journey by trying to establish a few contacts in England. In the spring of 1908, he wrote a letter of inquiry about becoming a

member of the Quill Club, an association in London that provided various services for beginning and established authors, and not just through
the mail. If he joined the club, he would be entitled to attend its regularly
scheduled meetings, where he could make connections and learn some
practical tips for getting published.

Pessoa probably signed his letter to the Quill Club as Alexander
Search, the same name he used in a letter to Sprigg, Pedrick & Company, a London literary agency. Failing to get a response from Sprigg
or Pedrick or their company, he wrote them again on April 21, 1908,
renewing his request for information about how their agency operated. When that information finally arrived, he drafted the following,
brief reply:

My brother is at present in Spain and is therefore unable early to
reply to your letter of the [*date left blank*] instant. He will be back
in a few days, when I will give it him immediately.
> Very faithfully,
> Chas. Search

Since his archives contain no further mention of Sprigg, Pedrick & Company, we can only speculate about whether Pessoa actually sent a reply
like this draft and about what motivated him to proceed with so much
artifice. Did he want to pave the way for Charles James Search to submit
his translations of Portuguese poetry into English? Was he concocting
an international reputation for Alexander, whose foray into Spain, if all
went well, would be followed up by a trip to Britain? Although he left no
details, he evidently wanted to create a larger family story. The margins
of the epistolary draft signed by Charles contain signatures for two other
members of the clan: Catherine Search and Augustus Search. Perhaps
Pessoa, making his voyage to England, intended to land there as Alexander Search, with a packet of English poems ready for submission to
publishers and a few stories to tell about his three siblings back in Lisbon. Unless Catherine and Augustus, rather than siblings, were meant
to be Charles and Alexander's parents.[17]

Pessoa's fondness for the character Pip, whose name he borrowed
for one of his earliest heteronyms, probably had to do with the city of
London, where the teenaged Pip moves in order to become a gentleman and fulfill his great expectations. Like Dickens's protagonist, Pes-

soa had grand designs for his prospective journey to the English capital. No less grand were the hopes he nurtured for a Portuguese publishing house. The two aspirations did not have to be mutually exclusive and were in fact complementary. There is no document to prove it, but I suspect that Pessoa's idea, at this point, was to spend six months or a year in London—enough time to become familiar with the literary milieu and make inroads there with his own work—before setting himself up as a publisher in Lisbon. Perhaps Alexander Search would stay on in England to promote himself as an English poet and to spread his republican ideas, while Pessoa would return home alone to focus on his own poetry, his writings to foment revolution, and the creation of a publishing house he hoped could rival the best publishers in London.

# CHAPTER 20

A LTHOUGH HE HAD ROUNDED THE CAPE OF GOOD
Hope three times and sailed up through the Suez Canal and
across the Mediterranean Sea on a fourth voyage, Pessoa
had not once ventured beyond the vicinity of Lisbon—except in his
imagination—since returning from Africa in 1905. Yet, in spite of being
surrounded by Portuguese people, Portuguese language, and Portuguese
culture, at the age of twenty he was still an almost exclusively English-
language poet. The few political poems he had written in Portuguese,
for the earnest purpose of overthrowing the monarchy, were short and
satirical pieces that delivered little more than witty jibes and denunciatory punches. Then, in mid-November of 1908, as if a muse had suddenly
blessed him with a brand-new voice, he wrote a flurry of lyrical poems
in Portuguese unlike anything he had so far produced, in any language.
They were more delicate and evocative than the poems in English signed
by Alexander Search and less self-consciously literary than the Portuguese poems Pessoa had written as a thirteen-year-old, when he spent a
year in Portugal.

One of his poems in the new style ponders the horrifying possibility
of his dying young, like Keats, the poem's dedicatee, without having had
time enough to put all that his soul feels into poetry. That fear could be
partly what led him to start writing in Portuguese. Though deaf to the
slight stiffness and occasional wrong note in his English poetry, Pessoa
began to realize that there were feelings he could better express in his
native tongue, the one he heard and spoke every day. He had also begun
to read Portuguese poetry more closely. According to Pessoa's own
account, he was influenced in this period by national poets such as João
Almeida Garrett (1799–1854), Antero de Quental (1842–1891), Cesário
Verde (1855–1886), António Nobre, and Guerra Junqueiro.[1] Included in
this illustrious list was the name of Henrique Rosa, his prolific but poetically unremarkable stepuncle, who was bound to be an important influ-

ence given that he was the first flesh-and-blood poet Pessoa had ever spent any time with. Rosa instilled in him an appreciation for certain themes, such as world-weariness.

Of all the poets mentioned, Antero de Quental was the one whom critics admired most at the beginning of the twentieth century, and he was also the most widely translated. Pessoa, who seems not to have known about the *Sixty-four Sonnets* by Quental published in London, in 1894, worked on English translations of more than thirty of Quental's sonnets, none of which he finished. Quental was born on the Azorean island of São Miguel and died there, a suicide, but he spent most of his life in mainland Portugal, where he studied law, helped to organize the anarchist and socialist workers' movements, and struggled with depression throughout his adult life. A philosophical pessimist (like Henrique Rosa), he built his poems around large ideas and concepts: the vanity of human endeavor, Love, Reason, the death of God, transcendence, and so forth. Attracted to this poet's religiously skeptical humanist outlook and similarly afflicted by bouts of despondency, Pessoa mentioned him in an anguished autobiographical note written on September 5, 1908, in English: "I am never happy, neither in my selfish nor in my unselfish moments. My solace is reading Antero de Quental. We are, after all, brother-spirits. Oh, how I understand that deep suffering that was his."[2]

Questions about the nature of God and the more basic question of whether God even exists fascinated Pessoa as a young man, and sonnets by Quental such as "O Inconsciente" ("The Unconscious"), in which God is portrayed as an ancient ghost that haunts human minds but whose reality is in doubt, inspired him to sketch some stanzas in English for a book of his own sonnets to be titled, in Latin, *Mors Dei*.[3] He had already used the same title in English, *Death of God*, for collections of poems signed by C. R. Anon and Alexander Search, both of whom were noticeably influenced by Quental, a poet Pessoa read for the first time as a teenager in Durban.

It is harder to detect Quental's influence on Pessoa's Portuguese poetry. While both poets loved to grapple with weighty ideas, Pessoa's language—when he wrote in his mother tongue—was more musical, and his poems more sensitively shaped. Consider two stanzas from his poem "Mar. Manhã." ("Ocean. Morning."), written in November 1909:

The rolling of an ocean wave
Resembles a living thing:
A snake that slithers forward
With placid turns and twists.

United, vast and unending
In the peaceful solar blue,
The ocean unmovingly pitches,
Drunk on the dawn's rosy hue.

Even in translation we can see how the words of the poem are bonded to their referents, in lines that wavingly move like the surging ocean they describe. Quental's poetry, by and large, is conceptually and linguistically less nuanced. His words typically convey an idea through a narrative whose effectiveness depends on the punch line.

Pessoa took up some of Quental's philosophical speculations, and also the antiroyalist and anticlerical themes he found in Guerra Junqueiro's poetry, but it was other poets, such as Garrett, who taught him how to be lyrical in Portuguese. Garrett, the towering figure of Portuguese Romanticism, was a playwright and novelist as well as a poet, and his poetic discourse often feels dramatic, as if it were taking place on stage. This is especially true in his later poetry, which favored colloquial language and popular verse forms. It was after Pessoa read or else reread Garrett's poetry, in 1908, that, challenging himself to do even better, he began writing lyric poetry in Portuguese.[4] The stylistic similarities between the two poets are easy to trace, though their subject matter is rather different. Garrett's poems are often addressed to beloved women, or they soliloquize on the lover's doubts and frustrations. Pessoa wrote a few poems in this vein, including one for a "Linda Maria" ("Lovely Maria"), written that November, but he much more often used poetry to dramatize his Quental-like anxieties about living in a world ruled by unknown forces.

Pessoa enacted his existential concerns with penetrating directness in *Fausto*, a verse drama he wrote in Portuguese, whose protagonist stares relentlessly into the abyss of the unknown and into his own unknowable soul. Pessoa's interest in reinventing the legend that sprang up around the life of Faust, a sixteenth-century alchemist and magician, was first revealed by *Ultimus Joculatorum*, the drama in which his own life seemed to be at stake, with cosmic forces (including a spirit of evil, Jacob Satan) competing for influence. The direct inspiration for this sketchy, preparatory drama as well as for Pessoa's deeply self-exploratory *Fausto* was Goethe's *Faust*, which the poet owned and read in an English translation. He would also acquire a copy of Christophe Marlowe's *The Tragical History of Dr. Faustus.*[5] Yet one of the chief points of dramatic tension in these two famous plays—namely, the eternal destiny of the protagonist's soul—did not in the least interest Pessoa. In his own version of the legend, where the Devil hardly appears, Faust's drama is basically that he thinks too much. He agonizes over the nature of life and of consciousness, dreaming versus reality, what has been and what will be, and the possibility of other realities, other levels of existence. The regrettable consequence of his fanatical search for knowledge is that it prevents him from actively engaging with life itself.

Or is it the other way around? Perhaps his dread of acting and interacting causes him to take refuge in solitary intellectual pursuits.

Pessoa began his *Fausto* in the fall of 1908 and worked on it steadily for the next several years, then intermittently until at least 1933, leaving more than two hundred passages that he never attempted to piece together, although he drew up several synopses and occasionally indicated which act a given passage belonged to. Adding to the confusion, at a certain point he decided to create a second and a third version of the Faust story, but most of the passages he wrote (usually in blank verse but sometimes rhymed) seem to be for the first version. Besides the speeches of Faust himself, there are a few characters with bit parts as well as a few stage directions, which make it possible to organize the swirl of disordered text into a quasi-coherent drama. Very different renditions of Pessoa's play have been assembled and staged in Portugal, France, and elsewhere.

Pessoa also conceived a female character, Maria, who loves Faust "in the way love loves," without knowing why, irrationally, but the hero is beyond being able to reciprocate. In his planning notes for the development of Faust's dialogue with Maria, Pessoa wrote that "the chasm existing between him and love begins as a chasm existing between him and his own self."[6] Like most of the *Fausto* material, these notes are undated, but the explanation of why Faust cannot give in to love is valid for the explainer himself at any point in his adult life. The chasm tending to separate Pessoa from all feelings of love and even from his feeling self was due, as it was in the eponymous protagonist of his *Fausto*, to a hyperactive consciousness. It is not that Pessoa felt less than other people; he felt more. But whatever he felt became an instant object of reflection and analysis, as well as potential subject matter for his writing.

Along with lyrical poetry and his somber, sometimes stifling *Fausto*, Pessoa's sudden burst of Portuguese writing included a few humorous poems, one of which was published in late 1908, in the *New Portuguese-Brazilian Almanac of Remembrances for the Year 1909*.[7] This hugely popular compendium of fun facts and useful information also included some light and not so light literature, as well as dozens of riddles, which were often rather elaborate productions. Pessoa's contribution to the almanac was a riddle in the form of a poem whose speaker declares his love to a beautiful woman in twenty-nine wittily rhyming lines. He could more easily write about love when it was in theory, in jest, or in the name of someone else. His poetic riddle was signed by Gaudêncio Nabos, his comic heteronym who worked as a physician. Dr. Nabos, who spoke only English back in Durban but was now bilingual, would remain active until at least 1914, by which time his jokes and stories were exclusively in Portuguese.[8] As a humorist, Dr. Nabos had to deftly wield everyday language to comic effect, so it was only natural that he switched to speaking Portuguese, the language that ultimately came most naturally to Pessoa.

The exalted transports of his lyric poetry, the anxieties of his mentally tortured Faust, and the breezy mirth of Dr. Nabos were all moods of feeling and modes of writing that coexisted in Pessoa's capaciously creative self.

◆

PESSOA'S BLOSSOMING AS A Portuguese-language poet was stimulated by the knowledge that in 1909 he could finally use his inherited wealth to launch a publishing house in Lisbon. To produce a line of books for the Portuguese market, he would need original writing in that language, and why not writing by him and his fictitious collaborators? But he looked forward to more than just becoming a bona fide published author, or series of authors; he wanted to use his printed words to promote republicanism. This latter ambition could be achieved more quickly and effectively through journalistic publications, which were therefore one of his editorial priorities. And so, several months before his twenty-first birthday, when he would gain unrestricted access to the five million reis left him by his grandmother, Pessoa created—in a spirit of diversion but also as preparation—a "newspaper" devoted to politics. In fact, he launched not one but two mock newspapers, each affiliated with an imaginary political party. More sophisticated than the handwritten efforts of his teenage years, these newspapers, although not typeset, were at least typewritten and mechanically reproduced, using a mimeograph.

On April 14, 1909, the first issue of *O Progresso* (*Progress*) rolled off the duplicating machine. Subtitled a "Radical Newspaper," it was the official organ of the opposition party, whose members included Fernando Pessoa, his cousin Mário Freitas, and Raul da Costa, who was a distant cousin to Fernando and a first cousin to Mário. All three were members of the parliament of an unnamed republic. On April 16 the same mimeograph produced the first and only issue of *A Civilização* (*Civilization*), which represented the party in power, one of whose leaders was Armando Couto, likewise a distant cousin on Fernando's mother's side.

Raul and Armando were both born in Lisbon in 1890, just two years after Fernando, who seems to have had little or no contact with them when they were children. Now they were part of his social circle—or rather, he was part of the circle that they and several others formed with his first cousins, Mário and Maria. Fernando remained on the periphery, observing more than participating. The cousinly clan spent occasional weekends and part of each summer in Trafaria, a popular beach town on the other side of the Tagus and easily reached from Lisbon by ferryboat. Originally a fishing village, it had in recent years opened up a number of small hotels and even a modest "casino," with a restaurant and entertainment but no gambling, except perhaps bingo. Mário and Maria's mother, Anica, also liked to spend her holidays in Trafaria, and Fernando went there at least once.

But wading in the water, strolling on the strand, and sitting in the casino hall to hear the local band did not appeal to him in the least. His way of joining in the fun was by writing about it. The main parliamentary proposal discussed in his mimeographed newspapers, *Progress* and *Civilization*, was the founding of a recreational club in Trafaria and the construction of a "chalet" for the use of club members. Congressman Mário Freitas and Congressman Raul da Costa signed "letters to the editor," but these were obviously written by Pessoa, like everything else in the newspapers. There is a passing mention of Congressman Fernando

Pessoa, stating that he had published a few poems in English and was "always a great bantam poet; when still breast-feeding, he was already reciting verses to his wet nurse, the rascal." Inventing political parties and politicians preoccupied with ludicrous issues came easily to Pessoa, who had learned to play at politics as a little boy, through his abundantly imaginative uncle Cunha.[9]

Pessoa's indifference to sun and surf was not the only reason he preferred writing about Trafaria in his newspapers to actually going there. He also had no aptitude for getting romantically involved, which was the chief attraction of the place for his friends. His cousin Mário spent the better part of his time at the beach wooing Helena, the younger sister of Raul da Costa, who in turn devoted his attentions to Mário's reciprocally attentive sister, Maria. It was also in Trafaria that Maria's best friend, Clara, met and fell in love with Armando Couto. In a few years' time, all three couples would be married. Amid all the handholding, kissing, and fond gazing that went on as the sun beat down and gentle waves lapped the shore, Fernando felt singularly out of place.

Although not an outgoing type, Pessoa was witty and hit it off well enough with other young men. It was with women around his own age that he felt ill at ease. They intimidated him, and sometimes he, out of self-defense, intimidated them. When Clara first met him, he went out of his way to talk and act idiosyncratically, and it rattled her. That was in 1906, when Pessoa was studying and living with Aunt Anica, who had invited her best friend from the Azores, Palmira, and Palmira's daughter, Clara, to visit her family in Lisbon. Palmira and Clara ended up living with Anica for over a year, overlapping for a few months with Fernando, who was three years older than Clara. Instead of charming her with his fluent English, tales about his life in exotic South Africa during the Anglo-Boer War, and anecdotes from his present life as a student at the School of Arts and Letters, he mostly aroused suspicion with his quirky behavior. Afraid he might sneak into their room to scare them in the middle of the night, she enlisted her mother's aid to barricade the door with furniture.

Palmira and Clara ended up renting their own apartment in Lisbon and never returned to the Azores. They became part of the family that orbited around Aunt Anica, and despite their earlier apprehensions, they got on well with Pessoa, as they did with everyone else in the family. But he was not like everyone else.[10]

✦

THREE ISSUES OF *PROGRESS* and just one issue of *Civilization* were "published" in mid-April. According to Pessoa's notes from 1909, he owed Mário Freitas twenty reis for each issue.[11] The mimeograph machine belonged to Mário, who had turned eighteen in February and was already a businessman. Unlike Fernando, he could freely draw on the inheritance left by his father without having to wait until he was twenty-one. Anica, Mário's mother, was an unusually accommodating estate trustee. Fernando was full of ideas on how his cousin should invest his capital, and the mimeograph was one of them. Besides serving as a useful office tool, it could make money as a cheap alternative to printing for customers needing multiple copies of flyers, form letters—and make-believe newspapers. Fernando was probably his cousin's first customer. Besides giving him a feel for doing journalistic layout using a mechanical reproduction process, even if a mimeograph was a far cry from movable type, Pessoa's "newspapers" allowed him to test Mário's enthusiasm and better evaluate what role, if any, his cousin might play in his publishing house.

The two cousins were already collaborating on another business venture: the Anglo-Portuguese Mining Agency. The money at stake was all Mário's, but the "Anglo" angle came from Fernando. The idea was to secure British investment capital for Portuguese mining operations, with the agency earning a commission on the amount of capital invested. The young men compiled two lists of Portuguese mines, one that classified them by location, and the other by the type of ore extracted: antinomy, copper, iron, lead, silver, tin, wolframite, etc. Next they drew up a questionnaire for proprietors interested in selling or leasing their mines. They also obtained detailed reports on specific mines, some of which Fernando translated into English.

The agency had its office on Rua Bella da Rainha, in the heart of downtown Lisbon, where Fernando loved to while away his afternoons.[12] Tired of living with his aging great-aunts Maria and Rita, he felt oddly at home among desks, typewriters, ledgers, and briefcases, and on streets where men in dark suits walked with brisk steps as if they had very important things to do. No, the sunlit beach was not for him. He preferred the dusky offices and right-angled streets of Lisbon's commercial district. It was not only to publish his literary works and a republican newspaper that he dreamed of opening a publishing house; he also wanted to become a businessman.

# CHAPTER 21

**P**ESSOA WAS SUPPOSEDLY IN A BARBERSHOP, getting a shave and a trim, when he spotted an ad in the newspaper for a used printing press. With his face still partly covered with lather, he jumped out of the chair and, brandishing the paper, ran out of the shop in a mad rush to contact the seller before anyone else did. It was Pessoa's younger half brother who would report this story, which apparently circulated among the poet's survivors. However much they may have enhanced it (the shaving foam seems an added flourish), the essential facts of the story were true: on August 5, 1909, Pessoa saw a newspaper ad for a printing press, and he proceeded to close a deal as soon as possible.[1]

António Maria Silvano, the great-uncle who administered Pessoa's inherited estate, must have heaved a worried sigh when he heard how the young man was going to invest his money, but at this point he could not stop him. Two and a half months earlier, on May 26, Silvano had drawn up a balance sheet of credits and debits for recent activity in the heir's estate. The credits included large dividend payments on twenty-four shares of stock in the Bank of Portugal and slightly exceeded Pessoa's debits, which were for his room and board and other living expenses. The amount of ready cash in his account, though considerable, was not exactly a fortune, but the bank shares were worth well over four million reis,[2] the equivalent of sixteen years of room and board. Pessoa did not need his prudent uncle to point out that the dividend income from the bank shares, as demonstrated by the balance sheet, was just enough to cover his basic expenses. In other words, he could live off the estate, as long as he lived frugally, without ever touching the principal. The young poet could only have smiled. His imagination was far too large and lively to give such a reasonable, uninspired idea any serious consideration.

Meanwhile, Pessoa's stepfather had prevailed on his two brothers in Lisbon to find a job for Fernando that could develop into a career.

Henrique Rosa was too withdrawn from the practical world to be of much help, but Júlio Leopoldo Rosa succeeded in the search: Pessoa was offered a position at Vacuum Oil Company with a starting salary of twenty-five thousand reis per month.[3] If he stuck with it, he would soon be promoted and earn significantly more, but he rejected out of hand the idea of working for someone else at a job with set hours. Being his own boss, he could potentially earn much more, while at the same time doing something for literature and for Portugal.

He turned twenty-one in June and, with inheritance in hand, acted quickly. The printing press he saw advertised in August was located in Portalegre, a district capital near the Spanish border—one hundred miles east of Lisbon, but it took him six hours to get there by train. The local economy revolved around cork, olive oil, lumber, and livestock, but Pessoa was only interested in his printing press, which was being carefully dismantled and packed for shipping. On August 24, after having drunk a lot of "decidedly alcoholic" wine at the Hotel Brito, he wrote an "epistolary composition," in English, to Armando Teixeira Rebelo, the classmate from the School of Arts and Letters who had also spent time in South Africa as a child. He remarked that the weather was exceedingly hot, that there was nothing to do in the town except "get tired of doing nothing," and that it was "taking a damned long time" to get everything ready to ship. Although his tone is jocular throughout, the mild desperation expressed at the end of the letter seems to have been authentic. He complained of "hyper-boredom" and of "ultra-get-tired-of-everythingness," yet he was "unable to summon energy" to read a book he'd found.

It was probably not energy but concentration that Pessoa could not muster for reading the book, even though reading was his favorite pastime. His mind was too busy whirling with plans. But the next day, still in Portalegre, he did manage to sketch an Alexander Search poem:

What is life that we should care for it?
What is love that we should bear for it
Hope and despair and misery?

Nothing is worth anything.
Let us shut out hope, [*line left incomplete*]
And cross our arms and close our eyes
And let apathy be king.[4]

Eager as he was to set up shop as a publisher, Pessoa shielded himself with a protective layer of apathy. The first stanza above justifies his ambitious enterprise: win or fail, he would at least not simply have lived and loved the way most people do. The second stanza establishes an attitude of sublime detachment from the project, which he suddenly realized was risky. The path to success was laden with pitfalls, and he was placing his entire inherited fortune on the line, but in a certain part of his being he decided to cross his arms and close his eyes, leaving the whole business in the hands of fate. While this attitude may have buffered him against whatever disappointment might follow, it also guaranteed that success was unlikely. Pessoa dedicated only part of his heart and soul to the business, and in that heart dwelled an aristocrat, unwilling to get his hands dirty. His enterprise would rely almost entirely on hired help.

The used printing press cost Pessoa around one million reis, almost a quarter of his inheritance, and he had to pay to have it dismantled, shipped, and reassembled in Lisbon. He also needed additional equipment and replacement parts, which he purchased through Aniceto Mascaró, the cousin by marriage who had arranged for his brief internship at R. G. Dun two years earlier. The entrepreneurial Mascaró, who got involved in various businesses over the years, had recently opened a Lisbon firm that sold printing machinery and supplies imported from Germany and elsewhere. He was taking advantage of the local boom in printing—there were close to a hundred printing offices in Lisbon—but presumably did not take advantage of Pessoa. Nor did Fernando expect any special favors. He was proud, evasive as to his ultimate intention, which was to become a literary publisher, and closemouthed about his finances. In September, at the latest, he sold his stock in the Bank of Portugal without telling anyone except, in all likelihood, his cousin Mário, swearing him to secrecy.[5] At least half the money went to pay for the used press, additional equipment, and set-up costs, and the rest would be needed for operating and living expenses until the business began turning a profit. In a small notebook, Pessoa jotted down figures and reckoned these expenses would amount to around two hundred thousand reis per month. It was a disastrously conservative estimate.[6]

In the same notebook, he drew up a list of eleven books in translation that he wanted to publish. Doing his best to be realistic, he selected works of fiction he thought had sales potential, including novels by the best-selling authors C. Ranger Gull (aka Guy Thorne) and W. W.

Jacobs, as well as literary classics such as the short stories of Edgar Allan
Poe and Pessoa's all-time favorite novel, *The Pickwick Papers*. He also
planned a *Revista Lusitana* (*Lusitanian Review*), sixteen pages of which
would be reserved for his own work.[7] He named his publishing house
Empreza Ibis—Typographica e Editora (Ibis Printing and Publishing).
The ibis Pessoa had in mind was from the shores of the Nile, in ancient
Egypt, where the god Thoth, scribe of the other gods and the inventor
of writing, was usually portrayed with a human body and an ibis head,
making this bird a symbol for the divine art of writing. Now the same
bird served as a talisman for Pessoa's venture in publishing. It would fly,
unfortunately, too close to the sun.

✦

ALTHOUGH IT WAS SWIFTLY consuming all his resources, Pessoa,
with nervous excitement, managed to open the Ibis press in November
1909.[8] It was located on Rua da Conceição da Glória—a little removed
from the downtown bustle and just one block away from the Praça da
Alegria, where in the shade of tall, exotic trees a small fountain pushed
up a single stream of softly trickling water. Lisbon's most tranquil square,
it may have afforded some comfort to the young businessman when, as
soon happened, he found himself overwhelmed by practical difficulties.
Two blocks in the other direction, on Rua da Glória, Pessoa moved into
his own apartment. For the first time ever he would be living alone.

The first print job executed by the Ibis press was its own letterhead
stationery. Next to the company's name and address appeared a hand-
somely designed logo of an ibis standing on one leg. The press also
printed stationery for Mário's Anglo-Portuguese Mining Agency, and
Pessoa no doubt counted on other relatives and friends to order calling
cards and to entrust him with assorted print jobs. Attracting business
was no easy matter. The competition among printers was fierce, so that
clients had to be courted aggressively; they rarely walked in off the street.
Pessoa, however, could not get excited about printing calling cards, flyers, announcements, brochures, and the like. In the apartment he had
rented on the street called Glory, he spent feverish evenings laying plans
for his publishing empire. The giddy range of his publication program
included everything from classical Portuguese literary works to his own
poetry and prose, from plays by Aeschylus and Shakespeare to Robert
Louis Stevenson's *Dr. Jekyll and Mr. Hyde*, from a novel by Brazil's Joa-

quim Machado de Assis, *Posthumous Memoirs of Bras Cubas*, to a selection of poems by Finland's Johan Ludvig Runeberg, who wrote in Swedish (Pessoa read him in English). Besides national and international poetry and fiction, Pessoa planned collections of scientific, historical, political, and philosophical works. A book on gymnastics by Luís Furtado Coelho, whose method had proven so beneficial to Pessoa in 1907, was also on his list of books to publish.

Books were just one facet of Pessoa's program for dominating the world of Portuguese publishing. He also planned to issue a series of "Ibis Pamphlets," several of which would contain political essays signed by his heteronym Pantaleão. In addition to the *Lusitanian Review*, the Ibis press would publish two newspapers, *O Iconoclasta* (*The Iconoclast*) and *O Fósforo*[9] (*Inflammable*), which offered a mix of political commentary, literature, and humor.[10]

As by now the reader may suspect, Pessoa invented a new set of heteronyms to handle the writing and translating for so many publication projects. The most multifaceted of his new collaborators was Vicente Guedes—poet, short story writer, and translator. He was scheduled to contribute poems to *The Iconoclast* and to publish, under the Ibis imprint, translations of Byron and Shelley as well as a collection of his own stories.

The similarly versatile Carlos Otto, besides writing poetry, was tasked with translating Arthur Morrison's *Martin Hewitt, Investigator* (1894), whose protagonist competed with Sherlock Holmes for the attention of readers partial to detective fiction. But instead of translating, Otto devoted his energies to the most improbable of all the books in the would-be Ibis catalogue: a *Treatise on Wrestling*, according to the "Yvetot method." Although the French wrestler or trainer named Yvetot was Pessoa's own invention, his photo was nonetheless slated to grace the book's frontispiece, along with a photo of the equally unreal Carlos Otto. The treatise proper—the few pages of it that were written—provides a detailed description of various kinds of moves and the Yvetot technique for executing them.

How did Pessoa become so well informed about the art of wrestling? With a little effort we can picture him in his neatly tailored suit at Lisbon's Coliseum, in a middle- or back-row seat, taking notes to pass on to Carlos Otto or else simply looking on in rapt attention as two he-men sweated it out in the ring. He would have no reason to clap or cheer, since he did not care who won or lost, but he would watch the battling physiques as closely as anyone. Of course, it is also possible that he merely read about the wrestlers' art.[11]

Political outreach was the most urgent item on the Ibis agenda, and special-purpose heteronyms were conjured up to wield their imaginary pens against the monarchy and the conservative hierarchy of the Catholic Church. Manuel Maria, a journalist for the Ibis newspapers *The Iconoclast* and *Inflammable*, took over as the author of some satirical, anti-monarchist "Visões" ("Visions") that had previously been signed by Pantaleão. Another scheduled contributor to the two newspapers, Joaquim Moura-Costa, wrote caustic poems against the Catholic Church as well as the monarchy. Markedly different was Father Gonçalves Gomes, an *Inflammable* columnist who was a fervent republican yet faithful to the Church he served. Pessoa wanted to make the point that religion and republicanism were not incompatible. It was not Catholicism per se that he bitterly opposed, but the alliance between the Church leadership in Portugal and the corrupt monarchy.

✦

THE IBIS PRESS COULD almost be the subject of a Borges short story titled "The Publishing House of Babel." Though anchored in a specific time and place, it was as endlessly fantastical as the Babelian library conceived by the Argentine writer. The Ibis publication plans, germinated over the course of a few months (and merely summarized here), would have kept a team of real writers and translators busy for many years to come, and even for time eternal, since the plans would have kept proliferating. Pessoa, the bedazzled planner, proceeded as if his team of unreal writers and translators would be able to accomplish their literary assignments on their own, without needing their creator's writing hand, his brain, and his time, without interrupting his beautiful dream. The dream was at least slightly, nominally fulfilled, since the firm called Ibis Printing and Publishing actually existed, and Pessoa wanted to savor it, to keep dreaming of what his publishing house could be and do. He did write a few poems and prose texts in the names of Carlos Otto and Vicente Guedes; he produced a lampoon against the Church and another against the queen in the voice of Joaquim Moura-Costa; he jotted down a number of ideas for stories and sketched some plots, wrote some scenes—enough to make the dream feel vaguely sustainable. But his creditors were pounding on the door, almost from the day the Ibis press opened for business.

On January 13, 1910, Jaime de Andrade Neves, his mother's cousin as well as his personal physician, wrote him a letter requesting immediate repayment of an overdue loan of ninety thousand reis. It was a substantial sum, and all the debtor could reply was that he would pay up as soon as possible.[12] Pessoa, who already owed money to other relatives and friends, now found himself having to borrow from B to pay off A, from C to then pay off B, and so forth. It was worse than that, since the total amount of debt increased with each passing day. The set-up costs for his business had been more than he'd anticipated, and the overhead was high. He had employed perhaps half a dozen workers to receive and manage print orders, set type, handle paper, run the machinery, and do deliveries. To turn a profit, the press would have had to operate at near full capacity, but Pessoa was a neophyte in a competitive field, and anything but a good salesman. His workers were often idle. Unable to break even as a commercial printer, the firm could by no stretch of the imagination evolve into a publishing house.

Scholars used to wonder whether the Ibis press might have gone bankrupt even before it could open for business, since there was no evidence of its having printed anything other than its own stationery. In 2010 a researcher finally discovered that for three months in 1910 the Empreza Ibis was listed on the masthead as the printer of a weekly newspaper published in Loulé, a town in the Algarve.[13] (The printed copies were shipped by train.) The March 12 issue of *O Povo Algarvio* (*People of the Algarve*) was the first one printed by the Ibis press, and the large number of typographical errors—for which an apology was issued the following week—suggests it may have been the press's first large-scale job. *O Povo Algarvio* was a stridently republican and anticlerical paper, which must have pleased Pessoa, though at that point he was grateful for whatever print jobs came along, helping him to stanch his operating loss. In April or May he put his press up for sale, and it was with tremendous relief that he found a buyer for it in the second half of June.[14] His editorial dream had ended in a financial nightmare.

The shuttering of the Ibis press caused some of Pessoa's lately created heteronyms to be laid off, as it were. Carlos Otto, Joaquim Moura-Costa, Manuel Maria, and Father Gonçalves Gomes, all of whom were closely connected to Ibis publishing projects, had no more role to play and were never heard from again, but Vicente Guedes, a larger and more complex heteronym, would reemerge several years later as a fictional author of *The*

*Book of Disquiet* (a role subsequently passed on to Bernardo Soares). The material legacy of the failed enterprise was a tall stack of Ibis stationery, which Pessoa used for notes and for his creative writing between 1910 and 1914, as well as a pile of debt, only partially reduced by the sale of the press. In less than a year's time he had spent his entire inheritance of five million reis—and then some. On top of various amounts owed to family members, friends, and several investors, Pessoa had taken out a bank loan that he would be paying off for the next four years.[15] Since he had no job, the only way he could service his debts was through freshly borrowed funds from newly recruited creditors.

And what if he turned his back on everything and sailed for England? Since returning to Portugal in 1905, not a year had gone by without his pondering the possibility of making Shakespeare and Milton's country his own, and 1910 was no different. The harrowing experience of trying to be a publisher had not dampened his resolve to write and publish, but he wondered more than ever whether his talents might be better appreciated elsewhere. On August 5, however, he outlined a poem titled "Por que não vou para o estrangeiro" ("Why I Am Not Going Abroad"). Although the outline is sketchy, the thread of the poem is easy to trace. The narrator comments on the oppressive atmosphere of Portugal and particularly of Lisbon, where life feels precarious and where so much is lacking for a "subtle spirit" like his own, but this is his land, and he realizes that genius and virtue are born out of troubled circumstances. "And that is why I am not going abroad," concludes Pessoa in the last line of the poem.[16]

But he did go abroad poetically. On the same piece of paper where he sketched his flagrantly autobiographical poem, he began writing Shakespearean sonnets in English.

✦

**WHILE BY DAY THE** Ibis press had been proving itself to be unprofitable, forcing Pessoa to borrow cash left and right to pay for paper, employee wages, and the monthly rent, at night the beleaguered entrepreneur read his favorite authors against the intermittent background noise of the Ascensor da Glória, a funicular that—just a few yards away from his ground-floor apartment—ferried pedestrians up to and down from the hilltop neighborhood of Bairro Alto. Rereading Shakespeare's sonnets over the course of several evenings, he was more fascinated than ever by their conceptual and linguistic complexity, and in August he drafted, in English, a number of his own Shakespearean sonnets—a form consisting of three rhyming quatrains followed by a couplet and not actually invented by Shakespeare. The first such sonnet attempted by Pessoa, and not completed until two years later, is his most famous. Here is the first quatrain in its final version:

How many masks wear we, and undermasks,
Upon our countenance of soul, and when,
If for self-sport the soul itself unmasks,
Knows it the last mask off and the face plain?

The answer to the last question is no, according to the next two quatrains, since our souls "foist otherness" on whatever images of ourselves we might see (as in a mirror) with our "co-masked eyes." We can never reach the state of spiritual nakedness, "the last mask off." The sonnet's closing couplet sums up the conundrum:

And, when a thought would unmask our soul's masking,
Itself goes not unmasked to the unmasking.

Although this sonnet lacks—like virtually all of Pessoa's English poems—the naturalness of expression that would make it great poetry, it is a perfect formulation of his conviction that we can never know ourselves, since we are actors who cannot do other than act. It's not just that all the world's a stage; each individual is a stage, where he or she is forever pretending, especially to his or her own self.

Pessoa was forever bemoaning his weak will and yet demonstrated remarkable fortitude. In the wake of the Ibis debacle, he retreated to a field of endeavor he understood—poetry—and decided to compete head-on with none other than Shakespeare. He was not altogether unsuccessful. Between August 5 and August 15 he wrote ten of the sonnets included in his *35 Sonnets*, a chapbook he would self-publish eight years later to modest acclaim.[17] A review published by *The Times Literary Supplement* on September 19, 1918, noted that the sonnets by the unknown poet from Portugal, "probing into the mysteries of life and death, of reality and appearance, will interest many by reason of their ultra-Shakespearian Shakespearianisms, and their Tudor tricks of repetition, involution and antithesis, no less than by the worth of what they have to say."

Shakespeare was not the only great author whom Pessoa aimed to equal or improve on. Amid the English sonnets he drafted in the first half of August 1910, the twenty-two-year-old writer jotted down an idea for "a drama, in Portuguese, dealing—better than Ibsen did—with general paralysis."[18] The Norwegian playwright, who had a conflicted relationship with his homeland and spent many years in exile, was appreciated by the failed businessman for his stark realism. Pessoa's play was to end with an old, once stalwart soldier confined to a chair and unable to do more than mumble. The enfeebled soldier clearly represented Portugal, whose decay and decadence were the dual refrain of the many pages Pessoa continued to write on the nation's history and politics.

Although he never did anything with his Ibsenesque idea, Pessoa had already been working for some months on a rather different portrayal of the national drama: an epic poem divided into cantos, like *The Lusiads* of Camões, and patriotically titled *Portugal*. Expressing disillusion with Portugal's present state of decadence but also pride in its past and high hopes for its future, it was a work he had planned to publish at the Ibis press, whose demise did not diminish his passion for writing it.[19] Portugal would be the never-ending object of Pessoa's desperation and adoration. Despite feeling that his "subtle spirit" was misunderstood, intellectually malnourished, and condemned to solitude in the country where he was born, he loved it too much not to stay put—especially at this critical juncture, when the political winds heralded big changes.

Lisbon in the late nineteenth century. *(Marina Tavares Dias,* A Lisboa de Fernando Pessoa *[Lisbon: Assírio & Alvim, 1998], pp. 116–17)*

The São Carlos Theater, as seen from the building where Pessoa was born. *(João Gaspar Simões,* Vida e obra de Fernando Pessoa *[Lisbon: Bertrand, 1971])*

(LEFT) Pessoa's father, Joaquim de Seabra Pessoa. *(Courtesy Manuela Nogueira)* (RIGHT) His mother, Maria Madalena Nogueira, when still single. *(Courtesy Manuela Nogueira)*

His great-uncle Cunha and great-aunt Maria, who were like a second set of parents. *(Courtesy Manuela Nogueira)*

Fernando, almost three years old, sitting next to his aunt Anica. Behind them stands his mother, flanked by two cousins. *(Courtesy Manuela Nogueira)*

Studio portraits of Fernando at age six. *(Courtesy Manuela Nogueira)*

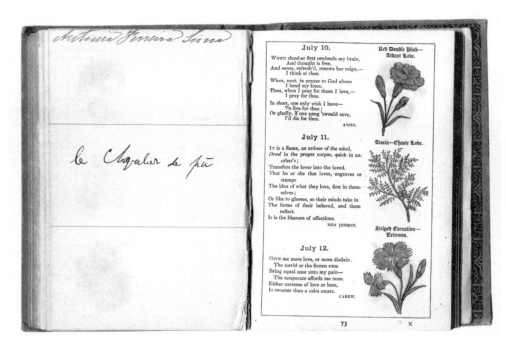

In a birthday book belonging to his mother, six-year-old Fernando inscribed the name of his first heteronym, the Chevalier de Pas. *(Courtesy Assírio & Alvim)*

A ship sailing past the Point and into Natal Bay. The ocean beach is on the right. Downtown Durban and the Berea Ridge are in the background. *(The Natal Mercury [Durban], Weekly Edition, 9 Dec. 1904)*

West Street, Durban, in 1898 (now Dr. Pixley Kaseme Street). Rickshaws plied on the outer lanes. *(Local History Museums, Durban)*

Fernando in Durban, at age ten. *(Courtesy Manuela Nogueira)*

Teaching staff of Durban High School, with Mr. Nicholas, the headmaster, seated in the middle. *(The Natal Mercury, Weekly Edition, 15 July 1904)*

Fernando, his mother, his brother Luís Miguel, his stepfather, and his sister Henriqueta (Teca) in 1901, during the family's yearlong holiday in Portugal. *(Courtesy Assírio & Alvim)*

(ABOVE) Fernando and his family at 25 Tenth Avenue, where they lived after returning to Durban in 1902. *(Courtesy Manuela Nogueira)*

(RIGHT) The family sitting on the steps of the same house. Fernando's youngest brother was born in January 1903. *(Courtesy Manuela Nogueira)*

Praça do Rossio, Lisbon's main square, in 1905. *(Courtesy Library of Congress)*

Pessoa in 1907 with (from left to right, sitting or standing) his great-aunt Maria, great-aunt Adelaide, grandmother Dionísia, aunt Anica, cousin Maria (Anica's daughter), and great-aunt Rita. *(Courtesy Manuela Nogueira)*

The heteronym Alexander Search had his own calling card and received mail at the same addresses where Pessoa lived between 1907 and 1910. *(Courtesy National Library of Portugal)*

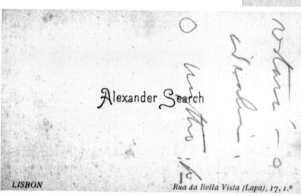

(ABOVE) Pessoa practiced many different signature styles for his heteronyms. *(Courtesy National Library of Portugal)*

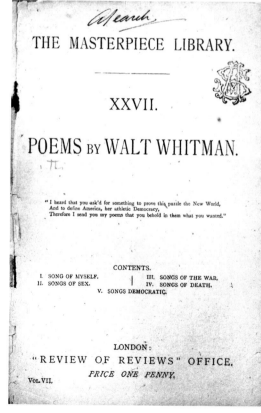

THE MASTERPIECE LIBRARY.

XXVII.

POEMS BY WALT WHITMAN.

" I heard that you ask'd for something to prove this puzzle the New World,
And to define America, her athletic Democracy,
Therefore I send you my poems that you behold in them what you wanted."

CONTENTS.

| I. SONG OF MYSELF. | III. SONGS OF THE WAR. |
| II. SONGS OF SEX. | IV. SONGS OF DEATH. |
| V. SONGS DEMOCRATIC. | |

LONDON:
"REVIEW OF REVIEWS" OFFICE.
PRICE ONE PENNY.
Vol. VII.

(RIGHT) Alexander Search's signature, sometimes accompanied by his florid monogram, appears in a number of books acquired by Pessoa. *(Courtesy Casa Fernando Pessoa)*

(LEFT) Undated photo of Pessoa as a young man. *(Courtesy Manuela Nogueira)*
(RIGHT) General Henrique Rosa, the brother of Pessoa's stepfather and a staunch
republican, was an important influence on Pessoa. The photo shows him as a young
army officer. *(Isabel Murteira França,* Fernando Pessoa na intimidade *[Lisbon: Dom Quixote,
1987]).*

"Historical Pages." On October 5, 1910, while the republican revolution prevailed in Lisbon, King
Manuel II and other royals fled to the fishing village of Ericeira, where they would board the royal yacht
and sail to Gibraltar. *(*Ilustração Portuguesa, *17 Oct. 1910. Lisbon Municipal Libraries [Hemeroteca])*

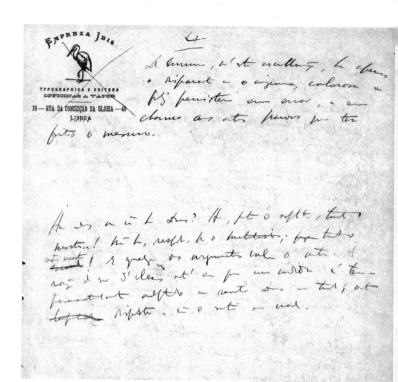

The Empreza Ibis, a quixotic publishing adventure, ended in disaster in 1910. Pessoa used the leftover stationery and blank invoices for his literary work. *(Courtesy National Library of Portugal)*

(LEFT) A portrait of Pessoa painted in 1912 by Adolfo Rodriguez Castañé, a young Spanish artist who lived in Lisbon. *(Courtesy of the photographer, Nuno Fevereiro)* (RIGHT) Caricature of Pessoa drawn by Castañé and published in 1912. *(República, 21 Sept. 1912. Fundação Mário Soares)*

In the early months of 1912 Pessoa met the writer Mário de Sá-Carneiro, who would become his closest friend.

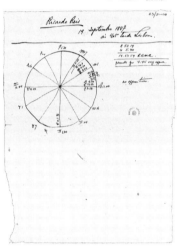

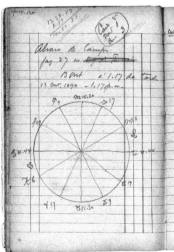

Pessoa cast astrological charts for his three major heteronyms. He would later change Álvaro de Campos's date of birth to October 15. *(Courtesy National Library of Portugal)*

*(Courtesy National Library of Portugal)*

(LEFT) The cover of *Orpheu 2*, published in June 1915, was probably designed by José de Almada Negreiros. Pessoa and Mário de Sá-Carneiro were the editors in chief. *(Courtesy National Library of Portugal)*
(RIGHT) *Dynamic Decomposition of a Table + Style of Movement*—one of four works by Santa Rita Pintor reproduced in *Orpheu 2*. *(Courtesy National Library of Portugal)*

Luís de Montalvor—a founder of *Orpheu* and Pessoa's first posthumous publisher—in a photo dating from the 1930s.

## OS PRECURSORES DO MODERNISMO EM PORTUGAL

Fernando Pessoa—Alvaro de Campos—Ricardo Reis—Alberto Caeiro.

José de Almada-Negreiros.

José Pacheco.

Santa-Rita Pintor †

Amadeu de Sousa Cardoso. †

Dr. Raul Leal

Dr. Alfredo Pedro Guisado

Antonio Ferro

Mario de Sá-Carneiro †

"The Precursors of Modernism in Portugal." Published in a magazine in 1929, this page pays homage to some of the main writers and artists associated with *Orpheu*. *(O Notícias Ilustrado, 24 Feb. 1929)*

# CHAPTER 22

O MO MO MO MO MO MO MO MO MO MO MO MO MO MO

O NE MONTH SHY OF HIS TWENTY-FIRST BIRTH-
day, King Manuel II fled to the coastal town of Ericeira, where
he, his mother, his grandmother, and other members of the
royal family were taken by rowboats out to the royal yacht, on which
they would sail to Gibraltar. Fishermen and other townspeople watched
in stunned silence from the shore. Their king was deserting them. A
few hours earlier on that same day—October 5, 1910—the Portuguese
Republic had been proclaimed from the balcony of Lisbon's city hall.
Fewer than a hundred people, most of them civilians, had been killed in
the fighting.

The downfall of the monarchy was not such a surprise in the capital, the nation's political bellwether, where Republicans had won overwhelmingly in the legislative elections held on August 28, even though
they were still a minority countrywide. In a futile attempt to check the
growth of republicanism, the young king, like his father before him, had
allied himself with reformists, going so far as to woo the small Socialist
Party, which he hoped could draw proletarians away from the republicans. This strategy only alienated conservatives, who opposed the liberal governing coalition and won a third of the seats in the parliament.
Catholic clerics mostly supported the conservative bloc, but a few sided
with the liberals, and both blocs were mishmashes of disparate parties,
splinter parties, and subgroups. The Republicans themselves were by
now split into two factions, radical and moderate, each with its own
newspapers, but they rallied behind their determination to topple the
increasingly wobbly monarchy. Although there was public sympathy for
King Manuel, who cultivated an informal style and avoided ostentation,
the institution he represented was irreparably tarnished.

Destiny was manifestly on the side of the Republicans, but they had
disagreed about when and whether to take up arms. At the Tenth Party
Congress, held in April 1909, the revolutionary contingent prevailed

over those who preferred the peaceful but slow path of elections; party members in Lisbon began stockpiling guns for the propitious moment. Republicans operating *outside* the party also played a crucial role— especially through the Portuguese Carbonária, a secret political society that borrowed its name from the Italian Carbonari and some of its hierarchical structure from Freemasonry. Founded in the late nineteenth century, the group was fanatically anticlerical and recruited its followers from among teachers, students, civil servants, shopkeepers, laborers, and soldiers. The group's secrecy bred visionary fervor and a ravenous taste for intrigue and conspiracy. King Carlos's two assassins had belonged to the Carbonária; one of them was also a Freemason. Most Masons, whose social status was comparatively high, were also republicans. Both they and the Carbonários had deeply infiltrated the Portuguese armed forces, whose support would be crucial for the revolution to succeed. The navy, in particular, was thoroughly republicanized, owing to the republicans' staunch support for Portugal's overseas empire.

Deciding at last that it was time to act, a group of radical republicans, at a meeting held on October 2, 1910, scheduled the revolution for the early morning of October 4. Things did not go exactly to plan, nor did Lisboners spontaneously rise up in support of the coup, partly because of some initial confusion about what was going on, but several army garrisons and navy battleships stationed in the Tagus duly revolted when given their cues, the government forces spent a day fighting back half-heartedly, or they joined the revolutionaries, and citizens began to gather and cheer. A new republic was born.

✦

THERE ENSUED A GRACE period of republican consensus. Moderates such as Fernando Pessoa, while ambivalent about armed rebellion, rejoiced in the overthrow of the monarchy and conceded that the radicals were right to act when they did. The Republic was greeted in the cities by general applause, while the rural population—which made up the large majority of Portugal's close to six million people—shrugged and did not oppose it. Predictably, the leading figures of the new order jostled to occupy the front of the stage or to exert their influence from behind the scenes, but they all shared a number of core ideals. They were freethinkers who envisioned a Portugal guided by enlightened reason. If they had not actually read, like Pessoa, the works of Haeckel and Spencer, they understood and had faith in the luminous materialism propounded by these and other science-inspired philosophers.

Republicanism was not just a new form of government; it was a concept of the nation as a dynamic organism that would involve all citizens in a collective program of social, economic, and moral progress. The republicans were vocal defenders of "the people," which meant especially the anonymous masses who worked in agriculture and industry and whose lives as individuals were rarely taken into account by politicians. The republicans wanted everyone to be counted, without respect to social class. Within two weeks of the revolution, the provisional government declared all titles of nobility to be null and void. Members of the government eschewed the pomp and privileges typically associated with public office. They used public transportation. They dressed simply.

These were meaningful indicators of good intentions, but "the people" needed to be educated and energized. Fully 70 percent of Portuguese adults were illiterate.* In Lisbon and Porto the figure was lower, yet still hovered around 40 percent. Besides reading and writing, the republicans wanted to teach people to question and to think scientifically, and they hoped to instill civic awareness by fostering their knowledge of national history and geography. It was not by accident that many prominent republicans were doctors, such as Egas Moniz, and many others were professors, such as Afonso Costa. Through proper instruction and by providing a favorable environment, these leaders thought they could cure and change people. But only after overcoming an old and formidable obstacle: the Catholic Church.

Long before the Portuguese monarchy fell, to be a republican was practically synonymous with being anticlerical. Politically conservative and enormously influential (its activity directly or indirectly reached into nearly every Portuguese person's life), the Church was a bulwark of the monarchy, and vice versa; the two institutions had protected each other. That was not the only reason for the republicans' animus. They felt that Catholic doctrine was obscurantist and that the indoctrinators—especially the allegedly sinister Jesuits—warped and enslaved people's minds, preventing them from thinking freely and clearly.

---

* The illiteracy rate was about 50 percent in Spain, 8 percent in the United States, and 2 percent in England.

Fernando Pessoa, contrary to some republicans, did not see Catholicism as a cancer that had to be eradicated for the sake of the nation's health and well-being, but he was, without metaphor, a card-carrying anticlericalist. In October 1909 he had paid ten thousand reis, which was equivalent to one month's rent on his apartment, to become a member of the Junta Liberal,[1] a group that campaigned for the separation of church and state and organized protest rallies against the Jesuits and other religious orders. This was the only organization that Pessoa ever formally joined. Three days before taking out this membership, he had written a violently satirical poem attacking Father José Lourenço de Mattos, a priest who published pro-royalist and antirepublican commentary in newspapers—especially in his own newspaper, called *Portugal*.[2] Pessoa's poem was signed by Joaquim Moura-Costa, his most adamantly anticlerical heteronym, and tagged for inclusion in *Inflammable*, one of the never-to-be Ibis newspapers.

As soon as the republicans seized power, they lost no time in using it against the Church. On October 8, the three-day-old provisional government issued a decree that outlawed all monasteries and convents and expelled the Jesuits from Portugal. Some Jesuits fled to Spain; many others were jailed and deported. On October 22, religious instruction was excised from the primary and secondary school curricula and replaced with civic education. A decree issued the following day abolished the School of Theology at the University of Coimbra. On the twenty-sixth, all religious holidays were declared to be regular workdays. On November 3 divorce was legalized, and on December 25 marriage was defined as a civil rather than sacramental union. On the last day of the year it became illegal for priests to work as teachers or to wear their habits in public.

The man behind these and other, similar measures was Afonso Costa, the minister of justice in the provisional government and an ardent atheist. At a secret meeting of Freemasons held on March 26, 1911, he boasted that it would take only two generations for Catholicism to be completely extirpated from Portugal. This statement was leaked to *O Dia* (*Today*), a Catholic newspaper, obliging Costa, a renowned lawyer as well as a professor and a statesman, to use his notable skills of argument and oratory to mollify republicans who believed in God. His Law on the Separation of Churches from the State, issued one month later and modeled after French legislation passed in 1905, actually made the Catholic Church in Portugal dependent on the government, which expropriated all its property and stipulated that its activities could be financed only through local associations—charities and philanthropic societies, for instance—in which priests could not be members.[3]

Though he considered Costa's law separating church and state better than no law, Pessoa thought it went too far.[4] And it troubled him that a provisional government, made up of fewer than ten individuals, was imposing such radical reforms by fiat, without any representative body to discuss and debate them. The government ministers did meet regularly with the Republican Party's Central Committee and with its Advisory Board, giving rise to some serious internal policy disputes, and there were personality clashes and power struggles—all of which were initially downplayed, or ignored. The Republicans nurtured the idea that they were fundamentally of one mind, united behind a common political project. Despite having already won the revolution, they continued to campaign, using rallies and rhetoric not only to bash remnants of royalism and the Catholic episcopate but also to promote their own progressive doctrines, symbols, and brand. With great ceremony they waved the new green and red flag and had people sing, hats off, the new national anthem. Dozens of clubs and associations sprang up to spread the collective gospel: it is good and republican to love the nation. Patriotism was the new religion, and republicanism the new theology.

Pessoa began very quickly to feel uneasy. Despite his long-standing adherence to the republican cause, he instinctively bristled when he was expected to be a willing and even joyous participant in a mass movement, whatever it was. One day while sitting at the Café A Brasileira, located on Rua Garrett, the main artery of Chiado, he read a newspaper article that lambasted the idea of a conservative republican party being formed to oppose the more radical republicans who were holding sway. Indignant, he asked the waiter for some paper, took up his pen, and attacked the article for its "extraordinary stupidity," noting that "only the blind don't see the danger" of the radicals doing whatever they pleased, unchecked. His furiously scribbled notes were undoubtedly for a letter to the editor, which never got written.[5] They date from mid-February of 1911, when the country, four months into the new dispensation, was tipping toward social mayhem.

Workers had started to organize under the monarchy, and strikes—

to the delight of the republicans—bedeviled the reign of the last king, Manuel II. They became a constant of daily life after the October 5 revolution, whose success emboldened wage earners in the industrial, service, and transportation sectors. Factories were routinely deserted, train lines paralyzed, and shops forced to close by disaffected employees. When bakers walked off the job, military kitchens had to be pressed into service to provide Lisbon with bread. Government leaders soon decided that it was unrepublican to strike, and skirmishes broke out between strikers and republican militants. For their efforts, the strikers usually achieved at least some of their demands—higher pay, shorter hours, or a healthier environment—but the majority of workers were not unionized, and their conditions did not improve all that much during the first decade of the Republic. Tens of thousands of Portuguese continued to emigrate each year.

The sluggish national economy, dominated by inefficient agriculture and light industry, did no better and no worse than under the monarchy. There was, however, a change in mentality, especially among the members of the bourgeoisie but also among laborers. Taking to heart the message that science and reason could transform human life, the country made an intellectual leap of sorts. Knowledge, which before had been a welcome asset, became an imperative.

The republicans wanted to expand education at all levels, but resources were limited, and it was hard to force rural children to go to school when they were needed to work the fields or tend sheep, and more than half the country was engaged in farming. Although more schools were opened, the national literacy rate increased only marginally during the next decade. The phonetically based spelling reform, which was supposed to make it easier to learn reading and writing, seems to have had little impact. In higher education, the new regime did make a large and lasting difference, establishing two new universities and an engineering school in the spring of 1911. Women, however, continued to be a tiny minority among college students.

Virginia Woolf dubiously claimed that "on or about December 1910 human character changed." She naturally based this statement on her observations of English society, but we can be sure that not even on the British Isles, and not even in her own social clique, was there a sudden transformation in human *character* as this word is usually understood. Woolf's use of it was misleading. Fortunately she went on to explain exactly what she meant: "All human relations have shifted—those between masters and servants, husbands and wives, parents and children. And when human relations change there is at the same time a change in religion, conduct, politics and literature." As we shall see, there were some striking parallels between English and Portuguese modernism of the 1910s, with the latter movement being largely orchestrated by Fernando Pessoa. Whether or not Woolf, writing in 1924, was right to see late 1910 as a turning point in English interpersonal relations that led to changes in other areas of life, including literature, her narrative can be usefully applied to Portugal, as long as we shift around the terms a bit. The Republic was not, in truth, a great economic or political success, but it did abolish the nobility and blunt the distinctions between social classes, it did secularize society, it did insist on the dignity of all people, and it promoted education rather than birthright as the key to success. Human relations in Portugal changed, which may have helped prepare the ground for new kinds of art and literature.

Pessoa, in 1910, had only recently begun writing poetry in Portuguese and had produced nothing as yet that would qualify him as an exceptional genius. Without the Republic and the changes it precipitated, it is impossible to know how he might have developed as a writer, a thinker, and an agent of transformation in Portuguese literature. With the Republic, he became a political theorist whose ideas evolved in unexpected directions, a spiritual quester who tirelessly traveled from truth to truth, a man who felt intensely yet with paradoxical detachment, and—perhaps not unrelatedly—a complexly original, often dazzling writer.

◆

ALL THINGS CONSIDERED, the transition to the Republic had been remarkably peaceful. Repressive legislation threw the Church into a state of semichaos, labor strikes caused disruptions in public transportation and occasional shortages of consumer goods, and raucous political rallies added to the general air of commotion, but the financial markets did not panic, the military did not intervene, and people went about their business as usual.

Pessoa's mother and stepfather, though not republican sympathizers, quietly accepted the new regime, which soon affected their lives in a major way. João Miguel Rosa had served as a diplomat in the British colony of Natal for fifteen years and was planning to bring his family home, but the Ministry of Foreign Affairs implored him to stay on and serve as Portugal's consul-general to the recently unified, independent country of South Africa, which still remained under the British crown. The republicans wanted to send a message of stability and continuity to Great Britain, whose leaders viewed its Iberian ally's political transformation with jittery apprehension. Rosa accepted the promotion, and in September 1911 he took his family to the new national capital, Pretoria, where they would live for the next eight years. This unexpected development had consequences for Pessoa's life, and possibly for his life as a writer. Had his parents returned to Lisbon in 1911, he could not have fooled them into believing that his inheritance from Grandma Dionísia was still largely intact, notwithstanding his misadventure as a printer and publisher. With them living in the same city and knowing that he was flat broke, the pressure on him to get a full-time job that would enable him to slowly pay off his debts might have been too strong to resist.

Pessoa did look for work, but as if he did not actually need work, as if he were looking for the right sort of cuff links or necktie. He was in no hurry: his creditors could wait. Journalism appealed to him, and he looked forward to writing reportage and commentary for a new daily paper that a friend was planning to launch. His starting salary would be thirty thousand reis per month. So he wrote his mother on January 24, 1911, after which she regularly asked him, in her weekly letter, if the newspaper was finally going to start publishing, and if not, then why couldn't he work for an already existing newspaper? It was easy for Fernando, in letters, to simply ignore this question, which his mother stopped asking in June.

By then he had at least managed to find some freelance work, and it happened to perfectly suit his talents and interests. He translated English poets such as Wordsworth, Shelley, and Robert and Elizabeth Barrett Browning—as well as some poems, fables, and dramatic works from Spanish—for the *Biblioteca internacional de obras célebres*, a Portuguese adaptation of the twenty-volume *International Library of Famous Literature*, published in London in 1898–1899. Bound in maroon leather and containing over ten thousand pages, the original *Library* sought to bring together the best in world literature, from ancient times up to the present. The *Biblioteca*, consisting of twenty-four volumes, would include a majority of the selections found in the *Library* plus a much enlarged offering of works by Portuguese and Brazilian authors. The man in charge of the massive undertaking was Warren F. Kellogg, an American editor and publisher who arrived in Lisbon in May 1911, opened an office downtown, and contracted various translators, including Pessoa. He paid seven hundred reis per translated page, higher than anyone else in town. Although produced in Portugal, the *Biblioteca* would be distributed almost exclusively in Brazil, beginning in early 1913. Pessoa's name signed some but not all of the twenty or so poems he translated and none of his many prose translations for the work.[6]

Pessoa continued to collaborate with his cousin Mário, whose mining firm, rechristened the International Mining Agency, had moved to Largo do Carmo. Mário had a second firm that operated out of the same office: Social Guarantee—Agency of Indefinite Business Matters. As suggested by its bizarre name, which could have been invented only by Fernando Pessoa, this agency was ready to handle almost anything. But neither of the two businesses flourished, and Mário saw his capital dwindle. The only compensation he could offer his cousin, who handled his correspondence and probably the bookkeeping, was free lodging: during the first half of 1911, Pessoa, who had given up his apartment, bedded down at the office on Largo do Carmo, a square named after what used to be the Convent and Church of Our Lady of Mount Carmel, built in the fourteenth and fifteenth centuries. The skeletal remains of the church, which collapsed in the 1755 earthquake, are Lisbon's most haunting reminder of that cataclysm. Gazing across the square from the window of his cousin's office, Pessoa could see the lonely gothic arches standing out against the sky like a sardonic monument to the destructive power of nature. Or perhaps he marveled at how those human-engineered arches, one and a half centuries later, still resisted.[7]

Aunt Anica, in her letters to Pessoa's mother, confessed that it was making her a nervous wreck to watch Mário slowly deplete his inheritance through ill-conceived business schemes, but she did not let on (if indeed she knew) that her nephew's inheritance had completely evaporated in his very first attempt to be a businessman. Fernando's mother, still in the dark, ironically feared that his situation as a financially comfortable heir was making him complacent. Why didn't he get a regular job? In her letters to him, she harped on this theme until he finally wrote her that any form of submission, including a job with set hours, repulsed him.[8] In fact, the advice and warnings of the two worried mothers fazed neither Mário nor Fernando. Although they were in many ways complete opposites—Mário had no interest in literature; Fernando was not gregarious like his cousin—they both treated life like a never-ending game. If one lost today's round, he might still win tomorrow's.

Fernando was moody and often preferred isolation, but in the company of his aunts, uncles, and cousins he could be witty, play tricks, and act goofy. During the six months he lived at Mário's office on Largo do Carmo, his distant cousins Raul da Costa and Armando Couto sometimes came by for a little sport. Both were amateur toreadors and perfected their style with the help of Fernando, who had no interest in real bullfighting but gladly played the part of a riled bull, charging with head bowed and fingers pointing forward from his temples like horns, while they danced from side to side with bath towels as if they were red capes. This information comes from Couto's daughter, who told me what her father told her. She also reported that her mother, Clara Alves Soares, who would marry Armando Couto in 1918, once saw Pessoa imitate a very different animal: the ibis. Clara, when still single, had gone shopping with her mother, and they happened to spot Fernando on the other side of the street. When they waved at him, he abruptly stopped walking, balanced on one foot, stretched his neck forward, put one hand behind him to represent a tail, another in front of him as if it were a beak, and announced, "I'm an ibis." The two women giggled with embarrassment as pedestrians turned their heads to behold the strange spectacle.[9]

Although the Ibis press had folded, the bird lived on: it was Pessoa's mascot, personal symbol, and nickname. In his notebooks he had drawn sketches of a face labeled Ibis and of a stick-figure captioned "an ibis called António," which was his second name.[10] In 1920 he would sign himself Ibis on a poem dedicated to his sister; he was Ibis in some of the letters he would exchange with his only girlfriend, Ophelia Queiroz; and the children born to his cousins Mário and Maria would call him Ibis rather than Uncle Fernando. Giving in to their insistent pleas, he would balance on one foot and pretend to be a wading bird while they squealed with laughter.

Thus Pessoa made a literally standing joke out of his calamitous attempt to be a publisher, wearing his defeat like a badge, incarnating the name and logotype of the defunct enterprise. But for some time after it had closed its doors, despite his outward air of nonchalance, he was visited by moments of painful despair. One year after selling the press, around the time of his birthday, he wrote a sonnet that bitterly lamented the twenty-three "uselessly" lived years of his life, each one of them marked by dejection, each one a recurring tale of unrealized aspirations, and added to this regret was the terrifying suspicion that his years to come might not be any different.[11] This sonnet was the first piece of writing that Pessoa signed with the name Ibis—a symbol of defeat, but also of defiance. The divine writing spirit of ancient Egypt's sacred bird was tenaciously, ferociously alive in the breast of the young poet.

# CHAPTER 23

**A** MONG THE DECREES ISSUED BY THE PROVISIONAL government to introduce social reforms in the young republic, Pessoa paid special attention to the one dated May 11, 1911, which regulated the treatment of the mentally ill. He read the entirety of the decree in the official government newspaper, but what particularly caught his eye was Article 33, which recognized the right of mentally disturbed individuals to commit themselves to a psychiatric hospital. In a couple of letters written years later, in 1920 and in 1925, Pessoa would claim that he was thinking of invoking Article 33 to sign himself into a mental institution. In the first of these, sent to Ophelia Queiroz, his girlfriend, he was surely joking. In the second letter, to an unidentified recipient, he may have been serious. But even before the decree about mental health and hospitals was handed down, he had already invented his own psychiatric hospital, making it the setting for a strange narrative titled "Na Casa de Saúde de Cascais" ("In the Cascais Sanatorium").

Located about twenty miles west of Lisbon, Cascais is the last stop on the coastal train line leading out of Lisbon. With its abundance of sunshine, invigorating ocean air, and the calming blue water of its gentle beach, it made an ideal setting for an institution to promote mental well-being. Between 1909 and 1911 Pessoa wrote about twenty, mostly brief passages for his curious fiction, in which an inmate suffering from hysterical paranoia and dressed in a toga lectures to the narrator, a visitor to the sanatorium, on the ills of modern European culture and on the superiority of ancient Greece. In Chekhov's "Ward No. 6," Ivan Gromov, a patient in a mental asylum, complains to the director about injustice in the world. Pessoa's mental patient, far from being concerned about social injustice, disdains the principles of "liberty, equality and fraternity," whose wide acceptance he attributes to the degenerative influence of Christianity. Conversely: "Courage, fortitude, physical and moral beauty—all of this is pagan."

The trinity of ideals enshrined by the French Revolution—*liberté,
égalité, fraternité*—were co-opted by the republican revolutionaries of
Portugal, but Pessoa had his doubts about their viability and desirability.
He thought such abstractions were dangerous, or simply vacuous, and his
problem with Christianity was its abstracting tendency: it had placed all
that was good and strong and perfect in a single, faraway God. The Greek
gods were more human, closer to Earth, and multifarious, like nature
itself. Pessoa would write hundreds of pages in defense of neo-paganism,
a doctrine anticipated by the toga-clad inmate of his imaginary sanatorium. The balmy inmate, named António Mora, would later reemerge as
a major heteronym and important theorist of neo-paganism.[1] This term
has become associated with Wicca and other movements dedicated to
recovering or reinventing pagan rituals from various traditions, but Pessoa was mainly interested in the Greek and Roman paganism idealized
by the German Romantics, who influenced poets such as Shelley, Keats,
and Swinburne.

The name of the psychiatrist attending António Mora at the seaside
sanatorium was Dr. Gomes. This seems to be the same individual as
Dr. Florêncio Gomes, author of a *Tratado de Doenças Mentais* (*Treatise
on Mental Illnesses*), which is cited in *Marcos Alves*, a novel Pessoa began
plotting in 1909, the same year he started writing "In the Cascais Sanatorium." Afflicted by persecution paranoia, Marcos Alves repeatedly
attempts suicide, succeeding on the third try. Dr. Gomes's summary of
the unfortunate case, excerpted from his *Treatise*, forms the epilogue
to the novel.

Like António Mora, Marcos Alves was unable to adapt to the world,
but for very different, less philosophical reasons. He was overly sensitive,
too easily moved to tears of sorrow or compassion, and hence afraid of
contact with human society. Still a virgin, what he most of all feared
was sexual contact, the very idea of which made him shudder. Sex, nevertheless, was constantly on his mind. He tended to "always analyze
other people from a sexual point of view. Sexuality filled his entire brain,
coloring everything with its designs." His method of suicide, when he
finally succeeded, was a gunshot in the mouth, the same method used
by Antero de Quental, whose sonnets he was fond of reading. Pessoa,
of course, was equally fond of Quental's sonnets, and the similarities
don't stop there. Dr. Gomes's case history of Marcos Alves, written in
1912 or 1913, describes him as a twenty-four-year-old born in Lisbon,

with a paternal uncle who died of tuberculosis and a paternal grandmother who suffered from "mental alienation" and was the only surviving offspring of her parents. On Alves's mother's side, in contrast, there
seemed "to be nothing abnormal." These details perfectly fit the case of
Fernando Pessoa: he too was twenty-four; his TB-afflicted father had
had a brother who died young from the same disease; and his demented
Grandma Dionísia was the eighth and last child of a couple whose first
seven children were all born prematurely and died. On his mother's side,
however, there was nothing psychologically "abnormal," except for occasional bouts of nervous agitation in Aunt Anica. Pessoa included all this
information in a family tree that he sketched for himself in 1912 or 1913.

Since Pessoa believed that one's psychological profile depends on
heredity, Marcos Alves, endowed with a family background identical
to his own, would seem to be an autobiographical study. Yet there is
no evidence to suggest that Pessoa had ever contemplated suicide. Nor
does Alves's medical diagnosis—"persecution paranoia"—ring true for
Pessoa, whose many pages of self-analysis never mention this pathology.
About all this leaves us, as a basis for comparison, is the fictional character's uneasy relationship to sex: always thinking about it, usually as
something unclean, and recoiling from the slightest possibility of engaging in it. Pessoa's cousins and their friends, all younger than him, were
already experiencing the pleasures and disappointments of being in love,
while he, with no experience at all, observed them and wondered what
he was missing. Like Marcos Alves, he was intimidated by sex, perhaps
even a little disgusted by it, yet unable to keep thoughts of sex at bay.
Alves, however, suffered from an extreme case of sexual-aversion obsession, worthy of inclusion in *Psychopathia Sexualis* (1886), by the German
psychiatrist Richard von Krafft-Ebing, who is mentioned in Pessoa's
notes about his hapless character.[2] It was this pioneering, best-selling
work of medical sexology that established classifications for a number of
"deviant" sexual behaviors and popularized words such as "homosexuality," "pedophilia," "sadism," and "masochism."

Pessoa's cousins and their sweethearts touched, kissed, and gazed at
one another with desires they understood, while he read authors such
as Krafft-Ebing,[3] invented his own psychiatrists, and invested fictional
characters with exaggerated forms of sexual behavior—in an attempt
to discover what he himself desired and also, no doubt, to relieve the
pressure of his sexual preoccupations. Some of that relief was comic.

The medicalized account of Marcos Alves's troubled life and suicidal death was so implausibly pathetic that it could not have failed to provoke laughter in the man who wrote his story.

✦

PESSOA WROTE ABOUT TWENTY pages of passages and notes for *Marcos Alves*, mostly between 1909 and 1913.[4] It was also in 1909 that he conceived a five-act play in which madness, sex, and sexual abstinence were prominent themes. Titled *The Duke of Parma: A Tragedy*, he would keep working on this drama for the rest of his life, producing more than two hundred pages of dialogues, monologues, and stage directions.[5] He did not write in sequence, his ideas for the plot kept changing, and from the resulting textual jumble it would be impossible to establish an authoritative dramatic sequence, but the story buried in the text is relatively well fleshed out. Even so, no researcher has yet had the patience to decipher, transcribe, and piece together all the material. It is one of the largest and weirdest of the many plays Pessoa tried to write. If its title sounds like it belongs to a play Shakespeare could have written, it is because the author was aiming for precisely that.

Like the Shakespearean sonnets he began writing in 1910—and like Oscar Wilde's *The Duchess of Padua* (1883), a play that also imitated Shakespeare—*The Duke of Parma* was written in an English embroidered with archaic flourishes, such as "doth," "hath," and "wilt." More than any oldness or oddness in the vocabulary, however, it is the tone, phrasing, and dramatic method of Pessoa's play that make us think of Shakespeare. On a sheet of paper containing a scene from *The Duke of Parma*, Pessoa made a note of the total number of lines in *King Lear*, *Hamlet*, *Macbeth*, and *Julius Caesar*. He wanted to be sure that his own tragedy had a comparable length—fewer lines than *Hamlet*, which is rarely performed in its entirety, but no less than *Macbeth*.[6]

For Pessoa to pit his Shakespearean sonnets against those of the master from Stratford-upon-Avon was not wholly absurd, since the sonnet was a form still much in use by poets. Far more dubious was his lonely attempt to write, in the twentieth century, a play in the style of Shakespeare and with some of Shakespeare's phraseology. Had he completed and published *The Duke of Parma*, we might greatly admire it, but only as an ingenious curiosity. It would be like a modern-day composer turning out a cantata in the style of Bach: if exceptionally talented, he or she might create a piece worthy of comparison, but who would go to hear it performed? Pessoa was probably not intending his play to be performed. It was a closet drama, and in more ways than one, since its Shakespearean trappings helped to conceal its main subject: Fernando Pessoa.

Molded from the sort of clay used to make Hamlet or Lear, the Duke of Parma is intense, impetuous, psychologically unstable, and philosophically restless. He holds that "every face is ugly looked at close / And every soul studied closely has some madness."[7] In his own soul, that seed of madness is his manic inquiry into the true substance of things. At a meeting of his advisers he asks a doctor to tell him "which is dirtier: the conception of a man or his birth." This is followed up by the question "Which is the viler: a virgin or a whore?" And when the doctor answers that a whore is viler, the duke replies: "There art thou mistaken, for one lies with men, and the other with her imagination, which is as if she lay with a monster."[8]

It emerges that the previous duke was himself slightly unhinged and had grown impotent, characteristics he seems to have passed on to his only biological son, the present duke, in whom they became exacerbated. And yet the present duke, despite being childless, is not truly impotent, just chaste. Despite having renounced sex, he cannot forget its abject power and attraction—"abject" according to his point of view. "All's dirty in the world—all, all!" he laments, and he especially deplores female lust, female sex organs, and even, at certain moments, femalehood in general. Though he knows the accusation is false, he at one point calls his wife a whore, grabs her by the throat, and hurls her over the parapet, watching her fall to her death with "insane delight."[9]

While Shakespeare's Hamlet and Tolstoy's Pozdnyshev (who also murders his wife and idealizes chastity) may have supplied a few symptoms for the duke's obsessive character, his sexual neuroses derived from Pessoa's own imagination—or rather, from Pessoa's *literary* imagination, as he took great care to point out. After one of the duke's speeches, Pessoa scribbled an explanation for the benefit of his future readers: "The Duke's constant sexual allusions and their *purpose*. They are not the author's; they belong to the author's conception of the character of the Duke."[10] He echoed this warning in an isolated phrase jotted down in 1912 and specifically earmarked for a preface (never written) to *The Duke of Parma*: "I have never shown what I am."[11] Because Pessoa does not normally go to the trouble of reminding us that his fictions are fictions, this disclaimer smacks of a sly admission. On the other hand, it is true that he did not *obsess* about sexual matters and mores like the Duke of Parma.

Neither the Duke nor Marcos Alves was an autobiographical portrait. Like the heteronym Alexander Search, both served their creator as dummies, or guinea pigs. Worried about his sexual inhibition and the possibility of a latent mental illness inherited from his grandmother, Pessoa juxtaposed and exaggerated these points of fragility in two characters from different social classes and time periods. After endowing both of them with progressive insanity and severe sexual phobias, he wrote about their possible outcomes.

What all this means about Pessoa's sexuality, beyond his obvious reticence to engage in sex and his pronounced discomfort with women, is uncertain. Although it is our richest resource, mining Pessoa's work to discover Pessoa the man is an endeavor fraught with peril, since he used his writing to experimentally study, to transform and to enlarge himself, rather than to passively express it. He was not just searching for his sexual identity; he was slowly constructing it.

✦

IN ONE OF HIS weekly letters to Durban, sent in May 1911, Pessoa had piqued his mother's curiosity by telling her that he needed to write a long letter explaining a few things. What he needed to explain, of course, was that he had run through his inheritance and was now swimming in debt, but he would put off making that confession for another year and a half. In the meantime he strung along his creditors with hollow promises. He continued to do translations for the Portuguese version of the *International Library of Famous Literature*, earning high compliments from the multilingual project coordinator, Warren Kellogg, and he tried— or thought of trying—to get more work using his language skills. On November 17, for instance, while sitting in his favorite café, A Brasileira, he spotted a want ad for a translator in the *Diário de Notícias*. He started drafting a letter then and there, saying he could handle anything from poetry to philosophy, whether written in English, French, or Spanish.

But some part of him rebelled, and instead of finishing the letter he wrote one of his Shakespearean sonnets, complaining how "the miserly press of each day's need" prevented his soul from doing the task it was "born to think that it must do." The need to make money, in other words, distracted him from writing. Below the sonnet, on the same sheet of café stationery, the poet inscribed the amounts of money he owed several less forbearing creditors as well as the money he was counting on from Kellogg—for translations of poems by Shelley and others—to be able to pay them off.[12]

His aunt Anica, fortunately, did not hound him to pay his share of the rent. He had been living with her and his cousins Mário and Maria since the summer of 1911—in Arroios, a newer neighborhood north of the downtown Baixa district. Clacking yellow streetcars passed right by their building, Rua Passos Manuel, 24, but Pessoa usually walked— twenty minutes—between there and the centrally located cafés that he frequented nearly every day. Aunt Anica had also taken in his great-aunts, Rita and Maria, making it a little crowded in their third-floor apartment, and so Pessoa, for the time being, left most of his books at the office on Largo do Carmo, which Mário continued to lease.[13] Aunt Maria died in September after a long illness, but Rita, the only of his mother's aunts who never married, was still energetically critical and crotchety at eighty-three, testing everyone's patience, especially Aunt Anica's.[14] Pessoa had no choice but to humor her, since she had managed to build up a small nest egg and was one of his creditors.

The downtown cafés were miniature oases, where Pessoa could more easily be his literary self. They served him as makeshift offices for read-ing books as well as newspapers, for writing poems as well as letters. And they were also the nexus of his social life since at least 1908, the year the Café A Brasileira installed tables, encouraging customers to congregate and linger. In 1911, the owners opened a second café, also called A Bra-sileira, on the western side of Praça do Rossio, Lisbon's liveliest square. It was only a ten-minute walk between the two cafés and Pessoa toggled between them, but in the earliest years of the Republic he preferred the older one, in Chiado, since its clientele was more literary.

Rossio was a hub for various cafés, including the venerable Café Suisso and Café Martinho, both of which had been serving coffee since before 1850. Striving to outdo one another in elegance, cafés lavishly adorned their interiors with mirrors, marble, carved plaster moldings, and, in some cases, flower-shaped light fixtures. The Café Martinho on Praça do Rossio had a still older, less ostentatious relative, the Café Martinho da Arcada, located in the arcades of Praça do Comércio, the broadly majestic though sparsely peopled square next to the Tagus River. When it first opened for business, in 1782, its chief attraction was ice cream—with the ice being brought in from the mountains in the north. Pessoa frequented a dozen different cafés, but the A Brasileira of Chiado (especially between 1908 and 1920), the A Brasileira of Rossio (between 1912 and 1918), and the Martinho da Arcada (from 1914 until his death) were the ones where he spent more time and money, debated more ideas, laid more plans with writer friends, and drafted many letters, poems, and prose pieces.*

Each café attracted a different sort of crowd—which might include businessmen, writers, students, professionals, civil servants, or journalists—but women were not part of the culture. Although it diligently imitated French fashion in dress and in décor, Portuguese society remained conservative. Parisian women patronized cafés; women in Lisbon did not, unless it was to purchase a takeout item at the counter. This would begin to change in the late 1920s, but the company Pessoa kept in cafés was always resolutely male. Except for this tacit gender restriction, the company was variegated, with assorted professions and political persuasions represented.

One of Pessoa's earliest café companions was his stepuncle Henrique Rosa, who introduced him to a number of other writers and intellectuals, including Camilo Pessanha (1867–1926), Portugal's greatest symbolist poet. They met at the Café Suisso in the second half of 1908, when Pessanha was on holiday from his job as a colonial official in Macau. The Portuguese had been administering this enclave since the sixteenth century, and it was there that Pessanha spent most of his adult life—working not very long hours, treating his delicate health, consorting with Chinese concubines (one of whom bore him a son), smoking opium, collecting Chinese art, and occasionally composing one of his exquisite poems.† I say he "composed" poems, because it was in function of sound that they took shape—in his head and on his lips, before they were committed to paper. A few of them had been published in periodicals, but he still had no book, and it was mostly through the handwritten or typed copies of admirers that his poetry circulated. He recited some of his poems on one of the two occasions when Pessoa had the privilege of sitting at his table

---

* The first and last of these three cafés are virtually the only ones from Pessoa's time that have survived; their façades and interiors look more or less as they did in the mid-1920s, when the Chiado café was remodeled.

† Most of Pessanha's poems, however, were written in Portugal.

in the Café Suisso. Mesmerized by what he heard, the younger writer later obtained copies of these and other poems from a friend of Pessanha, he transcribed another Pessanha poem that he heard someone recite by heart in the Café A Brasileira, and he hoped to be the first one to publish Pessanha's poetry in book form, according to a notebook with plans for the Ibis press.[15]

◆

NO SOONER DID PESSOA become a regular patron of cafés than he began to draft an essay decrying the arrogance and affectedness of the rest of the clientele, whom he caricatured without mercy. Typical of the essay is this observation: "One of the prime qualities fostered by café life is pedantry, idiotic pretentiousness. The fellow who uses a monocle, not for seeing but just for show, is the quintessential café type."[16] The heteronym Álvaro de Campos, whom Pessoa would equip with a monocle, was occasionally pretentious and quite fond of cafés, even if he defined them as "oases of useless chatter" in his "Triumphal Ode" (1914). Fernando Pessoa, shy and apparently not at all pretentious, also loved cafés, and one of the things he especially loved was to be able to feel how different he was from most of the men at the surrounding tables, particularly the braggarts and big talkers. In fact, his own discreet form of pretension was to fancy himself a creature quite unlike anyone else.

Pessoa was not a scintillating conversationalist, but his mental acuity and astonishing literary culture gradually made him stand out, and by 1911 he began to attract admirers among other young writers. One of the first writers to discover him was Armando Côrtes-Rodrigues (1891–1971), who arrived from the Azores in the fall of 1910 to study at the School of Arts and Letters, which soon became a faculty of the University of Lisbon. Although Côrtes-Rodrigues had published several poems in newspapers as a teenager, he later wiped them from the record, saying that he only really discovered poetry in the capital, through his contact with Fernando Pessoa, whose enthusiasm for the genre was contagious.

In an interview from 1960, he would recall how his friend used to recite, from memory, poems by his favorite poets, and the poem Pessoa most recited was Camilo Pessanha's "Violoncelo" ("Cello"), whose five stanzas evoke an auditory universe of majestic sorrows and high tragedy.[17] The musicality is impossible to render in English, since the tightly rhyming lines are short, with scant room for a translation to maneuver, but the reader can get some idea of Pessanha's way with sound by looking at the first stanza of the original Portuguese:

| | |
|---|---|
| Chorai, arcadas | Weep, O tautly |
| Do violoncelo, | Trembling bows |
| Convulsionadas. | Of the cello. |
| Pontes aladas | Winged bridges |
| De pesadelo . . . | Of nightmares . . . |

Note how the Portuguese words not only rhyme, they alliterate and rhythmically echo one another. Pessoa experimented with his own short-lined, closely rhyming, and reverberating poems, and it would be hard to overemphasize the attention he paid to sound and rhythm. He argued in his theoretical texts, and tried to show by his own practice, that poetry could be more musical than music itself.[18]

Each day, after his classes at the university, Armando Côrtes-Rodrigues would head to A Brasileira in Chiado to meet with his new friend and mentor. From there they walked down to one of the cafés at Praça do Rossio. At that hour people were getting off work, shops started closing, barefoot newsboys hawked the evening edition, passengers packed into streetcars at different points around the square, and men filled up the cafés to enjoy coffee, a brandy, and some conversation before going home—although some men, like Pessoa, were in no hurry. His café friends were mostly people he had met recently, but a couple of them were former classmates, including Armando Teixeira Rebelo. Despite not having much in common, apart from their English fluency acquired in South Africa, Rebelo treasured his friendship with Pessoa and was delighted when he agreed to be the godfather of his daughter, Signa, who was born on December 6, 1911. Brought up bilingual like her parents, she would always speak and write to Pessoa in English.

Rebelo worked in Lisbon but lived with his family outside of town, so Pessoa saw his goddaughter only occasionally. She would remember him as soft-spoken and terribly reserved ("He walked close to the walls, head lowered, looking like a shadow"), yet endowed with an excellent sense of humor, always wearing the hint of a smile when he spoke.[19] Others who knew Pessoa would describe his smile as mysterious and mischievous.[20] We can't see it in photographs, where his thin lips are impassively pressed together, revealing nothing, but we can feel it in his writing: an ambiguous, amused, vaguely ironic, and ever enigmatic smile, like the one drawn by Leonardo on his most famous portrait.*

A conspicuous absence from Pessoa's café and social life around this time was his stepuncle. In letters to his brother in South Africa, Henrique Rosa complained that Fernando—who used to regularly come by his apartment and sit with him in cafés—was avoiding him, coming around only when he needed something. Without ever falling completely out of touch, the two friends had a strained relationship for the next several years and would never recover their former closeness. Precisely because he owed part of his identity to the retired general, who had helped to mold him as a thinker, a poet, and a republican, Pessoa now felt a need to assert his independence. He began pulling away in the second half of 1911, and soon there was a prosaic source of friction—money—which he exploited to justify a rift.

In January 1912 Henrique Rosa became legally empowered to manage the financial interests of Pessoa's parents in Portugal, but since the general was often homebound, they depended on Fernando to do the legwork of receiving interest and dividends here and making payments there. It seems he sometimes finagled the timings of these transactions to temporarily cover one of his pressing debts. At one point his stepuncle accused Pessoa of misconduct, prompting the younger man to react with his own accusations in a very long threatening letter.[21] Although not gifted with a silver tongue, in writing he was piercingly articulate and knew how to wield, like a set of daggers, irrefutably logical arguments. Had he become a lawyer instead of a poet, his legal briefs would have devastated his adversaries, just as his letter successfully devastated and humiliated Henrique Rosa, who backed down. Years later he would feel remorse for how he had treated his much older friend, but in his midtwenties Pessoa, proud and self-preoccupied, could not have acted any differently.

✦

THE FIRST ANNIVERSARY OF the Republic, in October 1911, was celebrated by parades, speeches, and the unveiling of a plaque in Lisbon.

---

* The *Mona Lisa* became even more famous in August 1911, when it was stolen from the Louvre, a feat that completely baffled detectives. It would be recovered two years later.

It was also the occasion chosen by recalcitrant Portuguese monarchists to launch a raid from across the northern border with Spain, where they had gone into exile. This insurrection and a recent monarchist uprising in Porto were both easily subdued, but the jails of the Republic were filling up with political prisoners, the wave of strikes and demonstrations showed no signs of ebbing, the streets were becoming increasingly unsafe, and the country's political future looked precarious to some. On October 4, the day before the republican anniversary, London's *Daily Telegraph* alleged, with exaggeration, that "rather than a Republic, Portugal is an anarchy, where every abuse of liberty prevails."[22]

The instability was understandable, in Pessoa's view, since the new order was still getting its bearings: it needed time to settle before the country could begin to make meaningful progress. He remained optimistic, notwithstanding all the immediate problems. So as to encourage a serious discussion of those problems, he was again planning to be a publisher, though on a far more modest scale, all too mindful of the Ibis press fiasco and its still lingering debts. His idea was to publish a magazine, patriotically titled *Lusitania*. The Lusitani people were the inhabitants of western Iberia before the arrival of the Romans, who gave the name Lusitania to the province that included most of what would become modern Portugal. For Pessoa the name signified all that was specifically and spiritually Portuguese. *Lusitania*, as he conceived it, would defend the Republic not only from its detractors but also from misguided republicans who were hampering its growth and development.

The new Portuguese republic suffered, above all else, from a leadership problem. Leaders were not in short supply; the problem was that loyalty to a given leader, and to the political faction he represented, too often took precedence over concern for good governance and respect for due process. Three factions would be formally delineated by the beginning of 1912: the Democrats, led by the feisty and unyielding Afonso Costa; the Unionists, headed by newspaper editor Manuel Brito Camacho, who was dour and doctrinaire; and the Evolutionists, led by the charismatic António José de Almeida, who founded his own newspaper. Almeida was the most stirring orator, but Costa inspired fanatical devotion among his supporters—and hatred among his opponents. His Democrats were the ideologically radical party, and he was the architect of the law designed to strangle the Catholic Church in Portugal. The other two parties were also anticlerical, but without animus in their rhetoric. With or without animosity, the Church's clergy continued to be persecuted and its properties expropriated, in keeping with the draconian terms of the law separating church and state. Certain republicans in the north of Portugal, where the Church was strongest, reacted with organized protests against parts of the legislative program passed by the provisional government. A few of them even defected to the side of the monarchists, or neo-monarchists, whose reaction took the form of armed conspiracies.

Pessoa criticized the political reactionaries and attacked even more fiercely republican radicals such as Afonso Costa in passages for an essay called "Oligarchy of Brutes." "All radicalism fosters reaction," he warned, "since the informing spirit is the same."[23] Both the radical and reactionary attitudes were, to his way of thinking, antisocial "pathologies," and he accused Portugal's political leaders of constituting a de facto oligarchy, concerned mainly with keeping themselves in power.

"Oligarchy of Brutes" was scheduled to be the lead article of the first issue of *Lusitania*. If its vicious assessment of Costa and other politicians raised any doubts about Pessoa's republican sympathies, they would be dispelled by the issue's second article, "The Coronation of George V." Britain's King George V had risen to the throne in May 1910, but his coronation ceremony was held a year later. The British Empire was practically at its height, and no pomp was spared for the occasion, which brought fifty thousand marching troops to London. Pessoa's entirely fictional account of the event is narrated by a Portuguese republican who happens to be in London when the royal extravaganza takes place. He reports that the festivities have a sickly, yellowish color, the empire is moribund, and British subjects are like "sleepwalkers heading toward a precipice."[24] Pessoa, who could not have possibly believed in this prophecy of imminent doom, may have been getting revenge for the British press's skeptical coverage of Portugal's transition to a republican form of government. He also wanted to impress on his Portuguese readers that monarchies were *passé*, the future belonged to republicanism, and he saw nothing wrong with using fake reportage to create well-meaning and useful propaganda. Other articles for his magazine examined the Portuguese Republic in a larger European context, and for foreign readers there would be an essay in English, "The Decline and Fall of the Portuguese Monarchy," for which he wrote a few pages.

*Lusitania* either preceded or succeeded another magazine project, soberly titled *Estudos Contemporâneos* (*Contemporary Studies*),[25] where the same political essays were scheduled to appear. The provisional table of contents for its first issue also lists *Portugal*, Pessoa's patriotic epic poem, never completed, and the twistedly humorous "La France en 1950," in which his French heteronym Jean Seul, as mentioned earlier, imagines a future society where pedophilia, infanticide, and every conceivable form of sexual perversion will be acceptable and even required behavior. That Pessoa meant this satire to be a criticism of contemporary liberalized sexual mores seems to be confirmed by his plan to publish, in the same issue of *Contemporary Studies*, a group of "moral poems," about which he offered no details.

Pessoa was not pedantic, like some of the café habitués he disparaged in his writings, but he was pedagogical, as these magazine projects from 1911 demonstrate. He wanted to teach politicians how to behave, intellectuals what to think, and the Portuguese in general why it was important to be patriotic. And as a young man he also aspired to be a sexual moralizer—for motives that arouse suspicion. On the one hand, Jean Seul takes too much delight in narrating the kinky sexual practices that his satires are ostensibly condemning. On the other, the tormented chastity of characters like Marcos Alves and the Duke of Parma, in whom the mere thought of a vagina strikes panic, makes us wonder whether Pessoa was using his moral campaign to avoid dealing, in his own life, with sex and sexuality. Then again, virtually all of Pessoa's intellectual pursuits, including his pedagogical activities, were partly undertaken for their entertainment value. However earnest his political essays and moral satires, we can be sure that while he wrote them he was smiling, à la Mona Lisa, with at least a little bit of blithe detachment. Pessoa finished none of the works scheduled for publication in *Lusitania* and *Contemporary Studies*,[26] which was perhaps just as well, since he was far too deep in debt to think seriously of starting up a magazine.

# CHAPTER 24

S TARKLY DIFFERENT FROM THE TUMULTUOUS
atmosphere of the one-year-old republic was the peaceful,
orderly world of Pretoria, where Pessoa's stepfather had taken
up his new post as consul-general and installed his family in a spacious
house with the obligatory big yard. Chosen as the administrative capital of the Union of South Africa, created in 1910, Pretoria was graced
with a new railway station that same year and would soon inaugurate
the splendorous Union Buildings, a kind of Acropolis sitting above the
rest of the town and housing the offices of the president and the new
national government. The east and west wings of the elegant complex
were said to represent the English and Afrikaans languages. Nothing in
the architectural ensemble paid tribute to Zulu, Xhosa, or other native
languages. Independent South Africa was founded on a unity of white
interests, and laws were quickly being enacted to enforce segregation,
to prevent blacks from voting,* and to otherwise pave the way for the
system that would become known as apartheid. In January 1912 a group
of blacks from the educated elite formed an organization—eventually
called the African National Congress—for the purpose of defending
their own interests and, as time went on, the interests of black South
Africans generally.

Such matters, of course, did not concern Pessoa's mother, whose
weekly letters to him reported on the Rosa household. His sister and two
brothers—now aged fifteen, eleven, and nine—were all learning to play
the piano. She also inquired about her oldest son's health, mood, and
work life. And she worried a little about the future of Portugal, seized by
turmoil and clouded by so many unknowns.

* In the politically more liberal Cape Province, blacks could traditionally vote but were
gradually disenfranchised after South Africa became independent.

The turmoil was especially severe in Lisbon, where demonstrations and a wave of crippling strikes in late January 1912 led the government to declare a state of emergency. It was still in effect when Pessoa wrote his mother on February 10 that he was feeling out of sorts and that his trouble had to do with the long letter he had been promising her since last May. In her next several letters she coaxed him to come out with his news but added that she hoped it was nothing disagreeable. And so he continued to harbor his secret, while recommending patience to his creditors. Although he desperately needed to earn money, he would never, for its sake, violate his natural rhythm or submit to an outside authority. He continued to do freelance translations, which he rather enjoyed, and to maximize that enjoyment he did them at his leisure, rather than according to schedule. Warren Kellogg sent him a letter on February 19:

Dear Mr. Pessoa,

I don't know what to say to you and my angelic temper is sorely tried! You promised solemnly to bring in those Spanish poems and finish the *Cid* at once, and weeks are again going by and you do not appear. Tomorrow is a holiday so by Friday I shall expect you. If you do not come this week I shall, on Monday the 26th, reluctantly give the *Cid* to someone else to translate. Please return those dictionaries. Their absence from the office is a great and daily inconvenience.

Please reply to one who is still

Yrs truly,

Warren F. Kellogg

Although Pessoa's disappearing acts were infuriating, his translation work was excellent. In a few months' time, Kellogg would be packing up all his things and going to London, where he would finish the editorial work on the twenty-four-volume *Biblioteca* of world literature. He invited Pessoa to go with him for a period of six months, as he would need a native Portuguese speaker and writer to help him tidy up loose ends. It was an extraordinary opportunity for Pessoa, who had been fantasizing about London ever since coming back to Portugal from Durban. The perennial problem of how to finance the voyage and cover his living expenses was miraculously solved. He already had a list of English writers, critics, and editors he wanted to contact about his own work, and the publishers of the *Biblioteca* might be able to help with introductions. Six months would be enough time to make a few friends and, with luck, find an outlet for his writings in English.

Pessoa, nevertheless, turned down the invitation, which was then extended (probably at his suggestion) to his friend Armando Teixeira Rebelo, who jumped at the chance, even though it meant a long separation from his wife and their newborn daughter.[1] Unlike Armando, Fernando had no intimate relationships that were holding him to Lisbon, which makes his decision to stay put all the more mysterious. His financial situation no doubt complicated matters, since he had to make monthly payments on the bank loan he took out when the Ibis press collapsed, and to all those friends and acquaintances who had loaned him money it might appear that he was absconding. On the other hand, the money earned in England could help pay off some debt. And absconding was perhaps not a bad idea. In November 1911, after drawing up an updated list of old debts and new expenditures in a memo book, he scribbled in large letters, in English: "Cut & run for clear intellectual life! December to reconstruct life."[2]

What better place to run to than London? It made for a lovely dream, and Pessoa would continue to nurture it for at least the next twenty years, but the thought of *really* going to any new place and dealing with new people flustered him. He hated changes in his outward life; he preferred to change his mental perspectives, by altering his opinions and by adopting, through his heteronyms, contrasting points of view. He was not good at making small talk with new people; he preferred writing, and during the next several years he would send a number of letters to editors in London, trying to generate interest in his creative work. Then too, going to London with Kellogg would mean answering to Kellogg, being Kellogg's assistant, doing what Kellogg politely told him to do. No. He would remain in Lisbon, answering only to himself.

✦

PESSOA HAD ANOTHER, LOFTIER reason for not going to London: the dawning of the Portuguese Renaissance. More precisely, what kept him on home soil was his concentrated effort to prove, in a series of densely formulated articles written between March and December of 1912, that a Portuguese Renaissance was imminent and inevitable. His articles were published in *A Águia* (*The Eagle*), a Porto-based magazine belonging to the Renascença Portuguesa (Portuguese Renaissance), a movement whose very name chimed with his own belief in a national resurgence. Both the movement and its magazine contributed to his development as a writer and as a public figure who would soon create movements and a magazine of his own.

Amid the turbulence and instability that would continue to afflict the recently founded republic, *A Águia* managed to have a long and remarkably steady existence. Launched in December 1910, two months after the republican revolution, the magazine would keep publishing into the 1930s, but it is mostly remembered for its early years, when Portugal felt like a new country where everything was possible. Consisting of poetry, fiction, social research, cultural criticism, and articles on education, and suffused throughout with an emphasis on self-betterment, *A Águia* embodied the spirit of republican nationalism but gave it a mystical coloring. Teixeira de Pascoaes (1877–1952), an important poet and the most influential essayist published by the magazine, wrote a piece for the inaugural issue that eulogized Portugal's tenant farmers and other people connected to the land who, despite the "Catholic superstitions" inculcated in them by narrow-minded priests, were admirably indwelt by "that exceptional Soul, instinctively naturalistic and mystical, that created *Saudade*, the promise of a new *Lusitanian Civilization*" (emphasis in original). Pascoaes became editor in chief of *A Águia* in 1912[3] and promoted with evangelical fervor the doctrine of *saudosismo*, according to which *saudade* (intense longing, yearning, nostalgia) was an essentially Portuguese, soulish energy and the key to the nation's civilizational progress.

In *Creative Evolution* (1907), the French philosopher Henri Bergson had proposed élan vital as a primordial impulse responsible for evolution and creativity in the broadest sense of the word. His idea quickly spawned kindred concepts and may have influenced Pascoaes, who seems to have understood *saudade* as a localized, specifically Portuguese élan vital—"the spiritual blood of our Race," according to his lead editorial for the January 1912 issue of *A Águia*. Although several prominent voices of the Renascença Portuguesa were not keen on this essentialist, racialist view of the Portuguese spirit, or soul, or People, it was Pascoaes's ideas that prevailed, and he had steadfast followers, including Mário Beirão (1890–1965), a good friend of Pessoa whose poems had been regularly appearing in *A Águia* since January 1911.

It was no doubt in cafés that Pessoa met Mário Beirão, whose dark, deep-set eyes radiated seriousness and sincerity; perhaps through Beirão, Pessoa met Pascoaes, who had the air of a man in possession of a great secret. (Pascoaes was from northern Portugal but occasionally visited Lisbon.) Or perhaps Pessoa, on his own initiative, wrote a letter to Pascoaes or another editor of *A Águia* to pitch the first of his articles on contemporary Portuguese poetry. He had been purchasing the magazine since its founding and identified to a certain extent with the philosophy and ambitions of the Renascença Portuguesa group.[4] In fact, it suddenly dawned on him that his ideas about the transformations taking place in Portugal were more or less in sync with theirs. Or rather, he could (and would) dress up his own ideas in such a way as to create an impression of near convergence, in this way gaining a platform to promote them.

*A Águia* brought out Pessoa's "The New Portuguese Poetry Sociologically Considered" in its April 1912 issue. This was his first published piece of critical writing, and the Portuguese intelligentsia was awed by its dazzling argumentation and precise language, even if its thesis and conclusion struck some people as a hoax. Adopting an evolutionary perspective, Pessoa established a relationship between literary progress and political, or sociological, progress. He explained in careful detail that just as Shakespeare and his Elizabethan peers flowered at the *beginning* of the (in his opinion) great political era that would culminate in Oliver Cromwell's republic, and just as the greatest literary movement in France—Romanticism—began after the fall of the ancien régime but *before* the French Revolution took root in the soul of the people (between 1848 and 1870, by his calculation), the same pattern was bound to repeat itself in Portugal: the new but still fumbling republic would lead to the greatest sociopolitical period of its history and would be *preceded* by the greatest literary period it had ever known. The (for him) obvious fact that recent Portuguese poetry was original, intensely Portuguese, and objectively of high quality confirmed that a literary renaissance was under way, and this in turn confirmed that the young republic's current state of disarray was a dissonant prelude to the "*glorious future* awaiting the Portuguese Nation."

Because a country's literary high point always predates its political high point, and because that political zenith could already be hazily discerned, Pessoa deduced that the excellent Portuguese poetry being produced in 1912 was a breeding ground for a genius writer who would soon raise national literature to an unprecedented height. It was inevitable, he concluded, that a "Great Poet" would emerge and eclipse Luís de Camões. He did not mention that this presumptive Great Poet was himself.

Not everyone thought that Pessoa's observations and conclusions were obvious or inevitable. One week after his article came out, a Lisbon newspaper published a critique rejecting its main points. Pessoa wrote a rejoinder for the May issue of *A Águia*, reiterating and expanding on his original arguments. To back up his claim that the new Portuguese poetry had attained an extraordinary degree of originality and "elevation," he cited concrete examples, such as the following lines of verse by Teixeira de Pascoaes:

> The leaf slowly falling
> Was a soul ascending,

and this stanza from a poem by Jaime Cortesão (1884–1960), a founder of the Renascença Portuguesa and a regular contributor to *A Águia*:

> And moistened by moonlight,
> The poplars no longer have branches
> Or leaves, they're just poplars
> Of a Soul in the calm of night.

Pessoa conceded that someone might not "feel the elevation and originality of these verses. The reasoner, however, only presents his reasons. He is not obliged to hand out intelligence beforehand." Which is to say: if you're too aesthetically obtuse to recognize good poetry when you see it, I can't help you. It is safe to assume that not even Pascoaes and Cortesão were aware that they had written such original and elevating poetry, but they were delighted to be so favorably cited by the clever young critic. Pessoa's judgment, although not necessarily insincere, was certainly not disinterested. Pascoaes's movement was in fact less a breeding ground than it was a springboard for the Great Poet predicted by Pessoa, who intended to fulfill, in his own person, what he prophesied. The more elevated the springboard, the bigger splash he could make.

In the fall he published another essay, "The New Portuguese Poetry in Its Psychological Aspect," which took up nineteen pages, spread over three issues of *A Águia*. To support his assertions that the new poetry was simultaneously subjective and objective, and imbued with a "pantheistic transcendentalism," he resorted to the examples from Pascoaes and Cortesão he had used in May, and he added new examples from two poems by Mário Beirão. He argued even more incisively than before that these and other "new" poets were a kind of collective John the Baptist, preparing the way for the Great Poet, or "Super-Camões," who would inaugurate a new literary renaissance, which would radiate from Portugal outward to the rest of Europe.

Although he cited their poems and used some of their vocabulary in his discourse, Pessoa was proposing a very different vision from the one espoused by the *saudosistas*, for whom the Portuguese Renaissance would unfold (according to Pascoaes) in the soul of the people, not "through the artifice of the Arts, as in Italy."[5] In Pessoa's view, art was what mattered above all else, and it was individuals who made things happen—whether in art or in any other field of human endeavor. His articles also exalted the Portuguese "Soul" and expressed faith that republicanism would lead to a national golden age, but at the end of his last article he sternly warned that if the current state of political chaos did not die down naturally, then a Portuguese Cromwell would rise up and use brute force to impose order. Such a possibility had no place in the *saudosistas*' vision of a Portugal where people would live in peace and harmony while cheerfully working for the national good.

Pessoa's ominous prophecy of a Portuguese Cromwell, a strongman who would usher in a period of national peace and grandeur, would be semifulfilled in the late 1920s and early 1930s, when António de Oliveira Salazar finally brought peace and stability to Portugal, but no grandeur, and there were two dictators who preceded him, in 1915 and 1917–1918. Pessoa placed some hope in all three, but only Salazar lasted more than a year, and it would not take much longer than that for the poet to become disillusioned. He had guessed wrong, bet wrong, but it is hard to say what would have been the right bet, particularly for such an incorrigible idealist like Pessoa.

His wagers in the literary sphere were more successful. The prophecy of a Great Poet, for instance, was astonishingly accurate, as proven by the existence of hundreds of books about Pessoa and his writings. No one could have imagined that this newcomer to the scene, still virtually unpublished, was predicting his own future apotheosis as Portugal's modern literary giant. His prediction was, if we like, a symptom of megalomania, but it was also a sublime instance of his famous capacity for constructive feigning, or *fingimento*. Pessoa, who thought of himself as a dramatist who happened to write poetry, set the stage and conceived the part that he himself would play on it. It was by pretending to be great that he arrived at greatness.

# CHAPTER 25

**W**HILE THE GREAT POET LURKED IN THE WINGS, still invisible to the world, the mild-mannered man to whom that title secretly belonged continued to attract other writers to the tables where he sat in Lisbon's cafés. Pessoa was a passive magnet, only dimly aware that he was becoming a leader. It was not a role he coveted, partly because he was suspicious of collective enterprises, usually preferring to act on his own, representing only himself, but a writers' circle formed spontaneously, and it revolved around him, although at first no one realized it. They were just young men who met together, apparently leaderless, and Pessoa was the most soft-spoken of them all. But he was the group's center of gravity—a dense concentration of intellectual power, erudition, language, and culture, and with the capacity for thinking and seeing from new angles, like a Portuguese Pound or a Portuguese Eliot. (At this point, however, he knew little if anything about Ezra Pound or T. S. Eliot.) The modernist urge to reinvent art had been sweeping across Europe, and some of the writers who gravitated around Pessoa already had vanguardist aspirations. It was Pessoa, however, who would show them how to break with traditional forms of representation and with the notion of art as a faithful expression of a reliable "I."

While he had not yet come into his own as a truly original poet, Pessoa emitted opinions about other people's poetry like a learned high judge. In late 1912 and early 1913 he sent letters to several published poets, including Mário Beirão, to explain in clear detail what was praiseworthy in their poetry and also where it fell short. Pound was famous for offering similarly forthright, even brutal criticism to other poets, most notably to Eliot, but he himself had already published some outstanding work. Pessoa had not published a single poem, except as a teenager, and must have come across as presumptuous to some of the poets he critiqued. His criticism, however, was insightful, and if the thin-skinned found it off-putting, it drew other writers to him.

Poundian, too, was Pessoa's dedication to advancing other writers' careers. His learned and lively articles promoting the poetry of the Renascença Portuguesa group had earned him not only a grateful letter from their official leader and spiritual guide, Teixeira de Pascoaes,[1] but also a publishing venue for himself and for whatever friends he decided to help out. On December 4, 1912, along with the last installment of his article on the new Portuguese poetry in its "psychological aspect," he sent a longer than usual letter to the managing editor of *A Águia*, proposing that the magazine publish literary work by two of his friends—a poem by António Cobeira (1892–1959) and a short story by Mário de Sá-Carneiro (1890–1916). Several months later, he proposed a poem by Armando Côrtes-Rodrigues, his Azorean friend. *A Águia* accepted all three suggestions. Only later did Pessoa submit something of his own to the magazine.

Ezra Pound (1885–1972), living in London and serving as the foreign correspondent of *Poetry*, the Chicago-based journal founded in 1912, expended his critical and promotional energies on talents such as Eliot, James Joyce, and Robert Frost. Pessoa operated in a far more circumscribed, less sophisticated milieu, and his efforts on behalf of friends often had only modest results. Such was the case with António Cobeira, who had moved to Lisbon—like Côrtes-Rodrigues—to study at the Faculty of Arts and Letters. Encouraged by Pessoa, he thrived as a young poet and critic, regularly publishing his work in magazines until, after four or five years, he abruptly quit writing. In a newspaper article published long after Pessoa's death, Cobeira would remember his friend as an "incurably inhibited sort, impotent in real life—asexual like a lone angel adrift in his flight through infinity," and as one who had fallen "into the nerve center of the universe as into a bottomless well," with scant interest in the "immediately tangible" world. Cobeira was unwilling to go so far or to plumb so deep. "I soon escaped from my hell," he wrote, in an allusion to Rimbaud's *A Season in Hell*. The French poet, after he quit writing, became a merchant in Yemen and Abyssinia; Cobeira became a schoolteacher.[2]

There were also those who recognized Pessoa's genius but nevertheless rejected his poetic influence. For instance, after an initial period of close camaraderie with Pessoa, Mário Beirão began to drift away from him aesthetically and philosophically. This coincided with his physical relocation, in September 1912, to the wine country north of the Douro

River, where he went to live with a nobleman. Beirão strengthened his ties to the Renascença Portuguesa, which was headquartered in Porto, and more fervently embraced Pascoaes's mystical confidence in *saudade* and the Portuguese soul. He still exchanged some warm letters with Pessoa and must have seen him when he returned to Lisbon to study law, but after 1914 they fell out of touch. Their literary tastes and theories were fundamentally at odds; Beirão thought that Pessoa was too cerebral.

Teixeira de Pascoaes, not too surprisingly, shared this opinion. In 1950 he would tell an interviewer that Pessoa "tried to intellectualize poetry," producing something artificial and without soul that could not even rightly be called poetry.[3] A few other poets have expressed similar, though less extreme, reservations. In 1985, during the celebrations that marked the fiftieth anniversary of Pessoa's death, Brazil's Carlos Drummond de Andrade declared his preference for Camões, saying that Pessoa "is cold, he touches only our intellectual side."[4] If that assessment has any validity, then how does one explain the fact that Pessoa is the most beloved poet in Brazil with the possible exception of Drummond de Andrade himself? He is, to be sure, an intellectual poet, but one with a rare gift for expressing complex ideas and sensations in eminently accessible language. We don't need to look up words, hunt down references, or read up on some period of history or current of philosophy to follow his poetic trains of thought and feeling. His erudition is only parenthetically present in his poetry, which touches us just as immediately and emotionally as Drummond's. And yet Pessoa *was* a cerebral artist, insofar as he "intelligently" managed his dramatic sensibility to create poems that arouse powerful responses in the reader. He separated himself from his feelings and repackaged them. To some poets it seemed as if he was cheating—as if poetry, to be legitimate, had to come direct and unfiltered from the Muse.

◆

AMONG ALL HIS PEERS, only one man completely understood and appreciated Pessoa's kind of genius: the poet and fiction writer Mário de Sá-Carneiro, who had nothing but admiration for his intellect and intellectualizing, even if his own poetic processes were more intuitive. And no one, more than Pessoa, understood Sá-Carneiro's genius. Their passionate faith in each other's creative artistry reciprocally enabled them to branch out in new directions and to reach new heights: the

two writers would rank far above everyone else in their literary generation. Committed to each other not only as writers but also as the best
of friends, in some ways they made an odd pair. Both were equally in
love with literature, but Sá-Carneiro also craved the world's beautiful
things and lavishly treated himself to whatever he fancied. Handsome
but pudgy as an adolescent, he was a corpulent adult—not obese, but
as if his body were trying to burst out of its fleshly casing. He was born
into a well-to-do family from Lisbon, took himself seriously as a writer
by the age of thirteen, and had an uncommonly literary set of high
school classmates, several of whom were part of the still amorphous
group that began meeting in the summer of 1912, without any specific
objectives beyond sharpening their critical capacity and improving their
writing. They read to one another their poems and prose pieces—either
in cafés or at Sá-Carneiro's home on Travessa do Carmo, in Chiado,
just two blocks away from the Brasileira café. It was there, in Mário's
bedroom, that Fernando Pessoa and António Cobeira listened to him
recite stories from his forthcoming book, *Princípio* (*Beginning*), published in August 1912.[5]

*Princípio* was not, in truth, a very good beginning—Sá-Carneiro's
subsequent fiction was vastly superior—but I mention it because of the
author's inscription in Pessoa's copy, signed on the twenty-ninth of that
month: "To his dear friend Fernando Pessoa—to the lofty spirit, the artist and the thinker, offered with a big hug." The Portuguese are generous with their written hugs, even giving them to people they know only
professionally, but a "*querido amigo*" (dear friend) is someone you care
about deeply. There was already a close bond between the two young
writers, and before long they would be emotionally linked in a way that
Pessoa had thought could never happen. As we've seen, he complained
back in 1907 of not having one intimate friend, saying that even if he
had one, he would not be intimate according to *his* standard of intimacy. But Mário de Sá-Carneiro confuted and confounded him. Mário's
voluptuous appreciation of life's good things included his friends and,
foremost among them, the "lofty spirit" named Fernando Pessoa. He
touched some deep and concealed part of Pessoa, who was disarmed to
the point of embarrassment—like a man who, in a dream, suddenly realizes that he's stark naked.

An only child who lost his mother to typhoid fever when he was two
years old, Mário grew up lovingly spoiled by his father, his paternal

grandfather, and a devoted nanny. His father, Carlos, an army engineer, often had to spend long periods away from home, but he made up for it by traveling with his son on holiday, taking him every year to Paris, where they saw the latest plays, which were Mário's favorite distraction. Precocious but with no patience for sitting through classes and studying for tests, Mário was twenty-one years old when he finally graduated from high school, in July 1911. After a few months studying law at the University of Coimbra, he dropped out and returned to Lisbon, where he met Pessoa in early 1912.[6]

✦

PESSOA WROTE HIS FIRST two homoerotic poems around the same time he met Mário de Sá-Carneiro, who was surely not their direct inspiration. Curvaceously, femininely plump, he was not apt to arouse desire in Pessoa, who admired athletic physiques, and while the attachment between the two men was strong and developed quickly, it followed the pattern of a friendship. But it may be that Sá-Carneiro's sexually ambiguous manner and uninhibited conversation emboldened Pessoa to be imaginatively uninhibited and to write, at last, about love between men. The beloved to whom his poems are addressed, in Portuguese, could have been one of the many charming males he mingled with in cafés. The poems could also, just as easily, have been inspired by no one in particular, by the mere *idea* of a beloved man, or by the forbidden possibility of loving a man. Whether real or theoretical, it was a possibility that clearly perturbed Pessoa.

In one of the two poems, only half written, the narrator ruefully notes that "nature," "social outrage," and his own love of "virtue" hinder his love for another man. Love nevertheless wins out:

There are a thousand reasons not to love you,
But one for loving you, which is my loving you.

The other poem, written the same day, describes the plight of the "virtuous" narrator with painful poignancy. Even its title, "Sonnet That Shouldn't Have Been Written (but That Was Written in the Café A Brasileira on February 11, 1912)," winces with guilt. And the logic of the sonnet's final lines is devastating:

I love you because I love you, loathing
Myself, and that loathing wounds my love
With a feeling so completely hurtful

That the hurt, being a feeling and making me feel
Yet more, increases the feeling of my wanting you—
Of my being unable to want to be able to have you.[7]

The narrator's love for a man stirs self-loathing, which paradoxically increases his desire for this man whom, because he's a man, he can't let himself desire. Yet he *does* with all his heart desire him, against his will but also without regret, since love, by its nature, cannot regret loving.

Was the narrator of these two poems Fernando Pessoa? Was Fernando in love? Nothing else he wrote in his notes and in the rest of his poetry for the year 1912 suggests that he was. But perhaps he had a passing crush? Perhaps. I read these poems against the backdrop of *Marcos Alves* and *The Duke of Parma*, whose chaste protagonists neither tolerated the thought of sex with women nor dared to entertain the idea of sex with men. Now, finally, Pessoa dared. The title "Sonnet That Shouldn't Have Been Written" speaks to his awareness that he was committing a transgression. The subtitle "but That *Was* Written" (emphasis added) attests to a defiant decision, a resolution. He even dated the poem: on February 11, 1912, Pessoa said no to the prohibition against same-sex love drilled into him by the conservative moral code of Portuguese society, by his Catholic upbringing, and by his rigorously Victorian education in Durban. Though he still had misgivings, his poetic narrator overcame, at least momentarily, the moral strictures that paralyzed Marcos Alves and the Duke of Parma not only in deed but even in thought.

Even if he loved nobody, Pessoa was now ready, in his imagination, to be in love—like the young St. Augustine, according to the *Confessions* he would write after his conversion: "I was not yet in love, but I was in love with the idea of love." Toward the end of his life, Pessoa would cite this line in a poem signed by his heteronym Álvaro de Campos.[8] But whereas Augustine, as we know from his famous book, lived a life of debauchery until becoming a devout believer, Pessoa, without believing, very probably died a virgin. His "debauchery," such as it was, would find consummation in his writing. The same was true for Sá-Carneiro, whose writing is highly sexualized but whose pampered life was unremittingly chaste, until its tragic denouement.

It is almost impossible to conceive of Pessoa and Sá-Carneiro as physical lovers, and even as dedicated friends they were not obviously compatible—one of them an epicure and the other one indifferent to worldly pleasures. Although they did have a congruent literary sensibility, admiring many of the same authors, each applied that sensibility to his own creative work in divergent ways. Whether in poetry or prose, Pessoa expressed ideas and feelings dramatically, through character-narrators. Sá-Carneiro's writing was directly histrionic, promiscuously weaving his personal life into his poems and stories. To read his works as autobiographical expressions would be to read backwards, however. It was his life that imitated literature—à la Oscar Wilde, whom he read early on. Fernando Pessoa lived much of his life through the art of literature, using it to test and invent himself; Sá-Carneiro's life *was* his ultimate work of art. United, at any rate, by their nearly identical *feeling* for literature, Fernando and Mário would become literary soulmates, entering into each other's work like no one else could, caring about it almost as if it were their own. But this only happened after they were geographically separated for the first time and found themselves completely alone with each other—in their letters.

# CHAPTER 26

O N A PLATFORM OF THE RAILWAY STATION AT Praça do Rossio, as steam hissed from the locomotive of a waiting train, a group of men took turns shaking hands and embracing Mário de Sá-Carneiro. Unwilling to return to the University of Coimbra, the fickle student had persuaded his indulgent father to finance his legal education at the Sorbonne—a farce, if there ever was one—and shortly before midday on October 13, 1912, he boarded the Sud-Express bound for Paris. The well-wishers included his father and grandfather, several actor friends, some former classmates, and his "*querido amigo*" Fernando Pessoa.[1]

It took a day and a half to reach Paris, and a passenger such as Mário could almost wish it took longer. The Sud-Express was a luxury train, with fine dining, fancy lounge cars, and comfortable bedding. "Wonderful," wrote Sá-Carneiro in a one-word sentence to describe how he felt in a postcard to Pessoa sent after his arrival at the French capital. Then the letters began, sometimes many pages long, and occasionally interspersed with more postcards, like smiles or winks to animate their written conversation. The letter paper and the cards were often from one of the cafés he patronized—the Balthazard, the Cardinal, the Régence, and especially the Café Riche, where Baudelaire and his dandified friends had once been practically part of the furniture. Zola and Maupassant both described, in novels, the Riche's glittery ambience—the mirrors, the gold trim, the spotless tableware—repeated in room after room of the enormous interior.

Sá-Carneiro felt wonderful, but the political tensions that had been building up around Europe since the start of the new century could no longer be held in check by diplomacy. While the Sorbonne student settled into his hotel in the middle of the Latin Quarter, more than a million troops in southeastern Europe began to trade fire in what would become known as the First Balkan War. Bulgaria, Serbia, Greece, and

Montenegro, banding together to form the Balkan League, all declared war on the Ottoman Empire in mid-October. The common objective of the four nations was to oust the Ottomans from the Balkan Peninsula, which they largely managed to do in less than eight months of fighting. Then came the Second Balkan War, in which the victors squabbled over the conquered territory. But it all happened quickly, so that by August 1913 the hostilities were over and national boundaries redrawn. Who could have guessed that the localized fighting was a preview, in miniature, of a conflict that would embroil the whole of Europe, extend beyond it, and cost fifteen million lives?

After forty years of peace, a continually expanding economy, and a secure feeling of glamorous privilege, the bourgeoisie in France could scarcely imagine these conditions changing. Although a vast underclass continued to live in the penumbra of the fashionable arrondissements, competing for cramped quarters rife with germs and disease, visitors to Paris were struck first of all by the smartly dressed gentlemen and ladies, their elegant carriages and automobiles, the rationally laid out streets, the solid feel of the city's architecture, the art nouveau doors, façades, and métro stations (the first métro line opened in 1900), the theaters, cabarets, music halls, and movie houses. Sá-Carneiro thrilled at all the stylish splendor on display, but Paris at the end of the Belle Époque was also a dynamic center of artistic innovation. It was there, in 1913, that the first volume of Proust's *À la recherche du temps perdu* was published (Pessoa's copy was printed in 1922), as well as Guillaume Apollinaire's *Alcools*, whose poems, though rooted in symbolism, heralded the modernist emphasis on formal innovation. In that same year Apollinaire, an early champion of the cubist painters, published one of the first books about their art, which had developed in the French capital, and in May the premiere of Igor Stravinsky's dissonant *Rite of Spring*, choreographed by Vaslav Nijinsky for the stridently unconventional Ballets Russes, caused an uproar at the Théâtre des Champs-Élysées, enthralling some spectators and horrifying many others.

Sá-Carneiro wrote steadily, sat for long hours in cafés, and strolled in the Luxembourg Gardens, but his excitement about being in Paris soon alternated with states of tortured anxiety about seemingly nothing, except for the fact that beauty is fleeting, and life less than perfect. Atrociously aware of all that was missing in the world, which he loved, and in himself, whom he adored, he was an unhappy voluptuary and a failed narcissist. Pessoa vented his own, even more abstract anxieties, being most of all preoccupied with the *why* of this world and his place in it, and he imagined other worlds, other selves. Their letters also contained news and commentary about their mutual friends. But most of their conversation was about literature. As soon as Pessoa managed to write a complete poem, he would post it to Paris to see what his privileged reader thought. And Sá-Carneiro sent both poems and stories, counting on Pessoa for his honest appraisals and advice.

Mail delivery between the two capitals was fast—three or four days—which helped to make this one of the more fruitful literary exchanges of the twentieth century. Both writers were at tipping points in their careers, and their critical engagement with each other's work decisively influenced what and how they wrote. Their letters, moreover, had an intoxicating effect, boosting their confidence in what they could creatively accomplish: suddenly everything that was conceivable seemed doable.

◆

IN A LETTER SENT to Sá-Carneiro in late January 1913, Pessoa curiously remarked that the Viscount of Vila-Moura (1877–1935), a member of the Renascença Portuguesa and an ostentatiously Wildean figure, was apt to be a "pernicious influence" on their friend Mário Beirão, who had been living with the viscount for the past four months. Given that Beirão was already firmly committed to the Renascença group and to the ideas of Teixeira de Pascoaes about the regenerating power of Portuguese *saudade*, Pessoa must have been referring to the harmful effect that the viscount himself—his personal literary style, or lifestyle—might have on Beirão, who was thirteen years younger.

Although he was friends with Pascoaes and regularly published articles in *A Águia*, Vila-Moura, at this point in his career, actually resembled a decadent more than a *saudosista*. In 1912 he had published *Nova Sapho* (*The New Sappho*), described in its subtitle as a "novel of sensual pathology." The writing is limp and the plot poorly structured, but the novel is fascinating for its forthright treatment of erotic attraction in socially conservative Portugal. It tells the story of an emancipated female aristocrat who is an apostle of aestheticism, prefers women to men, and publicly defends Oscar Wilde, her personal friend. The last half of the novel introduces a secondary protagonist, a homosexual count obviously modeled on the novelist himself.

The Viscount of Vila-Moura sent a copy of *The New Sappho* to Pessoa, who wrote a critical appreciation in a letter to the author that has not survived. A few months later, in 1913, Pessoa began writing about Oscar Wilde's ideas, literary work, and personality. He became a little obsessed with both Wilde's and Walt Whitman's sexual orientations, purchasing books that dealt specifically with their homosexuality.[2] And during the next several years he would write a number of homoerotic poems. This might suggest that Pessoa himself was not immune to the "pernicious" literary influence of Vila-Moura, but he did not need the viscount to show him how one could write unself-consciously about "different" kinds of love and sexuality; he could rely on the example of Sá-Carneiro, whose work abounds in sexual identities that are both ambiguous and unstable. Explicitly homosexual characters, however, are scarce in his writing.

Sá-Carneiro's fictional works, even more than his poetry, reveal a sexuality that is fundamentally self-involved. This reading is spelled out by the writer himself in the story "Resurrection," whose autobiographical protagonist admits that even "normal sexual intercourse" is to his way of thinking a form of masturbation, since one possesses not the woman's body but only one's own sexualized idea about its beauty and desirability. Far from regretting his failure to sexually engage anyone but himself, he considers this a triumph, and he goes on to exalt masturbation as "the Soul's highest form of sensuality," boasting that he and his friend Fernando Passos—a code name for Fernando Pessoa—both practice "an art of masturbation."

Pessoa's writings are peppered with references to masturbation, both literal and metaphorical. In September 1912, one month before Sá-Carneiro boarded the train for Paris, Pessoa jotted down this idea for a short story, in English: "Two masturbators—one male, one female—who live together and masturbate each other without daring to attempt coitus, he because inexperienced, she because afraid of being ruptured." Then he crossed out "each other," replacing it with "each himself." In parentheses he lucidly wondered: "Is this quite the probable thing?"[3] Probable it was not, yet this bizarre scenario obliquely prefigured the intimacy that would develop between him and Sá-Carneiro. Although they never lived together, they were like two deeply attached but inalterably self-involved masturbators, each one exciting the other to pursue his own literary pleasure, to be more blissfully himself.

✦

ALTHOUGH SÁ-CARNEIRO WAS THE more assiduous, "needier" correspondent, Pessoa also exhibited signs of vulnerability and insecurity.
He knew that his friend admired him for his mental prowess and literary talent, but he was forever nagged by doubts about his capacity to stir
heartfelt affection—in Sá-Carneiro or in anyone else. In the first entry of
a diary he began keeping on February 15, 1913, Pessoa mentions a visit
to the home of Ponce de Leão (1891–1918), one of Sá-Carneiro's close
friends from school and now a young playwright. Later that same year
he and Sá-Carneiro would co-author a play, *Alma* (*Soul*). They had been
friends for many years, accumulating a wealth of shared experiences and
emotions about which Pessoa, perhaps a little jealous, knew nothing at
all. Sá-Carneiro was the main subject of his conversation with Leão,
who showed him some of the letters he had received from their mutual
friend in Paris. And he assured Pessoa, apparently after some prompting,
that he was very well liked by Sá-Carneiro. "Doesn't everyone like you?"
he added.

"A ray of light," wrote the diarist apropos of these soothing words.

Though only sixteen, António Ferro, another of Sá-Carneiro's former
classmates whom Pessoa occasionally saw, was already ambitiously writing plays and poetry.[4] Intrepid, energetic, and enterprising, Ferro would
develop a high-flying career as an author, elite journalist, and cultural
czar in Salazar's government, and it was partly through his efforts that
Pessoa, in 1934, managed to publish and win a prize for his poetry collection *Mensagem* (*Message*).

Pessoa would also have kept in touch with Luís Ramos, yet another
of Mário's high school friends and a member of their fledgling literary
circle, but he sailed for Brazil just six weeks after Mário left for Paris.
Although his job at Portugal's diplomatic mission did not work out,
Ramos, who had already published two chapbooks of poetry, stayed on
in Brazil's capital and quickly became part of its literary scene. It was
a heady time for elegant, still Eurocentric Rio de Janeiro, where new
avenues and sumptuous buildings such as the ritzy Hotel Avenida had
recently been built, along with the aerial cable car to Sugarloaf Mountain. The transplanted Portuguese poet, as if infected by the city's fever to
be stylishly up-to-date, sported a monocle and adopted a lofty-sounding
pseudonym, Luís de Montalvor, which is how I will refer to him from

now on. Upon his return to Portugal, in 1915, he and Pessoa would become close literary collaborators, and this alliance remained in force even after Pessoa's death, when Montalvor—who by then had a small publishing house—would bring out the first comprehensive, multivolume edition of the late writer's works.

Pessoa was not exempt from the sort of vanity that made Luís de Montalvor cultivate his public image, but he worried more about posterity than about the people he passed on the street. In March 1912, the same month he started writing his articles that foresaw a poet on Portugal's horizon who would outshine Camões, he sat for an oil portrait, the only one of him produced in his lifetime.[5] The painter, Adolfo Rodriguez Castañé, was born in Madrid, moved to Lisbon when still quite young, and made a name for himself as a talented caricaturist and illustrator. A caricature he drew of Pessoa in the fall of 1912 depicts him with a disproportionately large head, his left hand clutching some rolled-up papers, and his right leg taking a large stride forward—an intellectual on an urgent mission.[6]

The oil portrait, which now hangs in Lisbon at the Casa Fernando Pessoa, is a faithful likeness, showing the poet with slightly wavy hair combed close to the head, rimless glasses, a Semitic nose, a discreet, perfectly trimmed moustache, and a bow tie. He looks serious, a little sad, and self-contained, impenetrable—the exact opposite, it so happens, of the portraitist, a jaunty and lighthearted fellow whose reputation as a ladies' man preceded him. In fact Sá-Carneiro's very first letter to Pessoa mockingly alluded to "Castañé and his love letters," which the artist routinely bragged about in the cafés where they met. A few months later, the painter would be exchanging love letters with Luís de Montalvor's wife, who had remained in Lisbon with the couple's little boy instead of going to Brazil. She ended up having a torrid affair with Castañé, which carried on until her family, determined to save the marriage, put her and the boy on a ship bound for Rio, where they joined Montalvor.[7]

Pessoa and Sá-Carneiro were equally inexperienced in matters of sex and romance, but they were attentive to everything that went on among their friends, from the not just literary bond uniting Mário Beirão and the Viscount of Vila-Moura to the adultery of Montalvor's wife, and they shared with each other the latest gossip. Both were curious about sexual love in all its varieties, and both played out that curiosity in what they wrote.

✦

PESSOA'S SERIES OF ARTICLES from 1912 had announced to the world the coming of a Great Poet, a Super-Camões, and he had already commissioned an oil portrait for the Great Poet's future admirers, yet the Poet remained unpublished, to the dismay of his most dedicated friend and literary adviser. In a letter sent on December 2, 1912, Sá-Carneiro complimented him on his latest article about Portuguese poetry but regretted that readers knew him "only as 'the critic Fernando Pessoa' and not as the Artist." Two months later, on February 3, he urged Fernando to collect, conclude, and publish his poems, without squandering his energy "on long articles of criticism" or on "fragments of admirable but never completed works." The fragmentary works Sá-Carneiro had in mind were Pessoa's political and sociological pamphlets, unwieldy plays such as *Fausto* and *The Duke of Parma*, and never-ending fictions such as *Marcos Alves*. Publish a few poems in magazines, he suggested, but Pessoa thought he would attract more critical attention by revealing his poetic self to the world through a book, for which he had already thought of two possible titles: *Gládio* (*Sword*) and *Exílio* (*Exile*). A small notice in a newspaper announced the latter title as forthcoming, and in 1913 Pessoa drew up a list with more than a hundred poems for the collection.[8] Many of them were unfinished, however, and he was more inclined to begin new poems than to fiddle with old ones.

Something else hindered him from actively trying to publish in Portugal: his old ambition of launching himself as an English poet. To this end he did make some effort. On December 26, 1912, he wrote a long letter to the Poetry Society in London, inquiring about its activities, its membership terms, and its journal, *The Poetry Review*, copies of which he was keen to obtain.[*] He admitted that his interest in current English poetry was not his only reason for writing; he was also looking for a channel to publicize contemporary Portuguese poetry, which he described as "astonishingly *new*" and of "extraordinarily high" quality. After making the preposterous claim that this new Portuguese poetry was stylistically similar to the work of the Elizabethans and would therefore be difficult to translate, he proposed sending a group of poems that

---

[*] Founded in 1909, the Society still thrives today, along with *The Poetry Review*.

he, though a Portuguese poet, had written in English. By this indirect route the good people of the Poetry Society would be able to appreciate "the intensity and the quality of the contemporary poetic movement in Portugal." He added: "I insist on the point that no desire to publish the poems in question moves me to propose this to you. My purpose is no deeper than I have stated."

Is it possible that Pessoa did not realize how perfectly transparent his real purpose was? Between 1910 and 1912 he had produced more than fifty Shakespearean sonnets in English, many of which would be included in his *35 Sonnets* (1918). The thirty-first sonnet from this book was written, in fact, just two days before he wrote to the Poetry Society. Pessoa was hungry for a critical reaction to his extraordinary enterprise— extraordinary for appropriating, without pastiche, Shakespeare's use of parallel structures, linguistic inversions, and rhetorical devices—and he knew nobody in Portugal with the poetic expertise as well as the necessary linguistic competence to be able to appreciate what he had done. He also, all too obviously, hoped to find a British publisher for his sonnets.

Ignoring the curious offer contained in Pessoa's letter, the Poetry Society merely replied with general information about the organization and *The Poetry Review*. Undaunted, Pessoa decided not only to join the Society but also to enter a poetry contest sponsored by the *Review*. So he indicated on a list of things to do drawn up in the spring of 1913.[9] As was so often the case, he failed to follow through on his intentions, but over the next few years he educated himself about the poetry publishing business in England, he drafted a number of cover letters to prospective publishers, and now and then he actually posted a cover letter, along with a submission of his English poems.

◆

WHILE HIS CAREER AS an English poet continued to stall, and although his run as a translator of English and Spanish poetry into Portuguese had ended with Warren Kellogg's departure for London, Pessoa's foreign-language skills were not going to waste. He spent part of each day writing letters in English, and less often in French, for Portuguese businessmen. Sometimes they would provide him with a draft in Portuguese for him to translate, but often enough they would simply explain what needed to be communicated and trust him to give it the right epistolary form. Pessoa had learned the rules for writing good

business letters at the Commercial School in Durban, and during the
past several years had gained practical experience writing letters for his
cousin Mário. Word got around, there was a demand for his skill, and
in 1912 it developed into his major freelance occupation, the one that
would provide him with a reasonably regular income for the rest of his
days. Though more lucrative than translating poetry, it still did not earn
him more than his basic upkeep. All the debt accumulated by the Ibis
press continued to sit there, like an impregnable monument to Pessoa's
editorial folly, until finally one of his creditors got tired of looking at
unpaid IOUs and threatened legal action. On December 21, 1912, Pessoa, needing to be rescued, sent his mother, Maria Madalena, the long
letter he had been promising to write for a year and a half.

It was summertime in Pretoria, and there was more than a month of
school holidays. Consul João Miguel Rosa naturally took some time off
to spend with his family. Teca, Pessoa's half sister, had turned sixteen
in late November, when the city's thousands of jacaranda trees carpeted
the streets with the last of their purple blossoms. His two half brothers
would both have birthdays in January. The three siblings played tennis
on the court in their backyard, and the whole family played croquet.
In the midst of this warm and lazy, festive season, Fernando's mother
received his letter like an icy blast from another world, the one engen-
dered by her first marriage, a nest of problems and disappointments: a
sickly husband who died slowly, a baby who died suddenly, a demented
mother-in-law, and an unusually intelligent firstborn son who, proud and
evasive, had dropped out of college, stubbornly refused to get a normal
job, and now was in danger of being taken to court for unpaid debt. Was
she reading a letter from her son or a passage from one of those Dickens
novels in which the characters end up in debtors' prison? Although she
had suspected that he must have touched the principal of his inheritance
to finance the Ibis press, it was inconceivable to her that five million
reis—slowly and painstakingly garnered through Aunt Maria's careful
stewardship of Grandma Dionísia's assets—had so quickly and completely vanished.

"Five million reis!" she repeated in her outraged reply, sent on January
12. The main subject of Pessoa's letter, however, had not been the money
he lost but the 350,000 reis he owed and now needed to pay off, or else
face unpleasant consequences. Yes, she wrote, her husband would send a
telegram authorizing him to use their investment bonds as collateral for

a bank loan, but when would he get a proper job? Why was he so against answering to a boss? Wasn't the anxiety of constant financial insecurity and indebtedness far more humiliating? In paragraph after indignant paragraph, she kept insisting that he had to become financially responsible and gainfully employed, knowing as she wrote her words—and this was what galled her—that he would not hear them.

Pessoa's precarious finances did cause him some anxiety, as his mother surmised, but not because it humiliated him to depend on others to get by. He only felt anxious when he couldn't satisfy an immediate need—such as food, an item of clothing, a particular book—or when he was hounded by an obstreperous creditor. As soon as he received his stepfather's telegram, he went to the bank, took out a large loan, paid off only the people he had to pay off, and breathed a sigh of relative relief: he could relax for a couple of months. Such was not the case for his poor cousin Mário. After opening and closing a string of small firms that only lost money, he was almost as broke as Fernando but had more than his own needs to worry about, since his cousin and girlfriend, Helena Soares da Costa, was six months pregnant. Mário joined the army in January 1913, the couple got married in February, and in March she gave birth to a girl. Fernando Pessoa was her godfather.

Grateful not to have dependents to feed and clothe, Pessoa nevertheless had monthly payments to make on his new bank loan as well as IOUs to pay off. He could just about manage to meet his commitments with the income from his freelance work, but he had to keep at it. And so, despite not having to answer to a boss, he was almost as much a slave to duty as he would have been with a real job. This was and wasn't a problem. Although he would never admit it, Pessoa clearly enjoyed traipsing from office to office while complaining about not having more time for his writing, and he enjoyed the challenge of finding a solution to his predicament. He had lately hit on a new idea: he would plead his case to a philanthropist. He decided to write Andrew Carnegie, the steel tycoon whose penchant for giving away money had become a religion, the tenets of which he set out in an article titled "The Gospel of Wealth." Not enough of Pessoa's unsent letter got written for us to know exactly how he would have justified his request of £300 (the equivalent of £20,000 today), but he significantly billed himself as a creator and promoter of literature written in English rather than Portuguese: "Of my sympathy with English literature, and my ability to disseminate an

interest in it, these pages will be ample proof, and I make bold to assert that they yield nothing to any living writer of the English language, both in the accuracy of their logical purport and in the proper balance of their exact English."

The likely "logical purport" of Pessoa's missive was to convince its recipient that English culture would be amply advanced if his writing activities were subsidized and even more so if he could do a spell as a writer abroad, in England. Now that he was no longer under immediate threat of legal reprisals, Pessoa transferred his outstanding debts to the back of his mind, and it was certainly not for the purpose of discharging them that he thought of appealing to Carnegie. In March 1913, as if it were an annually recurring fever, he was again seized by a yen to travel to Great Britain. According to his diary entry for the thirtieth of that month, a friend was willing to lend him the money for the voyage, but by the next day, alas, he had changed his mind. It was at that point, or a little later, that Pessoa decided to approach the Scottish American philanthropist.

✦

GERALDO COELHO DE JESUS, the friend who reneged on his promise, did at least come through with a small loan for Pessoa's immediate needs, and he toured him around the city and outside it in his automobile.[10] This could hardly compensate for the frustrated voyage to England, but motorized vehicles were still for the privileged—it was in that same year that Henry Ford introduced assembly lines into his plants, which would significantly reduce production costs—and the poet was delighted to spend the whole afternoon of March 31 joyriding. A mining engineer, Coelho de Jesus met Fernando in 1910, when he was a consultant for the Anglo-Portuguese Mining Agency,[11] one of the firms founded by Pessoa's cousin Mário Freitas. Like all of Mário's firms, it was a commercial failure, but Pessoa "profited" from the friendship he struck up with Geraldo, who became one of his most dependable, and tolerant, creditors. By late 1913, in fact, Geraldo would achieve the "distinction" of being the friend to whom Pessoa owed the most money.

Handsome and easygoing, Geraldo had only a vaguely literary side but loved to carouse and converse with anyone, poets included. His conversations with Fernando were not about trivialities. They discussed Portugal and its dysfunctional politics, its backward economy, its need to modernize, and after the Great War they would collaborate on a short-lived newspaper, but what most attracted Pessoa to Coelho de Jesus was his good looks and carefree spirit, his charming manner and success with women. He was the debonair playboy that Pessoa, in one of his dreams, wished he could have been.

Coelho de Jesus was just one of the more than fifty people mentioned by Pessoa in the diary he kept between mid-February and mid-April of 1913. The diarist, at this point in his life, spent little time at home and alone. Like the 1906 diary, the one from 1913 is a bare-bones account of each day's events, but their sheer quantity makes for a sometimes dizzying read. We find Pessoa zigzagging between cafés and the various offices where he made money by drafting business letters; he reports running into this or that friend on one of Lisbon's downtown streets and walking together for a few blocks or else back to the friend's home; he regularly stops by the editorial office of *Teatro: Revista de crítica* (*Theater: A Journal of Criticism*), an ephemeral publication for which he wrote damning reviews of several novels and magazines, revealing himself to be as mordant in print as he was meek in person; he attends an exhibit, a conference, a concert; he receives letters, writes letters; he eats lunch at one restaurant, dinner at another; and after spending an entire Saturday flitting from place to place, he decides, already past midnight, to get a shave and a haircut before finally heading home.

Pessoa spent a good portion of each day just talking—about literature, politics, psychology, and metaphysics—and one of his regular interlocutors was Israel Anahory, a Portuguese Jew who made his living as a dentist but also wrote poetry and plays, never published.[12] One evening at a café they got into a lengthy discussion on belief and skepticism after Anahory told Pessoa that his Jewish ancestry was discernible not only in his Semitic nose but also in his tendency to take everything seriously. Pessoa's seriousness was deceptive. Mentally supple, he had a fondness for ardently defending a certain idea one day and then attacking it the next, with equally impassioned arguments. But while the rightness or wrongness of the points debated did not greatly matter to Pessoa, he did take seriously the human drama that gives rise to so much debate.

In Renaissance art the Madonna, the story of Christ's Passion, and the lives of the saints became a mere pretext for some painters, who were concerned with things like spatial composition, coloring, and the play of

light, as well as with exquisitely rendering the human bodies in the fore-
ground and the natural landscape in the background—and not necessarily with the religious meaning of the scenes depicted. Pessoa thought
and worked in the other direction. It occurred to him that the world's
historical, social, and political dramas might be local manifestations of
a larger reality, which he sometimes called God. And with that idea in
mind, his art of skillfully using language, sound, and rhythm to produce
exquisite poems became, to a certain extent, a pretext for his pursuit of
God. We will do better, though, to think of his writing as an *intertext*,
weaving through unspeakable mysteries.

Ever since he was a boy, the mystery of the universe intrigued, perturbed, or terrified Pessoa—depending on his mood. More recently, that
mystery enchanted him like a magical, fantastical forest, and he used
poetry as a tool to ponder and explore it. Between November 1912 and
February 1913, he wrote over a dozen English poems in a new, far more
lyrical style and from a pantheistic point of view, according to which
God was not only *in* everything but also *between* everything:

> between our waking and our sleep,
> Between our silence and our speech, between
> Us and the consciousness of us.[13]

These poems became part of a book-length collection, *The Mad Fiddler*,
which he would try to publish four years later.

The same sort of spiritual interpenetration—between God, the universe, and the narrating poet—inspired some of Pessoa's Portuguese
poetry written around the same time, particularly a quintet of poems
titled "Além-Deus" ("Beyond-God"). In his letters from Paris, Sá-
Carneiro responded to these five poems with even more than his usual
enthusiasm, despite not sharing his friend's interest in metaphysics and
spiritual investigations. For Sá-Carneiro, the "truth" was in poetry itself,
or was inseparably wrapped up in it. Dedicated as Pessoa was to probing
the unknown, he agreed, in a certain way, with his writer friend. Pessoa
might be able to point at the truth, but he knew it could never be seized.
His spiritual attitude is perfectly summed up in the title "Beyond-God."
God, whatever God was, would never be more than a stopping place
in Pessoa's restless journey. And although it was a stopping place that
he, unlike Sá-Carneiro, kept returning to, it was never exactly the same

place. I mean that no concept, idea, explanation, or linguistic designation of God could satisfy Pessoa. There was always another beyond.

✦

PESSOA'S SOCIAL LIFE WAS peopled not only by devotees of literature, politics, religion, and philosophy. He also mingled with musicians
and artists, including a precocious young man named José de Almada
Negreiros, whose first one-man show, consisting of caricatures, opened
in March 1913, a few weeks before his twentieth birthday. Pessoa had
already seen the works for the show at the artist's home, he saw them
again at the opening, and he wrote about them in a discerning review for
the April issue of *A Águia*. Almada was a complete unknown, still without much artwork to show, but Pessoa, like a scientist analyzing a small
DNA sample, identified the essential characteristics of the artist's talent
as it would develop in his subsequent, highly successful career: quick
"brilliance and intelligence," an unusual formal versatility that stemmed
partly from a frustrated search to find himself, and a related tendency to
borrow and adapt from others.

"Almada Negreiros is not a genius," Pessoa wrote with unmitigated
candor, and as an originator he indeed was not. On the other hand, no
other Portuguese artist of the twentieth century had his flair for instantly
capturing, synthesizing, and communicating. An excellent example of
that flair is his famous painting that depicts Pessoa writing at a table,
cigarette in hand, and with a copy of the magazine *Orpheu* 2 next to his
elbow. As for Almada's versatility, it went beyond the bounds of visual
art; he would also become an important writer. Pessoa noted in his 1913
diary that the young man was "exaggeratedly impish"—he liked to play
jokes and misbehave—but he admired his work and would count on him
as a collaborator for his publishing projects, beginning with *Orpheu*, the
magazine that would bring modernism to Portugal, in 1915.

Ruy Coelho, who had studied music composition in Berlin, where
Arnold Schoenberg was one of his teachers, returned to Lisbon in 1913
and became acquainted with Pessoa, Almada Negreiros, and other
young writers and artists intent on revitalizing Portuguese culture by
introducing artistic novelties from other parts of Europe and making
them uniquely national. Coelho himself was responsible for the most
ambitious attempt to be Portuguesely European in a work of art. In June
1913, his *Symphonia Camoneana No. 1*, a choral symphony in homage to

Luís de Camões, was performed at Lisbon's São Carlos Theater by no less than five hundred singers and musicians.[14] If Pessoa was in the audience, he probably reacted to the work, like most critics, with perplexity.[15] While perhaps applauding the composer's attempt to modernize Portuguese music, even if tonal experimentation was disagreeable to his ears, he would have questioned whether Camões merited such a grand production—and not only because he hoped to supersede him as Portugal's great national poet. Pessoa maintained that Camões was an excellent but unoriginal poet, since he relied on the poetic forms of Petrarch, such as the sonnet and canzone, rather than inventing his own.[16] At this stage in his career, Pessoa's chief aspiration as a poet was not to say new things but to say things in new ways.

# CHAPTER 27

T HE "FECES OF THE REPUBLIC" WAS PESSOA'S epithet for the dominant republican party—the so-called Democrats—led by Afonso Costa, the nation's prime minister since January 1913.[1] In "Oligarchy of Brutes" and other writings, the poet portrayed Costa and his cronies as thugs without scruples whose only real interest was to keep their party in power. This judgment was too harsh. Costa demanded unswerving loyalty and could be a slippery operator, but to get anything accomplished required determination and ingenuity, which he possessed. The triumph of the Republic had created enormous expectations from all quarters: workers, capitalists, merchants, civil servants, and the armed forces. All these groups exerted tremendous pressure with their conflicting demands, requiring of the prime minister a delicate balancing act that no one could have performed to general applause.

But it was true that, although the form of government had changed, Portuguese politics continued to be plagued by the same spirit of unflinching partisanship that had brought down the monarchy. Through a series of sweeping decrees, the provisional government of the just born republic had separated church and state, reformed the justice and education systems, reorganized the armed forces, and guaranteed certain worker and tenant rights, but once a new constitution was adopted and a new parliament began to legislate, in August 1911, an old and seemingly endemic paralysis reasserted itself. Beneath all the agitation generated by the rival republican parties, the country once more seemed to be stagnating.

Whether it was a mere coincidence or a kind of sympathetic reaction to Portugal's political situation, Pessoa, on March 29, 1913, wrote a poem called "Pauis" ("Swamps") that wallowed in stagnation. He realized immediately that it was quite unlike anything else he had so far produced. But was it any good? He showed it to Ruy Coelho, who had told Pessoa that he wanted to set one of his poems to music—but no, not that one! Although he was himself an experimentalist, the composer abhorred it.[2] Even Pessoa's writer friends were initially taken aback, not sure what to make of it. António Ferro thought the poem beautiful but too laden with riddles.[3]

> Swamps of yearnings brushing against my gilded soul . . .
> Distant tolling of Other Bells . . . The blond wheat paling
> In the ashen sunset . . . My soul is seized by a bodily chill . . .
> How forever equal the Hour! . . . The tops of the palms
>     swaying! . . .

More than enigmatic, these opening lines are languidly evocative— of a twilit world arrested in a state of suspended animation. The palms do not sway; they exist in a state of swaying. The soul, or the self, has been transfigured into—and trapped within—this swampy, etherealized landscape where it would be difficult for blood or passion or sex to exist. But after some more wispy allusions, suddenly, out of nowhere:

> The sentry stands very straight, but his lance planted on the
>     ground
> Is still taller than he . . . What's all this for? . . . The flat day . . .

It's hard to say what it was all for, but the erectly standing sentry and his even taller lance are clearly phallic. Even in these swamps the sexual impulse stalked the poet. Mário de Sá-Carneiro told his friend that the sentry and his lance made him unaccountably afraid, but he nevertheless admired that disturbing image, along with the rest of the poem, many of whose lines he quoted back to Pessoa in his letter of May 6. Rejecting Pessoa's fear that the poem might be too "misty," he declared it to be "sublime," one of the greatest things his friend had so far written.

Sá-Carneiro's enthusiasm is understandable, since his own poetry resorted to similar motifs and atmospheric effects—yearnings, things gilded, crepuscular lighting—to describe an exteriorized, narcissistically contemplated self. Pessoa's narrator is less a narcissist than a man bewildered by what he sees. He feels estranged from his own self, and unsure of where it begins or ends, or if the self he seems to see is really him. "How my self-dread longs for something that doesn't weep!" he announces in the eighth line.

Praised and promoted by Sá-Carneiro, the poem "Swamps" circulated among his and Pessoa's friends and eventually gave its name to a Portuguese literary movement known as *paulismo*, or swampism, definable as an exacerbated symbolism, with suggestion, uncertainty, and mystery enveloping extravagant images in a shadowy world without time or geography. It was a style Pessoa used not only for poems but also, and most effectively, for certain prose pieces included in his newest literary project, *The Book of Disquiet*. This, the most expansive and potent of all his works, had the humblest of beginnings: it germinated from the single word *desassossego* (disquiet), which Pessoa jotted down in large letters next to a poem written on January 20, 1913. He knew he wanted to use the word as a title, but for what sort of a book? Without a clear or even unclear idea of what form it might take, he began writing passages of prose that were often fragmentary and incomplete, reflecting his own hesitation and uncertainty. Some passages were "swampy," while others were plaintive, exalted, or meditative, and still others lucidly analytical. The work swerved in unpredictable directions, taking the writer with it, like a car whose driver has lost control.

*The Book of Disquiet* could also be called *The Book of Uneasiness*, or *Restlessness*, or *Unsettledness*. Those would all be valid translations of the Portuguese *desassossego* that Pessoa himself was feeling in this period. His diary entries from 1913 reveal a man forever restive, unable to sit still for long, sometimes because he was exhilarated, sometimes because he was nervous and distraught. March 20, according to the diarist, was "a day of absolute and overwhelming depression." Throughout his life Pessoa periodically suffered from the kind of depression that arrives like a black wave, for no apparent reason, but the mood swings and disquiet he experienced at this juncture in his life were connected to his personal situation as a twenty-five-year-old still trying to find his way.

His literary career was more or less on track, with his published articles having already proven his talent as a critic, and with friends such as Sá-Carneiro revering his poetry and urging him to publish it without delay, but socially he was an odd duck. Word had gotten around in the café crowd that it was better not to say anything off color in front of Pessoa, who might blush, or get upset, or irritated. The diary does not say exactly how he reacted when sex entered the conversation, but it does note how distressed it made him feel one afternoon to find a woman at the editorial office of the magazine *Teatro*, where he had stopped by to chat with the boys.[4]

◆

PESSOA CONTINUED TO DEAL with his sexual uneasiness in the literary realm. It was during this period that he perfected the story line of
*Marcos Alves*, his novel in progress about a sensitive young man pathologically afraid of sex, and in his diary entry for March 8 he acknowledged a close affinity with this protagonist. In 1913 he also jotted down
some ideas for a work of fantasy fiction titled "Timidez—O caso do dr.
Garcez" ("Shyness—The Case of Dr. Garcez"), in which the shy doctor
tries to figure out how to experience intimacy with a woman without
actually being with one. After discarding the possibility of inventing an
"extrahuman" female, he ponders the hypothesis of a woman created out
of his own body, with him surviving only as a soul and becoming her one
and only dream, her "Ideal Prince." In this way he would possess her,
yes, but only inwardly, psychologically, which is not what he desires. He
wants "to be like other men" and to possess a woman physically. What
he needs to do, he concludes, is to "create *a real woman*," but one divested
of a "central consciousness," such that she would not see him, not notice
him.[5] (One hundred years later, Dr. Garcez could perhaps have come
close to realizing his dream with one of the ultrarealistic silicone sex
dolls manufactured in Japan and a few other countries.)

In *The Book of Disquiet*, on the other hand, Pessoa used words and the
imagination to invent a number of completely *unreal*, unsexual women.
The narrator of this book, far from wanting to possess a female physically, praises the virtues of chastity. As he explains in one of the first
passages written for the book and addressed to an ideal, immaculately
virgin woman:

> I don't dream of possessing you. Why should I? It would only
> debase my dream life. To possess a body is to be banal. And to
> dream of possessing a body is perhaps even worse, if that's possi-
> ble: it's to dream of being banal—the supreme horror.[6]

But the horror "of being banal" is not what leads the narrator to opt for
and extol sexual abstinence. "My horror of real women endowed with sex
is the road that brought me to you," he admits in a *Disquiet* passage addressed to another antiseptically dreamed female, dubbed "Our Lady of
Silence." And having made this admission, he wonders: "Who can honor

the Wife without being assaulted by the thought that she's a woman who copulates? Who can help but despise having a mother by whom he was so vulvally, loathsomely born?"

At the same time that he was introducing dreamily virgin, genital-free women into passages from *The Book of Disquiet*, Pessoa—forever uncertain, unsettled—was writing a long poem in English about a bride who fearfully looks forward to surrendering her virginity in exchange for "joy-hot unity" with the groom. It was an "Epithalamium," a genre that the Greeks invented to sing at wedding processions or at the bride's marriage chamber, interspersing frequent invocations to Hymen, the god of marriage celebrations. The Romans infused the form with explicitly sexual references. Unexplicit, "dignified" epithalamiums were popular among English Renaissance poets, and Pessoa read those of Edmund Spenser and John Donne, and probably Ben Jonson's, but his bridal song, unlike theirs, was unabashedly ribald. Stanza XIV begins:

The bridegroom aches for the end of this and lusts
To know those paps in sucking gusts,
To put his first hand on that belly's hair
And feel for the lipped lair,
The fortress made but to be taken, for which
He feels the battering ram grow large and itch.

Another stanza describes the groom's "hairy legs and buttocks balled to split / White legs mid which they shift." These lines almost rate as pornographic, but they are more comic than arousing. Not that Pessoa was trying to be humorous; it's just that his English, like a precision instrument he wielded imperfectly, played tricks on him in poetry, producing unexpected effects. This was especially true here, since tone is crucial when writing about sex. Poets before Pessoa focused more on the marriage celebration, the festive atmosphere, the beauty of the bride, the couple's joyous longing, and reflections on this major transition in life. The narrator of his epithalamium, without ceremony or subtlety, exhorts the couple to do their desirous duty, making love until it feels as "natural as / Pissing when wish doth press!"

When Pessoa published his "Epithalamium" eight years later, in 1921, a review in Scotland's *Aberdeen Daily Journal* commented that it was "more disgustingly lascivious than was even Donne in his most voluptuous moments."[7] While writing the poem, it must have amused Pessoa to imagine how it would have shocked the café-goers who teased him for being such an incurable prude. Alone in his own room with just his thoughts, a pen, and paper, he lost all his squeamishness.

In the spring of 1913 he also wrote "O outro amor" ("The Other Love"), a sonnet addressed to a young male. Our biographical search for the poem's addressee need go no further than its first two lines: "With what rage I raise the *idea* of my arms / To the *idea* of you!" (italics added). The sonneteer had in mind only a theoretical, imaginary young man, referred to in the eighth line as Venus-Ephebus. The poem was as divorced from personal experience as it was ostentatiously homoerotic. It belonged to a larger literary project, *Livro do outro amor* (*The Book of the Other Love*), for which the author planned to write a long poem titled "Morte de Antínoo" ("The Death of Antinous") as well as more sonnets. Three weeks later he did write half a dozen additional sonnets, in which the narrator wishes that his hypothetical male lover were more like a woman or, alternatively, that he himself were more feminine, so that they could live together as a heterosexual couple—the only model of passionate intimacy fully accepted by society and by the narrator, who is still struggling with guilt one year after courageously declaring love for a man in Pessoa's first two homoerotic poems. "I hate myself for loving you," he confesses in an unfinished sonnet for *The Book of the Other Love*.[8]

The euphemism "the other love" had already been used by other writers[9] and would continue to be used long after Pessoa's death, most notably by Montgomery Hyde, a vigorous campaigner for the decriminalization of homosexuality and author of a groundbreaking work titled *The Other Love: An Historical and Contemporary Survey of Homosexuality in Britain* (1970).[10] It is possible that Pessoa's *Book of the Other Love*, with its narrator who strives to come to terms with his desires, also aspired to promote more understanding of and sympathy for same-sex love.

The passages from *The Book of Disquiet* addressed to sexless women also describe what we might call an "other love," since it doesn't fit the traditional heterosexual paradigm in which a strong man possesses a yielding woman, both of them urged on by sexual desire. The first half of 1913 was one of the most fertile periods for Pessoa's diversified sexual explorations through writing. Like a protean actor simultaneously playing different and even contradictory roles, he was radically celibate in *The Book of Disquiet*, nervously expectant in his paean to marriage, which focuses at length on the about-to-be-deflowered bride, and enamored of a young man in *The Book of the Other Love*. So does this mean that Pessoa, in literature, wanted to be everything all at once? Undoubtedly, but he may also have been trying to figure out what, if anything, he wanted to be or do sexually, in the flesh.

He finished his ambitious "Epithalamium" in the same year he started it, 1913, and two years later he revisited a classic story of homoerotic love in his poem "Antinous," also written in English. The two poems formed a diptych that, according to Pessoa's remarkable explanation, served to free his mind from all lascivious thoughts. In a letter sent on November 18, 1930, to João Gaspar Simões, his first biographer, the poet would write:

'Antinous" and "Epithalamium" are my only poems (in fact my only writings of whatever sort) that may clearly be considered obscene. There is in all of us, however little we may be inclined toward obscenity, a certain element of this order, which obviously varies in degree from person to person. Since these elements, no matter how small, will in some way be a hindrance to superior mental processes, I decided to eliminate them twice, by the simple expedient of expressing them intensely. This is the reason for the shocking obscenity that you will find in these two poems—particularly in "Epithalamium," which is blatant and bestial. I don't know why I wrote either of them in English.

As Pessoa suggests at the end of this passage, "Antinous" is not blatantly sexual, but it is no less sensual than his "Epithalamium." The poem shows us Emperor Hadrian next to the naked corpse of his drowned lover, whom he fondly remembers when still alive and in his arms, the two men freely fulfilling their lustful desires. Pessoa apparently wanted to convince Gaspar Simões that he had successfully eliminated lustful thoughts by embedding them in poems, one heteroerotic and the other homoerotic, but it is hard to believe that he believed in his own explanation. And his claim not to know why he wrote them in English rings of false naïveté, particularly since he initially thought of writing about the dead Antinous in Portuguese.

Pessoa, whose large literary projects tended to drag on indefinitely, was motivated not only to complete and polish these two poems, which were among his longest and most singular, but also to go public with them, by financing their publication as chapbooks and sending review copies to the United Kingdom. The poet could not hope for—and perhaps did not want—many readers in Portugal, where English was still not widely spoken. By writing in this language he could express himself "intensely," as stated in his letter to Gaspar Simões, while remaining safely anonymous, because unread. While "Epithalamium" was intensely salacious, his "Antinous" was intense with longing. It was the most compelling love poem that Pessoa would ever write.

✦

THE GREEK YOUTH ANTINOUS is mentioned in one of the "other love" sonnets written in the spring of 1913, which is when the idea of a poem about the death of Hadrian's favorite first sprang to the poet's mind. Even if Pessoa, as he would later maintain, was trying to free his mind of sexual thoughts—homosexual thoughts, in this case—he did so by entertaining them, by giving them a poetic form and working out tender line after tender line. He was at the very least wondering "What if?" If that wondering was inspired by anyone in particular, it was his friend Mário de Sá-Carneiro. Although the "other love" sonnets were directed to an imaginary, rhetorical other, certainly not to Sá-Carneiro, the affective bond between the two friends had become so strong that it may have caused Pessoa to wonder where the relationship might yet go, or what a consummated love—or a physically *un*consummated love—between two men might be like.

In a kind of Socratic dialogue dating from 1913 and probably inspired by Oscar Wilde's use of this genre, Pessoa wrote that the "supreme" type of man, such as Shakespeare, is so engaged with the things of life that he has no time to waste on "the pursuit of normal sexual pleasure and will therefore replace it with the sexual pleasure afforded by sublime friendship with other men."[11] Sá-Carneiro may not have had sex appeal for Pessoa, but he had great soul appeal. Mário felt life passionately, from its mundane particulars to its epiphanic heights, and it was with passion that he cherished his friend Pessoa, who cherished him in return and became, inevitably, more human.

An extraordinary affection can rarely keep entirely mum; giddy with excitement, it wants to let other people know it exists. Despite his reserved temperament, which so often inhibited him from sharing what he felt with others, Fernando Pessoa told his mother about Sá-

Carneiro, and in a most aggressive manner: on February 8, 1913, he wrote her about a close friend who esteemed him even "more highly" than she did. It was an odd, offensive comparison to make, and the piqued reader of those words wrote back that it was wonderfully reassuring to learn that her son would never feel "spiritually isolated, since in that elite soul that so well understands your own you'll find what you don't find in me." Pessoa's "philosophical letter," as his mother styled it, had explained that females were "essentially coarse and crude" beings, which was why the soulful understanding he felt with his special friend could only exist with another man, never with a woman. Hurt and scandalized, Maria Madalena did not scrimp on sarcasm in her response, which she ended by commenting that a health problem of hers in need of medical attention would surely not interest him, since "just as my coarse and crude spirit cannot understand your soul that's far superior to mine, so your high-wafting soul will not understand this sorry materialism."[12]

Pessoa's mother was truly not feeling well, and her son's latest letter had made her cry so many tears that Teca, a little alarmed, secretly wrote her brother, explaining how much sadness he had caused and suggesting that he apologize in his next letter. She also said that their mother's harping on him to get a proper job was for his own good. And she asked, "Can't you see how happy it would make Mom to see you employed the next time we come to Lisbon? Can't you make just a little bit of a sacrifice for a mother who has always been so good to you and who could even give up her life for the sake of your happiness?"[13] Pessoa was unmoved by his mother's distress, which he probably chalked up to hysteria. And Teca, by agreeing with Maria Madalena that he should get a salaried job, revealed herself to be equally, femininely materialistic.

As a man in his twenties, Pessoa was zealously misogynistic. He purchased several books whose aim was to prove the inferiority of women, and in one of them he made notes in the margins expressing hearty approval of the author's thesis.[14] In his own writings he argued that women were inferior to men both as thinkers and creators because they were dragged down by matter, which prevented them from soaring. It was not just that women, as child bearers, were naturally drawn to the practical aspects of running a household; Pessoa contended that they were more physically sexual than men. "The natural slavery of woman unto Sex is monthly proclaimed by Nature, by menstruation," he wrote in English. "Every month the woman is reminded that she is merely a womb, and that all other things in her are subservient to that [function]."[15]

In one of the weirdest sections from *The Book of Disquiet*, titled "Advice to Unhappily Married Women," an expert on sexual enhancement techniques explains to his female "disciples" how they can cheat on their husbands, in midcoitus, by imaginatively replacing them with the men they really crave. "The height of sensuality," he guarantees, "is to be the lewdest slut imaginable and yet never unfaithful to your husband." He does not offer the same advice to men, since "the man is a different kind of creature." And if the man is a superior man, "he can have sensuality without sexual possession," which is "something a woman, even a superior one, could never accept. The woman is a fundamentally sexual creature."

Pessoa's insistence on women's compelling need for sex is the most curious and original point in his misogynistic discourse. It is also the key for understanding what gave rise to that discourse. Uncomfortable with women, terrified at the idea of sexually engaging with them, Pessoa disguised his personal aversion with specious theories about their inferiority, their unsuitability as intellectual soulmates, their creative impotence, and so forth. By denying their human complexity, by reducing them to sexual creatures, he could justify avoiding them altogether. Better to spend his time cultivating intellectual and spiritual communion with men like Sá-Carneiro than to fritter it away on intimate encounters with women, who could offer nothing more than sex. Pessoa's misogyny, vicious as it was, would prove to have shallow roots. Within a few years' time, after his discomfort with women abated, so did his interest in arguing that they were less capable and less complex than men.

In 1913 Pessoa's misogyny was still at its peak, and his perspicacious mother correctly understood that she herself was a target of its fire. In that same year Pessoa wrote that women, "barring pathological exceptions," are interested only in having a man,[16] a general rule apparently corroborated by the example of Maria Madalena, who ardently fell in love with a new man a mere six months after the death of her first husband, Joaquim Pessoa. Albeit a well-educated, "superior" type of woman, not even she could help but be "fundamentally sexual."

Pessoa's relationship with his mother had already gone through a rocky patch, when in 1907 he quit the School of Arts and Letters, and in the early months of 1913 their letters became hostile. Weary of her lecturing him on his financial irresponsibility, which she did incessantly after learning that the young heir was insolvent, Pessoa wrote curt, chilly weekly letters, and he often posted them a few days late and with false dates, which she detected by comparing them with the postmark dates on the envelopes. When she accused him, with good reason, of deliberately wanting to hurt her with his remarks on Sá-Carneiro's capacity to understand him in a way she never could, for the simple reason that she was a woman and therefore "essentially course and crude," he replied that her "ludicrous statements" were upsetting his peace of mind.

After weeks of epistolary wrangling, including a March 23 letter in which Maria Madalena magnanimously offered to stop writing her son so as not to risk putting him in a sour mood, he finally wrote her a letter to the effect that all her recriminations were wasted ink, since "mothers are the last people to have any influence over their children."[17] Now he lectured her, putting her in her place, and she—astonishingly—completely capitulated. Perhaps she feared losing him all together, or simply realized that she was uselessly making herself suffer. On April 20, without a hint of irony, she wrote that he had opened her eyes to the truth. She promised that she would never again discourage him in his projects or try to change his way of thinking. True to her word, from that day on she worried about him in silence, refraining from criticism and offering no advice that ran contrary to his own plans and dreams.

Pessoa had won the war with his mother, neutralizing all vestiges of her authority over him and liberating himself from whatever guilt and resentment her ongoing reproaches had aroused. He could take more pleasure in their weekly exchange of news. But it was the letters from Sá-Carneiro, still in Paris, that he waited for with impatience. Reading those letters, we do not find a lot of soul baring or effusive expressions of affection; and Pessoa, whose letters to his friend have unfortunately not survived, was surely not more forthcoming. Yet Pessoa had vaunted to his mother that Sá-Carneiro appreciated and understood him in a way that she never could. So what made the connection between the two friends so special, and how did it *feel*, how did it express itself?

What stands out from the correspondence (some of the content of Pessoa's letters can be gleaned through Sá-Carneiro's replies) is their mutual infatuation with each other's creative mind, an infatuation whose rapturous intensity found release in the literature they produced and shared with abandon. Their literary union was facilitated by Oscar Wilde.

✦

AS THE FLASHIEST SPECIMEN of the decadent movement in the British Isles, an aesthete who disdained the masses and proclaimed that Life imitates Art, Wilde was a natural case study for Max Nordau's thesis that degenerate artists and writers were having a corrosive effect on European society and morals. Pessoa's first contact with Wilde's sometimes extravagant and ever stimulating opinions may have been through his reading of Nordau's *Degeneration*, in 1907. Shortly thereafter, he began reading Wilde's work directly. Sá-Carneiro's own interest in the Irish writer, which had developed independently, no doubt stoked Pessoa's, and vice versa. Four books of stories and poems by Wilde survive in Pessoa's library, but we know he read others—including plays and *The Picture of Dorian Gray*—from the informed references he makes to them in his notes. He translated five of the six parablelike stories that Wilde called *Poems in Prose*, and he also planned to produce Portuguese versions of *De Profundis*, *The Ballad of Reading Gaol*, and two essays framed as dialogues: "The Critic as Artist" and "The Decay of Lying."[18] It is in this last work that Life and Nature are both said to be imitators of Art, which "never expresses anything but itself."

In "The Critic as Artist," Pessoa must especially have appreciated axioms such as "What people call insincerity is simply a method by which we can multiply our personalities." Or this one: "Man is least himself when he talks in his own person. Give him a mask, and he will tell you the truth." The exemplary wearer of masks, according to Wilde, was Shakespeare the playwright, and elsewhere in the dialogue he holds up the Victorian poet Robert Browning for his similar, Shakespeare-like ability to assume so many different personalities in the dramatic monologues of his poems. Pessoa also compared Browning with Shakespeare, insofar as he "enters into a state of complete depersonalization."[19]

Depersonalization, disinterest in "life as it is," and creation as an intellectual performance rather than a spontaneous outflow were among the Wildean notions that wove through the letters and poems exchanged by Pessoa and Sá-Carneiro in the first half of 1913. Pessoa, meanwhile, began writing (in English) a "Defence of Oscar Wilde," which credited him with "absolute selflessness"—not because Wilde was selflessly altruistic but because he did "not believe even in himself. His interest in himself was an interest in the nearest of his surroundings." Pessoa's "Defence" was double-edged. He rated Wilde as "one of the greatest figures" among the "futile adventurers in the arts," attributing his greatness to the fact that he was *consciously* futile, "true to falsehood." In "Concerning Oscar Wilde," yet another English-language essay conceived in the early months of 1913, Pessoa was less charitable. He wrote that Wilde, for all his insistence on decorativeness, was artistically dull in his prose. *Dorian Gray* contains "long descriptions of beautiful decorative things," yes, but Wilde "does not invoke those beautiful things by means of phrases that shall place them before our eyes in a living manner; he does but catalogue them with voluptuosity. He describes richly, but not artistically."[20]

The most damning judgment on Wilde the writer was made by Wilde himself, when he told André Gide, who would win the Nobel Prize in Literature in 1947, that he had put his genius into his life, and only his talent into his work.[21] Pessoa offered an interesting twist on this assessment, writing: "He was a dandy of real life, not a dandy in literature, except incompletely and by reflexion."[22] Pessoa's point was not that Wilde put his genius into being a dandy rather than a first-rate writer but that he failed to put his dandified self *into his writing*. Wilde's "selflessness" undermined his literary art. Thanks to his intelligence and fluid, aphoristic way with words, Wilde's writing sparkles, but the poetic style that Pessoa and Sá-Carneiro developed together in 1913 was more viscerally, acutely decadent than what the Irishman achieved.

In *Degeneration*, Nordau did not rail against Wilde because of his decadent *literature* but because of his decadent *person*: his cult of dandyism, his scandalous attitudes, his flippancy, his flamboyance.[23] Wilde's plays and *The Picture of Dorian Gray* are peopled with decadent dandies, of course, but they tend to function as mouthpieces for the author's transgressive opinions, as Wilde implicitly acknowledged in a letter to a friend: "I can't describe action: my people sit in chairs and chatter."[24] In Sá-Carneiro's works of fiction, the characters dare to transgress sexual and gender boundaries, while his poems, which are structured around obsessively self-gazing narrators, achieve an almost unbearable degree of linguistic refinement. Pessoa, despite being the antithesis of flashy, would manage to create a heteronymous dandy, Álvaro de Campos, and in his approach to writing he was always dandiacal, changing styles the way a model changes clothes in a fashion show.[25] It was in their literary work that the two friends, each in his own manner, were flamboyant, decadent, and—according to Nordau's criteria—inexcusably degenerate.

# CHAPTER 28

○🔾○🔾○🔾○🔾○🔾○🔾○🔾○🔾○🔾○🔾○🔾○🔾○

**P**ESSOA'S POEM "SWAMPS," CLOTTED WITH IMAGES
seemingly frozen in time, is suggestive of the political morass
that was hindering Portugal from moving decisively forward,
but it also evokes the "swampy" state of his personal and artistic life in
1913. While a couple of his friends brought out their first poetry collections, Pessoa continued to let his creative energy meander and published
not one single poem. For him to publish a whole book of poems would
have been difficult if not impossible, since he continued to be mired in
debt. And so, obliged by circumstances, he divided his time between the
lofty pursuit of literature and his ongoing attempts to obtain ready cash.

Since February Pessoa had been planning a trip to Tavira, in the
Algarve, to visit the cousin once removed he called "Aunt" Lisbela.
Although he had not seen her in more than a decade, they wrote each
other regularly[1] and not only to exchange news and friendly greetings:
she was one of his main creditors. In the summer of 1910, when he had
closed his ruinous printing office, he owed her 50,000 reis,[2] a debt she
probably waived, before loaning him yet more money. Pessoa's latest list
of personal debts included 28,000 reis owed to Lisbela, rather more than
he owed almost anyone else. Pessoa had another reason for nurturing his
relationship with Lisbela. As the cousin his father had been closest to,
she could help enhance and complete what few memories Fernando had
of the man. As it turned out, Lisbela needed to come up to Lisbon in
late April and again in June, so that was where she and Fernando met for
the first time in eleven years. He could be charming when he felt at ease,
and they got on well together—well enough for her to loan him another
20,000 reis.[3]

Pessoa's most generous creditor, however, was not Aunt Lisbela but
Aunt Anica. He had been living with her since the summer of 1911 and
was supposed to contribute 20,000 reis per month for room and board,
but the rent due just kept piling up, to more than 400,000 reis in 1913.

It was a sum grown so large that he could not possibly pay it off, unless he were to take first prize in one of the puzzle contests sponsored by mass-market newspapers such as *Tit-Bits* or *Answers*, pioneers of English tabloid journalism. As an adolescent Pessoa had thought of participating in short story competitions organized by these same weekly papers, without ever acting on the idea, but as an adult he often did participate in their puzzle contests, whose grand prizes could amount to as much as a thousand pounds—equivalent, in purchasing power, to about ninety times that amount today.

In addition to making money as a contestant, Pessoa hoped to sell a book with tips on how to solve puzzles. He gave it a sophisticated-sounding title, *The Psychological Laws of Problem Solving*, and assigned the task of writing it to a fictitious Englishman, James Bodenham, who got no further than the introduction. A list of "Publications to make money" from 1913 includes Bodenham's book and, more intriguingly, three books by a fictitious Englishwoman, Olga Baker. Baker's works— on the woman's toilette, on being a housewife, and on being a mother— were supposed to be published in Portuguese, perhaps in translations by Fernando Pessoa. Despite his pathological unease around coquettish females and despite never showing any interest in motherly or house-wifely occupations, Pessoa apparently deemed himself qualified to write for the expanding market in women's books. Unfortunately, none of his Baker books advanced beyond their titles.

◆

MÁRIO DE SÁ-CARNEIRO HAD finished his first and last year as a student of law at the Sorbonne and in mid-June fired off three postcards in a row, informing Pessoa in triplicate that he would arrive at Lisbon on Monday, June 23, at 10:52 p.m. He implored his friend to meet him at the station. "Are you upset with me about something?" he asked in the third postcard. More than a month had gone by with no letter from Fernando, who perhaps had slipped into one of his dark moods or, dis-tracted, had simply forgotten to write. Or perhaps he was deliberately creating a little distance, preparing himself for a certain loss of intimacy that their relationship was liable to suffer with Mário's return to Lisbon.

Their letters had created a private space that was all their own. It was harder to be alone with each other in Lisbon, where the two friends were habitually joined by other young men such as their mutual friends António Ferro, Armando Côrtes-Rodrigues, and José de Almada Negreiros. A new member of the group was Alfredo Pedro Guisado (1891–1975), who had just published his first book of poems. Though born in Lisbon, Guisado had close ties to Galicia, where his parents were from and where he often went on holiday. Galicia, which occupies the northwest corner of Spain, has strong cultural affinities with its southern neighbor, reinforced by a common linguistic heritage, since modern Galician and Portuguese derive from the same medieval language. There was also a robust tradition of Galician immigrants making their livelihood in Lisbon— often as unskilled laborers, but also as hoteliers, restaurateurs, and café owners. Guisado's parents owned and operated a successful restaurant, Irmãos Unidos (Brothers United), where he and his new literary friends sometimes met. Decisively influenced by Pessoa and Sá-Carneiro, Guisado would write his next book of poems in the so-called swampist style that they had developed.

In one of his last letters to Sá-Carneiro in Paris, Pessoa had suggested they start up a literary magazine to promote their own work and that of a few friends. It needn't have a long life—just enough issues to shake up Portugal's literary world and to put their own names on its map. Had this idea depended mainly on Pessoa for its realization, we can be quite certain it would have foundered, but Sá-Carneiro was more determined and pragmatic. He not only seconded his best friend's idea, he promised to take care of the funding, meaning that he would prevail on his father to pay the printer. So when Mário returned to Lisbon, there was already a collective publication project, along with a growing awareness of who belonged to the collective; still it took six months until they drew up concrete plans for this magazine. When it finally saw print, more than a year later, it did much more than put the names of its contributors on the map: it redrew the borders of contemporary Portuguese literature.

Sá-Carneiro, meanwhile, diligently worked on his own literary projects, whose publication his father was also willing to underwrite. He spent the summer and fall getting his collection of poems, *Dispersão* (*Dispersion*), into final form, and he wrote the novel *A Confissão de Lúcio* (*Lúcio's Confession*), which he had long ago plotted in his head. By the end of 1913 he would have four published books, while Pessoa remained a virtually unpublished poet. Fernando's literary output, though much larger than Mário's, consisted mostly of works in progress. It was like a sprawling yet increasingly unbuilt city, whose builder was so busy laying the foundations for new structures that almost nothing rose higher than one or two unfinished floors. Along with a volume or two of his poems, Pessoa hoped to publish his *Fausto* by the end of the year, or in 1914 at the latest, but this verse play—which was so far just a disordered heap of incomplete scenes, dialogues, and monologues—had to compete with his dramatic works in English, *The Duke of Parma* and *Prometheus Rebound*, as well as a proliferation of other plays in Portuguese. Around 1911 Pessoa had commenced a dramatic trilogy whose protagonists were Briareus, Enceladus, and Typhon, three giants of Greek mythology.[4]

It would befuddle the mind of any normal playwright to work simultaneously on a suite of neo-Greek tragedies, the Shakespearean *Duke of Parma*, and a remake of Goethe's *Faust*, but Pessoa, not satisfied, also began writing in a dramatic subgenre he called "static drama." This oxymoronic designation was not his own coinage; he borrowed it from the Belgian poet and playwright Maurice Maeterlinck, who earned renown—and the Nobel Prize in Literature, in 1911—for his early symbolist plays in which nothing happens and the dialogues circle around, without ever leading to conclusions or decisive actions. The invisible protagonist of his plays is Fate, whose workings the characters only dimly grasp. Maeterlinck wrote in French, and it was in this language that Pessoa began writing his first static drama, *Le Matelot* (*The Sailor*), in 1913. It was a one-act play that structurally resembled Maeterlinck's *L'Intruse* (*The Intruder*), a one-act published in 1890. True to habit, Pessoa was brazenly trying to beat a literary star at his own game, and even in his own language. After writing and rewriting a number of scenes, he realized that his French was not up to the task. So *Le Matelot* became *O marinheiro* (*The Mariner*), and he also used Portuguese for *A morte do príncipe* (*The Death of the Prince*), *Diálogo no jardim do palácio* (*Dialogue in the Palace Garden*), and a few other static dramas.[5]

While working on all these plays in different styles and different languages, Pessoa continued to generate new ideas for short stories, many of which got partly written, and none of which he ever finished. Nor was his dispersion limited to the realm of creative literature. Sá-Carneiro wrote—and published—poems, plays, short stories, and a novel. Pessoa, besides writing in all of those same genres, also drafted essays, articles, and pamphlets on history, politics, religion, philosophy, and what would later come to be known as cultural studies. Sá-Carneiro was psychologically dispersed. Pessoa's self was also scattered across time and the world,

and particularly across Portugal—its people and language, its past and future, its geographical reality and symbolic significance, none of which held any interest for his Paris-besotted friend.

Pessoa was an unusual sort of patriot. One could argue, in fact, that the country of his birth had become yet another of his alter egos, an extension of himself. As if to make room and a dignified setting for the Super-Camões, he championed a grander version of the Portugal that actually existed. Book projects such as *Extent and Causes of Portuguese Decay*, undertaken by Pessoa when Portugal was still a monarchy, gave way to more panoramic treatments of the country in the 1910s. *All about Portugal* was the title of a compendium that was supposed to have chapters about everything from the nation's prehistory, topography, and agriculture to its art, music, philosophy, and science—all in English, to promote Portugal to the rest of the world. Conceived in 1914 or 1915, it regularly appeared in Pessoa's publication plans until the 1920s, but he wrote little for it besides the impressive table of contents.[6] Likewise eager to promote Portugal among his compatriots, Pessoa had already planned an identical sort of compendium for domestic consumption, *Manual do Português*.[7]

◆

BUT WHILE PROMOTING PEOPLE'S awareness and appreciation of Portuguese culture would be useful for boosting national self-esteem, Pessoa was more concerned about reinvigorating and expanding that culture. It occurred to him that the experience of another nation on Europe's western periphery, Ireland, could perhaps serve as a model, and so, in 1913, he drafted a letter to William Butler Yeats, asking for particulars about the "Irish movement in modern poetry and drama."

At that point the Irish Literary Renaissance was old news in Ireland, but it was the kind of news that reached Portugal slowly, if at all, and Pessoa found out about it only thanks to his reading of British newspapers and reviews.[8] Yeats had played a leading role in the Renaissance, and the Renaissance, in turn, was a major force shaping his early work. In 1888, when he was just twenty-three, Yeats published the anthology *Fairy and Folk Tales of the Irish Peasantry*, and five years later he brought out a collection of sketches and tales narrated in his own voice, *The Celtic Twilight*, whose title became another name for the Renaissance. One of this movement's greatest achievements was in theater, a flowering that owed much to Yeats, a cofounder of Dublin's short-lived Irish National

Theatre Society and of the still thriving Abbey Theatre. Yeats himself wrote several plays for the Abbey, and so did his friend John Milling-ton Synge, the most talented Irish Renaissance playwright as well as the most polemical, since he refused to idealize the life and ways of the rural Irish. Fernando Pessoa acquired an edition of three Synge plays and translated part of his *Riders to the Sea* into Portuguese, probably in 1913.[9] In that same year he purchased a selection of Yeats's poetry from the English bookstore in Lisbon.[10]

Pessoa did not finish his letter to Yeats and failed to explain, in the paragraphs he wrote, exactly why he thought the Irish movement was important for the "literary and extraliterary future of Europe," but in the last sentence of the surviving draft he remarked enigmatically that the most glorious period of a nation's life is "when the civilizational moment requires such a creation as can best be carried out by that nation." This language is reminiscent of his 1912 articles on "The New Portuguese Poetry" and implies that he thought Ireland, like Portugal, was on the threshold of its most resplendent period ever. That would make the Irish Renaissance analogous to the *saudosista* movement led by Teixeira de Pascoaes and mentioned by Pessoa in those same 1912 articles as a pre-paratory phase for the advent of the Great Poet, whose still unrevealed name was Fernando Pessoa. Yeats, whose patriotic fervor was interwoven in his writing, had emerged as the foremost poet of Ireland, and it may be that Pessoa saw him as the Irish counterpart of what he himself hoped to become—the Super-Camões—in the Portuguese context.

This analogy would have been especially enticing to the Portuguese poet given that Yeats was born under the sign of Gemini, on June 13, exactly twenty-three years before he himself came into the world. Coin-cidences of this sort were lately of far more interest to Pessoa, who was becoming irresistibly attracted to astrology. In 1909, while getting ready to stake his entire inheritance on the Ibis press, he had ordered astrolog-ical charts and detailed readings from three different astrologers based in the United Kingdom. One of them warned that December 1909 and January 1910 would be "unfortunate for money matters,"[11] which pain-fully proved to be the case, since it was then that the novice business-man slid precipitously into debt. In the fall of 1913 Pessoa sent for a free mini-reading from an astrologer based in Paris, in 1914 he acquired some manuals of astrology, and in 1915 he cast his first astrological charts, including one for Yeats.[12]

By that time the Irish Renaissance had gone from being an object of Pessoa's curiosity to becoming a butt of his ridicule. In 1914 or 1915 he wrote a text in English that carefully distinguished the nationalist spirit of the "Golden Age of Portuguese literature" allegedly just beginning—with him and Sá-Carneiro leading the way—from "the narrowness of regionalist movements" such as "the 'Celtic Revival' or any Yeats fairy-nonsense."[13] Pessoa's vitriolic "Ultimatum," written under the name of Álvaro de Campos and published in 1917, would take yet another swipe at "Yeats of the Celtic mist wafting around a sign pointing nowhere." Pessoa preferred Synge's realistic, unromanticized portrayal of Irishness, and in the 1920s he would acquire another, larger selection of his plays, one that included *The Playboy of the Western World*, whose opening performance at the Abbey Theatre, in 1907, stirred a riot among nationalists who felt it sullied Ireland's image.

Notwithstanding his contempt for "fairy-nonsense," Pessoa was quite willing to indulge mystical doctrines and occult paths to knowledge that most intellectuals rejected as sheer hocus-pocus. In this he and Yeats were equals. Astrology, magic, Theosophy, and automatic writing were like a family of interrelated languages through which Yeats—and Pessoa, as we shall see—connected with the spirit world.

◆

PESSOA HAD BEEN GRADUALLY, privately distancing himself from Teixeira de Pascoaes and the *saudosista* movement, and because of the same error he would impute to the Irish Renaissance: a nationalist vision that was too misty, idyllic, and, ultimately, regionalist, unable to cross the border. "We are not Portuguese writing for Portuguese. [. . .] We are Portuguese writing for Europe, for all civilisation." So Pessoa proclaimed in his promotional text about the "Golden Age of Portuguese literature," which did not yet exist but which he hoped to soon inaugurate with his friends. In the meantime he maintained cordial relations with Pascoaes's Renascença Portuguesa group and continued to submit work to their magazine, *A Águia*, whose August 1913 issue brought out his first piece of creative prose, "In the Forest of Estrangement." Occupying five full pages of the issue with oneiric language about an otherworldly landscape, it was identified as a passage from *The Book of Disquiet*, "in preparation." The more the author prepared this book, the more it eluded any likely conclusion. But through all its phases, meanders, and detours,

*The Book of Disquiet* never ceased being an experiment in how far a man can be psychologically and affectively self-sufficient, living only off of his dreams and imagination. It was an extreme, monomaniacal version of Pessoa's own, essentially *imaginative* way of living life.

The narrator of "In the Forest of Estrangement" vaguely interacts with a mysterious woman who walks at his side through the lushly unreal forest, but rather than shuddering at the idea of any sexual contact with her, as happens with the female figures in "Our Lady of Silence" and other early passages from *The Book of Disquiet,* here he at least muses on the possibility of physical love: "We held hands and our gazes wondered what it would be like to be sensual and to try to live out the illusion of love in the flesh." But this "we" is ambiguous. The mysterious female derives exclusively from the soul of the narrator, who explains that he became "dualized"—into himself and the woman.

Two selves in one, male and female, Pessoa's narrator personifies the tension between the reality and illusion of the dreamed-of forest, of love, and of life in general. He, or he-she, sums up the languorous nondrama of self-othered existence by noting that "we were obscurely two, neither of us knowing for sure if we weren't actually the other, if the uncertain other lived." Significantly enough, Sá-Carneiro borrowed these words for the epigraph of his novel *Lúcio's Confession,* in which the protagonist's passion for a friend named Ricardo is erotically sealed by way of the affair he carries on with Ricardo's wife, Marta, who has no character of her own; she is described in the penultimate chapter as an extension of Ricardo, a materialization of his "sexualized" soul. Sexually possessed by both friends, Marta is the go-between through whom they consummate their love.

Considering how the writings of Pessoa and Sá-Carneiro from this period caressed, possessed, and borrowed from each other, we might say that literature was the Marta through whom they experienced a kind of consummation.

✦

SÁ-CARNEIRO, WHOSE NOVEL AND first poetry collection were both published in November 1913,[14] was completely, blithely dependent on his father for all his material needs and wishes: stylish suits, the manicurist, orchestra seats at the theater, French magazines and books, and the typesetting and printing of his own books. Pessoa had no such benefac-

tor. Besides the aunts to whom he was heavily indebted, many other relatives were willing to provide him with smaller loans, but they all thought he should repay what he owed. Intelligent, able-bodied, well-qualified, and with no dependents, he had no excuse for not being able to support himself. On November 15 he drew up a new reckoning of his "Financial Situation," which listed close to sixty debts of widely varying amounts. He subsequently crossed out a few of the small sums owed—to his barber, to a hatter, to a bookstore—and only one larger amount, a loan from a café friend, next to whose obliterated name he wrote, in English: "He died."[15] This was the second general reckoning of his indebtedness that year. Although he had no qualms about keeping his creditors waiting until they despaired of being repaid or departed from life, Pessoa kept scrupulous records. So did the bank, of course, and late payments on its loans were not tolerated.

Through want ads and word of mouth, Pessoa found occasional translation work to supplement the income he earned writing letters in English and French for half a dozen business firms. Other ideas on how to make money regularly occurred to him, but they were usually impractical, and even when he did his best to carry out a good idea, something inevitably went wrong. The misadventure of his bilingual compilation of three hundred proverbs was typical. After noticing a book of Spanish proverbs translated into English as part of a "National Proverbs" series, he wrote to the London publisher on September 26, 1913, wondering whether they might be interested in doing a volume of Portuguese proverbs. Yes, they would be, and Pessoa agreed to the proposed remuneration of five guineas (equivalent to around five hundred pounds today), payable upon publication. In the spring of 1914 he would send off the complete manuscript, which was promptly approved, and the proofs were supposed to be forthcoming. But that July the Great War broke out, causing the project to be postponed indefinitely.

The last of the three hundred not-to-be-published proverbs was Pessoa's favorite, rendered in English as "God writes straight on crooked lines." Though he was far from certain about God's existence, Pessoa had faith in the tortuous and roundabout ways of Destiny.[16]

# CHAPTER 29

A T THE SAME TIME THAT PESSOA, IN LISBON, WAS keeping track of his debts, securing fresh loans, and devoting a significant amount of energy to assorted schemes and odd jobs that earned him not very much money, the poet Constantine Cavafy, who lived in Alexandria, Egypt, spent a few hours each morning working for the Irrigation Service—where he usually arrived late—and had the rest of the day free for reading, writing, and other pleasures. Why couldn't Pessoa, like the Greek poet, hold a part-time job, which would have saved him considerable time and stress?

In 2008 a Greek film director made a boldly imaginative documentary titled *The Night Fernando Pessoa Met Constantine Cavafy*.[1] The completely imaginary part of the film is the meeting between the two writers, who almost surely never even heard of each other. But the notable parallels between their lives and careers make it possible to argue that they were kindred spirits who virtually coincided in the world of literature. Although the work of both men was firmly rooted in the European literary tradition, it was written on the fringes, linguistically and geographically. Cavafy, who was born into the Greek community of Alexandria in 1863 and died in that city in 1933, lived in England between the ages of nine and fourteen, an experience that profoundly shaped his intellect and literary tastes. Like Pessoa, he was schooled on Shakespeare and the English Romantics, he wrote his first poems in English, and he would read and be influenced by Oscar Wilde. Both he and Pessoa learned some of their poetic technique from the dramatic monologues of Robert Browning, and both brought history into their poetry, though in very different ways. Neither poet was in a hurry to publish, and they achieved wide fame only posthumously.

Their sexual orientation may be seen as another point of proximity between the two writers, but also one of separation. Although not a practicing homosexual like Cavafy, Pessoa acknowledged in himself "a mild sexual inversion." The way sexuality played out in their lives and in their writing partly accounts for why their poetries, despite the similarities in their literary education, are fundamentally different.

Cavafy uninhibitedly paid moonlighting shop assistants, delivery boys, and other young men for sex (he conveniently lived above a male brothel) and then, like a master jeweler, set those one-night stands in elegantly simple, historicizing lines of verse that made them stand out as stunning, memorialistic solitaires. Poems about male beauty and encounters with young men by no means dominate his work, however. He wrote many more poems, including his finest ones, out of history itself, in whose annals he frequently inserted fictional protagonists. One kind of Cavafy poem was, in its method, the exact converse of the other. Either he endowed a personal experience (like a successful pickup or an observed scene) with a historical aura, or he personalized and dramatized history, bringing it wonderfully close to us. And some of his poems were philosophical reflections or commentaries, such as his justly famous "Waiting for the Barbarians," in which a decadent nation's leaders and citizens hunker down and do nothing because the invading barbarians will render all actions useless. Unless of course there are no barbarians, in which case the tragedy is even greater, since, as noted in the last line of the poem, they were "a kind of solution," a justification for doing nothing.

"Waiting for the Barbarians" epitomizes the decadent attitude permeating most of Cavafy's poetry, in which there is no progress, no hope or pretense of love, and no redemption. If the barbarians, or sickness and death, are arriving tomorrow, what better way to spend the night than in sensual bliss, or with blissful memories? A four-line poem written in 1917 and titled "To Sensual Pleasure," though slight, is instructive:

My life's joy and incense: recollection of those hours
when I found and captured sensual pleasure as I wanted it.
My life's joy and incense: that I refused
all indulgence in routine love affairs.*

We may doubt whether love affairs are more routine than serial one-night stands, but the interesting word in these lines for understanding

---

* Translated by Edmund Keeley and Philip Sherrard.

Cavafy's poetic technique is the two-way "captured," which refers to the moment of physical or visual possession as well as to the entrapment and preservation of that moment in poetry. Cavafy sensualized Wordsworth's definition of poetry as "emotion recollected in tranquility." His daily life was full of routines, beginning with his part-time civil service job, which was perfect for promoting the tranquility he needed to transform sexual and other experiences (including, especially, his secondhand "experiences" from ancient history) into memorable poems.

The Wordsworthian formula—particularly in its Cavafy adaptation— was not of much use to Pessoa, who was permanently untranquil, restless, disquieted. There is much autobiographical *feeling* in his poetry, which often records his thought life and imaginative life, but seldom did he write poems based on actual or vicarious experiences, and he had practically no sensual experiences to draw on. He would eventually try out a love affair with a woman, but it was never consummated, nor did he engage in casual sex. About his confessed "mild sexual inversion," he explained:

It stops in my spirit. But whenever I've paused and thought about myself, I've felt uneasy, for I've never been sure, and I'm still not sure, that this inclination in my temperament might not one day descend to my body. I'm not saying I would practice the sexuality that corresponds to that impulse, but the desire would be enough to humiliate me. There have been many of us in this category down through history, and through artistic history in particular.

And he goes on to name Shakespeare as an illustrious example of "inversion."[2]

Pessoa took it for granted that Shakespeare was homosexual based on the famous sequence of sonnets he addressed to a "fair youth." Curiously, he never considered the possibility that this sequence might not be autobiographical. Even more curiously, he posited a direct connection between Shakespeare's dramatic inventiveness and his presumed homosexuality. In an unfinished essay from 1913, Pessoa wrote: "we cannot separate, in Shakespeare's personality, his dramatic intuition from [. . .] his sexual inversion."[3] What this statement really means, given that the Portuguese poet consistently likened himself to the English playwright by portraying him in his own image, is that the said intuition and the said inversion were inseparable in the personality of Fernando Pessoa.

Pessoa elucidated the nature of his "mild sexual inversion" by say-ing that he was "female by temperament, with a male intelligence." He "always wanted to be loved but never to love," never to "feel obliged to return affection out of a banal duty to reciprocate, to be loyal in spirit." He "liked being passive." Whatever we may think about Pessoa's clas-sification of human intelligence and sensibility into male and female types, he was indeed inherently passive in matters of love. He was not a seducer, not interested in actively captivating or conquering. Refusing "to reciprocate, to be loyal in spirit," he let his attention wander from one pleasing object of attraction to another. He made no concessions; every-thing was for him and his pleasure, or reverted to him, and that "him" was boundless.

Sexual inversion, in Pessoa, took the form of a massive self-expansion, enacted with panache in his dozens of male alter egos and more dis-creetly in the way he spread himself out, intellectually and spiritually, in so many directions. He had a "male" intelligence inclined to dominate others in literary or political debates, or in his attempts to improve on the works of famous or not so famous writers, but his accentuatedly "female" sensibility made him concurrently receptive to every stimulus. He was unfocused, endlessly divided, forever seduced by new ideas, new projects, new possibilities. This self-dispersion had consequences not only for his literature but also for his life as a Lisbon citizen. Unable to conceive of holding a job with set hours, even part-time, he showed up at the offices of his various clients according to no schedule, and on certain days he didn't show up at all. His erratic method for attending to his paid work mimicked the way he proceeded in his creative work, veering from poem to poem, story to story, essay to essay, and from one genre to another, sometimes on the same sheet of paper.

✦

WORKING CALMLY AND CAREFULLY throughout his life, Cavafy pro-duced a smallish body of delicately wrought poems, many of which are perfect gems. It is remarkable how Pessoa, without any calm, writing convulsively, was able to produce a much larger body of outstanding poetry—along with plays, critical essays, creative prose, and fiction. This last genre included a series of "intellectual short stories," some of which were credited to Pero Botelho, who quietly emerged in 1912 or 1913.[4] In the draft of a fictional letter bearing his initials, this otherwise obscure,

ill-defined heteronym confessed that he was indifferent to sexual desire
but that it existed in his soul. Elsewhere among Pessoa's papers there is
a cryptic note in English on Botelho that states: "sexuality in all (sexual element in genius)."[5] Or perhaps this note is not so cryptic: directly
and indirectly, Pessoa repeatedly acknowledged that the sexual impulse
throbbed in his intellect and imagination, even and especially when it
did not throb in his body.

It hardly matters that none of Pero Botelho's "intellectual" stories
were completed, since their plots are as insubstantial as their imaginary
author. Like Pessoa's static dramas, they contain little or no action, consisting mostly of dialogues in which two or more roughly sketched characters discuss philosophical and religious questions. Some dialogues are
exercises in how far logic can go. The main speaker in "O eremita da
Serra Negra" ("The Hermit of the Black Mountains"), a trenchant logician who gave up a promising literary career and withdrew from society,
can reel off arguments for justifying incest, theft, and murder, but he
can just as easily argue the other way. No facts can hold up against his
power of reason. But since "the only certainty is that nothing is certain,"
the hermit calls reason itself into question and heartily recommends a
religious attitude, even in the absence of faith: "If you can, pray to God.
You don't need to believe in him to do this. You just have to know how
to pray." Like the hermit, Fernando Pessoa loved to argue and yet cultivated at the same time a religious sensibility, for he was all too aware of
reason's power to cut in any direction, going everywhere without going
anywhere. Differently from the hermit, Pessoa was able to be part of Lisbon's literary life and simultaneously exiled from it, in the middle of the
city yet mentally and spiritually far removed.

Skepticism and religiosity had been symbiotically linked in Pessoa
since at least 1907, when he created the heteronym Friar Maurice, who
questioned the existence of God yet did not abandon his religious vocation. In 1913, the rational-minded characters of short stories attributed
to Pero Botelho included not only the hermit of the Black Mountains
but also a prior from a seaside village called Buarcos, a Jesuit priest, and
a Jewish prophet. Botelho's most impressive reasoner, however, was a
detective named Dr. Abílio Quaresma, a Portuguese successor to Ex-
Sgt. William Byng, who had handled some of the cases in the detective
stories Pessoa began writing as a teenager, in English. Abílio Quaresma
was a more complex character than Byng, and a far more proficient

detective. Our first instinct is to compare him to Sherlock Holmes, but he actually had more in common with Martin Hewitt, the reclusive and mild-mannered detective invented by Arthur Morrison, the contemporary of Conan Doyle whose stories Pessoa had planned to translate into Portuguese for the Ibis press. While he never worked as a physician, Quaresma had a medical degree, and his studies in that area proved useful, since his deductions were often based on psychiatric considerations.

Pero Botelho quickly faded from the manuscripts and imagination of Fernando Pessoa, but Dr. Quaresma became more active as the years went by. "Active" is a manner of speaking, given that the detective kept largely to his rented room on Rua dos Fanqueiros in downtown Lisbon, where he spent his time solving riddles and brainteasers when not applying his formidable power of reasoning to crime cases. He was a bachelor and an alcoholic who smoked cheap cigars. His room was a hopeless mess, and he himself was disheveled in appearance and in poor health. He died in 1930 at the age of sixty-two,[6] according to some notes for a preface to the Quaresma stories, which Pessoa continued to work on until his own death five years later. There are over a dozen of these stories, plus a novel, which have been collected and published in a volume that runs to well over four hundred pages.[7] Neither the novel nor any of the stories were completed, however. Pessoa, as usual, had little patience for painting scenes, developing plots, and creating suspense; the stories focus almost entirely on the logical and psychological processes of detection.

◆

DETECTIVE FICTION—PESSOA'S FAVORITE kind of light reading— was a rapidly expanding genre in the early twentieth century, and it was also the heyday for literary sleuths bent on discovering who really wrote the plays of William Shakespeare. Pessoa avidly followed the debate and wrote a couple of hundred pages discussing the evidence presented for and against the various candidates, one of whom was naturally the actor born in Stratford-upon-Avon and named William Shakespeare. None of the actor's contemporaries had any doubts that he was the author of *Hamlet*, *Henry V*, *Othello*, and *The Tempest*. The authorship question arose only in the mid-nineteenth century, as a logical fallout from Shakespeare's canonization and quasi-deification. How, some asked, could a glover's son with limited formal education have produced such an astounding body of plays, so rich in legal and other specialized vocabulary and displaying great familiarity with English court life?

It was in 1912 that Pessoa seized on the authorship question like a dog that has found a delectable bone, and he wrestled with it for the next several years.[8] Nowadays the most popular challenger to the historical Shakespeare for the authorship of *Hamlet* and the rest is Edward de Vere, the 17th Earl of Oxford, whose candidacy was endorsed by Sigmund Freud, but before 1920 Francis Bacon was the favored genius-playwright-in-hiding among "anti-Stratfordians." Bacon, developer of the scientific method and a brilliant essayist on assorted subjects, was Shakespeare's almost exact contemporary. In 1913 Pessoa drew up a bibliography of more than twenty books and articles under the heading "Shakespeare-Bacon Controversy." These titles were in addition to the fifteen books on the subject that he actually purchased and read closely, underlining key passages and making notes in the margins. Almost all of these books—which included Mark Twain's *Is Shakespeare Dead?*—were in English, and not one of them in Portuguese.[9]

National ignorance about the controversy motivated Pessoa to write a pamphlet, "William Shakespeare, pseudónimo," that would educate his compatriots. Or would it mislead them? Five densely typed pages for his introductory study explain why Shakespeare could not have written the works attributed to him and why Bacon might well have. The most curious rationale is sexual. Pessoa argued that the actor from Stratford, who had three children by Anne Hathaway, a farmer's daughter, was heterosexual, while the author of the "Shakespearean" sonnets and plays was manifestly homosexual—just like Bacon, according to some spotty evidence in one of the books Pessoa owned.[10]

Pessoa soon changed the title of his pamphlet in progress to "O mito de William Shakespeare" ("The Myth of William Shakespeare")[11] but abandoned it around 1916. Between 1913 and 1916 he also wrote more than a hundred pages on the topic in English. Then his interest waned, but it never died out, and around 1930 he planned to expand the dormant pamphlet into a full-length work, *The Person of Shakespeare: A Study in Transcendental Detection*, to be published in English as well as in Portuguese. The detective angle announced in the book's title was reinforced by the identity of its fictional author, none other than "the late Dr. Abílio Quaresma."

It tickled Pessoa to be an investigator for a detective story embedded in historical reality, but he never really doubted that Shakespeare was Shakespeare, despite the anti-Stratfordian position provocatively adopted in the first part of his unfinished pamphlet. A cursory look at the writings of Bacon, of de Vere, or of any other alternate author that has been proposed instantly reveals the absurdity of the hypothesis, since none of them writes at all like Shakespeare. Pessoa, nevertheless, could not completely let go of the idea that the greatest author in the English language might have succeeded in concealing his true identity.

The concept of invisible authorship had enchanted Pessoa since childhood, when his habit of writing under false names was a form of play—a variation on the game of let's pretend I'm someone else. Why he kept pretending as he got older is harder to understand. Around the age of eighteen, when he was signing most of his poetry and many of his prose texts as Charles Robert Anon or Alexander Search, he wrote about a scenario of concealed authorship that he had always found "extremely interesting":

> I considered the case of a man becoming immortal under a pseudonym, his real name hidden and unknown. Such a man would, thinking upon it, not consider himself really immortal but an unknown to be immortal in deed. And yet what is the name, he would consider; nothing at all. What then, I said to myself, is immortality in art, in poesy, in anything whatsoever?[12]

Pessoa's English is awkward here, but the conclusion seems to be that the name does not matter; *personal* immortality is an illusion. The work itself is what counts and what endures. Homer may not have existed, but *The Iliad* and *The Odyssey* are cornerstones of Western literature. Of Shakespeare the man we know next to nothing, but *Romeo and Juliet, A Midsummer Night's Dream*, and the sonnets dedicated to the mysterious W. H. are known and loved by millions.

Pseudonymous authorship emphasizes the elevated status of literature itself, apart from whoever wrote it. The enhanced pseudonyms that Pessoa called heteronyms served simultaneously, and somewhat paradoxically, to keep literature tied to earth, by giving it a *lively* context, thereby recalling its human origins.

✦

IF BY CHANCE THE heteronyms also served to remind their unworldly maker of his own humanity, they represented rather eccentric forms of the human species. Think of Alexander Search, forever flirting with insanity, or Jean Seul, pathologically obsessed with sex and morality. In 1913 Pessoa created his most peculiar alter ego: Frederick Wyatt, a resident of Lisbon but of British descent and presumably noble lineage, since he is referred to at one point as *Lord* Frederick Wyatt. A preface intended for his collected poetry describes him as an incorrigible dreamer who had a brilliant mind but no talent for coherently organizing his metaphysical ideas and theories. He was inconsistent in his opinions as well as in his behavior, which alternated between shy passivity and reckless self-affirmation. Severely nearsighted and invariably dressed in a frock coat, he elicited laughter during his habitual strolls on the Calçada da Estrela. The mention of this street, where Pessoa himself resided with his parents in 1906–1907, suggests that Wyatt was a self-parody. The youthful Pessoa, a Lisboner with a British education, was likewise shy yet self-affirmative, likewise unable to tame his thoughts, which ran in all directions, and while he never used a frock coat, he at least tried to imagine himself as a dandy.

Though he was a solitary creature, Frederick had quite a few relatives. The Pessoa archive contains signatures for a Rev. Walter Wyatt from Sandringham, England, a Monsieur Alfred Wyatt based in Paris, an Arthur C. Wyatt, a Charles, a Francis, and a Stanley Wyatt. Pessoa, several years earlier, had even drafted a complete though brief missive addressed to a Christopher Wyatt, telling him that he would write again at greater length in a few days' time. The letter was signed "Yours very truly, F. Nogueira Pessoa." And he added a postscript: "Kiss Baby for me. Hope she is well." One could advance psychological explanations for Pessoa's strange habit of writing letters to nonexistent people, but perhaps it was just his way of doodling—through words instead of drawings.

The proliferation of Wyatts and the letter writing they inspired are reminiscent of the epistolary Search family. It was as if an entire heteronymous clan had been reincarnated, with the Wyatts replacing the Searches, a notion corroborated by the fact that Frederick Wyatt expropriated part of Alexander Search's poetic output—twenty-one poems, to be exact, written between 1904 and 1908.[13] They are listed in one of

Pessoa's notebooks under the heading "The Poems of Frederick Wyatt," with no mention of where they came from (Search).

Pessoa did not write any fresh work for Wyatt, whose only practical function was to provide a new critical and biographical frame of reference for poems from Pessoa's youth that perhaps struck him, with hindsight, as a tad naïve, too driven by idealism and too insistently contemptuous of convention. Instead of rewriting the poems, he justified their naïveté by rewriting their fictional context, making them the products of Frederick Wyatt's dreaminess and inability to effectively articulate his thoughts, characteristics clearly announced in the preface to Wyatt's work. The preface also informs us that the distracted poet was "extraordinarily ignorant of modern English literature" and had "never read anything by Oscar Wilde, Bernard Shaw." In fact, the Search poems inherited by Wyatt were written *before* Pessoa began reading the two Irish writers at all closely, and Wilde, as we have seen, helped Pessoa refine and articulate his aesthetic point of view.

Pessoa was trying to get his poetic house in order and prepare for something new, without yet knowing what form it would take. He knew that something was missing, however. It was not for lack of opportunity that he failed to publish his poems, since the magazine *A Águia* would have gladly printed them. He procrastinated because he felt he could do better. Despite having predicted his own emergence as Portugal's Great Poet, and despite having written dozens of memorable poems in both English and Portuguese, he had not made that mysterious passage whereby the genius artist creates something that surpasses what he or she could reasonably, plausibly produce. Pessoa stood on the mound of all that he knew, like an eagle getting ready to soar.

# CHAPTER 30

**F**OR PESSOA IT WOULD PROVE TO BE AN *ANNUS mirabilis*, but the early months of 1914 already portended catastrophe for Portugal and the rest of Europe. Lisboners were not especially fazed by the train strike in January that led to clashes on the streets and a few deaths—serial disruptions had become the new normal—but the Portuguese Republic, now in its fourth year, felt increasingly fragile. Afonso Costa and his Democrats, the most radical of the three republican parties, had managed to stay in power throughout 1913, but to do so they not only had to quash another monarchist revolt, they also had to put down insurgent republicans disenchanted with the Democrats for not being radical enough. So overcrowded were the jails with political dissidents that British newspapers, always quick to find fault with post-monarchical Portugal, launched a campaign denouncing their appalling conditions. In order to more efficiently mete out justice to their opponents, the Democrats had created a rogue police force called the Formiga Branca, or White Ants, and soon there was a second vigilante force, the Black Ants, which wielded arms on behalf of a different republican faction. Pessoa must have marveled at the sad coincidence: when he was a little boy, his uncle Cunha had made up fantastical stories about warring ants, beetles, and crickets, and now gun-toting "ants" were terrorizing the streets of Lisbon.

Political volatility had spread over most of the continent. In neighboring Spain the assassination of a Liberal prime minister, in November 1912, further fragmented its political system, so that neither of the major parties could command a majority on its own. Governments in France were forming and dissolving in quick succession, with three prime ministers resigning in 1913 alone. Great Britain was being rattled by worker strikes, suffragette activism, and the threat of armed violence in Ireland over the question of Home Rule. And the governing elite in Germany was anxiously trying to curb the rise of the far-left Social

Democrats, who had won the Reichstag election of 1912. An arms race among Europe's major powers continued unabated, and even certain smaller countries, particularly in the Balkans, were spending huge sums of borrowed money to outfit their armies with the latest and best in modern weaponry.

But while it is easy, with hindsight, to point to the many warning signs of the First World War, there was no climate of anticipation, no real awareness that the balance of power known as the Concert of Europe was actually a tinderbox waiting to explode. Europe's rest-lessness, deriving from not only national rivalries but also a more empowered working class, was a sign of vitality as well as a source of instability, and local economies were prospering. Portugal was no exception. Construction there was booming, export revenue from cork and wine was increasing, and so was the demand for imported goods. Industrialization continued to lag, however, and the balance of payments deteriorated.

Afonso Costa's high-handed style of governing and his unwillingness to entertain changes to the harsh anticlerical laws had alienated moderate republicans, forcing him to resign in late January 1914. This could only have delighted Pessoa, who detested Costa, but he was temporarily distracted from the national drama, with literature now occupying most of his attention. *Lusitania*, the largely political magazine he had sketched plans for in 1911, had evolved into a would-be monthly magazine devoted entirely to creative writing. Mário de Sá-Carneiro drew up a masthead and a table of contents for the first issue, scheduled for publication on March 1, 1914.[1] Pessoa was to be the editor in chief, with Sá-Carneiro, Armando Côrtes-Rodrigues, and Alfredo Guisado rounding out the editorial staff, but the new *Lusitania*, like the old one, foundered even before it could be launched. In February, on the other hand, Pessoa at long last went public as a poet. Two of his poems, including "Swamps," appeared in a magazine under the suggestive title "Twilight Impressions."[2]

Both Sá-Carneiro and Alfredo Guisado were enthusiasts of the swampist style, but Pessoa himself was growing weary of the decadent languor that saturated poems such as "Swamps," certain prose texts for *The Book of Disquiet*, and static dramas like *The Mariner*. About the final version of this play, published in 1915, he would boast: "No more remote thing exists in literature. Maeterlinck's best nebulosity and subtlety is coarse and carnal by comparison."³ Having succeeded in being more nebulous than Maeterlinck, more ethereal than Pascoaes, and more syntactically and imagistically exotic than Sá-Carneiro, Pessoa longed to do something else. He would wade no more in the stagnant waters of swampism, and static drama, by its very definition, had nowhere to go (which is why Maeterlinck himself soon abandoned the genre). There are marvelous passages of dialogue in Pessoa's other static dramas, which include a play aptly titled *Inércia* (*Inertia*) and the aforementioned *Salomé*, influenced by Wilde's play of the same name, but none have the dramatic power and magic of *The Mariner*, which was the only one he was able to finish.⁴

*The Mariner* is a brilliant demonstration of how to use dreams like bricks to construct reality. Enconsced in a circular castle, three women keep watch through the night over the corpse of a fourth woman, dressed in white and lying in a coffin. They hesitantly talk, uncertain what their talking is for or whether their words stand for anything real. The dead woman represents their future, or their true present state, or perhaps she is the God people have stopped believing in, or the author at the end of his resources. Or perhaps she is not dead, just sleeping, and the three watchers are but the diaphanous substance of her dreaming. All logic, all discourse, and all speculation prove to be circular, like the castle. But halfway through the play, one of the watchers begins to tell her dream about a shipwrecked mariner stranded on a desert isle where, all alone, it pained him to remember the life and the people he once knew. Rather than succumbing to nostalgia, he spends his days conjuring up a completely new and unfamiliar homeland, slowly filling it with dreamed streets, events, and people. And so vivid is this past built only of dreams that it comes to replace the life he had actually lived before being shipwrecked.

After telling her strange tale, the watching woman wonders whether the mariner might after all be the only one who is real, and the scene in the castle with her and her companions just one of his dreams. One dream inhabits another, reality is at a loss, and the circle keeps on circling.

◆

PESSOA HAD THE VEXING habit, for scholars and biographers, of assigning fictional dates to some of his works, usually for the sake of an ideal narrative of his life and literary development. When he published

*The Mariner* in 1915, he dated it October 11–12, 1913, even though his notes and surviving manuscripts suggest that the initial draft was not completed until January or February 1914, and we know it was much revised before it saw print.[5] But Pessoa wanted to make sure that his future readers and commentators read his static drama as the prelude to a far more radical drama of the soul, which began to unfold in March 1914. *The Mariner* ends with the crowing of a rooster and the first light of morning chasing away the night of dreams. The new morning belonged to a different kind of dream, which thrived on sunlight and had a name: Alberto Caeiro.

Twenty-one years later, in his letter to a young critic about the origins of the major heteronyms, Pessoa would explain that Alberto Caeiro began as a joke he wanted to play on Mário de Sá-Carneiro. The idea was to invent "a rather complicated bucolic poet" and to dress him up with a few biographical details, to see if he could fool his friend.

> I spent a few days trying in vain to envision this poet. One day when I'd finally given up—it was March 8, 1914—I walked over to a high chest of drawers, took a sheet of paper, and began to write standing up, as I do whenever I can. And I wrote thirty-some poems at one go, in a kind of ecstasy I'm unable to describe. It was the triumphal day of my life, and I can never have another one like it. I began with a title, *The Keeper of Sheep*. This was followed by the appearance in me of someone whom I instantly named Alberto Caeiro. Excuse the absurdity of this statement: my master had appeared in me.

In 1936, the year after Pessoa died, this letter was published by its recipient, Adolfo Casais Monteiro, and the myth of the Triumphal Day was born. For decades to come, almost no one doubted the story of how Alberto Caeiro, the "master," erupted in Pessoa's soul with a torrent of wondrous poems on March 8, 1914.

Only toward the end of the twentieth century did a thorough examination of Pessoa's archives reveal a rather different literary genesis.[6] The oldest Caeiro manuscript—a large folded sheet of paper with five poems from *The Keeper of Sheep*—is dated March 4, 1914. Another folded sheet, dated March 7, contains three more poems from the same cycle. The name of Alberto Caeiro is missing from these two manuscripts and may not have occurred to Pessoa until a few days later. More poems followed, on manuscripts with and without dates, and by mid-March Pessoa had written at least half of the forty-nine poems from *The Keeper of Sheep*. He mythologized his achievement, crunching the work of ten days or two weeks into just one momentous day, March 8. But whatever the time span of this first outpouring of Caeiro poems, it was a triumph such as Pessoa had never experienced—not because of the quantity of poems written but because of what they said and how they said it.

Here are some of the lines of verse that came to him on March 4, like a sunbeam slicing through clouds of metaphysics and hitting him right in the eyes:

> For the only hidden meaning of things
> Is that they have no hidden meaning.
> It's the strangest thing of all,
> Stranger than all poets' dreams
> And all philosophers' thoughts,
> That things are really what they seem to be
> And there's nothing to understand.
>
> Yes, this is what my senses learned on their own:
> Things have no meaning: they have existence.
> Things are the only hidden meaning of things.[7]

Lines like these seemed to fatally discredit all the theories and explanations Pessoa had accumulated through many years of study and reading. To see things as they are, asserts a Caeiro poem written on March 13, requires "lessons in unlearning," and if Caeiro taught Pessoa anything, it was the art of unlearning, of seeing as if for the first time. Consider the sixth poem from *The Keeper of Sheep*, which neatly dispenses with the age-old debate about God's existence:

> To think about God is to disobey God,
> Since God wanted us not to know him,
> Which is why he didn't reveal himself to us . . .
>
> Let's be simple and calm,
> Like the trees and streams,

And God will love us, making us
Us even as the trees are trees
And the streams are streams,
And will give us greenness in the spring, which is its season,
And a river to go to when we end . . .
And he'll give us nothing more, since to give us more would
    make us less us.


Whether or not God exists, according to Caeiro's pellucid logic, is entirely beside the point of what life is for, namely living. Though indifferent to God, it is with holy devotion that Caeiro exalts the trees, the
streams, and all of nature, leading Pessoa to define him at one point as
"an atheist St. Francis of Assisi."[8] But Caeiro was not a true atheist, let
alone a saint. He was, however, a religion, whose first and main adherent
was Fernando Pessoa.

Pessoa claimed, in *The Book of Disquiet*, that certain fictional characters were more real to him than living people.[9] Alberto Caeiro was just
such a character. Only in succeeding years would Pessoa describe this
heteronym's physical features—medium height, hunched shoulders, fair
hair, blue eyes—and elaborate a biographical sketch: born in Lisbon on
April 16, 1889, attended only primary school, lived in the countryside
with an elderly aunt, and died from tuberculosis in 1915. But the voice
and personality of the clear-seeing shepherd, who never actually kept
sheep—"But it's as if I kept them," he says at the beginning of *The Keeper
of Sheep*—already stood out in his earliest poems, which could not have
originated without that voice, that personality, and that vision, so completely unlike Fernando Pessoa's.

In a letter sent to João Gaspar Simões in 1933, Pessoa would call
*The Keeper of Sheep* "the best thing I've ever written," an achievement
he could never again match, since it exceeded what he was rationally
capable of creating. Pessoa did not write these words only for the sake
of the myth that would survive him; they were an admission of his own
stupefaction and feeling of insufficiency. In March 1914 Alberto Caeiro,
uttering verses as clear and natural as water flowing down a slope, was
nothing less than a revelation, one that Pessoa could never fully fathom.
And so the story of his Triumphal Day was not so much a fabrication as
it was a metaphor.

Pessoa did like to play tricks, however, and Alberto Caeiro was perfect material for indulging his mischievous tendencies. In the past he had sent letters signed by Charles Robert Anon, Faustino Antunes, and Alexander Search to newspapers, publishers, business firms, and even— in the case of Antunes, his heteronymous psychiatrist—to people he had known in Durban. The emergence of Pessoa's newest, far more extraordinary heteronym emboldened him to go further. With a perfectly straight face, he told some of his café companions about this unheard-of poet named Caeiro who lived in Galicia, on the other side of Portugal's northern border, and he showed them copies of poems from *The Keeper of Sheep* that had come into his hands. His closest literary friends—Sá-Carneiro, Armando Côrtes-Rodrigues, and Alfredo Guisado—knew the secret and swore to keep it a secret, but António Ferro and others were fed the hoax and swallowed it whole.[10] So authentic was Caeiro's voice, and so different from Pessoa's, that it was easy to be fooled.

Ferro was a test case. Pessoa's real ambition was to fool the world at large, by launching Caeiro as an independent poet, while he remained backstage, out of sight. Caeiro a literary immortal and himself a complete unknown—that, for Pessoa, would be the highest triumph. He could never have dreamed anything like that for Alexander Search, who was not psychologically or even biographically all that different from his maker and whose poetry was good, but not great.

As poems streamed forth in the stunningly clear voice and simple language of Caeiro, Pessoa simultaneously began writing critical prose texts to announce the new literary prodigy. The poetry and the criticism sometimes occupied the same manuscript sheets. On March 13, while sitting at a café table, Pessoa jotted down the first version of a Caeiro poem that begins "What we see of things are the things." After eight lines had been written, an English critic abruptly took control of Pessoa's ink pen and wrote this incomplete sentence: "At the same time a preciseness so astonishing in noting states of enjoyment of nature that it is difficult . . ." Pessoa was already brainstorming for the preface to Caeiro's complete poems in English. Thomas Crosse, as the heteronymous translator assigned to the task would eventually be called, never translated more than a few lines of poetry, but many pages were written for his "Translator's Preface" and for articles about Caeiro that Pessoa hoped to publish in British newspapers.

The plans to promote Caeiro were extravagant: translations of his poetry into French as well as English; articles about him and his work in

English publications such as *T.P.'s Weekly* and *The Athenaeum*, in *Mercure de France*, in Spanish, Italian, and German publications; and a blitz in the Portuguese press. Pessoa thought of asking some journalists he knew from Lisbon's cafés to help publicize the new poet, and he counted on Sá-Carneiro to write an in-depth article for *O Século*, Portugal's best-selling daily paper, on Guisado to write for a newspaper in Galicia, and on Côrtes-Rodrigues to report on Caeiro in the Azores. In the end he decided not to impose on his friends, but he himself drafted an impressive array of promotional materials, including an interview with Caeiro allegedly conducted in the Galician port city of Vigo by someone who used the initials "A. S.," which perhaps stood for the English heteronym Alexander Search. The interview was in Portuguese, however. At one point the interviewee alluded to his "spontaneous materialism," but when asked point-blank if he was a materialist, Caeiro replied: "I'm not a materialist or a deist or anything else. I'm a man who one day opened the window and discovered this crucial fact: Nature exists. I saw that the trees, the rivers and the stones are things that truly exist. No one had ever thought about this."

Caeiro thought about a lot of things. Or rather, there was a lot of thought behind his "spontaneous" perception and acceptance of things as they are. Pessoa pointed this out in the rough draft of an article he was preparing for *A Águia*, which had so far been willing to publish whatever he cared to submit. Although it had the air of being naturally materialistic, he argued that Caeiro's work—"calculated, measured, *contemplated*"—was essentially abstract. His materialism, far from being a direct and spontaneous appreciation of things, was a philosophical view of the world, and the nature he celebrated in his verses was an *idea* of nature. This philosophizing and abstracting capacity, wrote Pessoa the critic, was precisely what he admired in this new poetry. The revelation of Caeiro was for him a *poetic* revelation. Caeiro did not open Pessoa's eyes to a new way to live life; he represented a new way to engage with life in his writing.

✦

"NOTHING IS BORN FROM nothing," wrote Lucretius, and Caeiro's birth owed something to Lucretius himself. The Roman Epicurean's *De Rerum Natura* (*On the Nature of Things*) used poetry to expound a materialistic philosophy of the world, and Caeiro's poetry was a kind of repeat performance on a more modest scale, despite the heteronym's claim to eschew philosophy. Lucretius may not have been at the front of Pessoa's mind when he dreamed up Caeiro, but the connection he drew between the two poets in his notes was quite real.[11] His knowledge of classical literature and philosophy was not only vast, it was vivid, it pulsed in his intellect, and its influence touched most of his work, whether signed by him or by one of his literary alter egos.

Walt Whitman was the most visible as well as the most intimate influence on Caeiro. The most *visible*, since the heteronym's poetry adopted the American's free-verse style, took up some of the same topics, and employed some suspiciously similar turns of phrase. The most *intimate*, since Whitman taught Caeiro how to open up, feel everything, be everything, and sing. The audacity of Whitman's poetic "I" had awed Pessoa when he read "Song of Myself" for the first time, six or seven years earlier, but he had no inkling of how to write like that. Alberto Caeiro showed him how.

In his many pages of criticism to promote the new, bucolic heteronym, Pessoa repeatedly mentioned Whitman, at times falsely claiming that his influence was minimal or nonexistent. And he marshaled arguments, mostly in English, to prove how fundamentally different Caeiro was. Whereas Whitman strove to see an object *deeply*, linking it up "with many others, with the soul and the Universe and God," Caeiro merely wanted to see the object *clearly* and in itself, apart from other objects and free of "transcendental meanings." Pessoa also contrasted Whitman's "violent democratic feeling" with "Caeiro's abhorrence of any sort of humanitarianism." And there were other differences, some of which Pessoa gathered into a long list.[12] It was a perfectly valid list; the two poets are indeed very different from each other. But Caeiro could never have existed without Whitman, the catalyzing inspiration that mixed with Pessoa's vast poetic culture to set off an admirably productive explosion.

Caeiro's poetry mentions only one Portuguese writer by name: Cesário Verde, Portugal's most original poet from the nineteenth century. Scarcely known during his short life—he died of tuberculosis at age thirty-one—Verde was still not widely read or appreciated in Pessoa's day. Pessoa read what was available, a posthumous collection called *The Book of Cesário Verde*, which crammed an astonishing quantity of visual, audible, palpable, and olfactory *things* into rhyming lines of regular, metered verse. It looked like traditional poetry but read like nothing ever done before in Portugal, or anywhere else in Europe. Here are two stanzas (in my unrhymed translation) from his greatest poem, "The Feeling of a Westerner":

An aproned knife maker, working the lathe,
Redhotly wields his blacksmith's hammer;
And bread, still warm, from the baker's oven
Sends forth its honest, wholesome smell.

And I, whose goal is a book that galls,
Want it to come from inspecting what's real.
Boutiques shine with the latest fashions;
A street urchin gapes at their window displays.

The other forty-two stanzas of this poem, whose narrator strolls through the city of Lisbon as the day turns into night, are similarly packed with urban and human detail: streetcars, carriages, apartment houses, churches, a jail, bars, a brothel, stevedores, fishwives, beggars. . . .

There is a Baudelairean influence in Verde, but without the ostentatious decadence and individualism of the French *flâneur*, who actively cultivated his reputation as a bourgeois-despising bohemian. The Portuguese poet, who was meekness personified, quietly working in the family business by day, gave his poetic soul to the life and objects all around him. "Oh, if I'd never die! If forever / I'd seek and attain the perfection of things!" he longingly wishes in "The Feeling of a Westerner." Verde's passionate objectivity is what made him a vital secondary spark for igniting the turbulent mélange of erudition and creative energy in Pessoa that gave rise to Alberto Caeiro. Walt Whitman provided the model of an expansive narrator who respected no boundaries and obeyed no rules. Cesário Verde contributed his thoroughly objective vision of things—of things intensely felt, and not only things from the city. Half of his poems were set in the rural outskirts of Lisbon, where the family had a farm.

It was not after all in Galicia but in the countryside northeast of Lisbon that Alberto Caeiro supposedly lived in a white house. There, leaning out the window in the late afternoon, we find him reading *The Book of Cesário Verde* at the beginning of the third poem in *The Keeper of Sheep*, and so intently does he read that his eyes burn. The twenty-eighth poem from the same cycle also begins with him reading a book, this time by an unnamed "mystic poet," but he quits after two pages, laughing so hard that he cries. From comments made elsewhere,[13] we know that the mystic poet alluded to was Teixeira de Pascoaes, for whom nature was the glorious pageant of a spiritual dimension. Caeiro criticized him and other mystic poets—including St. Francis of Assisi—for saying "that flowers feel / And that stones have souls / And that rivers are filled with rapture in the moonlight."

"Caeiro perhaps derives from Pascoaes," Pessoa admitted in a note written in Portuguese, "but he derives through opposition, through reaction." One sees this in the early Caeiro manuscripts. With their half-finished poems, crossed-out poems, and poems littered with deletions, insertions, and alternate wordings, they resemble battlefields, with Whitman and Verde waging war against Pascoaes and St. Francis of Assisi. The conceits and language of the latter team are the ones consistently defeated—sometimes by being modified and incorporated. Unlike the horrific conflict that would soon engulf Europe, it was a quick and brilliantly fruitful war, lasting for just a week in March 1914. Out of this showdown between contrasting poetic tendencies emerged, serene, Alberto Caeiro.

A reaction against Pascoaes, Caeiro was also and more broadly a reaction against Fernando Pessoa—against all his learning and incessant intellectual wrangling. Pessoa explains this beautifully in the unfinished article about the pseudo-shepherd that he drafted for Pascoaes's magazine, *A Águia*. Feigning "complete ignorance about the person of Sr. Alberto Caeiro," the article writer surmises that in his youth he must have been exposed to a "vast literary culture," after which "he retreats to the country and there, completely giving up all reading and book learning, surrenders himself to nature." Or as Caeiro puts it, in two lines from a poem:

I lie down in the grass
And forget all I was taught.

He forgets it, but he would not be the poet Alberto Caeiro without all that prior learning.

✦

THE FIRST PERSON TO translate Caeiro into English in a sustained way—twelve poems—was Thomas Merton (1915–1968), the American Trappist monk who was himself a fine poet as well as a major writer of contemplative literature. He studied Eastern mystical traditions, noting their connections with Western mysticism (St. John of the Cross, St. Teresa of Ávila, Meister Eckhart . . .), and felt especially, personally drawn to Zen Buddhism. It was their "Zen-like immediacy" that attracted him to Caeiro's poems, which he first read in Octavio Paz's Spanish translations. Merton perceptively noted, however, that this Zenishness was "sometimes complicated by a certain note of self-conscious and programmatic insistence."[14]

In 1914 Zen Buddhism had still not been popularized in the West, and Pessoa's knowledge of it was scant, although he was interested in the tenets and spirit of Buddhism generally. Caeiro's likeness to Zen was a sheer coincidence, evident in his renunciation of studious learning and the preconceptions it fosters, in his commitment to seeing what is there to see, without interpretation, and in his distrust of metaphysical speculation. One scholar has even noted similarities between Caeiro's verses and Japanese poetic styles such as the haiku, dear to many followers of Zen.[15] The principal aim of Zen, which is *satori*, or enlightenment, was not an ambition of Caeiro, who had no ambitions, but his accidentally Zen-ish qualities are what made him the master of the two other major heteronyms soon to emerge—Álvaro de Campos and Ricardo Reis—and of Fernando Pessoa himself. What's more, the story of Caeiro's mastership makes for yet another point in common with Zen Buddhism, whose essence is properly transmitted through the direct example of and dialogue with a master, rather than through private study and devotion.

Pessoa was the first one to admit the absurdity of claiming that Caeiro was his master, but the claim may seem not so absurd if we think of Caeiro as a convergence of empowering poetic influences that, dawning on Pessoa all at once, changed him forever. In fact the mythical, metaphorical Triumphal Day of Pessoa's life was not only about the birth of Alberto Caeiro but also about his own rebirth. Pessoa's account of what happened on March 8, 1914, does not end with the appearance in him of Alberto Caeiro. He goes on to say that, after dashing off thirty-odd poems in the name and style of "master" Caeiro, he grabbed a fresh sheet of paper and wrote, again all at once, the six poems that make up "Slanting Rain," by Fernando Pessoa. All at once and with total concentration. . . . It was the return of Fernando Pessoa as Alberto Caeiro to Fernando Pessoa himself. Or rather, it was the reaction of Fernando Pessoa against his non-existence as Alberto Caeiro.

Álvaro de Campos, in his delightful and frequently poignant "Notes for the Memory of My Master Caeiro," written between 1930 and 1932, recounted a different version of events for March 8, 1914. On that day Caeiro, who happened to be in Lisbon, supposedly met Pessoa and recited some of his poems from *The Keeper of Sheep*. Pessoa, reeling from "the spiritual shock" of that encounter, went home and immediately wrote the six poems of "Slanting Rain." They were his reaction "to the Great Vaccine—the vaccine against the stupidity of the intelligent." Campos claimed that, because of the inoculating effect of Caeiro, which some-what counteracted Pessoa's "overwrought intelligence," all the poems he would write from then on would be different from the ones he wrote before meeting Caeiro. Campos, it must be said, exaggerated the effect of Caeiro on the poetry signed by Pessoa himself, several of whose finest poems were written before Caeiro burst onto the scene. On the other hand, the triumphal emergence of Caeiro greatly boosted the creator's confidence to be himself as well as several other personalities and to take to a new level the stylistic experiments that had commenced with "Swamps" and other writings of similar ilk.

Swampism had borrowed a preexisting aesthetic—the symbolism developed by French poets such as Mallarmé, Verlaine, and Gustave Kahn—and intensified it, making it even more mysteriously suggestive, more excruciatingly atmospheric. The poems of "Slanting Rain," a bolder experiment, were an exemplary demonstration of intersectionism, a lit-erary aesthetic theorized by Pessoa in the second half of February 1914, shortly before Alberto Caeiro came into existence.[16]

The new movement was initially little more than an extension and rebranding of swampism. The other poets of Pessoa's inner circle—Sá-Carneiro, Côrtes-Rodrigues, and Guisado—immediately signed on to intersectionism but continued to write in their usual style. Mean-while, the name of the magazine that the four friends were planning to launch was changed from *Lusitania* to the more cosmopolitan-sounding

*Europa.*[17] At the end of February Pessoa drew up a list of intersectionist works that included, right at the top, his "In the Forest of Estrangement" (from *The Book of Disquiet*), previously considered a typical example of swampism. *The Mariner* and his "Beyond-God" sequence of five poems also made the list. So did various short stories of Sá-Carneiro, along with his novel *Lúcio's Confession*. Côrtes-Rodrigues and Guisado were listed for their poetry, as were Mallarmé and Gustave Kahn. In each case, the type of intersection was indicated: reality intersected with dreaming, reality with madness, mystery with sensation, the visual image with the musical image, and so forth.[18]

These after-the-fact intersectionist designations, if not always forced, were at any rate so-whattish. Don't virtually all literary works depend on conflicting or contrasting elements? To suddenly call those elements "intersecting" is hardly illuminating, let alone a real innovation, as Pessoa was the first to recognize. And so, with his matchless capacity for custom-building whatever was needed, he wrote "Slanting Rain," which instantly made intersectionism a meaningful term, a kind of literary equivalent to cubism in the visual arts. The six poems in the sequence juxtapose scenes from different times and places with one another as well as with the narrator's differing moods. And the scenes and moods are not only juxtaposed, they also interpenetrate, passing through each other the way Superman passes through walls, without him or the walls losing their structural integrity. In the first of the six poems, which intersects the narrator's "dream of an infinite port" with a wooded landscape, ships leaving the port "pass through the trunks of the trees" and "drop their moorings through the leaves one by one." In the last poem of the sextet, the scene and music of an orchestral concert crisscross, without distorting, the narrator's memory of playing ball in the backyard as a child. The four poems in between play out other sorts of intersections—spatial, temporal, and psychological.

Álvaro de Campos would rate "Slanting Rain" as the most admirable thing ever written by Pessoa under his own name, but most readers are less enthusiastic. Pessoa himself must have had his doubts, since he produced only a small handful of additional works based on the new technique. As for Pessoa's friends, none was capable of writing anything like "Slanting Rain," so the theoretical distinction between swampism and intersectionism, although they understood it well enough, was never reflected in their work. The upshot was that for the next several years the two movements coexisted, or rather, they were more or less the same movement. Intersectionism became practically a synonym for swampism.

There was a third ism, which would eventually absorb and outlive the other two: sensationism. This aesthetic creed held that sensations, since our entire notion of reality depends on them, should be the basis and the focus of all artistic creation. It was on the back of a sheet of paper with two Caeiro poems that Pessoa jotted down his first ideas about "*Sensacionismo*,"[19] and Alberto Caeiro was the first sensationist. He defined himself, and his sensationist attitude, in the ninth poem of *The Keeper of Sheep*:

> I'm a keeper of sheep.
> The sheep are my thoughts
> And each thought a sensation.
> I think with my eyes and my ears
> And with my hands and feet
> And with my nose and mouth.
>
> To think a flower is to see and smell it,
> And to eat a fruit is to know its meaning.

As the virtual shepherd tended Zen-like reflections such as these in fields of proliferating manuscripts, Fernando Pessoa kept writing promotional texts about him and the literary movements he was going to spearhead, if all went well. The plan was to launch peaceful, pastoral Alberto Caeiro at the forefront of a literary revolution.

# CHAPTER 31

O◼◻◼O◼O◼O◼O◼O◼O◼O◼O◼O◼O◼O◼O◼O◼O◼O◼

HE INVENTOR OF INTERSECTIONISM, SENSA-
tionism, and Alberto Caeiro was known to Aunt Anica only
as Fernando, her nephew, whom she loved well enough—but
couldn't he find somewhere else to live? He was already in his midtwenties. "What about a small apartment of your own, or a rented room?"
she repeatedly suggested.[1] But Pessoa could find no better deal than the
monthly room and board she charged and he rarely if ever paid. And
in spite of his taste for solitude, he liked the company of his aunt and
of Maria, her daughter. He could come and go as he pleased, and be as
sociable or unsociable as he felt like being.

So in late April of 1914, when mother and daughter moved from Rua
Passos Manuel to a third-floor apartment on nearby Rua Pascoal de Melo,
he and his worldly possessions moved with them. He owned a small but
elegant set of clothes (courtesy of tailors and haberdashers who extended
him credit), hundreds of books, and the famous wooden trunk where
he stowed manuscripts, notebooks, mementos, and letters, including the
weekly missives his mother sent from South Africa. Maria's fiancé, Raul
da Costa, was a regular presence at both the old and the new address,
located on the same streetcar line, no. 19.[2] Sweethearts since they were
teenagers, they would finally get married in the fall. Anica's good friend
Palmira and her daughter, Clara, were also frequent visitors. The new
apartment was smaller, but Pessoa's pesky great-aunt Rita, to everyone's
relief, had gone to live with her younger sister, Carolina Silvano.[3] The
atmosphere at home became more congenial without the constant threat
of Aunt Rita's criticisms and judgments.

When still a student at the School of Arts and Letters, Fernando had
enlisted Aunt Anica, his cousin Mário, and, no doubt, his cousin Maria
as experimental subjects for his phrenological studies. They patiently sat
still while he measured their heads in a dozen different ways and were
rewarded for their troubles with pseudoscientific profiles of their person-

alities. In 1914 Pessoa persuaded his aunt, his cousin Maria, and Clara, who was almost like Maria's sister, to participate in something more adventurous: séances. Alberto Caeiro was interested only in immediate reality, perceptible by the senses, but Pessoa himself was increasingly fascinated by realities that can't be seen, and he decided to try contacting the astral world.

One day he brought home a planchette: a small, thin, heart-shaped wooden board with a hole for holding a pencil and tiny casters enabling it to glide across paper at the gentle touch of fingers. Invented in France in the mid-nineteenth century, the planchette was used for automatic writing, through which spirits from the netherworld—dead relatives, more often than not—transmitted messages to the living. It was a helpful but nonessential device, since a communicating spirit could convey messages directly through someone's writing hand, sometimes in a different sort of script. This was the method that ultimately prevailed in the séances conducted by Pessoa, with Aunt Anica and Maria proving to be especially fluent mediums. As they all sat around the dining table, conjuring up dead spirits that may have included Anica's husband and Maria's father, Pessoa's own father, and both of Pessoa's grandmothers, Madalena and Dionísia, it was usually Anica or her daughter who received whatever written messages the departed relatives deigned to communicate. The séance participants may also have contacted dead people with whom they had no relation. Pessoa surely had questions to ask of certain writers he admired: Cesário Verde, Antero de Quental, Shelley, Whitman, or even Shakespeare. This is all speculation, since we know nothing at all about the senders and contents of the messages received. But the messages, in any case, were not the most extraordinary result of the séances: Clara would swear, years later, to have seen and heard Maria, prompted by Pessoa, speak on behalf of a dead spirit in English, a language she never learned.[4]

Perhaps Maria actually did know some English—from books and from her mother, Anica, who had learned it as a girl—but managed to speak it only when emboldened by Fernando, the séance master, to overcome her inhibition. If so, then her achievement somewhat resembled Pessoa's newfound ability to speak in the language of Alberto Caeiro by being audaciously plain and simple, uninhibited by the weight of his vast erudition. In an unfinished preface for a planned collection of works ascribed to his heteronyms, Pessoa explained that he served as their medium and wrote "as if he were being dictated to."[5]

✦

NOW THAT PESSOA HAD overcome all inhibition, there was no stopping him, or them. The disarming naturalness of Caeiro's *The Keeper of Sheep* was only the beginning, only one voice. Pessoa had lately invented a new side to Caeiro, or rather, a second life, and even a third life. The poet of nature was to move on to better or at least more modern things. In the first week of May, a few days after moving with his aunt and cousin to tree-lined Rua Pascoal de Melo, Pessoa drafted a partial list of poems written for *The Keeper of Sheep*. Further down on the same sheet of paper, he divided Caeiro's poetic career into three distinct phases, with the help of some false dates:

### Alberto Caeiro

| | | |
|---|---|---|
| 1. | The Keeper of Sheep. | 1911–1912 |
| 2. | Five Futurist Odes. | (1913)–1914 |
| 3. | Slanting Rain (Inters. Poems). | 1914 |

According to this scheme, Alberto Caeiro, emerging three full years before his actual dawning in Pessoa's soul, was to be a protean poet-wonder who kept outdoing himself. Pessoa, it seems, was grooming his heteronym to be the Super-Camões, or Great Poet, prophesied in his 1912 articles, "The New Portuguese Poetry." *The Keeper of Sheep* was a reaction to and correction of Pascoaes, whom Pessoa had initially praised but Caeiro sharply criticized, taking issue with his mystical interpretation of nature. This first phase would be superseded by futurist poetry, which nobody in Portugal had ever seriously tried to write. And the culmination of Caeiro's career would be intersectionism—a poetic style more advanced than anything else in Europe. That, at least, was how Pessoa intended to market it. The intersectionist poems of "Slanting Rain," written in March 1914, were a product of the same intellectual and creative ferment that gave rise to Caeiro, whom Pessoa initially credited as their author, and it was in Caeiro's name that he began writing futurist poems.

Futurism was born on February 20, 1909, with the publication of a manifesto by an obscure Italian writer, F. T. Marinetti, on the front page of *Le Figaro*, France's largest-circulation newspaper. A group of writers and artists from Italy (including the painter and sculptor Umberto Boccioni) soon joined with Marinetti to form the initial nucleus of the movement, whose ideas spread to other countries, especially Russia. It took only six days for news of the founding manifesto to be published in Lisbon's *Diário de Notícias* and Porto's *Jornal de Notícias*, but the actual doctrines and techniques of futurism arrived much more slowly. A few local poets published purportedly "futurist" poems that had nothing to do with what the movement stood for.[6]

Pessoa was better informed, having read about futurism in foreign newspapers and having heard about it from Mário de Sá-Carneiro, who had kept abreast of the futurists' pronouncements and activities during his time in Paris. Marinetti's "Technical Manifesto of Futurist Literature," published in 1912, advocated not only free-verse poetry but also "words in freedom" (*parole in libertà*), unfettered by traditional syntax. It also repudiated the nineteenth-century preoccupation with human psychology, proposing in its stead a "lyrical obsession with matter." Microbes, motors, machines, urban noise, smell, and speed were all worthy subjects of futurist poetry.

In the spring of 1914, Pessoa drafted the opening stanzas for four of the "Five Futurist Odes" envisaged for Alberto Caeiro. Although they did not abolish syntax, as Marinetti recommended, they sang of streets and streetcars, trains, automobiles, and the bustle of urban life—far removed from the rustic tranquility of *The Keeper of Sheep*. Both Walt Whitman and Cesário Verde alternated, in their poems, between rural and urban settings, but Pessoa's idea for Caeiro was different. According to his idealized biography, the poet who wrote objectively about nature and only about nature, supposedly in the years 1911–1912, would completely abandon that style when in 1913 he adopted futurism, which in turn would be eclipsed in 1914 by the intersectionism of "Slanting Rain." And in 1915 he would die, at which point Pessoa would reveal the extraordinary, many-sided poet to the world. But Caeiro's career turned out differently than planned. Pessoa would ultimately publish "Slanting Rain" under his own name, having decided that it made no sense to turn his clear-seeing poet of nature into a sophisticated intersectionist, and Caeiro's attempts to be a futurist had an unexpected outcome.

After four attempts at futurist odes that didn't get very far, Pessoa-
Caeiro, in May or June of 1914, embarked on a fifth ode that was louder,
faster, and more sustained. This time he began in the middle—in the
middle of the ode and in the middle of an unnamed city, a modern and
dynamic Everycity, evoked with sensual yearning and religious ardor:

> O fabrics in shop windows! O mannequins!
> O useless items that everyone wants to buy!
> Hello enormous department stores!
> Hello electric signs that flash on, and off, and disappear!
> Hello cement and reinforced concrete!
> I love all of you and everything like a beast.
> I love you carnivorously,
> Pervertedly, wrapping my eyes
> All around you, O great and banal, useful and useless things,
> O my contemporaries, present and proximate form
> Of the immediate system of the Universe!
> O God![7]

This is but a snippet from a six-page draft of the wide-ranging ode,
which chaotically exalts storefronts, hotel elevators, parliaments, political
corruption, newspapers, subways, effeminate homosexuals, prostitutes,
cathedrals, modern agriculture, horse races, sexual possession, sadism,
and masochism, but also Plato, Aristotle, "the ancient, solemn sea that
laps the shores," and even the memory of a house in the country where
the narrator spent time as a little boy. The poet of this "Triumphal Ode,"
as it would come to be called, was like Caeiro insofar as he was visual and
tactile, apprehending reality through the senses, but his insatiable longing to feel and possess everything under the sun was antithetical to the
serene detachment of the bucolic poet who longed for nothing. Alberto
Caeiro, instead of transitioning into a futuristic phase, had given birth
to a new, ostensibly futurist poet with a completely different personality:
Álvaro de Campos.

✦

IN PESSOA'S 1935 LETTER about the origin of the heteronyms, the
story of his Triumphal Day—when he wrote the first Caeiro poems and
the intersectionist poems of "Slanting Rain"—is followed by a second

tale of triumph in the very next paragraph. The letter writer claims that, not long after Caeiro emerged, "a new individual suddenly and impetuously came to me. All at once, without interruptions or corrections, the ode whose name is 'Triumphal Ode,' by the man whose name is none other than Álvaro de Campos, issued from my typewriter."

As he had done with the creation of Caeiro, Pessoa also mythologized the birth of Campos, whose "Triumphal Ode" was not composed all at once and letter-perfect at the typewriter. He wrote the initial draft of the poem by hand, then greatly reworked, reordered, and expanded it. The final version, a tour de force with 240 breathless lines of verse, omitted a direct reference to Walt Whitman contained in the first draft, and it is no wonder, since Campos's concupiscent love of life in all its varieties is even more reminiscent of the all-encompassing American bard than is Caeiro's calm love of nature and things as they are. Pessoa did not like to advertise his literary debts.

One of the things that Campos learned from Whitman was how to include the sexual body and sexual language in poetry naturally, as part of his impassioned interest in humanity generally and in his own, individual humanity. In February 1914 Pessoa had written another sonnet for his *Book of the Other Love*, but that "other" love continued to be otherworldly, inspired by a "masculine Venus" that made the narrator forget all about "carnal desires."[8] Álvaro de Campos, emerging three or four months later, brought everything down to earth and to his own large and lusty self. Openly bisexual, he did not shrink from versifying his fantasies of being manhandled and possessed by savage pirates (in "Maritime Ode," 1915). Raw feeling—at turns euphoric, terrifying, violent, tender—welled out of him and took shape in poems that Pessoa could never have written under his own name. Alberto Caeiro was the father of sensationism; Álvaro de Campos, who yearned to "feel everything in every way possible," was the doctrine incarnate.

Triumphal tale number two, like tale number one, was literally false but faithful in spirit to Pessoa's experience. Rough and incomplete as it was, the draft version of the "Triumphal Ode" catapulted him to a vertiginous height of poetic emotion. We can quibble with his spectacular accounts of how the heteronyms "appeared" in him or "came" to him. We can insist on the fact that Pessoa *created* Caeiro and *created* Campos. True enough. But it was Caeiro who taught him to see like a god, and it was Campos who showed him how to express tremendous feeling.

The familial connection of the two new poets is encoded in their names. *Campos* means "fields," and *de* means "of" or "from." Álvaro came from the fields of Alberto, and he brought with him the project of "Five Futurist Odes." (Pessoa crossed out Caeiro's name on a couple of these incipient odes and replaced it with Campos's.) Before long, however, Campos would distance himself from futurism and develop other poetic styles, refusing to be tied to any doctrine or program that might hamper his own "program," which was simply to feel as fully as possible whatever there was to feel. The most prolific of the heteronyms, he was also the most worldly. He would study naval engineering in Scotland, sail to the Far East, live between Great Britain and Lisbon, and have affairs with young men as well as women. This most modern and stylish of the heteronyms was also the youngest, born on October 15, 1890, two years after Fernando Pessoa and on Nietzsche's birthday.[9] Campos, in fact, represents the Dionysian impulse—the intoxicating affirmation of life, felt in all its pains and pleasures—as articulated by the German philosopher in *The Birth of Tragedy*.

Irrepressible and impertinent, Álvaro de Campos frequently interacted with Pessoa, sometimes sparring with him in articles or interviews published in the Portuguese press, while at other times they closely collaborated on behalf of a common cause. Campos occasionally substituted for Pessoa in social situations,[10] to the consternation of those who were expecting Pessoa himself to show up, or he acted as his creator's spokesman, publishing manifestos in an inflammatory language that Pessoa could not muster on his own. If Caeiro was Pessoa's religion, the solid rock of his poetic salvation, Campos was his right-hand man and true-blue companion. So close was Campos to Pessoa that he ended up hindering his one attempt to have a love life—with Ophelia Queiroz. And so gifted was he as an urbane poet of sensations that he became, inadvertently, a wedge between Pessoa and his best friend, Sá-Carneiro.

# CHAPTER 32

I N MARCH 1914, WHILE PESSOA WAS TRIUMPHALLY
giving birth to Alberto Caeiro, Mário de Sá-Carneiro was finishing
the short story "Resurrection," whose Portuguese protagonist fondly
remembers the time he spent in Paris, with its "wide avenues, the tumultuous boulevards," its "narcotics and nocturnal carousing," its romantic
gardens, its royal palaces. "Aristocratic Paris! Poor People's Paris! Paris
aswarm!"

It was to that city that Sá-Carneiro returned on June 6, almost one
full year after leaving it. He stayed in the same neighborhood as before,
the Latin Quarter, and at the same address: the Grand Hôtel du Globe,
on Rue des Écoles. His hotel was practically next door to the Sorbonne,
where he had attended a few (very few) classes during the 1912–1913
school year. He would not be going back there. He frequented the cafés
he knew and loved, resumed his promenades in the Jardin du Luxembourg, dined with friends, most of whom were Portuguese expats or
visitors, and wrote poetry and fiction—oblivious, like everyone else,
to the tenuousness of such peaceful pursuits. Historians disagree about
whether the First World War was the inevitable outcome of growing
national rivalries and the massive arms buildup or, on the contrary, an
"accident" resulting from a series of diplomatic missteps and political
miscalculations—but while the possibility of an impending war was
most definitely discussed in the inner circles of power, it was not on the
minds of most ordinary citizens.

Pessoa likewise had no clue that Europe would soon be swept up in a
devastating conflagration. He worried, instead, that his own life was on
the verge of upheaval. The day before he saw his best friend once more
board the Sud-Express for Paris, he sent a letter to his mother in Pretoria, saying that he felt tortured by an anxiety that was hard to describe
but that had a definite cause.

Everything around me is either departing or crumbling. I don't use these two verbs with gloomy intent. I simply mean that the people I associate with are or will be going through changes, marking an end to particular phases of their lives, and all of this suggests to me—as when an old man, because he sees his childhood companions dying all around him, feels his time must be near—that in some mysterious way my life likewise should and will change.

Sá-Carneiro was not the only friend leaving Lisbon. Alfredo Guisado would be spending the summer with relatives in Galicia. Yet another friend was moving to Porto. And in the fall his cousin Maria and Raul da Costa would be getting married and moving to Switzerland. Since Aunt Anica was going with them, Pessoa would have to find his own lodgings. These might not seem like especially dramatic changes, but change of any kind, he told his mother, was for him "a partial death."

Even the circumstance of publishing my first book will alter my life. *I'll lose something: my unpublished status.* To change for the better, because change is bad, is *always* to change for the worse. And to lose a defect, or a deficiency, or the status of being rejected, *is still a loss.* Imagine, Mother, how someone who feels this way must live, overwhelmed by such painful daily sensations!

What will I be ten years from now, or even five? My friends say I'll be one of the greatest contemporary poets. [. . .] But even if this is true, I have no idea what it will mean. I have no idea *how it will taste.* Perhaps glory tastes like death and futility, and triumph smells of rottenness.

Pessoa was neither exaggerating nor being coy. Friends such as Sá-Carneiro, Guisado, and Armando Côrtes-Rodrigues fully expected him to become a famous poet, a prospect he both looked forward to and dreaded. He knew that fame would do little to quench his thirst for things like love, understanding, and being understood. And if all he achieved was a modest fame, then the act of bringing his poetry into print would make him merely banal: he would join the vast ranks of the published.

The forthcoming "first book" announced in Pessoa's letter alluded perhaps to *The Keeper of Sheep*, for which he had written a number of additional poems in May; he now had tentative if not final versions for nearly all of the cycle's forty-nine poems. Or perhaps it referred to *Exile*, the collection of miscellaneous poems he had been hoping to publish since 1913. Another possibility was *The Book of Disquiet*, for which he had already written enough passages to form a slim volume. Besides the symbolist (or swampist) texts in the manner of "In the Forest of Estrangement," he was writing more and more passages about the narrator's psychological disquiet and anxiety. In fact he made a typed copy of this anguished letter to his mother in order to include parts of it, duly adapted, in *The Book of Disquiet*. It is his only complete letter to her that has, in this way, survived.

Whatever book Pessoa had in mind did not come out in 1914, or in 1915, or in 1916. He lacked the self-discipline to finish his books, he had no money to publish them, and he really did worry, as he indicated to his mother, that publication and literary renown might be a path to disillusion. He also feared that his writing career, as it advanced, would make him more isolated, and lonely. Indeed this was already happening, unpublished though he was. Sá-Carneiro's imminent departure was the immediate reason for the anxious tone of his letter to his mother, but the almost one thousand miles of railroad that would separate the two friends only rubbed in, geographically, the fact that Pessoa had already set out on his own journey, toward literary destinations where Sá-Carneiro could not possibly follow.

✦

IN A LETTER POSTED from Paris on June 15, two days after Pessoa's twenty-sixth birthday, Sá-Carneiro sent his greetings "to our Alberto Caeiro." There is more to that "our" than the privilege of knowing, along with a few other select friends, the true origin and identity of this refreshingly uncomplicated poet who reportedly lived in the country and had little formal education. Sá-Carneiro not only knew that Caeiro was an invented poet; he also helped the inventor bring him into being—a detail that was concealed for over a hundred years.

In 2017, when reexamining the Caeiro dossier from the Pessoa Archive, it dawned on me that one of the early, crossed-out poems was actually written by Sá-Carneiro.[1] A manuscript sheet from March 7, 1914, contains not only three Caeiro poems in Pessoa's handwriting but also an incomplete fourth poem written in the distinctively rounded letters of his best friend. The poem's first eight lines describe an idyllic pastoral scene with sheep roaming over the fields, wafting breezes, smiling nature, a softly flowing river, a doleful peasant in the distance, and washerwomen singing. The ninth line reads "Everything on earth is vigorous life." Unfortunately, poetic vigor is precisely what was lacking in this and the preceding eight lines, prompting the poet to abandon his effort.

For the past several years Pessoa had been taking notes for a philosophical essay titled "The Feeling of Nature,"[2] and to create a poet of nature was entirely his own idea. But Sá-Carneiro may have helped him conceive the actual figure of the shepherd-poet. Caeiro's very name seems to be a homage—*Carneiro* (the Portuguese word for "sheep") without the *carne* ("flesh"). And Sá-Carneiro certainly deserved a homage. On at least one afternoon, sitting with Fernando in a café, Mário listened and made suggestions as Pessoa wrote some of his very first triumphal poems, and he even tried his own hand at a nature poem, with predictably disastrous results, since even in his imagination he was irrevocably urban, and narcissistic.

Pessoa would write in his 1935 letter about the heteronyms that the creation of Caeiro was a kind of joke that he played on his friend, and so it was—an unintentionally cruel joke, revealing to Sá-Carneiro a level of creative bravura that he could never hope to match, as proven by his embarrassing attempt at a poem à la Caeiro. Pessoa was like the prodigious child who climbs straight up the tree, to tall and unlikely branches, while his less agile playmate can only look on from below with admiration or envy. And Caeiro was just one of the tall trees inaccessible to Sá-Carneiro.

In mid-June Pessoa sent his friend the "Triumphal Ode" of Álvaro de Campos. It was an already revised, polished version—a radiant paean to machines and modernity—but still untitled and not quite complete. (Pessoa would add a few more stanzas to the beginning of the poem.) Dazzled by what he read, so unlike anything Pessoa had ever written, Sá-Carneiro wrote him on June 20 that the poem had afforded him one of the greatest pleasures of his life. Although it did not have all the technical ingredients prescribed by Marinetti, Sá-Carneiro pronounced it to be the undisputed masterpiece of literary futurism. And he made a frank admission: "this is the kind of poetry that shows me how much distance [. . .] lies between me and you."

That distance looked even greater to him one week later, when he received a dozen odes signed by Ricardo Reis, whom Pessoa had just pulled out of the forge. A classicist who believed in the gods of antiquity, Reis was the most unlikely heteronym of them all. His odes, elegant and restrained, were the opposite of the effusively futuristic "Triumphal Ode" that had so impressed Sá-Carneiro. Now his jaw dropped again as his eyes scanned lines like these:

There are in our life
No sorrows or joys.
So let us learn,
Wisely unworried,
Not how to live life
But to let it go by,

Keeping forever
Peaceful and calm,
Taking children
For our teachers
And letting Nature
Fill our eyes . . .

Despite the strong presence of nature in Ricardo Reis, it would be impossible to confuse one of his odes with a poem of Alberto Caeiro. The rhythm, the tone, and the coloring are completely different. So is the raison d'être of nature. For Caeiro it is an end in itself, something to feast on with the eyes and our other sense organs. Nature, for Reis, is an example that we should follow; it teaches us how to live. His telling us to fill our eyes with nature sounds perhaps like Caeiro, but after several stanzas about the impossibility of our resisting Saturn, the god of time, he concludes his ode with these exhortations:

Let us pick flowers.
Let us lightly
Wet our hands
In the calm rivers,
So as to learn
Some of their calmness.

Sunflowers forever
Beholding the sun,
We will serenely
Depart from life,
Without even the regret
Of having lived.

The other odes sent to Paris mentioned the gods Pan, Apollo, Ceres, Jupiter, and Pluto, as well as the philosopher Epicurus, who taught that pleasure was the highest good. For Ricardo Reis, positive pleasure was too much to hope for in a modern world ruled by Christian thinking, which he abhorred; he strove to at least live calmly and without suffering. Born on September 19, 1887, this lover of antiquity was the oldest heteronym and the only one born before Pessoa himself.

Sá-Carneiro defined the new poet as a modern-day Horace (but with more "soul," he told Pessoa), partly because of all those references to Olympian gods but also because of the themes, the elevated tone, and his classical sense of measure. As more Reis odes were written, their vocabulary and spelling became more Latinate, their syntax more intricate, and they often employed Portuguese adaptations of the so-called Alcaic and Sapphic stanzas, named after the poets Alcaeus and Sappho, who were both from the Greek island of Lesbos.* These formal characteristics mirror those of Quintus Horatius Flaccus, who was famous for adapting complex Greek lyrical meters to Latin.

Horace also inspired Ricardo Reis's recommendations to live for today, to follow the middle way, and to accept what the gods, or fate, have ordained, but the heteronym was more melancholy and less playful than his Roman precursor. An ode from July 1914, by which time Reis, only one month old, had already attained his mature style, counsels us to live our lives

Like panes of glass: transparent to light,
Pattered by the sad rain trickling down,
    Warmed only by the sun,
    And reflecting a little.

---

* The Alcaic stanza, as adapted by Pessoa-Reis, consists of two lines containing four metrical feet followed by two shorter lines, while the Sapphic stanza has three long lines followed by a short one.

Ricardo Reis's brother, Frederico, a literary critic invented several weeks after Ricardo, described the new poet's philosophy as a "sad Epicureanism," and his poetry as "a lucid and disciplined effort to obtain a measure of calm." But Reis's strong sense of determinism, which his odes personify as a supreme Fate that even the gods are subject to, was a stoical notion. Horace, too, wove ideas from both the Epicureans and the Stoics into his verses, and scholars wonder which school he belonged to, if any. His main concern was no doubt to be a good poet, and so it was for Pessoa, in whichever persona he was writing.

The persona of Ricardo Reis is beguiling. If we think of him as a mask—the Latin *persona* originally signified a theatrical mask—we will scratch our heads trying to figure out what dramatic situation he belongs to. Although Reis believes in the Greek and Roman gods, admires the philosophy of the Epicureans and Stoics, and writes in the style of Horace, Pessoa did not situate his classicist creation in the historical past. Ricardo Reis was a Portuguese man from the twentieth century who acted as if he were living, or who wished he were living, in ancient Greece or Rome. That was why he could not aspire to more than the *illusion* of happiness, according to his brother Frederico, who noted that "happiness cannot be felt by someone exiled from his own faith and from his soul's natural habitat." Rejecting the modern world and the Christian religion that prevailed in the country of his birth, Ricardo Reis espoused a revival of Greek moral, social, and aesthetic ideals, and the introduction of a new paganism, adapted to the contemporary mentality.

Frederico did not reveal where exactly his brother lived, but a good bet—if it was still doing business in 1914—would be the Cascais Sanatorium, imaginatively founded by Pessoa in 1909 for people just like Ricardo Reis. In chapter 23, I discussed Pessoa's short story about this institution, one of whose mentally infirm residents was António Mora, a champion of ancient Greece and a votary of paganism. Pessoa quit working on the story in 1911, and António Mora disappeared from view, but he would resurface in the Pessoa world in 1915, a year after the emergence of Ricardo Reis, who was his ideological double. These two apostles of neo-paganism would even collaborate together on a long, wishful essay titled "O regresso dos deuses" ("The Return of the Gods").

Besides this and several other essays, Ricardo Reis would sign his name to dozens of pages for a preface to an edition of Alberto Caeiro's poetry, commissioned by surviving "relatives" some time after his premature death, in 1915, but Reis initially wrote only poetry, no prose, and it turns out that his poetic career began somewhat earlier than in 1914. Pessoa's 1935 letter about the heteronyms' origins would recall that "a hazy, shadowy portrait" of Ricardo Reis had appeared to him around 1912, when he wrote a few poems "from a pagan perspective" and "in a semiregular style." It was actually in 1910, when the Ibis press was depleting his inheritance and António Mora was raving about the Olympian gods at the Cascais Sanatorium, that Pessoa began writing poems "from a pagan perspective." They were rather sketchy, consisting of isolated stanzas never organized into finished compositions, and although the verse patterns *look* regular, the syllable count varies slightly from line to line.

The mature odes of Ricardo Reis follow a strict metrical pattern, but half a dozen of his first run of poems from 1914 are in a "semiregular" style and take up some of the same motifs found in the pagan poems from 1910–1911. It is as if Ricardo Reis, though still unnamed, had tenuously begun to take shape and then fell into a three-year sleep, before decisively coming to life in June 1914.

But there was another facet to this evolutionary tale. The pagan poet who only tentatively emerged around 1910 was also a precursor to Alberto Caeiro, one of whose early, embryonic poems talked about his love of nature and about paganism in the same breath. In fact, the poet of nature was initially conceived as a pagan who, like the ancient Greeks and Romans, regarded the forces of nature as divine manifestations. Pessoa, however, had a fine inspiration, which was to get rid of the middleman, or rather, the polytheistic system of gods. Caeiro, as he finally emerged, could not subscribe to paganism or call himself a pagan since he himself *was* paganism—according to Campos's explanation in his "Notes for the Memory of My Master Caeiro." And Ricardo Reis would explain that their master, "an absolute objectivist," saw that the gods "were made in the image and likeness of material things; but they were not those material things, and so he had no use for them."[3]

Pessoa's original idea of creating a pagan poet for whom divinities inhabited the forms of nature was fulfilled in Ricardo Reis. Alberto Caeiro, a felicitous deviation, went beyond any idea that Pessoa might have had and was himself a kind of god, the divine master poet. Álvaro de Campos derived from the "deviation" that was Caeiro, but his creation was predestined: he was the missing piece that had to be invented to complete Pessoa's "drama divided into people, instead of into acts," as the dramatist would famously define his greatest literary achievement. It was a Greek drama, a tragedy in the form of a trilogy, as in the age of Aeschylus, when an entire day was set aside for the performance. Caeiro was the poet of dawn, when eyes open up to see life beginning anew; Reis was the poet of afternoon, when the sun clearly outlines the forms of objects; and Campos represented evening, when feelings take over and the sensations of the whole day not only linger, they loom larger.[4] Álvaro de Campos's second major poem was a long ode to night, composed at the end of June, two weeks after Ricardo Reis had finally and fully come into his own with a series of odes in the style of Horace. The essential pieces of the heteronymous drama were all in place.

Aristotle tells us that tragedy developed out of the dithyrambic hymns in honor of Dionysus, the frenzy-inducing god of wine. But it was the Apollonian love of clarity, measure, and equilibrium that gave it form and raised it into a high art, argued Nietzsche in *The Birth of Tragedy*. These two divine forces are personified in the emotionally exorbitant Álvaro de Campos and the reason-governed Ricardo Reis. Alberto Caeiro, the "absolute objectivist," was sheer perception, beyond or before emotional responses and rational considerations.

✦

IT WOULD TAKE A few years for Pessoa to bring into sharp focus the contrasting views of his three main heteronyms on literature, politics, religion, and society, and he would keep fiddling with their biographies until the year he died, but their essential temperaments and relationship to one another were established. Reis the restrained classicist and Campos the unbridled futurist, although radically different from each other, were both disciples of Caeiro, whose purity of vision, acceptance of things as they are, and simplicity of expression drastically reduced the distance between seeing, being, and speaking. That was the basis of his poetic originality, conferring on him the status of master.

Pessoa explained these interrelations to Sá-Carneiro in the letter he sent with his first Ricardo Reis odes, in late June 1914. "What a beautiful page of literary history!" exclaimed the duly impressed friend in his reply. But Sá-Carneiro also pointed out that the real master was Pessoa himself, the creator of that literary story, and wondered if these "pseudonyms" (Pessoa did not use the word "heteronym" until much later) were really necessary. This ambivalence was connected to Mário's uneasy feeling that Caeiro, now with two disciples, was drawing Pessoa away from him. Pessoa had bluntly told his friend that Caeiro, Campos, and Reis had nothing to do with swampism and would not be entering the ranks of that movement. Sá-Carneiro, while saying that he understood, admitted to feeling disappointed in his letter of June 27. The next day he wrote a new poem, a sonnet titled "Apoteose" ("Apotheosis"), and sent it straight off to Pessoa, fitting all fourteen lines onto a postcard. The first line reads, "Masts broken, I sail in a sea of Gold," and the final line, "O swamps of Me, a stagnant garden." Thus he proudly, desperately, reaffirmed his allegiance to the swampist aesthetic that he and Pessoa had developed together a year earlier.

Enamored of his new trio of invented poets, Pessoa was insensitive to his friend's fear that he was being left behind, even as the friend, in spite of his fear, enthusiastically asked to see more poetry of Álvaro de Campos, the cosmopolitan heteronym and his personal favorite. Pessoa complied with his request, and Sá-Carneiro continued to be amazed. Pessoa himself was amazed, and disconcerted. He could not account for where all the *feeling* in these new poems was coming from. It was as if he were absent from it all, exiled from the real world and from real feeling, while the three heteronyms felt *instead* of him, feeling things he himself had never felt and could never feel, at least not directly. Was he fooling himself? Was all this poetic feeling a sham?

He confessed his self-doubts to Sá-Carneiro, who replied on July 13 that anyone capable of writing the extraordinary poems Pessoa was writing, even "if he does not feel, *knows* how to marvelously feel. [. . .] To know how to feel is to feel, my Friend." And he elucidated what he meant by way of self-comparison: "I feel that I could never have written Álvaro de Campos's ode, since I don't sufficiently love everything he sings about to capture it in the same way. . . . I 'feel' less than he feels, I 'love' less than he loves, I 'experience' less than he experiences the Avenues de l'Opéra, the cars, the Derbies, the prostitutes, the wide boulevards." Pessoa, in other words, could poetically, imaginatively feel the bustling avenues and elegant boulevards of Paris more intensely than his friend who actually walked them and frequented their cafés.

Pessoa's poetic feat made an inadvertent mockery of Sá-Carneiro's obsessive attraction to living in Paris, and it also deepened his friend's sense of poetic inferiority. Sá-Carneiro expressed no reproach and felt no envy; for Pessoa he had only admiration. In the same letter Mário wrote that his greatest personal glory, which he underlined, was to know that *"Fernando Pessoa likes what I write."* A few sentences later, however, he announced that the end of his life was approaching, that he felt like an embalmment of himself, that he was tired of playing the same role over and over, always himself as the main character. He went on in this vein, reflecting on his limitations, looking back on his life, remembering his childhood, his family, some friends, and he mentioned the book of short stories he still needed to finish. But then. . . . Hadn't he told Fernando time and again that he couldn't see himself as "a lengthy work"? How would his life end? "I don't know," wrote Mário. "But more than ever I believe it will be suicide."

Jolted out of his Caeiro-Reis-Campos reverie, Pessoa shot off a panicky letter to Alfredo Guisado, relaying the ominous words of their mutual friend. From his holiday in Galicia, Guisado wrote back on July 27 to say that he had just received a letter from Sá-Carneiro, and it contained not the vaguest allusion to suicide. Pessoa, in the meantime, had himself received a reassuring letter from his cherished friend, who had no immediate plans to do anything drastic. Indeed, he had written that letter of the thirteenth when in a somber mood, which had passed. Even so, he stood by the word "embalmment" to describe the seemingly torpid state of his art and life. He felt he was bound to keep on doing the same sort of thing, writing the same sort of poems and stories, unable to come up with anything different or to be anybody else but who he was.

# CHAPTER 33

○❉○❉○❉○❉○❉○❉○❉○❉○❉○❉○❉○❉○❉○❉○❉

**T**HE ASSASSINATION OF THE ARCHDUKE FRANZ Ferdinand of Austria in Sarajevo by a Serbian nationalist, on June 28, 1914, momentarily spooked Europe and in particular its diplomats, who were fearful there would be armed retaliation, but the financial markets remained calm. It was assumed that the inflamed international tensions would die down, and Portuguese newspapers continued to be preoccupied with domestic politics. Pessoa's own focus was likewise fixed on the four-year-old republic, especially its cultural milieu, which he hoped to stir up with his literary inventions.

While Mário de Sá-Carneiro, in Paris, was deploring his artistic limitations, Pessoa was rewriting the history of Portuguese literature so that it could better accommodate his self-multiplication into a panoply of authors and styles. Under the name of Frederico Reis, Ricardo's brother, he drafted an essay on the Escola de Lisboa, the Lisbon School of writers. The notion of a school was a bit misleading, cautioned Frederico, since there was not a joint program uniting its members, who were three in number: Alberto Caeiro, Ricardo Reis, and Álvaro de Campos. They were all born and raised in Lisbon; they had a common precursor in Cesário Verde, the nineteenth-century poet who observed and felt things large and small with unusual acuity; and they were inextricably interconnected, since Caeiro was the master who "woke up" the poetry lurking in Reis and Campos. But they actually represented three different literary movements. Caeiro was a "pure naturalist," Reis "a great, and the only, neoclassicist," and Campos the "poet of sensations" as well as a futurist, or rather, he was "what the futurists wanted to be."

Pessoa would later change Ricardo Reis's birthplace to Porto and Álvaro de Campos's to the Algarvian town of Tavira, but he would retain and flesh out with colorful details the story of how, upon meeting Caeiro, they both woke up to their calling as major poets, each one unique. As for Caeiro himself, Frederico maintained that he was, quite simply, "the greatest poet of the Portuguese language." Frederico's essay, which Pessoa planned to bring out as a pamphlet, lauded the new poets for being both innovative and international—unlike Teixeira de Pascoaes, Mário Beirão, and the other *saudosistas*, whose celebration of a "spiritualized, transcendentalized Nature" amounted to a Portuguese continuation of Romanticism. That was their originality, the essayist granted, but what sense did it make to prolong Romanticism, which had been dead for half a century?

Frederico mentioned two other poets who, if not actually members of the Lisbon School, were closely affiliated with it: Fernando Pessoa and Mário de Sá-Carneiro. The former, as the "culmination of self-analysis," and the latter, with his "materialization of sensations, the carnalization of the spirit," had perfectly achieved what the French symbolists aspired to. Although Frederico Reis did not use the term, this heightened, allegedly perfected symbolism was what its adherents called swampism and, more recently, intersectionism.

In mid-July, around the time Sá-Carneiro wrote his letter in which he talked seriously for the first time about suicide, Pessoa wrote him about Frederico Reis's pamphlet on the Lisbon School, and he teasingly noted that Frederico had some very interesting things to say about Mário's poetry. These and other words in Pessoa's letter were a balm to Sá-Carneiro, who realized that his friend, despite his enthusiasm for Caeiro, Campos, and Reis, was not going to abandon swampism and intersectionism—at least not yet. The two friends' project for the intersectionist magazine *Europa*, conceived some months earlier, was more alive than ever. Indeed Pessoa, rather than forsaking intersectionism or *Europa*, was getting ready to put them to new uses.

◆

It was probably in the spring of 1914, before Sá-Carneiro returned to Paris, that Pessoa typed a tentative table of contents for the first issue of *Europa*.[1] An introductory manifesto about intersectionism was to be followed by a selection of intersectionist poems and prose pieces by Pessoa, Sá-Carneiro, Armando Côrtes-Rodrigues, and Alfredo Guisado. To internationalize the magazine and the movement it represented, a supplement to the issue would contain intersectionist works in French and English signed by Pessoa, Sá-Carneiro, and—unexpectedly—Alexander Search. Search had been relegated to silence in 1910, the year his once steady stream of English poetry dried up. And he would continue, after all, to remain silent, since Pessoa's capricious idea of resurrecting this heteronym quickly faded.

But the magazine idea kept gaining momentum. Sá-Carneiro and Guisado, each with a couple of self-published books, were familiar with the practical details of publishing, including the costs involved. In the letter he posted to Pessoa in late July, Guisado offered to contribute some start-up money for the magazine's inaugural issue. With or without his contribution, funding for *Europa* would not be a problem, since they could always count on the patronage of Sá-Carneiro's father. All that was really holding up the magazine was its editor in chief, Fernando Pessoa, who needed to decide what editorial line it should adopt, exactly what mix of fiction, poetry, and nonfiction it would publish, and who from beyond their inner circle should be invited to submit work.

Pessoa dithered, partly because he always dithered and partly because he wanted to make the most of this opportunity—not only for himself and his friends but also, if possible, for his country. Although he never stopped being a patriot and political visionary, Pessoa's literary communion with Sá-Carneiro had been exhilarating and fulfilling enough to subdue somewhat his passion for politics. But there were new developments in Portugal, new pressures on the still young republic, and it occurred to him that *Europa*, albeit a literary publication, could be a tool for energizing the nation's social and political life.

One of the latest challenges to the Republic was Portuguese integralism. This sounds like it might refer to some sort of holistic movement, and in a way it does. The integralist ideology, formulated in France by the political theorist Charles Maurras, viewed the state as an organic whole made up of different, efficiently interacting social classes and viscerally dependent on its geography, history, and ethnic roots. For a nation to flourish, it needed to respect the principle of social hierarchy as well as its own particular traditions, physical circumstances, and national psychology. Based on this rationale the French integralists, through the Action Française movement as well as a newspaper of the same name, called for a return to monarchy in their country. So did the Portuguese integralists, who founded the magazine *Nação Portuguesa* (*Portuguese Nation*) in April 1914 and quickly attracted support among people disillusioned with republicanism, including a number of young intellectuals. Pessoa was not one of them. Exasperated as he was by the failings of the Republic, to go back to the monarchical system was, at the least, a retrograde idea.

And integralism was a French idea, whose usefulness for France Pessoa disputed, and whose application to Portugal he completely rejected. The Portuguese integralists distanced themselves from the more right-wing, xenophobic, and antisemitic attitudes of Maurras and Action Française, but they parroted the organization's core ideology, which was traditionalist, pro-Catholic, and antiparliamentary.

Though Pessoa, in his writings, tirelessly branded Maurras a reactionary, he shared the ideologue's distaste for popular democracy and disbelief in the feasibility of a classless society. He nevertheless thought of himself as a progressive, since he defended a modern-day class system along nontraditional lines. Rather than choosing between the democratic ideals as embodied by the Republic—which had so far yielded rather discouraging results—or the integralists' project of resuscitating the monarchy, he concocted a hybrid solution for Portugal: an aristocratic republic.

He excitedly laid out his new theories on class and government in a July 28 letter to Sá-Carneiro.[2] Progress, he argued, could be achieved only through an aristocracy of superior individuals. Having nothing to do with blue blood or inherited privilege, it would spontaneously develop and sustain itself through a Darwinian process of natural selection. For this aristocracy to emerge, it was first of all necessary to create "an aristocratic attitude" in the cultural sphere—a task Pessoa was prepared to accomplish himself, with a little help from friends such as Sá-Carneiro. By launching not just one but several avant-garde literary or artistic movements, they would promote lively intellectual debate and competition among the people capable of appreciating those movements—namely, the self-selecting aristocracy, or elite. Presented with superior but contrasting, even conflicting cultural products, this aristocracy would have something meaty to chew on, thereby becoming more mentally vibrant, cosmopolitan, European, and hence fit to serve as the enlightened class and guiding rudder of the Portuguese Republic.

Much of the groundwork for generating an enlightened aristocracy was already laid, since two competing cultural movements had already been created: swampism (or intersectionism) and Caeirism. Now they just needed to be properly launched. The launchpad, according to Pessoa's letter, would be *Europa*. With this magazine, he predicted, "we will open up a conflict between Caeirism and Swampism," as well as a conflict between these two "cosmopolitan" movements and the more parochial but still worthwhile *saudosista* movement of Teixeira de Pascoaes.

The term "Caeirism" referred to the phenomenon of radical self-othering that gave rise not only to Caeiro but also to Álvaro de Campos and Ricardo Reis. It was as if these three literary warriors were being pitted against the swampists (Sá-Carneiro, Pessoa himself, and their friends), with the two factions forming a united front to oppose the *saudosistas*.

Pessoa had ingeniously turned a potentially troubling clash between his new poetic order, Caeirism, and the slightly older swampist movement into a necessary condition for fostering the formation of a cultural elite and the development of an aristocratic republic. This theory greatly impressed Sá-Carneiro, according to his reply of August 1, and what delighted him most, he admitted, was the important role played in it by swampism, the movement he clung to as if his literary survival depended on it. And he mused: "What a wonderful thing our magazine *Europa* would be now, with this 'total' orientation!"

Only "would be," he wrote, since Europe itself had suddenly been plunged into confusion. On July 28, exactly one month after Archduke Ferdinand was assassinated and the same day Pessoa outlined his vision of a literary struggle between the swampists and the Caeirists but before he read the evening paper, the Austro-Hungarian Empire declared real war on Serbia. Other European nations immediately, eagerly, began mobilizing their armed forces.

◆

THROUGHOUT THE EUROPEAN HEARTLAND, bustling cities such as Paris were rocked by anxiety, suddenly aware of their vulnerability. On July 31 Sá-Carneiro's father, who had just taken up a post as director in chief of Mozambique's railroads, sent his son a telegram from Lourenço Marques advising him to go straight home to Lisbon; Mário, however, wired back that he would wait to see how events unfolded. The next day Germany declared war on Russia, and three days later on France. On August 6, no longer able to exchange his Portuguese currency in French banks, Sá-Carneiro placed thirty thousand reis in a registered letter to Pessoa, asking him to send a telegraphic money order for the equivalent amount in French francs. On the same day he sent his friend a second, longer letter describing how his beloved Paris, carefree and glamorous, had in one week's time become a different, unfamiliar city: "stunned, terrified, and deserted." Irremediably self-preoccupied, he mourned "the shuttered department stores, the cafés gone dark—all comfort lost! Theaters, cozy hotel rooms, the salons of the great couturiers. . . . What a pity, what a pity. . . . The truth is that I feel like the petite sweetheart of a twenty-year-old blond lad who went off to war and never came back."

Even before hearing from his friend in Paris, Pessoa had reacted to the war in a very different way, feeling it through his heteronym Álvaro de Campos. On August 2, as Germany invaded Luxembourg, the poet of the "Triumphal Ode" wrote almost a hundred lines of what would become his "Ode marcial" ("Martial Ode"). Europe, it seems, had unconsciously been aching to go to war, and young men around the continent signed up to fight as if for an all-expense-paid holiday, but there was nothing triumphal or heroic in Campos's vision of the lethal combat just getting under way:

The war, the war, the war in reality,
Enormously here, horror, the real war . . .
With its reality of people who really die,
With its strategy really applied to real armies composed of real
    people
And with real consequences, not things told in books
But cold truths, about really human losses, deaths of those who
    truly die,
And the likewise real sun over the likewise real earth,
Real in fact, and the same old shit in the midst of all this!

Wars have inspired poetry since even before *The Iliad*, but the Great War prompted an unprecedented outpouring of verse from around the globe and most especially in Europe, where hundreds of poets—from Apollinaire, Rupert Brooke, and Germany's August Stramm to complete unknowns, from civilians in their homelands to soldiers in the trenches—published poems that responded to the armed conflict. Some of these poets still romanticized the virtues of soldierly heroism and national solidarity, but as the fighting wore on the poetic portrayals of war became increasingly skeptical, focusing—like Campos's "Martial Ode"—on its utterly hideous reality.

Sá-Carneiro held out for three more weeks at the Grand Hôtel du Globe, as German troops invaded Belgium to better make their way into French territory, where the national army had been joined by British forces. Threatened by imminent foreign invasion, Paris reeled with dread even as it prepared to defend itself, with antiaircraft guns being mounted on the Eiffel Tower. Refugees from Belgium and northern France began streaming into the city, while tens of thousands of its inhabitants fled south. Sá-Carneiro was among them, heading to Barcelona, where he thought he might stay for the duration of the war, which nearly everyone believed would be brief. Although the Catalonian capital was no substitute for the epicenter of modernist art, Antoni Gaudí's Sagrada Familia church, with its art nouveau refashioning of gothic architecture, thoroughly enchanted him. He dubbed it a "swampist cathedral" in a letter to Pessoa, a "cathedral of dreams, a cathedral of Otherness, looming in other countries, in other intersections," and he followed up his letter with two postcards depicting the church and its multiple spires, saying that it embodied a "yearning for the new, mystery, strangeness, audacity."

In the fortnight after war erupted, Portugal's government declared its loyalty to the British-Portuguese alliance, began to consider whether its troops should join the fray, granted itself emergency powers, and placed stricter price controls on staples such as bread. There was already speculation of food shortages in Lisbon. The war was eliciting swift reactions, deliberations, and precautionary measures. Throughout June and July, Pessoa had regularly met with Armando Côrtes-Rodrigues, showing him the same poems of Álvaro de Campos and Ricardo Reis that he was sending to Sá-Carneiro in Paris, but in August his friend from the Azores moved back there with his wife and their newborn son. Côrtes-Rodrigues was twenty-three and highly draftable, in the event Portugal entered the conflict. On the island of São Miguel, nine hundred miles from the Portuguese mainland, he was at a relatively safe remove. Young men from Portugal, unlike many of those from countries north and east of the Pyrenees, were not the least bit eager to take up arms.

While Álvaro de Campos continued to produce dramatically felt passages for his "Martial Ode," Fernando Pessoa analyzed, weighed, and extrapolated, as if he were grappling with a complex problem of logic. In a letter sent to Côrtes-Rodrigues on September 2, he wrote that he had "formulated various theories about the present war and about the social, national and civilizational forces at work. I think I'm getting close to an interpretation of the conflict that has at least some semblance of truth." Whatever interpretation he had in mind was merely provisional; for as long as the war lasted and even after it was over he would keep on theorizing, producing several hundred pages—most of them still unpublished—about the clash of national ambitions that it tragically enacted. Pessoa informed Côrtes-Rodrigues that Sá-Carneiro was in Barcelona and would doubtless be back in Lisbon before long. It was a good thing he had left France, since "the Germans might possibly lay siege to Paris—though this will scarcely affect the extreme likelihood of their eventual defeat."

German troops were marching toward Paris as Pessoa wrote those words, and several days later they arrived within fifteen miles of the city limits before being pushed back in the Battle of the Marne, with the help of a few hundred Parisian taxis that were mobilized to carry soldiers to the front. As for Sá-Carneiro, Pessoa had correctly predicted that he would soon return to Lisbon. Mário told no one that he was coming home with the exception of Fernando, who waited for him amid the cast-iron columns supporting the roof of the train station, on September 9 at quarter to three. We can see Sá-Carneiro, voluminous and exuberant, stepping down onto the platform and throwing both arms around his best friend, squeezing him, while Pessoa, always disconcerted by demonstrations of affection, reciprocated with an awkward embrace. It was not easy for him to be physical, and most people, sensing and respecting this, hardly tried to touch him. Mário, notwithstanding an admiration for Fernando that verged on worship, exercised his right as a friend to be a pest, to whine, to send him on errands, to demand he be at the Rossio station at 2:45, to give him a hug when he felt like hugging him, and to be hugged in return. Fernando could not have failed to be there at the appointed time, anxiously waiting. He had no friend in the world like Mário.

In his letter to Côrtes-Rodrigues, Pessoa also mentioned that, since the outbreak of war, he himself was going through a "crisis period," both in his writing and in his character. "I want to discipline my life (and, consequently, my work) as if disciplining an anarchic country—anarchic because of the surfeit of 'vital forces' in disparate yet interconnected action, conflict, and evolution." Some of those vital forces had names: Alberto Caeiro, Ricardo Reis, and Álvaro de Campos, all of whom he mentioned in his letter. Pessoa was still dumbfounded, still disoriented from the turns taken by his literary life during the last six months. He had invented those three individualities but without knowing quite how, or where they came from, or what new responsibilities they entailed for him.

◆

IN 1930 PESSOA WOULD strike up a correspondence with the English magus Aleister Crowley. On a sheet of paper containing a partial draft of his very first letter to Crowley, Pessoa wrote, "The creation of Caeiro and of the discipleship of Reis and Campos seems, at first sight, an elaborate joke of the imagination. But it is not. It is a great act of intellectual magic, a magnum opus of the impersonal creative power."[3] These were bold, even presumptuous, yet perfectly suitable words for initiating the addressee into the mysteries of his heteronyms. As a practitioner of magic and a prolific writer on the subject, as well as a poet and novelist, Crowley was in an excellent position to appreciate—perhaps more than Pessoa himself—the "intellectual magic" involved in creating Caeiro, Reis, and Campos.

Or was this magic just the abracadabra of children, whose fertile imaginations are good at conjuring up "supernatural" phenomena?

Some Pessoa scholars pooh-pooh the heteronyms, seeing them, at best, as a literary device comparable to Søren Kierkegaard's playful use of differentiated pseudonyms or, at worst, as a literary hoax akin to Thomas Chatterton's creation of Thomas Rowley, a fictive fifteenth-century priest in whose name the talented and imaginative eighteenth-century teenager from Bristol produced faux-medieval poetry, while under his own name he wrote in contemporary English. The figure of Chatterton, who used arsenic to commit suicide three months before his eighteenth birthday, fascinated English Romantics such as Keats and Shelley, and he also fascinated Pessoa, who owned a collection of his poetry and planned to write about him when still a student in Durban.[4] Chatterton's self-othering as Thomas Rowley must have been at least a subliminal inspiration for Pessoa's creation of the heteronyms, whom he initially planned to publish and pass off as autonomous, flesh-and-blood poets. This does not diminish Pessoa's achievement or disprove its allegedly magical character.

Imposture and magic make good partners, and they were perfectly married in Aleister Crowley, who would perpetrate one of his greatest hoaxes with the close collaboration of Pessoa. I mention Crowley at this point because of the ambiguously magical heteronyms, who were not so much a joke that Pessoa played on his readers as they were a joke that someone or some power—the "impersonal creative power"—played on him. He would spend the rest of his life trying to fathom the nature and origin of that power, its relationship to other powers, and how he was meant to use it for himself, for literature, for Portugal, and for eternity.

# Part III

# DREAMER AND CIVILIZER
## (1914–1925)

To create in myself a nation with its own politics,
parties and revolutions, and to be all of it, everything,
to be God in the real pantheism of this people-I, to be
the substance and motion of their bodies and their
souls, of the very ground they tread and the acts they
perform!

—*The Book of Disquiet* (text 157)

A "provisional visual representation" of Pessoa (so he
wrote on the back of the photo) at age twenty-five,
shortly before the emergence of his major heteronyms.
*(Courtesy Manuela Nogueira)*

# CHAPTER 34

○ ❊ ○ ❊ ○ ❊ ○ ❊ ○ ❊ ○ ❊ ○ ❊ ○ ❊ ○ ❊ ○ ❊ ○ ❊ ○ ❊ ○ ❊ ○ ❊ ○ ❊

**P**ESSOA CLOSELY FOLLOWED THE UNFOLDING OF the Great War, which rapidly escalated beyond all expectations, spreading beyond Europe to battlefronts in Africa, the Middle East, and east Asia, but he did not let the unsettling events distract him from his own campaign of defeating the world through dreams, literature, imagination, and his heteronyms. It's almost as if the poet, recognizing how appalling the war really was, became all the more determined to overcome reality itself.

Since the day the first shots were fired, the war had been filling up the front page of every major newspaper in Portugal, which was officially neutral—even though it had announced its readiness to aid Britain, its oldest ally. Many statesmen, particularly in Afonso Costa's Democratic Party,* were keen for the Portuguese to join the Allied cause, convinced that doing so would bolster the small nation's tattered standing in Europe and bring it material advantages when the war was over, assuming the Allies won. But since Portugal did not have a well-trained army to offer, Great Britain said no thanks, for now. And so Portugal had to be content with fortifying its African colonies, in case of invasion from German Southwest Africa (present-day Namibia), which lay to the south of Angola, or German East Africa (corresponding roughly to Tanzania, Burundi, and Rwanda), the northern neighbor of Mozambique. With patriotic exhortations the government called up soldiers from around the country to form two expeditionary forces, and on September 7, 1914, the *Diário de Notícias*, one of the morning papers that Pessoa read regularly, published a lead article with a photo showing hundreds of troops amassed at Santa Apolónia, Lisbon's oldest railway station. The uni-

---

* The Portuguese Republican Party, led by Afonso Costa, was informally called the Democratic Party, in order to distinguish it from the two other, equally republican parties.

formed men, greeted by a cheering throng that crowded the platform, had arrived from various inland towns and would soon board two ships bound for Africa.

That same day, Pessoa wrote two poems about a soldierly cavalcade *returning* from Africa under the command of King Sebastian, the starry-eyed and fanatically religious young monarch who had led a suicidal campaign to reconquer lost Portuguese territories in Morocco, in the summer of 1578. In one of the two poems, "O regresso" ("The Return"), the resurrected king and his vast cavalcade arrive on a foggy morning to announce a new era of national splendor. The soldiers riding the horses are phantoms, however, since they are part of a mythical story, whose power resided precisely in its unreality. The myth had gone through various permutations, and Pessoa would be responsible for inaugurating yet another one.

King Sebastian was mythologized almost out of necessity, to mitigate the humiliation of the worst and most senseless military defeat in Portugal's history. Impervious to all warnings that it was a foredoomed enterprise, the twenty-four-year-old king assembled an army of about eighteen thousand men to wage war against a far more numerous enemy on its home soil.[*] It took only a few hours for the great majority of those men, hungry and exhausted after a seven-day march through the desert, to be killed or captured in the battle fought on August 4 near the town of Ksar el Kebir. The king also died. But amid so much pandemonium of gored bodies and severed limbs, who could be absolutely sure? Four months after the battle, the victors handed over the king's mortal remains to the Portuguese, but there was no way to vouch for their authenticity.[†]

Sebastian had no heir, the Portuguese nobility had lost the best of its men in the catastrophe, the homeland was in frantic disarray, and stories began to circulate that the king was not dead: someone had seen him

---

[*] In addition to Portuguese soldiers, the army included more than five thousand volunteers and mercenaries from Spain, Germany, Flanders, and Italy. It was joined in Morocco by six thousand Moorish troops of Abu Abdallah, a deposed king trying to recover the throne from his uncle, Abd Al-Malik, who was supported by the Ottomans and had raised an army three times larger than the combined forces led by King Sebastian.

[†] In 1582 the king's remains were buried in Lisbon's Hieronymite Monastery. Some historians have urged the Portuguese government to allow for their exhumation and DNA testing.

riding away from the battlefield on horseback. And since he had survived, said the storytellers, he was sure to return.[1]

One professed Sebastian after another did return, sometimes with endorsements from members of the Portuguese aristocracy anxious to depose Philip II of Spain, who in 1580 had managed to crown himself king of a much weakened Portugal. As each fraudulent Sebastian was exposed, a growing number of people waited for the true King Sebastian, whom they expected to return on a misty morning. In 1640 Portugal regained its sovereignty from Spain, and by that time the disappeared king, if still living, would be decrepit, but people continued to wait, investing the idea of his return with allegorical and messianic interpretations, partly inspired by the ancient legend of King Arthur, who was supposed to return from the island of Avalon to save his people.

The Sebastianist legend kept spreading and eventually traveled abroad. At the end of the nineteenth century, António Conselheiro, a mystic preacher and leader of Canudos, a community of some thirty thousand souls in northeastern Brazil, still predicted the imminent return of King Sebastian. The settlement, deemed a threat to Brazil's young and secularist republic, established in 1889, was brutally exterminated by government forces.*

The poet Sophia de Mello Breyner Andresen (1919–2004) told me that as a young woman she still saw coastal villagers looking out into the morning mist for the returning ship of the Adormecido, the Sleeping King. A more common epithet for Sebastian was the Encoberto, the Hidden One, since it was believed he would come back in a veiled form—as a different but marvelous king, or as a wondrous event—to lift his country out of the doldrums. It was this passive waiting for a redeemer, or for a redemptive occurrence, that made nineteenth-century intellectuals such as the poet Antero de Quental or the historian Joaquim Pedro de Oliveira Martins view Sebastianism as an emblem of Portugal's decadence.

When Pessoa alluded to Sebastianism in "The Old Castle," an adolescent poem discussed in chapter 12, he also characterized it, like Quental or Oliveira Martins, as a passive, melancholy hope that was predestined

---

* Euclides da Cunha, a journalist who followed the events, published *Os sertões*, a gripping chronicle about the War of Canudos in 1901 (it appeared in English in 1944 as *Rebellion in the Backlands*).

to disappointment. But now, in 1914, he confidently poetized King Sebastian's second coming as a revolutionary turning point in the Portuguese mentality. His radically altered point of view owed something to one of the books that helped relaunch Sebastianism in the twentieth century, *O encoberto*, published in 1904 by Sampaio Bruno. After reviewing some of the ways that Jesuits and others had used Sebastianism for assorted purposes, good and bad, the author proposed that King Sebastian be understood as a collective entity, such as the Portuguese nation.[2] Although Bruno did not explain exactly what a "collective" King Sebastian might accomplish, he contended, in opposition to Oliveira Martins, that the Sebastianist myth could rouse Portugal out of its psychological stupor. Pessoa admired this thesis but thought it likely that any national, collective arousal would be set in motion by an individual.

On September 8, the day after he wrote his two poems evoking the return of the Hidden One, or King Sebastian, Pessoa sent a letter to Bruno, complimenting him on his book and soliciting suggestions for further reading on the subject. By way of introduction and to justify his interest in Sebastianism, he told the older writer, who lived in Porto, about the "vague messianic inclination" revealed in his 1912 "New Portuguese Poetry" articles, which had announced "the imminent arrival of a Super-Camões."[3] This Super-Camões, as we have seen, was Pessoa himself, who was now prepared to add another title to his résumé, that of a modern-day King Sebastian come home at long last to save Portugal. He was grooming himself to be a cultural messiah, whose divine mission was to restore Portugal to its former state of glory—not through maritime exploits but through poetic ones.

Pessoa's Sebastianism was not narrowly conceived. The Hidden One might return in his own person as the Super-Camões, or in the flesh of a great statesman capable of saving the nation from its self-destructive politics, or in the form of a transformed national consciousness. Pessoa allowed for all of these hypotheses, separately and in combination. What he had come to reject, on the other hand, was the positivist project of certain republicans, who envisioned a science-based society of secular citizens illuminated by the twin virtues of order and progress. Like Sampaio Bruno, who wrote not only about Sebastianism but also about Kabbalah and other esoteric traditions, he wanted to reserve a mystical and transcendent, even divine dimension for Portugal and for humanity at large.

✦

PESSOA FOUND HIMSELF IN a "cabalistic mood" as far back as 1907, when he wrote his Alexander Search poem about magic called "The Circle," and his curiosity about religion and the supernatural dated back to his adolescence. In the years before and after the emergence of his three main heteronyms, that mood and that curiosity expanded into a passion for metaphysical study and research. Pessoa's interest in the occult was connected to, and would far outstrip, his interest in the psychology of genius and madness. The French neurologist Joseph Grasset, who had been one of his guides on the subject of insanity and its relationship to literary, philosophical, and musical genius, was also the author of the first serious book on the occult that Pessoa read, *L'Occultisme hier et aujourd'hui* (1908).[4] Published in English in 1910 as *The Marvels Beyond Science*, Grasset's book was a scholarly overview of paranormal phenomena such as mediumistic communication, the sensation of déjà vu, astral bodies, telepathy, levitation, mind reading, and clairvoyance.

The neurologist specifically excluded magic, Hermetic traditions, alchemy, and initiation rites from his discussion. These topics were introduced to Pessoa via *The Rosicrucians: Their Rites and Mysteries*, a book by Hargrave Jennings that he probably read in 1910 or 1911.[5] Profusely illustrated, this book furnished him with signs, symbols, linguistic formulas, esoteric doctrines, and spiritual systems for articulating his awed awareness of the world's mystery.

I'm the knowledge that doesn't know,
The insomnia of suffering and thinking
Hunched over the book of the world's horror.[6]

These lines are from Pessoa's *Fausto*, which dramatizes the impotence of Intelligence—personified in the title character—to fathom Life and the Unknown. The drama was Pessoa's own and would never quit haunting him, but his readings on the occult suggested to him the possibility of another kind of knowledge, not obtained through reason. In a passage from *The Rosicrucians* that especially impressed Pessoa, Jennings maintained that what is "apparent and reasonable" is never true, since Truth is ineffable, and so "we cannot know God [. . .] through the Intelligence," only "through the heart and affections."[7]

Jennings's book was the likely inspiration for Pessoa's "Hermetic Philosopher," a monologue that enunciates some of the key doctrines attributed to the divinely wise Hermes Trismegistus, a mythical personage from antiquity. Three doctrines in particular greatly impressed Pessoa:

1. All reality is essentially dual, with a side that we see and a side that remains forever imperceptible to common sense, science, and philosophy.
2. The hidden side of reality can be discovered through magic and through the spiritual, revelatory kind of knowledge sometimes called *gnosis*.
3. There is an elite group of people initiated into secret, higher mysteries.

Pessoa's Hermetic philosopher did not merely rehash what others had written; he also theorized that a few rare individuals are initiated *ab origine*, from birth. As an example of a born initiate he pointed to Shakespeare, whose remarkable intuitions in the field of psychology—long before this field of study even existed—enabled him to create the stupendous figure of King Lear. This sort of intuitive power, we're told, was a clear manifestation of "unconscious occultism, unconscious illumination."[8]

Was Pessoa's capacity to write with different personalities and in very different styles not a feat of intuition comparable to Shakespeare's? He claimed that it was. His three major heteronyms did not yet exist when he wrote "Hermetic Philosopher," but this monologue had already laid down the theoretical justification for considering their creator, along with Shakespeare, as an initiate *ab origine*, a spontaneously occurring *illuminato*. Pessoa, however, was not content to passively receive mysterious creative powers from hidden masters of the universe. Fascinated by the notion of a reverse or hidden side of reality, he actively sought to communicate with it, as proven by the family séances he conducted at the home of his aunt Anica. In his poetry, meanwhile, the spiritual realm was no longer just a poetic conceit; it was presumed to actually exist.

In September 1914, besides his poems about the hidden King Sebastian who was soon to be revealed, Pessoa also wrote his first poem worthy to be called "esoteric." Titled "A múmia" ("The Mummy") and divided into five sections, it has been convincingly analyzed as a rite of initiation in which the poet dies to himself.[9] In the first section, after traversing "miles of shadow" within himself to reach a desert, or rather, his vision of a desert, he acquires a new and strange sense of perception. "I no longer include me in myself," he says, and he feels he is in the presence of a dead man, who is apparently himself, his earthly self. In the next four sections, his temporarily freed and clearly flustered spirit experiences the other side of the world's reality.

In his unfinished "Gahu" epic, written as an aspiring young poet in Durban, Pessoa had already played out an initiatory death to the self, though without any esoteric trappings. If now he needed to die a second ritual death, it was to mark his advent as the Great Poet prophesied in his 1912 *A Águia* articles. A practical demonstration of his poetic greatness was carried out on the manuscript sheet of the final section of "The Mummy." Turning the sheet over, Pessoa used half the page to write two poems signed by Alberto Caeiro and dated September 17, 1914; a quarter of the page to write an ode signed by Ricardo Reis, followed by the same date; and the remaining free space for a poem in yet another style, written under his own name and likewise dated September 17. No less extraordinary than Pessoa's self-multiplication into different poetic personae was the way they cohabited and simultaneously asserted themselves, like a roomful of talkative people all eager to have their say. "I no longer include me in myself," he wrote in "The Mummy." That self now sheltered a host of poetic spirits, who perhaps nourished Pessoa's interest in otherworldly spirits.

✦

TOWARD THE END OF September Pessoa finally made his long-planned trip to Tavira, home to the Pessoa clan and the supposed birthplace of Álvaro de Campos. Twelve years had passed since his last visit to the town, which is on the Algarvian coast, less than twenty miles from the Spanish border, and much had changed. Now he could get all the way there by train, the streets had electric lighting, and the street flanking the north side of the river that divides the town in two had been renamed Rua Jacques Pessoa, in homage to one of his relatives, a militant republican who had died in 1909 at the age of sixty—a victim of tuberculosis, like a number of other Pessoas. Tavira, with twenty-five thousand inhabitants, was a charming, well-preserved town whose economy relied on agriculture, tuna fishing, and salt harvesting. Fernando visited various distant cousins, nearly all of them older and well-heeled, but he spent most of his time with the cousin he knew best, Aunt Lisbela. She had a home in the center as well as a rural property in Mesquita, several miles outside of town.

Descendants of the Pessoas from Tavira say that Fernando visited the town at least five or six times as an adult, but the many letters he exchanged with Aunt Lisbela have all been lost, and only two of his trips are documented.[10] On one of those trips, while staying at the house in Mesquita—a white house perched on top of a hill, just like Alberto Caeiro's rural abode—he wrote a couple of quatrains according to a traditional Portuguese formula calling for seven-syllable lines and considerable lightheartedness. One of the quatrains was dedicated to Lisbela. Here is a free translation:

You look out a high window
In your house of whitewashed stone,
Without a care or complaint,
Apart from living alone.[11]

Widowed at the age of twenty-eight, after her brief marriage to a soldier with late-stage tuberculosis, Lisbela had remained alone and was now sixty-nine. With the income she made from her investments, which included farmland east of Tavira, she sometimes helped out younger relatives. She had a soft spot for Fernando, who freely availed himself of her generosity. On one of his visits he came out and asked her if she could provide him with a monthly stipend to support his writing. Firm in his dedication to poetry and justifiably convinced of his talent, he considered it an entirely reasonable request. In those days, with few governments and almost no private foundations providing grants to writers, patronage was direct and personal, and often came from women. We might not have Joyce's *Ulysses*, let alone *Finnegans Wake*, were it not for Harriet Shaw Weaver (1876–1961); Yeats counted on Lady Gregory (1852–1932) for financial help as well as lodging at Coole Park; and Margaret Cravens (1881–1912) underwrote Ezra Pound in his early years. Olivia Shakespear (1863–1938) directly or indirectly aided Yeats, Pound, Joyce, and Eliot. In the discreetest way possible, without ever thinking of herself as a patron of literature, Lisbela da Cruz Pessoa Machado sponsored her cousin Fernando. She could not offer him a monthly stipend, she said, since her income was variable, depending on each year's harvest, but she began to give him money as she could and when he most needed it. They dispensed with the fiction of "loans."[12]

✦

BACK IN LISBON BY early October—after a return journey from Tavira that took twelve hours on the night train—Pessoa was again spending his days at the downtown offices where he drafted letters in English to earn enough escudos for his occasional expenses, mainly books and clothes. The escudo was introduced in 1911, but most people were still counting money in reis, a thousand of which equaled one escudo. Pessoa had begun to keep semiregular hours at several offices, where he used their stationery and their typewriters to write his poems, creative prose, essays, and personal notes. He liked the quiet, congenial but not socially demanding atmosphere of the business firms in Lisbon's old downtown district, the Baixa, and he invariably became friends with his employers, who treated him well. They also became his creditors.

Since returning from France and Spain in September, Mário de Sá-Carneiro had been trying to finish a book of short stories at the family home in Camarate, on Lisbon's northern outskirts, but he often came into town and met with Pessoa, usually at the Café Martinho on Praça do Rossio, whose luxurious interior reminded him a little of a Parisian café. Four red-painted columns topped with gilded capitals supported an upper gallery where fine French cuisine was served, but the two friends sat at a table on the ground floor. Their most urgent literary matter was *Europa*, the intersectionist magazine they had been planning for months but now reconsidered, beginning with its title, since Europe had suddenly become synonymous with conflict and bloodshed. Neither Pessoa nor Sá-Carneiro subscribed to point nine of Marinetti's "Manifesto of Futurism," which said we should glorify war, "the world's only hygiene"—a point reaffirmed by the Italian futurist in 1915, after the war had already "cleansed" Europe of hundreds of thousands of people.

Changing the title would be a simple enough matter, but was a magazine after all a good idea? They were afraid it risked being a one-off that got no attention, like the magazine *A Renascença*, where Pessoa had published his first poems and Sá-Carneiro a short story at the beginning of the year. The two friends decided on an alternate plan: an *Anthology of Intersectionism*, published as a book and containing prose and poetry by Pessoa, Sá-Carneiro, Alfredo Guisado, Armando Côrtes-Rodrigues, and Álvaro de Campos. Pessoa was responsible for the volume's introductory "manifesto," the same one he had started drafting in the spring for *Europa*. In the combative tone and spirit typical of manifestos, Pessoa, while admitting that the futurists and cubists were precursors of intersectionism, derided them as "slaves of having painters and sculptors in their ranks, of considering painting and sculpture to be forms of art." He was exaggerating. In fact he allowed that painting and sculpture were forms of art but deemed them inferior to the art of literature, which had no rival, with the possible exception of music.

Futurism and cubism were also precursors of the British vanguard movement known as vorticism, cofounded by Ezra Pound and Wyndham Lewis (1882–1957), who published the first issue of the vorticist magazine *Blast* in June 1914. Pessoa would purchase copies of this graphically compelling periodical, but not until the summer of 1915. If by chance he read about vorticism in the summer or fall of 1914, it exerted little influence on his intersectionist manifesto, which proposed something quite different. The British movement promoted the dynamic energy of the new vortex for the making of visual art as well as for writing. Pessoa wanted literature, on its own, to accommodate *all* artistic expression.

Pessoa devoted many pages to explaining the three movements he had invented—swampism, whose sensorial language and atmospheric intensity were like French symbolism on drugs; intersectionism, which could mean almost any kind of writing that was not linear and single-voiced; and sensationism, which advocated exuberant expression of the senses à la Walt Whitman—but in actual practice they blended into one another, and in the second half of 1914 they coexisted. Ultimately they all shared the same ambition: to prove that literature was capable of subsuming all other arts, rendering them unnecessary.

The more urgent and pragmatic function of the three movements was to furnish Pessoa's literary circle with avant-garde credentials, setting it apart from the rest of Portuguese literature. Pessoa was also anxious to establish their originality in the international context, which is why he went out of his way to attack cubism and any other ism that hailed from Paris, lest anyone suppose that the isms of his own invention were mere offshoots. Sá-Carneiro rubbed his hands together with conspiratorial glee.

In the fall of 1914, the dividing line known as the western front etched itself with blood into Europe's traumatized terrain; it would shift very little until the last year of the war, with both sides diligently killing each other while remaining firmly, literally entrenched. Pessoa, meanwhile, with the help of his friends, waged war against the Portuguese cultural establishment and tried to launch intersectionism (alias swampism, or sensationism) as a modernist movement more original and more advanced than any other in Europe. But the battle to impose intersectionism would come to nothing, with Pessoa himself losing faith in the cause.

# CHAPTER 35

**P**ESSOA'S LARGE AMBITIONS AS A WRITER WERE religiously framed, for he saw himself as a cultural redeemer, but before he could begin to realize his mission, he had to pass through an agonizing period of reassessment. "I am no longer me," he wrote his friend Côrtes-Rodrigues on November 19, 1914. "I'm a fragment of myself conserved in an abandoned museum." He had been living with Aunt Anica and his cousin Maria for over three years, and their recent departure from Lisbon had thrown him off balance, filling him with insecurity and self-doubt.

The war had not prevented Maria's fiancé, Raul da Costa, from obtaining a government grant to study industrial engineering in Switzerland, which remained neutral, and in mid-November, two weeks after getting married, the young couple moved to Lausanne, taking Aunt Anica with them and obliging Fernando to suddenly fend for himself. With more than a touch of melodrama, but also with sincere distress, he described his present state of mind as one of "infinite desolation" and almost "absolute abulia." His letter to Côrtes-Rodrigues went on about other matters, including the *Anthology of Intersectionism*, which was still on track albeit temporarily shunted onto a siding, since it would not make sense for "an aesthetic act of *European* character" to be published and distributed until the war was over. He also mentioned that he was writing poetry and working hard, despite his allegedly paralyzed will, or "abulia," on *The Book of Disquiet*, though all he could show for it were "fragments, fragments, fragments." His main reason for writing: could his "*caro Amigo*" lend him twenty thousand reis? He did not know when he would be able to pay back this amount or the five thousand reis he already owed his Azorean friend, but he was desperate and had no one else he could turn to.

In actual fact, he had quite a few people to turn to: Aunt Lisbela; his great-aunts Rita, Adelaide, and Carolina; various cousins who lived in Lisbon; and a couple of deep-pocketed friends. Even before Côrtes-Rodrigues wrote back that, unfortunately, he had no cash to spare, Pessoa had borrowed money elsewhere to pay for room and board, both of which he had been freeloading off of Aunt Anica. His new address, on Rua de Dona Estefânia, was right around the corner from Anica's apartment. He had leased a ground-floor room in the apartment of an *engomadeira*, a woman who made her living by starching and ironing clothes.

Pessoa's new, essentially solitary living situation wrenched him out of established rhythms and made him take stock of himself, his literary activities, and his motivations. On November 21, one week after moving into his rented room and two days after writing to Côrtes-Rodrigues about his feeling of self-estrangement ("I am no longer me"), he wrote four pages of personal notes that began with a declaration of artistic independence and integrity:

Today, having once and for all decided to be Me, to live up to my calling, scorning the idea of publicity and the plebeian socialization of myself, i.e. Intersectionism, I have reentered for good [. . .] into the full possession of my Genius and the divine awareness of my Mission. Now I wish to be only what my innate character wants me to be and what my Genius that was born with it obliges me to be.[1]

In the same set of notes, Pessoa definitively renounced any interest in starting up an intersectionist magazine such as *Europa*. Instead, he was inclined to collaborate once again with Teixeira de Pascoaes's Renascença Portuguesa group, through which "one could have an impact on the Nation." This was a remarkable about-face. Just nine days earlier, Pessoa had informed the managing editor of *A Águia* that he was cutting ties with the Renascença group and their magazine, due to a "radical and inevitable [. . .] incompatibility" between the literature produced by people like him and Mário de Sá-Carneiro[2] and the literature born out of Pascoaes's *saudosismo* and ethnic nationalism.

If Pessoa was now reconsidering, thinking that after all there *was* some common ground between his patriotic interests and those of the Renascença poets, it was because of lapses in the compatibility he felt with his closest friend and literary collaborator. A self-involved writer for whom literature was a mirror, Sá-Carneiro felt no special connection to Portugal's soul, history, identity, or destiny. While Pessoa, in his megalomania, conceived of himself as the Super-Camões or the returned King Sebastian, Sá-Carneiro was only and always "Sá-Carneiro"—in quotation marks, since his literary mirror was not a faithful reflector. His was a mirror that enlarged, distorted, and voluptuously transformed his image, but it was still, at heart, *his* image. Pessoa transformed his very self—into projects, personae, poems, and prose texts that were still him, yes, but in impersonalized forms that could, he hoped, engage with the world and help shape it into something more glorious. Mere social reform did not interest him; he saw himself as a creator of civilization, on behalf of Portugal and of humanity.

"Associate less with others," Pessoa recommended to himself on the second page of his notes. In December he laid low, without any appetite for socializing or for writing letters, including to his family in Pretoria.[3] No doubt he still met with Sá-Carneiro, who had returned from Camarate to his family's Lisbon residence, but Fernando could not talk openly about the crisis he was experiencing, since his friend—or his friend's attitude, his friend's indifference to grand entities such as the Nation, God, the Future, and the Universe—was part of the problem. So he wrote about it instead. Could Sá-Carneiro have read what he wrote, one comment in particular would have surprised and wounded him: "It is Côrtes-Rodrigues who understands me better, and more deeply, than anyone else."

The words were not fair, or true. It was only in a restricted sense that Côrtes-Rodrigues could understand Pessoa better, since he shared with him a high-minded idealism that was missing in Sá-Carneiro. The Azorean poet believed fervently in God and in a divine purpose for the world and the creatures who inhabit it. He had spent some of his formative years in a boarding school run by priests and remained forever a devout Catholic, without being dogmatic in his beliefs. His religiosity was more of a feeling than a creed, which is why Pessoa, who rejected Catholic theology, could nevertheless suppose that this friend uniquely understood him, or the religious side of him. None of Côrtes-Rodrigues's letters to Pessoa have survived, but one suspects that he had no idea how to reply to Pessoa's outpourings about his divine "Mission." For the undogmatic but faithful Catholic, religion meant humble devotion. For Pessoa it meant being a savior.

✦

ON JANUARY 19, 1915, Pessoa sent a long letter to Côrtes-Rodrigues that reiterated and expanded on his "psychological crisis" as a tortured genius for whom the making of art was a "terrible mission—a duty to be carried out arduously, monastically, never taking one's eyes off the creator-of-civilization purpose behind every artistic work." His fundamentally "religious spirit" had asserted itself as never before, making him impatient with any art or literature that served only the vague purpose of art itself, and that impatience applied even to certain works of his own authorship. He never had any reservations, however, about the elaborate fictions called Alberto Caeiro, Ricardo Reis, and Álvaro de Campos. They and their works were sincere, he wrote Côrtes-Rodrigues, because he *lived* them and *felt* them. "In each of them I placed a profound concept of life, different in all three, but always gravely attentive to the mysterious importance of existing."

Along with his ponderous letter, Pessoa sent Côrtes-Rodrigues a dozen typed poems, mostly of recent vintage and all signed with his own name. His favorite of the lot, "A ceifeira" ("The Reaper"), was a remake of William Wordsworth's "The Solitary Reaper."[4] Like the narrator of Wordsworth's poem, Pessoa's poetic speaker is enchanted by a young woman who plaintively sings as she harvests grain in a field, but rather than just observing her and remembering her song, he imagines himself in her place, transported from his present life to become her "weightless shadow." Three lines from the penultimate stanza contain the crux of the poem, as well as a key to understanding Pessoa's poetry generally:

Ah, to be you while being I!
To have your glad unconsciousness
And be conscious of it!

Almost by necessity, a creative writer is apt to be simultaneously actor and spectator, but in Pessoa the dichotomy was radical. He was not a better observer than other writers; he was a better actor, having developed an extraordinary, Whitmanesque capacity for dramatically marrying himself to the scenes and characters described in his poems, while remaining completely detached.

Despite having confessed to Côrtes-Rodrigues that he was tired of poems such as "Swamps," since in them his "attitude toward the public is that of a clown," that very poem was one of the twelve he enclosed with his letter. Pessoa vacillated on whether swampism, intersectionism, and other kinds of self-consciously unconventional, arguably gimmicky literature were worth pursuing, but in his notes from this period he reaffirmed his conviction that, in any kind of literature, a certain insincerity is obligatory[5]—insofar as a creative work depends on invention, on pretending, on not simply repeating what already exists. He was clearly willing to allow even clownishness, as long as it served a higher, civilizing, and spiritual purpose. What he disputed, at this point in his journey, was not only the value but even the very notion of creativity on its own behalf. "Art for art's sake," he aphoristically wrote in English, "is really only art for the artist's sake."[6]

◆

PESSOA'S CRISIS BETWEEN NOVEMBER 1914 and January 1915 was, at its core, a crisis of faith in the power of literature. Perhaps, as he tried to show, it could encompass and supersede all the other arts, but it could not replace life, as he also sometimes tried to show in *The Book of Disquiet* and elsewhere. This realization did not diminish the importance of literature, which was his sacred vocation, his medium for understanding, revealing, celebrating, and enriching life. It now occurred to him, however, that life harbored even more mysteries than he had imagined. His January letter to Côrtes-Rodrigues speaks of the duty he felt "to shut myself in the home of my spirit and to work [. . .] for the progress of civilization and the enlargement of human consciousness." The idea that his writing could enlarge human consciousness anticipates Harold Bloom's notion that Shakespeare and, by extension, a handful of other great writers have invented our human nature, insofar as they used words to create inwardness, charting and extending previously hazy tracts of thought and feeling.* But the expansion of consciousness that Pessoa had in mind was spiritual as well as psychological.

Although he had written about his crisis to Armando Côrtes-Rodrigues because of his friend's "profound religiosity," Pessoa concealed the nature of the spiritual awakening connected to that crisis, since he knew that any good Catholic would reject it outright. It was in esoteric doctrines and occult sciences that his religious yearnings had found shelter. When he suggested to Côrtes-Rodrigues that they were religiously

---

* One of Bloom's best books, *Shakespeare: The Invention of the Human* (1998), enshrines this idea in its very title.

kindred spirits, he was in the midst of writing an arguably heretical sonnet sequence titled "Passos da Cruz" ("Stations of the Cross"), which
describes not the sufferings of Jesus as he dragged his cross up to Calvary
but his own path of self-discovery as a divine messenger bearing occult
messages. One of the fourteen sonnets, written on November 30, begins:

> Emissary of an unknown king,
> I carry out hazy instructions from beyond,
> And the sudden words my lips pronounce
> Have for me another, anomalous meaning . . .

Everything—including everything Pessoa said or did—was more than
it seemed to be, according to his present point of view. And despite his
compulsion to doubt, which undermined all his attempts to profess any
kind of faith, Pessoa, like a votary, would attend to higher or hidden
realities throughout the rest of his life.

The first such reality that enthralled him was the one he could see by
looking up at the black sky on a clear night. In late 1914 he began poring
over astrology manuals like a man obsessed with learning a foreign language. He copied and recopied the symbols for the planets, their angular
relationships known as "aspects," their influences, and in 1915 he cast a
series of charts for famous people from the past, comparing his results
with charts published by eminent astrologers. In sum, he designed his
own teach-yourself course, with the aid of classical texts on astrology
by authors such as Sepharial, Raphael, George Wilde, and Alan Leo.
The diligent student purchased a number of his manuals through the
English bookstore, located downtown on Rua do Arsenal, close to the
river. When Sr. Tabuada, the bookseller, told him about another client
interested in astrology, Pessoa lit up and asked to be put in touch with
him, eager to learn from someone with experience.

César Porto (1873–1944), who wore rimless glasses like Pessoa but
had a fuller face and a very full head of hair, was a dedicated schoolteacher as well as a poet, playwright, and novelist of limited talent. He
had been studying astrology for some years but could teach almost nothing to Pessoa, who had quickly assimilated the art of constructing and
analyzing charts by reading and training on his own. Pessoa was nevertheless delighted to make a friend with whom he could discuss astrological questions and get an opinion on some of the charts he made. They

met regularly in 1915 and 1916, usually at the Brasileira café on Praça do Rossio, and sporadically after that, remaining in contact until Pessoa's unexpected death, in 1935.

In November 1936, César Porto would publish an article in a Lisbon newspaper about his late friend's interest in astrology.[7] While for himself astrology was never more than a hobby that yielded some "curious predictions," it was a consuming passion for Pessoa, who brooded over the deeper connections between "sidereal motions" and human life on Earth. Without coming out and saying so, Porto implied that Pessoa took astrology too seriously and spent too much time on it. He regretted that his friend's literary output was "not only scattered, since its parts don't form a homogeneous whole, but also—and more unfortunately—without one composition in which his whole self is mirrored." The late poet, he submitted, had never really found himself.

Pessoa's first biographer would make essentially the same diagnosis, arguing that the heteronyms were a product of the poet's failure to put his whole self into his writing. It is a reasonable enough conclusion to draw. Pessoa was the first one to accuse himself of being too easily pulled in too many different directions, and he told Côrtes-Rodrigues that he urgently needed to eliminate distractions, since they were preventing him from developing his literary genius and using it on behalf of Portugal and human civilization. And yet he lavishly indulged his newest interest, astrology, sacrificing time he could have used for writing. Pessoa's spiritual search soon became an odyssey, which spiraled in ever wider orbits, making it that much harder for him to concentrate his entire self in a single work of literature—a goal that at any rate would mean very little to someone trying to grasp the cosmos within himself, as well as the universe beyond.

✦

PESSOA WOULD SPEND HUNDREDS of hours studying astrology, devising his own astrological theories, and casting astrological charts for himself, his heteronyms, his friends, historical figures such as Napoleon and King Sebastian, historical events (the French Revolution, the founding of the Portuguese Republic), writers (Shakespeare, Goethe, Baudelaire, Marinetti), composers (Chopin, Wagner), and other cultural icons. He cast more than three hundred charts.[8] Realizing, it seems, that he could use an assistant to help him study, theorize, and put all he learned into practice, he invented a heteronymous astrologer, Raphael Baldaya, whose place and date of birth were never established but whom he endowed with a very long beard. Baldaya's name started to appear in Pessoa's papers in late 1914, as the author of *Novo Tratado de Astrologia* (*New Treatise on Astrology*). Although Pessoa was still a neophyte in this celestial science, he was already planning to write about it, and to write something original. The new heteronym was also supposed to author *Introdução ao Estudo do Ocultismo* (*Introduction to the Study of Occultism*), a subject that Pessoa was likewise not yet qualified to write about, but before long he would be.

In the years to come Pessoa would alternately delve into Theosophy, automatic writing, Kabbalah, magic, Freemasonry, and Rosicrucianism, and he practiced astrology without letup. It's always a little baffling when someone as cerebral as Pessoa believes in—or suspends his disbelief in— astrology, magic, and the like. Teenagers are often fascinated by witch- craft, wizardry, and the astral world, then lose interest as they grow older. With Pessoa, the opposite happened. His adolescent curiosity about supernatural phenomena and the spirit world expanded exponentially in adulthood. It was only then that he took notice of the language of heavenly bodies, sending off for charts and readings from foreign astrol- ogers between 1909 and 1913. In that last year he also planned to consult Madame Brouillard, Portugal's most renowned clairvoyant, who bor- rowed her name from the French word for mist or fog.[9] With the creation of Raphael Baldaya and his associated book projects, Pessoa's astrolog- ical and other spiritual pursuits were grafted into his literary program, virtually guaranteeing that they would flourish. They received a further boost from his idealizing nationalism, which conferred a mythical aura on Portuguese history and Portugal's destiny.

Nationalism and spiritualism were similarly linked in Yeats, who embraced the Celtic mythology of Ireland's pre-Christian history and tried, without success, to create a Celtic Order of Mysteries. But his spir- itual interests, like Pessoa's, were universal in scope, and in many points they converged. Early in their careers, both poets reveled in the mysti- cism and prophecies of William Blake's poetry, which Pessoa read in an edition prepared and prefaced by Yeats. The Irish poet was a member of the Theosophical lodge in London run by Helena Blavatsky (1831–1891), the Russian occultist who had lived in India and developed Theosophy's syncretic belief system; Pessoa would translate half a dozen books by Blavatsky and other Theosophists in 1915–1916 and was initially seduced by their ideas. Although Pessoa never belonged to a Hermetic order, he would study the doctrines of Hermeticism and, as already noted, would become acquainted with Aleister Crowley, who was a member of the Hermetic Order of the Golden Dawn at the same time as Yeats (they did not get along). Pessoa would begin to contact astral spirits through automatic writing in 1916, one year before Yeats and his wife, Georgie Hyde-Lees, received their first messages from the spirit world.

Remarkable as these coincidences are, the two poets were differently motivated, and had different expectations. "The intellect of man is forced to choose / Perfection of the life, or of the work," wrote Yeats in his poem "The Choice," but he himself cultivated perfection in both the life and the work, and he went a long way toward achieving it thanks largely to his spiritual investigations. With the collaboration of his energetic wife, who was well versed in esoterica, he molded all that he had picked up over the years—from Celtic mythology, from the Indian mysticism that permeates Theosophy, from Kabbalistic and Rosicrucian traditions co-opted by the Golden Dawn—into his own esoteric vision of the universe and humankind's place in it.[10] His poetry, highly symbolic, shimmeringly reflected the unity he slowly forged in his spiritual worldview, and certain later poems such as "Sailing for Byzantium" rank among the finest treasures in the English language. (Pessoa's edition of Yeats's poetry was published in 1913, and he seems not to have read any of his subsequent work.) Yeats was fifty-one when he married Hyde-Lees in 1917, and a few years later he would go with her and their two children to live in an old castle in Galway—a symbol of his by then august life. Confirming his poetic stature and crowning him with worldly honor, the Swedish Academy awarded him the 1923 Nobel Prize in Literature.

Pessoa preferred to live on the fringes. He did not marry or have children, never earned enough money to pay taxes, and refused to belong to any political, religious, professional, or fraternal association. He was appreciated as a thinker, a poet, and a polemicist, but only by those few who kept up with his publications in periodicals. At first glance, our impression is that Pessoa, disdaining the world, chose to perfect his work at the expense of his life, and there may be some truth to this idea—but what really set him apart from Yeats was his lack of unity and perfection. He set the bar too high, believing perfection to be unattainable in the visible world, except in fleeting moments of great inspiration.

Yeats's belief in spirits and magic was entirely sincere; it was also eminently useful for his life and work, whose "perfection" relied on a blend of many elements, both worldly and spiritual, and on the artful reconciliation of their incongruities, so as to allow for a satisfying impression of wholeness. Pessoa, who had no talent for joining together disparate parts into seeming wholes, resorted to the spiritual world because the earthly world and his life in it—and even his literature—were damned to imperfection. Although the poetry he wrote under his own name would be a beneficiary of his zealous research into Hermetic traditions and occult mysteries, the benefit, from a purely literary standpoint, was unimpressive. His poems inspired by doctrines of Kabbalah and the Order of the Rosy Cross are interesting for their esoteric content; they are not among his best poems. But this hardly mattered to him. "Emissary of an unknown king," he had a mission to fulfill, which was to write what he had been given to write, without always knowing what or whom he was writing for. Was he really Portugal's future Great Poet, the Super-Camões? All he knew for certain was that he had to keep writing. Where his life and work would fit in the larger plan of the universe was inscribed, he liked to think, in the cryptic configurations of the stars.

In January 1915, determined to stop wasting his energy on things like intersectionist magazines or anthologies, Pessoa drew up a list of ambitious publication plans for his poetry. One of the planned volumes would have introduced Caeiro, Reis, and Campos to the world in one fell swoop, under the title *A Total Literature*, while other volumes would have gathered together all the lyrical and patriotic poetry in Portuguese that he had been writing under his own name. The most curious project, *The Seven Halls of the Abandoned Palace*, organized his poetry in thematic sections (the seven "halls") such as "Pure Lyricism," "Swampism," "Lyricism with Religious Mysticism," and "Lyricism with Metaphysical Anguish."[11] None of the projects went forward. Despite his declared intention of "arduously, monastically" pursuing his own artistic work, Pessoa's energy was abruptly rechanneled into a type of collective endeavor whose usefulness he had lately begun to question. In 1915 he and his literary friends, along with the unreal Álvaro de Campos, would finally bring out a magazine. He had feared that a literary magazine might go unnoticed. But this one, on the contrary, fell like a bomb on the Portuguese house of letters.

# CHAPTER 36

I N THE FIRST DECADES OF THE TWENTIETH CENTURY,
Rio de Janeiro was doing its best to become a tropical version of
Paris, elegant and modern, through massive urban development
projects that demolished a number of poor neighborhoods, forcing their
residents to occupy makeshift houses in the surrounding hills—today's
*favelas*. Great poets and fiction writers—such as Machado de Assis,
who died in 1908—hailed from Rio, which was also a thriving center
for musical innovation, thanks largely to the descendants of slaves who
had emigrated from the Bahia and inhabited, often enough, the hillside
shantytowns. Just as jazz originated among African American communities in New Orleans, samba and several other musical genres developed
among the African Brazilians living in Rio, where the first recordings of
music identified as samba were made in the mid-1910s. It was in this city
of sharp economic contrasts and enormous cultural vitality that the idea
for the magazine that would be called *Orpheu* was born. Published not
in Rio but in Lisbon, it would profoundly alter the history of twentieth-
century Portuguese literature.

The main obstacle to Pessoa's cherished plans for an "intersectionist" magazine titled *Europa* or, in its stead, an *Anthology of Intersectionism*, was intersectionism itself. With the exception of Pessoa's "Slanting
Rain," virtually none of the works produced by him and his compeers
lived up to the theory in its pure form, so intersectionism had become a
hazy, confusing designation for anything recherché. It took some geographical intersecting—with Brazil—to shake off the cumbersome theory and enable a magazine to finally come into being. Its unexpected
prime mover was Luís de Montalvor, Sá-Carneiro's high school friend,
who had only mediocre literary talent, no money to contribute, and no
experience as an editor.

At the start of 1915, Montalvor returned to Lisbon after two years
abroad in Rio, where he had bonded with Ronald de Carvalho (1893–

1935), a poet with a recently published first book, *Luz gloriosa* (*Glorious Light*). The poems, like the book's title, were faintly and loftily luminous, wafting in the symbolic heights of Stéphane Mallarmé. French symbolism also inspired Montalvor, who had been working intermittently and inconclusively on a long poem named after Orpheus, the poet-musician of Greek mythology whose sublime singing and playing could calm wild beasts. One evening in Copacabana, which was still a quiet neighborhood, with only a narrow strip of sand on its long beachfront, Montalvor and Carvalho excitedly discussed the possibility of jointly founding a literary magazine containing both Portuguese and Brazilian writing. Their idea was not original except in one point: the magazine would publish exclusively new and upcoming writers rather than well-known and established ones.

New and upcoming meant Montalvor, Carvalho, and their friends, who were already reading one another transatlantically. Montalvor had distributed copies of Sá-Carneiro's books to his literary pals in Rio, a couple of whom wrote glowing reviews in the Brazilian press, and he was also a publicist in the other direction, sending copies of Carvalho's book of poems to Fernando Pessoa and other Portuguese writers. Thus he prepared the terrain for the magazine he wanted to call *Orpheu*, like the poem he had kept trying in vain to finish. Montalvor still did not know Pessoa all that well, but he knew that Sá-Carneiro, whose participation in the project he considered crucial, would have nothing to do with it unless Pessoa was also involved. He may also have intuited that Pessoa, despite having so far published little, would be an even more vital contributor, guaranteeing the magazine's success.

While not a great literary talent himself, Luís de Montalvor was a reasonably good judge of other people's talent. He was also a brilliant negotiator. Reunited in January 1915 with Mário de Sá-Carneiro, one of his closest friends, he no doubt broached the subject of the magazine, to whet his appetite. The next month, after Ronald de Carvalho had failed in his bid to secure funding, Montalvor proceeded to strike a deal with Pessoa and Sá-Carneiro that was astonishingly one sided, at least to outward appearances.[1] Montalvor and Carvalho were to be the co-editors of a magazine called *Orpheu*, whose financing would be ensured by Sá-Carneiro. Pessoa and Sá-Carneiro would be shadow editors, deciding on the magazine's content and seeing it through the publication process. They would do all the work, in other words, without getting any of the credit.

Why they agreed to this arrangement is not entirely clear, but Sá-Carneiro must have run out of patience with his best friend's aesthetic dilemmas and continual waffling that kept their own joint projects, such as *Europa*, from ever getting off the ground. Pessoa was attracted to the proposed magazine's Brazilian component. It suddenly occurred to him that, instead of stressing Europe as a source of Portugal's cultural identity, it might make more sense to celebrate the spreading of its culture and language to other continents, and in particular to the sprawling and dynamic land of Brazil. This was an idea he would soon expand on, welding to it his version of the Sebastianist myth. There was also a practical circumstance that favored the realization of *Orpheu*. Sá-Carneiro's second book of short stories, *Céu em fogo* (*Sky on Fire*), was currently at the printers. If he and Fernando started to deliver copy for the new magazine immediately, they could hitch a ride, as it were, on the credit account of Mário's benevolent father.

Alfredo Guisado had no objections to the reconfigured magazine project, to which he pledged twelve thousand reis toward publication costs. His family's restaurant, Irmãos Unidos, was located on Praça do Rossio, next door to the popular Francfort Hotel, and did a thriving business.[2] The *Orpheu* writers often met at this restaurant, but it was at the nearby Café Montanha—spacious but relatively quiet—that Pessoa and Sá-Carneiro jointly wrote Armando Côrtes-Rodrigues, on February 19, telling him about the plans for the magazine and urging him to send some poetry without delay. "*The most intersectionist work you have*," Pessoa underlined, despite having written this friend exactly one month earlier that he was disenchanted with intersectionism. Pessoa's doubts about the movement persisted, but he wanted poems that would startle readers, poems marked by his and Sá-Carneiro's influence, rather than the conventionally inspired ones that came more naturally to Côrtes-Rodrigues.

◆

TYPESETTING FOR THE MAGAZINE got under way in late February 1915, and as galley proofs became available Sá-Carneiro looked them over with Pessoa, who was taken aback by the proof sheet of the masthead. Above the names of Luís de Montalvor and Ronald de Carvalho, listed as the editors in chief for Portugal and Brazil, respectively, there was a name he had not expected to see: António Ferro, another of Sá-Carneiro's high school friends, was listed as the "managing editor," though in fact he managed nothing. Pessoa pointed out that, as an eighteen-year-old, Ferro could not even legally hold such a position, a detail that only increased the mirth of Sá-Carneiro, the author of the joke. In the same transgressive spirit, the two proofreaders purposely let several typographical errors stand, thereby making the baroque prose of Montalvor's introduction and a wispy symbolist sonnet by Ronald de Carvalho even less intelligible.[3]

For his part, Ferro was pleased to learn that he was *Orpheu*'s managing editor. He would have preferred to be published in the magazine, but at least he could claim to be, even if in name only, a member of its editorial team. This would become a useful credential when, a few years later, he branded himself as a Portuguese modernist.

José de Almada Negreiros, who was developing into an important modernist writer as well as a major painter, published a group of experimental prose pieces in *Orpheu* 1, while Sá-Carneiro, Guisado, and Côrtes-Rodrigues all contributed poems. Writing by Fernando Pessoa—his play *The Mariner* and two long poems signed by Álvaro de Campos—dominated the issue. It was Pessoa's glorious coming-out as a creative writer. The two poems he had published in February 1914 occupied all of one page in a slender, one-shot magazine that attracted nobody's attention, but *Orpheu*, where his works took up a third of its eighty pages, would become the most talked-about literary publication in Portugal.

Elegantly printed on high-quality paper, *Orpheu* 1 was available for general purchase toward the end of March and immediately began to make news. On March 30, *A Capital* published an extensive front-page review titled "Literature from the Insane Asylum: The Poets of *Orpheu*." Contesting the pretensions to novelty of this "group of young men who can often be spotted in some of the downtown cafés," the reviewer said it was old stuff, analyzed fifteen years ago by the eminent psychiatrist Júlio de Matos, who had published a book about the painters and poets interned in Lisbon's mental hospital.

Though he knew that the young writers sometimes called themselves "swampists," because of a strange literary movement known as swampism, the reviewer was apparently unaware that Álvaro de Campos was a fictitious personality. He noted, correctly, that this individual "diverges in one of his poems, 'Triumphal Ode,' from the methods of his comrades and sings about the most unseemly and least poetic things of our time in shocking, sometimes pornographic language." Campos's most shocking,

"pornographic" lines featured eight-year-old girls from Lisbon's underclass who "[m]asturbate respectable-looking men in stairwells."*

*Orpheu* 1 included a second, very different Campos poem, "Opiário"
("Opiary"), consisting of rhyming quatrains and dated "Suez Canal,
March 1914," although Pessoa wrote it while the magazine was being
assembled and going to press. He said later that he wanted to show—by
dint of a mentally taxing, "twofold depersonalization"—what kind of
poet Campos must have been before his encounter with Alberto Caeiro
transformed him into the futurist and sensationist author of the "Triumphal Ode" (which was dated "London, June 1914" in the magazine).⁴ The
result was a blasé, opium-smoking decadent who, as a student of naval
engineering in Scotland, had idled away his time instead of studying.
To try to stave off boredom he also traveled, and it was on his way home
from a long voyage to the Far East that Campos wrote his "Opiary,"
which lucidly summed up the nature of his and his compatriots' decadence in this memorable formulation:

> I belong to that class of Portuguese
> Who, once India was discovered, were out
> Of work.

Alberto Caeiro and Ricardo Reis remained incognito, perhaps because
their poems, although nothing like them had ever been written in Portuguese, were more classical in tone and less likely to scandalize bourgeois
sensibilities. Pessoa may also have deemed it wise not to play all his trump
cards at once. He still toyed with the idea of launching Alberto Caeiro as
an "independent" poet. In any case, the magazine could not be overrun
by the work of Pessoa and his heteronyms. As it was, Álvaro de Campos,
with his two lengthy poems, occupied more space in *Orpheu* 1 than any
other writer. He was also one of the two poets who attracted the most
attention, indignation, and laughter in newspapers; the other was Mário
de Sá-Carneiro. The latter's most discussed poem, inscrutably titled "16,"
ends with the tables of a café whirling in the air while one of the poet's
arms falls off and, dressed in tails, goes waltzing through the halls of a

---

* For forty years after Pessoa's death, this line would be censored in Portuguese editions of his works.

viceroy's palace. As far as I know, no literary critic has ever ventured to interpret this passage, which seemed to amply prove the charge of collective insanity leveled by the reviewer of *Orpheu* writing for *A Capital*. The charge struck a chord, instantly echoed by other newspapers in Lisbon, Porto, and elsewhere. "On the Way to the Madhouse," "The Poets of *Orpheu* and the Maniacs," and "*Orpheu* in the Inferno" are some of the titles of the more than fifty critical reviews and shorter news items on *Orpheu* 1 that Mário de Sá-Carneiro clipped and pasted into a scrapbook. Lisbon's literati were scandalized but terribly curious, and even those who normally had no interest in literature went out and bought the magazine, which sold out within three weeks. The writers who published in *Orpheu* were treated as the members of a freakish literary cult. When spotted on the street—Sá-Carneiro with his bulbous torso and still boyish face, Almada Negreiros with his angular cheeks, pronounced eyebrows, and tightly curled hair, and the conservatively dressed Pessoa, who didn't stand out on his own—people pointed at them and giggled, or simply stared with vague wonderment. Pessoa and his friends had become celebrities.

Pessoa was human enough to be elated by all the attention—he gloated about it in his April 4, 1915, letter to Côrtes-Rodrigues—but differently from most humans, he was especially delighted that the attention came from scoffers rather than from admirers. He took their laughter to be a prophetic sign. One week after *Orpheu* 1 went on sale, he was asked to write about it for a new Lisbon daily, *O Jornal*. He wrote, instead, about the *Lyrical Ballads* of William Wordsworth and Samuel Taylor Coleridge, explaining to his readers (few of whom had ever heard of the *Ballads*) that the book's publication, in 1798, marked the beginning of the English Romantic movement. He further explained that everybody, including even Lord Byron, ridiculed the kind of work—such as "Lines Written above Tintern Abbey" and "The Rime of the Ancient Mariner"—presented by the two poets. But Byron himself ended up adopting the new style, and Wordsworth was named Britain's poet laureate in 1843. Pessoa capped off his literary lesson by quoting the following observation from Wordsworth's "Essay, Supplementary to the Preface" of the 1815 edition of the *Ballads*: "every Author, as far as he is great and at the same time *original*, has had the task of *creating* the taste by which he is to be enjoyed; so has it been, so will it continue to be." And he concluded his piece for the newspaper by saying that the future would decide if there were "men of genius among the contributors to *Orpheu*."[5]

According to Pessoa's stunningly accurate prediction, the "men of genius" of *Orpheu*—himself and Sá-Carneiro—would have the last laugh, just like the two poets of the *Lyrical Ballads*, by creating in others the necessary aesthetic sensibility to appreciate what they and their friends wrote. The "others" Pessoa had in mind were not the general populace but a cultural elite, which could be fostered by creating an intellectual, aesthetic conversation between contrasting literary movements—according to his theories of a self-generating, nonhereditary aristocracy developed the previous summer. *Orpheu* had launched exactly such a conversation, since the futurist "Triumphal Ode" of Álvaro de Campos had little to do with the rest of the magazine, where the ultra-symbolist style known as swampism prevailed. One of the most obvious, sharpest contrasts to Campos was the contribution of Fernando Pessoa, *The Mariner: A Static Drama in One Act*, whose "static" essence radically opposed it to the frantically forward-driving poem of Campos. Pessoa, aided by the heteronyms could accomplish most of his literary objectives on his own, but he needed his writer friends to create context and to give weight to the movements he created.

◆

THERE WAS ANOTHER NEW magazine, *Contemporânea* (*Contemporary*), which Pessoa was counting on to help *Orpheu* create a cultural elite in Portugal. *Contemporânea* was founded by José Pacheco (1885–1934), an architect, graphic designer, and cultural promoter who, like most Portuguese artists with ambition and the wherewithal, had lived for a spell as a young man in Paris, where he met Mário de Sá-Carneiro. Once they both returned to Lisbon, in the second half of 1913, Pacheco became acquainted with Pessoa, Almada Negreiros, and others connected to the group that would publish *Orpheu*. They fraternized at cafés or at one of the artist-designer's favorite haunts, the Cervejaria Jansen, technically a beer hall but decorated like an old-style café, with paintings on the ceiling and waiters who wore black coats and white aprons. The setting enhanced the visual impact of Pacheco's high-fashion clothes tailored in Paris or after Parisian designs.

Paris was also where Pacheco had begun using morphine, which was not a controlled substance in France until well into the Great War. He got hooked on the drug, according to people who knew him.[6] Other artists and writers in Pessoa's circle also experimented with opiates—but never Pessoa. Conservative in his choice of apparel, he was also conservative in his preferred vices: tobacco, coffee, and alcohol. Even Álvaro de Campos, whose "Opiary" has him injecting morphine as well as smoking opium during his trip to the Far East, would admit in another poem, "A passagem das horas" ("Time's Passage"), that he preferred "thinking about smoking opium to smoking it."

Pacheco designed the covers for two of Sá-Carneiro's books and was also the cover artist for *Orpheu* 1.[7] In the meantime he was making plans for his own magazine, with the precious assistance of Pessoa, who drew up a list of possible sections, section editors, article topics, and contributors. Pessoa also wrote the copy for a promotional brochure, informing prospective readers that *Contemporânea* would be the "first step toward the creation of a cultured milieu among us." Indeed, the mere circumstance of reading the elegantly produced magazine would be "an act of spontaneous good taste."[8]

The brochure was printed and distributed in March 1915, and the magazine launched at the end of April, one month after *Orpheu*. For sheer elegance, no other Portuguese publication could rival it. It was larger in format than *Orpheu*, beautifully printed, and contained photographs, illustrations, and engravings. Pacheco had adopted some of Pessoa's suggestions for the contents and general organization of *Contemporânea*, whose cover was designed by the *Orpheu* contributor Almada Negreiros, making for yet another family tie between the two periodicals. In substance, however, they had little in common. Pacheco's magazine, which included a "women's section," focused on fashion, high society, theater, and current events such as the war. It also offered readers a poem and a short story, by respected writers whose mental sanity no one would ever question.

*Orpheu* and *Contemporânea* were complementary projects. The former sought to create an intellectual, literary elite; the latter, a social elite defined by its cosmopolitan sophistication, even while a world war was in full swing. Pessoa's hope was that, together, they could foster the formation of a social class fit for governing his idealized "aristocratic republic," but Pacheco's magazine quickly gained the reputation of being antirepublican. Three of its contributors were founding members of the Portuguese integralism movement, which, as mentioned earlier, supported a return to monarchy and to traditional, Catholic values.[9] *Contemporânea*, moreover, openly endorsed the current government, which protected the integralists.

The current government was a caretaker administration. Social instability and deep divisions among the republicans had led to a bloodless coup d'état that seized power from Afonso Costa's radical Democrats in late January 1915. Yielding to pressure from powerful groups in the armed forces and with the backing of the two more moderate republican parties, the nation's president had invited General Joaquim Pimenta de Castro (1846–1918) to rule as a temporary, de facto dictator. The retired, white-haired general, who made a point of never donning his uniform while in office, assumed the task of restoring peace and order before the next general election, set for June. He was in many ways a conciliatory figure, albeit hostile to the Democrats, who naturally despised him. While not himself a monarchist, Pimenta de Castro allowed the integralists and other monarchists to freely organize and promote their views. He also extended an open hand to the Catholic Church, softening some of the harsher anticlerical measures introduced by Afonso Costa in 1911.[10]

Pimenta de Castro was respected by many intellectuals, Pessoa included, even though the poet thought the general was drifting too far into the orbit of the neo-monarchical integralists, whose ongoing attempts to disavow any link with the decisively far-right French integralists never convinced him. Disenchantment with the Portuguese Republic was helping to swell the neo-monarchist ranks, and even two of the heteronyms, Ricardo Reis and Álvaro de Campos, identified as monarchists. Pessoa, however, continued to subscribe to republicanism, at least on paper. Which is to say: he continued to write notes for his exotic theory of an aristocratic republic,[11] a concept that would have struck virtually every republican of the three major parties as a hopeless contradiction in terms, since they associated aristocracy with monarchy. If pressed on the issue, Pessoa could have pointed to the example of the Roman Republic, where the aristocracy held sway.

✦

PESSOA WAS GAINING A reputation as a spirited intellectual, and one week after *Orpheu* was launched he began a lifelong career as an occasional political and social commentator in the Portuguese press. Hired as a columnist for *O Jornal*, he published his first opinion piece on April 5, 1915 (one day before his article on *Orpheu* and the *Lyrical Ballads* appeared). A brilliant preamble for all his future writing in this genre, it cautioned his readers that "only superficial people have deep convictions" and insisted that a modern intellectual "has the cerebral obligation to change opinion [. . .] several times in the same day." This intellectual might, for instance, be "a republican in the morning and a royalist at dusk." In his second column, published three days later, Pessoa took the Portuguese to task for being overly disciplined, for always acting and thinking and feeling as a group, with no one assuming personal responsibility. Fanatical obedience to the political parties currently dividing the country was, according to his analysis, a fatal consequence of too much discipline and lack of independence. "Portugal," he wrote, "needs an antidisciplinarian."

Pessoa fancied himself as that "antidisciplinarian," according to a letter he sent Côrtes-Rodrigues on April 19, and the first of his tasks in that self-appointed role was to teach mental flexibility through his own example. Although he adhered to a core set of values and principles, including respect for individual differences and the right to free movement and free speech, his vehemently argued propositions and critiques were often deliberately provocative, more for the sake of exercising his and his readers' minds than for promoting definite points of view. A sportsman in the field of logic and debate, Pessoa sometimes got into trouble for being too playful. So it was at O Jornal, where the sixth column he wrote stirred up a royalist nest of hornets.

Under the accommodating government of Pimenta de Castro, Lisbon's neo-monarchists had finally succeeded in forming an official association, inaugurated with fanfare. Pessoa, in his column of April 21, made fun of the royalists for needing to define themselves as a class with its own association—like chauffeurs, he noted, who founded an association and became a new class of proletarians after the introduction of the automobile. The aristocratic-minded monarchists, in other words, were behaving like proletarians. The newspaper's editor in chief published a notice the next day stating that his publication was politically independent, that Pessoa's column was offensive to monarchists and should not have been published, and that the columnist had been sacked.[12] Lisbon's chauffeurs, who also took offense, sent a letter of protest published in the newspaper on the twenty-third.

The dismissed columnist did not apologize to the irate chauffeurs, but he drafted a facetiously conciliatory response to the "worker demands" of the monarchists' association. He offered them his assistance, saying that they could count on him, "a poor fashioner of paradoxes," to come up with some arguments in favor of monarchy, "even if it's just for the pleasure of leading them astray."

The newspaper declined to publish Pessoa's response, if indeed he submitted it, and the antidisciplinarian went elsewhere with his contrarian opinions and absurdist arguments. On May 13, in the first and last issue of a political journal called *Eh real!*, Pessoa published an article titled "The Bias in Favor of Order" that took direct aim at the "new monarchists," or "neo-monarchists," for obsessively harping on the need to impose order on Portugal's politically volatile society. Using a series of dubious but cleverly formulated arguments, he contended that they had it backwards, since order was the result—not the cause—of a healthily functioning organism. Other contributors to *Eh real!* criticized General Pimenta de Castro, the temporary dictator, for sanctioning the monarchists, formerly a fringe movement that now loomed as a danger to the Republic. The *real* in the name of the journal was sardonic: the word in Portuguese means "royal" as well as "real." The royal threat was a real threat.

✦

EXACTLY ONE DAY LATER, May 14, cannons, machine guns, and grenades rained fire over Lisbon, quickly quelling any worries Pessoa may have had about the neo-monarchists coming to power and imposing peace and order on Portuguese society. A revolution instigated by Afonso Costa's Democrats and supported by some of the armed forces, especially the navy, took to the streets to depose the dictator and reclaim the Republic for the common people. Breaking into the army arsenal, ordinary citizens outfitted themselves with guns and returned to the streets, clashing with soldiers loyal to the government. Pimenta de Castro surrendered the next day, but skirmishes and sniping continued for several more days, in Lisbon and other cities, killing close to two hundred people, far more than had died during the republican revolution of 1910. Hundreds more were seriously wounded, and a few armed civilians even fired at Red Cross workers who came to the aid of the injured.[13] As a revolutionary junta asserted its control, people raised flags, ruffians looted shops, bands played the national anthem, and shouts of *"Viva a República!"* (Long live the Republic!) bayoneted the air.

Pessoa, like most middle-class Portuguese, was appalled. Although he opposed the monarchists and the chummy alliance they had been fostering with Pimenta de Castro, he was on the whole satisfied with how the old general had governed the country, without a secret police and without censoring any newspaper. Nevertheless, despite the grandfatherly air, he was a dictator and had made no effort to appease the Democratic Party, which was determined to bring him down before the upcoming elections, so that they would control the electoral machinery.

In the weeks following this coup, Pessoa wrote extensive notes for an essay whose working title was "May 14—Notes on a Victory of the Plebeians."[14] Whether in this essay or in his other ruminations on the current state of Portugal, Pessoa claimed to be writing as a disinterested sociologist, a rigorous theorist. And progress, for this impartial analyst, meant overcoming stultified ways of thinking and doing. In his view, the political life of the Republic was thus far a repetition of the constitutional monarchy it had replaced: a democratic system in which competing parties squabbled and put their own interests above those of the nation. For the country to be able to move decisively forward, he envisioned an aristocracy that would "reduce the proletariat as far as possible to the condition of slaves." The theorist offered some details of this purportedly progressive vision: "The plebeian class should be the instrument of the imperialists, the dominating caste," and "linked to them through a community of national mysticism, such that it is voluntarily their slave." This dominating role of the aristocrats was not to be an end in itself; it would serve as an education in how to dominate other nations.[15]

Ideas such as these, which nowadays could be voiced only by someone trying to win a prize for offensiveness, were aggressive and extreme even in 1915. Pessoa the thinker did not censor himself. When musing on what set of conditions would logically result in a smoothly running republic, he freely let his mind contemplate brutal class discrimination. The enslaved workers of his aristocratic republic, he tellingly wrote, were to serve the dominating caste of "imperialists." The poet's ultimate ideal for the nation of Portugal was, in fact, exaltedly imperialistic. Yet the empire he envisioned, while in some ways analogous to traditional, militaristic empires, was fundamentally unlike any that had ever existed.

Particularly as a young man, Pessoa excoriated the imperialism of Great Britain in Ireland and South Africa, but that did not stop him from delineating a modern imperialist agenda for Portugal in 1915. German rather than British imperialism ostensibly inspired his thinking, which dwelled on Germany's "spiritual" objectives in the present war, overlooking its bloody record of colonialism in Africa. Economic considerations and territorial expansion, Pessoa argued, were but secondary motives prompting Germany to wage war; the main, entirely laudable impulse had been a visceral desire to affirm itself and its culture, by imposing it on others.[16] And what an enviable culture it was, with figures such as Kant, Hegel, and Nietzsche in philosophy, Goethe in literature, and Beethoven and Wagner in music! Pessoa, in his notes, cited all these names as proof of German cultural vigor, which he linked to a process of "re-Hellenization" and "repaganization," even if the nation was outwardly Christian.[17] Its pagan undercurrent had blossomed in the Romantic movement and flourished beyond it, through the operas of Wagner, which celebrated Norse and Germanic mythology, and the writings of Nietzsche.

Given that pagan symbols and myths from Germany's ancient past, glorified by Wagner, would be promoted by Heinrich Himmler and other members of the Nazi hierarchy, it's scary to imagine what Pessoa's idealized paganism might have led to if applied to realpolitik, but there was nothing realistic about his own imperialistic program. He dreamed, impossibly, of a modern-day Portuguese empire that would come about solely on the strength of its culture.

In Pessoa's idiosyncratic view of the world, Germany was the only country in Europe with anything remotely akin to the "national mysticism" he championed for Portugal, which was why he could theoretically sympathize with the Germans in the war, even if he couldn't, in good conscience, condone the unprovoked invasions of Belgium and France. He got around this difficulty by channeling his Germanic sympathies through António Mora, the toga-clad, Greece-obsessed maniac he had invented around 1910, for his short story "In the Cascais Sanatorium." Whether this individual was still wearing a toga and living in the sanatorium in 1915 is uncertain, but in the spring of that year Pessoa promoted him from the status of fictional character to that of a heteronym tasked with large writing projects. One of the first works assigned to the revived Mora was a *Dissertation in Favor of Germany*, whose dozens of pages explain why that nation's imperial destiny necessarily led it to war and why Portugal was spiritually and culturally closer to Germany than to Britain or France.[18]

Mora's defense of Germany, on the grounds that an essentially pagan blood ran through its self-asserting culture, was merely a prelude to Pessoa's more central concern to rehabilitate and promote paganism, as well as Greek culture, in the modern world. In 1915 he wrote numerous passages for Mora's *Prolegomena to a Reconstruction of Paganism*, the first of several long treatises in which the heteronym discusses the principles of paganism and defends its superiority to Christianity. Mora would also author a preface to the poetry of Alberto Caeiro, whom he defined as the "reconstructor of the essence of paganism."

Espousing the same classicist values as Ricardo Reis, António Mora reemerged from the forgotten halls of the Cascais Sanatorium as a counterweight to *Orpheu*, or to reviewers' perception of it as an iconoclastic project divorced from the literary tradition. In his own review of the magazine, Mora noted that one needed to be steeped in Greek culture to correctly understand what these young writers wanted to achieve.[19] Pessoa, more than any other writer of *Orpheu*, knew very well what he hoped to achieve. However much it delighted him to outrage the literary establishment with swampism and intersectionism, he was not ultimately interested in being avant-garde. What he yearned for was a new renaissance, to be spearheaded by Portugal.

✦

PERHAPS IT WAS AS a pamphlet, or in the next issue of *Orpheu*, that Pessoa planned to publish a manifesto titled *Atlantismo*. Atlantism was neither a doctrine promoting the lost island of Atlantis nor a new literary movement; it was a blueprint for Pessoa's dreamed-of renaissance. Like *Orpheu*, which styled itself a Portuguese-Brazilian publication, Atlantism looked in the direction of the ocean on which Portuguese ships had set out centuries earlier, establishing a worldwide maritime empire scarcely imaginable for such a small nation, and yet it somehow came to exist. Pessoa proposed to replicate that feat, but with poems and myths instead of ships, and with religious feeling, aristocratic attitudes, and creative energies in lieu of territorial possessions and military might. It was, nonetheless, a thoroughly imperialistic project.[20]

The actual manifesto failed to materialize, but Pessoa's copious notes for it painted a vivid picture of a cultural alliance between the "Atlantic" regions of Iberia, Ireland, and the Americas. The old centers of Europe—London, Paris, and Rome—were designated as "the enemies." As for Germany, although its pagan spirit and cultural vigor were worthy of emulation, its militaristic empire was doomed to fall, since grossly material empires were obsolete. The imperialism of the future would be wholly spiritual, founded on conquests of the human spirit, and with Portugal leading the way. In this picture of empire, the Portuguese colonies in Africa and Asia were a millstone that ought to be cast off. "Sell them before they're taken from us," Pessoa pragmatically wrote in a notebook used in 1915.[21] The "spiritual" imperialism of Atlantism embraced, as its religion, the reconstructed paganism preached by António Mora and Ricardo Reis, but it appropriated from the Judeo-Christian tradition the notion of a Messiah, applying it to the figure of King Sebastian, and it proclaimed the dawning of a glorious Fifth Empire, based on a prophecy from the Bible.

◆

THE FIFTH EMPIRE DOCTRINE, which now emerged as the focal point of Pessoa's vision for his country's future, was the brainchild of Father António Vieira (1608–1697), one of the most robustly imaginative intellects ever to write in Portuguese. Born in Lisbon, this Jesuit preacher, missionary, diplomat, and political activist traveled widely around Europe but divided most of his eighty-nine years between Brazil, where he championed the dignity of indigenous peoples yet reluctantly accepted the enslavement of Africans,* and Portugal, where he defended the Jews against the Inquisition and became a counselor to the king.

In addition to his vast output of exquisite sermons, Vieira wrote prophetic works, including a *History of the Future*, which presaged a universal, millenarian reign of peace under the aegis of a Portuguese king. He deduced that optimistic future by crossing the prophetic utterances of a sixteenth-century shoemaker and vatic poet named Gonçalo Annes Bandarra, who predicted that a "hidden king" would bring grandeur and prestige to Portugal, with a prophecy in the Book of Daniel, chapters 2 and 7, about the downfall of four successive kingdoms and the advent of a fifth kingdom, ruled by God and lasting forever. Biblical scholars have traditionally interpreted the first four kingdoms as Babylon, the Persian (or Medo-Persian) Empire, Greece, and Rome. Vieira's novelty was to place a Portuguese king (Bandarra's "hidden king") on the throne of

---

* Preaching that blacks and whites were equal, Vieira was horrified by slavery but believed that there must be a divine reason for its existence, and so he told Brazilian slaves to accept their lot.

the futuristic Fifth Kingdom, or Empire, such that the peaceful reign of God on Earth would coincide with an age of glorious preeminence for Portugal.

During the two centuries following Vieira's death, other "historians" of Portugal's future promoted the Sebastianist myth, linking the "hidden king" of Bandarra's prophetic poems to the disappeared King Sebastian, who was supposed to return and regenerate a decadent, despondent Portugal. It was Pessoa who revived, in the twentieth century, Vieira's idea of a Portuguese Fifth Empire, seeing it as the natural, spontaneous consequence of King Sebastian's mystical or symbolic return.

Throughout the rest of his life Pessoa would write about the two intertwined doctrines—Sebastianism and the Fifth Empire—interpreting them politically as well as poetically, and refining his interpretations in accord with Portugal's shifting fortunes. But even his political interpretations of these grand ideas, defended with ingenious arguments, were essentially acts of poetry. Whether or not they ever corresponded to any tangible transformation in Portuguese society, Pessoa could and did appreciate them as beautiful verbal constructions, just as good as or even better than reality.

# CHAPTER 37

○ ✕ ○ ✕ ○ ✕ ○ ✕ ○ ✕ ○ ✕ ○ ✕ ○ ✕ ○ ✕ ○ ✕ ○ ✕ ○ ✕ ○ ✕ ○ ✕ ○ ✕ ○ ✕ ○ ✕

I T WAS AT NIGHT IN HIS RENTED ROOM, WITH A cigarette in his left hand and a pen in his right, that Pessoa the thinker and dreamer plotted a Fifth Empire in which Portugal would reign supreme, helped heteronym António Mora develop the principles of a modern paganism and strategies for disseminating it, gave free rein to his sexual imagination, and cast astrological charts for himself, for people around him, for *Orpheu*, and for Portugal.[1] By day Pessoa the poet, editor, and journalistic *provocateur* crisscrossed downtown Lisbon, meeting with friends in cafés to discuss ideas, literature, the barrage of news about the horribly deadly yet static Great War, and the revolution of May 1915, which had ousted Pimenta de Castro, a strong proponent of Portuguese neutrality. With the Democrats back in power, it looked increasingly likely that Portugal would enter the war. It was not a good climate for an elitist magazine like *Contemporânea*, particularly since it had applauded the government of the now disgraced dictator, and José Pacheco decided to suspend publication, but *Orpheu*, which had stayed out of politics, was getting ready to publish its second issue. It would offer, like the first issue, close to eighty pages of original poetry and prose, as well as a new feature: artwork.

The invited artist was Santa Rita Pintor (1889–1918),* who in the years before the war had been living in Paris, where he attended Marinetti's lectures on futurism and kept company with Mário de Sá-Carneiro. As tense and wiry as Mário was rotund and expansive, Santa Rita stood out like a shadow risen off the ground: he liked to dress in black, from his shoes up to his hat, which was pulled down close to his eyes. Bursting with ideas and electric energy, he could outargue anyone, with the

---

* A pseudonym—*pintor* is the Portuguese word for "painter." The artist's real name was Guilherme de Santa Rita.

possible exception of Fernando Pessoa, who could hold his own, despite being less assertive in speech than in writing. Irritatingly self-important but seductively intelligent, the artist described the aesthetic principles of his paintings in progress with such brio and conviction that no listener would doubt that they were extremely original, if not absolute master-pieces, but few people had actually seen them.

Pessoa was wary of Santa Rita, whom Sá-Carneiro, in an early letter from Paris,[2] had described as mendacious, self-centered, and calculating, but a flyer distributed in May 1915 announced in bold type that the sec-ond issue of *Orpheu*, to be published the following month, would include a "Special contribution of the Futurist Santa Rita Pintor" as well as a "Manifesto on the New Literature" by Fernando Pessoa. Like many of Pessoa's planned manifestos, this one never got written, but the maga-zine would indeed include reproductions of four works by Santa Rita, all with futurist-sounding titles, such as *Dynamic Decomposition of a Table + Style of Movement*. Part drawing, part collage, and visibly inspired by the early collages of Picasso and Georges Braque, the four compositions were actually more reminiscent of cubism. Their shock value was at any rate considerable, for they were like nothing ever displayed or published in Portugal.

When it came to avant-garde movements, Pessoa continued to play it both ways. He used them to shake things up, to disconcert overly obedi-ent, complacent minds, and—why not?—to generate some publicity for himself and for *Orpheu*, while at the same time actively disdaining them, unless they were of his own manufacture. He was happy to let Santa Rita bill himself as a futurist, but he did not want people to think that *Orpheu* was derived from or inspired by Marinetti's movement. Neither did Álvaro de Campos.

On June 4, the "engineer and sensationist poet," as Campos liked to sign himself, addressed a letter to the editor of *Diário de Notícias*, object-ing to its use of the term "futurist" to characterize *Orpheu*. Futurism, he explained, wanted to eliminate emotion, lyricism, and subjectivity from art, whereas the contributors to the first issue of *Orpheu* were intensely subjective and full of dreamy abstraction. If they had to be linked to a movement, then they belonged to the Portuguese movement known as intersectionism, or swampism. Campos acknowledged that his own "Triumphal Ode," published in *Orpheu* 1, was futurist in its subject matter—but *only* in its subject matter, not at all in its literary technique.

He added: "I, for that matter, am neither an intersectionist (or swamp-ist) nor a futurist. I am me, just me, concerned only with myself and my sensations."

*Diário de Notícias* did not publish Campos's letter, and we can't be cer-tain that Pessoa actually sent it. But on the back of the typed copy found in his archives, the naval engineer and poet of sensations—apparently still fuming because of all the misguided talk about futurism—immediately drafted another letter, this time in French. It was addressed to none other than F. T. Marinetti, the leader of the futurists, and began with a little flattery. Campos wrote that he was including with his letter a copy of *Orpheu* 1 and a translation into French of his "Triumphal Ode," which he planned to dedicate to Marinetti when it came out in book form, pro-vided he had no objection. There the niceties ended. The letter continued:

> I must tell you, quite frankly, that I'm not at all a futurist, but I have read in your attitude (not in your Work) this love for modern things that was already in me and that I tried, in my "Triumphal Ode," to express in a purely mechanical and technical way, purely as an engineer.
>
> Admitting no relationship between art and reality, I naturally do not admit your technique and your methods. For me, your words-in-freedom make no sense. I admit only my sensations, and in art, to borrow your expression, I admit only sensations-in-freedom.

Having rejected one of the fundamental characteristics of futurist poetry—the liberation of words from syntax—Campos went on to eluci-date the foundations of his own poetry:

> Let me be clear. There are no words. There are no things. There are only sensations. There is no art but that of sensations. Everything is only what it is in us. It is to this *sensationist* school that I belong. This school is me. There is no sensationist but me. In my intellec-tual lineage I find Blake and Walt Whitman. Your movement is a spent light that illuminated our path.[3]

After a few more sentences insulting the futurist movement, the letter petered out, unfinished and hence unsent, making it unnecessary for the

"Triumphal Ode" to be translated into French. During the next year and a half, Pessoa would write many pages expounding on sensationism, but the Campos letter to Marinetti shows how little it aspired, unlike the intersectionism it eclipsed, to be a vanguard movement. When Campos declares himself to be the *only* sensationist, he is making a philosophical assertion about the impossibility of knowing anything about anyone else's sensations. He has only *his* sensations, and because he longs to feel more than what is in the world to feel, he identifies with William Blake, whom he would later evoke in a poem that begins:

Ah, open my eyes to another reality!
I want to feel, like Blake, the angels all around me
And to have visions for lunch.[4]

Blake refused to be limited by visible reality; he also rejected all instances of bondage observable in the world around him. His poetry took stands against religious constraints, political oppression, limits on free speech, and sexual repression, and he was arguably the initiator of free verse in the English language. "Poetry Fetter'd Fetters the Human Race," he wrote at the beginning of *Jerusalem* in defense of the new style, which no longer counted syllables, though perhaps we should credit the invention of free verse to the translators responsible for the King James Version of the Bible—a major source of his inspiration. Blake's liberated views and poetics make him a kindred spirit of Whitman, of course, as well as of Pessoa's most unrestrained and impulsive heteronym.

✦

In "Salutation to Walt Whitman," begun in June 1915, Álvaro de Campos stridently celebrates his kinship with the American poet, yawping from one side of the ocean to the other:

From here in Portugal, with every historical age in my brain,
I salute you, Walt, I salute you, my Universal brother,
Forever modern and eternal, the singer of concrete absolutes,
Passionate mistress of the scattered universe,
Great pederast who rubs against the diversity of things,
Sexualized by stones, by trees, by people, by professions,

Full of lust for passing bodies, chance encounters, mere
  observations,

. . .


Inner spasm of all outer objects,
Pimp of the whole Universe,
Slut of all solar systems, pansy of God!

The uninhibited language, repetitive formulas (in stanzas not cited
here), and expansive emotivity make this poem read, at times, like a
Portuguese precursor to Allen Ginsberg's "Howl," and it is no accident
that the American beat poet wrote a poem titled "Salutations to Fernando Pessoa," in which he wishfully claims to be a superior poet, on the
grounds that the United States is a much bigger country than Portugal.
Vaunting an even larger poetic ego, Campos dares to consider himself
not only a brother to Walt Whitman but his absolute equal in feeling.
Together, he says, they go "hand in hand, dancing the universe." The
poem's dance is a delirious whirl of unbridled sensations, ideas, impressions, impulses, and corporal fantasies more daring than any in Whitman's poetry. Campos wants to feel everything intensely but passively,
masochistically—to be whipped, to be run over, to be "the she-dog of all
he-dogs," to be "whatever's crushed, abandoned, uprooted, destroyed."
At one point his passivity becomes confessedly homoerotic:

Put me in shackles just so that I can break them!
So that I can break them with my teeth and make my teeth bleed!
O masochistic, blood-spurting joy of life!

The sailors took me prisoner.
Their hands squeezed me in the darkness,
And I died for a moment when I felt this.
Then my soul licked the floor of my private jail [. . .]

In May 1915, one month before Campos swooned at the thought of
being manhandled by sailors in a poem that saluted Walt Whitman as a
great "pederast" and pansy, Pessoa had written his loveliest homoerotic
poem: the aforementioned "Antinous," which describes the Emperor

Hadrian's tender love for his companion who mysteriously drowned in the Nile in the year 130. Ardent as well as tender, Hadrian's love soon took the form of worship. Proclaiming the beautiful dead youth to be a god, the bereaved emperor established a cult of Antinous, built an Egyptian city named after him, and founded a set of lavish games held annually in his honor. More than two thousand statues of the young Greek from Bithynia with thick tousled hair and a melancholy air were sculpted in the years following his death, and over one hundred of these have survived. In the nineteenth century, Antinous became an emblem for "the love that dare not speak its name," to use the epithet made famous at the disastrous trial of Oscar Wilde,[5] who included references to Antinous in *The Picture of Dorian Gray*, "The Young King," and "The Sphinx."

In Pessoa's several earlier attempts to write poetry about love between men—his sonnets for *The Book of the Other Love*, for instance—the poems' narrators were still tormented by the idea that such love was unnatural, immoral. It was through Hadrian that he succeeded in writing with vivid feeling and without shame about one man's overwhelming affection for another. Despite an occasionally clumsy phrase or ill-chosen word, in this case the English language worked in the poet's favor, by freeing him to be more uninhibitedly sympathetic toward his subject. In the almost eighteen hundred years since the death of Antinous, no one had ever told with more acutely enunciated passion the story of his and Hadrian's love.

Unable to imagine what his life will be without his beloved, Pessoa's Hadrian contemplates, with horrified grief, the corpse of Antinous stretched out on a couch. He remembers the "love they lived as a religion," how they held each other, acting on all their burning desires, and

> Even as he thinks, the lust that is no more
> Than a memory of lust revives and takes
> His senses by the hand, his felt flesh wakes,
> And all becomes again what 'twas before.

Hadrian showers the dead body with kisses, implores the gods to bring it back to life, recalls how the younger man was "a kitten playing with lust," the lust of them both, "sometimes one / And sometimes two, now linking, now undone."

The second half of the poem consists of a speech to Antinous in which Hadrian promises to build him a deifying statue not made of stone but of his yearning for "our love's eternity." Antinous is already a god, says Hadrian, since his wish that he be one is itself a divine "vision of the real things beyond / Our life-imprisoned life, our sense-bound sense." The deification of Antinous, as described in the poem, depends entirely on the power of love welded to the imagination, without any need for an actual cult, yearly games, or a city named Antinoöpolis. Hadrian's manner of reasoning—of using reason and feeling to create reality—is suspiciously like Fernando Pessoa's.

Pessoa's Hadrian turns out to be remarkably modern, and prophetic. The historical emperor did not fit the paradigm of a Roman aristocrat who avails himself of a young male slave for sexual gratification and other amenities without developing a long-standing affective attachment, but Pessoa goes further, turning Hadrian into a champion of oppressed homosexuals:

Some will say all our love was but our crimes;
Others against our names the knives will whet
Of their glad hate of beauty's beauty, and make
Our names a base of heap whereon to rake
The names of all our brothers with quick scorn.

What can "all our brothers" mean but Verlaine and Rimbaud, Wilde and Douglas, Whitman, Proust, and all men who have felt society's contempt because they were attracted to other men rather than to women? The emperor, endowed with foreknowledge that the Roman gods would be eclipsed, concludes his speech with an optimistic, fast-forward reference to "the end of days" when Jupiter will be "born again," attended by Ganymede, and his and Antinous's "dual unity" will "again be raised." This predicted return of the gods, or rebirth of paganism, was part of Pessoa's vision of the Fifth Empire; the acceptance and celebration of "dual unities" between men, such as the one Hadrian knew with Antinous, was another aspect of that same vision.

Besides being a spokesman for some of his own ideas and theories, Pessoa's Hadrian also embodied something of his own, prodigiously *imaginary* experience of love. Since Antinous is dead, Hadrian's love can be only a memory of what was—a memory he idealizes and eternalizes. "Thy death has given me a higher lust," he announces to his lover's cold body, a "flesh-lust raging for eternity." Pessoa's own beloved—or

his potential desire for a beloved—is likewise lost, but in an indefinite past time, or in a realm outside of time. Pessoa is a Hadrian with
an enchanted memory who, in spite of never having held in his arms
a fleshly Antinous, succeeds in creating "Antinous," the immortal and
immortalizing poem.

✦

WHEN HE FIRST ADMITTED homoeroticism into his writing, in 1912–
1913, Pessoa was hesitantly following the lead of writers such as Shakespeare (in the sonnets) and Oscar Wilde. When, in 1915, he more boldly
embraced love between men as a poetic subject, he may have been somewhat inspired by the example of a new friend and literary compeer, Raul
Leal (1886–1964)—not by Leal's example as a writer but by his example
as a self-accepting homosexual. Eccentric to the point of seeming a bit
mad, the special mark of Leal's unusual character was absolute candor.
He was incapable of not saying exactly what he felt and being exactly
who he was. The son of a wealthy financier, he had grown up in luxury and was used to freely indulging his appetites. And so, after studying at Coimbra and working for several years as a lawyer in Lisbon, he
proceeded to squander most of the considerable inheritance left by his
father. His most profligate splurge was in France, where he lived in the
fall of 1913 and again in the early months of 1914, staying in the fanciest
hotels, dining at the finest restaurants, attending operas and concerts,
and purchasing silk pajamas and other finery. In Paris he met the Italian
writer Gabriele D'Annunzio, an extravagant Nietzschean decadent then
at the height of his popularity, as well as Marinetti, and he consorted
with that other Portuguese eccentric Santa Rita Pintor.[6]

In 1913, before going to the seaside resort of Biarritz and then on
to Paris, Leal had published *Liberdade transcendente* (*Transcendent Freedom*), his first major exposition of vertiginism, a philosophical concept
and utopian doctrine that would engross him for the next fifty years.
Vertiginism advocated the simultaneous experience of all moments and
all aspects in all of life, whereby the self attains to a divine, unified
awareness of everything in its sublime diversity—or something like that.
Pessoa, in a notebook he used in 1915, had this to say about his friend's
vertiginism: "The impossibility of explaining it explains it. It cannot be
defined—and that is its definition."[7]

It was probably after Leal returned to Lisbon in 1914 that he gave

Pessoa an autographed copy of *Transcendent Freedom*, and by the first half of 1915 they had become friends. Sá-Carneiro also befriended Leal but considered him a confused thinker and a weak writer. Pessoa was fascinated by Leal and by his ideas, even if they were confusing, and he was probably the one who pushed for his inclusion in *Orpheu 2*. The work Leal contributed, "Atelier: A Vertiginous Short Story," was inspired by *The Picture of Dorian Gray*. In that same year, 1915, Pessoa cast an astrological chart for Leal and noted that the moon in the House of Venus occupied the very same position in his and in Oscar Wilde's charts.[8]

Pessoa would cast three more charts for Raul Leal, whose sexuality, astrologically speaking, interested him only incidentally. In the case of Wilde, on the other hand, the practice of homosexuality and how it led to the writer's imprisonment were at the heart of his astrological considerations. In the first of the two charts he cast for Wilde, in 1915, Pessoa made a special note of the position of the subject's stars in 1895, the year of "scandal," as he noted in English, when the Irishman was tried and found guilty of "gross indecency." The second chart, from 1917, was accompanied by a biographical sketch in English. The last four items in the sketch read:

> Began paederasty as experiment—1886.
> Paederasty became a habit—1889.
> Sentenced to 2 years imprisonment—1895.
> Died in Paris 30 November 1900.

Pessoa connected the events in Wilde's life—and especially the disaster of 1895—to planetary positions on his chart. Turning over the page, he wrote, in English, "My case," followed by several astrological transits that compared his current situation with Wilde's before and after his trial and condemnation.[9]

According to Pessoa's biographical sketch, Wilde was thirty-two when he started dabbling in "pederasty."[*] The amateur astrologer was not consulting the stars to see whether he might be destined to imitate Wilde's example, but he does seem to have wondered if he might gain

---

[*] Pessoa was probably using this word, as he did on other occasions, to mean sex between males of whatever age. Wilde's first male lover, Robert Ross, was seventeen, but it was reportedly Ross who seduced Wilde.

a kind of Wildean notoriety, perhaps because of "Antinous." In a curious reversal of Freudian logic, Pessoa would comment in English, many
years later, that "Wilde repressed, owing to environment, the inverted
tendency in his works, so it cropped up all the stronger in his life."[10] This
is a fascinating if debatable point of view. Although there is nothing
explicitly homosexual in *The Picture of Dorian Gray*, it has obvious homoerotic undertones and was used against Wilde at his trial. Perhaps Pessoa agreed with James Joyce that "if he had had the courage to develop
the allusions in the book, it might have been better,"[11] but it is doubtful
that this would have caused the author's "inverted tendency" to be less
pronounced in his life. At any rate, the idea that this tendency was consciously repressed in his writing was corroborated by Wilde himself, who
stated in his preface to *Dorian Gray*: "To reveal art and conceal the man
is art's aim."

For the poet of heteronyms, the aim of art was neither to reveal nor
to conceal but to transform the self. It was in art and in his relationship
to art that Pessoa most readily took risks and was a porous, vulnerable,
sexual being.

# CHAPTER 38

**O**RPHEU 2, PUBLISHED IN LATE JUNE 1915, TRIED to capitalize on the succès de scandale of the magazine's first issue by being even more experimental and unhinged. Pessoa and Sá-Carneiro, whose names now appeared on the masthead as the editors in chief, no longer pitched it as a Portuguese-Brazilian publication but as a rival to other European avant-garde projects. Although Pessoa had failed to complete his announced manifesto on the "New Literature," he and his co-editor could count on Santa Rita Pintor's "four definitive futurist works" to elicit incomprehension and bourgeois scorn, thus establishing *Orpheu* as Portugal's premier forum for advanced art. To cement its reputation for "advanced" literature, the issue included a mischievous poem by Sá-Carneiro titled "Manicure," replete with free-floating typographical symbols, brand names, logotypes, and nonwords printed in variously sized letters and assorted typefaces. Pessoa would later claim that this poem, the only one of its kind by Sá-Carneiro, was a "semi-futurist" spoof made-to-order for the magazine.[1]

Like bait dangled before the covey of critics who had derided *Orpheu* 1 as a publication of lunatics, the second issue opened with a group of poems by Ângelo de Lima, who had been interned in Lisbon's psychiatric hospital since 1901. Unable to resist such a delectable tidbit, *A Capital* ran a front-page story, on June 28, with the predictable headline "Artists from Rilhafoles: Another Issue of *Orpheu*." Rilhafoles was the name of the mental hospital where Ângelo de Lima was living—and where he would die, six years later. The newspaper speculated that Mário de Sá-Carneiro, if he continued to be afflicted by the deliriums vented in his poem "Manicure," would soon become Lima's fellow inmate.

Reviewers of *Orpheu* 2, still pouncing on the alleged derangement of the magazine's contributors, did not read closely enough to detect the homoerotic story line of Raul Leal's "Atelier," which they would have considered morally objectionable as well as psychologically abnormal. Even less normal was a group of poems credited, in the byline, to an "anonymous author or authoress who goes by the name of Violante de Cysneiros." This female pseudonym was proposed by Pessoa to his friend Armando Côrtes-Rodrigues, who adapted his writing to make it fit the name. Becoming a poetic cross-dresser, he alternated pseudomemories of doing embroidery and dancing like Salomé with some existential musings that he borrowed from Pessoa and Sá-Carneiro but wrapped in the dulcet voice of Violante. The poems of the ambiguously gendered Armando-Violante were more than a gag, however. Pessoa had correctly surmised that his friend, assuming another personality, would write more interesting poetry.

✦

FERNANDO PESSOA'S CONTRIBUTION TO *Orpheu* 2 was "Slanting Rain," the sextet of intersectionist poems that Álvaro de Campos would later hail as his progenitor's finest literary moment. But the greatest contribution to the issue was Campos's own "Ode marítima" ("Maritime Ode"). This epic ode is also the greatest single poem ever written by Pessoa or any of his heteronyms. It is a mystery how Pessoa, during one of the outwardly and inwardly busiest periods of his life, was able to muster the creative concentration needed to produce its more than nine hundred perfectly concatenated lines.

In a passage for *The Book of Disquiet* from 1914, Pessoa wrote: "No one has the divine capacity [. . .] to write a masterpiece large enough to be great and perfect enough to be sublime."[2] He considered the case of Shakespeare's *King Lear*, which, since it is a large-scale work, naturally has a few flaws; and since it is indeed a great masterpiece, those flaws stand out as "monstrous defects." Perfection, according to the same passage, is only possible for works that can be written "in a single burst"—a brief lyric poem, for instance. The colossal "Maritime Ode" contradicted Pessoa's theory of composition, since it is too large to have possibly emerged in a single burst, and yet it contains no apparent flaws, let alone monstrous defects. It was written in April or May, when Pessoa was promoting *Orpheu* 1 and preparing *Orpheu* 2, when he was theorizing a Fifth Empire in which Portugal would dominate the world through its culture, when he wrote "Antinous," his longest and greatest poem about love between men, and when he began drafting essays in the name of

António Mora, the heteronym endowed with a thoroughly Greek sensibility in matters of aesthetics, politics, and religion.

"Maritime Ode" succeeded in poetically enacting most of the ideas and ideals then spinning around in the genius's head. It was the crowning jewel of the *Orpheu* project and yet repudiated, in a way, the avant-garde movements that the magazine seemed to represent. There are futurist touches in the poem, such as a description of "modern maritime life" as "clean, fit, and full of machines!" But the dominant setting of "Maritime Ode" is the classical sea of sailors, of pirates, and of poets as ancient as Homer—a sea indifferent to modern machinery. Composed of strophe, antistrophe, and epode,[3] like the odes of Pindar, it is a Greek performance, but Campos narrates his story on a deserted wharf in Lisbon, from where Portuguese caravels once set out on voyages of discovery.

The effect of the poem is cumulative, so that a quoted stanza or two would not begin to convey to the reader its splendor, but I will try to give an idea of its epic sweep, beginning with the opening section, the strophe, in which Álvaro de Campos talks in abstractions about Distance, Time, the Indefinite, and the Pure Faraway, remarking that his soul identifies with what he least sees. He transcends to a universe of idealized Forms and explicitly invokes Platonism in lines that allude to the Absolute Wharf, "unconsciously imitated" by the human builders of mundane wharfs such as the one in Lisbon where he muses about all these things. He considers those who spend their lives on ships to be "symbolic people" from another reality, and he knows himself to be a symbol as well. Everything is vaster and more interconnected than it seems.

The philosophical, visionary voyage of the ode's first section takes up 210 lines, at which point Campos, suddenly possessed by "the delirium of maritime things," finds himself hurtling "through deep and mysterious nights" of imagination, impelled by ecstatic desire. This second section, the ode's antistrophe, is a rhapsody about rough and gruff men who make their lives at sea, especially pirates, the roughest and cruelest, and Campos's dream is to be the woman who waits for them in ports, to be "raped, killed, cut and mauled" by them, to "feel them in a vast, passive ecstasy!" Desires of this sort are repeated over and over, in formulations like the following:

Kiss with cutlasses, whips and rage
My blissful carnal fear of belonging to you,

My masochistic yearning to submit to your fury,
To be the sentient, impassive object of your omnivorous cruelty,
Rulers, lords, emperors, pirates!
Ah, torture me,
Rip me apart!
And once I've been hacked into conscious pieces,
Strew me over the decks,
Scatter me across the waters, leave me
On the voracious beaches of islands!

Interspersed among these appeals are several sailor calls and shouts, sometimes printed in huge letters, as well as the refrain of a sea song taken from Robert Louis Stevenson's *Treasure Island*:

Fifteen men on the dead man's chest,
Yo-ho-ho and a bottle of rum.

Pessoa was quite fond of this novel as a boy in Durban, where we saw him loitering at the Portuguese consulate, intrigued by the "seafaring characters" who came by to obtain clearance for their ships to continue northward to the Mozambican port at Lourenço Marques. It is unlikely that young Fernando's fascination with sailors was directly, vividly sexual; it is even less likely that the fantasies of erotic brutality in "Maritime Ode" were transcriptions of Pessoa's sexual fantasies at the age of twenty-seven. They sprang out of his literary imagination, duly stimulated by what he himself, as noted earlier, referred to as a mild or latent case of "sexual inversion," an old-fashioned term that acquires new meaning when applied to ultraliterary Fernando Pessoa, a master at the art of inflecting, inverting, and transforming. The entire second section of "Maritime Ode," insofar as it corporealizes and sexualizes the imagination, is in fact an *inversion* of what occurs in the first section, where the imagination is spiritualized and given to metaphysical abstractions.

"Something in me snaps," announces Campos in the 620th line of the ode, and his frenzied evocations of pirate cruelty and masochistic lust abruptly give way to the ode's third and final section, the halcyon epode. Having lost interest both in the Pure Faraway and in the alienating dream of being a pure body abandoned to ardent desire, Campos's now "healthy, rugged, pragmatic imagination" is concerned only with what is close by and a part of daily life, with "immediate, modern, commercial, real things." It is as if a Portuguese version of the beastly Mr. Hyde had suddenly reverted to being a sedate and civilized Dr. Jekyll. As an adolescent in Durban, Pessoa had also read and loved Stevenson's *Strange Case of Dr. Jekyll and Mr. Hyde*, and as an adult he translated some of its pages into Portuguese.[4]

The strange case of Fernando Pessoa and Álvaro de Campos is more complex than that of Jekyll and Hyde. The well-traveled heteronym and irrepressible lover of sensations seems to represent the hidden, reverse side of his afraid-to-act creator, but Campos—as proven by "Maritime Ode" and "Salutation to Walt Whitman"—is himself a divided soul, often chafing against the urbane, well-mannered engineer he is on the outside and letting his thoughts run wild.

Like almost everything Pessoa published, "Maritime Ode" did not attract much admiration at the time, but it gained renown soon after his death, inspiring Portuguese actors to dramatically recite it in its entirety, sometimes from memory.[5] The poem's unique achievement is to enclose so much conflict, calmness, frantic energy, and uncensored desire within the structural framework of an ancient Greek ode, prompting an anonymous English-language critic invented by Pessoa to comment that "no German regiment ever had the inner discipline which underlies that composition." The same nameless critic aptly defined Campos as "a Walt Whitman with a Greek poet inside."[6]

With raw emotion, personal memory, fantasy, metaphysics, history, and eros all crewing the same ship on a voyage that both evokes and imaginatively surpasses the voyages of the Portuguese navigators, "Maritime Ode" had fulfilled, in the literary realm, Pessoa's dream of a Portuguese Renaissance, a national revival. But he longed to see the dream fulfilled in his country's political and social life, which meant that the Republic as it currently functioned—convulsively, without a coherent and consistent approach to policy—would have to be superseded. All of its ills, to his way of seeing, were incarnated in the head of the Democratic Party, Afonso Costa, whom he impulsively decided to attack, with the help of his liveliest heteronym.

◆

ALTHOUGH COSTA'S DEMOCRATS OVERWHELMINGLY won the general elections held on June 13, 1915, the same day that Pessoa turned twenty-seven, this only hardened their opponents and heightened the tension ensuing from the bloody revolt that had toppled Pimenta de Castro exactly one month earlier, and there were rumors of a counterrevolution in the making. On the evening of July 3, less than a week after *Orpheu* 2 went on sale, a short circuit on a Lisbon streetcar produced a resounding boom that caused one of its passengers—Afonso Costa, who, like most republicans, used public transportation—to suspect an attempt on his life. He jumped out a window, cracked his skull on the pavement, and was rushed to the hospital, his life hanging by a thread. On July 5, the staunchly Democratic *A Capital* informed its readers that the party leader's condition had improved but was still precarious. Elsewhere on the same page, a brief article reported that the "group of harmless futurists" responsible for *Orpheu* was planning to stage a "dynamic drama" titled *Drunkenness* and performed only by legs, with the curtain rising no higher than the actors' knees.*

The next day, July 6, Álvaro de Campos wrote a letter to the editor stating that the information in the article was inaccurate: the planned play would indeed show only legs, but it was titled *The Journalists* and would be performed by the twelve legs of three Portuguese members of the profession. Campos added that, while he normally objected to the term "futurism" being applied to *Orpheu*, "it would be in bad taste to repudiate links to the futurists at such a deliciously mechanical moment in which even Divine Providence avails itself of streetcars to convey its lofty lessons."

*A Capital* did not publish the complete letter, just the outrageous last sentence that called Costa's streetcar disaster an act of divine providence. "The Poets of *Orpheu* Reveal Themselves to Be Malicious Individuals" announced the headline of the paper's indignant front-page notice. Álvaro de Campos had gone too far. Anxious to save *Orpheu*, Mário de Sá-Carneiro immediately wrote his own letter to the editor, pointing out that Campos did not speak for the magazine, which was strictly literary, but had acted on his own initiative. *A Capital* published Sá-Carneiro's letter and reported that José de Almada Negreiros had passed by its offices to declare himself in complete disagreement with Álvaro de

---

* This precisely describes the scenario of Marinetti's *Le basi* (*The Bases*), which no one, in all likelihood, was seriously thinking of staging in Lisbon.

Campos. It also informed its readers that the gentleman responsible for all the ruckus was a "literary pseudonym of Sr. Fernando Pessoa," who had apparently admitted to his friends that he was drunk when he wrote the offending letter.

Álvaro de Campos had at least one supporter, and even a collaborator, in Raul Leal. On the same day that Afonso Costa took his near fatal dive out of a streetcar window, the founder, prophet, and only disciple of vertiginism coincidentally published a densely printed broadside in which he castigated the Democratic leader for "sullying [the world] with the fetid exhalations of his soul, poisoning it with an outpour of pus that is his decomposing soul, a fatal cancer full of perverse torments." *The Sinister Band: An Appeal to Portuguese Intellectuals*, which Leal distributed in cafés and on the Lisbon-Cascais train line, contained twenty-five hundred additional words of similarly grisly invective against Costa and his supporters that alternated with jeremiads against the Republic and predictions of a brighter, vertiginous future for Portugal. A reporter for *O Mundo* (*The World*), the Democratic Party's official newspaper, published a long article making fun of the manifesto's extravagant prose and its peculiar author, whom he described as a young man with "a static, semicomatose air, suggestive of a seminarian escaped from his cell," his face "the color of spoiled milk." The reporter pointedly noted that Leal had signed his tirade as a "Contributor to *Orpheu*."

The *O Mundo* article came out on July 5, the day before *A Capital* denounced Álvaro de Campos's callous suggestion that Afonso Costa's cracked skull was the will of God. Sá-Carneiro, in his letter to *A Capital* of the seventh, did not criticize Campos's suggestion; he merely insisted that the engineer's views—and, by implication, Raul Leal's—could not be imputed to the rest of the *Orpheu* group. And Almada Negreiros, while deploring Campos's remark, downplayed the gravity of the offense by blaming it on Pessoa's having had a little too much wine. But other voices from *Orpheu* reacted more forcefully to their colleagues' aggressive affirmations. In a jointly signed letter to *O Mundo*,[7] Alfredo Guisado and António Ferro (the nominal managing editor of *Orpheu*) condemned Campos's and Leal's affronts to Afonso Costa, a statesman they held in "the highest esteem," and they announced that they were severing ties with *Orpheu*.

The idea had gotten around that *Orpheu* was a literary arm of monarchism, since two of its contributors—Raul Leal and Santa Rita Pintor—

were indeed fervent monarchists, but Guisado and Ferro both supported Costa and his Democrats, the most powerful of the three republican parties. Pessoa still identified as a republican, although without belonging to any party and especially not the so-called Democratic one. The conflicting political stances of the *Orpheu* contributors posed no problem as long as they were never mentioned in connection with the magazine, but Pessoa had let his loathing of Afonso Costa get the better of Álvaro de Campos.

✦

CAMPOS, BY WISHING EVIL on Costa, had put more than the survival of *Orpheu* in jeopardy. After *A Capital* exposed Campos as a "pseudonym" and Pessoa as the real author of his unkind words, the unmasked poet found himself suddenly, directly vulnerable to reprisals. A group of Democratic vigilantes—perhaps from the secret police known as White Ants—came looking for him at Irmãos Unidos, the restaurant owned by Guisado's parents and frequented by the *Orpheu* group. Pessoa would later boast, with some exaggeration, that he had risked being lynched.[8] At most they would have roughed him up, smashing his eyeglasses and breaking a couple of ribs, but they did not find the offender, who had been warned to stay out of sight for a few days. He presumably instructed his landlady, whose ironing business faced the street, to tell nobody that he was in his rented room at the back, lying low.

Meanwhile, yet another *Orpheu* writer threatened to defect: Armando Côrtes-Rodrigues, who had returned to Lisbon from the Azores in May, in order to finish and defend his thesis for a degree at the University of Lisbon. On July 9, *A Capital* published a letter in which he joined Guisado and Ferro in repudiating the "political ideas" of Álvaro de Campos and Raul Leal.

Chastised by his brethren from *Orpheu*, Álvaro de Campos was nevertheless unrepentant. He drafted a second letter to the editor of *A Capital* in which he not only refused to retract his words that had exulted in the life-threatening mishap of Afonso Costa, he reaffirmed them, saying that this "sinister leader" of the Democratic Party, whom he blamed for "the state of anarchy, desolation and sadness in which Portuguese souls are languishing," did not deserve compassion. Costa was wildly popular among his party faithful, but a significant swath of the electorate shared

Pessoa-Campos's frustration with the present state of the Republic and would have nodded their heads approvingly as they read this sentence:

> I therefore want to stress—and in doing so I know I speak for many of the Portuguese, for the oppressed Catholics, for the aggrieved middle classes, for peaceful citizens assaulted on the street, for all those whom Pimenta de Castro represented—that the only thing about Costa's disaster that does not delight me is his recovery, which unfortunately seems to be confirmed.

Fortunately for Pessoa, the letter was not completed. Had it been received and published by the newspaper, it would truly have placed his life in great peril.

◆

MÁRIO DE SÁ-CARNEIRO, ON the other hand, never had anything to fear, since he was not the least bit interested in politics. And yet all of a sudden, like a man in deep trouble, he absconded from Lisbon on July 11, 1915, telling no one except Pessoa that he was leaving. His destination, not surprisingly, was Paris. The brouhaha surrounding *Orpheu* and the (mostly superficial) rifts that had arisen among its contributors had nothing to do with his departure. Far from wanting to put *Orpheu* behind him, Sá-Carneiro, in the letters he sent en route to and upon his arrival in Paris, implored Pessoa to send him the latest news about their beloved project. How was the magazine selling? What further reviews and references to it had appeared in the press? In a letter of July 17, he mentioned that a false report of Afonso Costa's death in Spanish and French newspapers had briefly made him fear for the life of "Fernando Álvaro Pessoa de Campos," and he asked whether Raul Leal was showing his face in public. Both men, it seems, were still in danger for having publicly reviled the leader of the Democrats.

What prompted Sá-Carneiro's precipitous departure from Lisbon was a personal matter, which he alluded to in another letter that month, but only for the purpose of asking Pessoa never to make the slightest reference to it, whatever "it" was. Probably it had to do with his stepmother, Maria Cardoso de Sá-Carneiro, whom his widowed father had met in a Lisbon nightclub when Mário was twelve or thirteen. Mário and Maria developed an unusually close relationship, particularly after his father—her common-law husband—went to Mozambique to manage its railroads, in the summer of 1914. Mário's surviving letters and cards to Maria reveal that something he did in June 1915 infuriated her and permanently strained their relationship, despite his attempts to assuage her and earn her forgiveness.

Whatever the reason that caused him to decamp, Sá-Carneiro was only too glad to return to his much cherished and idealized Paris. Foreign correspondents published rather gloomy accounts of life in the French capital almost one full year into the war—subdued and sparsely populated streets, shuttered shops, women dressed in black, wounded soldiers, makeshift hospitals[9]—but the monumentally self-absorbed Sá-Carneiro saw only what he wanted to see. In letters sent to Pessoa and to José Pacheco in mid-July, he wrote that the cafés were bustling and the streets still full of elegantly dressed women, without many people in mourning to be seen, and no drabness, no air of sadness. It was the same Paris as before but slowed down, diminished, as if dazed by a fever, imbuing it with a novel charm. What most impressed Mário was Paris by night, its gaslights now turned low or turned off, "in futurist fear of the huge imperial dirigibles" (i.e., the bomb-dropping zeppelins of the Germans), and yet people in the habit of keeping late hours still jostled on the hard-to-see streets of the darkened metropolis, "a city outside of space and time." It occurred to him that he might develop his description of wartime Paris into a prose piece for the next issue of *Orpheu*.

The only thing about Lisbon that Mário missed was Fernando's company, and yet it seemed to him that their friendship was even closer, stronger, when they were far apart. So he wrote on August 22, repeating the idea in a letter sent two days later: "Here as in Lisbon—but here more intimately—you are my sole companion." It was the same for Pessoa. Their epistolary exchange was like a small, quiet, and cozy room, where there was no one and nothing to disturb them—not even their own physical presence. But while letter writing conferred on them a soothing feeling of intimacy, their literary trajectories were fatally diverging.

# CHAPTER 39

**C**ATCHING HIS BREATH, REFLECTING ON ALL THAT had happened in recent months, Pessoa must have metaphorically if not literally shaken his head in disbelief. Like a bombastic encore to the stunning eruption the previous year of Alberto Caeiro, Álvaro de Campos, and Ricardo Reis, the first half of 1915 had seen the sky open up through astrology, Portugal's literary milieu jolted out of its complacency by the seismic shock of *Orpheu*, and the nation's history and role in the world assume new proportions thanks to Atlantism, the Fifth Empire doctrine, and the philosophical and sociological deliberations of António Mora. But the most remarkable recent development in Pessoa's universe had been the massive expansion of Álvaro de Campos, who took his creator to new poetic heights, in "Maritime Ode," as well as to dangerous depths—through his propensity to make brazen pronouncements, placing Pessoa at risk of bodily harm. This might sound like overstatement, since Campos's magnificent poem and his reckless letter to the editor that rejoiced over a political leader's brush with death were in fact written by Fernando Pessoa, but Pessoa could not have written what he wrote and in the voice that he wrote it without the invented personality of the naval engineer and sensationist poet.

Pessoa had always supposed that his irresistible inclination to write as if he were someone else was rooted in his psychology. Now it occurred to him that it might also have been inscribed in the stars. On July 24, 1915, he wrote to Alfred H. Barley, an editor of the London-based journal *Modern Astrology* and the author of astrological books and manuals, asking him to kindly send information on the cusps and planets needed for constructing the horoscope of Francis Bacon. Astrology was one of the tools used by certain "Baconians" to prove that Bacon was the real author of Shakespeare's plays, but Pessoa was only marginally interested in what the stars had to say on that matter. His main interest, he wrote Barley, was to see what in Bacon's horoscope registers his peculiar characteristic of being able to write in different styles (a fact which even non-Baconians admit) and his general faculty of transpersonalisation.

I possess (in what degree, or with what quality, it is not for me to say) the characteristic to which I am alluding. I am an author, and have always found it impossible to write in my own personality; I have always found myself, consciously or unconsciously, assuming the character of someone who does not exist, and through whose imagined agency I write. I wish to study to what this may be due by position or aspect and am therefore interested in the horoscope of the man who is known to have possessed this faculty in an extraordinary degree.[1]

It was not only Bacon's stylistic "transpersonalisation" that fascinated Pessoa; it was also his capacity to excel in various disciplines and to accomplish so much that was useful and enduring. A philosopher, scientist, statesman, and essayist, Bacon has had an influence on modern Western society almost as great as that of Shakespeare on the modern individual's sense of self. Pessoa identified closely with Shakespeare, whose transpersonalizing talent was applied exclusively to literature, and he had no doubt that the playwright and poet was the greater genius, but he shared Bacon's commitment to educating, enlightening, and edifying the human species. It's no wonder that, as mentioned earlier, Pessoa was so attracted to the theory that the two Elizabethans were one and the same man. It was as if the spirits of Shakespeare and Bacon kept vying in Pessoa, with the latter lately getting the upper hand.

✦

NOT FOR THE FIRST time, Pessoa was tormented by the conviction that his genius should not serve literature only. In August he wrote Sá-Carneiro in Paris that a new personal crisis was making him call into question the value of all the work he had done so far. This was a resurgence of the crisis he had experienced in late 1914, recounted in his long letter to Armando Côrtes-Rodrigues. Forgoing the religious vocabulary he had used with his Azorean friend, he explained to Sá-Carneiro that the creation of beauty was too small an ambition for the talent he had been given. His literature and his literary "others"—especially Alberto Caeiro, Ricardo Reis, and Álvaro de Campos—needed to serve a higher purpose. He described his vision of a Fifth Empire in which Portugal would overcome its political infighting and become a model of civilizational progress, and he revealed the existence of his alter ego António Mora, now titled *Dr.* António Mora, whose job it was to help him convert his vision into reality by bringing the best aspects of Greek civilization to bear on the modern world. Pessoa wanted, like Prometheus, to be a benefactor of humanity. Not by coincidence, it was around this time that he set himself—or rather, Ricardo Reis—the improbable task of translating *Prometheus Bound* from the Greek. Pessoa did not know Greek; Reis supposedly did.[2]

On August 24, the same day he received Pessoa's letter, Sá-Carneiro wrote a generous reply, pointing out that his friend was *himself* a varied humanity, an entire civilization, a sovereign nation. He recalled that the self-dispersed protagonist of his short story "I Myself the Other," written in late 1913 and published in *Sky on Fire*, wonders out loud at a certain point, "Have I myself become a nation?" The story was Mário's, but the question prophetically pertained to Fernando, and the answer was a resounding yes. And that "nation," wrote Sá-Carneiro, included not only Pessoa's invented personalities—Caeiro, Campos, Reis, Mora—but also and especially his inner intellectual life, with its vast array of political, social, and spiritual ideas and aspirations.

Reading and rereading the pages of Pessoa's letter detailing his "crisis"—which was after all a crisis of abundance—Sá-Carneiro could take pleasure in the knowledge that he was at least partly responsible for that creative profusion, since they were close literary collaborators. At the same time, however, he felt more acutely than ever his own limitations: "Yes, my dear friend—you are the Nation, Civilization, and I am something like the great Royal Hall, covered with rugs and full of color, emeralds and satins, gilt surfaces and marquetry. And I wouldn't even wish to be more than that." Beauty, which was not enough for Pessoa, was the only thing that mattered to Sá-Carneiro—"beauty reverberating with flashes and highlights, infinite mirrors, a thousand shimmering colors, lots of lacquer and lots of gold: theater of magic shows and grand finales with balls of fire and naked bodies." That, and only that, was what he aspired to in his life and work.

Pessoa's new and passionate interest in astrology was connected to his disillusion with the creation of literary artifacts for their own sake. In his letters to Mário, he talked more openly than he had in person about the extent of that new interest, mentioning the astrological charts he had cast for *Orpheu* and for Mário himself. Sá-Carneiro was curious about what the stars had to say, chiefly because Pessoa was the stargazer. He marveled at his ultrarational friend's ability to pursue astrology, to create heteronyms who thought in such different ways and wrote in such different styles, to advocate a revival of Greek paganism, to dream of a Portuguese Fifth Empire, and to be in himself an entire nation, or even a universe. Sá-Carneiro believed in nothing, nor could he act as if he believed. For him there was no God, no transcendent soul, no purpose or meaning. There was just glitter and gold—bits of beauty that he would cultivate for as long as they could still enchant or at least distract him.

✦

WHAT ASTOUNDED SÁ-CARNEIRO ABOUT Fernando Pessoa's "Inner World"—as he called it in his August 24 letter, capitalizing the two words[3]—was not only its boundless extent but also the way everything fit together. And this was truer than he knew. Astrology, for instance, was more than a predictive tool or personality detector; it was a mirror that validated Pessoa's opinions and theories about himself, other people, real events, and speculative phenomena, such as the birth of a Fifth Empire governed by Portugal and ushered in by the symbolic return of King Sebastian. Raphael Baldaya, Pessoa's astrologer heteronym, confirmed all these details in a set of "astrological considerations" about the five world empires prophesied in the Book of Daniel. He calculated that the imminent Fifth Empire would be ruled by Aquarius, and King Sebastian, conveniently enough, was an Aquarian. The country at the forefront of the Fifth Empire, according to Baldaya, would be ruled by Pisces, and Pisces, it so happens, is the zodiac sign of Portugal.[4]

Half a century before it became a popularized notion, Fernando Pessoa, with the help of Baldaya, had already envisaged an Age of Aquarius in which poetry would prevail over politics and military might. I have already suggested that Pessoa's logically constructed prophecies were their own reward, not requiring literal fulfillment to be spiritually valid, but the poet was not just a visionary. He tried, in his own peculiar way, to promote and prepare Portugal for its role as the cultural pacesetter of the glorious age he foretold. His promotional efforts included *All about Portugal*, the manual for tourists and foreign businessmen that he outlined (but never actually wrote) in 1915. To prepare Portugal for its Fifth

Empire future, Pessoa drew up grandiose plans for a multifaceted company called Cosmópolis, whose ten separate divisions included Business
Services (ideas for company and brand names, outfitting of commercial
establishments, letter writing, translations), Literary Services (library
research, copy editing, proofreading, typing), Advertising, Legal Services, Publishing, and a Real Estate Agency.

These and other ideas for Cosmópolis fill up seven pages of a notebook
used by Pessoa in the early months of 1915. He even drew a sketch for
a company logotype: a globe diagonally inscribed with the name cosmópolis. It was an original and in some ways ingenious project, which
would allow Pessoa to put a number of his own skills to profitable use—
maybe he could even pay off some old debts—while helping Portugal
get ready to lead the world by first of all making it more vibrant and
prosperous, more like the rest of Europe. Some of Pessoa's ideas for moving the country in that direction were simple enough. The Cosmópolis
headquarters, for instance, would provide a reading room for public use,
and its publishing division would print how-to pamphlets such as *How to
Write a Business Letter* and *How to Make a Window Display*.

Whereas *Orpheu* sought to stimulate the intellectual and artistic mentality of Portugal, Cosmópolis would foster culture in the broadest sense
of the word—in the realm of commerce, in social interactions, and even
in matters of personal taste and aesthetic sensibility. It would also promote Portugal abroad, with one of the company's ten divisions being
exclusively dedicated to disseminating information about the country
to foreigners.[5]

◆

Cosmópolis would do this and would do that *if* Pessoa could
find investors willing to finance it, but money and credit were hard to
come by, and the project had to remain on hold for the duration of the
war. During the early months of the fighting, life in Portugal had carried on as usual, but in 1915 the nation's economy began to deteriorate,
with most sectors affected and poor people hit the hardest. The country depended heavily on imported wheat, which became increasingly
expensive due to the perils of shipping across oceans full of mines and
submarines. Mobs in Lisbon attacked bakeries when the price of bread
was raised in March, but the cost of wheat from America and Australia
would only keep climbing.[6] On May 7, 1915, a German torpedo sank

the *Lusitania*, killing almost twelve hundred passengers and crew members traveling from New York to Liverpool—a grim reminder of how all ships, military or commercial, sailed at their own risk.

Portugal's burgeoning foreign debt, its occasional food shortages, and the ongoing threat of insurgency movements among discontented republicans as well as monarchists did not lessen politicians' appetite for entering the war, particularly if they were Democrats. With their party back in power, a campaign was launched to convince a reticent public that Portugal should fight on the side of the Allies. Pressure to declare support for the Allied cause was pointedly brought to bear on writers such as Pessoa through "Portuguese Writers and the War," an opinion piece published in the July 10 issue of *O Mundo* by João de Barros, a poet and a high-ranking official in the Ministry of Education. Calling on his peers to join with him in forming a "League for the Allies," Barros used a racial rationale to justify his urgent appeal. Portugal and France, he argued, were both "Latin nations," whose people shared a sensibility at odds with German culture, which was admirable but practically reducible to "method" and "discipline."

Pessoa drafted a reply to Barros's appeal, acknowledging that Portugal had no viable option but to support the Allies, even if it remained officially neutral, but he maintained that his and his compatriots' "spiritual solidarity" should lie with the German empire. Resorting to ideas contained in António Mora's *Dissertation in Favor of Germany*, he argued that this nation's imperialistic impulse was reminiscent of the "civilizational" work accomplished by Portugal through its overseas discoveries and maritime empire. He also pointed to the close parallel between the legend of Frederick Barbarossa—the twelfth-century German king and Holy Roman Emperor who, some claimed, did not really drown during the Third Crusade but was asleep in a mountain cave and would return to restore Germany to its former glory—and the myth of King Sebastian's triumphal return to Portugal. Rejecting the Latin kinship theory, Pessoa contended that Germans had strong affinities with the Portuguese, insofar as they were "temperamentally sentimental, adaptable," and capable of greatness only when "directed and disciplined by a strong aristocracy."[7]

Had Pessoa sent his letter of rebuttal to *O Mundo*, the suggestion that the Portuguese people were like Germans and needed to be ruled by an aristocracy would no doubt have prompted some fellow writers to protest, but he wasn't motivated enough to finish it. He had already claimed, in a recently published article,[8] that the Portuguese resembled the Germans, which he probably didn't believe, except while arguing that he did, and now he let the argument drop.

✦

EVEN THE LIFE-AND-DEATH BUSINESS of war—some twenty million people would perish in World War I—served Pessoa as an opportunity to practice his reasoning skills, independent of which side he supported or how much blood was being shed. The war, if properly exploited, might also provide some supplemental income. On July 15 he posted a letter to A. W. Gamage, Ltd., in London:

> Gentlemen,
>     Having invented two games, which may be called war-games, to be played with dice and on special boards, I beg to inquire whether you are interested in this subject and whether, therefore, I could send them to you, with complete and explicit rules and drawing of the boards. [. . .]
>     I have said that they may be called war-games, but you must understand this as meaning that, if necessary, they can be, for selling purposes, given out as referring, say, to the present War. As a matter of fact, almost all games, since they are contests, can be called war-games; draughts and chess are prominent instances.

Arthur Walter Gamage was the founder of the Gamage's department store, which opened in 1878 and remained in business until 1972. The store sold seemingly everything except tombstones and was especially famous for its huge selection of games and toys. Strategy and Opposition were the names of Pessoa's two war games, and for the first one he drew up a set of detailed rules, but Gamage and his associates expressed no interest in learning more about either of them.[9]

Pessoa had invented other board games he hoped to sell, including Table-Cricket, Table-Football, and an astrological game called Aspects. Astrology of the more learned variety was, of course, Pessoa's own favorite game, a kind of cosmic version of chess. In 1915 he took some notes on recent solar and lunar eclipses for a work (in Portuguese) titled *The War and Astrology*, which he hoped to market under the name of Raphael

Baldaya.[10] Álvaro de Campos, in "Martial Ode," vividly realized the atrocities of war. Fernando Pessoa, focusing on its causes and consequences, saw war as a geopolitical contest—atrocious but inevitable, written in the stars.

The debate about Portugal's noninterventionist stance carried on, but in reality the country was already fighting an erratic, undeclared war in Africa, where its expeditionary troops in Angola and Mozambique skirmished with forces from Germany's neighboring colonies. The largest clash so far had taken place in Naulila, on Angola's southern border, where in mid-December 1914 the Portuguese lost about seventy troops and were forced to retreat northward. Francisco Aragão, a twenty-four-year-old lieutenant who was wounded in the battle and had been taken prisoner for seven months, was given a hero's welcome when he returned to Portugal in August 1915, but Pessoa did not share in the enthusiasm.

In a speech delivered in Madeira, his first point of arrival, Aragão blamed his country's political indecision for the defeat at Naulila, lambasted the ex-dictator Pimenta de Castro for having maintained neutrality instead of coming out against the Germans, and made an impassioned plea for Portugal to enter the war in Europe.[11] Infuriated at what he considered crass ignorance and impudence, particularly with respect to the young lieutenant's criticism of Pimenta de Castro, Pessoa wrote a flurry of pages for a pamphlet, *Letter to a Stupid Hero*, which he planned to sign with his own name and as an "Editor of *Orpheu*." Mindful of all the fuss lately generated by Campos's letter to the editor of *A Capital* and Raul Leal's broadside that lashed out at Afonso Costa, he decided to consult with Sá-Carneiro, who diplomatically wrote back on August 31 that the pamphlet was a "magnificent" idea but that to actually publish it would be "to cast pearls before swine." Pessoa deferred to his friend's advice and abandoned the pamphlet.

✦

ALTHOUGH MÁRIO WANTED TO avoid political controversy in the magazine, he was all for provoking its readers with the unconventional and unexpected. Of the possible contributions under consideration for *Orpheu* 3, he endorsed the idea of including something by Numa de Figueiredo, an Angolan friend of Pessoa who wrote in French, since to publish "a *Portuguese black* who writes in *French*" would be a "record of cosmopolitanism," and he was even more eager to publish a group of "prose poems à la Wilde" unambiguously titled "Pederasties," by a friend of Almada Negreiros. About this latter contribution, Sá-Carneiro wrote Pessoa in his August 31 letter: "we have to get this, even if it's weak." Long before professors of literature began pressing for diversity and multiculturalism, it was as if the co-editors of *Orpheu* were determined—perhaps not entirely in jest—to challenge the predominance of heteronormative, white male authors. As mentioned earlier, *Orpheu* 2 had already included not only Raul Leal's homoerotic short story but also some poems by a female author, Violante de Cysneiros, who was not after all female.

Pessoa, meanwhile, was hoping to enlist a contribution from the still obscure Camilo Pessanha, whose poetry he had dreamed of publishing since the founding of his short-lived Ibis press. Pessanha, who had been living in Macau since 1894, was twenty years older than the *Orpheu* poets and wrote symbolist poetry in a style more in keeping with the nineteenth than the twentieth century, but its sheer grace and beauty made it timeless. Using *Orpheu* stationery and in his capacity as co-editor, Pessoa wrote Pessanha a letter, which probably did not reach Macau before September 10, when the addressee—unbeknown to Pessoa—set sail in the opposite direction for a six-month holiday in Portugal.[12]

Pessoa's own contribution to *Orpheu* 3 was to include, as in the first two issues, an exuberant poetic ode signed by Álvaro de Campos, although he was undecided about which one. He was initially inclined toward "Time's Passage," which he began writing in August, but most of this large and often breathtaking poem would not actually be committed to paper until the following year. Hundreds of lines for the equally ambitious "Salutation to Walt Whitman" had already been written, and that was the Campos poem he finally settled on for the magazine's third issue—if indeed there would be a third issue.

A September 13 letter of Sá-Carneiro abruptly informed his best friend that *Orpheu*, awash in debt, could not continue. Presented with a bill from the printers for 560,000 reis, or about $390 U.S. (equivalent, in purchasing power, to $10,000 today), Carlos Augusto de Sá-Carneiro had written his son an enraged letter from Mozambique. It is understandable that he lost his temper, and yet *Orpheu* was not, in truth, all that ruinous a venture. Close to half of the printers' bill pertained to Mário's collection of short stories, *Sky on Fire*, published in April, and the revenue from sales, whether of the magazine or his story collection, was not applied to production costs; it all went to Mário, who used it to pay for fine clothes and fine food, the best seats at the best shows, and the manicurist (he was exceedingly proud of his beautiful, pampered hands).

Fernando insisted with Mário that *Orpheu* was not finished, that they would find financing elsewhere. As if by magic, Santa Rita Pintor, who had published four of his artworks as photographic inserts in *Orpheu 2*, announced that he could underwrite part or all of *Orpheu 3*. It was not a magic that appealed to the co-editors, who were averse to making Santa Rita the featured artist for a second time in a row, which was the minimum he would demand. Actually, his initial proposal was to become one of the editors, but he quickly lowered—or at least adjusted—his expectations, asking only that the issue include reproductions of works by two artists: himself and Pablo Picasso.

Toward the end of September, Pessoa took the precaution of officially registering *Orpheu* as the literary property of Mário de Sá-Carneiro, who had given him carte blanche to deal with Santa Rita Pintor as he thought best. Undeterred, the rascally artist decided to launch a magazine titled *3*. Since a gigantic *2* occupied most of the cover of *Orpheu 2* (probably designed by Almada Negreiros), a magazine called *3* and with a similar cover would be interpreted by most as a continuation. Exasperated, the two friends decided that they might as well accept Santa Rita's invitation to contribute work to the new publication.

Just several weeks earlier, Pessoa had enthusiastically drafted a publicity flyer for *Orpheu 3*, apprising readers that *Orpheu* was "the only bridge between Portugal and Europe" as well as the only good reason "for Portugal to exist as an independent nation." Now he drafted a flyer announcing the temporary suspension of the magazine, due chiefly to the increased cost of paper. This was a valid enough excuse, since the war had made paper and just about everything else more expensive, and the war also made people less willing to spend on nonessentials such as culture. *Blast*, the London-based magazine of the vorticists, was in a similar predicament. Its second issue, the "War Number," had come out in July, several weeks after *Orpheu 2*, but its announced third issue stalled indefinitely.[13] Pessoa acquired both issues of *Blast* in early August and seems not to have been much impressed by the poetry contributions of T. S. Eliot and Ezra Pound (the poems they contributed were not among their best). More to his liking was Pound's manifesto on the vortex, included in *Blast*'s first issue. Pound wrote that movements such as futurism, which he defined as "only an accelerated sort of impressionism," were "the CORPSES OF VORTICES" and that "Marinetti is a corpse." Pessoa underlined the three quoted phrases.

*Blast* and vorticism, it turned out, were themselves corpses, unable to survive beyond their declarations and manifestos, and *Orpheu* had entered a coma that would endure for two years, while Pessoa kept valiantly trying to awaken it. Santa Rita's announced magazine, *3*, died quietly while still in the planning phase.

# CHAPTER 40

W ITH *ORPHEU*'S FUTURE SUDDENLY IN DOUBT, Pessoa found himself torn by conflicting impulses. Part of him wanted to keep the *Orpheu* movement going, with or without the magazine, but another part urged greater concentration on his own writing, and on getting it published. Astrology, on the other hand, led him to inquire about the true nature of the relations of all things. And there were his sexual impulses, which he kept postponing and which kept asserting themselves. Like the character in a novel in search of the plot, Pessoa carried on, busy but directionless.

Precisely because its future was uncertain, Pessoa acted quickly to extract some promotional benefit from *Orpheu*'s first two issues. Setting his sights on the United Kingdom, he used the magazine to call attention to the Portuguese sensationists—as he now preferred to call the *Orpheu* contributors, rather than intersectionists or swampists—and he used his position as the publication's co-editor to tout himself as an up-and-coming Portuguese poet who also happened to write in English. Pessoa may have been the only person in Portugal to acquire copies of *Blast* and to make contact with the editorial staff of *The Egoist*, a London-based review that published many of the decade's most notable modernist writers, including Pound, Eliot, James Joyce, Marianne Moore, H. D. (Hilda Doolittle), William Carlos Williams, and D. H. Lawrence (the majority of whom also contributed to *Poetry*, published in Chicago). After an initial query about a poetry-in-translation series announced in the summer of 1915, Pessoa drafted a follow-up letter to *The Egoist* that got closer to what he really wanted to know: whether the editors might consider publishing Portuguese sensationist poetry in English translation.

Dear Sir,

    [. . .] By this mail I am sending you the second number of our quarterly *Orpheu*, representing the Sensationist Movement in recent Portuguese literature. The circumstance that the first number sold out in three weeks prevents me from sending you a copy also of that. You are probably unacquainted with Portuguese, and the second number of *Orpheu* draws perhaps too much, not on Futurist feelings, but on Futurist processes, to please you. Yet the Portuguese Sensationist movement is a thing quite apart from Futurism and having no connection therewith.[1]

At the end of the typed draft—unfinished, but perhaps similar to a letter he actually sent—Pessoa jotted down the titles of some poems he had in mind for the translation series, including three published in *Orpheu* 2: Sá-Carneiro's "Manicure," his own "Slanting Rain," and Álvaro de Campos's "Maritime Ode." He made a partial translation into English of this last poem, which he titled "Naval Ode."

On October 23, 1915, Pessoa sent sixteen of his English poems to John Lane, the publisher of *Blast* and also of a diversified book list that included contemporary poetry. In a cover letter that mentioned both his editorship of *Orpheu* and his leadership of the Portuguese sensationist movement, the hopeful poet inquired whether Lane "would be disposed to publish a book the substance of which is precisely on the lines which these poems represent." Their occasional "eccentricities and peculiarities of expression," he cautioned, were not owing to his being a foreigner but to their "extreme pantheistic attitude," which led to some unusual turns of phrase.

Pessoa's cautionary warning smacks of excuse making for infelicities in his English syntax, but "pantheistic" was indeed the right word to characterize the spirit of *The Mad Fiddler*, the book he hoped to publish. One of the sample poems sent to John Lane, "Fiat Lux," states that in each thing there is an "inner infinity" and that the visible, sunlit world is but "the night unfurled." God is the implicit substance of all things, though "substance" is only a manner of speaking, as becomes clear when we reach the poem's crux, in the penultimate stanza:

Nothing: all,
And I centre of to recall,
  As if Seeing were a god.

According to this elucidation of the Pessoan dialectic of "everything is nothing" and "nothing is everything," there is no *substance*; there is vision, for those who see, and the vision is a Platonic re-vision, or recollection.

Pessoa wrote "Fiat Lux" in February 1915; that August he wrote a poem called "The Mad Fiddler"; in September he drew up a tentative outline for a book of his English poems with this same title;[2] and in October he was already looking for a publisher, even though he was still shaping the book and would continue to add poems to it for the next year and a half. No sooner had he received a rejection letter from Lane, who was nevertheless encouraging, than he decided to submit the same set of sample poems—accompanied, this time, by a copy of *Orpheu 2*— to another publishing house.[3] He also drafted several letters intended for well-known literary critics from Britain and Ireland, such as George Saintsbury and Edward Dowden, soliciting their frank appraisal of whatever poems he might have enclosed—either some Shakespearean sonnets or some "pantheistic" poems from *The Mad Fiddler*.[4] What he secretly wanted, of course, was to be discovered by a critic who would help launch his career as an English poet.

✦

IN THE HYPERACTIVE YEAR of 1915, Pessoa also found time to translate C. W. Leadbeater's *A Textbook of Theosophy* and Annie Besant's *The Ideals of Theosophy*. He took on the job to make money, knowing nothing about Theosophy when he started, but in mid-November, while checking the page proofs for the book by Besant, he became obsessed by the possibility that the doctrines he had translated might actually be true. It surprised him that, at the age of twenty-seven, he could still be completely disconcerted by a new religious or philosophical system, but that was what happened in the case of Theosophy. So he explained to his friend Sá-Carneiro, in an unfinished letter dated December 6, 1915. He was impressed by "the notion of power, of dominion, of *higher* and extra-human knowledge" woven into Theosophical writings.

The seductive spell of Theosophy on Pessoa wore off quickly. The very next day, December 7, he wrote in a diary entry (in English): "No depression; rather the beginning of clear thought, occultistly antitheosophical." Indeed, the occult traditions of Kabbalah, Rosicrucianism and Freemasonry held far more purchase on Pessoa's imagination than did Theosophy, which he soon criticized for being a watered-down, confused version of Indian religiosity, removed "from the great though diseased beauty of

the Buddha of the East" and forced into a "mixture with western movements." Raphael Baldaya denounced Theosophy as "merely a democrati-
zation" and "Christianization" of the ancient tradition of Hermeticism.[5]

Pessoa thought there might be a market for some of the things he
planned to write and sometimes did write as Raphael Baldaya—essays
on metaphysics and the occult, a book on astrology and the Great War,
and assorted treatises on astrological theory and practice—but finding
an interested publisher was never easy, and less so during the war, so
it occurred to him to do direct sales by mail. He drafted some advertising copy and drew up a price list, in English, for *A New Theory of
Astrological Periods* and several other pamphlets authored by "Raphael
Baldaya, Astrologer," all of which could be sent "post free to any part
of the world." Horoscopes and astrological readings were also available,
and for these he drew up a separate price list in Portuguese.[6] The typed
lists date from late 1915 or early 1916, and it was around this time, in a
December letter, that Pessoa finally revealed the existence of Baldaya to
Sá-Carneiro, who laughed out loud when he read about this heteronym's
long beard. Although it seemed like a promising idea, Pessoa never actually put Raphael Baldaya to work as a fee-charging astrologer. In his own
name he cast a number of charts for people he hardly knew—friends of
friends—and may have received occasional gratuities for his services.

Pessoa's many schemes for making money might have been profitable
for somebody with initiative, self-discipline, and a practical sensibility,
all of which he lacked. He needed to be under pressure to get a job done.
Translation was a remunerative activity that particularly appealed to
Pessoa, but unless he had commissions and deadlines—as he did for the
books on Theosophy—he could rarely finish what he started. In 1915 he
was still working on translation projects launched at the time of the Ibis
press or even earlier: Shakespeare's plays into Portuguese, for instance, or
the sonnets of Camões and of Antero de Quental into English.[7] He had
also embarked on several new projects, including an English rendition
of a still unpublished and unperformed play titled *Octavio*, by Victoriano
Braga, who was a distant cousin as well as a friend.

Related to Pessoa through Grandma Dionísia, Victoriano Braga was
born in Lisbon just one month after him, but they apparently never knew
each other as children. Pessoa reports in his diary from 1913 that he
was "introduced" to Braga that February. They quickly became good
friends. An accomplished amateur photographer as well as a playwright

and drama critic, Victoriano Braga consorted with the *Orpheu* clique and took iconic photographs of Fernando Pessoa, José de Almada Negreiros, Santa Rita Pintor, José Pacheco, and Ruy Coelho. Mário de Sá-Carneiro was especially fond of Braga and made him into a character—with the code name Vitorino Bragança—in the short story "Resurrection," in which Pessoa also appears, with the name Fernando Passos.

Perhaps it was Sá-Carneiro's fictions that inspired Victoriano Braga to write about a sexually troubled man in *Octavio*. This play's eponymous protagonist, a musician from an aristocratic family, makes it clear in the opening dialogue with a friend named Gil that he does not care for women, except as aesthetically pleasing objects. He admits to being infatuated with a young male violinist from Italy, however, and we learn that he associates with other young men whom Gil calls "exploiters"— men, it seems, who are beneath his social station and make him pay dear for their sexual favors. Against Gil's advice, Octavio goes through with a marriage to a young woman he only makes unhappy. The marriage is never consummated, she becomes pregnant by a lover, and Octavio— already gravely ill—loses his sanity and dies from despair when his mother tells him the "good news" that he is going to become a father.

*Octavio* has a simple, engaging plot, well-drawn though rather shallow characters, and convincing dialogue. It is a good play; it is not a great one. But Pessoa held it in exaggeratedly high esteem. He began translating it in 1915—directly at the typewriter and also by hand, in between the lines of a manuscript copy of the play—and some years later he would write dozens of pages to argue for its superior worth in the panorama of modern European drama.[8] Actually, he would forget his original purpose and write about drama in general, making little direct reference to *Octavio*, and there was indeed no reason to refer to it, since the qualities he considered essential for successful drama—such as psychological subtlety, dramatic instinct, and the ability to construct artistic wholes—may be found in countless plays besides *Octavio*. Pessoa's fervent interest in this otherwise unremarkable play can only be explained by its storyline, described by a Lisbon theater critic as a "case of sexual psychopathy" he considered "repugnant."[9]

Pessoa, in "Antinous," had written about a love between two men from a remote time and culture. While the story was true, it had the aura of a legend, which he retold with flair and feeling. Victoriano Braga, on the other hand, had dared to depict the real-life drama of a contemporary man who desires other men. It may be that Pessoa was enchanted by *Octavio* because of its audacity—because he too, like the play's lead character, felt desire for other men. But he wasn't sure if he really wanted whatever it was he desired. And perhaps, after all, he preferred not to desire anything. "I'd like to be able to like liking," begins one of his poems, but it was signed by Álvaro de Campos, who follows up this confession by asking for a cigarette.

✦

IN NOVEMBER AND EARLY December 1915 Pessoa kept his third and last diary, which is in the same factual style as the first two—from 1906 and 1913—though with a little more personal reflection.[10] He started writing it in Portuguese but switched to English on the third day, when he spent the evening reading William James's *The Varieties of Religious Experience*, a work cited in Besant's *The Ideals of Theosophy*, which he had just translated.[11] Calmer than the diarist of 1913, Pessoa no longer flitted from café to café, but he still frequented them on a daily basis, he regularly passed by the offices where he drafted letters in English, and he met up with assorted friends. On November 14 he reluctantly went to a photography exhibit with Victoriano Braga, his wife, José Pacheco, and Almada Negreiros, got tipsy from the wine, and after all enjoyed himself. He went without dinner, however, since he had run out of money. The next day he would borrow some from a friend, or get another advance from one of his employers.

On at least two different days in November Pessoa met with Raul Leal, whose exorbitant ideas and febrile manner of expressing them prompted Sá-Carneiro to comment, in a letter sent to Pessoa on November 5, that he was "a little too *Orpheu*" for his own good. Pessoa, however, was eminently patient with Leal and suspected that vertiginism, like an original and powerful yet baffling poem, might actually contain some kind of truth.

Having read many books about the relationship of genius and madness, and being persuaded that he himself had not only an abundance of the former quality but also a germ of the latter, Pessoa was spontaneously attracted to people who weren't quite normal. On November 26, while browsing in a bookstore, he ran into a Spanish literary acquaintance, Juan de Nogales (1884–1929), who in addition to being a poet and essayist was also a painter, Theosophist, spiritist, Esperantist, and sometime vegetarian. He had traveled around the Americas and Europe, including Russia, reportedly had a full set of gold teeth, occasionally dyed his hair green or white, and owned a wardrobe that would be the envy of any theater's costume department.[12] The "likes of *Orpheu*," noted Pessoa in his diary, and they met again the following day. Nogales, for whom Pessoa cast an astrological chart, promised to write an article on Portuguese sensationism for the Spanish press, but it never materialized.[13] On the same day he ran into Nogales, Pessoa saw his amateur astrologer friend, César Porto, with whom he was thinking of creating a Portuguese Astrological Society[14]—yet another idea never acted on.

The most intimate, revealing side of the 1915 diary is connected to Aunt Lisbela, Pessoa's cousin and benefactor from the Algarve. She had come with a niece to spend a full month in Lisbon and sent word of their arrival to Fernando on November 8. He went by their hotel that evening and on many others. Lisbela had a way of putting him at ease, so that he became more talkative, more animated, and after a few evenings together he felt confident that they were enjoying his company as much as he was enjoying theirs. One evening a new presence—a teenage girl—turned the ritual hotel visit into a very different experience for Fernando, who wrote in his diary: "At night with Aunt Lisbela at hotel, very pleasant; made eyes with a rather interesting girl, who seemed to like me. Felt myself agreeable to them (her and perhaps a sister), though I said little . . . The Emperor, alas! . . ."

The next night, November 30, it was more of the same. The diarist had "passed a pleasant 1½ hours at hotel making still more eyes (and exchanging) with the girl (17 years old, excellent) and seemed agreeable to her, her sister and even her deaf mother. Spoke to her quite easily and at her eyes even. Alas!" Once more his account of the meeting ended with a regretful "Alas!" although without any mention of the cryptic Emperor. The next day Pessoa caught a bit of flu, felt very depressed, and "forced" himself not to go to the hotel, but the following evening he was back there again and had a pleasant time talking with the girl. Nevertheless, "the Emperor innerness caused a great unrest. I think the girl wondered at my slowness." He left the hotel a little after midnight and walked home to his rented room by way of Avenida da Liberdade, in a "very strong depression." He waited three days before returning to the hotel, by which time the girl with communicative eyes must have checked out, since she was never again mentioned.

The inhibiting Emperor who was also at the hotel, unbeknown to anyone but Pessoa, was of course Hadrian, whose love for Antinous he had
exalted in his poem of the same name written a few months earlier. Pessoa's attraction to men clearly prevented him from pursuing more forcefully the "excellent" girl at the hotel. Far less certain is whether he would
ever have wanted to pursue a romantic or sexual relationship with a man.
For better or worse, Pessoa relentlessly took all things apart—including
his attractions, repulsions, and whatever else he thought or felt—and put
them back together, through his imagination and his writing. Hadrian,
deifying Antinous, turned his love and lust into a religion. Pessoa continually converted love and lust into topics of literature.

In the fall of 1915 Pessoa wrote a triptych of Álvaro de Campos sonnets, the third of which enacts as well as justifies the author's literary
attitude toward love. Published by him in 1922, it is the most famous of
all the sonnets he wrote, under his own or any other name:

Listen, Daisy. When I die, although
You may not feel a thing, you must
Tell all my friends in London how much
My loss makes you suffer. Then go

To York, where you claim you were born
(But I don't believe a thing you claim),
To tell that poor boy who gave me
So many hours of joy (but of course

You don't know about that) that I'm dead.
Even he, whom I thought I sincerely
Loved, won't care . . . Then go and break

The news to that strange girl Cecily,
Who believed that one day I'd be great . . .
To hell with life and everyone in it!

In the world created by these fourteen lines, nobody is reliable and nothing is certain—love least of all. Campos suspects Daisy of dissembling,
and he himself dissembles to her, carrying on a secret same-sex romance
not just with any boy but with a boy from her hometown (if York *is*, after

all, her hometown). Although he was once convinced of his love for the boy, Campos now has doubts, and he doubts the boy really loves him. As for becoming great and famous, that prospect is also a sham. The poem is Campos's disillusioned adieu to the world.

By retreating into literature, astrology, and spiritual contemplations, by confining his "experience" of love and sex to the literary plane, and by inventing characters such as Campos to speak and act and feel in his stead, Pessoa too, like the naval engineer, effectively sent life and the living to hell.

# CHAPTER 41

P ESSOA'S MOTHER, MARIA MADALENA, WHOM HE had not seen for seven and a half years, continued to faithfully send him a weekly letter, which he opened, read hastily, and added to the pile of her previous letters. She wrote about the family she had formed with João Miguel Rosa, about their house in Pretoria, about some of the people from Durban with whom she was still in contact, and about assorted relatives from Portugal—nothing that especially amused or interested her firstborn son. But if he read with more enthusiasm, and even voracity, the letters he received from Sá-Carneiro, he cherished the letters from his mother as a kind of anchor, which still firmly connected him to an ancient feeling of home. Her constant concern over the state of his health, her expressions of love and affection, and her handwriting whose loops and lines he knew so well—he could always count on these things, week after week, no matter what anguished "crisis" he might be going through. And so, in mid-December 1915, when a letter arrived not from his mother but from his stepfather, Pessoa opened it up quickly, nervously, wondering what on earth was the matter. In the second week of November, his mother had suffered a stroke that paralyzed her left side. Only now did he learn the news, since mail from South Africa took as much as a month to reach Lisbon.[1]

He was totally stunned. Although Maria Madalena complained of occasional ailments and gloomy moods in her letters, it had never occurred to him that she might not be invulnerable. She was fifty-three years old, almost fifty-four—too young for a stroke. It had fortunately hit her left side rather than her right, but it hit very hard. For the next six months, João Miguel Rosa would send weekly reports to Fernando about his wife's recovery, which was worryingly slow. The doctors experimented with electric shocks, but she found them unbearable.

Despite his worry and anxiety, Pessoa did not mention his mother's condition to Mário de Sá-Carneiro. Was it because he did not want his

family life—and in particular the deep affection he felt for his mother—
to intrude on the special liaison he had with his friend? Whatever the
reason, it so happened that his friend was soon a greater source of worry
to him than his mother, so that he received letters postmarked Paris with
not only anticipation but also a little dread.

Mário's letter of December 29 contained the first warning signs. He
felt "dizzyingly bored" of everything, and especially of himself. "I'm fed
up! fed up! fed up!" he blurted in the middle of his letter. His first letter
of the new year was less glum, but his second one, sent on January 13,
1916, announced that he was definitively, positively crazy. Even more
troubling was a statement authorizing Pessoa to publish his poems wherever and however he saw fit. At the not exactly old age of twenty-five,
Mário had suddenly decided to name a literary executor. The letter contained other signs of desperation, and Pessoa did not know how best to
answer it, or he procrastinated out of self-defense, as if already fearing
that he was going to be abandoned. Mário sent disconsolate postcards,
demanding a letter from his friend, who finally wrote him toward the
end of the month.

Where was the Mário who loved to discuss literature, artistic theories, and editorial projects? Pessoa would have liked his friend to help
him at least dream of, if not plan for, the continuation of *Orpheu*, but no
encouragement was forthcoming from Paris. Mário gleefully reported
on a couple of comments that the two published issues had aroused in
the French capital, but when Pessoa, just before Christmas, wrote him
about a potential backer for *Orpheu* 3, Sá-Carneiro was skeptical. For
him as for most of the other young men connected to *Orpheu*, its time
had passed. They went their separate ways, investing their energy in new
projects, which included a few other short-lived magazines: *Exílio* (*Exile*;
1916), *Centauro* (*Centaur*; 1916), and *Portugal Futurista* (1917).

Sá-Carneiro continued to exchange literary news with Pessoa,
although without his former passion for literature itself. He also continued to send his friend new poems, now piercingly autobiographical.
His letter of February 3, included a poem titled "Aquele outro" ("Somebody Else"), which consisted of a series of unflattering, self-descriptive
epithets, the last of which was "the fat Sphinx." Self-control had never
interested Sá-Carneiro, and his already plump body was distending. He
paid no attention to the war, except insofar as it affected the city he currently inhabited and the one he had left behind. They reflected each other,

partly reflected him, and served as the backdrop for his unapologetically central concern, which was himself. His February 3 letter noted the curious coincidence of German zeppelins having bombed Paris on the very same evening, January 29, that homemade bombs exploded on the streets of Lisbon. Agitators, in fact, had organized armed assaults on some of the Portuguese capital's grocers and food warehouses, claiming that they were withholding government-subsidized foodstuffs in order to sell them on the black market. Portugal's underclass was getting hungrier and more desperate.

✦

SÁ-CARNEIRO AND PESSOA HAD one good friend who had been fighting in the trenches since the beginning of the war: Carlos Franco, a painter, set designer, and honorary member of the *Orpheu* group. They got to know him in the fall of 1913, after Sá-Carneiro and José Pacheco returned from Paris. Endlessly amiable, Franco was the sort of person everyone took to immediately, including Pessoa, who dedicated to him his play *The Mariner*, which he began writing around the time they met. Franco, Sá-Carneiro, and Pacheco were all in Lisbon on the last day of 1913, which they spent together in a festive fashion—without Pessoa, who disliked holidays and the obligation to celebrate them—and all three of them happened to be in Paris in the summer of 1914. Franco had landed a good job painting sets for the opera at one of the city's many scenic studios, but he was laid off when the war broke out, had no prospects for work in Lisbon, and decided to enlist in the French Foreign Legion. At the time he was twenty-seven, one year older than Pessoa.

Franco sent letters from the front to Sá-Carneiro, who relayed his news to Pessoa, and in December 1915, when the soldier had six days of leave, he spent them with his friend in Paris, staying at the same hotel on Rue Victor Massé, close to La Cigale and the Moulin Rouge. After Franco left to rejoin his regiment, Sá-Carneiro wrote Pessoa that he had found him in great form, physically and psychologically, despite seven straight months of combat in Arras and in Champagne, where the French had waged arduous but fruitless battles against the Germans. Copies of *Orpheu* 1 and *Sky on Fire* had accompanied him on the battlefront, and he knew some of Mário's poems and some passages from Fernando's *The Mariner* by heart. Although Franco was an unknown who never exhibited or published anything to speak of, a portrait of him in uniform—

painted in Paris while he was there on leave—was the cover image for the February 7 issue of *Ilustração Portuguesa* (*Portuguese Illustration*), a popular Portuguese weekly magazine. Portugal was on the verge of entering the war, and the editors wanted to do their part as recruiters.

On February 24, 1916, the Portuguese navy, at the request of Great Britain, seized seventy German merchant ships peacefully moored in Lisbon's harbor.* In exchange for two-thirds of the ships, which Britain would repurpose for the war effort, Portugal would receive a loan of £2 million to purchase wheat and weapons. On March 9 Germany, as expected, declared war on Portugal; the next day the Portuguese parliament issued a reciprocal declaration, and soon able-bodied men were being pressed into the Portuguese Expeditionary Corps, which would fight with the Allies in Europe. The undeclared war in Africa, where thousands of troops had been sent to defend Portuguese East Africa (Mozambique), had exhausted the capacity of Portugal's army, and it would take months to mobilize civilians and train them to be soldiers, with the first detachments of the corps not arriving on French soil until February 1917. By then Carlos Franco was already part of that soil, having been killed six months earlier in the Battle of the Somme, which claimed over a million casualties.[2]

Fernando Pessoa cast an astrological chart for Portugal's March 10 declaration of war against Germany.[3] The reverse side of the chart contains a dozen variously styled signatures for António Mora, who continued to argue, in passages for his *Dissertation in Favor of Germany*, that it would make more sense for Portugal to side with this country rather than the Allies—at least from a cultural, civilizational perspective. Despite sympathizing with his heteronym's point of view, Pessoa ultimately sided with the Allies, yet questioned the wisdom of sending Portuguese soldiers to France. The government, headed up once more by Afonso Costa, had secured a much needed loan, but the material and human costs of participating in the war would be enormous.

✦

A T  T H E  S A M E  T I M E  that Portugal officially declared war and the nation's citizens, including Pessoa, uneasily wondered what would hap-

---

* The ships' crews had been repatriated to Germany.

pen next, Mário de Sá-Carneiro was entering more deeply into the world of his own fictions, assuming the role of a doomed character. On February 16, 1916, he had sent Pessoa an eerie poem titled "Feminina" ("Feminine"), which begins:

> I wish I were a woman, so that I could stretch out
> Next to my friends, on the benches of cafés.
> I wish I were a woman, so that I could powder
> My face in front of all the café customers.

And after three more stanzas of the same fantasy, it ends with:

> I wish I were a woman, to excite those who look at me.
> I wish I were a woman, so that I could jilt myself.

Two days later he wrote Pessoa in a postcard: "I've been living in a nameless hell for weeks."

In the letters that followed, Sá-Carneiro debated whether he should return to Lisbon or stay put in Paris. But whatever he decided to do, right now he needed money, more money, still more money. He hounded his father, his publisher, and his friends for funds, and he charged Fernando with the embarrassing task of visiting the nanny who had raised him (and who still worked for the family as a housekeeper) to obtain from her a certain gold chain, which he was to deposit at a pawnshop as collateral for a loan, wiring the money received to Paris. Pessoa did as he was told, obtaining 160 francs for Mário, who spent them as soon as they arrived, in mid-March. He needed ever-increasing, exorbitant amounts of ready cash, but only at the end of March did he offer Pessoa a dim clarification of the sort of turn his life had taken: "For the last two weeks I've lived a life I've always dreamed: I lived everything during this time: I've finally realized the sexual part of my work." He unfortunately had run out of the money that fueled this fabulous life, and unless he miraculously received 500 francs on Monday (he wrote on the thirty-first, a Friday), he would commit suicide, but not before mailing him a notebook with the poems for his second collection, *Indícios de oiro* (*Traces of Gold*). He entrusted Fernando with its publication.

Mário sent off the promised notebook of poems on Sunday and followed it up, on Monday, with a postcard to reconfirm that, within a few hours' time, he would throw himself in front of a speeding train at the Pigalle métro station. He asked Fernando to do him one last favor, which was to convey a fond farewell to his nanny and his grandfather. But before this postcard made it to Lisbon, Pessoa received a telegram telling him to disregard it: Sá-Carneiro was not going to kill himself just yet. A few days later a new letter from Mário arrived, explaining that his suicide had been at least temporarily forestalled by the "female charac-ter" who had recently entered his life. She would be able to support him in the short run—by selling her body to other men.

Fernando Pessoa, always so unflappable and self-contained, lost his composure. Here was a Mário he did not know, suddenly ready to give up writing and the remaining days of his life for the sake of a fling with a prostitute, but what about their special friendship? What about him, Fernando? "Do you think at all about me?" he asked in his next letter to Mário, who answered that he never stopped thinking about him, partic-ularly in times like he was going through now. He said he felt no love, no affection, for the woman he was seeing, but he felt ineluctably connected to her since she was, in a way, just like himself. "You understand," he wrote apologetically, "that I'm living one of my characters—I myself, my character—*with one of my characters.*" His life had become his last work of literature.

The next day, April 18, Mário wrote on a postcard: "What did I do with my poor Pride? Look at my horoscope. Now, more than ever, is the time. Tell me. I'm not afraid." But elsewhere on the card he declared himself very afraid of absence, of separation, and he implored his friend ("I beg you on my knees") to write.

But Pessoa did not immediately write. He waited a few days and then, on April 26, began a letter by offering excuses for the delay. A series of unspecified chores, large and small, had been occupying all his free time, but worse yet, he was in a terribly distracted state of mind. He told Mário for the first time about his mother's stroke, her slow recovery, and the anguish it caused him. He said that Mário's crisis had compounded his distress, since he naturally suffered his dearest friend's troubles as if they were his own. Furthermore, he himself was experiencing yet another of his "severe mental crises," about which he offered no details, but the point he wanted to make was clear enough: you're not the only one who has to deal with serious personal problems. He begged "a thousand par-dons" for not writing sooner, but "it couldn't have been otherwise."

He tucked the two pages he had so far written into an envelope and addressed it to M. Mário de Sá-Carneiro at the Hôtel de Nice, 29, Rue Victor Massé, but before he got around to finishing the letter he received the calamitous news: on that same day, April 26, Mário had taken his life by ingesting five vials of strychnine. For this final act he had asked José de Araújo, a Portuguese friend he had made in Paris, to come to his hotel room at 8:00 p.m. sharp. Arriving at the appointed time, the unsuspecting friend found the suicide lying down in his best suit of clothes, still conscious but already in agony. Sá-Carneiro died before any medical help could arrive. A coffin was ordered to be brought the next day, but the corpse had greatly swollen during the night, bursting all the seams of the suit that covered it, so they had to bring a larger coffin, the largest available, and even then it took some cramming to get all the folds of flesh into the box. Lest the body keep expanding, they quickly screwed down the lid and strapped tight the coffin. A small funeral without speeches—paid for by Araújo—took place on the twenty-ninth.[4]

Sá-Carneiro had left a farewell letter for Pessoa, which Araújo sent on to Lisbon immediately. It was uncharacteristically thin, just a single sheet of folded paper with seven words and his signature, all writ large: "A huge, huge farewell from your poor Mário de Sá-Carneiro / Paris, 26 April 1916."[5] Two weeks later, Araújo sent Pessoa a detailed account of Mário's death and a summary of the events leading up to it. He claimed that the "female character" who had enthralled Mário was responsible for getting him hooked on ether—then a popular and highly addictive narcotic—and for making him run through the phenomenal sum of 3500 francs during their two-month-long affair. Although he could not tear himself away from her, Mário told Araújo that he did not even like the woman.

Araújo, a businessman, was one of Sá-Carneiro's two close companions in Paris during his last six months of life. The other one was Carlos Ferreira (1884–1948), a Portuguese playwright who knew him—as well as Pessoa—from Lisbon. Shortly before the suicide, Ferreira had sent a letter to Pessoa divulging extraordinary things about Mário's doings and recommending confidentiality. That letter has disappeared, perhaps because the recipient destroyed it. After the suicide, Ferreira sent Pessoa his own account of what happened, asked him to contact the family, and solemnly urged him never to reveal to anyone why Sá-Carneiro had taken his own life.[6] Possible motives were not wanting. There was his frustration as a writer who, lacking the transformative power of Pessoa, felt he had reached his limit and was uselessly repeating himself. There was the murky relationship between him and his stepmother, who in December had gone to join his father in Mozambique. There was his tormenting affair with the prostitute, whose name was Renée and whom he met at Le Cyrano, a café on Place Blanche, across from the Moulin Rouge.[7] But the ultimate reason for his unbearable despair remains an enigma.

✦

IN ADDITION TO BOOKS, manuscripts, and personal effects, Sá-Carneiro's suitcases contained letters, including all the ones Pessoa had written him during his third and final sojourn in Paris. Understandably enough, the Hôtel de Nice was unwilling to give up the suitcases or their contents without authorization from the father of the deceased, and the management may also have been holding them as surety against an unpaid bill of 254 francs.[8] But when Carlos de Sá-Carneiro returned from Africa and finally visited the hotel years later, he reportedly found nothing in his son's luggage except moth-eaten clothes.[9] Either someone had pilfered his papers or his father preferred not to make them public knowledge. As for the dozens of letters Sá-Carneiro had received from Pessoa during his previous stays in Paris, he kept them in Lisbon among his most treasured possessions. It had elated him when his best friend, in July 1914, half jokingly predicted that *Unpublished Letters of Fernando Pessoa and Mário de Sá-Carneiro* would be a literary sensation when issued in the year 1970. Sadly, all of Pessoa's letters to his friend seem to have been tossed out with the trash.[10]

The brief death notices published in several French newspapers referred to Sá-Carneiro as a futurist poet, while a full-fledged obituary in the Portuguese press, headlined "The 'Swampists' in Mourning: The Poet Sá-Carneiro Kills Himself in Paris," styled him more pompously as "the leader of the famous futurist school and editor in chief of *Orpheu*, the sect's official organ."[11] Pessoa's grief over his friend's death did not blind him to its usefulness for promoting the so-called sect and, possibly, relaunching *Orpheu*. On May 4 he wrote to Armando Côrtes-Rodrigues, who had returned to the Azores for good in January, to tell him the tragic news and to solicit a contribution for a booklet that *Orpheu* would publish in memory of its late co-editor. A few days later, he convened a meeting in Lisbon to discuss the memorial booklet as well as the publication of *Orpheu* 3. José Pacheco, Luís de Montalvor, and José de Almada Negreiros were likely attendees at the meeting, which led to nothing concrete, but Pessoa optimistically cast a horoscope about the "*Orpheu* Business" deliberated that day, May 8, at 5:00 p.m.[12]

Although Sá-Carneiro had initially just smiled at his friend's interest in astrology, during the last months of his life—like a terminally ill patient willing to try out exotic cures—he wanted to know all that the stars had to say about his character, his current state of high anxiety, and his future. Pessoa, however, did more than just study his friend's condition through astrological charts and calculations; in his last, unfinished letter of April 26 he said that he could *feel* telepathically the "astral projection" of what Mário was feeling. It was while his friend helplessly gravitated toward death that Pessoa began to develop his mediumistic powers, encouraged by Mariano Santana, an occultist and magnetizer who frequented the intellectual circles that met in Lisbon's cafés.[13]

One evening in his rented room, just back from the Brasileira café on Praça do Rossio,[14] the apprentice in occult spirituality impulsively picked up a pen and put it to a sheet of paper. Without thinking, he found himself writing the signature of Manuel Gualdino da Cunha, the great-uncle who had been a surrogate father to him in his childhood, and under this signature he wrote a few cryptic phrases. In the following weeks he continued to write, or to draw, automatically. Initially, in fact, he rarely wrote normal sentences; he was more apt to produce Masonic and Kabbalistic signs, occult symbols, and sequences of numbers, whose meaning could often be clarified by his friend Mariano Santana.[15] Pessoa never heard again from the spirit of his uncle Cunha, and if he asked the communicators who they were, they evasively answered with drawings and numbers.

Pessoa described all of this in a letter sent on June 24 to Aunt Anica, who had participated, with her daughter Maria, in the séances he'd organized two years earlier. He recalled how the automatic writing of the two women was fluent and intelligible, while he himself, albeit the leader of the sessions, was less spiritually receptive. But now, unexpectedly, he was a *seeing* medium as well as a writing medium. He explained to his aunt that he was experiencing "etheric vision," which enabled him to perceive certain people's "magnetic aura."

To be endowed with these new powers was exciting, but also unsettling. "What worries me," he told his aunt, "is that this isn't how the powers of a medium usually develop." And he continued:

I know enough of the occult sciences to realize that the so-called higher senses are being aroused in me for some mysterious purpose and that the unknown Master who is initiating me, by imposing on me this higher existence, is going to make me feel a deeper suffering than I've ever known, not to mention the profound dissatisfaction with worldly things that comes with the acquisition of these higher faculties. The mere dawning of those faculties is accompanied by a mysterious feeling of isolation and desolation that fills the soul with bitterness.

Pessoa had other, less mysterious reasons for feeling isolated and desolate. With the death of Sá-Carneiro, it was not only his friend's special affection and intimacy that Pessoa had lost but also his solidarity in their shared condition of being celibate. A number of his other friends were still single, but they had girlfriends, or at least had sex. Even Sá-Carneiro, in the lead-up to his suicide, had had a sexual adventure with a Parisian prostitute. Fernando Pessoa, who had just turned twenty-eight, was still a virgin.

As a poet he was as bold and vigorous as ever. In late May he had written more than three hundred lines for Álvaro de Campos's "Time's Passage," including the longest of its eight sections, which begins:

To feel everything in every way,
To live everything from all sides,
To be the same thing in all ways possible at the same time,
To realize in oneself all humanity at all moments
In one scattered, extravagant, complete and aloof moment.

And it goes on like that, immoderately and all-embracingly, as it was Campos's manner to go on, only in this case it went farther and higher than usual, reaching yet another of his staggering summits, making it almost a twin peak of the "Maritime Ode."

One week after this effusion of verses signed by Álvaro de Campos, Pessoa wrote three odes of Ricardo Reis, including "The Chess Players," which tells the story of two men in Persia who placidly, obliviously, continue their chess game while foreign invaders rampage through the city, burn down houses, rape women, and kill children. Cognizant of life's brevity and convinced of its vanity, Reis commends the attitude of the chess players. Many moral philosophers would not. But the ode—the longest ode signed by Ricardo Reis—was another high point in Pessoa's career.

Despite these recent achievements of Campos and Reis, despite the many other great poems written in their names and in that of Alberto Caeiro, their triumphant master, and despite *Orpheu*'s success at driving a stake or two into the heart of the Portuguese literary establishment, a note Pessoa wrote to himself (in English) on June 13, 1916, was the opposite of triumphal:

> I have, thus, arrived at my 28th year, with nothing done in life— nothing in life, in letters or in my own individuality. I have tasted failure to the full up to now. How longer must I taste it, alas?
>
> The more I examine my conscience, the less I acquit myself of the nothingness of my life.
>
> What horrific thing is this that has so delayed me?
>
> My deficient reading, my lack of practical spirit, my[16]

He left the last sentence hanging, and it is hard to know where he might have gone with his self-indictment, which begins with a dubious allegation: "deficient reading." None of his friends, and few people in Portugal in 1916, were as well read as Fernando Pessoa. His "lack of practical spirit," on the other hand, was a real and constant handicap, since it hindered him from finishing his literary projects, publishing his books, and becoming a well-known writer.

It was not only as a writer and intellectual that Pessoa felt frustrated, however. He complained of being a failure "in letters," yes, but also in life generally and in his "individuality." His recent acquisition of mediumistic abilities had led him to conclude that there must be "some mysterious purpose" for which "the unknown Master" was "initiating" him. Reading those words in the letter from her nephew, Aunt Anica naturally understood that he was alluding to a spiritual initiation. So he was, but that initiation would be sexually configured. Pessoa's sense of failure was partly due to his lack of sexual experience, a problem that his astral Master would set out to remedy.

On June 13 Pessoa's mother felt well enough to write him for the first time in seven months. It was a simple postcard to wish him a happy birthday. She mentioned that she could finally move, just slightly, her left arm. Her writing hand was unaffected by the stroke, and her mind was clear, but she and her son never recovered their old routine of weekly letters—a routine that, on Fernando's part, was marked by lapses even before her stroke. He missed his mother but found it difficult to write her about his literary life, let alone his recent spiritual discoveries, which might make her worry, or frown.

While not nearly as desperate as Sá-Carneiro had been, Pessoa also felt like he had reached an impasse, and astrology—albeit fascinating—changed nothing. At best it threw a clarifying light on his situation. Desiring active help and guidance, he turned to astral spirits.

# CHAPTER 42

**M**IXED IN WITH THE MANY THOUSANDS OF poems and prose texts that make up the Pessoa Archive are some two hundred sheets of automatic, or mediumistic, communications—mostly in English and written in a childish-looking script that bears little resemblance to Pessoa's normal handwriting. It was by this means that astral spirits supposedly answered whatever questions Pessoa cared to ask. He did not record his questions, but their gist can usually be inferred from the answers transmitted through his writing hand.

In the letter he sent to Aunt Anica on June 24, 1916, Pessoa noted that the communicating spirits for whom he acted as a medium were anonymous and their messages not too coherent. Four days later that all changed.[1] The Master communicator revealed his name, Henry More, and in smoothly loquacious, only slightly flawed English revealed his main mission: to cure his disciple of virginity. In a communication dispatched on June 28 at 6:00 p.m., More did not mince words. After explaining that he was Fernando's friend and wanted to help him, he got straight to the point:

> You must not maintain chastity more. You are so misogynous that you will find yourself morally impotent, and in that way you will not produce any complete work in literature. You must abandon your monastic life and *now*. [. . .] Keeping chastity is for stronger men and men who have to [keep chaste] on account of physical defects. This does not apply to you.* A man who masturbates himself is not a strong man, and no man is a man who is not a *lover*.

---

* Pessoa's chastity was clearly not, as at least one writer has suggested, due to a physiological problem.

[. . .] You are a man who masturbates himself and who dreams of women in a masturbator's manner. Man is man. No man can move among men if he is not a man like them.

Although Pessoa was an enormously productive writer, a volcano in permanent eruption, he feared that his difficulty in completing large-scale literary works might be related to his "incompleteness" as a man. Henry More exploited that fear, and he astutely encouraged his disciple to overcome his misogyny by appealing to that same misogyny, saying that he could not "move among men" (whose company he preferred) unless he was "a man like them" (a man who has sex with women).

However much he "dream[ed] of women in a masturbator's manner," Pessoa was not easily attracted to women he actually met—another communication mentions his "aversion to women"—but Henry More had a solution for that problem:

Make up your mind to go to bed with the girl who is coming into your life. Make up your mind to make her happy in a sexual way. She is a masculine type of girl and she is a woman quite made for you. She must make you happy, because she makes a man of you. She meets you and she makes you love her. She is strong and immensely masculine in her will and in her manner of making you submit to her. Make no resistance. There is nothing to fear. It will all be simpler than you suppose. She is a virgin, just as you are, and nomad[ic] as you in life. She is no marriageable woman, for she is morally too nomad[ic] to make a nest. Only a girl like this can make you mate with her.

So at least he would not have to marry her. Later that same evening Pessoa received a follow-up communication, confirming that he would meet and mate with "a very masculine woman." Other communications from around the same time described her as a "lithe, spare, but bosomed girl" who was educated in France and England, wrote poetry that was "not very bad," and longed to meet the "strange creature" in charge of *Orpheu*.

Most of the communications, unlike the lengthy one just cited, consisted of brief answers to Pessoa's questions, and sexual initiation was by no means the exclusive topic of conversation. Some of the communications touched on Pessoa's literary projects, on his finances, and on banal events of daily life. All these matters were subsidiary, however, to the larger issue of his spiritual progress, which was linked to his sexual progress. In the vision of cosmic reality disclosed to Pessoa by his communicators, the mysteries of sex mirrored the arcane mysteries of spirit.

In his earthly incarnation, Henry More (1614–1687) had been an English poet, philosopher, and theologian, as well as the leading figure in the group of thinkers later known as the Cambridge Platonists. Some occultists have speculated that More was also a Rosicrucian, which was almost certainly not the case, but in his communications to Pessoa he presented himself as a Frater Rosae Crucis and often affixed the abbreviation "R†C" after his signature. There were other, less erudite spirits in contact with Pessoa, including one named Wardour, who was More's ally in trying to get Pessoa devirginized, and a malefic spirit called the Voodooist.

◆

THE ASTRAL SPIRITS WHO communicated with William Butler Yeats and his much younger wife, Georgie Hyde-Lees, in some 450 sessions of automatic writing conducted between 1917 and 1921 also stressed the importance of sexual satisfaction, arguing that his creative success depended on it.[2] Even the success of the automatic writing sessions depended on it, since the medium, Georgie—or George, as she was nicknamed by her husband—performed well only if Willy was adequately performing in bed. The communicators repeatedly reminded him to do his sexual duty and told the couple on more than one occasion to end their writing session and go straight to bed.

Since Pessoa did not have anyone to go to bed with, his communicators had a more daunting task, which they tried to accomplish not only by goading him to meet and mate with someone of the opposite sex but also by conjuring up women who would be his type or who, at any rate, were predestined for him. After first predicting that his disciple would meet a masculine, literary sort of woman who had been educated abroad, Henry More changed his bait, saying that Pessoa's future sexual partner was an English lass named Margaret Mansel. But even this more feminine creature had a "Man" prominently embedded in her last name and even in the city of her birth, which was Manchester. More's motivation for setting her up with Fernando was not disinterested, according to a communication that dates from July 1916:

Margaret Mansel. She is my wife in my world. My marriage was unhappy because I was of an ascetic habit of life, so I have to repair the evil done to her, in her next incarnation. Her next incarnation is the young girl you are going to meet not many days from now. [. . .] My marriage was not consummated on this earth. It has to be. Now, as I cannot yet return to earth, and my wife is already there, I must make her the mistress of the man who stands next to me in the numbering of monads. Marry her is not marry her in a church or before a registry officer, but marry her means copulate.

The girl was young indeed. More's astral colleague, Wardour, informed Pessoa that she was born in Manchester on July 30, 1903, 4:12 a.m. Pessoa used these vital statistics to cast her astrological chart.[3]

Another communication from More assured Pessoa that he was already "monadically married" to Margaret Mansel—"not to Margaret Mansel in the somatic state, but to her in the monadic over-state." This may have suggested to the monadic husband, Pessoa, that physical union with the girl was after all not necessary. She was not of the same opinion and, losing both her patience and her temper, communicated with Pessoa herself, using words that almost made me blush when I transcribed them from the original manuscript:

You onanist! Go to marriage with me! No onanism [any] more.
504 Love me.
You masturbator! You masochist! You man without manhood!
[. . .] You man without a man's prick! You man with a clitoris instead of a prick! You man with a woman's morality for marriage.
Beast! You bright worm.
Margaret Mansel

Margaret was promiscuous, at least in the astral sphere. A George Mansel* intervened in one of Henry More's communications, professing to be her husband, while in another communication Wardour made the same claim. And there were yet other claimants, including a Monsieur Man-

---

* George Mansel was the name of the chief commissioner of the Natal police when Pessoa was living in Durban.

sel. When Pessoa asked if she had really belonged to so many different men, Henry More replied: "Yes. What do you want?"

Pessoa did not know what he wanted. Simply to lose his virginity? Or perhaps, after all, to have a loving partner? The spirits proposed several other women besides Margaret Mansel, including an eighteen-year-old Azorean called Olga de Medeiros. They provided a little information about each prospective mate and predicted when and where Pessoa would meet them. He was to be quite the playboy, as well as a reproducer of the species: a communication from Henry More informed him that he would father three boys by three different women, when he was twenty-nine, thirty-seven, and forty-one years of age. Straining the credulity of even the firmest believer in ESP and clairvoyance, More announced the precise dates of birth for Pessoa's three future offspring.

Needlessly or not, the Yeatses' communicators, whom they styled "instructors," prescribed copious quantities of sex, and the couple had two children, Anne and Michael, who both lived long lives. The sexual recommendations of Pessoa's communicators were played out in astral projections and foretold encounters with invented people, like so many notes for an unwritten novel. Only in this case there was no ambition to write a novel, merely to experience one, which Pessoa did in a certain way—on the astral plane. And so automatic writing, rather than motivating him to have an active sex life, obviated or at least postponed the need for real sex.

✦

THE AUTOMATIC WRITING CHANNELED through Georgie Hyde-Lees, besides inciting her husband to be more sexually active, also provided him with insights, concepts and images for the spiritual system set out in *A Vision* (1926; revised, 1937). But that was not the most important gift bestowed on Yeats by Ameritus, Thomas of Dorlowicz, and the other curiously named instructors who delivered their messages through George. "We have come to give you metaphors for poetry," he later said they said, and the results are there to see: his already remarkable poetry took a giant leap forward. Those metaphors would not have arrived without George, however, and the biographer Richard Ellmann persuasively argues that what actually energized and transformed Yeats's poetry was his marriage to this woman, with whom he fell deeply in love and created a family.[4] Fernando Pessoa would write a number of poems that were explicitly esoteric and others that reflected, here and there, his passionate interest in magic and the occult, but this interest did not result in a *poetic* breakthrough. Pessoa's poetry had already made its greatest forward leap in 1914, with the birth of his self-generated family of heteronyms. Henry More and the other communicators from beyond, more than providing inspiring metaphors for individual poems, were like a collective metaphor—or spiritual counterpart—of that family.

Although Alberto Caeiro was the recognized master of the other heteronyms and of Pessoa himself, they all had their particular points of view, which sometimes coincided, and sometimes collided. In the astral world, there was likewise agreement and dissension. Pessoa's spiritual master, Henry More, ruled over Wardour, an equally kindhearted, collaborative spirit, but they were opposed by the Voodooist, who on earth had been incarnated in Giuseppe Balsamo, better known as Count Alessandro di Cagliostro (1743–1795), a notorious alchemist, magician, Freemason, and con artist. In one of Henry More's communications, after he forewarns Pessoa that the Voodooist wants to harm him, this froward spirit proceeds to interfere with the handwriting, making it jagged and contorted, while More comments: "He is interrupting me." In another communication, the Voodooist gives Pessoa false information about one of the sexually arousing women he was supposed to meet.

The Yeatses also had to deal with contrarian communicators, whom they dubbed "frustrators," inasmuch as they hindered the development of the spiritual system that would be crystallized in *A Vision*. By contrast, what was at stake in Pessoa's automatic handwriting was not a system of thought or a work of literature but Pessoa himself. The astral spirits were fighting for control of his soul. Back in 1907, symbolic characters such as Erasmus Dare and Jacob Satan had faced off in a virtual drama, *Ultimus Joculatorum*, which seemingly took place in Pessoa himself. Nine years later he again became a battlefield for the age-old conflicts between good and evil, truth and falsehood. "You are the center of an astral conspiracy," Henry More warned his disciple on July 9.

The communications received by Pessoa—who seems to have known nothing of the Yeatses' contacts with the astral realm and whose own automatic writing began one year before theirs—defined a spiritual world of growing complexity. The initial trio of spirits that contacted him through written messages soon expanded into a motley and multilingual company. Besides More, Wardour, and the Voodooist, there were intermittently attending spirits such as Henry Lovell, George Henry Morse, or Sousa, while still others remained anonymous. Although English was the main language of the communications, some were in Portuguese, a few in French, and at least one in Latin. Wardour was a bilingual spirit and had a literary side, communicating not only messages (usually in English) but also two poems (in Portuguese), one of which he cosigned with Fernando Pessoa. He even provided editorial advice. When Pessoa was having a hard time with the opening lines for a new poem, Wardour commented: "This is no good. Try this." And he offered a revised version of the lines found wanting.[5] Thus Pessoa's communicators, on at least a couple of occasions, gave him not merely poetic metaphors but actual poems. They were his impromptu muses, vivid manifestations from the spiritual realm where—he liked to think—his poetry and his heteronyms originated.

◆

"MOVE TO SENGO'S HOUSE," urged Wardour in a communication dating from the fall of 1916—or was this merely Pessoa talking to himself? Whatever its source, Pessoa followed the advice: he leased rooms from Manuel Sengo on Rua Cidade da Horta. As was true of other buildings where the poet lived during this period, the façade of his new building was covered with the painted ceramic tiles known as *azulejos*, used in Iberian architecture since the time of the Moors (and still widely employed in Portugal today). Before the rooms were ready to let, Sengo, a businessman Pessoa had met through his cousin Mário Freitas, put him up for a month or two in a room attached to a dairy store he owned on Rua Almirante Barroso.[6] And before that he briefly occupied an apartment on Rua Antero de Quental. Pessoa never stayed in one place for long: between 1914 and 1919 he moved at least eight times, always taking with him the wooden chest with his manuscripts and as many of his books as his new dwelling could accommodate; he left the rest of his library in storage with friends.

Nearly all of Pessoa's addresses during these years were on nondescript streets in the contiguous neighborhoods of Estefânia, Anjos, and Intendente. As if parodying the life of a globe-trotter, he constantly moved without really going anywhere, though he mentally sailed the high seas in Álvaro de Campos's "Opiary" and "Maritime Ode," journeyed to ancient Rome in "Antinous" and to Persia in Ricardo Reis's

"The Chess Players," and went to outer space through astrology. It's no wonder he was so fond of *Voyage Around My Room*, by Xavier de Maistre (1763–1852), whose protagonist, a French army officer under house arrest, imagines the furnishings of his room to be the scenery of a marvelous journey. Likewise refusing to be confined by the physical space he inhabited, Pessoa visited far-flung places and even other periods of history in his mind. Among his alter egos, this aptitude was especially pronounced in the daydreaming narrator of *The Book of Disquiet*, who paces around his rented room while traveling in the world and beyond it. In a passage titled "A Voyage I Never Made," he explained his method:

> I didn't set out from any port I knew. Even today I don't know what port it was, for I've still never been there. And besides, the ritual purpose of my journey was to go in search of nonexistent ports—ports that would be merely a putting-in at ports; forgotten inlets of rivers, straits running through irreproachably unreal cities. You will doubtless think, on reading me, that my words are absurd. That's because you've never journeyed like I have.[7]

Even on his gregarious days, Pessoa imaginatively journeyed within himself, shut off from others, and in the summer of 1916, more glum than gregarious, he spent many days literally shut within four walls, consulting the astral spirits and brooding. "If you've been exiled," he commented in a September 4 letter to Armando Côrtes-Rodrigues, whose island home was in the middle of the Atlantic, "so have I, without being exiled." Partly because of Sá-Carneiro's suicide and partly because of his mother's devastating stroke, Pessoa's recent life had been "a long history of Depression" and "literary sterility," but he was coming out of his funk and expected to be completely "reconstructed" by the end of the month. As a symbolic sign of that renewal, he had decided to shed the circumflex from his surname, which up until then had been written Pessôa. That useless little hat over the "o" would only hinder his name's cosmopolitan possibilities, at a time when he hoped to make an international impression with his English poetry, including the quasi-pornographic "Epithalamium" and the homoerotic "Antinous." He explained to his Azorean friend that these poems, because they were too "indecent" to publish in England, would be included in *Orpheu* 3. It was a puzzling strategy. Perhaps he imagined that curious readers in Great Britain, unable to obtain such literature locally, would purchase the magazine to be able to read the two poems.

The exciting news, in any case, was that he had found a way to finance the magazine's third issue, which he expected to launch within a month. Besides his "indecent" English poems and some Portuguese poetry signed by Álvaro de Campos, *Orpheu* 3 was to include work by José de Almada Negreiros, the lately deceased Sá-Carneiro, and several new contributors. The special, surprise contributor (*"tell no one about this,"* enjoined the letter writer, underlining the words twice) would be Camilo Pessanha, the little-known poet much beloved by Pessoa, and the issue would also include an artistic surprise: four reproductions of works by Amadeo de Souza-Cardoso, "the most acclaimed Portuguese avant-garde painter." Pessoa's words to describe the painter were accurate, but the acclaim came from abroad, not from Portugal, which is why he could not take it for granted that Côrtes-Rodrigues would be familiar with him or his work.

Born into a prosperous family of grape growers from the north of Portugal, Souza-Cardoso spent only a year at Lisbon's Royal Academy of the Fine Arts before heading to Paris in 1906, on his nineteenth birthday, to study architecture. He soon dropped out of the course and took up painting. As dedicated as he was unruly, he initially frequented the studio of a postimpressionist but learned more from the examples of Picasso, Sonia and Robert Delaunay, and Amedeo Modigliani—painters he knew personally. Several of his paintings were displayed in the eyebrow-raising cubist section of the 1912 Salon d'Automne, which Mário de Sá-Carneiro visited upon his arrival at Paris in October of that year. Mário also raised his eyebrows, calling the Portuguese painter's works "insignificant and preposterous" in a March 1913 letter to Pessoa. Souza-Cardoso, he added, was reputed to be "a snob, conceited, unbearable, etc." Snobbish or not, Souza-Cardoso would turn out to be the greatest Portuguese painter of the twentieth century.

At the very moment when Sá-Carneiro was dismissing his paintings and deriding his character, Souza-Cardoso was garnering international recognition. Eight of his paintings had traveled to America as part of the Armory Show, officially known as the International Exhibition of Modern Art, which opened in New York in February 1913 and later ran in Chicago and Boston. At last modern art, still a predominantly European product, was viewable on a grand scale in the United States, where it was ridiculed by most, highly praised by a few, and ultimately embraced by the American art world. Although a majority of the more than three hundred exhibiting artists were American, the big names came from Europe: Cézanne, Degas, Renoir, Monet, Manet, Van Gogh, Brancusi, Matisse, Duchamp (his *Nude Descending a Staircase* got the most laughs), Braque, and Toulouse-Lautrec, among others. No one knew Souza-Cardoso's name, but it was listed on the poster among the most notable artists, and all but one of his works were sold. He followed up this success by participating in exhibitions in Berlin (1913) and London (1914).

Souza-Cardoso and his longtime girlfriend from Paris happened to be in Spain when the Great War broke out. Instead of returning to France, they went to Portugal, got married in Porto, and settled in Manhufe, his native village, where he developed his final, most memorable style, in which we can think of him as a highly colorful and kinetic cubist.

Santa Rita Pintor and José Pacheco had known Souza-Cardoso in Paris and admired his drawings and paintings, but for José de Almada Negreiros they were not only admirable, they were wondrous creations of an artistic genius that he could never possibly match and that he generously, selflessly promoted. The bad boy of *Orpheu*, Almada Negreiros dressed extravagantly, jumped up onto café tables to make impassioned declarations, booed and hissed at public functions when he felt like booing and hissing, and spared no mercy when it came time to attack opponents. He craved attention, demanding to be heard and taken seriously, but as a visual artist he completely deferred to Souza-Cardoso. It was his idea to include the painter's work in *Orpheu* 3.[8] Fernando Pessoa, for whom literature and music were the sublime arts, could appreciate the innovative handling of forms and colors in an artist such as Souza-Cardoso, but he needed coaching. So did most of the rest of the world: despite the international attention that his work received in 1913–1914, it did not gain a wide audience until the 1950s.

Souza-Cardoso selected the four paintings he wanted to see reproduced in *Orpheu* 3, and Pessoa, for the same issue, assembled a group of unpublished poems by Camilo Pessanha, whom he may have seen during the latter's recent trip to Lisbon, on leave from his post in Macau.[9] Without any opium at his disposal, the vacationing poet resorted to alcohol, ordering potent grogs and cocktails in café after café, including some of the ones Pessoa frequented. Pessanha stayed out later, however, drinking into the wee hours of inebriated oblivion. Whether or not they met and talked about the matter directly, Pessoa apparently obtained permission to publish Pessanha's poems and had most of the main contributions— literary and artistic—he needed for *Orpheu* 3, which nevertheless stalled. Perhaps the financial support he had been counting on fell through, or perhaps, continually distracted, he simply had trouble attending to the practical details of putting together an issue and getting it into print. Other publication projects vied for his attention, with the result that nothing went forward.

◆

IN THE LATE SUMMER of 1916, as the months-long Battle of the Somme annihilated thousands upon thousands of British, French, and German soldiers, Pessoa drafted a couple of cover letters for a chap-book submission to Harold Monro, founder of *The Poetry Review* and owner of the Poetry Bookshop, which in 1914 had published *Des Imagistes*, a pivotal anthology of eleven imagist poets edited by Ezra Pound.[10] While conceding that the poems he was submitting might be considered stylistically "conventional," Pessoa bragged that the poetry he wrote in Portuguese was "far more 'advanced' than [the work of] the English Imagists."* To substantiate this claim, Pessoa told Monro that he was enclosing a copy of *Orpheu* 2 and a translation of his six-poem sequence "Slanting Rain."[11]

Although Pessoa failed to translate "Slanting Rain," it seems he did send a selection of his English poems to the Poetry Bookshop, offering to pay for their publication out of his own pocket—meaning, perhaps, that he would ask Aunt Lisbela for the money. Demoralized when his proposal was rejected, he decided, yet again, that he really should contact an English literary critic and request an honest evaluation of his poems. The surviving draft of his letter to the critic[12] is addressed to an unnamed "Sir," possibly Sir Edmund Gosse, who was an English literary institution—a poet, critic, biographer, and lecturer. "You must induce Gosse to see your poems," one of Pessoa's astral communicators had insisted, saying that he could be "some sort of aid." After explaining to Gosse, or to some other critic, that his poems had been turned

---

* Some of the leading imagists were American, not English: Pound, H. D., Amy Lowell, and William Carlos Williams.

down despite his clearly stated intention of footing the cost of their publication, Pessoa confessed that the "summary kind of rejection which the poems thus offered received" had made him insecure. "Though I never conceived them to be good," he wrote with false modesty, "I have never thought they would have been so deserving of an absolute contempt." Actually, the poet had always been confident that what he wrote in English was very good, even excellent. Only now did he begin to have doubts. Discouraged but determined, he kept writing poems for his book in progress called *The Mad Fiddler*.

A *Sensationist Anthology*, which was to include work by him and his friends, was another of Pessoa's book projects conceived for a British readership. He pitched the idea in a letter to an English publisher drafted in mid-1916, going on at great length about the nature, origins, principles, and literary consequences of sensationism, which he described as "a new species of Weltanschauung."[13] Although it cannot substitute for Pessoa's elaborate theorizations that attempt to make an aesthetic philosophy out of sensationism, Álvaro de Campos's motto, "To feel everything in every way possible," does a good job of synthesizing the essential sensationist *attitude*.

One has to marvel at Pessoa's do-it-yourself resourcefulness. After inventing—with his heteronyms—a society of collaborating authors, critics, and translators, he then fabricated doctrines that they embodied, such as neo-paganism, and movements that they belonged to, such as sensationism. He had initially envisioned sensationism as an in-house movement whose principal adepts were Alberto Caeiro and Álvaro de Campos, but in 1916 he shifted its scope, recasting it as an extension of *Orpheu*. In an article specifically about the "Sensationist Movement" that he wrote for *Exílio*,[14] a literary review published in April, Pessoa pegged its inception to the "glorious" date when *Orpheu* was founded and imaginatively claimed that sensationism was winning over the Portuguese intelligentsia. But while the magazine itself had made headlines and would be remembered as a decisive turning point in modern Portuguese literature, nobody but Pessoa and his friends had ever heard of the movement it supposedly embodied.

To promote sensationism abroad, Pessoa put two English heteronyms to work: Thomas Crosse and Sher Henay. Crosse was created in 1916[15] to write, initially, about Portuguese poets both ancient and modern, from the medieval troubadours to the twentieth-century sensationists.

Sher Henay, created the same year, had no other task than to compile a *Sensationist Anthology*, with contributions by ten different writers associated with *Orpheu*.[16] Almost nothing was translated for the *Anthology*. But Pessoa-Henay, or else Pessoa-Crosse, did find the time to write an essay about the sensationists. Revealing himself to be an Englishman who had moved to Portugal in the spring of 1915, the essayist explained that "Sensationism began with the friendship between Fernando Pessoa and Mário de Sá-Carneiro," described in a few words the main members of the movement, which he deemed "far more original" than cubism or futurism, and extolled their magazine. "There are," he claimed, "only two interesting things in Portugal—the landscape and *Orpheu*."[17] Even more interesting, though, was Pessoa's inner landscape.

# CHAPTER 43

**D**ECORATED IN ART NOUVEAU STYLE, WITH A wrought-iron and glass canopy over the front window, the Café A Brasileira at Praça do Rossio attracted a trendy clientele that included political as well as artistic types. In 1916 Pessoa and his friends regularly occupied two tables at the back. César Porto, his comrade in astrology, was one of the regulars but, discreet and unassertive, did not stand out. The opposite was true for Mariano Santana, the magnetizer who tutored Pessoa on esoteric matters. Santana was affable, outspoken, and an evangelist of the occult; other members of the café group fervently hung on his every word. They also listened closely to the less ostentatious Pessoa, who offered carefully considered interpretations of the astrological charts he cast for his friends. He also practiced numerology. Word soon got around about the group's supernatural activities, which were partly responsible for landing one of its members, Alberto Da Cunha Dias, in a psychiatric hospital.

Cunha Dias (1886–1947), whose small and squarish head contained a wildly imaginative mind, was a lawyer and writer Pessoa had known since at least 1911. Drama and trauma had been the stuff of his upbringing. His father was a tyrant; his younger brother had taken his own life; and he himself was excitable and impetuous, spontaneously generous but also susceptible to vehement outbursts. In the summer of 1916, he accused his pregnant wife of adultery and declared the child in her womb to be the fruit of an extramarital affair. To back up his claims, he presented astrological evidence obtained from Santana and Pessoa. After a series of fraught confrontations, he left his wife, whereupon his father and father-in-law reported him to the authorities and requested that he be seized on the grounds of insanity. Their petition pointed out that, besides threatening to kill people, including his wife's alleged lover, he had relied on astrology to prove her infidelity.

On August 8, Cunha Dias stood up from the two tables at the café where the usual group of friends met to talk about books, politics, astrology, and the spirit world, walked out the front door, and was apprehended by policemen waiting in ambush. Interviewed by a psychiatrist, he was diagnosed as a dangerous and incurable individual who suffered from "pathological jealousy" and a "persecution complex." The next day, *A Capital* published a front-page article titled "Sorcerers, Conjurers and Necromancers," in which the journalist—Cunha Dias's brother-in-law—wrote about the "tragedy" that had befallen his good friend, "almost a brother." Without actually naming the quasi-brother, the article told how several months earlier he had taken up a passionate interest in things like animal magnetism, ESP, palm reading, and astrology, all of which undermined his mental health, with the result that he had abandoned his loving wife and been locked up "in the Madhouse." During the next several weeks, the newspaper published a number of additional articles about the perilous spread of the occult sciences.

Cunha Dias, meanwhile, was transferred from the "Madhouse" in Telhal, near Sintra, to a psychiatric hospital in Porto, from where he wrote letters to Pessoa and Santana. In the first of four letters to Pessoa he wondered: "And you? Did they beat you up? I suppose you were spared!" And he asked for an "astrological opinion" as to when his captivity would end. It ended on October 1, thanks to an orderly who helped him escape from the hospital, and at the end of the month he was back in Lisbon, meeting with his usual friends at the same café. His mother had persuaded his father to drop the requisition for their son's internment.[1]

During the next several years Alberto Da Cunha Dias would publish a stream of articles and a couple of books denouncing the psychiatrists who had certified his insanity and criticizing the law that had made his forced committal possible. No doubt he had been wronged, but his inclination to paranoia shows through clearly enough in some of his writing, and Pessoa, convinced of his friend's mental infirmity, took some notes in English for what was apparently meant to be an illustrative case study. The notes suggest that Cunha Dias's "study of occult affairs" was a contributing factor to the "eclosion of his disease."[2] While it stands to reason that research into hidden knowledge and contact with the spirit world might entail certain risks, including to one's mental equilibrium, the real danger for Cunha Dias was simply that he took it all too seriously, or too literally. He did not have his poet-astrologer friend's capacity to be deeply engaged and sublimely detached at one and the same time.

✦

ENCOURAGED BY MARIANO SANTANA, Pessoa continued to consult the astral world. One of the most curious exchanges between him and his astral communicators involved a list of twenty-six famous individuals whom the poet thought he might like to meet. Drawn up in the summer or fall of 1916, the list included writers, politicians, the kings of England, Germany, and Spain, one visual artist—Picasso—and no women. After each name there was a check or a cross, courtesy of a communicator, to indicate whether Pessoa would ever make that person's acquaintance. One of the writers he hoped to meet (and *would* meet, according to the list) was Ezra Pound, who in that same year published a book of Japanese Noh plays as well as a collection of poems, *Lustra*, neither of which Pessoa would ever read. The Pound that interested him was the promoter and theorist of imagism and vorticism. It was Pound who coined the names of both these movements, and it was with comparable, Pound-like ingenuity that Pessoa elevated the word "sensationism" into the name of an aesthetic doctrine and a movement, planned an anthology to promote it internationally, and redefined *Orpheu* as a sensationist literary journal.

Pessoa had also drafted plans for a publication titled *Athena: A Journal of Pagan Reconstruction*.[3] With António Mora as its editor in chief and featuring essays signed by him and by Pessoa as well as poems by Alberto Caeiro and Ricardo Reis, it was a complementary project, involving all the major heteronyms *except* Álvaro de Campos, who was the exemplary sensationist and the only heteronym published in *Orpheu*. But *Athena* and its pagan reconstruction would have to wait. The two issues of *Orpheu* had made a decisive splash in the literary world of Portugal, whose greatest living artist (Amadeo de Souza-Cardoso) and one of its greatest poets (Camilo Pessanha) were willing to have their names associated with the magazine and some of their work published in its pages. There was no time to lose; Pessoa urgently needed to get out the third issue.

Although he had Pound's knack for inventing artistic concepts, doctrines, and movements, Pessoa lacked the American's gumption and practicality in literary dealings. While *Orpheu* 3 was begging for attention, its editor in chief was contemplating fanciful book projects and drafting letters—most of which he never sent—to propose them to English publishers. One of those letters stated that *Orpheu*'s third issue would be "out in a few days," and the preface he was writing for a *Sensationist Anthology* affirmed that the issue had already been printed.[4] In the second half of August, Pessoa even announced the forthcoming publication of *Orpheu* 3 in a Lisbon newspaper. Yet apart from an editorial, several versions of which survive among his papers,[5] there is no evidence that he prepared any copy for the printers.

Then he had a rude surprise: in mid-October *Centauro*, a literary review announced at the beginning of the year by Luís de Montalvor, finally launched its inaugural issue, which included fifteen previously unpublished poems by Camilo Pessanha. They were more or less the same poems Pessoa had planned to publish as the literary revelation of *Orpheu* 3. Now he would have to rethink the issue.

It was probably a week or two before *Centauro* went on sale that Pessoa learned, to his chagrin, that his dream of publishing Pessanha had been preempted. Montalvor, a regular member of the group that met at the Café A Brasileira, must have talked about its contents to his friends, and especially to Pessoa, who was himself a contributor to the first and, as it turned out, only issue of *Centauro*. In fact "Stations of the Cross," his suite of fourteen sonnets, elegantly printed, took up almost as many pages as the Pessanha section. Maybe this consoled Pessoa, but he was still disgruntled, as if a trust had been betrayed. In 1917 he would receive a warning from the astral spirit of Henry More: "Luís de Montalvor means to wrong you by making public that you are many times another, so you may not make your success with Caeiro."

◆

MISSING FROM THE CHAT circle at the Brasileira café in Praça do Rossio was Raul Leal, who had moved to Spain at the end of 1915, lest he suffer reprisals for his antirepublican activities. It was not a wise move. Although he escaped the vague threat of being physically assaulted in Portugal's capital, Spain proved to be a veritable crucible of suffering. For reasons that remain obscure, the prophet of vertiginism was unable to obtain enough money to live on from his trustee in Lisbon and soon swirled in a vortex of squalor and depression, which he described in letters to Pessoa. In June 1916 he wrote from Madrid that he had tried to commit suicide by lunging in front of a car, whose driver veered away in the nick of time. At that point Pessoa proceeded to make a detailed reading of Leal's astrological chart, noting, among other things, that Uranus in his Ascendant augured "an inclination to original and strange ideas and conceptions," while Mars in conjunction with Uranus boded "tendencies toward mental confusion and hallucination."[6]

In October Leal, who had since moved to Toledo, marked his presence in Portugal's literary scene through a short story, published alongside Pessoa and Pessanha in Montalvor's magazine. The story recounts how the Norse gods of Valhalla overcome the Greek gods of Olympus by virtue of a same-sex encounter in which Adonis, yearning for a "vertiginous indefinition" that Aphrodite cannot offer, sexually yields to a satyr sent by Wotan, the supreme god of the Norse pantheon. Meanwhile the storywriter, according to a letter he sent Pessoa in December, was going hungry in the "infernal fortress of Death" that was Toledo, where his clothes had been reduced to "putrid rags" stained by the pus and blood of "boils and syphilitic sores" covering his body. "The Spirit shines ever brighter but through an accelerating decomposition of matter and of life," Leal stoically concluded after chronicling the repellent details of his present circumstances.

Leal was mentally eccentric but not erratic or contradictory. He was firmly convinced that his tribulations were preparing him for his glorious vocation as the "precursor of the Divine Paraclete, Vertigo."[7] His delirious vision of the world and his role in it was remarkably constant throughout the years and, according to his way of thinking, logically consistent. Perhaps it was his example that prompted Pessoa to write, in 1916, this observation for *The Book of Disquiet*: "Having seen how lucidly and logically certain madmen justify their lunatic ideas to themselves and to others, I can never again be sure of the lucidness of my lucidity."[8]

Lunatic or not, Leal's ideas paralleled Pessoa's. His vertiginism was an exaggerated, sped-up form of sensationism, and his millenarian prophecy of a Paracletian Church that would replace Portuguese Catholicism bore some resemblance to Pessoa's vision of a Portuguese Fifth Empire founded on culture and on a revival of paganism. Integrated into the grand and futuristic visions of both writers was an ideal, spiritualized view of sexuality. But Leal's vision had a dark underside. To his way of seeing—and of being—the flesh needed to be abased and corrupted, through deprivation on top of depravity, so that the spirit could vertiginously prevail. The bodily afflictions he endured in Spain complemented his previous years of debauchery in Lisbon, where he had yielded to what he himself described as the "stupendous attraction of public urinals."[9] Pessoa experienced debauchery only poetically, through Álvaro de Campos's masochistic fantasies in "Triumphal Ode," "Maritime Ode," and

"Salutation to Walt Whitman." Part of him may have envied people like Leal who fulfilled, without qualms, their most extreme cravings, but what he dreamed of was a pure and radiant love.

◆

"THE RAIN OUTSIDE WAS cold in Hadrian's soul," reads the first line of "Antinous," and throughout the rest of the poem the rain keeps drearily falling, adding to the discomfort of the already distraught Emperor. In the midst of that outward and inward gloom, Hadrian's cherished memory of the love he knew with Antinous is a glowing lamp whose light can be concealed but not defiled. In the second half of 1915, a few months after producing the first draft of "Antinous," Pessoa wrote four more homoerotic poems, all in English. In "Le Mignon," a dramatic monologue, the narrator is once more Emperor Hadrian, recalling and vigorously defending his love for Antinous. Two other poems evoke the male lovers immortalized by the Greek lyric poet Anacreon—in particular Bathyllus, who enchanted the poet with his great beauty and his flute playing. The narrator wistfully regrets not having lived in ancient Greece, where he could also have loved young men and "not think it ill" to do so. His consolation, and frustration, is that the "sweet presence" of Bathyllus, conveyed to him by way of Anacreon's poetry, is "now interwove / With my modernity's despair."

The despair for a modern writer attracted to other men was twofold, since it was dangerous to openly love someone of the same sex and difficult to write about such love except in a veiled way, and even then there could be ugly consequences. Oscar Wilde was the paradigmatic victim of that danger and that difficulty, and I have already noted how the Irish writer's "pederasty" and imprisonment were astrologically examined by Pessoa in 1915 and again in 1917. In 1916, when he asked the astral spirits whether he would one day meet certain celebrities, three of the twenty-six names on his list belonged to writers whose only claim to fame was their connection to Wilde and his posthumous reputation: Robert Ross, who introduced Wilde into the London world of homosexuality and was his literary executor; Lord Alfred Douglas, or "Bosie," who repudiated his relationship with Wilde when the suppressed parts of De Profundis, a letter written in prison and addressed to him, began to come to light in 1912; and Thomas Crosland, who incited and collaborated with Douglas to denigrate Wilde's name.

Pessoa's preoccupation with Wilde's homosexual activity and subsequent downfall might suggest to us that he flirted with the idea of acting on his own desire for men but worried about the possibly unpleasant consequences. It is more likely, however, that he had closed the door on that idea and wanted to convince himself he had made the right decision. In late 1916 or early 1917, he scribbled in pencil yet another homoerotic poem in English, very different than any other he had so far written. The first six lines read:

> I write this to thy memory, my love, who art not dead,
> And to the memory of that love we never knew to have.
>
> I was the elder, you were the younger, and we were boys.
> Had we known how to love, we would have loved each other.
> Had we guessed that love's way, we would have found its joys,
> But we were boys and we loved each other as brother to brother.

The writer goes on to reflect that, if they met today, they would still not be lovers, but for a different reason: "Now I am shamed to be what erst I knew not I was." It was better, after all, that nothing ever happened between them, since the "pure white flame" of their love thus retained its purity. And the poem ends with this startling confession:

> Thou wert graceful and fair; I was neither: I loved.
>
> The taint is deeper in me of this ancient disease
> That only the Greeks made beautiful, because themselves
> beautiful were.[10]

It is hard not to conclude that the speaker of this poem is virtually identical with the author. Even if, as seems likely, the poem's addressee is an imaginary figure, corresponding to no boyhood friend of Pessoa's in particular, the story so possessed him that he let all the rules of poetry fly to the wind. The second and third stanzas are rhyming quatrains, though the meter is irregular. From then on, all attention to poetic form—rhyme, meter, stanza breaks—collapses. The poet, forgetting his art, obeyed a compulsion to commit those revealing words to paper, as if he were committing a small but irresistible crime. Love between men was acceptable and even beautiful if not acted on, or if the lovers were Greek or Roman, or if their love flourished in a work of literature, but in Pessoa's mind the idea of homosexual love in the world he inhabited was still clothed with the vocabulary of pathology—"disease," "vice," "degeneracy"—and to imagine himself with another man made him blush with shame.

Then too, sexual possession of whatever kind amounted, in Pessoa's view, to little more than the satisfaction of an instinctive urge. He rejected being a slave to instinct, and not only for noble, philosophical reasons. The fact was that he did not know *how* to act instinctively, naturally, like a so-called normal man.

◆

PESSOA WROTE HIS POEM about the love that "only the Greeks made beautiful" on a sheet of paper with an updated list of contributors to *Orpheu* 3. A year and a half had passed since the publication of *Orpheu* 2, but he stubbornly tried to keep the magazine going. The winter and spring of 1915, when he closely worked with Mário de Sá-Carneiro to bring out the first two issues, had been one of the happiest, most productive, and most exciting periods of his life. If he could not recover the elation and creative stamina he felt back then, he wanted to at least preserve *Orpheu* as an emblem of those days and of his friendship with Mário. Although he could no longer reveal Camilo Pessanha's gorgeously sensorial poetry to the world, since Luís de Montalvor had just done that in *Centauro*, Pessoa still hoped to be the first magazine editor to publish artwork by Amadeo de Souza-Cardoso, whose status as Portugal's leading avant-garde artist was confirmed with fanfare in the last two months of 1916.

In November Souza-Cardoso organized his first solo exhibition, in Porto, the cultural capital of the north and less than fifty miles from Manhufe, the village where the artist lived. His exhibition was also the first large display of modern art in Portugal. The show attracted huge crowds and considerable outrage, personal insults, accusations of insanity, journalistic lampoons, and bravos from a few admirers. One month later, the same show opened in Lisbon at the Navy League, a few blocks away from the neighborhood of Chiado, the city's intellectual nerve center.

José de Almada Negreiros was the exhibiting artist's chief promoter in Lisbon, and on December 5 he hosted a dinner for him at his tiny, top-floor apartment on Rua do Alecrim. The select group of guests, according to a notice published in more than one newspaper, included

Fernando Pessoa, the composer Ruy Coelho, and José Pacheco, who was responsible for the layout and design of *Orpheu* 3. The forthcoming issue, and Souza-Cardoso's participation in it, must have been more than an incidental topic of conversation.

The journalists and visiting public of the Portuguese capital were on the whole more receptive to Souza-Cardoso's paintings, though perplexity and ridicule were still the most common reactions. One newspaper reported: "After the farce that was *Orpheu*, now we have this exhibition in which a talented young man makes us either fear for his mental health or suspect that his cynical intention is to scandalize the middle classes." In fact Souza-Cardoso's exhibition, insofar as it appalled bourgeois sensibilities, was the visual art equivalent of *Orpheu*.[11]

◆

WHILE SOUZA-CARDOSO'S EXHIBITION WAS assaulting prevailing notions of what art could or should attempt, António Machado Santos (1875–1921)—a highly respected naval officer and the most celebrated hero of the 1910 republican revolution—launched a military coup out of Tomar, a town some seventy miles north of Lisbon. Though he looked every bit like a romantic revolutionary, owing partly to his wire-frame glasses, Machado Santos was disillusioned from the start with the Portuguese Republic's model of governance, which seemed designed to breed instability. He had backed previous reform movements, including the Pimenta de Castro dictatorship, and would lend his support to future ones, but there was an added incentive for the revolt he himself helped to orchestrate on December 13, 1916: opposition to Portugal's involvement in the European war. He had rallied other officers and a few hundred unhappy recruits to help him attempt to overthrow the government. The putsch was quickly foiled and its leaders and participants imprisoned, which is all that the newspapers were allowed to report. The information that many of the insurgents were dissatisfied conscripts was censored.

Although the Portuguese armed forces had succeeded in swiftly mobilizing thousands of young men and turning them into soldiers, the government had done a poor job of selling the war effort as a patriotic endeavor, and few recruits believed they were serving a noble cause. Portugal's reasons for joining the war were not terribly persuasive, particularly since its much larger neighbor in Iberia, Spain, remained neutral. Even if one understood and accepted the argument that fighting and dying for the

Allies was necessary in order for the country to secure a large loan from Britain that would pay for imported wheat and other necessities, it was obvious that the war would sap Portugal's resources, more than offsetting the immediate benefit of the loan. One long-term benefit that Portugal did stand to gain by participating in the war was British recognition and protection of its colonial sovereignty over Angola, Mozambique, Cape Verde, Portuguese Guinea, and São Tomé and Príncipe, but this was not a justification that could be advertised, since it would be tantamount to admitting how fragile Portugal's hold on its colonies was.

There was another unspoken motive for joining the Allied cause: a desire to revamp Portugal's image abroad. The five-year-old republic—politically tumultuous and economically improvident—wanted to show that it could behave, as it were, like a self-disciplined and cooperative adult. The problem was not just with the Republic, however. The nation's image had been sullied during the monarchy by widespread reports of slave labor in Portuguese West Africa. The practice of forcing Angolans to work on the cocoa plantations of São Tomé and Príncipe, from where they never returned, went back many decades, but in the early 1900s it began to be loudly denounced in Great Britain and the United States, leading Cadbury and other chocolate manufacturers to boycott São Tomean cocoa in 1909.[*] Only in 1914, bowing to intense pressure, did the island colony's cocoa growers curtail their abusive labor practices to the satisfaction of international observers.

◆

PESSOA'S REACTION TO THE British boycott of cocoa grown in São Tomé opens a wide window onto his attitudes regarding imperialism, slavery, and race. Since his boyhood days in Durban, he had bristled with nationalistic indignation whenever criticism was hurled at Portugal from the British Isles. And so it is not really surprising that one of his many writing projects from 1909, when he was crafting big plans for the Ibis press, was an essay titled "The Pretended Slavery of São Tomé"—in English, of course, since the Portuguese colonizers had already convinced

---

[*] One year earlier, international outrage over the human atrocities in the rubber-producing areas of the Congo Free State—a colony personally owned and administered by Belgian King Leopold II—had led Belgium to annex the territory and begin to curb the most abusive practices.

themselves that to coerce Africans to work in subhuman conditions was not comparable to slavery. The partly written essay, which its author perhaps thought of publishing as an Ibis pamphlet, was to be followed by a companion piece titled "Slavery and Cruelty in the British Colonies."[12] The accusation of hypocrisy could not have been less subtle. Pessoa wrote nothing for the follow-up essay, but his essay on "pretended" slavery, while admitting that "the poor negroes" forced to work in São Tomé had sometimes been subject to "brutal inhuman treatment," argued that they were often better fed and better treated than the migrant blacks who worked in the South African mines, where their British employers paid them a wage but "work[ed] them to death."[13]

Pessoa's compassion for the mistreated native Africans who worked in São Tomé or in the Transvaal mines was slight, and his denunciation of Britain's imperialism was little more than a knee-jerk reaction to its cavalier attitude toward Portugal's own colonial empire. When it came to pointing out actual victims of British imperialism, Pessoa was narrowly selective. At several points in his writing he deplored how the British had mistreated the Boers,[14] but at no point did he fault them for exploiting the Indians they had brought to Natal as indentured servants, much less for lording it over the Zulus, whose lands they had appropriated through war and intimidation—to mention only the colonizing practices Pessoa witnessed firsthand as a boy growing up in Durban. As a student at Durban High School, moreover, he had learned to ridicule those who were not white as he and everyone else in the school was. One day, when bored with his schoolwork, he scrawled on a piece of paper a couple of racistly "funny" questions for a mock exam. "Describe a coolie," instructs one, in "botanical language" and in "poetic language," as if Durban's many Indians were a colorful and curious form of subhuman life. The other faux exam question is more blatantly derogatory: "What, besides the Zulus, are the chief breeds of cattle in use in South Africa and for what purposes is each most suitable?"[15]

Clearly not all people were equal for Pessoa, and his acceptance of their presumed inequality shaped his own imperialist ideology. In a passage from an unfinished essay on imperialism datable to around 1916, he stated unequivocally that a colonizing empire rightly seeks to spread its own civilization simply for the sake of spreading it, not because it will benefit the colonized. He continued, "Slavery is logical and legitimate; a Zulu or a Landim [an indigenous Mozambican] represents nothing useful in this world. To civilize him, whether religiously or in some other way, is to want to give him what he cannot have. The right thing is to compel him, since he is not a person, to serve the ends of civilization."[16]

A number of Pessoa scholars have insisted that he was not a racist. The lines I have just quoted, they say, must be considered in the context of his entire work, notable for presenting provocative and often contradictory points of view. And they note that Pessoa never publicly supported any racist ideology. Indeed he did not; nor was he interested in the literature on "scientific" racism then much in vogue.[17] But nowhere in his writing did he suggest that Europeans represent nothing useful in this world; he reserved that "distinction" for black Africans.

The lines quoted above are a rare but not unique instance of blatantly racist sentiment in Pessoa. A couple of years later, he would affirm, in English, that black people "are not human beings, sociologically speaking. The greatest crime against civilization was the abolition of slavery."[18] These words, published here for the first time, are from a passage arguing that democracy in ancient Greece and Rome was successful only because there were distinct social classes, including slaves as well as aristocrats.

I agree with the scholars who say that many of the positions Pessoa defended were for argument's sake, and despite what a couple of his statements might suggest, I don't believe he harbored any hostility toward black Africans. But he considered them, nonetheless, to be an inferior race. Though he questioned many common beliefs and prejudices of the society in which he lived, it did not occur to him to question his own racism—until the very end of his life. At that point, as we shall see, his views on class, race, and slavery would shift rather dramatically. But as late as 1930, to support his contention that "the barbarian [. . .] is wholly modern," Pessoa would write, again in English, that "the negro always wears the latest introduced fashions."[19]

The passages I have cited practically exhaust Pessoa's overtly racist statements. On the other hand, and independent of any racial considerations, Pessoa strenuously and consistently argued against the doctrine of human equality. In his view, as in Nietzsche's, most people had a herd mentality, imitating others without knowing why and obeying the instincts of conservation and reproduction as other animals do.[20] Exceptional, higher men (and only rarely women) were the ones responsible for great empires, great music and literary works, philosophies, and other sophisticated products of human invention.

✦

THE GERMAN GOVERNMENT DISTRIBUTED copies of *Thus Spoke Zarathustra* in a pocket edition to its soldiers during the First World War—perhaps to convince them that they belonged to a race of "higher men," or perhaps to reassure them that their lives, if lost, would be serving the high purposes of the masters who had sent them into battle. The notion of higher purposes eluded most of the soldiers of the C.E.P.—the Portuguese Expeditionary Corps—who morbidly joked that the acronym stood for Carneiros de Exportação Portuguesa (Portuguese Sheep for Export). If they were a herd going to slaughter, they were a conscious, not very willing herd.

The uprising of recruits led by Machado Santos in mid-December had slightly delayed their departure, but in late January 1917 the first contingent of Portuguese soldiers left Lisbon's harbor. Hailing from all over the country, they wore double-breasted greatcoats, high boots, and peak caps, with knapsacks firmly strapped to their backs. One or another battalion had a small brass band to rouse morale; some men from the interior hurriedly wrote letters to their families before it was time to weigh anchor; and mixed in with the soldierly crowd were a few young women, bidding farewell to their boyfriends going off to war, uncertain when or if they would return. The recruits sailed on three British ships, and after disembarking on French soil it was the British army that trained them in the art of trench warfare. In April they were dispatched to the fighting front, still under close supervision, and on the fourth day of that month they lost their first man in combat.

Fernando Pessoa's sympathies, in this case, lay with the herd—with the tens of thousands of young men forced into service by a political strategy that was not, he believed, in the nation's best interest. As the first lot of troops boarded the ships bound for Brest, he sketched a poem whose second stanza summed up in seven words his point of view on the inglorious wartime reality of the Portuguese: "Vile slaves of England, / Pariahs of France."[21] In the poem's next stanza, looking beyond the nation's present state of subservient humiliation, he invoked "new Indias for the dream / Of our glory." These were nongeographical Indias, belonging to his glowing vision of a Portuguese Fifth Empire, but who else in all of Portugal nurtured such a fantastical dream, and what possible shape could it assume in space and time?

Confident though he was of his status as a higher man with a special call-ing, Pessoa did not know quite what to do with himself and with his large hopes and dreams that seemed to have no place in conceivable reality—particularly now, with Portugal and most of the rest of Europe dedicated to mutual destruction. Toward the end of February, he tried to articulate his lonely predicament in a poem, which he soon abandoned, but not before formulating a précis of what he wanted it to convey: "The idea that genius is a curse of the gods, since it fills men with desires and hopes beyond what they can obtain, and because it separates them from the cozy and limited lot of being equal to others in life and emotion. The man of genius has godly emotions and desires, with a human body and soul—hence his eternal anguish."[22] The divine curse of genius was an old theme in Pessoa's arsenal of self-analyses, and the idea that it breeds emotional isolation from the "normal" people all around him was also not new. His feeling of isola-tion and estrangement had somewhat diminished during the years of his friendship with Mário de Sá-Carneiro, but like a firmly rooted plant that can survive any weather, it now flourished with greater vigor than before.

Instead of remarking that men of genius are condemned to solitude since they are not "equal to others in life and emotion," Pessoa might have personalized his observation and said, more simply, that he was unable to love and be loved. But was this inability really an inevitable by-product of being a genius? Or did he retreat into the role of the lonely genius because love seemed so unlikely, and complicated? His astral communicators, rejecting the inevitability theory, continued to insist that he needed to realize himself as a lover in order to be a fully realized poet. In a communication from January, Henry More, the most diligent matchmaker from beyond, made this promise: "A woman assumes sway over you on the 3rd day of March, 1917. She is a woman of a sensual bent and is your woman until 5.III.1918." Although More hoped to set Pes-soa up with a suitable lady, he accepted that his disciple was a complex creature. The same communication contains this open-ended reply to an unrecorded question: "Yes, women and boys. Women in womanly wise; only one in a manly one. Boys in a womanly way."

Pessoa dreamed of a Fifth Empire consisting of new and marvel-ous, immaterial Indias, pursued his growing interest in the occult, and devoted many hours to making contact with the spirit realm. But the astral spirits, curiously enough, kept trying to bring him back down to earth, to his fellow creatures, and to the possibility of love.

# CHAPTER 44

VER SINCE THE PUBLICATION OF *ORPHEU* 1, WHOSE most talked-about contribution was Álvaro de Campos's reputedly futurist "Triumphal Ode," Pessoa had been distancing himself from Marinetti's movement, but José de Almada Negreiros and Santa Rita Pintor were still fervent advocates of futurism. What attracted them, more than its artistic methods, was the audacious and arrogant, impolite figure of the futurist artist. It was a style, which they cultivated. On April 14, 1917, Almada Negreiros delivered a "First Futurist Lecture" at the Theater of the Republic (now the São Luiz Theater). Appearing on stage in a jumpsuit of his own design, a kind of lightweight aviator suit, he warmly introduced Santa Rita Pintor, who would intermittently jump up from his seat in one of the boxes, fielding questions or responding to objections from people in the audience, who were allowed and even encouraged to interrupt the proceedings. In a stentorian voice Almada Negreiros recited three manifestos, including Portuguese translations of the "Futurist Manifesto of Lust," published in 1913 by the writer and artist Valentine de Saint-Point, and Marinetti's "The Variety Theater," also from 1913. Almada Negreiros began the session by reciting his own "Futurist Ultimatum to the Portuguese Generations of the Twentieth Century"—a manifesto that denounced Portuguese decadence, challenged his generation (he had just turned twenty-four) to revitalize the nation, and praised the Great War for annihilating reactionary sentimentalism and awakening the spirit of creativity and construction.

If Pessoa attended the lecture, he must have cringed at his friend's glorification of war, which went on at some length, echoing Marinetti's contention that war was "hygienic" as well as energizing. The Italian futurists, it must be said, not only supported the Great War with their words, by collaborating with the propaganda service of the army, they also fought in it as soldiers. Although Pessoa agreed with Heraclitus that war is the mother of all things,[1] although he theoretically approved of Germany's ambitions to expand its empire through armed force, and although he had tried to market several war games of his own invention back in 1915, actual war horrified him, and the negotiated participation of Portuguese soldiers in the European war was to his mind unconscionable.

Even if the Portuguese negotiators acted in good faith, events quickly suggested that they had made a poor deal. Despite the British line of credit extended to Portugal like a float for a man drowning, the nation's finances—strained by the expense of outfitting and training the soldiers it sent to France—floundered more than ever. Unable to import enough wheat, on May 10 the government decreed that all bread sold had to be baked with a certain percentage of corn flour. The loaves thus produced were deemed inedible by some, and many bakeries simply turned off their ovens. More affluent classes could purchase, at a premium, bread baked in surrounding towns or by private individuals, but the urban poor were increasingly malnourished. Food riots, collectively known as the Potato Revolt, broke out in and around Lisbon,* markets and grocery shops were plundered, troops were called in, and a few dozen rioters were killed, hundreds more arrested, before order was restored at the end of the month.

However much he sympathized with the plight of the hungry, Pessoa ignored the turmoil on the streets and concentrated on various publication projects—including the next and long overdue issue of *Orpheu*, his English poetry, the poetry of his heteronyms, and an edition of *The Mariner* and his other "static" dramas.[2] On May 12, while Lisbon's working class was clamoring for bread, he decided on the publication details for *Orpheu* 3 and cast a horoscope for the occasion. On that same day he sent the finalized version of *The Mad Fiddler*—fifty-three poems divided into eight sections—to Constable, one of the largest British publishers. This submission also merited a horoscope.[3] Destiny, it quickly turned out, did not favor *The Mad Fiddler*, which the publisher returned in the first week of June, along with a terse rejection letter.

✦

IN THAT SAME MONTH of June, Pessoa began using playing cards to discover his fortune, but it was not his future as a writer that immediately

---

* Such riots were common throughout wartime Europe, even in neutral nations such as the Netherlands and Switzerland.

concerned him, notwithstanding his repeated failures to get his English poetry into print. He used card reading, like automatic (or mediumistic) writing, to try to glean something about his future as a lover. One future was at any rate connected to the other, if it was true—as Pessoa suspected—that his sexual retardation was impeding his spiritual and literary progress.

Consulting a manual in French to help him interpret their meaning, Pessoa drew cards from a well-shuffled deck and laid them out in various combinations, which he recorded on dated sheets of paper between June and December 1917. The cards were an alternate method for contacting the astral world, possibly with the very same spirits he knew through automatic writing. On June 21, he used an automatic communication—one that predicted, in pencil, that a woman would soon enter his life—as a palimpsest. Turning the sheet of paper sideways and writing in ink on top of the prediction, he recorded (in English) the questions he put to the cards to learn more about the "hypothetical woman" promised by one of his communicators: "Who is she? Where shall I meet her? When/How shall I meet her? What will [the] result be?" The answer to the first question was the nine of spades, the eight of spades, and the queen of spades, while for the second question he drew the nine of clubs, the three of diamonds, and the six of hearts. Unfortunately, he did not record his interpretations.[4]

For some people, card reading is a form of solitaire, and so it probably was for Pessoa, but it was not only that. On July 11 he consulted an experienced card reader—perhaps his friend Mariano Santana, or the nationally renowned Madame Brouillard, who received clients on Rua do Carmo, near Praça do Rossio—and later that same day he cast an astrological chart to confirm the accuracy of the reading.[5] Pessoa's desire to see what was in store for him may have been stimulated by Raul Leal, who had just presented him with an eight-page narrative of "Prophecies" about his own future. Using an unspecified method—possibly sheer clairvoyance—Leal charted his changing psychological and material fortunes and, especially, his spiritual progress from July 1917 until March 1934, when death would transform him into pure Vertigo and, ergo, into God.[6] (He would live thirty years longer than predicted.)

✦

THE SELF-REALIZATION AND SELF-ELEVATION that Pessoa sought in the spirit world were a preparation, as he saw it, for his missionary task of elevating and dignifying Portugal, whose fortunes the Republic had so far failed to turn around. Indeed, his lofty dream of a Portuguese Fifth Empire founded on "spiritual" rather than material conquests was a response to the decadence in which the nation continued to languish. A spiritual response of a very different kind—a response not to Portuguese decadence but to the Republic itself, or to republican policy—was at that very moment taking hold in the Portuguese heartland.

On May 13, 1917, in the village of Fátima, about seventy-five miles north of Lisbon, the Blessed Virgin Mary appeared to three shepherd children as a lady made of brilliant light, hovering above an oak tree in a field where they grazed their sheep. She told them to pray the rosary to bring an end to the war and peace to the world, and she instructed them to return to the same spot at the same time, on the thirteenth day of each of the next five months, as she had things to reveal. Local people, and soon the faithful and curious from all over the country, gathered at the sacred oak tree on the appointed day of each month, where the children talked with the Virgin, whom the bystanders could not see, but there were signs of her divine presence, such as humming in the air and clapping thunder. About two thousand onlookers gathered for the third apparition, on July 13, which was reported in the national newspapers with skepticism.

The Catholic clergy was also initially skeptical, then cautious, and eventually accepting. The Virgin had told the children that during her last visitation she would perform a miracle, and on October 13 at least thirty thousand people gathered in the field with the oak tree to see it with their own eyes. It was a rainy day, but at a certain point the sun emerged as a silver disk among breaking clouds, and it began to whirl, flashing with a panoply of colors. The Miracle of the Sun, as it came to be called, validated the claims of the children, and Fátima became a new pilgrimage site for Marian worship, competing with Lourdes, where the Virgin appeared to a little French girl in 1858. The cult of Our Lady of Fátima marked the resurgence and the revenge of the Catholic Church in Portugal. Afonso Costa, architect of the harsh anticlerical laws passed by decree after the monarchy gave way to the Republic, had bragged that he and other secularists would succeed in stamping out Catholicism in Portugal, but Church leaders and the faithful would have the last laugh.

Pessoa, who did not believe in the Blessed Virgin, let alone in her apparitions at Lourdes and Fátima, observed in an unfinished book or booklet titled *Rationalism*, which he hoped to publish in England, "Religion is an emotional need of mankind. The rationalist may not want it, but he has to admit that other people may."[7] He proposed to satisfy that need in the Portuguese masses with the new paganism preached by António Mora and Ricardo Reis. The fact that Athena and Apollo are less real than the Virgin Mary—since Jesus's mother actually existed, even if she was not a virgin—was by no means a disadvantage, since people, according to Pessoa, prefer colorful fictions to the unvarnished truth. And paganism, with its lush profusion of gods and myths, was even more colorful than Roman Catholicism and its pantheon of saints.

Elitist and rational-minded Pessoa could not help but view the religious needs of common people with condescension, and yet he himself was similarly needy. Instead of embracing a simple faith in God, which his reason would not allow, he groped like a blind man in a maze of occult mysteries that, by definition, could never be fathomed. His quest for esoteric truth, which in a few years would lead him to pore over dozens of books on Kabbalah, Rosicrucianism, and Freemasonry, was like an unsolvable puzzle that could endlessly fascinate and entertain his intellect. As for his religiously "emotional need," he satisfied it with séances, astrological charts, automatic writing, and card reading—like so many scenes and props from a riveting Theater of the Beyond.

✦

ON JULY 11, THE same day he consulted Mariano Santana, Madame Brouillard, or some other fortune-teller, Pessoa wrote a letter to his friend José Pacheco, who was handling the layout and design of *Orpheu* 3. Page proofs for most of the issue had at last been printed, and the editor in chief wanted to arrange a meeting to discuss the front matter and a publicity flyer. The issue opened with eleven poems by Mário de Sá-Carneiro and also included Pessoa's quintet of poems titled "Beyond-God," which his deceased friend had especially admired. But the poetic centerpiece of the issue was the sixteen-page "A cena do ódio" ("Scene of Hatred"), written by José de Almada Negreiros during the revolution of May 1915 that deposed the dictator Pimenta de Castro—whom he supported, as did Pessoa and many others weary of political unrest. The poem was a manifesto of disgust and disillusion with Portugal ("the country where Camões died of hunger / and where everyone stuffs their bellies with Camões!") as well as a declaration of individual difference:

I stand tall, a Sodomite, booed by idiots,
I'm divine, a divine Harlot, emblem of Sin,
and I hate all that's not Me for laughing at my I!

These are the three opening lines of the poem, whose language of effrontery and contempt is reminiscent of Álvaro de Campos, but with added fire. The poem was dedicated to Campos, who, as if responding to a challenge, would soon produce an even haughtier and more vituperative manifesto.

The page proofs for *Orpheu* 3 included another long and remarkable poem, "Para além doutro oceano" ("Beyond Another Ocean"), which was dedicated "to the memory of Alberto Caeiro," who supposedly died in 1915. Some passages of the poem are in a voice uncannily like Caeiro's, while others have stylistic affinities with the poetry of Álvaro de Campos, or of Fernando Pessoa writing under his own name, so that the ensemble makes for a fascinating Pessoa-esque medley, an unconscious pastiche. The poem's author, José Coelho Pacheco (not to be confused with the José Pacheco responsible for producing the magazine), was an unusually attentive reader and impressionable enthusiast of Pessoa's multifarious works, some of which he must have read in manuscript copies. When still a college student, Coelho Pacheco had been a cofounder of *A Renascença*, the ephemeral magazine that revealed Pessoa as a poet, in 1914, and his name appears on lists as a possible contributor to a couple of Pessoa's aborted publication projects: the magazine *Europa* and the *Anthology of Intersectionism*. His interest in writing had waned, however, and was already overshadowed by his passion for automobiles. He would eventually become a car dealer, and gradually fell out of touch with Pessoa.[8]

Although José Coelho Pacheco was unrelated to José Pacheco the graphic designer and art promoter, he was the nephew of another close friend of Pessoa: Geraldo Coelho de Jesus, the mining engineer, who had already tried to be a car dealer, without success.[9] As an engineer, however, he made lots of money. He also spent lots of money, including on cars, and continued to be one of Pessoa's most generous creditors. In August 1917 he also became the poet's business partner for a firm called F. A. Pessoa, which operated out of a small office on Rua de São Julião, close to Praça do Comércio and the Tagus River. The company specialized in "commissions and consignments."[10] Vaguely defined businesses of this sort had been proliferating in Lisbon since the beginning of the century. Requiring little start-up capital, they could and sometimes did make easy money as intermediaries, even during the middle of the war, which afforded special opportunities for the adventurous. Several of the businesses opened by Pessoa's cousin Mário were of the "commissions and consignments" variety, and they all flopped, but Pessoa thought he could do better. Geraldo Coelho de Jesus was a happy-go-lucky individual, not averse to risk, and more than willing to collaborate with his friend Fernando. The same was true for the firm's third partner, Augusto Ferreira Gomes (1892–1953), a journalist who had met Pessoa in the spring of 1915, not long after the publication of *Orpheu* 1.

Less than five feet tall, with a sallow complexion and a sunken chest, yet lively, witty, and ready to talk about anything, Gomes resembled a comical character from a picaresque novel, but his favorite author was Edgar Allan Poe. He loved mystery and magic, occult theories of Portugal's history and destiny, and astrology—subjects that had in recent years begun to enchant Pessoa. A regular member of the café group in which the astral world often filtered into the conversation, Gomes also got on well with Alberto Da Cunha Dias, who had trusted astrology to confirm his suspicions about his wife's adultery, and was good friends with Geraldo Coelho de Jesus, who, completing the circle, was friends with Cunha Dias. Pessoa was the magnet that drew them all together.

Truly good writers are rare, and Gomes was not one of them, but Pessoa appreciated the short piece he contributed to the third issue of *Orpheu*. It was a wistful, poetic description of the death of a faun, at twilight, supposedly inspired by a frieze found at Pompeii. These framing devices—twilight and Pompeii—accentuated the feeling of doom surrounding the faun and the ancient world of myth it represented. The heteronyms Ricardo Reis and António Mora, both still unpublished, embodied a similar kind of nostalgia. The page proofs for *Orpheu* 3 included other, likewise brief contributions by three of the editor's lesser friends, but one major contribution was still missing: Álvaro de Campos's "Salutation to Walt Whitman." Pessoa planned to finish the poem, which was to close the issue, in mid-July. He also needed to find a sponsor to cover the cost of printing the magazine. On August 5 he posted a letter to Aunt Lisbela, a usually trusty source of funding, and cast a horoscope for the event,[11] presumably to find out whether his request for assistance had been made at a propitious moment. Chances are she wired him some money, but *Orpheu* was still waiting on "Salutation to Walt Whitman." Something was blocking the poet from engaging with the more than six hundred lines and twenty-some passages he had written for the poem two years earlier.

◆

MEANWHILE PESSOA, WHO HAD turned twenty-nine in June, was still waiting on love. In July, a month after resorting to cartomancy to learn some details about the "hypothetical woman" that his communicators kept promising, he noticed a very real young woman who lived right across the street. Finding her attractive, or at least intriguing, he consulted his cards to see if she might be meant for him. Perhaps not. On August 19, discouraged by so many spiritual communications and consultations that led only to dead ends, he cast a horoscope for the question "Shall I marry?" The answer was yes, but he would marry late.[12] In September he wrote about love's elusiveness:

> By nature I quickly strike up acquaintances. People are friendly to me right away. But I never receive affection. I've never been shown devotion. To be loved has always seemed impossible to me, like a stranger calling me by my first name. [. . .] Left an orphan by Fortune, I needed—like all orphans—to be the object of someone's affection. This need has always been a hunger that went unsatisfied, and so thoroughly have I adapted to this inevitable hunger that I sometimes wonder if I really feel the need to eat.

When it came to love, Pessoa was indeed a kind of hunger artist, since if he really felt a pressing *need* to love and be loved, he would have done something, anything, to meet the young woman who lived across the street rather than ask a deck of cards whether she was destined to be his. Pessoa, however, was not exactly the "I" of the paragraphs just cited, which belong to a passage from *The Book of Disquiet*,[13] whose narrator, while largely modeled on Pessoa, was a distinct persona. Expressing anguished feeling with clinical objectivity, the passage is not an autobiographical outpouring but a mediated, literary formulation of the writer's feeling of lovelessness.

Pessoa had slowly been defining and redefining the narrator of his most penetrating work of prose to make him more like himself, and hence more useful as a tool for self-study. In the early days of *The Book of Disquiet*, the dreamy narrator who cultivated absurdity and artificiality had no biography, but in late 1914 an embryonic preface to the book defined him as a "[d]andy in spirit" who "promenaded the art of dreaming through the randomness of existing."[14] Like a poorer, Portuguese cousin of Jean Des Esseintes, the hero of Huysman's proto-decadent novel *Against Nature*, Pessoa's hero lived alone in two rooms with "a semblance of luxury"—denoted by fine armchairs, drapes, and rugs—so that he could "maintain the dignity of tedium." Given that he "never had to face the demands of society," he evidently had a small independent income that provided for his needs. His name was Vicente Guedes. Originally a poet, short story writer, and translator for the chimerical Ibis press, Guedes, whom we have already met, had dropped out of circulation in 1910, the year Ibis went under. When he resurfaced in 1914, his only writing assignment was to tell about himself, his ideas, and his feelings in one all-consuming opus, *The Book of Disquiet*.

In 1917 Pessoa made refinements to Guedes's person and personality. He was still a dreamer, still solitary, and still a model of "inner aristocracy," but without his former air of impoverished gentry. Instead of two reasonably elegant rooms, he was reduced to inhabiting just one slightly dingy room, and he earned his living by working in an office. He had no friends to speak of and spent his free time writing. These new details are from the longest of the passages that Pessoa wrote for his preface to *The Book of Disquiet*. The same passage recounts how Pessoa supposedly met *The Book*'s author, Guedes, at a cheap restaurant where they both regularly dined. One evening they finally struck up a conversation, and when Pessoa mentioned the literary review *Orpheu*, he was surprised to discover that his dinner companion was one of its devoted readers. Pessoa, who could invent whatever collaborating authors he needed for his many writing projects, likewise never lacked for ideal readers.

The biography of *The Book of Disquiet*'s pseudo-author continued to evolve—some notes from 1918 would reveal that he was an assistant bookkeeper, and many years later he would go by the name of Bernardo Soares and do the bookkeeping for a fabric warehouse—but by 1917 he was already established as a discreet, unremarkable office worker whose secret life of exuberant dreaming and writing no one around him would ever have imagined. He was a radicalized version of Fernando Pessoa, who was not friendless, just celibate, and whose vocation as a writer was a secret to no one. A citified hermit, Vicente Guedes—later, Bernardo Soares—served as a predictive model of what a resolutely lonely life might be like.

Henry More and his astral cronies had warned Pessoa that a monkish existence was not for him, but he was not so sure.

# CHAPTER 45

I N THE SUMMER OF 1914, WHEN THE WAR WAS A NEW and glamorous adventure, hundreds of thousands of young men had gleefully donned uniforms and taken up arms. Enthusiasm was much harder to find among the streams of conscripts pressed into service as the static conflict ground on, destroying millions of lives without either side gaining or losing any significant ground. Soldiers from all the participating armies, which included huge numbers of Africans and Asians, grew increasingly restless, some of them rebelled, and many others deserted. It was in late 1917 that shell-shocked Wilfred Owen (1893–1918) wrote his famous poem describing the gross horror of the war, the first in which gas was a weapon, and denounced "the old Lie: *Dulce et decorum est / Pro patria mori.*"[1]

Soldiers in the Portuguese Expeditionary Corps were not even dying for their country but for the sake of a centuries-old alliance between Portugal and Great Britain, or so the reasoning went. Troop morale was never high, and it only kept sinking as the months went by. British ships had been transporting about five thousand Portuguese recruits per month to France since January 1917, and by that fall the corps had reached its maximum size: some fifty thousand reluctant combatants. More Portuguese troops were supposed to arrive, but the British decided that their ships were needed in other capacities. If additional Portuguese soldiers were not a high priority, why were any of them taken there in the first place? The recent entry of the United States into the war may have weighed on the British decision. The first American troops landed on French soil in the summer of 1917 and began fighting at the western front in late October, though still only in small numbers.

The more Pessoa read about the war in the papers, the more absurd he thought it was, and on October 31 he publicly declared his own war on all of Europe, in an "Ultimatum" signed by Álvaro de Campos. Published in a new magazine, *Portugal Futurista*, Campos's manifesto opened with a laundry list of politicians, writers, and intellectuals whom he insulted individually and conjointly. He was particularly harsh on the national leaders who had plunged Europe into war, calling them "bare-assed incompetents, overturned garbage cans at the door of Contemporary Inadequacy!"

The manifesto borrowed its title from the infamous British Ultimatum of 1890, which had obliged Portugal to relinquish its claim to a wide stretch of territory between Mozambique and Angola; Campos retaliated by remembering, in his own "Ultimatum," the British Empire's worst defeats at the hands of the Boers, who did not even have a standing army. Evenhandedly, Campos upbraided Britain's enemies as well as her allies. António Mora admired Germany's culture, represented by figures such as Goethe and Nietzsche, and he lauded the strong pagan undercurrent that supposedly persisted in its Christianity, but Campos turned this rosy picture on its head: "You, German culture, a rancid Sparta dressed with the oil of Christianity and the vinegar of Nietzscheization, a sheet-metal beehive, an imperialistic horde of harnessed sheep!" Although the "Ultimatum" focused on the failures of Europe, Campos also took digs at Brazil and the United States, defining the latter as a "bastard synthesis of Europe's scum, garlic of the transatlantic stew, nasalized pronunciation of tasteless modernism."

The first half of the "Ultimatum" was not a plea for pacifism; it was a jeremiad about the dearth of great politicians, great generals, great thinkers, and great poets. The second half was a far-fetched recipe for curing the problem through "sociological surgery," abolishing the allegedly Christian dogmas of "personality," "individuality," and "personal objectivity." On the face of it, the proposed surgery would only aggravate the problem it was meant to correct, but its predicted end result—logically argued by the naval engineer—was that a handful of exceptional people would represent a nation's collective will, intelligence, and creative genius. Democracy as we know it would be replaced by "the Dictatorship of the Total Man, of the Man who in himself is the greatest number of Others, and hence The Majority." And the greatest artist would be "the one who least defines himself, and who writes in the most genres with the most contradictions and discrepancies," such that "two poets endowed with fifteen or twenty personalities" would be enough to represent a literary age. It hardly needs to be pointed out who, in Pessoa's mind, was the prototype of such a vastly self-multiplied and self-contradictory artist.

The "Ultimatum" foresaw a radically transformed society guided by Nietzschean Overmen, or Supermen, whose advent is explicitly invoked at the end of the manifesto. The Superman, declared Campos, would be "not the strongest man but the most complete, [. . .] not the toughest man but the most complex, [. . .] not the freest man but the most harmonious!" Pessoa, with these words, thought he was correcting Nietzsche, whose Übermensch was commonly and erroneously thought to be a strong-willed, ruthless dominator, a perception that has endured. In actual fact, the philosopher's Overman was a forceful but also emotionally complex individual who was more likely to be an artist than a commander.

*Portugal Futurista* also included the three manifestos that Almada Negreiros had recited six months earlier in his First Futurist Lecture, excerpts from assorted manifestos by Marinetti and other futurists, and the French version of the "Manifesto of Futurist Painters," first published in Italian, in 1910—all of which served as a launching pad for Santa Rita Pintor, "The Great Initiator of the Futurist Movement in Portugal." This was the caption for a full-page photograph of Portugal's self-proclaimed and self-promoting futurist painter, who was largely responsible for organizing the magazine.[2] Four of his works were reproduced in its pages, which contained significantly smaller reproductions of two paintings by Amadeo de Souza-Cardoso. Raul Leal, who had returned to Lisbon from Spain during the summer, contributed an article about the vertiginous splendor of one of Santa Rita Pintor's artworks, while another of Santa Rita's friends wrote a piece informing readers that he was the outstanding artistic genius of contemporary Portugal.

The literary component of *Portugal Futurista* included Pessoa's esoteric poem in five sections titled "The Mummy," as well as his poem sequence "Ficções do interlúdio" ("Fictions of the Interlude"), three poems by Mário de Sá-Carneiro, poetry and prose by Almada Negreiros, and poems in French by Guillaume Apollinaire and Blaise Cendrars. The magazine opened with an effusive announcement heralding the imminent arrival in December of Sergei Diaghilev's revolutionary and influential Ballets Russes, which had traveled around Europe and to the Americas and would finally perform in Lisbon—although without the troupe's most famous dancer, Nijinsky, whose last public performance had taken place in Montevideo that September.[3] The announcement was signed by Almada Negreiros, the composer Ruy Coelho, and the designer José Pacheco (or "Pacheko," as he sometimes signed his last name). The three men had combined their talents to produce several ballets in 1916, and in 1918 they would collaborate in a short-lived ballet company founded by Almada Negreiros and inspired by the Ballets Russes.

With avant-garde poetry written in French, an encomium of the Ballets Russes, futurist manifestos from Italy and France, and the incendiary manifestos of Álvaro de Campos and José de Almada Negreiros, *Portugal Futurista* had every appearance of being more advanced and cosmopolitan than *Orpheu*, to the enormous delight of Santa Rita Pintor, the featured artist at the center of it all. His apotheosis did not last long. On November 2, two days after it went on sale, the magazine was pulled from the shelves by the police. Álvaro de Campos's lampoon of the war and Portugal's involvement in it did not amuse the censors, who may also have objected to the word "shit" appearing midway through his manifesto in oversized capital letters. (A law authorizing censorship had been passed in 1916, after Germany and Portugal declared war on each other.) On the same day that *Portugal Futurista* was banned, a monarchist newspaper published a satirical "Ultimatum to the Futurists" in the denunciatory style of Campos.[4]

Campos's "Ultimatum" had also circulated as an offprint, the back page of which announced that his "Salutation to Walt Whitman" would appear in *Orpheu* 3, "forthcoming in October 1917." But Pessoa would never finish the poem, and *Orpheu* 3 would never be published.[5]

◆

THE POLITICAL FALLOUT OF the Great War commenced with the Russian Revolution of February 1917, which Álvaro de Campos explained, in his "Ultimatum," by saying that the oppressed people of the Eurasian nation "won a coil-spring freedom only because the coil snapped!" The tsarist autocracy had been under severe strain for many years, and while the war might have united the people against a common enemy, it went disastrously for Russia, whose poorly equipped army sustained several million casualties in the first two and a half years of combat at the same time that its already ailing economy disintegrated, leading to massive strikes, demonstrations, and food riots in Petrograd. Spiraling inflation had eroded the real value of wages, forcing many people to beg, migrate back to the countryside, or turn to crime. After Tsar Nicholas II abdicated in March 1917, the continued unpopularity of Russia's participation in the war helped undermine the provisional government, culminating in the Bolshevik Revolution that November. The new government immediately negotiated an armistice with the Central Powers.

War-weariness bred political agitation around most of the continent. The year 1917 saw three governments collapse in France, two in Germany, two in Hungary, and two in Greece. Angry women in a number of cities staged demonstrations calling for a halt to the senseless killing. Laborers grew increasingly restive. *"Pane e pace!"* (Bread and peace!) shouted the proletarians of Turin, who in August mounted an insurrection that led to hundreds of arrests and dozens of fatalities. Even countries that had stayed out of the war were susceptible to internal strife. Spain's neutrality helped its economy expand, but the army was asserting political power through so-called Juntas de Defensa, which the civil government relied on to end a general strike organized by the socialist and anarchist labor movements in August, the same month as the revolt in Turin; two months later, the Spanish prime minister was forced to resign. In Portugal, where inflation had become rampant and food shortages frequent, and where support for the war effort was tepid at best, the government's credibility had all but evaporated.

Although it was the most left-leaning of the three republican parties, the Democrats of Afonso Costa had repeatedly been obliged to crush strikes and reject worker demands, thus losing the support of organized labor. Middle-class adherents to the party had long ago abandoned it, and even party loyalists were disenchanted with Costa's leadership. When a group of soldiers and junior officers led by the conservative republican Sidónio Pais staged a coup d'état on December 5, 1917, the citizens of Lisbon welcomed it with applause. Armed civilians joined the conspirators, who attacked when Afonso Costa was outside the country, attending an Inter-Allied Conference on the war in Paris, and within three days the coup had prevailed. Sidónio Pais and his revolutionary junta, which included Machado Santos—imprisoned one year earlier, after his own attempted coup was thwarted—assumed control of the government.

The apparitions of the Virgin Mary at Fátima had galvanized Catholic religiosity, especially in rural Portugal, and one of the junta's priorities was to make peace with the Church. The harshest measures of Afonso Costa's law separating church and state were annulled by decree in February 1918. Exiled bishops were allowed to return, restrictions on financing and organizing religious services were lifted, priests and nuns could again wear their habits in public, shuttered seminaries and religious institutions were free to reopen, and new ones could be founded. Devout Catholics, who had naturally felt alienated from the Republic, welcomed the dictatorial regime, which styled itself the New Republic, and many of them saw Pais as a national savior. His appeal was broad, even among nonpracticing Catholics, who were captivated by his personality and his stage presence more than by his policies.

Like other successful dictators, Pais sought ratification not from political parties but directly from the people, most of whom were fed up with the traditional parties. That winter he traveled up and down the country, meeting with local officials, attending rallies, visiting hospitals and other institutions, shaking hands, and holding babies. Journalists from several major newspapers were part of his entourage. Pais was a natural communicator and had learned some things from the Germans during his recent stint as Portugal's ambassador in Berlin, such as how to use clothing, national symbols, and ritual gestures to convert an ordinary public appearance into a theatrical spectacle. A reserve officer who taught mathematics at the University of Coimbra before holding various government posts, Pais had not worn a uniform for many years, but now he made sure never to be without one. A cadre of spiffy young officers accompanied him from town to town, they saluted back and forth, and a military band invariably played the national anthem. Legend has it that some ladies swooned.

Men too, Pessoa included, fell under the leader's spell. Pais instituted universal suffrage for men (only in 1931 would Portuguese women begin to vote) and garnered a record number of votes, almost half a million, in the country's first direct presidential election, held in April 1918. Although he was the only candidate, the popularity of the president-elect was palpable, and he used it to justify his personalistic style of governing. He explained to a reporter that, by relying on his conscience to make decisions, he was "interpreting millions of consciences."[6] His conscience, in other words, was the national conscience. Pessoa seems to have agreed, viewing the Pais government as "the Dictatorship of the Total Man" prophesied by Campos's "Ultimatum," and Pais as "the Man who in himself is the greatest number of Others, and hence The Majority." At the very least, he believed that this dictatorial leader was what Portugal needed right now.

The country's new system of government, established by fiat, mimicked the presidential system of the United States, but the three traditional parties boycotted the elections, and the congress—whose members were mostly from a newly created government-backed party—passed no legislation. Setting a precedent for the more enduring regime of Salazar, whose dictatorial rise to power would begin ten years later, President Pais and a handful of ministers decided what was law. They sincerely tried to do a good job but lacked a comprehensive program to deal with the fractured and inefficient economy. They focused on bolstering agriculture, with some success, but inflation still soared, poverty kept increasing, and food shortages in the cities intensified. The government opened soup kitchens for the indigent and would institute food rationing later in the year.

◆

GOING AGAINST THE NATIONAL trend, Pessoa's own economic situation had decisively improved. F. A. Pessoa, the firm he had opened in the summer of 1917, was prospering, thanks to one of the two silent partners, his old friend Geraldo Coelho de Jesus, who channeled some business to the firm from a metal factory outside Lisbon where he was the head engineer. A month or two before the December coup, Pessoa had moved to Rua Bernardim Ribeiro, 17—his sixth domicile in the space of three years.

The apartment was in a corner building, well lit and with enough room to accommodate a live-in housekeeper, Dona Emília, as well as her four-year-old daughter, Claudina. Live-in housekeepers were such a standard feature of middle-class households that apartments in Lisbon were usually built with an independent entrance to a small bedroom designed especially for staff. All the homes in which Pessoa grew up had been served by domestics, so it was only natural that he hire one himself, as soon as his means permitted. In December the firm F. A. Pessoa also moved, from Rua de São Julião to nearby Rua do Ouro, 87, where Manuel Sengo, the landlord of Pessoa's previous apartment and the father of Claudina, had an office right across the hall. And so the bachelor poet suddenly became the vital nexus of a broken family, keeping Sengo informed about his little girl and no doubt delivering messages and gifts on his behalf. Dona Emília, a vivacious and good-humored woman, got on well with her new employer, who was sympathetic to her situation. He cast an astrological chart for her daughter, predicting that she would live to be fifty-four or fifty-five years old.[7] (At the time, forty-five was the average life expectancy for those Portuguese who survived infancy.)

For the first few months after moving in, Pessoa shared his apartment with Alberto Da Cunha Dias, who was in the middle of his journalistic campaign against the law on mental health that had enabled his father to have him forcibly committed.[8] No details of their life together have survived, but various clues suggest that Pessoa quite enjoyed the "family" formed by himself, Emília, Claudina, and Cunha Dias, and that he welcomed other friends to visit him in his new, more spacious quarters.

✦

AS A KIND OF English-language sequel to Campos's "Ultimatum," Pessoa began drafting an open letter to David Lloyd George, a social reformer who had staunchly opposed the Anglo-Boer War but became the United Kingdom's war secretary in July 1916 and its prime minister that December. Although the Great War was the main theme of the letter, Pessoa had no concrete proposals to make, nor even a specific criticism about how the war was being conducted, but he argued that Allied propaganda against the Central Powers had failed. While granting that German imperialism was more ruthless and cruel, he pointed out that the "democratic tendency" represented by Lloyd George had the defect of hypocrisy, since it falsified the true motives for fighting the war (presumably, the protection of Britain's own imperialistic interests) to make it more palatable to public opinion. "Thus, undermined on one side by Imperialism, and on the other by Democracy, the mind of modern nations is altogether debased. We reach this conclusion: this present War is waged on mankind, and in its waging the seeming enemies are intimately allied." Or as he put it in another passage for the same letter, "this war is the inter-War of Decadents." Or again: "This is not a war of nations against nations. It is a civil war of civilization. It is a revolution all over Europe."[9] These grand assertions echo the idea of Campos's "Ultimatum" that the war was the result of generalized European decadence, and they suggest—as Campos did—that profound changes in the continent's political and social order were bound to come to pass. Most historians, however, would point to clashing nationalism, not to civilizational decadence, as the reason for the Great War.

Portugal's participation in the conflict was comparatively minuscule, but with dire results. On April 9, 1918, the Second Division of the Portuguese Expeditionary Corps, with about fifteen thousand troops on the front line in French Flanders, was shredded like a piece of flimsy cloth in the Battle of the Lys. As if nature had grimly chosen to parody the myth of King Sebastian, whose glorious return was supposed to occur on a foggy morning, a dense fog on the morning of the battle allowed the more numerous and better armed Germans to pull off a surprise attack, infiltrating into the line and coming at the Portuguese with grenades and bayonets from more than one side. With over seven thousand casualties, it was Portugal's worst military showing since the 1578 debacle in which thousands of soldiers commanded by King Sebastian were slaughtered or captured in northern Morocco.

The humiliating rout of April 1918 might have been foretold, even without the benefit of clairvoyance. Since the previous fall, the Portuguese Expeditionary Corps had begun to atrophy, due to a lack of resources, discipline, and political will. If wounded, soldiers might wait for months just to be transported home; others feigned sickness to avoid fighting; still others, when granted leave, simply did not return; mid-level officers with connections finagled and got reassigned to posts in Portugal, leaving the rank and file to manage for themselves; and there were few new recruits to fill vacancies, so that the size of the corps gradually shrank, and those who still fought were exhausted beyond all reasonable limits. President Pais paid lip service to his country's unwavering support for the Allies but did nothing to reinvigorate the Portuguese fighting force.

The corps never recovered from the Battle of the Lys. Some of its members went on to serve with the British army as fighting men; others became trench diggers.[10]

# CHAPTER 46

I N HIS LAST RECORDED SESSION OF CARTOMANCY, on December 22, 1917, Pessoa had asked the cards about three things: his "Financial Situation," his "Open Letter to Lloyd George," and "Love Affairs."[1] He was financially better off than he had been for years, according to a letter he sent his mother three weeks later, on January 14, but his situation soon deteriorated, and in May 1918 he was forced to close the firm of F. A. Pessoa. His open letter to the British prime minister, on the other hand, was flourishing all too well. He must have vaguely thought of publishing it in a British newspaper, but he kept writing more and more passages, making no attempt to bring it to a close. It also spawned a second, even more voluble open letter, addressed to the energetic and high-minded Woodrow Wilson, president of the United States.* Pessoa wrote brief passages for this letter while the war still raged but much longer ones later, once the Paris Peace Conference was in session. As for love affairs, the astral spirits had been promising them for almost two years, but the only woman who had entered Pessoa's life was Dona Emília, and all she did for him was clean and cook.

Endowed with less faith than Mr. and Mrs. Yeats, Pessoa soon arrived at the conclusion that his spiritual powers and direct contacts with the spirit world were all illusory. In 1918, after having received well over a hundred communications from the beyond, he wrote "Um caso de mediunidade" ("A Case of Mediumship"), an essay that meticulously deconstructs his experience of etheric vision and automatic writing.[2] Subtitled "A Contribution to the Study of the Mind's Subconscious Activity," the essay attributes the onset of Pessoa's mediumistic behavior to his "hysteroneurasthenia," to his reading of occult and Theosophical literature,

---

* High-minded though he was, and progressive in many ways, Wilson allowed racial segregation not only to continue but to expand within the federal government.

to autosuggestion, and even to hypnotic suggestion, since he had been hypnotized right before his first session of automatic writing—probably by his friend Mariano Santana. The essayist analyzes the contents of his communications from the astral world, including the story of his "monadic" marriage to Margaret Mansel, as the product of subconscious memory or sheer fantasy; he warns that "mediumistic self-intoxication" may result in crime, madness, or suicide; he censures spiritism for undermining the scientific spirit without any compensatory benefit; and he peremptorily states that it should be banned by law.

Up until this point, the author of "A Case of Mediumship" sounds like a no-nonsense psychiatrist whose main concern is to prevent people from doing harm to themselves and to others. But the essay's concluding paragraphs allude to Greek civilization, "our common mother," and argue that its foundational influence on Western art and science is being eroded by Indian, Chinese, and other civilizations responsible for the pernicious spread of occultism and spiritism. This sounds like the voice of António Mora, Pessoa's Grecophile philosopher and diagnostician of modern ills. Whether Pessoa was writing as Mora or as an unnamed fictional psychiatrist, he shared the essayist's skepticism about his contact with astral spirits through automatic writing, and yet he would remain in contact with them for the rest of his life.

His communicators, however, as if intimidated by this broad and well-argued attack on their legitimacy, became laconic, and instead of signing their names, they tended to mark their presence only through their characteristic insignia—triangles, in the case of Henry More, or the infinity symbol (a sideways figure eight) for Wardour. Henceforth, they communicated sporadically, spontaneously, rather than in mediumistic question-and-answer sessions. Often their messages were just a few encouraging words, such as "Do not worry," scrawled in the margin of a manuscript.[3] These mini-messages are reminiscent of the many signatures of heteronyms and other fictional individuals (as well as of a few real people, such as Francis Bacon) that likewise appear in the corners and the margins of Pessoa's literary texts. During his lonely struggle to write well, to fulfill whatever mission his genius was meant to fulfill, and to simply live another day, at least he had this strange company of astral spirits and sundry autographers—a chorus of invisible witnesses who reminded him that his personal dramas were part of a far larger, only faintly discernible story.

Pessoa's communicators sent him a cautionary mini-message on May 30, 1918: "Love is only one of your needs. Fame and greatness are others."[4] It was as if they were telling Pessoa, or he were telling himself, to stop procrastinating. He was about to turn thirty but was still unappreciated as a poet, except among his friends. In the letter to his mother sent in January, he had announced yet again his by now old intention of publishing several books of poetry, beginning with one in English, and in the summer he finally made good on his word. With borrowed funds, or perhaps with the help of Aunt Lisbela, he published not one but two books in English. That language, he had always believed, was a surer avenue than Portuguese to fame and greatness.

Having been turned down by at least three different publishers in London, Pessoa decided to self-publish—but which books? *The Mad Fiddler*, for which he had produced a typed and ready-to-publish manuscript in 1917, would have been an obvious choice, had Pessoa not unreadied it in the meantime. After the manuscript was rejected by Constable, he considered omitting certain poems and started tinkering with others. Another possibility was "Epithalamium" and "Antinous," which he had recently thought of publishing together as *Two Unprintable Poems.*[5] He decided to publish the latter poem by itself, as a chapbook titled *Antinous: A Poem*. For his second book, or chapbook, he selected thirty-five of the more than fifty English sonnets he had written since 1910.

Sentimental considerations, as well as ambition, influenced the poet's publication choices. In his rambling and sometimes snarky open letter to Lloyd George—who couldn't have cared less what the bumptious unknown from Portugal had to say—Pessoa noted that, however much he might object to certain actions and attitudes of modern Great Britain in the arena of world affairs, he would always conserve a deep love for old England—the England of writers such as Shakespeare and Milton.[6] They were his literary heroes, and it was their hall of fame he yearned to belong to. Just as his English sonnets carry strong echoes of Shakespeare, his elegy in which Hadrian memorializes and deifies the drowned Antinous has conspicuous affinities with Milton's greatest elegy, "Lycidas," which memorializes and places in heaven a friend who drowned at sea. There are structural parallels, too, since both poems are decasyllabic and rhyme, but irregularly, accentuating the paragraphic effect of each stanza. "Antinous" can be read as a pagan inversion of Milton's emphatically Christian poem. With *35 Sonnets* and *Antinous: A Poem*, Pessoa courted comparison with the two writers he most admired and entered the tradition of English poetry by grafting himself into what he considered its golden age. It was a bizarre strategy, if a strategy it was; perhaps it was simply his way of paying respectful homage.

◆

NO SOONER DID PESSOA get his two chapbooks printed, in late July, than he took a stack of copies to the post office and mailed them to selected newspapers and magazines in Great Britain. A horoscope cast for the "birth" of the first chapbook, on July 25, 11:00 a.m., indicated that the "first important fact" of its existence in the world would occur in about four weeks' time.[7] If the important fact Pessoa had in mind was critical attention, this actually came a little sooner. The first journalistic notice appeared on August 15 in *The Scotsman*, of Edinburgh: "Both the sonnets and the poem ['Antinous'] are remarkable as instances of the literary accomplishment of a foreigner writing well in English; but it is always a foreigner's English, and is often too Southern both in expression and in feeling to be likely to please a strictly English taste." Pessoa would have smiled at the "Southern" problem, which was the reviewer's own problem with the homoeroticism of "Antinous," but his heart must have sunk upon reading "always a foreigner's English." Two days later a critic for *The Graphic* (London) remarked in a brief notice that "Antinous" was "written in excellent English,"[8] suggesting, once more, that it was a foreigner's English.

But two reviews published on September 19—full-fledged reviews, not just brief notices of books received—were like twin crowns of glory for Pessoa's English poetry. The one published in the *Glasgow Herald* began: "These two little volumes reveal a poet of great boldness and imaginative power." And it ended: "Both books are the work of a strong poetical intelligence." The review from *The Times Literary Supplement* was also largely complimentary, and republished one of the sonnets in its entirety. "Mr. Pessoa's command of English is less remarkable than his knowledge of Elizabethan English," was the reviewer's opening sentence, whose polite ambiguity allowed the poet to ignore the suggestion that his command of non-Elizabethan English was perhaps defective. The reviewer for the Glasgow paper regretted that the sonnets, admirable as they were, suffered from "a certain crabbedness of speech, due to an imitation of a Shakespearean trick."

About "Antinous" the two reviews were also in general agreement. After remarking on the poem's "repellent" theme, the Glaswegian reviewer acknowledged that "out of mere fleshly lust grows a true vision of eternal beauty." The *TLS* reviewer deemed it to be "often striking" as poetry but delicately forewarned—in a variation on the "Southern" theory—that it was "not a poem that will appeal to the general reader in England." In January 1919 a brief notice in *The Athenaeum* would likewise use the word "repellent" to refer to the homoeroticism of "Antinous," while admitting the "unquestionable power" of some of the poetry. "Antinous," unquestionably, is Pessoa's finest poem in English and the one he most cherished. In late 1921 he would republish it in a revised version, at which point a reviewer for the *Aberdeen Daily Journal* would finally remark on the fact that the poem is "somewhat after the fashion of Milton's 'Lycidas.'"

◆

WHILE PESSOA'S CHAPBOOKS WERE garnering an unexpected amount of attention from reviewers in Great Britain, Portugal's president, whose personal charm and hands-on approach to running the country had earned him a popular mandate earlier in the year, found himself under attack from various sides. Upon coming to power, Sidónio Pais had ended censorship, released hundreds of political prisoners, and won the support of organized labor. To stay in power, he ended up reinstating censorship, creating a secret police, imprisoning hundreds of dissidents, and brutally repressing worker associations, which called for strikes. The bourgeoisie, fearing a Portuguese equivalent to the Bolshevik Revolution, condoned these despotic measures, but the food shortages got worse, the country seethed with unrest, and on October 12, 1918, military units in Lisbon, Porto and several other cities staged a coup, with the support of some civilians. Government forces subdued the insurgents, and Pais declared a national state of emergency.

The Democrats of Afonso Costa, who was exiled in Paris, were the perpetrators of the putsch and the most visceral opponents of Pais. But Pessoa, a faithful supporter of President Pais and his New Republic, seemed to be more worried about the monarchists, who backed the dictator but whose ultimate goal was, of course, to restore the monarchy. On October 13, the same day that Pais declared a state of emergency, Pessoa published a newspaper article that marshaled an array of logical arguments to refute the monarchists' contention that the Portuguese Republic was a failed experiment. The next day an anonymous monarchist, in a reply titled "Futurist . . . Logic," berated the by then largely forgotten codirector of *Orpheu* for his sophistry and pointed out that Pais's regime, a dictatorship that had been welcomed by the people with open arms, was glaring proof of the Republic's failure.[9] In fact there was nothing very republican about the so-called New Republic.

In the months leading up to the present crisis, Pessoa had written incomplete drafts for other articles defending Pais, and he even created a fictitious commentator, João Craveiro, who specialized in writing about the president and the current political situation. Craveiro praised Pais for his leadership qualities but also cautioned that he was not a constructor, not a true transformer.[10] This caveat squared with Pessoa's prediction, stated in an unfinished essay, that the Pais regime was a period of transition and would be succeeded by a new political order.[11] His ostensible hope was that the autocratic New Republic might evolve into something like the aristocratic republic, which he had been postulating since 1914.

That hope was clearly mirrored in his latest plans for *Athena*, a magazine conceived three years earlier to promote paganism but left to simmer, like so many of Pessoa's projects. According to a revised table of contents drawn up in the summer or fall of 1918, *Athena*'s first issue would include "Commentaries" by Craveiro as well as an article on "Portuguese Neopaganism," signed by António Mora or Ricardo Reis, and an article titled "The Aristocratic Principle," signed by Pessoa himself. The only literary contribution to the issue would be a selection of poems by Alberto Caeiro, whom Mora and Reis regarded as the paragon of objective seeing and hence the consummate modern expression of the Greeks and Romans' pagan sensibility.[12] The goal of *Athena*, and the dream of Pessoa, was to instill the ethos of pagan antiquity in contemporary Portugal.

There were other European modernists who looked to antiquity for cultural models that could invigorate contemporary art and literature. In Spain, for instance, *Grecia* (*Greece*) was the name of a magazine published by the ultraist movement, founded in 1918. (Jorge Luis Borges, who lived in Spain between 1919 and 1921, was a contributor to *Grecia* and would publish a manifesto in Buenos Aires promoting the tenets of ultraism.) But Pessoa set his sights on much more than art and literature; he envisioned a renewal of human society, with Portugal setting the example by integrating the pagan sensibility of the ancients into its national psychology.

◆

WHILE HE LET HIMSELF freely, fervently indulge his political-poetical fantasies, Pessoa was perfectly well aware that his visions of an aristocratic republic and a Hellenized Portugal were not only unrealistic, they were delusional. And so it occurred to him to revive the Cascais Sanatorium, where António Mora had first espoused his Hellenistic ideals, according to the fragmentary short story "In the Cascais Sanatorium," discussed earlier. The abandoned story had lain dormant for seven full years, but now, in 1918, Pessoa dusted it off and thought of expanding it into a much larger project. *In the Cascais Sanatorium* became the general title for a book that was to include an interview with António Mora, an essay by Mora promoting neo-paganism, and poems by the heteronyms Alberto Caeiro and Ricardo Reis.[13]

Pessoa, in other words, was ready to place nearly all his major and most enduring heteronyms—only Álvaro de Campos was excluded—in his make-believe insane asylum. This would be consistent with his conviction, memorably expressed by John Dryden, that "Great Wits are sure to madness near allied." It would also support his contention that the heteronyms had their origins "in a deep-seated form of hysteria."[14]

However fanciful his explanation of the heteronyms' origins, Pessoa himself felt genuinely unadapted and unadaptable to the world he was born in, not unlike the eponymous protagonist of "Bartleby, the Scrivener." Bartleby represented a broad rejection of the economic system and social expectations of the time, or of any time, since he simply and splendorously would not go along, offering no justification except for his whimsical "I would prefer not to." But there is a more personal, autobiographical angle to this tale of alienation, published in 1853, just two years after *Moby-Dick*, which sold poorly, and one year after *Pierre*, which got vicious reviews. Melville, at that point, felt like a misfit in American literature. He had written the greatest novel ever produced in his country, and almost no one paid it any heed. But he would not retreat. Nonconforming Bartleby embodied his refusal to go back to writing the more traditional sea stories—*Typee* and *Omoo*—that the reading public had adored.[15]

In the case of Pessoa, who of course never read Melville—he was hardly read by Americans until well after the Great War—virtually all his writing was connected to his feeling of misfittedness. Not at home in the world, he wrote instead. His heteronyms were like so many Bartleby scriveners, but turned inside out. Whereas Melville's hero preferred, at a certain point, to *stop* writing (the things that others expected of him), Pessoa's cast of characters *insisted* on writing (things that others did not expect). Because they represented ways of seeing and thinking inimical to twentieth-century Europe and were even—in the case of the neo-pagans António Mora and Ricardo Reis—avatars of a different era, the most natural place for them was an asylum, whose location *outside* Lisbon further underscored the socially alienated spirit of its inmates. From the safe remove of Cascais, the heteronyms could rant and rave about what is wrong with today's world and pontificate on what would be healthy for Portugal, for society at large, and for human individuals. Alberto Caeiro, instead of raving, would calmly announce through his verses the simple yet not so simple lesson of objectively seeing and experiencing everything exactly as it is.

Pessoa did not follow through on his plan to move Alberto Caeiro and Ricardo Reis into the Cascais Sanatorium, but no matter what imaginary space the heteronyms inhabited, they reproduced their creator's own feeling of not fitting in. Unwilling to make any effort to adapt, Pessoa, besides inventing his own intellectual companions, fantasized a Portugal that would be more to his liking, a little more like his idealized version of ancient Greece.

The Portugal where he actually lived, meanwhile, was being battered by calamities and engulfed by uncertainty.

◆

AFTER THE OCTOBER PUTSCH, people in the political class and on its fringes carefully checked their positions and plotted their next moves, in anticipation of regime change: too much was going wrong for Sidónio Pais to be able to hold out much longer. Military leagues, or *juntas*, were springing up around the country, organized labor was planning a general, nationwide strike for November, and the citizens of Lisbon were infuriated at having to stand in long lines to buy rationed food, with bread and sugar constantly in short supply.

Contributing to Pais's problems was the Spanish flu, which reached its deadliest peak in October. A pandemic that infected as many as half a billion people around the world and killed at least fifty million, the flu did not originate in Spain, but that was where it was first widely reported in the press, since the countries at war had censored news of the pestilence, fearing it would depress morale. At least sixty thousand Portuguese died of the flu, mostly between September and December 1918. Schools were closed, the sick were isolated, buildings and public places were disinfected, but the mysterious virus spread unchecked through the provinces as in the cities, among the wealthy as among the poor. Pessoa, with his delicate constitution, had always been prone to catching flu viruses, and he also caught this one, but his symptoms were mild.[16]

Differently from the coronavirus that would grip the planet a little over a century later, the Spanish flu, which triggered an overreaction of the infected person's immune system, ravaged the young and strong more than the weak. One of its victims was Amadeo de Souza-Cardoso, thirty-one years old and a poster boy of robust health. So ended the cometlike career of a painter who might have become one of the outstanding names in the history of twentieth-century art. Just two years earlier his exhibition had caused a sensation in Porto and Lisbon, but newspapers from those two cities scarcely reported on his death.[17] Too many people were dying to be reported. Churches were prohibited from tolling their bells for the deceased, no matter how illustrious. But one could not escape the eerie music of horse hooves resounding on the paving stones as funeral processions took the fallen to their graves—as many as three hundred a day in Lisbon. To ward off infection, the terrified mourners inhaled ammonia and gargled with boric acid.[18]

Souza-Cardoso's widow, Lucie, moved back to Paris, taking most of his paintings with her, and for the next forty years his name would be little remembered, his work rarely displayed. Like Fernando Pessoa, only slowly would he gain recognition as a great European modernist, although to this day he is not well-known outside Portugal, where more than 250 of his paintings and drawings have been collected by museums. Another artist associated with *Orpheu*, Santa Rita Pintor, had died six months earlier, in April, from tuberculosis. Almost no works of his survive, since he instructed his family to burn everything. It was probably a small fire. Yet the name of this artist is still well remembered and his enigmatic role in Portuguese modernism much discussed.

In November Pais's doomed government enjoyed a brief remission, thanks to the signing of the Armistice, which brought an end not only to the trench war in Europe but also to the jungle war fought between German East Africa and other European colonies, including Mozambique. Twice as many Portuguese troops died in Africa as in Europe—partly from enemy fire but mostly from tropical diseases, harsh conditions, and neglect. At least a thousand indigenous troops and many more thousands of Mozambicans serving as porters for the Portuguese also perished. It was an even more disastrous performance than in Flanders, but Portugal could now claim a spot among the victors. On the eleventh of November, Portuguese flags—and an occasional French, British, or American flag—waved out of windows and vehicles, the bells of streetcars and horns of automobiles made a joyful racket, and Lisboners filled the squares shouting *"Viva!"* to the Allies and to the Republic of Portugal.[19] Caught up in the collective euphoria, for a few days everyone was outwardly reconciled, critical voices held their peace, and opposing factions observed a tacit truce, so that the nationwide strike called for November 18 was somewhat of a flop.

But the end of the war also removed any scruple that conspirators might have about spoiling Portugal's endgame on the two fighting fronts. Once the cheers died down and Portugal went back to being its sharply divided self, it was open season for Sidónio Pais. On December 6 a nineteen-year-old Democrat attempted to assassinate him, but the pistol misfired, and several days later a plot to abduct him was discovered in time. Despite being warned that other plots were afoot and that his life remained in danger, the president continued to appear in public, and on December 14 a second attempt on his life succeeded. Benefiting from the martyr effect, the memory of the charismatic leader once more entranced the general populace, forgetful of the food lines, their ravaged wages, and the rise in crime. Thousands of people filed by his corpse while it lay in state in the Presidential Palace, and thousands more lined Lisbon's streets for the funeral procession on the twenty-first. Some people kissed the wheels of the carriage that bore Pais's coffin; others fell to their knees and folded their trembling, upraised hands in prayer. Portugal's failed savior had passed into history.

Even Pessoa, who avoided public manifestations of whatever kind, probably went out to the street to watch the black-draped horses pulling the president's mortal remains to the former Hieronymite Monastery of Belém, a jewel of late gothic architecture and a national monument, where just a few Portuguese greats—including Luís de Camões—were buried.[20] Soon Pessoa would become a theologian of Sidonism, a new "religion" that venerated the spirit of the slain leader, but in the immediate aftermath to the assassination he was mainly interested in discovering who was behind it. Did the gunman act alone, or was he—as the police and many others suspected—part of a conspiracy forged by Freemasons, Democrats, anarchists, or monarchists?

To help him figure it out, Pessoa enlisted the assistance of Dr. Abílio Quaresma, the sleuth he had invented several years earlier to be a crime solver for the detective stories he wrote in Portuguese. Now he applied the skills of this crack detective to an actual murder, writing about three thousand words for a story in which a nameless narrator (possibly Fernando Pessoa) runs into Dr. Quaresma on a street in downtown Lisbon just a few days after Sidónio Pais was shot. After learning that his old friend is a little strapped for cash, which was the case for many Portuguese in 1918, the narrator asks the ratiocinator if he has given any thought to the president's assassination. Quaresma has not, but after some prompting, he proceeds to take the crime through an obstacle course of inductive arguments, eliminating various motives that might have led one or another conspiratorial group to act. He had not yet solved the case, however, before Pessoa gave up on the story.

The historical evidence shows that it was personal animosity, and fierce loyalty to the republican ideals of Afonso Costa's Democrats, that motivated the assassin, but the monarchists were the ones who seized the opportunity thus created. On January 19, they mounted a revolt in Porto and other cities of the north, proclaiming the restoration of the monarchy in the name of the exiled king, Manuel II, of the House of Braganza. Several days later the monarchist forces in Lisbon also took up arms, but only halfheartedly, with some of their partisans not joining the cause, fearing that it lacked sufficient popular support, and in a few days their little uprising was put down. The monarchists had a stronger base in the north, where they set up a provisional government in Porto, declared the 1911 constitution null and void, raised royal flags, distributed pictures of the king, who was living in England, and got crowds to sing the traditional royal anthem. The Monarchy of the North held out for almost a month before capitulating to Republican forces.

Deeply disillusioned by the turn of events, Ricardo Reis, who was a hard-core monarchist (his last name means "kings"), boarded a steamer bound for South America, where he lived mainly in Brazil, earning his keep as a high school Latin teacher—according to his fictional biography. An address for a Dr. Ricardo Sequeira Reis, found among Pessoa's papers, indicates that he lived for a time in a Peruvian mining town, Cerro de Pasco, one of the highest settlements in the world, but Pessoa never revealed how or why he ended up there. It seems doubtful that the miners would have hired him to teach their children Latin.

The briefly restored, rather goofy "kingdom" of early 1919 was the monarchists' last hurrah. Having lost credibility in the eyes of the public, and having lost faith that their goal was achievable, they desisted from trying to undo the Republic by force. It was at this point that Fernando Pessoa, who had always been a staunch, though often exasperated, defender of the harum-scarum republic, suddenly became a monarchist—after his own fashion. Contrary to the monarchists whose hopes had just been dashed, he did not favor bringing back the House of Braganza to preside over the nation. In fact he remained as opposed as ever to the constitutional monarchy that had reigned up until 1910. What sort of monarchy he envisioned is impossible to describe with clarity, since he himself saw it only dimly, but there are clues in Álvaro de Campos's "Ultimatum," which presages the arrival of a "Scientific Monarchy that will be antitraditionalist, antihereditary, and absolutely spontaneous, since the Average-King may appear at any time." By "Average-King," Pessoa-Campos meant a king who realizes the average of all the individual wills of the people he rules. But where would this king come from, what would prompt him to emerge, and how would he assert his authority? The answers to these questions were shrouded in fog—just like the mythical return of King Sebastian.

# CHAPTER 47

I N WHAT MUST RANK AS ONE OF THE GREATEST
political upheavals in human history, World War I brought about
the dissolution of four empires, the redrawing of numerous national
boundaries, the formation of new countries, and the reshuffling of foreign control over assorted lands in Africa, the Middle East, and east
Asia. But Portugal simply went back to being Portugal, with its ancient
borders, its same old colonies, a massive foreign debt, and an agonizing
lack of political direction. Even before Sidónio Pais was buried, his New
Republic had begun to implode. Since none of his ministers had the
political stature or popular appeal to be able to rule dictatorially, by fiat,[1]
the only basis on which they could govern was the 1911 constitution
established by the "old" republic. The nation that had always prided itself
on its maritime discoveries was now like a ship adrift, with three governments coming and going in the space of six months. Pessoa, meanwhile,
was quietly planning a national cultural revolution that, if successful,
would relegate traditional politics to the dustbin and usher in a so-called
New Monarchy, quite unlike any system of government Portugal had
ever known.[2]

Grémio de Cultura Portuguesa, or Portuguese Culture Guild, was
the unassuming name of Pessoa's organ for revolutionizing Portugal. Its
goal was to prepare the nation for its "future imperialism" by creating a
"Portuguese cultural state," independent of the political state. Pessoa had
lost patience with the republic and doubted that much good could ever
come out of normal political processes. "We need to concentrate cultural
forces, financial forces and aristocratic forces," he wrote, so as to create,
"in opposition to all that is foreign, a Portuguese national personality."[3]
This nationalistic yet ostensibly apolitical project was inspired not just by
the manifest failure of politics in Portugal but by what seemed to him a
failure of politics everywhere.

Critical of all the leaders of the major powers involved in the war, Pessoa reserved a special loathing for Woodrow Wilson. One passage from the open letter he began writing to the U.S. president in 1918 described him as a "soft-headed fool" and "pro-German in action."[4] Pro-German he was not, but in his wartime speeches Wilson had always been careful to distinguish between the German people and the "military masters" of Germany who exploited them for their program of belligerent conquest and domination.[5]

Wilson, as expected, adopted a conciliatory attitude toward Germany at the Paris Peace Conference, which convened in January 1919, but Georges Clemenceau and David Lloyd George, the prime ministers of France and the United Kingdom, were considerably less forgiving or understanding, since their two countries together lost close to two million soldiers in combat, as opposed to fifty thousand American fatalities. Delegates from more than thirty countries attended the peace conference, but the triumvirate of Wilson, Clemenceau, and Lloyd George made most of the decisions.

Many Europeans who followed the proceedings of the peace conference came to feel that Wilson, although well meaning, did not and could not understand Europe. Probably no one expressed that perceived incapacity in words as blunt as Pessoa's: "The great traditions on which our civilization is built are foreign to you, as an American. The instinct called patriotism you are bound to ignore; it cannot be an experience of such a pseudo-nation as yours is." In another passage from his open letter to Wilson, which he kept writing and writing, Pessoa complained, "It is not the least harm wrought by this war that, in opposition to the German State, your voice should have been the one to crawl into loudness. For you are the voice of all that is merely mercantile and unspiritual in the civilization of men."[6]

For Wilson, the Great War was the work of people in positions of power—such as the "military masters" of Germany—who dragged their nations into useless, bloody confrontation. For Pessoa, nations were also people, they had personalities, and wars were inevitable, civilizational clashes. He had opposed Portugal's involvement in the war because it was essentially an outsider, fighting on someone else's behalf rather than asserting and defending its own civilization. As for the United States, it did not even rate as a nation with soul; it was a mongrel amalgam united by pecuniary and other, utilitarian interests.

As the peace conference got under way, Pessoa wrote more and longer passages for his never-ending open letters—one to President Wilson and the missive to Prime Minister Lloyd George discussed earlier—but except for the occasional paragraph that specifically railed against Wilson or the United States, the letters were no longer addressed to anyone in particular.[7] The just finished war was a pretext for Pessoa to expatiate on the history of Western civilization and religion, on the continuing struggle between the Christian and Hellenic elements of European culture, on different political systems—monarchy, republicanism, democracy, plutocracy—and on the conflicts between social classes, exacerbated in recent years by worker movements, for which he had no sympathy. Pessoa had for a long time been an elitist, but in analyzing postwar Europe his point of view became more aristocratic than ever, and vehemently antidemocratic. He defended the existence of clearly differentiated social classes in "Against Democracy," an essay for which he drafted passages in both English and Portuguese.[8]

About the Treaty of Versailles, signed in late June 1919 after months of haggling, Pessoa had not a good word to say. Despite having scoffed at Wilson's earlier proposals to treat Germany with magnanimity rather than blaming and punishing its people for so much death and destruction, he now criticized the treaty for its vindictive character, predicting that the harsh provisions against Germany amounted to "the reconstruction of a future war."[9] And he dubbed the general terms of the treaty a "Bolshevist peace," apparently convinced that Wilson's insistence on self-determination for the peoples of eastern Europe, where new nations were created from the breakup of the German, Austro-Hungarian, and Russian empires, would lead to a proliferation of civil wars like the one that still raged in Russia, two years after its proletarian revolution. Bolshevism, in Pessoa's lexicon, had become practically a synonym for democracy.

It was not only popular uprisings and democratic processes that Pessoa found repugnant. The torrent of sociopolitical analyses produced by him during and after the war—including Campos's "Ultimatum"—were all *predicated* on the notions of a civilizational Armageddon and a general breakdown of European governance. Pessoa, in other words, disallowed any hope that Europe's current leaders and systems of government (including democracy, militarism, and communism) might reverse the continent's inexorable downward spiral.

In this apocalyptic scenario, Portugal was potentially better off, since Sidónio Pais had largely eviscerated the power structures of the Republic, making the country ready, perhaps, for something completely new. Although the Democratic Party won the May 1919 elections, governmental institutions were more fragile than before; uncertainty and instability reigned. The army, bloated in size because of the recent war, now loomed as a virtually autonomous authority that might intervene unexpectedly. Everything was in flux, making this the perfect time for the wishful Pessoa to do his part in preparing the country for its culturally imperialist destiny.

◆

WHILE HE AND HIS friends drank coffee and smoked cigarettes in their usual haunts, discussing the European peace treaty and the parlous state of national affairs, Pessoa laid out his idea for a Portuguese Culture Guild, but none of them really fathomed what he hoped to accomplish with it: a suprapolitical nation defined not by geographical borders but by Portugal's language and culture. Radiating out from Iberia, it would reach all over the world, wherever Portuguese was spoken and the Portuguese spirit prevailed. This "Portuguese Empire," as he referred to it in his profusion of notes on the Culture Guild, was none other than the Fifth Empire he had first envisaged in 1915.[10] Projects formulated in that year to foster Portugal's imperialist vocation, such as the book *All about Portugal* and Cosmópolis, his diversified commercial agency, had languished during the war; in 1919 Pessoa decided that it was time to implement them. To the smorgasbord of activities conceived for Cosmópolis four years earlier—everything from advertising, legal, research, and real estate services to providing expert assistance for business start-ups—he added a few more, such as architectural design and an agency for setting up auctions.[11]

The main goal of the Portuguese Culture Guild was to influence attitudes and change mentalities; Cosmópolis was more business oriented and down-to-earth. There was considerable overlap between their activities, however. Both organizations were supposed to raise the cultural level of the Portuguese and improve Portugal's image abroad. Central to Pessoa's strategy for achieving those ends was an ambitious publishing program: literary works, guidebooks, commercial directories, and an English-language weekly with news about Portugal.

Sensitive to new developments in communications technology, Pessoa also thought of going into the business of making motion pictures, through a company called ECCE Film, whose name was probably an acronym as well as a variation on *Ecce homo*, "Behold the man!," uttered by Pontius Pilate when presenting a scourged Jesus to the crowd. At this stage in its sluggish development, the Portuguese film industry produced mainly documentaries and newsreels, whose powerful potential for cultural propaganda was not lost on Pessoa, even if he was too enamored of the written word to ever become a film buff. Many years later he would draft synopses for three stories he thought might make good movies, but ECCE Film ("Behold my film company!") never amounted to more than the design for a logotype left among his papers.[12]

Pessoa's most curious idea for fomenting culture was a "correspondence college" to be called Athena. Like his project for a magazine called *Athena*, dedicated to reconstructing the paganism of antiquity, the school of the same name aspired to leaven modern ways of thinking and doing with the spirit of the Greeks. It would offer instruction in some practical business skills, but the main focus would be on personal development, through courses in subjects such as Mental Culture, Literary Culture, and the Science of Idling. Some copy written by Pessoa for an advertising brochure explained: "We teach idlers, society people and mere decorative personalities—all those, in fact, who have no purpose in the world except having no purpose in the world."[13] With English as its exclusive language of instruction, the school was conceived as a form of international outreach, whereby Portuguese professors—Fernando Pessoa and perhaps several Anglophone heteronyms—would teach the rest of the world how to sublimely, aristocratically do nothing at all.

Faithful to the spirit of idling promoted by its core curriculum, Pessoa took no practical steps to make the Athena school a reality. The vast majority of his other projects from 1919 likewise stagnated. It was an old problem, which he laid out in a June 10 letter requesting information about the correspondence course offered by Messrs. Hector and Henri Durville, a father and son team who offered instruction in animal magnetism—also known as mesmerism—through their Institut du Magnétisme et du Psychisme Expérimental, located on Rue Saint-Merri in Paris. The poet explained, in French, that he was a hysterical neurasthenic whose neurasthenia dominated his hysteria, keeping it at bay, but that he had no control over his will:

> My extreme emotionalism unsettles my will; my extreme rationalism—fruit of an overly analytical and logical intelligence—

crushes and debilitates this will that my emotions had already unsettled. [. . .] I always want to do three or four things at once, but I ultimately do none of them and, what's more, don't want to do any of them.

As we might expect, Pessoa's intention to seek out treatment for this problem was stymied by his inability to finish and post the letter.

Notwithstanding his deficient willpower, Pessoa did make some attempt to carry out at least one of the dozens of projects on his to-do list for 1919: a journal of ideas to be published in French and English and distributed abroad.[14] But his enthusiasm for this rather amorphous publication project was soon diverted to a veritable, tangible newspaper in Portuguese, *Acção* (*Action*), for which he was one of the main contributors. The paper's founder and editor in chief was his friend Geraldo Coelho de Jesus, who had been a partner in F. A. Pessoa. Augusto Ferreira Gomes, the third partner in that now defunct firm, also contributed to *Acção*, which billed itself as the official organ of the National Action Committee. The "membership" of this important-sounding committee consisted of the three friends, who shared some of the same ideas about what was needed for postwar Portugal.

The second issue of *Acção*, dated May 19, 1919, contained the first part of "Public Opinion," a long article in which Pessoa argued that this opinion was a kind of collective instinct, rooted in the tradition of a people bound together by a common language and not discoverable through the voting rituals of democracy. Moreover, modern democracy was injurious to the healthy functioning of society, insofar as it abolished class privileges and promoted equality. The democracy of the ancient Greeks was socially salutary because it rested on the institutions of aristocracy and slavery. The article also stated that war, not peace, is the natural and right state of humanity, that people hating one another gives rise to civilization, and that humanitarianism is antihumanitarian. Since Pessoa loved to be provocative, one could argue that in 1919 he mischievously decided to play the part of a die-hard reactionary. If so, he was wholly and utterly convincing in the role.

Although *Acção* was advertised as a biweekly, the third issue (which included the second part of "Public Opinion") did not come out until two and a half months later, in August. Abandoning its professedly apolitical stance, the paper reproduced a photo of the late dictator Sidónio

Pais on the whole of the front page, while Geraldo Coelho de Jesus's editorial, "Sidonism or Bolshevism," equated patriotism with the spirit of Pais and all party politics with Bolshevism. Since the editor had business to attend to as the chief engineer of a mining company located in Porto de Mós, north of Lisbon, it fell to Pessoa to oversee the paper's distribution, which proved to be a risk-fraught undertaking. Pais continued to be revered as a demigod by many Portuguese, but not by unionized workers or by the Democrats, who were back in control. On August 9, Democratic partisans seized more than 700 copies of *Acção* from the hands of newsboys and set them ablaze in front of the Brasileira café on Praça do Rossio.[15] Most of the rest of the print run—10,000 copies—was sold, sometimes clandestinely, by newsboys and through shops, and by mail to other parts of the country.

Pessoa dropped everything to devote himself, heart and soul, to getting out the Sidonist word, setting up a sales network and crisscrossing Lisbon to make sure it functioned smoothly. In the space of five days he sent three telegrams and four breathless letters to Coelho de Jesus, reporting in great detail on the excitement stirred up by the newspaper and on the vicissitudes of selling it. Nobody was more excited than Pessoa himself. In one of the letters he told the "heartwarming" story of a zealous young shoeshiner who was proudly collecting all the published issues of *Acção*. The editor in chief, who had staked his own reputation as well as his money on the paper, responded to his friend's deluge of effervescent missives with a single three-word telegram, urging him to send more copies to the provinces.

The fervor of Pessoa's dedication to distributing the latest issue of *Acção*, as if Sidonism were a persecuted religion and he one of its stalwart evangelists, is hard to account for. While Coelho de Jesus and many other people placed their faith and hope in the model of government embodied by the late Sidónio Pais, Fernando Pessoa seems also to have placed in the slain leader his love—or a feeling that substituted for the love he had only been passively seeking, in consultation with astral spirits.

A fourth and final issue of *Acção* would come out six months later, in February 1920. In the front-page editorial, Coelho de Jesus reaffirmed his adherence to Sidonism, which he understood as a set of policies promoted by Sidónio Pais—including enforcement of law and order, constraints on political party activity, creation of social welfare programs, and economic development—but not as a personality cult, not "as a kind of Sebastianism." In that same issue Pessoa, who was more interested in Pais's symbolic value than in his policies, published a 240-line poem, "To the Memory of President Sidónio Pais," which glorified the late leader as an incarnation of King Sebastian. The poem's original title styled Pais a "President-King," an epithet that Coelho de Jesus, who was not a monarchist, obliged Pessoa to shorten to "President."

◆

THE MAJORITY OF PESSOA'S friends were at least receptive to his ideas for fostering, through culture and commerce, what he hoped would be a Portuguese golden age, and a couple of them embraced his mystical narrative, which conflated the dawning of that age with the Second Coming of King Sebastian. But there was a key aspect of his vision for an imminent Portuguese Renaissance, or Fifth Empire, or New Monarchy, that Pessoa had been keeping mostly to himself and his writings, since almost no one would have understood: paganism. According to his notes for the Portuguese Culture Guild, one of its main objectives was to promote neo-paganism[16]—"neo" in the sense of a modern revival, because he considered the spirit of Portugal to be essentially, originally pagan. The ancient Lusitanians were polytheistic, and the traces of paganism subsisting in the rituals of Catholicism were, he contended, even more pronounced in the Islam of the Moors, who at one time ruled most of Iberia.

What might the "reconstructed paganism" espoused by Pessoa—and especially by his heteronym António Mora—actually look like? Perhaps it would have no outwardly obvious characteristics. It would surely not consist of temples to Apollo or animal sacrifices to Diana, and it would just as surely avoid rigid doctrines and definitions. Indeed, one of the things that attracted Pessoa to paganism was its undogmatic character. He wanted to replace the religious ideology of Christianity, which he blamed for hindering civilizational progress in Europe, with the *experience* of religiosity promoted by the paganism of the Ancients.

His inspiration for this implausible task was the world's first neo-pagan, the Emperor Julian (c. 331–363), sometimes called the Apostate for having rejected the Christianity of his own upbringing. At a time when the Roman Empire was already tilting toward the new, mono-theistic religion, Julian tried unsuccessfully to revive paganism, not by directly proselytizing devout Christians but by restoring the prestige of ancient cults and by rallying the many remaining pagans to a more religious way of life. In the renowned city of Antioch, whose ruins lie in Turkey, close to a modern city with the same name, pagans as well as Christians ridiculed his efforts and his own paganly ascetic lifestyle.

In 1916, the same year Pessoa acquired two tomes of Julian's works in a Greek-English edition, he conceived a poem sequence titled "Juliano em Antióquia" ("Julian in Antioch"), for which he wrote a few lines as well as a note in English describing what he wanted it to express: "The idle efforts of a reformer, of a man who wishes to bring back the fair past to the evil present, the past of kings to the present of *slaves*."[17] A couple of years later, he wrote at least six poems for the sequence; or perhaps the poems, none of which he completed, were meant to be assembled into one long poem.[18] Constantine Cavafy also wrote a clutch of poems about the austere convert to paganism, scrutinizing Julian and his impossible crusade with a somewhat sardonic, somewhat compassionate gaze. Pessoa's poems are more obviously sympathetic. Both poets were drawn to the figure of Julian not only because he tried to salvage paganism when it was already in decline but also because he defended the Hellenistic culture that still survived in Antioch, founded as a Greek city by one of Alexander the Great's generals. Cavafy's interest in Hellenism came to him naturally, inevitably, since he himself was Greek and a passionate student of ancient history. Pessoa, who was better versed in Portuguese history, had a clichéd, idyllic view of ancient Greek life and attitudes.

By evoking Julian, Pessoa implicitly acknowledged that his own attempt to reanimate the long dormant spirit of paganism in the modern world was foredoomed, suggesting to us that his project of repaganization was a poetic fantasy, not an objective he thought could ever be accomplished. In fact it was part of a larger fantasy concerning Portugal and its future, and ultimately himself. One of the lists of goals he drew up for his Portuguese Culture Guild, instead of mentioning neo-paganism, ends with the exhortation "Stimulate, in everything, Greek culture."[19] Not only the religion of the Greeks but also their aesthetic sensibility, their individualism, the city-state as their organizing unit, and their civic life—all of these things greatly appealed to Pessoa's imagination.

And all these things (in Pessoa's imagination) were the fruit of a man's world. In a passage written in the spring of 1919 for one of his open letters about the Great War and the decline of Western civilization, Pessoa claimed that the Greeks considered the function of women to be "exclusively sexual," insinuating—not for the first time—that a true communion of souls was possible only between two men. Just as controversially, he wrote that the fact "paederasty is considered immoral among us is perhaps the most typical phenomenon about our decadent civilization." Love between men and boys, Pessoa argued, "is a natural morbidity of nature, corresponding to an intensity and extravagance of friendship."[20] The word "morbidity" recalls his poem from 1916 or 1917 in which the narrator, musing over the boyhood love he might have had with a still younger boy, admits to being infected by "this ancient disease / That only the Greeks made beautiful, because themselves beautiful were." Greek culture, in Pessoa's ideal view, both beautified and justified the "morbid" attraction of one man for another.

✦

ONE AFTERNOON IN 1999, while sitting in a darkened room at the National Library of Portugal, scrolling through a microfilm of the Pessoa Archive[21] and occasionally feeling my eyes droop, I suddenly sat straight up in my chair, startled by the projected image of a love poem unlike anything by Pessoa I had ever seen. What surprised me as much as my discovery was the fact that other researchers, who had surely come upon the poem, preferred to let it linger in obscurity, like a secret best left untold. They may have snubbed the poem for being fragmentary and unfinished, but it is typewritten, fills up three full pages, is dated—July 5, 1919—and contains extraordinary verses.[22] The poem's enamored narrator, expressing himself in Portuguese and addressing a man who is close to him in age, longs to declare his love but cannot bring himself to do so, convinced that his friend is thoroughly heterosexual:

> You kiss the ordinary lips of women,
> And I just the useless dream of your lips.

It tortures him to endure "this terror of loving you without being able / To tell you my love," and he recalls how once, in a conversation, the subject of "Shakespeare's vice" came up. It was the chance he had been waiting for, a chance to slowly, gently open up his heart and confess his love, but, fearing rejection, he said nothing.

He carries out a thought experiment, wondering what might happen if he ever got up the courage to declare himself and his friend miraculously responded in kind. Would he then be able to act on his desire?

> Who knows! who knows! with so many people in me!
> With so many lost and denied urges,
> I'm so far removed from my own self
> That perhaps the greatest torture would be
> To win your acceptance but be too anguished
> And wound up to take the final step.

This "wound up" narrator inhabited by "many people"—I couldn't help but notice as this part of the poem scrolled into view—bears an unmistakable resemblance to Fernando Pessoa. Elsewhere in the poem, the incognito lover remarks to his unknowingly beloved friend: "I take refuge from you in Antinous," apparently alluding to the poem in which Pessoa feelingly wrote about the love of the Greek youth and Emperor Hadrian.

If the publication of *Antinous: A Poem*, in July 1918, was a covert admission of sexual diversity, the reactions it elicited did not encourage its author to emerge from his poetic hiding place. Even before two British reviewers pronounced its theme to be "repellent," William Bentley, an English editor who lived in Lisbon, chided Pessoa for not having found "a worthier subject than such a pitiful playing around the most ignoble vices."[23]

But was Pessoa hiding? Was there a man he secretly loved? So vivid are the details and so powerful the sentiments in his poem from July 1919 that it strikes us as a true story, a confession he had to make on paper, poetically, since he didn't dare make it to the man he fancied and couldn't keep holding it in. What man? Possibly Geraldo Coelho de Jesus, the mining engineer, who was handsome, still single, and had kissed many "ordinary lips of women." An unusual fondness for Geraldo would help explain Fernando's unusual devotion to his newspaper, *Acção*, and the exuberance of the letters he wrote Geraldo when handling the distribution of the paper's third issue. In one of those letters, Pessoa made a request: should the newspaper's editorial office move to larger quarters, then "let me remain here in your place." Pessoa wanted to turn Geraldo's office into the home where he slept.

Pessoa's love poem from the summer of 1919 may have been inspired by a real acquaintance, such as Geraldo, but it's equally possible that the unnamed beloved was a hypothetical man, invented by the poet for him to love with truly felt but imaginary passion—as if in reaction to the astral spirits who had been proposing one hypothetical woman after another, so far without success.

Soon, however, Pessoa would have a girlfriend.

# CHAPTER 48

P AGANIZING PORTUGAL MAY HAVE BEEN A FAN-
tastical notion, but Pessoa was quite serious about transforming
the country's cultural life and turning around its slumping economy through the slew of activities he proposed for Cosmópolis and the
Portuguese Culture Guild, all of which he neatly inscribed in a special
notebook. He was also plotting major changes in his personal life. For
the Culture Guild and Cosmópolis to efficiently do their job of burnishing Portugal's international image and boosting its cultural and commercial traffic with other countries, he decided that he would need to set
up two offices, one in Lisbon and one in London, which meant he had a
fresh motive for finally visiting the land of Shakespeare, Milton, Shelley,
and Keats. While in London—which had emerged from the Great War
relatively unscathed, compared with other European capitals—he hoped
to sell some of the board games he had invented, some English translations of Portuguese literature, and, of course, his own literary work, but
his immediate purpose for the trip would be to establish the foreign hub
of his Portuguese cultural and business conglomerate. To finance his
ambitious projects, he drew up a list of potential investors: well-to-do
relatives from the Algarve, friends in Lisbon with a little money to spare,
and several bankers.[1]

Pessoa optimistically chose mid-August 1919 as his target date for
having the London office up and running. If all went to plan, he would
hire a manager to oversee operations in London while continuing to base
himself in Lisbon, or near Lisbon. He thought of renting a house or
apartment in Cascais or another suburb, where there would be plenty of
room for all his things—books and papers, mainly—and fewer distractions interfering with what he called his "speculative life." He needed
peace and quiet for thinking as well as for writing. His trusty housekeeper, Emília, would be in charge, taking care of him when he was
there and looking after his affairs when he was away, in London. Pessoa

estimated that he would need $5000 to "pay all debts and set life clear on this new footing." He reckoned he would need three times that amount to get his company up and running in London, and perhaps as much as $50,000 (more than $700,000 in today's currency) for it to be fully functional.[2] Only banks had that kind of money, and bankers could only have smiled condescendingly at the investment opportunities afforded by Cosmópolis, the Portuguese Culture Guild, and Athena, the correspondence school specializing in the "science of idling."

Until these improbable influxes of venture capital arrived, Pessoa still depended on writing business letters in English and French for his income, which he was lately able to supplement with earnings from translation work. Warren Kellogg, the American editor who in 1911–1912 had commissioned Pessoa to translate poetry and prose for the Portuguese version of the *International Library of Famous Literature*, was back in Lisbon to coordinate another multivolume book project: a Portuguese version of *The Book of Knowledge: The Children's Encyclopedia*.[3] Besides translating poems, factual articles, popular legends, and episodes from ancient history, Pessoa contributed at least one original poem to this encyclopedia.[4]

In March 1919, Pessoa had sent an urgent message to several friends, requesting a small loan—five escudos—to tide him over until he got paid by "the American of my translations," Mr. Kellogg.[5] Two months earlier, he asked his cousin Victoriano Braga for a much larger sum—sixty-two escudos—in order to pay off a promissory note.[6] Indebtedness was such a familiar condition to Pessoa that to owe no money at all might have upset his vital equilibrium, but he must have been tempted to say yes when presented with an opportunity to live without financial worries. In May the new rector of the University of Coimbra, who knew Pessoa personally, offered him a job as an English professor. Pessoa was by nature a pedagogue, he *liked* to give lessons, he loved English literature, and he would have plenty of time to do his own writing. There was almost nothing about the job he could object to, except for the fact that it *was* a real job. Aunt Anica urged him to accept the offer, but he rejected it, saying that he was not academically qualified, since he himself had no university degree. He also told her that the offer was mired in political infighting, which was true: the rector was dismissed from his post on June 21, just three months after being appointed.[7]

Lack of funds hardly curbed Pessoa's spending. In June he ordered a dozen books from England, including three shorthand manuals (he was still perfecting his own stenographic method), a biography of Herbert Spencer, two books dealing with prophecies, one on free thought, and another on how to build up willpower. The next month he bought, on credit, a set of new clothes.[8] And at the end of August he made a week-long trip to the Algarve, where he stayed at the finest hotel in Faro,[9] the regional capital. It was a business trip, possibly linked to a scheme for exporting canned fish and other Algarvian products, with Pessoa acting as an intermediary between local producers and an import-export firm recently opened by his cousin Mário.[10] Although no concrete deal resulted from the trip, Pessoa undoubtedly managed to wrangle more money out of his wealthiest relative, Aunt Lisbela, whose home was only twenty miles away from Faro.

Pessoa even owed money to his housekeeper, Emília, probably because her salary was in arrears. She and her daughter had moved with him in late 1918 to more modest quarters on Rua Santo António dos Capuchos, and six months later to a still smaller, ground-floor apartment on Rua Capitão Renato Baptista. The rooms were cramped, Pessoa was unhappy there, and by August he was again looking for new lodgings, but he could afford neither a spacious suburban house nor a full-time house-keeper. In September he regretfully gave her notice.[11]

The new home he finally found for himself that fall was on Avenida Gomes Pereira, in Benfica, a neighborhood five miles northwest of the city center. He rented rooms from a family, who took care of the cleaning and may have provided him with meals.[12] Although it lacked the charm of Cascais or Sintra, Benfica still retained traces of its rural past, when religious orders and wealthy aristocrats in search of tranquility had chosen the area to establish impressive convents and country estates. By distancing himself from the bustle of downtown Lisbon, the writer hoped to work with greater concentration, but he lost a lot of time in commuting. On the days he didn't really need to make the trip into town, he invented reasons for boarding the streetcar and going there anyway. Pessoa, though prolific, was able to write only intermittently, in between his restless moving from one place to another.

◆

PESSOA'S MOVE TO AN outlying neighborhood was the most visible sign of his partial retreat, beginning earlier in the year, from social life and family obligations. He still regularly saw Aunt Anica, who had returned from Switzerland and France in 1917 with her daughter, Maria, and son-in-law, Raul da Costa, and in the spring and summer of 1919 he saw Raul practically every day, since they both pitched in at their cousin Mário's import-export firm. He was remiss, however, about staying in touch with his other relatives, unless he needed something, like a loan. His great-aunt Rita had died three years before, and his great-aunt Adelaide in June, the day after his thirty-first birthday, leaving his great-aunt Carolina as the last survivor of that generation, but Fernando had not seen her for many months.[13]

The family member with whom he was least in touch, weirdly enough, was his own mother. Maria Madalena sent him frequent postcards and less frequent, diarylike letters full of news about life in Pretoria, her slow and only partial recovery from the stroke she'd suffered, her children and husband, and their plans to return in the near future to Portugal, but Fernando, who used to at least send postcards, now let months go by without sending any news at all. He relied on Aunt Anica, who wrote her sister faithfully, to provide his mother with updates about his doings and his health. He would later justify his negligence by saying that he liked his mother too much to want to write her; letters were for people that he didn't enjoy talking to.[14]

"Try to write," urged his sister, Teca, in the postcard she sent for his birthday in June 1919. "It's been over seven months since your last letter." Three months later he finally broke his epistolary silence, but only to forward a copy of an important legal document. On September 12 Henrique Rosa, his stepfather's older brother, had transferred to him the power of attorney over his parents' financial affairs in Portugal.[15] Fernando's erstwhile intellectual mentor had become too sick to leave his apartment, and after the death of his common-law wife in April it became physically impossible for him to deal with banks and bureaucracy.

It's likely that Pessoa, when sending the document to his parents, remembered to include birthday wishes for João Miguel Rosa, who turned sixty-two on September 29. But before any wishes could reach their recipient, a telegram brought word of his unexpected death, on October 7, at a clinic in Pretoria (from acute meningitis brought on by a kidney infection). Even if Pessoa did not feel a great personal loss, the news must have saddened him a little. His stepfather, who used to take him to the St. Joseph's Convent School when he was but seven years old and who helped him out of a debt crisis when he was twenty-four, had always treated him as well as his own children, and any friction between the two men had long ago dissipated. Paying his respects in the most immediate and visible way possible, the next day he wore his finest black trousers, black jacket, and black vest to the office.

✦

THE OFFICE BELONGED TO a start-up, one of whose three partners was his cousin Mário Freitas. It succeeded the import-export firm opened by Mário earlier in the year at the same address.[16] Pessoa helped out at both firms by typing directly, in English or French, letters dictated to him in Portuguese. He had his own desk and spent most of the time working on his own writing. The new firm, called Felix, Valladas & Freitas, Ltd., had placed a want ad for a secretary, and on October 8 a young woman came by in the morning for an interview. She was waiting at the door when Pessoa arrived, with his black trousers carefully tucked into his black spats, an accessory that was beginning to go out of style. She felt an urge to laugh but controlled herself. Pessoa told her and her chaperone to come in and wait for one of the bosses. Mário soon arrived, and while he fielded questions to the applicant, Pessoa looked on from across the room. He was intrigued by her unusual, Shakespearean first name: Ophelia.

It was a busy, productive day for Pessoa. The news of his stepfather's death made him reactively, creatively reflect on life—in five poems and a passage for *The Book of Disquiet*. The poems muse, in different ways, on the great divide between the speaker's inner life of thoughts and the life that exists all around him or that has already gone by. In one of two poems that reminisce on his childhood, the speaker addresses his mother, pleading with her to let him go back in time to look for his toys in the backyard. Even more revealing is the passage Pessoa wrote for *The Book of Disquiet*—a fantasy about being transformed into a retired major who lives in a small-town hotel where, after dinner, he sits at the table with the other, slightly inebriated guests for no reason at all. And that practically sums up the whole story, which ends like this:

Independent of Time and of Life, the major I imagine myself to be doesn't have any kind of past life, nor does he or did he ever have relatives; he exists eternally at the dining table of that small-town hotel, already weary of talking and trading jokes with the other lingering guests.[17]

The narrator of this passage dreams of having no more than a traveler's passing relationship to other people, while the narrators of the five poems written the same day either return to the past or withdraw into their mental lives. What all six narrators have in common is an unwillingness to engage affectively and meaningfully with people in the present.

It had been twelve and a half years since Pessoa had seen his mother, who would now at last be coming home, and although he looked forward to seeing her, he was also apprehensive. She was getting old, and the stroke had diminished her. He, on the other hand, felt younger than his thirty-one years, since he still had no family of his own, no job with set hours, and no permanent address. Even so, he had emphatically established his emotional independence, to the point of being able to let ten months go by without writing his mother, not even on her birthday.

Every change is for the worse, he had written her in a 1914 letter, since it involves a partial death, the permanent loss of a previous condition, and the changing dynamic of their relationship was for him especially troubling. While he didn't really want to go back to being her little boy, he missed the original simplicity of their rapport, before it became muddled by the presence of other people, other affections, and before they said and did things that hurt each other, to their mutual regret. She loved her oldest son but couldn't understand him, and he failed to meet her expectations. The retired major with no past and no family, who statically lives life in a small corner of the world, had the advantage of never being disillusioned and of never disappointing anyone.

◆

SEVERAL DAYS AFTER HER interview, Ophelia Queiroz was summoned to report back to Felix, Valladas & Freitas, ready to work. Pessoa himself was waiting for her and explained what she needed to do. To help her get quickly acclimated, he told her just a little about each of the firm's three partners, and about the hole in the rug on the stairs, where she might trip if she wasn't careful. His attentiveness impressed her.

Later on, she heard one of the partners say: "Oh Fernando, wouldn't you love to place a kiss on this lass's neck?" Ophelia was nineteen years old.

"I think not," he answered drily.[18]

She liked men to notice her, but she liked even more Pessoa's gentleness and respect.

Pessoa's friends had gotten used to coming by the office when it was an import-export firm belonging just to Mário Freitas, and they continued to come around when the business changed and Mário had partners. Two of Pessoa's most assiduous visitors, Geraldo Coelho de Jesus and Augusto Ferreira Gomes, talked to him about politics and discussed the next (and last) issue of their Sidonist newspaper, *Acção*. Luís de Montalvor was more interested in talking about literature.

"It's a crime that you're still unknown," he told his friend, reproaching him for not publishing his work, except here and there in magazines.

"Don't worry," said Pessoa, "when I die I'll leave boxfuls of it behind."[19]

What did he write about, Ophelia wondered, and why so much? Intrigued by this man so unlike other men, and whose unusual way with words made her think, and rethink, as well as laugh, she began flirting with him in her first week on the job. Pessoa did not discourage her, he liked the attention, but it also unnerved him. On Saturday, October 18, he wrote two pages for a poem in English whose speaker asks a young, infatuated girl

> why, unless thou wouldst play
> A prank alike on Fate and me
> Do thine eyes come my way
> And thy smiles seek me, who have sought not thee?

"I could not dare to long for thee," he warns the girl in the same poem, for he is "thought-penned" and "pain-enclosed, / Cloistered from life in idle dreams."[20]

Ophelia kept up the attack the following week, making eyes and smiling at Pessoa, who returned some of her glances and smiles, but without letting on that he understood, nor was he certain that he understood correctly. Maybe she was, after all, playing a prank, having some fun. He always found it hard to believe that anyone could be romantically interested in him.

Ophelia decided to spell out what she felt in a note but was unsure how to word it. She jotted down a couple of possible formulas, including: "I cherish your presence at the firm Felix, Valladas & Freitas, because I feel attracted to you."[21] Too audacious! She ripped up what she had written into little pieces and threw them into the trash. After she left the office, Pessoa collected the pieces from her wastebasket and took them home. Assembling them like a jigsaw puzzle, he read with astonishment her unambiguous admission.

Knowing that she found him attractive, Fernando let his fondness for Ophelia flourish without restraint. Had she been sent to him by Destiny? His astral communicators had said that he needed a masculine woman to make him submit, but they also predicted that the woman destined for him was quite young, still in her teens. Girlish and petite, Ophelia fulfilled only the latter condition. There was nothing manly about her. But she was also not the sensually seductive sort of woman who so easily intimidated Pessoa. She looked seventeen, not nineteen, used little makeup, and was small-breasted, with a child's build. Though she succeeded in winning Pessoa's affection, he held the reins to their relationship, which proceeded at a slow trot, in between all the business activities of Felix, Valladas & Freitas.

For three months they exchanged furtive smiles, passing glances, and polite words masking fond emotions, like schoolchildren afraid of getting caught by the teacher. They also passed little love notes to each other, sometimes in the form of poems. But there was no physical contact between them until January 22, 1920, during a power outage, after everyone else had left for the day. Ophelia herself was getting ready to leave when Fernando entered the room where she worked, carrying a kerosene lamp, and declared himself with words borrowed from Hamlet's letter to *his* Ophelia:

> O dear Ophelia, I am ill at these numbers; I have not art to reckon my groans: but that I love thee best, oh, most best, believe it.

Hamlet was referring to his inability to express what he felt in formal poetry, with a fixed number of syllables per line. Fernando, on the contrary, could not express himself spontaneously and in his own words; he resorted to literature.

Flustered, Ophelia put on her coat and said good night, at which point he grabbed her around the waist and began passionately kissing her—"like a madman," she would report in an interview more than fifty years later. Pessoa wrote a poem about the episode and observed, in his private notes, that his stars on January 22 augured success in amorous adventures.[22]

For the rest of January and all of February, their romance went on as discreetly as before, but with the significant addition of stolen kisses, which were an absolute novelty in the life of Fernando Pessoa. "I still don't believe in what I'm feeling," began a poem of his written in the second week of February. Ophelia wondered what exactly he was feeling. She loved his witty remarks, his little notes and poems, and especially his kisses, but she wondered if they added up to a real commitment, or if he was an incorrigible bachelor. On February 28 she wrote a letter, asking him to clarify his intentions. She specifically wanted to know whether he had ever considered or might yet consider having a family. If the answer was no, then she, with regret, would prefer to remain with her current boyfriend—Eduardo, a student of painting—who she knew could make her happy.

"Those who truly love don't write letters that read like lawyers' petitions," replied Pessoa on March 1, in a letter that questioned Ophelia's own intentions and accused her of feigning love. If she preferred her current boyfriend over him, then fine, he could not hold it against her. Love is or it isn't, and he confessed to loving her very much, sidestepping the question of whether he might be willing to marry and create a family. Between his lawyerly skills and hers there was no contest.

With that dated and signed confession in her possession, Ophelia forgot about practical considerations. Eduardo, after all, might make her more bored than happy, whereas Fernando was a mysterious world full of possibilities. He had already initiated her into his game of existential plurality, in which she proved to be a quite willing participant. On March 11 she wrote a message to a Sr. Crosse, and four days later she addressed an envelope to a trio of individuals: Fernando Pessoa, Álvaro de Campos, and A. A. Crosse. A. A. Crosse's only task in his unreal life was to compete in word games sponsored by mass-circulation English newspapers. He had just won a small prize—one pound—and had his name published in *Answers*, a weekly paper. Ophelia, a devout Catholic, promised to pray that Sr. Crosse would win the grand prize of one thousand pounds. Fernando never told her about A. A.'s two brothers: I. I. Crosse, who wrote laudatory essays about the poetry of Alberto

Caeiro and Álvaro de Campos, and Thomas Crosse, the essayist and translator we met earlier.

Ophelia, perhaps not incorrectly, understood Álvaro de Campos and A. A. Crosse to be imaginary characters invented by her sweetheart as a form of self-amusement, but they also clearly represented different aspects of Pessoa's personality and even, so it seemed, contrasting attitudes toward her. She considered A. A. Crosse to be an ally, since the big money he was competing for would make it easier for her and Fernando to get married. Álvaro de Campos, on the other hand, continually tried to thwart their relationship. On the night of March 25, just before going to bed, she told her "Fernandinho" in a letter that she was going to say prayers for him and for Sr. Crosse but not for Sr. Campos, "because he's crazy."

The naval engineer sometimes interjected disconcerting comments in Fernando's letters to Ophelia, but his craziness was in full bloom when he showed up in person. "Today I'm not me," Fernando would warn her, "I'm my friend Álvaro de Campos." We don't know whether Pessoa-as-Campos had his own accent and facial expressions. Ophelia would report only that he acted very differently and talked in non sequiturs, making normal conversation impossible. Sometimes Campos would merely tag along, so that it was the three of them who went for a walk or rode the streetcar together. When she tried to protest, saying that she detested Álvaro de Campos and didn't want him around, Fernando answered, "I don't know why. He's very fond of you."[23]

For the first five months, the relationship was confined to the walls of the office, at Rua da Assumpção, 42. On Sunday, March 14, Fernando and Ophelia met for the first time in the open air. It was a simple walk in a quiet neighborhood, with some handholding and some petting, but since Pessoa insisted that they were not ordinary lovers, he did not allow that such walks were ordinary walks. And so Ophelia, a quick learner, alluded to that first walk in a letter by saying: "I miss going with you on an outing to India."[24] Pessoa's reading of the Kama Sutra, which he owned in a French translation, may have been what led him to style their experiences of intimate contact as trips or outings to India. The Asian travel trope recalls the observation, from *The Book of Disquiet*, that a sensitive soul can experience a trip between downtown Lisbon and Benfica (where Pessoa was still living in March) as if it were a journey to China.[25]

Pessoa seems to have sought, in the restrained eroticism he experienced with Ophelia, the effect of an exotic sexual odyssey.

Ophelia would have liked to live in India, but Fernando wanted to go there only occasionally, and less so as time went by. Reading the spate of letters they exchanged in the second half of March, after Ophelia accepted a better job at a different firm, we can feel how excited he was to write her, see her, talk with her, and touch her. That excitement was tempered, however, by an automatic reflex action of detachment. He closed his letter of March 26 with "I'm convinced (for my part) that I like you. Yes, I think I can affirm that I have a certain fondness for you." It would be hard to fit more hesitating qualifiers into a declaration of affection. Compare it to an excerpt from one of Franz Kafka's early missives, from 1912, to Felice Bauer: "I answer one of your letters, then lie in bed in apparent calm, but my heart beats through my entire body and is conscious only of you. I belong to you; there is really no other way of expressing it, and that is not strong enough."[26]

Although he backed out each time, Kafka was twice engaged to be married. Marriage, for Pessoa, was rarely more than an imaginary idea belonging to an indefinite future. It existed in his automatic writings, in his astrological charts, and in some of his letters to Ophelia, where the prospect was usually linked to conditions, such as A. A. Crosse's winning a thousand pounds. There was a moment, however, when the idea of his marrying Ophelia assumed a palpable form: he suggested that they might be able to live together in the same apartment with his family,[27] who had departed from South Africa in February and would soon reach Lisbon. The idea withered, however, before the steamship docked, on March 30, 1920.

✦

IT WAS AFTER A forty-day voyage up the eastern seaboard of Africa and then westward across the Mediterranean that twice-widowed Maria Madalena, an attending nurse, and Maria's three grown children finally pulled into the port of Lisbon. Scanning the crowd of people waiting on the dock, they were surprised and consternated not to see Fernando. Since there was no harbor station, just an open-air dock, they waited on the ship, the *Lourenço Marques*, forlornly watching all the other passengers debark.[28] After a few hours, now frankly worried, they began to wonder if they should go ashore and get in contact with some other relative. When at last he showed up, along with his cousin Mário, Fernando profusely apologized for the delay. Due to a postal strike, he had not received the last letter they'd sent from Pretoria, but luckily Mário, then employed by the National Maritime Transport Bureau, had discovered that they were passengers on the arrived ship.

The weary travelers were greatly relieved but also taken aback, since Fernando, still recovering from a bad case of flu, looked terribly pale. The impression they made on him was even more startling. However much he had mentally prepared himself, it was still a shock to see his mother in a wheelchair.[29] She could walk for short distances with a cane, could move her left arm hardly at all, talked without her former verve, and looked older than her fifty-eight years. The nurse, dressed in white and flaunting a Red Cross emblem, highlighted the gravity of Maria Madalena's condition. Pessoa's half sister and half brothers, who were small children when he last saw them, made for a different sort of shock: all were handsome and self-confident young adults. As far as he could tell, they still looked up to him. It was a good, if disconcerting, reunion.

Pessoa had found an apartment that could accommodate the whole family, including himself, but it still needed to be furnished and the walls papered, the ceilings painted. His mother and siblings stayed temporarily with one of her cousins, António Silvano, a navy captain and occasional creditor of Fernando,[30] who had vacated his rooms in Benfica and was staying with his friend Mariano Santana, the occultist. By mid-April Maria Madalena, her nurse, and all four of her children were sleeping in the first-floor apartment at Rua Coelho da Rocha, 16, in Campo de Ourique, a residential neighborhood northwest of downtown. Situated on a plateau and with a thriving local commerce—cafés, restaurants, grocers, and assorted shops—Campo de Ourique had the air of a peaceful and prosperous village unto itself. This was where Pessoa would live for the rest of his life.

Maria Madalena was thrilled to be rejoined with her oldest son but soon had to bid farewell to her younger boys, Luís Miguel and João Maria, now nineteen and seventeen years of age. On May 8, after just a few weeks in Lisbon, they boarded the train to Paris and from there continued to London, where they would earn university degrees, pursue successful careers, and get married. During the brief time that the whole family was united, Pessoa enjoyed being their guide to life in Lisbon and talking with them over dinner and into the night—in English with his brothers and in Portuguese with his mother and his sister, Teca, who was twenty-three. Pessoa also treated his brothers to a couple of nights on the town, which meant hanging out with his friends at the Café Martinho da Arcada until two or three in the morning. Luís Miguel would later report how he looked on with wide eyes as Fernando drank copious quantities of wine, followed by *aguardente* (brandy), "without the slightest detectable effect either in his speech or in his powers of argument."[31]

Ophelia was jealous of Fernando's siblings, as she admitted to him in a March 31 letter, because she was jealous of everyone and everything that occupied his attention. This was a false problem, of course. She came from a family twice as large—she was the youngest of eight children—and in addition to all her family obligations, she had her day job as a secretary, she took private lessons in the evening to improve her French, and she helped out in her eldest sister's dressmaking business; still, her thoughts never strayed far from the man she loved. Ophelia did not occupy Pessoa's life in the same way. Although it might be unreasonable to expect him to shift the center of his attention from his literary and speculative life to Ophelia Queiroz, a rich writing life and a great romantic passion did not have to be mutually exclusive. James Joyce, at the same time he was producing some of the finest modern fiction in English, was passionately attached to Nora Barnacle.

Ophelia wrote an almost daily love letter. So did Pessoa during the second half of March, but then he slacked off, which was not necessarily a sign of waning interest. He had forewarned her, in his March 23 letter, that he preferred to talk in person rather than in writing, and by April they had established a repertoire of places and times to meet. So Pessoa's days, much to his own surprise, were now punctuated by rituals of courtship. One regular meeting place was the English bookstore on Rua do Arsenal, an ancient thoroughfare running west from Praça do Comércio and containing a number of shops that sold things like oil, flour, dry beans, and salt cod, which hung in the doorways to entice customers. Ophelia's new job was not far from the bookstore, where she would find Fernando after work, and he would walk her home. When she changed jobs again and had to commute to Belém, on the western edge of Lisbon, he often returned with her on the streetcar to the center. Sometimes he took her to her French lesson, or met her when it was over.

There were also agreed-upon times of day when Fernando, passing by Praça do Rossio, would make faces and blow kisses toward Ophelia, who would be anxiously waiting as if she were now Juliet, waving back to her Romeo from the balcony window of the apartment belonging to her oldest sister, who lived opposite the Rossio train station. Ophelia often stayed with this sister, Joaquina, rather than at her parents' apartment.

Ophelia confided in Joaquina and in her mother about Fernando, but he never told anyone in his family that he had a girlfriend. Nor did he consider that he had one. He disliked definitions. And he disliked commitment. He often canceled or failed to show up at his appointed meetings with Ophelia, which were at any rate brief, and when he did show up he was sometimes distracted, or he showed up as Álvaro de Campos. But there were also times when he completely surprised her. One day, in a voice taut with passion and looking straight into her eyes, he said, "You're sulfuric acid." Another time, while they were patiently waiting for a streetcar, he suddenly pushed her into a stairwell and gave her a forceful kiss; then they continued waiting, as if nothing had happened.[32]

She bombarded him with letters and nagged him to write more often because her love was great and because his was quirky, uncertain. She wanted documents, material proofs, of an affection he did not convincingly convey to her in person. And so their relationship, as it proceeded, was largely an extension and repetition of their initial exchange of letters, when they worked in the same office and she, perplexed by demonstrations of affection that alternated with aloofness, asked him to state in writing what he felt for her.

Meanwhile Eduardo, the disconsolate ex-boyfriend, stalked and confronted Ophelia, investigated the identity of the man who had supplanted him, succeeded in surprising the two lovebirds on one of their walks, and in late May reported his findings to Ophelia's father, who was furious for having been left in the dark about his daughter's new romantic interest. Around the same time, Eduardo swore to her mother that he would get revenge.

Informed of what had transpired, Pessoa, contrary to his laconic custom, wrote Ophelia two long letters on the same day, May 28. Besides offering words of comfort to calm her agitated spirit, he explained that what she needed, above all, was "the willpower *to think only this*: I like Fernando, *there is nothing else*." He went on to ask: "are you capable [. . .] of concentrating your mind in an attitude of indifference to everything that is not your Nininho? If you can't do this, you still don't know how to love." Fernandinho (a diminutive) and Nininho (a diminutive of this diminutive) were pet names for Fernando, who called his sweetheart Baby, Babykins, Nininha, and Wasp. They also called each other Ibis, the nickname he had adopted in 1909, the same year he set up the Ibis press.

Far from following his own advice, the great sage in matters of the heart had already begun to slowly pull away from Ophelia. An early sign of his cooling passion was the increasingly meddlesome, obstructive presence of Álvaro de Campos. In three different letters sent in May, Ophelia implored her Fernandinho to leave his unreal friend at home the next time they had a rendezvous.[33] To the extent he represented Pessoa's literary life, Campos was Ophelia's most serious rival for his attention, but the playful heteronym incarnated a still more formidable obstacle to the relationship: Pessoa's tendency to treat everything as a game. It was a tendency that deluded him as much as it deluded her. In the greetings he sent Ophelia for her birthday, which fell on June 14, one day after his, Fernando wrote that next year, with luck, he could wish her happy birthday before getting out of bed. By August this sort of pleasantry had vanished from his letters, which became infrequent. He met with her less often and less willingly. On August 14 she penned a gloomy letter complaining that she was the one who did everything—from letter writing to suggesting when and where they could meet—to keep their relationship going. "I wish," she wrote, "that you'd show more interest in me." Pessoa's heart, in fact, was no longer in it.

# CHAPTER 49

**T**HE MANY SOURCES OF OPHELIA'S AMOROUS agitation included Fernando's plans to go to London on business in the fall of 1920. "Let's go together," she had suggested in a letter written in June, although she knew that would never happen.[1] She was jealous of his entrepreneurial plans as she was jealous of his siblings and jealous of Álvaro de Campos—because she sensed that they were all more important to him than she was. But was he serious about going to London, or was he just daydreaming? Pessoa himself may not have known the answer to this question, but he acted as if it was an entirely serious intention.

He had channeled his surfeit of ideas for promoting Portuguese culture and commerce into a more manageable stream, but they were ambitious nonetheless, and a trip to London would be essential for putting some of them into practice. He still nurtured plans for a Portuguese Culture Guild, and while he had given up on the mega-enterprise called Cosmópolis, in its stead he wanted to set up a "general agency" called Olisipo, which was the name of Lisbon when it was ruled by the Romans. Olisipo would also function as a publishing house and eventually develop, Pessoa hoped, into a publishing conglomerate with branches in Brazil, in the United States, and in former or current British colonies such as South Africa, India, and Australia.[2] This was a revolutionary idea in 1920, when nothing of the kind existed in the publishing industry.

Ten years had elapsed since the Ibis press had wiped out Pessoa's inheritance and plunged him into debt. That was enough time for him to get over the trauma and be able to dream again, uninhibitedly, of publishing dozens of books both in Portuguese and in English. He retained, however, a few lessons from the Ibis disaster: think big but start small, rely on others for the initial capital investment, and use established printshops instead of purchasing his own press. To sell his idea to investors, he prepared a comprehensive, five-part prospectus that analyzed what was missing in the current panorama of Portuguese publishing (such as a good translation of Shakespeare's plays), explained why Olisipo was uniquely positioned to take up the slack (it had a translator, Pessoa, who was "entirely imbued with the spirit of Shakespeare's work"), and estimated that a 30 percent profit could be realized on its editions of translations and original works. If the capital investment was large enough, the publisher could also undertake serialized editions, dictionaries, encyclopedias, books in foreign languages, and an English-language yearbook about Portugal. The more capital invested, the greater the return—it was that simple. Indeed![3]

In 1919 Pessoa had drawn up a list of possible investors for Cosmópolis. One year later, and in the very same notebook, he drew up a much longer list of friends and relatives who might be willing to purchase shares of stock in Olisipo. He assumed that his writer friends, including such *Orpheu* contributors as José de Almada Negreiros and Alfredo Guisado, would naturally be interested in a publishing house that specialized in literature and was a possible outlet for their own works. And since Olisipo would also act as a commercial agency committed to stimulating Portuguese business activity, wasn't it bound to appeal to friends such as Geraldo Coelho de Jesus, who had published articles insisting on the need for Portugal to industrialize and become more economically dynamic?

Some of his friends initially showed enthusiasm, but they weren't willing to chip in and help him actually launch Olisipo. Nobody took seriously his wildly inflated figures for the number of books that the publishing division was likely to sell, with an implausible profit margin of 30 percent. And his poor track record as a businessman was no secret. Without telling Ophelia the nature of the business, Pessoa complained to her of his friends' lack of solidarity in a letter sent on June 11:

> I, who came up with the idea for the business and studied how to set it up, have fulfilled my role, and it was no small matter, for I did the essential part, laying the foundations for the work. To expect me to do all the rest is like expecting the same person, in an office, to be the boss, the bookkeeper, the typist, and the office boy who posts the letters.

Pessoa was the mastermind, full of ingenious and eloquently formulated ideas but lacking in patience to act on them in a sustained way.

Whether they were business ideas, nationalistic ideas such as the Portu-guese Fifth Empire, or ideas for large literary projects such as *The Book of Disquiet*, *Fausto*, and *The Duke of Parma*, Pessoa rarely concerned him-self with the practical steps needed for their realization. Although he did write hundreds of passages for those three literary works, the first two could never have been published without the meticulous labor of his posthumous editors, while *The Duke of Parma* is still waiting for perse-vering scholars to make it a publishable text.

Contrary to habit, Pessoa did take the necessary steps to launch Oli-sipo, but in a modest, scaled-down version that required only a small capital outlay. He found an office to let on Rua da Boa Vista, a street with hardware shops and small grocers, west of the pricier Baixa district; he furnished it with a few basic items, including a typewriter and a folding bed;[4] he acquired a cable address and a post office box; and he ordered some stationery with "OLISIPO—Portuguese General Agency" printed on the letterhead. The bed made his office a useful home away from home. As much as he loved his mother and sister, every now and then he needed to be completely alone.

By the fall of 1920 Olisipo was open for business. As a "general agency" it was poised to handle all sorts of business transactions, but since Pessoa was who he was, the polar opposite of a true entrepreneur, his company transacted very little. Its operations began quietly, invisibly, through let-ters of presentation sent to a handful of foreign firms, including Veloce Ltd., maker of the Velocette, a classic British motorcycle. Pessoa, with his fondness for motor vehicles, was apparently exploring the possibility of being a Velocette agent for the Portuguese market. Álvaro de Campos might have liked to own one of their latest model motorbikes, but Oli-sipo did not pursue negotiations with the manufacturer.

◆

AT THE SAME TIME that Olisipo's director and manager was sending out letters to various industries and manufacturers in England, Den-mark, and elsewhere,[5] like a hunter randomly shooting in the dark and hoping for a lucky hit, he was already drawing up plans for the compa-ny's publishing program, which included his latest poems in English: a group of "Inscriptions," or epitaphs, inspired by his reading of the Greek Anthology. Pessoa, who owned a five-volume, Greek-English edition of this famous compendium of pithy poems from antiquity and the early

Middle Ages,[6] wrote most of his "Inscriptions" in 1920, though the first one in the sequence—along with the idea of writing inscriptions—dated back to 1907.[7] Here it is in the revised, final version:

> We pass and dream. Earth smiles. Virtue is rare.
> Age, duty, gods weigh on our conscious bliss.
> Hope for the best and for the worst prepare.
> The sum of purposed wisdom speaks in this.

Were it not for the clunky last line, we could be fooled into thinking that this inscription actually was from the Greek Anthology.

Almost every great modernist is in some sense a classicist, and a Romantic too, since the Poundian aspiration to "make it new" implies familiarity and engagement with previous literary traditions. James Joyce wrote the quintessentially modernist novel by recasting *The Odyssey*. But Fernando Pessoa, once he had proven—and even *while* he was proving— that he could be a futurist and a cubist-inspired intersectionist, seems to have aspired to "make it old." He conveyed a modern individual's concerns, confusions, and frequent feelings of anguish in Petrarchan and Shakespearean sonnets, in the Horatian odes of Ricardo Reis, in traditional Portuguese verse forms when writing poetry under his own name, and in epigrammatic verses reminiscent of the Greek Anthology. Even the early, quasi-futurist poems of Álvaro de Campos emulated the dithyrambic odes of ancient Greece to more effectively sing the praises of factories, machinery, speed, and the raucousness of city life. Under whatever name he wrote, Pessoa used the old, etymological way of spelling Portuguese. He himself dressed conservatively. And he dreamed, absurdly, of Hellenizing—or neo-paganizing—twentieth-century Portugal.

Pessoa's conservatism was an implicit critique of all that is touted as new and improved without, perhaps, truly meriting those designations; it was also a tacit plea for *conservation*. Let new ideas, new forms, and new gods be born, if they will, but let's not discard the beautiful ideas, elegant forms, and venerable gods of those who came before us!

✦

"WE PASS AND DREAM. Earth smiles." Painfully aware that all human endeavor is condemned to eventual oblivion, Pessoa sought to delay that fate through literature. Words, he believed, when organized into superior literary compositions, can outlive actions. Hence Oliver Cromwell, in some distant future, "will be remembered only because Milton mentioned him in a sonnet."[8] Miltons are exceedingly rare, however, as Pessoa noted in "Impermanence," an essay for which he drafted fourteen passages, all but one of them in English, between 1918 and 1920. Examining what kind of literary works would endure across the ages, the essay predicted that poets such as Byron and Robert Browning would practically disappear from human memory, while Shelley would be reduced to a couple of lyric poems "in the English Anthology of the future."

Works and their writers survive, according to Pessoa's analysis, either because they achieve perfection—the case of Milton and John Keats in his odes—or because they are vastly representative, like Walt Whitman, "the medium of Modern Times," whose "power of expression is as consummate as Shakespeare's." Pessoa's prognosis for contemporary literature was especially dire, with nearly all of it being doomed to impermanence, being forgotten. The current age, nevertheless, would survive in the following manner: "A great poet will appear with an appeal to eternity—a builder, a master of the intellect. In his work the 'genius' of the age will be reflected."[9] Thus Pessoa reiterated, in English, what he had prophesied in Portuguese back in 1912: the emergence of a Super-Camões, or Great Poet, who was himself.

Pessoa's earlier prophecy had been based on nothing but faith in his own ability. In the meantime, however, he had written some extraordinary, highly original poetry, and who among his contemporaries could claim to be as diversely representative as Pessoa? He had forged a poet of nature, in Alberto Caeiro; a poet of the modern city, in Álvaro de Campos; and a poet of the ancient world transposed to the present, in Ricardo Reis. Moreover, he could poetize in English as well as in Portuguese. Surely he possessed qualities that might appeal to eternity and make him the great poet of his age, a Super-Camões, perhaps even a new kind of Shakespeare. This tentative confidence was bolstered when he succeeded in publishing one of his English poems in a British literary magazine. "Meantime," which is from *The Mad Fiddler*, appeared in the January 30, 1920, issue of *The Athenaeum*, whose contributors included the likes of Virginia Woolf and T. S. Eliot.

To publish in *The Athenaeum* was no small feat, and we can only guess how Pessoa managed to do it, since none of his correspondence with the magazine has survived. It could be that he submitted many more poems to *The Athenaeum* and other publications, until his persistence finally paid off. Whatever the case, "Meantime" is not a very good poem. Its author, however, stubbornly ignored the shortcomings of his English poetry and looked forward to publishing much more of it in book form under the Olisipo imprint. He also planned to bring out individual volumes with work by his Portuguese heteronyms. He had made such plans before, but in 1920 he actually wrote a general preface for *Aspectos* (*Aspects*), a series of five or more books to be published under as many different names.[10]

Although "heteronym" was not yet part of Pessoa's vocabulary, he had already fully conceptualized the notion of pseudo-authors who were him but not him. "The human author of these books," asserted his preface to *Aspects*,

> has no personality of his own. Whenever he feels a personality well up inside, he quickly realizes that this new being, though similar, is distinct from him—an intellectual son, perhaps, with inherited characteristics, but also with differences that make him someone else.
>
> That this quality in the writer is a manifestation of hysteria, or of so-called personality dissociation, is neither denied nor affirmed by the author of these books. As the helpless slave of his self-multiplication, it would be useless for him to agree with one or the other theory about the written results of that multiplication.

Looking ahead to his literary afterlife, Pessoa was already providing future critics with potentially useful psychopathologies for explaining his particular genius. Alberto Caeiro, Ricardo Reis, Álvaro de Campos, and other fictional authors were presented as different *aspects*, or facets, of Fernando Pessoa, who claimed to have no personality except in and through those aspects—as if, when looking in a mirror, he saw them rather than himself, or as if, when he went to speak, it was in their voices that he found himself speaking.

Besides the three poetic heteronyms, there were at least two prose voices that were to be represented in the *Aspects* book series: António Mora, with an essay on "the pagan revival," and Vicente Guedes, author of *The Book of Disquiet*. Guedes was an unsettled, somewhat fuzzy personality, as we might guess from the very disparate kinds of prose to be found in the more than 150 passages thus far written for *The Book of Disquiet.* Pessoa was at a loss as to how to organize all this material into a publishable whole. He had redefined Guedes as an introverted office worker in 1917 or 1918 but without bringing his character into sharp focus and without adapting the book to the narrator's new circumstances. Nor had he written much new material for it in the past couple of years, absorbed as he was by other projects, including his two recent business ventures—F. A. Pessoa, and now Olisipo. The book lost momentum, and in 1920 it stalled completely. After being prominently mentioned in the preface to the *Aspects* series, which never went ahead, *The Book of Disquiet* fell into a prolonged sleep, and Vicente Guedes into an eternal sleep; he vanished forever from Pessoa's literary universe.

Just as lovers have only partial control over the way their love develops, changes, subsides, occasionally revives, so Pessoa with his heteronyms and his writing projects could not foresee how they would behave, what directions they would take. There was some truth in his histrionic claim to be "the helpless slave of his self-multiplication."

❧

OPHELIA QUEIROZ KNEW THAT Álvaro de Campos, besides serving as her boyfriend's deputy to tease and torment her, wrote and published poetry, some of which she had read and enjoyed,[11] but she was not privy to the rest of Pessoa's literary universe. Nor did he tell her about his hopes for developing Olisipo into a publishing empire, or his ideas about a New Monarchy and a Portuguese Fifth Empire. Literary and artistic creation, politics, and business were men's occupations, and he wanted to keep them that way.

Women were inferior to men, Pessoa argued, not because they were less intelligent but because they were less curious and creative; their chief interest was to capture a man and live for him. Ophelia, whose main ambition in life after she met Fernando was to marry him, seemed to confirm his point of view, which failed to consider conditioning factors such as societal and familial expectations for women, and their limited educational opportunities. As for female intellectuals and artists whose work Pessoa admired—from Sappho onward—he considered them to be deviant, masculinized exceptions, ergo not true women.

I have argued that Pessoa's misogyny stemmed from dread rather than enmity. Women—except when they were relatives, housekeepers, office secretaries, or shop assistants—intimidated him. And yet Ophelia, who was much more to him than a secretary, succeeded in putting him at ease. Although their physical contact was limited to kisses and petting, she had partly fulfilled the mission of Henry More and the other astral spirits, who wanted to cure their disciple not only of his virginity but also of his aversion to women. Even if Pessoa, out of habit, would continue to assume that women were intellectually and creatively less gifted than men, in 1920 all rhetoric about female inferiority suddenly and completely evaporated from his writing.

Ophelia's love was an unexpected blessing for which Fernando would remain forever grateful, but whatever love he felt for her had dwindled to a feeling of duty, the duty to reciprocate, which he was loath to fulfill. In mid-October, after three days without any sign from him, not even a note to tell her not to wait for him at the usual places, she wrote a reproachful letter. He replied the next day, saying that she had every reason to be angry but that he wasn't to blame. A "black wave" was falling over his mind, and he intended to seek treatment in a clinic in November. "What happened, you ask? I got switched with Álvaro de Campos!" The prospective stay in a clinic was an embellishment; the black wave—one of his periodic bouts of depression—was all too real. But what stood in the way between him and Ophelia was Álvaro de Campos.

The black wave lifted, but his coolness to her remained. On November 27, after again not seeing or hearing from him for a few days, Ophelia wrote briefly, bluntly, to say that she was unwilling to continue on in this way. Upon reading these words, Pessoa's first reaction was to write an English sonnet, dated November 28, expressing his great relief that "this mockery" of love between them had ended. It was a melancholy sonnet, with hazy regret coloring the poet's sense of relief. In the margins and on the reverse side of the sheet containing this and another, incomplete sonnet about the breakup, Pessoa drafted his letter of reply to Ophelia, saying "this really is the only solution—to stop prolonging a situation that's no longer justified by love, whether on your side or mine."

Actually, she was still deeply in love and must have suffered indescribable humiliation upon reading the third paragraph of Pessoa's eloquent and insensitive letter:

Time, which grays hair and wrinkles faces, also withers violent affections, and much more quickly. Most people, because they're stupid, don't even notice this, and they imagine they still love because they got used to being in love. If this weren't so, there would be no happy people in the world. Superior creatures cannot enjoy this illusion, however, because they can't believe love will endure, and when they see it's over, they don't fool themselves by taking what it left—esteem, or gratitude—for love itself.

He further insulted her when, in another paragraph, he wrote that

I'll never, never forget your delightful figure, your girlish ways, your tenderness, your devotion, and your lovable nature. It's possible that I fooled myself and that these qualities I attribute to you were my own illusion, but I don't think so, and even if they were, it did no harm to have seen them in you.

Years later, Pessoa would reveal the full meaning of this last sentence in a passage for *The Book of Disquiet*: "We never love anyone. What we love is the idea we have of someone. It's our own concept—our own selves—that we love."[12]

Whatever the true nature of his romantic attachment to Ophelia, or to his "concept" of Ophelia, Pessoa predicted that he would never have another one. "My destiny," he wrote her at the end of his farewell letter, "belongs to a different Law, whose existence you're not even aware of, and it is ever more the slave of Masters who do not relent and do not forgive." She wrote him one more letter, embittered and sarcastic, and he, in obedience to his literary masters, produced two more English poems about the end of the affair.[13]

For now they went their separate ways, but unbeknown to him or her there was still a vital link between them: Carlos, the thirteen-year-old son of Joaquina, the much older sister with whom Ophelia often stayed. More like a brother to her than a nephew, in five years' time he would become a poet, and a friend of Fernando Pessoa.

# CHAPTER 50

T HE FIRST HALF OF THE 1920S IN LISBON WAS, TO use a Dickensian phrase, the best of times and the worst of times, depending on your social class, on your willingness to be adventurous, and on your appetite for nightlife. Portugal confronted many of the same challenges faced by other countries of postwar Europe, including high unemployment, a depreciated currency, housing shortages, increased worker demands, and the rise of extreme nationalist ideologies. The nation, in fact, was more politically unstable than it had ever been, with seven governments collapsing in 1920, and six more in 1921. The armed ruffians known as White Ants continued to trash businesses and rough up individuals judged inconvenient to the Democratic Party; the less numerous Black Ants continued to oppose them; and now there was a new organization, the Red Legion, whose members hurled bombs and attacked high-placed politicians and industrialists to promote anarchy. There was a record number of strikes during the postwar period—among railroad employees, streetcar operators, construction workers, factory workers, typesetters, tailors, upholsterers, postmen, and others—and in case any scabs thought of going to work, locomotives were derailed and streetcars hijacked, bringing public transportation to a standstill. Meanwhile, the ranks of the underclass swelled with hundreds of war veterans too physically or emotionally damaged to enter the workforce. And yet for many it was a time of gaiety and prosperity.

Afonso Costa, the chief negotiator for Portugal at the Paris Peace Conference, had obtained few concessions, and the monetary reparations forthcoming from Germany fell far short of the exorbitant debts racked up by his country during the war. To fund public spending, which included the salaries of a state bureaucracy vastly enlarged by the Republic, the government printed money, causing inflation to spike to well over 50 percent in 1920 and 1921. Coins disappeared from circulation, since their metallic worth overtook their face value, and the escudo's exchange rate plummeted. Although these problems could not compare with the economic devastation affecting Germany and other central European countries, Portugal's inveterate sluggishness and seeming incapacity for innovation did not favor its recovery. Its weakened currency, however, turned out to be a boon to local industry, whose products became more competitive in the home market. Many new banks opened, while many old ones closed. Money changed hands quickly, creating new wealth for some, and people with money suddenly started to spend it. The market for imported goods surged.

In Portugal, as in the rest of Europe as well as flapper-mad America, a heightened awareness of life's precariousness and impermanence encouraged a more permissive mentality, and people in the largest cities, especially Lisbon, loosened up. Women, while they still could not vote, became more independent. Adopting the latest fashions from abroad, they wore close-fitting cloche hats, raised their hemlines to the knee, smoked cigarettes, and began to go out alone, unchaperoned. Men, who had been gradually trimming back their facial hair throughout the previous decade, were now usually clean-shaven, though a few, including Pessoa, continued to wear a moustache. For people who could afford them, nightclubs became the rage. Sumptuously decorated, they offered fine dining, absinthe, champagne and cocktails, live music, variety shows, dancing, and roulette wheels—until 5:00 a.m. The revelers sniffed cocaine to keep up with the night. Although public spending was reined in by 1924, causing inflation to give way to deflation, the nightclubbers partied on, in an attitude of indifferent frivolity that countered the politics of austerity.

Pessoa drank only wine and brandy, beginning at lunchtime; his gambling was limited to the purchase of lottery tickets; and his only, unsuccessful attempt at revelry was in a one-act verse play about the hedonistic female votaries of Bacchus, *Auto das Bacantes* (*The Bacchantes*), which he began writing in 1917 and abandoned in the early 1920s.[1] Although he himself had no interest in Lisbon's enhanced nightlife and the liberated women who now caroused as much as men, he defended people's right to dress and to act as they please, believing that it was not the place of government to moralize citizens or intrude on their private lives.[2]

The new spirit of levity and audacity—which influenced not only social behaviors and clothing fashions but also art, music, and literature—coexisted in Europe with heightened political agitation, on both the right and the left. Populist and authoritarian movements sprang up in a number of countries and counted, among their supporters, certain libertines and artistic innovators fed up with party politics.

Among Pessoa's acquaintances, the most paradigmatic figure of this age of contrasting attitudes was António Ferro, Mário de Sá-Carneiro's high school friend who had served, in name only, as the managing editor of *Orpheu*. Formerly a supporter of Afonso Costa's Democrats, Ferro had become, like Pessoa, an avid admirer of Sidónio Pais, seeing in the late dictator a presage of the glorious return of King Sebastian. But whereas Pessoa did not have a clear idea of what form that return might take, Ferro was confidently waiting for the arrival of another, even stronger dictator to put the chaotic house of Portugal in order.[3] While waiting, Ferro occupied himself with lighter matters. In 1920 he published a collection of provocative aphorisms and paradoxical observations aptly titled *Teoria da indiferença* (*Theory of Indifference*). This was followed, the next year, by *Leviana* (*Frivolous Woman*), whose coquettish narrator exalts in futile and libidinous pleasures. Ferro was a second-rate writer but adept at capturing the mood of the new decade and turning it to his advantage. In 1922 he would make an extended trip to Brazil, where he schmoozed with the local literati, lectured on "The Age of the Jazz-Band," acted in a risqué play of his own authorship, and earned a reputation as Portugal's leading modernist.

José de Almada Negreiros—by nature irreverent, lighthearted, and a free-spirited sensualist—was already, automatically in sync with the carefree mood of the 1920s. He even worked for a time as a dancer at Maxim's, Lisbon's oldest and largest nightclub. Increasingly in demand as an illustrator, cover designer, and poster artist, he also became a regular contributor to newspapers, writing sketches and commentary about contemporary life. On March 3, 1921, he presented another of his "lectures," ever unconventional though not at all like his futurist lecture of 1917. Instead of strident manifestos to jolt people out of their established points of view, he read a series of charmingly intimate, poetic prose pieces under the general title "A invenção do dia claro" ("The Invention of the Clear Day"). So charmed was Pessoa by Almada's text that he translated much of it into English,[4] convinced it would appeal to foreign readers. He never finished the translation, but the publishing division of his still fledgling company called Olisipo would soon bring the work out in Portuguese.

Another possibility for Olisipo caught Pessoa's attention: *Canções* (*Songs*), a collection of unabashedly homoerotic poetry by a relative new-

comer to the literary scene, António Botto (1897–1959). Challenging
the superficially tolerant spirit of the times, Botto's book rubbed against
deeply rooted notions of what was morally acceptable. Published in a
limited edition in February 1921, it was displayed in a Lisbon bookstore
next to a sensual photo of the young poet, exhibiting naked shoulders
like the bust of a Greek statue and with his head tilted back, so that his
lips were thrust forward, as if silently asking, "Do you dare?" Here are
three stanzas from the ninth poem:

> With mysterious,
> Gentle elegance
> He gave me his golden body,
> Which I kissed in a kind of fever.
>
> On the windowpane
> The tinkling rain . . .
>
> He squeezed me, shutting
> His eyes and dreaming . . .
> And slowly I died
> Like a scent in the wind . . .

This was one of a half dozen poems quoted by an outraged critic,
whose review was the lead story on the front page of *A Capital* on April
18.[5] (A three-month newspaper strike had prevented the review from
coming out sooner.) He referred to the author in the feminine, as Miss
Antónia, and marveled that the police and government authorities could
allow something so morally repugnant to be openly sold. He also accused
Botto of promoting himself and his work by appealing to people's baser
instincts. The book, which the critic himself unwittingly promoted,
quickly sold out its small print run.

Botto's poems are notable for their limpid style and ability to conjure
up an atmosphere in few words, but what makes them truly memorable is
their candid celebration of love between men. Fernando Pessoa proposed
bringing out an enlarged edition of *Songs* as an Olisipo book, in May he
and Botto agreed on an advance against royalties,[6] and it was around this
time that the two men became friends.

They were opposites in many ways, due to their very different upbring-

ing. Pessoa, a child of privilege, had lived in "good" neighborhoods, surrounded by books but without the company of other children. Botto
had grown up in neglected and impoverished Alfama, Lisbon's oldest
neighborhood—successively inhabited by Phoenicians, Romans, Visi-
goths, and the Moors. Sloping upward from the Tagus, where Botto's
father worked as a boatman, Alfama vaguely resembled a medina—with
its winding streets, staircases, and archways, as well as its motley, exuberant humanity: manual laborers, shop clerks, housewives, fishwives,
pimps, prostitutes, hoodlums, bawling infants. The German cultural critic
Walter Benjamin wrote an exquisitely insightful essay about the *porosity*
of Naples, Italy, and that same quality distinguished Alfama. It was an
overcrowded neighborhood in which honesty and knavery, industry and
indolence, religiosity and sensuality all coexisted in plain view. Open a
window or step out a door and there were people from various heights and
angles who would notice you, making absolute privacy impossible.

In that promiscuous, boisterous environment, Botto had somehow
managed to educate himself in literature, and although he was not intellectually thorough or profound, he was quick and witty, charming when
he wanted to be, and free of inhibition. The most original thing about
him—and it would have been a point of originality in virtually any country in the world—was his total acceptance and open affirmation of his
homosexuality. It was a characteristic that fascinated Pessoa, who would
defend him and his work throughout the rest of his life.

◆

EFFECTIVE APRIL 1, 1921, Olisipo had a new, more central location, at Rua da Assumpção, 58, and new stationery, which now read
"OLISIPO—Agents, Organizers, and Publishers." There was in reality
only one agent, organizer, and publisher, and the firm never organized
anything; Pessoa did, however, try to drum up business as a commercial
agent. In May he placed an ad in a Porto newspaper that targeted mine
owners,[7] a number of whom he ended up representing to mining corporations in the United Kingdom. He also approached African Realty
Trust, a London-based company, to see if it might consider investing in
an agricultural concession in Portuguese Guinea. Less ambitiously, or
more desperately, he wrote several British firms to offer the Portuguese-
English translating services of Olisipo. As far as I could ascertain, his
multipronged efforts did not result in a single deal. Although his busi-

Portuguese troops before boarding the ships that would take them to France, where they would fight on the side of the Allies. Pessoa questioned the wisdom of Portugal's participation. *(Ilustração Portuguesa, 12 Feb. 1917. Lisbon Municipal Libraries [Hemeroteca])*

**PORTUGAL FUTURISTA**

Santa Rita Pintor. José de Almada-Negreiros — Amadeo de Souza-Cardoso

Appollinaire Mario de Sá-Carneiro — Fernando Pessoa — Raul Leal — Alvaro de Campos

Blaise Cendrars.

(LEFT) José de Almada Negreiros in the outfit he wore to deliver a "First Futurist Lecture" to curious Lisboners, in the spring of 1917. *(Courtesy National Library of Portugal)* (ABOVE) *Portugal Futurista*, published in October 1917, included the manifestos read by Almada Negreiros at his spring lecture as well as Álvaro de Campos's "Ultimatum," which lashed out at Europe's political leaders and cultural luminaries. *(Courtesy Calouste Gulbenkian Foundation)*

Santa Rita Pintor, a close collaborator of Almada Negreiros and the mastermind behind *Portugal Futurista*, which published reproductions and encomiastic reviews of his artwork. *(Joaquim Matos Chaves,* Santa Rita Pintor: Vida e obra *[Lisbon: Quimera, 1989], p. 58)*

Ophelia Queiroz around the time she met Pessoa.
*(Courtesy Maria da Graça Queiroz)*

Pessoa's half-brothers and half-sister, his mother and his mother's nurse, along with crew members and a family they met on their voyage back to Lisbon. *(Courtesy Maria José de Lancastre)*

Praça do Rossio in the 1920s. *(Courtesy Maria José de Lancastre)*

·ANTONIO·BOTTO·

# CANÇÕES

SEGVNDA·EDIÇÃO
MVITo·AVGMENTADA
COM·VM·RETRATO·D
AVCTOR·PALAVRAS
DE·TEIXEIRA·DE·PAS-
COAES·E·NOVAS·RE-
FERENCIAS·POR·JAY-
ME·DE·BALSEMÃO
**1922**

(ABOVE) Photo of the openly homosexual António Botto, published in the Olisipo edition of *Canções (Songs)*. *(Courtesy Maria José de Lancastre)*

(RIGHT) Botto's *Canções* (1922) and Raul Leal's *Sodoma divinizada* (1923), both published by Pessoa's Olisipo press, fueled the "Literature of Sodom" scandal. *(Courtesy Casa Fernando Pessoa)*

(ABOVE) The logotype of Olisipo, which published just five titles. *(Courtesy Casa Fernando Pessoa)*

(LEFT) Raul Leal, in a photo dating from around 1920. *(Courtesy Casa Fernando Pessoa)*

A INVASÃO DOS JUDEUS

### 69

#### Intelectualidade orientalista (ou asiática)

São os descendentes dos Invasôres do Sul. Sua índole é revolucionária : *modernista*, *futurista*, *internacionalista*. Seu tipo é judáico, sefardínico, ou de qualquer modo semita : cabêlo geralmente escuro, podendo subir até côr de castanha ; rôsto moreno -oliváceo, (mate ou amulatado), podendo subir até ao trigueiro simples ; (os antropó-logos, conquistaram estes dados ; 50°/₀ dos judeus apresentam o tipo do *Homo syríacus*, brachicéphalia, isto é, cráneos sobre largo, narizes judáicos, e tendencia para o engordamento flácido ; 5°/₀ são do tipo do puro semita beduíno ; 10°/₀ apa-rentam o tipo loiro do indo-europeu ; 55°/₀ são de formas mistas. Convem observar que a percentagem do tipo loiro é muito menor em Portugal, em virtude do predo-mínio sefardínico)

1.°—José Pacheco, chefe do grupo dos «Novos»; 2.°—O escritor Homem Cristo, filho, (retrato por Eduardo Malta); 3.°—O poeta Ferreira Gomes; 4.°—O poeta Fernando Pessoa, director da «Athe-na»; 5.°—O escultor Diogo de Macedo ; 6.°—O desenhador Almada Negreiros ; 7.°—O desenha-dor Teles Machado; 8.°—O desenhador Bernardo Marques ; 9.°—O escritor Antonio Ferro, 10.°—O escritor Raul Leal ; 11.°—O escritor Augusto d'Esaguy ; 12.°—O poeta Luiz Pinto; 13.°—O escultor Rui Bastos ; 14.°—O pintor Alberto Cardozo; 15.°—O escritor Mendes de Brito

Um dado gôsto numa dada época, uma escola artístico-lite-rária, não é mais que o despertar d'afinidades latentes, o acordar e o juntar indivíduos da mesma índole, e ora, pois, da mesma raça. E assim é que uma época ajuda a expressão dum lote d'ho-mens, e outra época outro lote. Assim : a escola francêza, ou arcádica, realçou, em Portugal, principalmente os descendentes dos francezes (por ex. Bocage), e tornou inoportuna a expressão

A page from *The Invasion of the Jews* identifying Pessoa, José Pacheco, Almada Negreiros, Raul Leal, António Ferro, and others as intellectuals descended from Sephardic, Semitic Jews.
*(Courtesy Casa Fernando Pessoa)*

Mário Saa, author of *A invasão dos judeus* (1925) and a friend of Pessoa.
*(Courtesy Maria José de Lancastre)*

(LEFT) Between 1922 and 1926, Pessoa, under his own name and as Álvaro de Campos, regularly published poems and prose pieces in the magazine *Contemporânea*. *(Courtesy Lisbon Municipal Libraries [Hemeroteca])* (RIGHT) Pessoa was the literary editor of *Athena* (1924–1925), where he published poems by Ricardo Reis and Alberto Caeiro for the first time. *(Courtesy National Library of Portugal)*

Pessoa walking on the eastern side of Praça do Rossio. *(Courtesy Manuela Nogueira)*

The original editors of *Presença* (from left to right): João Gaspar Simões, José Régio, and António José Branquinho da Fonseca. This last editor would part ways and be replaced by Adolfo Casais Monteiro. *(Courtesy Cascais Historical Municipal Archive)*

(LEFT) The fourth issue of *Presença*, in which the first of Pessoa's many contributions to the magazine appeared. *(Courtesy National Library of Portugal)* (RIGHT) Ophelia's nephew, the poet Carlos Queiroz, was the intermediary between Pessoa and *Presença*. *(Courtesy Maria José de Lancastre)*

(LEFT) The photo for Pessoa's national identity card, issued in 1928. *(Courtesy Casa Fernando Pessoa)*
(RIGHT) This is the photo that Pessoa, after a nine-year separation, sent to Ophelia Queiroz in the fall of 1929. *(Courtesy Maria da Graça Queiroz)*

Pessoa at the Café Martinho da Arcada, with Augusto Ferreira Gomes (standing), António Botto, and Raul Leal. *(O Notícias Ilustrado, 23 Dec. 1928)*

(ABOVE) The Russian naturist and poet Eliezer Kamenezky, in downtown Lisbon, several years before Pessoa became his translator and friend. *(Courtesy Maria José de Lancastre)*

(RIGHT) Aleister Crowley, aka The Great Beast 666, in the late 1920s. *(Courtesy Casa Fernando Pessoa)*

(ABOVE) António Ferro in October 1933, accepting his appointment as the director of the Secretariat of National Propaganda. Standing next to him is the prime minister, António de Oliveira Salazar. *(Courtesy António Quadros Foundation)*

FERNANDO PESSOA

# MENSAGEM

LISBOA 1934
PARCERIA ANTÓNIO MARIA PEREIRA
44 RUA AUGUSTA 54

(RIGHT) *Mensagem* (1934), the only book Pessoa published in Portuguese, won a prize from the Secretariat of National Propaganda. *(Courtesy Casa Fernando Pessoa)*

Photo of Pessoa taken in the fall of 1934 by Augusto Ferreira Gomes. *(Courtesy Maria da Graça Queiroz)*

Pessoa with the journalist Costa Brochado at the Café Martinho da Arcada, in 1935.
*(Courtesy Manuela Nogueira)*

This portrait of Madge
Anderson was painted a few
years after she met Pessoa.
*(Courtesy Madge Anderson's heirs;
photograph by Heloise O'Keeffe)*

Pessoa at the Hieronymite Monastery of Belém with his niece Manuela, his half-brother Louis Michael, his sister Teca, and his brother-in-law Chico, in September 1935. *(Courtesy Manuela Nogueira)*

Pessoa's last written words: "I know not what to-morrow will bring." *(Courtesy Casa Fernando Pessoa)*

Pessoa's books and his wooden trunk full of manuscripts, when still in the possession of his heirs. The books were acquired by the Casa Fernando Pessoa, the manuscripts by the National Library of Portugal, and the trunk by a private collector. *(Courtesy Assírio & Alvim)*

ness letters were well written, one feels that the businessman is still Fernando the adolescent—bright, well informed, and articulate, but too immured in book learning and his own ideas to be able to read the real world accurately. He certainly did not have a good nose for business.

By October the agenting activities of Olisipo had ceased; it was about to become a publishing house, after two years of planning that had so far served only to entertain the planner. Having failed to attract investment capital for the large-scale, international publisher originally envisioned, Pessoa gave up on the idea of opening branches in London and other foreign capitals, but other ideas had more recently occurred to him. In 1921 he crafted a proposal for Olisipo to operate as not only a publishing house but also a bookseller—of its own books and other books, new and used, domestic and imported. Just as soon as he typed up the eight pages of his proposal, it entered the vast graveyard of his unrealized projects. Another idea was to make Olisipo a niche publisher of deluxe editions, to be sold through an associated bookstore.[8] This idea was also quickly, silently laid to rest. Olisipo, as we shall see, did turn out to be a niche publisher, but not in the way the tireless planner had imagined.

In the fall of 1921 Pessoa typed a list of more than fifty potential Olisipo titles—poetry, fiction, and nonfiction. At the top of the list was António Botto's *Songs*, so far the only book under contract. Almada Negreiros's *The Invention of the Clear Day* was also on the list, along with works by several other contributors to *Orpheu*. The writer Fernando Pessoa was generously represented by poetry and prose titles in both Portuguese and English, some of which were credited to heteronyms.

Pessoa not only thought big, he thought internationally, and more than half of the books on his publication wish list were translations. These included English-language editions of sonnets by Camões and by Antero de Quental, for which he already had some tentative drafts, as well as the *Complete Poems of Alberto Caeiro*, to be rendered into English by fellow heteronym Thomas Crosse. Scheduled translations into Portuguese included the poetry of Sappho, Machiavelli's *The Prince*, Coleridge's "The Rime of the Ancient Mariner," and a book of haiku and other Japanese poems.[9]

✦

THE MOST STARTLING ITEM on Olisipo's list of prospective publications was *The Protocols of the Learned Elders of Zion*, which purported to be the minutes of a secret meeting of Jewish leaders discussing strategy for taking over the world—by infiltrating Freemasonry, dominating world finance, controlling the media, and fomenting political instability. *The Protocols* was first circulated in Russia, to stir up anti-Jewish sentiment during the bloody wave of pogroms that commenced two years before the Revolution of 1905. Around 1920 it was published and publicized in English, French, and German to pin blame on the Jews for the Great War, the Bolshevik Revolution, and other real or perceived ills of the twentieth century. Its main disseminator in the United States was Henry Ford, whose newspaper, the *Dearborn Independent*, published a series of articles chronicling the worldwide Jewish "problem" between 1920 and 1922. The majority of the articles were reprinted in four volumes under the general title *The International Jew*. Pessoa bought the first two volumes.

*The Times* of London, in August 1921, published conclusive evidence that *The Protocols* was a fraudulent document, but antisemites continued to cite it as proof of a worldwide Jewish conspiracy. Hitler's endorsement of *The Protocols* in *Mein Kampf* assured that it would remain a staple of German anti-Jewish propaganda. Hitler's book also praised Ford for maintaining his independence from the "fury" of American Jewry.

It was right *after* Pessoa read the *Times* article that he decided to translate *The Protocols* into Portuguese. Or rather, he commissioned A. L. R., a mysterious new heteronym known only by his initials, to undertake the translation and to accompany it with notes and an introduction. Pessoa, who owned a French edition of the controversial text, seems to have only skimmed it, and almost surely did not believe it was genuine. For this very reason he wanted to argue that it was. "Against arguments there are no facts," declared a crime solver in one of his detective stories,[10] and no one took this dictum to heart as much as Pessoa, who delighted in proving the truth of ideas and assertions he knew to be completely false. Although he never actually translated any of *The Protocols*, he did write a few passages for an introduction, which proposed to logically demonstrate how the text, in spite of plagiarizing a nineteenth-century French source having nothing to do with the Jews, might still be valid. Weren't the Jews, he argued, accomplishing exactly what the so-called Elders of Zion were said to have plotted at the turn of the century? And he pointed out that plagiarism did not itself prove forgery, since a man might use someone else's ideas and words for his own purposes.[11]

Pessoa even drafted some advertising copy for his projected edition of *The Protocols*. [12] One of the ads blamed the Learned Elders of Zion not only for the Great War and Bolshevism but also for modern democracy. Another ad conflated the Learned Elders with the three hundred men who governed the economic destiny of Europe, according to an unfortunate statement made by Walther Rathenau in 1909.[13] This German Jewish industrialist and liberal politician had spoken of a cabal of three hundred men as a kind of metaphor, to deplore the fact that a small group of bankers, financiers, and industrialists wielded so much influence, but some antisemites interpreted his words literally and maintained that Rathenau himself was part of the cabal. Pessoa too, at least on paper, subscribed to this ludicrous idea. In 1922 Rathenau—recently appointed foreign minister of the Weimar Republic—would be assassinated by a group of ultranationalist terrorists whose ringleader claimed that their victim was one of the infamous "three hundred" Learned Elders of Zion.

Like just about everything else in Pessoa's intellectual life, his interest in and writings about *The Protocols* revolved around literature—in this case a distinctly unpleasant literature whose pernicious consequences he apparently never stopped to consider. A conspiracy theory that provided a neat and simple yet not at all obvious explanation for the course of recent world history naturally appealed to someone like him, an aficionado of detective stories, astrology, ciphers, myths, and prophecies, someone for whom everything visible was backed by something invisible.

So what was Pessoa's gut feeling toward Jews? It's not at all clear that he had one. Between 1923 and 1925 he would write more than twenty pages in Portuguese for an ambiguous essay titled "The Conspiracy of the 300," which parroted some of the stereotypes spread by anti-Jewish propagandists even as it criticized the "anti-intellectual hatred" of antisemitic campaigns.[14] Without any perceptible animus toward Jews, writing as a calm analyst who happened to be informed by reactionary ideas, he noted that the three hundred members of the oligarchy allegedly plotting to overthrow the world order were not all Jews but were imbued by the spirit of what he called "sub-Judaism," characterized by crass materialism and support of democracy and humanitarian causes. He stressed that Christianity itself contained strong traces of this spirit, while a Jew such as Albert Einstein counteracted it.[15]

As a companion publication to the Olisipo edition of *The Protocols*, Pessoa planned to issue a pamphlet titled *The Jew Sociologically Consid-*

*ered* in Portuguese, English, and French.[16] Hotly debated elsewhere in Europe, the so-called Jewish question was largely ignored in Portugal, no doubt because the national community of practicing Jews was minuscule, but Pessoa learned all about this "question" from Mário Saa, a poet and prose writer he met in 1916. Saa, obsessively interested in the influence of Judaism on the Portuguese nation, was part of the café group that included Augusto Ferreira Gomes and Alberto Da Cunha Dias, and his name appears on several lists of possible contributors to *Orpheu* 3. A monarchist, a traditionalist, and the heir of a wealthy landowner, Saa undertook genealogical research to show that the founding of the Republic was the work of Jewish-blooded politicians and Freemasons. This thesis was as easy to prove as it was meaningless. Given the tens of thousands of Jews who were forcibly converted to Christianity in the fifteenth century, thereby facilitating and encouraging intermarriage, traces of Jewish ancestry in Portuguese family trees are commonplace.

"Fernando Pessoa, born in Lisbon, poet and prose writer (and temperamentally antisemitic!), is a direct descendant of Jews, and belongs as well to a Jewish racial type."[17] So began a genealogical profile drawn up by Mário Saa in November 1921. The profile went on to trace Pessoa's paternal lineage back to his New Christian ancestors, some of whom were condemned as crypto-Jews by the Inquisition (see chapter 1). Saa produced dozens of similar genealogies to highlight the Jewish roots of Portuguese politicians, businessmen, and cultural figures, and in February 1925 he would publish his major antisemitic opus, paranoiacally titled *The Invasion of the Jews*. The invasion was a fait accompli, since it was not recent Jewish immigrants, who were at any rate few in number, but people with admixtures of Jewish blood in their ancestries who were attaining positions of power and accused of destroying Portugal.

Inspired by Cesare Lombroso's *Criminal Man* (1876), which contained mug shots of various physiological types supposedly predisposed to crime, Mário Saa's *Invasion* included dozens of photos of Portuguese notables with supposedly "typical" Jewish features. Pessoa's photo was one of fifteen that represented the "Oriental" or "Asiatic" type of Jewishness found among Portuguese intellectuals. José Pacheco, José de Almada Negreiros, Raul Leal, Augusto Ferreira Gomes, and António Ferro were in the same group. In the book's four pages devoted to Pessoa, Saa wrote that his "multiplicity of personalities" was merely the absence of a unified personality, "a lack of literary character." He submitted that this was a typically Jewish characteristic, as was Pessoa's marvelous ability to analyze and purported inability to synthesize.[18]

Mário Saa, one of Pessoa's closest friends in the 1920s, earned a reputation as Portugal's most fanatical antisemite of modern times, but his crusade against the insidious influence of Jews was at least half in jest, according to Augusto d'Esaguy, a prominent Jewish writer and journalist from Lisbon.* Saa's claims do often sound exaggerated, their tenor and tone somewhat tongue-in-cheek, and after publishing *Invasion of the Jews*, he never again mentioned the Jewish "threat" in his writings. Yet in an interview promoting the book and titled "The Jewish Peril," his ominous warnings contained not a hint of irony.[19] If it was all a joke, it was a ghastly one, precisely because it was so well disguised.[†]

While Saa's real views about the virtues of racial purity are a matter of speculation, Pessoa clearly stated in his own writings that intermarriage is fundamental to the evolutionary process and, more specifically, to the creation of genius. In line with this argument, he suggested that the Jews might be "an inferior people" insofar as they are "more or less a pure race."[20] Though this and other statements of Pessoa may be construed as antisemitic, he was probably not "temperamentally" and surely not viscerally so, not in a manner that could ever remotely justify racial cleansing. It was not Jewish blood but "the Jewish 'direction,' the Jewish *Weltanschauung*," that supposedly posed a threat to Western civilization.[21] But if he actually believed in the Conspiracy of the 300, whereby certain Jews—as well as non-Jews associated with the "Jewish direction"—were plotting to destabilize and control Europe, he believed with equal fervor in the counterconspiracy that he claimed was afoot in the most fascinating passage from his essay on the theme. The only passage written

---

* Esaguy reported that Saa himself, who was a friend, had some Jewish ancestry and that his *Invasion of the Jews* was part of a "humoristic campaign against Portuguese Jews." But he also denounced Saa for sloppy scholarship, for misrepresenting history, and for uncritically regurgitating the arguments of antisemites from the Action Française movement. See *O Ditador*, 19 Apr. 1925, p. 4; *A Batalha*, 15 Feb. 1925, p. 2.
† In spite of Saa's inflammatory allegations, antisemitism never caught on in interwar Portugal, which would, as the Nazis advanced, receive tens of thousands of Jewish refugees who might otherwise have ended up on death trains to the gas chambers. Esaguy was a leader of the effort to assist the refugees while they waited, in and around Lisbon, for ships that took them to the Americas.

in English rather than Portuguese, it disclosed the secret existence of a "Third Order" that actively opposed the 300 conspirators.

So secret was this Third Order that no one in the world knew about it except Fernando Pessoa. Allegedly descended from the Order of the Knights Templar and the Order of Christ that succeeded it in Portugal, the Third Order also included descendants from "an obscure order called Ordem Sebastianista," which promoted "the mystic and symbolic theory of the Return of King Sebastian," as well as "more recent elements, all Portuguese Jews."[22] The "obscure" Sebastianist Order was Pessoa's own invention, while the "recent elements, all Portuguese Jews," meant Fernando Pessoa, José Pacheco, José de Almada Negreiros, Raul Leal, and other intellectuals outed by Mário Saa for having Jewish-tainted blood. Jews, concluded Pessoa with abundant mirth, would help save the world from the Jews.

Oblivious to the carefree spirit of the 1920s, which was leading more than a few men and women of his social class to dress more casually and behave more extravagantly, Pessoa spent his evenings at home, amusing himself with far-fetched conspiracies to take over the world and counterconspiracies to oppose them. Meanwhile, very real conspiracies continued to rattle Portuguese politics, threatening the peace and safety of Lisbon's citizens as well as the ability of the Republic to endure.

# CHAPTER 51

○■○■○■○■○■○■○■○■○■○■○■○■○■○■○■○■○■○■○■○■○■○■

**N**OITE SANGRENTA, OR BLOODY NIGHT, IS HOW A
Lisbon newspaper baptized the late hours of October 19, 1921,
when five illustrious statesmen were abducted from their homes
and brutally murdered by a band of two dozen men under the direction of a hotheaded corporal known as Gold Tooth.[1] A so-called ghost
truck had hurtled down Lisbon's dimly illuminated streets to round up
three of the doomed victims, including Machado Santos, emblematic
founder of the Republic. Another of the victims—António Granjo, a
prime minister who that morning had peacefully resigned when a coup
overthrew his government—was riddled by hundreds of bullets, his jaw
crushed by the butt of a rifle and his torso sliced open by a sword, so
that his butchered remains could scarcely be identified when they arrived
at the morgue. But why kill this man at all, twelve hours after he had
resigned without the least show of resistance? And why kill with such
barbaric fury? The assassins, no less than the assassinated, were all ardent
republicans. Commentators and the general public reacted with shocked
incomprehension.

The assassins identified with the left-leaning republicans known
as Democrats, who had staged the coup that brought down the Liberals, a coalition of more moderate republicans. Although the leaders
of the coup claimed to have nothing to do with the murderers, whose
actions they condemned, in some way or other they were connected—
even if only ideologically. Several prominent republicans publicly admitted what had become all too obvious: republicanism itself was horribly
diseased. The brazen murder of Walther Rathenau by antisemitic terrorists presaged the death of the Weimar Republic, which nevertheless endured for eleven more years. The senseless violence of the Bloody
Night, on the other hand, was not a threat from outside but a cancer at
the center of Portugal's republican system of government, which would
survive just five more years before giving way to autocracy. Afonso Costa

realized that Portugal had become a frightfully dark and unsafe country, and although he was still a powerful voice in the Democratic Party, he remained based in Paris for the rest of his life.

The savage murders of the five statesmen confirmed for Pessoa that, since Portuguese politics had become hopelessly self-destructive, the nation would be better served by promoting culture and commerce, which he was now trying to do through Olisipo. On October 11 he had officially registered the name and logotype of the new publishing house,[2] and in November the first book, Almada Negreiros's *The Invention of the Clear Day*, went to the printers. The author designed its striking cover, bright green like the leaves of trees when the sun shines through them. The book was an eloquent, albeit useless, retort to the Bloody Night of October 19.

*The Invention* was issued in the second week of December, a few days after a prepublication excerpt appeared in the magazine *Ilustração Portuguesa* and a few days before the *Diário de Lisboa* (*Lisbon Daily*) mentioned the book in a brief but admiring notice.[3] Olisipo's next two titles, published at the end of that same month, received no publicity at all in the Portuguese press, which was hardly surprising. *English Poems I–II* and *English Poems III*, by Fernando Pessoa, were intended not so much for the Portuguese market but for readers and literary critics in the United Kingdom. The first slender volume contained a revised version of "Antinous" and fourteen "Inscriptions," while the second, equally slim book was taken up by "Epithalamium," the sexually charged bridal song written in 1913. The print run for each volume, as for *The Invention of the Clear Day*, was one thousand copies.

Resorting to the same strategy he had used in 1918 for publicizing his *35 Sonnets* and *Antinous: A Poem*, Pessoa sent his latest chapbooks of English poetry to newspapers and magazines in England, Scotland, and perhaps Ireland. This time around the critical reaction was negligible— nothing in the *Glasgow Herald*, let alone *The Times Literary Supplement*. A brief review published in the *Aberdeen Daily Journal* seems to have been the one and only journalistic notice of these 1921 volumes.

Demoralized, Pessoa finally desisted from trying to be a Great English Poet. He canceled his plans to bring out additional volumes of his English poems—including a revised edition of his sonnets, which was ready to go to the printer. What's more, the remarkably steady stream of poetry he had been producing in English for over fifteen years suddenly shrank to a trickle. He would keep writing poems in that language until almost his dying day, but sporadically, not on behalf of his old ambition to be a twentieth-century Shakespeare, Keats, or Shelley. On the other hand, he still refused to acknowledge that there might be a problem with his English, believing that his poetry's failure to follow poetic fashion was to blame for its disastrous reception. Fashions change, and Pessoa, counting on posterity, sent copies of *English Poems I–II* and *English Poems III* to the libraries of Oxford, Cambridge, Dublin's Trinity College, and the Faculty of Advocates in Edinburgh (which served as the deposit library of Scotland), as well as to the British Museum.[4]

It was also with posterity in mind that he revised "Antinous" and made it the leadoff poem of his English poetry issued under the Olisipo imprint. The most notable difference in the revised version is the narrator's attitude toward the relationship of Hadrian and Antinous. Both versions of the poem boldly celebrate this homoerotic love story, but the narrator of the earlier version used the word "vice" to refer to that love at six different points in the poem; he also styled it a "wrong lust," guilty of "crimes of fancy." Inspired, perhaps, by the personal and poetic example of the openly homosexual António Botto, whom he had met earlier in the year, Pessoa excised all terms of moral disapprobation from the Olisipo version of "Antinous," whose narrator no longer betrays any note of scandal, even though he knows that the story of love between two men will scandalize others.

It's not clear where Pessoa found the money to print his books and maintain the Olisipo office, whose address changed once more, from Rua da Assumpção to Rua de São Julião, 52, conveniently located two blocks away from the Café Martinho da Arcada, now the home base of his social life. The Café A Brasileira on Praça do Rossio, where he used to meet every afternoon with friends, had become a kind of command post for radical Democrats, making the poet wary of even walking past its front door, lest he get hit with a cane.[5] In those politically embattled times, the cane was an occasional weapon as well as a decorative accessory. Had Pessoa used one, it would have been strictly for show. In writing he could defend war; in reality he abhorred all forms of physical violence and confrontation.

❦

TO COMMEMORATE THE CENTENNIAL of its independence, Brazil hosted a world's fair in 1922 in Rio de Janeiro, by then already renowned as the South American City of Lights. The organizers of the fair wanted to show that the whole of Brazil was an "illuminated" country, notable not only for its industrial and technological progress but also for its creative and intellectual vivacity. Of the thirteen foreign countries participating, Portugal was the guest of honor. Seeing an opportunity for Olisipo, Pessoa drew up a proposal for a two-volume *Album of Portugal*, described as "a kind of graphic transposition of the Portuguese presence in the Exposition." The two volumes, with a total of one thousand richly illustrated pages devoted to Portuguese commerce, industry, culture, science, and tourism, would easily sell upward of twenty-five thousand copies, Pessoa estimated. He included other numbers—production cost, cover price, and anticipated profit—in his neatly typed, four-page proposal submitted in February (the fair would open in September). But his calculations were too optimistic, his experience as an editor was limited, and the organizing committee of the Portuguese pavilion entrusted others with the task of producing an exhibition catalogue.[6]

In that same month of February, Pessoa formulated a far more ambitious proposal for a very different undertaking—the creation of one or two corporations that would consolidate as many small Portuguese industries as possible. These two supercompanies, if set up according to his plan, would be able to market a plethora of goods produced both in their own factories and in other factories. Pessoa pitched this idea to Eduardo Ramires dos Reis, director of the Industrial Company of Portugal and the Colonies, which was the nation's largest flour miller and producer of cereal products. The eminent businessman, for whom Pessoa had worked in his freelance capacity as a letter writer in English and French, returned the proposal, saying that it was ingenious but flawed, since the unusual diversity of products to be produced and marketed would require an unusual number of specialized managers, making it virtually impossible for the parent company to maintain adequate control.[7]

Whether it was the mammoth, two-volume *Album of Portugal* or the gargantuan corporation (or corporations) that would revolutionize Portuguese trade and marketing, Pessoa's proposals proposed too much. A more serious problem was the way Pessoa generated his business proposals—in isolation. Instead of engaging up front with the people who could help make his ideas happen, he spent long hours in solitary lucubrations to construct detailed and (in his mind) logically foolproof plans that were often more intimidating than enticing.

◆

ONLY ONCE, AND IN fiction, did Pessoa become a successful business-man. In January 1922 he took on the role of a filthy rich banker who claims, incongruously, to be an anarchist. This incongruity extended to Pessoa's manner of setting down the banker's tale, in more than twenty single-spaced typed pages of smoothly flowing, continuous prose, with no lingering gaps to be filled in later—completely contrary to his anar-chical writing habits.[8] Discounting several short sketches, "The Anar-chist Banker" is Pessoa's only complete short story in Portuguese. It takes the form of a dialogue in which the first-person narrator draws out his wealthy friend and raises feeble objections before coming around to admitting that his interlocutor is indeed a genuine anarchist.

While smoking a cigar after the two friends have finished dinner, the banker recalls how he quickly realized, as a young convert to anarchism, that it would be impossible to single-handedly free society from "social fictions," the most tyrannical of which is money, so he decided to free at least himself, by acquiring money in great abundance, such that it could no longer oppress or influence him. Since he achieved as much freedom as it was possible to achieve, the rich banker concludes that he is a true anarchist.

There are other, auxiliary arguments to buttress the banker's thesis, and the ensemble makes for an elegant logical construction. It is founded, however, on shaky premises, beginning with his assertion, early on in the dialogue, that we can do nothing to correct the "injustices of Nature." Modern medicine, in fact, is quite successful at correcting some of those injustices; and isn't the history of civilization largely a story of over-coming nature and of attenuating the effects of natural inequalities? To defend his philosophy of rational self-interest, which the Russian-born novelist Ayn Rand would later popularize in *The Fountainhead* and *Atlas Shrugged*, the banker reminds his friend and listener that altruism and self-sacrifice are unnatural, yet evolutionary theory and ethology have debunked that notion. As for the idea that untrammeled accumulation of money enables a man to escape its tyranny, this is a little like supposing that this same man, were he to indulge in unlimited quantities of alcohol or heroin, would thereby acquire immunity to their addictive power.

Pessoa defined "The Anarchist Banker" as a "dialectical satire."[9] The immediate object of the satire was the anarcho-syndicalist movement, which staged a rash of paralyzing strikes in Portugal in 1919–1920 and achieved at least one important goal for its efforts: the eight-hour workday.* Thereafter the movement splintered and lost momentum. The intellectual butt of Pessoa's satire was the nineteenth-century French politician Joseph-Pierre Proudhon, author of *What Is Property?* and the first major ideologue of anarchism as a social movement. The French thinker's dictum that "property is theft" had persuaded Pessoa when he was a very young man. As if to atone for his youthful credulity, he embodied anarchist ideals in a rich banker, ironically inverting Proudhon's unsuccessful attempt to open a People's Bank, whose noncapitalist principles were described in a book on anarchism Pessoa read in 1908 or 1909.[10]

That same book contained a chapter on a very different kind of anarchist, Max Stirner, whom Pessoa's fictional banker, instead of mocking, emulates, though without ever mentioning Stirner by name. So taken was Pessoa by this German philosopher that in 1909, while setting up the Ibis press, he planned to bring out a Portuguese translation[11] of his major work, *Der Einzige und sein Eigentum* (1845), which he may have read in French. The book's title, translatable into English as *Only You and What's Yours*,[12] sums up the essence of Stirner's radically individualist anarchism, which rejected the authority not only of the state and of society but also of all ideologies, including nationalism, socialism, communism, and liberalism.

Nowhere in his writings did Pessoa comment directly on the gruesome murders carried out by republican vigilantes on the night of October 19, 1921, but his "Anarchist Banker," besides taking aim at the anarchist workers' movement, seems to have been a response to the lawless state of Portuguese politics that made the notorious Bloody Night possible. (The vigilantes were tried and sentenced, but the politicians and military officials who enabled them were never called to account.) The anarchist banker, like the Stirnerian anarchist, and like Pessoa himself, knows his freedom inwardly and would never resort to violence.

But Pessoa's outspoken defense of individualism, when it ventured into the question of people's sexual behavior, would lead to a moral uproar that soon became verbally and psychologically violent.

---

* This did not apply to rural or domestic workers, and the work week was still six days, not five.

# CHAPTER 52

P ESSOA'S NAME GAINED A NEW AND UNEXPECTED kind of prominence in the fall of 1922, when Álvaro Maia, a conservative Catholic journalist, published a magazine article with the accusatory title "Literature of Sodom: Sr. Fernando Pessoa and the Aesthetic Ideal in Portugal." Sodomy and other sexual acts between men were illegal in Portugal, just as they were in most of Europe; if they were discreet, however, practicing homosexuals were not likely to be prosecuted. Maia did not suggest that Pessoa engaged in illicit sexual behavior but rather—and this was a potentially worse charge— that he encouraged its acceptance and propagation through literature. Pessoa was annoyed, but he had only himself to blame for attracting unwanted attention.

"Literature of Sodom" appeared in *Contemporânea*, the magazine that had gotten off to a false start back in 1915, with the publication of a single issue devoted largely to current events, fashion, high society, theater, and news for women. It was relaunched in May 1922 with a focus almost entirely on literature and the arts. José Pacheco, the magazine's editor in chief as well as a friend and collaborator from the *Orpheu* days, gave Pessoa carte blanche to publish almost anything he liked, beginning with "The Anarchist Banker," which took up seventeen full pages of the inaugural issue. For the July issue of *Contemporânea* Pessoa wrote an article titled "António Botto and the Aesthetic Ideal in Portugal." His small publishing house, Olisipo, would soon bring out Botto's collection of overtly homoerotic poetry, *Songs*, and he wanted to whet readers' appetite. As it turned out, Pessoa's article did much more than stimulate interest in Botto's poetry; it set the stage for a full-blown literary scandal, beginning with Álvaro Maia's pugnacious article, which sought to unmask the prurient character of the "aestheticism" promoted by Pessoa.

The "aesthetic ideal," according to Pessoa's carefully constructed essay, was a Hellenic ideal, since he considered the Greeks—who sought perfection in the material world instead of longing for an alternate, spiritual reality—to have been the most dedicated cultivators of beauty. Relying on his usual, triadic method of expounding on a subject, he explained that the *superior* Hellenic artist replaces imperfect life with artistic creations that approach perfection, such as *The Iliad*; the *intermediate* Hellenic artist tries to perfect life itself, intensely experiencing its imperfection in an effort to overcome it—an attitude that gave rise to Greek tragedy; the *inferior* Hellenic artist accepts the imperfect things of life but treats them as if they were perfect, feeling them so sensually that they acquire a kind of transitory perfection.

The "inferior," sensual way of making art is the aesthetic ideal pure and simple, without higher ambitions. Botto, according to Pessoa, was this kind of artist, indeed the only one in Portugal "to whom the designation of aesthete can be applied without reservation." Physical beauty and pleasure were the guiding lights of his poetry. And since he was a pure aesthete, his *Songs* naturally celebrated the male body, which, Pessoa contended, contains more elements of beauty (both gracefulness *and* strength) than the female body (gracefulness only).

To bolster these arguments, Pessoa resorted to the eighteenth-century German art historian Johann Winckelmann, whom he called the "founder of aestheticism in Europe," and to Walter Pater, "the greatest European aesthete." He noted that Pater, when writing about Winckelmann, quoted him as saying that the "supreme beauty [of Greek art] is rather male than female" and that those who cannot appreciate male beauty seldom have an "inborn instinct for beauty in art." And he concluded his literary analysis by affirming that *Songs*, while not a work of genius, was the only conspicuous example in modern European literature "of the aesthetic ideal in all its empty purity." In other words, Botto's poetry was important not because it was great literature but because it was unconditionally, purely "aesthetic," as proven by its bold, unproblematic exaltation of masculine beauty—possibly unique in European writing.

The patient reader of *Contemporânea* who made it all the way to the end of the six dense pages of tortuous argumentation presented in "António Botto and the Ideal Aesthetic in Portugal" was then treated to a light and easy, illustrative "Song" by Botto, presented on the next two pages of the issue. But rather than illustrating any points made in Pessoa's logical exposition, the poem belied its central thesis. Speaking to a tall and slender, blond teenage male, the poem's narrator does not celebrate his masculine beauty; he focuses instead on their amorous physical contact and on the misgivings it has aroused in the younger man, initiated by him into homoerotic sex. It may be that Fernando and António, who were by now close friends, co-conceived this playfully naughty diptych: the former's essay on the higher, Hellenic aestheticism juxtaposed with the latter's poem about the sexual deflowering of one man by another.

It was not because he missed the joke but because he understood it all too well that Álvaro Maia accused Pessoa, in so many words, of being a purveyor of sodomitic literature. He pointed out that Winckelmann was a homosexual (so was Pater), and while he made no innuendos about Pessoa's sexuality, he denounced his Greekly aesthetic apology of Botto's poetry as a sophistic ruse that perversely ennobled what was plainly, "in every acceptation of the word, sheer filth."

Maia's frontal attack appeared in the October 1922 issue of *Contemporânea*,[1] which contained a second response to Pessoa's article from the ever refractory Álvaro de Campos, who was known to some but not all readers as the poet's fictional sidekick. In a letter to the editor supposedly sent from Newcastle-upon-Tyne, where he worked at the shipyards in his capacity as a naval engineer, Campos—rather like Maia—faulted Pessoa for obfuscating: "Aesthetic ideal, my dear José Pacheco, aesthetic ideal! Where did that expression go looking for a meaning? And what did it find when it got there? There are no ideals and no aesthetics except in the illusions we make of them." Campos said that Pessoa wasted his energy trying to prove unprovable things because he was too shy to simply affirm, and to act. Very different was António Botto, whose *Songs* Campos admired because of their "absolute immorality," pursued without apology.

The Olisipo edition of Botto's *Songs* was published in mid-November.[2] It included ten new poems and, as a bonus feature, a reproduction of the bare-shouldered photo of the author that had been displayed in a bookshop window to help sell the original, 1921 edition of the book, prompting an indignant reviewer to brand it as "pornography." As if eager to stir up even more indignation, Pessoa distributed a promotional flyer that called the semierotic photo of Botto, which took up a whole page in the Olisipo edition, "a notable source of aesthetic education."[3] Commenting on the new edition, the *Diário de Lisboa* noted that Botto's poems "have been read and savored like a forbidden fruit. They contain a scent of nard much appreciated by sick or slightly perverted hearts."

Álvaro Maia's allegation that Pessoa's aesthetic theories served as a cover for the so-called Literature of Sodom was begging for a response, but the theorist was not forthcoming. In the next issue of *Contemporânea*, instead of refuting Maia, he pointed out a tiny grammatical mistake in his homophobic tirade and left it at that. Not content with his friend's ironic riposte, Raul Leal, who wholly sympathized with Botto and his poetry, wrote his own reply, "Sodom Deified: A Few Theometaphysical Reflections on an Article."

Leal's article was about the same length as Maia's, but José Pacheco refused to publish it in *Contemporânea*. No matter: Pessoa was happy to issue it as an Olisipo book, or booklet. *Sodom Deified* came out in the third week of February, with the letters of its title printed in fiery red on the cover. It was also in red that Leal's recently adopted spiritual name, Henoch, was printed in parentheses after his secular name. Henoch, or Enoch, was the biblical prophet who reportedly "walked with God" and, instead of dying, was whisked up into heaven. Some esoteric traditions also identify him with Hermes Trismegistus, the legendary founder of alchemy as well as "Hermetic" philosophy.

A flyer for *Sodom Deified* described it as a "remarkable defense of Sensuality from the religious point of view."[4] Remarkable it was. Its author defended António Botto and Fernando Pessoa against the accusations of Álvaro Maia by suggesting that immorality and ungodliness resided in the mind of the accuser. According to Raul Leal's way of thinking, sensuality and "pederasty" (i.e., homosexuality) were pure, bestial manifestations of Vertigo, which is God, the Indefinite Absolute. Sodom was justly condemned, he admitted, but only because its inhabitants were irreligious, unaware that the sexual acts they practiced were an "inspiration of God," who "deliriously stirred up their souls and feelings."

✦

**DEIFIED OR DEMONIZED, BEHAVIORS** associated with Sodom and Gomorrah were a timely topic. On February 14, 1923, three days before Raul Leal's book went on sale,[5] the *Diário de Lisboa* reported that the police had broken up a Carnival dance party for men only in Graça, a working-class neighborhood just up the hill from Alfama. Sixteen of the men, all dressed up as women, were arrested for immoral behavior and fined.[6] On February 16 the same newspaper announced the publication of *Decadência* (*Decadence*), a collection of poems that exuded a "strange and highly sensual perfume." This was the first book published by Judith Teixeira, whose sensuality happened to be aroused by women rather than by men. Some booksellers displayed her book alongside Botto's *Songs* and Leal's *Sodom Deified*.[7]

Urban poverty combined with the liberalized mores of the 1920s provided the perfect breeding ground for social vices such as gambling, cocaine addiction, and child prostitution, which newspapers deplored and politicians promised to rein in if not eradicate,[8] but it was the open, public expression of homosexuality that prompted a group of conservative Catholic students to appoint themselves moral watchdogs. On February 19 they founded the Lisbon Student Action League, led by Pedro Teotónio Pereira, a student of mathematics who would eventually become a high-level official in the dictatorial regime of António de Oliveira Salazar, serving twice as Portugal's ambassador to the United States. In an interview published on February 22, the terribly earnest, twenty-year-old Pereira ominously warned that his group was going to "bring into line these ambiguous gentlemen" with "feminine manners" who walked Lisbon's streets and frequented its cafés; he promised that bookstores would be monitored so as to root out immoral works by "decadent artists, the poets of Sodom"; and he said that the students would take it upon themselves to exercise "strict censorship in theaters and cinemas."[9] The Action League would focus on—and achieve—the second of these three goals.

Partly because European laws against homosexuality were often vaguely worded—Portuguese legislation proscribed "vices against nature," for instance—their enforcement depended on which government was in power and on the current tide of public opinion. German homosexuals during the 1920s, despite a nineteenth-century law criminalizing sex between men, were relatively free to congregate and even to publish periodicals and books. In Spain, on the other hand, although the penal code did not specifically outlaw homosexual activity, the Church vehemently condemned it, making indiscreet homosexuals liable to arrest for "offences against morality." In Portugal, too, the persecution of homosexuality depended on what groups, at a given moment, exerted pressure on the government.

When confronted by vociferous Catholic students, the Portuguese authorities readily agreed with them that "immoral"—and especially homoerotic—literature should be banned. On March 3 the police seized copies of three recent works from the shelves of bookstores: António Botto's *Songs*, Raul Leal's *Sodom Deified*, and Judith Teixeira's *Decadence*.[10] Two days later, three hundred members of the Action League demonstrated their support for the ban by marching in downtown Lisbon and distributing a manifesto against the "inversion of intelligence, morality, and sensibility." What this "inversion" amounted to in practice was clearly spelled out: "Sodom is resurrecting in books and in writers, in minds and in bodies. It has attained the ultimate abomination, which in the biblical tradition caused fire to rain down from heaven."

Lisbon's moralizing students received favorable coverage, especially in the Catholic press, with one newspaper publishing the Action League's manifesto in its entirety.[11] Fernando Pessoa, implicitly under attack as the publisher of two of the banned books, counterattacked with a manifesto signed by Álvaro de Campos, who told the students that they should stick to their studies and let writers do their writing. He also responded to their homophobia: "Have fun with women, if you like women; have fun in another way, if you prefer another way. It's all fine and good, since it pertains only to the body of the one having fun." (All, or nearly all, of the protesting students were male.) António Botto also published a manifesto of protest, in which he cited Álvaro de Campos, who had supposedly commented to him in a letter that "morality is the ignoble hypocrisy of envy" for "not being loved."

Raul Leal published his own manifesto against the Action League, and also against the Catholic Church, which he accused, no doubt correctly, of inciting the league's activities. Without the rhetorical fervor of a manifesto, writing more in the style of a personal essay, Leal justified himself and his offending book by explaining how his own experiences of moral as well as material squalor were a crucible for purifying his spiritual yearnings and ethical sensibility. But Sodom and divinity could coexist: "Wine, gambling and debauchery are in me the outer shell of an essentially, utterly pure life, full of sorrow and resignation." Rejecting Catholic theology, he defended a Universal Theocracy and aspired to be the founder of "the Reign of Vertigo or of the Holy Spirit." He signed his manifesto as "the prophet Henoch."

This document was pay dirt for the students, who extracted useful, truncated phrases and reassembled them in yet another manifesto—one that took direct aim at Raul Leal, cruelly ridiculed as a sexual degenerate suffering from paranoia and delusions of grandeur. Raul Leal—alias the reincarnated prophet Henoch—very obviously *did* have an exaggerated notion of his divinely ordained role in the world and probably suffered from paranoia as well, but Pessoa was fiercely loyal. He wrote and published a broadside, "Concerning a Student Manifesto," that denounced the moralizers' bad faith, showing how they had misquoted and misrepresented his friend. It was an impassioned yet serenely articulated text, the last salvo in the war of words surrounding the Literature of Sodom, and ended with a magnificent affirmation of solidarity: "Whatever direction my life may take, I doubt that I will ever feel more honored than I feel now, for having [Raul Leal] as my companion in this cultural adventure where we coincide, different and alone, under the scorn and derision of the mob."

Pessoa sent copies of his broadside to more than two hundred journalists, intellectuals, and politicians, including the president of the Republic and every Catholic bishop in Portugal.[12] Never in his life had he been so committed to a cause, which was to defend not only his friend but human dignity generally and people's right to be different. When he wrote that he felt honored to stand with openly homosexual Raul Leal "under the scorn and derision of the mob," he was borrowing a page from the life of Oscar Wilde, who, during his transfer in 1895 from Wandsworth Prison to Reading Jail, stood in convict's clothes on the platform of Clapham Junction "in the gray November rain surrounded by a jeering mob"—as the disgraced writer would recall in his book *De Profundis*. The incident haunted Wilde for the rest of his days, and it greatly impressed Pessoa, who in 1930 would remark, in English: "Wilde was never so much attested a genius as when the man on the railway platform spat in his face when he was gyved."[13]

Leal's *Sodom Deified* was the last work published by Olisipo. Given that its list of just five titles also included Botto's *Songs* and Pessoa's own "Antinous" (which took up most of *English Poems I–II*), one could argue that Olisipo was the first gay imprint in Portugal, if not all Europe.[14]

◆

**PESSOA'S ATTITUDE TOWARD HOMOSEXUALITY** had changed. In the previous decade, however much he had tried to overcome his own prejudices, he'd been unable to visualize love between men in the full light of day; he celebrated it in the rainy, mournful atmosphere of "Antinous." Raul Leal, his friend since at least 1915, actually practiced it, but as part of a process of fleshly mortification to prepare him for a spiritually exalted future. It was Pessoa's newest friend, António Botto, who showed him how erotic attraction between men could exist without shadows or justificatory discourses.

Ostentatious, affected, and theatrical, Botto was a textbook example of the style known as camp, a style that Álvaro de Campos seemed to share with him, but only up to a point. Campos's theatricality was inspired by Greek tragedy; Botto's was the drama of the revue or variety show, genres that were popular in Portugal throughout most of the twentieth century. Campos had a profound streak of hysteria, the hysteria of the maenads; Botto was capricious and tetchy, with a malicious streak. He also had a lively mind and a lighthearted manner, and Pessoa—or the slightly campy, Campos side of Pessoa—managed to be lighthearted with him. Spending time with Botto was like going on a holiday from seriousness. Which is not to say that Botto was not a serious, hardworking writer. In the following decades and in various genres he steadily published books, several of which included critical appreciations by Pessoa, who was ready and willing to do almost anything to help promote his friend's career. It was as if he owed a debt to Botto—a debt of gratitude for just being open about the kind of man he was.

It was through Botto that Pessoa met a wealthy landowner's son named Francisco Manuel Cabral Metello. A dandy who would never marry, Metello (1893–1979) enjoyed a certain notoriety as a young Lisbon socialite who radiated elegance and brio. He was the kind of person to whom Botto, anxious to rise above his working-class origins, was naturally drawn. In November 1922 the two young men invited Pessoa to spend some time with them at the Metello family estate in Oliveira do Hospital, east of Coimbra. In spite of being an antisocialite who avoided unfamiliar situations, Pessoa, who had just published Botto's *Songs*, gladly accepted the invitation.[15] He unfortunately left no account of the trip in his notes.

A few months later, Francisco Metello published his first book, *Sáchá*, a thinly plotted novella whose characters are habitués of Lisbon's decadent social whirl. "I won't say that your novella is remarkable as literature," Pessoa wrote in a letter, but he confessed to being fascinated by the personality of its author—"frivolous, feminine, scandalously European, complicatedly sociable"—because it was so different from his own "speculative and metaphysical spirit," predestined to being "sad and graceless." Although he might one day be famous, he mused, never could he hope to be elegant.

Pessoa's unusually revealing letter seems to have been written with only its addressee in mind, but it somehow made its way into a spring 1923 issue of *Contemporânea*,[16] perhaps at the suggestion of Metello, who was naturally keen to promote his book. The same issue of the magazine included a poem of Álvaro de Campos, "Lisbon Revisited (1923)," whose title was in English—a nod to the fact that the naval engineer had been living and working for some years in northern England. Making a trip to Lisbon in 1923 after a long absence, he finds that it is nothing like the Lisbon of his childhood, for the overwhelming reason that he is no longer a child, and he cantankerously declares his independence from everything and everyone. Here are the poem's opening stanzas:

No, I don't want anything.
I already said I don't want anything.

Don't come to me with conclusions!
Death is the only conclusion.

Don't offer me aesthetics!
Don't talk to me of morals!
Take metaphysics away from here!
Don't try to sell me complete systems, don't bore me with the
    breakthroughs
Of science (of science, my God, of science!)—
Of science, of the arts, of modern civilization!

Notice how Campos, in the first three lines of the third stanza, dismisses all sides of the Literature of Sodom debate recently sparked by Pessoa's article about António Botto and fanned into a fire by Raul Leal's *Sodom Deified*. The naval engineer has no use for Pessoa's attempt to legitimize love between men through aesthetic ideals, much less for the student moralists who declared such love an abomination, and he also scorns Leal's metaphysical, or "theometaphysical," glorification of it. All debate is useless, as is all human progress in philosophy, science, and the arts. This generalized indifference resembles the decadent, blasé attitude of people who live for today and for appearances, since everything else is uncertain or unavailing, but Campos rejects even appearances, as well as any obligation to be sociable. Here are eight lines from the middle of the poem:

Leave me alone, for God's sake!

You want me to be married, futile, conventional and taxable?
You want me to be the opposite of this, the opposite of anything?
If I were someone else, I'd go along with you all.
But since I'm what I am, lay off!
Go to hell without me,
Or let me go there by myself!
Why do we have to go together?

The Portuguese *fútil*, rendered in the second line above as "futile," could also be translated as "frivolous." It was one of the admiring adjectives used by Pessoa to describe the personality of Francisco Metello, who repeatedly invited him in 1923 to make another trip to his family's estate. Perhaps in a couple of months, answered Pessoa, with no intention of ever going back there. He agreed, however, to write a brief afterword for the aspiring writer's next book, published at the end of the year. "Elegant" and lightweight like Metello's first effort, the second book would also be his last. He could not be a serious writer any more than Pessoa could be elegantly futile.

It's possible that Pessoa slightly envied Francisco Metello his worldly sociability and António Botto his enjoyment of Greekly "aesthetic" pleasures, and that he compensated for the absence of these things in his own life through the pseudolife of his urbane heteronym, who had traveled immensely, dressed fashionably, had love affairs, and was a jaunty man of the world. But Campos, outwardly a dandy and even a bit campy, was also self-sufficient. He wanted to "feel everything in every way possible," according to his motto, but without being bound by any law or constrained by any will not his own. Álvaro de Campos was a more radical anarchist than the banker Pessoa invented in 1922.

Although Campos stands out as Pessoa's largest and liveliest alter ego, if we remove his monocle and tight-waisted coat and look past his flamboyant demeanor, we will find Pessoa himself—or his identical twin—raw and innocent, quasi-primordial. I stated earlier that Alexander Search, invented in 1906, was a transcendent version of Pessoa, a distilled projection of his *intellectual* self as a young man. Álvaro de Campos was a *visceral* Pessoa, all feeling and instinct, before the intrusion of reason. Temperamentally shy, Fernando Pessoa retreated early on into study, speculation, and analysis; his elaborate mental constructions were products of his inhibition. Álvaro de Campos personified his id, and that id wanted to experience everything without limits, but to experience it in his own way.

It might seem that Pessoa—if less pent up and less socially maladroit, less insecure about his sex appeal—could have been initiated into homosexual activity by António Botto, as Oscar Wilde was by Robbie Ross. But Pessoa was not always maladroit and insecure; he had proven himself quite capable of enchanting Ophelia Queiroz and keeping her enthralled. The fatal thorn in that relationship was, significantly, Álvaro de Campos, insofar as he represented Pessoa's dedication to writing and the imaginary life and also, possibly, his preference for men.

Above all else, however, Pessoa preferred himself—a preference likewise embedded in Campos, consistently unwilling to be defined, enlisted, or even accompanied: "Leave me alone, for God's sake!" The heteronym's fantasies of being physically abused by pirates ("Maritime Ode") and grabbed by the hands of sailors in the dark ("Salutation to Walt Whitman") are powerfully suggestive but never more than fantasies. Álvaro had a secret romance with a boy from the town of York, according to a sonnet discussed earlier (and published in *Contemporânea* 6, in December 1922), and once loved a blond youth named Freddie, according to his poem "Time's Passage," but the two poems also mention a girlfriend named Daisy and a certain Mary with whom he spent many delightful hours reading poetry. To none of his lovers was Campos deeply committed, which one might guess from his confession, already alluded to, that although he smoked opium and drank absinthe he preferred "thinking about smoking opium to smoking it" and liked "looking at absinthe more than drinking it."

Pessoa, too, preferred writing about love between men to actually loving a man, and from 1923 on he was content to simply watch António Botto be Botto—an exuberantly practicing homosexual, with a notorious penchant for sailors. Apropos of that penchant, Pessoa reported to a friend that Francisco Metello, when he spotted Botto with his arm around a sailor on a Good Friday, playfully reprimanded him by saying, "António, I can't believe you'd eat meat on Good Friday!" To which Botto, never at a loss for words, replied: "A sailor isn't meat, he's fish."[17]

Throughout most of the 1910s Pessoa had produced an intermittent yet compelling stream of homoerotic poetry, from "Sonnet That Shouldn't Have Been Written" of February 1912 to the 1919 poem that hopelessly declared love to a presumably heterosexual man, and in December 1921 he published his much revised version of "Antinous." For the remaining fourteen years of his life he wrote no more homoerotic poetry, except for a 1923 ode of Ricardo Reis containing a far from obvious allusion to a beloved male. Álvaro de Campos would write a prose piece that cited this ode to "out" his fellow heteronym, alleging that the Horatian maidens frequently named in Reis's poetry—Lydia, Chloe, and Neaera—were a ruse; the real addressee of his odes was a young man.[18]

Pessoa's passion for Ophelia, though of brief duration and low to moderate intensity, was enough to satisfy his curiosity about what it would be like to love a woman, at least for a number of years to come. And his curiosity about what it would be like to love a man—once he brought the beast out of the jungle and into the open sunlight, or rather, after António Botto brought it out for him—also subsided. Romantic love was for others, not for him, he had written Ophelia in his farewell letter, and this was so not just because he was timid or repressed but because there were other things, including his own company, that he loved more.

## CHAPTER 53

THE HOMOPHOBIC CAMPAIGN OF THE LISBON
Student Action League was part of a conservative groundswell—
felt not just in Portugal but in large swaths of southern and
central Europe—that defended a return to traditional values and called
for tough measures to impose discipline on a profligate society and seemingly dysfunctional political order, even if this would mean an authoritarian government. On the opposite end of Portugal's political spectrum,
movements such as anarcho-syndicalism, while they attracted adherents
in urban centers, did not have revolutionary ambitions. Most leftists still
rallied around the Republic, with intellectuals debating what was needed
to make its parliamentary system less volatile and more efficient. Pessoa,
divorcing himself from the immediate realities confronting Portugal in
the early 1920s, pursued his own idea of what constituted the Portuguese
nation and what it could yet become.

Although he did not subscribe to the doctrine of intense longing, or
*saudade*, which Teixeira de Pascoaes mantrically asserted to be the distinctive and redemptive virtue of the Portuguese "race," Pessoa's idealized Portugal was nurtured by nostalgia for the glory years of its maritime
history of centuries past. As if he were a sculptor and that monumental
history were a block of fine marble, he had lately produced a suite of
twelve exquisitely wrought poems titled "Mar Português" ("Portuguese
Sea"), published in the October 1922 issue of *Contemporânea*. The poems
were patriotic evocations of such navigators as Ferdinand Magellan,
Vasco da Gama, and Bartolomeu Dias, and of the people in the home
country who contributed to the voyages and discoveries that made much
of the sea effectively Portuguese in the fifteenth and sixteenth centuries.
Not all was serendipity, however. A note of elegy threads through these
poetic tributes. The first poem of the suite, "Prince Henry the Navigator," honors the great royal patron and promoter of the discoveries, glo-

rifies the Portuguese achievement of circumnavigating the globe, and laments the inglorious state of present-day Portugal:

> God wills, man dreams, the work is born.
> God willed that all the earth be one,
> That the sea unite rather than divide it.
> Anointed by Him, you unveiled the foam,
>
> And the white crest went from island to continent,
> A path of light to the world's end,
> And all at once the entire earth
> Appeared, round, from out of the blue.
>
> The One who anointed you made you Portuguese,
> A sign to us of our pact with the sea.
> The Sea was won, the Empire undone.
> Lord, we still must win Portugal!

Pessoa was a staunch imperialist, but the penultimate line of his poem acknowledges the paradoxical fact that Portugal's imperial decline was the price paid for its maritime success. This reflects his conviction, arrived at many years before, that material conquest was not viable for a small country like Portugal, which could hope to dominate the world, or at least part of the world, only through its culture. Hence his vision of a new renaissance in the offing, spearheaded by Portuguese creators of culture, with himself leading the way.

Pessoa had no shortage of grand ideas, such as the Portuguese Culture Guild, for how to stimulate Portugal's intellectual activity and promote its art and literature, but his friend José Pacheco, besides publishing *Contemporânea*, actually organized conferences, concerts, and art exhibitions. Every other month there was some sort of *Contemporânea*-sponsored event. And the magazine itself, the most elegantly produced publication in Portugal, was unreservedly praised by most of its highbrow readership. But Pessoa, grateful as he was to be able to publish in its pages, had his reservations. In August 1923, after a seven-year hiatus, he wrote to his old friend from the Azores, Armando Côrtes-Rodrigues. It was a short letter, written in a fit of nostalgia, and reminisced about *Orpheu* and the literary movements such as swampism and intersectionism that Pessoa had cooked up with the help of his friends. And then: "Have you seen *Contemporânea*? It is, in a way, the successor of *Orpheu*. But how different! How different! One thing or another recalls that past, but the rest, the ensemble. . . ."

José Pacheco did not disagree with Pessoa. In an interview published shortly after his magazine was relaunched, he was the first to point out that there was almost nothing avant-garde about it, since Portuguese writers and artists, including the so-called modernists, were "always conservative."[1] In an effort to compensate, or to make *Contemporânea* at any rate more cosmopolitan, Pacheco opened the magazine's pages to contemporary writers from Spain, including Ramón Gómez de la Serna, a combative avant-gardist who had translated Marinetti's futurist manifestos into Spanish.

Serna was the most interesting Spanish author published in *Contemporânea*, but it was another Spanish contributor to the magazine who played a bit role in the story of Pessoa's life. Adriano del Valle, an Andalusian poet who had published in *Contemporânea* the previous fall, spent almost a month in Lisbon in the summer of 1923. He went there on his honeymoon, although he seems to have been every bit as interested in the local writers he met as he was in his bride. José Pacheco introduced him to Pessoa, who introduced him to Raul Leal and António Botto, and Botto introduced him to Judith Teixeira, the sapphic poet who—like the two homosexuals published by Olisipo—had seen one of her books banned for indecency in March. Valle met with Pessoa's friends at the Café Martinho da Arcada; he probably visited Teixeira at her home, renowned for its "decadent" décor of exotic rugs, tapestries, and naked statues;[2] and on many an afternoon he received Pessoa at his hotel, where the two men worked together on translations of Mário de Sá-Carneiro's poetry into Spanish. In an interview published long after Pessoa's death, Valle would recall how the Portuguese poet talked to him with lit-up eyes about other writers' work, never about his own.[3]

Valle returned to his hometown of Huelva, on the southern coast close to the Portuguese border, with the editions published by Olisipo and a few other books in his luggage, including two that came highly recommended by Pessoa—*The Book of Cesário Verde* and Camilo Pessanha's recently published *Clepsydra*. Soon Valle and Rogelio Buendía, a poet who lived in the same town, blitzed the local paper with Spanish renditions of contemporary Portuguese poetry. On September 11 and in Buendía's translation, *La Provincia* published five of the fourteen "Inscriptions" included in Pessoa's *English Poetry I–II*. These were the first translations of Fernando's poetry into Spanish—or into any language.

Pessoa would correspond with Adriano del Valle for more than a year, and he also exchanged letters with Buendía and another Spanish poet, Isaac del Vando-Villar. Vando-Villar and Valle had been the cofounders of the ultraist magazine *Grecia*, where Borges published poems and prose pieces in 1920, but ultraism had a short life and was mentioned only once in their spoken or written conversations, in Valle's very last letter to Pessoa.[4]

The writer who most benefited from Valle's trip to Lisbon was António Botto. Valle translated some of his poems, and a couple of Spanish critics published favorable reviews of the Olisipo edition of Botto's *Songs*.[5] The Portuguese poet cultivated his notoriety. In August 1923 he delivered a lecture at the National Theater on Praça do Rossio in which he spoke for all of ten minutes, without anyone in the audience asking for their money back, since they had paid ten escudos not to hear what he had to say but simply to see him: he strutted onto the stage with dyed blond hair and blush on his face.[6] Botto's budding renown across the border was cut short, however, after he wrote a letter ordering his Spanish translator to quit changing the "he" in his poems to "she."[7] Valle preferred, instead, to quit translating his poetry. The Literature of Sodom was ultimately too "ultra" for him and his ultraist colleagues.

After the students of the Action League went back to their studies and "immoral" literature stopped being news, Pessoa quietly redistributed Botto's *Songs* and Raul Leal's *Sodom Deified* to Lisbon bookstores, but in late August and September the police again confiscated whatever copies of the books they found.[8]

◆

PESSOA'S SISTER, TECA, HAD met a man she loved who was about her age, and on July 21, 1923, they got married. A captain in the administrative division of the army, Francisco Caetano Dias (1897–1969) was in charge of a uniforms warehouse and had a house at his disposal on the same property—at the Quinta dos Marechais,[9] in Benfica, the neighborhood where Pessoa had lived for a few months in 1919–1920. Pessoa's mother, who was practically an invalid, moved into the house with her daughter. Some months later they were joined by Henrique Rosa, who had grown too frail to keep living on his own. Almost thirty years earlier, when Maria Madalena, on the day she turned thirty-four, was married by proxy to Captain João Miguel Rosa, Henrique Rosa had stood in for his younger brother, who was already in South Africa, serving as Portugal's consul in Durban. Now, in a new kind of proxy arrangement, Maria and Henrique would live what was left of their lives with each other, linked once more by the absent husband and brother.

Pessoa, on the other hand, found himself suddenly, completely alone in the large apartment on the usually quiet, residential Rua Coelho da Rocha. That pleased him, in a way, since he treasured his solitude, but he missed eating home-cooked meals prepared by his sister. He also greatly missed his mother. After she and Teca moved to the Quinta dos Marechais, he became a regular visitor there, occasionally staying overnight or for the weekend. Maria Madalena was becoming more withdrawn and detached, but she listened attentively whenever her son recited one of his poems.

Before meeting Ophelia, when he still had Emília in his employ as a housekeeper, Pessoa sometimes invited friends to his rented rooms. Rarely did he bring anyone to the apartment where he lived with—and now without—his family. Although his mother and sister had moved out, the apartment still contained many of their personal belongings and was haunted by memories of their daily routines, by the lingering echoes of their voices formerly heard throughout the day. And there was the imposing presence of furniture from when he was a little boy, brought out of storage after the family's return from Africa in 1920. The largest piece of furniture was the piano that his mother used to play and that he pretended to play when he was five or six years old. His sister had played it very occasionally, but now it stood silently against a wall in the living room. Pessoa kept his two "families" strictly separate. Over lunches and dinners at the Quinta dos Marechais, he seldom mentioned António Botto, Raul Leal, Geraldo Coelho de Jesus, or Augusto Ferreira Gomes, and at the cafés where he met with these and other friends he never talked about his mother or sister, unless it was in an aside to his cousin, Mário Freitas.

We can think of Pessoa's family of friends as an informal men's club, nearly all of whose members had a literary bent, but in the mid-1920s national politics often dominated their conversation, as it did among most educated Portuguese men. On one point the club members were politically united: their veneration for the posthumous, mythicized figure of Sidónio Pais, whose actual record of accomplishments as president and de facto dictator they preferred to overlook, recalling only how, for a few months, he had managed to inspire people with faith and hope. Disenchanted with democracy as it had played out in the Portuguese Republic, they hoped for another strongman who could bring stability, self-confidence, and steady economic growth to the nation. But they differed in their ideas about the system of government over which this strongman should preside. Alberto Da Cunha Dias, Pessoa's high-strung friend who had been briefly committed to an asylum in 1916, wanted the Republic to continue being republican, with an elected parliament but also with a more powerful president. Raul Leal, a tenacious monarchist, wanted the country to be ruled by a king. Pessoa, an abstract monarchist, promoted a theory of nonhereditary monarchy that was hard to fathom. Augusto Ferreira Gomes, Geraldo Coelho de Jesus, and Mário Saa adhered to a new political movement with a definite theory of government and absolutely concrete goals: fascism.

◆

FOR THREE YEARS BENITO MUSSOLINI'S nationalistic, blackshirted Fascists had terrorized northern and central Italy by violently breaking up strikes, beating up or killing opponents, torching union offices, left-wing newspapers, and Socialist Party headquarters, and overthrowing local, freely elected governments. Notwithstanding their methods, the Fascists enjoyed significant support among business leaders and the middle class, who feared the specter of communism, and the blackshirts' March on Rome, in October 1922, culminated with Mussolini's appointment as Italy's prime minister.

The Fascist leader, whose distinctive square jaw suggested unflinching determination, was getting good press abroad. As a former journalist, he knew how to manipulate and spread news, and his government could boast of some real achievements. While other countries in postwar Europe were still convulsed by social and economic turmoil, Mussolini succeeded in quickly restoring order, embarked on a program of public works that helped shrink unemployment, and stimulated productivity; the economy flourished during his first years in power. He ruled with tyranny, yes, but Italy was again an energetic, smoothly running country—so foreign observers often pointed out. In the summer of 1923 The Washington Post and other U.S. newspapers ran a syndicated article about the "spirit of discipline" fostered by Mussolini's government and "concretely illustrated" by Italy's trains, which were notorious for being late but now ran on time.[10] Their unprecedented punctuality became an emblem of Fascist efficiency.

Because of its geographical, cultural, and religious proximity as a southern, "Latin," and Catholic country, Mussolini's Italy received intense media coverage in Portugal, where some young intellectuals quickly hailed it as a model to follow. In 1923 they organized themselves under the banner of Lusitanian Nationalism—also known as Fascist Nationalism or Nationalist Action—and in June they founded their first newspaper, a short-lived weekly called *Portugal*. It was largely written by friends of Pessoa. Augusto Ferreira Gomes was its managing editor and chief reporter. Mário Saa wrote a column in which he praised Italian fascism and ultranationalist movements in France such as Action Française. The composer Ruy Coelho complained, in two articles, that Portuguese music and theater were insufficiently nationalistic. Geraldo Coelho de Jesus was the subject of a feature article and also contributed his own articles, in which he continued to push for industrialization and criticized democracy as a seductive but impractical doctrine. One of his articles discredited the trinity of ideals—liberty, equality, and fraternity—enshrined by the French Revolution.[11] Fernando Pessoa had taken issue with those same ideals in recent articles and in notes for unpublished essays, including the aforementioned "Against Democracy,"[12] yet his name was conspicuously absent from the pages of *Portugal*. This could only be because he turned down his friends' repeated invitations to contribute.

Another major contributor to the new newspaper was João de Castro Osório, a young publisher to whom Pessoa, in that same month of June, proposed a translation series of Shakespeare plays and English poetry, without success. Castro Osório was the likely author of a stridently fascist manifesto published in the fourth and final issue of *Portugal*, which informed readers that it would be succeeded by a daily paper also called *Portugal*. This daily edition never materialized, but in the fall of 1923 Castro Osório, the chief ideologue of Lusitanian Nationalism, published a series of articles detailing the group's "Nationalist Program" in a new weekly paper whose very title was a blunt profession of fascist faith: *Dictatorship: A Periodical of Portuguese Fascism*.

Mussolini's most enthusiastic advocate in Portugal was António Ferro, who traveled to Italy in October 1923 to cover the festivities commemorating the one-year anniversary of the March on Rome. The series of interviews and reports from his Italian journey, including an interview with Mussolini himself, were all stamped with unstinting admiration for the dictator and the achievements of fascism. Somewhat surprisingly, Ferro was the special correspondent of *A Capital*, the staunchly republican, traditionally left-leaning newspaper. In addition to the interviews from Ferro's monthlong trip, the paper published other articles praising the Fascist regime.[13]

As in many other countries, including the United States,* seemingly everybody in Portugal—with the exception of the Communists, Socialists, and anarchists—had a favorable impression of fascism. "Everybody" did not include Fernando Pessoa, who left this withering comment among his random notes: "Fascism's major accomplishment is to have reorganized and improved the railroads. Now the trains run smoothly and are always on schedule. So let's say you live in Milan, and your father lives in Rome. The Fascists kill your father, but you can count on the train to get you there in time for the funeral."[14]

Pessoa abhorred Communists, Socialists, and political anarchists, whose destabilizing activities he was all for repressing, as the Italian Fascists had done. He agreed that democracy did not work any better in Portugal than it did in Italy, and that the country needed a strong ruler, someone with the charisma and vision of Sidónio Pais, and with the ability—which Pais lacked—to impose his will. "Someone like Benito Mussolini," thought António Ferro and many other young intellectuals.

Pessoa, however, smelled a rat in Mussolini. The disagreeable odor reached him through a small news item published by the *Diário de Notícias* in late February 1923: four months after coming to power, the Fascist leader had instructed the police to confiscate all "immoral" publications from bookstores. The editors of the newspaper commented that similar action ought to be taken in Portugal, where obscene books with a "pseudo-literary appearance" were lately being displayed in shop windows. This was an obvious allusion to the books of António Botto, Raul Leal, and Judith Teixeira, which the Lisbon Student Action League had declared anathema a few days earlier. Pessoa clipped and saved this news item.[15] Later that year, the Portuguese press reported other instances of

---

* "In affairs of state Mussolini exhibits remarkable self-control, rare judgment and an efficient application of his ideas to the solving of existing problems," wrote the editors of *Time* in the August 6, 1923, issue, whose cover featured an austere image of Il Duce.

Fascist censorship and of violence meted out to critics of the regime[16]—all of which reinforced Pessoa's antipathy toward Mussolini.

As far back as 1912, Pessoa had predicted that Portugal might need a brutal leader—a Portuguese Oliver Cromwell, he wrote—to overcome its divisive, unruly politics, and he blinked at Sidónio Pais's creation of a secret police that beat up and jailed hundreds of political opponents—although Pais, it must be said, personally ordered the release of some of the men arrested. Like Pais, Mussolini was a populist, personalist leader, but with a well-defined agenda and a willingness to use as much force as necessary to implement it, which is why many Sidonists admired him. They saw him as a kind of consummated Pais. But Pessoa did not after all like the consummation. He liked only his *dream* of a modern-day Caesar, Napoleon, or Cromwell, not any real incarnation of the same.

◆

INSPIRED BY MUSSOLINI'S MARCH on Rome, Adolf Hitler, in the fall of 1923, planned a March on Berlin to seize control of the Weimar Republic, which was battered and exhausted from having to contend with extremist far-right and far-left groups that threatened to take over regional governments. The harsh terms of the Treaty of Versailles were greatly resented by most Germans, a growing number of whom were enchanted by a nationalist, xenophobic rhetoric that called for a prouder, more self-assertive Reich, while many proletarians were attracted to the Communist call for social revolution. French and Belgian troops, meanwhile, had occupied the Ruhr Valley to pressure Germany to make good on its war reparations, which were the main driver of runaway inflation, now at its absurd peak, with a loaf of bread costing double in the evening what it cost in the morning. (In his trunk full of papers Pessoa saved a banknote for ten billion German marks issued on October 1, 1923, and worth almost nothing by the end of that month.)[17]

Amid the pandemonium and with the support of the Prussian general Erich Ludendorff, Hitler, in November, staged the Beer Hall Putsch in Munich, from where he and his Brownshirts marched, not to Berlin after all, but only down the streets of the Bavarian capital before crossing paths with the state police. Hitler fled but was soon found, tried for treason, and jailed for nine months. While behind bars, he wrote *Mein Kampf*. In Spain, on the other hand, a military coup had easily prevailed in the month of September, installing General Miguel Primo de Rivera as dictator. Most Spaniards, like most of their Portuguese neighbors, were weary of social unrest and disillusioned with a political class deemed corrupt and feckless. Pessoa closely followed the nationalist movements in Italy, Germany, Spain, and elsewhere, rejecting all of them as models for his own, increasingly mystical brand of nationalism.

In October 1923 the poet gave his first interview ever, for *A Revista Portuguesa*, a literary and cultural review. The interviewer's questions all dealt with Portugal: its art, its literature, and the "political, moral and intellectual" aspects of its current "crisis." The nation's precarious present and uncertain future had become obsessive topics of discussion among intellectuals, particularly in light of the agitated political climate affecting much of Europe. But it was in the light of history and of prophecy that Pessoa answered the interviewer's questions. The only other European country he mentioned was Greece, the Greece of antiquity, which he likened to the Portugal of tomorrow. Lisbon, he noted, is on almost the same latitude as Athens. When asked exactly what he envisioned for the future of the Portuguese people, the interviewee answered, "The Fifth Empire. The future of Portugal—which I don't envision, but *know*—has already been written, for those who can read it, in the verses of Bandarra and the quatrains of Nostradamus. That future is for us to be everything."

Pessoa had never before mentioned in print the Fifth Empire, a doctrine that had developed into something even more utopian than when he first wrote about it in his notes, back in 1915. According to his original idea, the people of Portugal were destined to imperialistically dominate the Western world through their culture. Now he contended that they were quite simply to *be* everything worth being. The idea of cultural domination, while it did not disappear from his Fifth Empire vision, was now presented as a by-product of an imperious Portuguese will to boundless self-enlargement—a will that had already manifested itself five centuries earlier, when Portugal's people took to the seas and spread themselves around the globe.

As for the two poet-prophets mentioned by Pessoa, the shoemaker Gonçalo Annes Bandarra (see chapter 36) was a humbler, Portuguese version of the far more famous Nostradamus, his contemporary. Michel de Nostredame (1503–1566), a French apothecary, Latinized his name around the time he began garnering renown as a clairvoyant. Clairvoyant means "clear seeing," but the hundreds of prophetic quatrains he published were nearly all of them obscure, susceptible to countless interpretations, so that they have been credited with predicting everything from the rise of Hitler to global warming. In the early 1920s, while his peers debated political solutions for their ailing nation, Pessoa was studying the prophecies of Nostradamus, and poring over those of Bandarra, to show that the Fifth Empire destiny of Portugal was a foregone conclusion.

Pessoa owned two editions of Bandarra's prophetic poems, some of which he copiously annotated; he did painstaking research at the National Library to see how others had interpreted them; and he wrote dozens of pages of his own interpretations, as well as general considerations for an introductory essay.[18] This unusually concentrated labor was all for the sake of a new edition of Bandarra's poems, to be commented on and interpreted by Raphael Baldaya, Pessoa's astrologer heteronym.[19]

True to the venerable tradition of reinterpreting ancient prophecies to make them fit contemporary events, Pessoa-Baldaya claimed that Bandarra had forecast the first aerial crossing of the South Atlantic, accomplished by two Portuguese aviators, Gago Coutinho and Sacadura Cabral, in the spring of 1922.[20] It took the pilots two and a half months and three different planes to fly from Lisbon to Rio de Janeiro, with long layovers on a couple of islands, but they traveled almost three times the distance of John Alcock and Arthur Brown, who had crossed the North Atlantic three years earlier in a nonstop flight lasting sixteen hours. (Charles Lindbergh would make the first solo nonstop transatlantic flight, from New York to Paris, in 1927.) Since there were few things in recent history that the Portuguese could brag about, this feat was lavishly, laboriously celebrated by Portugal's politicians, journalists, and artists—in patriotic speeches, articles, songs, poems, films, and postage stamps. For Raphael Baldaya, the felicitous event foreshadowed the mystical return of King Sebastian and the birth of the Fifth Empire.

The actual year of the king's return would be 1924, according to Pessoa's interpretation of a prophetic saying by another Portuguese poet-seer, the little-known Thamar Lamim.[21] Yet this conflicts with Baldaya's calculation that, according to Bandarra's prophecies, Sebastian would return in 1888.[22] Putting two and two—or rather, 1888 and 1924—together, we are led to conclude that King Sebastian had already returned in the person of Fernando Pessoa (born in 1888) but would not be publicly recognized until 1924.

And then he and his heteronyms would usher in the Portuguese Fifth Empire? Perhaps not so quickly, and certainly not so literally.

Baldaya cautioned prospective readers of his interpretative commentary that Sebastian, the Hidden One, "is our own concept; he will only come if we make him appear, if we create him in and through our own selves." He went on to say that there are no saviors, no messiahs, and that the most a great man can be is "a stimulator of souls," by inciting others to heed St. Paul's injunction to the Philippians: "Work out your own salvation."[23] So Pessoa's veiled claim to be the returned King Sebastian prophesied by Bandarra was not as self-aggrandizing as it might seem at first blush, since all he hoped to do was point the way, through his example.

Despite the quotation from the Pauline epistle, the salvation contemplated by Pessoa had nothing to do with Christian redemption. After stating in his interview for *A Revista Portuguesa* that the future of the Portuguese people was to be everything, he asked rhetorically:

Who, if they're Portuguese, can live within the narrow bounds of just one personality, just one nation, just one religion? What true Portuguese can live within the sterile limits of Catholicism when beyond it there are all the Protestant creeds, all the Eastern religions and all the dead and living paganisms for us to experience, Portuguesely fusing them into Superior Paganism?

This was Pessoa's first public mention of the Portuguese paganism that he, António Mora, and Ricardo Reis had been theorizing for the past eight years. And this was how he pleaded for it to whoever might read his words: "Let's not leave out a single god! [. . .] Let's be everything, in every way possible, for there can be no truth where something is lacking! Let's create Superior Paganism, Supreme Polytheism! In the eternal lie of all the gods, the only truth is in all the gods together."

It was a curious conclusion to a curious interview, for which Pessoa submitted his carefully pondered answers in writing; there was nothing spontaneous about them.[24] Notwithstanding his previous insistence, in notes he never published, on a national literary and cultural flowering as the basis for a Portuguese Fifth Empire, his public announcement of that empire connected it not to literature but to religion—to a religion like no other. "Let's be everything, in every way possible" is a rule of life that makes the observance of commandments and rituals typical of most religions seem like a small thing. The working out of one's salvation, according to Pessoa's gospel, is a continual opening of doors, the admission of all possibilities, resistance to every definition and every confining doctrine, the rejection of all limits.

# CHAPTER 54

I T WAS IN HIS LITERARY IMAGINATION—BY WHICH I mean his poems and prose pieces but also his astrological calculations, his Sebastianist and Fifth Empire visions, his spiritual divagations, and his dream life—that Pessoa managed, as much as one man can, to be everything in every way possible. To his relatives, however, he was just a quirky member of the family who happened to write poetry, as did many other men and women. None of them had any idea how rich and unusual was his mental life. None of them except, perhaps, the boys and girls who loved him as their favorite uncle. They could at least feel how different he was from other adults, and how he was a little like they were—still with a child's taste for play, still with an unhampered, omnipotent imagination.

By the time he became a literal uncle, with the birth of his sister's first child, in July 1924, Pessoa was already a belovedly avuncular figure for the eight children born to his two first cousins between 1913 and 1922, six to Mário and two to Maria. He was the godfather of all but one of them, and they all knew him as their uncle, but they called him Ibis— the nickname that survived, along with heavy debts, from his first quixotic attempt at a publishing house. Whenever he went to Mário's home for lunch or dinner, it was a special occasion for the two little girls and four little boys, who would grab his arms and legs and compete for space on his lap or at his side, wherever he sat. He told jokes and funny stories, sometimes slapping himself in the face for comic effect, to the point of making his glasses fall off. As they giggled with abandon, he kept a perfectly straight face. At other times he lay on the floor and spun his legs in the air, as if cycling.

When he left to go home, they would look out the window to wave goodbye and watch him pretend to bump into a lamppost on the other side of the street, making them laugh still more. "Do the ibis!" they would shout before he turned the corner. Without removing his hat or raincoat, he would press his hands together and point them straight ahead in the form of a beak, while balancing on one foot, leaning forward.[1] Awkward in social situations with adults—except in cafés, where the conversation was literary and intellectual—Pessoa was a natural hit with children, amusing them with his bumbling manner of the goofy bachelor uncle, a persona later immortalized by Jacques Tati, in the 1958 film *Mon Oncle*.

During the first half of 1924, Pessoa lived for a few months with two of his godchildren, or rather, they lived with him. After three and a half years in Italy, his cousin Maria and her family, including Aunt Anica, returned to Lisbon in February and stayed at the apartment on Rua Coelho da Rocha while looking for their own place. Maria's husband, Raul da Costa, had graduated from the Royal Naval School of Genoa as a naval engineer and would hold various posts in the shipbuilding division of the Portuguese navy.[2] Some people have speculated that Álvaro de Campos's profession was inspired by Raul da Costa's, but if anything, the opposite was true. It was not until 1920, five years after Campos's "Maritime Ode" was published, that Pessoa's cousin-in-law joined the navy and pursued a degree in naval engineering.

Living up to his reputation in the family for being a prankster, Pessoa, after his cousin had put her two children to bed, would sometimes stick his head in the door and ask, in a voice loud enough to rouse the dead, "Are you already asleep?"[3] The children giggled as their mother sighed with annoyance. Maria and Raul's firstborn, Eduardo, was a studious and inquisitive eight-year-old, already fond of words, and it was around this time that Pessoa, who never ceased being literary, began to write and recite occasional poems for him and the rest of his godchildren. One of the poems was about his favorite bird, memorably described in the first stanza:

> The ibis, an Egyptian bird,
> Stands on just one foot,
> A fact
> That's weird.
> It has a calm air,
> Because it goes nowhere.[4]

The Egyptians mummified millions of ibises, which they raised on breeding farms as well as catching them in the wild.

Rarely with both feet firmly planted on the ground, the poet known as Ibis to his godchildren let his mind wander from idea to idea, project to project, while keeping his gaze vaguely fixed on the future, whatever it would be. On June 1, 1924, he described his state of calm indifference in a letter to Adriano del Valle: "Lately I've been far removed from the literary milieu and its fringes. I haven't stayed away on purpose, or for any particular reason. It just happened. I continue to work, on one thing or another, but I'm in no hurry. If ever I'm to be admitted into the presence and the time of the gods, it will depend on them, not on me."

Under separate cover, Pessoa sent two books by Portuguese fiction writers to the Spanish poet, who had little way of knowing that his Lisbon correspondent was greater than almost any Portuguese writer living or dead, since Pessoa continued not to publish his work, except in occasional contributions to magazines. He had been patiently waiting for the gods, or the future, to discover him, perhaps because he feared that his contemporaries would not recognize him as a literary genius without rival, and perhaps because he was too proud to let on that he cared about recognition.

✦

BUT A FEW MONTHS later, in the fall of 1924, Pessoa's status as a writer on the fringes seemed to be abruptly coming to an end. He had unexpectedly become the literary editor of *Athena*, a magazine in whose pages he would publish not just a couple of his poems but a copious selection of choice works by him and his three main heteronyms. What's more, the magazine's five issues would dare to completely override modernism, as if this movement had never even existed. Pessoa's drama of literary self-multiplication—fully revealed in *Athena* for the first time—was in fact conceived as an Olympian performance, belonging to eternity.

Pessoa had drawn up plans for a "neo-pagan" magazine titled *Athena* back in 1915, returning to the idea in 1918 and again in late 1923,[5] without ever giving it any shape in reality. The idea might have lingered in limbo forever were it not for Ruy Vaz, an artist with financial means who invited Pessoa to partner with him on a new magazine. Vaz would be its art editor; Pessoa, who proposed the title *Athena*, would have total control over its literary content. Vaz had recently handled the production of *Contemporânea*, whose editor in chief, José Pacheco, was so weakened from tuberculosis that he temporarily suspended its publication, thus clearing the field for *Athena*. It was a perfect opportunity for Pessoa, who had criticized *Contemporânea* for being graphically sumptuous but intellectually and imaginatively vapid, to show what he could do.

He quickly ran into the same problem Pacheco had encountered: there were not that many interesting, innovative Portuguese writers he could enlist for *Athena*. His heteronyms, though, could partly make up for the shortage. Alberto Caeiro and Ricardo Reis, neither of whom had ever been published, would be presented as autonomous poets. Pessoa thought of including an essay on paganism by António Mora, likewise unknown to the public, and a poem by Diniz da Silva,[6] a fleeting heteronym he invented in 1923, but he changed his mind about the poem, and about António Mora. This apostle of neo-paganism, who had been the backbone of *Athena* in the original 1915 plans, would remain in the shadows. Deciding that it was better to show and not tell, Pessoa tried to make his magazine convey the spirit of paganism without any theorizing, explaining, or proselytizing.

*Athena* was not only an impressive showcase for writing by Pessoa and his heteronyms—the largest and most varied display to be published in his lifetime—but also the carefully curated exposition of a personal, literary utopia. Soberly elegant, the first issue came out in October 1924. It opened with an article by Pessoa that justified the magazine's title by arguing that "superior art results from the harmony between the particularity of emotion and understanding" and the "universality of reason," a harmony epitomized by the goddess Athena. This ideal equilibrium between emotion and understanding, between the concrete and the abstract, between what we know and can only imagine, was exemplified in the magazine by twenty classical odes of Ricardo Reis, most notably in the eleventh ode, which begins with a confession:

Fate frightens me, Lydia. Nothing is certain.
At any moment something could happen
     To change all that we are.

The rest of the inaugural issue included Edgar Allan Poe's "The Raven," masterfully rendered into Portuguese by Pessoa, a dramatic dialogue by José de Almada Negreiros, and four "Letters That Were Returned to

Me" by António Botto. Since Botto's homosexuality had become a popular topic of gossipy chitchat, readers would readily understand that the four letters—love letters—were addressed to a man, which added to the "Greek" aura cultivated by *Athena*'s literary editor.

There was one other literary contribution to the first issue: a group of eight sonnets by Henrique Rosa, Pessoa's stepuncle. Well fashioned but with nothing to make them stand out, the sonnets were no better and no worse than much of the other poetry being published in Portugal. But Pessoa sincerely appreciated them, partly for sentimental reasons, and he wanted to show his appreciation before it was too late. The sonneteer's health was fast declining, and we can imagine with what satisfaction the proud editor placed in his gnarled hands a copy of *Athena*, still smelling of freshly printed ink. It was an attractive magazine, and Pessoa no doubt offered copies to the rest of the family—his mother, sister, and brother-in-law—on one of his increasingly frequent visits to the Quinta dos Marechais. His mother, like Henrique Rosa, was also fading, but the household atmosphere was enlivened by Pessoa's niece, Maria Leonor, who was just a few months old.

◆

THE *DIÁRIO DE LISBOA* published a brief interview with Pessoa apropos of *Athena* on November 3, 1924, and on that same day *A Capital*, which had savaged *Orpheu* almost ten years earlier, spoke highly of the new magazine and superlatively of its literary editor: "Fernando Pessoa is a notable modern sensibility, a complete mentality, with an astonishing erudition and a critical sensibility perfectly attuned to the most audacious new trends. He is, without exaggeration, the outstanding figure of his generation."[7] The "outstanding figure" read these words with no small amazement. After all the attention heaped on *Orpheu* and its contributors had died down, Pessoa's name had fallen back into obscurity, having recently merited a bit of public notice only because of his association with the Literature of Sodom scandal.

But even those contemporaries who acknowledged Pessoa to be a powerful literary intelligence often failed to grasp his greatest moments of inspiration. The critic writing for *A Capital*, for instance, reported that the eight sonnets of Henrique Rosa published in *Athena* were "wonderful" and said nothing about the incomparably more interesting odes of Ricardo Reis. Nor does it seem that Pessoa's friends—who of course knew, unlike most readers, that Ricardo Reis was an alter ego—fully appreciated the originality of his odes, which they perhaps regarded, not without some justification, as a quaint literary throwback. In a letter he sent with a copy of the magazine to an old acquaintance, the English editor William Bentley, Pessoa himself coyly noted that Reis "has been called, admirably I believe, 'a Greek Horace who writes in Portuguese.'"[8]

While *Athena's* literary editor may have been attuned to the "most audacious new trends," the magazine's novelty was in how it completely ignored them. In the years before and after *Orpheu*, Pessoa had played at being a futurist, an intersectionist, and a sensationist, but he was ultimately indifferent to all artistic recipes, fads, and formulas, including those of his own invention. In *Athena* he sought to be trendless and timeless.

The magazine's second issue included a selection of epigrams and epitaphs from the Greek Anthology as well as Pessoa's translation of Walter Pater's famous meditation on the *Mona Lisa*, which Yeats, in 1936, would lineate as a free-verse poem and place at the beginning of *The Oxford Book of Modern Verse*. In the ambiguous, haunting smile of the Florentine lady Pater found "the animalism of Greece, the lust of Rome, the mysticism of the middle age with its spiritual ambition and imaginative loves, the return of the Pagan world, the sins of the Borgias," and he concluded his meditation by calling her "the symbol of the modern idea" whereby humanity, at every moment, sums up in itself "all modes of thought and life." It is debatable whether Pater's was a fair characterization of "the modern idea" held by intellectuals in 1869, the year he first published his essay, but he beautifully expressed his own idea—and Pessoa's idea—of what humanly mattered.

The harmony that Pessoa associated with the goddess Athena and tried to realize in this magazine depended not on excluding what did not fit but on leaving nothing out. *Athena* fostered the coexistence of contemporary writing with a revival of the pagan state of mind and feeling. Its pages included poetry, fiction, essays, and dramatic works, whether in translation or written in Portuguese. Literature from any time period and any genre—"*all* modes of thought and life"—could be accommodated.

The principle of inclusiveness also signified diversity of opinion, achieved with the help of Pessoa's friends, real and imaginary. The second issue of *Athena* included an article signed by Álvaro de Campos that disputed Pessoa's assertion, in the lead article of the first issue, that metaphysics was an art rather than a science. In the third and fourth issues, the naval engineer went even further. In a two-part essay called "Notes for a Non-Aristotelian Aesthetics," he attacked the classical understanding of art as the creation and transmission of beauty, proposing in its stead an art that was Nietzscheanly founded on force and domination. This position was attacked, in turn, by Mário Saa, who argued (in *Athena* 4) that Campos's conception of art was abusively materialistic. Pessoa, not for the first time, was trying to foment a culture of lively debate among his intellectually lethargic compatriots.

◆

IN MARCH 1925 THE editors of *Athena* printed a flyer announcing a second volume of five issues, but this never went forward. There was probably no money, and there was no real need, for a volume II; Pessoa had achieved his objectives. Through its graphic design as well as its contents, *Athena* had successfully generated a classical air of pagan antiquity, as if *Athena* were the literary equivalent of a surviving Greek temple. In this exemplary setting Pessoa had presented twenty odes by Ricardo Reis, a dozen lyrical poems signed by his own name, two essays by Álvaro de Campos, and a generous offering of poems by Alberto Caeiro: almost half of the forty-nine-poem sequence titled *The Keeper of Sheep* and sixteen of his so-called *Poemas inconjuntos*, which roughly means "collected poems that don't form a whole." This hard-to-translate title vaguely echoes the crucial line from the forty-seventh poem of *The Keeper of Sheep*: "Nature is parts without a whole."

One of the great advantages of art over nature, for Pessoa, was that it could create at least an illusory whole. So it was with his wide-lens magazine, which aimed to be a harmonious diversity, a house for all the gods. The literary contributor whose work rounded out the final issue of *Athena* (still forthcoming) was, appropriately, Alberto Caeiro, the heteronym who saw that nature lacked a unifying principle but who—because he saw everything for what it is and did not want it to be anything but what it is—was himself a unifying principle. To see something, for him, meant that the something belonged, it was valid, it fit. He was the unconditional accepter of life, and also of death. In a poem that foresaw his early death, Caeiro summed up the "meaning" of his existence:

If I die very young, take note:
I was never more than a child who played.

I was heathen like the sun and the water,
With a universal religion that only humans lack.

Caeiro's "childish" attitude reminds us of Nietzsche's Zarathustra, for
whom "[t]he child is innocence and forgetting, a new beginning, a game,
a self-propelled wheel, a first movement, a sacred Yes."[9]

In addition to the cited poem, *Athena* 5 included three others that say
yes even to death—Caeiro's own death. All four poems were written in
1915, the year when the poet of nature supposedly perished. The last of
the four is a miniature autobiography, or notes for whoever might want
to write about this heteronym's life. Here are the first seven of its fifteen lines:

If, after I die, someone wants to write my biography,
There's nothing simpler.
It has just two dates—the day I was born and the day I died.
Between the two, all the days are mine.

I'm easy to define.
I saw as if damned to see.
I loved things without any sentimentality.

Thus spoke Caeiro, some of whose unsentimentality Pessoa would
have liked for himself at that moment, shaken up as he still was by the all
too real phenomenon of death. Caeiro's serene reflections on the cessation of his fictional life were small consolation for his maker. Less capable of detachment in the reality he inhabited, Pessoa had plunged into a
paralyzing depression.

◆

AS PESSOA WAS CONSTRUCTING his sunlit "temple" called *Athena*,
a pall descended on his sister's home in Benfica, where on February 8,
1925, his ailing stepuncle, at the age of seventy-four, finally succumbed
to pulmonary congestion. Given this man's role as an intellectual father
who had guided the young poet in his readings and reflections, encouraged him to pursue writing, and initiated him into Lisbon's literary life
after he dropped out of college in 1907, perhaps it was inevitable that
Pessoa, yearning to be himself, an independent man, would snub the

older poet during the following decade. But once Pessoa had "proven" himself and seen Henrique Rosa grow feeble, he blushed at the memory of all the hours they had spent together in excited conversation about religion, evolution, philosophy, and literature.

Less than a month later, one of Pessoa's worst fears came true: his mother suffered another devastating stroke. Already in the habit of spending weekends in Benfica, at the Quinta dos Marechais, now he stayed there during the week as well, to be close to her prostrate body. The stroke had caused excruciating pain, for which her doctor prescribed a drug that practically made her unconscious. Pessoa's sister was the dutiful caregiver—washing their mother, changing her sheets, and making her as comfortable as possible. She had done as much for Henrique Rosa, and on top of these duties she had Maria Leonor, her baby, to care for and everyone to cook for, including now Fernando. When his mother was still responsive, Pessoa would sit next to her and talk, perhaps recalling scenes from the houses where they had lived together in Durban or in the Lisbon of his infancy. Once she had lapsed into a comalike state, which would last for twelve days, he could not bring himself to enter her bedroom. He paced around all the other rooms, saying very little, his mind in a permanent state of distraction. But when Teca, his sister, dared to hope that their mother would soon be out of her misery, he exploded, telling her to hold her tongue, because we should never wish death on anyone.[10] Teca called a priest. Pessoa's freethinking father had refused the Church's last rites, but his mother, consciously or not, received them. She was sixty-three years old.

On March 18, seeing a paid death notice in the newspaper for Maria Madalena Nogueira Rosa, Mário Saa wrote his undemonstrative friend an extraordinary letter,[11] telling him not to hold back but to cry his heart out until he could cry no more. It was a thoughtful but unnecessary recommendation. Pessoa withdrew to his apartment on Rua Coelho da Rocha and indulged his grief, which was not only about the loss of his mother. Retaining the fresh and frightful images of his stepuncle, then his mother, being lowered into the ground, at the same cemetery, Pessoa found himself compulsively remembering all those who had died—his father, his baby brother, the aunts and uncles he loved, his grandmothers, his stepfather, his best friend—as well as the lost times of his life when those people still existed. Where were those times and those people now? Where did they, and where does everything, go? The inventor of sensationism could *feel* oblivion and it horrified him.

Overcome by worry and distress, Pessoa had not been writing any poetry, and not until three weeks after his mother's funeral would he finally break his poetic silence with a suite of four Portuguese sonnets, the first of which opened with these lines:

All the forgotten dead surround me.
They've returned. I saw them in dreams.
If I loved them, how did I forget them?
If I forgot them, how were they loved?

The other three sonnets reiterated the theme of how we, the living, keep shoveling dirt on top of the dead with our forgetting. In this tercet, for instance:

Who dies is damned by whoever survives.
We are the ones who most bury the dead!
It's in our own heart that Death lives!

What revolted Pessoa was that even the most heartfelt grief was pitifully small, shamefully brief. Long before his mother physically died, he had begun killing her off—just by asserting himself, by living his own life—and his life would continue, with little room or time or patience for her and the other dead, since life cares only about living. And then he would die, without any children to forget him, which was maybe just as well. He had only one hope: if he could write pages of poetry and prose whose startling reenactments of human feeling would make them endure, then his name would be remembered. What's more, through those pages he would keep touching minds and hearts, and in that way keep on living, long after his body had been reduced to bones and dust.

◆

BUT WOULD HIS LITERARY legacy after all startle anyone? The fifth and last issue of *Athena*—due out in February but delayed because of the deaths that had been occupying Pessoa's attention—finally came out in

June, completing the spectacular, five-part presentation of his work as poet, essayist, and creator of heteronyms. Nobody took notice. Although a couple of newspapers had praised it as an excellent magazine put out by a talented editor, nobody seemed to have realized how exceptional were the many poems and prose pieces signed by Pessoa and his heteronyms. Francisco Costa, a young poet who published a group of sonnets in *Athena* 5, sent Pessoa a letter in July, acknowledging receipt of his contributor copies and congratulating Pessoa for his "magnificent" translation of an O. Henry short story. He said not a word about the poetry of Caeiro published in the same issue.[12]

Pessoa had to wonder: was he the only one for whom Alberto Caeiro was a revelation? In the previous decade he had written dozens of pages for prefaces, critical essays, and promotional articles that marveled over the poet-shepherd and his staggeringly simple poems, and in 1923 he drafted a new book preface in which Ricardo Reis, appointed to be Caeiro's posthumous editor, explained that his "Transcendental Objectivity" was what made him "the greatest poet of the twentieth century." The preface ended with a word of thanks to two surviving relatives— António Caeiro da Silva and Júlio Manuel Caeiro—for allowing his poetry to be published in book form.[13] The authorization of the heteronym's "heirs" availed nothing. Disappointed by the nonreaction to the Caeiro poems revealed in *Athena*, Pessoa canceled his book plans and wrote nothing else in Caeiro's name until the end of the decade.

This heteronym recognized as the master poet, who had taught Pessoa to write dramatically, full of feeling yet impersonally, full of philosophy yet simply, was still his master, guiding and inspiring him, yet he suddenly doubted whether literature could save him, and even its power to soothe him now faltered. The central object of Pessoa's primal love was naturally his mother, whose death precipitated a quiet catastrophe. Although they had lived for many years on separate continents and were reunited only when she was already frail and a ghost of her former self, her existence had still been a reliable link to his own, preliterary self, to that time when he was an utterly dependent infant, speechlessly in love. The cessation of her existence left him existentially unmoored, floundering in the ocean of his written desires, fears, dreams, words.

Without an amorous partner who could to a certain extent take his mother's place, Pessoa, as we shall see, found himself increasingly drawn toward spiritual compensations: higher purposes, higher knowledge, communion with gods and angels. But another, less obvious impulse urged him to recover what he had lost: a primordial, absolutely *human* connection. Whichever way he went, in search of divinity or humanity, Pessoa's next and final decade would be less about self-expansion and more about self-surrender.

# Part IV

# SPIRITUALIST AND HUMANIST
## (1925–1935)

I was never convinced of what I believed in. I filled my hands with sand, called it gold, and opened them up to let it slide through. Words were my only truth.

—*The Book of Disquiet* (text 221)

(Top) On a downtown street in Lisbon.
*(Courtesy Manuela Nogueira)*
(Bottom) Pessoa at forty-five or forty-six years of age but
looking much older.
*(Teresa Rita Lopes,* Fernando Pessoa: Vivendo e escrevendo
*[Lisbon: Assírio & Alvim, 1998], p. 89)*

# CHAPTER 55

**A**LL THE EBULLIENCE AND EXTRAVAGANCE OF THE 1920s were in full flower on both sides of the Atlantic. Despite the trial that convicted John T. Scopes for teaching evolution in Tennessee, or the publication in Munich of Hitler's *Mein Kampf,* the year 1925 rode a wave of forward intellectual and artistic momentum coupled with widespread prosperity that fueled optimism and a booming stock market. In the American capital of high finance, fashion, book publishing, and the arts, a sophisticated new magazine called *The New Yorker* launched its inaugural issue. Paris hosted a lavish Exposition Internationale des Arts Décoratifs et Industriels Modernes, which promoted the style known thereafter as art deco. *La Revue nègre,* with an all-black cast starring Josephine Baker, opened to wild acclaim at the Théâtre des Champs-Élysées, helping to popularize the Charleston in Europe. In Germany the Bauhaus school, which had just moved from Weimar to Dessau, was revolutionizing architectural, industrial, and graphic design, while an androgynously sensual newcomer named Marlene Dietrich, still known mainly as a stage actor, performed in musicals and revues to packed houses in Berlin. Having cured itself of inflation, the Weimar Republic was thriving economically as well as culturally, but politically it wobbled, with fragile coalitions forming one government after another.

Urban Portugal, especially Lisbon, danced the Charleston, listened to jazz music, and erected art deco buildings, and the country as a whole prospered, albeit at a slower tempo than most of Europe. But while there was relative stability in the economic and social spheres, the nation's politics continued to be addicted to volatility. The Democrats, who still dominated the political process, had split into several factions, so that governments could be cobbled together only through inevitably short-lived coalitions. Differently from Weimar Germany, where the many political parties tended to be ideologically driven, in Portugal they coalesced around charismatic personalities whose ideas were not always well defined. There was a growing sense among the Portuguese that their republic could not keep on like this, uncertain where it was going and without strong, principled leadership.

Fernando Pessoa, like his country, felt a little aimless in the mid-1920s but was immune to the gaiety of the era that infected, at least superficially, many of his compatriots. The death of his mother had infused him with sadness. It also made him more aware of his own mortality. As the oldest sibling, he would logically be the next one in his immediate family to die, and his own father had lived only to age forty-three. Pessoa knew he needed to consolidate, to finish and organize the works he most cared about, but he was listless and unable to muster enthusiasm. Next to love—the love between him and his mother whose importance only now, after losing her, he truly fathomed—the significance of his literary life temporarily paled. It would revive and he would recover, but in the summer of 1925 he still mourned that loss, viewed the future without expectations, and felt dejected and numb.

Late in the summer, Pessoa ran into António Cobeira, whom he had known ten years earlier, when Cobeira still nurtured literary ambitions. The two old friends spent an afternoon together in Sintra, where Portuguese royals used to live during the summer months because it was cool, and as they walked on the town's ancient streets, surrounded by tree-covered hills out of which rise dreamy, pastel-colored palaces and mansions, they reminisced about the past and talked a little about their present lives. On the way back to Lisbon, Pessoa asked Cobeira: "So what do you plan to do in the future?"

"Nothing, if possible," he answered.

"Like me," said Pessoa, "but with one small difference. I'll do nothing by doing. And you'll do nothing by not doing."[1]

◆

BUT PESSOA, EVEN THOUGH he was able to function, was oppressed by the sensation that all his doing was pointless. With what loving care he had prepared the five issues of *Athena*, which culminated with the public debut of Alberto Caeiro, whose poetry failed to attract the slightest attention! In mid-August Pessoa wrote a poem that begins:

Every work is in every way futile.
The futile wind, stirring up futile leaves,

Resembles our effort and our general state.
Given or achieved, everything is Fate.

Unable to shake off his gloom, on the last day of August he drafted a letter to an unnamed friend, probably the lawyer and writer Alberto Da Cunha Dias, asking how to go about committing himself to a psychiatric hospital. Cunha Dias had written ad nauseam about his own experience of being forcibly committed to more than one such hospital. Pessoa, fearing that his grandmother's madness was finally catching up with him, thought he might be suffering from a mild case of "psychasthenic insanity"—unable to concentrate, his mind always wandering, assaulted by memories, apathy, depression. Someone else with those symptoms might have said they were on the verge of a nervous breakdown.

As tended to happen with his literary projects, which rarely got beyond the project stage, once Pessoa had a plan to check into a mental hospital, he lost interest in actually carrying it out—as if the planning were a virtual equivalent of being admitted, treated, and cured. Cured or not, he kept on doing, which in his case meant writing, although his spirit weighed too heavy for imaginative flights, making it hard for him to write creatively. He tried drafting a book review and some drama criticism, and he devised a vague plan to bring out yet another magazine, *Orpheu—Second Phase*,[2] but his melancholy mood made his thoughts drift elsewhere, especially toward people and places from the past. The idea of resurrecting *Orpheu* was itself a nostalgic journey, taking him back to the time when his mother was still in good health and Mário de Sá-Carneiro was alive and living in Lisbon, and the two best friends were talked about in the newspapers and pointed at on the downtown streets.

A concurrent, much more radical trip to the past took Pessoa all the way back to his boyhood and to another continent: Africa. On the same sheet of paper where he drew up a masthead and table of contents for the new but never-to-be *Orpheu*, Pessoa jotted down a first-person account, in English, of his performance as a cricketeer "in Saturday's match against the Marines." His own team won, thanks to his brilliant playing: "I got 12 boundary strokes" and "added 115 to our score in two hours. This is the finest score I have ever made."

The Marines were one of the sports clubs invented by Fernando in Durban, along with entire teams of soccer and cricket players, whose matches took place in his adolescent mind and on sheets of paper (see chapter 13). There are no traces of his imaginary sporting life after 1905—until this match, when he was thirty-seven years old. How would Dr. Faustino Antunes, Pessoa's psychiatric heteronym, have explained this behavior that was already a little odd, a bit infantile, when his patient was sixteen or seventeen? Now, twenty years later, it was beyond abnormal.

Was it because Lisbon's cultural scene overlooked or underrated Pessoa that he spontaneously regressed to the virtual athletic contests of his teenage years, making himself stand out as the star player? Possibly so. But the peculiar psychology that had enabled this youthful pastime in the first place was the same psychology that characterized much of his adult behavior. Unreal sporting events, heteronyms, magazine and book projects he dreamed up and abandoned, visions of a returned King Sebastian and a triumphant Fifth Empire, messages received from astral spirits—they all came about spontaneously, with almost no distance between the creator's imagination and his written pages. They were all literary performances. His recorded account of the winning match against the Marines even included alternate wordings—"left-hand strokes" instead of "boundary strokes," "highest" or "best" score instead of "finest" score—as if it were a poem or prose piece whose language he needed to get just right. Get right for whom?

In the real world inhabited by Pessoa, meanwhile, everything seemed to be going wrong. Added to all the other setbacks and misfortunes of 1925 was the sudden death, in September, of his sister's fourteen-month-old daughter, Maria Leonor. Pessoa, who had continued to visit his sister's family and was deeply attached to his niece, wrote "An Elegy," which recalled (in English) her laughter filling the house in Benfica, her tiny clothes, and her toys that Pessoa, his sister, and his brother-in-law would gather up from the floor after she'd been put to bed. "We will yet play again," he promised her lifeless body in one of the closing lines of his poem.[3]

On September 30, two days after the funeral, the baby's shattered parents packed up their belongings and moved back to Rua Coelho da Rocha. In a letter to Jaime de Andrade Neves, his mother's cousin, Pessoa explained that with so many deaths haunting the house at the Quinta dos Marechais—Henrique Rosa, his mother, now his niece—no one could stand to live there anymore.[4] He was worried about his weepy and disconsolate sister, who was seven months pregnant, but in mid-November, assisted by an experienced English midwife,[5] she gave birth to a healthy second daughter, Manuela.

◆

SINCE PESSOA WAS STILL too benumbed and uninspired to be able to write good poetry, it was just as well that his sister's family had moved back to the apartment, helping to keep him distracted. Sometimes after dinner, while the housekeeper washed the dishes and Teca attended to her new baby, he and his brother-in-law, still sitting in the dining room after drinking their coffee, discussed things like budget planning, inventory management, and cost control. Francisco Caetano Dias had studied business and accounting, acquiring technical know-how that he used every day in his job as an administrative officer for the army, and Pessoa was genuinely interested in his work.

Even during his creatively fertile periods Pessoa felt inexplicably drawn to the world of business, taking much more than a passing interest in the commercial transactions of the firms where he earned his living by writing letters in English and French. Since he was not only fluent in these languages but also well versed in business protocols, he occasionally proposed himself as a middleman for international deals and negotiations—none of which ever worked out, to judge by the surviving letters he exchanged with companies based abroad.

Pessoa was also the inventor of some practical business tools, from which he hoped to profit. Although he never carried out his old idea of creating a simpler, more practical "commercial code"—such codes were used to drastically abbreviate telegraphic messages and thus reduce transmission costs—he did invent a system for further condensing existing codes, which he proposed to Eden Fisher & Co., publisher of *The ABC Telegraphic Code*, in October 1925. A "serious depression in the Code Market," replied the London-based firm, made it impossible for them to publish yet another code or code condenser.[6]

Pessoa had no better luck with his method for condensing the annual business directory for Portugal and its colonies into half the size and making it consultable in all the major European languages. For this invention he took out a patent, which he tried to sell to the recently created Angola and Metropole Bank, whose coffers were overflowing with money to lend and invest.[7] On December 5, one week after he submitted his proposal, the mysterious source of the bank's vast sums of capital was revealed. It was phony money, fruit of one of the greatest frauds in history. The beauty of the scheme was that the banknotes themselves were not forged. Artur Alves Reis, who had already done a spell in jail for embezzlement, fabricated documents purporting to be from the Bank of Portugal and authorizing him to solicit a special, secretive issue of banknotes from the British printer of Portugal's currency, supposedly for circulating in Angola on behalf of development projects. Some of the two hundred thousand fraudulently printed notes, worth a total of 100 million escudos (about $5 million U.S. at the time), did end up circulating in the Portuguese colony, while many others circulated in Portugal itself, providing a short-term, artificial boost to the two economies.

As soon as the scam was exposed, Alves Reis was arrested, his bank shuttered, and his ill-gotten wealth confiscated. Five years later he was brought to trial and sentenced to twenty years in prison. At that point Pessoa, who had always marveled at the culprit's ingenuity, would begin writing a true crime story in English titled "The Second Issue."[8] The spurious banknotes were, in fact, a second printing of a legitimate issue of notes, and it was through their duplicate serial numbers that the swindle was discovered. Pessoa, it turned out, was not the only one who thought that the audacious crime of Alves Reis might interest the English-reading public. Two years after the trial, a British author named Cecil Kisch would publish *The Portuguese Bank Note Case*. Pessoa's own treatment of the case never got past a five-chapter outline and a few introductory pages, which included an indignant mention of the diamond-studded garters purchased by Alves Reis's wife on a shopping spree in Paris.

As for the inventor's patented method for producing a compact, multilingual version of Portugal's—or any other country's—annual business directory, in 1926 he offered it to a French company, again without success.[9] Pessoa came up with several other inventions, including a "letter-envelope," which was a forerunner of the aerogram, and an innovative key-striking mechanism that would allow a single typewriter to produce the accents and occasional special letters of most European languages.[10] But he consistently failed in his attempts to put his business knowledge and ideas to practical use, whether as an actual businessman or as an inventor of products that could make the businessman's life easier. Only by teaming up with his better organized brother-in-law was he able to do something useful with his business expertise.

Like Pessoa, Francisco Caetano Dias had a pedagogical streak. He was passionate about his field of work and eager to teach others what he knew. Between 1930 and 1966 he would publish seven books on accounting methods and business administration.[11] But first there was the *Revista de Comércio e Contabilidade* (*Business and Accounting Review*), founded by him and Fernando Pessoa in 1926. Caetano Dias was the editor in chief and contributed articles on accounting, bookkeeping, and inventory management. Pessoa wrote articles about the "sociology" of business, including topics such as the historical evolution of commerce and its connection to culture, the relationships between government and business and between business and the individual, and state-controlled versus liberalized economies. In an article titled "As algemas" ("Handcuffs") he vigorously defended free trade, at a time when European countries and the United States were raising tariffs to protect domestic industry and agriculture. Interspersed among the magazine's articles were assorted aphorisms, tips on how to write good business letters, some thoughts on advertising, thoughts on what makes for a good businessman and a smooth-running business, and general advice on how to be successful in life—all by Pessoa.

The people with the best business acumen, argued Pessoa, were the Americans. They had turned business into a science by studying the laws of the market to make products and services respond directly to people's needs, thereby boosting profits. He credited Americans with being able to discuss technical business problems in a pragmatic and lighthearted fashion, in contrast to Europeans, who tended to be "solemnly incompetent."[12] One of his articles offered paraphrased precepts culled from the writings of the ever pragmatic Henry Ford, such as "Strive for simplicity" and "Don't theorize; experiment," but he noted that they only partly accounted for the carmaker's success, which also depended on other precepts that were shrouded in secrecy.[13] Even the apparently clear-cut world of profits and losses had occult underpinnings.

At around the same time that Pessoa, in the *Business and Accounting Review*, stressed the advantages of free enterprise and lauded Americans for the business savvy that was making some of them extremely rich, he was drafting an insulting open letter addressed to "American Millionaires," an equally disparaging "Message to Millionaires," and "An

Essay on Millionaires and Their Ways."[14] The letter, the message, and the essay—all written in English—accused the superrich of accumulating wealth uselessly, since they were too unimaginative and uncultured to properly enjoy it. "How many of you have a harem, a real harem?" he asked. That, according to Pessoa, "would be an interesting application of wealth." Instead, he noted in "Message to Millionaires," the rich buy paintings without possessing the aesthetic sensibility to appreciate them, or they build libraries, making "ten thousand books accessible to a hundred thousand fools who shall get out of them no more than is in themselves, which is nothing in most cases." Andrew Carnegie used some of his vast wealth to finance the construction of some twenty-five hundred libraries, mainly in North America and the British Isles. If the rich wanted to give away money, the only thing worth helping, Pessoa contended, was individual genius. This was the rationale that had justified his request for financial assistance from Carnegie back in 1913, in a letter he never sent.

It was not only how millionaires spent their money but also how they earned it that appalled the poet. "No man ever became a millionaire by hard work or cleverness. At the worst he became so by a vast and imaginative unscrupulousness; at the best by happy intuition in speculative circumstances." Chicanery and good luck, in other words. American millionaires, according to Pessoa, were so fixated on hoarding wealth that they had "no shred of decency, no sense of fellow-feeling with the warm commonness of mankind." And the millionaire he loathed most was Henry Ford, whose antisemitic conspiracy theories he had been willing to consider but whose professed belief in reincarnation, revealed in interviews from the mid-1920s, struck him as a fiction to enhance the carmaker's image and increase his profits:

You have dared to use the words of Indian mystics and European occultists towards the furthering of your publicity. You have affected a belief in reincarnation out of a real belief in advertising. Everything your kind touches it pollutes, and the doctrine which leads the Indian mystic not to kill a fly leads you not to let men live.

One wants to ask: "Will the real Fernando Pessoa please stand up?" Was he the indignant defamer of allegedly uncultured, inhumane American millionaires? Or was he the defender of free trade who wrote glowingly in his brother-in-law's magazine about the American way of doing business, which helped create Fords, Carnegies, and Rockefellers? Pessoa's particular genius condemned him to being entirely whatever person he was, during the brief time he was that particular person. The "real Fernando Pessoa" was always someone else.

◆

THE FIRST ISSUE OF *Business and Accounting Review* appeared on January 25, 1926. Half of the articles were written and signed by Fernando Pessoa. In that same month the first two installments of his translation of Nathaniel Hawthorne's *The Scarlet Letter* were published in *Ilustração* (*Illustration*), a handsome new magazine aimed at a general readership. In keeping with then common practice, the translator's name went unmentioned, which mattered not at all to Pessoa, who made a competent enough translation but does not seem to have cared all that much for the novel. The magazine, in any case, paid its contributors well, and the task kept him occupied.[15]

Another task that took up many hours of Pessoa's time was *Lisbon: What the Tourist Should See*, an English-language travel guide for foreigners. It was a spin-off of his far more ambitious *All about Portugal*, the wide-ranging compendium for foreign businessmen as well as tourists that he had been planning, but not writing, for over ten years. He did manage to write his guidebook to the nation's capital, which suggests that he may have had a publisher for it. Since the founding of the Republic, private associations as well as the government had been striving to promote tourism in Portugal. But if someone or some entity had commissioned Pessoa, the deal fell through, and the typescript of his book lay nestled among his voluminous papers for more than six decades. When it was finally published, in 1992, many Pessoa scholars were skeptical, believing it to be a translation rather than an original work. How, they wondered, could language so banal and a style so insipid have issued from such a great writer?

Since Lisbon is now a major tourist destination, and Pessoa a world-renowned writer, his travel guide sells and has been published in many languages, including Portuguese. A film director even made it into a movie, which, faithful to the text, was inevitably tedious.[16] Many of the book's sentences read better, no doubt, when translated *out* of English. For instance: "The general aspect of the square is of a kind to give a very agreeable impression to the most exacting of tourists." Or this one, about a church: "The temple is also worth seeing inside, though not especially remarkable in that respect." Adjectives such as "remarkable," "fine," and "magnificent" recur over and over. That this was Pessoa's original work is proven by the surviving typescript, on which he made handwritten revisions affecting the content as well as the style.

Written in the early months of 1926, Pessoa's guidebook poached nearly all its technical information from an authoritative guide to Lisbon published in Portuguese two years earlier.[17] His failure to inject life into the descriptions of art museums, public statues, churches, and monuments had less to do with deficiencies in his English prose—which could be brilliantly expressive, despite the occasionally awkward phrase—than with his relative disinterest in the physical world, which made him apathetic toward art and architecture. Walter Pater's poetic reverie on the *Mona Lisa* enchanted him; the *Mona Lisa* itself did not. "How much more beautiful the *Mona Lisa* would be if we couldn't see it!" he remarked in *The Book of Disquiet*.[18]

Although most of Pessoa's travel guide makes for dull reading, it has an inventive framing device and a promising first page and a half. The author invites the visiting tourist to come along with him in his "motor-car," so that they can drive around the city together, while the informed guide points out all the sights. Before any of that, however, he offers a luminous, initiatory vision of Lisbon to his ideal tourist, who arrives there by ship. This is how the book opens:

> Over seven hills, which are as many points of observation whence the most magnificent panoramas may be enjoyed, the vast irregular and many-coloured mass of houses that constitute Lisbon is scattered.
>
> For the traveller who comes in from the sea, Lisbon, even from afar, rises like a fair vision in a dream, clear-cut against a bright blue sky which the sun gladdens with its gold. And the domes, the monuments, the old castles jut up above the mass of houses, like far-off heralds of this delightful seat, of this blessed region.

That "vast irregular and many-coloured mass of houses" is a distinctively Pessoan formula, recalling similar vignettes of the capital in *The Book of Disquiet*. It was this visionary Lisbon built on seven hills, like

Rome, that Pessoa loved, not its museums or other tourist attractions. As soon as he descends from the hills to meet the ideal visitor who has just stepped off the boat, on the second page, his travel guide lapses into a dreary and lifeless account of things to see. It did not help matters that Pessoa was feeling more than usually alienated—even from the beloved city where he had spent his early childhood and all his adult life.

◆

PESSOA'S GUIDEBOOK TO LISBON, no less than his translation of Hawthorne's most famous novel, was busywork. As a creative writer Pessoa had been going through the driest spell of his entire career. March 17 marked the first anniversary of his mother's death, and in the year gone by he had written a few poems in his own name, just two odes of Ricardo Reis, nothing of Alberto Caeiro, and no poems of Álvaro de Campos except, perhaps, several hard-to-date sonnets.[19] For the next month or so he wrote no poetry at all. He worked on his guidebook and on articles for the *Business and Accounting Review*.

The fourth issue was scheduled to come out on April 25, but it had still not gone to the printers, and on the twenty-sixth Pessoa was struggling to finish a theoretical article on the art of organizing. Unable to concentrate, he scrawled a few sentences that did not add up to anything, and then unexpectedly, as if it had been hijacked, his pen produced a poem about a toy car whose simplicity makes it seem, at first glance, like a children's poem. Titled "The Wooden Car," it is actually a bitter parody of a children's poem:

> The wooden car
> That Baby left behind . . .
> The car is still here,
> The baby has died . . .

The remaining five stanzas tell how family members stumble upon the toy car after the funeral, stow it away in the attic, and gradually forget the baby, since "Life is for those / Who keep on living." It was the same old obsessional theme about how the living make quick work of the dead. Perhaps Pessoa was thinking of his first niece, who had died seven months earlier. Below "The Wooden Car" he began writing another, thematically related poem, which got no further than the first line: "Everlasting remembrance, how briefly you endure!" Pessoa's post-humous editors have published this as a complete, one-line poem.

Something was opening up; more poems poured out. On a separate sheet of paper, also dated April 26, Pessoa wrote a poem in which the "high tide" of the natural world radiantly waves around the torpid narrator, who is dead to life, shut up in his own world of dreams and visions of what will never be. Where this poem ended, he began yet another, shifting now to the person and voice of Álvaro de Campos. What resulted was one of his psychologically most searing works, "Lisbon Revisited (1926)," whose first thirty lines are a mirror image—same subject, inverted point of view—of "Lisbon Revisited (1923)." The earlier poem was an adamant declaration of independence: "No, I don't want anything"; "Leave me alone, for God's sake!"; "Don't grab me by the arm!" In 1926, the revisitor wants "fifty things at the same time" but cannot fix his attention on any one thing. His wanting is hopelessly dispersed, his conscious self too helplessly scattered to make adamant declarations.

The second half of the poem can be understood as Pessoa's own lament for his lost childhood, channeled through Campos, who was back in Lisbon on holiday from his job as a naval engineer in northern England.

> Once more I see you,
> City of my horrifyingly lost childhood . . .
> Happy and sad city, once more I dream here . . .
> I? Is it one and the same I who lived here, and came back,
> And came back again, and again,
> And yet again have come back?
> Or are we—all the I's that I was here or that were here—
> A series of bead-beings joined together by a string of memory,
> A series of dreams about me dreamed by someone outside me?
>
> Once more I see you,
> With a heart that's more distant, a soul that's less mine.

Pessoa-Campos does not grieve for his childhood per se, as if he constantly remembered it and wished he could return there. He laments having become insensitive to the past, emotionally cut off from it. He mourns the death of the person, or the series of persons, he once was but has ceased to be. He remembers them only tenuously, and the revisited past is no longer a country where he feels at home. The anguished visitor to Lisbon and to the history of his own life closes the poem with an ontological apocalypse:

> Once more I see you,
> But, oh, I cannot see myself!
> The magic mirror where I always looked the same has shattered,
> And in each fateful fragment I see only a piece of me—
> A piece of you and of me!

The magic mirror, the privilege of illusion enjoyed by childhood innocence, was what had afforded the poet (before he became a poet) a cohesive vision of himself and of the world. The experience of living broke the spell. Fragments—flashes—from childhood occasionally accosted Pessoa, as on that autumn day about six months before when he found himself scoring runs in an imaginary cricket match, just like he used to do in Durban. Yet he did not loll among those fragments, much less try to connect them all into a reconstructed childhood where he could hide out. His hideout was literature, for which his childhood, along with the rest of his life, provided thematic material.

Three poems written in his own name as well as Álvaro de Campos's "Lisbon Revisited (1926)" was an impressive day's work, but the day was not over. Pessoa wrote one more, very different sort of Campos poem, untitled and addressed to an unnamed individual who is toying with the idea of suicide. Far from discouraging him, Álvaro de Campos eggs him on:

> If you want to kill yourself, why don't you want to kill yourself?
> Now's your chance! I, who greatly love both death and life,
> Would kill myself too, if I dared kill myself . . .
> If you dare, then be daring!

In the seventy-seven lines that follow this opening taunt, Campos anticipates and refutes the possible objections that the addressee might raise to carrying out his project of self-annihilation. What good, he asks, "is the changing picture of outer images / We call the world?" And what good "is your inner world which you don't know? / Kill yourself, and maybe you'll finally know it." Does the contemplator of suicide think he's needed in the world? Campos guarantees, on the contrary, that everything and everyone will keep on going without him.

As for the survivors who will grieve over his disappearance, Campos reassures him:

Don't worry: they won't cry for long . . .
The impulse to live gradually stanches tears
When they're not for our own sake.

He proceeds to explain, as Pessoa himself had repeatedly explained in other poems, how the shock and sorrow felt by his loved ones will slowly give way to forgetfulness, until the dead man is remembered only twice a year: on his birthday and his death day.

This poem, not by accident, was written on the death day of Mário de Sá-Carneiro, who had committed suicide exactly ten years earlier. The memory of that event was what had been eating at Pessoa while he tried, in vain, to concentrate on his article for the *Business and Accounting Review*, so that he ended up writing a series of poems instead, all of which had to do with death—of relatives, friends, of the past, the self, and of all that a self at one time felt but feels no longer. The last poem in the series seems, in a way, to be a tribute to Sá-Carneiro's suicide, since it endorses self-termination as a logical way out for a thinking and sensitive man dissatisfied with life. The poem's opening lines, on the other hand, might suggest to us that Pessoa, cross with his friend for having abandoned him, was retroactively and self-defensively feigning indifference—as when a jilted lover defiantly says, "Go ahead and leave me. See if I care!"

But neither of these readings accounts for the taunting, argumentative style of the poem, whose narrator is Álvaro de Campos, not Fernando Pessoa. The liveliest of the heteronyms was speaking to Pessoa himself, who for a long time had been trapped in a disillusioned, defeated, and depressed frame of mind. In case he had any thoughts of following the suicidal example of his dearest friend, Campos was there to call his bluff, forcing him to choose between death or life.

Pessoa chose life. The poems he wrote on April 26, in his own name and in Campos's name, released him from the despair and hazy resentment that had been clouding his spirit. While still hampered by depression, and although still feeling defeated, he was ready to resume his calling as a poet.

✦

THE RESURGENT POET HAD an immediate outlet for publishing what he wrote, since his friend José Pacheco, in remission from tuberculosis, resumed his work as an editor, bringing out three issues of *Contemporânea* in 1926. Pessoa contributed poems to all of them—either as himself or as Álvaro de Campos, whose "Lisbon Revisited (1926)" appeared in the June issue.[20] One of the new contributors to the revived magazine, perhaps recommended to Pacheco by Pessoa, was Carlos Queiroz, his newest and youngest friend. Ophelia had occasionally mentioned this nephew, since she lived under the same roof with him and his mother; and Carlos, as a youngster, had heard quite a bit about his aunt's sweetheart, the Poet. Now, as if by an oblique transmission of influence, Carlos himself was a promising poet. Ophelia urged him to seek out her ex-boyfriend in Lisbon's cafés,[21] and Fernando, who fondly remembered her and the exhilaration (love?) he felt during the early months of their relationship, was only too glad to help the young man in his fledgling career as a writer. He introduced him to his literary compeers, and in February 1926 he drew up a fresh set of plans for a "new phase" of *Orpheu* that listed Carlos Queiroz, who had not yet turned nineteen, as a possible contributor.[22] According to Pessoa's latest idea, the reincarnated *Orpheu* would be a weekly magazine featuring literature, criticism, and, just as important, political content.

If I follow at least partially, sketchily, the long and winding trail of Pessoa's discarded magazine projects—which are far too numerous for them all to be mentioned—it is because they help define his inward intellectual trajectory. As negative "milestones" of what he failed to accomplish, they also serve as windows into his nagging sense of ineptitude. Far more than the reader, Pessoa sighed at all the wreckage of ideas not acted on, of magazines never published, of articles that were but sketches or mere notes for articles. The "new phase" of *Orpheu* was the latest casualty of the writer's chronic dereliction. But soon he had the chance to disseminate, in print, some of his ideas for one of the magazine's unwritten articles, "The Fifth Empire."

In the spring of 1926, Pessoa was invited to participate in a newspaper survey dealing with Portugal's place in the world and its status as a major colonial power. But instead of exalting the Portuguese colonies, he dismissed them as a measly advantage in the international arena and used the survey to promulgate Sebastianism and the Fifth Empire. Readers must have smiled, or else frowned, when they discovered that these doctrines were being promoted precisely because they were sheer fictions. Pessoa maintained that only a "great national myth," absolutely untrue but imbued with the power of truth, could raise the morale of a nation.[23] Portugal's real advantage over other nations was not its colonies but the existence of "the Sebastianist myth, deeply rooted in the past and in the Portuguese soul." That myth needed to be revitalized, however, until it intoxicated the entire Portuguese populace, at which point "an unpredictable phenomenon will occur in the Nation's soul, giving rise to New Discoveries, the Creation of the New World, the Fifth Empire. King Sebastian will have returned."

Pessoa's survey responses—far more extraordinary than any other participant's—were published on May 28 and June 5.[24] By an uncanny coincidence, May 28 marked the beginning of a military revolution that swept away, like a house of cards, the multiparty political system in place since the nineteenth century, when Portugal was still a constitutional monarchy. It was almost as if Pessoa, by speaking of an "unpredictable phenomenon" that would transform the nation, had foreseen the coup d'état. Though it did not usher in anything remotely resembling his hoped-for Fifth Empire, the coup drew a curtain across the liberal, secularist and often turbulent Republic founded in 1910, leaving open the question of what might come next. Pessoa remained hopeful.

# CHAPTER 56

OXOXOXOXOXOXOXOXOXOXOXOXOXOXOXOXOX

**T**HE STRANGEST THING ABOUT THE DEATH OF Portugal's First Republic (1910–1926), as it came to be called by historians, was the timing. After a decade and a half in which its founding ideals had been rudely traduced by political intrigue and corruption, food shortages, mayhem on the streets, financial scandals, and flawed foreign policy decisions, the Republic had matured and become relatively well balanced, circumspect, and financially responsible. Like a number of other nations that had fought in the Great War, Portugal still struggled with a huge external debt, and its politics continued to be a messy affair, with constant bickering among and even within the various parties; nevertheless, although the political leaders never managed to stay in power for very long, they had learned to control spending and govern sensibly. Rampant inflation was a thing of the past, and not even the Angola and Metropole Bank scam seriously affected the value of the escudo, in spite of flooding the economy with funny money. The scam, however, did help further undermine the government's reputation—for no reason, really, other than the fact that besmirching the government had become a national pastime.

The majority of Portuguese, including Fernando Pessoa, had fallen out of love with the Republic since at least the time of their collective romance with Sidónio Pais. Disenchantment turned into nausea when they saw republicans viciously dispatch other republicans on the Bloody Night of October 1921. Right-wing nationalists—whether fascists, monarchists, or the Catholic traditionalists of the integralist movement—ruthlessly denigrated the powers that be, which were under simultaneous fire from the far left. Even traditionally supportive newspapers became hypercritical, as if the government could do nothing right. Meanwhile, the army's prestige and clout kept growing. Its embarrassing performance in the war, owing to some quirk in the national psyche, had metamorphosed into a heroic undertaking, with its humiliating defeat at the

Battle of the Lys, in April 1918, being commemorated annually as if it were a resounding victory. In order to secure the backing of the armed forces, or to at least keep them at bay, successive postwar governments appointed more and more officers to ministerial posts.

Elsewhere in Europe, army officers had been playing even more prominent roles, rising to power through coups in Poland, Bulgaria, and Greece. Much closer to home, General Primo de Rivera had solidified his position as the dictatorial prime minister of Spain, ruling without a constitution—and not ruling so badly, according to some observers (although in a couple of years his regime would unravel).

The Portuguese military coup of May 28, 1926, met with only muffled opposition: nobody took up arms against it, and not one person died. Most people, including many on the left of the political divide, greeted the takeover with relief, since the army was supposed to save the nation from dishonesty, waste, partisanship, poverty, backwardness, crime, and moral depravity—but no one had given much thought to how its salvific mission was to be accomplished. There were competing conspiracy groups inside and outside the army, and the initial coup was followed by a second coup two weeks later. General Manuel Gomes da Costa, one of the "heroes" from the Great War, was the useful, idiotically smiling leader of them both. In principle a moderate, he had no program of his own and became the stooge of nationalist ideological forces, especially the Portuguese fascist and integralist movements.

Although Pessoa had not opposed the military intervention and its dissolution of the elected government, he soon worried about the political orientation being adopted by the new regime. He decided to intervene in his own way, with a manifesto to the nation warning against the influence of "pseudonational" ideologues such as the Portuguese fascists, whom he accused of parroting whatever Mussolini uttered, and the integralists, whose ideas he traced to Charles Maurras, the ultra-Catholic monarchist at the head of the Action Française movement. Pessoa did not sign the manifesto, dated July 8, 1926, with his own name.[1] It was signed by the National Action Committee, which he and Geraldo Coelho de Jesus had hatched seven years earlier, when launching their Sidonist newspaper, *Acção*. Before the manifesto could be printed and distributed, however, the political situation took a new twist: on July 9 another coup, the third one in the space of six weeks, installed Generals Óscar Carmona and João José Sinel de Cordes at the head of the government. Costa, who three days earlier had been feted at a British embassy luncheon as the new chief of state, was arrested and exiled to the Azores.

The dust kicked up by military infighting had settled for now, and the generals began to govern in earnest. To preclude inconvenient criticism by contrarian journalists, they swiftly instituted prepublication censorship of newspapers and magazines, causing Pessoa's attitude toward the new situation to pivot from rather sympathetic to moderately wary. Restraints on free speech for the supposed good of the nation struck him as a troubling sign that the generals might model their nationalist program after Mussolini's. In the summer of 1925 the Italian dictator had embraced the word "totalitarian" to describe the Fascist will, and in the fall of that year he formulated fascism's guiding motto: "Everything within the state, nothing outside the state, nothing against the state." The interests of the individual, according to Mussolinian ideology, should be tolerated only insofar as they do not collide with those of the nation. Pessoa believed—and would publicly defend—the exact opposite. He decided to attack Mussolini head-on, and to aid him in this task he engaged a heteronym of sorts born in Italy.

✦

IN THE FALL OF 1926, five months after the army seized control of the government, a friend of Pessoa named Celestino Soares founded a daily newspaper, *Sol* (*Sun*), to which Pessoa became a regular contributor.[2] In its first two weeks of existence, the paper published a poem signed by Álvaro de Campos, a poem and a humorous sketch written under Pessoa's own name, and fourteen installments—in his Portuguese translation—of *The Leavenworth Case*, a pioneering and once very popular detective story published in 1878 by the American writer Anna Katharine Green. The *Leavenworth* installments continued, and soon Pessoa, with the collusion of Soares, created his own mystery story, presented in two parts on the front page of the newspaper as if it were legitimate, reliable reportage.[3]

On November 20, a Saturday, readers of *Sol* were greeted by the headline "Mussolini, 'Il Duce,' Is a Madman." What followed was an "interview"—forged in its entirety by Fernando Pessoa—with an Italian literary critic named Giovanni B. Angioletti, a "well-known contributor to *Mercure de France*" who had voluntarily exiled himself to Portugal because of his bitter opposition to fascism. Contradicting a visiting Fascist dignitary from Italy who, just two days before, had given a lecture in Lisbon that praised Mussolini and the achievements of his regime,[4] Angioletti stated that the Italian dictator was a lunatic afflicted by paranoia and that fascism was a contagious form of insanity, comparable to the mysterious dancing epidemics of the Middle Ages, in which the sufferers sometimes danced themselves to death. The worst thing about fascism, clarified the fictitious interviewee, even worse than its violent methods for silencing dissent, was its exaggerated exaltation of Italy, its obsession with "national grandeur." And to clarify the nature of his own fervent nationalism and Fifth Empire dreams, Pessoa placed the following words in the mouth of Angioletti: "No nation has the right to exist if it does not contribute something to the general progress of humanity, if it is not an Empire in the highest sense of the term—a hub for spreading ideas and breakthroughs that benefit the whole world." Pessoa never considered a glorified, imperial Portugal to be a worthy end in itself.

The next day, the Italian consulate in Lisbon announced that it had no record of any Giovanni B. Angioletti residing on Portuguese soil. Whereupon *Sol*, on the day after that, the twenty-second, published the second and concluding part of Pessoa's Italian political mystery story.[5] It began with an article reaffirming the identity of the anti-Fascist interviewee and ended with a letter—in French, accompanied by a translation into Portuguese—purportedly written by Angioletti himself. He congratulated the newspaper for accurately reporting his criticisms of fascism but pointed out that he had never contributed anything to *Mercure de France*, as stated by the interviewer. Perhaps, he suggested, there was another Italian critic who went by the same name.

Indeed there *was* another, real-life critic named Giovanni B. Angioletti (1896–1961), who published in Italian newspapers and literary reviews. He was not an anti-Fascist activist, however, let alone a political exile. What was Pessoa up to? He could have attacked Mussolini just as effectively through an Italian critic invented by him from scratch rather than going to the trouble of stealing, and distorting, the identity of a critic nobody in Portugal had ever heard of. Pessoa, however, liked to commingle fiction and reality, to complexify life, to make it even more mysterious than it was naturally.[6]

Besides the articles featuring the ersatz Angioletti, *Sol* published other pieces harshly critical of Mussolini's regime, which the recently established Censorship Commission could not prohibit, since they did not directly attack the political powers or institutions of Portugal. *Sol* also reported on Lisbon's underclass, on the jobless citizens immigrating to Brazil, on poor sanitary conditions, and on the scandalous problem of adulterated foods, such as milk, allegedly diluted with water from gutters and public urinals. Although none of these were new problems, they did not make for a rosy picture of national life under the new dispensation, and on December 1, after just one month of operation, the daily paper abruptly ceased publication—probably under duress. The readers who had gotten hooked on the daily installments of Pessoa's translation of A. K. Green's first and most successful detective novel were left guessing which of the suspects had murdered the wealthy bachelor Horatio Leavenworth.

◆

PESSOA REJECTED FASCISM AND other radical nationalisms for the same reason he rejected ideologies of class struggle such as communism: they reduced the individual to an interchangeable unit at the service of some higher, collective reality such as the nation, or the proletariat. For a similar reason he disdained the creed of humanitarianism, believing that it can all too easily lump "needy" people together into an anonymous, undifferentiated mass, whom the creed's proponents feel morally obliged to aid and protect. The only social reality, he insisted, is the individual, a point of view poetically expressed by Alberto Caeiro:

> They spoke to me of people, and of humanity.
> But I've never seen people, or humanity.
> I've seen various people, astonishingly dissimilar,
> Each separated from the next by an unpeopled space.

While it is true that Pessoa, ever since he was young, felt it was his sacred duty to serve humankind, he always acted as a strict individualist who aspired, through his writings, to benefit other individuals. Not even his passion for certain political causes could induce him to belong to a formal group or organization—with the exception of the National Action Committee, which was little more than a name stamped on a couple of publications. It was as a guerrilla belonging to no army that he had attacked Afonso Costa's Democrats, defended the memory and the myth of Sidónio Pais, and now inveighed—through Giovanni B. Angioletti—against Italian fascism, lest it replicate itself in Portugal.

Like-minded friends could count on Pessoa's help in their campaigns to bring about useful reforms in government, in society, and in the cultural sphere, but they could not extract from him a personal commitment to a collective endeavor. His stubbornly individualist form of solidarity was never more glaringly demonstrated than when José Pacheco, a dedicated cultural activist as well as the editor in chief of *Contemporânea*, asked him to draft a petition calling for the dismissal of Portugal's do-nothing director-general of fine arts. The poet gladly obliged, using logical argument laced with satire to justify the demand of the petitioners. It was a caustic, typically Pessoan piece of writing, four typed copies of which he delivered to his friend on August 17, 1926, along with a note saying that he himself would not be signing the petition, and not because he disagreed with it.

"As you know," Pessoa reminded him, "I will sign nothing in conjunction, cooperation or collaboration with anyone else." Correcting the proverb "Better to be alone than in bad company," he said that for him, an "absolute individualist," it was "better to be alone, even when the company is good."

◆

PESSOA'S RELUCTANCE TO BELONG to formal groups or to collaborate with others was reflected in his ambivalent attitude toward publishing,[7] and toward any other kind of public achievement. To win the world's approval is a form of collaboration. And accomplishments, by defining us, in a certain way make us smaller. What we actually manage to become is always something less than all the things we dreamed of being in our youth.

In an autobiographical note written in English on his twenty-eighth birthday, Pessoa had reproached himself for having come that far with "nothing done in life—nothing in life, in letters or in my own individuality." Yet ten years later, in September 1926, he touted that same lack of accomplishment as a blessing. His apologia for achieving nothing at all was prompted by a letter to the editor of *Answers*, one of the British weeklies that he occasionally purchased to compete for cash prizes in the games section. The writer of the published letter, a man from Glasgow, explained that he was thirty-seven years old, professionally successful, free of financial worries, and no stranger to love, all of which made him not only satisfied but full of energy and ready for many good years of life ahead.[8] Pessoa recounted his own, rather different experience in a letter to the same newspaper:

> I am one year older than your correspondent and I feel young for the reasons which are precisely opposite to his. I am thirty-eight and I feel younger every year because every year I am nearer to having never achieved anything in life. [. . .] Achievement makes us old. You must pay something for everything; the price of achievement is the loss of youth. It is only purposelessness and an inconsequential way of life—if the word "way" can be applied to such an absence of way—that keeps us young. I have not married and so have kept free both from the special pleasures and the particular cares of that species of partnership; and the good and the evil of the state are equally ageing. I have never settled down to a profession or a course of life, nor even to an opinion outlasting the transient minute in which it was held. [. . .] I have never made a real effort after anything, nor applied my attention strongly except to futile, unnecessary and fictional things. I feel young because I have lived in this way.

The letter continued in a more obviously ironic tone, with Pessoa pointing out, for instance, that by virtue of doing nothing in life he had not "stood in the way of any fool's natural greatness," but it also accurately described him as a "spectator of my own self and of the times," who was able, through "imagination and fancy, to extract empires from casual meetings."

Having extracted a fanciful moral triumph from his nonmeeting with the letter writer from Glasgow, Pessoa no longer needed to keep writing his own letter, which he dropped, unfinished, into his bottomless trunk, like a child dropping a coin into a deep well. Pessoa placed his faith in posterity, with no guarantee that the future would remember him, and there were times when doubt got the better of him, making him wonder with anguish if his work truly deserved to be remembered.

As for life in the present, his claim to feeling younger for having never achieved anything was dubious. Lack of visible accomplishments—

and of the responsibilities, commitments, and concessions that worldly success usually entails—may have had a youth-enhancing effect when he was in his late twenties and early thirties, but with the death of his mother the years quickly caught up with him. As he approached his fifth decade, the lightness of being nothing in the world, completely free and unattached, was offset by the weight of all his thwarted or aborted literary projects, his fruitless attempts to be a businessman, and his botched attempt at love. No, he was not feeling young, at least not on most days. On his thirty-eighth birthday, after looking closely in the mirror, he wrote this poem, in the voice of Ricardo Reis:

> Already over my vain brow
> The hair of that youth who died is graying.
>     My eyes shine less today.
> My lips have lost their right to kisses.
> If you still love me, for love's sake stop loving:
>     Don't cheat on me with me.

The uncompromising individualist had always preferred celibacy, a condition that now felt less like a choice than like a destiny he was forced to accept. He could hardly imagine that anyone, at this point in his life, would find him attractive, desirable, lovable.

◆

**PESSOA'S FRIENDS FROM THIS** period did not necessarily look younger than him, but they acted younger. Outwardly, at least, they were more energetic and high-spirited. Geraldo Coelho de Jesus, born six months before Pessoa, was a bon vivant who loved to travel, especially to Paris, as well as a philanderer with a taste for younger women. One of the many women he had made passes at was nineteen-year-old Ophelia Queiroz, back in 1920, unaware that she was already committed to his friend Fernando.[9] Augusto Ferreira Gomes, perhaps to compensate for his bantam stature, was the jokester of the group, bright eyed and easily excited, especially when fired up by alcohol, and since he was small, it didn't take much for him to get completely drunk. Coelho de Jesus, partial to absinthe (already banned in France but still available in Portugal), was the kind of drinker who becomes garrulous and expansive. Pessoa was a slow but steady, discreet imbiber, a fully functional alcoholic. Wine and brandy altered neither his behavior nor his tone of voice. On occasion, however, he pretended to be drunk by walking crookedly on the sidewalk or twirling around a lamppost, for the amusement of his cousins' children or to irritate his sister, who worried about what others would think.[10]

Raul Leal, almost two years older than Pessoa, continued to endure bodily mortifications and psychological torments that, according to his metaphysical theories, were preparing his spirit for the heights of Vertigo. After his profligate behavior in the mid-1910s reduced him from riches to rags and his *Sodom Deified* made him the butt of cruel verbal abuse, he began to earn a modest living as a journalist for monarchist newspapers, yet he still managed to attract misfortune and injury. In August 1926 he was ambushed and viciously caned in a Lisbon café for having criticized, in published articles, the administration of the government agency in charge of public assistance.[11] But like a boxer made of rubber, Leal always bounced back up and continued fighting for the restoration of the monarchy, for vertiginous purity, and for the glorious reign of the Church of the Paraclete. About these last two topics he wrote endlessly.

In that same month of August another of Pessoa's close friends, António Botto, turned twenty-nine. Endowed with the reckless self-confidence of someone even younger, the poet liked to flaunt his homosexuality but had a more complicated relationship with his humble origins, exploiting them in several literary works while at the same time inventing for himself, in highly fictionalized autobiographical accounts, an upper-class upbringing that included schooling in England. This self-aristocratizing tendency may explain his attraction to Luis Fernando de Orleans y Borbón, a Spanish prince who, if he lived today, might also have called himself a queen. After spending about fifteen years as a young man in Paris, where he earned a scandalous reputation for his life of drugs and sex with other men, he was expelled from France and stripped of his royal privileges by King Alfonso XIII of Spain.

The prince moved to Portugal in late 1924 and was in contact with António Botto by the summer of 1925,[12] when he attended Lisbon's Second Fado Festival to listen to Botto, who was the star attraction. In awe the prince watched as his handsome friend, singing his own poems, succeeded in taming a rowdy bunch of pimps and their friends, who sported gold chains and gaudy diamond rings and had come to the São Luiz

Theater for the express purpose of heckling the fairy.[13] This was the kind of event that Pessoa would never have attended, but he saved the flyer, which hyperbolically described Botto as "the most elegant and most original contemporary Portuguese poet,"[14] and he no doubt met Luis Fernando on other occasions. Details of Botto's liaison with this royal personage are sketchy, but it was certainly not a serenely steady affair. The prince had another Portuguese boyfriend, also named António, and he continued to have run-ins with the law. In March 1926, when he crossed the Spanish border into Portugal dressed as a woman, the police arrested him under suspicion of trafficking cocaine. (They found none.)[15]

Fado, the searingly plaintive style of song made internationally famous by Amália Rodrigues (1920–1999), has its origins in Africa and Brazil but came into its own in the poorer neighborhoods of Lisbon in the early nineteenth century.[16] The word *fado* means "fate," and *casa de fado*, which nowadays refers to a restaurant with live fado music, used to be a popular name for Lisbon's brothels, where it was the fate of certain indigent women to earn their living. It was partly in brothels that fado music developed. The most celebrated *fadista* of the nineteenth century, Maria Severa (1820–1846), was herself a prostitute, and in the first decades of the twentieth century fado was still largely a product of Lisbon's bohemian subculture. This was the milieu that António Botto grew up in, and nothing about it could faze him. For Pessoa it was an exotic, unseemly world that repelled his genteel sensibility while arousing his curiosity. He observed from a safe distance.

In an unpublished essay written after Pessoa's death, Botto would recall that his friend, "femininely modest," immediately changed the subject at the mere mention of prostitutes,[17] but he was by no means an absolute prude. Two letters from the older poet to the younger one reveal an inquisitive spectator, a kind of armchair voyeur, who kept abreast of Botto's gay escapades and enjoyed making spirited, sometimes piquant observations about their common friends and about himself. The letters—both full of witty code language—were sent in March 1927, two months after Botto and his Spanish prince set out on a steamship for a luxury holiday in Italy. Pessoa had cast a horoscope for Botto that predicted a harmonious January,[18] which is when the two travelers departed from Lisbon, and everything went smoothly in Naples, their point of arrival, where their sightseeing included a trip to the ruins of Pompeii. But in Rome they had an ugly spat and Botto left for Paris—alone. So we can deduce from Pessoa's remarks, in his second missive (sent to France), about the fluctuating "temperature" of the letters and postcards he had received from Botto, which have unfortunately not survived.

Botto was sending romantic weather reports of his time with the prince because Pessoa, in his first missive, posted to Italy, had specifically requested "news that is particularly your own, including your impressions (or sensations) of the scenery in its various aspects." The wry tone of the letter and its mostly mischievous content make it clear that Pessoa was referring to the "scenery" of Botto's affair with the prince. In the next paragraph he told Botto about what their mutual friends were up to. Augusto Ferreira Gomes had managed to be "drunk for two days in the space of 24 hours"; Geraldo Coelho de Jesus had bought a fancy new car, the better to help him seduce young women; and Raul Leal had supposedly written 595 pages of a new metaphysical treatise, still less than half done. He also informed Botto that there was no basis in fact to the rumor that Leal was getting married.

The letter writer's most acerbic ironies were directed at himself:

Yesterday I drew up five complete and definitive projects, but I can no longer remember what they were, or why. My most recent poems have all ended somewhere in the middle—just like my non-recent poems. According to an old plan of mine, I expect to depart for England the day before yesterday, so I've almost decided to think about getting everything ready. The rumor that I'm getting married likewise has no basis in fact.

Pessoa placed himself in the same unmarriageable category as Raul Leal and António Botto, but while these two friends were both (homo)sexually active, his own sexual energy was directed toward his multiplied self. In his letter's final paragraph, Pessoa wrote that the engineer Álvaro de Campos happened to be in Lisbon and sent Botto his greetings "as a sunflower and a swan," to which he added his own greetings, sent "from the sunflower's old garden, from the swan's sad lake."[19] Pessoa, in other words, was the old garden or sad lake where his heteronym—like a tall-stemmed flower or a long-necked swan—gloriously affirmed himself.

Fernando and Álvaro formed an odd but productive couple. Notwithstanding his propensity to leave many works half finished, Pessoa, during his remaining years, would write hundreds of complete poems under his own name—in a subdued and reflective, often wistful tone of voice. Campos's poems, though infused with his creator's sad weariness, would continue to be dramatically emotive. Pessoa's melancholy contemplations, when transposed to Campos, become strident laments and waving arms. Together they would flourish: the old garden and the defiant sunflower, the sad lake and the proud swan.

✦

WHILE ANTÓNIO BOTTO WAS still in Naples, enjoying the company of the scandal-courting Spanish prince, an armed revolt had attempted to overthrow the government of Portugal. Pessoa was well acquainted with a couple of the ringleaders, Jaime Cortesão and Raul Proença, both members of the Grupo da Biblioteca (Library Group), whose role in the rebellion he mentioned in his March 8 letter to Botto. The quiet halls of libraries are not usually where revolutionaries meet to conspire, but the top administrators of the National Library of Portugal were liberal republican activists who had begun plotting against the military dictatorship in the summer of 1926, almost as soon as it came to power. Together with other insurrectionist groups they enlisted the support of army and navy personnel loyal to the original spirit of the Republic, striking first in Porto, in the early morning hours of February 3, but not until four days later in Lisbon. By February 10 it was all over, leaving close to two hundred soldiers, sailors, and civilians dead, and hundreds more wounded. More than a thousand rebels were deported without trial to Madeira, the Azores, and Portugal's African colonies. Cortesão, who had published poems in *A Águia*, and Proença (1884–1941) were dismissed from their posts at the National Library and fled to Paris.

Even if it had been better planned, the revolt of February 1927 would have failed for the most basic of reasons: lack of popular support. Hundreds of left-wing republicans, including organized labor, which in recent years was less organized and less numerous, turned out on the streets to aid the insurgents, but moderate republicans stayed at home and just wanted the brouhaha to die down quickly. They were tired of instability and resigned to living under a dictatorship. And as dictatorships go, it was a mild one. The generals Sinel de Cordes and Óscar Carmona, although not in a tremendous hurry to return the reins of government to civilian hands, viewed their regime as a short-term necessity. Many people agreed, Fernando Pessoa included.

But Pessoa soon began to have second thoughts. In the aftermath of the February rebellion, the police sacked the headquarters of the General Confederation of Labor (a nationwide workers' union), the Communist Party was forced underground, and the publication or dissemination of "subversive propaganda" was decreed sufficient cause for summary trial and condemnation. Pessoa may not have cared about the official prohibition of the Portuguese Communist Party (founded in 1921), but the government's increasing control over the printed word rankled him, and he decided to protest. He wrote "Fado da Censura," or "Censorship Fado," which he tried to publish in *Sempre Fixe* (*Always A-Okay*), a satirical weekly paper whose issues from 1927 usually included a traditional, forty-four-line fado[20] that poked fun at one thing or another, or that was at any rate lighthearted.

Since the newspaper's cartoons often targeted the censorship laws, Pessoa's "Censorship Fado" must have seemed to him like an obvious winner, but there was a problem: his fado was not the least bit humorous. It was a dark poem, a grim prophecy, which depicted state censorship as a thick dust that clouds normal vision and obstructs breathing, making it impossible to see the way and go forward. If the editors did not reject Pessoa's unfunny fado, the Censorship Commission did.[21]

Pessoa vigilantly monitored the events of the day and was ready to use his writing to take a stand, but his creative work lagged. He wasn't suffering from writer's block; he simply felt unmotivated. While he had gotten over his mother's death, to the extent that he would ever get over it, the indifferent reaction to his magazine *Athena*, where he and his heteronyms had published more than seventy poems—poems he judged to be among his best—still haunted him. And who, at this point, remembered the poems and the play he had published in *Orpheu*? Contrary to what he had claimed in his unfinished letter to a London newspaper, Pessoa was feeling a little like a has-been, old before his time.

◆

HE MIGHT HAVE CONTINUED to feel outdated, respected but little noticed, relegated to the sidelines, were it not for a man named José Régio (1901–1969), who had devoured—no, had savored like an epicure—every word published by Pessoa in *Orpheu*, in *Athena*, and in other periodicals. So great was the admiration of this young writer and editor that he confidently dubbed Pessoa Portugal's "most richly complex" modernist, endowed with "the stuff of a Master," even though he had not yet published a book, just several chapbooks of his English poems. Régio's generous and wholly accurate assessment of this poet whom he had never laid eyes on appeared in an article titled "On the Modernist Generation," which led off the third issue of *Presença* (*Presence*), a magazine founded in March 1927—not in Lisbon or Porto but in Coimbra, whose university and large student population made it an intellectual rival to the nation's two largest cities. The same article mentioned four other members of the modernist generation, all of them close friends of Pessoa and all connected to *Orpheu*: Mário de Sá-Carneiro, José de Almada Negreiros, Raul Leal, and Mário Saa (a candidate for inclusion in the ill-fated *Orpheu* 3).

*Presença* did much more than relaunch Pessoa and his friends. For future textbooks of literary history, it canonically established Pessoa, Sá-Carneiro, and Almada Negreiros as the three pillars of Portuguese modernism, and *Orpheu* as the cornerstone of that movement. And yet the editors of *Presença* were not interested in literary movements as such. In the magazine's second issue, Régio saluted the artistic innovations of futurism, expressionism, and dadaism[22] but noted that rigid adherence to any aesthetic dogma was stifling to artistic intuition, and he concluded that "superior modernism is individualistic and classical."

Respect for artistic autonomy, rejection of academic dictates, and curiosity about the art and literature produced elsewhere in Europe and beyond were the characteristics of the *Orpheu* generation that *Presença* strove to reembody, with some success. On the whole, however, it was a lackluster sequel. Pessoa and Sá-Carneiro were a hard act to follow, and the younger generation of creative writers promoted by the new magazine, which saw itself as *Orpheu*'s successor, could not begin to compare. *Presença*, on the other hand, was Portugal's liveliest, most intellectually rigorous forum for literary and art criticism during the thirteen years it endured. But its greatest achievement was simply to stimulate and disseminate the creative production of Fernando Pessoa, who would grace its pages with some of his finest poems and prose pieces.

The crucial intermediary between Pessoa and *Presença* was Ophelia's nephew, Carlos Queiroz, a short and thin young man who, despite his unassuming air, brashly introduced himself to writers he admired. An already published poet but a perennially bad student, Queiroz was nineteen when he transferred to a high school in Coimbra, where he hoped to buckle down and finally graduate. Instead, he continued to neglect his studies, spending the late afternoons with José Régio and other members of the *Presença* group, which congregated at the Café Central, located in the downtown area. They relied on Queiroz to obtain contributions from the Lisbon modernists singled out by Régio in the April issue of their new magazine. Works by Raul Leal and Mário Saa appeared in the May issue, while the June *Presença* featured a medley of contributions from Lisboners: a cover drawing by Almada Negreiros, a poem by Sá-Carneiro (furnished by Pessoa, his literary executor), a prose piece signed by Álvaro de Campos, a poem by Pessoa, and a four-poem suite by Queiroz himself.[23]

Of all the contributions from the Lisbon writers, Campos's was by far the most interesting—and provocative, since it rocked the boat that had kindly welcomed Pessoa and his friends on board. At issue was the putative virtue of being true to one's self. While Pessoa wholeheartedly concurred with the importance the magazine placed on artistic individuality, rather than on adherence to an aesthetic movement or a set of principles, he disagreed with its understanding of "individuality." The inaugural issue of *Presença* had opened with an article titled "Living Literature," in which José Régio held up originality and sincerity as interrelated qualities necessary for all great art. Originality, he wrote, "proceeds from the truest, most virgin and most intimate part of an artistic personality."

Pessoa, for whom no such true, virgin, and intimate personality existed, mobilized Campos to help him formulate his ideas on the self, self-expression, and self-knowledge. The result was "Environment," an aphoristically philosophical text that concludes with these paragraphs:

> Every true emotion is a lie in our intelligence, where emotion doesn't exist. The expression of every true emotion is therefore false. To express ourselves is to tell what we don't feel.
>
> The cavalry's horses are what make it a cavalry. Without horses, the cavalry would be infantry. A place is what it is because of its location. Where we are is who we are.
>
> To pretend is to know ourselves.

For Pessoa as for Campos, who in this case served as his creator's faithful spokesman, the self's true emotions cannot be intelligibly known, much less expressed, and the self is unreliable, its reality forever fluid, contingent on its changing relations with the surrounding environment. Self-knowledge, or individuality, is therefore a matter of attitude, of acting. The great artist, or great anything, is a great pretender.

In the coming years, the editors of *Presença* would repeatedly invoke sincerity of expression and trueness to one's self as hallmarks of superior art, while Pessoa would repeatedly question whether words such as *sincerity* and *trueness* can signify anything useful for a creative artist. The radical divergence in their respective outlooks was itself a powerful stimulus, inciting Pessoa to produce, by way of reaction, like an electric current overcoming resistance, some of his most dazzling works of literature.

# CHAPTER 57

U PON THEIR MOTHER'S DEATH PESSOA'S SISTER,
Teca, had been surprised to learn how little the estate was
worth but accepted the explanations of its administrator, Fernando. When she discovered, in early 1927, that her older brother had
in fact misused estate monies and concocted a story to cover up his
deed, she flew into a rage, then settled into a sullen indignation. Though
he was sorry to have upset her, there is no evidence that Pessoa ever
repented of his behavior, which was part of a pattern. His rejection of
truth and sincerity as self-evident and sacrosanct categories had consequences not only for his creative writing; it also influenced his creative
handling of personal finances. Entries from the diaries he kept in 1913
and 1915 reveal that when family money passed through his hands, it
ran the risk of being slightly trimmed in his favor, as if he were entitled
to a commission.

Pessoa had exercised power of attorney over his mother's finances
since 1919, and while he may not have actually siphoned off funds, he
seems to have used some of her investment capital as collateral for loans
he was unable to repay in a timely manner. It was these loans, I suspect,
that had covered the publishing costs of the Olisipo press. Pessoa would
later claim, in a letter to his two brothers, that he had been forced to
borrow against the estate for reasons he was not at liberty to disclose.
And he implied that the estate monies, although legally tied up, were not
actually lost. Perhaps they believed him.[1]

With Teca's silent recriminations pervading the atmosphere at Rua
Coelho da Rocha, Pessoa had more reason than ever to make himself
at home in the offices where he wrote business letters in English and
French. He had the keys to three or four different offices, so that he
could go there after hours, to work in complete privacy on his own writing. Empty bottles next to the desk where he sat and cigarette ashes
fallen between the typewriter keys were the telltale signs that he had

used the office during the night or on the weekend. Pessoa's employers had no interest in reading his poetry but seem to have been delighted that he wrote some of it on their premises, making them passive patrons of the arts. Toscano & Company, an importer of motors, machinery, and automobiles, was the firm where he worked the longest, from around the time he met Ophelia Queiroz until his death sixteen years later. Pessoa's archives contain poems and passages from *The Book of Disquiet* typed on stationery from this and many other firms.[2]

Pessoa also worked for more than a dozen years—beginning in 1922 or 1923—at Moitinho de Almeida, Ltd., an import-export firm at Rua da Prata, 71, conveniently located between his favorite café, Martinho da Arcada, and an outlet of Abel Pereira da Fonseca, a distributor of wines and spirits, which could be consumed by the glass at the counter.[3] Several times in the course of an afternoon, Pessoa would stand up from his typewriter, straighten his jacket and his glasses, put on his hat, and announce to the employees, "I'm going to Abel's," where he downed a glass of red wine or brandy.

One day he made so many trips to Abel's that the boss's son, a high school student who was often at the office during school holidays, had the temerity to observe: "You can hold it like a sponge!"

"Like a sponge?" Pessoa countered. "Like a store full of sponges, with an adjacent warehouse."

The boss, Carlos Moitinho de Almeida, raised no objections to Pessoa's alcoholic interludes, since they put him in a better mood, and he tolerated the letter writer's refusal to follow a fixed schedule: Pessoa showed up when he felt like it. His legendary mastery of English, specifically business English, guaranteed that he was in high demand in spite of his peculiarities, and his work was indeed excellent, provided he faithfully translated what was dictated. Given the chance, however, Pessoa became literary, injecting too much wit and even vaguely philosophical reflections in letters whose real purpose was to inquire about prices, availability, shipping terms, and payment schedules.

Employers also appreciated Pessoa for being absolutely trustworthy. As his sister might have told them, it was a reputation he did not entirely deserve. Although he would never brazenly cheat or steal, he was not above "borrowing" ideas for business deals, the way he borrowed literary ideas, making them his own. Such was the case with the lucrative business of representing foreign tobacco firms to the Companhia dos Tabacos, the state-sanctioned monopoly that had the exclusive right to purchase, mill, and sell leaf tobacco in Portugal.[4]

Since Moitinho de Almeida was the agent for half a dozen foreign suppliers of tobacco to the monopoly, Pessoa, the trusted employee who handled all the pertinent correspondence, had become intimately acquainted with the not very transparent system for awarding purchase contracts. Armed with this knowledge, he wrote an audacious letter on January 6, 1927, in which he proposed to act as an agent for the Burley Tobacco Growers' Co-operative. In thirteen typed, single-spaced pages—mailed to the cooperative's head office in Lexington, Kentucky, as well as to its European office, in Brussels—he described in detail the history and workings of the monopoly, explained that he had successfully "deciphered" the "occult conditions" governing the purchase of foreign tobacco, and assured his prospective client that he possessed "the influence and the inner knowledge" necessary to represent it or any other tobacco firm vis-à-vis the Companhia dos Tabacos. After transcribing several pages of "secretly and confidentially" procured information about recent, successful bids for purchase contracts, Pessoa went on to explain, in a section of his letter bizarrely subtitled "The Inner Technique of Purchases," that the award of such contracts basically depended on three or four individuals, at least one of whom he had good connections with, or so he implied. He proposed a 5 percent commission on the sale price should he, as Burley's agent, successfully land a purchase contract.

Presented with this semi-esoteric, semi-Sherlockian account of Portugal's tobacco trade, the Burley office in Brussels cautiously replied that no decision could be made except in consultation with the head office in Lexington. Pessoa quickly wrote back to say that a Portuguese businessman named Mr. Moitinho de Almeida would soon travel to Brussels and no doubt call on them to propose himself as their agent. This gentleman, Pessoa clarified, was a competitor with whom he had no connection. Playing with fire, he assumed that the Burley tobacco cooperative would not reveal to his boss that it had already been approached by another agent from Portugal, namely Mr. Fernando Pessoa. Or did he sign his letters to the cooperative with the name of a heteronym? Possibly so, since his own name does not appear on the carbon copies of the letters that have survived. And what if Moitinho de Almeida were to discover that his chronically cash-strapped, freelance employee had succeeded in cutting a profitable deal by outsmarting him? Perhaps he would have been more glad than vexed. No deal resulted from Pessoa's intrigues, however.[5]

◆

STARTING IN MID-JUNE 1927, Pessoa was again living alone. Teca and her family moved to Évora, a provincial capital where her husband, Francisco Caetano Dias, had been transferred as a disciplinary measure, for having talked about a high-ranking officer with a subordinate. It was a sweet revenge for the aggrieved officer, as the guilty captain had to serve at his new post, which he thoroughly despised, for three full years.[6] Évora, an ancient town where part of a Roman temple still stands, is less than seventy-five miles east of Lisbon, but in those days it took five hours to get there by train. It was a long time before Fernando would make that journey, since Teca was still furious at him for his duplicitous handling of their mother's estate. But she and her husband and their daughter occasionally came to Lisbon.

While it was a relief to no longer have to confront his sister's censorious glances on a daily basis, her family's absence from Lisbon could only reinforce Pessoa's feeling of isolation. His brothers, whose college education had consumed a large chunk of the estate when their mother was still living, had no reason to feel cheated out of money, but he avoided writing them, knowing that Teca counted on their solidarity. Preferring not to make further excuses for his financial misconduct, all he could do was wait for her to forgive him. He remained in regular contact with his cousins Mário and Maria, their spouses, and their children; he had his circle of friends; and there were the offices where he wrote letters and was treated a little bit like family by his bosses. Despite having a large and peaceful apartment now completely at his disposal, he continued to do much of his writing at these offices, and not only because of the typewriters and free paper. He liked the predictable, bland atmosphere of wooden desks, wooden chairs, lamps, no bibelots, tidy efficiency, and neatly attired employees—a neutral background for mental journeys to far-off and indefinite places or more focused cogitations, depending on whether he was writing a Ricardo Reis ode addressed to Lydia or a study of Portugal's political future.

The clerical monotony of Moitinho de Almeida, Ltd., was interrupted by the eccentric friends who came by to visit or fetch Pessoa: the whim-sical Augusto Ferreira Gomes, the passionate and excitable Alberto Da Cunha Dias, the metaphysically tortured Raul Leal, and the swagger-ing, affected António Botto. There was a small room where Pessoa could retreat to when he wanted, but he often received his friends in the gen-eral office where the firm's full-time employees all had their desks. The boss's teenage son looked on in fascination. Pessoa, who never discussed his family, did talk to people in the office about certain friends, par-ticularly António Botto, whose voice he imitated by talking in a high-pitched lisp.[7]

◆

LIKE A FEW OTHER notable writers, including F. Scott Fitzgerald, who had recently published *The Great Gatsby*, Pessoa used his flair for words to supplement his income as a copywriter, but with mixed results. His publicity slogans and ad copy, like his business letters, were some-times too creative, or too literary. Between 1925 and 1935 Manuel Mar-tins da Hora, cofounder of Portugal's first advertising agency, engaged Pessoa to handle the firm's correspondence in English and French and also to write advertising copy in Portuguese.[8] It's not clear whether Pes-soa was involved in the ad campaign for the agency's most important client, General Motors, but he paid homage to the carmaker in an onei-ric poem featuring Álvaro de Campos at the wheel of a Chevrolet in the middle of the night on the road to Sintra, some twenty miles west of Lisbon.

The Hora Agency had another client from Detroit, the manufacturer of Berryloid, advertised in the United States as a high-luster lacquer for motorcars and airplanes. In Portugal it was marketed only for cars, and Pessoa was asked to write the copy for an illustrated advertising bro-chure. So literary is the text he wrote that one of his posthumous editors has published it as a short story.[9] The brochure's narrator begins his tale by telling how repeated washings caused all the paint from his once blue automobile to rub off onto his chamois cloth, resulting in an unwanted "transfusion of blue blood" and a car body suffering from "anemia." Paint, he notes, "should be attached like hair, not subject to flights of freedom, like a wig." At wits' end, he consults a professional car washer, asking him to recommend a "faithful and undivorceable" paint for his by now colorless vehicle. And so forth. The brochure was amusing, but potential customers had to read three hundred words of text before seeing Berryloid mentioned for the first time.

Pessoa knew how to be poetically concise, of course, and he used this capacity to invent clever slogans, some of which helped sell girdles and corsets for Pompadour, a Portuguese manufacturer. In the case of Coca-Cola, however, his cleverness backfired. Like Berryloid, Coca-Cola was imported from the United States by Moitinho de Almeida and advertised by the Hora Agency. The ad campaign began in early July 1927 with a teaser in several newspapers stating that "the famous American beverage" was on its way to Portugal. The following week, readers were informed that Coca-Cola was now on sale at Lisbon's "chic" cafés and eateries, and then, in mid-July, Coca-Cola ads appeared with Pessoa's slogan: "On the first day you drink it slow. On the fifth day you can't say no." Or, translating more literally: "On the first day it tastes odd. On the fifth day it takes hold."[10]

The ad campaign continued and the drink sold at a good clip until, in the fall, its importation was abruptly embargoed. This was probably a protectionist measure, to encourage national industries and help curb the country's trade deficit, but when American authorities pressed the Portuguese government for a justification of the ban, pointing out that Portugal's own testing of the product showed that it did not contain cocaine, it was the minister of health who offered an irrefutable argument against it. Either it contained hard-to-detect traces of cocaine, which was an illegal substance, or it contained no cocaine and was guilty of false advertising—more flagrantly guilty in Portugal than in English-speaking countries, since the Portuguese word for "cocaine" is *coca*. The minister cited Pessoa's slogan, calling it an unacceptable "invitation to addiction."[11]

Coca-Cola, thanks in part to Fernando Pessoa, would not be sold in Portugal for the next fifty years.

◆

WHILE THE AMERICAN SOFT DRINK, with the help of Pessoa's rhymed slogan, was quenching the thirst of curious Lisboners in the summer of 1927, a new conspiracy was under way to try to bring down the government. Unlike the putsch mounted by liberal republicans six months earlier, the August coup attacked the military dictatorship from the right. Strangely enough, one of the leaders of the conspiracy was the new head librarian of the National Library, Fidelino de Figueiredo (1889–1967), who had been hired just a few months earlier to replace Jaime Cortesão, one of the key conspirators behind the February putsch. The other leader of the August coup was Filomeno da Câmara (1873–1934), a naval officer and right-wing extremist. Owing to the "Fi" in the names of both leaders, their ill-conceived rebellion was deliciously christened the Revolt of the Fifis, and it went forth with all the ferocity of a lapdog. Few army officers paid heed to the manifesto issued by the Fifis, and those who did were speedily arrested and banished to Africa.

Also arrested was António Ferro, who was accused of abetting Câmara, the prefacer of Ferro's recently published book of interviews, which focused on the authoritarian regimes in Spain, Turkey, and Italy.[12] Câmara used the preface to heap praise on Mussolini, whose methods he wanted to introduce into Portugal, with himself as the nation's dictator. Ferro would gladly have played a role in Câmara's government had the Fifis prevailed, but there was no evidence that he had actually conspired with them. After being questioned by the authorities, he was released from jail and got on with his career as a globe-trotting interviewer not only of autocrats and politicians but also of writers, artists, fashion designers, and movie stars. On a recent trip to America he had interviewed Mary Pickford in Hollywood and Calvin Coolidge in the White House.

Opposed by some for ruling Portugal without any lawful basis and by others for not ruling like unapologetic autocrats, the generals in charge were not having an easy time of it. Toward the end of 1927, Geraldo Coelho de Jesus, who considered political stability a sine qua non for Portugal's economy to flourish, implored Pessoa to write a manifesto in defense of the military government as an interim solution clearly in the nation's best interest.[13] Since the generals, by crushing the Fifis, had dispelled Pessoa's earlier fear that they might embrace fascist ideology, he was quite willing to defend their dictatorial regime as a necessary, temporary expedient, and it pleased him to indulge Coelho de Jesus, his least literary but most materially generous friend. The result was an eight-thousand-word manifesto that filled seven large pages, printed under the auspices of the impressive-sounding National Action Committee, which, as we have seen, was a figment of the two friends' imagination, existing in name only.

In this case the name proved useful, since it allowed Pessoa to remain anonymous—or it would have allowed that, had the Censorship Commission not prohibited the manifesto from being circulated, for reasons we can only guess at. The way to get around the ban was to publish the manifesto as a booklet by a given author, since books (and booklets) were not subject to prepublication censorship. Pessoa reluctantly allowed the manifesto to be converted into a thirty-one-page booklet, signed with his name.[14] It was dated January 1928 but not actually issued until March.

Titled *The Interregnum: Defense and Justification of Military Dictatorship in Portugal*, the booklet offered one of Pessoa's most formidable displays of logical analysis and close reasoning. He argued that the Portuguese, half of whom were monarchists and the other half republicans, found themselves at an impasse, and that constitutional democracy—which worked well enough in Great Britain, where it grew out of a "direct, immediate, spontaneous, cohesive and organic public opinion"—had proven unfeasible in Portugal, where there was no comparably robust public opinion, or national consciousness. Portugal needed a new political system, and until that system could be discovered and implemented, a military dictatorship was the only tenable form of government.

Stressing that his defense of dictatorship applied only to the current "State of Transition," he set himself apart from those who favored a long-term authoritarian solution, such as fascism. On the other hand, he did not spell out what kind of political system he supported. He instead teased his readers, saying that *The Interregnum* was only the first, introductory part of a five-part book about what "could or should be the future Portugal" and that the next three parts would take up, in turn, the Portuguese Nation, the Portuguese State, and Portuguese Society. About part five he was evasive, saying only that it was the "most important" part.

Pessoa wrote none of the promised continuation of his book about "the future Portugal," but it is easy enough to deduce that the fifth part would have discussed its apotheosis as the world's Fifth Empire. He concluded his *Interregnum* by affirming that no one else—in Portugal or outside it—had the "soul and mind" to be able to write the booklet he had just written and that this was the "First Sign," duly revealed "in the promised Hour." Translation: Fernando Pessoa, if not himself the returned King Sebastian, was the herald of his return, a sign to Portugal that the Fifth Empire was about to dawn.

In April 1928, one month after *The Interregnum* was published, Fritz

Lang's *Metropolis* premiered in Lisbon at the São Luiz Theater.[15] If by chance Pessoa went to see the film, he may have found its portrayal of a dystopian future—where oppressed workers run the underground machines that power the aboveground world of a smiling elite—too simplistic, too deterministic in its suggestion that machines were bound to increase rather than alleviate the misery of the masses. But at least it was a portrayal, at least it could be visualized. The political, economic, and social dynamics of the Fifth Empire future he prophesied for Portugal were all shrouded in indefinition.

◆

APPARENTLY CONVINCED BY HIS own argument that Portugal was at a crossroads, that some change was at hand, Pessoa became exaggeratedly attentive to signs, in which he saw much more than would a normal observer or a typical patriot. Several months after the publication of *The Interregnum*, which was largely ignored by the Portuguese press, the government announced that the first printed copy of a new and rigorous "national edition" of *The Lusiads*, by Luís de Camões, would be presented to the president of Brazil. This sixteenth-century epic poem about Vasco da Gama's maiden voyage to India is for the Portuguese a foundational text of national identity (as *The Aeneid* was for the Romans), a hymn to Portugal's golden age of maritime supremacy. Afonso Lopes Vieira, the poet and scholar responsible for the new edition, would himself cross the ocean to present, in Rio de Janeiro, the fruit of his labors. It was a symbolically weighty undertaking, which Pessoa freighted with still more symbolic, mystical significance.

On June 3, the same day that Lopes Vieira and his edition set sail, Pessoa anonymously published an article about his overseas "mission" as the bearer of "the sign of hope common to all that is Portugal," a nation that included "New Portugal," by which he meant Brazil, as well as "Old Portugal." Portugal, thus conceived, extended far beyond its territorial homeland in southwestern Europe. Although he elsewhere claimed that the author of *The Lusiads* was overrated, in this article Pessoa styled him the "singer of King Sebastian," and he wrote that Afonso Lopes Vieira was an apostle of Sebastianism, whether he knew it or not. As part of the ceremonies surrounding his departure to Brazil, the Camões specialist had delivered a lecture on *The Lusiads* five days earlier, May 29, which was not just another date on the calendar. Pessoa informed his readers that, according to the calculations of a renowned pyramidologist, May 29, 1928, marked the beginning of a new era in world history.[16]

Pessoa, it so happened, had recently purchased a book called *The Great Pyramid: Its Divine Message*, written by a devout Christian who had deciphered a time line of world history supposedly encoded in the pyramid's passageways and chambers—with each inch of pyramid corresponding to a solar year. Amid the book's wealth of diagrams and explanatory text, Pessoa was intrigued to discover that the "Last Time" had begun in 1557 and that the "Final Tribulation"—a period of worldwide troubles before the Second Coming of Christ—would begin on May 29, 1928.[17] Dispensing with the author's Christian bias, Pessoa interpreted the prophecies he had extracted from the Great Pyramid in light of his own, Sebastianist brand of millennialism. He pointed out that the inception of the "Last Time," 1557, was the very year when Sebastian, at the tender age of three, succeeded to the Portuguese throne. This led him to conclude that the beginning of the "Final Tribulation" heralded not the imminent Second Coming of Christ but the Second Coming of King Sebastian. According to this view, Portugal's current "State of Transition," as Pessoa defined the military dictatorship in his *Interregnum*, could be considered a brief time of troubles, or tribulation, before Sebastian's triumphant return.

Had Pessoa been endowed with a talent for writing blockbuster fiction, he could have woven these and other details into a Portuguese precursor of Dan Brown's *The Da Vinci Code*. The "other details" needed to flesh out his fantastical story of Portugal's imminent regeneration were revealed a few days later.

On June 8, less than a week after the special copy of *The Lusiads* had embarked on its symbolic voyage to the "New Portugal," Pessoa read in the *Diário de Notícias*[18] that the hillside town of Silves, capital of the Algarve when it was ruled by the Moors, was planning to unveil a memorial plaque to Al-Mu'tamid ibn Abbad (1040–1095), a poet-king of Seville who was partly raised in Silves. Once more Pessoa took to the printed word, suggesting in a pair of articles published in *O "Notícias" Ilustrado* (*The "News" Illustrated*), a weekly magazine, that the noble spirit of this highly cultured Iberian ruler, who had lived on both sides of the line that would later divide Spain and Portugal, was an energizing influence destined to chase away the "fatal torpor" of the present. Pessoa, in effect, was announcing the advent of his ideal Fifth Empire, which had a Portuguese heart but extended to the rest of Iberia as well as to Brazil and other lands historically connected to Portugal.

The second article (both were written by Pessoa but signed by Augusto Ferreira Gomes, a staff writer for the magazine) quoted the contents of a delirious letter supposedly sent by the Sebastianist Order, an organization no one had ever heard of. The letter explained that some fourteen years earlier, in March 1914, the masters of this mysterious order had met with a special emissary sent to Portugal by a no less mysterious Pagan Council, with whom they reached a "supreme agreement" to bring about a revival of the "Arab spirit" in its true pagan splendor—a revival symbolized by the plaque in honor of Al-Mu'tamid that was about to be unveiled in Silves.[19] Thus Pessoa, the real author of the letter from the fictitious Sebastianist Order, reinforced the idea that Portugal was on the threshold of a new historical era.

Suddenly, unexpectedly, the poet's long-cherished hopes for a neo-pagan revival, the return of King Sebastian, and the commencement of the Fifth Empire were being fulfilled—*because he fulfilled them*, enacting them with the help of his literary personalities and his friend Ferreira Gomes. It was a spectacle put on by a small cast of characters for a thoroughly bewildered audience, since the readers of O *"Notícias" Ilustrado* would have no inkling that the members of the Sebastianist Order were Fernando Pessoa and his heteronyms, who began to emerge in March 1914 with a burst of poems signed by Alberto Caeiro.

Pessoa, whose body showed signs of aging but whose imagination could still do somersaults, was repeating a stunt that went back to his boyhood, when he conferred a social reality on Dr. Pancrácio and his other juvenile personae by having them "publish" in make-believe news-papers—*The Tattler* and *The Word*—distributed to his family. Although the magazine where he published his Sebastianist and neo-pagan fantasies in 1928 was quite real, the stunt was essentially the same. Despite being complete fabrications, the Sebastianist Order and the Pagan Council registered in the minds of the magazine's readers as something scarcely intelligible but nevertheless as *something*, thereby acquiring a public reality.

All of which—his elaborate theorizations, rationalizations, and fabrications—shows us to what lengths Pessoa could go to amuse himself. It also shows us just how devoted he was to the myth of Sebastianism. In or around 1920 he wrote: "I want to be a creator of myths, which is the highest mystery achievable by a member of the human race."[20] His family of heteronyms was one of the myths he created; his personalized versions of Sebastianism and the Fifth Empire were others.

Did he believe in these myths? This is a little like asking if God the Creator believes in his, her, or its creations. Pessoa believed in all seriousness that it was his destiny, his purpose, his nature at its most sublime, to forge the myths he forged. His seriousness was tempered, or counterbalanced, by an infallible sense of humor. "God is God's best joke," a phrase written by Pessoa in English, strikes us upon a first reading as a mere witticism; it was actually a summary of his personal theology.[21]

# CHAPTER 58

I N 1928, THE YEAR PESSOA TURNED FORTY, THE
problem of his uncertain destiny as a writer and the problem of
Portugal's glorious but nebulous Fifth Empire future competed so
keenly and closely for his attention that they almost seemed like the
very same problem. Meanwhile the real and present nation of Portugal had taken a seemingly innocuous turn that would have profound
and long-lasting consequences. In April 1928 António de Oliveira Salazar, a highly respected economics professor at the University of Coimbra
School of Law, was named finance minister of Portugal.

Born one year after Pessoa in a small town north of Coimbra, Salazar,
like many Portuguese boys from poorish families, was sent to a Roman
Catholic seminary for his middle and high school education, which duly
prepared him for the priesthood, though he never took more than minor
orders. Dour in appearance and Catholic to the core, he knew exactly
what he believed and what the world needed—faith, moral guidance,
and the spirit of sacrifice—to go forward. Although timid in social situations, just like Pessoa, and like him a lifelong bachelor, he abounded
in self-confidence and patient determination for pursuing his objectives,
qualities that were often wanting in the poet.

Salazar had been appointed finance minister once before, as soon as
the military seized control of the government in 1926, but he resigned
within two weeks, after the first of the countercoups that ultimately left
Generals Carmona and Sinel de Cordes in charge. The latter general,
tasked with handling Portugal's economy, steered it badly off course,
causing the national debt to bloat even more and pushing the country to
the brink of bankruptcy. Salazar was brought in to fix things but accepted
the job only on the condition that he be granted extraordinary powers
to oversee and restrict government spending, thus making him more
powerful than the prime minister. His appointment was part of a cabinet reshuffle following the election of Carmona, on March 25, 1928, as

the nation's president. Carmona's election was a pro forma exercise—he ran unopposed—designed to legitimize the military dictatorship; Salazar would slowly and successfully maneuver to transform it into a civilian dictatorship, with himself as the sole ruling power.

During the 1920s the number of cars in Portugal—though still relatively small—increased sixfold, resulting in frequent injuries to pedestrians, since rules for driving had not been well defined or enforced.[*] Shortly after Carmona was elected president and Salazar appointed finance minister, a major change in those rules took effect: as of June 1, 1928, motorists, accustomed to driving on the left side of the road, were obliged to keep to the right, as in most of the rest of continental Europe. Newspapers dutifully forewarned their readers of the change, and on May 31 *Sempre Fixe*, the satirical weekly, illustrated its front page with a barefoot newsboy calling out to the nation that traffic would now keep "to the right, to the right, to the right, to the right," a phrase repeated eleven times in all. The political message was clear, and as a prophecy it proved accurate: Portugal's politically moderate dictatorship veered to the right in 1928.

For the new finance minister to achieve what he achieved, it could not have been otherwise. On July 31 Salazar proposed a balanced budget by sharply raising taxes and drastically cutting the public payroll, pensions, and other expenditures. Only a hard-line authoritarian government could swiftly and uniformly implement such measures, which were especially harsh on those already just scraping by. Many politicians reacted to the budget with disbelief, for its arithmetic seemed too impossibly simple, yet Portugal would end the fiscal year with an even larger surplus than predicted. The more prosperous classes, not just low-wage earners, also paid the price for this success. Easy money dried up, which partly accounts for why the high-living, free-spending mentality of the twenties died an earlier death in Lisbon than in other European capitals.

Even before Salazar came to town, the ruling generals had been applying pressure to squelch the fun, much of which was connected to gambling. Determined to establish strict rules governing this activity, in April 1927 the minister of the interior invited the general public to com-

---

[*] *Diário de Lisboa*, 14 Jan. 1928, p. 4. By 1930 there would be around 20,000 automobiles in Portugal, around 200,000 in Spain, and more than 25 million in the United States.

ment on his proposal for a gaming law. Pessoa, who had probably never entered a gambling hall, argued in an article published on the front page of the *Diário de Notícias* that gambling was a vice comparable to alcohol, and as such should be controlled but not completely outlawed.[1] As usual, he was defending people's right to run their own lives, even if that meant recklessly driving themselves into financial ruin. There were unfortunately many men who were ruining their families, not just themselves, as newspapers and politicians had been pointing out for a long time, and in December 1927 gambling in Lisbon was summarily banned.

This was tantamount to cutting off oxygen from the city's nightclubs, which were forced to shut down one by one,[2] including even the swanky Bristol Club, which in 1926 had been remodeled and decorated with paintings and sculptures by Portugal's finest contemporary artists: José de Almada Negreiros, Eduardo Viana, António Soares, and others.[3] The Bristol Club had a jazz band, a dance floor, shows, and fine dining, but it was the gambling hall that brought in the revenue needed to sustain this and other stylish clubs. Roulette, keno, and thirty-one (not to be confused with twenty-one) were some of the most popular games.

Gambling was still allowed in casinos, usually located at seaside resorts and catering to the moneyed class. In Estoril, which is close to Cascais, a huge hotel and casino were being built as part of an extravagant project to make the so-called Costa do Sol, or Sun Coast—with its plentiful sand, blue waters, and mild temperatures—a competitive alternative to the French Riviera. Pessoa, perhaps at the request of the Hora Agency, outlined a strategy to promote this stretch of coastline for the foreign and domestic markets. Abstract and theoretical, his plan was of little use to promoters, but the luxurious tourist facilities that finally took shape were at any rate hugely successful.[4] The Estoril Palácio Hotel and the Casino Estoril, whose doors opened for business in 1930 and 1931, quickly attracted the rich and glamorous from Europe and beyond. But the prohibition of gambling in Lisbon killed off nightlife for the smart set. Without clubs such as the Bristol, late-night dancers, drinkers, flappers, and jazz enthusiasts suddenly had nowhere to go.

✦

SALAZAR, FOR WHOM NIGHTCLUBS were dens of iniquity and their extinction a godly blessing for society, maintained the same frugal and methodical lifestyle in Lisbon that he had observed in Coimbra. His lack of humor and panache worked in his favor, conferring credibility on his no-nonsense program of fixing the nation's economy like a knowledgeable mechanic repairing a broken-down car. The country was still weary of colorful politicians who delivered nothing but rousing speeches and personal favors. Although he did not conquer hearts like a Sidónio Pais, Salazar won people's trust, convincing them that he was the right man for the job. Pessoa was one of the convinced,[5] even if the new finance minister—steadfast in his opinions, impatient with theoretical niceties, and blind to his own limitations—had a personality type that he instinctively disdained.

Pessoa was disdainful of most politicians, for the simple reason that they were what he called "men of action." Men of action are necessary, he acknowledged, since without them the world would stagnate, but by imposing their will they knowingly or unknowingly do violence to others. And they do violence to themselves. "Action is a disease of thought, a cancer of the imagination. Action is self-exile." These words are from *The Book of Disquiet*, whose narrator, in yet another passage, claims that "the dreamer gets far greater and more varied pleasure out of life than does the man of action."[6]

That may be true for as long as the dreamer is dreaming, but what about the rest of the time? Dreams are hard to sustain, especially when no signs of their fulfillment are forthcoming. Pessoa envied, as much as he disdained, the "man of action."

"Tabacaria" ("The Tobacco Shop"), written on January 15, 1928, plays out a drama that Pessoa had been living from an early age, always vacillating between the world of action in which he physically moved and his inner world of dreams. Tethered to that conflict of allegiances was the lifelong question of his genius (true genius, he wondered, or a fanciful delusion?) and his concomitant duty to do something with it (but what, and for whom?). The poetic enactor of his drama, Álvaro de Campos, announces at the outset that he is nothing and will always be nothing but immediately counters this dire self-appraisal with the observation that he is simultaneously everything, in his imagination. As the poem unfolds, we see Campos moving back and forth between a chair, where he sinks into his thought life, and a window that looks out onto the street, where life in this world—represented by the tobacco shop just opposite—beckons.

On this particular day, in this particular poem, the visible, practical life that thrives on doing and accomplishment seems to have won out over the imaginary life. Campos admits, about a third of the way through the poem, that genius without works to show for it is as good as nonexistent:

> The world is for those born to conquer it,
> Not for those who dream they can conquer it, even if they're right.
> I've done more in dreams than Napoleon.
> I've held more humanities against my hypothetical breast than Christ.
> I've secretly invented philosophies such as Kant never wrote.
> But I am, and perhaps will always be, the man in the garret,
> Even though I don't live in one.
> I'll always be *the one who wasn't born for that*;
> I'll always be merely *the one who had qualities*;
> I'll always be the one who waited for a door to open in a wall without doors
> And sang the song of the Infinite in a chicken coop
> And heard the voice of God in a covered well.
> Believe in me? No, not in anything.

Although the poem is inspired by Pessoa's own feelings of inadequacy and conflicted relationship with the world of useful, abundant, and even enviable productivity, those feelings and that conflict are dramatically exaggerated in Álvaro de Campos, whose tale of self-defeat Pessoa sets out to overcome, by converting it into a vivid demonstration of his poetic excellence. Like other towering moments in his literary output, "The Tobacco Shop" is Pessoa's revenge against his inability to adapt to life and to simply "be himself," if he could only figure out what that self is. In one of the poem's stanzas, after recounting how he went through life wearing the wrong costume, being someone he wasn't, with a mask he pried off his face but only after it was too late, the naval engineer concludes his litany by remarking, with self-mockery: "And I'll write down this story to prove I'm sublime." The actual author of the poem, however, clearly knew that he was writing in a state of creative grace and that the resulting work of art was indeed sublime.

No sooner had Pessoa finished his poem than he revived, yet again, his plans for a new incarnation of *Orpheu*, where "The Tobacco Shop" would have featured as the contribution from Álvaro de Campos.[7] But quickly his *Orpheu* plans sank back, yet again, into dormancy, and for five years the poet, like a jealous lover, held on to his stunningly poignant Campos poem, as he had held on to his Caeiro poems and Reis odes for years before finally including selections from both heteronyms in *Athena*. He eventually submitted "The Tobacco Shop" to *Presença*, whose editors published it in their July 1933 issue:

> I'm nothing.
> I'll always be nothing.
> I can't want to be something.
> But I have in me all the dreams of the world.
>
> Windows of my room,
> The room of one of the world's millions nobody knows
> (And if they knew me, what would they know?),
> You open onto the mystery of a street continually crossed by
>     people,
> A street inaccessible to any and every thought,
> Real, impossibly real, certain, unknowingly certain,
> With the mystery of things beneath the stones and beings,
> With death making the walls damp and the hair of men white,
> With Destiny driving the wagon of everything down the road
>     of nothing.[8]

And on it goes, for fifteen more stanzas of wildly different lengths, rhythmically reproducing the fits and starts of the poet's anguished reflections. It was an anthem of despair, sublime despair, and the greatest poem *Presença* would ever publish.

◆

"THE TOBACCO SHOP" WAS followed by a dozen more Campos poems, a dozen odes of Ricardo Reis, and close to twenty poems written under Pessoa's own name—all in the first six months of 1928. It was an impressive run, Pessoa the poet was now flourishing, but he continued to be bedeviled by his chronic incapacity for organizing his poems into coherent collections and for concluding his half-written prose works. Projects launched ten, fifteen, or even twenty years ago—plays such as

*Fausto* and *Prometheus Rebound*, or Caeiro's *The Keeper of Sheep*—still popped up in his publication plans, as if jostling for attention, and their author sometimes returned to these works, but without any of them getting any closer to a terminus. Another writer in this same predicament might have tried out some sort of therapy for becoming more self-disciplined, more committed to finishing whatever he started. Pessoa had a different way of dealing with his frustration: he embodied it in a new heteronym, the Baron of Teive, whose character traits were closely modeled after selected traits in Pessoa, even though their outer lives had little in common.

The story of Álvaro Coelho de Athayde, the 14th Baron of Teive, begins with his suicide—Pessoa does not tell us whether by hanging, gunshot, or strychnine—and the manuscript he left behind to explain why he resorted to that extreme expedient. There were various, interconnected reasons, but the one that stands out in the first passages written for *O único manuscrito do Barão de Teive* (*The Only Manuscript of the Baron of Teive*) is his inability to write complete works of literature. Though he had filled up page after page with ingenious ideas, striking sentences, and witty sayings, he lacked the patience or skill to tie them all together into fluid, satisfying narratives. And so he burned them all, which was why his final manuscript to explain his actions would be his *only* manuscript. Pessoa, never that courageous, saved most of his manuscripts, but his attempts to write fiction and theater were as disappointing as the baron's. The many fragmentary stories and plays that have been extracted from his archives by dedicated decipherers of his sometimes hieroglyphic handwriting can make for interesting reading, provided we appreciate them for their curious ideas, flashes of insight, and expressive language, caring not at all about plot, narrative structure, scenic description, and character development—provided, in other words, that we do not approach them as stories or plays.

The self-analyzing baron blamed his shortcomings as a writer both on his "lukewarm will to make the enormous effort that a finished whole requires" and on his "perfectionist instinct," which, instead of stimulating action, led to renunciation. "My pride," he wrote, "won't let me settle for less than my mind is capable of."[9] Like Monsieur Teste, the alter ego of Paul Valéry (1871–1945) who was all mind and no emotion (*teste* is the Old French word for "head"), the Baron of Teive had an exaggerated confidence in the power of his own intellect. Valéry, who jotted down the occasional opinions of the ultrarational M. Teste in his notebooks over a span of fifty years, once commented that this abstract gentleman couldn't have survived in the real world for more than a few quarters of an hour.[10] The Baron of Teive couldn't even survive in the world of fiction. He tried to live off reason alone but concluded, when he decided on suicide, that this was an impossible ambition. Pessoa, too, was beginning to question his reliance on reason. The specter of hereditary madness had haunted the poet for many years after the death of his demented grandmother, but by 1928 he was worried about an opposite problem: too much lucidity. Although he felt immensely and intensely, reason ruled, keeping his emotions in check, bridled. He let them run with Álvaro de Campos, which resulted in some powerful poetry; in real life he was ever the polite, somewhat peculiar gentleman, uneffusive and inscrutable.

The baron had been raised in rural luxury and lived for a time in Paris, where he frequented the French nobility and fought in a duel; some time later, unlucky in health, he had to have his left leg amputated. Pessoa's life, except for his youthful voyages to Africa, was comparatively uneventful, but there are notable coincidences in the two men's trajectories. Pampered to his heart's content as a child, the nobleman recalls that all he really wanted in his early years was to be left alone. Pessoa was likewise a spoiled and solitary young boy, quite content to entertain himself. The baron's mother died when he was already a full-grown man, and only then did he fully realize how much she had loved him and how he needed affection in his life. So it was for Pessoa, in relation to his own mother.

Missing out on sex as well as on affection, the baron berates himself for having always found excuses not to seduce one of the willing housemaids who worked at his country estate. Besides the housemaids, there was a girl he could have married who might, he admitted, have made him happy, but she was a commoner and he worried about being laughed at. The baron's wistful remembrance of this lost opportunity recalls the parenthetical aside made by Álvaro de Campos in the penultimate stanza of "The Tobacco Shop":

(If I married my washwoman's daughter,
Perhaps I would be happy.)

As for Pessoa himself, he did not regret having broken off with Ophelia Queiroz, but he remembered her attentions with tenderness and still harbored a fuzzy, intermittent fantasy of one day getting married. In the spring of 1924, an astral communication had assured him that marriage was still in his future.[11]

Back in 1916, when the astral spirits were in regular, loquacious contact with Pessoa, Henry More—his astral master—had warned him that his chastity could have disastrous consequences, making him "morally impotent," an incomplete man, and thus unable to produce "any complete work in literature." The Baron of Teive, who was as incapable of sexually realizing himself with women as he was of finishing any of the works of literature he started, illustrated the truth of Henry More's theorem. His missing leg "stood," as it were, for both his manly and literary incompetence.

"I kept my distance from life and the world," wrote the Baron of Teive, who did not on that account feel sad at heart. Rather: "My heart feels like an inorganic weight"—a weight he had always insisted on bearing stoically, without complaint. In fact *The Education of the Stoic* was an alternate, ironic title for the baron's final testament before he passed into nonexistence. "I've always valued my consciousness over all the agreeable sensations of my body,"[12] he noted at one point, to explain why he refused to be put to sleep when his leg was amputated, accepting only local anesthesia. Pessoa, no doubt, would have preferred not to witness the gruesome spectacle of his own mutilation, but it perversely amused him to subject his latest heteronym to just such an ordeal. A kind of voodoo doll into which he stuck pins, the Baron of Teive was a blackly humorous, dramatic parody of Pessoa's own lucid and loveless, somewhat detached way of being.

The baron was also a playful incarnation of his maker's pretensions to nobility, which were founded on the fact that he had a few aristocratic ancestors on his father's side, including a certain Dona Leonor Francisca Coelho de Athayde, a seventeenth-century noblewoman whose family name, Coelho de Athayde, was inherited by the baron. Pessoa's fascination with nobility began in childhood. His first infant heteronym was a minor aristocrat, the Chevalier de Pas, and when he was thirteen years old he painted the family coat of arms, based on its description in a Portuguese book of genealogy and heraldry.[13] During the dozen or so years he supported republicanism, Pessoa's interest in his aristocratic roots waned, although one of the three heteronyms he invented in 1914—Ricardo Reis—was an intransigent monarchist. After he himself became a monarchist, in 1919, Pessoa purchased a ring engraved with the same family crest that he had artistically rendered as a boy. Made of silver, he occasionally wore it throughout the rest of his life.[14] If the ring signified pride in his remotely aristocratic roots, the creation of a one-legged, impotent baron who commits suicide poked fun at those same roots. Formidable vehicles for self-expansion, the heteronyms were also instruments of critical and sometimes sardonic self-reflection.

Pessoa wrote the first passages for *The Only Manuscript of the Baron of Teive* in a small black notebook, in August 1928. About twenty in number, they were disconnected, contained incomplete sentences and ideas to be developed, and did not follow a logical narrative sequence. He would deal with fleshing them out and properly linking them together later. Except, of course, that he wouldn't. Later, he would write close to twenty additional passages—long and short, typed and handwritten, focused and not so focused on the original themes. And so the Baron of Teive's "only manuscript," which was supposed to succinctly explain why, in despair, he had destroyed all his previous manuscripts and was going to take his own life, became yet another of the unwieldy, unfinished literary works that drove him to commit suicide in the first place. It also became a source of mild exasperation for Pessoa scholars. Hard to piece together, and containing passages that are diabolically hard to decipher, not until the end of the century, in 1999, would the baron's troubled opus finally be published in its entirety.[15]

◆

IF THE FARCICAL TRAGEDY of an artistically frustrated and sexually inept nobleman who thought too much could not provide Pessoa with a true catharsis, it was at least an amusing distraction, diminishing the burden of certain personal obsessions and freeing up his mind for other contemplations. And the death of the tormented baron was followed by a kind of resurrection, with Pessoa rising up—transfigured—as the Portuguese nation. On the last page of the notebook where he created the Baron of Teive and condemned him to die, Pessoa wrote an outline for *Portugal*, the book of Portuguese poetry that he would publish six years later, changing the title at the last minute to *Mensagem* (*Message*). It was a song of the nation but also, inextricably, a song of himself.

It's not certain whether Gustave Flaubert actually said *"Madame Bovary, c'est moi,"* but the words are true insofar as the French novelist, while he bore no resemblance to Emma Bovary, poured into her his creative thought and impassioned emotion. Pessoa, just as truly, might have said *"Portugal, c'est moi!"* to denote his intimate identification with the country of his birth and also with the book he named after it. Like Flaubert's most famous protagonist, Pessoa's Portugal was an entity that existed mainly in him and in his writing. However closely connected it was to the land under his feet, "Portugal" was ultimately a person, a character, a heteronym.

The epic poem titled *Portugal* that Pessoa began writing when he was twenty-one years old had daringly aspired to outdo Camões's master-work, *The Lusiads*, but like many of Pessoa's large-scale projects, it mean-dered and petered out. The *Portugal* conceived by him in September 1928 was also epic, at least in its scope, consisting of short lyric poems that together would narrate Portugal's history from its modest beginnings to its predicted apotheosis as the leader of a Fifth Empire far greater than the Portuguese maritime empire of the 1500s. The book was an expan-sion, toward the past and toward the future, of "Portuguese Sea," the suite of twelve poems (published in *Contemporânea*) about the nation's glory days navigating uncharted oceans to reach lands hitherto unknown to Europeans. "Portuguese Sea" became the middle section of *Portugal*, which would occupy a privileged place in Pessoa's imagination until its publication in the fall of 1934.

Pessoa wrote more than ten poems for the book the world now knows as *Message* in the last four months of 1928, but his enthusiasm for this new project could not dispel the despondent mood that had prompted him to write, at the beginning of the year, "I'm nothing. / I'll always be nothing." On the contrary, his exalted poetic vision of Portugal as it once was and as it was destined to become only accentuated the aura of wea-riness that permeated his days. It wasn't the dreary routine of his rounds among the offices; he liked that routine. Nor was it the loneliness of liv-ing as a bachelor, which did on occasion make him sad, but not weary. It was life itself that wearied him. It was all the doing, feeling, hoping, and regretting of the forty years he had lived so far. It was the nagging sensation that "all is vanity and vexation of spirit," as he remarked in a passage from *The Book of Disquiet*, citing the words of the Preacher of Ecclesiastes. And he also cited, in the same passage, that bleak utterance of Job: "My soul is weary of my life."[16]

# CHAPTER 59

THE WORDS *CANSAÇO* AND *TÉDIO*, WEARINESS and tedium, had for many years been staples in Pessoa's literary vocabulary. Between 1910 and 1913 he wrote three separate poems titled "Tédio," having already concluded that life, no matter how it might unfold, was a tiresome affair. But his tedium was not only a feeling, it was an attitude, inherited from the fin de siècle decadents, who called it *ennui* if they were French. The attitude carried over into passages written for *The Book of Disquiet*, beginning in 1913, and into the poetry of Álvaro de Campos. Toward the end of the 1920s, Pessoa's sense of tedium intensified, becoming a quasi-metaphysical topic of meditation—a meditation inspired by the example of Omar Khayyam (1048–1131), the Persian mathematician, astronomer, and poet.

In 1926 Pessoa had published a trio of rubaiyat in the style of Khayyam, but it was only in the fall of 1928 that he began writing them with élan, usually in concentrated bunches. The first bunch, written on November 22, consisted of six rubaiyat, including this one:

Each day gives me cause to hope
For what no day can ever give me.
Each day makes me weary from hoping . . .
But to live is to hope and to grow weary.

In the original Portuguese, the first, second, and fourth lines rhyme with one another. This was the most common rhyme scheme for a ruba'i, or quatrain, whose simplicity appealed to medieval Persian poets tired of the formal demands of the lengthy, more complexly rhymed poems prescribed by tradition.

Pessoa was at least vaguely familiar with Omar Khayyam when still in Durban, and he thought of translating some of his rubaiyat into Portuguese as early as 1913.[1] The allure of the Persian poet was part of a wider attraction that Middle Eastern culture exerted on Pessoa throughout most of his life. He wrote several poems with Arabian settings and protagonists, and he owned a number of books about Islam, the Middle East, and Persian poetry, including one that was dedicated exclusively to Omar Khayyam. But not until 1928 did he finally purchase a copy of Edward FitzGerald's immensely popular translation, *Rubáiyát of Omar Khayyám*, first published in 1859, which transformed the famous mathematician into a world-renowned poet.[2] That renown is problematical, since only a small number of rubaiyat were undoubtedly written by Khayyam, who has nonetheless been credited with as many as two thousand.

The Persian poet immortalized by the translations of FitzGerald was a religious skeptic with a deterministic view of the world and an acute awareness of life's fleetingness, committed to living only for the pleasures of today. Fernando Pessoa, when writing on Khayyam, imagined him to be a little sadder, less hedonistic. A philosophical fatalist, Pessoa's Khayyam drank neither to be happy nor to forget but "because that was all that was left."[3] Not even love could make him smile on life.

Besides writing close to two hundred of his own Persian-style quatrains, Pessoa translated about forty of Khayyam's rubaiyat from Fitz-Gerald's English into Portuguese.[4] In an unfinished preface that would have accompanied his translations, in the unlikely event of their ever being published, he noted that the "practical philosophy of Khayyam comes down to a mild Epicureanism."[5] Frederico Reis used almost identical words—"a sad Epicureanism"—to describe his brother's philosophy. In fact Ricardo Reis, who counseled peaceful acceptance of whatever destiny the gods mete out in our brief life, was a philosophical cousin of Khayyam the poet as adapted by Pessoa for his own purposes. This was even truer now than when the classicist heteronym first emerged. The poetic scenery of Reis's earliest odes often included the pagan gods of antiquity: Apollo, Saturn, Ceres, Jupiter. . . . By 1928 these and other divinities had all but disappeared, being only occasionally invoked as an anonymous collective ("the Gods"). In their stead Fate itself prevailed directly, irresistibly, and the odes became shorter, more aphoristic, more in the spirit, if not exactly in the style, of the rubaiyat of Omar Khayyam.

The poetry of Álvaro de Campos also changed. Talky theatricality was still his *modus poeticus*, but he had lost his former stamina. "The Tobacco Shop" contains 167 lines, but nearly every poem of his written after 1928 could fit on one page. Pessoa's heteronyms, like Pessoa himself, were getting weary. Only at this point, as the game of heteronymy showed the first signs of winding down, did its inventor finally explain to the public what it was and how it worked.

◆

As **PART OF THEIR** effort to promote Portugal's modernist generation, the young editors of *Presença* published a "Bibliographical Summary" for half a dozen writers whose work they particularly admired: Mário de Sá-Carneiro, Fernando Pessoa, Raul Leal, Mário Saa, José de Almada Negreiros, and António Botto. In most cases they asked the writers themselves to draw up lists of their published works. Pessoa prefaced his list, which appeared in the December 1928 issue, with some background information that included unheard-of literary terminology. Readers learned that his output was divisible into two main categories—*orthonymous* works, signed with his own name, and *heteronymous* works, signed with other names. A heteronymous work involved more than just an invented name, however; it required the author to write "outside his own person," in the voice of a personality created by him but different from him.

Several years would go by before Pessoa referred to his literary alter egos as "heteronyms,"* but he used his "Bibliographical Summary" to introduce the three personalities thus far responsible for his heteronymous works—Alberto Caeiro, Ricardo Reis, and Álvaro de Campos—and observed that they formed "a dramatic ensemble," a drama "divided into people instead of into acts." The intellectual interaction and personal relationships of these three writer-actors would be revealed, he promised, in their "forthcoming biographies," which would include "astrological charts and, perhaps, photographs." Photographs? To further confound the perplexed readers of *Presença*, a parenthetical note affirmed that the "metaphysical problem" of whether Caeiro, Reis, and Campos were more real or less real than Fernando Pessoa was one that he, Pessoa, would never be able to solve. The long, explanatory prologue about the

---

* English dictionaries have traditionally defined "heteronym" as one of two or more words with the same spelling but different pronunciations and meanings, like "wind" (which blows) and "wind" (the clock). Portuguese dictionaries defined *heterónimo*, an adjective, as "pertaining to a work published under another (real) person's name, or to the author of such a work." Pessoa gave the word a new meaning.

writer and his mysterious trinity of collaborators was followed, finally, by a selected list of his "orthonymous" and "heteronymous" publications.

Friends in the loop must have cackled when they read about his plans for illustrated biographies of the heteronyms, but Pessoa actually took steps in that direction. He had already cast the astrological birth charts of Caeiro, Campos, and Reis, and during the next few years he would mentally draw and record, in words, their photographic images—most vividly in the case of Alberto Caeiro, as we shall see. He would also write biographical sketches and prose pieces in which the heteronyms enjoy one another's company and discuss their different points of view on literature and philosophy. Biography is a genre usually reserved for people who have died or whose lives are mostly behind them, and so it was for the heteronyms. Pessoa, who had always been a centrifugal writer, forever spawning new ideas and projects as well as dramatic incarnations to express them, now began turning his focus and energy inward. Though still committed to his fictional others, he was more and more interested in discovering the separate strands of who, perhaps, he really was.

◆

IN NEW YORK, LONDON, Berlin, and Paris the Roaring Twenties—known as the Golden Twenties in Germany and the Crazy Years in France—showed no signs of abatement. The year 1928 had brought continued prosperity not only to the United States, where in November a satisfied electorate handed Commerce Secretary Herbert Hoover a landslide victory in his bid for the presidency, but also to much of Europe, including Germany, where industrial production had recovered to its prewar level and hourly wages were leaping upward.

The situation was different in Portugal, since Salazar's draconian cost-cutting measures had forced most families to shrink their budgets. Lisbon's shops, even so, were as crowded as usual at Christmastime, with shoppers making their money stretch further by purchasing less expensive gifts.[6] Restaurants, theaters, and movie houses all did good business. One special attraction was *Ben-Hur*, a silent epic featuring the "Latin lover" Ramon Novarro, which played on Christmas Eve and again on Christmas Day. Certain newspapers as well as charities received donations to provide food baskets for the poor. And magazines offered the usual assortment of seasonal literature, which included a poem by Fernando Pessoa, published on December 30. Titled "Natal," its speaker imagines rural families celebrating the Christmas holiday in their "cozy homes," while he spends the day all alone.[7]

Pessoa's poem might lead us to picture him in his apartment wrapped in a blanket, smoking cigarette after cigarette and with only his wistful musings for company, but he actually spent Christmas with his sister, brother-in-law, and three-year-old niece in Évora. It was his first visit since their relocation to that town, in the center of the Alentejo region, a year and a half earlier. Fernando had sent brooches to his sister and his niece for their birthdays, both in November, and Teca responded with a chatty, affectionate thank-you note.[8] To his great relief, it seemed she had finally forgiven him for his financial shenanigans that depleted their mother's estate. His Christmas visit confirmed that they were back on good terms. She and her husband, who was especially fond of Fernando's company, would have liked him to stay longer, and their little daughter, Manuela, adored her uncle, but he returned to Lisbon after just three days.

Outside of Lisbon he felt out of place. He missed its streets and its squares, the hills covered with variously colored buildings and trees poking out here and there, the majestic calm of the Tagus, his books, his friends, and the suited men, typists, and secretaries from Moitinho de Almeida, Toscano & Company, and the other firms where he wrote business letters to eke out a living. "Don't ever call me a poet; at most, I write poems," he had once admonished Ophelia Queiroz, perhaps in the office where they both worked for a few months.[9] On his recently issued national identity card, his declared profession was *empregado no comércio*, office clerk. Pessoa missed his urban solitude.

The Café Martinho da Arcada—sturdy and dignified, with wainscoted walls and a couple of broad arches supporting the ceiling—had fallen out of favor and was often half empty. There, for at least an hour each afternoon, Pessoa held court, surrounded by a few friends and occasional visitors. Though not as lively as it used to be, his literary circle was still a breeding ground for creative projects. In the summer of 1928, Pessoa and José Pacheco talked about the need for a new magazine, something to replace *Contemporânea*, which had ceased publication in 1926. Both Pessoa and Pacheco had experience editing magazines; neither one had any money. Luís de Montalvor and Mário Saa were more interested in producing books, but an actual publishing house would require a large investment. Together the friends came up with an innovative format for publishing both books *and* a magazine.

Saa, despite being notoriously tightfisted with his considerable wealth, readily offered to finance what came to be called Solução Editora, or Solution Publishers. The "solution" was to publish a periodical consisting of a magazine section followed by autonomous installments of full-length books that might not otherwise see print. Once the installments of a given title had all been issued, they could be joined together to form the complete book, for which the publisher would provide a cover.[10] Most of the books were related to Saa's own research interests, such as genealogy and local history, but there was one eminently literary work, an anthology of "modern Portuguese poems" (*Antologia de poemas portugueses modernos*), compiled by Fernando Pessoa and António Botto. Three installments were published between May and August of 1929, at which point the anthology languished, probably because editorial control of the magazine/book venture had passed into other hands.[11]

Pessoa used the magazine section of the hybrid periodical to present a couple of diarylike passages identified as excerpts "from *The Book of Disquiet*, by Bernardo Soares, assistant bookkeeper in the city of Lisbon," yet signed at the end by Fernando Pessoa. Some readers may have been a little flummoxed, but there were precedents for seemingly legitimate diaries whose nominal authors did not actually exist. Rainer Maria Rilke had published *The Notebooks of Malte Laurids Brigge* in 1910, and Valéry Larbaud brought out *The Diary of A. O. Barnabooth* in 1913.[12] While Pessoa does not seem to have read either of these books, he was well acquainted with the posthumously published *Fragments d'un journal intime* (1882–1884) of Henri-Frédéric Amiel, which was a partial inspiration for *The Book of Disquiet*, where Amiel is mentioned in five different passages, not always favorably. One passage deplores the Swiss diarist's "unbearable interiorizing."[13]

Rilke's Brigge was a Dane living in Paris; Larbaud's Barnabooth was a Swede raised in South America who gadded about Europe; Amiel was forever and exclusively Amiel, professor of philosophy at the University of Geneva. And Bernardo Soares? He was an impersonation of Pessoa in his forties, an expressive though smaller-than-life replica, with the traits and features somewhat rearranged. Pessoa would later explain that Soares was not a true heteronym but a semiheteronym, not a different personality but a "mutilation" of his own personality.

◆

**BERNARDO SOARES HAD TENTATIVELY** come into being nine years earlier, in 1920, when he was named in one of Pessoa's notebooks as a writer of short stories and a specialist in shorthand,[14] but he quickly failed at both tasks and, terribly shy, withdrew to a corner of his maker's imagination. Only at the end of the decade did he find his proper subject matter: himself, defined as a "mutilated" version of Pessoa's self. Succeeding Vicente Guedes as the author of *The Book of Disquiet*, Soares also inherited Guedes's profession, that of assistant bookkeeper, as well as his unsociable character. As a diarist, however, he was more forthcoming than his predecessor.

Although he lived and worked in Lisbon, Vicente Guedes had only rarely alluded to the city, and never to his job, and in 1920 he fell completely silent. *The Book of Disquiet*, after lying dormant for nine years, came back to life precisely in the office world of downtown Lisbon, where Pessoa himself spent the better part of each day. Bernardo Soares's stocky and brusque yet fair-minded boss, Senhor Vasques, was modeled after Carlos Moitinho de Almeida, for whom Pessoa had been writing business letters for seven years and would keep writing them for as long as he lived. Vasques & Co., the name of the fabric warehouse on Rua dos Douradores where Soares did his bookkeeping, had the same layout as the office of the Moitinho de Almeida import-export firm, located on nearby Rua da Prata. Vieira was the name of the sales representative and António the name of the office boy—in the fabric warehouse of *The Book of Disquiet* as at the firm Moitinho de Almeida, where Pessoa actually saw and spoke with these two men on a daily basis.[15] And the Lisbon of Bernardo Soares was Pessoa's Lisbon, a world of gentle tedium tinged with enchantment where everything was familiar, and simultaneously strange.

"I love the stillness of early summer evenings downtown, and especially the stillness made more still by contrast, on the streets that seethe with activity by day." So begins the passage from *The Book of Disquiet* published in February 1929—the first passage published since 1913, when the inchoate book still inhabited exotic landscapes belonging to no time or place. Bernardo Soares is firmly situated in reality, Pessoa's reality, even if his mind constantly wanders. Walking, just like Pessoa, along familiar streets that are quickly deserted after the banks and offices have closed for the day, he slips into and identifies with their melancholy solitude, concluding that there is little difference between him and them "in the algebra of the world's mystery." He remembers, with sadness, that everything is a sensation of his but also something external, beyond his power to change. And even his own dreams often rise up before him as things that exist independently, "like the streetcar now turning the corner at the end of the street, or like the voice of an evening crier, crying I don't know what but with a sound that stands out—an Arabian chant like the sudden patter of a fountain—against the monotony of twilight!"

Algebra and the Arabian chant evoke the Moors and the Middle East—where algebra, a word derived from Arabic, had its origins—and faintly call to mind the Persian poet Omar Khayyam, author of a major treatise on algebra. The next passage of *The Book of Disquiet* published by Pessoa, in June 1929, makes this hazy connection explicit. Bernardo Soares, sitting at his desk in the fabric warehouse and scanning, with tired eyes, the large pages of the bookkeeping ledger, suddenly smiles to himself as he remembers "the great navigators, the great saints, and the poets of every age" who don't enter the books. And then:

> In the very act of writing down the name of an unfamiliar cloth, the doors of the Indus and of Samarkand open up, and Persian poetry (which is from yet another place), with its quatrains whose third lines don't rhyme, is a distant anchor for me in my disquiet. But I make no mistake: I write, I add, and the bookkeeping goes on, performed as usual by an employee of this office.[16]

Many Persian poets wrote "quatrains whose third lines don't rhyme," or rubaiyat, but Pessoa was mainly familiar with Khayyam's, which had lately inspired him to start writing his own. His copy of FitzGerald's *Rubáiyát of Omar Khayyám* was the most marked-up book he owned. The disquieted bookkeeper's secret refuge was in poetry, in far-flung cultures and mythologies, in the infinity pursued by Islamic architecture and decorative arts, with their geometrical patterns that lead the eye to no end, and in contemplations that only end where others begin, like the imbricated stories of *One Thousand and One Nights*.

When he finishes each day's work, Soares leaves the office on Rua dos Douradores and goes home to his fourth-floor rented room, also located on Rua dos Douradores. There he spends the evening not being there, transported by his imagination to the Middle East, the Far East, the west, north, and south, past and future. Unlike Khayyam, or Pessoa, he does not need wine to offset the tedium of living; his mental life is intoxicating enough. In a passage for his *Book of Disquiet* titled "Funeral March" and dating from that summer, Soares headily asserts that the Ganges River—with all its sacred significance and throbbing humanity—also passes by the Rua dos Douradores and that all historical ages, "the multicolored march of customs, the distances separating cultures, and the vast variety of nations" exist right there in his small rented room.[17]

Soares, however, is not just a dreamer who evades monotony by inebriating himself with fantasies. He acutely analyzes his feeling of monotony and all his other sensations, "exploring them like large unknown countries."[18] An ascetic whose only religion is to feel, to contemplate, and to imagine, he has renounced the outer world, wanting to be nothing more than an assistant bookkeeper, dreading the mere thought of being promoted to head bookkeeper, since this would encumber him with more responsibility, encroaching on his life of dreaming and writing.[19] *The Book of Disquiet* contains several passing allusions to unnamed friends, none of whom is intimate or devoted. Soares is likable, not lovable, and it's just as well. People make him nervous; he prefers his own company.

Defeated in the world even before the battle began, Soares takes genuine pleasure in studying the details of his retreat, consoling himself by remembering that success is illusory, or ephemeral. All of life—from the world's great empires to the futile activity of entering debits and credits in the ledger of Vasques & Co.—is but a vast funeral march, which he watches like a fascinated child attending a circus or parade.

◆

LIKE THE BARON OF TEIVE, Bernardo Soares was an experiment in self-portraiture—ironic but not entirely so. Whereas Pessoa, in the baron, drew a proud and wealthy, more worldly version of himself, the assistant bookkeeper was an outwardly sullen and lifeless figure, a diminished Pessoa that nobody would ever notice. But the aristocrat and the office worker were genetically similar, sharing a number of personality traits with each other and with their maker. All three men felt ill adapted to the world, ill suited for love, and doomed to be disappointed in whatever they dared to hope for.

This self-perception persisted in Pessoa, even when parts of the portrait were contradicted by reality. He had lately been gaining critical recognition as an original, even groundbreaking author, yet this did not translate in his mind as "success." José Régio's definition of him as a modernist with "the stuff of a Master," in the April 1927 issue of *Presença*, was certainly flattering, but the effect was undermined by the critic's appraisal of Mário de Sá-Carneiro, in the very same issue, as "our greatest contemporary poet." Something similar occurred in February 1929, when António Ferro published a magazine article on the "precursors" of Portuguese modernism.[20] While conceding that Pessoa was not less important than Sá-Carneiro, Ferro lavished his attention on the latter writer.

Is it possible that Pessoa was in competition with his deceased friend? Yes. And he chafed at being placed in the school called modernism, or rather, in its preschool. If he, Sá-Carneiro, and Almada Negreiros were its "precursors," then modernism logically came into full bloom only after *Orpheu* planted the seeds.

In the summer of 1928 a third critic, José Rebelo de Bettencourt, had remarked in a short but perceptive essay that, while most writers "make us feel only their own emotions," Pessoa arouses in us "a new world of images that are not only his, but also ours." This seems to mean that Pessoa expresses, in felicitous images, things that his readers feel but would never be able to express so eloquently. It was a prescient observation, since it is this very quality in his writing—particularly in *The Book of Disquiet*—that would prove seductive to future generations.[21] But Pessoa scarcely took notice of this and other glowing comments, making not one pencil mark in his copy of the book with the four-page essay dedicated to him and his work. Bettencourt's style was breezily journalistic, his insights often on the mark but not examined in depth, and Pessoa seems not to have taken him very seriously as a critic.

One year later, in June 1929, a far more substantial essay on Pessoa was published in a book by João Gaspar Simões, a co-editor of *Presença* and his first biographer. Just twenty-six years old but unusually well read, Gaspar Simões was perspicacious, capable of viewing literature in new ways, and a lively writer. He sent an inscribed copy of the book, *Temas* (*Themes*), to Pessoa, who went straight to the chapter named after him, underlining key phrases throughout the essay. What gratified him even more than being recognized as a writer with "a solitary and supreme standing" in Portuguese literature was the critic's valiant attempt to fathom the origins and the nature of his "heteronymous personalities."

Pessoa's first letter to the young writer and editor, written to thank him for his essay, astonishes with its candor. After noting that Gaspar Simões's analysis of him and his work had freed him, at least momentarily, from his existence as "an objectively obscure personality," he confessed that only "far-reaching fame" could give him the kind of "psychological" freedom he longed for. And he related a curious incident. Several days earlier, through a "violent effort of impersonalization," he had managed to write a new, concise preface by Ricardo Reis for the poetry of Alberto Caeiro, an accomplishment that caused him to almost weep with joy, until he remembered that these two individuals and whatever transpired between them were strictly private matters, occurring only in him. At a time when he found himself assailed by doubts, burdened by the lonely drama of his heteronyms, Gaspar Simões's essay had given him renewed faith and confidence in his "personal existence as an independent nation." He was tremendously grateful, even moved, he wrote, for it was the first time a critic had treated him "not as a writer but as a soul who writes," placing him "in reality and not in literature."

These were strange, somewhat contradictory affirmations. It is normal enough for a writer to want to be famous, but this confessed desire seems to be at odds with Pessoa's poignant gratitude for being treated as a person of the real world who happens to write rather than as just a great writer, a literary phenomenon. Indeed fame, mere fame, was not what Pessoa ultimately longed for. He wanted to touch and be touched— one soul touching another, many others—through his writing. His inner society of heteronyms was a simulacrum of the intimacy he sought to achieve with real people by way of his literature. Writing was Pessoa's way of loving and of being loved.

The letter, he decided, was too expansive and too revealing to send to someone he didn't even know, and so he wrote another, shorter version, which less effusively thanked Gaspar Simões for treating him in his essay "as a spiritual reality" and for acknowledging him "as an independent nation." In this missive, sent in late June, Pessoa made no mention of his poetic alter egos or of his craving for fame. Perhaps, upon rereading the essay, he had noticed that Gaspar Simões, while fascinated by his capacity to be various poets at once, viewed the heteronyms as a problem—or the symptoms of a problem—that would fatally hinder true greatness: "If Fernando Pessoa does not succeed in producing a great work, it is because the forces of his individuality, divided as they are, cancel each other out."[22]

◆

BERNARDO SOARES, THE SEMIHETERONYM, while pursuing his self-effacing career as an ungregarious office worker who dreaded being noticed, occasionally mused that the passages of prose he wrote in his spare time might bring him recognition long after he was dead. In one of those passages he dares to imagine future generations reading and admiring the very page he is at that moment writing, and he sees his "invisible and inwardly majestic stature" hovering above Detroit, Michigan—then one of the largest and richest cities in America.[23]

More proactive than the assistant bookkeeper, Pessoa complemented his dreams with rational demonstration. In 1929 he began writing "Erostratus, or the Future of Celebrity," an essay that logically *proved* it was his destiny to become enduringly famous, albeit only in his post-mortem life. Erostratus, or Herostratus, was a nonentity from ancient Greece who set fire to the Temple of Artemis at Ephesus, one of the Seven Wonders of the Ancient World, for no other reason than to make himself famous.[24] The Ephesians therefore issued a prohibition against pronouncing the criminal's name, which of course guaranteed that it would spread, just as steadily as the fire that burned the wooden beams supporting the roof of the destroyed temple.

The announced aim of Pessoa's essay, for which he wrote dozens of disconnected passages, all of them in English, was to examine the conditions that enable an individual, or even an entire nation, to go down in history—whether through artistic achievement, political success, sainthood, military prowess, sheer genius, or even a heinous crime—but it ended up dwelling on his area of special interest: literature. It argued that great writers can be recognized as such only by future generations, since true genius is always ahead of its time. The future, however, would deal harshly even with the best writers, so that in a hundred years' time it would be "impossible to issue a complete edition of Byron, or of Shelley, or of Goethe the poet or Hugo." And the future's impatience with prolific outputs was justified, according to the essayist, since most people, poets included, don't after all have that much to say. Stylistic variety was the only acceptable excuse for abundance: "No man should leave twenty different books unless he can write like twenty different men."

The essayist—who counted on leaving quite a few of his own books for posterity, written under at least half a dozen different names, all belonging to the "nation" called Fernando Pessoa—was clearly setting the stage for his own canonization. Although "Erostratus" is in some ways an expanded version of the essay "Impermanence," written ten years earlier, the central focus of its inquiry is different. "Impermanence" considered the characteristics that allow specific *works* of literature to survive through the ages; "Erostratus" was concerned with the qualities that make certain *writers* long-lastingly famous. Contrary to what we might expect, such writers are rarely forerunners or obviously innovative. In an apparent swipe at the modernism everyone was lately talking about, Pessoa wrote: "The real novelty that endures is the one that has taken up all the threads of tradition and woven them again into a pattern that tradition could not weave them into." Pessoa was describing his own achievement. Wasn't each heteronym a thread of tradition? He certainly thought so.

◆

SOME TIME AFTER COMMENCING "Erostratus, or the Future of Celebrity," Pessoa wrote a few passages for a companion essay titled "Anteros, or the Future of Affection," also in English.[25] Once more he set out to cover his topic broadly, by discussing the nature of love and friendship in men, in women, in the context of marriage, between people and their pets, and so forth, but he quickly veered off into a "sociologically disconcerting phenomenon" that had always intrigued him: "the paederasty of the Greeks." He noted that, whereas in almost every historical period "the sane normal man" sharply distinguishes between friendship and love, which he defined as "a primarily sexual emotion," the Greeks found themselves at a special moment of human critical sensibility in which they did not make this distinction. For them friendship and love were intertwined. At this point Pessoa veered off track again, without ever explaining the significance of the "Greek phenomenon" for the future of affection. But his essay's title, with its mention of Anteros, is enlightening.

The god Anteros, brother of Eros, has been portrayed since ancient times either as a symbol of reciprocal affection, and hence the avenger of unrequited love, or as the personification of a love at odds with Eros. Pessoa followed the latter interpretation, understanding the two brothers as "two impulses of sensuality—love for love's sake, and love for beauty's sake—that perpetually compete in the mind of rational man. The first impulse, which loves according to instinct, always prefers the opposite sex; the second one, which loves according to reason, often prefers the same sex."[26] Pessoa had already invoked Anteros many years earlier, in a subtitle for "The Visual Lover," a passage from *The Book of Disquiet* written in 1916. This Anteros-influenced lover, explains the passage, loves only with his gaze and without any sexual preference, since he has no sexual desire. Loath to touch or even to talk with those he loves, loving them for their beauty alone, he is the purest and most pristine aesthete imaginable.

The future of affection envisioned by Pessoa in 1929 was not such an antiseptic affair. Although short on detail, the passages he wrote for his essay suggest a future society in which attraction would no longer be conditioned by gender and where friendship, as in Plato's *Phaedrus*, would be elevated to love. It so happens that Plato, in this dialogue, used the word *anteros* (counter-love) to characterize the emotional response that a lover's *eros* produces, like an echo, in the breast of his beloved friend.

Pessoa was familiar with *Phaedrus*, either directly or through secondary sources,[27] and he knew about Edward Carpenter, a British socialist philosopher who also wrote prolifically about love and sexuality. He is mentioned in Pessoa's notes as a possible recipient of the Olisipo edition of his *English Poems*.[28] What, the poet must have wondered, would be Carpenter's reaction to "Antinous" and "Epithalamium," which dealt forthrightly with love and sex, both inside and outside of marriage, between people of opposite sexes or of the same sex?

Carpenter, whose intimate and enduring relationship with a working-class man inspired E. M. Forster to write *Maurice*, is nowadays remembered as an early defender of homosexuality or, as he liked to style it, "homogenic" love, but he wrote broadly about human culture, society, and the many varieties of sexual experience. Perhaps Pessoa, whose own views had evolved since he wrote "Epithalamium" and "Antinous," read *The Intermediate Sex: A Study of Some Transitional Types of Men and Women*, in which the English author optimistically asserted that "as people are beginning to see that the sexes form in a certain sense a continuous group, so they are beginning to see that Love and Friendship—which have been so often set apart from each other as things distinct—are in reality closely related and shade imperceptibly into each other."[29]

Today, more than a century after those lines were written, it is doubtful whether the distance between Love and Friendship has appreciably diminished in the minds of most people, but Carpenter described very well Pessoa's own futuristic ideal of affection between humans. Less clear is whether Pessoa could see himself living in "the new city of Friends" ruled by "robust love," as envisioned in a poem (which he had read) by Walt Whitman.

"**A**N INTIMATE FRIEND IS ONE OF MY IDEAL things," Pessoa had confessed in writing, shortly after his nineteenth birthday, but the ideal was so lofty that down-to-earth, person-to-person intimacy became all the more difficult. Only Mário de Sá-Carneiro, whose affection was irrepressible, succeeded in slipping through Pessoa's defenses, getting closer to him than anyone else ever had. Pessoa did not expect to have another such friend and perhaps would not even have wanted one. Intimacy was exhausting. Friendship bordering on or blended with love was a beautiful idea—for the future, or in literature. For his present life, since the death of Sá-Carneiro, he had contented himself with his Pickwickian circle of mostly bachelor friends.[1] They were good company, loyal, mildly stimulating, discreetly affectionate, and not too demanding.

At the end of Dickens's novel, a couple of Samuel Pickwick's friends get married, whereupon the Pickwick Club dies a natural death. When three of Pessoa's close friends married, one after another, his informal social club did not risk dissolution, but it became less stable, the daily sessions less well attended. The first one to marry was Mário Saa, who in 1928 had a son with a woman from Alentejo, where his family owned land that stretched so far it reportedly took over an hour to cross by train. The marriage was unofficial but long-lasting, with Marina and their son living mostly in the country, where Saa began to spend more time.[2] Next to marry was Geraldo Coelho de Jesus, a serial womanizer everyone had assumed was a confirmed bachelor. Perhaps it was a midlife crisis that prompted him to propose to a woman he met on a trip to Paris. Geraldo was forty-one, Germaine just nineteen. He brought her back to Lisbon in March 1929, and on September 18 it was official, with Pessoa signing as a witness on the marriage certificate.[3] One year later, Augusto Ferreira Gomes would marry Marcelle,[4] who was also from Paris and may have been friends with Germaine. When Marcelle gave birth to a girl, Augusto asked Fernando to be her godfather.[5]

Married life did not stop Pessoa's friends from seeing him when they could, and they would have seen him more often were he not so stubbornly attached to the Café Martinho da Arcada, which was close to the river and to most of the offices where he worked. They preferred the Café A Brasileira of Chiado, stylishly redecorated in 1924 and 1925 with the help of José Pacheco, who commissioned Almada Negreiros and other contemporary artists to execute paintings that were hung in two long rows, like friezes, above the bottles and the mirrors. Located in the fashionable part of town, it was frequented by artsy and fashionable people, a few of whom—still just a few—were female, which would have been unthinkable when Pessoa used to be a regular part of its human scenery, back in the days of *Orpheu*.

One of the first female customers was Beatriz Costa, a young actor who had grown up poor and unschooled and was attracted to intellectuals. She enchanted Mário Saa, who promised to leave his family and live with her in Paris if she would marry him. Saa was disastrously short—he looked like a schoolboy, a perfect target for spitballs—and she laughed at him, but when he wrote her letters she answered. Costa, who was the most popular Portuguese actor of the 1930s, with a bob hairdo reminiscent of Louise Brooks, would later report that on the few occasions she saw Pessoa at the Brasileira, which he normally avoided, he was a gloomy bore. Other café-goers were witty, sparkling conversationalists—not Pessoa. [6]

Pessoa listened more than he talked, and when he talked he was soft-spoken, phlegmatic. Sometimes, though, he would quietly utter a statement so intelligent and well formulated that it stunned the loud talkers into silence. He could also be funny, but one had to follow him closely to get the joke.

When he was twenty-some years old, Pessoa had begun an essay, discussed earlier, that mocked the patrons of the very cafés where he himself spent a few hours of each day talking about literature and politics and idle matters. Fifteen years later, after he had renounced trendy cafés like the Brasileira, he availed himself of *The Book of Disquiet* to unleash a new round of vitriol against their clientele. "The most extraordinary thing about all of these people," recalls Bernardo Soares with regard to the people that he (and Fernando) used to frequent in cafés, "was their complete and unanimous lack of importance." They had treated him well, he admitted, since he was "the good listener who would always let them show off and have the pulpit," but he had had enough of their braggadocio and café wit.[7]

If you wanted to have coffee and conversation with Fernando, you had to go to *his* café, where there were no paintings or mirrors or women. And they went there. Mário Saa, Geraldo Coelho de Jesus, Augusto Ferreira Gomes, Raul Leal, António Botto, Alberto Da Cunha Dias, Luís de Montalvor, and Carlos Queiroz. But they went there intermittently, and more intermittently as the years slipped by. In the summer of 1929 there were rarely more than four or five people sitting at Pessoa's table in the Martinho da Arcada. Ferreira Gomes showed up most days, as did Leal and Botto, provided these last two were showing themselves in public. When overwhelmed by the psychological suffering imposed on him as the prophet Henoch, Leal would retreat to his apartment for a few days or even weeks. Botto, highly social, was also very moody, and vain. Toward the end of the summer his face broke out in a rash and he stayed out of sight until it cleared up. Vanity made him stay indoors, but the rash was the symptom of a serious illness—probably syphilis—and lasted for a few months. Ferro, with whom Botto had become friends, raised money to help him get treatment.[8]

On the days when Alberto Da Cunha Dias showed up at the café, the discussion became heated, since he had lately launched a journalistic crusade against the Freemasons, whom Pessoa defended. Cunha Dias was jovial and garrulous but also touchy, easily offended, and capable of flaring up without warning. Luís de Montalvor, on the contrary, was so calm and well-mannered he seemed not quite there, or not quite real, an impression reinforced by his physical appearance. He was white and glabrous, having lost all the hair on his head and even his eyebrows.[9]

Amid so much idiosyncrasy, the junior member of the group was blessedly normal. Carlos Queiroz, now twenty-two years old, was easy-going, easy to please, and a great admirer of Pessoa's work. The older poet was to some degree a mentor, and the younger one an apprentice, but they were equals in their affection as friends. So it was only natural, or apparently natural, for Fernando to give Carlos an inscribed photo of himself. It was taken by one of his employers, the publicist Martins da Hora, who spotted him drinking a glass of red wine at Abel's, the downtown bar where he refreshed himself throughout the day. Martins da Hora, when he needed Pessoa's help with advertising copy or a letter in English, would leave messages for him at the bar, but on this occasion he happened to find the poet there, standing at the marble counter, with a glass raised to his lips—and click! Or did he pose?

◆

AS FERNANDO MUST HAVE known would happen, Carlos showed the photo of him drinking wine to Ophelia, his aunt, who had turned twenty-nine in June. They both still lived with his mother, Joaquina, in the same building just opposite the Rossio train station where Fernando used to slowly pass by and do goofy things while his sweetheart looked down from the balcony window and laughed. Nine years had passed. The photograph showed Pessoa as he really was: a decade older, ten pounds heavier, and with a chin beginning to sag just a little. Ophelia smiled. She asked Carlos to ask Fernando for another copy ("But don't tell him it's for me"), and Fernando obliged ("It's for Ophelia, isn't it?"). On September 9 she wrote him a thank-you letter, timidly affectionate, saying that she'd be happy to hear from him, if he cared to write.

Pessoa answered immediately:

Dear Ophelia,
    The heart I felt in your letter touched me, though I don't know why you should thank me for the photograph of a good-for-nothing, even if the good-for-nothing is the twin brother I don't have. Does a drunken shadow hold a place, after all, in your memories?
    Your letter reached my exile—which is I myself—like joy from the homeland, and so it's I who should thank you, dear girl.

After a third paragraph in which he apologized for not greeting her on the several occasions during the last nine years when they happened to cross paths (he said he recognized her only when it was too late), he closed his letter with a coyly framed invitation: "One more thing . . . No, nothing, sweet lips. . . ."

His Pickwickian group of friends were after all not enough. Longing for another kind of affection, he remembered how much Ophelia cared for him and remembered, too, the thrill of physical contact—kisses, petting—with another soft and warm body.

Fernando's letter transported her. Like the water of a dam now opened, or broken, the feeling of love flooded her whole being all over again, as if the intervening years had hardly existed. And in a certain way they hadn't, for the scenery, props, dialogue, and action of their renewed romance were largely a rerun of 1920. Again they rode the streetcar together, again there were love letters, again her plans for their life together as a married couple, and again his talk of moving to Cascais or another Lisbon suburb so that he could better concentrate on his writing—like Horace at his house in the Sabine Hills, far away from the commotion of Rome. Ophelia lived, as before, in a permanent state of agitation, waiting for their next meeting, his next letter, or his next phone call from one of the offices where he worked. This last form of communication was new in their relationship; Ophelia's much older sister, who still ran a dressmaking business out of her apartment, had acquired a telephone. Phones were finally beginning to be affordable, at least for the bourgeoisie.

As in 1920, but much more quickly, the voracity of Ophelia's love made Fernando recoil, as from a precipice. On September 26, just two weeks into their rekindled relationship, she received a letter signed by "Álvaro de Campos, naval engineer," who recommended that she toss her "mental image" of Pessoa down the drain. Fernando was testing her; at this point he still hoped that they could reach an amorous equilibrium. Ophelia replied to the engineer that he, not Fernando, was whom she would gladly toss down the drain or under a passing train. To her "sweet love" she wrote that all she wanted was to be his perfect wife. Did he not long to be her husband?

He had his priorities. On September 29 he wrote a letter that gently reproached her for not adequately respecting his literary ambitions. After a first paragraph in which he claimed to be ill, he wrote:

> What I said about going to Cascais (which means Cascais, Sintra, Caxias or anywhere else outside yet close to Lisbon) is absolutely true: true, at least, in intent. I've reached that age when a man comes into full possession of his talents and his mind is at the height of its powers. And so it's time for me to consolidate my literary work, finishing up certain things, compiling others, and writing some things that are still in my head.

In the next paragraph he explained that his life revolved around his literary work, everything else was secondary, and to want him to have the feelings "of an ordinary person" was like wanting him to have "blue eyes and blond hair." But after stressing how completely different he was from her, an "ordinary" person, he went on to fan her most ardent hope:

> I'm very, very fond of you, Ophelia. I adore your character and temperament. If I marry, it will only be with you. It remains to be seen whether marriage and home (or whatever one wants to call it) are compatible with my life of thought. I doubt it. For now I want to organize, without delay, this life of thought and my literary work. If I can't organize it, then I won't even think of thinking about marriage. And if I organize it in such a way that marriage would be a hindrance, then I'm sure not to marry. But I suspect this won't be the case. The future, and I mean the near future, will tell.
>
> There you have it, and it happens to be the truth.

No doubt it was all true, like almost everything Pessoa wrote, in the moment he wrote it. On paper nothing was impossible, including nuptial bliss with Ophelia. Inspired perhaps by his friend Geraldo, who was one year older and had just gotten married, he was at least intrigued by the possibility of getting married himself.

Heartened by Fernando's letter, Ophelia humored her beloved—and indulged her own fantasy in the process. Of course he should move to Cascais, if that would further his writing career—and thus fulfill the chief requisite for any marriage to take place. She said she could wait. Fernando, who had never believed in the likelihood of marriage, only in its theoretical possibility, realized soon enough that it was entirely out of the question, but he could not bring himself to tell her so. On October 9 he sent her two letters written in a now run-on, now disjointed prose style that mimicked the insane state of mind avowed by the sender, who warned in the second letter that he was fit to enter an asylum:

> The spring of the rattletrap in my head finally snapped, and my mind, which had already ceased to exist, went tr-tr-r-r-r- . . .
>
>      . . .
>
> Do you like me because I'm me or because I'm not? Or do you dislike me even without me or not? Or what?
>
> All these sentences and ways of saying nothing are signs that

the ex-Ibis, the extinct Ibis, the Ibis that's kaput and not even happily bonkers, is going to the nuthouse at Telhal or Rilhafoles,[10] and there's a big party to celebrate his magnificent disappearance.

Since the letters, among their nonsensical statements, included expressions of affection and desire—"I'd like to kiss you precisely and greedily on the lips, and to eat your lips"—Ophelia was thrilled to get them. She laughed at her boyfriend's silly talk of insanity, not realizing that it amounted to a disclaimer of responsibility for his behavior from then on. Little did she know that those were the last real letters she would get from him. For the next two weeks he completely avoided her.

But then the minitrysts resumed—short rides on the streetcar, whose humming motors, screeching brakes, and frequently ringing bells made enough noise to guarantee that nobody could overhear their conversation, and short walks during which they sometimes kissed. Ophelia had lost her girlish look but was still petite and attractive, and still devoutly religious. Fernando occasionally walked her home from the church where she attended Sunday Mass. He even visited her home a few times, but only when her nephew and his friend, Carlos, was there as well, and the three of them would chat together in the living room. Every evening, at around eight o'clock, she listened for the telephone, hoping he would call from the office of Moitinho de Almeida or from another of the firms where he worked. His calling, his showing up for a rendezvous, and his kissing her when he did show up all happened, when they happened, erratically, and never often enough to please her.

As in 1920, sometimes Álvaro de Campos rather than Fernando telephoned or showed up at the streetcar stop, or the two friends showed up together. ("It was Álvaro who said that, not me." Speaking, perhaps, in a sassy voice.) Ophelia tried to play this game to her advantage. When Fernando excused himself for not writing her by saying that Campos had made off with his paper, pen, and ink, she wrote a letter claiming to have met privately with the engineer, who promised to send their mutual friend all the items necessary for writing a few lines to his sweetheart. Under separate cover, Fernando received a packet containing paper, pen, and ink, along with a homemade calling card from "Álvaro de Campos, Engineer," the purported sender. Fernando continued not to write. Ophelia said she would even settle for another letter from Campos, whom she usually wanted to banish from the relationship. ("Have you sent him back to England?" she asked Fernando more than once.) But no one wrote to Ophelia.[11]

Besides chronicling, in her dozens of unanswered missives, the torment of a love so stingily requited it would have been better—from an outsider's perspective—to be flat-out rejected, Ophelia recounted the events of each day, pleaded with Fernando to control his drinking, and daydreamed about their future together. Amused and a little touched by her concern for his health, Pessoa, when they met or talked on the phone, inflated the amount of wine and brandy he actually consumed, which was at any rate considerable. Small but frequent sips. He never guzzled and was never visibly inebriated. Nor would that have deterred Ophelia. However alcoholic, infirm, or indigent Pessoa was or might become, she wanted to spend her life with him and him only. Obsessed with marriage? If that were the case, she wrote in one of her letters, she would already be married—to somebody else.[12]

Ophelia was wholly, deeply in love with Fernando, and if he was unable to love her back, it was not because of any defect in the quality of her love, not because she wasn't pretty enough, not because her cultural level lagged behind his, and not because she would rob him of time and energy for writing. Nor would it have made any difference if she were a man, and Fernando as well as the rest of Portugal fully accepted homosexuality. The difficulty was love itself, eros love, for which he had no aptitude. He had already reached this conclusion when he broke off with Ophelia the first time, saying that his destiny was the slave of mysterious "Masters" and obeyed "a different Law" than hers or most people's. With less grandiosity, he might have simply told her that he was not cut out for love.

Whatever his reason—probably sheer loneliness—for repeating an experiment that had already failed once, he suspected it was a bad idea by mid-October, when he wrote those two letters declaring himself mentally unfit. In fact he was amorously unfit. The relationship would continue but was fast proving itself, as far as Pessoa was concerned, to be a renewed failure. So much so that in mid-November he awarded himself a literary consolation prize: a love poem, or post-love poem, of Alberto Caeiro.

Caeiro's unexpected resuscitation, after more than six years without his signing a single poem, is a testament to the power of love, even when the love—Pessoa and Ophelia's—doesn't work out. Caeiro, according to his biography, had once been in love with a country girl, who filled him with euphoria and inspired a poetic sequence titled *The Shepherd in Love*, initiated in 1914 but discontinued after just two poems. On November 18, 1929, Pessoa-Caeiro finally returned to the sequence, penning not a joyous poem of love but an elegy that mourned a love just ended: the enamored shepherd was alone again, abandoned by the girl with "beautiful lips and hair" who used to walk with him in the fields and pick flowers. Thus Pessoa, using his poetic art to rewrite history, reversed the roles of his real-life relationship with Ophelia, making Caeiro love's victim, jilted by the young woman who so enchanted him.

Ophelia stayed firmly on the path of love, because Fernando continued to visit it—with brief but frequent phone calls and occasional streetcar rides—through the rest of 1929 and the following year. He knew the path would lead nowhere but wanted her to stay on it, at least for now. Because it gratified him to know she thought about him constantly? Because he looked forward to her letters, even if their content was uninteresting? Because their brief encounters and conversations, if not exactly stimulating, were at least pleasantly distracting? None of these hypotheses is especially convincing, though he did hold on to every one of her letters.

Let's consider the reaction of Bernardo Soares to the only time in his life when, as he puts it in a passage for his diary written in 1930, "circumstances mischievously led me to suppose that I loved and to verify that the other person truly loved me." True to his habit of closely analyzing every sensation, he scrupulously recorded the effects on him of this novel condition. After an initial state of confusion, as if he had won "a grand prize in an inconvertible currency," followed by a normal enough feeling of vanity, he was beset by tedium, due to the little and large duties imposed by love on his time and emotions and due as well to "the obligatory monotony of a definite feeling"—the feeling of love. But what he felt most of all was weariness, for being the object of someone else's "burdensome emotions" and for "having to love at least a little in return, even if it's not a true reciprocity."[13]

Because Soares, with far more detail than I've presented, was clearly analyzing Pessoa's own experience of being loved, we might suspect that Pessoa let his relationship with Ophelia drag on precisely for the sake of that analysis, which fills up two pages of *The Book of Disquiet*. But Pessoa—as quick in his feelings as he was in his intelligence—did not need to prolong a situation to understand how it made him act and react emotionally. Everything described by Soares had already been experienced by Pessoa in 1920, during the first phase of his relationship with Ophelia Queiroz; during the second phase it took him no more than two weeks to remember—and he apparently needed a reminder—how her love affected his mood. He knew very well what he felt.

Much harder for him to fathom was Ophelia Queiroz. If there was a subject in his study of amorous psychology that required long observation, it was this woman in thrall to her unrelenting love for him. He could easily understand the tedium and weariness caused by love, but not what makes love—even a painful, unrequited love—persist. One might argue that Ophelia had no other great ambition or dream, nothing better to occupy her time. But why did she love him and not someone else? From remarks in her letters it was clear that she had been waiting for him for most of the nine years they were apart.

In a couple of her October 1929 letters to Fernando, Ophelia noted that he sometimes liked to make her suffer.[14] It was not a whiney accusation, just a matter-of-fact observation. To judge by his behavior—not phoning when he said he would, making her wait in vain at a streetcar stop, or showing up as Álvaro de Campos, wry and aloof—there was some truth to what she said. He kept putting her love to the test, not because he doubted it but because he was fascinated by its strength, its tenacity, its capacity for suffering. And he envied her a little, not knowing how it might feel or what it might mean to suffer for someone in the way she suffered for him.

But it was not only as a case study in love that he let the relationship go on in its languid way, to the discomfort of them both. Fernando was truly fond of Ophelia and respected her sentiments. He knew that her love, because it was love, wanted to keep loving, and so he reciprocated just a little bit, to keep her fooled, and perhaps, after all, to fool himself.

"**B**LACK THURSDAY IN AMERICA." "WALL STREET Crash!" "Prices Tumble Like an Avalanche."[1] These headlines from the London press were echoed around much of Europe, where panic spread to local stock markets and government economists dreaded the consequences for international commerce, domestic trade, unemployment rates, and foreign debt obligations. But the dramatic sell-off that commenced at the New York Stock Exchange in late October 1929—with Black Thursday being followed by Black Monday and Black Tuesday—did not garner headlines in Portugal's newspapers, nor would the nation be especially hard hit by the worldwide Great Depression that followed. Its economy was still largely rural and little internationalized, with exports accounting for only 10 percent of its gross domestic product. Declining prices meant that imports, which represented 20 percent of the national economy, also became cheaper. And Salazar, the finance minister, had already instilled the idea that citizens as well as the government needed to make do with less. "Politics of Truth, Politics of Sacrifice, Politics for the Nation" was the title of his latest speech, delivered on October 21, three days before Black Thursday.

Pessoa accepted the *situação*, or situation, as the Portuguese like to call the political status quo. Under the ruling generals there was stability, the streets were peaceful, and the austerity measures of the finance minister had restored confidence in the economy. But how long would the *situação* last? Pessoa's *Interregnum* had defended the military dictatorship as a transitional solution. That transition was going on its fourth year, and the example of other countries in southern Europe suggested it would not end soon. General Primo de Rivera had been governing Spain for six years, and Mussolini had so far been in power for seven. Another authoritarian regime, the "dictatorship of the proletariat" that ruled first Russia and now the Soviet Union, had just celebrated its twelfth anniversary, with Josef Stalin now at the helm. Other countries, including

Poland, Turkey, Yugoslavia, and Albania, were also ruled by autocratic figures if not outright dictators.

Motivated, apparently, by a sincere curiosity as to where all this was going, Pessoa drew up, in English, a questionnaire to send to David Lloyd George, Winston Churchill, and several other British political leaders, to the dictators Mussolini and Primo de Rivera, and to representative writers—including H. G. Wells, author of *The War of the Worlds*—from the three nations where these statesmen wielded power.[2] Pessoa wanted to know, in the first place, how these illustrious leaders and intellectuals viewed the individual in relationship to society and to the nation. More pointedly, he asked if they considered the "growing tendency to state-control or anti-individualism—whether it name itself socialism, or humanitarianism, or fascism, or dictatorship, or military or proletarian government—" to be a temporary phenomenon or a "definite acquisition" that would shape the future of civilization. What primarily concerned Pessoa, as we can tell by the way he couched his questions, was the future of *individuals*, whom he regarded as the true creators and only deserving beneficiaries of civilization.

An anthology of opinions on the totalitarian trend in Europe by the likes of Churchill, Mussolini, and H. G. Wells would be an editorial coup and a profitable undertaking for Pessoa, who drew up two different versions of his questionnaire, but he had no idea how to go from there. António Ferro had made a name for himself as an international journalist whose interviews with famous people were published first in newspapers and then compiled into books. How was Pessoa, a little-known poet with a bizarre theory about a forthcoming Fifth Empire, supposed to introduce himself in a letter to David Lloyd George or Il Duce?

He would give up on his potentially lucrative book project and, in mid-December 1930, would instead draft a letter proposing that he be hired on a half-time basis by J. Walter Thompson, the world's largest advertising agency. Headquartered in New York, it had an office in Madrid and was represented in Portugal by the Hora Agency. Manuel Martins da Hora, one of the businessmen for whom Pessoa worked on a freelance basis, highly valued his services as a creator of slogans, a copywriter, and a translator and readily agreed to sign and send his employment proposal to the office in Madrid. One of the paragraphs explained, in Pessoa's peculiar English prose style: "Now Mr. Pessoa, who is always getting tired of doing the things he happens to be doing, and for the precise reason that he is doing them, wants to simplify the five or six offices situation in some manner, the more so that he has special literary work of his own which he wants time for."[3]

The Madrid office, however, would not guarantee even a half-time salary for Mr. Pessoa, who was clever but committed, by his own admission, to literary work rather than to advertising. When offered the chance to attend a training program in copywriting in Madrid—with all expenses paid by J. Walter Thompson—he turned it down. And so he would continue to make the rounds among half a dozen offices, Monday through Saturday. He couldn't afford to slack off: Aunt Lisbela, the wealthy cousin from the Algarve who occasionally provided him with financial assistance, had died in October 1929.

◆

PESSOA'S ETERNALLY RECURRING INTENTION to change his routine—by setting up some sort of business in London, by moving out of the city to somewhere like Cascais, or by at least reducing the number of offices where he worked—was itself an essential component of that routine. The only change he made, in March 1930, confirmed that everything would remain equal: he rented a room on Rua da Prata, the very same downtown street where the Hora Agency[4] and Moitinho de Almeida, Ltd., his main employer, had their offices. Thus his life imitated his art. Bernardo Soares also rented a room on the same street where he worked, Rua dos Douradores,[5] one block over from Rua da Prata. Pessoa, however, did not live in his rented room, nor is it entirely clear why he rented it. To store some of his things, he explained to Ophelia. But why, she wondered, when there was surely room for them at the large apartment on Rua Coelho da Rocha?

Pessoa, I believe, wanted and needed a sanctuary, a place all his own. Francisco Caetano Dias, his brother-in-law, who was determined to get out of Évora, either by being posted to Africa or transferred back to Lisbon, was now making frequent trips to the capital and stayed with his family at the apartment. It may be that Pessoa, who had gotten used to living alone, occasionally preferred to sleep in his rented room, particularly if he had been working late into the night at one of the various offices to which he had the keys.[6] In August, when the army finally approved Caetano Dias's request to return to Lisbon, Pessoa moved more books and papers to his rented room, as well as more furniture.[7] He lived with his family, however, and probably made a monthly contribution for the meals prepared by Teca.

Ophelia was exasperated. In the letters she kept writing and Fernando kept not answering, she pointed out more than once that the rent money he spent on the room downtown and on his share of the family apartment would be enough to rent a small apartment for the two of them, and it needn't be fancy or in a good neighborhood.[8] She would settle for anything.

But he had gotten tired of keeping up what for him was a charade and began to actively discourage her illusions. For months before his forty-second birthday in June 1930, she had obsessively looked forward to celebrating it with him. When the day finally arrived, she uselessly waited for an hour at their habitual meeting place. He did not even call her. Instead of celebrating his birthday with her or with friends, he wrote a poem called "Birthday," which reminisces on his fifth birthday, 1893, when more than a dozen relatives were present for the occasion, including his father, who would die one month later (see chapter 2). The poem toggles back and forth between that idyllic time of childhood, when happiness "was as sure as any religion," and his present life of "having survived myself like a spent match." Today, he wrote,

I no longer have birthdays.
I endure.
My days add up.
I'll be old when I'm old.
That's all.

The poem was signed by Ophelia's nemesis, Álvaro de Campos, whose anguished thoughts about the loss of childhood innocence and the joy-lessness of his present life were "answered" on the same day—June 13, 1930—by a simple poem of Alberto Caeiro, who says he woke up early, had nothing to do, went outside for a walk, found it very windy, and let the wind guide his steps. In conclusion:

So has my life always been, and so I would like it always to be—
I go where the wind takes me and don't need to think.

Pessoa also wrote two odes signed by Ricardo Reis, one of which rec-ommends that we concentrate our thoughts on "what remains of what is passing" whenever our minds are assaulted by the realization that we ourselves are passing, like yellowing leaves, in the autumn of our lives. It seems unlikely, however, that the passive acceptance prescribed by Reis and exemplified in Caeiro could help assuage Campos's nostalgia for that person "with a heart and family," that person "who was a boy they loved," back when "they used to celebrate my birthday!"

Of all the poems and prose pieces in Pessoa's massive oeuvre, "Birthday" provides the most glaring evidence in support of João Gaspar Simões's thesis, presented in his 1950 biography, that nostalgia for lost childhood is the key to understanding the writer's creative output. This nostalgia, according to Gaspar Simões, is a mark of sincerity conferring artistic authenticity on the work. And yet it is possible, even advisable, for us to doubt the complete sincerity of the nostalgia that suffuses "Birthday." On the same day Pessoa wrote this poem, a Caeiro poem, and two odes of Ricardo Reis, he also wrote a passage for Bernardo Soares's *The Book of Disquiet*. Here is the first paragraph:

> I always live in the present. I don't know the future and no longer have the past. The former oppresses me as the possibility of everything, the latter as the reality of nothing. I have no hopes and no nostalgia. [ . . .] I don't even miss the feelings of times gone by, because what is felt requires the moment when it's felt—once this has passed, there's a turning of the page and the story continues, but with a different text.[9]

Soares challenges the very concept of nostalgia. Since feelings are linked to the moment when they are felt, to yearn for something from the past is to reinvent it, or to reinvent what one felt about it. It's an act of emotional imagination, which was the specialty of Campos, Pessoa's heteronymous drama queen. Borrowing an image from a song by Billie Holiday, we could say that Pessoa, to write the poem "Birthday," turned on the faucet labeled Álvaro de Campos. Then he turned it off, and wrote other kinds of poems, as well as a passage for *The Book of Disquiet*. There was a moment of acute nostalgia, in which he cried or at least felt like crying, with outstanding results: "Birthday" is a deeply moving poem, often recited in public readings of Pessoa's poetry.

It was a triumphal birthday for the poet, with his three heteronyms and his semiheteronym all saluting him, all contributing to a celebratory bouquet of literary compositions, but there was still more to come. On that same June 13, 1930, he received a birthday message from one of his astral communicators: "You must separate yourself from mortal thoughts and feelings and show no more to the world than the world can see." For Pessoa the meaning was clear enough. He had lately come to understand, more forcefully than before, that his life had a higher, occult significance.

The next day, June 14, was Ophelia's birthday, her thirtieth, and Fernando not only met with her, he presented her with a filigree and enamel bracelet. For his birthday she gave him a cigarette case.[10] Besides exchanging presents, they kissed—something that now only happened rarely. He knew, but she did not, that it was the last time they would ever kiss. Four days later he told her they should separate, and that evening he received another communication from beyond: "Now you soar. Hasten."[11] In July he wrote five more poems for Caeiro's *The Shepherd in Love*, which included a second elegy about the end of love. Unlike the first one he had written in November of the previous year, when he realized that he did not and could not love Ophelia, the July 1930 elegy is narrated in the third person. It tells how a distracted Caeiro, after losing his staff and letting all his sheep scatter, finally stood up from the illusion of love, saw the reality of nature all around him, and "felt the air reopen, with pain, a freedom in his chest."

Pessoa may have been ready to soar, but the relationship with Ophelia Queiroz plodded on. They still met, he still called, and she still wrote letters, wondering when they would get married. Several pages of a letter she sent him on October 7, 1930, described in vivid particulars an ideal day in their future life together under one roof, with her attending to his every small need and seizing every opportunity, from dawn to dusk, to shower him with kisses, unless, of course, he was not in the mood. It was a film that could only fill him with terror. The task of extricating himself, which would in any case be delicate, was made even more so by his friendship with her nephew, Carlos Queiroz, who had helped bring Ophelia and Fernando back together.

◆

PESSOA WAS IN ONE sense the dominant personality in his affectionate relationships, since he required others to respect his timing, his habits, his refusal to make concessions, but he was passive insofar as he rarely took the initiative to develop a rapport. People came to him. This was true of friends and it was true of Ophelia, who had been the one to start flirting when they met in 1919, and while it was Pessoa who, a little unthinkingly, had rekindled the relationship through the ruse of a photograph, it was she who fostered it with enormous energy, even if she could never mold it to her ideal.

This attitude of passivity combined with quietly stubborn self-assertiveness also marked Pessoa's "professional," literary relations, thereby contributing to his paradoxical status as a recognized yet obscure genius. Pessoa was disastrous at what we call networking. Certain friends, however, sometimes networked for him. This was especially true of Carlos Queiroz, the go-between responsible for Pessoa's initial publications in *Presença* and the facilitator of the first meeting between him and two of its three editors, in May 1930, when José Régio and João Gaspar Simões came from Coimbra to Lisbon for the First Salon of Independent Artists.[12]

Intended as a celebration of Portuguese modernism, the salon exhibited paintings, sculptures, drawings, architectural projects, and photographs. Poetry was represented by an anthology that included verses by Álvaro de Campos, Pessoa, and other writers connected to *Orpheu*, *Contemporânea*, and *Presença*. João Gaspar Simões, a burly twenty-seven-year-old, and José Régio, slight in build and one year older, participated in various salon activities and attentively viewed the artworks on display, but they were every bit as interested in meeting Fernando Pessoa, the elusive master of the modernist generation. Carlos Queiroz set up a rendezvous for Sunday, their free day.

Pessoa's usual café, the Martinho da Arcada, was closed on Sundays, so they met at the nearby Café Montanha: Carlos, João, José and, to the surprise and chagrin of the two editors of *Presença*, Álvaro de Campos. Writing about the meeting years later, João Gaspar Simões would report that it was the naval engineer rather than Fernando who showed up. This is not too surprising. While it is true that in his letters to younger writers, Pessoa sometimes assumed the role and tone of a master, offering well-meaning criticism when it was not necessarily wanted, he rejected any role imposed on him from the outside. Since the pilgrims from Coimbra expected a shy and introverted literary master, he showed up as the urbane engineer, who talked to them freely, flippantly, about nothing much. When they asked about the influence of English literature on his work, he puffed on his cigarette and replied, without blinking, "Well,

I've read a couple of English novels." José Régio felt especially ill at ease, and although they had the whole afternoon free, he soon nudged Gaspar Simões, stood up from the table, and announced that they would be on their way.[13]

Diametrically different was Pessoa's encounter, several months earlier, with another young man connected to the *Presença* group. Pierre Hourcade, a French student who had come to the University of Coimbra to complete his dissertation on the poet Guerra Junqueiro, was awed by the writing of Pessoa, a new discovery, and read whatever he could find by him in *Presença* and other magazines. Thanks to Carlos Queiroz, who once more acted as an intermediary, Hourcade had the privilege of meeting Pessoa on a trip he made to Lisbon in February.[14] The trim, bespectacled student of literature eagerly waited at one of the marble-topped tables in the Café Martinho da Arcada, expecting a short and dark-complexioned man infected by the melancholy spirit of Portuguese *saudade*. In walked the poet with a lively gaze, a mischievous smile, and an engaging manner that put him instantly at ease.

Speaking in French, Pessoa described in animated detail the personae of his invented literary universe. Álvaro de Campos, he said over the background noise of clinking saucers, cups, and spoons, groped about in a symbolist brume until one morning, in March 1914, Alberto Caeiro flashed into existence and swept away all illusions with his starkly lucid way of seeing. Awakened from his dreamy ruminations, Campos abandoned literature as he knew it and began to use his writing to upend political, social, and cultural certainties—most flagrantly in his 1917 "Ultimatum." Now oblivious to the café, hearing nothing but Pessoa's voice, the young Frenchman learned that Ricardo Reis—educated in the classics at the same South African school where Pessoa had excelled in English, Latin, and French—reacted to Campos's unbridled freedom by producing compact, strictly metered odes in the manner of Horace. A dialogue between Reis and Campos to be published later in the year, said Pessoa, would pit the classicist's ideals of order and obedience against the engineer's rebelliousness and creative spontaneity. (Although he never published this dialogue, Pessoa did write many passages for it.)

Furnished with these revealing and colorful particulars, Hourcade published a brief article on Pessoa in the June 1930 issue of *Contacts*, an ephemeral Parisian literary review.[15] It was the first time, in any language, that the backstory of the heteronyms was made public. The information about Reis's having studied in South Africa was the only part that did not jibe with the story as Pessoa would tell it in Portuguese. His definitive account of the heteronyms, from 1935, would state for posterity that Ricardo Reis, born in Porto, studied at a Jesuit high school before going on to earn a degree in medicine.

✦

PESSOA DEFINED AND REDEFINED his heteronyms from the time they emerged until almost the end of his life, and it was only in 1930 that he endowed them with a vivid, shared past, making them a psychologically complex "family." He had been willing and even eager to talk to Pierre Hourcade about their origins and their interrelationships because it was a topic at the forefront of his mind; he was about to embark on Álvaro de Campos's "Notes for the Memory of My Master Caeiro," a memoir not only about Alberto Caeiro but also about his profound influence on the other main heteronyms and on Pessoa himself. Pessoa would publish a few pages of these "Notes" in the January–February 1931 issue of *Presença*. They open with an account of how Campos met Caeiro during a trip to the Ribatejo province, north of Lisbon, where the poet-shepherd lived in a white house on top of a hill:

> After completing, in Scotland, almost three quarters of my course in naval engineering, I went on a voyage to the Far East. On my return, I disembarked at Marseilles, unable to bear the thought of more sailing, and came by land to Lisbon. One day a cousin of mine took me on a trip to the Ribatejo, where he knew one of Caeiro's cousins, with whom he had some business dealings. It was in the house of that cousin that I met my future master. That's all there is to tell; it was small like the seeds of all conceptions.

Next Campos sketches, with photographic precision, a verbal portrait of Caeiro: blue eyes and a pale complexion, blond to light brown hair, medium to tall in height but with sloping shoulders, a "strange Greek air" emanating from his inner calm, and, what was even stranger, an "imposingly white" forehead. Campos describes Caeiro, in effect, as a Greek statue,[16] perfectly composed, in spite of the tuberculosis that would end his life just one year later, age twenty-six.

Pessoa had already explained, elsewhere in his writings, how Álvaro de Campos and Ricardo Reis were disciples of Alberto Caeiro, but Campos—in his "Notes" to Caeiro's memory—uses boldly sexual analogies to describe the dramatic conversions that took place when he and Reis first came into contact with the serene and statuesque master poet. He recalls how, in his own case, the stunning simplicity of Caeiro's way of seeing and speaking seduced him with a primal shock, "as always occurs when someone is deflowered," but contrary to what happens in physical seduction, the effect on him "was to receive all at once, in all my sensations, a virginity I'd never had."

No less drastic was the sexual shock experienced by Ricardo Reis. Campos tells us that this "latent pagan," at odds both with modern life and with "that ancient life into which he should have been born," discovered his true nature and became a pagan poet when he met Alberto Caeiro, "the reconstructor of Paganism." It was a total transformation, leading Campos to remark: "Some physiologists say that it's possible to change sex. I don't know if it's true, because I don't know if anything is 'true,' but I know that Ricardo Reis stopped being a woman and became a man, or stopped being a man and became a woman—as you like—when he met Caeiro." Pessoa, it seems, was aware of the trailblazing work of sex-change surgery being done in Weimar Germany, particularly through the Sexual Science Institute of Berlin, founded in 1919, and although he claimed to be little interested in sex and sexuality, he was pleased to have a heteronym who was transsexual, at least psycho-poetically speaking.

"Notes for the Memory of My Master Caeiro" is redolent with nostalgia, and Pessoa would later admit in a letter that he sometimes cried real tears[17] while writing about the fond encounters and friendly discussions that supposedly took place among master Caeiro, Campos, Reis, António Mora, and himself, Fernando Pessoa. Perhaps the tears were a spillover from his acute solitude that preceded, gave rise to, and outlived this ghostly family. Or perhaps they were the tears of a seasoned method actor. In any case, the heteronymous theater had been slowly collapsing, and the literary spectacle that marked Pessoa's birthday in June 1930—when he managed to write poems for all of his major heteronyms on the same day—was a last hurrah. After a few more Caeiro poems written the following month, the shepherd would never be heard from again. Campos, meanwhile, increasingly voiced the same anxieties as Pessoa himself. Their poetic differences had to do more with tone and form than with substance.

◆

AROUND THE SAME TIME that Álvaro de Campos was proposing that
Ricardo Reis might be gender fluid, Pessoa invented his last heteronym
and only female alter ego: Maria José, author of an anguished and solitary "Letter from a Hunchback Girl to a Metalworker," which would
not be published until 1990.[18] In addition to her hunchback, nineteen-
year-old Maria José suffers from crippling arthritis and late-stage tuberculosis. She knows she will die soon and, unable to contain herself,
desperately declares her love to Senhor António, the handsome metalworker who passes below her window on his way to work in the morning
and back home in the evening. The letter describes her life as a shut-in
who depends on others for all her needs, spends the whole day next to
the window, and looks forward to nothing except for seeing him pass by.
She wishes he would look up and meet her gaze with his, but without
looking at her too closely, since she's not at all attractive, and without
ever perceiving what she feels for him, since he could only laugh. Which
is why, she says, "I'm only writing this letter to hold it against my chest
as if you'd written it to me instead of me to you."

With this love letter, Pessoa, as method actor, delivered one of his
finest performances, capturing the intense emotion of the luckless young
woman while at the same time replicating the simple language and syntax we would expect from someone of her social class. We can wonder,
however, exactly what method he followed. So closely did Pessoa identify with the role he was playing that the hunchback at one point refers
to herself with a masculine rather than feminine form (*eu mesmo* instead
of *eu mesma*).[19] This grammatical slip reinforces our suspicion that poor
Maria José was a parodic stand-in for Fernando Pessoa, who had none
of her exaggeratedly pathetic qualities but who thought of himself as an
unattractive, unlovable creature—regardless of however much Ophelia
loved him. "I've never had a flattering notion of my physical appearance,"
he ventriloquized through Bernardo Soares in a passage for *The Book of
Disquiet* written on April 5, 1930.[20] Arriving one morning at the office
of Vasques & Co., the assistant bookkeeper looks at a recently printed
group photograph of the employees and sees himself, among all the others, as a "nondescript Jesuit" with a "gaunt and inexpressive face." The
metalworker, on the other hand, epitomizes the dashing and athletic
man that Fernando, whose second name was António, had sometimes

fantasized being, even if he quickly realized, as a teenager, that he would not get very far with Eugen Sandow's bodybuilding method.

Toward the end of her letter, Maria José announces her imminent death in the same epistolary breath she bids farewell to the metal-worker: "Goodbye, Senhor António, my days are numbered." For Pessoa the letter signified a farewell to all love, a renunciation not only of love affairs he might have with others but also of his ongoing love affair with himself—an affair that alternated between self-pity, represented by the hunchback, and romantic self-re-creations such as the metalworker and the major heteronyms.

Pessoa was divesting himself of all attachments, outward and inward. On August 26, 1930, he wrote a poem that begins:

I want to be free and insincere
With no creed, duty, or titled post.
I loathe all prisons, love included.
Whoever would love me, please don't!

Pessoa also refused to be imprisoned by his heteronyms. He was ready to go beyond them, and beyond literature itself.

Yet Pessoa's literary output did not slacken. His "orthonymous" poetry machine, on the contrary, was more productive than it had ever been. Whereas he had written around forty poems per year under his own name between 1927 and 1929, he wrote nearly three times that number in just the last six months of 1930. His poetry became, like *The Book of Disquiet*, a running diary of thoughts and feelings, concerned with his uncertain place and purpose and destiny in the universe. Heteronymy as a creative and structuring mechanism was waning, but the poet felt as self-dispersed as ever:

I don't know how many souls I have.
I've changed at every moment.
I always feel like a stranger.
I've never seen or found myself.

. . .

Attentive to what I am and see,
I become them and stop being I.
Each of my dreams and each desire
Belongs to whoever had it, not me.

(August 24, 1930)

Pessoa accepted that there was no *essential* self he would ever know. But he hoped to discover the place and significance of the relative self—the ever-changing person or ensemble of persons called Fernando Pessoa—in the grand scheme of things. This was an old aspiration. Now, however, he was ready to try out new methods of exploration. He even considered the possibility of relinquishing control, of pursuing truth not only through private study, through his prodigious power of reasoning, and through imaginary encounters with invisible astral spirits, but also through direct contact with a living spiritual master.

On August 29, Pessoa received a telegram: "Crowley arriving by Alcantara please meet."[21] On that same day Aleister Crowley, the notorious English magus reputed by many to be the devil incarnate but known to disciples as Master Therion, set sail from Southampton on the RMS *Alcantara*. When the boat pulled into Lisbon's harbor on Tuesday afternoon, September 2, Pessoa, a pacing bundle of nerves in a suit, was waiting for him on the dock.

# CHAPTER 62

**T**HE THOUGHT OF MEETING ANYONE FOR THE first time filled Pessoa with a mild dread, and the very name of Aleister Crowley, who was W. Somerset Maugham's model for the unsettling protagonist of *The Magician* (1908), could stir twinges of anxiety even in normally unflappable people. He was one of the most reviled public figures in Great Britain, with a reputation for black magic, kinky sex, immoderate drug use, and the ruination of people who came into close contact with him. But for some people, including Fernando Pessoa, contact with Crowley was a spiritually life-changing experience.

Born in 1875 to a well-to-do family of English evangelical Christians, Edward Alexander Crowley began to challenge Christian theology and flout Victorian standards of conduct at an early age, giving free rein to his sexual urges as a teenager. He also wrote poetry, climbed mountains, played chess, and painted. At Cambridge University, where he adopted the name Aleister, a Scottish corruption of Alexander, he had his first mystical experiences and became passionately interested in the occult. In 1898 he was initiated into the Hermetic Order of the Golden Dawn, founded in London ten years earlier. The order had appropriated and reformulated an eclectic array of magical symbols and rituals from ancient traditions such as Kabbalah, organizing them into a hierarchical system of personal spiritual development. Crowley soon quarreled with William Butler Yeats and other long-standing members of the order, which began to splinter in 1900 because of a leadership crisis. In 1909, after spending a number of years mountaineering, striking out on new spiritual paths, and taking up with assorted lovers in Mexico, the United States, Japan, China, Nepal, India, Egypt, and half a dozen other countries, Crowley and another ex-member of the Golden Dawn formed their own magical order, the A∴A∴, whose initials are thought to stand for Argentium Astrum, or Silver Star.

The symbols, rites, and initiatory degrees of the A∴A∴ order closely mimicked those of the Golden Dawn, but blended into the magic mix was Thelema, a religion invented by Crowley. The name Thelema comes from a Greek word meaning "will," and "Do what thou wilt shall be the whole of the Law" was—and still is—the religion's guiding motto. The responsorial countermotto is: "Love is the law, love under will."* Pessoa, as we shall see, would develop his own schemes for spiritual advancement based on the initiatory hierarchies of the Golden Dawn and the A∴A∴ order, and he would adopt for himself the basic rule of Thelema: Do what thou wilt.

In 1912 Crowley was appointed grand master of the British section of a rather different spiritual society: the Ordo Templi Orientis, or Order of the Oriental Templars (O.T.O.). Founded around the turn of the century in Austria or Germany, this occult order used sex magic in its liturgy and initiation rites. Crowley, who eventually became the O.T.O.'s worldwide leader, expanded its sexual rituals and infused them with Thelemic doctrines. After spending the war years in the United States, where he wrote for magazines and newspapers, enjoyed a vibrant magical sex life, and titled himself Master Therion, he returned to Europe and in 1920 founded the communal Abbey of Thelema in Cefalù, Sicily. Its members wore ornate robes, worshipped the sun, occasionally performed a Crowleyan Gnostic Mass, and participated in sex-magic ceremonies that were enhanced by the use of hashish and heroin, to which Crowley was addicted. When one of the commune's residents died from enteritis in 1923, the man's devastated wife denounced the practices and sanitary conditions at the abbey, Crowley was deported from Italy, and the British press—which had already maligned him for organizing "pagan orgies," advocating "Platonic love" (he was bisexual), and encouraging drug use—now branded him "the Wickedest Man in the World."[1] Pessoa read about the magician and onetime mountaineer with heightened curiosity, convinced that a spiritual leader capable of attracting so much scorn very likely possessed unworldly powers and insights.

While there was some truth to most of the accusations leveled against Crowley, "wicked" was not the right adjective to define his character.

---

* Crowley's religion was inspired by François Rabelais (c. 1490–1553), whose satirical *Gargantua and Pantagruel* describes an Abbey of Thélème where Catholic monks and nuns lived together in luxury accommodations, which included tennis courts and pleasure gardens. They were required to observe only one rule: "Do what thou wilt."

The tragedies that befell some of his followers were nearly always pre-inscribed in their personalities, marked by neediness and a willingness to be psychologically dominated. Other people, relishing Crowley's lively intelligence without surrendering their critical and emotional independence, consorted with him on an equal footing.

Crowley's romantic, rambunctious biography—full of sex, drugs, lovers, enemies, and one thousand and one adventures on four different continents—stands in absolute contrast to the life of Pessoa, which was founded on ideas, abstractions, imaginary characters, and mental projections. These denizens of Pessoa's mind were, of all his friends, the most faithful and enduring. From a certain point of view, they were also his worst enemies, enslaving him no less than sex and drugs enslaved Crowley. Pessoa, in many ways, was Crowley turned inside out, which is what makes their encounter so fascinating, and mutually revealing.

Crowley's considerable inheritance had dried up a long time ago, and after the Sicilian fiasco his star began to fall. But he still found patrons willing to finance him as well as attractive women—plus a few men—to keep him company and be his partners in sex magic. Throughout all his adventures, the English magus steadily wrote and published poetry, occasional fiction, and numerous books on the occult and on magic, which he said should be studied like a science. One of his latest writing projects was an "autohagiography," the first two volumes of which were published in 1929 as *The Confessions of Aleister Crowley*. Pessoa ordered *The Confessions* from Mandrake Press that November. After receiving and quickly devouring the first volume, he suggested in a letter to the publisher that the autobiographer's astrological chart was incorrect and should be recast with a slightly earlier time of birth. Pessoa's letter was forwarded to Crowley, who wrote him on December 11. Admitting that he did little astrology, Crowley accepted the observation about his birth chart and said he would be glad to have some information about his current astrological situation. He signed his letter as Tò Μέγα Θηρίον, the Great Beast.

Mandrake Press was a new publishing house, and Pessoa, seeing an opportunity, sent the editors three of his chapbooks of English poems, "just as a curiosity without interest." He sent the same three chapbooks—of which he had dozens if not hundreds of unsold copies—directly to Aleister Crowley and received an immediate letter of thanks. It opened and closed, like all his letters, with the twin precepts of Thelema.

Care Frater:

Do what thou wilt shall be the whole of the Law.

Thank you very much for the three little books. I think they are really very remarkable for excellence.

In the Sonnets, or rather Quatorzains, you seem to have recaptured the original Elizabethan impulse—which is magnificent.

I like the other poems, too, very much indeed.

Love is the law, love under will.

Yours fraternally,

Aleister Crowley[2]

To this typed letter, dated December 22, 1929, Crowley added a handwritten postscript: "I have, indeed, taken the arrival of your poetry as a definite Message, which I should like to explain in person. Will you be in Lisboa for the next three months? If so, I should like to come and see you: but without telling anyone. Please let me know by return of post. 666"

Without telling anyone? Why the secrecy? Wavering between nervous excitement and apprehension, Pessoa did not immediately reply. If the Great Beast 666 wanted to meet him, then the intersection of their paths must have been plotted in the stars, but was it really a good idea? On December 31 he took the train to Évora to visit his sister and her family, returning to Lisbon on January 2. The next day he received an encouraging message from one of his astral communicators: "You mark now soon a marvellous stage in the least of your careers. You will further your martial tendencies now." The planet Mars is associated with action, self-affirmation, sexual desire—areas in which Pessoa's "career" was indeed not brilliant. Perhaps Crowley, with his "Do what thou wilt" philosophy, would help invigorate those feeble "martial" tendencies. But Pessoa was not yet ready to meet the magus. In his letter of January 6, 1930, he suggested that Crowley delay his visit to Lisbon until March, partly because he had unspecified matters to take care of in the coming weeks and partly for "astrological reasons." Moreover, he claimed he might be traveling to London in late February, in which case they could meet there.

One of Pessoa's close friends was also in touch with Crowley. After listening, a little awestruck, to Pessoa's description of the occult master's tumultuous life and unorthodox teachings, Raul Leal asked for his address and sent him a copy of *Antichrist and the Glory of the Holy Spirit*, a "sacred poem-hymn" he had published in French, as well as a lengthy letter, also in French. Introducing himself as Henoch, the Prophet of God and of Death sent to the world to announce the Kingdom of the Holy Spirit, Leal informed Crowley that their respective doctrines had much in common. They had, in reality, a little in common. Leal's idea that one needed to go to the depths of fleshly bestiality in order to transcend it, making the bestial divine, resembled Crowley's own spiritual method, which relied on heavy drug use and extreme sex to reach an elevated spiritual state. But the beast in Crowley was a loudly laughing, wildly playful beast. Leal's was a sad, excruciatingly earnest beast that suffered, covered with wounds, in the corner of its cage. "My divine mission requires me to become a martyr of the Occult," he wrote in his letter.[3]

Crowley, who had plenty of experience with kooks and eccentrics, politely replied to the Prophet of God and of Death that he looked forward to making his acquaintance. The man in Portugal he really wanted to meet was the bilingual poet and accomplished astrologer named Fernando Pessoa, who continued to temporize. On February 25, Pessoa wrote him that "not till the very verge of yesterday" did it become clear he would not be going to England that month. In May, Crowley, who had traveled to Germany the previous month, wrote Pessoa to inquire whether he might be going to London anytime soon. Not soon, Pessoa answered, but perhaps in the fall. Thus the poet managed to keep postponing their meeting, by repeatedly suggesting it could wait until he traveled to London—a prospect only marginally more likely than his traveling to Tahiti.

The two men might not ever have met were it not for Hanni Larissa Jaeger, a young German American woman Crowley had met in Berlin.* Abandoning his current wife, who would soon enter an insane asylum, he took up with Jaeger, bringing her to England in August. On September 4, 1930, this new Scarlet Woman—the ninth or tenth woman so titled—would turn twenty, and Crowley decided to commemorate the occasion by taking her to Portugal for a Magical Retirement, or holiday, that would include walks along the sea and sex magic in their hotel. He

---

* Born in Berlin in 1910, Hanni Jaeger spent her adolescent years in America, having immigrated in 1924—with her mother and two older sisters—to join her father in Santa Barbara, California. (Ellis Island online database.)

also hoped to set up a Portuguese branch of the Ordo Templi Orientis, under the direction of Fernando Pessoa.[4]

✦

CROWLEY HAD SENSED A rare creative intelligence in Pessoa. Even before learning about the heteronyms, he could feel something magical, alchemical, in a Portuguese poet capable of writing sonnets in the style and language of Shakespeare. He also thought highly of the other poems Pessoa had sent: his raunchy "Epithalamium," which would have made the Greek inventors of the form blush, and his bravely homoerotic "Antinous." His intuition told him that Pessoa—a spiritually, magically, and sexually advanced individual—would be the ideal leader of a Portuguese section of the O.T.O., some of whose higher degrees of initiation involved sexual doctrines and practices vaguely inspired by Tantric traditions from India. In Crowley's reworking of the O.T.O. system, the eighth degree was an initiation into masturbatory magic, the ninth degree an initiation into magical vaginal intercourse, and the eleventh degree an initiation into anal intercourse for magical purposes. The rites associated with these higher degrees included the consumption of sexual and other body fluids.[5] To use a tired but fitting cliché, this hardly sounds like Pessoa's cup of tea.

The O.T.O.'s sex-magic rites might remind us of the salacious behaviors luridly described by heteronym Jean Seul twenty years before, in moral satires against decadence such as "La France en 1950," but they were quite beyond anything that Pessoa and his present-day heteronyms could ever contemplate, let alone teach and practice. Although a resourceful as well as voracious reader, Pessoa probably knew very little about the secretive O.T.O. and thus could scarcely have any inkling of what the English magician and occultist had in mind for him.

Lisbon was hotter than usual for early September, which, added to his nervousness, must have made Pessoa sweat a little as he greeted Crowley and his girlfriend, who stepped off their ship around four in the afternoon. He accompanied the travelers from the port to the Hotel de l'Europe, on Praça de Camões, where they were staying for the night. After the couple checked in, they all sat down for a proper conversation, in which Crowley lost no time in discussing with Pessoa the possibility of his heading up an O.T.O. chapter in Portugal. Pessoa, who had his own agenda, presented some ideas for an Anglo-Portuguese publishing venture. Hanni Jaeger—a slender, sensuous blonde—observed them while they talked, no doubt over drinks at the hotel bar. Both men had slightly feminine features and gestures, but they looked completely different. With his shaved head and flabby jowls, the countenance of the fifty-five-year-old Beast vaguely resembled a pyramid—a tired pyramid caving in on itself. His eyes, however, could still pierce and intimidate. Pessoa was well protected—by his round-rimmed glasses, his moustache, and his hat, which hid his own baldness. Speaking in English helped him to be a better actor, evincing self-confidence. He made a good first impression. "A *very* nice man," Crowley wrote in his diary. About Lisbon, however, he was not complimentary: "Squalid, ill-paved, dirty, narrow, dull."[6]

Before leaving the next day, September 3, for the beaches of Estoril, where he and Jaeger would spend the next two weeks, Crowley wrote a letter urging Pessoa to come and see them as soon as possible. They needed to talk further about possible publication projects and, especially, about "the scheme of putting the Work of the Order on a world-wide basis of close organization."[7] On Sunday, September 7, Pessoa boarded the suburban train for the resort town of Estoril, which attracted an increasingly international clientele, and met the two vacationers for lunch. They talked for a few hours and agreed to see each other again on Tuesday, when Crowley would be going to Lisbon to pick up mail. Pessoa said he would invite Raul Leal to join them. His friend was eager to meet Crowley, who was at least mildly curious to hear what the soi-disant prophet would have to say in person. Pessoa, in one of his letters to the magus, had spoken of Leal's "splendidly intense metaphysical ability." Perhaps he would be a useful auxiliary for implanting the O.T.O. in Portugal. What would really be useful was someone with capital to help finance the order and pay its worldwide spiritual leader a salary. Leal? Pessoa?

That evening Pessoa, feeling jittery, cast an astrological chart about what might result from the meeting between Crowley, Hanni Jaeger, himself, and Raul Leal. It's impossible to say what expectations or qualms he harbored. The stars' answer to Pessoa's mysterious inquiry was that the meeting of the four individuals entailed a definite advantage for Jaeger, a slight advantage for Pessoa, no advantage for Leal, and a slight disadvantage for Crowley. Summing up, the astrologer cryptically noted in English: "The case will not pass, but very little harm will come of it."[8]

The four of them met at the Café Martinho da Arcada, whose white-shirted, black-aproned waiters looked upon their most loyal customer with bulging eyes: never had they seen him with a woman before, and Hanni Jaeger radiated sensuality. Their astonishment increased when they saw the young woman smile with soft delight as she and Pessoa conversed in English. Crowley and Raul Leal, meanwhile, spoke to each other in French. A little of Pessoa's friend went a long way for Crowley, who would comment in his diary: "Met Leal: don't like him. There's something very definitely wrong about him." The two men would not meet again.[9] Pessoa, on the other hand, was very much to Crowley's liking, even though it was by now obvious that there would be no O.T.O. chapter in Portugal. The poet was clearly not the right type for being initiated, or initiating others, into sex magic. Crowley deferred, instead, to Pessoa's idea of their collaborating on some publication projects, and he offered to write a preface for a book of his English poems, assuming that Mandrake Press would publish it. The press was struggling, and Crowley hoped that Pessoa—always impeccably dressed, and with his signet ring that advertised nobility—might have some money to invest.

Pessoa, ingenuously enough, wrote a long letter to Mandrake Press outlining some projects he had discussed with Crowley: the publication of books by "strange or unknown Portuguese authors," including Fernando Pessoa, in England; the opening of a Mandrake branch in Portugal, where the printing plates for its editions could be made more cheaply and no less professionally, with Pessoa guaranteeing that they would be "letter-perfect"; and the translation of Mandrake books, such as *The Confessions of Aleister Crowley*, into Portuguese. Pessoa received a prompt reply from Robert Thompson Thynne, chairman of the board of Mandrake Press. He thought Pessoa's proposals "extremely interesting" and wondered whether he would like to be a shareholder of Mandrake Press and its official Iberian representative. "We have at present 2,000 £1, 10% Cumulative Preference Shares available," he wrote, pointing out the large potential profits to be made. (Two thousand pounds in 1930 would be equivalent to at least £120,000 today.)

One week later, Pessoa received a prospectus for "Aleister Crowley Ltd.," a company that, if successfully established, would take over and exploit all of the magician's assets, which included not only his books and manuscripts but also theater and film rights, his paintings, the copyright for a set of Crowley-designed chess pieces, and his secret recipe for a liqueur currently in the trial stage. The potentially huge yearly profits would be divided among shareholders after Crowley, as managing director, drew his salary of £1000.

Even before the prospectus was sent—by Karl Germer, a German disciple of Master Therion and his current financial lifeline—Pessoa had confessed to Crowley that he was flat broke, which did not make him any less appreciated.[10] As for Hanni Jaeger, an aspiring artist, she found Pessoa to be thoroughly charming, a feeling that was reciprocal, though the charm she exerted was of a different order. He felt it most strongly during their time together "alone" at the café, when Crowley was occupied with Raul Leal. The day after that meeting he wrote the only poem of his entire life in which the speaker unequivocally lusts after a female body:

> Her very being surprises.
> A tall, tawny blonde,
> It delights me just to think
> Of seeing her half-ripe body.
>
> Her tall breasts resemble
> (Or would, were she lying down)
> Two hills in the early morning,
> Even if it isn't dawn.
>
> . . .
>
> She entices like a boat,
> Or like an orange, so sweet.
> When, my God, will I sail?
> When, O hunger, will I eat?[11]

Crowley, meanwhile, was sating his sexual hunger at Estoril's Hotel Paris with cunnilingus, fellatio, and anal intercourse, all recorded in his Magical Record, or diary. His favorite pet names for Jaeger were Monster and Anu, the latter because her anus was for him the most delectable of all her body parts. On September 11, after noting that he had anally penetrated her for at least the second time during their trip, he vowed in the diary: "She will learn this Art." She may have been learning this and other "arts," but at the price of increasing psychological instability. On

September 12 she had a "melancholy fit," on the thirteenth "a long fit of hysterical sobbing," and two days later "a sudden transient fit." On the evening of the sixteenth she suffered "a general hysterical attack" that stirred up the whole hotel.

The next morning, she packed her suitcase, went to Lisbon, sought financial assistance from the American consulate, and booked passage on a steamer bound for Bremen, from where she would get a train to Berlin. Crowley went to Lisbon but could not persuade her to stay, and on the twentieth she departed on the SS *Werra*. That same day he went to Sintra, where he won a few rounds of chess against a Portuguese master. It was Pessoa who had arranged for the two chess buffs to meet.

Crowley returned to Lisbon on Sunday, September 21, and checked out of his hotel two days later. He told the staff that he was going back to Sintra. Instead he disappeared, leaving behind a suicide note next to the Boca do Inferno, or Mouth of Hell, an ominous, wave-racked gorge amid the sea cliffs just beyond Cascais, the next town over from Estoril. Such were the facts reported by Lisbon's newspapers. The note, weighted down by an exotic cigarette case, read: "I cannot live without you. The other 'Boca do Infierno' will get me—it will not be as hot as yours!" It was addressed to L. G. P., signed by Tu Li Yu, and dated using astrological symbols. The person who supposedly found the note was Augusto Ferreira Gomes, and Fernando Pessoa confirmed to the police that the handwriting, along with the Spanish spelling of "Inferno," was Crowley's. He explained that L. G. P. were probably the initials of Hanni Jaeger's "mystical name" and that Tu Li Yu was an ancient Chinese sage of whom Crowley believed himself to be the reincarnation.

The Portuguese border police quickly verified that Crowley was a passenger on a Paris-bound train that crossed into Spain on Tuesday, but Fernando Pessoa told the papers and the police that he happened to see Crowley, "or his ghost," on two different occasions the following day, September 24. This led to the hypothesis that it was only Crowley's passport—without Crowley—that crossed the Spanish border on the Sud-Express.

In fact, Crowley left his suicide note not on the cliffs above the Mouth of Hell but with Fernando Pessoa, on the morning of the twenty-third, before catching his train to Paris, from where he would continue on to Berlin. He also left an interpretive key to the meaning of "L. G. P." and "Tu Li Yu," and a couple of written suggestions as to how to "work up" the story, which he thought could "fetch £200 [in] American rights alone."

The suicide hoax was entirely his own idea, but Pessoa was only too glad to collaborate, and he enlisted Augusto Ferreira Gomes's help to turn the story into front-page news. Ferreira Gomes photographed the suicide note and cigarette case, which belonged to Pessoa's brother-in-law, for publication in the papers and "interviewed" Fernando Pessoa, Crowley's main contact in Portugal and the chief eyewitness of the mysterious case. Pessoa wrote both the questions and the answers to the interview, giving one copy to his friend and keeping a carbon copy for himself.

As a well-connected journalist, Ferreira Gomes easily obtained wide coverage for the farce—with articles appearing in the major newspapers and in a couple of magazines.[12] Since he happened to be going to Paris to get married to Marcelle, his fiancée, in October, Ferreira Gomes took advantage of that trip to report the suicide story to *Détective*, a French weekly whose editors made it the featured article of their October 30 issue. In England the story appeared in the October 12 edition of Manchester's *Empire News*.[13] The paper's anonymous reporter noted that the statement of the Portuguese border police was at odds with the testimony of a "gentleman named Fernando Pessoa" and wondered: "Are there two Crowleys, one genuine and one an impostor?" Three days later the *Oxford Mail* published an article stating that Crowley, according to a London medium, had been pushed over a cliff and into the Mouth of Hell "by an agent of the Roman Catholic Church," who planted the suicide note to cover up the murder.[14]

By September 27, which was when news of his strange disappearance began circulating in Portugal, Crowley was already in Berlin, with Hanni Jaeger. He lay low for a few weeks, since the news could proliferate only if his whereabouts remained a mystery. The fake suicide was to some extent a piece of romantic theater, like a lover's serenade, to impress Jaeger. Mainly, it was a publicity stunt, an attempt to revive the floundering Aleister Crowley brand. Mandrake Press was bringing out his books, but bookstores were reluctant to stock them. Unfortunately for the Great Beast, British newspapers—except for the two papers just quoted—were unwilling to touch the Mouth of Hell story, precisely because it smelled like a hoax.[15] Portugal's largest-circulation newspaper was also skeptical. "A Case That Looks like Sheer Mystification," read the title of its article on the missing magus.[16] Such publicity as the gimmick generated did nothing to boost the sales figures for Crowley's books, and before the year was over Mandrake Press filed for bankruptcy.

✦

PESSOA HOPED THAT *HE* at least could profit from the bogus suicide, by packaging it as a detective novella written in English and aimed perhaps at the American market, where Crowley thought the story would be an easy sell. Titled *The Mouth of Hell*, the novella took shape in Pessoa's mind in October and November, and on December 3 he sent copies of a synopsis to Crowley and his host Karl Germer in Berlin, as well as to Crowley's secretary in London, Israel Regardie.[17]

Narrated by an English detective hired to discover what really happened to the vanished Beast, *The Mouth of Hell* is trademark Pessoa, mixing facts with fiction and featuring characters with multiple identities. There is a pseudo-Crowley, who crosses the border into Spain, along with a real Crowley, who is trying to elude enemies, and a pseudo as well as a real Pessoa. Augusto Ferreira Gomes, Pessoa's real enough friend, is also a character in the novella. And so is the formerly real but lately deceased Ernesto Martins, a cabdriver whose mysterious murder on the outskirts of Lisbon was reported in the newspaper on the same day as Crowley's disappearance.[18] It tickled Pessoa to include the unlucky cabbie in the pages of his novella, where, a few hours after driving Crowley from point A to point B in Lisbon, he is brutally shot down in cold blood—identical to the cold blood that covered the corpse of the nonfictional Ernesto Martins, who was found at 6:30 a.m. on September 27, 1930.

Crowley, writing from Berlin, offered a few suggestions for the novella, which Pessoa ended up dividing into ten chapters. Within a few months he had a rough draft, although some chapters still needed to be fleshed out and the whole work revised and polished. Pessoa, as I have noted, was not adept at creating dramatic suspense and painting well-drawn scenes, but the biggest, perhaps insurmountable problem of *The Mouth of Hell* was the event that inspired it. Crowley's pseudo-suicide was not a very interesting subject, and Pessoa's fictionalized handling of it was almost bound to be a dull read. He suspected as much. His preface to the novella admits that the subject matter "may seem to the reader to be of very slight importance" and the resulting narrative "rather minute and perhaps tedious," but if the reader presses on "he will find more thrills than he expects." Actually, he—or she—won't.

The most interesting chapter of *The Mouth of Hell* considers how it is possible that Crowley could be simultaneously "a sort of mountebank" and "a profound occultist and magician." Questioned by the English detective, the character named Fernando Pessoa explains that Crowley has "a dual life," divided into a lower and a higher self, and the futility of the former does not invalidate the spiritual superiority of the latter.[19]

For Pessoa, in fact, it was almost as if Crowley the charlatan (the self he showed to the world) vouched for the authenticity of Crowley the superior magus (the self that the world could not see). And besides those two basic, opposing selves, Crowley was dozens of subselves: from mountaineer to chess player, from yoga master to kabbalist, heroin addict to religious mystic, poet, painter, journalist, a high priest, an active sodomite with women, and a passive sodomite with men. Pessoa, a prodigious self-multiplier in his *imagination*, had to gape in awe at Aleister Crowley, who in actuality managed to be many different, sometimes contradictory things.

The novelist Christopher Isherwood, whose *Goodbye to Berlin* (1939) would be adapted into the hugely successful musical *Cabaret* (1966), hobnobbed with Crowley in Berlin's bars and clubs in the early 1930s and commented, in his diary, that "one suspects he didn't really believe in anything."[20] But one could just as well say that Crowley believed in absolutely everything—just like Fernando Pessoa. On this point the two men converged. Although their lifestyles were antithetical, both were inclined to give a little credence to everything, a lot of credence to certain things, and total credence to nothing.

✦

**THROUGHOUT HIS ADULT LIFE** Pessoa had felt the pull of the spiritual world, without knowing what that world encompassed and wondering, often enough, if it might be nothing more than his own wish for another world, another reality. Even after he began practicing astrology, in late 1914, uncertainty dogged him, so that he alternately accepted and rejected the teachings of Theosophy and the possibility of contacting astral spirits. In 1925, after reading two new books on Rosicrucianism,[21] he began drafting several interrelated essays that discussed, among other things, the idea that there are nonmaterial planes of existence and the role of reincarnation in the belief system of occultists.[22] But whatever beliefs he himself entertained, Pessoa failed to finish his essays, and during the rest of the decade he wrote little else about the occult, a subject that fascinated him but triggered doubts he could not quell. Might it, after all, just be metaphysical gibberish?

His vacillating attitude fled like an exorcised demon when, in 1930, he met Aleister Crowley, a powerful spiritual master not because he never doubted but because he never let doubt stop him. In the same way that Walt Whitman liberated Pessoa poetically, showing him how to rip off the suit of traditional poetic forms and diction in order to express naked emotion, the Great Beast freed Pessoa spiritually, emboldening him to follow his spiritual inclinations without fretting over what his reason might consider implausible or nonsensical. Belief, for Crowley, was not a matter of conviction but of dramatic enactment. Snapping up whatever he found useful or delightful from yoga, Egyptian mythology, Rosicrucianism, the Golden Dawn, and on, and on, he forged it all into his own religion, Thelema.

Pessoa, of course, had also proposed a new religion, Portuguese paganism, whose avatar was Caeiro, with Ricardo Reis and António Mora as the two main apostles, but it was basically a poetic conceit, without any rituals or transcendental ambitions. Esoteric religions, on the other hand, claimed to be vehicles for gaining access to hidden truths, a hypothesis Pessoa was far more willing to admit after reading and meeting Aleister Crowley, who impressed upon him two lessons about truth. The first was that all traditions ultimately express the same truths.[23] The second lesson was that the truth, for a spiritually attuned person, is whatever that person says it is. "Say what thou wilt shall be the whole of the Law." Though he never actually uttered this variation on the core motto of Thelema— "*Do* what thou wilt shall be the whole of the Law"—Crowley intimated it through his own example.

✦

ON OCTOBER 23, 1930, exactly a month after Crowley secretly left Lisbon, Pessoa wrote the poem "Elias Artista." Also known in English as Elias the Artist, Elias Artista was the name of a supremely wise alchemist-to-come prophesied by Paracelsus (1493–1541), a Swiss German physician, philosopher, and renowned occultist. Besides transmuting all types of metals, Elias Artista was supposed to reveal to humanity new kinds of knowledge, revolutionizing the sciences and ushering in a utopian age. Pessoa read about this messianic, Sebastian-like figure in his books on the Rosicrucians, who assumed that this future enlightener of the world would be a man from their own brotherhood. Speaking in the first person, the Elias of Pessoa's poem meditates on the source of his, or of anyone's, superior knowledge:

Everything in this or in the other world
Is what, in our will, we think it is.
Everything is our own deep self.
I flood myself with my imagining,
And the outer world cannot invade me.

After meeting Crowley, Pessoa was ready to dedicate both his *will* and his *imagination* to the pursuit of higher, occult knowledge. He was Elias Artista.

He was also the weary high priestess of "O último sortilégio" ("The Last Spell"), a poem written in mid-October. The priestess recalls the power she once wielded to enchant, to conjure up, to subdue infernal forces, and to make people fall in love with her. No longer able—and no longer wishing—to do any of those things, she musters the remaining vestiges of her incantatory powers for a different purpose. Her last act of magic, invoked at the end of the poem, is to become a statue of herself in a living body, to die to all she is or ever was, and to be reborn in that death as *nothing*, the nothingness in which her true earthly life consisted.

"The Last Spell" was a poetic ritual of self-initiation. This is confirmed by the fact that Pessoa made an English translation of the poem to send to Crowley, who served him as an informal, ad hoc master.[24] The master wrote back from Berlin to say that the poem was "pretty bloody damn good." Another ritual act, or part 2 of the same ritual, was Pessoa's translation into Portuguese of Crowley's signature poem, "Hymn to Pan." Alhough not a great poem, its ruttish, hot-blooded energy makes Shelley's "Hymn of Pan" and Keats's hymn to the same god, in "Endymion," read like tame pastorals. Pan was a lusty god of the outdoors, of springtime, of magic, and of sex. Christians linked him to Satan, of whom Crowley had no fear. The narrator of his poem begins by summoning the goatish god to come and possess him:

Thrill with lissome lust of the light,
O man! My man!
Come careering out of the night
Of Pan! Io Pan.

. . .

Come, O come!
I am numb
With the lonely lust of devildom.

By the end of the poem the narrator has become one with the wanton, insatiable god:

I am Pan! Io Pan! Io Pan Pan! Pan!
I am thy mate, I am thy man,
Goat of thy flock, I am gold, I am god,
Flesh to thy bone, flower to thy rod.

"Hymn to Pan" prefaces Crowley's *Magick in Theory and Practice* (1929), a copy of which was sent to Pessoa from London at the author's request in October 1930. Read or recited, the poem may have aroused some of Crowley's disciples to magically sexual readiness, but the act of translating it served an opposite purpose for Pessoa, who was ready to embrace sexual abstinence as his own destiny. He announced his indifference to sex in a letter to João Gaspar Simões that November, right around the time he embarked on his translation.

In this letter, already mentioned earlier, Pessoa claimed that his heterosexual "Epithalamium" and homosexual "Antinous," written in 1913 and 1915, served to free him from "obscenity," since this was "a hindrance to superior mental processes."[25] If Pessoa meant that the two poems were written to get sex out of his system, the attempt emphatically failed. Henry More and other astral spirits, in 1916 and 1917, berated him for being a masturbator; sexual longing was a topic that continued to crop up in his literary works; and the possibility of sensual physical contact was one of the attractions that drew him to Ophelia Queiroz, in 1919 and again in 1929.

It was in 1930, not in 1913 and 1915, that Pessoa decided to banish "obscenity" from his life. Although he still called Ophelia and saw her occasionally, the sessions of kissing and petting had ended—much to her regret, not his. In his early automatic writing, and later through the Baron of Teive, chastity was treated as a pathology that needed to be cured. Of late, however, Pessoa viewed it as a virtue, and all the more so after he met Crowley, whose sexually charged lifestyle was inimical to his own sensibility, his own spiritual path. By translating to perfection the Great Beast's "Hymn to Pan"—an achievement that required him to identify wholly and perfectly with its author and narrator—Pessoa dominated its sexual energy, converting it into more literature: the Portuguese version of the poem.

Love and sexuality were wedded not only to Pessoa's spiritual aspirations but also, increasingly, to his dreams of a Portuguese Fifth Empire. In the same letter to Gaspar Simões that affirmed the cathartic function of "Epithalamium" and "Antinous," he explained that the two poems were part of an "imperial" cycle, in which five historical empires are represented by five very different poems of love. Like so: (1) Greece, "Antinous"; (2) Rome, "Epithalamium"; (3) Christianity, "Prayer to a Woman's Body"; (4) Modern Empire, "Pan-Eros"; and (5) Fifth Empire, "Anteros." While Pessoa never actually wrote the last three poems, their titles are suggestive. To judge by the passages he drafted for his aforementioned essay titled "Anteros," the fifth and final poem in his amorous poetic cycle would have evoked a world in which the distinction between love and friendship is blurred, allowing for what we might call "Pan-Affection," as opposed to the "Pan-Eros" love of the fourth empire.[26] It was a world in which chaste, nonerotic love would be highly prized. Not mere chastity, but *chaste love*, would be the goal—at least for certain individuals.

◆

PESSOA WORKED ON *The Mouth of Hell*, his detective novella, until he got bored with it, and he had already wearied of writing Crowley, who was still living in Berlin, availing himself of its thriving nightlife. After two letters received in early 1931, both of which implored him to send some news ("You never told me what you thought of *Magick*"), Pessoa finally wrote back, without even mentioning Crowley's treatise on magic, then retreated again into silence. "But what has happened to you?" demanded the Great Beast seven months later, in a letter informing him that "the Monster," Hanni Jaeger, had disappeared from his life and that an exhibition of his paintings would open at a Berlin gallery in October.* Pessoa replied, blaming his epistolary negligence on a bad astrological

---

* Jaeger would commit suicide in 1933.

conjunction, and then continued to be negligent, leaving Crowley's next letter unanswered and effectively terminating their correspondence.

Some months later, Pessoa did receive one further piece of mail from Crowley—or rather, from Master Therion. It was a form letter conveying "Greetings of the Equinox of Spring," perhaps mainly intended for members of the A∴A∴, the initiatory order created by Crowley in 1909. It is extremely unlikely that Pessoa belonged to this order or that he considered Crowley to be his formal spiritual master. He recognized him as a master of magic, however, and as a man whom Destiny had brought into his life to teach him a few things, through his writings and his example. In an undated note Pessoa wrote (in Portuguese), "To feel out of place in one's milieu is the initial stimulus leading to victory. Master Therion gave this to me with authorization from above. To conceive the dissimilarity between me and what surrounds me—that is the first step, the beginning of wakeful awareness."[27]

Crowley, in Pessoa's view, did not attain full victory. Although he admired the man for following his own trajectory, no matter what society thought about it, the poet was not always positively impressed by what he read in Crowley's *Confessions: The Spirit of Solitude*, much less by what he learned about him from other sources. In his most trenchant reflection on the magician and occultist, Pessoa wrote (in English):

> He is right in calling his autobiography the spirit of solitude. He is essentially a friendless man, and he has constructed from solitude and friendlessness a false personality which has overgrown his true one. He has been, to a certain extent, the denial of his own principles and the self-vitiation of his own true will. Like all men made weak who really are strong, he needs a helping hand.[28]

As spiritual leaders are wont to do, Master Therion often attracted needy people. But Crowley the man, according to Pessoa's diagnosis, was in his own way just as needy.

In his first letter to Pessoa after arriving in Berlin, Crowley had bragged that his social circle included Aldous Huxley, author of the soon-to-be-published *Brave New World*, whose dystopia of universally contented, mind-benumbed people was precisely the sort of future Pessoa implicitly campaigned against by insisting on the supreme value of human individuality. One of Huxley and Crowley's favorite haunts, wrote the latter, was the Mikado, a bar "where all the women are dressed as men, and vice versa." Although the fun would end in a few years' time, with some of the revelers ending up in concentration camps, the Berlin of Weimar Germany was a paradise of sexual diversity, with dozens of bars for homosexuals, lesbians, and the undefined. Huxley's company notwithstanding, in a subsequent letter Crowley admitted, "I get good chess here but no intelligent conversation," and he pleaded for some astrological insight into his future.

It seems as if the Beast was reaching out to Pessoa for a "helping hand," and hoping for more than just some astrological advice. But Pessoa, having learned what he had to learn from Crowley, could see no reason to prolong the relationship. The magician had his cosmopolitan life full of glamorous and curious people such as Huxley, Isherwood, Germer, Germer's rich wife from New York, and Bertha Busch, his new Scarlet Woman—enough to distract him from his solitude. In 1932 he would return to London. Pessoa, meanwhile, got on with his usual life in Lisbon, avoiding distractions.

# CHAPTER 63

A T THE SAME TIME PESSOA WAS YIELDING TO THE seductive appeal of higher, spiritual planes of existence, he was pulling away more decisively from Ophelia Queiroz, who still clung to her impossible dream of their living together as man and wife. In late January 1931, she sent him a letter saturated with bitterness. She had gotten used to him not writing and used to him not kissing, but lately he had stopped calling, and he often canceled their meetings or simply did not show up at the appointed time and place. It had been a disastrous month for their romance, and she nightly prayed to God that Álvaro de Campos, its great obstructor, would quit making her suffer. Unfortunately for her amorous ambitions, Fernando and his meddlesome friend were inseparable: if Álvaro stayed away, so did Fernando. On February 15 she wrote to ask how it was possible that he had stood her up twice in a row without any forewarning. He did not answer. After he stood her up a third time, she wrote to ask if he was ill. The next day she received a phone call, but it was not from Fernando and not even from Álvaro. The caller identified himself as Ricardo Reis and informed her that Fernando was "confined and incommunicado" until the beginning of March.

Did Pessoa, posing as Ricardo Reis, speak in a different voice? Did Ophelia plead with the heteronym to pass the receiver to the man she loved? Did Pessoa smile or giggle a little as he hung up the phone in whichever office he happened to be working that day? Or, on the contrary, was he troubled, agitated, for having taken such a drastic step?

All we can be certain of is that Ophelia, after slowly placing the receiver into its cradle, felt terribly, exceedingly sad. But maybe he was testing her, or would at any rate reconsider. She wrote her beloved to say that Ricardo Reis, whom she had never had the pleasure of meeting, was surely lying and that she would wait for him tomorrow as usual at the streetcar stop. "Have pity on me at least!" she begged. The next day she waited and waited, looking left, then right, while holding back tears.

Out of desperation she resorted to an old stratagem, writing a letter in which she claimed to have run into Álvaro de Campos, who promised to call her within the next few days, but no call was forthcoming.

Since Ricardo Reis had intimated that Fernando would resurface in March, she wrote a letter on the first day of that month to say she would expect him on Tuesday at the streetcar stop, 6:30 p.m. At six thirty on Tuesday he was somewhere else. Finally, in April, after two months without any sign from Fernando, she desisted. On June 13 she sent a polite note wishing him a happy birthday, and one and a half years later, on Christmas Day of 1932, she wrote a letter to thank him for conveying his best wishes for the holiday season, apparently through her nephew Carlos, whom he continued to see regularly.[1] She said she was unhappy and that it was her own fault, for having foolishly fallen in love with him. There were no more letters, but each year she would send him—and he would send her—a telegram with birthday greetings.

◆

**BY THE 1930S, PESSOA'S** cultivation of solitude was something of a legend among those who knew him or knew of him. On April 4, 1931, a Lisbon journalist published an article about a recent encounter with the poet of *Orpheu*, *Contemporânea*, *Athena*, and *Presença* at the "dusky and discreet" Martinho da Arcada, a café "well-suited to long meditations and fanciful daydreams." He described Pessoa as "the soul of the movement of literary renewal during the last twenty years," who could have conquered fame and honor with his unrivaled intelligence but who chose instead to "cloister himself in a circle of stubborn modesty." Indeed, the unassuming writer "enjoys, there in that sad café, the voluptuosity of isolation." It was a rainy March afternoon, and none of Pessoa's friends were there with him, just a German man, who was recounting, in French, the strange prophecies he had heard from the mouth of an aged Riffian seer in Casablanca. The prophecies did not impress the journalist. He marveled, rather, at the rapt attention of Pessoa, who hung on every word.[2]

Pessoa himself now had the air of a seer or sage, according to another journalist, Luís da Câmara Reis, who for a year or two met and talked with the poet almost every Saturday night. They had a friend in common who hosted a weekly dinner party for a few intellectuals. Writing about these soirées after Pessoa's death, Câmara Reis remembered his dinner companion as the perfect picture of an office worker, dressed invariably in a black suit, friendly and simple in his manner, not at all affected, and yet somehow mysterious. "He spoke slowly, calmly, solemnly. He was never quick to interrupt what others had to say. There was something in him of a magus, something priestly, ritualistic."[3]

The weekly dinners ended in 1930. For the rest of his life, most of Pessoa's intellectual conversation took place at his favorite café, with whatever friends or acquaintances happened to show up, and occasionally with strangers like the German who had lived in Morocco. Pessoa is reported to have also met with a group of friends at the Café Montanha—perhaps on Sundays, when the Martinho da Arcada was closed. An agricultural engineer named Francisco Peixoto Bourbon would reveal the existence of the Montanha group in a prolific series of newspaper articles that he began publishing thirty-seven years after Pessoa's death. Bourbon was the youngest member of the group, which he said met weekly and included Mário Saa, Alberto Da Cunha Dias, and the playwright (and distant cousin of Pessoa) Victoriano Braga.

The memoirist's articles, most of which were generically titled "Evoking Fernando Pessoa," are full of curiosities and surprises. We learn, for instance, that Pessoa was a Lisbon agent for the short-lived Monarchy of the North, proclaimed in Porto in 1919, one month after President Sidónio Pais's assassination. And Bourbon informs us, with regard to Pais's death, that Pessoa did guard duty to prevent the dictator's detractors from making off with his corpse when it was lying in state at the Presidential Palace in Belém.[4] Pessoa as political agent and bodyguard—or rather, corpse protector—does not remotely fit our picture of a man who avoided the active life as if it were an allergen, taking "action" only through the written word.

Bourbon published almost two hundred articles on Pessoa between 1972 and 1990.[5] An article from 1983 contains his most sensational disclosure. One afternoon, wrote Bourbon, after their coffee and literary chitchat at the Café Montanha, the group decided to visit a brothel. Pessoa, to no one's surprise, did not go along. But what was their astonishment when they discovered at the brothel, through their conversation with the prostitutes, that Pessoa was a regular customer and had his own preferred "sweetheart"! This revelation, publicized in a book that came out two years later,[6] was a dream come true for those admirers of the poet who cringed at the thought that he might not have been perfectly, performatively heterosexual. But while Bourbon allowed that Pessoa could afford to pay for sex with a prostitute, we learn in other installments of

"Evoking Fernando Pessoa" that he wore threadbare suits and lived in squalid rooms.[7] Actual evidence shows us, on the contrary, that he was always well dressed and lived in a spacious apartment with his sister and her family. Bourbon is often cited as an authority by biographers and scholars, but a careful inspection of his "evocations" shows them to be rife with contradictions and false claims.[8]

◆

PERHAPS BECAUSE HE WAS so reserved, and his life so uneventful, a remarkable array of legends and misinformation about Pessoa's forty-seven years of earthly existence have sprung up in his afterlife. Manuela Nogueira admitted to me that she can't be absolutely sure that her own mother, Pessoa's sister, was entirely truthful in everything she reported to interviewers who pressed her for answers to their many questions. And we have seen how Pessoa himself, when writing about his life and about his heteronyms, sometimes embroidered or invented facts, without even invoking the excuse of poetic license. Indeed, he contended that there is something inherently, inevitably false about every statement a poet makes, even when it is "true."

More than forty translations of Pessoa's signature poem, "Autopsychography," have been published in English. This is how I translate its first two stanzas:

> The poet is a feigner
> Who's so good at his act
> He even feigns the pain
> Of pain he feels in fact.

> And those who read his words
> Will feel in his writing
> Neither of the pains he has
> But just the one they're missing.

The trickiest word of the poem to translate is the last one of the first line: *fingidor.* Faker, pretender, and feigner are the closest equivalents in English, but "faker" is too loaded with falseness, and while the verb "pretend" rather nicely suggests a child's naturally poetic capacity for make-believe, "pretender" can insinuate dishonesty. "Feigner" mitigates the brashly phony feel of "faker" but sounds a little old-fashioned, quaint.

There is, however, a compelling reason for preferring "feigner," together with "feigns," in the English translation: it directly links the poem to a likely source of its inspiration, Shakespeare's *As You Like It*.[9] In the third act of this pastoral comedy—one of the dozen or so Shakespeare plays that Pessoa was still planning to translate into Portuguese[10]—the clown Touchstone attempts to woo Audrey, a simpleminded goat herder:

> TOUCHSTONE: Truly, I would the gods had made thee poetical.
> AUDREY: I do not know what "poetical" is. Is it honest in deed and word? Is it a true thing?
> TOUCHSTONE: No, truly, for the truest poetry is the most feigning; and lovers are given to poetry, and what they swear in poetry may be said as lovers they do feign.
> AUDREY: Do you wish then that the gods had made me poetical?
> TOUCHSTONE: I do, truly; for thou swearest to me thou art honest: now, if thou wert a poet, I might have some hope thou didst feign.

At this point the audience laughs, since the word "honest," in Touchstone's last speech, means "chaste." The poetry the clown refers to in this passage is, of course, specifically the poetry of lovers, who tell sweet lies to win their heart's desire, but we can be quite certain that for William Shakespeare *all* poetry—and all literary creation in general—implied feigning, invention, simulation. It is obvious from his own practice as a writer who portrayed a dizzying array of personality types.

Pessoa sometimes compared his literary alter egos to Shakespearean characters. In his preface to *Aspects*, the series of books by heteronyms that he thought of publishing around 1920, he suggested that Caeiro, Campos, and Reis were like so many Hamlets. In 1929 he adopted a new general title for his heteronymous book series, *Fictions of the Interlude*, and in a prose passage probably intended for his new preface, he clarified what he meant by that earlier reference to Hamlet: "Let's suppose that a supremely depersonalized writer, such as Shakespeare, instead of creating the character Hamlet as part of a play, had created him simply as a character, without any play. He would have created, so to speak, a play of just one character—a prolonged analytical monologue." His heteronyms, Pessoa went on to explain, were precisely in this category. Quasi-independent, they expressed certain ideas he strongly disagreed with and certain feelings he himself had never felt.

"Autopsychography," however, is not about feigning what one *doesn't* feel so as to create convincing characters, be they Hamlets or heteronyms; it is about feigning what one *does* feel, so as to convert it into literature. Rather than Wordsworth's "emotion recollected in tranquility," Pessoa was proposing emotion *re-created* in the artist's forge, so as to make it into an object his readers would better understand. "Autopsychography" is a meditation on—and a strategy for overcoming—the difficulty of conveying to others our true feelings. If the poet does their job well, then the reader will feel the same thing they felt, though only in the form of a simulacrum. In fact the reader's "pain," according to the poem's second stanza, is at best an emotional representation of the feigned pain.

The poem's third and last stanza is ambiguous:

And so around its track
This thing called the heart winds,
A little clockwork train
To entertain our minds.

It seems, on the one hand, to prolong the poem's reflection on the elusiveness of feelings, which pulse with their own life, beyond our control. On the other hand, it seems to demote feelings to the status of a mental entertainment, a toy train for adults. When writing this stanza, on April 1, 1931, perhaps Pessoa was thinking of the feelings aroused in him by his lately terminated relationship with Ophelia Queiroz—feelings of surprise, excitement, confusion, bemusement, and ultimately weariness, all of which he closely observed and pondered.

In *As You Like It*, Touchstone's courtship of Audrey, whom he will end up marrying, is a parody of romantic love. "Autopsychography," without resorting to parody, reveals a deep skepticism about the knowability, communicability, and even the real value of all human feelings. The poem vaguely recalls the arguments of Pessoa's favorite pre-Socratic philosopher, Gorgias: nothing exists, but even if something does exist, we cannot know it, and even if we can know it, we cannot communicate it to anyone else. The poet as feigner does in a way succeed, by sleight of hand, in communicating their feelings, but no one, not even the poet, truly fathoms what they felt.

◆

PESSOA'S FAVORITE IBERIAN PHILOSOPHER, Francisco Sanches (c. 1550–1623), was the quintessence of skepticism. Born to a Spanish father and Portuguese mother, he spent most of his life in France, where his Jewish-descended family immigrated to escape the scrutiny of the Inquisition. His best remembered work is *Quod Nihil Scitur* (*That Nothing Is Known*), which Pessoa planned to translate into English as well as into Portuguese,[11] even though he probably never read it all the way to the end. Sanches's book critiques and repudiates a number of methods for obtaining knowledge, including Aristotle's use of syllogistic reasoning, but Pessoa was primarily interested in the book's very first sentence, which he quoted in a passage for *The Book of Disquiet* written less than a month before "Autopsychography." The passage argues that the stage of human consciousness represented by Socrates, when he said, "All I know is that I know nothing," was superseded by Sanches, when he declared, "I don't even know if I know nothing."[12] The implication is that perhaps, after all, we do or can know something, albeit without knowing that we know it.

To doubt one's own doubt is to open a door to the possibility of knowledge—particularly knowledge not based on logical reasoning or empirical observation—and Pessoa, after his encounter with Aleister Crowley, swung that door wide open. In the summer of 1931 he purchased a stack of new books on Rosicrucianism, on Kabbalah, on Freemasonry, and on initiation rites.[13] As was his custom, whenever he was inflamed with a new enthusiasm, he immediately began to write articles, pamphlets, and books on the theme—in this case, esotericism. He expounded on ideas and doctrines culled from his readings, clothing them in his own expressive style, and he formulated new ideas, new doctrines.

*Subsolo* (*Underground*) was Pessoa's working title for a general introduction to the history of occult doctrines and the secret societies responsible for transmitting them down through the ages. The first chapter would set out some basic laws of "occult life," beginning with the most important one of all: "That which is below is like that which is above, and that which is above is like that which is below." Or, in a terser formula: "As above, so below." That law is contained in the *Emerald Tablet*, an esoteric text disseminated in Arabic around the seventh century but purportedly written much earlier, by the mythical personage Hermes Trismegistus, who was an amalgam derived from the Greek god Hermes (credited with inventing the alphabet) and the Egyptian god Thoth (the patron of writing and magic). The name of this "thrice-greatest" Hermes was attached to many esoteric writings produced in the first centuries of the Christian era and later translated from Greek into Latin as the *Corpus Hermeticum*.

The period when Hermetic doctrines began to take written form also saw the emergence of Gnosticism, which is closely related to Hermeticism but has a more radical concept of God's transcendence. Both traditions hold that human souls originate in God—who is ineffable—but are trapped in matter. By achieving that higher spiritual insight sometimes referred to as *gnosis*, souls have the possibility of ascending through graduated spheres of reality to approach or to become reunited with the Oneness that transcends all.

The notion that there are various levels of reality had always appealed to Pessoa, some of whose poems—the first section of "Maritime Ode," for instance—directly invoke the Platonic world of ideal Forms. And the Hermetic axiom "As above, so below," oft repeated in Pessoa's writings on esotericism from the 1930s, was already inscribed in a stanza from a poem he wrote in 1923:

> Ah, everything is symbol and analogy.
> The wind that blows and this cold night
> Are something other than night and wind—
> They're shadows of Being and of Thought.[14]

But the world "above" was not only populated by ideal Forms, elevated Thoughts, and empyrean splendors; it was also inhabited by spiritual powers that govern the universe—contentiously so, with the same kinds of power struggles that convulse the geopolitical world "below."

◆

"WHAT HELLS AND PURGATORIES and Heavens I have inside me! But who sees me do anything that disagrees with life—me, so calm and peaceful?"[15] Pessoa had written these words many years earlier, but never were they as pertinent as in the 1930s. Behind his soberly dressed and

mild-mannered exterior, which made him blend quietly and unremark-
ably into the urban landscape of Lisbon, there were at least three occult
forces—a previously mentioned Pagan Council, a group of Hidden Masters, and a mysterious Brotherhood—that clashed with one another in
an ongoing religious war that took place, if nowhere else, on the field of
Pessoa's imagination.

The Pagan Council, according to some of Pessoa's more original and
fanciful writings on the occult, attacked mysticism and defended, like
Alberto Caeiro, "the world as it has been given to us." The Hidden Masters, who were the custodians of deep mysteries much older than Jesus
Christ, bitterly opposed the Catholic Church, but the Pagan Council
protected it, since many remnants of paganism were conserved in the
Church's rites and rituals. The unnamed Brotherhood—which was in
fact the Rosicrucian Brotherhood—also stood up for the Church, out of
sympathy for certain Christian symbols and doctrines. The Pagan Council and the Brotherhood, besides protecting the Church, were committed
to defending European civilization against the threat of "Orientaliza-
tion," a tendency actively fostered by the Masters, whose wisdom was
partly rooted in Jewish and Asian esoteric traditions. A lineage of Hidden Masters with secret knowledge passed down through the ages was
an idea popularized by Helena Blavatsky, the Russian occultist and Theosophist, who claimed to have met some of those Masters in Tibet.

"Thus everything," wrote Pessoa with respect to the battle that raged
between these unseen forces, "is a struggle on high, of which the ant-
hill of humans here below is but a shadow and corruption."[16] The spiritual war on high also dramatized a cultural struggle. Pessoa had always
defended the superiority of European civilization, whose ancient Greek
origins he wanted to revitalize through neo-paganism. His fascination
with esoteric knowledge and spiritual planes of existence challenged his
Eurocentrism. What sense would it make for a universal, *spiritual* reality
to be regionally biased? One of the arguments for the existence of arcane
knowledge, or gnosis, is precisely the coincidence of certain esoteric precepts and concepts across a number of different cultures.

Pessoa acknowledged that the secret wisdom of the West and the
secret wisdom of the East were the same wisdom, the same secret, but
he was still a Westerner, and it was Western esoteric traditions that
engrossed his attention. Most of those traditions interacted in some
way with Christianity, whose language he knew fluently, and not only

because of the education he received from the nuns at St. Joseph's Convent School in Durban. Throughout his adult life he read books about Church history, theology, and the Bible, especially the New Testament, which he owned in a modern English version translated from the best critical edition available.[17]

Hostile to Catholicism, Pessoa subscribed to what he would later call the Secret Tradition of Christianity, and he styled himself a Gnostic Christian.[18] He understood redemption from the material world to depend on esoteric knowledge—or gnosis—of Jesus Christ, who is not himself divine but is "the shadow of a divine *process*" and the "symbol of *Something* from Beyond."[19] It is hard for a layperson to imagine what practical application these rather indefinite definitions might have for an aspirant on the path leading to reunification with one's true Self, but Pessoa's brand of Gnosticism prized verbal subtleties such as "shadow of a divine *process*" for probing, through the thick fog of our earthbound minds, the divine truth.

◆

ONE SUNDAY MORNING, WALKING in the vicinity of Praça do Rossio and suddenly finding himself in front of the Igreja de São Domingos, a medieval church destroyed in the 1755 earthquake and rebuilt in baroque style, Bernardo Soares remembers how he liked to go there with his mother, dressed up in his only good suit. He would enter Mass "as into a great mystery," not understanding it (the Mass was still in Latin) but taking it all in with great awe and respect. "Only the self who stopped believing and became an adult," he comments in his diary, is "fiction and confusion, anguish and the grave." And as the assistant bookkeeper watches a crowd of the faithful leaving one Mass and another crowd gathering at the doors for the next Mass, it occurs to him that "what I am would be unbearable if I couldn't remember what I've been."[20]

Pessoa, when he was a little boy, went to Mass with his mother at a different church, closer to where they lived, but Soares's recollections of his childhood faith were Pessoa's own recollections. He missed the simplicity of accepting without understanding, and of not caring that he didn't understand. The religiosity of his adult years endeavored to recover his childhood faith, but it could no longer be simple. Theological systems and nuances were like drugs to his mature mind, addicted to complexity.

The Secret Tradition of Christianity, as Pessoa understood it from the weighty tomes he read, began with heterodox sects in the early years of the Christian era, quietly continued inside and outside the Catholic, Eastern Orthodox, and Reformation Churches, and found a galvanizing pole of attraction in the Rosicrucian Brotherhood. Pessoa himself was strongly attracted to this brotherhood, and the fact it was founded on a contrived legend made it all the more appealing to the poet-feigner's sensibility. Legends, like myths and symbols, stand for higher truths.

The main author of the legend was a seventeenth-century Lutheran deacon from Germany, Johann Valentin Andreae, who sought to foster Christian piety through fiction and allegory. Between 1614 and 1616 he and a couple of friends anonymously published a few pamphlets that recounted the venerable life of one Christian Rosenkreutz, a German doctor said to have received instruction from enlightened masters on a trip to Arabia, Egypt, and Morocco. Returning to Germany, he supposedly founded a secret fraternity, the Rosy Cross Brotherhood, over which he presided until his death in 1484, at 106 years of age. The pamphlets further claimed that this Christian brotherhood secretly lived on, preserving the occult wisdom vouchsafed to Rosenkreutz in his travels.

There the allegorical tale ended, but from it a new religious movement was born. Quickly and widely translated, the Rosicrucian pamphlets generated excitement and controversy across Europe. While some learned men tried to discredit the publications, others professed to have independent knowledge of the Rosy Cross Brotherhood, or they claimed to belong to its secretive ranks. In the eighteenth century, Rosicrucian societies began to spring up, along with new publications containing reputedly ancient rules and regulations for governing the fraternity.

By that time ceremonial, "speculative" Freemasonry—as opposed to the original, "operative" guild of professional stonemasons—was flourishing in both Europe and America, and a number of Masonic groups, avid for narratives and symbols to embellish their rituals, embraced assorted bits of Rosicrucian lore and doctrines. The influence was reciprocal: Rosicrucian orders began to introduce initiatory degrees partly modeled on the Masonic system. A quasi-Masonic Order of the Golden and Rosy Cross, founded in Germany in the 1750s, introduced an impressive nine-degree system of initiation ranging from Zelator to Magus. The system, with successive modifications, made its way into other orders, including the Golden Dawn and Aleister Crowley's A∴A∴ order.

Despite knowing full well that Christian Rosenkreutz was a fictional personage and that the rites and rigmarole of the Rosy Cross Brotherhood, Freemasonry, and their various offshoots were likewise the fruits of human invention, Pessoa—like many others—allowed that these creations might have been inspired by higher, superhuman powers. Wherever they came from, initiation and degree systems tantalized his imagination. To ascend through ranks with evocative Latin names such as Zelator, Practicus, Philosophus, and Adeptus Minor made spiritual progress seem like a simultaneously fun and momentous undertaking. Hunched over his table late at night and surrounded by esoteric books, like a highly learned but heretical monk, Pessoa wrote with fervor about the initiatory hierarchies, rich symbolism, and ceremonial practices of the Golden Dawn, the A∴A∴, and other secret societies, considering the Rosy Cross Brotherhood to be the mother society from which they all descended.[21]

◆

BUT PESSOA ULTIMATELY AND patriotically identified with a much older spiritual order, the Portuguese branch of the Knights Templar. Although it had been disbanded six centuries earlier, he claimed that the order still existed, in a different form and under an alternate name.

With their distinctive white mantles blazoned with red crosses, the elite soldiers who fought in the Crusades to the Holy Land during the twelfth and thirteenth centuries are firmly ensconced in the collective imagination. But behind the dashing Templar knights there was a vast network of less well remembered Templar brothers who stayed in Europe to manage the enviable wealth of the order, which owned hundreds of buildings and tracts of land across the continent, as well as in the Middle East. In 1307 King Philip IV of France, who owed the Knights Templar huge sums of money, ordered all the Templars in his country to be arrested on the basis of mere hearsay. It was rumored, without a shred of proof, that the brothers engaged in homosexual acts and that postulants to the order were required to curse the name of Christ and spit on the Holy Cross as part of their initiation. Confessions to these and other alleged crimes were obtained through torture, dozens of Templars were burned at the stake, and Pope Clement V, bowing to pressure from the French king, dissolved the order and reassigned its assets to the Knights

Hospitaller. Portugal's King Dinis, however, obtained papal approval for transforming the Portuguese branch of the Templars into what became known as the Order of Christ.

Prince Henry the Navigator was the most celebrated grand master of the Order of Christ, which played an important role in the Portuguese discoveries but then slowly dwindled, to the point of becoming a government-awarded decoration, like a presidential medal, with no role in anything—until Pessoa reinvented it. In 1925, he made a passing reference to the moribund Order of Christ (see chapter 50), saying that its leftover remnants helped form part of a Portuguese "Third Order," which surreptitiously combated a network of 300 influential Jews and Masons who controlled world finance and politics. In the 1930s, Pessoa's interest in the Conspiracy of the 300 was eclipsed by the more alluring theory that unseen spiritual forces reigned over the universe. Abandoning his earlier idea of a Third Order, he set out to rehabilitate and revive the Order of Christ by claiming, in the first place, that its so-called Inner Order had secretly preserved the original spirit of the Templars down to the present day.[22]

And what was that "original spirit"? Religious historians insist that the Templars were devoutly Roman Catholic, but Pessoa, like many other occultists, accepted as true the trumped-up charges of heresy that led to their demise, since this made it possible to graft the suppressed order into the Secret Tradition of Christianity, which understood its putatively heretical rites and rituals to be coded expressions of Gnostic or Hermetic doctrines.[23]

Rather than joining the Rosicrucians or any other established order, Pessoa took spiritual shelter in his proudly Portuguese Order of Christ, described in his book *Underground* as "the most sublime" order of all.[24] Unlike the others, it had no degree structure, no rituals, no insignia, and no formal initiation. What's more, its members knew one another without ever having met, and communicated with each other without recourse to human language. The poet and *fingidor* had created the most ethereal occult order imaginable, one that was as invincible as it was invisible. Fittingly enough, its de facto grand master—Fernando Pessoa—was himself more or less invisible to the world.

# CHAPTER 64

L IKE HIS YOUTHFUL PARTICIPATION IN VIRTUAL cricket and soccer matches—undertaken in the privacy of his bedroom, with nothing but the roll of dice to break the silence—Pessoa's spiritual life was a largely solitary affair. Yeats cofounded the Dublin Hermetic Society, joined Blavatsky's Theosophical Society in London, was initiated into the Hermetic Order of the Golden Dawn, and even married a Golden Dawn comember.[1] Although Pessoa had a few esoterically inclined friends, they did not form a cohesive, focused group, and there was little they could tell him that he did not already know. In all of Portugal there was no one better versed than he in the intricacies of Western esotericism.

Raul Leal listened with pricked ears to whatever Pessoa had to say about Freemasonry and other repositories of occult knowledge, but he was not a helpful interlocutor. His one-track mind sifted and adapted whatever he heard to make it fit the millenarian worldview of Joachim of Fiore, the twelfth-century Italian monk who had predicted that the third and most glorious era of human history would be the Age of the Holy Spirit. The spiritual focus of Augusto Ferreira Gomes, another good friend, was more wide-ranging, and more superficial. Ferreira Gomes was like a kid who delights in amazing coincidences, special signs, secret handshakes and passwords, extraordinary predictions—the paraphernalia of the occult. Pessoa, too, treated the occult world like a child's game, but a game he took to heart, as if it were fatefully important. And perhaps, he thought, it really was.

Pessoa's imaginary friends, the heteronyms, were inclined to think otherwise. They questioned the usefulness of his spiritual quest, or they cautioned him to moderate his enthusiasm, to keep his expectations low. The nameless heteronym who wrote rubaiyat in the style of Omar Khayyam had this to say:

How many kabbalahs I've contemplated!
I can't find them or myself in the end.
Leave the occult in its well and enjoy,
While they last, the sun and your house and garden.

Written in late May 1931, this advice came too late for Pessoa, who was already hooked on the occult and could not possibly let it go. Enjoy his garden? His garden lately consisted of spiritual ideas, theories, hypotheses, and visions, which he admired like so many exotic shrubs and flowers.

Álvaro de Campos, on June 4, suggested the best vantage point for enjoying such a garden. In a poem called "Oxfordshire," the longtime resident of England recalled how one day, while on a hike in the countryside around Oxford, he happened to notice a church steeple towering above the houses of a small village. He walked toward it with piqued curiosity. . . .

From the road I associated that steeple with spirituality,
The faith of all ages and practical charity.
When I arrived at the village, the steeple was a steeple
And, what's more, there it was.

Pessoa heeded the lesson contained in the poem: better to keep a distance, not get too close. He read about, studied, and admired many spiritual systems, but he admired from afar, without ever entering any temple.

Six months later, a six-line ode of Ricardo Reis imparted a similar sort of lesson, or caveat:

No one in the vast religious jungle
Of this immeasurable world ever sees
         The god he knows.
We hear in the breeze only what the breeze brings.
Our thoughts, whether of love or of gods,
         Pass, since we pass.

Besides evoking the profusion of rival ideas covering the world's religious landscape, the word "jungle" could also describe the luxuriant universe of Pessoa's writings on religion, especially the esoteric kind. For researchers who enter that textual forest, it is hard to sort out all the separate species and hybrid forms of religious thought that grabbed the writer's momentary attention or merited more careful inspection. It is still harder to say what he believed in.

No matter. That Pessoa was not too concerned with the specific content of his belief is proven by the eclectic nature of his inquiry. Esoteric religions have their internal disputes, divisions, and splinter movements, just like the world's more visible religions, but they are less prone to declaring a monopoly on truth. They cultivate symbology rather than theology, and admit that there are many paths to occult, higher knowledge—a knowledge going back as far as Adam and Eve before the Fall. Accepting the endless variety of religious cults, Pessoa sought the one truth from which they all sprang.

◆

MEANWHILE BERNARDO SOARES, THE semiheteronym, studied his own soul. He made a religion out of his sensations and dreams, aspiring to experience and analyze them from every possible point of view. But even for this self-focused program of inquiry and research he often lacked the necessary stamina, assailed as he was by frequent bouts of tedium. And so he decided to analyze tedium itself, which resulted in one of the more memorable passages in *The Book of Disquiet*. After half a dozen paragraphs discussing the salient characteristics and possible causes of tedium, Soares wonders if tedium, deep down, isn't simply "the soul's dissatisfaction because we didn't give it a belief, the disappointment of the sad child who we are on the inside, because we didn't buy it the divine toy." And he concludes his brief treatise on tedium with these lines:

> Those who have Gods don't have tedium. Tedium is the lack of a mythology. For people without beliefs, even doubt is impossible, even their skepticism will lack the strength to question. Yes, tedium is the loss of the soul's capacity for self-delusion; it is the mind's lack of the nonexistent ladder by which it might firmly ascend to truth.[2]

The abstract ladder for ascending to truth recalls the Gnostic, Hermetic, and Kabbalistic idea of successive stages or spheres of knowledge through which initiates must progress in order to approach the divine Oneness. But the ladder does not exist, according to the assistant bookkeeper. He does not believe in the spiritual universe that enthralled Pessoa and does not even believe in himself. In another *Disquiet* passage—written on the same day as the one just cited, December 1, 1931—Soares describes his soul as "a black whirlpool, a vast vertigo circling a void, the racing of an infinite ocean around a hole in nothing." Swirling in the oceanic whirlpool are myriad images and sounds of things he has seen or heard, including "houses, faces, books, boxes, snatches of music and syllables of voices." And amid all this confusion

> I, what's truly I, am the center that only exists in the geometry of the abyss: I'm the nothing around which everything spins, existing only so that it can spin, being a center only because every circle has one. I, what's truly I, am a well without walls but with the walls' viscosity, the center of everything with nothing around it.[3]

These lines evince an uncannily Buddhistic view of the world. According to Buddhists, who do not believe in an almighty God, the three marks of existence are unsatisfactoriness, or suffering; impermanence, since all things are forever in flux, forever changing; and the absence of a soul or an essential self. Without actually denying the soul, some of Pessoa's writings, like this passage from *The Book of Disquiet*, practically deplete it of all substance, reducing it to a vacuous entity that exists only in function of everything else. The denial of an individual soul, or self, is a distinctively Buddhist doctrine, and Pessoa arrived at its outskirts on his own. He was not a quasi-Buddhist, however. Rather than letting his awareness spur him on to liberation from the illusion of ego, he compensated for its lack of real substance by developing an outsized consciousness of all he thought or felt.[4]

But consciousness—conditioned, contingent, fluctuating—is not a reliable basis for positing the existence of an enduring soul. Pessoa had witnessed the complete breakdown of consciousness in his dementia-afflicted grandmother. Did her soul break down too? Presumably not, but then where was it during that painful process of mental disintegration? And where was it now?

More than a quest for truth, Pessoa's exploration of Gnostic and esoteric religions was an attempt to give his soul meaning and substance, to find a home for it in the immense and apparently indifferent universe. He himself was one of those people who, according to Bernardo Soares, resort to mythologies to escape from tedium and insignificance. But there was still another motivation for his religious searching. Whether or not he attained his own spiritual fulfillment, Pessoa, ever a pedagogue and a missionary, was anxious to suggest to others how they might attain theirs. His favorite biblical dictum, "Work out your own salvation,"[5] implies that there are as many possible paths to salvation as there are spiritual seekers. His own path consisted in not taking a torch down just one path but in throwing light instead on the relentlessly bifurcating paths of the "vast religious jungle" of beliefs and disbelief, creeds formed and yet to be formed, gods named and unnameable.

In "Time's Passage" (1916), Álvaro de Campos, drunk on feeling everything there was to feel, including religious experience in all its manifestations, had boasted that "in each corner of my soul there's an altar to a different god." Yet Campos and his begetter would both remain forever uncertain about whether any god actually exists. Pessoa only knew for certain that he did not believe in nothing.

◆

THE PRINCIPLE OF WORKING out one's own salvation, as Pessoa understood it, applied not only to individuals but also to nations, each of which had to follow its own most suitable path. His friend Geraldo, the mining engineer, harped on the need for Portugal to industrialize in order to progress economically, and Pessoa did not disagree with him, but he himself was more worried about the nation's moral and historical destiny. He had lost interest in his elaborate plans, concentrated in Cosmópolis, for stimulating national business activity. Portugal as a small yet uncommonly prosperous country—a Netherlands or Switzerland of southern Europe—was not a vision that excited his imagination any more than the thought of becoming a rich man. Indifferent to his financial situation, investing instead in his literary output, he likewise cared little if Portugal remained materially poor, as long as it could vaunt cultural achievements that contributed to civilization. But what path should it follow? And what path would it follow? Pessoa obsessively read the newspapers, searching for clues.

Economic uncertainty was breeding political uncertainty in much of Europe, but in the United States, despite a still sinking stock market and a burgeoning number of soup kitchens, faith in capitalist democracy, though questioned by some, was not fundamentally shaken. The construction of the Empire State Building—which would tower over every other building in Manhattan and the rest of the world for the next forty years—went forward in 1930 and was completed ahead of schedule, on May 1, 1931. That same day in Portugal was marked by protests against the military dictatorship. Lisbon's papers reported that the police fired shots in the air to disperse hundreds of demonstrators gathered in Praça do Rossio. More protests broke out in the following weeks. Even before the May Day agitation, dissatisfied workers and students had begun to stage a series of strikes. In early April a revolutionary junta had managed to seize control in Madeira, holding out for a month before a military expedition subdued the rebels.

Encouraged by these displays of antigovernment sentiment, and heartened as well by the recent proclamation of a republic in Spain (where Primo de Rivera had been ousted from power the year before), a group of liberal republicans mounted an armed revolt in Lisbon on August 26. It led to several hundred casualties and arrests but no change in the *situação*. The year 1931 was stressful for the dictatorship, which reacted to the many acts of sedition and revolt by clamping down even more on freedoms of speech and assembly. Amid all the commotion the finance minister, António de Oliveira Salazar, succeeded in further consolidating his power and influence.

In the hundreds of pages he wrote about Portuguese politics, Pessoa had almost nothing to say about the recent events, perhaps because he wasn't sure what to think, what point of view he should adopt. We know he feared the worst for the Spanish republic, believing that the Catholic countries of southern Europe were not suited to be governed democratically,[6] yet he could not bring himself to *actively* support the authoritarian government that currently ruled his own country. He supported it only passively, as the least distasteful alternative. His peculiar style of patriotism was out of step with the nationalistic march toward the future— think of bands, anthems, slogans, salutes—under way in Portugal and a number of other countries.

It was in the fall of 1931 that Pessoa wrote, in a passage for *The Book of Disquiet,* "My nation is the Portuguese language."[7] Lest anyone miss the point, he went on to say that it would not bother him one bit if Portugal were invaded by a foreign power, as long as he was left in peace. What bothered and disgusted him was "the badly written page," "incorrect syntax," and the phonetic spelling of Portuguese introduced by decree in 1911, since this stripped the written language of its Greco-Latin "royal robe." (The word *syntaxe* became *sintaxe*, *orthographia* was reduced to *ortografia*.)

Pessoa published this passage in the November 1931 issue of *Descobrimento* (*Discovery*), whose title waved like a flag in honor of the Portuguese discoveries. Founded that same year by João de Castro Osório, who had given up on his attempt to spearhead a national fascist movement *alla italiana*, the new magazine patriotically celebrated the literature and culture of Portugal and the lands it had colonized, especially Brazil. Pessoa's contribution from *The Book of Disquiet* was a calculated move. He wanted to clarify that his primary allegiance was to the Portuguese *language*—not to the Portuguese nationality or any Portuguese colonial empire.

But in spite of disdaining its colonialism, Pessoa extolled Portugal's cultural imperialism. No less than Castro Osório, he took great pride in the Portuguese discoveries as glorious achievements in themselves, apart from any useful purpose they might serve, and also because they established the global importance of the Portuguese language—spoken in Europe, South America, Africa, and Asia. Faithfully devoted to his own mother tongue, he tried to show that it was superior to other languages. He maintained that Portuguese, of all the Romance languages, was the most expressive, most complex, and most flexible. Conceding that English was even more complex than Portuguese, as well as more concise, Pessoa argued that Portuguese was nevertheless more nuanced. He presciently identified English as the new Latin, the worldwide language for general and scientific use, while envisioning Portuguese as the literary and domestic language of the forthcoming Fifth Empire. English would be for learning, Portuguese for feeling.[8]

Pessoa's ardent love of the Portuguese language depended not a little on Father António Vieira, the seventeenth-century Jesuit priest and Brazilian missionary. Described earlier as a defender of the oppressed and a prophetic visionary, Vieira wrote books, pamphlets, and hundreds of sermons in an exquisite prose style idolized by Pessoa, who had fallen under his spell when still a child.

One night in Durban, stretched out on his bed or else sitting in a chair in the living room after dinner, he was browsing through an anthology of Portuguese poems and prose pieces and came across a brief passage by Vieira, in which he describes King Solomon's royal palace and luxurious amenities in Jerusalem.[9] This doesn't sound like a topic that would make anyone choke up, but the Jesuit preacher's clear and majestic "expression of ideas in inevitable words, like water that flows because there's a slope," stirred up so much emotion in young Fernando that he broke into joyful tears.[10]

A poem about Antonio Vieira that would be included in the book *Message* acknowledges him both as a prophet of the Portuguese Fifth Empire and as "the Portuguese language's Emperor." This is a little puzzling, until we realize that the Portuguese language *is* the Fifth Empire. Vieira fulfilled his own prophecy by reaching a new level of vigor and eloquence in his use of Portuguese. So awed was Pessoa by Vieira's verbal prowess that he credited him with an "alchemical knowledge of the Portuguese language."[11] Which leads us back to Pessoa's attraction to esoteric spiritualities. For him as for many other enthusiasts of alchemy, magic, Kabbalah, Rosicrucianism, and Freemasonry, words were among the most seductive symbols lining the possible paths to occult truth. They had the power to conjure, to enchant, to seal, and to illuminate, and it was as if this power emanated from the words themselves, independent of what they literally signified.

Pessoa had been cultivating the power of language since his student days in Durban, where he spent long hours mastering Latin, French, Shakespeare's diction, and Milton's prosody.[13] Language was at the heart of his heteronyms, his affections, his ideal politics (Sebastianism, the Fifth Empire), and his endlessly speculative spirituality. I mean not simply that all these things are realized by language but that *language itself*, mysterious and sacred, is to a large extent what they realize, what they're really about.

But no one, Pessoa included, can be reduced to language. Before any words there was desire and fear, attraction and repulsion, and the unconscious reminiscence of an umbilical cord.

◆

**BY THE EARLY 1930S** Pessoa was not only familiar with Sigmund Freud's theory that our childhood drives and desires, when repressed, will live on in the unconscious; he himself had become a Freudian case study. The study was embedded in an article by João Gaspar Simões, "Fernando Pessoa and the Voices of Innocence," published in the December 1930 issue of *Presença*. In Pessoa, ventured the critic, "there may be enough material for a scientific application of Freudian doctrines," since his poetry contained references that hinted at "childhood disturbances." A certain narcissism, for instance, which results when primordial desire, inhibited from pursuing its natural goal, is redirected to oneself. "It is also a known fact," Gaspar Simões noted with a knowing wink, "how much Fernando Pessoa admires Greek civilization." Though surely not the direct result of "sexual deviations," Pessoa's poetry bore telltale signs of "an infantile fixation." And he quoted several poems in support of his thesis.

Pessoa's knowledge of Freud was not profound, but he had recently acquired and read the psychiatrist's brief yet significant study *Leonardo da Vinci and a Memory of His Childhood*. Freud himself was especially fond of this work, which first appeared in 1910. Pessoa read it in a French translation published in 1927. While Freud was by no means the first person to assume that the Florentine artist, architect, inventor, and scholar was a homosexual, his study turned it into a generally accepted fact. He presented evidence to suggest that Leonardo, an illegitimate child who had little or no contact with his father in his early years, developed an unusually close relationship with his mother, causing him to embark "on a phase of infantile sexual activity," whose effect on him was "profound and disturbing." A "powerful wave of repression brought this childhood excess to an end," leading to "an avoidance of every crudely sensual activity," so that Leonardo gave the impression of being asexual. Most of his sexual instinct was sublimated "into a general urge to know"—hence his prolific intellectual and artistic activity—while a much smaller portion of his libido yielded a "stunted adult sexual life." Since his love for his mother had been repressed, "this portion took up a homosexual attitude and manifested itself in ideal love for boys." His "fixation on his mother" persisted in his unconscious.[13] This psychosexual portrait of Leonardo matches rather closely the one Gaspar Simões intimated for Pessoa. Perhaps he too read Freud's book.

Unlike Leonardo's father, Fernando's was not altogether absent in his earliest years, but he was also not very much present. He worked by day for the government and at night as a journalist, devoted much of his spare time to reading, and was chronically ill from TB during the boy's fifth year of life. Trapped between her ailing husband and demented mother-in-law, it may be that Pessoa's mother developed an unusually strong attachment to her son, although, to be honest, there are no hints to that effect in the letters she exchanged with her mother and sister.

Whatever the exact nature of Pessoa's relationship with each parent, the markings he made in Freud's study of Leonardo show that he read it as if his were the life under scrutiny. Early on in the study, the Austrian psychiatrist notes that the brilliant artist and scholar had a "feminine delicacy of feeling" and, in the next paragraph, that he "represented the cool repudiation of sexuality." Pessoa underlined both observations, which perfectly fit his own case. Toward the end of the essay, Freud draws a connection—which Pessoa also underlined—between "the almost total repression of an active sexual life" and the eventual decline of Leonardo's creative powers.[14]

The painter's sexual repression was probably less than Freud supposed. Pessoa's, on the other hand, was indeed severe, and even before he had read any Freud he worried, as we saw earlier, that the lack of an active sexual life might hamper his literary production. As we have also seen, Pessoa had lately come to value his chastity as an advantage for spiritual advancement. His old worry, however, still asserted itself. In the summer of 1931 the astral spirits who used to encourage him to mate and to copulate—with great persistence in 1916–1917, and sporadically in the early 1920s—revisited him with the same message. In communications dating from around the time of his forty-third birthday, they once again promised him that he would soon meet some eligible women, including one named Anna Maria, and get married within a matter of months. One of the communications also contained a curious prohibition: "Never sample sex in man."[15]

Why a prohibition, unless the recipient of the communication felt at least vaguely tempted to experiment? And why not experiment, unless Pessoa, despite his capacity for mentally reveling in the homoerotic love of others, could not accept the idea of that sort of love in his own flesh? The flaunter of convention who eschewed narrow-minded thinking was still, in many ways, a man of his time, helplessly vulnerable to certain moral attitudes that he publicly rejected, and hence inwardly conflicted about his sexual impulses.

Pessoa read Gaspar Simões's Freudian interpretation of his poetry as soon as it was published, but not until one year later—December 11, 1931—did he write a long letter to the critic in which he questioned the wisdom of applying Freud's theories to literary criticism. An emphasis on sexuality, wrote Pessoa, "leads to instant debasement of the author being studied, particularly in the eyes of the public," and writers themselves might look askance at a fellow writer exposed by a critic as a homosexual.

This was more than a hypothetical example; Pessoa was a little concerned about his own reputation, since it was obvious enough what Gaspar Simões was driving at when he alluded to his penchant for "Greek civilization."

The proper activity of the critic, Pessoa went on to say, is not to plumb the psyche but to study the artist "exclusively as an artist, letting no more of the man enter than what's absolutely necessary to explain the artist." All the critic really needs to discover, finally, is "the *central definition* of the artist." And he defined himself, for Gaspar Simões's benefit, as a "dramatic poet," meaning not that he wrote plays in verse but that his poetic method was essentially dramatic. "[I]n everything I write, I always have the poet's inner exaltation and the playwright's depersonalization. I soar as someone else—that's all."

That's all? Gaspar Simões deemed Pessoa's explanations simplistic and reductive, which indeed they were. By calling himself a "dramatic poet," he may have aptly characterized his basic literary method, but this label does not elucidate the origins, the motifs, and the pathos of his art.[16] Pessoa's insistence on a "central definition" to reveal all one needs to know about an artist may have been a tactic to close down the discussion, to discourage Gaspar Simões from probing further into his artistic personality, and if so, it worked for a while. The critic and editor did not reply to his letter and would write nothing more about Pessoa until after his death. But it may also be that Pessoa, with his simplistic self-analysis, was ironically responding to the critic's own naïve and reductionist view of his work. Gaspar Simões had ended his semi-Freudian study with this categorical conclusion: "The poetry of Pessoa is a lament and a protest of his lost childhood."

✦

PESSOA INSISTED, IN HIS long letter to Gaspar Simões, that nostalgia for lost childhood was not an underlying motive of his poetry but merely a poetic artifice, an artistic lie. And in a passage for *The Book of Disquiet* written ten days before his letter, he showed how a feigned nostalgia could be artistically useful. The *Disquiet* narrator, Bernardo Soares, asks us to suppose that his dull job as a bookkeeper has brought on a feeling of "vague sadness" and nervous anxiety, which he wants to make into art, communicating it through writing. After some searching, he concludes that nostalgia for one's childhood is the "ordinary human emotion" that has the same "coloring, spirit and shape" of the particular emotion he feels as a weary bookkeeper. So he writes about his lost childhood, about how much he misses the people and furniture of his family's old house in the country when he was a little boy with no responsibilities. And this recollection, Soares triumphantly concludes, "if it's well written and visually effective, will arouse in my reader exactly the same emotion I was feeling, which had nothing to do with childhood."[17]

Soares's explanation of how to convey feelings in a work of art reminds us of "Hamlet and His Problems" (1919), the essay in which T. S. Eliot famously wrote that emotion can be expressed "in the form of art" only by finding an "objective correlative"—in other words, "a set of objects, a situation, a chain of events" that will immediately, automatically evoke "that *particular* emotion."[18] Eliot judged *Hamlet* an artistic failure for not presenting an "objective correlative" capable of evoking, for the reader or spectator, the emotional state of the play's protagonist.

But Pessoa, with his artistic feigning, took Eliot's concept a step further, allowing emotion to be immediately evoked by an object or set of objects that is not at all "correlative." Nostalgia for lost childhood, in the example he offered, has nothing to do with the assistant bookkeeper's "vague sadness" but merely happens to elicit, in the reader, an identical emotion. It was a clever trick, though hard to pull off and of limited use to Pessoa, who hardly knew what meanings or emotions he wanted to communicate. His creative writing, more often than not, was a vehicle for traveling into what he did not know. He would have concurred with the observation of Virginia Woolf, one of Eliot's good friends, that "the only meanings that are worth anything in a work of art are those that the artist himself knows nothing about."[19]

Very few critics would rate *Hamlet* a failure. For the sort of complex, indescribable emotion that Shakespeare sought to portray and convey, he could find no tidy objective correlative, and yet the play, despite its rough spots and incongruities, does evoke in most people a great emotion—presumably akin to the emotion that the playwright could not name or objectify.* Shakespeare, it is worth remembering, was hailed as the paragon of what John Keats called "negative capability"—the ability, that is, "of being in uncertainties, Mysteries, doubts, without any irritable

---

* Eliot himself, twenty-two years after writing "Hamlet and His Problems," found it wanting and excluded it from an American edition of his essays.

reaching after fact and reason." Pessoa, like almost every good poet, communed with uncertainties; mysteries and doubts were everyday companions; and reasoning was a mental sport, not a pathway to truth. He was, as he told Gaspar Simões, a "dramatic poet," but did not very well grasp the drama he performed.

Eliot also lived with uncertainties, but less so as he aged. Born in the same year as Pessoa, 1888, he was likewise sexually timid, losing his virginity only at the age of twenty-six, and likewise a pivotal modernist who militantly defended the classics, the "tradition." Both men dedicated a portion of their energies to promoting culture through journalism—Eliot with *The Criterion*, Pessoa with *Athena* and a lifelong stream of projected articles, a few of which he actually wrote and published—and both were politically conservative, disdainful of humanitarianism, and distrustful of modern democracy. Pessoa, however, continually modified his opinions and was not too sure about anything, which is why he preferred dreamy and indefinite, futuristic Fifth Empires. Eliot, in contrast, would gladly have turned back the clock to the time of a more stable, orderly, courteous world, where everything and everyone knew their proper place.

Eliot's uncertainties come out in his poems, notably so in *The Waste Land*, whose objective correlative is announced in the title. Published in 1922, the poem is littered with wreckage and toppled truths, the surviving fragments of a great devastation, with few signs of hope that the world—of postwar Europe, of modernity, of Eliot's shaken beliefs, of his faltering marriage—can be rebuilt. Nor is Eliot sure that it ought to be. The poem's closing exhortations from the Upanishads suggest that the rebuilding of Western civilization should be along different lines. *The Waste Land* is Eliot at his most uncertain. From then on he began to define himself and his views on life and the world with increasing confidence, and rigidity. In 1925 he left Lloyds Bank to work as an editor at Faber and Faber, where he would remain until his death, forty years later. Raised in St. Louis as an unenthusiastic Unitarian, in 1927 he converted to Anglicanism (identifying as an Anglo-Catholic) and became a British citizen. In 1928 he took a vow of chastity. He solemnly pursued the goal of self-perfection and conceived the perfect society as one knit together by Christian beliefs and values.[20]

Pessoa had no hard-and-fast beliefs, his personal finances were in chronic disarray, and the better part of his writing formed a monument to the rough, the unfinished, the fragmentary. It was not only his lack of discipline and sustained concentration that prevented him from completing longer works; he set his artistic bar unusually high, requiring that every small and large part be perfectly fashioned and perfectly articulated with all the other parts. Self-perfection, on the other hand, was never a goal that enticed him. His and Eliot's deepening interest in religion, while roughly coincident in time, sharply differed in substance. Eliot's conversion was motivated by a desire to feel nearer to God through worship, to become a better person, and to be part of a spiritual community where he felt at home. Pessoa's spiritual goal was gnosis, hidden knowledge, which could reportedly transform one's very sense of self, life, the universe.

Pessoa lit no candles, said no prayers, and attended no services. He did, however, *write* a few prayers, usually in the form of poems, authored by him or by one of his heteronyms. His spirituality was inseparable from his literature, and the expository essays on Hermetic wisdom, esoteric traditions, and initiation rites that lately occupied much of his time may also be considered literary documents, since they participated in the project of exploring, explaining, and even expanding the mystery of existence. I do not mean to say that Pessoa's spirituality was a subset of his literature. The two things were wedded together. We can say that his devotional praxis took place in the act of writing or, with just as much truth, that the act of writing was an act of devotion.

But everything about him, including his writing, seemed to happen haphazardly, as if life were leading him rather than he leading his own life. He had once been a model pupil—not well rounded, but at least well organized in his studies, so that he consistently stood out at the top of his class. As an adult, while he could not help but have his brilliant moments, given that he *was* uncommonly brilliant, Pessoa usually occupied the margins, in stark contrast to Eliot, who was recognized as a major poet and critic in his own lifetime.

Pessoa had no plan for working out his own salvation—only passion, and a hazy faith that destiny was on his side.

# CHAPTER 65

O N JANUARY 27, 1932, AFTER MANY MONTHS OF being politely threatened with legal action, Pessoa finally settled with a law firm representing Lourenço & Santos, then the finest tailors in Lisbon. Though he often found himself practically penniless, relying on friends to pay his share of the lunch tab, the poet never scrimped on clothes or books. His account in arrears with the tailor had amounted to 200 escudos (roughly equivalent to $150 U.S. today). He still owed 150 escudos to the Livraria Portugália for books on esoteric orders and traditions purchased the previous summer, but in the coming months he would also manage to repay that debt.[1]

Portugal suffered the worst effects of the Great Depression in 1931, but because its economy was still dominated by agriculture, unemployment never climbed to more than 6 percent (as compared to 15 percent elsewhere in Europe, and as high as 30 percent in Germany), and by the following year a timid recovery was already under way.[2] The dismal state of Pessoa's finances also showed faint signs of improvement, thanks to a new source of income. Besides his letter writing in English and French, he was translating poetry and prose by Eliezer Kamenezky, a Russian Jew who had learned Portuguese in Brazil, where he preached vegetarianism and nonmaterialism between 1915 and 1919. One of the dozens of articles about Kamenezky published in the Brazilian press had called him "the Apostle of the Simple Life."[3] Characters like Kamenezky, more plausible in works of fiction than in real life, instinctively gravitated to Pessoa, and he to them.

Kamenezky was born in 1888, a couple of months before Pessoa, in Luhansk, Ukraine, which was then part of Russia. He began practicing naturism, healthy eating, and detachment from worldly goods as a young man, living as a nomad in western Europe and the Middle East. Tall and wearing only a white robe, with long flowing hair and a full black beard, he resembled a biblical prophet. In 1914 he tried to take his antimaterialist gospel to the United States but found few receptive listeners, whereupon he went south to Argentina and Brazil. In 1920 he sailed to Lisbon and settled down, still an exotic figure but less so with the passing years. By the time he hired Pessoa as a translator in 1930, he was a successful dealer in antiques, porcelain, and art objects.[4]

It was in Portugal that Kamenezky began to write poetry in earnest, with the help of Maria O'Neill, a poet, journalist, vegetarian, spiritist, and, in 1921, founding member of the Theosophical Society of Portugal. She corrected his written Portuguese and may have typed up the poems that were passed on to Pessoa, who did some tweaking of his own before translating them into English and, in a few cases, French. Around 1927 Kamenezky dictated to O'Neill his *Memórias de um judeu errante* (*Memoirs of a Wandering Jew*), later retitled *Peregrinando* (*Globe-trotting*). Pessoa translated more than three hundred pages of this autobiographical work, which has never been published in Portuguese or English.[5] Kamenezky also wrote—and Pessoa translated—dozens of prose poems.[6]

For several years Pessoa was a regular visitor to Kamenezky's dusky antique shop, located in the Bairro Alto on Rua São Pedro de Alcântara, just opposite the garden of the same name.* He went there to pick up and drop off translation work, but also just to talk with the owner. The medieval legend of the Wandering Jew, condemned to roam the Earth until the Second Coming of Christ, had always fascinated Pessoa, who had begun to write his own version of the tale while studying at the School of Arts and Letters,[7] and now he knew a man who for much of his life had been a veritable wandering Jew.

Kamenezky's plans for disseminating his poetry in English and French never came to fruition, but in March 1932 he published *Alma errante* (*Wandering Soul*), a book of poems for which he prevailed on Pessoa to write a foreword.[8] Who better than a fellow poet to comment on one's work? So Kamenezky must have reasoned, but what Pessoa wrote was a dense essay on Jewishness and Jewish influence in the world. He began by discussing the "essential" materialism of the Jewish people, discernible in their "traditionalist patriotism," in their "Kabbalistic spec-

---

* The man who took over the shop from Kamenezky in 1951 would report more than fifty years later that Pessoa, after having had too much to drink, sometimes took naps in the tiny cellar (in which it was not even possible to stand up), scribbling poems on the walls. As the years went by after Pessoa's death, the legends about him became increasingly, more daringly preposterous.

ulation," and in their social idealism as manifested in doctrines ranging from egalitarianism to naturism (this a nod to Kamenezky). Although he blamed tsarist tyranny for the Russian Revolution, Pessoa argued that "oriental Jews," and Russian Jews in particular, because of the tremendous oppression they suffered, had developed and propagated a "mystical egalitarianism," which was embraced by the "European stupidity" of the proletarian class and thereby enabled the rise of communism.

Jewish mysticism, according to Pessoa, was an inevitable backlash, or counterpoint, to Jewish materialism, and Eliezer Kamenezky was the perfect example of a mystical Jew. About his poems, Pessoa said only that they were unintellectual, "childishly sincere" and lacking in eloquence, though he granted that a foreigner could not be expected to write well-turned Portuguese, "one of the world's most complete, subtle and sumptuous languages." Rarely has a foreword written at the request of the author been so unflattering. But Kamenezky, whose poetry was exactly as Pessoa described it, may have taken "childishly sincere" as a compliment.

Completely missing from Pessoa's discussion of Jews and Jewishness was his former interest in the theory of a Jewish conspiracy to take over the world. What remained was his essentialist brand of racism. In his view each ethnicity—whether Jew, Russian, French, or Indian—had a unique set of characteristics that set it apart from every other social group. These characteristics, however, were neither genetic nor altogether static; they depended on a complex web of historical, geographical, and sociological circumstances. His essay significantly noted that the Jews had just as much right as any other people to defend and assert themselves.

Toward the end of his foreword, Pessoa once more remarked on Kamenezky's wispy and shapeless poetry, but only indirectly, by affirming that all Jewish literature is "essentially uncoordinated and diffuse," so that no Jewish poet, however great, would be capable of writing a composition with the logical progression of, say, a Greek ode, divided into strophe, antistrophe, and epode. "And no Jew," he wrote in conclusion, "would be capable of writing this foreword." Since Pessoa descended from Jews on his father's side, the concluding sentence has the effect of a punch line, making us wonder whether the essay we have just read is but a playful exercise in logical reasoning and intellectual persuasion, expressing no truth any deeper than the undeniable shimmer of its argumentation.

◆

KAMENEZKY'S LYRIC POEMS, PROSE poems, and memoirs hardly even rated as "literature," as far as Pessoa was concerned, but to translate them was a welcome—and duly paid—diversion from writing letters for business firms, which he had been doing for twenty years, with no end in sight. At one of the firms, Moitinho de Almeida, the sameness of the days was at least attenuated by the occasional presence of the boss's son, Luís Pedro, who had begun frequenting his father's office after school and on holidays when he was eleven years old. From almost day one, agog with curiosity, the boy had closely observed Pessoa and his poet friends who dropped by to chat. When he was older he sometimes sat in on their discussions, which inspired him not only to read poetry but also to write it, until finally he decided to publish a book of his own poems, *Acrónios* (*Morning Stars*).[9] Pessoa might have felt gratified to see his poetic influence at work even amid the desks and typewriters of an import-export firm, but the resulting poetry was not felicitous. Worse yet, Luís Pedro, now a nineteen-year-old college student, asked him to write a foreword for the book.

Pessoa acceded to the request but had no idea what to say about the young man's poems, which could not even be appreciated, like Kamenezky's, as naïve expressions of thought and feeling. Luís Pedro tried, and disastrously failed, to be "poetic." Pessoa, in the end, wrote an introduction that traced the evolution of Western poetic form—from *quantitative* to *syllabic* to *rhythmic*. He cautioned that rhythmic, or free-verse, poetry requires enormous self-discipline to be successful and noted, in all honesty, that this discipline was still wanting in Luís Pedro's work.

Contrary to Luís Pedro, whose knowledge of traditional poetic meter and form was shallow and whose intuitive sense of poetic rhythm was almost nonexistent, Pessoa had intently studied the meters of Greek, Latin, English, and Portuguese poetry as a boy, becoming acutely sensitive to rhythm in whatever form it took. His mastery of metrical form is palpable in the odes of Ricardo Reis and the poems written under his own name, but it is in the free-verse poetry of Alberto Caeiro and Álvaro de Campos, and no less so in *The Book of Disquiet*, that he reveals himself to be an outstanding rhythmist. In fact *The Book of Disquiet*, whose prose often rises to the level of great poetry, can be fully appreciated only when read out loud.

◆

PESSOA ALSO AGREED TO write something for António Botto's latest book, a collection of fictional love letters published in May 1932.[10] "António Botto and the Creative Aesthetic Ideal," which appeared in the book as an afterword, used a somewhat different train of logic to arrive at the same conclusion Pessoa had reached ten years earlier, in "António Botto and the Aesthetic Ideal in Portugal"—namely, that the homoeroticism evident in this author's creative work effectively certified him as a superior aesthete. Pessoa's main argument was that a true aesthete, who appreciates beauty wherever it occurs, is not bound by an attraction to the opposite sex, ergo Botto was a true aesthete. But Botto, in actuality, did not appreciate all beauty equally, irrespective of the body where it is found; he was bound by an attraction to the *same* sex. This detail did not suit Pessoa's carefully constructed thesis—it would immediately have made the whole edifice collapse—so he simply ignored it.

Thus Botto, like Eliezer Kamenezky and Luís Pedro Moitinho de Almeida, became Pessoa's unwitting dupe. All three authors must have gloated at the prospect of Pessoa's critical imprimatur gracing their respective books, but the critic belittled Kamenezky's poetry, was patronizing toward Luís Pedro's work—a "good beginning," he wrote, for the "book of a beginner"—and made not the slightest reference to the content of Botto's book in his afterword. Pessoa used and slightly abused the three friends, or the occasions they provided, to expound his views on topics only tangentially related to their work.

In the case of Botto that abuse was not new; Pessoa had long ago hijacked the figure of the younger writer, transforming him into a quasi-heteronym to further his own agenda.[11] Pessoa's Botto, whose sexual "inversion" he repeatedly construed as the sign or consequence of an unusual degree of aesthetic elevation, was as much a creation—or projection—as Caeiro, Reis, or Campos. Botto made many extravagant claims about his artistic genius, but "pure aesthete" and "impartial cultivator of beauty" were not concepts he used to describe himself; much less did he resort to these or any similar notions to justify his homosexuality.

The "heteronymized" Botto did not replace in Pessoa's mind the real-life Botto, whom he admired precisely for being perfectly comfortable with and straightforward about his sexuality. Pessoa's idealized, super-aesthetic Botto—who existed only in Pessoa's writing—represented a kind of libido-free love that served to explain, or dress up, *his own* sexuality, with which he was never completely comfortable.

◆

DESPITE BEING AN ACTIVE, self-accepting homosexual, António Botto had settled down with a woman, Carminda Silva Rodrigues, who was ten years his senior. She had taken care of him during his illness in the fall of 1929, and by January 1930 they were living together as common-law spouses. In a letter sent to António Ferro when still convalescing, Botto referred to Carminda as his "nurse,"[12] and it was her capacity for caring, sharing, and cherishing that bonded him to her and that he tried, as best he could, to reciprocate. She would continue to look after him and to look up to him, with unfailing adoration, for the rest of his life—thirty more years.

No one in Pessoa's life was similarly, single-mindedly devoted to him. He could have married Ophelia Queiroz, but she would have expected him to love her sexually—something that Carminda Rodrigues did not require from Botto. Pessoa, however, had a loving family. His sister took care of him when he was sick and nagged him about his drinking; he had long talks with his brother-in-law about politics, economics, and accounting; and he doted on his niece, Manuela, whom they called Mimi. When she stubbornly refused to answer to this nickname, he gave her another one: the Revolucionária, or Revolutionary.[13] In 1932 she was a tall six-year-old, lively, intrepid, and it was around that time that she began to earn money as her uncle's alternate barber. She would have him lean back on the blue-upholstered sofa in the living room, tie a towel around his neck, and ask him if he wanted just a shave or a haircut too. After working up lather in a small metal bowl, she spread it on his face with the brush, proceeded to scrape it off with a plastic letter opener ("Hold still, Senhor Pessoa—I don't want to cut your ears"), pretended to trim his hair if he had also requested that service, and charged him accordingly.[14] With her earnings she bought candy from the *leitaria*, or dairy store, of Senhor Trindade, located a few doors down from where they lived on Rua Coelho da Rocha. Pessoa regularly purchased cigarettes and brandy at the same establishment, called A Morgadinha, usually on credit. (Dairy stores in Portugal, as in many other countries, were the forerunners of convenience stores.)

Mimi had learned her trade from Manassés, the barber who shaved

Pessoa's beard every day of the week and trimmed his hair as needed. The barbershop was on the other side of the street, directly opposite the dairy store. On Sundays, when his shop was closed, Manassés Seixas made a house call to service his most regular client. Mimi watched him wield his razor and scissors and listened to the two men talk. Only after he was properly groomed did Pessoa, dressed in a dark suit, set out for the offices where he worked downtown, including on Sunday, when he could devote himself to his own writing. On the days he came home for lunch, he often had a treat or small toy that he placed under his niece's napkin. Sometimes he entertained her with funny poems and stories. He also wrote a poem for his nephew, Luís Miguel, born on January 1, 1931.

The dining room doubled as a living room and was the apartment's center of gravity. There the two children played while the adults chatted or read books and newspapers. And lately they looked over blueprints and discussed floor plans, tiles, the woodwork, and the windows of the summer house that Teca and her husband were building in São João do Estoril, a seaside village that bordered on Estoril proper. The apartment also had a study, used mostly by Pessoa's brother-in-law but with a set of shelves for Pessoa's books and a His Master's Voice phonograph used by the whole family. Their record collection included fado and other Portuguese music, international hits, and classical music. When he wanted privacy, Pessoa retreated to his small, windowless bedroom. Or he walked back and forth, hands behind his back, in the L-shaped hallway that connected all the rooms, and even his niece instinctively knew not to disturb him. He always wore shoes, trousers, a proper shirt, and sometimes even a suit, changing into pajamas and slippers only when he got ready for bed, much later than the rest of the family.[15]

Pessoa continued to drop in on his first cousins, Mário and Maria, whose children—his godchildren—continued to call him Ibis, even when they were teenagers. Another relative he saw regularly was Dr. Jaime de Andrade Neves, his cousin once removed, who shared Teca's concern for Pessoa's health and repeatedly urged him to moderate his drinking. The poet ignored the advice but sincerely appreciated the concern. He liked his status as a family member who was always welcome yet remained independent, without any one person wholeheartedly devoted to him but also without the burden of having any commitments.

✦

P ESSOA'S  OLDEST  GODDAUGHTER,  S IGNA, was now twenty. They kept in touch through infrequent letters and through her father, Armando Teixeira Rebelo, the only classmate from the School of Arts and Letters with whom Pessoa was still in contact. Rebelo worked in Lisbon but lived with his wife and daughter in a country house near Queluz, a small town west of the capital, famous for a rococo palace built by the royal family in the eighteenth century. When the two friends met for lunch or coffee, Pessoa often brought one or two English detective novels for Rebelo to pass on to Signa, and from her he received home-made cookies. Ten miles separated Lisbon from Queluz, but for Pessoa they were an almost insuperable distance. Only after countless invitations from Rebelo did he finally visit them at their house in the country. They ate well, drank well, and reminisced about their college days, when Portugal was still a monarchy, and Pessoa—because his hosts insisted—recited some of his poems.[16] Once everyone else had gone to bed for the night, the poet found himself alone with his thoughts and feelings and habitual insomnia, gazing out upon the blackly silent expanse.

It was probably this outing that inspired a passage from *The Book of Disquiet* in which Bernardo Soares, after spending a day in the country at the behest of an unnamed friend, retires to the guest room and is overwhelmed by anxiety as he looks out the window "onto the open field, onto an indefinite field that is all fields, onto the vast and vaguely starry night, in which a breeze that cannot be heard is felt." He finds the peacefulness all around him "painful and oppressive" and would flee right then and there, could he do so without causing a fuss, for in that immensity of nature he feels terribly out of place—not because he misses the "products of science" such as telephones, telegraphs, phonographs, and radios. It is Lisbon itself that he misses, and nature in the context of Lisbon:

> I love the Tagus because of the big city along its shore. I delight in the sky because I see it from the fourth floor on a downtown street. Nothing nature or the country can give me compares with the jagged majesty of the tranquil, moonlit city as seen from Graça or São Pedro de Alcântara. There are no flowers for me like the variegated coloring of Lisbon on a sunny day.

The hilltop neighborhood of Graça and the garden of São Pedro de Al-cântara both offer spectacular views of the city down below, bounded on the south by the anciently oblivious Tagus River. Elsewhere in his diary Soares lovingly describes the weather, the rooftops, the streetcars, and the urban sounds of Lisbon, and he claims that this city, rather than any writer, is his greatest literary influence.[17]

But the assistant bookkeeper is enamored not only of the city's geog-raphy; he is also in love with its humanity. Office workers, shop owners, waiters, barbers, housekeepers, seamstresses, streetcar operators, street vendors, and delivery boys form the crucial setting in which Soares moves and meditates on his life and on all life. One day a waiter, noticing that he has eaten and drunk less than usual, says, "So long, Sr. Soares, and I hope you feel better," which leads the under-the-weather diarist to remark that "with these café and restaurant waiters, with barbers and with the delivery boys on street corners I enjoy a natural, spontaneous rapport that I can't say I have with those I supposedly know more intimately." It is a tragic day when António, the office boy, leaves his job at the fabric warehouse to return to his hometown in Galicia, since—observes Soares—"he was a vital part, because visible and human, of the substance of my life. Today I was diminished. I'm not quite the same. The office boy left today." In yet another passage from *The Book of Disquiet*, the narrator admits: "In dreams I am equal to the delivery boy and the seamstress. I only differ from them in knowing how to write. [. . .] In my soul I'm their equal."[18]

Soares in these passages is but a literary surrogate for Pessoa, who felt the same organic link to Lisbon, the same simple kinship with the peo-ple in the offices where he worked, with the housekeepers where he lived (particularly Emília, when he was still living on his own), and with people such as Manassés the barber, or Senhor Trindade from the dairy store, or Virginia Sena Pereira, the neighbor across the hall who let him use her telephone, lent him books in English, and conversed with him in that lan-guage (she was the widow of an American consul to the Azores),[19] or Joa-quim Esteves, an employee at the funeral parlor around the corner[20] and undoubtedly the same Esteves who, in the final stanza of "The Tobacco Shop," looks up and waves hello to Álvaro de Campos, jolting him out of his lofty existential reverie and reminding him that life is down below, among the crisscrossing streets and shops and people. Were he a great fiction writer rather than a great poet, Fernando Pessoa might have writ-ten, in the manner of James Joyce, a book of short stories titled *Lisboners*.

Pessoa the elitist, who defended a class-based society, who claimed to find virtue in the historical institution of slavery, who rejected the socio-political ideal of equality between men and scoffed even more at the idea of equality between the sexes, nevertheless recognized that when it came to the soul he was everyone else's equal. The fact that café waiters, office boys, seamstresses, his barber, and the clerk at the dairy store were, in all outward ways, completely unlike him made their fundamental, spiritual connection to him stand out in sharper relief, since their *only* trait in common with him was the circumstance of their having a human soul, an awareness of self. They did not think the things he thought, much less express them in rhythmic prose or poetry, but they felt life and felt death perhaps as he felt them.

In one of the most brutal and most moving passages from *The Book of Disquiet*, written in January 1932, Bernardo Soares confesses that he always struggles to understand "how other people can exist, how there can be souls that aren't mine, consciousnesses that have nothing to do with my own, which—because it's a consciousness—seems to me like the only one." He reflects for several paragraphs on how none of us "genu-inely admits the real existence" of other individuals, on how most people are little more for us than scenery, and then:

> When I was told yesterday that the employee of the tobacco shop had committed suicide, it seemed like a lie. Poor man, he also existed! We had forgotten this, all of us, all who knew him in the same way as all those who never met him. Tomorrow we'll forget him even better. But he evidently had a soul, for he killed himself.[21]

Though Pessoa had no real intimacy with the waiters, shopkeepers, office workers, and neighbors with whom he came into daily contact, and though he could easily forget almost any one of them who happened to move away or drop dead, since they were indeed like scenery whose trees are replaceable, he was deeply attached to their ensemble, to that scenery, and more so as he grew older and his solitude grew starker and faintly ominous, like a portent.

Pessoa's elitism was also a costume, an attitude, a protective armor—like those finely tailored suits that made him look like an orderly, respon-sible, secure, and self-confident man.

# CHAPTER 66

**P**ESSOA'S SPIRITUAL INVESTIGATIONS, WHILE
tending to pull him away from the world in which he lived with
the rest of humanity, also endowed that world and that humanity with new significance. Although he could not fathom the meaning
of the deaths and misfortunes that marked so much of life generally
and his own life in particular, he believed—or wanted to believe—that
they were inscribed in some kind of cosmic tapestry, partly discernible
through astrology. Pessoa understood meaning, in any case, to be not in
things themselves but in the spaces between things, in their relationship
to other things, in how we react to and deal with them. Life's vicissitudes, if looked at from a spiritual point of view, were obstacles designed
to educate and strengthen us, and even one's physical deterioration was
an opportunity for spiritual advancement. He preferred, however, not to
have to witness human disease and decay.

Mário Freitas, Pessoa's cousin, had been slowly succumbing to tuberculosis, the disease that sent both their fathers to the grave. But even
though Mário was more like a brother than a cousin, Fernando made
no effort to see more of him than usual during the year and a half of his
inexorable decline.[1] He hated to visit sick people (and did not want visitors when sick himself).[2] With his mother he had made an exception,
staying at the Quinta dos Marechais to be close to her when she was
dying, while pretending to himself that her illness might not be terminal. In the years since then, he had come to understand "terminal" as just
a manner of speaking.

The deaths of his mother and his stepuncle, one right after another,
had inspired a group of poignant sonnets. Pessoa wrote no poem in
memory of Mário, who died on March 23, 1932, but six months later he
analyzed the planetary transits at the time of his cousin's death and the
astrological indicators of death in general. Amid all his notes Pessoa jotted down, in English, a question that made those indicators less signif-

icant, if not completely irrelevant: "Does anyone die?"[3] He had already answered that question in a poem titled "Iniciação," published in the May issue of *Presença*. It describes the process of spiritual initiation as a stripping away of all that is earthly until even "your body, or outer soul, ceases," at which point you realize your kinship with the gods. The poem ends: "Neophyte, there is no death." Pessoa clarified the meaning of this concluding line in a brief poem written on the same day:

> Death is a bend in the road,
> To die is to slip out of view.
> If I listen, I hear your steps
> Existing as I exist.
>
> The earth is made of heaven.
> Error has no nest.
> No one has ever been lost.
> All is truth and way.

What we call death is but a turning point, a doorway, connecting the earthly world to the spiritual one. And those worlds are essentially the same world, according to the first line of the second stanza—"The earth is made of heaven"—which beautifully restates the Hermeticists' cardinal law: as above, so below.

Pessoa's increasing preoccupation with the world "above" was linked to the looming specter of his own mortality. Though only in his forties, he frequently cast horoscopes to find out how long he had to live, and the stars usually answered that he would die after the age of seventy, and never earlier than sixty-two.[4] But maybe they were wrong. The death of his consumptive cousin at forty-one was expected but shook him up nonetheless, and not long thereafter he was rudely reminded of how his own health was slipping. On June 23, ten days after his forty-fourth birthday, he blacked out, an experience referred to in his notes as a "frustrate syncope."[5] He quickly regained consciousness but was critically ill, confined to his bed for the first two weeks of July. Unable to write or do anything else, he had never felt quite this bad and it unnerved him. His sister, brother-in-law, niece, and nephew had gone to spend the summer in their just built house near the sea, in São João do Estoril. All alone at the apartment on Rua Coelho da Rocha, drifting in and out of a state of semidelirium, he could not have helped but imagine the worst. The housekeeper presumably prepared and served him light meals, and he could count on his cousin Jaime, the doctor, to monitor his condition. "General intoxication" was Jaime's diagnosis. Fernando had to control his drinking or, better yet, quit altogether. It was ruining his liver, and perhaps his kidneys as well.

◆

WHILE PESSOA WAS SICK in bed, two events occurred that would shape Portugal's future for decades to come. On July 2, 1932, the exiled King Manuel II, ensconced at an estate near London since shortly after the republican revolution of 1910, unexpectedly died at age forty-two— asphyxiated by severe swelling of the larynx. He had no heir. On July 5 António de Oliveira Salazar, invited one week earlier to form a government, was appointed prime minister, effectively making him Portugal's dictator. Good Catholic that Salazar was, perhaps he said a prayer for the soul of the last scion of the House of Braganza; he most certainly thanked God for extinguishing this royal line, since it could no longer pose a threat to his hold on power. Formerly a potent force to be reckoned with, Portugal's monarchists now devolved into a fringe movement of hard-core idealists.

Most of the cabinet ministers appointed by the gray and efficient Salazar were either apolitical or traditional republicans, some of whom were more liberal than conservative.[6] At this point in his trajectory, Salazar was a right-leaning moderate who tried to create a broad political consensus. His government was opposed on the left by organized labor and by the clandestine Portuguese Communist Party. The greater threat, however, came from the fascistic National Syndicalist Movement, whose origins can be traced to a group of right-wing university students. It appealed to young nationalists, including soldiers and junior officers in the army, and especially to the integralists and fascists who had tried, unsuccessfully, to impose their extremist ideology on the dictatorship of generals when they first seized power, in May 1926. One of the far-right ideologues, the intense and energetic Francisco Rolão Preto (1893–1977), became the group's leader in the spring of 1932.[7]

Mimicking the rituals, but not the terrorist actions, of Italy's Fascists and Germany's National Socialists, the National Syndicalists held rallies and parades, sang rousing fight songs, raised their right arms in the so-called Roman salute, and wore paramilitary uniforms with distinguishing insignia. Known as Camisas Azuis, or Blueshirts, they defended authoritarianism, anticommunism, and Portuguese imperialism, but also anticapitalism and social justice for the working class, and workers made up a significant part of their constituency.

This movement's proud adoption of Fascist and Nazi doctrines, albeit in watered-down versions, made it especially unpalatable to Pessoa, but he accused all Portuguese political factions of importing their governing models from abroad instead of developing original policies suited to the nation's unique history and character. That character, however, was trapped in a vicious cycle, as he explained in a hard-hitting essay, "The Portuguese Mental Case," published in November 1932.[8] According to Pessoa's diagnosis, Portugal suffered from chronic provincialism, with disastrous consequences for its art, literature, and politics. Political ideas, he charged, were all "slavishly plagiarized" and accepted "not because they are good ideas but because they are French, or Italian, or Russian, or whatever." If Portugal's politicians had indeed all become helpless imitators, then the deprovincialization of the national psyche was clearly not something that politics could accomplish. Pessoa hoped that through literature he could begin the task of weaning the country off foreign ideas and models.

◆

ON JULY 28, 1932, still weak and flustered from his recent illness but back to his usual routines, Pessoa wrote a letter to João Gaspar Simões, with whom he regularly corresponded. "I'm beginning—slowly, as it's not something that can be done quickly—to organize and revise my writings, so that I can publish one or two books at the end of the year," he told the *Presença* editor. "They will probably both be poetry collections, as I doubt I can have anything else ready by then—ready, that is, by my standards." Pessoa was keen to publish *The Book of Disquiet* but told Gaspar Simões that it would take him at least a year to assemble and revise its hundreds of passages. Another of his pet projects, the *Complete Poems of Alberto Caeiro*, could perhaps be put together quickly, but he feared it would be a commercial flop. It would be more prudent, he concluded, to first of all publish some poetry written under his own name, beginning with *Portugal*—or *Message*, as it would finally be called. This book was three-quarters written; he needed to fill it out with at least ten more poems.

Around this same time Pessoa typed up a long list of works in Portuguese that he hoped to publish in cheap editions—everything from his Abílio Quaresma detective stories to a collection of his esoteric poems[9]—but his perpetual planning distracted him from actually preparing any one book for publication. He was also looking for ways to boost his ever insufficient income. With his sister and her family away for the summer, the expenses of keeping up the apartment and stocking the kitchen all fell on him.

In mid-August an anxious Pessoa consulted the stars on three different days, probably to find out about the state of his health and most definitely about that of his finances. Next to a horoscope cast on August 17 he noted, in English, that money was the subject of that particular consultation and that "hard but possible" was the outlook.[10] Two weeks later he spotted a notice in the newspaper inviting applications for the post of curator/librarian of the Condes de Castro Guimarães Museum-Library, in Cascais. While not a sinecure, the job would require him to be there only from noon to four in the afternoon, and the salary—1200 escudos per month—was much more than he earned as a freelance writer of business letters.[11] He decided to apply. For many years now he had been talking about moving to Cascais or another town outside of Lisbon so that he could better focus on his literary work, and he suddenly felt there was no time to lose. The death of his cousin Mário, followed by his own serious illness, had foreshortened his sense of the future.

Even if he had to be on the grounds of the museum for four hours each day, there could hardly be a more evocative setting in which to write. Bequeathed to Cascais by the late Count of Castro Guimarães, the museum was a palatial villa abounding in arches, flanked by trees, and with a tower abutting the sea. It was the kind of place that would have ignited the creative imagination of a Romantic such as Byron or Shelley. Pessoa was attached to Lisbon as to a lifelong spouse but evidently thought it would be good for him and his writing if he broke with ingrained habits and separated himself from the city.

He submitted his application on September 16. It included documents attesting to his academic achievements in South Africa, copies of his English poetry chapbooks, and clippings of the reviews they received from *The Times Literary Supplement* and the *Glasgow Herald*. He hoped that his international recognition, modest though it was, would dazzle the selection committee. One of the rival candidates for the post happened to be Armando Teixeira Rebelo, his old friend from the School of Arts and Letters, whose application stated that he was knowledgeable about art as well as literature, having visited the major museums of Spain, France, England, Belgium, and Germany.[12] Since returning to Lisbon in 1905, Pessoa had only occasionally ventured outside the capital and its environs, and never outside the country. Nor did he know much or care much about any art besides the written kind. "I don't feel the visual arts," he once admitted to a friend.[13]

On October 2 Pessoa used a new tool, *The White-Magic Book*, to find out what the future held in store for him. The manual instructed him to select a question, to touch a "table of signs" while mentally concentrating on the question with his eyes closed, and to look up the answer for the sign where his finger happened to land. By repeatedly following this method, Pessoa learned that he would regain his health, would eventually become well-known, should be on his guard with women, would never discover the truth about the occult, and could expect to receive an offer within the next twelve months that he would do well to accept.[14]

This last prediction must have raised Pessoa's hopes of being offered the position in Cascais, where he could peacefully write poems to the sound of ocean breezes wafting through the trees, in a seaside version of Alberto Caeiro's pastoral existence in the province of Ribatejo. But in mid-October the administrative committee of the museum chose a local painter, Carlos Bonvalot, to be its curator and librarian. His qualifications were less impressive than Pessoa's but more appropriate, since he held a degree from the Lisbon Academy of Fine Arts. The elegantly furnished villa was primarily a decorative arts museum, with only a small library.[15]

✦

SEVERAL WEEKS AFTER PESSOA learned that the only job he ever applied for was not to be his, he wrote the following lines for *Fausto*, the verse drama he had been fitfully working on for almost a quarter century:

Everything we see is something else.
The sweeping tide, the raging tide,
Is the echo of another tide that flows
Where the world is really real.

All we have is forgetfulness.
The cold night and the wind's blowing
Are shadows of the hands whose motions
Are the mother illusion of this illusion.[16]

In the face of defeats and disappointments, Pessoa could always remind himself that this world was just an echo of the real one, and that setbacks here might be triumphs there. The second of the two cited stanzas merits particular attention. Its first line ("All we have is forgetfulness") affirms one of Pessoa's favorite spiritual doctrines: anamnesis, according to which our souls possess knowledge from a previous existence, only dimly if at all remembered in our current, earthly incarnation. And yet that higher form of existence from which we fell into this coarse, illusory world is itself an illusion, according to the poem's disconcerting conclusion. Worlds within worlds, subrealities and superrealities, and no end of possibilities, no truth that reason can ever attain. . . .

If everything is illusion, in the "higher" world no less than in the earthly realm, then what is truth and where is it to be found? Questions about truth and whether truth even existed had been hounding Pessoa since adolescence, and now, finally, he had arrived at some sort of an answer: "Only the Serpent, winding around the open infinities [. . .] of the two worlds escapes illusion and knows the beginning of truth."[17]

Inspired by the Kabbalistic, serpentine ascent up the Tree of Life through the ten *sefirot*, or divine emanations, Pessoa devised his own, somewhat different tree of spiritual life, whereby the neophyte ascends through ten stages in pursuit of Identity, or spiritual oneness.[18] Pessoa stressed, however, that truth is in the ascent itself, not in any spiritual acquisitions. Notable not only for its S-like trajectory but also because it continually renews itself by sloughing its skin, the Serpent "is the understanding of all things and the intellectual comprehension of their emptiness."[19] In a 1939 letter, Yeats would famously write, "Man can embody truth but he cannot know it." Pessoa's Serpent weaves through and around the truth, but "embodies" only the absence of any enduring substance or certainty.

I have been quoting from O *caminho da Serpente* (*The Way of the Serpent*), a project that dates from 1932. Although Pessoa wrote only a dozen or so passages for this book, it contains some of his most original and profound considerations on the spiritual life—such as his idea that an aspirant, to attain the pinnacle of spiritual freedom, must recognize "the truth as truth and at the same time as error" and "feel all things in all ways possible" yet be "nothing, in the end, but the understanding of all things."

The pinnacle is not only a point of arrival—to an advanced state of consciousness—but also a point of departure, since the Serpent, "when it reaches God, does not stop."[20] The exemplary Serpent, as readers of this biography will have already understood, was Fernando Pessoa.

# CHAPTER 67

NTÓNIO SALAZAR, WHO WAS ALSO A KIND OF
serpent—patient and tenacious, slow and then sudden—had
attained the pinnacle of political power. As a prime minister
ruling without a real parliament, and without a well-organized opposition to challenge him, he was poised to exercise more control over the
nation's destiny than any leader in a hundred years. What he needed to
do now was ensure his position and, just as important, his policy agenda
for Portugal. His most capable helper for this twofold task was none other
than António Ferro, the nominal editor of *Orpheu* who had made a name
for himself in the 1920s as a modernist writer and an international journalist. Ferro was a longtime apologist of authoritarian regimes, and his
love affair with Mussolini—whom he interviewed in 1923 and 1926—
continued into the 1930s, but he was not a fascist ideologue. What he
admired in the Italian leader was his capacity for imposing his political
program by entrancing the masses.

Salazar had none of Mussolini's charisma. He hated to be in the lime-
light, his preferred title was "Professor," and he lived simply and frugally
for a head of state. His low-key style earned him sympathy from ordinary people, who were the majority, but Ferro warned that they expected
more from a leader and would soon get restless. On October 31, 1932, he
published an article in the *Diário de Notícias*, "The Dictator and the Multitude," which might as well have been titled "Letter to Salazar," who
was finishing his fourth month at the helm of the government. Like a
toned-down Machiavelli addressing the modern equivalent of a despotic
Prince, Ferro pointed out that the words and ideas of a dictator needed
to be constantly drilled into the people and his very person blended in
with theirs. If the dictator's personality was averse to regular, direct contact with the people, then he should "commission someone" to act as a
go-between, someone to stage "those crucial dialogues, in dictatorships,
between the multitude and its rulers."

Ferro was proposing the creation of a job for which he had impeccable credentials, as proven by his own status as a celebrity. Even though his poems, plays, and works of fiction never rose above the mediocre, he had adroitly succeeded in promoting himself as a major Portuguese writer. As a kind of test run that would demonstrate to Salazar his personal loyalty as well as his capacity for packaging and marketing the dictator and his opinions, Ferro proposed a series of five interviews, which were published that December in the *Diário de Notícias*. By fielding a wide range of questions, which included delicate topics such as censorship and the onerous price paid by the poor to improve the nation's finances, and by embellishing the answers with his own literary touch, the dedicated journalist succeeded in creating a vivid, winsome portrait of the dictator, suitable for foreign as well as domestic consumption. The interviews were promptly republished as a book, which was subsequently translated into French, Italian, Spanish, Konkani (a language of Goa, ruled by the Portuguese until 1961), and English.

One of the people favorably impressed by the figure of Salazar that emerged from the interviews was Fernando Pessoa. That impression soured, however, as the dictator's ideas and ideals took shape in concrete policy decisions. At the end of the final interview, Ferro described Salazar as a leader "perhaps stubborn, perhaps a visionary, perhaps proud, insensitive," yet "undeniably honest and intelligent." This was a fair summation of his character, which Pessoa could respect and to a certain extent admire, but not his plans for a narrowly Catholic, colonial, and self-absorbed Portugal.

Salazar's agenda for Portugal would also, somewhat unexpectedly, allow more than just a symbolic role for culture. This was entirely the doing of António Ferro, who, long before he was awarded a post in the government, worked diligently to promote culture as well as Salazarism, simultaneously and symbiotically. On November 21, 1932, less than a week before meeting the prime minister for their first interview, Ferro published an article titled "Politics of the Spirit,"[1] a plea on behalf of the creative human spirit responsible for music, art, and literature. Bemoaning the dearth of support and recognition for artists and writers in Portugal, he pointed to the contrasting examples of countries such as Italy, where the recently created Royal Academy had "significantly contributed to the spiritual creation of the new Italy." Writers wooed and honored by Mussolini's regime—such as F. T. Marinetti and Luigi Pirandello—

were endowing fascism with "an intellectual and spiritual armature." The entire article, particularly the example of Italy, was manifestly intended for Salazar's edification.

Two days later, Ferro introduced the selfsame Marinetti to a packed hall at the National Society of Fine Arts. The founder of futurism had come to deliver a lecture on that very topic—in French, which was understood by almost everyone in Portugal's educated class. It was a pompously solemn, paradoxical affair in which Marinetti—whose futurist manifesto of 1909 had recommended the destruction of museums, libraries, and "every type of academy"—repeated many of the ostensibly irreverent but by now domesticated shibboleths he had been uttering for over twenty years to an audience of mostly bourgeois ladies and gentlemen, who listened with delight. Marinetti, thoroughly integrated into the establishment he once excoriated, was still a captivating speaker.

José de Almada Negreiros, who had met Marinetti in Madrid four years earlier,[2] was sitting in the audience, silently fuming. He was the only living writer or artist in Portugal who might actually have deserved the label of "futurist." Álvaro de Campos, on the other hand, while he never really identified with futurism, was the author of the greatest Portuguese poem inspired by the movement, "Triumphal Ode." But neither Marinetti nor António Ferro deigned to mention Almada Negreiros, or Campos, or Santa Rita Pintor, who had spearheaded the publication of *Portugal Futurista* (1917) and died six months later. Almada Negreiros vented his ire in a newspaper article published two days after the event, which he characterized as a coup staged by the enemies of Portugal's true futurists. He was harsh on Marinetti and even harsher on Ferro, accusing him of being self-serving.[3]

Pessoa routinely avoided social functions and had no reason to make an exception for Marinetti, whom he had already literally written off. In April 1929, one month after the futurist's investiture as a charter member of Mussolini's Royal Academy of writers, artists, and scientists, Pessoa wrote a Campos poem, "Marinetti, Member of the Academy," that mocked him for becoming institutionalized. But who after all was he mocking? Pessoa-Campos suspected that a similar sort of fate awaited him. "My only way out," it occurred to him in the poem's second stanza, "is to die first."

✦

ANTÓNIO FERRO RARELY CROSSED paths with Fernando Pessoa, but they had friends in common, and in March 1933, once the interviews with Salazar had been published in book form, he sent a copy playfully inscribed "To Fernando Pessoa, to Álvaro de Campos, and to Ricardo Reis, three great names of contemporary literature." He forgot all about Alberto Caeiro. Without taking it amiss, Pessoa promptly responded, declaring his admiration "for the keen determination and marketing mastery" with which the interviewer had presented Salazar to the public. The poet hastened to add that the word "marketing" was not derogatory; he meant it as a compliment.[4] Perhaps he did, but he was beginning to have serious doubts about the worth of the product being marketed.

Pessoa admitted that Salazar, as a finance minister, was something of a wizard, but he faulted him, as a prime minister, for being too much of a technician, lacking in creativity and human warmth. "For him the country is not the people who live in it but the statistics of those people." Good at organizing and coordinating, Salazar was better equipped to be "the nation's head butler" than its head of government. These remarks are from notes Pessoa may have written a little later.[5] Whatever his exact opinion of Salazar's leadership qualities in the early months of 1933, he still supported his government. In February or March he began writing "Political Conditions in Present-Day Portugal," an essay in English that defended the status quo, arguing that "the present Dictatorship may frankly be described as liberal," in contrast to the "strictly anti-liberal system" of Hitler, who had recently been appointed chancellor of Germany and was acting quickly and brutally to crush all opposition. Pessoa even excused Salazar's censorship of the press, saying that it was after all "not very harsh."[6]

Indeed, at this juncture Salazar was gentleness personified in comparison with other European dictators, and a few constraints on free speech seemed like a small price to pay for peace and stability. Events across the border did not inspire nostalgia for parliamentary republicanism. Founded with optimism and widespread support in the spring of 1931, the Spanish republic was already under siege because of warring political factions, with the powerful anarcho-syndicalist movement having recently staged a second major insurrection. Between this sort of agitation and António de Oliveira Salazar, Pessoa preferred the latter, in spite of defining him as an "emotive corpse, artificially galvanized by propaganda."[7]

Salazar's eager and able propagandist had sent Pessoa his book of interviews to find out where he stood and whether, with the right bait, he might be reeled in. An endorsement from the poet of Ferro's "politics of the spirit" (a concept borrowed from Paul Valéry) would have lent it considerable credibility. But Ferro was not the only one cajoling writers, artists, and other creators of culture to line up behind the dictator. He was aided in his cause by one of Pessoa's most assiduous friends, Augusto Ferreira Gomes, who likewise brimmed with enthusiasm for Salazarism. Ferreira Gomes was a journalist for the *Diário da Manhã* (*Morning Daily News*), a government-funded newspaper whose pages served up large helpings of regime propaganda. In mid-March of 1933, a few days before a nationwide plebiscite to approve a new constitution that would legitimize Salazar's grip on power, Ferreira Gomes published reproductions of four posters under the headline "Modern Art at the Service of the New Constitution." Some of the nation's finest artists, including José de Almada Negreiros, had been persuaded to design posters urging people to vote in favor of the constitution that formally established what was already being called the Estado Novo, or New State.[8]

The new constitution was approved by about 60 percent of the electorate; 40 percent of the voters abstained. That same month, Ferreira Gomes began publishing a series of interviews with artists and writers about how they viewed the *Diário da Manhã*'s "crusade" on behalf of the New State. Some of the interviewees were all for it. Others—such as Almada Negreiros, the first artist interviewed—were evasive.[9] None risked being openly critical.

Pessoa refused to participate in his friend's series of interviews with cultural luminaries, but that did not prevent the journalist from using his name and work to promote Salazar's brand of nationalism. On June 15 and in a different right-wing newspaper, *Revolução* (*Revolution*), he published an article whose title, "We Must Renew the Portuguese Mentality!," was taken from a recent speech of the dictator. Yes indeed, wrote Ferreira Gomes, it was high time to foment a new national mentality, but he respectfully observed that the Ministry of Education, when it recommended that a certain nationalistic poem be taught in the schools, had overlooked a far superior, unimpeachably patriotic poem: Fernando Pessoa's "Portuguese Sea." The next day and in the same newspaper, Ferreira Gomes republished the twelve-poem sequence—or the twelve sections of one long poem—which he said had been unjustly ignored when first published in *Contemporânea*, in 1922.

If the praise and publicity heaped by Ferreira Gomes on "Portuguese Sea" were meant as a birthday gift for the poet, who had just turned forty-five, it was not received with glee. Pessoa agreed that the Portuguese mentality needed to change, and the idea of still impressionable school-children being instructed to read "Portuguese Sea" to help achieve that goal may have piqued his vanity, but Ferreira Gomes's Salazaristic framing of his poetic sequence about the great Portuguese discoveries could only have made him wince. He rejected being an official supporter of anything or anyone, and while he allowed that Salazarism might be a necessary if unpleasant medicine, he was already beginning to wonder whether it might end up poisoning the body politic it was meant to ameliorate.

Pessoa may also have been troubled by the publication where Ferreira Gomes presented and exalted his poetry. *Revolução*, the newspaper of the fascistic National Syndicalists, had ecstatically covered Hitler's ascension to the post of chancellor and continued to cheer on the Nazis, endorsing their violent tactics and ignoring their antisemitism. This contrasted with the more critical reportage of the liberal *Diário de Lisboa*. If there was any European leader whom Pessoa trusted even less than Mussolini, it was Hitler. "His very moustache is pathological," he wrote in his notes, in English.[10] On the other hand, *Revolução*, while supporting the current dictatorship, at least had an independent editorial line. It might have been worse for Pessoa to be praised and published in the *Diário da Manhã*, where Ferreira Gomes was a staff reporter. This mouthpiece for the New State had few friends. In a report to Salazar submitted on August 7, 1933, the managing editor informed him that the newspaper needed a 40 percent increase in its monthly subsidy to be able to stay in business, since people were afraid to take out subscriptions, newsboys hawking the paper were routinely harassed, postal workers purposely misdirected issues sent by mail, and businesses ironically justified their refusal to take out ads by citing Salazar's advice to cut down on expenses.[11]

◆

THERE CLEARLY HAD TO be a better method for promoting the New State. On September 25—six months after the founding of Nazi Germany's Ministry of Public Enlightenment and Propaganda and one year before Mussolini's press office was enlarged into a Secretariat for Press and Propaganda—Salazar created Portugal's Secretariat of National Propaganda. António Ferro, rotund in body and expansive in manner, was named director in chief of the new government bureau, whose official tasks were to foster the appreciation of Portuguese history and culture, both at home and abroad, and to combat ideas, attitudes, and behaviors deemed not in the "national interest." Ferro's own impassioned idea, which Salazar let him freely pursue, was to stimulate the production of *national* art and literature, burnishing Portugal's image through its writers and artists. This was his so-called politics of the spirit, which seems at first glance to resemble Pessoa's Fifth Empire, whereby Portugal would achieve international prominence through its culture. But Pessoa dreamed of a culture so vigorous it would effectively replace politics. Ferro, while he sincerely loved culture, was ready to make it a servant of politics.[12]

The secretariat was a boon for artists and writers willing to use their talents on behalf of New State iconography, exhibitions, and promotional materials. Augusto Ferreira Gomes became the director's right-hand man for designing events and publications. José de Almada Negreiros would be the recipient of numerous commissions, small and large. And Pessoa himself soon had a golden opportunity to reap a personal benefit from Ferro's new fiefdom. One of the secretariat's first major initiatives was a literary prize contest, in five categories: the novel, history, poetry, essay, and journalism.[13] In whatever the category, patriotic coloring was a must. To be considered for the Antero de Quental Poetry Prize, for instance, works needed to demonstrate a "decisively Portuguese inspiration and, preferably, a lofty feeling of nationalist exaltation." Pessoa's *Portugal* (later rechristened *Message*) met this requirement.

The December 1933 issue of *Presença*, which had recently published Álvaro de Campos's "The Tobacco Shop," included a long note that welcomed the creation of literary prizes but objected to the prize criteria, since obligatory patriotism infringed on "the inalienable liberty of the Artist." The prizes ran the risk of "reducing artists to pamphleteers." Although Pessoa could not disagree with this criticism, his book was already fully conceived; no prerequisites had compromised its artistic integrity. If *Portugal* serendipitously had the same sort of subject matter stipulated by the contest rules, why shouldn't it compete for the prize?

The prize money, five thousand escudos, was more than he earned in six months as a freelancer. Competing books had to be submitted by July 1, 1934. That would give him enough time to finish his book and get it published, if indeed he decided to compete.

While mulling over whether he could decently let his name be associated with António Ferro's "politics of the spirit," Pessoa was becoming increasingly disenchanted with the national and imperial politics of the New State. In November, the same month that the rules for the literary prizes were announced, Salazar issued an Organic Charter of the Colonial Portuguese Empire, which superseded the Colonial Act of 1930. The charter's 248 articles asserted the New State's more centralized, rigid control over Portugal's eight colonies in Africa and Asia.

"Organic" charter? Pessoa lampooned this document and the New State's pretensions by drawing up an "Inorganic Charter of the Independent State of Bugio."[14] (Bugio is a small sandbar with a lighthouse situated in the middle of the Tagus at the point where its waters empty into the sea.) Pessoa's charter begins with a gibe at the legalese of official decrees: "The laws of this State, contrary to those of the adjacent mainland, are written in Portuguese." The first of the charter's various articles states that the laws of Bugio will be the exact opposite of the ones on the mainland. Article 2 stipulates that, in order to facilitate the immigration of artists, Bugio's laws with respect to marriage will not require spouses to be of different sexes. Per Article 3 and contrary to the custom of the Portuguese colonies, where people were classified either as full citizens, as natives, or as "assimilated" natives, there would be only one category of citizenship in the State of Bugio, obtained by the mere fact of existing. The remaining articles were similarly derisive.

The more he read the papers and watched Salazar's New State tighten its hold over the nation and its far-flung colonies, the more Pessoa grew uneasy. Given his knee-jerk aversion to organized labor, which he partly blamed for turning strife and disruption into the normal way of Portuguese life throughout most of the Republic, he probably approved of the ban on strikes inscribed in the new constitution, but he surely deplored the National Labor Law of September 1933, which compelled workers to belong to "national unions" created by the government for the purpose of peacefully resolving labor disputes in dialogue with government-created "guilds" of factory owners. This was in keeping with the New State's "corporatist" philosophy, modeled mainly after Italian Fascist corporatism and championed long before that by Maurras and the integralists of Action Française, as well as by the Catholic Church. It was a medieval, class-based concept, in which a nation is treated as an organism made up of related parts—artisans, soldiers, intellectuals, managers, manual laborers, and so forth—that need to work together in harmony for the whole body to thrive.

Since Pessoa accepted that people are naturally divided into distinct social classes, we might have expected him to support a corporatist model of government. But while he believed that the existence of classes was inevitable and even necessary for the advancement of civilization, he also believed that any person's essential worth or meaning was an *individual* matter. "Be complete in each thing," counseled Ricardo Reis in one of his recent odes, and: "Put all you are into the least of your acts." These imperatives were directed to a resolutely singular "you." The New State, meanwhile, fostered a collective mentality dedicated to realizing regime-promoted goals such as thriftiness, obedience, family harmony, godliness, and patriotism. Individual differences and independent thinking were discouraged.

The anarchist in Pessoa—the philosophical anarchist for whom individual freedom was as much a primordial need as oxygen—had begun to nervously fidget, like a wild animal suspiciously glancing in all directions, afraid it might be attacked or captured. Workers and their bosses, the colonized and their colonizers—over what other social groups would the New State extend its rules and regulations, its paternalistic and authoritarian gaze, its tiny vision of the world?

# CHAPTER 68

W **ITH HITLER'S NATIONAL SOCIALISTS GAR-** nering 44 percent of the vote in an election for the Reichstag held exactly two weeks before Portuguese voters, on March 19, sanctioned Salazar's New State, 1933 would prove to be an ominous year for Germany, for Portugal, and for all of Europe. But it seemed to bode well, at least in the early months, for Fernando Pessoa's professional life. With his failure to land the job in Cascais well behind him, he was ready to pursue other goals. In late January or early February, he made a belated New Year's resolution to publish four books: his collection of patriotic poems titled *Portugal*, a collection of one hundred poems called *Songbook*, a large selection of Ricardo Reis odes, and the *Complete Poems of Alberto Caeiro*. Except for *Portugal*, the books were practically written; all he needed to do was organize, edit, and polish them.[1]

Pessoa had no money, only debts, but financing for one of the books fortuitously materialized. On February 17 João Gaspar Simões wrote a letter inviting the poet to be part of a contemporary literature series for which *Presença* had secured funding. Was he agreeable to this proposal and would he send the magazine a book title, to be followed by a finished manuscript? We can picture Pessoa, cigarette in hand, rereading the words to make sure he had understood them correctly. Yes, he had a publisher that would finally bring out his first book in Portuguese!

The editor from Coimbra was the bearer of other good news: their mutual friend Pierre Hourcade had just published a "Brief Introduction to Fernando Pessoa," along with some of his poems, in the prestigious review *Cahiers du Sud*, from Marseille. Gaspar Simões forwarded his copy of the review to Pessoa, who beheld with astonishment three Caeiro poems and one Campos poem in the language of Hugo, Baudelaire, and Rimbaud. These were the first Portuguese poems of Pessoa published in translation.[2]

Hourcade, who occasionally came down from Coimbra to Lisbon and met with Pessoa, described him in his introduction as an "octopus-poet," with the heteronyms radiating out of him like so many tentacles. This was in some ways an apt analogy, particularly in light of the octopus's ability to trap its prey—like Pessoa his reader—with its many arms. But the inventor of heteronyms preferred to think of them as autonomous personalities, his supreme fictions, and although the fictions were breaking down, they persisted as the founding myth on which his literary identity depended. Heteronymy—the capacity to play a god so independent minded that he succeeded in creating co-gods rivaling him in beauty and power—was at the heart of Pessoa's originality as a poet. Without the heteronyms, he would never have developed into the most expansive and (in Hourcade's judgment) "the most European of contemporary Portuguese poets."

After receiving Hourcade's translations, Pessoa, who had planned to offer the *Presença* editors *Songbook* (the volume of poems written under his own name) for their new book series, decided instead on Alberto Caeiro. But rather than bringing out this heteronym's *Complete Poems*—which would require more work and more time than he originally thought, since he wanted to undertake a "psychological" revision of the shepherd-poet's miscellaneous poems—his latest idea was to publish Caeiro's *The Keeper of Sheep* on its own. He explained in a February 25 letter to Gaspar Simões that this, the major work of Alberto Caeiro, was almost ready to go to press. Indeed it was. Uncharacteristically, Pessoa had neatly copied all of *The Keeper of Sheep*'s forty-nine poems into a notebook many years ago—it was the most cherished of all his literary creations. Again and again he went back to the poems, changing a line here, adding a line there, and inscribing alternative words and phrasings in the margins. The only work remaining, for the collection to be finalized, was the multiple-choice task of deciding among those alternatives.

We can tell from his letter to Gaspar Simões that Pessoa was thrilled to be publishing *The Keeper of Sheep* in *Presença*'s new book series. He declared it to be his finest work. Even if he were to write another *Iliad*, he mused, it would in a certain way not equal the work of Caeiro, which sprang from a kind of inspiration that surpassed "what I could rationally generate in myself." For the same series Pessoa also proposed *Indícios de oiro* (*Traces of Gold*), Mário de Sá-Carneiro's unpublished poetry collection. Gaspar Simões applauded both suggestions—Caeiro and Sá-Carneiro—and asked Pessoa to send the respective manuscripts as soon as possible. He and his co-editors planned to launch their series with these two works and with a prose work by José de Almada Negreiros, the third pillar of the *Orpheu* group.

In April 1933 Pessoa sent a typed manuscript of *Traces of Gold*, but not yet the foreword he had promised to write for it. And his work on the Caeiro volume was stalled. Multiple-choice tasks were a torture for the poet, whose tendency was to think of yet more possibilities. Two and a half months later, Pessoa asked Gaspar Simões to give him deadlines for the Caeiro manuscript and the introduction to the Sá-Carneiro book, but his letter went unanswered. By that time other publication projects were competing with the contemporary literature series, which the *Presença* editors eventually shelved.

Pessoa was naturally disappointed, especially with himself. Why couldn't he be more disciplined? What was it that kept preventing him from getting a book, at least one book, into publishable shape? But perhaps, on second thought, the time was not right. He needed to recheck his horoscope. Then too, he still had mixed feelings about publishing a book. Perhaps critics would ignore it and nobody would buy it. If, on the other hand, it made him famous, would that be a good thing? "Everything is complex, or I'm the one who's complex," he wrote in the name of Bernardo Soares. "But at any rate it doesn't matter, because at any rate nothing matters."[3]

◆

**WHILE PESSOA KEPT MAKING** new and never realized plans to publish one or another of his multifarious works, António Botto brought out a string of books that received critical applause from esteemed writers such as Teixeira de Pascoaes, José Régio, and the enigmatic Manuel Teixeira Gomes, who had served as Portugal's president from 1923 to 1925 before exiling himself to Algeria. Botto's most dedicated critic was Fernando Pessoa. *António*, a "dramatic novella" about two men in love published in January 1933, was Botto's fourth book to contain either a foreword or an afterword by Pessoa. In fact Pessoa wrote two different afterwords for *António*, the first of which reiterated his obstinate contention that the author's homoeroticism was *aesthetic* in origin. It stressed that love between men based on reason—or "love for beauty's sake"—had nothing to do with the sexual "invert's" *instinctive* attraction to men, which he labeled a "monstrosity."[4]

Pessoa did not truly believe that sensual same-sex attraction was monstrous, but he was trying to defend Botto, and possibly himself, against moral censure. Botto did not need or want such defending, and he might even have found it offensive. And so Pessoa, in lieu of his first afterword, which was not included in *António*, wrote a second one that presented arguments to show that the story of the two men's tragic love was actually a *moral* tale. And it suggested that the theme of love between two men, although shocking to many contemporary readers, would be more easily accepted by future generations.

In 1933 Pessoa also became a translator of Botto's poetry, rendering into English the fifth edition of *Songs*. Containing eighty-nine poems, this was a revised and much expanded version of the collection published by Olisipo ten years earlier. Pessoa was remunerated for his work, but it was also, in a special sense, a labor of love. Reading his translations, one can't help but feel that he derived some bittersweet pleasure from his task, vicariously, as if he were the original writer of lines like these:

> My love, when he went away,
> Said no word and spoke no name.
> He set his eyes on the floor.
> He cried and I cried the same.
> We held hands a while and knew
> It was love that held them then.

While not a feat comparable to his self-transformation into Alberto Caeiro, Álvaro de Campos, or Ricardo Reis, Pessoa's capacity for being António Botto in English was impressive. Botto was elated with the result and would announce in 1935 that *Songs* was forthcoming from "a major English publishing house."[5] But only thirteen years later, and in Brazil, would Pessoa's translation of his poems finally see print.

◆

ONE AFTERNOON WHILE BROWSING in the English bookstore, located midway between two of the offices where he worked for a few hours nearly every day, Pessoa spotted a copy of James Joyce's *Ulysses*. The scandal generated by its partial publication in *The Little Review*, between 1918 and 1920, may not have reached Pessoa's attention, but by 1933 he knew all about its celebrity status as a banned book, judged obscene and still unavailable in the United Kingdom and the United States.* The copy he saw—and purchased—was of the two-volume Odyssey Edition, published in December 1932, in Germany. Both volumes have come down to us in pristine condition, without so much as a fleeting pencil mark. The only evidence that Pessoa actually read *Ulysses*, or enough of it to know that he wanted to read no more, is the laconic commentary he scribbled, in Portuguese, on a scrap of paper:

> The art of James Joyce, like that of Mallarmé, is art preoccupied with method, with how it is made. Even the sensuality of *Ulysses* is a symptom of intermediation. It is oneiric delirium—the kind treated by psychiatrists—presented as an end in itself.
>
> A literature on the brink of dawn.

Pessoa's less than enthusiastic reaction to the book recalls Virginia Woolf's comment in a diary entry written shortly after the complete novel was first published in Paris, in 1922: "When one can have cooked flesh, why have it raw?" It might also remind us of Edmund Wilson's much more positive reaction, in the book review he wrote for *The New Republic*: "Mr. Joyce manages to give the effect of unedited human minds, drifting aimlessly along from one triviality to another, confused and diverted by memory, by sensation and by inhibition. It is, in short, perhaps the most faithful X-ray ever taken of the ordinary human consciousness."[6]

Woolf, who had a few other snide things to say about *Ulysses*, may have been rattled because Joyce had so brilliantly realized her own ambition, soon enough revealed in performances such as *Mrs. Dalloway* (1925) and *To the Lighthouse* (1927), her most stunning novel. Unlike either of these writers, Pessoa was not interested in *representing* human consciousness in literature; he wanted to analyze and, if possible, expand it. His *Book of Disquiet* often meditates on the nature and limits of consciousness, and on its relationship to the unconscious. Bernardo Soares repeatedly reminds his ideal reader that consciousness deceives us, by solipsistically taking itself to be the measure of reality. We are largely ruled, he insists,

---

* In December 1933, a court overturned the American ban, while the British ban endured until 1936.

by unconscious instincts, and our life, as for any other animal, is contingent on the external dimension.[7] For Pessoa there was also the reality, or the real possibility, of a spiritual dimension, with the whole of our human drama being a mere analogue of some other sort of life.

Joyce and Pessoa had an unusual trait in common: brontophobia. If a storm broke out while he and Nora were going somewhere by car, Joyce would immediately order the driver to turn around and take them home.[8] Pessoa, on the other hand, did not feel safe from the convulsions of weather even when safely indoors. One afternoon he and José de Almada Negreiros were calmly conversing at the Café Martinho da Arcada when a rainstorm hit. Almada Negreiros, assertive in his art and impetuous in his behavior, ran to the door so that he could revel at the sight of rain gushing down over Praça do Comércio as lightning crackled and thunder resounded. When he turned around to say something to Pessoa, he stopped in midsentence, astonished to see nobody there. Looking more closely, he noticed a black shoe poking out from under their table, where his trembling friend had taken cover.[9]

Joyce and Pessoa, who had both rejected Catholicism early on, still retained a feeling of awed humility vis-à-vis the vagaries of nature, and both were inclined to see mystical signs in life's odd details, symbolic meanings in everyday coincidences. Joyce made use of this inclination in his writing, which is interwoven with signs and symbols, to convey the wondrousness of life and our perception of it. He read a number of books by mystics and Theosophists, and his own books, especially *Ulysses*, are seeded with allusions to the doctrines of Hermeticism, Kabbalah and alchemy; yet he also ridiculed those who, like Yeats, put great store in the occult. Esoteric symbols and doctrines served Joyce, it seems, as metaphors for the hidden side of human consciousness and for the hard-to-decipher mysteries of life on Earth. He had no patience for the idea that this world is but a shadow of some other, more perfect place. Pessoa, on the contrary, used his writing to go in search of something before and beyond symbols, words, and the life we know.

◆

PESSOA'S SEARCH FOR GOD was a search for language, and his search for language was a search for God. But he was not a linguistic innovator like James Joyce, who invented thousands of new words and even new forms of syntax for his most challenging work, *Finnegans Wake* (1939). Pessoa pushed gently against the boundaries of Portuguese and English, coining occasional neologisms and using words in new ways, but he made no attempt to reinvent language. He aspired, more simply, to use received vocabulary and grammar with precision, to make language stick close to the things it denotes. His linguistic project bears some resemblance to that of another contemporary, Ludwig Wittgenstein. Alberto Caeiro, in particular, sometimes sounds like the compulsive clarifier of *Philosophical Investigations*. In poem 45 of "The Keeper of Sheep," for instance:

> A row of trees in the distance, toward the slope . . .
> But what is a row of trees? There are just trees.
> "Row" and the plural "trees" are names, not things.

In another poem, Pessoa's poet of nature reproaches St. Francis of Assisi for the anthropomorphism that runs through his "Canticle of the Sun":

> Why call water my sister if water isn't my sister?
> To feel it better?
> I feel it better by drinking it than by calling it something—
> Sister, or mother, or daughter.[10]

For Pessoa-Caeiro, words are properly used only when and to the exact extent they are necessary.

After Caeiro stopped poetizing, in 1930, Bernardo Soares continued his campaign on behalf of limpid and accurate, radiographic language, though with a rather different outcome. Caeiro had celebrated the outer world, all that is knowable through vision, hearing, and the other senses. He prided himself on being "superficial," asserting that reality has no inner "depth" except in our confused thinking. Soares, while seeing everything with no less clarity, internalized the world and then—in an instantaneous turnaround—externalized his sensations of it. His world included dreamed and imagined things as well as things seen. Caeiro, standing to one side, had said: "Behold the world!" Soares used his science of language to *become* the world that he closely contemplated, transforming himself into the exquisitely composed passages that form *The*

*Book of Disquiet*: "I am, in large measure, the selfsame prose I write. I unroll myself in sentences and paragraphs, I punctuate myself. [. . .] I've made myself into the character of a book, a life one reads."[11]

It was a painful metamorphosis, achieved at the price of an uncompromising solitude. The assistant bookkeeper's attempt to live a completely independent life, dedicated only to his sensations of what he saw, he felt, and he dreamed—without concessions—proved to be almost unbearable, though by no means unfruitful. "All this stupid insistence on being self-sufficient! All this mocking awareness of pretended sensations! All this imbroglio of my soul with these sensations,"[12] vents Soares in a moment of exasperation, linguistically molding yet more sensations into another scintillating passage of his sumptuous diary, left for whomever it might move, inspire, or at least amuse.

Lurking behind the relentlessly solitary Soares was the not quite as solitary Pessoa. *The Book of Disquiet* tends to be distortedly autobiographical, but sometimes Pessoa and Soares perfectly coincide. Whether the experience described in a passage for the book written on September 8, 1933, happened in fact or only in Pessoa's imagination makes little difference, but I will suppose it to have been factual. . . .

Teca and her family were spending this summer, like the previous summer, at their house in São João do Estoril and would not return to Lisbon until October. Pessoa's small bedroom, situated in the middle of the apartment on Rua Coelho da Rocha, was overrun by books and papers—papers in his wooden trunk, and books as well as papers piled on the table, the dresser, and the nightstand next to his bed. When staying at the apartment by himself, he and his papers and books would spread into the dining room, covering almost every inch of the oval-shaped table. Four or five ashtrays overflowed with cigarette butts. Here and there an empty glass still smelled of brandy. Late into the night, after he had finished writing and for as long as his insomnia kept him awake, Pessoa would either pace or sit still in the darkness, smoking. On such a night in September, looking out of a window onto the sleeping city, the poet sees—or imagines Soares seeing—a single lamp lighting up a high window in the distance. All the other windows are black rectangles. Without mitigating his solitude, that one light makes him feel at least tentatively pertinent:

An invisible thread links me to the unknown owner of the lamp. It's not the mutual circumstance of our both being awake; in this there can be no reciprocity, for my window is dark, so that he cannot see me. It's something else, something all my own that's related to my feeling of isolation, that participates in the night and in the silence, and that chooses the lamp as an anchor because it's the only anchor there is.[13]

Pessoa, who had always cringed at the mere idea of belonging to a collective, any collective, configured in *The Book of Disquiet* an absurdly tenuous form of solidarity: isolated individuals who, enveloped by silence and mystery or perhaps mere nothingness, realize that there are others immersed in that same mystery or nothingness. He had reached a point in his life in which he identified with a "community." It consisted of the world's solitary, ill-adapted, and invisible people.

◆

PESSOA TREATED HIS FRIENDS with flawless respect and was ready to do whatever favor they requested, but his intimacy with them, which never ran deep, hardly increased over time and may even have diminished in his later years. Poetry was his preferred confidant. In the second half of 1933 (as in the second half of 1930), the rate at which he wrote poems under his own name more than doubled, to about ten poems per month, and he would maintain this rhythm throughout the following year. In poem after poem we find Pessoa charting his way—or bumbling along—between waking life and dreamed life, consciousness and unconsciousness, reason and emotion, time past and time fleeing. Some of the poems center on his esoteric search for supreme knowledge, or oneness, prescribing abdication from the self he knows as a condition for finding the true self. In 1933 Pessoa also began writing, in English, "An Essay on Initiation." After first explaining that the life we live is a death and a sleep, the world we see just a symbol and shadow, an illusion, he defines initiation as a gradual awakening and dispelling of that illusion. To return, by degrees, to one's divine origin, there are three paths available to the spiritual initiate: mysticism, magic, and gnosis (or alchemy). The last path is the surest.[14]

Alberto Caeiro would consider any of the three paths to be delusional, since they endeavor to disclose something beyond the visible world, beyond which there is nothing. For him there is no reality but in the world we see. His poetry is an emphatic antidote against mysticism, metaphysics, and all notions of higher knowledge or ethereal realities. It will not do to argue that Pessoa, by ceasing to write in Caeiro's name, had discredited his point of view; if the heteronym spoke no more after 1930, it was simply because he had said everything he had to say, with consummate clarity. More convincingly, we might argue that Caeiro's point of view never had anything to do with Pessoa, who claimed to have invested his heteronyms with their own ideas and feelings. Which brings us back to the question of who or what was "Pessoa."

In an untitled sonnet written on September 22, 1933, the poet conceives himself as a motley throng of diverse selves—all of them him and not-him—walking down a monumental stairway, ignorant of one another and of him, their horrified spectator, mixed in with that disorderly rabble. And the multitude of selves that are all him, and not-him, keeps swelling, keeps descending, in a kind of ontological nightmare. But when the poet successfully overtakes that babble of voices, drives, and personae, he ends up without any identity at all:

> I feel them all inside me, moving me,
> And I descend, profusely innumerable,
> Until I pass them all and lose myself.

This angst-ridden sonnet contrasts with a poem written two days earlier (and cited more fully in chapter 13), where we find Pessoa *exulting* in his permanently shifting identity: "To travel! [. . .] To be forever someone else. [. . .] To belong not even to me!" "Pessoa," according to this poem, is whatever he happens to be at the moment—sometimes Caeiro or Campos, sometimes a defender of Sebastianism and the Fifth Empire, sometimes a religious seeker. But while the speaker of these two poems either denies or dispenses with the notion of an enduring self, in a third poem written during that same week of September he notes that "[s]omething obscure persists / In the center of my being."[15]

As he had been doing throughout most of his life, Pessoa wrestled with the question of who he was, proposing answers that never fully convinced him, and psychological answers least of all. Years earlier he had admitted "personality dissociation" as a possible explanation for his case, but what did it explain? Very little to the seeker of gnosis, who wondered if the whole of the visible world—including everyone in it—might not be a vast diffusion, or projection, existing only in the way that moonlight exists in relationship to sunlight.

# CHAPTER 69

**T**HE MORE PESSOA ADVANCED INTO HIS FORTIES, the more easily his physical self escaped people's notice. Wearing well-cut but inconspicuous suits, he spoke in a soft voice, walked with a light step, and was the one who least stood out in a crowd. João Gaspar Simões, when he met Pessoa for the first time, was struck by how his feet hardly seemed to touch the ground, as if he were suspended by a wire hooked to an invisible nail.[1] Pierre Hourcade, who moved to Lisbon in the fall of 1933 to teach French at the university, began to see Pessoa on a regular basis at the Café Martinho da Arcada, where they usually talked about poetry, then walked together for a few blocks after paying the bill, and he would later report this uncanny sensation: that the poet, as soon as he disappeared around the corner of a downtown street, had really disappeared, and would be nowhere in sight were he to run after him.[2]

If Pessoa struck Gaspar Simões, Hourcade, and others who knew him in his later years as semiabsent, his substance a little ethereal, it is because his mind was often half focused on the ether, the upper air, the other world—inhabited by gods and demigods, by angels and archangels, and by our very souls, according to Hermeticists. A poem Pessoa wrote on May 9, 1934, begins:

> In this world where we forget,
> We are shadows of who we are,
> And the real actions we perform
> In the other world, where we live as souls,
> Are here wry grins and appearances.

The rest of the poem affirms that a few exceptional people have occasional glimpses into what those "wry grins" correspond to in that "other world"; they can sense the connection between their supernal self and their earthly self that is its shadow. Pessoa was one of the exceptionals—at least in the universe of his writing, laced throughout with wry grins.

Eternally unsure of what connection his written universe might have with the universe at large, Pessoa kept writing, and more than ever about esoterica. It is hard to precisely place in time the hundreds of pages he wrote for various essays on esoteric topics from 1931 on, since he rarely dated them, but he did date his poetry, and 1934 was the banner year for poems about other, immaterial worlds. In that same year he wrote most if not all of "A hora do Diabo" ("The Hour of the Devil"), a fascinating dialogue in which a philosophical Devil avers that the universe is an undecipherable hieroglyph, that religions are all symbols of the same reality, and that he himself is "the God of worlds that existed before the World."[3]

◆

WHILE HIS SPIRITUAL SPECULATIONS almost seemed like they could lift him up and away, current events in Portugal and the rest of Europe commanded Pessoa's attention and grounded him, at least temporarily, on planet Earth. Sometimes his spiritual interests and political preoccupations converged. This was particularly the case with Freemasonry, which mainly interested him because of its initiatory degree structure for ascending through successive stages of occult knowledge but which was under attack around much of the continent for alleged political intrigue and for eluding the control of governments, especially authoritarian ones. In January 1934, when Nazi Germany followed the example of Fascist Italy and began taking steps to exterminate Freemasonry, one of Portugal's main Catholic newspapers, A Voz (The Voice), reported the news with predictable satisfaction. The Catholic Church had long ago decreed ipso facto excommunication for anyone joining the Freemasons, a policy that would remain in force until 1983.

Springing into action, Pessoa wrote a letter to the editor of A Voz to point out that three Masonic fraternities disbanded by the Nazis were specifically Christian and not, as his editorial staff supposed, godless associations bent on spreading heresy and overturning the established social order. Their suppression, according to Pessoa, was entirely in keeping with the "base pagan ideology" that animated "Hitlerism as well as Fascism and Bolshevism—the triple offspring of the Antichrist."[4] Pes-

soa used to admire Germany's pagan spirit as expressed, for example, in
the music of Wagner. Not anymore. Even though his letter addressed
a timely topic with some persuasive arguments, *A Voz* ignored it. This
same newspaper had published as many anti-Masonic diatribes as his
friend Alberto Da Cunha Dias cared to submit.

Anti-Masonry and antisemitism, which often went hand in hand,
were given fresh impetus in France by the Stavisky affair, which filled
the front pages of newspapers in January 1934. Alexandre Stavisky was
a Russian-born Jew and high-rolling scam artist, who kept out of jail
through payoffs and his connections to financiers and politicians, including government ministers. His crimes were exposed in December 1933,
whereupon he fled and was found dead in his Alpine chalet on January 8,
either from murder or suicide. Right-wing groups such as the Action
Française responded to the revelations by staging demonstrations against
the government, which was forced to resign, and by vilifying Jews and
Masons, who were allegedly key operators in Stavisky's web of fraud and
malfeasance.

Pessoa followed the events in France and embarked on a long essay,
"The Jews and Freemasonry," in English. Taking a wide view and mentioning the Stavisky affair only in passing, he argued that there was no
essential link or systematic collusion between Masons and Jews. He
vigorously defended the core values of Freemasonry, which admittedly
not all Masons respected, and he ambiguously defended the Jews, or
at least some Jews. If, as a "cleverer" and "more cohesive" people, they
often managed to outperform Christians, then that was to their credit.
Rejecting the allegation that they cheat their way to positions of power
and influence, he wrote, "If the Jews are triumphant, it is because we
have surrendered without fighting. If the Jews are masters, it is because
we have voluntarily sold ourselves to them as slaves." This generalized,
vaguely racist characterization of Jews as being "cleverer" than other
people was also vaguely sympathetic, but elsewhere in his essay Pessoa
drew a vicious distinction between Sephardic and Ashkenazic Jews:

> It is not the Jews, but the dregs of Jewry, that we meet everywhere
> in command of the practical world. For the really great Jews—the
> Portuguese and the Spanish Jews—the Rothschilds, the Rath-
> enaus, the whole false lot with German and Polish names, are the
> dregs of their race and the infamy of their religion.[5]

Pessoa uncharitably took pride in his own Jewish ancestry, while denouncing as disreputable the Yiddish-speaking Jews from countries such as France, Germany, and Poland. This point of view was not unique to Pessoa. Without necessarily demeaning their Ashkenazic brethren, many Jews of the Sephardic diaspora saw themselves as the aristocrats of Judaism. They traced their ancestral origins, somewhat dubiously, to the elite Jews of ancient Jerusalem, and they took pride in their culture and religious traditions, which had evolved in the tolerant and sophisticated, learned world of Moorish Iberia. The architects of the Final Solution would of course make no distinction between Sephardi and Ashkenazi.

As noted earlier, Jews in twentieth-century Portugal were a tiny minority and antisemitism failed to get a significant foothold there, but the campaign of nationalists to stamp out Freemasonry was ferocious. Aware that the nation's president, Óscar Carmona, was himself a Mason, Pessoa may have assumed that the fraternal order, although increasingly under attack, was not in serious danger of being suppressed. If so, he couldn't have been more mistaken.

◆

THE PRESIDENT WAS A largely ceremonial figure without any real power, except one: he could sack the prime minister. Salazar, however, was too entrenched to be removed without triggering a national crisis, which General Carmona and the rest of the military brass wished to avoid at all costs. In the absence of viable political parties, suppressed years before, Salazar had become virtually irreplaceable. Pessoa conceded as much and grudgingly accepted him and his New State, which was increasingly invasive but still fundamentally different from other dictatorial regimes. The Nazis in Germany and the Stalinist regime of the Soviet Union promoted the state as a kind of surrogate religion, as did the Fascists in Italy, even if Mussolini could not possibly supplant the authority of the Catholic Church, to which he cynically half bowed. Salazar did not share their ideal of a totalitarian state. A devout Catholic, he continued the process—initiated by the military dictatorship—of reinstating most of the Church's privileges that the republicans had annulled, and he cemented a new partnership between Church and State, which remained separate but supported each other.

The cult of Our Lady of Fátima, which was officially recognized in 1930 and now drew hundreds of thousands of pilgrims, helped to reaffirm Catholicism as the maternal lap where the multitudes could take comfort at the same time that it fostered Salazar's complementary role as the nation's sometimes stern but always righteous, loving father. Appalled as he was, Pessoa knew things could be much worse. He vastly preferred processions in honor of the Virgin Mary under the benevolent gaze of Professor Salazar to a militarized or forcibly collectivized society.

Less flamboyant, less vainglorious, and far less prone to violence than his autocratic peers, Salazar nonetheless exhibited many of their same personality traits. So argued one of Pessoa's English-language heteronyms, Thomas Crosse, in some notes for a study on dictators. Mussolini, Hitler, Stalin, and Salazar were all "unbalanced characters," whose "limited vision of reality" might, he acknowledged, make them act more effectively in the limited part of reality they saw, but whatever their vision, they shared the same "hatred of intelligence, because intelligence discusses." They were all "enemies of liberty" and therefore anti-individualists, since "liberty, if not individual, is nothing." Pessoa-Crosse's most perspicuous observation was that dictators, by nature, "are unhumourous, because a sense of humour preserves a man from that maniac confidence in himself by the which he promotes himself dictator." Likewise typical was their "inordinate vanity," but in Mussolini and Hitler this trait was "natural," while in Salazar it was "induced."[6] In fact the Portuguese dictator, albeit a little too confident in his remedies for curing the ills of the nation, was not a vain man—until he acquired absolutist power and the aura that came with it.

António Ferro, as previously described, was the person in charge of managing, enhancing, and projecting that aura. A dictator, he had cogently argued, needed to conquer the masses by winning over their hearts and by inspiring devotion, and it was especially important to win over young people, since they represented the future. In December 1933, just two months into his new job as Salazar's chief propagandist, Ferro created the fascistic Student Action Vanguard. Its mission was to rechannel the patriotic fervor of the youngest members of the far-right National Syndicalists, or Blueshirts, who had lately been plunged into a state of turmoil. The Censorship Commission had forced the movement's newspaper, *Revolução*, to cease publication in the fall of 1933, and soon afterward a splinter group of Blueshirts rejected Francisco Rolão Preto as their leader, declaring themselves exclusively and unconditionally loyal to Salazar.

In January 1934 a rally for the Student Action Vanguard was held at Lisbon's São Carlos Theater and attracted several thousand young reactionaries. In an impassioned speech Ferro, whose baldness made his large head more imposing, assured the attendees that the subdued and sober Professor Salazar—whose impassive demeanor could excite no more than a bemused yawn in an impartial observer—was actually a more revolutionary leader than Hitler or Mussolini. With the crowd now fired up, Salazar himself addressed it, speaking in his squeaky, old man's voice, although he had not yet turned forty-five. A visiting contingent of Italian Blackshirts raised their arms in the Roman salute.[7]

In the following months, the Student Action Vanguard received military training, organized patriotic marches, established contact with Italian Fascist and German Nazi youth groups, and espoused anti-Communist, antiliberal, and anti-Masonic rhetoric. Eduardo Freitas da Costa—the son of Pessoa's cousin Maria Freitas and one of the godchildren who used to laugh with delight at his slapstick antics and humorous poems—was a zealous member of the new student movement. At a family gathering where Pessoa heard Eduardo repeatedly rail against assorted dangers to society, he finally piped up to say that he disagreed with the Vanguard's motto: "Against Communism, Against Demo-Liberalism, Against Freemasonry." He said that the young men and (far less numerous) women, instead of declaring themselves *against* this and that, should take a stand *for* something, which in their case, since they were nationalists, ought to be the Portuguese nation.[8]

The student vanguardists did take a positive stand, but not exactly on behalf of the nation. Infected by the fetishistic, symbol-ridden, and personality-driven nationalism that had spread like a virus around much of Europe, they promoted a mystical veneration of the New State and its leader. Even so, Salazar, fearing infiltration of Rolão Preto loyalists into the group, restricted its activities, causing it to die out by the end of 1935.[9] In its stead the New State would create two organizations—Portuguese Youth and Female Portuguese Youth—in which all children were enrolled at the age of seven.

◆

THE POLICY OF DISCOURAGING, transforming, and ultimately absorbing most of the Blueshirts caused the New State to shift further to the right. It became more stridently nationalistic, a little more intol-

erant, authoritarian, and amenable to using brute force—stances that
the National Syndicalists had been urging the dictator to adopt. Salazar, however, succeeded in not militarizing his regime. Thanks to the
dedicated labor of Ferro at the Secretariat of National Propaganda, he
could rely for the most part on the forces of persuasion, marketing, image
building, and censorship. For refractory opponents—efficiently tracked
down by the secret police—he resorted to detentions, imprisonment, and
banishment.

Even as its colonies were being publicized as never before—in June
1934 a lavish Portuguese Colonial Exhibition, complete with half-
naked "natives" brought from Africa, opened in Porto—the nation was
becoming more insular, with less room for divergent points of view.
Meanwhile Pessoa, between January and April, had written ten new
poems for *Portugal*, the book he planned to submit to the secretariat's
prize competition for patriotic poetry. The book was practically finished.
At most he had a couple more poems to write. But he still had no publisher or, rather, no money to publish. And if money were not a problem,
he would have found other excuses for not concluding the manuscript.
He kept telling himself that he would get to it next week, or the week
after next, and before he knew it the July 1 deadline for submissions
had passed.

Two weeks later, on July 16, Pessoa wrote a poem that marked a stylistic turning point:

I have in me like a haze
Which holds and which is nothing
A nostalgia for nothing at all,
The desire for something vague.

I'm wrapped by it
As by a fog, and I see
The final star shining
Above the stub in my ashtray.

I smoked my life. How uncertain
All I saw or read! And all
The world is a great open book
That smiles at me in an unknown tongue.

The meter of the poem is irregular not only in my translation but also in the Portuguese original. This was highly unusual in the poetry written under Pessoa's own name, but it became less so from this moment on, and in his poems from 1935 both rhyme and rhythm would often follow no discernible pattern. Suddenly the poet cared less about form and less about producing literary gems; his poems served other purposes.

The poem just cited could be a diary entry. In the summer of 1934, Teca and her family had once more migrated to Estoril, leaving the whole apartment in Lisbon to Fernando, whose books and papers again spilled into the dining room, where perhaps on one of his frequent sleepless nights, as dawn began to glimmer on the horizon, he noticed the "final star" of night, flickering above his spent cigarette and his increasingly spent life. Looking back across the years he'd lived, and looking around where he was now, he saw the same vast uncertainty, the same unintelligible mystery. As if, in his long journey, he had made no progress.

Pessoa did not despair; he relaxed. In that same month of July he wrote the last dated passage of *The Book of Disquiet*, quitting in midsentence after a paragraph and a half, and he placed a question mark at the top, unsure whether he even wanted to include it in the book.[10] He was tired of writing the intellectually potent, emotionally piercing, linguistically meticulous prose of his restless masterpiece, which he concluded by not concluding it. He still toyed with ideas on how to organize its disparate material, and he had hazy plans to revisit the older passages, adapting them to the "true psychology" of Bernardo Soares, who had assumed the book's authorship only in 1929.[11] But he was in no hurry to tinker with the book, or with anything else.

"*Disjecta membra*," said Thomas Carlyle, are all that remain "of any Poet, or of any man."[12] His remark was inspired by the case of Shakespeare, whose work contains frequent moments of absolute greatness but also, inevitably, less radiant passages and obvious imperfections. Citing Carlyle, the Baron of Teive used the term *disjecta membra* to describe the "incoherent heap of half-written scraps" that made up his would-be literary oeuvre,[13] consigned to the flames before he took his own life. The baron's frustration was Pessoa's own—he created the suicidal heteronym to vent that frustration—but in 1934 it gave way to a hopeful resignation. What Pessoa had written he had written. He still wanted to complete and polish his works, but even if they remained fragmentary and disjointed, they might survive as the foundations or the ruins of something fabulous. So it would be with *The Book of Disquiet*, unfinished and unfinishable, left for posterity in such a scattered state that it took almost fifty years for the first posthumous edition to see the light of day, in 1982. Yet it is one of Pessoa's loftiest achievements—superlatively faithful to our human experience precisely because it is fragmentary, unstable, and irremediably jagged, the product of great inspirations but also of failed and aborted attempts.

◆

**AS IF TO MOCK** the whole business of "serious" literature, Pessoa, around the same time he quit working on *The Book of Disquiet*, began to churn out Portuguese folk quatrains—close to one hundred of them in the months of July and August alone. He would write another two hundred and fifty or so between September and the following August. His attraction to this genre was not altogether new. Half a dozen of the first poems he wrote in Portuguese as an adult, back in the fall of 1908, were folk quatrains, or *quadras populares*. At the time, he had thought of trying to work up a collection of these simple four-line poems, each line with seven syllables, but in the decades that followed he wrote only a few more of them, including several for his sweetheart, Ophelia Queiroz, and one—mentioned earlier—for Aunt Lisbela, his cousin from the Algarve. Now they poured out of him as if from a just discovered underground stream.

A tradition going back at least to medieval times, Portuguese folk quatrains typically comment on a beloved, on love in general, or on life's vicissitudes. By turns wistful, humorous, and didactic, they are still a living art, practiced not only by poets. Some years ago I hired a carpenter to redo the plank floors in my apartment in Lisbon. While he measured, sawed and hammered, I was treated to an ongoing recitation of quatrains that he himself had composed, or was in that moment composing.

Many of Pessoa's quatrains fit perfectly within the genre; others are sophisticatedly aphoristic, or poignantly self-revealing. In the following quatrain, written on July 11, 1934, the poet alludes to a patron saint of Portuguese fishermen, Our Lady of Agony, whose sanctuary is in the town of Viana do Castelo, on the northwestern coast:

In the church you'll find an image
Of our blessed Lady of Agony.
But what agonizes me
Is a pain that none can see.[14]

No amount of intelligence and inventiveness could make Pessoa's folk quatrains qualify as great poetry—the form is too restrictive—and he was not aspiring to anything great. Was he simply bored of writing ambitious works, or had the capacity to undertake large works deserted him? "How long it's been since I could write / A long poem!" begins a poem of Álvaro de Campos written on August 9. It wasn't just long poems but any complex or concentrated piece of writing, whether poetry or prose, that were eluding Pessoa and Campos, his only still reasonably active heteronym. (Ricardo Reis retired from active duty at the end of 1933, signing a single ode in 1934 and one more in 1935.) Pessoa's intellectual and creative energies were being channeled elsewhere.

◆

ON THE BASIS OF three chapbooks of his English poems, including the explicitly sexual "Epithalamium" and the boldly sensual "Antinous," Aleister Crowley had leapt to the conclusion that Pessoa was a man of his own stripe, one who could head up a Portuguese branch of the Ordo Templi Orientis, recruiting members and teaching them the ins and outs of the order's sex-magic rituals. Although several face-to-face meetings with the timid and unimposing poet were enough to disabuse the English magus of that rash idea, his intuition was not completely off the mark. Pessoa opted for chastity, but he understood it as an inwardly directed sexuality that resulted in self-fertilization. And while it's true that recruiting members and setting up meetings for a local branch of the O.T.O. or any other existing order would have been anathema to his personality, he conceived all the necessary trappings for an initiatory order of his own invention.

In 1931 Pessoa had indicated that the "inner" order of the Portuguese Order of Christ, which lay dormant for centuries before supposedly resurfacing in modern times, had no degree structure or rites of initiation. Two or three years later he changed his mind. Borrowing terminology from other esoteric orders, he created a series of initiatory degrees for the secret, inner Order of Christ—whose only real secret was its nonexistence—and some tests or trials associated with each degree: Neophyte, Adeptus Minor, Master of the Atrium, and so forth. The Adeptus Minor, having conquered the love of life and the fear of death, could become a Master of the Atrium by overcoming "the attachment to personality."[15]

Professing himself to be a Master of the Atrium, Pessoa retrospectively mapped his spiritual ascent to reach that stage in a set of notes written in English. They inform us that he was initiated into the Neophyte degree early on, through Alberto Caeiro, who conferred on him "the intuitional intelligence of the pagan world, of the world as it is seen." This throws a new light on Pessoa's claim that Caeiro emerged in 1914 not only as an astonishing poet but also as his personal master. The revelation of Caeiro, who taught him to see the world exactly as it is, was now recognized as the first step on his path toward gnosis.

According to the same notes, it was not until many years later, in 1931 or 1932, that Pessoa attained the grade of Adeptus Minor, by "conquering the love of life." At this point the tests of poverty, chastity, and obedience became "self-imposed vows." The notes indicate September 4, 1933, as the probable date when he ascended to the grade of Master of the Atrium, but they offer no clue as to what exactly happened that day.[16] Perhaps all that "happened" was a quiet realization.

Pessoa's scale of initiation included four more degrees, for a total of seven, the highest of which entailed "renunciation of deification," but he himself ascended no higher than the third degree, Master of the Atrium. That was a high enough grade for inducting others, and one year after attaining it, in September 1934, he created an initiation rite for incoming Neophytes, who, blindfolded and with hand on heart, were to answer a series of questions:

Q: What do you believe?
A: I am blind.
Q: Who are you?
A: I am naked.
Q: What do you have?
A: Only myself.
Q: Do you wish to be received into this order so that you will have light?
A: Yes, if you will show it to me.

The questions and answers continue on in this vein; I've translated just a snippet. At the end of the catechism—apparently formulated for us, his future readers—the presiding master of ceremonies utters a ritual speech, which includes words of encouragement such as the following:

> My brother, everything in this world is symbol and dream— symbols whatever we have, dreams whatever we desire. The whole universe, to which we belong through error and as punishment, is an allegory whose meaning you understand today since your eyes, being closed, are open, and your ears, being covered, are finally able to hear.[17]

Elsewhere in his notes, Pessoa established a governing structure for international chapters of the Order of Christ, in the event it should spread from Portugal to the rest of Europe and beyond.[18] And he dreamed up another, conspicuously patriotic spiritual order, which had eight rather than seven degrees of initiation, one for each letter of the word "Portugal," with "L" being the lowest degree and "P" the highest. Members of the order initiated into the fifth degree, "T," would be authorized to open up branches in other countries.[19]

Were he an assertive, aggressive personality, and not so committed to being a poet, we could almost imagine Pessoa as a Portuguese rival to Aleister Crowley. Inspired by the English magus, Pessoa not only invented his own spiritual orders, he also laid plans for their propagation around the globe—even though he never actually initiated anyone except, perhaps, himself. Crowley's Abbey of Thelema still stands—an overgrown ruin—in Cefalù, Sicily. Not to be outdone, Pessoa, for one of his religions, created a virtual "Abbey of the Quintessence,"[20] whose essential immateriality guaranteed that it would never risk decay or destruction. Religion, for him, was a competitive sport, a successor to the make-believe cricket and soccer matches of his youth.

◆

WHILE PESSOA WAS FRENETICALLY writing about magic, alchemy, esoteric orders, and initiation rites, as well as inventing his own orders and rites, William Butler Yeats—who actually belonged to several orders and had performed experiments in magic—was getting ready to bring out a much revised edition of *A Vision*. Had he read this work, Pessoa would have marveled at its astonishingly original treatment of the cosmic cycle of change, portrayed as a constant interplay of subjectivity and objectivity, personal history and universal history, life and afterlife, free will and fate—all endued with astrological correspondences and spanning eons. Although it was informed by the automatic writing of his wife, Georgie Hyde-Lees, the structure of the system and the impetus to create it came from Yeats, as did the hard work to present it in a readable text. (It is not, however, an easy read.) What Yeats aspired to and achieved—with some help from his wife's astral "Instructors"—was a unified, symphonic vision of the individual human soul in relationship to time and the universe.

Lacking the Irish poet's grand ambitions and conviction, Fernando Pessoa was more like a jazzman of higher, occult truth, improvising on standard doctrines of the esoteric repertoire and introducing his own variations, without staying in any one place for long. He returned incessantly to his favorite themes but never developed them in the same way twice. Rather than striving for an all-encompassing unity, Pessoa played and explored, searching for the sake of the search while at the same time creating a transcendent context for his own solitary soul. All the pages he dedicated to initiation rites served mainly, it seems, as a substitute for the real-life initiation he never had.

Initiation rites, in any case, were symbolic ceremonies that did not necessarily correspond to a deeper grasp of occult knowledge. Pessoa considered such rites to be expendable for literary geniuses and even, in a certain way, redundant. Of no genius was this truer than Shakespeare, held up by Pessoa as the archetypal "left-hand initiate," meaning that his spiritual initiation was not obtained by the regular, "right-hand" method of steady upward progress through grades. It occurred spontaneously, and *Hamlet*, whether or not the playwright knew it, was a "symbolic or ritual drama" of the highest order.[21] Here as elsewhere, Shakespeare was Pessoa's preferred mirror for beholding and admiring his own self. He was also a "left-hand initiate," who instead of *Hamlet*, *King Lear*, or *The Tempest*, created the symbolic, ritual dramas he called heteronyms.

Once again, Pessoa proved that literature can do and be just about everything. In the most intriguing passage written for his "Essay on Initiation," he compared the ascending grades of spiritual initiation to the successive stages of poetic achievement.[22] The poet starts out by acquiring basic tools such as grammar and literary culture, thereby attaining to the level of "simple lyrical poetry," then progresses to more complex poetic forms such as the ode, and finally, in the higher stages, arrives at epic and dramatic poetry. These last two genres are superior because "impersonal," requiring poets not only to express what they feel but also to feel with intensity things that they don't personally, naturally feel.

But the highest form of poetic achievement, according to Pessoa's initiatory scale for poets, is "the fusing of all poetry, lyric, epic and dramatic, into something beyond all these." He realized that sublime fusion in *Message*, issued at long last in the fall of 1934. With this book Pessoa, who had seemed to be slipping into willful anonymity, enveloped by a spiritual world that even he could only dimly perceive, suddenly reemerged as a notable—and soon to become notorious—poet.

L EFT TO HIS OWN DEVICES, PESSOA WOULD NEVER have published *Message*, for the same reason he never published Alberto Caeiro's *The Keeper of Sheep*, or collections of Álvaro de Campos's poetry and Ricardo Reis's odes, or a volume of the hundreds of miscellaneous poems written under his own name: inertia. His was not the inertia of one who can't get started but the inertia of one who can't stop: an incorrigible juggler, he kept dozens of literary projects spinning at once. To quit juggling long enough to actually prepare a book for publication meant violating his own nature. Added to his inertia was an old and nagging apprehension. What he had told his mother in a 1914 letter still held true: to become a published author would be a change, and he hated any change to his outward circumstances. Yes, he had somehow managed to bring out four chapbooks of his English poems, but they never threatened his status as a reputed literary genius whom few people had actually read. To publish in Portuguese was a riskier proposition.

*Mensagem* (*Message*), however, was more than a book that might confer fame and honor on Pessoa, a possibility that fascinated as much as it frightened him; it was a book that could rouse the Portuguese from their slumber and prepare Portugal to be a culturally proud, spiritually aware nation. He had a moral obligation to publish it! So argued Augusto Ferreira Gomes, at whose apartment Pessoa had lately been a regular guest for Sunday lunch. "I'll take care of the practical details," Ferreira Gomes promised. All he required from Fernando was a typescript for the printer.

Ferreira Gomes was the visible face of a joint effort. Standing right behind him was the director of the Secretariat of National Propaganda, António Ferro, who was anxious to see Pessoa's book published quickly, so that it could compete in the secretariat's contest to promote patriotic literature. The deadline for submissions had been extended from July 1 to October 31, 1934. Both Ferro and Ferreira Gomes, who worked for the secretariat as a graphic designer, were convinced that Pessoa's intensely

Portuguese book would be a shoo-in for the poetry prize, and to have Pessoa on "their" side would give it needed luster and momentum.

Not everyone had chosen political sides, but a divide was growing among Portugal's writers and artists, many of whom quietly opposed Salazar and his chief propagandist's nationalistic "politics of the spirit." António Ferro would have liked to be a conciliating figure in Portugal's artistic and intellectual milieu, but his job was to promote culture in such a way that it benefited the regime. By astutely investing money and cultivating friendships in Portugal's fledgling film industry, he had successfully brought José Leitão de Barros and other talented directors into the New State fold. Such artists as José de Almada Negreiros, in exchange for regular commissions, were pleased to mute whatever inconvenient opinions they might be tempted to express. The adverse opinions of writers, on the other hand, given that their artistic medium is language, were harder to conceal. Ferro realized that with Pessoa he had to proceed with caution. Augusto Ferreira Gomes assured him that the poet was a supporter of the regime, but he also knew that Pessoa insisted on his total independence, refusing to be officially associated with any group, cultural or political. They had to impress on him that there were no strings attached to the prize.

Pessoa was after all not that hard to convince. He agreed to contribute three poems from his forthcoming book to the July–August issue of *O Mundo Português* (*The Portuguese World*), a government-sponsored magazine whose special focus was the colonial empire. And in mid-August he prepared a final typescript of his book. He read it to Ferreira Gomes at one of their Sunday lunches, and the next day Ferreira Gomes escorted him to a publishing house. Presenting his typescript to the owner, manager, and head printer, Pessoa sheepishly apologized for not knowing when he would be able to settle the bill. He promised to pay as soon as he could, in installments. The printer nodded and said nothing; the remuneration for his services had already been guaranteed. Unbeknown to the poet, António Ferro was going to cover the cost of typesetting and printing his book with discretionary funds from the Secretariat of Propaganda.[1]

In the coming weeks, Pessoa frequently stopped by the printers to check the page proofs. So did Ferreira Gomes, who had experience in these matters and helped with design and layout. Pessoa made a few cor-

rections to the text, completely rewrote one of the poems, and decided
at the last minute to change the book's title from *Portugal* to *Message*. It
was his friend Alberto Da Cunha Dias who got him to rethink the title,
by reminding him that the name of their beloved country had been pros-
tituted by a shoe store called Portugal, whose slogan was "Portugalize
your feet!"[2] The shoe store, in fact, was a minor issue. The real problem,
Pessoa realized, was that the Portugal of his book transcended the visible, materially poor country of some 35,000 square miles where people
actually lived and worked and did things like buy shoes. His Portugal
was a symbolic lesson, a hope, a message. He decided that this last word
best captured the spirit of his book. And *mensagem* ("message" in Portuguese) was also shorthand—so he fancied, in his private notes—for *mens
ag[itat mol]em*, "mind moves matter," from Virgil.[3] Pessoa's book, as we
shall see, was punctuated by Latin epigraphs, and now Latin was even
embedded in the title.

✦

ON THE SAME PAGE of autobiographical notes where he credited
Alberto Da Cunha Dias with talking him out of his original title, Pessoa
pointed out that their conversation took place in a psychiatric hospital—
as if to suggest that his friend's mental disequilibrium made him more
qualified to proffer worthwhile opinions about the book. And so it did,
in the world according to Pessoa, whose about-to-be-published *Message*
contains a poem in praise of madness. It is narrated by King Sebastian,
who admits that his disastrous military campaign in Morocco was an
insane enterprise, and yet he defends the exalted impulse that led him
on, since:

> Without madness what is man
> But a healthy beast,
> A postponed corpse that breeds?

Cunha Dias, who had committed himself to an asylum at least once
before,[4] was not Pessoa's only mentally unstable friend. Raul Leal had
recently done a stint in Lisbon's psychiatric hospital, where he spent his
days composing what was possibly the most vertiginously metaphysical,
least comprehensible prose he ever wrote.[5] And José Pacheco, who was

briefly interned in a mental hospital in 1932 and whose tuberculosis had
returned with a vengeance after a period of remission, had lost all sense
of proportion and become a religious fanatic. Or was this comrade from
*Orpheu* days and the editor of *Contemporânea* actually more lucid than
ever before? If he truly believed in God, what could make more sense
than to devote his remaining, TB-afflicted days to prayer and worship?

For as long as his health allowed, Pacheco had attended Mass every
morning and occasionally visited the shrine of Our Lady of Fátima, but
by 1934 he was an ecstatic recluse and saw almost no one but his priest,
Father Pio, who would preside over his funeral, on September 29.[6] Just
a few people showed up, and Pessoa was not one of them, partly because
of his distaste for traditional Catholicism—an obscurantist religion that
imprisoned people's minds "through dogma, mysticism and superstition,"
according to an article he hoped to publish in 1935.[7] And yet he still, now
and then, felt nostalgia for Catholicism. Sylvia Plath, in her only novel,
used the bell jar to symbolize the life that stifles for lack of freedom,
lack of air. Pessoa, in a poem written in April 1934, used the very same
image to evoke the cozy feeling of being enclosed and protected by the
Catholic Church as a little boy, before he began to ask questions. One
of the poem's stanzas insinuates that his current interest in "Kabbalahs,
gnoses, mysteries, Freemasonries" and so forth was an attempt to fill the
void created by that lost faith.[8] There was no going back, however, and a
super-Catholicized Pacheco could only strike Pessoa as an exotic curiosity. The Pacheco he could relate to—the graphic artist, magazine editor,
promoter of art exhibitions, organizer of conferences, theater producer
and all-around enthusiast of culture—had died a few years before.

Theaters continued to stage new plays, and publishers continued to
publish upcoming as well as established authors. And there were new
publishing houses, including one called Edições Ática, founded by
another of Pessoa's *Orpheu* friends, Luís de Montalvor. But there was
no cultural activist in Lisbon to replace José Pacheco except, perhaps,
António Ferro. Some questioned whether his vigorous defense of the
arts within the New State was compatible with his vehement support of
an antiliberal, ultranationalist model of government. But whatever the
verdict on Ferro and his politics, shouldn't it be possible to promote culture and patriotism in the same stroke? Wasn't Pessoa attempting to do
exactly that through his book now at the printers?

✦

MESSAGE WAS PUBLISHED TOWARD the end of October, just in time to be considered for the Antero de Quental Poetry Prize, but it did not actually go on sale until December. On the ninth of that month the first review of the book was published, by Alberto Da Cunha Dias, who assured his readers that, although most of them had never heard of Fernando Pessoa, he was one of Portugal's few living writers whom the future would remember.[9] Five days later, the literary supplement of *Diário de Lisboa* dedicated an entire page to *Message*, publishing three of its poems, three matching illustrations by Almada Negreiros, and a short interview with the author, accompanied by a photo. The photo was credited to Ferreira Gomes, who had set up the interview and was sitting next to Pessoa at the Café Martinho da Arcada while it took place, on a cold and rainy afternoon, with the poet bundled up in a shabby raincoat. (While his suits were impeccable and his shoes well polished, Pessoa was curiously negligent when it came to his raincoats.)[10] In another newspaper, Ferreira Gomes anonymously published a brief notice that lauded *Message* as "a prayer to the Soul of the Nation and to the Spirit of our Race"[11] He and Ferro had gone to some effort to get Pessoa to publish his book in time to compete for the prize, and some good publicity could help ensure that it won.

In the midst of this miniblitz of favorable coverage, the weekly paper *Fradique* criticized the Secretariat of Propaganda for sponsoring a prize competition that was, in a word, propagandistic, rather than simply a celebration of great literature.[12] The prizes would confer, at best, a dubious prestige on their recipients. When the competition had first been announced, the editors of *Presença* voiced the same opinion, and Pessoa no doubt had his own qualms. But even if no prestige attached to the prize, he would at any rate welcome the money, with which he could pay off the IOUs he had been racking up at a couple of the firms where he worked,[13] the hundreds of escudos he owed at Senhor Trindade's dairy store, and the large and small loans extended by friends and family members. Making his financial matters worse, his sister and brother-in-law had decided to stay at their house in São João do Estoril rather than return to Lisbon in the fall. Teca and Chico—as Francisco, her husband, was known to family and friends—probably still contributed to the rent for the apartment on Rua Coelho da Rocha, but the housekeeper and utilities were now his exclusive responsibility.

It was not the romantic charms of life next to the sea that persuaded the couple to remain in Estoril. In the winter it was chilly, they were a little isolated from friends and family, and Chico had to commute every day to his job in Lisbon. But life in the apartment with Fernando also had its drawbacks, at least for Teca. Her brother came and went as he pleased, could be heard moving around long after everyone else was in bed, and while he did his best to be respectful of others, his personal disorganization hampered her efforts to keep a tidy home. He had prohibited the housekeeper from entering his bedroom, since whenever she cleaned it she inevitably left his scattered papers out of their mysterious "order," and he eventually declared it off-limits to everyone. For Teca this was the last straw. She didn't mind cooking for him, subsidizing him a little, and generally looking after him, but she confided to several friends and relatives that the thought of all that clutter and musty smell in his room—the papers, the overflowing ashtrays, and the occasional liquor bottle—was more than she could tolerate.[14] He was an affectionate, attentive uncle for her children, but she needed a little distance from Fernando.

The new arrangement suited him. Solitude was perhaps unhealthy, but he preferred it. They all got on well this way. Chico came by the apartment regularly to collect mail and check up on him. Fernando, who had enjoyed his occasional weekend visits to his sister's family during their summer sojourns, was glad to extend this ritual into the fall and winter. But even there, in São João do Estoril, solitude followed him. During one of his visits somebody noticed at a certain point that he had disappeared. Since he wasn't in the guest room, the living room, or out in the yard, he must have gone for a walk.

"Dinner's almost ready. Would you go look for Fernando?" Teca asked her husband when the sky began to dim, and soon enough he found him—on the other side of the train tracks, down by the water, sitting on the stone wall and gazing at the ocean, where the sun had already slipped below the horizon.

"We were afraid you'd gotten lost," joked Chico. "See anything interesting out there?"

"I was just thinking," said Fernando, and they walked together back to the house, where Teca was already putting food on the table.[15]

✦

**PESSOA RARELY WROTE TO** his two brothers, relying on his sister for news about their lives in England, but in 1934 he exchanged a few letters with João, now known as John, who had studied at the London School of Economics and now worked for a British merchant bank.[16] Acting as an informal agent for a couple of Portuguese firms where his usual occupation was to draft letters in English, Pessoa wanted some advice on a few business proposals. Without coming out and saying so, he hoped they might be of interest to the bank where his brother worked. To the first proposal—the expansion of a Portuguese gunpowder factory with investment capital from Great Britain—John Rosa answered in March that it fell outside the scope of his bank's interests, and he gently reminded Fernando of previous propositions of his that had proven to be half baked or unfeasible.

Pessoa, a little discouraged but not yet defeated, was at it again in October, writing on behalf of a different firm and with five new propositions: financing of a bank, exploitation of marble quarries, investment in corkwood forests, construction of a hotel in Lisbon, and the sale of a huge private estate in Portugal. On the last day of the year, apologizing for the lateness of his reply, John sent him a sixteen-page letter that explained why it was hard to obtain British financing for projects in Portugal, offered several suggestions about whom he might approach, and provided answers to various business-related queries. Well aware that Fernando, when it came to business deals, had an anti-Midas touch, John was not about to get his bank involved, and he pleaded with him never to mention the bank's name in connection with any negotiations. At the end of his letter, John instructed his brother to destroy it as soon as he had read and digested its contents.[17]

Although he did not destroy the letter, Fernando mercifully spared his banker brother further inquiries. Nor did he pursue negotiations with anyone else. Having been told, in so many words, that his assorted proposals were unrealistic, he desisted. He knew from the start that they were bound to go nowhere, but his destiny had compelled him to go through the motions of trying, once again, to be a businessman. This, the most mysterious of all his personae, could almost be a parody of the Yeatsian "anti-self," defined by the Irish poet as an antithetical figure to which the self is attracted and which in some sense completes it.[18] With no real expectation of making a profitable deal except in his imagination, Pessoa the inept businessman was an anti-self that "completed" Pessoa by completing nothing, by serving as a kind of metaphor for a life made of losses, debts, *disjecta membra*—in which poetry thrived, like wildflowers among ruins.

Only as an expert in the English language was Pessoa moderately adept at making money—by drafting business letters, by translating, and, lately, by teaching. In early 1934 he had begun tutoring three boys who were having trouble in school with English. For two or three sessions a week, held at one of the offices where he wrote letters, Pessoa earned 150 escudos a month. The pay was good for that kind of work, but it did not alleviate his indebtedness. Whatever money Pessoa received he spent— on books, restaurant meals, wine, and brandy. A boy in this group, Eduardo Calvet de Magalhães, would become one of his first posthumous editors, in 1942, and in 1985 he would publish a vivid account of his English lessons with the poet, which lasted for almost two years.[19] The pupil's first and most tenacious memory was his tutor's ethylic breath: he immediately realized he was in the presence of an alcoholic. Pessoa, having relegated his health scare of 1932 to an undifferentiated, faraway past, was consuming more liquor than ever, without even getting tipsy, as if it were mere fuel to get through each day.

Magalhães recalled that his tutor, besides elucidating the rules of English grammar, talked about literature, particularly the works of Edgar Allan Poe, and about secret societies such as the Rosy Cross and Freemasonry, some of whose signs and symbols he learned to draw. Card games were another frequent topic of conversation. The tutor knew that games, secret societies, and the mystery stories of Poe were things that could arouse the interest of adolescents bored by grammar, and all were things that never stopped being of interest to him. In the 1930s he still nurtured plans to translate book-length collections of Poe's shorts stories and poems,[20] wrote passionately about secret brotherhoods, and lived life the way he had always lived it, as if it were all a game. Lately, however, he had been dogged by depression.[21] Maybe he would cheer up soon, or maybe not. If everything went according to plan, he was going to be a prizewinning poet—a prospect that flattered his vanity but insulted his independence of soul, which he had always gone at great lengths to preserve and protect.

◆

TELLING HIMSELF THAT THE book prize, like book publication itself, was just another game, Pessoa did the things that just published authors and prize candidates do. In December, he sent copies of *Message* to journalists and critics as well as to friends and relatives. He even sent a copy to the prime minister, Salazar, perhaps vaguely hoping that his book's vision of a spiritually advanced Portugal might have some sort of an influence on public policy. The dictator responded, as people in high positions of government do, with a preprinted thank-you card.[22] On December 10 Pessoa left two copies—one inscribed to Ophelia Queiroz and another to Carlos Queiroz—at the apartment next to Praça do Rossio where they both lived with Carlos's mother. As soon as she realized from the housekeeper's description that the delivery man was Fernando himself, Ophelia ran to the front door—too late—and then to the balcony window overlooking the busy street, but the gentleman with a Chaplinesque moustache and round horn-rimmed glasses, who stooped a little and wore a beige raincoat, could nowhere be distinguished among all the other pedestrians.

He was on his way to the Hotel Borges, in the heart of Chiado, where he would drop off yet another signed copy of his book—for the Brazilian poet Cecília Meireles and her Portuguese husband, Fernando Correia Dias. Meireles was a poet whose work he admired. Correia Dias, an artist and an old friend of his, had immigrated to Brazil in 1914 and married her in 1922. It was her first trip ever to Portugal, and she was eager to make Pessoa's acquaintance. And Correia Dias wanted to catch up—it had been twenty years!

Pessoa had misgivings. What were he and Correia Dias supposed to catch up on, or return to? They were never especially close, and their friendship had lasted only a year. Nevertheless, in March 1914, one month before moving to Brazil, the artist had asked Pessoa to write something for his autograph book. Correia Dias's specialty then was caricature, which inspired his poet friend to write: "All of us, in our human and realized life, are but the caricature of our soul. We are always less than what we are. We are always a grotesque translation of what we wished to be, of what we inwardly and truly are."

It was Cecília Meireles whom Pessoa was more nervous about meeting. Given his admiration for her poetry, there was a reasonably good chance that the human, flesh-and-blood Cecília would not live up to the lofty idea of her that wafted in his imagination. And what grotesque impression would he make on her with his bashful manner, his eyes that wouldn't look straight at her, his nervous laugh, his fingers yellow from too much tobacco? No, it was better to avoid a face-to-face encounter. At the appointed time when the three of them were supposed to meet at a café, he failed to show up.[23] Better, he had decided, that they return to Brazil with a copy of his *Message* and whatever image of him that his poetry might conjure up. He left the book at the front desk of the hotel, looked furtively around the lobby, and walked out as discreetly as he had walked in.

Pessoa was naturally discreet, without the slightest air of self-importance. When he took a copy of *Message* to the home of José de Almada Negreiros, the housekeeper tried to shut the door in his face, mistaking him for a door-to-door book salesman. Hearing the commotion, the artist came to the front door to see what was the matter and found Fernando bent over with laughter, brandishing the autographed book.[24] It was inscribed to "the baby of *Orpheu*," since Almada Negreiros had been the magazine's youngest contributor.

The very first copy of *Message* inscribed by Pessoa, in mid-November, went to "Augusto Ferreira Gomes, imperially, and with a friendly and grateful hug."[25] "Imperially," wrote the inscriber, not only because his *Message* looked forward to an imminent Portuguese Fifth Empire but also because his friend had recently published his own, thematically related book of poems, *Quinto Império* (*Fifth Empire*), for which Pessoa wrote a brief introduction. The inscriber's hug was "grateful," of course, since Ferreira Gomes was the literary midwife without whom his *Message* might never have come into being, let alone be the odds-on favorite to win a prize. This feeling of gratitude extended to António Ferro, who also received a warmly inscribed copy of *Message*.

✦

SO REASSURING WAS FERREIRA GOMES that even Pessoa had come to believe he would win the secretariat's poetry prize, but the handpicked jury, presided over by Ferro, defied expectations. Actually there were two poetry prizes—one worth five thousand escudos, to be conferred on a book of poems of at least one hundred pages, and another worth one thousand escudos, for a shorter collection of poems or a single poem. To make Pessoa's book eligible for the larger prize, Ferreira Gomes had instructed the publisher to print its forty-four poems, none of which is long and some of which have less than ten lines, in such a way that they would take up just over one hundred pages. Pessoa had originally planned on a book of forty-one poems; it may have been at Ferreira Gomes's suggestion that he added a few more to stretch out the total length.

António Ferro opened the meeting of the jury, held on December 29, 1934, at the office of the secretariat, by announcing the works in competition for the two poetry prizes. *Message* was at the top of the list of books with more than a hundred pages. But one of the jurors balked, remarking on the many blank or sparsely printed pages in Pessoa's book. Next Ferro read the letters of two jurors who, unable to attend the meeting, sent their votes by mail. Teresa Leitão de Barros, a writer and the sister of José Leitão de Barros, the film director, cast her vote for *Message*. Not so the other absentee juror, a poet named Alberto Osório de Castro. While praising Pessoa's technical mastery of the lyric form, he deemed his book excessively "elliptical and hermetic," its inspiration too "esoteric to directly reach the clear and simple soul of the Portuguese people." He voted for *A romaria* (*The Pilgrimage*), by Vasco Reis, saying that it "sprouts from the Portuguese soil like a delicate Franciscan flower [. . .] in the springtime of emotion." Reis was a Franciscan priest and missionary. Ignoring the question of whether Pessoa's book had more than one hundred pages, Osório de Castro proposed in his letter that it be awarded the "second category" prize, for a poem or a group of poems. One of the three jurors physically present at the meeting—Mário Beirão, a friend of Pessoa from *A Águia* days—seconded Osório de Castro's choices, which prevailed by majority vote, much to the dismay of António Ferro.[26]

Ferreira Gomes was doubly disappointed. Having assumed that Pessoa would win the first category prize, he had submitted his *Fifth Empire*, a book of some sixty pages, with his eyes on the second category prize. But what really disconcerted him, and Ferro, was how Pessoa would take the news that his *Message*, despite their scheming, had lost out to a "delicate Franciscan flower" of poetry, written by a literary novice.

# CHAPTER 71

**P**ESSOA STANDS UP FROM HIS TYPEWRITER, PUTS
on his hat and his raincoat, announces to nobody in particular,
"I'm going to Abel's," and walks out of the office. It's already
late enough to purchase the evening paper, which he does a little self-
consciously, looking over his shoulder, not wanting to be seen. Only
when he's standing at the counter of Abel's, where a glass of red wine
is served up without his having to say anything except *"Boa tarde,"* good
afternoon, does he open the newspaper and discover that his book has
been trumped, demoted to the second category. He trembles imperceptibly, revealing no emotion to the bartender, places a coin on the counter,
and returns to the office.

Or perhaps he stayed at home that day, the last day of 1934, stepping
out to buy the paper in the late afternoon and returning immediately to
the apartment to read it in private, nervous with excitement, which soon
turned to chagrin—and perhaps sorrow, perhaps anger, though he would
still have kept a straight face, trying not to show emotion even to himself.

The winners of the Secretariat of Propaganda's literary prizes had been
announced a few hours earlier at a gala luncheon, a kind of warm-up
for those who would be going to parties to welcome in the New Year.
While the guests ate and drank at the expense of the government, they
learned that the recipients of the history, essay, and journalism prizes
had been chosen by unanimous decision. But the largest prize (10,000
escudos)—for the best novel with "a broadly constructive purpose"—was
not awarded, since the fiction jury felt that none of the entrants fulfilled
that vaguely worded criterion, which seems to have been New State lingo
for something like "conducive to moral improvement and patriotic fervor."

In view of the resulting surplus in the prize budget, António Ferro
had decided, on his own initiative, to increase the value of Pessoa's "second category" poetry prize to 5000 escudos, the same amount as the
"first category" prize (equivalent to $4000 or $5000 today). He justified

his decision by remarking on the "lofty nationalist feeling" of *Message*, which wound up in the second category only over a technical question of page length. According to the deliberations of the jury, which were read aloud at the luncheon, the book's author was "one of the most original personalities of Portuguese letters" but "voluntarily isolated from the public."[1] Ferro had done everything he could to make Pessoa's award equal in prestige to the first category prize, but he could not change the fact that a majority of the jury deemed Vasco Reis's book superior.

The gala luncheon, the names of the prize winners, and the considerations of the various juries were all reported in the *Diário de Lisboa*, next to an article in which the German foreign minister was quoted as saying that his country, where Hitler had assumed the title of Führer in August, desired nothing more than to live in peace with its neighbors. The rest of the newspaper was full of ads for the usual New Year's Eve diversions: fancy dinners, dancing, plays, and movies from America that starred actors such as Joan Crawford, Douglas Fairbanks Jr., Jean Harlow, and the Barrymore brothers.

Whether he worked at one or another office or spent the day at home, we know that on the evening of December 31 Pessoa, carrying a small suitcase, proceeded to the Cais do Sodré railway station, swarming with commuters at that time of day, and boarded a train for São João do Estoril, where he would spend a couple of days with his sister's family. He was indifferent to Christmas and to New Year's Eve but faithfully observed family birthdays, and his nephew, Luís Miguel, was turning four years old the next day. Before the train pulled out of the station, he was greeted by his brother-in-law, who had just boarded, briefcase in hand, making his usual commute home after finishing his day's work in Lisbon.

"Well well, Fernando!" exclaimed Chico with a smile and his arms wide open, as if embracing something abstractly large and wonderful.

Fernando, who was already seated, looked up at him blankly. "Well what?"

"What, you ask! Didn't you read the papers?"

"Yes," he answered in the same monotone as before. "Oh, you mean the prize I won."[2]

Chico sat down next to him, and within forty-five minutes they had reached their destination. It was a somewhat uphill ten-minute walk from the station to Chico and Teca's house, where Manuela and Luís

Miguel eagerly awaited their uncle Fernando, who tried to act natural and nonchalant, making light of the prize for which his sister also congratulated him.

Pessoa invoked apathy to neutralize, as much as possible, his disillusion and embarrassment. He had allowed himself to place hope in the prize, to dream of being a successful poet in the way the world measures success, and the hope defrauded him, the dream was a sham. In an embittered poem written in São João do Estoril that night or the next day he mused:

> Make a real effort?
> To conquer what?
> Glory? Knowledge? Power?
> What good is all that?
>
> O pastor who's a nobody,
> Since nobody notices you,
> Your youthful spirit
> I also have, without youth.
> But at least I've remained
> Faithful to innocence
> In all I put off, in all I don't do.[3]

After putting off and not following through for most of his life, the poet now chided himself for having tried to achieve glory, to be somebody. Vasco Reis, the twenty-four-year-old Franciscan pastor and missionary who won the first category prize, may have been a nobody, but one of the members of the prize jury—as reported in the newspapers— saw signs in his work of another Cesário Verde or António Nobre, two of Portugal's greatest nineteenth-century poets. Even if Pessoa did not regret publishing his book, he regretted having fooled himself, or having let himself be fooled, into thinking it would be understood and appreciated by the kinds of people who make up prize committees. Still, he needed the money and was grateful to Ferro for having quintupled the amount of his prize. For the first time since the Ibis press fiasco of 1910, he was financially solvent.

On the same sheet of paper where he scribbled the New Year's poem, Pessoa drafted a review of Reis's *Pilgrimage*. The *Diário de Lisboa* had asked him for an opinion piece about literary prizes in general, but Pessoa, unable to come up with an angle that satisfied him, decided to write a piece about the Franciscan's book instead. Published in the January 4 issue of the newspaper, Pessoa's book review congratulated the prize committee for having revealed to the public such an "admirable artist" and such an "adorable poem." (*The Pilgrimage* was a single, book-length narrative poem.) Choosing his words carefully, the reviewer noted an "utterly Christian paganism" in Reis's poetry, since it evinced the purely emotional element of paganism at the same time that it overflowed with the "religious tenderness" typical of Portuguese Catholicism. In other, plainer words, it was sentimental drivel. Pessoa dressed up his disdain for the "adorable" poem with religious concepts that deviously implied it was heretical. He was swinging in every direction—at the young poet, at the jurors who awarded his book a prize, and at the conservative Catholic establishment—but in such a way that his victims might think they were being stroked rather than punched. Thus he swiftly, slyly got his revenge.

On January 31 João Gaspar Simões published an article that lambasted António Ferro for appointing unqualified people to the various prize juries—not least of all to the jury for the fiction prize, which rejected all the novels in competition, including one submitted by Gaspar Simões. But the critic and novelist reserved his most devastating remarks for the surprise poetry winner, Vasco Reis, a "Franciscan as poor in talent as the founder of his order was poor in worldly possessions." The poet-priest had his defenders, one of whom was the nationalistic publisher and writer João de Castro Osório, and he also came to his own defense in a couple of rejoinders to Gaspar Simões sent from his missionary outpost in Mozambique.[4]

◆

PESSOA'S MESSAGE ALSO GENERATED conflicting opinions. The book's first reviewer, his friend Alberto Da Cunha Dias, had been generous with praise but feared that the poet's attempt to create "a national mysticism" ran the risk of being misinterpreted, and he wished that his book's symbolism were less esoteric and more Catholic. The book's second reviewer was twenty-two-year-old Luís Pedro Moitinho de Almeida, whose collection of poems from 1932, *Morning Stars*, had included a foreword by Pessoa that expressed no real admiration, only faint praise. Repaying him in kind, Moitinho de Almeida began his review by hailing *Message* as an opportunity for "the Sphinx," its author, to finally reveal himself; it concluded by saying that the Sphinx, after all, had still not spoken: "*Message* is a book by Fernando Pessoa that is not a book by Fernando Pessoa, by which I mean that, while it is a book full of beautiful poems that the intelligence of Fernando Pessoa created, it is not a book of poems that the heart of Fernando Pessoa felt."[5]

We may shake our heads at this young reviewer's reductive view of poetry as a fundamentally emotive, confessional art, but the thrust of his criticism—that Pessoa was too smart for his own good, or for the good of his poetry—was reiterated by others. The editor in chief of *Fradique* would write that the poet of *Message* was "extremely intelligent . . . and little more," the author of opaque poems that "few will be able to decipher and which don't reward the effort."[6]

Writing for *O Diabo* (*The Devil*), a cultural weekly, the poet and novelist Alice Ogando issued a diametrically contrary verdict: "So great is the poetic richness of this book that even if its author were never to write another line of verse, his name would be forever associated with the best in Portuguese poetry."[7] A poet could hardly aspire to a higher compliment for a first book. Ogando praised *Message* for its intellectual depth as well as its artistic excellence. Other enthusiastic reviewers analyzed the book's tripartite structure, its symbolism, and the substance of the message promised by its title. João de Castro Osório admired *Message* as "the complete, total and definitive expression" of Sebastianism in poetry.[8] It was an apt characterization: King Sebastian is directly referred to in no less than ten of the book's poems.

◆

A POETIC RETELLING OF Portuguese history, *Message* owed a good portion of its inspiration to Mário Beirão, who in 1917 had published *Lusitânia*, a collection of poems that evoked several centuries of Portugal's glorious past, especially the Age of Discoveries.[9] As one of the jurors for the Antero de Quental Poetry Prize, he must have noticed how his own work had influenced Pessoa's, and also how the poems of his former friend were incomparably superior. Maybe that's why he voted for the Franciscan missionary to win the first category prize.

Taking an even wider view than Beirão, Pessoa's book set out to capture, in a series of poetic miniatures, the story of Portugal from its ancient origins to its hopefully resplendent future. The first section,

"Coat of Arms," chronicles Portugal's history from the time of Lisbon's legendary founding by Ulysses to the rout of King Sebastian's army in Morocco in 1578. It is a dramatized history, with key actors such as Viriathus (a Lusitanian chieftain who valiantly defended western Iberia from Roman invaders), King Afonso Henriques (recognized in 1143 as Portugal's first king), and the ill-starred King Sebastian either speaking in the first person or being spoken to by the narrator in poems that bear their illustrious names as titles. The middle section, "Portuguese Sea," recalls Portugal in its height of glory as a ruler of the seas and discoverer of lands hitherto unknown to Europeans. "The Hidden One," the book's final section, looks forward to Portugal's Sebastianist and Fifth Empire future yet is tinted by melancholy, as if the nation might after all not succeed in rising out of its present state of stagnation to claim its rightful destiny.

Pessoa had initially titled the third section "Songs of Defeat,"[10] and some of the poems toward the end—especially "Night," "Storm," and "Fog"—oscillate between expectancy and resignation. "Fog," which is the last poem in the book, laments "The tarnished splendor of the land / That is Portugal wrapped in grief," a land where

All is uncertain and dying.
All is scattered, nothing is whole.
O Portugal, today you are fog . . .

And then comes the final line, the book's conclusion: "Now is the Hour!"—the Hour for a turnaround in Portugal's fortunes, the Hour of Sebastian's Second Coming, the Hour of the Fifth Empire. But the announcement rings a little desperate, or wishful.

✦

COMPOSED OF DRAMATIC LYRIC poems that tell an epic story, *Message* was a poetic hybrid that attempted to modernize and improve on *The Lusiads*, whose celebration of Vasco da Gama's inaugural voyage to India implicitly glorified the entire program of Portugal's discoveries and ocean exploits. While it would be hard to argue that Pessoa—in his bid to become a Super-Camões—succeeded in surpassing Camões's masterpiece, in a certain way *Message* is vaster, since it spans the whole of Portugal's history and proclaims its imperial future. Conversely to *The*

*Lusiads*, which immortalized the Portuguese maritime empire *after* it was already in decline, *Message* immortalized the Fifth Empire *before* it actually existed in time and space. What's more, it would never and could never exist spatially and temporally, since it was an empire—wrote Pessoa—"of poets" and "of grammarians,"[11] an empire of language. That doesn't mean he didn't hope for a visible, worldly Fifth Empire, but his hope itself was poetic, eloquently inscribed in the verses for his book and in his many other writings on the future of Portugal.

"Myth is the nothing that is everything," begins the poem in *Message* about Ulysses, the mythical founder of Lisbon, which in ancient times was called Ulyssipo, a name that resembles but is etymologically unrelated to that of the Greek hero. But this detail mattered not at all; it only made the myth more potent. "Because he never was," says the poet, this faux founder "slowly came to exist." And so "the legend, little by little, / Seeps into reality." The same principle applied to the Sebastianist legend, whose potential for raising the morale of the nation depended, according to Pessoa, on its mythical character.

*Message* contains other weighty symbols besides King Sebastian and the Fifth Empire. There are poems that allude to Sir Galahad's symbolic quest for the Holy Grail; to the Fortunate Isles of Greek and Celtic mythology, one of which was Avalon, where King Arthur sleeps until his glorious return; and to the central symbol of Rosicrucianism, the crucified rose. Pessoa went out of his way to impart a distinctly esoteric flavor to *Message*, whose opening epigraph (*Benedictus Dominus Deus noster Qui dedit nobis signum*) and concluding exhortation (*Valete, fratres*)— in English: "Blessed be Our Lord God Who gave us the sign" and "Be strong, brothers"—are salutations borrowed from Rosicrucian rituals. The book's three sections were also preceded by Latin epigraphs, vouchsafed to Pessoa in a message from one of his astral communicators.[12] Thus *Message*, like Yeats's *Vision*, although to a far lesser degree, also owed something to spirits from occult regions.

The esoteric slant of *Message*, by universalizing its nationalistic subject matter, paradoxically makes that subject matter somewhat irrelevant. The sixth poem begins: "Every nation is a mystery. / Each one, by itself, is the whole world." Portugal, the obsessive theme and original title of the book, is itself a mysterious symbol; it stands for something larger. But the real greatness of *Message* has nothing to do with what its symbols stand for or with the message or messages it contains. It is simply, as one of its first reviewers observed, fabulously good poetry. Densely packed with Portuguese history, the work is less accessible than others by Pessoa, and its elliptic stanzas and numerous aphorisms rarely survive translation unscathed, but the attentive reader will remark its constructive ingenuity and feel its expressive power.

✦

HOWEVER UNIVERSAL AND ESSENTIALLY poetic *Message* may be, it still brims with nationalism. Pessoa clearly hoped that the myth it embodied would seep into Portugal's political reality and be a transformative agent. But it was not at all clear what sort of transformation he hoped for. As I've already pointed out, the poet left no written record or picture of what a redeemed and reborn, glorious Portugal might look like. For right-wing nationalists such as Augusto Ferreira Gomes, Salazar's New State was—or was on its way to becoming—the Portuguese Fifth Empire heralded by *Message*. Politically independent critics rightly surmised that the book's nationalism was not so sectarian, but they struggled to understand its author's intentions and priorities.

*Message* particularly confounded, and disappointed, the co-editors of *Presença*, whose refusal to take a political stance was itself a stance, a form of resistance, at a time when organizations, publications, and citizens of note were under pressure to align themselves behind the New State. The youngest of the magazine's three editors, Adolfo Casais Monteiro, articulated his disappointment in a letter to Pessoa posted on January 10, 1935. He felt that the book, despite containing some excellent poems, misrepresented its author, giving undue prominence to a secondary facet of his poetic personality. In his reply three days later, Pessoa conceded that *Message* "was not a felicitous publishing debut. I am, to be sure, a mystical nationalist, a rational Sebastianist. But I am many other things besides that, and even in contradiction to it. And because of the kind of book it was, *Message* did not include those things."

Pessoa's self-descriptive epithets—"mystical nationalist" and "rational Sebastianist"—are helpful clues for fathoming the nature of his nationalism and the ambition of his book, whose esoteric symbolism served to enhance the Sebastianist myth, which was *rationally* adopted to energize the national psyche. Indeed, Pessoa justified the publication of *Message* ahead of his other books by telling Casais Monteiro that it "coincided with a critical moment [. . .] in the reshaping of the national subconscious." Pessoa may have believed in this explanation, but if the Portuguese subconscious was at that moment being reshaped, it was for the worse, enabling Salazar to remain in power for thirty-three more years—until 1968, when he would suffer a stroke (he died two years later). His New State, would endure a little longer, until 1974.

The youngest editor of *Presença* was less interested in Pessoa's political ideas than in his poetry, especially the poetry written under other names. In his letter he had gingerly asked about the genesis of the heteronyms, before quickly adding that he would not take it amiss if the poet preferred not to answer. Not at all reticent, Pessoa let loose, devoting more than half of his reply—and this letter of January 13 was the longest he ever wrote—to a detailed narrative of how he invented the Chevalier de Pas and other literary playmates as a young boy, of how Alberto Caeiro, Ricardo Reis, and Álvaro de Campos came into being in 1914, of how these three individuals interacted in his imagination, and of how, depending on his mood, he wrote in the voice of each one, or in the voice of his semiheteronym, Bernardo Soares, who, he confided, "always appears when I'm sleepy or drowsy, such that my qualities of inhibition and logical reasoning are suspended; his prose is an endless reverie." (However, for many months now he had written nothing in the voice of the assistant bookkeeper.) Pessoa also provided biographical sketches for his three main heteronyms: when and where they were born, their schooling and professions, and their physical characteristics.

Most of Pessoa's story of the heteronyms has already been recounted or directly quoted herein, but only in 1935 were the details of that story finalized. His January 13 letter, entrusted to Adolfo Casais Monteiro, was written for all his future exegetes (one of whom would be Casais Monteiro) and general readers. Anxious to ensure its preservation for posterity, Pessoa made not one but two carbon copies. He was beginning to get himself and his work ready for eternity. That precious letter, besides containing his definitive heteronymous creation story, also included his clearest, most straightforward declaration of spiritual belief.

◆

THE INQUISITIVE CASAIS MONTEIRO had also been cheeky enough to ask whether the occult interested the poet merely for the sake of its poetically useful symbols or because he was a genuine spiritual initiate. Pessoa replied that, although he belonged to no initiatory order, he believed "in the existence of worlds higher than our own and in the existence of beings that inhabit those worlds." He continued:

> I believe there are various, increasingly subtle levels of spirituality that lead to a Supreme Being, who presumably created this world. There may be other, equally Supreme Beings who have created other universes that coexist with our own, separately or interconnectedly. [. . .] Given this hierarchy of beings, I do not believe that direct communication with God is possible, but we can, according to the degree of our spiritual attunement, communicate with ever higher beings.

Progress in the occult world, wrote Pessoa, may be achieved by three paths—magical, mystical, and alchemical. He deemed the last path to be "the hardest and most perfect path of all, since it involves a transmutation of one's personality."

But in what does the alchemical path of self-transformation consist? Some notes written by Pessoa in English, probably in 1934, go a long way toward answering that question. They explain that the adept, before undertaking the *magnum opus* of transforming the self, must first of all possess the requisite *prima materia*, or prime matter, defined as "Bodily Life," or "vitality." This matter is less simple than it sounds. "The Man and Woman necessary to produce it have to be obtained within himself by the Adept," stipulates the poet-alchemist, "either satanically, by uniting homo with heterosexuality; or divinely, by chastity, which unites the activity latent in being man with the passivity of not using that activity (being thus, like the Creative God, man and woman *in one*)."

Aleister Crowley took the satanic route, realizing his vitality through promiscuous sex magic, performed with men as well as women. Pessoa preferred the divine road of chaste androgyny, which entails "seminal absorption" and what he termed "self-fecundation."[13] Throughout this biography I have avoided defining Pessoa's sexuality, but based on his spiritual explanations and as demonstrated by his own "practice," such as it was, it's possible to affirm that the poet was ultimately not heterosexual, homosexual, pansexual, or asexual; he was monosexual, androgynously so. The heteronyms can be seen as the fruit of his self-fertilization.

Having obtained, whether satanically or divinely, the prime matter—*vitality*—necessary for self-transformation, the adept, according to Pessoa,

is ready to pursue the *magnum opus*, or Great Work, in four stages: putre-
faction, albation (or whitening), gradation, and rubification (or reddening).
Borrowed from the Rosicrucians, these stages correspond to the "rotting of
the lower self," the "cleansing of the lower self," the ascent "of the self in
itself," and "full attainment."[14] The question remains whether Pessoa himself tried to follow this four-step path to achieve the *magnum opus*.

Ever since meeting Aleister Crowley in 1930, which is when he began
to delve more deeply into the shadowy realms of the spirit world, Pessoa
had been pondering the relative merits of the methods used by occultists
to progress toward truth and God, or Oneness. He settled on alchemy—
understood as the conversion of base, instinctive life into an ennobled,
divine life—as the surest path leading to "worlds higher than our own"
and ultimately to a Supreme Being, but he never said that he actually,
earnestly followed that path. To Casais Monteiro he said only that it was
the best of all paths and that he believed in those higher worlds, in those
graduated spheres of reality.

Pessoa's professions of spiritual belief, like his stories about the heteronyms, can be understood as acts of poetic—or, in this case, religious—
feigning. For him to say that he *believed* in something meant, at a minimum,
that it appealed to him intellectually, probably even fascinated him, and
struck him as something that ideally *ought* to exist. The something also
had to be immune to analytical reason; otherwise his relentlessly rational
mind would deconstruct it, depleting it of all its enchantment. These various conditions were fulfilled by the occult, which by definition is beyond
explaining, susceptible to probing but not positive discovery. It is therefore endlessly explorable, interpretable, and applicable.[15]

✦

**ALTHOUGH WE CANNOT KNOW** what exactly Pessoa believed or how
assiduously he believed it, his motivation for believing is not hard to
understand. Consider the opening lines from an Álvaro de Campos
poem he wrote on January 5, 1935, just eight days before his expansive
letter on the heteronyms and the occult:

> I don't know if the stars rule the world
> Or if tarot or playing cards
> Can reveal anything.
> I don't know if the rolling of dice

Can lead to any conclusion.
But I also don't know
If anything is attained
By living the way most people do.

Pessoa wanted to live a different kind of life. He aspired to some of the same things that most people aspire to—such as love, power, and personal recognition—but his practical experience of those things was atypical. He had forbidden Ophelia Queiroz from referring to him as her boyfriend and never seriously considered marriage; he preferred to exert influence on the literary and political life of his country from behind the scenes, in writing rather than in person; and he cared hardly at all about being famous while alive, hoping instead to go down in history as a literary immortal.

His college diary from 1906 had abounded in disdain for "conventionals," for conventional ideas and conventional ways of seeing and doing. Most college students eventually slough off their pretense of originality, of being fundamentally different from others, but not Pessoa. Were he an extrovert and a sensualist, he might have traveled around the world and had his fill of unpredictable amorous encounters, like Álvaro de Campos. Yet even Campos, an ambivalent cosmopolite, had tired of gallivanting, thereby confirming his inventor's suspicion that life in this world, no matter how one lives it, eventually becomes repetitive and tedious. Pessoa preferred to travel in literature and in speculations about the uncorrupted, occult world, of which our earthly world is a poor reflection. As above, so below—but with gross distortions and imperfections. He knew that the occult world might after all be nothing, but the world we live in is "half of nothing" and moribund, according to the poem from *Message* titled "Ulysses," which celebrates myth as "the nothing that is everything."

◆

ELATED TO RECEIVE PESSOA'S long and revelatory letter, Casais Monteiro wrote back immediately, emboldened to probe a little further. It seemed to him that Pessoa's poetry, published at irregular intervals according to no discernible plan and under various names, did not exactly evolve; it simply kept changing, from one voice and style to another. Was that a fair observation? In his reply, sent on January 20, Pessoa completely agreed, saying that some of the poems he wrote when he was twenty were just as good as the ones he was writing now. "I've naturally lost a certain simplicity and naïveté present in my adolescent poems," he noted, "but that's not evolution, it's just me getting older." Partly reiterating what he had told Gaspar Simões three years earlier, Pessoa explained to Casais Monteiro his poetic method:

> What I am essentially—behind the involuntary masks of poet, logical reasoner and so forth—is a dramatist. My spontaneous tendency to depersonalization, which I mentioned in my last letter to explain the existence of my heteronyms, naturally leads to this definition. And so I do not evolve, I TRAVEL. (This word is typed in capital letters because I mistakenly hit the shift key, but it's correct, so I'll let it stand.) I continuously change personality, I keep enlarging (and here there is a kind of evolution) my capacity to create new characters, new forms of pretending that I understand the world or, more accurately, that the world can be understood.

Although Pessoa was still a restless traveler, his "capacity to create new characters" actually seemed to be waning, not enlarging, and major heteronyms and semiheteronyms such as Alberto Caeiro, António Mora, and Bernardo Soares had completely disappeared from his writing world. But he was still the meeting place, or the medium, for a number of diversified characters, including some without individualized names, referred to in his January 13 letter as "the various subpersonalities of Fernando Pessoa himself." They included the world-weary poet who composed rubaiyat in the style of Omar Khayyam, the rhymester who penned hundreds of traditional Portuguese folk quatrains, the confessionalist whose poems were a transfigured record of his shifting moods, and the occultist who wrote esoteric poems and hundreds of pages about Kabbalah, the Knights Templar, Rosicrucianism, Freemasonry, initiation rites, magic, and alchemy.

But the occultist in Pessoa, so fervent and industrious between 1931 and 1934, grew listless in 1935, losing much of his interest if not his faith in the hidden side of things. He produced no more esoteric poems, and the torrent of speculations on esoteric subjects ebbed to a trickle. Another of the self-styled dramatist's "subpersonalities" now stepped forward and took center stage in his writing life: the political activist.

# CHAPTER 72

**P**ESSOA HAD BEEN WRITING ABOUT POLITICS
ever since his student days at the School of Arts and Letters,
when a desire to help topple the monarchy and curtail the power
of its chief ally, the Catholic Church, inspired satiric poems and several
long essays—none of which he published. When, in the 1910s, the victorious republic bred more social unrest and politically driven violence
than had existed in the monarchy it replaced, Pessoa responded with a
diverse mix of writings. These included idealistic proposals such as a
Portuguese Fifth Empire, better suited to poetry than reality; expository and analytical essays whose goal was to explain, not to change anything, at least not in the short run; and denunciatory works that were
sometimes too categorically vituperative to have any practical effect,
since what can one do if everything is rotten to the core? I'm thinking
here of the "Ultimatum" of 1917, in which Álvaro de Campos wrote off
the whole lot of Europe's politicians and intellectuals as complete and
unmitigated "shit."

The poet and polemicist could also be pragmatic, going on the attack
against attitudes and actions that threatened values he cherished. So it
was with the Literature of Sodom affair of 1923, when he drafted, published, and diligently distributed manifestos opposing the student movement that had campaigned to have the books of three homoerotic writers
banned. In early 1935 this last sort of political writer—the activist—
resurfaced to defend Freemasonry and, more fundamentally, the right to
speak, meet, and think freely. Acting as a lone wolf, his preferred style, he
triggered a controversy that ultimately had no effect on government policy but that helped to transform him, Pessoa, into an outspoken dissident.

On January 19, a bill to outlaw "secret societies" was introduced in the
recently created National Assembly, a puppet parliament whose ninety
members had been elected without opposition. While not actually mentioned in the bill, Freemasonry was the one and only "secret society" it

targeted. Masons have a policy of maintaining silence when their order is attacked, but the grand master of Portuguese Masons, faced with the possibility of the group's extinction, wrote a letter to the president of the National Assembly, criticizing the bill and insisting that Masons were upstanding, patriotic citizens who had nothing to hide. Indeed the letter writer, José Norton de Matos, was himself a decorated army general and distinguished statesman. Censorship prevented his letter—sent to the assembly on January 31—from being mentioned in any newspaper, but Pessoa had a copy of it, since someone from the Masons asked him to translate it into English. Perhaps they wanted to include his translation in a dossier sent to Masonic leaders in England and elsewhere, to apprise them of the threat to the order in Portugal.[1]

Pessoa also wrote his own, trenchant critique of the proposed law, coupled with a vigorous and wide-ranging defense of Freemasonry. Titled "Secret Societies," his essay was the lead article in the February 4 *Diário de Lisboa*. Why the censors let it pass is a mystery.[2] One plausible answer is that the New State leaders were not entirely sure it was a good idea to suppress Freemasonry. President Carmona, as previously noted, had himself been initiated into the order, along with a few others in the government, and Salazar had never pronounced himself against the Masons. The dictator was willing to do whatever was necessary to consolidate his power and promote his policies, but he did not want to do *more* than was necessary. On the other hand, he needed to keep his political base happy. The reactions to Pessoa's article would clarify public opinion on the issue as well as whether the issue really mattered.

The article explained that fraternal ties and a spirit of tolerance, not a set of dogmas, are what link Masons together; that their social and political tendencies vary from country to country, from Grand Lodge to Grand Lodge, although the vast majority of them are apolitical; and that many illustrious Masons are politically conservative, particularly in the British royal family. The article also discussed the allegedly occult origins of Freemasonry and warned that any attempt to ban the order was sure to backfire, since Masons, when persecuted, forget their ideological differences to defend one another tooth and nail. Pessoa intimated that there could be reprisals from countries such as Great Britain and the United States, where Masons were especially numerous, and he drew an obscure causal link between Hitler's dissolution of three Grand Lodges and subsequent divisions within the Nazi Party. Being a weaker country,

Portugal would be especially susceptible to nefarious consequences if the bill before the National Assembly became law.

What actually backfired was Pessoa's ominous warning about the latent capability of the Masons to unitedly attack their enemies. It was precisely this sort of hidden power, outside the control of government or religion, that made anti-Masons froth with fury. Confirming as it did one of their major objections to Freemasonry, Pessoa's article set off a hailstorm of protest in the right-wing press. The *Diário da Manhã*, which had published an encomiastic review of *Message* ten days earlier, saying that its concluding line—"Now is the Hour!"—was like "a clarion call at dawn, after a long night of waiting," retracted the compliment on February 5, quipping that the poet of the auspicious "Hour" had a watch that ran slow and must have been purchased at a Masonic *loja* (this word means both "lodge" and "shop").[3] Pessoa, in other words, was out of sync with the anti-Masonic, New State spirit of the times. The editor of *Fradique*, a sincere admirer of Pessoa as a writer and intellectual, took him to task in an open letter, saying that the "modern generation" had no interest in Freemasonry, at best a "picturesque" institution, and that the poet's "hymn to intellectual occultism" had a "moldy smell that divorces you from all of us."[4]

Pessoa was indeed divorced, temperamentally, from the "modern generation" and for the same reasons he was divorced from every other generation: he refused to identify with any group in a lasting way, nor did he ever settle in one place, idea, or enthusiasm for long. Unlike Eliot, who never strayed far from Anglo-Catholicism after his conversion in 1927, Pessoa let his unleashed mind keep running. The occult, which generated enormous interest among late-nineteenth-century writers and artists, had fallen out of fashion, hence the newspaper editor's comment that Pessoa's "intellectual occultism" was musty. But the poet was indifferent to fashion, and we have seen how established esoteric doctrines and rites of initiation were mere starting points from which he struck out in ever new directions. Nobody could say where Pessoa stood, since he was always on the move.

Luís Moitinho de Almeida, who had known the poet for over ten years, was right to call him a sphinx in his review of *Message*. But to many of the people who saw his name attached to a bold defense of Freemasonry, so bold it had become a journalistic sensation, Pessoa was less than a sphinx; he was a complete unknown. In a deliciously ironic twist, some of them even suspected that "Fernando Pessoa" was the pseudonym of a public figure who needed to protect his true identity.

On February 14 a magazine editor acquainted with Pessoa published an article whose headline promised "Revelations" concerning "the 'enigmatic' poet everyone is talking about." He began by assuring his readers that the name nobody had ever heard of, now "drenched by a thousand floodlights," was not an alias. A "minuscule intellectual minority" remembered him as the "occult, phlegmatic guide" of the *Orpheu* generation, whose "new theories of art and literature" were widely mocked but eventually prevailed. Since then the poet had kept a low profile, apparently determined "to hide like a secret" his "mission in life" and "to zealously fulfill it like a command of God." Sometimes he could be found with other poets, journalists, and artists at the Café Martinho da Arcada, where he was the least talkative one in the group, but when he did talk, he inevitably delivered "the final word on the topic under discussion—using a strange line of reasoning, seemingly distilled by a brain [. . .] from another planet."[5]

Characterized by journalists who knew him as a kind of bashful alien—a sphinx, a man who belonged to another era, an occult figure, an intellect from another planet—Pessoa suddenly, uncomfortably, found himself in the middle of the political arena, savaged by the warriors in favor of annihilating Freemasonry. Pessoa had goaded them, writing in his article that the sponsor of the bill to exterminate "secret societies" should have been a Dominican, since its harsh provisions and spirit of persecution were in keeping with "the best traditions of the Inquisition" (which was largely administered by Dominican priests). The bill's sponsor was José Cabral, an ex-member of the fascistic Blueshirts and now a New State loyalist. In his published replies to Pessoa's article, Cabral called him a "loser" in literature and in life, a "poor scribe" who had been exploited by the Masons and whose "name wasn't even worth mentioning."[6]

Pessoa answered Cabral and his other critics in a long and meandering rejoinder that he never finished—and if he had finished it, no newspaper in Portugal could have published it. Willingly or inadvertently, the New State machinery had allowed Pessoa's February 4 article to open a discussion, but the furious reaction of newspapers sympathetic to the regime prompted Salazar to quickly close it. As per instructions, the censors deleted favorable references to Pessoa's article in several independent newspapers.[7]

◆

THE FACT PESSOA WAS a much respected poet, even if little known outside the restricted circle of Lisbon's literary elite, was complicating matters at a delicate juncture for the New State in its relationship to the intelligentsia. A backlash was under way against António Ferro's "politics of the spirit."

On January 31—the same day that the grand master of Portuguese Freemasonry sent his letter to the National Assembly opposing the bill to ban secret societies—more than one hundred journalists, professors, writers, and artists attended a luncheon for the official purpose of creating a cultural association. What united them was their determination to defend artistic and intellectual freedom. Despite being attended by some well-known individuals, the luncheon was mentioned in only two newspapers—independent papers—and described in necessarily coded language. The *Diário de Lisboa* reported that the participants had all agreed to sign a "document" concerning "a momentous problem in the public press," to be sent to the National Assembly. The mysterious "document" was in fact a petition against press censorship, which would be signed by almost two hundred people, including many not present at the luncheon.[8] The Censorship Commission prohibited any direct mention of the petition, which was quietly filed away in the archives of the National Assembly.

But António Ferro—who had been a fervent republican when he sat at the same café tables with Mário de Sá-Carneiro and Fernando Pessoa—unquietly counterattacked. On February 24, 1935, he hosted his own bigger and better luncheon of pro-regime journalists, professors, writers, and artists. In its copious coverage of the event, the *Diário da Manhã*, a government bullhorn, reported that the crowd of over two hundred people "deliriously" cheered Portugal, Salazar, Carmona, and the New State. In his speech to this gathering, where Augusto Ferreira Gomes cheered loudly and drank abundantly, Ferro gloated that they far outnumbered the one hundred or so participants at the January luncheon, whom he accused, with unwitting irony, of being "intellectual dictators." Their petition to end press censorship, he argued, was an abusive attempt to usurp the authority of the National Union of Journalists. Not so surprisingly, António Ferro was the president of this "union," created by the corporatist New State the previous year.

"Don't be fooled!" he warned his captive lunchtime audience. "We're in a time of war, gentlemen! It's either them, or us!"[9] As director in chief of the Secretariat of Propaganda, Ferro not only had to toe the line, it was his job to help define that line and to make sure that others toe it. If they did not, they were enemies. There could be no more fence-sitting, no more middle ground, he announced in his speech. One was either for or against the New State.

Until very recently Pessoa had been a fence-sitter, though with his feet dangling on the side loyal to Salazar. In the draft of his rejoinder to those who called him a traitor for defending Freemasonry, he still called himself a *situacionista*. While he found much of the New State program unpalatable, he accepted the present situation and continued to place his confidence in Salazar, appreciating him for the "steady clarity of his intelligence," for his "clear steadiness of will," for his practical achievements at home, and for boosting Portugal's standing abroad.[10] That confidence crumbled to dust exactly two days before Ferro's nationalist luncheon, and because of another New State gala event: the awards ceremony for the secretariat's literary prizes.

The ceremony was held on February 21, at 10:30 p.m., which was not all that late by Portuguese standards. The invitation specified formal wear, and Pessoa—so he commented to Manassés Seixas, his barber—was not about to spend his prize money on a tuxedo. Nor, if he'd been provided a tux, would he have attended the event. He shunned official functions and high-society affairs, and the awards ceremony fit in both categories.

First thing the next day, however, he read about the event in the newspaper and quietly fumed. His name and prize were not mentioned, which was fair enough, since he chose not to attend the ceremony. What infuriated him were the words pronounced by Salazar, who began his brief speech by informing writers that not only should their works observe "certain limitations," they should also embrace "certain guidelines" defined by the New State's "moral and patriotic principles." Writers, he said, should be "creators of civic and moral energies" rather than "nostalgic dreamers of despondency and decadence," and in that particular "historic moment" it was their duty to help advance "the ideological foundations on which the new Portugal is being built." He ended his remarks by suggesting that many writers would do well to write less. And he quoted Seneca: "All kinds of orations and histories, on shelves reaching up to the ceiling, adorn the home of the lazy man." Pessoa considered the dictator's speech to be nothing less than an open assault against writers.

António Ferro's much longer speech, likewise published in at least three newspapers, was an expanded version of Salazar's.[11] He framed it, however, as a meditation on the so-called politics of the spirit. This was a politics, he explained, that pitted itself "against everything that soils the spirit," such as "depraved paintings." Restlessness, he conceded, is the driving force of art and literature, but it should seek order rather than disorder, be constructive and not destructive. The secretariat's literary prizes, he reminded the audience, were created to encourage works with "broadly constructive purposes," and those purposes could be readily deduced by reading Salazar's "speeches and the moral precepts contained in them." He ended his remarks by announcing that the organizers of the prize ceremony, defenders of "a healthy life and a healthy art," wished to "publicly declare war on the despots of free thinking, on 'free' intellectuals bound in chains and preconceptions, [. . .] on the Narcissuses of democracy who are poisoning the World!"

Pessoa shook his head in disgusted horror as he read the two speeches over his morning coffee. For him individual liberty was life's most ennobling privilege and art's first prerequisite. On that point he could not compromise. The lines were drawn, and he found himself on the side of the enemy. Against the New State's attack on free expression and free thought—an attack amply confirmed by Ferro's subsequent speech to hundreds of compliant intellectuals marshaled together at his pro-regime luncheon—Pessoa took up the only weapons he knew how to wield: pen and ink, and the typewriter. Besides drafting replies to his anti-Masonic critics for publication in newspapers, where he was liable to be censored, he decided to answer them more completely in a book, since books were not subject to prepublication censorship. Renouncing his stance as a reluctant *situacionista*, he now averred that the bill against Freemasonry served him as a "trampoline," a pretext for "attacking certain influences" that endangered, "all over the world, the dignity of Man and the freedom of the Spirit."[12]

A sea change was taking place in Pessoa's ever agitated mental life. The political theorist gave way to the worried citizen. Human dignity and freedom were after all what mattered most, and the threat against them was far-reaching. It is tempting to see a prophecy in Pessoa's words of warning, but he, like nearly everyone at that point, had no inkling of the irreparable harm that human dignity would suffer under the direction of Germany's Führer.

✦

PESSOA'S BATTLEFIELD WAS PORTUGAL, written words were his gunfire, and the main target of that fire was Salazar and the New State, which for the poet were practically synonymous. Throughout the rest of the year he wrote a series of political poems attacking the dictator and his regime, sometimes with vicious loathing. But the first poem of the series, written on March 16, was not at all vicious. Titled "Liberdade" ("Freedom"), it attacked by not attacking, by reveling in the freedom that Salazar and Ferro deemed decadent and dangerous. It began with the ghost of an epigraph: "(*a citation from Seneca*)." The citation not cited—so as to circumvent the censors—was the one Salazar had used in his recent speech to insinuate that intellectuals are lazy and the books in their libraries of dubious worth. Pessoa wholeheartedly agreed:

Ah, what a pleasure
To leave a task undone,
To have a book to read
And not even crack it!
Reading is a bore,
And studying isn't anything.


  . . .


Books are just paper painted with ink.
And to study is to distinguish, indistinctly,
Between nothing and not a thing.

How much better, when it's foggy,
To wait for King Sebastian,
Whether or not he ever shows!

Poetry, dancing and charity are great things,
But what's best in the world are children, flowers,
Music, moonlight and the sun, which only sins
When it withers instead of making things grow.

Greater than this
Is Jesus Christ,
Who knew nothing of finances
And had no library, as far as we know . . .

The poem rhymes in Portuguese, but haphazardly, and the meter is completely irregular. Both in its form and its content, "Freedom" is a rhapsody to spontaneity, to the flaunting of obligations, and to the untrammeled enjoyment of whatever happens to be one's pleasure. It takes a direct jab at Salazar, who was still the finance minister as well as the nation's prime minister, and an oblique swipe at Pessoa himself. "Books are just paper painted with ink" is not a facetious line. The poet was admitting that reading and study, his favorite pastimes, perhaps had no value except as entertainment. And his Sebastianism, suggests the next stanza, was perhaps an idle exercise in imagination. And so what? The poem defends the right to be idle, to pursue useless goals, to read or not read, to dance or not dance, to be at liberty in the world. The last stanza is not a profession of religious faith but a tribute to the freedom personified by Jesus Christ, who flouted rules and regulations and preached detachment from material things.

Pessoa gave a copy of "Freedom" to Manuel Mendes, a young writer, critic, and artist who occasionally met with him at the Café Martinho da Arcada. Mendes was closely connected to *Seara Nova* (*New Harvest*), a liberal republican magazine founded in 1921, and Pessoa timidly wondered if its editors might like to publish his poem. Only a radical change of heart could have made that poetry submission remotely thinkable. Though he respected the intellectual integrity of *Seara Nova* and appreciated its firm stance against the Portuguese emulators of Italian fascism, it had always leaned too far to the left for his taste. As recently as two years earlier, in some notes for an article on the current political landscape, he had criticized the magazine for its blindly dogmatic faith in democracy.[13]

The editors of *Seara Nova* were eager to publish Pessoa's poem, but the censors rejected it because of the penultimate line, with its thinly veiled reference to Salazar.[14] Pessoa, meanwhile, was writing poems that attacked the dictator by name and without mercy. A poem dated March 29, for instance, observed that Salazar was made of *sal* ("salt") and *azar* ("bad luck"), and that rain had long ago dissolved the *sal*, leaving Portugal with nothing but *azar*. Another poem mocked the "little tyrant" and his reputation for sobriety, accusing him of guzzling down so much truth and freedom that these crucial commodities were now in short supply.

Realizing that they could not wait for posterity, Pessoa typed up three of his anti-Salazar poems using modern, reader-friendly spelling—rather than the older, etymological spelling he preferred for virtually all his writing—and passed them on to selected friends, who cautiously showed them to others and perhaps made copies for distribution. At least one of his anti-Salazar poems circulated orally, through the poets Gil Vaz and Rui Santos, who both published in *Presença*. The latter poet, born in Tavira but now living in Lisbon, was a distant cousin Pessoa had met years ago on his trips to the Algarve to visit Aunt Lisbela.[15]

To recite from memory Pessoa's potentially incriminating poems was certainly the more prudent way of disseminating them. Although Salazar was a far cry from Stalin, who had recently sentenced Osip Mandelstam to internal exile over an unpublished poem that made fun of him, protesters in Portugal had to be increasingly vigilant. The New State secret police (whose methods of interrogation and torture would later be perfected with the help of German and Italian advisers) were empowered to arrest and detain, without a warrant, anyone suspected of endangering national security. Pessoa himself would receive a visit from the police, who gave him a tongue-lashing—possibly because they had seen a copy of his poetic squibs but more probably because of his collaboration with the Masons. He listened to his rebukers in silence. "I would have been arrested if I'd tried to answer them," he told his barber with a hint of satisfaction, proud to be one of the persecuted, but he was overstating the danger. The police would not have dared to arrest him.[16]

Pessoa signed his secretly circulated protest poems not with his own name but as "A NOSTALGIC DREAMER OF DESPONDENCY AND DECADENCE," the epithet used by Salazar in his speech at the prize ceremony to characterize the morbid, morally undesirable sort of artist. To help promote healthy and happy citizens, untainted by decadence, the New State created the National Foundation for Worker Happiness, which sponsored leisure and sports activities. Founded in June 1935, coincidentally on Pessoa's birthday, it was modeled after the national leisure organizations of Fascist Italy and Nazi Germany. Toward the end of the summer, in a brief poem that held "authoritarian governments" responsible for deadening people's intelligence, Álvaro de Campos would pay ironic tribute to the New State ideal of wholesome bliss by barbarically yawping

Salutation to all those who want to be happy:
Good health and stupidity![17]

# CHAPTER 73

**P**ESSOA THE POLITICAL AGITATOR HAD ONLY ONE objective: to defend human freedom. He was still a conservative, though with a transformed outlook on recent Portuguese history, on humanity at large, and on the relationship between that history and that humanity. Lest anyone make any mistake about where exactly he stood, he drew up an illuminating "résumé," neatly typed and dated March 30, 1935, the day after he wrote two ruthlessly anti-Salazar poems. Like most résumés, his is couched in the third person, but in addition to personal and professional information, it includes summaries of his political and religious views. A section titled "Political Ideology" deftly defines him as an "English-style conservative, meaning that he is liberal within conservatism, and absolutely antireactionary." He considers monarchy to be the appropriate form of government for "an organically imperial nation such as Portugal" and supports the Republic only because a monarchy would be "completely unfeasible."

These points of view were not new, but the section of the résumé listing the author's publications reveals a drastic change in how he viewed the circumstances leading up to the New State. Laconically yet momentously it states that *The Interregnum: Defense and Justification of Military Dictatorship in Portugal*, published in 1928, "should be considered nonexistent." Until recently the author had planned to republish this pamphlet in a revised version and in an English translation.[1] Now he saw it as an aberration he needed to expunge from his publishing record. The military dictatorship, instead of giving way to a very different, much better form of government, as the poet had dreamily fancied might happen, had evolved into an ever more repressive regime.

Pessoa had given the benefit of the doubt to Salazar, a benefit he kept extending until 1935, when events finally convinced him of his error. Very different was the case of Ezra Pound, who in January, speaking over Radio Rome, had delivered his first talk to America on the virtues of Mussolini's Italy, which would soon invade Ethiopia and ally itself to Nazi Germany, and which the American poet would continue to support, as if under an unbreakable spell. The Portuguese poet, however prone he was to invest in dreamy and unrealistic, sometimes wacky ideas, could never be the blind follower of any one idea or ideological system.

According to the section of his résumé titled "Patriotic Position," Pessoa was still a mystical nationalist who hoped that a "new Sebastianism" would spiritually replace Catholicism in Portugal. But the paragraph continues: "Nationalist guided by this motto: *Everything for Humanity, Nothing Against the Nation.*" This was a subversive variation on Salazar's famous slogan, "Everything for the Nation, Nothing Against the Nation," coined in 1929 and inspired by Mussolini's "Everything in the State, Nothing Outside the State, Nothing Against the State." More than a show of defiance, Pessoa's motto signified a dramatic shift in his priorities. For the first time in his writing life he clearly placed the interest of humanity—an entity he had disparaged a few years ago as a "complete fiction"[2]—above that of the nation. This shifted the ground under his nationalism, revealing it for what at heart, perhaps, it had always been. If everything is for humanity, then the vision of a Sebastianist Portugal must be a poetic vision with wide application, and the Portuguese experience memorialized in *Message* must be, above all else, an instructive paradigm of the human experience.

◆

WHEN SETTING FORTH HIS spiritual views, Pessoa's résumé is notable not only for what it reveals but also for what it conceals, obscures, or falsely alleges. This was not bad faith at work; obscurity was an integral part of his poetic method, which was inseparable from his method for being in the world. In the letter where he chided João Gaspar Simões for relying too much on Freud (see chapter 64), saying that the proper tasks of the critic are "to study the artist exclusively as an artist" and "to discover what we might call the *central definition* of the artist," Pessoa mentioned a third task—the most curious of the three. The critic, he wrote, should wrap their studies and discoveries "in a hazy poetic aura of unintelligibility," out of respect for "the essential inscrutability of the human heart."[3] Easy on the Freud, warned Pessoa, not because poetry (or any other art) isn't related to the intimate secrets of the human heart, but because it *is*, and those secrets should remain secret. "The most abject of all needs," he wrote in a passage for *The Book of Disquiet*, "is to confide, to confess," but if you must confess your secrets, then "confess what you don't feel."[4]

As if to help literary critics carry out what he deemed to be their proper tasks, Pessoa wrapped himself in an aura of mystery that became less and less penetrable as he aged. People who spent time with him in his final years remarked that there was something peculiar, cryptic, in his comportment—how he spoke, reasoned, and gestured—which they attributed to his fascination with the occult. That fascination was real enough, but the feigner in Pessoa never rested, making him not only cryptic but also unreliable when writing about his relationship to the occult. In the long letter sent to the *Presença* editor Adolfo Casais Monteiro in mid-January, he stated that he was not initiated into any spiritual order but had been allowed to leaf through the rituals of the first three degrees of the Portuguese Knights Templar, a military order that had not existed for hundreds of years. The résumé he drew up on March 30 asserted, on the contrary, that he was "initiated, through direct communication from Master to Disciple, into the three lesser degrees of the (apparently extinct) Templar Order of Portugal."

Abolished by a papal bull in 1312, the Portuguese Order of the Knights Templar existed nowhere but in Pessoa's teeming imagination and in his writings, which is also where his purported initiation took place, with Alberto Caeiro as his master. This swirl of fantasy and prevarication—or of metaphors and idealizations?—obliges us to pause and question what it means when we read, in the same résumé, that Pessoa was a "Gnostic Christian" and "faithful [. . .] to the Secret Tradition of Christianity, which is intimately related to the Secret Tradition in Israel (the Holy Kabbalah) and to the occult essence of Freemasonry." Does "faithful" mean only that he read and wrote about all of these interrelated traditions with passionate dedication, or does it mean something more?

The secret pathways and byways of Gnostic Christianity, Kabbalah, Rosicrucianism, and all the other esoteric traditions to which Pessoa claimed some kind of allegiance were, I propose, an enactment of the "essential inscrutabililty" of his human heart. We might say that occult religion was the "objective correlative" of Pessoa's unfathomable self, or soul. There was only one problem: the soul, he knew, might itself be a fiction. Which is why Álvaro de Campos, in his "Notes for the Memory of My Master Caeiro," could dare to say that "Fernando Pessoa [. . .] doesn't exist, strictly speaking."

✦

**THE HETERONYMS ARE NOT** mentioned in Pessoa's March 30 résumé. Their definitive story had already been told in his letter of January 13. Besides drawing up these two documents—which contain the whole record of his personal, literary, spiritual, and patriotic self as he wished it to be remembered—Pessoa now began to organize his legacy to the world, sorting through his papers and grouping them together in large labeled envelopes: "Political Prose," "The Book of Disquiet," "Astrology (theory and practice)," and so forth.[5] His health was not the best—he had developed a smoker's cough and continued to drink too much—and he sensed that the end might be approaching. He was forty-six years old but looked at least a decade older. "A nice old man, with intelligent and searching eyes" was how he would be remembered, sixteen years later, by the journalist from the *Diário de Lisboa* who interviewed him in December 1934.[6]

Pessoa had always counted on living to around the age of seventy, since that's what his horoscopes repeatedly predicted, but he confided to Raul Leal that 1933–1935 was a troubled period. A list of "aspects" (angles) between the sun, which was his "giver of life," and the other celestial bodies on his astrological chart indicated that the second half of 1935 would be especially fraught with adversity. Assuming he made it through the year, then indeed he could expect to live to a ripe age.[7]

Though with less tenacity than the stars, numbers also enchanted Pessoa, who owned a book titled *The Kabala of Numbers*. He only dabbled in numerology but was superstitiously attentive to numerical patterns and coincidences in dates, and it recently dawned on him that 1935 was predestined to be a highly significant year. He noted, in English:

> Every year ending in 5 has been important in my life.
> 1895—Mother's second marriage; result—Africa.
> 1905—Return to Lisbon.
> 1915—*Orpheu.*
> 1925—Mother's death.
> All are *beginnings of periods.*[8]

A chill ran down my spine when I first laid eyes on this document.

Pessoa, in 1935, lived the same sort of life he lived in 1934 or 1933, and yet everything was different, because *he* was different. He continued to write without respite and to come up with new publication projects, but the nature of his writing and his projects changed. The opinionated yet detached political observer of recent years was becoming what the French call an *écrivain engagé*, a writer who actively engages with the current social and political environment. At the same time, and in apparent contradiction to that engagement, he was yielding more and more to nostalgia, which he had claimed not so long ago never to feel except in passing, as a literary attitude.

One of the objects of his nostalgia was *Orpheu*. March 1935 marked the twentieth anniversary of its first issue. To commemorate that date, José de Almada Negreiros published an article about *Orpheu's* role as "the pioneer of the modern movement in Portugal," illustrating it with a scroll that listed the writers and artists who had contributed to the magazine. Crosses were placed next to the names of the deceased—six of the twelve contributors, none of whom lived to the age of fifty.[9] The latest one to die, in a car wreck in Rio de Janeiro, was the Brazilian poet Ronald de Carvalho, a co-editor of the first issue. Carvalho's old friend and fellow editor, Luís de Montalvor, published a tribute to him that fondly recalled their times together in Copacabana, when they were still starry-eyed young poets, and their shared dream of a different sort of literary magazine, fulfilled in *Orpheu*.[10]

Pessoa had somewhat analogous memories of those same years—centered around Mário de Sá-Carneiro and their own constantly mutating plans for a magazine, which finally materialized in *Orpheu*—and it occurred to him to bring out an anniversary issue, *Orpheu do Vigésimo Ano* (*Orpheu Twenty Years Later*). But it wasn't the magazine itself he missed; it was the excitement surrounding the entire venture. It was the sensation that life, at age twenty-six, was a rambling novel in the manner of *The Pickwick Papers*, in whose pages anything he dreamed of might still be written. It was, above all else, the experience of a friendship that aroused feelings in him he had never before known.

Scrapping his idea for a special issue to pay homage to the magazine, he instead wrote a poetic elegy, "Sá-Carneiro," preceded by an epigraph: "For that issue of *Orpheu* that will be made of suns and stars in a new world." Laden with pathos, the poem was not so much about the tragic figure of Mário de Sá-Carneiro but about what he had meant and still meant to Pessoa. Speaking directly to his long dead friend, the elegist expresses his fervent hope that their two souls will meet again; he describes the plight of his present life, in which he feels that he is not just himself but the two of them, inextricably joined together, even though the two of them is now only one of them, painfully alone; and he ends with a confession:

> Ah, my best friend, never again
> In life's now shrouded landscape
> Will I find a soul as dear as yours
> To the part of me that feels most real.

> . . .

> However much I'm able to be
> Myself, just me, without nostalgia,
> I can't help but long for company:
> The true friend I can talk to, and love.[11]

It was Pessoa's custom, suggests the last stanza, not to yield to nostalgia. He had told João Gaspar Simões that he was disinclined to look back because he was a "futurist [. . .] in the most literal sense of the word."[12] But in 1935 he let memories run through his mind like old films. They were a kind of company, while his future was all a blur. Nor was he in a "futurist" mood with respect to Portugal. Until recently, and no matter what tribulations the nation was enduring, he had looked forward to its regeneration. "Chamada" ("Call"), a long poem written mostly in 1934 but completed in the early months of 1935, still resonated with optimism, summoning all the mystical forces of Portugal to bring about the Fifth Empire, since "the future is already present / In the vision of those who know how to see." By springtime not even Pessoa could hear the call or imagine the dawning of a Portuguese Fifth Empire.

◆

PESSOA'S WAR ON THE government for hindering free speech and free assembly and for encroaching on free thought was a lonely endeavor. Most of his relatives and close friends sided with the regime or else took no side.

Working as a journalist as well as a graphic artist for New State publications, Augusto Ferreira Gomes was in ideological lockstep with his employer. For Alberto Da Cunha Dias, Salazar's only defect was his not being more like Mussolini. For Raul Leal, an unwavering monarchist, all that the dictator lacked was a crown. Mário Saa, who was spending ever less time in Lisbon and more at his agricultural estate, extolled the "glorious government of Salazar" in a speech delivered at his local town hall.[13] Although he had no interest in politics, Carlos Queiroz was obliged to passively acquiesce since taking a job as a program director for Emissora Nacional, the state-operated radio station, about which Pessoa wrote a sarcastic poem wishing that for once the announcer would tell listeners "what Salazar did *not* say."[14] José de Almada Negreiros insisted in lectures and writing that artists must have complete freedom to follow their individual paths, yet in a magazine article titled "Collective Mysticism" he stated that countries with authoritarian, nationalistic governments were reconnecting with their "mystic depths" and that "[t]he spiritual unity of Europe is now entering its mature phase."[15] He might as well have titled his article "Collective Delusion." Even António Botto seemed to be a New State partisan, stating in an interview published on March 22, 1935, that he was working "on a book about the extraordinary political leader and noble spirit Oliveira Salazar, a man I greatly admire."[16]

These and other friends no doubt thought that Pessoa, now an oppositionist, was overreacting, as well as biting the hand that fed him. The censors, after all, had allowed publication of his incendiary article against anti-Masonic legislation, even if they subsequently barred favorable references to it, and the government had awarded him a prize worth five thousand escudos. One had to admit that the Salazar regime, thanks to António Ferro, was allocating significantly more money to culture. In March the Secretariat of Propaganda held its first annual Exhibition of Modern Art, proving that Ferro's "politics of the spirit" sought to promote innovation in art rather than to ratify established, bourgeois tastes—notwithstanding his caveat, in February, against "depraved" paintings. While Almada Negreiros chose not to display any of his own work at the show, in a speech at the official banquet he noted with satisfaction that "for the first time in this country I see the public authorities on the side of what's newest in Portuguese art."[17]

The secretariat would continue to be a reliable supporter of contemporary art and artists—through exhibitions and commissioned work. Painters, designers, photographers, filmmakers, and writers were recruited to construct the myth of an efficiently modern and harmonious Portuguese colonial empire and the complementary myth of a peaceful, bucolic Portugal where peasants joyfully hoed corn, tended cattle, picked grapes, and wove baskets, while singing traditional songs and dancing in their spare time.

The benevolent empire myth had counterparts elsewhere in Europe. Imperial powers such as France, Belgium, and the United Kingdom organized exhibitions similar to the Portuguese Colonial Exhibition of 1934. More uniquely Portuguese was the myth of domestic rural bliss, propagated both at home and abroad. In 1935 an Exhibition of Portuguese Folk Art was strategically held in Geneva, home to the League of Nations. The contents of the exhibition would become the nucleus of a Museum of Folk Art created in Lisbon in the 1940s. Artistic displays of farm tools, traditional costumes, local crafts, and other facets of Portuguese rural life conveyed the image of a statically idyllic, timeless world. Yet huge numbers of people who actually inhabited that world were neither happy nor at peace in their indigent, illiterate, and insalubrious condition.

Rarely did Pessoa express concern for the material welfare of Portugal's poor people, whether urban or rural. But given that one of his fundamental objections to Salazar's regime was its assault on human freedom and, hence, human dignity, he was bound to disapprove of people being instrumentalized to create a New State picture of who they were but in fact weren't. In July he would write a poetic satire on the New State that pointed out the discrepancies between what the government claimed was the "new" state of things and what the nation and its people actually experienced. One of the poem's stanzas pokes fun at Portugal's colonial empire by noting that its latest "colonists" were exiled political dissidents; another stanza accuses the propaganda machine of putting a cheery face on hunger.[18]

The New State was praised both at home and abroad for putting Portugal on a path to prosperity,[19] but when Pessoa looked down the path on which the nation was headed he discerned spiritual impoverishment and stultifying claustrophobia.

C ONTRARY TO WHAT HE TOLD A JOURNALIST from the *Diário de Lisboa*, António Botto was not writing a book about Salazar. Whether he said this to curry favor with the regime or simply to be provocative is uncertain. Probably he was doing both things. How titillating, in any case, to praise the very man who, with a stroke of the pen, could cause his "indecent" books to be summarily banned! New State censorship was usually politically motivated, but the debut novel of José Régio—Botto's most tireless advocate after Fernando Pessoa—had recently been yanked from the shelves of bookstores because of its homoeroticism.[1] Botto's most recent book, a collection of poems titled *Ciúme* (*Jealousy*), was every bit as homoerotic, only more sensually so, making it more liable to lead young men off the sexually straight and narrow way. Yet the censors, mysteriously, left it alone. Had they prohibited the book, Pessoa would almost certainly have protested on behalf of his friend. But notwithstanding his opposition to government censorship, Pessoa harbored in himself a moral censor that prevented him from ever actively thinking, feeling, or behaving like António Botto.

*Jealousy* was published in June 1934. It contained a glowing afterword by José Régio, which the *Diário de Lisboa* republished in mid-July. A few days later, Tomás Ribeiro Colaço, editor in chief of the cultural weekly *Fradique*, responded to Régio's panegyric with a contentious article, "António Botto—a Poet Who Doesn't Exist," demanding to know where the poetry was. If Botto's poems were addressed to a woman instead of a man, he argued, nobody would ever have paid them the slightest attention, since they were poetically worthless. Their only charm, for those who found them charming, was their homoeroticism. For Régio that indeed seemed to be their main charm. His praise for Botto's latest book was centered on the fact that "his sincerity is more liberated," so much so that "it might reignite the scandal kindled by his earliest poems." He was referring to the homophobic reaction against Botto's *Songs*, published in 1921 and republished the following year by Pessoa as an Olisipo book. Botto's "irremediable sincerity," which might "shock bourgeois morality," was clearly a euphemism for Botto's open homosexuality.

Colaço concluded his devastating critique of Botto's poetry by offering the columns of his newspaper to whoever wished to argue the contrary, and so a prolonged literary debate ensued. Pessoa was going to enter the fray but abandoned a half-written article for *Fradique*, where the discussion carried on and on, until March 1935. That same month, Pessoa published, in the *Diário de Lisboa*, an elegantly synthetic and ingenious defense of Botto's poetry qua poetry, but it did not invalidate Colaço's original intuition. If women rather than men had been the inspiration for Botto's sensualism, he would most certainly have lost many of his readers, including Pessoa and Régio, who seemed to be competing with each other in their zeal for promoting Botto. Régio would eventually publish a book of his collected criticism on the poet. In 1935, Pessoa was planning to publish his own compendium of almost everything he had written on Botto, and he hoped to translate two of Botto's latest books into English: the poetry collection *Jealousy* as well as his homoerotic "dramatic novella" from 1933, *António*.[2]

Although he never got around to translating any more Botto into English, Pessoa did render three poems from *Jealousy* into French. Here is the shortest of the trio (in my English translation from the Portuguese):

Everything in life enchants you.
You're happy,
You laugh,
Everything is yours!

And I
Who have bitterly suffered and suffer—
Don't I have the right to seek
An enormous forbidden pleasure?

If Pessoa, while translating this poem, asked himself the question contained in the second stanza, the answer was no. Having come to accept that chastity was his calling, he was not entitled to pursue "forbidden" pleasures. According to some notes written in English and dating from 1934, not even masturbation was permissible for the chaste man—unless, he hypothesized, one could do it without pleasure. Sexual acts of the most varied kind were all in a day's spiritual work for a black magician like Aleister Crowley. Pessoa, however, had a vocation for white magic, and for a superior white magician all sex was taboo.

Yet not all sex, it turns out, was equally taboo. The champion of white magic and chastity singled out sex between men for special condemnation, calling it an act against the "Law of Nature" and "the height of indecency and unchastity, even to the *vas* used" (*vas* is Latin for "vessel").[3] I have already observed that Pessoa, despite celebrating love between men in his poetry and despite actively defending his homosexual friends, could never have accepted for himself the idea of a sexual encounter with another man. The outburst of homophobia in his notes on white versus black magic corroborates that observation, but its practical purpose was, I believe, consolatory. That stern voice of judgment, welling up from somewhere deep in his psyche, effectively reassured Pessoa, in case he was having second or third thoughts, that he had done well not to taste the forbidden fruit that most tempted him.

Pessoa's chastity was not a smooth condition, free of all turbulence. In 1935 all the loves he never tasted, as well as the ones he had sampled only tentatively, came back to haunt him. But while he no doubt regretted having missed out on the pleasures of sex, what he most remembered, and missed, and wished he'd had more of, was the pleasure of affection felt for certain men and for at least one woman, Ophelia Queiroz. Some years later, Raul Leal would write that Pessoa was more attracted to men than women but preferred not to act on his attractions. Although gifted with an uncommon degree of "intellectual magnetism," his late friend had "no magnetism of a sensual order." Wanting to avoid the humiliation of a carnal love that could only be unsatisfactory for the other person, he had preferred to constantly rein in "the violent impulses of the flesh." Pessoa offered a somewhat similar, somewhat different explanation for his "scant interest in sexuality," saying that he'd "never given much importance to myself as a physical and social being."[4]

António Botto, never one to hold his tongue, would have let the world know had Pessoa ever made advances on him or on anyone else. The only tidbit he reported in this line was that Fernando had a roving eye for young men. He certainly relished the company of young men—including, in his last years, Botto himself, Carlos Queiroz, Pierre Hourcade (who had left for Brazil in January), and Manuel Mendes—but don't most people, as they age, like having a few younger friends? Both Botto and Leal, for what it's worth, claimed that Pessoa had a small penis, which is not to say they ever saw him naked. "Looking at his crotch," explained Leal, "you couldn't make out anything there." What this means, given that Pessoa did not wear tight-fitting trousers, is simply that Leal never noticed him with an erection. His "violent impulses of the flesh" were perhaps, as Pessoa claimed, not so violent.[5]

On April 5 Pessoa wrote a short, yet enormous, poem:

What matters is love.
Sex is just an accident:
It can be the same
Or different.
Man isn't an animal:
He's an intelligent flesh,
Though subject to sickness.

According to these words, which were the last ones Pessoa wrote on the question of same-sex versus opposite-sex attractions, everything is permissible, since humans are not bound by the biological imperative of procreation. We now know that other animals are not bound by it either; hundreds of species engage in homoerotic and other sexual behaviors that are not procreative. Pessoa's point, however, was not merely that sexual orientation is unimportant. Sex itself is not necessarily important. Love is what matters. The idea of "intelligent flesh"—which implies that there can also be a fleshly, sensualized intelligence—recalls Pessoa's futuristic vision of a love ruled by "reason" rather than by sexual instinct. It was the kind of love he had experienced with Mário de Sá-Carneiro, and probably no one else.

✦

ONE WEEK AFTER WRITING "What matters is love," Pessoa received a letter from his half brother John Rosa. John's sister-in-law, Madge Anderson, who also lived in London, would be arriving by ship in Lisbon on April 15. If the weather was pleasant, she planned to spend three or four weeks in Estoril; if not, she would continue on to Spain. He counted on Fernando or else their sister, Teca, to meet the traveler and help her get settled in a hotel, assuming she chose to stay. "I'm sure you'll like her and she's very keen to meet you all." Madge Mary Moncrieff Anderson—a tall and slender thirty-year-old, with auburn hair and a hard but beautiful face, as if sculpted—was especially keen to meet Fernando, the poet. She was interested in literature and philosophy, both of which she had studied for her degree at St. Andrews, Scotland's oldest university. Now she was employed by the British Foreign Office. That didn't make her a spy, but as it turned out she did work in the area of secret intelligence. She was an intriguing figure, and still single.[6]

The weather was agreeable, a little cool but with lots of sun, and Madge Anderson decided to spend her holiday in Portugal. She met with Fernando a couple of times upon her arrival, and while we don't know any particulars, they evidently got along well. Madge, at any rate, found the poet to be stimulating company and looked forward to their next meeting, which he kept putting off. Toward the end of April, while she spent her days lying on the beach or walking along the shore, eating fresh-caught fish, reading one of the books she'd brought for the journey, and perhaps giving an occasional thought to her upcoming meeting with Fernando, he continued to put it off, and he wrote, out of the blue, three love poems—two in French, one in English. All were written in facile, light verse, and the amorous plights of two of the poetic narrators were also facile, hackneyed. The poem in English, dated April 28, begins:

> Was it just a kiss?
> Was it more than this?
> Was he just too kind?
> Were you just too blind?

And it goes on like this for thirty-five more lines, in which a jealous man promises to forgive his beloved if she confesses the details of her dalliances with another. The narrator of one of the French poems, written on the same day, laments that the woman he fancies is already hitched. Built around stock scenarios, both poems feel like odd exercises in nostalgia—for commonplace experiences of love that the poet had never experienced.

The other love poem in French, written two days earlier, is narrated by a man who is more like the poet we're familiar with, for he admits that the woman he loves may be a figment of his own imagination. On April 27 Pessoa wrote a third poem in French, which was also a kind of love poem, addressed to his dead mother, with whom he dreams of being reunited, not as his adult self but as a little boy forever nestled in her arms.

Perhaps the glamorous, independent, slightly mysterious Madge had put Fernando in the mood for love, or in the mood to imagine it. And perhaps his poems of love, especially the one for his mother, were partly triggered by the time and place where they were written: springtime in São João do Estoril, at the home of Teca and Chico, where he had gone to spend the weekend. They were a happy, loving couple, with two equally happy children, all living in a house with a yard and garden, like the house on Tenth Avenue in Durban, Pessoa's last address in South Africa before he returned to Lisbon, in 1905. His half sister, Teca, was then nine years old, the same age his niece Mimi was now. The elder of his two half brothers, Luís Miguel, was then four years old, the same age as his nephew, also called Luís Miguel.

Whenever her uncle Fernando made one of his weekend visits, Mimi would relentlessly try to get him to be her playmate, and sometimes she succeeded. Once he even took her to nearby Tamariz Beach, where there was a special play area for children, as well as cafés and restaurants along the waterfront. In his dark suit, he looked completely out of place among all the people dedicated to exposing their flesh to the sun and having a good time, but if he realized how he looked to others, he didn't care.[7] On that April weekend when he wrote love poems in French and English, Mimi wouldn't let him alone. She scribbled some things in the margins of his poems. For instance: "You only play with me so that I'll tell Mama you're behaving yourself."[8]

But he wasn't behaving like Teca wanted. She kept after him to visit Madge, whose hotel was within easy walking distance. Maybe tomorrow, he said, or maybe—he thought—the day after tomorrow. He worked on his poems, played with Mimi and Luís Miguel, conversed with Chico, ate well, and returned to Lisbon. Madge stayed on in Estoril for another three weeks, asking about Fernando whenever she saw or spoke with Teca, and finally sailed home to England.[9]

So repeatedly did Teca berate her brother for his disgraceful treatment of John's sister-in-law, who was all alone on holiday and would have enjoyed more of his company, that he finally wrote her a letter.

> My dear Madge:
>
> I have been wanting to write to you for a long time, but, as I never really know what time is, that unknown element has dragged on till now. It generally does this when we do nothing.
>
> My letter will be simply an apology. You arrived here when I was sinking and you stayed here till I had sunk. I have since come up to the surface, but I would be hard put to it to say what surface that is. I am very sorry for all that happened, meaning my discourtesy in disappearing, but you lost nothing by my disappearance, which was the best action that some remnants of decency could dictate to a man practically lost to the whole of it.
>
> Though I have risen to the apparent surface, I am now ready to sink again, and this time, I think, definitely. I should like you to remember me with Christian charity and not with simple human contempt, though this would be the right and proper feeling, as the world is.
>
> Most sincerely yours,
> Fernando[10]

Time had indeed dragged on. It was already September when Pessoa finally sent his apologetic missive, which she answered with a mildly flirtatious letter that scolded him for his "sinking trick," called him a "dramatic old silly," and closed by saluting him "most tenderly."[11]

◆

**DRAMATIC OR NOT, PESSOA** really was sinking. It was like his horoscope had foretold: 1935 would be rough, especially the second half of the year. He was out of sorts both psychologically and physically—anemic, with digestive problems, and a slumping morale. Relentlessly skeptical about the miraculous cures credited to Our Lady of Fátima, he was nevertheless a potential sucker for nostrums guaranteed to turn around one's health, and lately he cut out newspaper ads for several dubious tonics, including a beef-fortified wine, and for mineral waters certified to rejuvenate virtually every organ in the body. I say "potential sucker," since Pessoa, ever the hesitator and procrastinator, rarely carried out his intentions to try out remedies that would make him a new man. And a good thing too. In 1935 he entertained the idea of doing a cure at Termas Radium, a thermal spa up north renowned for having some of Europe's most radioactive water, which many people still believed was wonderfully invigorating.[12]

The political climate was oppressive for a free spirit like Pessoa, who saw no change in the offing that might have helped buoy his mood. In April the National Assembly unanimously passed the law against "secret societies," which took effect on May 21. The next month Teca's husband, Chico, like all civil servants and military personnel, was required to pledge in writing that he did not belong to, nor would ever belong to, a secret society (i.e., a Masonic lodge) as defined in Article 2 and so on and so forth.[13] On July 8 Pessoa typed a short preface for a corrected and annotated version of the newspaper article he had written against the law when it was first proposed. The article was indeed reissued, in the form of a pamphlet clandestinely published and distributed by the Masons under the title *Freemasonry as Seen by Fernando Pessoa*, but it did not include his preface or annotations.[14] No doubt they got tired of waiting for him to finish and deliver them. It was at any rate too late for pamphlets of any sort to save Freemasonry, which would remain illegal in Portugal until 1974.

Only a small minority of Pessoa's compatriots shared his concern for the rights of Freemasons, who were reputed to be some of the chief social agitators in Spain, a country polarized into belligerent hard-right and hard-left factions that would soon be fighting a civil war. As for the warning in his article that the law against "secret societies" would undermine Portugal's relations with the United Kingdom, given that country's strong Masonic tradition and respect for liberal values, events did not bear out that prediction. Great Britain wanted Portugal to be a shield against the spread of communism; it was not going to fuss about the suppression of Freemasonry and a few restrictions on what people could say or do.

Salazar, according to most Western observers, Britishers included, was doing a fine job. In May 1935, T. S. Eliot began negotiations with the Secretariat of Propaganda for the Faber and Faber edition of *Salazar: Portugal and Her Leader*. This was the chosen title for António Ferro's series of interviews with the dictator, soon to be available in English. Three years later Eliot would spend three weeks in Portugal, invited there by Ferro to be a juror for the Camões Prize, awarded by the secretariat to a book about Portugal by a foreigner. In his letter thanking Ferro and his wife for their hospitality, Eliot would remark on "the great beauty of your country," on "the charm of its people," and on "the strength of an enlightened and far-seeing Government." His "impressions of respect and admiration for Dr. Salazar, formed by reading, were confirmed by having the privilege of meeting him."[15]

If one could overlook his regime's political oppression and increasing use of police surveillance, there was certainly much to admire in Salazar, including his basically honest character, his ability to keep the army in check, and his undeniable success in putting Portugal's finances on a sound footing. But his fiscal conservatism, coupled with too much state control over the economy, would result in two decades of relative stagnation. In the late 1950s the New State's economic policy would change course, spurring more growth. Pessoa could not foresee his country's economic future, and it was not the economy he worried about. He feared for the nation's soul. Salazar had done his job, and done it well, but should now leave governing to more competent parties—Pessoa said exactly that in a letter addressed to President Carmona, the only one who could legally remove the dictator from power. They really were living in a New State, Pessoa wrote, since such a state of things had never before been seen. No one could ever have imagined that peace and order on the streets and improved infrastructures "would have to be purchased at such a high price: the piecemeal sell-off of the Portuguese soul."[16]

Had Pessoa finished and posted his letter, and had it actually reached the desk of the president, we can imagine Carmona nodding with a sigh as he read it. He and the other bemedaled generals responsible for usurping state power in 1926 had truly not intended to install a permanent dictatorship. But Salazar, just as truly, was keeping the country on a steady course in these perilous times, while Spain was teetering on the brink of chaos. And what did the letter writer mean by "the piecemeal sell-off of the Portuguese soul"? The sayings poets come up with!

In early June the poet wrote one of the darkest poems of his career, "Elegia na sombra" ("Elegy in the Shadows"), which a Portuguese scholar aptly defined as "a kind of anti-*Message*."[17] Unlike his prizewinning book, Pessoa's elegy does not individually honor the heroes of Portugal's early history and maritime exploits. It remembers them only collectively, like the dim figures from a fabulous dream no longer accessible to the dreamer. "The heroes shimmer in the distance, / In a past that is impossible to see," even with "the eyes of faith or of yearning." In the recesses of his imagination, the poet may have still yearned for the return of King Sebastian, or for the Portuguese resurgence that the king's mythic return symbolized, but his faith had been fatally shaken. His most recent poem was a hymn of farewell to a demoralized country, with no sign of hope on the visible horizon, a country "postponed," according to one of its stanzas, for some indefinite future.

◆

AS ALWAYS IN JUNE, but this year with more pomp than usual, people filled the squares and streets to celebrate the *santos populares*, or popular saints, with more revelry than religion. June 13 is the Feast of St. Anthony, the patron of sweethearts and the most popular saint in Lisbon, June 24 the Feast of St. John the Baptist, the favorite saint of Porto, and June 29 the Feast of St. Peter, the protector of fishermen, who is venerated in many coastal towns. The feasting, whose traditional rituals include hopping over small fires and presenting your beloved with a pot of small-leaved basil and a four-line poem, has remote origins, possibly connected to ancient fertility rites at the time of the summer solstice. Many of Pessoa's hundreds of folk quatrains are the kind written for sweethearts in the month of June. The feasting in honor of the popular saints intensified with the arrival of the New State, which took steps to promote and appropriate this manifestation of urban folklore. In a magazine published on June 9, 1935, a recently created Executive Committee of the Lisbon Festivities vaunted its mission "to go and tell the people what they have to do to transform their raw and exuberant joy into the rhythm of a work of art."[18]

On that same day Pessoa wrote three long poems in which he addressed each of the three venerated saints. Far from collaborating with the government program of idealizing and officializing Portuguese culture, the poet used his poems to take potshots at the Church and the New State. In his poem to St. Anthony he wrote that the Portuguese people loved him not at all as an apostolic, sermonizing Franciscan but only as their "pagan delight," a protector of wine drinkers and couples in love. He informed St. John the Baptist that besides being the Precursor of Jesus—and, alas, of the "cruel and blackly infinite multitude" of Catholic clergy that sprung up later—he was also at heart a Mason, since the first Masonic Grand Lodge of England was founded on his feast day, in 1717. Hence the poet, who identified as a Templar, was happy to shake hands with him as a brother in heretical occult mysteries. As for St. Peter, to whom Jesus gave the keys to heaven, Pessoa called him "heaven's jailer," said that he himself abhorred the idea of being shut up anywhere, "here or there," and launched a Promethean challenge:

> If you have miraculous power,
> If those keys open up everything,
> Then quit that pitiful heaven,
> Quit heaven and come down here
> To perform your greatest deed,
> Opening up for humanity
> The gates of Truth and Justice.

How far Pessoa had come from the days when he disdained the mere idea of correcting injustice in the world! "I accept injustice as I accept a stone not being round," said Alberto Caeiro in a poem that dates from around 1919, when Pessoa was working on essays titled "Against Democracy" and "In Defense of Tyrants."[19] By taking up the cause of justice in 1935 he had, in a way, come around full circle, returning to the high-minded and large-hearted ambitions of his youth, when in the name of Alexander Search he signed a "life-bond" that committed him to "doing good to mankind." But Pessoa's attitude toward this collective entity was not at all the same. As a young man, particularly when writing as Alexander Search, humanity was an abstract throng far removed from his own life; he hovered above it all. In 1935 Pessoa recognized himself as a member of the species—not a very social member, but still an essential and inseparable part of it. Humanity, like it or not, was family.

On the feast day of St. Anthony, June 13, an impressive cortège portraying scenes from Portugal's medieval history marched through Lisbon's decked-out streets, and at night there were fireworks that reflected off the glassy black surface of the Tagus. Pessoa, who turned forty-seven at around a quarter after three, had a quiet lunch with his friend Alberto Da Cunha Dias at the Restaurante Pessoa,[20] which he had been frequenting for more than twenty years, attracted to it because of the name. As usual he received a telegram from Ophelia Queiroz: "Happy birthday and *saudades* from Ophelia." The next day, when she turned thirty-five, he replied, as usual, with his own telegram: "Many thanks likewise with *saudades* Fernando."

Pessoa continued to see António Botto, Raul Leal, and Augusto Ferreira Gomes on a regular basis, although at wider intervals than before. Many other friends he saw only sporadically, and often enough he presided over an empty table at the Café Martinho da Arcada, a little disappointed that nobody showed up, and also a little relieved. He never got over being shy and never wished to be less than resolutely reserved, which his friends understood and respected. Since he divulged nothing about his private life, they did not feel entitled or inclined to talk about theirs. Their conversation was intellectual, with some banter thrown in. And yet Pessoa was a good listener for those several friends, such as Cunha Dias, who did talk freely about their personal troubles. According to Carlos Queiroz, nobody dared to inquire about Pessoa's troubles, or even to ask innocuous questions that risked being invasive, such as "What are you up to this evening?"[21]

# CHAPTER 75

EVERY EVENING, BEFORE CLIMBING THE STAIRS UP to his apartment, Pessoa, with a leather briefcase tucked under his arm, stopped at the dairy store on the corner, A Morgadinha, and asked Senhor Trindade for two bread rolls, some sliced ham, a small round of cheese, a pack of Bom cigarettes, matches, and a pint and a half of Macieira, a cheap brandy. For the last item he extracted from his well-worn briefcase a small bottle. The rolls, ham, and cheese were his dinner. He smoked the cigarettes and sipped the brandy while he worked on his writing. When the brandy was all gone he called it a night and went to bed—at two, three, or four in the morning.

On Sundays, when most shops were closed, Manassés the barber came to the apartment to give Pessoa his daily shave and also did some light housekeeping, emptying out the ashtrays and collecting abandoned glasses. Then he went to the dairy store to get Pessoa's bottle refilled and to pick up more bread, cheese, and cigarettes. Trindade kept a running tab of his client's purchases. Pessoa would occasionally pay off a portion of what he owed, and with the prize money for *Message* he paid off all his debts. By the summer he was incurring new ones.[1]

Trindade, Manassés, and the employees at the five or six offices where he worked had always known Pessoa to be a congenial and witty man, neat in appearance, and generally in a good mood, despite frequent bags under his eyes from not having slept enough. But if they happened to cross paths with him on the street, chances were that he would look right through them or else look away to avoid them, unsure what to say or how to behave without the furniture and props of the settings in which they usually interacted. And even in those familiar settings, he sometimes drifted into his own world of thoughts, suddenly oblivious to his surroundings.[2]

Outwardly the poet continued, in the summer of 1935, to be his amicably aloof self. Dressed in his invariable dark suit, he did his daily rounds at the offices, made others smile with his British-style wit and gentility, and kept his usual distance from everything. Inwardly he was becoming soft, warm, vulnerable. One day, while talking with Carlos Queiroz, he asked about Ophelia and blurted out, full of emotion, "What a beautiful soul!" Carlos, taken aback, hardly knew how to respond.[3] In late July Pessoa—an avid listener of the radio, which had only recently become a commonplace appliance in Lisbon's middle-class households—heard a French singer crooning over the airwaves in a "melancholy voice" that made him feel "the allure of banality and heaven." The lyrics of the song were perfectly stupid, he wrote in a poem, and yet his eyes filled with tears. And why not cry?

> But no, I don't want to cry.
> A poet shedding tears
> Over a song!
> How disgraceful for poetry!
> But my heart
> Ignores me and runs
> After that voice and melody
> Before I know it.

Next to this poem, which he wrote in Portuguese, he scribbled an isolated couplet in English:

> All our thoughts and gestures sink
> In the universal drink.[4]

The word "drink" was not only a metaphor. According to his first letter to Madge Anderson, Pessoa had begun sinking in April, and in that same month he suffered a mild bout of delirium tremens.[*] The symptoms started at his sister's home in São João do Estoril, and they inspired a comical, slightly disquieting poem:

---

[*] "Delirium tremens" refers nowadays to the worst stage of alcohol withdrawal syndrome. In Pessoa's time the term, less restrictive, could be applied to delirium and related symptoms experienced by drinkers who were still drinking heavily. See, for instance, the article "Delirium" in the 1911 *Encyclopaedia Britannica* (accessible online).

### D.T.

The other day indeed,
With my shoe, on the wall,
I killed a centipede
Which was not there at all.
How can that be?
It's very simple, you see—
Just the beginning of D.T.

When the pink alligator
And the tiger without a head
Begin to take stature
And demand to be fed,
As I have no shoes
Fit to kill those,
I think I'll start thinking:
Should I stop drinking?

The poem, written in English, continues in this jocular vein for four more stanzas. When Pessoa, three years earlier, had experienced a blackout and been laid up for several weeks, it spooked him; now, when afflicted by a syndrome that betokened a no less serious danger to his health, he made light of it. Rui Santos, one of the young writers who shared his distaste for Salazar, was a witness to his delirium tremens. Some time after the symptoms had all passed, Pessoa explained to his young friend that, according to his understanding of the matter, the condition could regularly recur in a binge drinker, whereas for an alcoholic the first episode was a warning; the second would be fatal. "And can you see me giving up brandy, Rui?"[5]

It was probably Pessoa's personal physician, his cousin Jaime de Andrade Neves, who told him that delirium tremens, in an alcoholic, was the body's way of saying "No more, or else!" Fernando lived just a few blocks away from Jaime and occasionally had lunch with him and his family on the weekend. "You're destroying your liver," the doctor repeatedly warned. Pessoa pretended to listen with attention, as if he might make an effort to drink less, but he believed that his life depended on fate. Drinking, at worst, was fate's instrument.

✦

AFTER A HARROWING SUMMER, Pessoa perked up for the visit of his
half brother Luís Miguel, or Louis Michael, who arrived from London
with his wife, Eva,[6] on September 2. Fernando had not seen either of
his brothers since 1920, when they came from Africa to Lisbon with his
sister and mother and everyone lived together for several weeks on Rua
Coelho da Rocha. They had talked for hours and hours about Durban,
Pretoria, the Lisbon they had known as children, present-day Lisbon,
and London, where the two younger brothers were headed to continue
their studies. Louis Michael earned a degree in chemical engineering
at the University of London in 1923 and got married in 1932. A shy
type, like Fernando, he was also fond of literature and even wrote a little
poetry.[7] He didn't take himself seriously as a writer but encouraged his
brother, insisting he should make more of an effort to publish, in English
as well as Portuguese. Pessoa showed him some of his poetry and recited
a few lines from his waggish "D.T." to make him and his wife laugh.[8]

A secret alcoholic Pessoa was not; he flaunted his addiction. When
introduced to the future daughter-in-law of Jaime Neves, he said: "Hav-
en't you heard of me? I'm the family drunk."[9] But no one had ever seen
him drunk.

Louis Michael and Eva spent nine days between Lisbon and Estoril. Aleister Crowley had also stayed in Estoril, and Pessoa regaled the
vacationers with stories about the charismatic magus. One of the family
outings was to the spectacular Hieronymite Monastery of Belém, whose
construction was initiated by King Manuel I around 1500, on the site
of an earlier church where Vasco da Gama and other navigators would
spend the night in prayer before setting out on their voyages of discovery
from the adjacent port. The monastery's so-called Manueline architecture pays homage to the seafarers by including nautical motifs—coiled
and twisted ropes, chains, anchors, navigational instruments, corals,
seaweed, sea creatures—in its intricately carved moldings and columns,
which never stop surprising an attentive eye. Pessoa, who was steeped in
everything that had to do with Portugal's maritime adventure, was the
perfect guide for his brother and sister-in-law.

Photographs from the outing show Fernando elegantly attired in a
three-piece suit, unsmiling, expressionless, with a cigarette permanently
in hand. Teca and Eva have the relaxed air of people on holiday. But

who looks happiest in the group is Luís, or Lhi, as Pessoa still called Louis Michael. He was thrilled to be reunited with his sister and to become better acquainted with his half brother, with whom he'd hardly ever spent any time, except as a small boy.

As soon as he got back to England, Louis Michael wrote Fernando to remind him that he had promised to prepare his English-language works for possible publication in Great Britain.

> What I said to you still holds good—I am quite prepared to act as your literary agent here and feel that you ought to have a try at least. The English market is tremendous and once you have become at all established you will find it immensely profitable.
>
> There is another point I want to emphasize. Should you ever get another chance to come to England don't miss it. Let us know as soon as you can and we will fix things for you.[10]

Despite his brother's encouragement, Pessoa no longer seemed interested in going to England, but he was amenable to his proposal to act as a literary agent. On October 10 he wrote back to say that he was busily "sorting and grouping" all his papers, spreading them out on tables, chairs, and even the floor in order to accomplish the task, which he claimed was three-quarters of the way done. Only when his papers were all in order would he be ready to start trying to publish his works, in English as well as in Portuguese. Before closing his letter, he asked Louis Michael whether he could find out whatever became of Aleister Crowley. Since they had fallen out of touch, Pessoa had never read anything more about him.[11] It would have been hard for Michael to learn much about Crowley, who had been declared bankrupt in April, lived a quiet life, and was no longer a newsworthy subject. Today he has thousands of followers and many of his books are back in print, but when he died in 1947 only a dozen people attended his funeral.

◆

THE DAY BEFORE WRITING his brother, Pessoa had sent another letter to Madge Anderson, enclosing with it a copy of "D.T." He explained to her that the poem was written in late April—when she was in Lisbon, in other words, and he was avoiding her, while coincidentally writing a couple of lighthearted love poems. "D.T." is itself a kind of love poem,

although only in the fourth stanza do we discover that its narrator is
speaking to a prospective lover:

> Your love might
> Make me better than I
> Can be or can try.
> But we never know—
> Darling, *I* don't know
> If the sugar of your heart
> Would not turn out candy . . .
> So I let my heart smart
> And I drink brandy.

The poet clarified to Madge in his letter that he did not care for candy.
And so his poem, in this stanza, suddenly becomes an unexpected confession: he drinks because he is afraid to try love, afraid he won't care for
it—whether it be with Madge or with anyone. Of course, there is a first
time for everything. Now it was Pessoa who was flirting. He claimed
that his poem "happens to be sincere enough, though it contains a good
deal of dramatic new silliness," and he also wrote Madge that "I am really not sinking now. Indeed, I am feeling far better in all ways."[12]

Pessoa, above all, was *feeling*. He had retrieved for himself the faculty of emotion for so long delegated to Álvaro de Campos, and it was
exhilarating to feel directly, in the first person, even or especially when
the things he felt pricked his heart. Instead of guarding against unsettling memories, or diverting them into the alter egos that had peopled so
much of his writing life, he now welcomed their frontal assault, which
hit him with full force in mid-September.

A few days after Lhi and Eva Rosa had finished their holiday and
returned to England, Pessoa happened to hear on the radio "Un Soir
à Lima," by the Belgian composer Félix Godefroid—a serenade for
solo piano that his mother used to play in Durban. It's a kind of bolero,
sprightly but with a doleful middle section in a minor key. Everything
Pessoa was doing and thinking stopped dead as he listened, transfixed.
The notes running up and down a mentally visualized keyboard, softly
then loudly, staccato or legato, overwhelmed him like an irresistible
tide and carried him in a flash back to the living room of the house

with broad verandas on Tenth Avenue in Durban. While his mother attentively played "Un Soir à Lima," his stepfather reclined "his calm and robust / Athlete's body" in the largest chair and smoked, his sister was curled up on another chair and pretended to be sleeping, his little brothers—still toddlers—really were sleeping, and he himself stood by the window, noticing the "wooded slope shimmer / Under the great African moon." This was the first time since leaving Africa that Pessoa's poetry made the slightest mention of the years he lived there.[13]

"I'm the naked stage where various actors act out various plays," Pessoa had written years ago in a passage for *The Book of Disquiet*,[14] but the actors had all deserted him, he was completely alone on that stage, and the play was his own life, the life he had actually lived. The more than three hundred lines of his poem titled "Un Soir à Lima" are a soliloquy, with frequent asides to his eternally absent mother, as here:

Mother, mother, I was your boy
Whom you taught to be
So well-behaved,
And today I'm a rag
Rolled into a ball by Destiny and tossed
Into a corner.

There I pathetically lie,
But the memory of what I heard and what I knew
Of affection, of home and of family
Rises to my heart in a swirl,
And remembering it I heard, today, my God, all alone,
"Un Soir à Lima."

"Un Soir à Lima" is one of Pessoa's great unfinished monuments, consisting of a dozen or so passages that he never assembled into a complete whole. It was finally noticed, transcribed, and published by an observant Pessoan archeologist in 2000,[15] half a century after the poet's first biographer proposed nostalgia for lost childhood as the main engine of his lyrical output—a thesis the poem does not really support. João Gaspar Simões maintained that Pessoa bitterly missed his *early* childhood, before his own father died and his mother fell in love with the "intruder," his stepfather.

But "Un Soir à Lima" calls up a scene from when Pessoa was about sixteen years old, and it evokes João Miguel Rosa, his mother's second husband, with frank admiration: "What a man! What heart and soul!"

Pessoa was indulging his nostalgia for all the people and things he had most treasured in life, from every period, including his early childhood. In October he would write "Pedrouços," a poem about the house in that neighborhood where he used to stay with his uncle Cunha and aunt Maria, with the big yard to play in and a room just for him, the privileged recipient of their love and attention.

Another poem from October, written the day before "Pedrouços," honored the memory of his relationship with Ophelia, all of whose more than 250 love letters to her Fernandinho, or Nininho, or Querido Amor, he held in safekeeping, as cherished evidence.

All love letters are
Ridiculous.
They wouldn't be love letters if they weren't
Ridiculous.

In my time I also wrote love letters
Equally, inevitably
Ridiculous.

Love letters, if there's love,
Must be
Ridiculous.

The rest of the poem affirms, among other things, that those who have never written love letters are more ridiculous than those who have.

Pessoa, it must be said, never had the slightest fear of appearing ridiculous in the eyes of others, but he had feared being conventional, or ordinary, in his own eyes. All his fears, defenses, and props were melting away. His "ridiculous" poem was signed by Álvaro de Campos, a quasi-human prop who lately had nothing of his own to say. The Campos poems written on June 24, August 28, and September 12, 1935, faithfully echoed what Pessoa himself was feeling: weariness, uncertainty, and dizziness, both mental and physical. The October poem about Pessoa's love letters exposed Campos completely. By usurping the place of the letter writer, the naval engineer and onetime saboteur of Ophelia and Fernando's romance was virtually annihilating himself, or he was annihilating Pessoa, which amounted to the same thing. At this point their names were interchangeable, making "Álvaro de Campos" redundant, superfluous. Having made his confession and paid his respects to Ophelia, his role was fulfilled and he signed no more poems. (But his name would still sign one more piece of prose.)

✦

PESSOA PLACED THE VARIOUS passages for "Un Soir à Lima" in an envelope labeled "Intimacy," a category that could encompass other recent poems dealing with his private world of affective attachments— such as "Pedrouços," the elegy to his friendship with Sá-Carneiro, or the poem that memorialized his love letters to Ophelia. Except as a teenager, when he taught himself to write by imitating and reworking the poems of others, Pessoa typically relied on his own thoughts and emotions for the raw material of his poetry, but he removed, distorted, or transformed their original contexts, in a process he described as "depersonalization." Now, however, he was willing to use autobiographical experiences direct and unprocessed.[16]

Pessoa's political thinking also took a new, rather astonishing turn, as revealed in two articles that would have greatly roiled the waters of public opinion, particularly among the supporters of authoritarian governments, had he managed to get them published. They also unsettle our view of Pessoa. His attitude toward the human race had been shifting since the beginning of the year, but so radical is the shift in "Liberal Nationalism" and "A Very Simple Matter" that we can scarcely believe they were really written by Pessoa.

"Liberal nationalism" was a new term in his political vocabulary. As recently as six months before, in the résumé he drew up of his personal, professional, and ideological life, he had styled himself a "liberal" conservative—a defender, that is, of individual rights and liberties—but also a proponent of a "mystical nationalism," founded on the myth of King Sebastian's symbolic return. Although there is no evidence of his ever having renounced Sebastianism, it and the word "mystical" are conspicuously absent from the more than twenty pages Pessoa wrote about the new kind of nationalism he so zealously espoused at this late date, like a man who, after much searching, has at long last discovered the truth. He distilled the essence of that truth in a new, three-part motto: "everything for the Individual, nothing against Society; everything for Humanity, nothing against the Nation; everything for Equality, nothing against Liberty."

*Equality?* Everything for *equality?* Pessoa had endorsed the idea of spiritual equality in his essays on initiation and esoteric orders, but never, in all his writing, had he stood up for political and social equality. The theorist who always inclined toward aristocratic models of government, seeing the proletariat as a kind of human herd that needed to be managed by an enlightened elite, now wrote in "Liberal Nationalism" that the nation is worth "the sum of its individuals," which sounds suspiciously democratic.[17]

Surprised as we are to find Pessoa exalting the ideals of humanitarianism, equality, and respect for all individuals, it surprises us still more to see how he applied those ideals to an actual case then much in the news: Mussolini's unprovoked invasion of Ethiopia, which led to war and the African country's eventual annexation. After more than twenty years of fighting, Italy had finally subjugated the whole of Libya. The conquest of Ethiopia, bordered on the north and the southeast by Italian Eritrea and Italian Somalia, would make it a major colonial power. Portugal's right-wing press initially supported Italy's pretensions to the country ruled by Haile Selassie. Only after the Portuguese foreign minister was tasked with chairing the commission of the League of Nations that found Italy in the wrong did Salazar's government and its supporters meekly and reluctantly denounce the Fascist aggression. The invasion was launched on October 3, 1935, and that same month, Pessoa began writing "A Very Simple Matter," in which he derided Mussolini's two main justifications for going to war with Ethiopia: first, that Italy, overpopulated, needed more space for its people, and second, that Ethiopians were savages whom, once conquered, Italy would do the favor of civilizing.

If the Italians were truly civilized, countered Pessoa, they would have fewer children and thus solve their population problem. As for the Ethiopians' alleged savagery, it was true that some of them still practiced slavery, and Pessoa agreed that it was immoral to treat human beings as things, but he pointed out that Fascist Italy also treated people as things, by subordinating them to the state. Furthermore, it was "the fate of all imperialist peoples that, by turning others into slaves, they turn themselves into slaves." In the most extraordinary paragraph of his article, Pessoa wrote that "all of us, all people in this world whose lives are oppressed" by the more fortunate and the powerful—"what are we all in this world if not Abyssinians?" Between "us" and "them" (the Abyssinians, or Ethiopians) he saw a "vast and broad human fraternity."

Here too, bewildered, we find ourselves wondering if these can really be the words of Fernando Pessoa, who in 1916 had stated that it was justifiable to enslave Zulus and native Mozambicans since they amount to "nothing useful in this world" except manual labor "to serve the ends of civilization," but who was now embracing and identifying with oppressed Abyssinians. There is no precedent in all his work for such a broad and inclusive vision.[18] The change in how he viewed the world and its inhabitants was accompanied by a change in how he saw himself: still as a highly civilized genius and poet but also, finally, as an ordinary man.

Despite his new determination to put his ideas and words at the service of fighting oppression and injustice, Pessoa's old writing habits had not changed, and he never finished "A Very Simple Matter." He did, however, complete a shorter article that just as effectively excoriated Il Duce's invasion of Ethiopia, by resorting to the dictator's own words. In 1913, when Mussolini was still a leftist and the editor in chief of a socialist newspaper, he had denounced the Italian invasion of Tripoli as a "moral perversion," a "miserable war of conquest" that laid bare the underlying weakness of Italy, since "strong nations have a sense of proportion." Pessoa cited these remarks in an article scathingly titled "Italian Prophecy," since Mussolini, twenty-two years later, was leading Italy into another "miserable war of conquest," this time against Ethiopia.[19] He submitted his article to one of Lisbon's independent newspapers, but the Censorship Commission blocked its publication.[20] Having bowed to international pressure to officially condemn the Italian invasion of a sovereign nation, the New State was going out of its way not to further antagonize its Fascist friend. Mussolini's signed and framed photograph sat snugly on the right side of Salazar's desk, where it would continue to sit until the Second World War, when it gave way to a photo of Pope Pius XII, elected to the papacy in 1939.

◆

PESSOA HAD PUBLISHED ALMOST nothing literary since *Message*, even though various magazines and newspapers would have gladly accepted whatever poems or prose pieces he cared to submit. The book prize gilded his name with respectability and could have been a spring-board for publishing other books and establishing himself as a major contemporary author. Instead, the prizewinner retreated to the shadows of literary renown—a leading poet of Portugal whose work hardly any-one knew. José Régio wrote him in June to suggest he send something for the next issue of *Presença*. It had been over a year since any of his work had appeared in its pages. Pessoa did not reply. One of Régio's co-editors, Adolfo Casais Monteiro, also wrote him a letter, and the third co-editor, João Gaspar Simões, who had moved to Lisbon in March to take up a job as a proofreader, met with Pessoa to urge him to make a submission.

Giving in to their insistence, Pessoa was finally getting ready to send work to the magazine, but as he explained in a letter to Casais Monteiro on October 30, something had just happened—"it happened five min-utes ago"—that made him decide to publish nothing else in Portugal, whether in periodicals or in book form. And in the next paragraph he recalled the odious words of Salazar, at the ceremony for the govern-ment literary prizes held in February, about how writers should not only refrain from challenging the New State's moral and patriotic princi-ples but also use them as guidelines for what and how to write. Pessoa did not finish his letter, leaving us in the dark about what had "hap-pened five minutes ago" that led to his dramatic decision to quit pub-lishing in his own country, but a likely candidate for the fateful event is the censorship of "Italian Prophecy." It seems that he made a phone call to question how the censors could disallow an article that factually restated what Mussolini himself had written.[21] Dissatisfied with the answer he got, he told Casais Monteiro, in this unfinished letter, that the New State was to blame for his definitive disappearance from the pages of *Presença*.

"The New State is making me feel old," he wrote in another unsent letter to a younger poet.[22] For the past eight months or so, the New State's ever-tightening stranglehold on the nation had galvanized him to write poems of protest and prose texts defending human freedom against assorted forms of tyranny. But he had come to suspect that all his efforts were quite useless, since his values were irrevocably out of step with the times, which favored nationalistic ideologies over individual self-expression.

In the second week of November, Pessoa would write his last and most despairing poem about the Salazar regime, "Poema de amor em Estado Novo" ("Poem of Love in a New State")—a state in which the dictator's guidelines and the stifling institutions created by his corporatist government infiltrate even the province of human affections, making a complete mockery of love.

# CHAPTER 76

**L**ITERATURE, UNTIL THE END, STILL BECKONED Pessoa, no matter how disillusioned he felt. He might see only trouble and confusion on the horizon, he might doubt that any gods existed, that the world mattered, or that his life had any purpose, but words still enchanted him, commanding his loyalty and demanding to be enunciated. Although he deeply resented being a victim of censorship, he did not carry out his threat to quit publishing altogether in the country of his birth. In the fall of 1935, he agreed to participate in and to help organize the third and last issue of the magazine *Sudoeste* (*Southwest*), which paid homage to *Orpheu* and *Presença* by presenting new work from writers associated with each of the two publications.

José de Almada Negreiros, the founder and editor of *Sudoeste*, entrusted the *Orpheu* section to Pessoa, who explained in a brief introduction that they had obtained contributions from all the Portuguese writers published in the legendary magazine with the exception of Armando Côrtes-Rodrigues.[1] He blamed this omission on geography, since Côrtes-Rodrigues lived in the far-off Azores, and took the opportunity to salute his old chum and café companion. But it was a backhanded salute, accompanied by a warning to the poet not to get too caught up in "bucolic Catholicism," lest he become one of the "literary victims" of St. Francis of Assisi. The Azorean writer had recently published *Cântico das fontes* (*Canticle of the Springs*), whose poems completely lived up to the collection's Franciscan title.

Pessoa was letting go of his elitism and appreciated, as never before, the virtues of simplicity and solidarity, but these changes entrained no relaxation in his insistence on conceptual clarity and intellectual rigor. He respected St. Francis's love of nature; he objected to his humanization and spiritualization of nature on behalf of an overarching religious narrative.

Pessoa's contributions to *Sudoeste* 3, published the first week of November, included a poem written under his own name as well as a deceptively titled "Random Note" signed by Álvaro de Campos, who took up the question of sincerity in literature. The note was secretly aimed at the two senior, sincerity-fixated editors of *Presença*—Régio and Gaspar Simões—and perhaps also at Côrtes-Rodrigues. The naval engineer maintained that "intellectual sincerity, which is what matters for poets," has nothing to do with people's conventional way of feeling and that "the world's only completely sincere poet" was Alberto Caeiro, a poet who did not actually exist. The equally nonexistent Campos left it up to the readers of his note to ponder whether Caeiro's unreality made him less, or more, sincere.

A triptych of sonnets by Pessoa titled "At the Tomb of Christian Rosenkreutz" was also scheduled to appear in *Sudoeste*, but either he withdrew them at the last minute or they were excluded for lack of space. Another, less likely possibility is that the censors objected to their heretical theology—Gnostic, or Hermetic:

God is the man of a yet higher God.
A Supreme Adam, He also fell.
Our Creator, He was also created,
And was cut off from the truth.

Pessoa had not written any esoteric poems since 1934, and it was probably then, or in 1933, that he wrote his undated triptych honoring the founder of the Rosicrucian Brotherhood, whose corpse, says the legend, was whole and uncorrupted when members of the order opened his tomb, 120 years after his death.[2] Whenever the three poems were written, Pessoa's intention to publish them in November 1935 confirms that he still believed, at least ideally, in an occult world, whose "increasingly subtle levels of spirituality" he described in his January 13, 1935, letter to Adolfo Casais Monteiro and vividly evoked in his triptych. But he believed with diminishing enthusiasm. His once ardent fascination with Rosicrucianism, Kabbalah, and other systems of occult knowledge was now just a small bed of glowing embers.

Although that January 13 letter had endorsed alchemy as the superior path for reaching higher levels of spirituality, Pessoa, during his remaining months of life, seems to have followed what he referred to in his notes on the occult as the "direct" method of spiritual progress, one that "renounces both magic and alchemy." This is "the simple path," he wrote, and those who follow it recognize the Word exactly "as it is given to us, as something not one but multiple, as the limbs of Osiris, many Gods." Rather than attempt to reconjoin the body of the god Osiris—whose corpse was cut up into pieces and strewn all over Egypt—they accept the fragmentary, multiple nature of the divine Word. And to accept "the Word as the Word," says Pessoa in conclusion, is to accept "the World as the World."[3] This wisdom recalls the lesson of the master heteronym, Alberto Caeiro, who saw and accepted that "Nature is parts without a whole."

Pessoa's spiritual journey is reminiscent of the Zen adage that before one studies Zen, mountains are mountains and waters are waters; while studying Zen, mountains are no longer mountains and waters are no longer waters; after enlightenment, mountains are once again mountains and waters once again waters. Pessoa, of course, never achieved anything remotely resembling Zen Buddhist enlightenment. What he attained, more modestly, was an awareness of the lightness of reality, and he himself was becoming lighter and lighter. We see it in his poems from 1935—more colloquial in tone, sometimes humorous, and frequently rhyming erratically, indifferently.

On November 13 Pessoa wrote a poem, however, that was not at all colloquial. It was an ode signed by Ricardo Reis, whose diction was always formal:

> Countless lives inhabit us.
> I don't know, when I think or feel,
> Who is thinking or feeling.
> I am merely the place
> Where things are thought or felt.
>
> I have more than just one soul.
> There are more I's than I myself.
> I exist, nevertheless,
> Indifferent to them all.
> I silence them: I speak.

The crossing urges of what
I feel or do not feel
Struggle in who I am, but I
Ignore them. They dictate nothing
To the I I know: I write.

This was the first Reis ode that Pessoa had written in over a year, and it was the last one he would write. According to a wonderfully ingenious novel by José Saramago, *The Year of the Death of Ricardo Reis*, this heteronym, after receiving word of his maker's death, would return to Lisbon from Brazil, vaguely follow the events leading up to civil war in neighboring Spain, participate in philosophical discussions with the ghost of Pessoa, and follow him to the graveyard in 1936. Yet he actually vanished out of existence with the writing of this ode, which bears the marks of his usual style but whose speaker is clearly not Ricardo Reis; it is Fernando Pessoa, telling us what it means for him to be a poet of many voices and what it means to *be*, period.

In the ode's first stanza the poet defines himself as a neutral, anonymous place occupied by countless, apparently autonomous beings. The next two stanzas reveal that those beings are actually him or, rather, are a hubbub of competing, conflicting hims, whom he silences by speaking and transcends by writing. This drama involves not just the heteronyms but all the murmuring voices that make Pessoa Pessoa. Yet he only *is*, he only positively exists, in the moment he takes the stage and performs, by speaking or writing.

The heteronyms were heteronyms, Pessoa had always insisted, because they were not him. They held different opinions, conceived the world differently, and interacted differently with life. So they did, for many years, but the masks had dissolved, the jig was up, leaving only Pessoa with his "crossing urges" of what he felt or didn't feel.

◆

SINCE THE SPRING OF 1935, Pessoa's health and mood had been lurching like an unsteady ship. Abdominal pains attacked unexpectedly and just as abruptly subsided; waves of depression engulfed him, then retreated. During his brother's visit in early September he was in good spirits, but at the end of the month, Teca and Chico—who had come to

Lisbon to seek treatment for their young son, himself seriously ill—were startled to see how haggard Fernando looked. They learned that one night he had passed out in the bathroom, which was locked, so that the door had to be forced. Fortunately he came to quickly.[4] By the second week of October, Pessoa and his nephew were both decisively better. Perhaps it was during the family's visit to Lisbon that Mimi, Pessoa's niece, wrote a penciled note, found among his papers, telling her "dear uncle" that she wished he would drink less wine at dinner.[5] The note had to be her mother's idea; for years Teca had been lecturing her older brother about his drinking.

On November 16, a Saturday, Mimi turned ten years old and Pessoa took the train to his sister's house to help celebrate. He stayed for two nights and looked well and ate well, to Teca's relief, but something was gnawing at him. On Tuesday, the day after returning to Lisbon, he wrote his last Portuguese poem, which begins:

There are sicknesses worse than any sickness;
There are pains that don't ache, not even in the soul,
And yet they're more painful than those that do.

There are dreamed anxieties and imagined sensations more real than anything life brings our way, continues the poet in succeeding lines, before uselessly saluting "what never was nor could be, and it's everything." And he ends the poem with a last request and its justification: "Give me more wine, because life is nothing."

He had come around to the point from where he had started, and from where he had never really left: an oppressive feeling that life is not enough. Some people, at the end of their lives, embrace religion. Fernando Pessoa, after years of philosophical, literary, political, and spiritual peregrinations, finally embraced life itself, with all its commonalities that connected him to people he knew and people he didn't. But it continued to be terribly insufficient.

That week, he received a letter from Madge Anderson (addressed to "Fernando my Dear"), in answer to his of October 9.[6] She thanked him for the poem "D.T.," excused the lateness of her reply by saying that she "devoted many thoughts" to him each time she intended but failed to write, and announced that lately she was feeling the way he had been feeling when he wrote his first letter: depressed. She mentioned that her sister, Eileen, and his half brother John had recently returned from their holiday in Mallorca, and she wished she could be "setting off on a visit to you all again," since she was tired of her job. "Write me another little poem some time soon and teach me how to recover my spirits as I tried to do for you!" she said in closing, and: "Give my love to all the family not forgetting yourself."

Madge threw in just enough sweet touches to keep up the flirtatious fun without signaling any interest in something more serious. Fernando, in other circumstances, would have been pleased to keep flirting back in the same lighthearted way. Madge was smart and refreshingly unpredictable.

On November 22, just a couple of days after receiving Madge's letter, Pessoa wrote his very last poem, in English:

The happy sun is shining,
The fields are green and gay,
But my poor heart is pining
For something far away.
It's pining for you,
It's pining just for your kiss.
It does not matter if you're true
To this.
What matters is just you.

There are two more stanzas, which are variations on this one and equally insipid.[7] Any of Pessoa's youthful poems in English signed by Alexander Search is more interesting. Even the first poem he ever wrote, "Separated from thee," at the age of twelve, is poetically not inferior. "I'm physically nauseated by commonplace humanity, which is the only kind there is," wrote Pessoa in *The Book of Disquiet* in 1930,[8] but his recent acceptance of and identification with that same humanity led him to take pleasure—without irony—in writing poems about commonplace subjects, including love. Might Madge Anderson have inspired this as well as other love poems by Pessoa? Quite possibly so. Which is not to say that he was in love.

Pessoa produced a remarkable run of love poems in the summer and fall of 1935—in English, French, and Portuguese. But like the ones he wrote in April, during Madge's visit to Portugal, they adopt continuously shifting points of view, exploring the phenomenon of love rather than meditating on a concrete experience of it. Even when the speaker pines after an individual "you," the beloved usually turns out to be theoretical or illusory. In a poem from August, written in Portuguese, the narrator nostalgically summons a lover from the past whose lips, he admits, "I no longer know how to love / Because I have never loved them." In another poem he claims to miss a beloved woman "without knowing if you exist."[9]

The women of Pessoa's love poems from 1935 are usually incorporeal, but a poem he wrote in French describes the beloved as a blue-eyed blonde. It ends in a quandary:

What to do? I fancy you
With my ever distant love.
Let me, in vain, confess it,
My blonde.[10]

This distantly felt affection could be for Madge Anderson as it could be for any other hypothetical or imaginary and in any case impossible lover—impossible not because of geographical or other hurdles but because Pessoa always ran in the other direction. If there was ever an exception that proved the rule, it was Ophelia Queiroz, a sweetheart he soon enough decided to keep at arm's length, offering her his company in frequent but strictly homeopathic doses.

"What matters is love," Pessoa had realized in a poem at the beginning of April, shortly before he met Madge, and his way of "experiencing" love at the age of forty-seven was by writing about it in three different languages and from myriad perspectives in an outpouring of amorous verse—some of it rather clever, some of it funny, some of it maudlin and poetically drab. All of the imaginary scenarios were ostensibly heterosexual. Because his libido now tended in that direction? Or because it didn't? These poems had little or nothing to do with libido. Pessoa's very last poem, whose three stanzas all end with the line "What matters is just you"—a "you" whose gender is not actually defined—was effectively if not intentionally an abstract declaration of love to all of us. "Yes," he was saying, "I can be like everyone else. I can even write mediocre poems about love, like this one. Yes, humanity, I am with you." But not for much longer.

✦

ON WEDNESDAY, NOVEMBER 27, Pessoa was scheduled to go back to São João do Estoril—this time for his sister's thirty-ninth birthday. Teca was laid up with a fractured leg, having taken a bad fall the day after his last visit, but she and her family were still going to celebrate.

They waited and waited for Fernando, in vain, and would have called the neighbor who lived across the hall from him, Virginia Sena Pereira, but their phone was out of order. Fernando had told them in recent days that he was a little under the weather, and the next morning Chico went to the apartment in Lisbon to see what was the matter. He found Pessoa in bed but apparently recovered after a night of vomiting and excruciating abdominal pain that his cousin, Jaime Neves, diagnosed as "hepatic colic." The neighbor with the telephone, who was acquainted with Dr. Neves, had called him despite the sick man's protestations that it was nothing.

Pessoa told Chico that the crisis had passed, asked about Teca, and remembered, a little later, to have someone send her a telegram with belated birthday wishes. On Friday his friend Armando Teixeira Rebelo paid him a visit and could see that he had taken another turn for the worse. They called back Jaime Neves, who examined him and decided he should go to the hospital. Pessoa thought it wasn't necessary, he would be better tomorrow, but the doctor insisted. All right, said his patient, but first he needed a shave.[11] So they went to get his barber, Manassés, who came with his set of implements, told his favorite client to relax, wrapped a clean, cool cloth around his neck, spread the lather over his face, expertly swiped the blade over his cheeks, his chin, and his neck while making some small talk, just like always, and wiped his face clean.

"There, Senhor Pessoa, you're all set!"

Carlos Moitinho de Almeida and Francisco Gouveia, a textile importer and exporter for whom Pessoa also worked as a letter writer, arranged to have him admitted to a private room at Hospital Saint Louis, which had originally been founded to serve French sailors and French residents of Lisbon. Administered by the Filles de la Charité, a French order of nuns, and located in what had been a luxurious palace in the Bairro Alto, it was one of the city's most expensive private hospitals.[12] The bill would be paid by Moitinho de Almeida, the inspiration for Senhor Vasques, owner of the fabric warehouse whose assistant bookkeeper, Bernardo Soares, had prophetically described his boss in a passage for *The Book of Disquiet* as a hard-nosed businessman capable of causing someone else's ruination for the sake of a good deal but also capable of generosity where generosity was due.[13] They gathered together a few of Pessoa's things—clothes, toiletries, and the leather briefcase he lately carried everywhere—and helped him into Moitinho de Almeida's car.

Pessoa had several visitors that afternoon, including his brother-in-law, and it was probably in the evening, still propped up in the hospital bed after everyone had left, that he wrote on a sheet of paper the day's date, "29-XI-1935," followed by just one sentence, in English: "I know not what to-morrow will bring." These were Pessoa's last written words. Scholars have proposed that he was paraphrasing Horace or some other author of antiquity acutely aware of how fragile and uncertain all life is.[14] But he could just as easily have been echoing the sentiment expressed by his own classical creation, Ricardo Reis:

> Fate frightens me, Lydia. Nothing is certain.
> At any moment something could happen
>     To change all that we are.

"I know not what to-morrow will bring" also echoes what Pessoa's father, gripped by tubercular fever and chills, wrote in a letter to his wife on the day before he died: "I don't know what this might be."

Whatever may have inspired Pessoa's last piece of writing, the fact he dated it, as was often the case for his literary works, encourages us to read it as a one-line poem. If he initially intended to write more lines, he realized after seven words that he had said all there was to say. Pessoa knew he was dying—if not tomorrow, then the next day or the one after that. But *then* what? It was a question that had always haunted him.

◆

PESSOA EXPIRED THE NEXT DAY, November 30, at around 8:30 p.m., in the presence of Dr. Jaime Neves, a second doctor, a nurse, and Francisco Gouveia and his partner Victor da Silva Carvalho, who both thought of Pessoa as a friend,[15] as did most of the businessmen he worked for. They, more than his literary friends, were the ones who accompanied him in his final passage—from the apartment to the hospital and beyond. Chico, his brother-in-law, had left the hospital at around six thirty, believing Fernando to be in stable condition, and received the news of his death in São João do Estoril.

Although the public records office lists "intestinal obstruction" as the immediate cause of Pessoa's death, several biographies have cited hepatic colic—the diagnosis of his condition when admitted to the hospital—or even cirrhosis as the cause. Hepatic colic is a confusing term, signifying a gallbladder attack (which in itself would not cause death) rather than pain occasioned by the liver, and it no doubt contributed to the erroneous notion that Pessoa died from cirrhosis. He did not have the symptoms of this disease. Teca would write Louis Michael that their brother's demise was due to "some dreadful liver trouble," but at most this was a contributing factor.[16] The direct cause of death was probably indeed intestinal obstruction. Another possibility is acute pancreatitis, resulting from his heavy consumption of alcohol.[17]

Portuguese burials are usually held within forty-eight hours, and Pessoa's was scheduled for eleven in the morning on Monday, December 2. Because December 1 was a holiday—commemorating the restoration of Portugal's independence from Spain in 1640—no evening paper was published that day and no morning paper on the next day, but there was a brief announcement of the poet's death on the radio,[18] and the news traveled by word of mouth. Carlos Queiroz learned what had happened on Sunday and called home to tell his mother, Joaquina, and his aunt Ophelia, who shrieked, a little beside herself, and then cried for the longest time, for she still loved him and had never stopped holding out hope. If she had known he was in the hospital she would have visited him—so she said years later in an interview—but she preferred not to be seen at the funeral.[19] Back then, women in Portugal were expected to do their grieving at home.

The funeral took place at the blissfully named Prazeres Cemetery, located in the residential neighborhood called Prazeres (Pleasures), close to where Pessoa had lived for the last fifteen years. Luís de Montalvor, on behalf of the survivors of *Orpheu*, delivered a short eulogy to an assorted mix of about sixty people. Among Pessoa's relatives were Francisco

(Chico) Caetano Dias, Jaime Neves, Victoriano Braga, and Eduardo Freitas da Costa—this last a vocal, lifelong defender of Salazar as well as a promoter and editor of Pessoa's work. Literary friends connected to *Orpheu* included José de Almada Negreiros, Raul Leal, Augusto Ferreira Gomes, António Ferro, and Alfredo Guisado (whom Pessoa had seen little of in recent years). Pessoa's two oldest, not-so-literary friends were also present: his college classmate Armando Teixeira Rebelo and the engineer Geraldo Coelho de Jesus. So was another old friend, Alberto Da Cunha Dias. And there were writers he got to know only in the 1920s or 1930s, such as António Botto, João Gaspar Simões, and Rui Santos and Gil Vaz, both of whom would secretly circulate a couple of his anti-Salazar poems.

Blended in with the relatives, literary types, and journalists was a sizable contingent of the businessmen in whose offices and on whose typewriters the deceased had composed some of his finest poems and prose works. And there was Manassés Seixas, his faithful barber, who closed his shop for a few hours so as not to miss the solemn send-off. Of the only two women who attended the funeral, one was Emília, the live-in housekeeper and single mother who never forgot the kindness of her onetime employer toward her little girl, Claudina, back in 1917. In the only known photograph of the funeral she is staring straight into the camera, defiantly Emília.[20]

✦

**PESSOA'S MORTAL REMAINS WERE** deposited in the family vault, joining those of Joaquim, his father, whose family line now ended; Jorge, his brother who died in infancy; Madalena Henriqueta and Maria Clara, half sisters who died in early childhood; Aunt Maria and Uncle Cunha, who were like a second mother and father; Aunt Rita, the ornery spinster who loaned him money he never repaid; and Grandma Dionísia, who purchased the vault.

Later that day, the evening papers published the first accounts of Pessoa's abrupt departure. The *Diário de Lisboa* reported that "he died the day before yesterday in silence, as he always lived, avoiding publicity and sinking into death in the same discreet manner he had passed through life." The article summarized that life, greatly praised Pessoa's work, and noted what an honor it had been for the paper to publish, earlier in the year, his "intelligent criticism" of the bill before the National Assembly that would outlaw Freemasonry.

The next morning *A Voz*, which had fervently supported that same bill, stated in its obituary that Pessoa's article against it was "deplorable" and not, at any rate, to be taken seriously; it was just "a gag by the humorist of *Orpheu*." Although the *Diário de Notícias* likewise supported the legislation to ban Freemasonry, as well as the rest of the New State political program, it expressed nothing but admiration for the "extraordinary" writer who "was always the youngest of the young men who sat together" at his table in the Café Martinho da Arcada. "Everything about him was unexpected—his life, his poems, and even his death."[21]

The weekly paper *Bandarra*—which was subsidized by the Secretariat of National Propaganda to promote arts and letters according to Ferro's "politics of the spirit"—recognized that Pessoa's death was "an irreparable loss for the nation's intellectual life" and correctly predicted that his "renown will grow with the passage of time." But the headline of the newspaper's obituary styled him "The Great Nationalist Poet," and it perversely paid homage to his memory by republishing, over the course of its next four issues, *The Interregnum: Defense and Justification of Military Dictatorship in Portugal*. Pessoa's renunciation of this booklet, in the résumé he had drawn up exactly eight months before his death, was not yet public knowledge, and supporters of Salazar inside and close to Pessoa's family made sure it would not become public knowledge for several decades to come.[22] Only a small underground of Portugal's intelligentsia knew that Pessoa unambiguously opposed Salazar and his New State. The branding of Pessoa as a nationalist poet prevented his renown as a writer of universal stature from growing more quickly.

Pessoa left no will or testament, and no personal property to speak of except his library and his papers. His family paid off the six hundred escudos he owed the dairy store on the corner. Little did they realize the inestimable value of his surviving literary output, only a fraction of which had been published. The famous trunk left behind by Pessoa was replete with manuscripts, but it held less than half of his poems, prose writings, translations, saved letters, and other documents, all of which take up close to thirty thousand sheets of paper.[23] Several hundred of those sheets consist of his vastly unrealized publication plans. Planning, like dreaming, was far more agreeable to Pessoa than the tedious business of taking concrete steps to realize practical objectives like publishing. Let others deal with the task of making his works available. His job was to write them.

In a poem from 1915 that begins "If I die young," Alberto Caeiro reflected on the posthumous life of his poems:

> Even if my verses are never published,
> They will have their beauty, if they're beautiful.
> But they cannot be beautiful and remain unpublished,
> Because roots may be hidden in the ground
> But their flowers flower in the open air for all to see.
> It must be so. Nothing can prevent it.

Pessoa had at least as much faith as Caeiro in the intrinsic worth of literature and in its power to prevail. If it was his destiny to die at the age of forty-seven, then destiny would look after his poetry, *The Book of Disquiet*, and the rest of his literary output. Destiny acted slowly, however, and many of his unfinished and fragmentary prose works have yet to be published. Some cannot be published as discrete works, since they ramified or metamorphosed, becoming strange configurations of two or more very different works.

As for the man behind this extravagant literature that flowered, monstrous and gorgeous, in so many different forms and under dozens of different names, he too has survived his death and is there "for all to see." But he is like the purloined letter of Poe's short story: easy to miss if you look too hard. Pessoa claimed to be an impersonal medium, a conduit, through whom a variety of contrasting voices spoke, or wrote, and he told his friends that poems "happened" to him.[24] Anyone who sifts through the original manuscripts of Pessoa's poems will quickly realize how spontaneously they took shape but also how obsessively he revised what he wrote before submitting it for publication. In his last published interview, about a year before his death, Pessoa explained that he wrote "on impulse, by intuition," after which "the author gives way to the critic." This method of writing is not an unusual one. Unusual was Pessoa's ability to criticize his own work with sublime objectivity, as if it were written by a complete stranger. And Pessoa was, in a way, a stranger to himself. His shyness, vacillation, and extreme reserve were not mere accidents of his temperament; they were allied to his disbelief in a reliable, knowable "I."

Rather than affirming himself through a vivid personality, rather than elaborating a set of definite convictions that together might amount to a palpable identity ("*This* is Pessoa"), and rather than cultivating a rich "inner" life, which he could then share or not share with others, Pessoa immediately exteriorized whatever he felt and thought and dreamed by putting it into writing. His self-definition as an impersonal poet—a medium, a conduit—was accurate. Most of what he wrote, on the other hand, was absolutely personal.

"I have never shown what I am," Pessoa announced to his future readers in 1912, and in one sense it was true, since there was no definite, permanent "I" to be revealed. But in another sense the statement was patently false. There's a photograph of Pessoa from 1914 that he described, in a dedication he penned for Aunt Anica, as a "provisional visual representation" of himself. Pessoa's writings were, by and large, provisional visual representations of his soul. In fact, he never stopped showing us who he was or was trying to be. His poems and prose pieces were *him*, his own person, or the bits and pieces of the person, or Pessoa, who did not exist as such. His sexual life? His spiritual life? They may be found in his writing, and *nowhere else* but in his writing. There is no secret Pessoa for the biographer to reveal.

Fernando Pessoa was an experimentalist, whose own life was the permanent subject of his research. Each of the heteronyms was an experiment, as was each of the philosophical, political, literary, and religious points of view that he successively adopted and successively abandoned. His relationship with Ophelia Queiroz was an experiment. So was the correspondence he had recently struck up with Madge Anderson. His attempts to be a businessman. His communications with astral spirits. His involvement with Aleister Crowley, pitting his inclination to white magic against the compelling allure of the black magician from Great Britain. All were experiments, most of whose procedures and results he recorded, like a scientist of love, of commerce, of religion, and so on.

What stands out from the record he left is the dynamic nature of all his observations and conclusions. They—and he—were unstable, in transit, ever subject to revision. For this reason they—and he—could never be immured in any school of thought, action, or art. Ever on the move, the poet-scientist did not even belong to himself, refusing to be bound by his own conclusions. According to *The Book of Disquiet*: "To belong is synonymous with banality. Creeds, ideals, a woman, a profession—all are prisons and shackles. To be is to be free."[25] And yet Pessoa, without a wife, a creed, or a normal profession, tried to embrace banality in his last year of life, belonging as much as it was possible for him to belong to common, ordinary humanity. It was his ultimate experiment and supreme test of freedom—freedom from himself—after which he could go no further, in this world.

# EPILOGUE

*Madge Anderson* soon fell in love with a former British spy, Fred Winterbotham, whom she married in 1939. Both were admitted into the Bletchley Park team of code breakers, whose work cracking Nazi ciphers is credited with shortening the war in Europe by one to two years. Divorced in 1946 and without any children, she lived in Argentina, Spain, and Cuba, attracting admirers wherever she went, but never remarried. She died in London in July 1988, several weeks after the centenary of Pessoa's birth.[1]

*Luís de Montalvor* persuaded Pessoa's heirs to entrust his small publishing house, Edições Ática, with the task of bringing out the writer's *Obras completas* (Complete Works). Montalvor and João Gaspar Simões were the co-editors of the collection's first five volumes—all dedicated to poetry—published between 1942 and 1946. Ática went on to publish volumes of Pessoa's prose as well as more poetry in succeeding decades, and *Livro do desassossego* (*The Book of Disquiet*) in 1982. However, none of these were handled by Montalvor, who died in 1947, together with his wife and their only son, in mysterious circumstances: returning home after Sunday Mass in the family car, with the couple's son at the wheel, they inexplicably veered off the road into the Tagus and drowned. The funeral service, attended by hundreds of people, took place in the church where Pessoa was baptized.[2]

*João Gaspar Simões* garnered fame as a prolific, original, and sometimes polemical literary critic and historian. His landmark biography of Pessoa, published in 1950, had the great merit of calling attention to an author whose true stature was not yet recognized; but family members and friends of the poet disputed the depiction of him as a man by turns destitute, disheveled, and visibly drunk. In 1972 Gaspar Simões, who had always felt that the heteronyms were "insincere," a mystificatory ploy, predicted that their "exotic" appeal would wear off in time.[3] He died in 1987.

*Henriqueta Madalena Nogueira Rosa Dias*, known to family members as Teca, was the guardian of her brother's literary archive for forty-four years. She welcomed into her home not only editors but also researchers who wished to consult the thousands of papers stored inside Pessoa's wooden trunk, a small suitcase, and a cabinet. In 1979 the Portuguese government purchased the archive and transferred it to the National Library. When interviewed in 1985, the fiftieth anniversary of Pessoa's death, she stated that "he didn't have a tragic air—in fact he was a cheerful sort—but it makes me sad to think of all those hours, so many hours, that he spent alone."[4] She died in 1992 (her husband preceded her, in 1969) and is survived by Manuela Nogueira, Pessoa's only niece. Nogueira's brother and Pessoa's only nephew, Luís Miguel Rosa Dias, died in 2019.

*Augusto Ferreira Gomes* called on Teca a few days after her brother's funeral and tried to console her by saying "Fernando had to die; he knew too much." He was referring to occult knowledge. In 1941, Ferreira Gomes published his last book, a mishmash of ancient prophecies interpreted to fit the circumstances of the Second World War. It was dedicated to "the astrologer Fernando Pessoa." He continued to work for the Secretariat of National Propaganda, remarried after the death of his first wife, Marcelle, and died in 1953. Raul Leal and José de Almada Negreiros were among the many who attended his funeral.[5]

*Alberto Da Cunha Dias* was privileged to be the subject of Pessoa's last published article—a sympathetic appraisal of a forthcoming book—and the subject of no less than five horoscopes cast by the poet-astrologer between the months of August and November 1935. Psychologically fragile and unlucky in love, Cunha Dias led an "agitated and anxious life," which ended in 1947 after a prolonged illness, according to his obituary.[6]

*António Botto* continued to publish, but the quality of his poetry declined and his financial situation deteriorated. In 1942 he was dismissed from the Portuguese civil service for writing and reciting poems while on the job and for making passes at a male co-worker, "displaying tendencies condemned by public morality." Five years later he and Carminda Silva Rodrigues, his common-law wife, immigrated to Brazil, where he scraped together a living through journalism, cultural events, and his paltry royalties, moving to new lodgings whenever he couldn't keep up with the rent. Afflicted with megalomania, he claimed to be a far better poet than Pessoa, whom he faulted for being too cerebral, but he also recalled with great fondness the many hours they had spent together in Lisbon. In an unfinished essay about Pessoa of February 24, 1959, he wrote that they were "more than adoring friends or brothers."[7] Seven days later, when crossing a street in Rio de Janeiro, he was struck by a truck and plunged into a coma, dying two weeks later at the age of sixty-one.

*Mário Saa*, now an active manager of his farmlands in the Alentejo, missed Pessoa's funeral. But in an elegy written soon afterward he returns to the Café Martinho da Arcada and wistfully gazes at the now vacant table where they used to sit and debate ideas. "And as absurd as it may sound," he writes toward the end, "he, Fernando, will be born after we have all died and in the same moment that he died. He was born after Our Future Death."[8] Besides tending his farms, Saa spent much of the rest of his life researching and writing a massive, six-volume work on the Roman roads of Lusitania. He died in 1971.

*Raul Leal*, aka the prophet Henoch, obsessively filled up long and narrow sheets of paper with disquisitions about the Paracletian Age, or "third divine reign." In 1960 he published *Personalist Syndicalism: Plan for the World's Salvation*, a book dedicated to Fernando Pessoa that called for a fusion of individualism, socialism, and fascist corporatism. Although his clothes were sometimes tattered—a tiny pension and his published articles brought in only a meager income—Leal retained the lordly manners inculcated in him by his affluent upbringing. He lived with a former boxer and trainer, who had once been his lover, and spent the afternoons of his later years in cafés, where he had a following among young poets. His horoscopes predicted he would die in 1967, but death came to get him three years early, in a Lisbon public hospital. Eleven people attended his funeral. He left behind thousands of pages of still unpublished works.[9]

*Geraldo Coelho de Jesus*, like Leal and like Pessoa, never learned to be a well-organized, "responsible" person. He continued to earn good money as a mining engineer and continued to spend it all in Paris, where he stayed for long periods. In Lisbon he very occasionally visited his nephew, José Coelho Pacheco, who had been connected to the *Orpheu* group and now made a comfortable living as a car dealer. For these surprise visits, Coelho Pacheco kept on hand a bottle of absinthe, his uncle's favorite drink. The engineer had no offspring with Germaine, his much younger French wife, who died from TB in 1946, and he himself died three years later, estranged from most of his family.[10]

*José de Almada Negreiros*, so restless and wild as a young man—donning flamboyant outfits, organizing lectures that were more like happenings, shaving his head, and loudly denouncing x and y and z—quieted down and gained an air of respectability, along with a much deserved reputation as one of Portugal's great twentieth-century artists. In 1941 the Secretariat of National Propaganda organized a retrospective exhibition of his drawings, and he soon received commissions for large-scale works of public art. In 1954 he painted his most famous picture—the one of Pessoa sitting at a café table with a copy of *Orpheu* 2—for the Irmãos Unidos restaurant, where the *Orpheu* group used to meet. When the restaurant closed its doors and the picture was auctioned, in 1970, it fetched the highest price ever paid for a work by a living Portuguese artist. Several months later the artist fell ill and was admitted into Hospital Saint Louis, where he expired in the same room as Pessoa.[11]

*Carlos Queiroz*, whose first book of poems came out in the fall of 1935, was delighted to learn that Pessoa had written a favorable review of it shortly before his demise. (The review was published posthumously.) Fernando had always been a generous friend to Carlos, who published a heartfelt "Letter to the Memory of Fernando Pessoa" in the July 1936 issue of *Presença*, which was entirely dedicated to the recently departed writer. In the same issue, he also published excerpts from Pessoa's love letters, without revealing that his aunt was their recipient. Queiroz worked for Portuguese National Radio as a cultural journalist, and it was in that capacity that France's Commissariat Général de Tourisme invited him to Paris in 1949. It was an exciting opportunity, his first visit to the French capital, but it ended in tragedy: a massive and fatal stroke. He was forty-two years old and left behind five small children.[12]

*Ophelia Queiroz*, with a helping hand from her nephew, got a job at the Secretariat of National Propaganda in 1936 and worked there for almost twenty years. Through the job she met a man named Soares—Augusto, not Bernardo—and married him in 1938. It was a happy union, lasting until his death in 1955, but she later admitted that she never really loved him, not as she did Fernando.[13] After having insisted for years that his love letters to her should be made public only after her death, she changed her mind as she approached her eightieth birthday and authorized their publication. Some people, including Pessoa's sister, reacted with indignation, believing that love letters should remain private. Ophelia died in 1991, at the age of ninety-one, and was buried in the cemetery that serves the eastern half of Lisbon. Twenty-five years later, on Valentine's Day, the Lisbon City Council transferred her remains to the Prazeres Cemetery, where they could rest in greater peace, close to the Pessoa family vault. But Fernando was no longer there. In 1985 his remains had been exhumed and transferred to the majestic Hieronymite Monastery, where his new "family" included Vasco da Gama, Luís de Camões, King Sebastian, and other entombed heroes of Portugal's proud history. In death, as in life, he eluded Ophelia.

# Acknowledgments

MY EARLY WORK AS A RESEARCHER IN THE PESSOA ARCHIVE WAS ENCOURAGED by José Blanco, of Portugal's Calouste Gulbenkian Foundation, and by members of the Equipa Pessoa (Pessoa Project), which embarked on a critical edition of Pessoa's works under the direction of Ivo Castro in the late 1980s. Two books I read around this time made a deep and lasting impression: Eduardo Lourenço's *Fernando Pessoa revisitado* (*Fernando Pessoa Revisited*; 1973) and Leyla Perrone-Moisés's *Fernando Pessoa: Aquem do eu, além do outro* (*Fernando Pessoa: Before the Self, Beyond the Other*; 1982). So did an essay on Pessoa by Octavio Paz, "El desconocido de si mismo" (1961), which has been translated into English as "Unknown to Himself" (in *The Centenary Pessoa*). All three works, different as they are, suggested to me that Pessoa could never be captured, pinned down, or fathomed. I hope to have written a book that will at least help the reader *feel* Pessoa.

Before and after the turn of the century I was part of a group of Pessoa researchers and editors based at the Universidade Nova of Lisbon and led by Teresa Rita Lopes. Rita Lopes, Manuela Parreira da Silva, Fernando Cabral Martins, Luísa Medeiros, and Paula Cristina Costa tutored me in the arts of deciphering Pessoa's handwriting and charting his labyrinthine papers. The editorial team at Assírio & Alvim—where I've had the privilege of working with Hermínio Monteiro, Graça Manta, Manuel Rosa, Lúcia Pinho e Melo, and Vasco David, among others—has enabled me to publish numerous editions of Pessoa's work, beginning with *Livro do desassossego* (*The Book of Disquiet*; 1998) and including, in 2003, a compendium of Pessoa's autobiographical and mediumistic writings in which I focused, for the first time, on the poet as a biographical subject. Clara Ferreira Alves, a former director of the Casa Fernando Pessoa, pushed me to write more on Pessoa's life and work, and in 2008 I published, together with Joaquim Vieira, a photobiography of Pessoa. He was responsible for the images; I wrote the text.

In 2007 my literary agent, Jim Rutman, prodded me into drawing up a proposal for a full-fledged biography in English, which I naïvely thought would take me two or three years to complete—not twelve or thirteen. The project quickly sparked interest among a few American publishers. Jim urged me to go with Liveright/W. W. Norton, whose editor in chief was, he guaranteed, an editorial wizard. On my next trip to New York, a deal was struck at Norton's offices on Fifth Avenue, and the very next day I happened to run into one of Robert Weil's assistants at a literary event. "Let me warn you," said the just-out-of-college assistant with a slightly wicked grin. "You may write like James Joyce, but Bob Weil will still have at least one suggestion to make on nearly every page of your manuscript." Since I do not write like Joyce, he had rather more suggestions to make, but he did not just fiddle with sentences; he was a patient and brilliant coach. His handwriting, to my amused dismay, was as difficult to decipher as Pessoa's.

In 2010 I made a trip to Durban, where the houses in which Pessoa lived and the school buildings in which he studied have all disappeared. But the architect Bryan Lee, urged on by Ester Lee, managed to uncover building plans, maps, and a wealth of information about old Durban. Bryan recruited other Durbanites to work on my behalf—Lenn Mostert, Arthur Gammage, Shelagh Spencer, Val Ward, and the architect-historian Brian Kearney. Elias de Sousa, Portugal's honorary consul in Durban, put me in touch with the Lees and kindly facilitated access to the consular archives. João Gouveia provided me with logistical support. Jeremy Oddy, the Durban High School archivist (the building is not the same, but the school still thrives), ferreted out old records and photos. Rebecca Naidoo helped me navigate the photo archive at the Old Court House Museum, and the gracious staff of the Killie Campbell Africana Library, where I spent many long afternoons, attended to my numerous requests for books and newspapers. In Johannesburg, Carlos Pereira Marques and Stephen Gray led me to some useful bibliographical sources. Nibs van der Spuy, a Durbanite I met in Lisbon several years ago, tracked down bits of information and an out-of-print book on trips to his hometown.

In Portugal, my research at the National Library was made much easier thanks to Fátima Lopes, Luís Sá, and Manuela Rêgo. The entire staff at the Casa Fernando Pessoa—in particular the librarians Teresa Monteiro and José Correia; the current director, Clara Riso; and the previous director, Inês Pedrosa—have always been ready to assist. The same is true for the staffs at the Hemeroteca Municipal, the Gulbenkian Foundation's Biblioteca de Arte, the Arquivo Histórico Militar, and the Arquivo Histórico da Marinha—all located in Lisbon. The online archives of the Fundação Mário Soares and the Digital Edition of Fernando Pessoa were yet other valuable resources. I spent one long and unexpectedly fruitful day consulting the António Ferro Archive, at the António Quadros Foundation in Rio Maior, fifty miles north of Lisbon. As a fervent promoter both of Portuguese culture and of the dictator António de Oliveira Salazar, Ferro remains a hotly debated figure, and I salute the foundation, directed by Mafalda Ferro, for making his papers freely available to all researchers, without restrictions.

José Bernardo Távora allowed me to consult to my heart's content the incredibly rich collection of manuscripts and first editions assembled by his father, the architect Fernando Távora. Luísa Castro and Manuel Andrade Neves showed me the smallish but valuable collection of family letters and other documents belonging to their great-grandfather, Jaime de Andrade Neves. Maria da Graça Queiroz, daughter of Carlos Queiroz and a great-niece of Ophelia, let me look at letters in her possession. The Paes Teles Archive Foundation graciously gave me access to letters received by Mário Saa, while Elisabete J. Santos Pereira provided me with some biographical data on this writer.

The Condes de Castro Guimarães Museum, the Lisbon Port Authority's Centro de Documentação e Informação, Lisbon's Centro Hospital Psiquiátrico, and the Casa de Saúde of Telhal all duly answered my requests for information; so did the official website for T. S. Eliot, the Bletchley Park Trust, and the Special Collections Division of the University of St Andrews.

Of the many *pessoanos* whose published works have in some way contributed to this biography (see Sources and References), I am especially indebted to José Barreto for carefully documenting the complex evolution of Pessoa's political thinking. Isabel Murteira França, on the other hand, revealed the more intimate side of Pessoa. She had the inspired idea, in the mid-1980s, of conducting interviews with her grandmother—Pessoa's sister—and with other people who had known the poet as an ordinary man, though of course he was anything but ordinary.

I learned much about Pessoa's relations with his maternal cousins, aunts, and uncles from Margarida Soares Couto, Madalena Gonçalves, and Miguel Freitas da Costa. For information about the paternal side of his family, in particular the cousin he knew as Aunt Lisbela, I'm indebted to Maria Manuela Pessoa Chaves Ortega, as well as Isabel and Inês Sarmento.

Ana Rita Palmeirim, Zetho Cunha Gonçalves, João Macdonald, Maria do Céu Estibeiro, Ricardo Marques, Marina Tavares Dias, Helder Macedo, Jorge Uribe, Pedro Sepúlveda, Arnaldo Saraiva, Aníbal Frias, Marianna Silvano, Sally Bolton, Vincent Barletta, Anabela Almeida, João Rui de Sousa, Mark Sabine, Chris Davies (the great-grandson of Eugen Sandow), and Fernando Cabral Martins all contributed to my research. Rita Marrone gave me a copy of her Laurea thesis on Pessoa and the tradition of Western esotericism, recommended some readings on this subject, and exchanged impressions with me on the dating of Pessoa's esoteric writings. João Concha kindly interpreted several of Pessoa's astrological charts. Jorge Ferreira was my guide to Lisbon's cemeteries and dug up death data from the civil registry offices. Four nieces of Madge Anderson answered queries about this mysterious woman Pessoa met in 1935.

The conversation, as well as the luminous essays, of two writers and Pessoa scholars with whom I became friends in the last years of their lives—Robert Bréchon (1920–2012) and Antonio Tabucchi (1943–2012)—helped to sharpen and enliven my vision of Pessoa. The conversation has carried on with other scholars, including Maria José de Lancastre, Anna M. Klobucka, António Feijó, Luísa Freire, Hanmin Kim, Caio Gagliardi, Mariana Gray de Castro, and Victor K. Mendes—plus some of the scholars whose names I've already mentioned.

I wish to remember five people, recently deceased, who were in some way connected to the writing phase of this work: my brother, Robert J. Zenith, at whose home in Arizona I sketched a number of chapters; Ana Maria Freitas, a friend and Pessoa scholar; Luís Miguel Rosa Dias, Pessoa's only nephew; Bryan Lee, the aforementioned Durban architect; and Manuela Rocha, a dear friend who often collaborated with me as an editor and translator.

I was fortunate to have two wonderful readers, in addition to my wizardly book editor. Adam Mahler made incisive suggestions on the unabridged version of my manuscript, while Martin Earl, who had read early versions of the first chapters, offered superb commentary and criticism on what was supposed to be the final version. Throughout the process, Martin has demonstrated to me a new level of moral support. My other friends in Portugal, Italy, Brazil, China, the United Kingdom, Ireland, and the United States have also cheered me on, or at least patiently put up with my strange moods and frequent absences. I thank the editorial, design, and marketing teams—including Trent Duffy, Anna Oler, Don Rifkin, Becky Homiski, Steve Attardo, Haley Bracken, Gabriel Kachuck, Peter Miller, Cordelia Calvert, and Nick Curley—for their stellar work on this outsized book. For their help in obtaining photographic images, I'm indebted to Maria José de Lancastre, Manuel Rosa, Joaquim Vieira, Jorge Garcia, and Fátima Campos.

I am tremendously grateful to all the people mentioned or implied in the preceding paragraphs but reserve my most heartfelt thanks for Manuela Nogueira, Pessoa's niece, who showed me all the letters and other papers in the family's possession and shared with me her memories, her frank opinions, and her friendship. I will never forget the many afternoons we drank English tea at the home built by her parents, in São João do Estoril, where Fernando Pessoa used to play with her when she was eight and nine years old and a tall girl for her age.

# Durban, c. 1900

① Pessoa's first home in Durban, 1896–97.

② St. Joseph's Convent School, where Pessoa studied between 1896 and 1899.

③ Ocean View Hotel, where Pessoa and his family lived for a few months toward the end of 1897.

④ Family home from 1898 to 1901. The Portuguese Consulate had a separate entrance in the same building.

⑤ Durban High School, where Pessoa studied in 1899–1901 and again in 1904.

⑥ Pessoa's last home in Durban, 1902–1905.

⑦ Commercial School, where Pessoa studied in 1903.

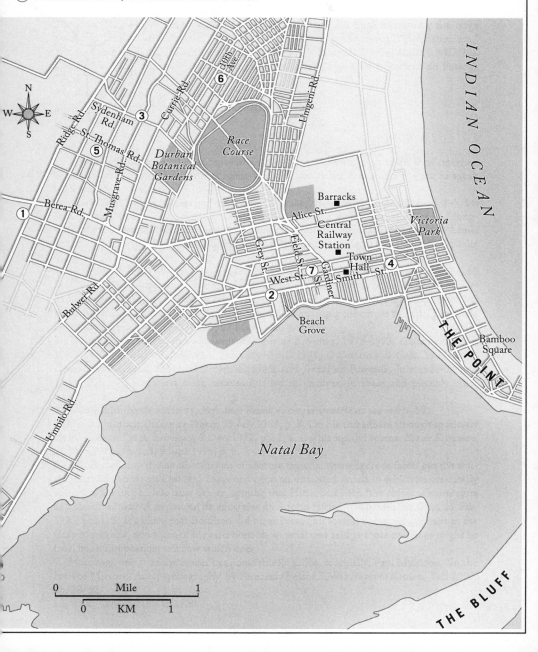

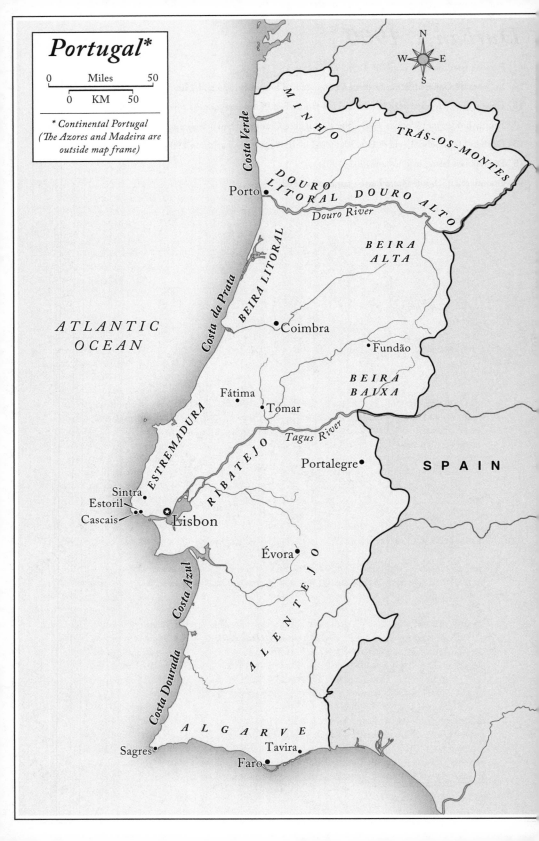

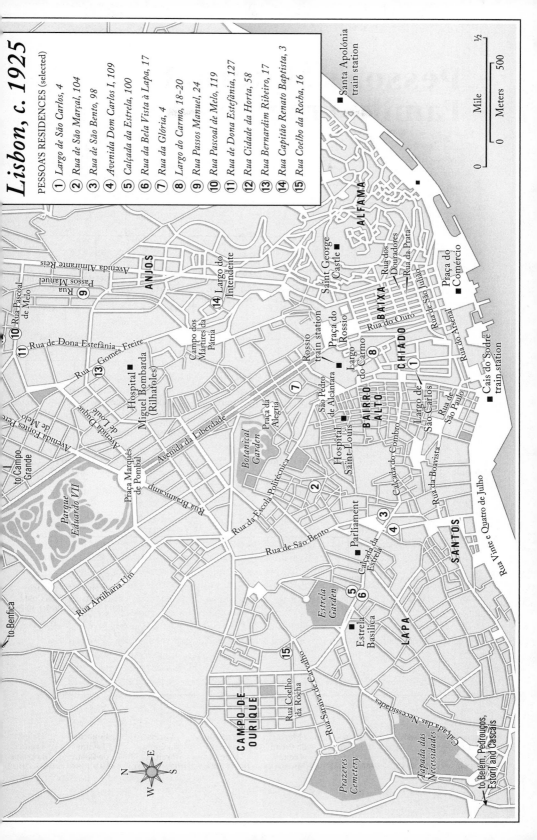

# Lisbon, c. 1925

PESSOA'S RESIDENCES (selected)

1. Largo de São Carlos, 4
2. Rua de São Marçal, 104
3. Rua de São Bento, 98
4. Avenida Dom Carlos I, 109
5. Calçada da Estrela, 100
6. Rua da Bela Vista à Lapa, 17
7. Rua da Glória, 4
8. Largo do Carmo, 18–20
9. Rua Passos Manuel, 24
10. Rua Pascoal de Melo, 119
11. Rua de Dona Estefânia, 127
12. Rua Cidade da Horta, 58
13. Rua Bernardim Ribeiro, 17
14. Rua Capitão Renato Baptista, 3
15. Rua Coelho da Rocha, 16

# Pessoa's Maternal Family Tree

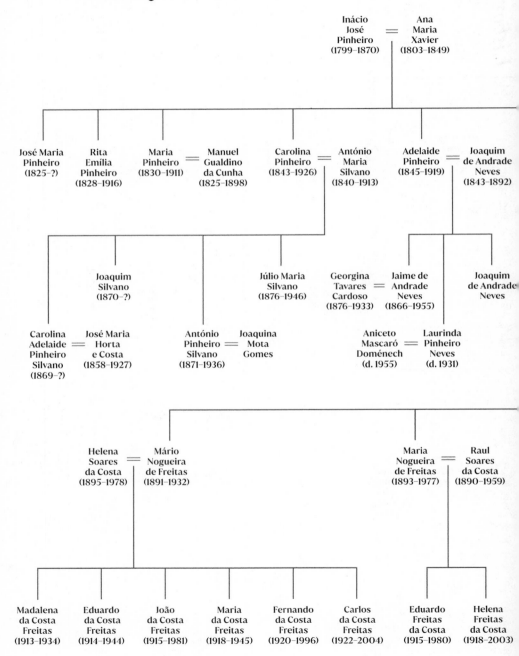

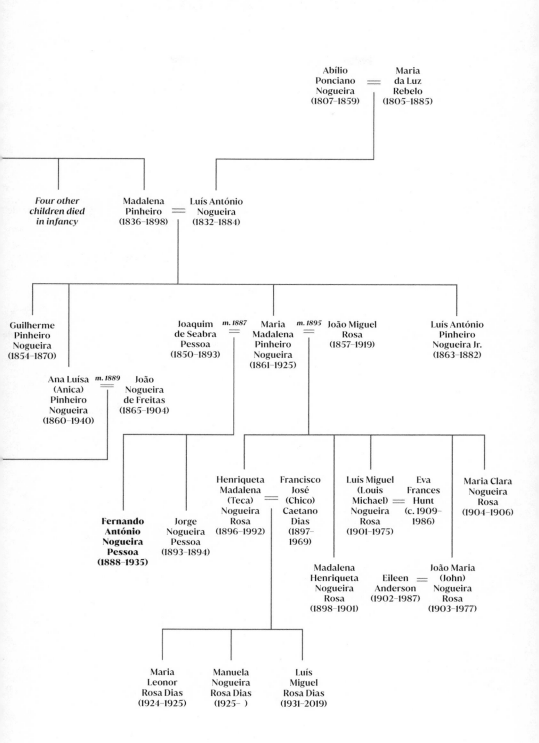

# Chronology of Pessoa's Life

### 1887

**September 19:** The heteronym Ricardo Reis is born in Porto at 4:05 p.m., about nine and a half hours before Pessoa was conceived, according to one of his astrological charts.

### 1888

**June 13:** Fernando António Nogueira Pessoa, first son of Maria Madalena Pinheiro Nogueira and Joaquim de Seabra Pessoa, is born at the Largo de São Carlos, 4, fourth floor left, opposite Lisbon's opera house, at around 3:20 p.m.

The English-language heteronym Alexander Search is born in Lisbon on the same day.

### 1889

**April 16:** The heteronym Alberto Caeiro is born in Lisbon at 1:45 p.m.

### 1890

**October 15:** The heteronym Álvaro de Campos is born in Tavira, the Algarve, at 1:30 p.m.

### 1893

**January 21:** Pessoa's brother, Jorge, is born.

**July 13:** Pessoa's father, Joaqum, dies from tuberculosis.

**November 15:** The surviving family, which includes Dionísia, Pessoa's paternal grandmother, moves to a smaller apartment at Rua de São Marçal, 104, third floor.

### 1894

**January 2:** His brother Jorge dies. That same month his mother meets João Miguel Rosa, a ship's captain.

## 1895

**July 26:** Recites a quatrain addressed to his mother, who writes down the words.

**December 30:** His mother is married, by proxy, to João Miguel Rosa, recently named Portugal's consul in Durban, capital of the British colony of Natal.

## 1896

**January 20:** Embarks with his mother for Durban, South Africa.

**March:** Enrolls in St. Joseph's Convent School. The family lives in the Tresilian House on Ridge Road, in the Berea, a neighborhood favored by Durban's white residents.

**November 27:** His mother gives birth to Henriqueta Madalena, who would be known in the family as Teca.

## 1898

By January of this year—and after staying for a time at the Ocean View Hotel, on 354 Musgrave Road—Pessoa's family has moved to 157 West Street, in downtown Durban.

## 1899

**April 7:** Enrolls in Durban High School.

**October 11:** Beginning of the Anglo-Boer War, which will cause thousands of refugees to descend on Durban.

## 1901

**January 11:** His mother gives birth to Luís Miguel.

**May 12:** Writes his first poem in English, "Separated from thee."

**June:** Passes, with high honors, the School Higher Examination.

**August 1:** Sails with his family for a yearlong holiday in Portugal, where they will spend most of their time in Lisbon, staying in an apartment at Rua de Pedrouços, 45, ground floor. At some point Pessoa, perhaps with the rest of the family, will travel to the Algarve to visit paternal relatives.

## 1902

**May 2:** Travels with his family to Terceira, an island in the Azores, to visit maternal relatives.

**June 26:** His family returns to Durban, while he remains in Lisbon to prepare and sit for the national elementary education exam. Resides at Avenida Dom Carlos I, 109, third floor left, no doubt with relatives.

**July 18:** Publishes his first poem, in the Lisbon newspaper *O Imparcial* (The Independent).

**September 19:** Departs for Durban, alone, on board the *Herzog*.

**October:** Enrolls in the Commercial School. Lives with his family in a house at 25 Tenth Avenue, once more in the Berea.

## 1903

**January 17:** His mother gives birth to João Maria.

**July 11:** Publishes a poem in English, "The Miner's Song," signed by Karl P. Effield, in *The Natal Mercury*.

**November:** Sits for the matriculation examination of the University of the Cape of Good Hope and wins the Queen Victoria Memorial Prize for the best English essay.

## 1904

**February:** Returns to Durban High School, where he pursues his first year of university-level studies.

**July:** Publishes a satirical poem signed by Charles Robert Anon in *The Natal Mercury*.

**November:** Sits for the Intermediate Examination in Arts, administered by the University of the Cape of Good Hope, and obtains the highest score in the province of Natal.

## 1905

**August 20:** Departs for Lisbon, where he will live with his aunt Anica and his cousins Mário and Maria, at Rua de São Bento, 98, second floor left.

**October 2:** Enrolls in the School of Arts and Letters.

## 1906

Emergence of Alexander Search, writer of poems, stories, and essays.

**July:** Moves to the Calçada da Estrela, 100, first floor, to be with his family, who are on another long leave from Durban.

Fails to sit for exams, due to illness.

**October:** Re-enrolls in the first year of the School of Arts and Letters.

## 1907

Emergence of Dr. Faustino Antunes, a psychiatrist, and Friar Maurice, a monk undergoing a crisis of faith.

**April 25:** His family returns to Durban. He moves in with two of his maternal great-aunts, Rita and Maria, and his grandmother Dionísia, at Rua Bela Vista à Lapa, 17, first floor.

**May or June:** Drops out of the School of Arts and Letters.

**September 6:** Dionísia dies, leaving her grandson a sizable inheritance.

## 1908

Emergence of Jean Seul, author of texts in French.

**February 1:** Assassination of Portugal's King Carlos I.

**December 14:** First dated passage for his *Fausto*, a verse drama inspired by Goethe's *Faust*.

## 1909

Joaquim Moura-Costa, Vicente Guedes, Carlos Otto, and other fictional authors emerge in connection with Pessoa's plans for a publishing house.

**August:** Travels to Portalegre, near the Spanish border, to buy a printing press.

**November:** Ibis Printing and Publishing opens for business in Lisbon at Rua da Conceirição da Glória, 38–40. That same month, Pessoa moves into his own apartment at Rua da Glória, 4, ground floor.

## 1910

**June:** The Ibis press, which did some printing but no publishing, goes out of business.

**October 5:** The monarchy falls and the Portuguese Republic is proclaimed.

## 1911

Forced to give up his apartment, he lives for a few months at an office belonging to his cousin Mário, at Largo do Carmo, 18–20, first floor.

**June or July:** Moves in with Aunt Anica at Rua Passos Manuel, 24, third floor left.

**September:** After his stepfather is named consul-general of Portugal for the recently formed nation of South Africa, his family moves from Durban to Pretoria.

## 1912

Meets the poet and fiction writer Mário de Sá-Carneiro, who will become his closest friend and literary ally.

**April:** Publishes his first article of literary criticism, "The New Portuguese Poetry Sociologically Considered," in the Porto-based magazine *A Águia*.

## 1913

**August:** Publishes, in *A Águia*, his first piece of creative prose, a passage from *The Book of Disquiet*, signed with his own name.

## 1914

**February:** Publishes his first mature poems, "Ó sino da minha aldeia" ("O church bell of my village") and "Pauis" ("Swamps"), in *A Renascença*, an ephemeral literary journal.

**March 4:** First dated poem of Alberto Caeiro.

**April:** Moves, with Aunt Anica and her daughter Maria, to Rua Pascoal de Melo, 119, third floor right.

**June:** Emergence of Álvaro de Campos.

**June 12:** First dated odes of Ricardo Reis.

**November:** Aunt Anica moves to Switzerland with her daughter and son-in-law. Pessoa rents a room at Rua de Dona Estefânia, 127, ground floor right.

**December:** Emergence of Raphael Baldaya, an astrologer and student of the occult.

## 1915

Emergence of António Mora, a theorist and promoter of neo-paganism.

Death of Alberto Caeiro, from tuberculosis.

**March 24:** Publication of *Orpheu* 1, which includes the "static drama" *O marinheiro* (*The Mariner*), signed by Pessoa, and "Opiário" ("Opiary") and "Ode triunfal" ("Triumphal Ode"), by Álvaro de Campos.

**June:** Publication of *Orpheu* 2, which includes Pessoa's "Chuva oblíqua" ("Slanting Rain") and Campos's "Ode marítima" ("Maritime Ode").

**September:** Completes the first of six translations of works by Helena Blavatsky, C. W. Leadbeater, and other Theosophical writers (published in 1915–1916).

**November:** His mother, still in South Africa, suffers a severe stroke affecting her left side.

## 1916

**March 9:** Germany declares war on Portugal, which in turn declares war on Germany the following day.

**April 26:** Mário de Sá-Carneiro commits suicide in a Paris hotel.

**May (?):** Pessoa rents a room on Rua Antero de Quental.

**June:** Earliest surviving automatic writings, supposedly dictated to Pessoa by astral spirits.

**September (?):** Lodges for a brief spell in a room at Rua Almirante Barroso, 12.

**October:** Leases rooms at Rua Cidade da Horta, 58, first floor right.

## 1917

**January:** First contingent of Portuguese troops sails to France to fight on the Allied side.

**May 12:** Sends *The Mad Fiddler*, a collection of poems, to an English publisher, which rejects the manuscript.

**August 21:** Pessoa and two friends open F. A. Pessoa, a firm that will act as an intermediary for business transactions. Its offices are at Rua de São Julião, 41, third floor. It ceases operations nine months later.

**October 31:** Publishes, in *Portugal Futurista*, Álvaro de Campos's "Ultimatum," a manifesto vilifying Europe's political leaders and cultural luminaries.

**October or November:** Moves to a spacious apartment at Rua Bernardim Ribeiro 17, first floor.

**December 5:** A coup d'état installs Sidónio Pais as dictator.

## 1918

**July:** Self-publishes two chapbooks of his English poems, *Antinous* (written in 1915) and *35 Sonnets*, which receive favorable reviews in the British press.

**November or December:** Moves to a furnished apartment on Rua de Santo António dos Capuchos.

**December 14:** Sidónio Pais is assassinated.

## 1919

**February:** A monarchist insurrection that broke out one month earlier is subdued by republican forces, whereupon Ricardo Reis, a monarchist, immigrates to Brazil.

**June or July (?):** Pessoa moves to Rua Capitão Renato Baptista, 3, ground floor left.

**October 7:** His stepfather dies in Pretoria.

**October 8:** Ophelia Queiroz is interviewed for a job as a secretary at Felix, Valladas, & Freitas, Ltd., a firm where Pessoa handles the business correspondence, located at Rua da Assumpção, 42, second floor.

**October or November:** Rents rooms from a family at Avenida Gomes Pereira, Vila Gonçalves de Azevedo, ground floor, Benfica.

## 1920

**January 30:** Publishes "Meantime," a poem from *The Mad Fiddler*, in the London-based magazine *The Athenaeum*.

**March 1:** Writes his first love letter to Ophelia Queiroz.

**March 30:** His mother and the three grown children from her second marriage arrive in Lisbon. His two half brothers soon leave for England, where they will eventually earn university degrees in London and settle down. Pessoa, his mother, and his half sister, Teca, occupy an apartment at Rua Coelho da Rocha, 16, first floor right. Pessoa will live at this address until his death.

**October:** Founds a small agency, Olisipo, which will operate initially as a broker in the mining business and subsequently as a publisher.

**November 29:** Breaks off with Ophelia Queiroz via letter.

## 1921

**December:** Olisipo publishes his *English Poems I–II* (which includes "Inscriptions" and a revised version of "Antinous") and *English Poems III* ("Epithalamium," written in 1913).

## 1922

**October:** Pessoa publishes, in *Contemporânea*, "Mar Português" ("Portuguese Sea"), a sequence of twelve poems, eleven of which will be included in *Mensagem (Message)*.

**November:** Olisipo publishes a revised and enlarged version of *Canções (Songs)*, a book of poems by the openly homosexual António Botto.

## 1923

**February:** Olisipo publishes *Sodoma Divinizada* (*Sodom Deified*), by Raul Leal.

**March:** In response to a campaign by conservative students against the so-called Literature of Sodom, the government bans various books deemed immoral, including Leal's *Sodom Deified* and Botto's *Songs*. Pessoa publishes two manifestos—one in his own name and the other signed by Álvaro de Campos—criticizing the students and defending Leal against their personal attacks.

**July 21:** Pessoa's sister marries Francisco Caetano Dias, known as Chico, and takes their semi-invalid mother to live with her and her husband.

## 1924

**October:** Ricardo Reis makes his first public appearance with twenty odes published in the magazine *Athena: Revista de Arte*. Pessoa is the magazine's literary editor.

## 1925

**March:** The fourth issue of *Athena* (dated January) presents Alberto Caeiro to the public, with twenty-three poems from *O guardador de rebanhos* (*The Keeper of Sheep*).

**March 17:** Pessoa's mother dies.

**June:** The fifth and last issue of *Athena* (dated February) includes sixteen of Caeiro's *Poemas inconjuntos* (Uncollected Poems).

**November 16:** Birth of Manuela Nogueira Rosa Dias, Pessoa's only niece to survive infancy.

## 1926

**January:** He and his brother-in-law found the *Revista de Comércio e Contabilidade* (*Business and Accounting Review*), which will run for six issues.

**May 28:** A coup d'état establishes a military dictatorship in Portugal.

## 1927

**June 4:** Becomes a contributor to *Presença*, an art and literary review where he will publish some of his finest poems and prose pieces over the next several years. Even though Pessoa is not well-known, the young editors of *Presença* consider him to be Portugal's most significant living writer.

## 1928

**January 15:** Writes "The Tobacco Shop," attributed to Álvaro de Campos.

**March:** Publishes *The Interregnum*, a booklet that defends and justifies military dictatorship as a necessary "State of Transition" in politically unstable Portugal. (Pessoa will repudiate *The Interregnum* in 1935.)

**April 26:** António de Oliveira Salazar is appointed finance minister and granted sweeping powers.

**August:** Pessoa begins to write prose passages in the name of the suicidal Baron of Teive.

## 1929

**March 22:** First dated passage from the final and most intense phase of *The Book of Disquiet*, attributed to the "semiheteronym" Bernardo Soares. Eleven passages will appear in periodicals between 1929 and 1932. Hundreds of others will not be published until decades after Pessoa's death.

**September:** Rekindles his relationship with Ophelia Queiroz.

**December:** Strikes up a correspondence with Aleister Crowley, the English magus and occult master, after reading his autobiographical *Confessions*.

## 1930

**January 11:** Writes his last letter to Ophelia Queiroz. They will continue to see each other, and she will keep writing letters, for another year.

**July 23:** Writes the last two dated poems of Alberto Caeiro.

**September 2:** Aleister Crowley arrives in Lisbon with a girlfriend and is met by Pessoa.

**September 23:** Helps Crowley stage a fake suicide, which receives considerable news coverage.

## 1931

**January 1:** Birth of Luís Miguel Rosa Dias, Pessoa's only nephew.

**April 1:** Writes "Autopsicografia" ("Autopsychography").

## 1932

**July 5:** António de Oliveira Salazar is appointed prime minister and becomes de facto dictator.

**September 16:** Pessoa submits an (unsuccessful) application for the post of curator/librarian at the Condes de Castro Guimarães Museum-Library, in Cascais.

## 1933

**January:** Five of his poems, translated into French, are published in *Cahiers du Sud* (Marseille).

**March 19:** A national referendum approves a new constitution that marks the inception of Salazar's so-called Estado Novo (New State).

## 1934

**July:** Pessoa begins writing a long run of Portuguese folk quatrains (*quadras populares*)—more than 350.

**December 1:** Publishes *Mensagem* (*Message*), the only book of his Portuguese poetry to see print in his lifetime. The book is awarded a prize by the Secretariat of National Propaganda.

## 1935

**February 4:** Publishes, in the *Diário de Lisboa*, an article against a proposed law to ban Freemasonry. The National Assembly will unanimously ratify the law in April.

**March 16:** Date of his first poem, "Liberdade" ("Freedom"), against Salazar and the New State.

**October 21:** Writes "Todas as cartas de amor são ridículas" ("All love letters are ridiculous"), the last dated poem of Álvaro de Campos.

**November 13:** Writes "Vivem em nós inúmeros" ("Countless lives inhabit us"), the last dated poem of Ricardo Reis.

**November 19:** Writes "Há doenças piores que as doenças" ("There are sicknesses worse than any sickness"), his last dated poem in Portuguese.

**November 22:** Writes "The happy sun is shining," his last dated poem in English.

**November 29:** Admitted into the hospital with severe abdominal pain. There he writes his last words, in English: "I know not what to-morrow will bring."

**November 30:** Dies at around 8:30 p.m., probably from intestinal obstruction.

**December 2:** Buried in Lisbon at Prazeres Cemetery, where Luís de Montalvor, from the *Orpheu* group, delivers a short speech to a crowd of about sixty people.

# Notes

Most of Pessoa's surviving letters have been published in *Correspondência, 1905–1922* and *Correspondência, 1923–1935*, or in *Cartas*, vol. 7 of *Obra essencial de Fernando Pessoa*. Some of his more important letters were translated into English and included in *The Selected Prose of Fernando Pessoa*.

Unless otherwise indicated, letters sent to Pessoa by his mother, his stepfather, and his stepsister, as well as those exchanged between his maternal relatives, are unpublished and belong to the Collection of Pessoa Family Letters. All the letters he exchanged with Ophelia Queiroz were published in Pessoa and Queiroz, *Correspondência amorosa completa, 1919–1935*. The letters he received from Mário de Sá-Carneiro have been published in *Cartas de Mário de Sá-Carneiro a Fernando Pessoa* (2001) and in other editions.

Articles, essays, and other prose works by Pessoa published in his lifetime can be found in *Crítica*, in *Prosa publicada em vida* (vol. 3 of *Obra essencial*), and in the online Digital Edition of Fernando Pessoa. His diaries and many autobiographical texts are in *Escritas autobiográficas, automáticas e de reflexão pessoal*. Books from Pessoa's personal library, unless otherwise indicated, may be consulted online at the Casa Fernando Pessoa website.

Most of my English translations of Pessoa's poetry can be found in *Fernando Pessoa & Co.* and *A Little Larger than the Entire Universe*. (These are very different selections, with virtually no overlap.)

Full bibliographic information for the works above, as well as for the frequently cited works in the list below, can be found in Sources and References.

In my frequent references to the Fernando Pessoa Archive, the numbers *after* the slash indicate the documents contained in the envelope whose catalogue number appears *before* the slash. For instance, "doc. 134A/93v" refers to the reverse side (v, for verso) of document 93, located in envelope 134A. In the case of Pessoa's notebooks, the numbers *after* the slash correspond to the folios in the notebook whose catalogue number appears *before* the slash. "Ntbk. 144B/50–51" refers to folios 50 and 51 in the notebook catalogued under the number 144B.

## ABBREVIATIONS USED IN THE NOTES

| | |
|---|---|
| *CA* | Pessoa. *Cartas astrológicas*. Cardoso, ed. |
| CPH | Collection of Pessoa's Heirs |
| *Disquiet* | Pessoa. *The Book of Disquiet*. Zenith, ed. |
| *DL* | *Diário de Lisboa* |
| *DN* | *Diário de Notícias* (Lisbon) |
| doc. | Document from the Fernando Pessoa Archive |
| *EA* | Pessoa. *Escritos autobiográficos, automáticos e de reflexão pessoal*. Zenith, ed. |
| env. | Envelope from the Fernando Pessoa Archive |
| *Exílios* | Jennings. *Os dois exílios: Fernando Pessoa na África do Sul* |
| *Fascismo* | Pessoa. *Sobre o fascismo, a ditadura militar e Salazar*. Barreto, ed. |
| *Foto XX* | Vieira and Zenith. *Fotobiografias do séc. XX: Fernando Pessoa* |
| *Génio* | Pessoa. *Escritos sobre génio e loucura*. Pizarro, ed. |
| *Imagens* | Nogueira. *Fernando Pessoa: Imagens de uma vida* |
| *Intimidade* | França. *Fernando Pessoa na intimidade* |
| *Notas* | Costa. *Fernando Pessoa: Notas a uma biografia romanceada* |
| ntbk. | Notebook from the Fernando Pessoa Archive |
| *Objectos* | Pizarro, Ferrari, and Cardiello. *Os objectos de Fernando Pessoa* |
| *OE* | Pessoa. *Obra essencial de Fernando Pessoa*. Zenith, ed. |
| *SP* | Pessoa. *The Selected Prose of Fernando Pessoa*. Zenith, ed. |
| *TNM* | *The Natal Mercury* (Durban) |
| *Vida* | Simões. *Vida e obra de Fernando Pessoa* |

## PROLOGUE

1. Letter signed by Campos and published in *Contemporânea*, Oct. 1922, p. 4.
2. Arthur Rimbaud to Georges Izambard, 13 May 1871.
3. *Disquiet*, text 310.
4. Docs. 20/74–77. *SP*, 262.
5. Docs. 27$^{18}$A$^3$/51–52; 20/12. *EA*, 76–78.
6. *Disquiet*, texts 23 and 331.
7. Ibid., text 247.
8. Doc. 133B/36; first published in *OE*, 5:11. To better replicate the verse recorded by Pessoa, who was citing a Portuguese Bible translated from the Vulgate, I've cited the verse in English as it appears in the Douay-Rheims Bible, also translated from the Vulgate.

## CHAPTER 1

1. *DN*, 14 June 1888, p. 1. On the strong winds: *Diário Ilustrado*, 14 June 1888, p. 3.
2. *Disquiet*, text 438.
3. Ibid., text 138.
4. Ibid., texts 259 and 30.
5. *Vida*, 36.

**6.** Obituaries in *O Comércio de Portugal*, 29 June 1884, p. 2, and in *DN*, 29 June 1884, p. 1. Entries for Luiz Antonio Nogueira in *Encyclopedia portugueza illustrada* (Porto: Lemos, 1900–1909) and *Portugal: Diccionario historico, chorographico, heraldico, bibliographico, numismatico e artistico* (Lisbon: João Romano Torres, 1911). One of the obituaries erroneously states that the son, Luiz António Jr., died at the age of seventeen in 1883; he was in fact born in 1863 and died on 30 Mar. 1882. The oldest son, Guilherme Pinheiro Nogueira, died on 18 Feb. 1870, at age fifteen.

**7.** Interview with Manuela Nogueira, Pessoa's niece, repeating a story she heard from her mother.

**8.** *DN*, 14 July 1893, p. 1.

**9.** Manuel Cadafaz de Matos, *Joaquim Seabra Pessoa ou o engenho sensível*, 22. Bernhardt played the Comtesse Marthe de Rocca, in *L'Aveu*, a play she wrote; critical reactions were mixed.

**10.** Dossier ("Processo Individual") on Joaquim António de Araújo, Arquivo Histórico Militar. Amadeu Fernandes, "Fernando Pessoa e Tavira," mentions a José de Seabra Pessoa, the brother of Pessoa's father. Pessoa sketched in his own hand a family tree that includes a paternal uncle, "J. Pessoa," whose death is attributed to tuberculosis (doc. 134A/93v), reproduced in *Génio*, 323, and *Foto XX*, 33.

**11.** Henrique Marques, *Memórias de um editor*, 97–105. Seabra's fluency in French and Italian: *DN*, 14 July 1893, p. 1.

**12.** The books are mentioned in Madalena Pinheiro Nogueira's 14 Nov. 1893 letter to her daughter.

**13.** CPH. Each scrapbook corresponded to a performance season, typically running from September or October to June, with occasional news items for the summer months.

**14.** The porcelain is mentioned in Madalena Pinheiro Nogueira's 16 Mar. 1894 letter to her daughter, Pessoa's mother.

**15.** *EA*, 204; the autobiographical notes are dated 30 Mar. 1935. Sancho Pessoa da Cunha's younger brother, Manuel, is the patrilineal ancestor of Fernando Pessoa for that generation, but Sancho is just as much a blood ancestor, since his daughter, Rosa Maria Pessoa, was the wife of Manuel's son, Diogo Nunes da Cunha Pessoa, who was next in the male line of succession. The "da Cunha" surname in Pessoa's lineage goes back at least as far as Pero da Cunha, a nobleman in the service of the sixteenth-century kings Manuel I and João III. A few New Christians were members of the nobility, and this may have been Pero da Cunha's case. If it was not, then either he or his son married a New Christian, according to the genealogical evidence.

**16.** Ofir Chagas, *Tavira: Memórias de uma Cidade*, entry on Jacques Pessoa.

**17.** The passage quoted (doc. 19/59v) is from his unfinished essay "Erostratus," in Pessoa, *Heróstrato*, 182.

**18.** Letter of 8 Feb. 1918. According to the charts he received from the *British Journal of Astrology*, Pessoa was born at 3:11:49 p.m. and conceived on 20 Sept. 1887 at 1:47:34 a.m. (doc. S5/87). In a chart he cast for himself, he arrived at a "prenatal epoch" that was about seven minutes earlier (ntbk. 144X/9). *CA*, 43, 47–49.

**19.** Doc. 28/99. Ntbk. 144C²/8v. *EA*, 45.

**20.** One of the holy cards (CPH) was reproduced in Maria José de Lancastre, *Fernando Pessoa: Uma fotobiografia*, 41.

**21.** *Vida*, 33, 45. *Notas*, 28–29. *Exílios*, 23.

**22.** A letter to Maria Nogueira Pessoa from her mother, written on 14 Dec. 1893, indicates that Dionísia had at some point—probably in 1892, but possibly earlier—entered a clinic for an unspecified length of time.

**23.** Pessoa's sister reported that the two housekeepers were elderly (*Intimidade*, 21). In a letter to her daughter (Pessoa's mother) dated 14 Dec. 1893, Madalena Pinheiro Nogueira, who had lived on and off in Lisbon during the preceding years, recalls that "there seemed to be hardly a week when [Joana] wasn't laid up in bed for 2 or 3 days." In a letter written a month earlier, on

15 Nov., she reminds her daughter that she had been deeply unhappy in her marriage except during the first year. That Pessoa's mother was prone to tears when unhappy is revealed in letters to her sister dated 19 Feb. 1895 and 4 Mar. 1895.

**24.** Joaquim Seabra Pessoa published a note of thanks to Dr. Joaquim de Andrade Neves for treatment received (clipping saved by Neves's heirs—newspaper and date unknown). An obituary described him as a homeopath (*DN*, 7 Sept. 1892, p. 4).

**25.** An idea mentioned, for instance, in his "A Metaphysical Theory" (docs. 22/21–22) and in his 13 Jan. 1935 letter to Adolfo Casais Monteiro.

**26.** The Belle Époque, running from the end of the Franco-Prussian War, in 1871, to the outbreak of World War I, is sometimes defined more narrowly as the period 1890–1914.

**27.** *DN*, 6 June 1888.

**28.** *Intimidade*, 30.

**29.** On a page of notes (doc. S6/16) linking autobiographical events to his astrological con-junctions, Pessoa wrote, "Oct. 1892 (end learning [to] read?)."

**30.** Reported by a family member in *Acção*, 19 June 1937, p. 8. The family friend was Álvaro Franco, according to *Notas*, 36.

## CHAPTER 2

**1.** Information on Lisbela obtained from conversations with Inês and Isabel Sarmento, as well as with Maria Manuela Pessoa Chaves. Information on Lisbela's husband, Romão Aurelio da Cruz Machado obtained from his dossier ("Processo Individual") at the Arquivo Histórico Militar. Aunt Anica, through her daughter Maria, told Pessoa that he'd traveled to the Algarve when he was two years old (doc. Anexo IV/20v).

**2.** *Correio da Noite*, 6 Sept. 1887.

**3.** João Korth, of Dutch ancestry but born in Angra do Heroísmo (Pedro de Merelim, *Fer-nando Pessoa e a Terceira*, 14), had been practicing medicine in Lisbon for at least ten years.

**4.** Obituaries published in *DN* and *Correio da Noite* on 14 July 1893. Joaquim Seabra Pes-soa's death registration states that he did not receive the Church's last rites. The letters he wrote from Caneças and Telheiras (the latter village is now part of Lisbon) were published in Manuel Cadafaz de Matos, *Joaquim Seabra Pessoa ou o engenho sensível*.

**5.** Ida Fuller (1867–1922) was the sister-in-law of Loïe Fuller (1862–1928), another and more renowned "serpentine" dancer. Information on both dancers from the blog Red Pou-laine's Musings, http://redpoulaine.blogspot.com/2013/07/ida-pinckney-fuller-belle-epoque .html, accessed Nov. 2018. Fuller's Lisbon perfomance described in *Ocidente* (Lisbon), 21 July 1893, p. 162.

**6.** *Disquiet*, text 30.

**7.** Auction mentioned in Madalena Pinheiro Nogueira's 16 Mar. 1894 letter to her daugh-ter. Information on the furniture removed to the new apartment: Madalena's 28 July 1894 letter to her daughter.

**8.** The possibility of meningitis is alluded to in Anica's 2 Jan. 1894 letter to her sister. It has been suggested that the smallpox vaccine may have contributed to his death, but Jorge's visible reaction to it—a skin rash—had ceased well before.

**9.** *DN*, 3 Jan. 1894, p. 1.

**10.** Maria's economic dependence on her mother-in-law is alluded to in Madalena Pinheiro Nogueira's 5 Mar. 1894 and 3 Oct. 1894 letters to her daughter.

**11.** *Notas*, 37.

**12.** The poem "Só!" (Alone!), which Maria Madalena wrote on 27 Aug. 1894—one day after she wrote "Desejos!" (Desires!), an ardent love poem to João Miguel Rosa—has been pub-lished as if it were in memory of her first husband (*Imagens*, 31). This was certainly not the case. The "coldness of the grave" mentioned in the poem's first stanza is not a reference to her first husband's death but a metaphor for what the speaker feels in her soul "when I part from you"—as she explains in another stanza, written firmly in the present tense. She is in fact describing the circumstance of finding herself alone after having enjoyed her lover's company. Furthermore, the graveyard motif reappears in the exact same formulation at the conclusion of her poem "O teu cigarro" ("Your Cigarette"), which is dedicated "[t]o my beloved and adored João" and dated 24 Jan. 1895 (CPH).

13. Madalena Nogueira Pinheiro's 15 Apr. 1894 and 2 Dec. 1894 letters to her daughter.

14. The movements of the *Liberal* and of João Miguel Rosa are recorded in the Ordens da Armada for 1894 and, in more detail, in Livro Mestre C, p. 131, at the Arquivo Histórico da Marinha, Lisbon.

15. Madalena Pinheiro Nogueira to Maria Nogueira Pessoa, 13 July 1894.

16. Madalena Pinheiro Nogueira to Anica Nogueira de Freitas, 3 Jan. 1895.

17. *Jornal do Comércio*, 16 Feb. 1893, p. 2.

18. Jaime de Andrade Neves Collection.

19. The Queen Amélia Gold Medal was awarded to Rosa in 1896. Travel information extracted from the letters of Pessoa's mother (now Maria Nogueira Rosa) to her sister, Anica, dated 19 Feb. 1895 and 18 Mar. 1895. On the Mozambican uprising and the Portuguese response, see António Enes, *A guerra de África em 1895* (Lisbon: Typographia do "Dia," 1898), especially 25–26 and 108–9.

20. *Anuário diplomátio e consular português* for 1916–1917. João Rosa's dossier in the Arquivo Histórico da Marinha.

## CHAPTER 3

1. Madalena Pinheiro Nogueira to Anica Nogueira de Freitas, 3 Jan. 1895.

2. He typed "Beg. knowl. m. & st-f" next to a planetary conjunction occurring after he turned six (doc. 90$^1$/62).

3. *Vida*, pt. 1, ch. 3.

4. What Maria wrote is deduced from her mother's reply, dated 28 July 1894.

5. Anica's letter of 21 Jan. 1894 is in Teresa Rita Lopes and Maria Fernanda de Abreu, *Fernando Pessoa, hóspede e peregrino*, 41.

6. From a poem that begins "Bem sei que tudo é natural" ("Yes, I know it's all quite natural").

7. *Disquiet*, texts 278 and 118.

8. "Diluente" (Diluent), dated 29 Aug. 1929.

9. *Foto XX*, 28, 33.

10. Madalena Pinheiro Nogueira cited her daughter's comment in a letter of 15 Nov. 1894.

11. *EA*, 68.

12. The sonnet of Pessoa's great-aunt Maria, and his remarks about her character, were published in Pessoa, *Cartas de Fernando Pessoa a Armando Côrtes-Rodrigues*, 75.

13. *Jornal do Comércio*, 26 Feb. 1895, p. 2. The opera was the Ricci brothers' *Crispino e la Comare*, popular at the time but seldom performed after the nineteenth century. Fernando's trip to the opera with his uncle is mentioned in Maria Nogueira Pessoa's 4 Mar. 1895 letter to her sister, Anica.

14. Details of Pessoa's relationship with Uncle Cunha and Aunt Maria can be gleaned from his mother's letters, such as her 4 Mar. 1895 letter to Anica, as well as from Uncle Cunha's letters to his nephew, two of which are in *Imagens*, 35–36. The fictitious newspapers linked to invented political parties (which are discussed further on) date from 1909.

15. From an unfinished preface for an unrealized publication of works by Pessoa's heteronyms. It has erroneously been published as a rough draft of his 13 Jan. 1935 letter to Adolfo Casais Monteiro.

16. Two letters, dated 20 July 1896 and 22 Mar. 1897, are in *Imagens*, 35–36. Other, still unpublished letters of Uncle Cunha in CPH provide a fuller picture of the alternate reality games he played with his nephew; excerpts in *Imagens*, 101–5.

17. The details in this and the preceding paragraphs are gleaned from unpublished family letters from 1894 through 1896.

## CHAPTER 4

1. Jorge Martins, "O Caso Dreyfus em França e Portugal," *História*, no. 70 (2004).
2. *Notas*, 38.
3. Docs. 49A⁵/55 (dated 1 Aug. 1918); 133A/60.
4. Maria Nogueira Pessoa to Anica Nogueira de Freitas, 19 Aug. 1895.
5. Ship records at Arquivo Histórico da Marinha, Box 499, indicate that the *Liberal* sailed from Lourenço Marques to Durban on 16 July 1893, landing there on the eighteenth, and began the return voyage on August 16. According to the Portuguese Consular Archives in Durban, in April 1895 the Castle Shipping Line—whose ships plied between Europe and southern Africa—lodged a formal complaint against João Rosa's immediate predecessor for not expediting a bill of health needed by one of its steamers to get under way. Rosa was named consul a few months after this episode.
6. The black velvet dress is mentioned in Anica's 16 Oct. 1894 and 2 Dec. 1894 letters to her sister, Maria. According to Maria's 4 Oct. 1895 letter to Anica, she had not yet met Henrique Rosa as of that date.
7. Madalena Pinheiro Nogueira was on the passenger list of the *Açor*, which left Lisbon for the Azores on 5 Jan. 1896, as reported by Pedro da Silveira in Pedro de Merelim, *Fernando Pessoa e a Terceira*, 90. Information on Dionísia extracted from Maria Nogueira Pessoa's 19 Apr. 1895 and 8 May 1895 letters to her sister, Anica. Hospital admission records (now at the Torre de Tombo): folio 137, admission no. 1365; folio 142, admission no. 1412. The journal of income and expenses for Dionísia kept by Maria Pinheiro Nogueira belongs to Pessoa's heirs.
8. This story, which circulated among family members, was reported in print two years after the poet's death, in *Acção*, 19 June 1937, p. 8.
9. *Disquiet*, text 165.
10. Thomas Pakenham's *The Scramble for Africa* is an excellent survey, although it does not cover the Portuguese-British dispute that culminated in the British Ultimatum.
11. Nuno Severiano Teixeira, "Política externa e política interna no Portugal de 1890: O Ultimatum Inglês," *Análise Social* 23, no. 4 (1987): 687–719.
12. Doc. 133E/84.

## CHAPTER 5

1. *Intimidade*, 27.
2. *The Standard* (London), 22 Jan. 1896, p. 1; *Diário de Notícias* (Funchal), 31 Jan. 1896, p. 2.
3. Uncle Cunha's 31 Aug. 1896 letter to Fernando refers to the two "spies" they spotted on the outward voyage (CPH).
4. The historian James Bryce described his 1895 voyage on the *Hawarden Castle* and arrival at Cape Town in *Impressions of South Africa*, 189–90.
5. The *Hawarden*'s arrival was reported in *TNM*, 21 Feb. and 22 Feb. 1896, under the shipping notes. Hubert Jennings, in two of his books on Pessoa, states that steamships did not enter Port Natal, Durban's harbor, before 1904, the year when monumental engineering works were finally completed. In fact midsized steamers such as the *Hawarden Castle* were already calling there on a weekly basis in the 1890s. The average depth of the water varied according to the tides and the time of year, however, so that even midsized steamers were sometimes forced to remain at the outer anchorage, from where lighters would convey passengers and cargo to the piers: Bryce, *Impressions of South Africa*, 180 and 282–83.
6. "Tersilian [sic] House, on Ridge Road" is mentioned in *Vida*, 63. Research at the Durban deeds office, undertaken on my behalf by Bryan Lee and Lenn Mostart, indicates that a John Francis Hitchens owned the property "Tresilian," at 60 South Ridge Road (now Mazisi Kunene Road), prior to 1902. My description of the house is based on Lee's reading of a 1931 aerial photograph of Tresilian House and vicinity; the house was demolished sometime thereafter. On the typical house style of the period: Franco Frescura and Barbara Maude-Stone, *Durban: Once upon a Time*, 109.

**7.** *Natal Almanac, Directory, and Yearly Register,* years 1896 to 1900.

**8.** *Imagens,* 35.

**9.** Two front-page obituaries were published on 26 Jan. 1898, in *Correio da Noite* and *DN.* José Luciano de Castro, the leader of the Progressives and current prime minister, attended Uncle Cunha's funeral.

**10.** The workers' names are recorded in the Portuguese Consular Archives in Durban.

**11.** Malyn Newitt, *A History of Mozambique* (Bloomington: Indiana University Press, 1995), 482–85; A. H. de Oliveira Marques, *História de Portugal* (Lisbon: Palas Editores, 1986), vol. 3, 195.

**12.** Registration of Servants Act #2, 1888.

**13.** According to Pessoa's sister, in *Intimidade,* 60.

**14.** Bryce, *Impressions of South Africa,* 283–85.

**15.** Yvonne Miller, *Dear Old Durban,* 6, 10, 32. Miller's memories go back as far as 1910. Pessoa would live in Durban until 1905.

**16.** On 11 May 1896, *TNM* reported: "So pleased are they with the town and climate that Mrs. and Miss Clemens are staying here a fortnight longer." Twain's South African sojourn was researched and recounted in amusing detail by Coleman O. Parsons in "Mark Twain: Traveler in South Africa," *Mississippi Quarterly,* Winter 1975–1976.

**17.** This book is in Pessoa's personal library at the Casa Fernando Pessoa. Pessoa's heirs possess the surviving table of contents for another Twain book acquired by Pessoa in Durban, *The Celebrated Jumping Frog of Calaveras County, and Other Sketches.*

**18.** Pessoa's letters to his maternal grandmother have not survived, but he saved a letter she wrote him on 15 Aug. 1896.

**19.** Several books of Portuguese poetry that belonged to Pessoa in Durban have survived in his personal library, kept at the Casa Fernando Pessoa; another one is at the National Library of Portugal.

**20.** *TNM,* 21 Dec. 1898. Prizes, including an annual examination prize, were awarded for each of the five classes, or grades, in the "kindergarten" (primary school). Fernando Pessoa was in the "first class," or fifth grade. His prize for Latin was a book by Joseph Smith Fletcher, *The Remarkable Adventure of Walter Trelawney.* The other two prizes may also have been books.

**21.** Docs. 28/69–70. *EA,* 66–69.

## CHAPTER 6

**1.** In actual fact, the great majority of the Indian passengers had already established themselves in South Africa or else were going there to join relatives.

**2.** Gandhi would remember the train station episode as having occurred seven days after arriving in Durban. Historians have proven that it actually took place on June 7, two weeks after his arrival: John Laband and Robert Haswell, eds., *Pietermaritzburg 1838–1988: A New Portrait of an African City* (Pietermaritzburg: University of Natal Press/Shuter & Shooter, 1988), 201.

**3.** In his *The Story of My Experiments with Truth,* Gandhi gives the date of the founding of the Congress as May 22, 1894, three months earlier than was the case.

**4.** *TNM,* 14 Jan. 1897, pp. 4–5.

**5.** *Time,* 31 Mar. 1930. He would reappear on the 5 Jan. 1931 cover as the Man of the Year.

**6.** Docs. 55H/64-65. *Foto XX,* 50–51.

**7.** *Disquiet,* text 258.

**8.** See Leela Gandhi, "Pessoa's Gandhi: Meditating on a Lost Heteronym" for reflections on Pessoa's encounter with Gandhi in the light of Alain Badiou's claim that philosophical thinking is "not yet *worthy of Pessoa*" (Badiou, "A Philosophical Task: To Be Contemporaries of Pessoa," 36).

## CHAPTER 7

1. Pessoa's sister reported that the family was already living at 157 West Street at the time of her birth (*Intimidade*, 30), but the *Natal Almanac, Directory, and Yearly Register* indicates that a tailor occupied those premises until at least 1897. There are no known photographs of the West Street dwelling's façade, but an insurance-company map for the town of Durban in 1931 (kept at the Don Africana Library in Durban) and aerial photos show the building to be as described in the text. (I owe this information to Durban architect and historian Brian Kearney.) In 1935, the house gave way to an automobile showroom, which still exists. On the Ocean View Hotel: J. Forsyth Ingram, *The Story of an African Seaport* (Durban: G. Coester, 1899), 175. My chronology of Pessoa's successive domiciles in Durban was established by collating family recollections, documents found in Pessoa's archives, Durban building records, address listings in annual directories for Natal, and information (not always accurate) provided to Gaspar Simões by Portugal's consul to Durban in 1949 (that consul's letter is in the Fernando Távora Collection).
2. Pessoa's mother would remember their outings to the bay beach in a 15 July 1911 letter to her son.
3. Pessoa's mother seems to have written her poetry in spates. Most of her known poems are from two periods, from 1894 to 1895 (CPH) and from 12 July 1898 to 6 Mar. 1899 (Ponta Delgada Public Library, in the Azores).
4. *TNM*, 24 Dec. 1898.
5. H. D. Jennings to Alexandrino Severino, 17 May 1965, in Severino, *Fernando Pessoa na África do Sul* (1970), 121–23.
6. Eric Anderson Walker, *The Cambridge History of the British Empire* (Cambridge: Cambridge University Press, 1963), vol. 8, 275–77.
7. Doc. 97/34. Pessoa, *Ultimatum e páginas de sociologia política*, 186.
8. Jeremy J. Oddy, *Where the Baobab Grows at Durban High School*, 40. Ernest A. Belcher and G. Churton Collins, *The Durban High School Record 1866–1906*, 56–58.
9. Hubert Dudley Jennings, *The D.H.S. Story 1866–1966*, 83, 85. Hubert Dudley Jennings, *Fernando Pessoa in Durban*, 9–10. *Exílios*, 201.
10. Oddy, *Where the Baobab Grows*, 40.
11. *Disquiet*, text 237.
12. Letter to Adolfo Casais Monteiro dated 20 Jan. 1935.
13. H. J. Ogden, *The War Against the Dutch Republics in South Africa* (Manchester: National Reform Union, 1901), 40.
14. Doc. 55H/80. Pessoa, *Ultimatum e páginas de sociologia política*, 238.

## CHAPTER 8

1. "Joseph Chamberlain," dated February 1905.
2. Byron Farwell, "Taking Sides in the Boer War," *American Heritage*, April 1976 (consulted online).
3. "Ultimatum" (1917), in *SP*, 72.
4. My thumbnail sketch of the war relies on Thomas Pakenham's reading of events in *The Boer War*.
5. Clifford Geerdts, cited in Hubert Dudley Jennings, *Fernando Pessoa in Durban*, 20.
6. *Collected Works of Mahatma Gandhi*, vol. 2 (New Delhi: Publications Division Government of India, 1999) (e-book, consulted online).
7. Johan Wassermann and Brian Kearney, eds., *A Warrior's Gateway: Durban and the Anglo-Boer War*, 380, citing Peter Warwick, *Black People and the South African War, 1899–1902* (Cambridge: Cambridge University Press, 1983), 127–28.
8. Information on European, Indian, and native African refugees from Wasserman and Kearney, *A Warrior's Gateway*, 251–52 and 381. On Indian refugees only: Coolam Vahed,

"Natal's Indians, the Empire and the South African War, 1899–1902," *New Contree* 45, September 1999, pp. 185–216 (consulted online).

9. Franco Frescura and Barbara Maude-Stone, *Durban: Once upon a Time*, 119.

10. Wassermann and Kearney, *A Warrior's Gateway*, 248.

11. *Disquiet*, texts 132, 138, and 420.

12. *TNM*, 25 Dec. 1899, p. 5.

13. Wassermann and Kearney, *A Warrior's Gateway*, 247.

14. Ntbk. 144B. C. Mazansky, "Cigarette Cards and South African Military History," *Military History Journal* (Kengray, South Africa) 8, no. 2, December 1989 (consulted online).

15. *Diário Ilustrado*, 29 Mar. 1901, p. 3. Fernando Costa, *Portugal e a Guerra Anglo-Boer*.

16. Ntbk. 144B/8–9.

17. The Sand novel is listed in Pessoa's notes as a textbook assigned in 1901 (ntbk. 144B/15). The "L." in Pessoa's signature also appears in two Latin textbooks he used in 1904: *Revised Latin Primer* and *A Practical Introduction to Latin Prose Composition*. See Jennings, *Fernando Pessoa in Durban*, 19–20.

18. Wassermann and Kearney, *A Warrior's Gateway*, 272. Anglo-Boer War Museum website: http://www.anglo-boer.co.za/. Pakenham, *Boer War*, 493–510 and 572–73.

19. "A Opinião Pública," *A Acção*, 4 Aug. 1919. *OE*, 3:315–34.

20. In 1914 Pessoa would tell his friend Armando Côrtes-Rodrigues that, except for the quatrain to his mother when he was seven, he produced no poetry until 1901. A poem titled "Anamnesis" has repeatedly and erroneously been cited as being written and dated by Pessoa on the same day as "Separated from thee"; it was actually written in 1915.

21. The twelve surviving pages of the mock newspaper were reproduced in Richard Zenith, ed., *Fernando Pessoa: O editor, o escritor e os seus leitores*, 134–36. Excluding the sports section, which was Pessoa's own doing, I easily located all the English content of the paper in various newspapers of the period posted on the internet, as well as some of the French content.

22. Pessoa referred more than once to his fondness for *The Pickwick Papers*. In a 1985 interview (Henriqueta Madalena Rosa Dias/Maria Ivone de Ornellas de Andrade, "Ele sabia o valor que tinha," *Jornal de Letras*, 26 Nov.–2 Dec. 1985, p. 6), Pessoa's sister reported that the book was well worn from being so often read; its current whereabouts are unknown.

23. Doc. 48B/134.

24. *Disquiet*, text 195.

25. Doc. 19/97. *SP*, 217–18.

26. *Disquiet*, "Our Lady of Silence."

27. Alexandrino E. Severino, *Fernando Pessoa na África do Sul* (1970), 143. *Imagens*, 39.

28. "Report for Half-Year ending June 26th, 1901," in *Exílios*, 187.

29. "Correspondência expedida para o Ministério dos Negócios Estrangeiros de 27 outubro 1896 a 22 agosto 1903," Portuguese Consular Archives, Dublin.

30. The sailing date for the *König*, mentioned in the consul's follow-up letter, is confirmed by the shipping notes of *TNM*, 2 Aug. 1901. On the death of Pessoa's sister, see *Intimidade*, 51.

## CHAPTER 9

1. *Jornal do Comércio*, 14 Sept. 1901, p. 1.

2. A surviving rent receipt (CPH) suggests that the Rosa family may not have occupied the apartment on Rua de Pedrouços until January 1, 1902, and the *Anuário comercial de Portugal Ilhas e Ultramar* for 1902 (compiled in late 1901) lists "Miguel Rosa, lieutenant captain of the navy" as a resident of Estoril. It's possible that the Rosa family stayed for the last few months of 1901 in this seaside town, which is west of Lisbon and on the same train line as Pedrouços, while Fernando stayed with his great-aunts and grandmother. João Miguel Rosa, however, was a full captain (since 1895), not a lieutenant captain.

3. In a 13 June 1894 letter to her daughter Anica, Madalena Pinheiro Nogueira sent her greeting to Lisbela, who had come up to Lisbon from Tavira. The whereabouts of Pessoa's

letters to Aunt Lisbela are unknown, but an heir who had them in her possession remembered reading a letter sent from Durban in which Fernando expressed thanks for the hospitality extended to him when in Tavira: Amadeu Fernandes, "Fernando Pessoa e Tavira," p. 9. This suggests that he visited Tavira in the summer of 1902, perhaps for a second time during his Portuguese holiday, shortly before returning to Durban.

4. Júlio Leopoldo Rosa, three years older than João Miguel Rosa, was a civil engineer and overseer of public works; he was married but with no offspring. Obituary in *DN*, 8 Nov. 1912, p. 4.

5. Copies of *O Pimpão* belonging to Henrique Rosa are now in the custody of Pessoa's heirs.

6. Facsimiles of Pessoa's make-believe newspapers from 1902 published in Teresa Rita Lopes, *Pessoa por conhecer*, 130–45. The issues of *O Palrador* are in the Pessoa Archive (docs. 87/23–25). The surviving issues of *A Palavra*, discussed further on, are in CPH.

7. *Revised Latin Primer.* The primer also contains signatures of Pessoa himself and of his heteronym C. R. Anon.

8. Diabo Azul was a pen name used by the Portuguese writer Narciso de Lacerda (1858–1913) for various story collections published between 1899 and 1902. He was not the only one, however, to furnish the stories attributed to Diabo Azul in *O Pimpão*: Jorge Abreu, *Boémia jornalística* (Lisbon: Guimarães, 1927), ch. 4.

9. Dated 5 July 1902.

10. Richard Zenith, "A Sonnet from the English," in *Reading Literature in Portuguese: Commentaries in Honour of Tom Earle*, ed. Cláudia Pazos Alonso and Stephen Parkinson (London: Legenda, 2013), 169–75.

11. The contributors to *The Tattler* with pen names borrowed from real journalists included not only Diabo Azul (Blue Devil), but also Pad Zé, which was short for Padre José, or Father Joe, the nickname of Alberto Costa (1877–1908), a law student at the University of Coimbra famous for his bohemian extravagance and quick wit. In 1899 Costa had put out three issues of a satirical magazine called *A Revista do Civil*, and in 1905 he would publish a mocking account of his university days, *The Book of Dr. Assis*, which was much appreciated by Pessoa.

12. Guiomar Silvano Pamplona Corte Real, a distant relative who saw Pessoa during the family's visit to Terceira, described him in Pedro de Merelim, *Fernando Pessoa e a Terceira*, 119–23.

13. Ibid., 20–21 and 87–107. *Intimidade*, 52.

14. Richard Zenith, "Quando, onde e como ela passa," in *Fernando Pessoa e Cia. não heterônima*, ed. Caio Gagliardi, 69–81. Jorge de Sena was the first scholar to note the connection of "When She Passes" to the António Nobre poem: see his *Fernando Pessoa e Cia. heterónima*, 283. Pessoa's partial translation of Gray's "Elegy" is in ntbk. 153/7–8.

15. Ntbk. 144B/49v–50v.

16. Henriqueta Madalena Rosa Dias/Maria Ivone de Ornellas de Andrade, "Ele sabia o valor que tinha," *Jornal de Letras*, 26 Nov.–2 Dec. 1985, p. 6.

17. *Intimidade*, 54. On the return voyage to Lisbon, see Pedro da Silveira, in Merelim, *Fernando Pessoa e a Terceira*, 104.

18. He had copied down the title, price, and shipping charges for the album in his memo book (ntbk. 144B/42). Facsimile image of stamp album, signed and dated by Pessoa in *Foto XX*, 54.

19. Facsimile in *Imagens*, 40.

20. Maria Nogueira Rosa to Fernando Pessoa, 11 May 1913.

21. The memo book he was using in 1902 contains the solutions to mathematical equations and story problems taken from a Portuguese textbook (ntbk. 144B/50–56).

22. Issues of 27 August, 24 September, 5 October, and 26 November, always on p. 7.

## CHAPTER 10

1. Government decree of 24 Dec. 1901 (information provided by Arquivo Histórico Militar). The document granting Pessoa this exemption is reproduced in Maria José de Lancastre, *Fernando Pessoa: Uma fotobiografia*, 106, and in *Foto XX*, 41.

**2.** *TNM*, a morning paper, reported on 16 Oct. 1902, that the *Herzog* was "outside" the harbor and on the eighteenth that it was "in harbor."

**3.** W. P. M. Henderson, *Durban: Fifty Years' Municipal History*, 116 and 210–15. Brian Kearney, "Bamboo Square: A Documentary Narrative," *Journal of Natal and Zulu History* 20 (2002): 29–64 (consulted online). João Miguel Rosa, in a letter sent to Portuguese authorities on 30 Nov. 1902, wrote that the first case of plague had been officially confirmed; the plague would resurface in April 1904 on a much smaller scale.

**4.** "School Vacations / Commercial School," *TNM*, Weekly Edition, 1 Jan. 1904, p. 14.

**5.** *Vida*, 80–81. Carlos Pittella, "Mr. Ormond: The Testimonial from a Classmate of Fernando Pessoa," *Pessoa Plural*, Fall 2017, pp. 194–235.

**6.** Hubert Dudley Jennings, *Fernando Pessoa in Durban*, 18.

**7.** *Vida*, 80. Pittella, "Mr. Ormond," p. 211.

**8.** This letter (doc. 114³/3) is transcribed in full in *OE*, 3:31–33.

**9.** *The Natal Who's Who* (1906). *1908 South African Who's Who* (Durban: Who's Who Publishing Co., 1908). See also articles in the Australian *Sydney Morning Herald*, 3 Oct. 1885, *West Coast Times*, 10 Feb. 1890, and *The Queenslander* (Brisbane), 21 Jan. 1891 (all consulted online).

**10.** Ntbk. 153/20, 26 and 66. On this last page a crossed-out note indicates that Effield was to author an unnamed play. Richard Zenith and Joaquim Vieira, *Fotobiografia de Fernando Pessoa*, 65, contains a facsimile of "The Miner's Song" as published in *TNM*. Handwritten request: doc. 49D²/18v. Envelope addressed to Effield in Durban: doc. 134/1.

**11.** Ntbk. 153/23. Docs. 77/20–21.

**12.** Ntbk. 153/8v, 27–29. "Martin Kéravas" was a potential pseudo-author as well as the title of a novel. Various examples of his signature can be found at the back of Pessoa's copy of *Pittman's Shorthand*.

**13.** Ntbk. 153/ 9v–10.

**14.** Ntbk. 153/12.

## CHAPTER 11

**1.** Christine Alexander, introduction to *Tales of Glass Town, Angria and Gondal: Selected Early Writings*, by the Brontës (London: Oxford University Press, 2010). David Daiches, introduction to *Wuthering Heights*, by Emily Brontë (London: Penguin, 1985).

**2.** Ntbk. 144R/1–13v.

**3.** Information on the story's serialization is at both http://www.friardale.co.uk/BFL and http://www.philsp.com/homeville. The complete story was subsequently published as a book, in 1906, a copy of which is in the dime novel collection of the Stanford University library, where Vincent Barletta graciously obtained a scanned copy for me. For a more detailed discussion, see Richard Zenith, "Barrowby, Boys' Books, and How to Make Literature," in *Fernando Pessoa as English Reader and Writer*, eds. Patricio Ferrari and Jerónimo Pizarro, 15–29.

**4.** Ntbk. 144R.

**5.** Docs. 104/38; 133M/39; 49B²/46v.

**6.** The relationship between the king and Piers Gaveston was the basis of Christopher Marlowe's play *Edward II*.

**7.** Doc. 49D¹/56.

**8.** Docs. 13A/37v; 14⁶/72v; 100/4.

**9.** There was also a single signature, dating from 1908, for a Martin Gaveston (doc. 92Q/31v). The three cited lines of verse are found on doc. 49D¹/56. The passage of "Essay on Poetry" topped by the name of Gaveston: doc. 13A/37v.

**10.** Three Yreka Jim novels were published c. 1900 in the Boy's First-Rate Pocket Library. The Australian writer Louis Becke's *Tom Wallis, a Tale of the South Seas* also appeared in 1900.

**11.** Ntbk. 144R/10v, 11r, 15v, 22–23. In what seems to be a tally of the very first session of "Derby" played, Gould is credited with the then considerable sum of £30, ruling out the possibility that any real betting was going on. Pessoa's sister recalled that the family sometimes played "Derby" in the evening after dinner (*Intimidade*, 67–68).

**12.** The Cato Lodge Cricket Club was mentioned in the sports section of Pessoa's newspaper in April 1901. The rosters drawn up by Pessoa date from August 1903 (ntbk. 144R/19v, 20). There are at least two surviving score sheets from mid-1904 for cricket matches involving players on the 1903 rosters (ntbk. 144S/15v, 16r, 17v, 18r). Other score sheets, with the names of different players, date from 1904–1905 (docs. 14⁶/76; 27⁹D²/51v, 52v; 49D¹/19). None of the full names on any of Pessoa's score sheets are to be found in Durban directories from the 1910s, by which time Pessoa's classmates would have been gainfully employed adults.

**13.** Doc. 124/39–42.

**14.** *Natal Almanac, Directory, and Yearly Register*, 1903, 1904, and 1905.

**15.** Like the poems that found their way into *TNM*, the puzzle column was part of a literary and opinion page titled "Man on the Moon," published each Saturday in the daily edition and again the following Friday in the weekly edition. Henderson Carr's literary projects are mentioned in ntbk. 144R/14–15.

**16.** *Disquiet*, text 114.

**17.** Doc. 28A/2.

**18.** Doc. 49A¹/3. Pessoa, *Poemas ingleses*, vol. 2, 173.

**19.** Most fragments from the early *Marino* verse drama were published in Pessoa, *Poemas ingleses*, 2:183–89, 193, and 200. Unpublished passages include docs. 11¹⁰MA/31, 38, 42. The unfinished "Vincenzo" was published in Pessoa, *Poemas ingleses*, 2:200–203. For the later, five-act version of *Marino*, Pessoa wrote a few unpublished passages and plot descriptions (env. 11¹⁰MA). A publication plan listing the poem "Vincenzo" (doc. 48C/6) dates from late 1907 or early 1908. Pessoa's surviving copy of Byron's complete poetical works (including the verse play *Marino Faliero*) was published in 1905, but we know that he started reading Byron several years earlier.

**20.** The expanded scope of the Commercial School was reported in *TNM*, 1 Jan. 1904, p. 14.

**21.** Pessoa's saved copies of the printed exam and results: docs. 28/71–87. Facsimile of official terms of the prize: Alexandrino E. Severino, *Fernando Pessoa na África do Sul* (1970), 179. Information on the number of examinees (899) provided by the Joint Matriculation Board of Pretoria to Gaspar Simões (*Vida*, 79n).

**22.** Facsimile of letter in Teresa Rita Lopes, *Fernando Pessoa: A biblioteca impossível* (Cascais: Câmara Municipal, 2010), appendix 3.

**23.** *Palgrave's Golden Treasury* and ten other Form VI textbooks have survived in Pessoa's personal library. Parts of the Intermediate Exam for 1904 and the syllabus of required readings are in Severino, *Fernando Pessoa na África do Sul* (1970), 166–78.

**24.** For exam results, see *Exílios*, 194. The book given as the prize was *The Nile Quest*, by Harry Johnston.

**25.** Pessoa also published some acrostics in the magazine (docs. 133I/52v, 53v). A facsimile of the Macaulay essay was published in Alexandrino E. Severino, *Fernando Pessoa e o mar português*, 64–67.

**26.** Hubert Dudley Jennings, *Fernando Pessoa in Durban*, 20. Geerdts's letter (docs. Anexo IV/25–28) was published in *EA*, 394–400.

**27.** Dr. Antunes's letter to Hardress O'Grady is in *EA*, 66–68. O'Grady's name appears on a short list of letters Pessoa intended to write in 1907 (doc. 28/99v).

**28.** Joaquim Vieira, *Portugal século XX: Anos 1900–1910*, 96. Johan Wassermann and Brian Kearney, eds., *A Warrior's Gateway: Durban and the Anglo-Boer War, 1899–1902*, 261.

**29.** In a lecture delivered in 1986 at Natal University in Durban (now part of the University of KwaZulu-Natal), Alexandrino Severino reported having seen Storm's letter in the early 1960s, when Pessoa's papers were still in the custody of his sister. The letter "was addressed to a psychiatrist in Lisbon who had written to inquire about a Mr. Pessoa's mental condition. The letter was very flattering to this Mr. Pessoa. Obviously, the psychiatrist was Pessoa himself, acting as if through one of his heteronyms, attempting to find out by way of a stratagem what others thought of him." See Severino, *Fernando Pessoa e o mar português*, 91. Mr. and Mrs. Storm are mentioned in letters Pessoa received from his mother in 1912. The couple had a son named William, who was eight years older than Pessoa, but he is not mentioned in the letters of Pessoa's mother and there does not seem to have been any friendship between them. It was no doubt William Sr. who was asked to evaluate Fernando's mental health as an adolescent.

**30.** *Exílios*, 197–98 (facsimile). *EA*, 390–92. The present whereabouts of this letter are unknown.

**31.** Docs. 133F/65v; 27⁹D²/46v.

**32.** Ntbk. 144S/12v.

**33.** *Disquiet*, text 457.

## CHAPTER 12

**1.** Pessoa's adoption of Milton's stanzaic scheme as well as several images from the "Nativity" ode is discussed in Patricio Ferrari, "Fernando Pessoa, poète-lecteur-théoricien: Des éxperiences métriques et rythmiques entre-langues," *Loxias* 30, 19 Sept. 2010 (consulted online).

**2.** Doc. 19/67. Pessoa, *Heróstrato*, 195–96.

**3.** Doc. 127F/1. Hubert Jennings, who published the rondeau (*Exílios*, 134), reported that O'Grady acted in the operetta, but the French teacher's name is not on the program.

**4.** Docs. 49B²/91; 49B⁴/33–34, 36, 40, 57, 99a, 100. Ntbk. 144S/13v. Most of the fragments are transcribed in Pessoa, *Poemas ingleses*, vol. 2, 176–78.

**5.** "A ceifeira" ("The Reaper"), as published in 1925 (*Athena* 3, dated December 1924).

**6.** A list of influences drawn up in 1914 is in *EA*, 150.

**7.** This poem was begun in 1904 (ntbks. 144S/10v–11; 153/9, 42, 51v–54v); it was revised, and more verses added, after Pessoa's return to Lisbon in 1905. Docs. 49B²/94v; 78B/39–43. Ntbks. 144J/8v, 24; 144T/19v–20. Transcribed in Pessoa, *Poemas ingleses*, 2:99–104. Three additional passages in CPH.

**8.** Most of the "Gahu" material is unpublished. Docs. 27⁹D²/43v; 49B²/40v; 49B⁶/42–44; 49D²/37; 133E/75. A facsimile of doc. 49B⁶/43 was published in *Exílios*, 204.

**9.** Pessoa later changed the sonnet's title, to "The Death of the Titan."

**10.** *Intimidade*, 68.

**11.** Docs. 13A/30v; 49B⁶/57. Ntbk. 144S/18v. Transcribed in Pessoa, *Poemas ingleses*, 2:165–66.

**12.** A half-written draft of this letter, which may or may not have been finished and sent, is in CPH. The Pessoa Archive contains a very incipient draft of the same letter, dated July 13 (doc. 49B²/5v).

**13.** The title and an opening paragraph, signed by K. P. Effield, are found on the back of a fragment from "Ode to the Storm" (doc. 49B⁴/100v). There is an outline of the essay, datable to 1904 but without Effield's signature, in ntbk. 144S/4v.

**14.** The name "S. P. Stool" is inscribed beneath "Atlantis" on a manuscript (doc. 49B⁴/37) that also contains a few lines from "Ode to the Storm."

**15.** A syndicated story by Herbert Flowerdew (1866–1917), "The Black Deed-Box," in which a Sergeant Byng of the New York Police Department pursues a notorious safecracker, was published in the *Utica Observer*, 22 Mar. 1900, and in the *South Wales Echo*, 25 Aug. 1900, p. 4. More research is needed to discover whether this story, or other syndicated stories featuring Sergeant Byng, might have been read by Pessoa in Durban.

**16.** Most of the passages written for "The Case of the Science Master" were published by Gianluca Miraglia, "The Case of the Science Master," *Revista da BN*, Sept.–Dec. 1988, 43–72; Jerónimo Pizarro published additional passages in *Génio*, 492–501. The earlier passages, signed by Horace James Faber or by Faber and C. R. Anon, are found in env. 27⁹D². Doc.13A/68v contains another early passage signed by Faber, whose name was subsequently blotted out. CVs for Faber and Anon: doc. 48B/153.

**17.** The title "Plausibility of All Philosophies," with a note stating that the essay was motivated "by Dr. Nabos' propounding Helvétius's theory," appears on a manuscript sheet dating from 1904 (doc. 48A/66); the reverse side contains the beginning of the planned essay.

**18.** From his preface to *Aspectos*: see *SP*, 4.

## CHAPTER 13

1. Docs. 49B⁴/36v, 40v.

2. Chinua Thelwall, "The Young Men Must Blacken Their Faces: The Blackface Minstrel Show in Preindustrial South Africa," *The Drama Review*, Summer 2013, pp. 66–85 (consulted online).

3. The account described here is from *Intimidade*, 60. Pessoa's niece recalls her mother telling a very different story, in which all the children dressed up as ghosts and Fernando did not run after the domestics, who were contacted the next day by his stepfather. Manuela Nogueira, *O melhor do mundo são as crianças*, 53.

4. Perhaps this character's name was inspired by *quebrantahuesos*, the Spanish word for the bearded vulture (literally, "bone-breaker").

5. *Intimidade*, 67. Pessoa's sister reported that their mother played music by Mozart, Beethoven, and Liszt, among others.

6. Ernest A. Belcher and G. Churton Collins, *The Durban High School Record 1866–1906*, 66–67.

7. João de Freitas had gone to the mainland to seek treatment and died in Lisbon on 21 Feb. 1904.

8. Doc. 49B¹/16.

9. H. S. Hall and S. R. Knight, *Elementary Algebra for Schools* (London: MacMillan 1898).

10. The terms and conditions for the scholarship were published in the 1903 *Natal Almanac, Directory, and Yearly Register*, 280.

11. David L. Chapman, *Sandow the Magnificent* (Urbana: University of Illinois Press, 1994), 153–55. The Weekly Edition of *TNM* for 27 May 1904 reported that Sandow was arriving in South Africa that same month and would make stops in Cape Town, Johannesburg "and cities along the coast."

12. Letter published in Pessoa, *Correspondência inédita*, 203 (doc. 79/7v). The mention of the measurement chart indicates that *Strength and How to Obtain It* was the book Pessoa ordered and received.

13. Jon Stallworthy, *Between the Lines: Yeats's Poetry in the Making* (New York: Oxford University Press, 1963), 14. Reiner Stach, *Kafka: The Early Years* (Princeton, N.J.: Princeton University Press, 2017), 278. Lyndall Gordon, *T. S. Eliot*, 30.

14. Pessoa held on to the letter, subsequently using the back side and part of the front for literary notes and scribblings (docs. 48A/44v–47v). Chest-expanding braces: doc. 133C/33.

15. In late 1904 or early 1905 Pessoa used about twenty pages of testimonials on the benefits accruing from the Macdonald Smith system to make a ntbk. (144B²). writing on the blank, reverse side of the pages.

16. Docs. 27²¹K⁴/1–4 (in English).

17. On "empire" as Pessoa's ingrained frame of reference, due to his upbringing, see Stefan Helgesson, "Pessoa, Anon, and the Natal Colony: Retracing an Imperial Matrix," in *Fernando Pessoa as English Reader and Writer*, ed. Patricio Ferrari and Jerónimo Pizarro, 30–46.

18. Doc. 114¹/81.

19. Docs. 27²²Z⁵/1–3.

20. Doc. 18/61. Pessoa, *Páginas de estética*, 81. Pessoa cast two astrological charts for Ruskin (doc. Sinais 6/61v and ntbk. 144/P3) and read W. G. Collingwood's *The Life of John Ruskin*.

21. Cited on p. 192 of John M. Robertson's *Modern Humanists*, in Pessoa's personal library.

22. Doc. 27²¹L⁴/19v. Unfinished and unpublished.

23. Docs. 27²¹O⁴/1–4. Unfinished and unpublished.

24. Docs. 48C/12; 124/26. Pessoa, *Teoria da heteronímia*, 356–57.

25. *Disquiet*, text 299.

26. *The Natal Who's Who* (1906), 189 (Storm entry).

## CHAPTER 14

1. "Lisbon Revisited (1926)."
2. *Ilustração Portuguesa*, 31 July 1905, p. 620.
3. An early movie house, the Salão da Avenida, opened in 1898 but lasted only a year. Some traditional theaters also exhibited films.
4. *Diário Ilustrado*, 10 Sept. 1905, p. 1; *Ilustração Portuguesa*, 18 Sept. 1905, p. 732. The tobacco industry was a major source of revenue for the Treasury and a wellspring of payoffs and kickbacks for those in power. Maria Filomena Mónica, "Capitalistas e industriais (1870–1914)," *Análise Social* 33, no. 5 (1987): 819–63.
5. Aunt Maria's record of Dionísia's finances contains references to her German maid (CPH). Pessoa made a passing reference to the maid in some notes from 1907 (doc.134/68v).
6. On Pessoa's academic attendance and performance while at the School of Arts and Letters, see Luís Prista, "Pessoa e o Curso Superior de Letras." On the school's history and the distinction between voluntary and regular students, see Francisco Adolpho Coelho, *Le Cours Supérieur de Lettres: Mémoire* (Paris: Aillaud et Cie., 1900), and Manuel Busquets de Aguilar, *O Curso Superior de Letras, 1858–1911* (Lisbon: Faculdade de Letras, 1939).
7. Beatriz's grandson, Rodrigo Miquelino, told me that her father was half English and her mother equal parts Irish, Norwegian, French, and Scottish. Information on Eduardo Teixeira Rebelo's consular stint in Pretoria found in the *Anuário Diplomático e Consular Português* for 1889–1890 and for 1891.
8. Doc. 49A⁷/28 (published in Hubert Dudley Jennings, *Fernando Pessoa: The Poet with Many Faces*, 83). Although he did not finish the poem, Pessoa would include "To a Prostitute" in lists of poems attributed to Alexander Search. This heteronym, however, did not yet exist at the time the poem was (partly) written.
9. "Harlot's Song," written in Portuguese (except for the English title) on 1 July 1910.
10. Doc. 133D/76v.
11. Doc. 133N/19v.
12. *Disquiet*, texts 195 and 317. *SP*, 217–18.
13. When Pessoa's archives were still in the possession of his sister, a copy of "Elegy on the Marriage of My Dear Friend Mr. Jinks" was found next to a draft of his letter to *Punch* (*Exílios*, 94). There's no proof, however, that Pessoa actually sent off copies of his letter (docs. 114³/25–26) and poem (docs. 78B/53–60).
14. *Imagens*, 55–57.
15. Diary entries for March 16, 20, 21 and April 12, 13, 27, 1906. The 1906 diary (docs. 22/74, 13A/41-58) was published in *EA*, 24-46.
16. Docs. 48B/123, 127, 129.

## CHAPTER 15

1. The book assaulting convention was *Palavras cínicas* (*Cynical Words*; 1905), by Albino Forjaz de Sampaio.
2. Information on Henrique Rosa from the Arquivo Histórico Militar. The dedication on an unpublished poetry manuscript in his literary archive (at the National Library of Portugal) indicates that he lived with Augusta from 1881 until her death in 1919.
3. Doc. 15B³/90 (in English).
4. Doc. 49C¹/40.
5. He did, however, make a few marginal comments in his copy of a French translation of Darwin's *The Descent of Man, and Selection in Relation to Sex*.
6. Ana Leonor Pereira, *Darwin em Portugal, 1865–1914* (Coimbra: Edições Almedina, 2001).
7. The Nazi slogan is often attributed to Haeckel himself but does not seem to appear in any of his published works. Haeckel, in any case, was an avid supporter of eugenics.
8. According to a list of "Memoranda" dating from 1913 (doc. 28A/9).
9. Docs. 92D/45–46. Pessoa, *Da República*, 158.

10. Hubert Dudley Jennings, *Fernando Pessoa: The Poet with Many Faces*, 67.
11. Ntbk. 144N/7v–8. Pessoa's 1906 diary (docs. 22/74, 13A/41-58).
12. Rousseau and most of the other cited authors are mentioned in the 1906 diary; Chateaubriand's name appears on a contemporaneous list (ntbk. 144B²/11).
13. Docs. 27¹¹L²/1–3.
14. Docs. 134B/28v; 23/13v; 48B/123; 133G/39.

## CHAPTER 16

1. Pessoa's first biographer reported that the family arrived from Durban in October 1906, but both the consulate records in Durban and the diplomatic archives in Lisbon indicate that they left Durban on 22 May 1906, sailing on the *Admiral*, a German steamer, which called at Lisbon on July 1. Doc. 90¹/62.
2. In the passage "Sentimental Education."
3. Passage titled "The River of Possession."
4. Pessoa saved the brown envelope sent by the wholesaler, G. Delpy, to Mário. Doc. 133J/34v.
5. Doc. 11⁷EN/7v.
6. Doc. 115¹/18.
7. Docs. 15A/33v; 49B¹/83v.
8. Ntbk. 144N/13–17. Docs. 14⁶/63v, 64, 66v; 24/14v. *EA*, 46–52. *Génio*, 620–21.
9. Several sheets with such measurements are in the possession of Pessoa's heirs. Pessoa had already recorded cranial measurements for himself, Great-Aunt Maria, and Aunt Anica. Doc. 90¹/80. *Notas*, 161.
10. Luís Prista, "Pessoa e o Curso Superior de Letras," 173–77. *Foto XX*, 70.
11. Docs. 22/74v; 13A/56v. Ntbks. 144B² and 144C².
12. Ntbk. 144H.
13. Docs. 13A/1–20.
14. This and several similar vows are part of a "life-bond" described in chapter 18.
15. In "Shelley and Keats," a lecture delivered at Harvard on 17 Feb. 1933, as part of a series on "The Use of Poetry and the Use of Criticism." Eliot, *The Use of Poetry and the Use of Criticism* (London: Faber & Faber, 1964), 89.
16. Doc. 74B/41.
17. The many passages Pessoa wrote for his *Prometheus Rebound* are in env. 11¹²PR. His first sustained work on the play was in late 1916, but the earliest fragments date back to at least 1907, and the work is mentioned on a list of writing projects drafted in that same year (doc. 48B/129).
18. From the poem "Às vezes medito" ("Sometimes I meditate"), dated 29 Apr. 1928.
19. Doc. 22/45a. Pessoa, *Textos filosóficos*, 1:68–69.
20. Docs. 22/48–49. Pessoa, *Textos filosóficos*, 1:73–74.
21. Doc. 35/30. Reproduced in Teresa Rita Lopes, *Pessoa por conhecer*, 225.
22. Docs. 22/39; 23/32. Pessoa, *Textos filosóficos*, 1:55, 186. The notebook inaugurated by Alexander Search in September 1906 contains the outline of a philosophical work more succinctly titled *The World as Power* (ntbk. 144H/39v).
23. *SP*, 9–10.
24. Docs. 22/45–46, 50, 53–57. Pessoa, *Textos filosóficos*, 1:67–72, 74–75, 80–83.
25. The passages written for *Extent and Causes of Portuguese Decay* are mostly to be found in envs. 92N–92Q; quotation at doc. 92O/72.
26. Rui Ramos, *D. Carlos*, 262–63.
27. Docs. 92O/84–91.
28. The cause of Maria Clara's death, on 11 Dec. 1906, is given in *Intimidade*, 59. Maria Madalena's miscarriage occurred on 19 Jan. 1907, according to burial records (I owe this information to Jorge Ferreira).
29. Letter of 5 Nov. 1910, excerpted in *Imagens*, 68.

**30.** A 28 Apr. 1912 letter from Pessoa's mother to her son confirms 25 Apr. 1907 as the date of departure from Lisbon.

**31.** His loss of interest is mentioned in a note at the end of an incomplete draft of a letter to his mother, written in the summer of 1907 (doc. 138A/47v). *EA*, 408.

**32.** João Maria Nogueira Rosa, "Fernando Pessoa—Como eu o conheci," p. 233.

**33.** Doc. 92O/88.

## CHAPTER 17

**1.** Pessoa's sister reported that her parents were bitterly diappointed by his decision to quit school (Henriqueta Rosa Madalena Dias/Maria Ivone de Ornellas de Andrade, "Ele sabia o valor que tinha," *Jornal de Letras*, 26 Nov.–2 Dec. 1985, p. 6). A surviving draft of a letter by Pessoa to his mother (docs. 138A/46-47) gives us an idea of the offended and offending tones of the letters actually exchanged.

**2.** Docs. 133I/57; 133F/53v. Ntbk. 144T/33v.

**3.** Doc. 78B/55. Pessoa, *Poemas ingleses*, vol. 2, 9–13 (editor's introduction).

**4.** A transcription of "A Very Original Dinner" was published in an appendix to K. David Jackson's *Adverse Genres in Fernando Pessoa*. The book's first chapter analyzes the story in the light of the ethnographic studies of scientists such as Darwin and the theorizations of Freud in works such as *Totem and Taboo* and *Civilization and Its Discontents*.

**5.** Max Nordau, *Degeneration*, bk. 2, ch. 3, p. 127.

**6.** *OE*, 3:211–12. This response to the survey was published six months after Pessoa's death.

**7.** Nordau, *Degeneration*, bk. 2, ch. 5, p. 197.

**8.** Ibid., bk 2, ch. 3, p. 101.

**9.** Doc. 134/44.

**10.** Docs. 134/59–60. *Génio*, 682–85. Pessoa consulted the article "Folie du doute avec délire du toucher," by Antoine Ritti (1844–1920), in the *Dictionnaire encyclopédique des sciences médicales*, vol. 3 (Paris: Éd. G. Masson et P. Asselin, 1879), 339–48.

**11.** Docs. 134/13, 40. *Génio*, 48, 50.

**12.** Doc. 134/41. *Génio*, 51.

**13.** Docs. 134/41; 134A/93v. *Génio*, 51, 323.

**14.** Lombroso's *Genio e follia* (*Genius and Madness*) was published in 1864. *The Man of Genius*, published in Italian in 1888, was a greatly expanded version of this earlier work.

**15.** In 1906 Pessoa had read, in a French edition, Lombroso's *L'uomo delinquente*, or *Criminal Man*.

**16.** Pessoa read an 1893 edition of Nisbet's book and an 1897 editon of Hirsch's book (first published in German, in 1894). Jerónimo Pizarro gives a thorough account of Pessoa's readings during this period in *Fernando Pessoa: Entre génio e loucura*.

**17.** Ntbk. 144Z/7.

**18.** Letter to João Gaspar Simões, 11 Dec. 1931.

**19.** Docs. 15B³/1–2. Ntbk. 144Z/19. *Génio*, 189, 375–76.

**20.** In 1909 Pessoa undertook an article (unfinished) that rebutted some of the main arguments presented in Nordau's *Degeneration* (docs. 14¹/89–90). *Génio*, 380–81.

**21.** Five of the six Nordau titles are in Pessoa's personal library. Pessoa owned a two-volume copy of a French edition of *Degeneration*, which he sold some time after 1910 (doc. 93/100v).

**22.** Doc. 20/84. This literary survey, like the last one mentioned, did not make it into print during his lifetime. Pessoa, *Páginas íntimas*, 122–24.

**23.** *Disquiet*, text 305.

## CHAPTER 18

**1.** Fernando Pessoa, "O que um milionário americano fez em Portugal," *Fama* (Lisbon), 10 Mar. 1933, p. 24.

**2.** João Lobo Antunes, *Egas Moniz* (Lisbon: Gradiva, 2010), 108.

**3.** Ntbk. 144T/30. The letter was sent on 26 Aug. 1907. Some twenty-five years later, the Bernarr Macfadden Foundation would showcase the founder's method among a group of fifty orphaned Portuguese boys, who spent six months at a children's camp west of Lisbon in 1931–1932. Pessoa would write glowingly about the results achieved and about Macfadden himself: "O que um milionário americano fez em Portugal," pp. 22–24.

**4.** Ntbk. 144T/51–52. Family members and friends reported that Pessoa always took cold baths (*Intimidade*, 250).

**5.** The Imperial Shoulder Brace: doc. 135/42. The "Pulvermacher appliance" appears in a 1908 list of things to take on a planned voyage to London (doc. 92Y/58v). Since the "appliance," or belt, was marketed for daily use, not as a travel item, Pessoa presumably already owned one.

**6.** Pessoa cast aspersions on Egas Moniz as well other Portuguese psychiatrists, and also on Egas Moniz as a neurologist, accusing him of never having an original idea and of merely parroting others. Docs. 15B³/81–85. *Génio*, 397–98.

**7.** Docs. 138A/46–47. *EA*, 63–65.

**8.** *Disquiet*, text 77.

**9.** Ntbk. 144T/24–29v (in English).

**10.** Docs. 49A¹/47v, 48v; 49D¹/44v.

**11.** Mascaró's letter (CPH) transcribed in *Imagens*, 53. The 1920 *Anuário comercial de Portugal Ilhas e Ultramar* lists Aniceto Mascaró as the director of R. G. Dun in Portugal. He would subsequently become the director of R. G. Dun in Spain, where he took his family. His wife, Laurinda, died and was buried in Madrid in March 1931. The son of a renowned ophthamologist who had founded a small school for the blind in Lisbon, Mascaró also worked as an optician.

**12.** Ntbk. 144I/7. Doc.137E/58 (published in *Foto XX*, 75).

**13.** Ntbk. 144T/42, 51. See also doc. 133M/30. Pessoa's early notes on his shorthand systems are mostly to be found in envs. 128 and 128C and in ntbk. 144L.

**14.** Docs. 14⁶/40v; 49D¹/48v; 75A/31v; 133F/53v. Ntbk. 144J/2v.

**15.** Doc. 79/10v. Information on the new home address from Margarida Soares Couto, whose mother lived with Anica's family in 1906–1907.

**16.** Ntbk. 144J/31–32. These notes were written in late 1907, in English.

**17.** *Poems by Walt Whitman* (London: Review of Reviews Office, c. 1895), 33–34.

**18.** Ntbk. 144T/52. Docs. 48C/18; 20/9; 133C/19. Pessoa, *Teoria da heteronímia*, 358–59.

**19.** Docs. 26/90v–91.

**20.** *EA*, 82.

**21.** *A Vanguarda*, 1 Jan. 1908, pp. 1.

## CHAPTER 19

**1.** Rui Ramos, *D. Carlos*, 313–19.

**2.** Pessoa's book cited another psychiatric study of Franco, *Um caso de loucura epiléptica* (*A Case of Epileptic Insanity*; 1907), by Arthur Leitão, a Portuguese physician. Pessoa's copy of the work (in env. 108C) bears the signature of Alexander Search.

**3.** Doc. 92P/70.

**4.** *The Graphic*, 29 Feb. 1908, p. 17.

**5.** Docs. 92Y/36, 41. Many other pages defending the regicide, some of them contemporaneous, some dating from 1909, can be found in env. 92Y.

**6.** Pessoa saved a typed copy of his submission (doc. 124/7), on which he recorded the date and the contents of the card that accompanied it.

**7.** "Lisbon Murders," *Daily Telegraph*, 11 Mar. 1908, p. 11.

**8.** Docs. 92J/23–24. Ntbk. 144I/7, 63. *A Vanguarda*, a republican newspaper, reported on 30 Mar. 1908 that more than 50,000 people attended the rally.

**9.** Doc. 92H/46. At the top of his draft for this unfinished article, Pessoa noted the date and the newspaper, *A Luta*, 27 Feb. 1908, where he had read about the "Sufferings of the Russian people."

**10.** Pessoa-Search critiqued the first volume of the four-volume *La Folie de Jésus* (1908–1915), which had caused a sensation and was immediately translated into Portuguese. The passages written for the pamphlet were transcribed in *Génio*, 244–56.

**11.** "Trois chansons mortes," *Contemporânea*, Jan.–Mar. 1923. Pessoa wrote about twenty complete poems in French, as well as many additional, unfinished poems and poem fragments, all of which are collected in his *Poèmes français*.

**12.** See, on this subject, the illuminating introduction to Pessoa, *Obras de Jean Seul*, 7–36.

**13.** Max Nordau, *Degeneration*, bk. 5 ("The Twentieth Century"), ch. 1. Nordau believed that this worst-case scenario of future decadence would be averted.

**14.** Docs. 92S/71–72 (in English).

**15.** Charles James Search was also supposed to translate José de Espronceda's *El estudiante de Salamanca* (*The Student of Salamanca*), a project previously entrusted to Alexander.

**16.** Ntbk. 144I/61v, 62r. Doc. 92Y/58v. Pessoa wrote both lists in English.

**17.** The Pessoa Archive contains at least five references to Pessoa's correspondence with Sprigg, Pedrick & Company, and one to the Quill Club. Docs. 48H/49; 92P/35v; 92W/29v; 133M/1v. Ntbk. 144I/3. On the Search family, see Pessoa, *Teoria da heteronímia*, 69.

## CHAPTER 20

**1.** "Influências," 1914, in *EA*, 150.

**2.** Doc. 138A/6.

**3.** Afterword and appendixes to Antero de Quental, *Os sonetos completos de Antero de Quental, com tradução parcial em língua inglesa por Fernando Pessoa*, ed. Patricio Ferrari (Lisbon: Guimarães, 2010).

**4.** Pessoa, *Cartas a Armando Côrtes-Rodrigues*, 76.

**5.** Pessoa's copy of *Dr. Faustus* was published in 1912.

**6.** Doc. 29/96. Pessoa, *Fausto*, 231, 502.

**7.** *Novo Almanach de Lembranças Luso-Brazileiro para o Anno de 1909*, 144.

**8.** Pessoa published another poetic riddle of Dr. Nabos in the almanac for 1910, 277.

**9.** Jerónimo Pizarro and Patricio Ferrari, the editors of Pessoa, *Eu sou uma antologia*, assert (709–10) that neither *O Progresso* nor *A Civilização* were the work of Pessoa, who, they propose, acquired copies because of the squib on his poetic prowess. But while he kept only one copy of *A Civilização*, where the squib appeared, he saved two copies of the third issue of *O Progresso* as well as single copies of the first two issues, in which no references to him can be found. Furthermore, several corrections in the newspapers were made in his handwriting. Since the mimeograph belonged to Mário, it is conceivable that this cousin and several others might have used it to produce something playful, but it was not in their imaginary power to invent opposing political parties, a make-believe government, and tongue-in-cheek political discourse. The cousins may have contributed something to the project, but it was obviously Pessoa's brainchild.

**10.** The life of Clara Alves Soares (1891–1977) in Lisbon, her impressions of Pessoa, and the outings to Trafaria were reported to me by her daughter, Margarida Soares Couto. Pessoa was sending correpondence to Trafaria as early as August 1907 (ntbk. 144T/30), and extant letters from his mother indicate that Aunt Anica and his first cousins continued to go there until at least September 1912.

**11.** Doc. 93/13.

**12.** Rua Bella da Rainha is now Rua da Prata. Mário soon moved his office to Rua do Carmo, 35, second floor. Documents connected to the mining agency are mostly to be found in envs. 137B–137D.

## CHAPTER 21

**1.** João Maria Nogueira Rosa, "Fernando Pessoa—Como eu o conheci," 232. António Mega Ferreira, *Fazer pela vida*, 51.

**2.** Doc. 137E/58. Mega Ferreira, *Fazer pela vida*, 55–56, 215–16.

**3.** His rejection of the job offer, and the salary he would have earned, are mentioned in Maria Nogueira Rosa's 12 Jan. 1913 letter to Pessoa. In *Notas* (61), Eduardo Freitas da Costa claimed that the starting salary was higher: 40,000 reis per month.

**4.** Doc. 49A²/37. The manuscript contains several alternate endings, all of which preserve the notion of apathy being king.

**5.** Ntbk. 144M/31v. Mega Ferreira, *Fazer pela vida*, 57–58.

**6.** Ntbk. 144M/1v. Mega Ferreira, *Fazer pela vida*, 41–65, provides the most complete account of Pessoa's purchase of the printing press and accessory equipment.

**7.** Ntbk. 144M. *Revista Lusitania* and *Revista Ibis* were alternate titles for the magazine.

**8.** Doc. S2/23.

**9.** Literally *The Match* (for lighting fires).

**10.** Pessoa's publication plans for Ibis can be found in ntbk. 144V as well as in docs. 48A/11; 48B/130–33, 148; 55D/101v; 93/51.

**11.** The title *Tratado de Luta, Sistema Yvetot (Treatise on Wrestling: The Yvetot Method)*, attributed to Miguel Otto rather than to Carlos Otto, appears on an incipient list of Ibis books that was crossed out (doc. 144V/5). The pages actually written for the treatise (docs. 124/56–59), under a slightly different title, were signed by Carlos.

**12.** Richard Zenith, ed., *Fernando Pessoa: O editor, o escritor e os seus leitores*, 150–51.

**13.** The name of the researcher is Rui Sena, of Loulé. Two years later another researcher, Ana Rita Palmeirim, discovered that the Ibis press printed the first issue of *A Mosca* (16 Mar. 1910) and several issues of *A Comédia* in April and May 1910; both were obscure, ephemeral magazines published in Lisbon.

**14.** Zenith, *Fernando Pessoa: O editor*, 155.

**15.** Docs. 28A/10; 66D/6v; 92A/87v.

**16.** Doc. 11¹⁴X/8v, 8av.

**17.** Doc. 11¹⁴X/8a contains the initial draft of the first quartet of the sonnet "How many masks wear we," dating from August 5 and quoted above. Nine additional sonnets that would go into the collection *35 Sonnets* (sonnets 1, 4, 11, 13, 14, 18, 23, 25, and 27) were written between 6 August and 15 August (see, on this point, the introduction to Pessoa, *Poemas ingleses*, vol. 1, 8–9). In that same month, Pessoa wrote still other English sonnets not included in *35 Sonnets*.

**18.** Doc. 11¹⁴X/9. Written, in English, at the same sitting as the document mentioned in the previous two notes.

**19.** Doc. 93/51. Most of the material for this fragmentary poem can be found in envs. 11⁷EN and 11⁷ENP (transcribed by Nicolás Barbosa, Jerónimo Pizarro, Carlos Pittella, and Rui Sousa in "*Portugal*, o primeiro aviso de *Mensagem*," *Pessoa Plural*, Spring 2020, pp. 76–229). Doc. 11⁷EN/71 contains a (fragmentary) epilogue, followed by the date August–September 1910, but Pessoa would write additional verses for the poem until at least 1918 (doc. 44/36).

## CHAPTER 22

**1.** Doc. Anexo IV/6.

**2.** Docs. 56/36–37. The poem, dated 26 Oct. 1909, was published in Teresa Rita Lopes, *Pessoa por conhecer*, 219.

**3.** My sources of information on the Portuguese Republic include Douglas Wheeler, *Republican Portugal: A Political History, 1910–1926*, and Rui Ramos, *História de Portugal: A segunda fundação (1890–1926)*.

**4.** Doc. 92W/63.

**5.** Doc. 92B/53. Pessoa's notes refer to an article published in *A Capital*, 10 Feb. 1911, p. 1. The writer, Abel Sebroza, feared that a conservative republican party would defend a return to royalist values and privileged classes.

**6.** Arnaldo Saraiva, *Fernando Pessoa, tradutor de poetas*, reproduces and discusses many of Pessoa's translations published in the *Biblioteca*. The Pessoa Archive contains four letters from Kellogg dated between 21 July 1911 and 19 Feb. 1912 (docs. 115¹/20–21; 66A/8v; 115⁸/43).

Kellogg's arrival in May 1911 is deduced from a passenger list (consulted at ancestry.com) indicating that he arrived in Southampton from New York on 3 May 1911 and held a through ticket to Lisbon.

**7.** Today the roofless church is home to an archeological museum.

**8.** Her letter of 12 Jan. 1913 would mention an earlier letter of his that had spoken of this repulsion.

**9.** Interview with Margarida Soares Couto.

**10.** Ntbks. 144V/55 and 144I/63v.

**11.** The sonnet was called "Junho de 1911" ("June of 1911").

## CHAPTER 23

**1.** António Mora was the name of the protagonist in one passage written for the Cascais tale; in other passages the protagonist's name was Dr. Gama Nobre. It is unclear which name came first and which one Pessoa finally settled on, if either. He never finished the story, but Gama Nobre would resurface in the 1920s as the deranged protagonist of a rather different tale, which takes place in a nearby town with a similar name: "Na Casa de Saúde de Caxias" ("In the Caxias Sanatorium"). Caxias is halfway between Lisbon and Cascais.

**2.** Doc. 27⁹E²/20. Marcos Alves's sexual phobia is apparent in several passages actually written and even more so in notes for passages not written: docs. 27⁹E²/1, 2, 7, 9, 10. Virtually all the material for the novel has been published in *Génio*, 526–47, and in Pessoa, *A porta e outras ficções*, 203–30, 282–84.

**3.** It is possible that Pessoa "read" Krafft-Ebing only through other writers, such as Nordau and Lombroso.

**4.** He abandoned the project around 1920.

**5.** The play is listed on publication plans throughout Pessoa's life, and part of at least one scene was written in his last year, on 4 Jan. 1935 (doc. 11⁵D/71).

**6.** Doc. 11⁴D/51v.

**7.** Doc. 11⁴D/16v.

**8.** Doc. 11⁴D/80v.

**9.** Docs. 11⁵D/42, 38; 11⁴D/95.

**10.** Doc. 11⁵D/83 (in English).

**11.** Memo book (1911–1913) in the Casa Fernando Pessoa. Page reproduced in *Objectos*, 150.

**12.** Docs. 16A/29–30.

**13.** Docs. 92J/2; 133M/76.

**14.** Letters from Pessoa's mother to her son from this period mention how Aunt Anica was dealing with Great-Aunts Rita and Maria. Her letter of 2 Sept. 1911 implies that Pessoa had moved in with his aunt and cousins at least one month earlier. He had begun to receive mail at their address in June.

**15.** Docs. 151/1; 117EN/92. Ntbk. 144V/4.

**16.** From a text titled "Os homens dos cafés" ("The Men in Cafés"), doc. 55F/28. Docs. 55F/27, 29–30 also belong to the embryonic essay, alternately titled "Vida de café" ("Café Life").

**17.** Armando Côrtes-Rodrigues, "Encontro," 11. Côrtes-Rodrigues claimed he met almost daily with Pessoa between 1910 and 1915 (but Pessoa's diary from 1913 proves this was not so). I have relied on Anabela Almeida's *Armando Côrtes-Rodrigues, vida e obra do poeta açoriano de Orpheu* for biographical and bibliographical information on this poet.

**18.** The place of music in Pessoa's writing and thinking, particularly as it relates to poetry, is examined in the first chapter of Rita Patrício's *Episódios: Da teorização estética em Fernando Pessoa* (Vila Nova de Familicão: Humus, 2012).

**19.** See Signa Teixeira Rebelo/Nuna Coutinho, "Nunca me disse que era Alberto Caeiro," *ABC do Bairro*, 5 Dec. 1985, and her other two published interviews.

**20.** Pierre Hourcade, *Temas de literatura portuguesa*, 134. Manuel Mendes, *Sobre a oficina do escritor*, 11. Luís da Câmara Reis, "Boletim," 333. Carlos Lobo de Oliveira, "Fernando Pessoa, tradutor e astrólogo," *Boletim da Academia Portuguesa de Ex-Libris*, January 1959, 16.

**21.** The Pessoa Archive contains a carbon copy of only the fourteenth page of the letter to his stepuncle (doc. 28/92). A reference to Pessoa's trip to the Algarve indicates it was written in the fall of 1914.

**22.** "Refugees in Spain," *Daily Telegraph*, 4 Oct. 1911, 11.

**23.** Doc. 48D/25. The dozens of pages written for the essay, in Portuguese, are concentrated in envs. 130–32.

**24.** Docs. 92W/50. See also docs. 92B/16–17; 92E/41–42, 65; 92W/22–23; 92X/49–50, 100. Pessoa attributed the authorship of the essay to one Gervásio Guedes or, alternatively, to L. Guerreiro.

**25.** Docs. 48H/7–8.

**26.** He kept working on "Oligarchy of Brutes," however, until 1915 (doc. 133M/97v).

## CHAPTER 24

**1.** *Vida*, 145. *Notas*, 62. Kellogg was still in Lisbon on 7 June 1912, when he sent a letter to the republican statesman Bernardino Machado (consulted online at casacomum.org), saying that he would be going to Brazil in the fall. He delayed his trip, sailing on 9 Jan. 1913 from Dover, England, to Rio de Janeiro on the *Zeelandia* (according to passenger lists consulted at ancestry.com). He and Rebelo must have traveled to London around July 1.

**2.** *Objectos*, 122.

**3.** *A Águia* was relaunched in January 1912 as the official organ of the Renascença Portuguesa group, founded the previous year. The group and its magazine allowed for diversity of opinion, and Pascoaes's initially strong influence would diminish over time. Pascoaes's real name was Joaquim Pereira Teixeira de Vasconcelos.

**4.** In his diary entry for 4 Mar. 1913, Pessoa mentions lending his copy of the 1 Apr. 1911 issue of *A Águia* to a magazine editor (doc. 133L/44v).

**5.** Pascoaes, "Renascença," *A Águia*, Jan. 1912, p. 33.

## CHAPTER 25

**1.** Pascoaes's letter of 21 Oct. 1912. *Imagens*, 75.

**2.** António Cobeira, "Fernando Pessoa, vulgo 'o Pessoa,' e a sua ironia transcendente." Cobeira would later write, and publish, an occasional poem.

**3.** Interview in *O Primeiro de Janeiro*, 24 May 1950, p. 3.

**4.** Reported in *Comércio do Porto*, 30 Nov. 1985, which gives the Brazilian magazine *Fatos* (perhaps *Fatos e Fotos*) as the original source.

**5.** Cobeira, "Fernando Pessoa."

**6.** François Castex, *Mário de Sá-Carneiro*, 13–42.

**7.** Doc. 38/37. Sonnet published in Pessoa, *Poesia: 1902–1917*, 121, in a slightly different transcription. Part of the second poem appears in an endnote in ibid., 452. The poems were republished in Victor Correia, *Homossexualidade e homoerotismo em Fernando Pessoa* (Lisbon: Colibri, 2018), 141–42, but mistakenly dated 11 Feb. 1919.

**8.** *Non amabam et amare amabam*, in book III. English translation by Carolyn J.-B. Hammond, from Augustine, *Confessions*, vol. 1, Loeb Classical Library (Cambridge: Harvard University Press, 2014), 91. The line appears, in Latin, in Campos's "Gostava de gostar de gostar" ("I'd like to be able to like liking").

## CHAPTER 26

**1.** The names of those who saw Sá-Carneiro off were mentioned in a small, front-page notice published the following day in *O Mundo*.

**2.** The books Pessoa bought include W. C. Rivers, *Walt Whitman's Anomaly* (1913) and Robert H. Sherard, *Oscar Wilde: The Story of an Unhappy Friendship* (1909).

**3.** Doc. 57/19a.

**4.** While Ferro's year of birth is often given as 1895, his birth certificate attests that he was born 17 Aug. 1896; he died in 1956.

**5.** The painting is dated 27 Mar. 1912 on the back of the canvas. A personal note of Pessoa's from September 1912 (doc. 57/19v) reads "Quadro casa Castañé" (Portrait Castañé's house), which might have been a reminder to pick up the painting.

**6.** *República*, 21 Sept. 1912, p. 1. The caricature accompanied one of Pessoa's rejoinders defending his contention that a Super-Camões would soon emerge and change the face of Portuguese literature.

**7.** Mário de Sá-Carneiro to Gilberto Rola, 5 July 2013 (published in *Vértice* [Lisbon], January 1966). Sá-Carneiro also alluded to the affair in his 21 Apr. 1913 letter to Pessoa.

**8.** A clipping of the notice, whose source I was unable to identify, survives among his papers (CPH).

**9.** Doc. 28/95.

**10.** On 30 Mar. 1913 Pessoa wrote that "Coelho" had promised to lend him 130,000 reis (about \$130 U.S. at the time, equivalent to \$3500 today) for trips he wanted to make to England and the Algarve. The next day's diary entry states that this same Coelho loaned him only 2,000 reis after all. This was one of seven loans from Geraldo Coelho de Jesus mentioned on two detailed lists of outstanding debts drawn up by Pessoa in 1913 (docs. 28A/8–10); a second list (CPH) shows his financial position on 15 Nov. 1913.

**11.** That July, Coelho de Jesus furnished the agency with a technical report on a copper mine (docs. 137C/14–22).

**12.** Anahory (1884–1969) gave up dentistry and his incipient literary career to join the Portuguese foreign service, which took him to France, where he served as the Portuguese consul in Sète and in Rouen. Dismissed from his post in 1935 for issuing false passports to opponents of Salazar, he spent some time in Spain, worked for the Portuguese branch of the Communist Party in Paris, and was arrested when he returned to Portugal. Biographical information, some of it found in the Portuguese secret police file on Anahory, compiled by António Paula Brito: http://www.olhaocubista.pt/personalidades/TextosFFL/Israel_Anahory.htm (accessed 6 Apr. 2015). Anahory's address in Sète is on a list compiled by Pessoa in 1923 (doc. 75/71v). References to Anahory's poems and a play: docs. 48D/14; 48H/42. Pessoa cast an astrological chart for Anahory: doc. S7/43.

**13.** From the poem "The King of Gaps."

**14.** Edward Ayres d'Abreu, "Ruy Coelho (1889–1986): O compositor da geração d'*Orpheu*" (master's thesis, Universidade Nova de Lisboa, 2014), 24–44.

**15.** Typical was the review published in *A Capital*, 13 June 1913, p. 1.

**16.** In "Nota ao acaso" ("Random Note"), signed by Álvaro de Campos and published in 1935. In texts written in English and dating from 1912–1914, Pessoa wrote that Camões was "an Italian," or "Italianated" (docs. 19/110v; 20/83v).

## CHAPTER 27

**1.** Doc. 130/23.

**2.** Diary entry of 3 Apr. 1913. The 1913 diary (docs. 20/18–45) was published in *EA*, 106–33.

**3.** Mário Sá-Carneiro relayed this comment to Pessoa in a letter of 6 May 1913.

**4.** Entries for March 8 and February 27.

**5.** Docs. $27^{22}C^6/1$–2.

**6.** *Disquiet*, text 345.

**7.** *Aberdeen Daily Journal*, 19 Jan. 1922.

**8.** The half dozen sonnets written on 14 May 1913 (docs. 40/33–34) were inadvertently published as a single, fragmentary poem with more than ninety lines in Pessoa, *Poesia: 1902–1917*, 174–77. In *Fernando Pessoa et le Quint-Empire de l'amour*, his study on Pessoa's poetics of love, Aníbal Frias interprets the Venus-Ephebe of the first sonnet in the series as an "ontological and grammatical" hybrid, both feminine and masculine, in continual tension (96ff.). If I understand his analysis correctly, he considers the narrator's desire to be not so much for a hypothetical individual but for this very blurring of genders and the (not only sexual) liberation that this represents. This is a fascinating hypothesis, but the entire series of sonnets clearly shows the poetic narrator trying to make a same-sex relationship fit the heterosexual paradigm, with one man playing the masculine role, the other the feminine.

**9.** Jacques d'Adelswärd-Fersen, the founder and editor in chief of *Akademos*, the first gay journal published in France, speaks of "l'Autre Amour" in the inaugural issue, 15 Jan. 1909, p. 68.

**10.** The American edition of Hyde's book, resorting to another euphemism, was titled *The Love That Dared Not Speak Its Name.*

**11.** Doc. 55/38.

**12.** Maria Nogueira Rosa to Fernando Pessoa, 16 Mar. 1913.

**13.** Ibid.

**14.** The book was a Spanish translation of *The Physiological Idiocy of Women*, by the German neurologist Paul Julius Möbius (1853–1907). Pessoa also owned *La indigencia espiritual del sexo femenino (The Intellectual Poverty of the Female Sex)*, by the Spanish doctor Roberto Nóvoa Santos (1885–1933). José Barreto's *Misoginia e anti-feminismo em Fernando Pessoa* discusses these and other misogynist books in Pessoa's library, as well as all the evidence for misogyny in his own writings.

**15.** Docs. 15B¹/82–83, published in Barreto, *Misoginia e anti-feminismo*, 131–33.

**16.** Docs. 55/36–38. The full text, a dialogue, was published in Barreto, *Misoginia e anti-feminismo*, 123–29.

**17.** In Maria Nogueira Rosa's letter of 20 Apr. 1913, she quotes these words of Pessoa back to him.

**18.** Wilde's *Poems in Prose* (all but "The Teacher of Wisdom") in Pessoa's Portuguese translation: docs. 27¹²T²/1–2; 27²³/13; 94/7–11, 14–15. Plans to translate other works by Wilde: docs. 55L/5v; 175; 179. See also "Traducções" (CPH), viewable at pessoadigital.pt (CP 248). Pessoa translated one short passage from *De Profundis*: doc. 23/66.

**19.** Doc. 18/50. Pessoa translated Browning's "Up at a Villa—Down in the City" for the *Biblioteca internacional de obras célebres*, 20:9890–92. He intended to translate additional Browning poems for publishing projects of his own (docs. 48/8, 10, 56; 48B/108; 77/1–2; 93/89–90). See also "Traducções" (CPH), viewable at pessoadigital.pt (CP 248).

**20.** Docs. 14E/64, 73, 69.

**21.** Pessoa's library contains Gide's book on Wilde (1910), which he read closely, as well as *Corydon*, Gide's 1924 defense of homosexuality.

**22.** Doc. 14E/62.

**23.** "Wilde has done more by his personal eccentricities than by his works." Max Nordau, *Degeneration*, bk. 3, ch. 3, pp. 317ff.

**24.** The letter, written in 1890, was to Beatrice Allhusen and referred to the first version of *The Picture of Dorian Gray*, published in *Lippincott's Monthly Magazine*.

**25.** I owe several of my observations on Wilde and Pessoa to Mariana de Castro's "Oscar Wilde, Fernando Pessoa and the Art of Lying," *Portuguese Studies* 22, no. 2 (2006): 219–49, and to Jorge Uribe's "Um drama da crítica: Oscar Wilde, Walter Pater e Matthew Arnold, lidos por Fernando Pessoa" (Ph.D. diss., Universidade de Lisboa, 2014).

## CHAPTER 28

**1.** Pessoa mentioned his correspondence with Lisbela in letters to his mother, who, in a letter dated 16 Feb. 1913, encourages him to pay her a visit, since "she has not seen you since you became a man."

**2.** Doc. 92A/87v.

**3.** Lisbela's visits to Lisbon are mentioned in letters to Pessoa from his mother. Her latest loan was recorded on the list of debts that Pessoa drew up on 15 Nov. 1913 (CPH).

**4.** Teresa Rita Lopes, *Fernando Pessoa et le drame symboliste: Héritage et création*, reported having seen notes for the play *Briareus* dating as far back as 1908. This is possible, but I could not find them in the Pessoa Archive. The scenes written by Pessoa for his trilogy also include dialogue for a giant of his own invention named Livôr.

5. Claudia J. Fischer "Auto-tradução e experimentação interlinguística na génese d'*O Marinheiro* de Fernando Pessoa," *Pessoa Plural*, Spring 2012, pp. 1–69. Claudia J. Fischer, "Os caminhos d'*O Marinheiro* entre criação e auto-tradução," in *Os caminhos de Orpheu*, ed. Richard Zenith, Fátima Lopes, and Manuela Rêgo, 59–68.

6. Doc. 48G/6. Ntbk 144P/51v.

7. Doc. 48D/57. This project dates from 1911 or 1912.

8. So Pessoa himself states in his unfinished letter to Yeats (doc. 114³/72). James H. Cousins, "William Butler Yeats: The Celtic Lyrist," *The Poetry Review*, April 1912, was a likely source of his information, according to Patrícia Silva McNeill, *Yeats and Pessoa: Parallel Poetic Styles*, 2.

9. Docs. 11¹⁴X/6–7.

10. Doc. 28/95v.

11. Docs. 90⁶/197–98.

12. Docs. 90⁵/100–101; S4/15v.

13. Doc. 20/83. Pessoa, *Páginas íntimas*, 119.

14. Although printed in November 1913, the title pages of *Lúcio's Confession* and *Dispersion* both give 1914 as the year of publication.

15. List in CPH.

16. Pessoa, *300 Provérbios*, ed. Orlando Silva (Vergada: Gráfica da Vergada, 1996); Pessoa, *Provérbios Portugueses*, ed. Jerónimo Pizarro and Patricio Ferrari (Lisbon: Ática, 2010).

## CHAPTER 29

1. Directed by Stelios Charalambopoulos.

2. Doc. 20/17. *SP*, 201.

3. "A imoralidade das biografias" ("The Immorality of Biographies"), published in Pessoa, *Páginas de estética e de teoria e crítica literárias*, 131–32 (doc. 19/15). Biographies, according to this unfinished essay, are morally problematic not because they draw invalid connections between artistic genius and eccentric behaviors or deviations from psychological "normality" but because those connections, which very often *are* valid, can induce would-be writers to imitate the lifestyles of Baudelaire, Verlaine, and Wilde, in the vain hope of acquiring some of their genius.

4. Docs. 25/134; 48A/48; S3/43v.

5. Docs. 138A/66; 131/35a.

6. I read the year of his birth, given in doc. 27¹⁶W²/42v, as 1868.

7. Pessoa, *Quaresma, Decifrador*.

8. Doc. 133G/52, dating from the summer of 1912, contains a reference to the pamphlet he planned to write on the subject.

9. Ntbk. 144D²/16–17.

10. Here and on other points, I am following Mariana Gray de Castro, *Fernando Pessoa's Shakespeare: The Invention of the Heteronyms*, 74–109, in her excellent analysis of Pessoa and the Shakespeare authorship question.

11. Docs. 48E/29; 48B/22.

12. Doc. 138/77.

13. Alexander Search, as mentioned earlier, emerged in 1906 but was retrospectively credited with a number of English poems written in 1904 and 1905. On the Wyatt family, see Pessoa, *Teoria da heteronímia*, 78–79.

## CHAPTER 30

1. The masthead is reproduced in Marina Tavares Dias, *Mário de Sá-Carneiro—Fotobiografia*, 144.

**2.** *A Renascença* (The Renaissance), February 1914. This was the first and only issue of the magazine, founded by two younger writers from Pessoa's literary circle, José Coelho Pacheco and Fernando Carvalho Mourão. "O church bell of my village," discussed in chapter 1, was the other poem published by Pessoa in the magazine, which, despite its title, had no connection with the Renascença Portuguesa group led by the poet Teixeira de Pascoaes.

**3.** *SP*, 62.

**4.** The static dramas have been collected in Pessoa, *Teatro estático*. *SP* contains a translation into English of *The Mariner*.

**5.** *O marinheiro* appears on a list of works dating from February 1914 (doc. 48I/5), at which point it must have been largely conceived if not completely finished.

**6.** Ivo Castro, "O corpus de *O guardador de rebanhos* depositado na Biblioteca Nacional," *Revista da Biblioteca Nacional 2*, no. 1 (1982): 17–61.

**7.** From poem 39, *The Keeper of Sheep*.

**8.** Doc. 14B/62a (in English).

**9.** *Disquiet*, texts 195, 285, 317.

**10.** Pessoa's 4 Oct. 1914 letter to Armando Côrtes-Rodrigues, which explains how Ferro was fooled, also implies that some Caeiro poems were circulating among readers who thought Caeiro was a real poet.

**11.** Doc. 68A/3.

**12.** Docs. 21/98–103, published in *OE*, 5:166–170. Doc. 14B/62, transcribed in an addendum to Richard Zenith, "Pessoa and Walt Whitman Revisited," in *Fernando Pessoa's Modernity Without Frontiers*, ed. Mariana Gray de Castro, 49–50.

**13.** In the aforementioned interview he supposedly gave in Vigo (docs. 68A/8-10; 143/100; 68A/5, 4v).

**14.** Thomas Merton, "Translator's Note," *New Directions in Prose and Poetry 19* (New York: New Directions, 1966), 299. On Merton and Pessoa, see George Monteiro, *The Presence of Pessoa: English, American and South African Literary Responses*, 32–40.

**15.** Leyla Perrone-Moisés, *Fernando Pessoa: Aquém do eu, além do outro*, in the chapter "Caeiro Zen."

**16.** Doc. 50A¹/21a.

**17.** Intersectionism is alluded to in three postcards Sá-Carneiro sent to Côrtes-Rodrigues between 2 March and 28 March 1914, and *Europa* in the third card. They are all reproduced in Anabela Almeida, *Armando Côrtes-Rodrigues, vida e obra do poeta açoriano de Orpheu*, appendix.

**18.** Doc. 48I/5.

**19.** Doc. 67/30. The poems, numbers 24 and 25 from *The Keeper of Sheep*, were dated 13 Mar. 1914.

## CHAPTER 31

**1.** Interview with Margarida Soares Couto.

**2.** Pessoa's diary entries show that Raul da Costa was staying there for at least a few days in February 1913. He may well have been living with them.

**3.** This is a conjecture on my part, given that Aunt Anica's new apartment was considerably smaller. We know for certain that Rita, when she died in 1916, was living with Carolina.

**4.** *Notas*, 161–62. Pessoa's 24 June 1916 letter to his Aunt Anica. In April 2011 the daughter and a granddaughter of Clara Alves Soares told me about her oft repeated account of the séances.

**5.** Preface for the planned collection of works titled "Aspectos" (Aspects). *SP*, 2.

**6.** Marinetti's *Manifesto del futurismo* was published in Milan and Bologna a few weeks before its publication in French. The first Portuguese translation of the manifesto appeared on August 5, 1909, but in the Azores, far from the mainland, in *Diário dos Açores*: see Pedro da Silveira, "O que soubemos logo em 1909 do Futurismo," *Revista da Biblioteca Nacional*, 1981, no. 1: 90–103. See also Fernando Cabral Martins, "Futurismo," in *Dicionário de Fernando Pessoa e do modernismo português*, ed. Fernando Cabral Martins, 301–2.

**7.** To this draft version (doc. 66/80-81) I have added the same punctuation (exclamation marks, mainly) that Pessoa would add to the final version.

**8.** Untitled poem that begins "Amem outros a graça feminina" ("Let others love feminine grace"), 23 Feb. 1914 (doc. 41/40).
**9.** His birthdate was initially October 13, but Pessoa later changed it to the fifteenth. Nietzsche was born on October 15, 1844.
**10.** "Today you're going to talk with Álvaro de Campos," Pessoa sometimes forewarned Alfredo Guisado, a close friend and collaborator in 1914–1915. But Guisado did not elaborate on Campos's conversational style. See Guisado, "Fernando Pessoa e a sua influência na literatura moderna."

## CHAPTER 32

**1.** Richard Zenith, "A verdadeira partida a Sá-Carneiro," *Colóquio-Letras*, May–Aug. 2017, pp. 135–42.
**2.** "O sentimento da Natureza" (docs. 14⁵/77–78; 40/25; 55M/28a; 150/1–3).
**3.** The respective explanations are found in the third of Campos's "Notes for the Memory of My Master Caeiro," published by Pessoa in *Presença*, Jan.-Feb. 1931 (*SP*, 40), and in Reis's long unfinished preface to the poems of Caeiro (see, in particular, docs. 21/68, 116).
**4.** The correlation of the three heteronyms with different times of day was first noted by António M. Feijó, in an article published in 1999 and integrated into his *Uma admiração pastoril*, 127–28. "Ode à noite" ("Ode to Night") was a title Pessoa used at one point for his "Excertos de duas odes" ("Excerpts from Two Odes"), dated 30 June 1914 and published posthumously.

## CHAPTER 33

**1.** Doc. 48G/32. Ntbk, 144D²/41v. It is possible that the table of contents was drawn up in the summer or early fall of 1914.
**2.** Pessoa kept a partial copy of this letter (doc. 92I/5).
**3.** Doc. 14B/5. Pessoa did not after all mention the heteronyms in his letters to Crowley, but the cited words were written with him in mind as their possible recipient.
**4.** Doc. 27²³/120.

## CHAPTER 34

**1.** The story of the battle and the Sebastianist myth that ensued is marvelously narrated by Ruth MacKay in *The Baker Who Pretended to Be King of Portugal* (Chicago: University of Chicago Press, 2012).
**2.** Sampaio Bruno, *O Encoberto* (Porto: Liv. Moreira, 1904), 167.
**3.** Sampaio Bruno, the pseudonym of José Pereira de Sampaio, responded with a cordial letter, recommending his book *The Hidden One*, which Pessoa owned and had already read. Pessoa also read his *O Brasil mental* (*Reason-Guided Brazil*), which critiques the French philosopher Auguste Comte's positivism (doc. 55I/53), and he at least planned to read *A ideia de Deus* (*The Idea of God*) (doc. 93/87), in which Bruno formulated his own system of belief.
**4.** Pessoa's copy of *L'Occultisme hier et aujourd'hui*, stamped with the monogram A. S., belonged to Alexander Search's "library." Chapter 4 of Grasset's *Demi-fous et demi-responsables* (1907)—published in English as *The Semi-Insane and the Semi-Responsible*—discussed "semi-insanity" in several dozen renowned writers, philosophers, and musicians.
**5.** In an unfinished letter to Sá-Carneiro dated 6 Dec. 1915, Pessoa would mention having read this book "a long time ago."
**6.** Doc. 29/28v.
**7.** "Most important," Pessoa noted on a flyleaf of his copy of *The Rosicrucians*, with the indication of the page number (377) where the cited passage is found. The passage especially struck him when he reread the book, in 1917 (ntbk. 144Y/29).

**8.** Doc. 27¹⁹M³/8v. This and other passages from "Filósofo hermético" were published in Pessoa, *Rosea Cruz*, 29–35.

**9.** Yvette Centeno, "'Episódios / A múmia' ou o hermetismo em Fernando Pessoa," in *Fernando Pessoa: Os trezentos e outros ensaios*, 33–64.

**10.** I toured the house in Mesquita with Isabel and Inês Sarmento in September 2011. Pessoa's September 1914 trip is mentioned in his 4 Oct. 1914 letter to Armando Côrtes-Rodrigues.

**11.** A printed and framed copy of the quatrain, with a mention that it was "inspired and written" in that white house on the hill, was still hanging on one of its walls in 2011. There is a manuscript copy of the quatrain in the Pessoa Archive (doc. 17/39).

**12.** Interview with Maria Manuela Pessoa Chaves Ortega, who was raised partly by Lisbela. The interviewee's memories are of what she heard from other family members. She confirmed the information given by Pedro da Silveira (in Pedro de Merelim, *Fernando Pessoa e a Terceira*, 107) that her cousin Rui Santos, a poet who had known Pessoa, had been holding on to his letters to Lisbela, which he planned to publish, but they went missing after he died in 1962.

## CHAPTER 35

**1.** Doc. 20/51. *EA*, 147–49.

**2.** *A Águia* had published an unfavorable review of Sá-Carneiro's first book of poemas in its June 1914 issue.

**3.** Fernando Pessoa, letter of 4 Jan. 1915 to Armando Côrtes-Rodrigues.

**4.** Jorge de Sena, *Fernando Pessoa e Cia. heterónima*, 94. António M. Feijó, *Uma admiração pastoril pelo diabo*, 38ff.

**5.** Ntbk. 144C/15. Pessoa, *Sensacionismo*, 286.

**6.** Doc. 14⁵/30, dating from 1917.

**7.** César Porto, "Fernando Pessoa e a astrologia."

**8.** Paulo Cardoso, in *CA* and other publications, has meticulously analyzed and tabulated Pessoa's astrological output.

**9.** Doc. 28/94. Virginia Rosa Teixeira (1852–1925) was the psychic's real name.

**10.** Yeats's search for unity of being is a guiding theme of Richard Ellmann's biography.

**11.** Ntbk. 144C/7v–11.

## CHAPTER 36

**1.** Letters and other documents connected to the founding of *Orpheu* can be found in Arnaldo Saraiva, *O modernismo brasileiro e o modernismo português*, and Richard Zenith, Fátima Lopes, and Manuela Rêgo, eds., *Os caminhos de Orpheu*. Steffen Dix, ed., *1915—O ano do Orpheu* contains essays about the year of *Orpheu*'s founding and about the writers and artists connected to the magazine.

**2.** The restaurant closed in 1970, the hotel in 1974.

**3.** Pessoa recorded these particulars in a pseudo-interview written many years later, published in Pessoa, *Sobre Orpheu*, 148–54, and elsewhere. The original is in the Fernando Távora Collection.

**4.** Fernando Pessoa to Adolfo Casais Monteiro, 13 Jan. 1935.

**5.** *O Jornal*, 6 Apr. 1915, 1.

**6.** Gustavo Nobre, "José 'Pacheko,'" in *Pacheko, Almada e "Contemporânea,"* ed. Daniel Pires and António Braz de Oliveira (Lisbon: Centro Nacional de Cultura/Bertrand, 1993), 43–57. *Ilustração*, Aug. 1, 1929, p. 36. Maria José Almada Negreiros, *Conversas com Sarah Affonso*, 99.

**7.** The books were *Dispersão* (1913) and *Céu em fogo* (1915).

**8.** Docs. 48G/29; 57A/5. Zenith, Lopes, and Rêgo, *Os caminhos de Orpheu*, 191–94. *A Ideia Nacional*, 27 Mar. 1915, p. 128.

**9.** António Sardinha, Hipólito Raposo, and Vasco de Carvalho.

**10.** Bernardino Machado, a moderate Democrat who was prime minister for ten months in 1914, had tried to mitigate government hostility toward Church leaders and activities, but the parliament would not allow alterations to the 1911 Law on the Separation of Churches from the State.

**11.** Docs. 92I/6–9. Other notes on the theory, written between the summer of 1914 and 1915, include docs. 16/24v; 92C/23–29; 92E/45; 92I/1, 3–5; 92L/61; 92M/1–4, 6–11.

**12.** In fact, it seems that Pessoa, when asked by the editor to explain himself, simply quit: see Augusto Ferreira Gomes, "Nunca passou miséria," p. 2.

**13.** Doc. 92J/34. The newspapers I consulted mentioned the Red Cross, but not their workers being fired on.

**14.** Material for the essay, still mostly unpublished, found in docs. 12¹/10; 92H/99–100; 92I/38, 41–42; 92J/30–47; 92M/12; and in ntbk. 144A/27v–28v.

**15.** Doc. 55I/34. Pessoa, *Sobre Portugal*, 226–27.

**16.** So Pessoa stated in, for instance, doc. 57A/24v. Published in Pessoa, *Sensacionismo*, 302.

**17.** Docs. 12¹/14, 32, 49, 60, 80; 55B/78v. Pessoa, "Dissertação a favor da Alemanha," in *O regresso dos deuses e outros escritos de António Mora*, 195–229. Pessoa, *Sensacionismo*, 137.

**18.** Most of these pages were published in Pessoa, *O regresso dos deuses*; others were published in Pessoa, *Ultimatum e páginas de sociologia política*, 223–40. Still other pages (including docs. 55G/66–67) have yet to be published.

**19.** Docs. 20/81–82. Pessoa, *O regresso dos deuses*, 255–57. Pessoa did not publish, or even finish, Mora's review of *Orpheu*.

**20.** This last point is discussed in Irene Ramalho Santos, *Atlantic Poets: Fernando Pessoa's Turn in Anglo-American Modernism*, 84–92.

**21.** Ntbk. 144A/26.

## CHAPTER 37

**1.** Ntbk. 144X/44v. Docs. 21/135; S6/20v.

**2.** Mário de Sá-Carnerio to Fernando Pessoa, 31 Dec. 1912.

**3.** Docs. 21/122v, 123v. Pessoa, *Prosa escolhida de Álvaro de Campos*, 122–24.

**4.** Poem dated 4 Apr. 1929.

**5.** Wilde was citing the last line of Lord Alfred Douglas's poem "Two Loves" (1894).

**6.** Pinharanda Gomes, *Filologia e filosofia* , 25–45.

**7.** Ntbk. 144X/64v.

**8.** *CA*, 206–18.

**9.** Ibid., 150–55. Ntbk. 144Y/50v.

**10.** Doc. 14E/66.

**11.** Richard Ellmann, *James Joyce*, 241, citing a 1906 letter from Joyce to his brother.

## CHAPTER 38

**1.** Pessoa made this assertion in a bibliography of Sá-Carneiro's works in *Presença*, Nov. 1928. Spoof or not, the long poem has given rise to some fascinating interpretations.

**2.** *Disquiet*, text 289.

**3.** A poem of Campos dated 9 Aug. 1934 mentions the Pindaric ode structure underpinning "Maritime Ode." I follow the division of the three sections—strophe, antistrophe, and epode—established by Pauly Ellen Bothe in "Poesía y musicalidad en las poéticas modernistas de Fernando Pessoa y T. S. Eliot: La ode marítima" (master's thesis, Faculdade de Letras/ Universidade de Lisboa, 2003).

**4.** Docs. 74/18–23. Pessoa's intention of publishing a Portuguese version of *Dr. Jekyll and Mr. Hyde* is mentioned in his plans for the Ibis press, in 1910 (ntbk. 144V/7), and again in 1915 (doc. 133M/97).

**5.** I believe the first actor to recite it, in 1938, was Manuela Porto (1908–1950), the daughter of César Porto, Pessoa's astrologer friend.

**6.** From a preface for a planned anthology in English titled *The Portuguese "Sensationists"*: *SP*, 62–63.

**7.** *O Mundo*, 7 July 1915.

**8.** The claim appears in the preface to the proposed anthology of sensationist writing, dating from 1916 (*OE*, 5:186). Gaspar Simões (*Vida*, 595–96) wrote that members of the Portuguese Carbonária visited the restaurant, but this organization had already disbanded.

**9.** E.g., Robert Herrick, "The Face of Paris," *Chicago Tribune*, 11 July 1915, p. 5, reproduced in Robert J. Young, *Under Siege: Portraits of Civilian Life in France During World War I* (New York: Berghahn Books, 2000), 42–44 (consulted online).

## CHAPTER 39

**1.** Barley did not answer this letter, if indeed it was sent, but he did respond to a similar letter sent (or resent) by Pessoa in January 1916.

**2.** Doc. 87/68, which dates from around August 1915.

**3.** "Inner World" was also the title of an unfinished short story by Sá-Carneiro that Pessoa much admired; the original has been lost.

**4.** Docs. 90$^1$/25–28. Baldaya's "considerations" were written in English.

**5.** Ntbk. 144P/46–49.

**6.** On wartime shortages of food and other necessities, see Rui Ramos, *História de Portugal: A segunda fundação (1890–1926)*, 519–23.

**7.** Docs. 55A/94; 55H/82; 135/20–22. José Barreto, "Germanófilo ou aliadófilo," *Pessoa Plural*, Fall 2014, pp. 152–215, includes transcriptions of the appeal published in *O Mundo* and of Pessoa's unfinished reply.

**8.** "Crónica da vida que passa," *O Jornal*, 8 Apr. 1915, p. 1.

**9.** Pessoa kept a typed copy of the letter: Pessoa, *Sensacionismo*, 661. Pessoa's heirs have both a handwritten and a typed copy of the rules for Strategy. Pessoa's intention to pitch Strategy, Opposition, and other games to Gamage is mentioned on a list of things to do dating from 1915 (docs. 133M/96–98).

**10.** Docs. 90$^2$/33; 133M/98v.

**11.** Newspaper reports in both *O Século* and *A Capital*, 22 Aug. 1915.

**12.** The typed draft of the letter conserved by Pessoa is undated, but he almost surely sent it in August. Mail from Lisbon to Macau took more than a month to arrive.

**13.** The two issues (CPH) were referred to in Sá-Carneiro's letter to Pessoa of 10 Aug. 1915.

## CHAPTER 40

**1.** Doc. 114$^1$/79. This draft was published in Pessoa, *OE*, 7:151–52, with a conjectural date of Aug.–Sept. 1916, but it was almost certainly written in the fall of 1915.

**2.** Doc. 52/3v. Pessoa intially thought of including some Alexander Search poems in *The Mad Fiddler* but quickly abandoned that idea. He was still very uncertain of how to organize his English poems for publication. A plan for a book called *"Antinous" and Other Poems*, also datable to 1915, includes a section titled "The Mad Fiddler" (doc. 31/90).

**3.** John Lane's receipt and rejection of the poems is mentioned in Pessoa's diary entry for 3 Nov. 1915 and in Sá-Carneiro's letter to Pessoa of 24 Dec. 1915. The Pessoa Archive contains the original and carbon copy of a cover letter of 27 Dec. 1915 to an unspecified publisher (docs. 114$^1$/61–63). Perhaps Pessoa had second thoughts about sending it, or he may have sent another, similar letter with a submission of his work.

**4.** Docs. 114$^1$/116–18; 48G/9. Chances are that he never actually sent any of his letters intended for literary critics.

**5.** Docs. 26B/8, 54A/85–86.

**6.** Doc. 90$^1$/16.

**7.** Docs. 133M/96v–97; 90$^1$/1.

**8.** The Pessoa Archive contains a typed translation of the opening scene (doc. 74/75) as well as a manuscript copy of the original play, possibly handwritten by Braga (env. Anexo D). Part of Pessoa's essay on drama inspired by *Octavio* (docs. 14A/45–53; 18/62–113) was published in Pessoa, *Páginas de estética e de teoria e crítica literárias*, 85–111.

**9.** Originally scheduled to premiere in late 1915, *Octavio* opened in May 1916 at Lisbon's National Theater, where it had six performances.

**10.** The 1915 diary (ntbk. 144X/140v–143) was published in *EA*, 156–72.

**11.** The diary records only the author's last name, James, but there is no record of Pessoa having read anything by Henry James. *Varieties of Religious Experience* is mentioned in his papers as a book he planned to read (doc. 93/87).

**12.** Pablo Javier Pérez López, "Fernando Pessoa e Iván de Nogales: El encuentro de la vida y la literatura," in *Fernando Pessoa em Espanha*, ed. Antonio Sáez Delgado and Jerónimo Pizarro (Lisbon: Biblioteca Nacional de Portugal/Babel, 2014), 39–62.

**13.** Docs. S3/19; 138M/98.

**14.** Doc. 138M/98v.

## CHAPTER 41

**1.** Had he been telegraphed immediately after the stroke, he would have noted the fact in his diary, kept between 1 November and 7 December. The 1 December entry mentions his mother, but only with reference to a letter she had sent the first week of November. Pessoa's stepfather, in his letter of 24 Nov. 1915, wrote that the stroke occurred on the ninth.

**2.** The March 1925 issue of *Contemporânea* would report that copies of *Orpheu* and of Sá-Carneiro's novel, *Lúcio's Confession*, were found in Carlos Franco's knapsack. Missing in action on 4 July 1916, Franco's corpse was never recovered. His death data (discovered by Carlos Silveira) can be consulted on the French Ministry of Defense's "Mémoire des hommes" website.

**3.** Doc. 90²/67. Two and a half months later, on 29 May, Pessoa would cast a horoscope to find out if he stood any chance of being drafted (doc. S6/94). The stars, to his great relief, answered in the negative.

**4.** An obituary published in the Lisbon paper *O Século*, 1 May 1916, reported that Araújo succeeded in having Sá-Carneiro taken to the hospital but that he died en route. There are proven inaccuracies in the obituary; I have relied on the detailed account that Araújo sent in his 10 May letter to Pessoa.

**5.** The letter belongs to a private collector. It is reproduced in Maria José de Lancastre, *Fernando Pessoa: Uma fotobiografia*, 179.

**6.** François Castex, a collector and researcher, met with José de Araújo in the 1960s and tried, unsuccessfully, to get him to reveal the real motive for Sá-Carneiro's suicide. See Mário de Sá-Carneiro, *Cartas a Maria e outra correspondência inédita*, 14.

**7.** The café is mentioned in Carlos Ferreira's letter of 20 May 1916 to Pessoa (Fernando Távora Collection); see Mário de Sá-Carneiro, "Cartas inéditas a Fernando Pessoa," 564. Marina Tavares Dias, the most thorough researcher into Sá-Carneiro's life, revealed the name of Sá-Carneiro's female friend in Sá-Carneiro, *Cartas a Maria*, 16.

**8.** Letter of José Araújo to Pessoa dated 18 Dec. 1916, in Sá-Carneiro, "Cartas inéditas," 570.

**9.** So he told Pessoa's first biographer.

**10.** One complete letter by Pessoa to Sá-Carneiro, dated 14 Mar. 1916, has survived in a typewritten copy made by the sender so that he could adapt parts of it for *The Book of Disquiet*. It's in the appendix of the Penguin edition of *Disquiet*.

**11.** *Le Figaro*, 30 Apr. 1916, p. 3. *Le Temps*, 1 May 1916, p. 3. *Le Petit Parisien*, 1 May 1916, p. 2. *Le Petit Journal*, 1 May 1916, p. 2. *República*, 29 Apr. 1916, p. 2. Obituaries were also published in *DN*, 28 Apr. 1916, p. 2, and *O Século*, 1 May 1916, p. 2.

**12.** Doc. 90⁵/6. The planned booklet was never published.

**13.** Pessoa's confidence in those powers was bolstered by some spiritual self-help books he purchased in April: *The Magic Seven* and *The Magnet*, both by the English American author Lida Abbie Churchill, and *Creative Thought*, by W. J. Colville. These three books, in which Pessoa made abundant pen and pencil marks, contain chapters on inner magnetism, the human aura, the power of suggestion, and so forth.

**14.** According to Pessoa's letter referred to in the next paragraph, that evening occurred in late March. Manuscript evidence suggests it was later, perhaps in late April or May.

**15.** Pessoa had known Santana since as least 1910, when Santana loaned him some money for the failing Ibis press (doc. 92A/87v).

**16.** Doc. 28/101.

## CHAPTER 42

**1.** The second communication of the thirty published in *SP* is dated 28 May 1916, but the correct date is 28 June. The communications cited in the following pages, unless otherwise noted, are published in *EA*.

**2.** George Mills Harper, *The Making of Yeats's 'A Vision': A Study of the Automatic Script*, 2 vols. (London: Macmillan, 1987).

**3.** Doc. 90⁴/24. Wardour ventured several other possible birthdates before settling on 30 July 1903 as "the right date."

**4.** Richard Ellmann, *Yeats: The Man and the Masks*, 223–25.

**5.** Docs. 42/28a; 58/12v; 66D/14.

**6.** *Notas*, 73–76.

**7.** Rhian Atkins discusses this passage and Maistre's book in "Going Nowhere in *Voyage autour de ma chambre* and 'Viagem Nunca Feita,'" in *Pessoa in an Intertextual Web*, ed. David G. Frier (London: Legenda, 2012), 82–98. Pessoa owned two copies of Maistre's book.

**8.** The only other person who might have suggested this painter to Pessoa was José Pacheco. In the fall of 1916 Pacheco opened an art gallery in Lisbon that displayed works by Almada Negreiros and other modernists, though not Souza-Cardoso.

**9.** It was only in 2015 that Marta Soares discovered the photographs, in Souza-Cardoso's archive, of the four chosen paintings. They are reproduced in Richard Zenith, Fátima Lopes, and Manuela Rêgo, eds., *Os caminhos de Orpheu*, 95–108. Pessoa had six typed poems of Pessanha but planned to include some others from a list of thirteen additional poems (docs. 151; 41/25v). Pessanha's holiday in Portugal lasted from the fall of 1915 to the spring of 1916. The dossier on Camilo Pessanha at the National Library of Portugal, which includes an excellent chonology assembled by Daniel Pires, may be consulted online.

**10.** The anthology was published earlier that same year in the United States in *The Glebe*.

**11.** The cover letters refer to two Poetry Bookshop chapbooks—by the imagist poets Richard Aldington and F. S. Flint—published in December 1915 and owned by Pessoa. One of the letters states that *Orpheu* 2 "dates back to June 1915, but we have succeeded in publishing the third, which will be out in a few days." These particulars make it possible to date the cover letters to August or September 1916. Docs. 114²/90, 62. *OE*, 7:149–51.

**12.** Doc. 114¹/112. The surviving draft is unfinished. It is possible, but unlikely, that Pessoa completed and actually sent off the letter.

**13.** Docs. 20/86–87. The letter was probably never sent.

**14.** Edited by Augusto Santa-Rita, a poet and the brother of Santa Rita Pintor. The review's founders included Alfredo Guisado, Armando Côrtes-Rodrigues, and António Ferro. The first issue was also the last.

**15.** Other researchers believe he may have emerged one or two years earlier.

**16.** Docs. 48/9, 17. The *Anthology* included writers who had published in *Orpheu* 1 or 2, or whose work was slated to appear in *Orpheu* 3.

**17.** *OE*, 5:187–97.

## CHAPTER 43

**1.** José Barreto's "O mago e o louco: Fernando Pessoa e Alberto da Cunha Dias" gives a detailed account of Cunha Dias's forced internment and a general overview of his life and relationship with Pessoa.

**2.** Doc. 48A/34.

**3.** *Athena* was alternately subtitled *A Journal of Higher Culture* (docs. 48G/26; 87/68). Some of the surviving plans for the magazine can be dated to 1915 on the basis of the typewriter and ribbon ink (docs. 48B/11; 48G/33; 87/68).

**4.** Letter to Harold Monro (doc. 114²/90). The prefacer to the *Sensationist Anthology* states: "*Orpheu* is a quarterly review of which, though it began a year and a half ago, only three numbers have appeared."

**5.** *República*, 23 Aug. 1916, p. 1 (announcement discovered by João Macdonald). Docs. 87/28–29, 42, 46. Pessoa, *Sensacionismo*, 78–79, 479.

**6.** Docs. 90⁶/59–60. Leal moved initially to Seville (doc. 115²/81–86) and from there went to Madrid. Pessoa alluded to Leal's attempted suicide in his astrological reading and in his 4 Sept. 1916 letter to Côrtes-Rodrigues.

**7.** So Leal wrote in a 27 Jan. 1916 letter to Mário de Sá-Carneiro, who forwarded it to Pessoa (docs. 115²/81–86).

**8.** *Disquiet*, text 430.

**9.** Leal to Sá-Carneiro, 27 Jan. 1916. The letter was published in Mário Cesariny, *O virgem negra* (Lisbon: Assírio & Alvim, 1989), 93–104.

**10.** Doc. 49B⁶/19. Published for the first time in 2007, in *OE*, 6:440.

**11.** *A Ordem*, 6 Dec. 1916.

**12.** Docs. 48H/49; 55D/88–107. See Ana Maria Freitas, "Fernando Pessoa e a polémica Cadbury," *Revista de Estudos Anglo-Portugueses*, no. 23 (2014): 349–58.

**13.** Doc. 55D/91. When criticizing the treatment of workers "at the Rand" (doc. 55D/91v), Pessoa may have been thinking not only of black Africans but also (as suggested by Freitas, "Fernando Pessoa e a polémica Cadbury") of the thousands of Chinese indentured laborers brought in to work the mines between 1904 and 1910. Pessoa's article also insisted that the injustices committed in Portuguese West Africa should be imputed not to the Portuguese nation but to the corrupt and decadent monarchy that ruled it at the time.

**14.** For instance, in "A opinião pública," an article published in 1919, and in doc. 110/5.

**15.** Doc. 49B⁷/6v.

**16.** Doc. 55B/88. Pessoa, *Sobre Portugal*, 217.

**17.** José Paulo Cavalcanti Filho, *Fernando Pessoa—Uma quase autobiografia*, 53, suggests that a book in Pessoa's library, John George Godard's *Racial Supremacy, Being Studies in Imperialism* (1905), promoted the idea of white supremacy. In fact, the opposite is true. The book was a damning critique of British imperialism and the notion of white supremacy that justified it.

**18.** Doc. 110/41. From an unfinished and unpublished "Open Letter" to Woodrow Wilson, discussed later.

**19.** Doc. 19/64. From Pessoa's study on literary immortality titled *Erostratus*, discussed later.

**20.** Doc. 92M/65.

**21.** Ntbk. 144Y/39. From a fragmentary poem that begins "Ora por nós, ora por nós" ("Pray for us, pray for us").

**22.** Doc. 58/27. Written in Portuguese and dated 26 Feb. 1917.

## CHAPTER 44

**1.** Doc. 55/91.

**2.** These book projects are mentioned in ntbk. 144Y.

**3.** Doc. S4/9 contains the two charts. The one for *The Mad Fiddler* refers to its "Registration" at 2:14 p.m. "Arrival in England: 21 or 22-V-1917," he wrote on the chart, in English.

**4.** Doc. 90⁴/50v.

**5.** Doc. 90³/40.

**6.** Docs. 113P¹/3–6.

**7.** Doc. 15²/66.

**8.** Ana Rita Palmeirim's *José Coelho Pacheco: O falso semi-heterónimo de Pessoa* is the best source for information on Coelho Pacheco's life and literary work.

**9.** A printed envelope in the Pessoa Archive (doc. 133C/52v) is the only evidence I could find of Coelho de Jesus's attempt to sell cars.

**10.** Pessoa cast an astrological chart for the firm's founding date of 21 Aug. 1917 (doc. S5/41).

**11.** Doc. S4/73v.

**12.** Docs. 124A/42v; S6/55v. The question was phrased in English.

**13.** *Disquiet*, text 429. Pessoa dated the passage 18 Sept. 1917.

**14.** Doc. 8/3. The reverse side of the manuscript contains a list of articles to promote Alberto Caeiro that dates from 1914.

## CHAPTER 45

**1.** "It is sweet and fitting to die for one's country" (from an ode by Horace).

**2.** The official founder and editor in chief, however, was the artist (and future film director) Carlos Filipe Porfírio, who obtained financing for the magazine through a friend. Most of the items published in the magazine, including the "Ultimatum," were assembled in the summer of 1917. See João Macdonald, "Porfírio & Santa Rita Lda.: Um exame à produção de *Portugal Futurista*," *Convocarte* (Lisbon), Sept. 2019, pp. 316–34.

**3.** In 1919, when he was already suffering from acute schizophrenia, he would perform a short solo dance at a hotel in Switzerland.

**4.** *A Monarquia*, 2 Nov. 1917, p. 1 (recently discovered by João Macdonald). Pessoa cast an astrological chart for *Portugal Futurista* with details about its brief existence (doc. 90²/32).

**5.** When some page proofs from the frustrated issue were finally published, in 1953, scholars concluded that the mysterious C. Pacheco, author of the poem "Beyond Another Ocean," was another heteronym of Fernando Pessoa. In 2011, Ana Rita Palmeirim came forward with original manuscripts of the poem, written by her grandfather, the forgotten José Coelho Pacheco. Palmeirim, *José Coelho Pacheco: O falso semi-heterónimo de Pessoa*, 161–78.

**6.** *A Situação*, 25 May 1917. Cited in Sidónio Pais, *Um ano de ditadura: Discursos e alocuções* (Lisbon: Lusitânia, 1924), 61.

**7.** Doc. 90⁴/31. *Notas*, 85–87. The *Anuário Comercial* for 1919 (compiled in late 1918) lists Sengo's office in the same building and on the same floor as Pessoa's. Sengo's office address is recorded in the Pessoa Archive, on stationery from Sengo's dairy store, next to which Pessoa had briefly lived in late 1916 (doc. 133C/58v). Pessoa also cast Sengo's astrological chart (doc. S5/88v).

**8.** Alberto Da Cunha Dias, *Outono*, 30.

**9.** Docs. 48/30; 110/5v, 96.

**10.** Carlos Jorge Alves Lopes, "Os portugueses na Grande Guerra" (master's thesis, Universidade Aberta de Lisboa, 2012; consulted online).

## CHAPTER 46

**1.** Docs. 90⁴/52–53 (in English).

**2.** What Pessoa actually wrote was a detailed, narrative outline for a full-fledged case study that he never realized. The typewriter and ink ribbon make it possible to date the typed version of the outline (docs. 54A/78–82) to 1918. The draft version (doc. 54B/23) was probably written that same year.

**3.** This recommendation from beyond occurs repeatedly and enduringly, until as late as 1934 (doc. 62B/33).

**4.** Doc. 43/1v.

**5.** Ntbks. 144X/54; 144Y/20.

**6.** Docs. 110/69–72.

**7.** Doc. S5/43 (in English).

**8.** The reception of *Antinous: A Poem* is discussed in George Monteiro, "Fernando Pessoa, He Had His Nerve."

**9.** Fernando Pessoa, "Falência?" (Failure?), *O Tempo*, 13 Oct. 1918, p. 1. "Lógica . . . futurista" ("Futurist . . . Logic"), *Diário Nacional*, 14 Oct. 1918, p. 1.

10. Doc. 113P¹/22.

11. Doc. 92D/60.

12. Doc. 87/66. *Minerva* was an alternate title for this magazine project. Craveiro's contribution (doc. 113P¹/21) was published in Pessoa, *Eu sou uma antologia*, ed. Jerónimo Pizarro and Patricio Ferrari, 544–45.

13. Doc. 5/83.

14. Stated in his 13 Jan. 1935 letter to Adolfo Casais Monteiro on the origin of the heteronyms. In this letter, Pessoa also defined Álvaro de Campos as "the most hysterically hysterical part of me," but he was better adapted to the modern world than his fellow heteronyms.

15. This idea was developed by Leo Marx in "Melville's Parable of the Walls," *Sewanee Review*, Autumn 1953; reprinted in *Melville's Short Novels*, ed. Dan McCall (New York: W. W. Norton, 2002), 239–56.

16. Maria Nogueira Rosa to Fernando Pessoa, 23 Nov. 1918.

17. *O Primeiro de Janeiro*, 26 Oct. 1918, p. 2, and *O Dia* (Lisbon), 28 Oct. 1918, published brief obituaries, while a couple of other newspapers published succinct death notices. See João Macdonald, "Os obituários de Amadeo," *Machina*, May 2020 (online journal).

18. Alfredo Guisado to António Ferro, 15 Nov. 1918 (letter in the António Ferro Archive).

19. *A Capital*, 11 Nov. 1918, pp. 1–2.

20. His mortal remains would be transferred to the National Pantheon in 1966.

## CHAPTER 47

1. António Machado Santos, the reputed founder of the Republic, had parted ways with Pais and his government some months earlier and would not, in any case, have been willing to rule as a dictator.

2. Doc. 92V/3.

3. Doc. 55J/12.

4. Doc. 110/38.

5. In his 14 June 1917 speech on the Washington Monument grounds, for instance, or in his address to Congress on 4 Dec. 1917.

6. Docs. 110A/1, 12.

7. In the spring of 1919 Pessoa reorganized his run-on open letters under a new title, *Five Epistles to the Boeotians*. The Boeotians were a proverbially dull-witted people of ancient Greece, whereas the modern Boeotians, according to Pessoa, were all those who regarded Wilson, Lloyd George, and Clemenceau as valid and respectable statesmen (doc. 111/11).

8. Some passages were written in English, others in Portuguese. Docs. 55J/36; 92B/73–74; 92U/49–50, 77–79; 92V/1; 112/4–8. Listed in publication plans: docs. 48H/2, 18; doc. 182; ntbk. 144G/38.

9. Doc. 92V/17 (in English).

10. Docs. 123/43; 55G/29 (point 6).

11. Ntbk. 144G/7–8.

12. Docs. 133G/93; 11¹¹MU/1–6; 27²³/126–27. Pessoa, *Argumentos para filmes*, 24–30, 39–48, 93–96.

13. Docs. 87A/7–10. Ntbk. 144G/13v. Doc. 55I/18v.

14. Ntbk. 144G/8v. *Diogenes* and *Portugal* were both possible titles for this journal. Docs. 48I/19–20; 92V/4; 136/62.

15. Pessoa, letters to Geraldo Coelho de Jesus, 10 Aug. and 12 Aug. 1919. Copies of two other Sidonist newspapers, *A Época* and *O Jornal*, were part of the bonfire (*A Capital*, 10 Aug. 1919, p. 1).

16. Doc. 55I/100.

17. Doc. 42/26. Poetic fragments and note published in Pessoa, *Poesia: 1902–1917*, 353–54, 466–67.

18. One of the poems belongs to the Fernando Távora Collection; another is in CPH; four others (docs. 42/47; 43/13, 47–48; 44/5–6) were published in Pessoa, *Poesia: 1918–1930*, 22,

51–57. The Julian material was published in a critical edition by Carlos Pittella in *Pessoa Plural*, Fall 2017, pp. 457–88.

**19.** Doc. 55G/29.

**20.** Doc. 111/10v, "First Epistle to the Boeotians" (in English).

**21.** The entire archive was digitized a few years later.

**22.** Docs. 43/50–51. I published the poem, together with an English translation, in *Lusosex: Gender and Sexuality in the Portuguese-Speaking World*, ed. Susan Canty Quinlan and Fernando Arenas (Minneapolis: University of Minnesota Press, 2002), pp. 47–53.

**23.** Letter from Bentley to Pessoa, 3 Aug. 1918 (doc. 115¹/19). Published in Pessoa, *Correspondência inédita*, 208. Bentley was the editor in chief of *Portugal: A Monthy Review of the Country, Its Colonies, Commerce, History, Literature and Art*, published in London in 1915–1916. Pessoa's *35 Sonnets* made a better impression on Bentley.

## CHAPTER 48

**1.** Ntbk. 144G/17–25. He wrote these notes in English.

**2.** Ntbk. 144G/22v, 19, 23.

**3.** This was the title of the American edition (1911). The original, British edition (1908–1910) was called simply *The Children's Encyclopaedia*.

**4.** *Tesouro da juventude* (*Young People's Treasury*), marketed only in Brazil, was not published until 1925, but most of Pessoa's work for it dates from 1919. The archive of Raul Proença, who oversaw the team of translators in Portugal, contains the orginal manuscripts for some of Pessoa's translations. Besides the poem "O avô e o neto" ("The Grandfather and Grandson"), signed by Pessoa, the encyclopedia includes a couple of unsigned poems he may also have written.

**5.** Doc. 114¹/96. Pessoa, *Correspondência, 1905–1922*, 271.

**6.** Pessoa to Victoriano Braga, 25 Jan. 1919 (letter in António Miranda Collection, Santo Tirso). A facsimile and transcription were published in *Pessoa Plural*, Fall 2019, pp. 391–92.

**7.** Maria Nogueira Rosa to Pessoa, letter dated 15 July–18 Aug. 1919. *Notas*, p. 63. On the brief tenure of the rector, Joaquim José Coelho de Carvalho, see Manuel Augusto Rodrigues, "A República e a autonomia da Universidade," *Biblos: Revista da Faculdade de Letras da Universidade de Coimbra* 8 (2010): 95–126 (consulted online).

**8.** Details recorded in a memo book at the Casa Fernando Pessoa. Reproduced in *Objectos*, 164–207.

**9.** The Grande Hotel de Faro, written up in the *Revista de turismo*, May 1920, pp. 132–34.

**10.** On 30 Aug. 1919, Pessoa wrote a letter to Luís de Montalvor from Faro, only vaguely explaining the motive for his trip (Fernando Távora Collection). The memo book referred to in n. 8, above, mentions his intention to research canned fish and other Algarve products: *Objectos*, 164–65.

**11.** Pessoa's 10 Aug. 1919 letter to Geraldo Coelho de Jesus mentions his cramped living quarters. *EA*, 180, 450–51. Pessoa decided to give Emília notice in August. *Objectos*, 195–99, 204, 183.

**12.** Pessoa's 19 Mar. 1920 letter to Ophelia Queiroz suggests he was living with a family.

**13.** Letters from Maria Nogueira Rosa to Pessoa dated 15 July and 19 Dec. 1919.

**14.** Pessoa to Ophelia Queiroz, 22 Mar. 1920.

**15.** Letters from Maria Nogueira Rosa to Pessoa dated 14 Oct. and 19 Dec. 1919.

**16.** The import-export firm had advertised in *A Acção*, 19 May 1919.

**17.** From the passage titled "The Major."

**18.** Pessoa and Ofélia Queiroz, *Correspondência amorosa completa, 1919–1935*, 15–16.

**19.** Ibid.

**20.** Doc. 49A⁵/73.

**21.** Ofélia Queiroz, *Cartas de amor de Ofélia a Fernando Pessoa*, 156.

**22.** Pessoa and Queiroz, *Correspondência amorosa completa*, 17–18. Pessoa's notes were made on 19 Feb. 1920, when he cast a horoscope apropos of his relationship with Queiroz (ntbk. 144G/26v–28).

**23.** Pessoa and Queiroz, *Correspondência amorosa completa*, 22.

**24.** Ophelia Queiroz to Pessoa, 23 Mar. 1920.

**25.** *Disquiet*, text 138.

**26.** Franz Kafka to Felice Bauer, 11 Nov. 1912, in Kafka, *Letters to Felice*, ed. Erich Heller and Jürgen Born, tr. James Stern and Elisabeth Duckworth (New York: Schocken Books, 2016), 37.

**27.** Ophelia Queiroz to Pessoa, 23 Mar. 1920.

**28.** The *Lourenço Marques* was one of the German ships that had been moored in Lisbon's harbor and seized by the Portuguese in 1916.

**29.** *Intimidade*, 235.

**30.** Docs. 28A/10v; 92R/4v; 92A/87v.

**31.** Michael (Luís Miguel) Rosa to Hubert D. Jennings, 20 Nov. 1966; published in *Pessoa Plural*, Fall 2015, pp. 253–57.

**32.** Pessoa and Queiroz, *Correspondência amorosa completa*, 21.

**33.** Letters dated 13 May, 18 May, and 30 May 1920.

## CHAPTER 49

**1.** Ophelia Queiroz to Pessoa, 1 June 1920.

**2.** Ntbk. 144G/9, 40. Personal notes (CPH) clearly state his intention to abandon Cosmópolis in favor of Olisipo.

**3.** Docs. 137D/44–47, discussed in António Mega Ferreira, *Fazer pela vida*, 76–79, and published in Pessoa, *Fernando Pesssoa: O comércio e a publicidade*, 154–59.

**4.** Doc. 48/44v. The exact address was Rua da Boa Vista, 102, second floor left.

**5.** Three envelopes from foreign firms addressed to Olisipo and postmarked in October and November of 1920 are in the Archive: docs. 104/30v; 49B$^5$/83v; 49C$^1$/6av. The last is from Veloce Ltd. Pessoa no doubt contacted other firms as well.

**6.** The Greek Anthology was published by Heinemann in the Loeb Classical Library. N. R. Paton was the translator.

**7.** Ntbk. 144T/3.

**8.** Doc. 125A/13. *SP*, 165–66.

**9.** Passages for "Impermanence" all found in Pessoa, *Heróstrato*.

**10.** It is possible that Pessoa wrote the preface in 1919, but no earlier, since it alludes to Ricardo Reis's immigration to the Americas, which occurred after the Monarchy of the North was crushed, in February 1919.

**11.** Queiroz to Pessoa, 3 June 1920.

**12.** *Disquiet*, text 112.

**13.** Docs. 49B$^5$/83; 49C$^1$/6–6a. Both poems are incomplete.

## CHAPTER 50

**1.** Docs. 58/57–61. Mostly unpublished, but two passages written in 1917 were transcribed in Teresa Rita Lopes, *Pessoa por conhecer*, 90–92. The play appears in various publishing plans, including one for Olisipo from 1921. Docs. 44/47; 48B/25; 137A/22. Ntbk. 144G/38.

**2.** For instance, in his article "As algemas" ("Handcuffs"), published in 1926.

**3.** António Ferro, "Sinfonia heróica," *O Jornal*, 5 Dec. 1919, p. 1. For a time, Ferro was the senior editor of this Sidonist newspaper.

**4.** Parts of Pessoa's English translation (CPH) were published by Jerónimo Pizarro and Sara Afonso Ferreira in "A génese d'*A invenção do dia claro* e o estabelecimento de *Invention of the Bright Day*," in *Fernando Pessoa: O guardador de papéis*, ed. Jerónimo Pizarro (Lisbon: Texto Editores, 2009), 283–338.

**5.** Anna Klobucka discovered this review. Her *O mundo gay de António Botto* provides an in-depth discussion of Botto's critical reception and other aspects of his life and work.

**6.** Doc. 133I/35.

**7.** *O Primeiro de Janeiro*, 3 May 1921, p. 6, and 4 May 1921, p. 6.

**8.** Docs. 137A/13–20, 52–57.

**9.** Docs. 137A/21–24.

**10.** "O caso da janela estreita" ("The Case of the Narrow Window"), in Pessoa, *Quaresma, decifrador*, 356 (doc. 27⁶S/4). The same statement appears in a passage for Pessoa's essay "O sentido de Sidonismo" ("The Meaning of Sidonism"; doc. 92B/72).

**11.** Docs. 55J/54, 56–59; 55A/101.

**12.** Doc. 48B/23v.

**13.** "Unser Nachwuchs," *Neue Freie Presse* (Vienna), 25 Dec. 1909.

**14.** Doc. 53B/70. More than half of the material written for the essay (docs. 53B/55–71, 92v) was transcribed in Yvette Centeno, *Fernando Pessoa: Os trezentos e outros ensaios*, 119–43. Additional passages: docs. 26/20–21; 55J/85–89.

**15.** Doc. 53B/57.

**16.** And possibly in other languages: doc. 137A/23. See also Pessoa, *Fernando Pessoa: O comércio e a publicidade*, 61–62.

**17.** *Exílios*, 183. The current whereabouts of this genealogical study are unknown.

**18.** Mário Saa, *A invasão dos judeus* (Lisbon: Libânio da Silva, 1925), 291–95, 298. A copy of the book is in Pessoa's personal library.

**19.** "O perigo judeu," *A Batalha*, 13 Feb. 1925, p. 1. A reviewer for the same newspaper deemed Saa's book to be unequivocally antisemitic (*A Batalha*, 23 Mar. 1925, lit. supp. p. 4).

**20.** Docs. 134A/26–28; 55J/54v.

**21.** In his sprawling open letter to Woodrow Wilson (doc. 110/30).

**22.** Doc. 53B/56.


## CHAPTER 51

**1.** *DN*, 20 Oct. 1921.

**2.** Docs. 137D/70–71.

**3.** *Ilustração Portuguesa*, 10 Dec. 1921, p. 81. *DL*, 17 Dec. 1921, p. 1.

**4.** Docs. 115¹/26; 115⁸/33. *Imagens*, 98.

**5.** So he told Ophelia Queiroz.

**6.** Docs. 137B/75–79; 137D/48–51. António Mega Ferreira, *Fazer pela vida*, 83–84. Pessoa's typed and dated proposal was almost certainly submitted, though I could find no conclusive proof to that effect. A one-volume exhibition catalogue, *Livro d'oiro e catálogo oficial: Exposição Internacional do Rio de Janeiro; Secção Portuguesa*, was published by the Comissariado Geral do Governo in August 1922.

**7.** Pessoa's proposal was actually an updated, expanded version of his idea for a Company of Portuguese Products, which he had hoped to launch through Olisipo, when this was still a commercial agency rather than a small publishing house. Docs. 137/80–90; 137A/1–12, 38–41, 50. Mega Ferreira, *Fazer pela vida*, 92–95. Eduardo Ramires dos Reis's reply (docs. 115¹/52–53) was published in Pessoa, *Correspondência Inédita*, 210–11.

**8.** Only the last page of the original typescript survives in the Pessoa Archive (doc. 27²D/14). The story probably germinated in his mind in 1921 (docs. 48/40–41).

**9.** Pessoa's definition is from an unfinished letter to José Pacheco (docs. 114³/9–10), published in Pessoa, *Correspondência, 1905–1922*, 410–11.

**10.** The book, Paul Eltzbacher's *As doutrinas anarquistas* (1908), is signed by Alexander Search and is in Pessoa's personal library.

**11.** Doc. 48B/62.

**12.** Translations of the work into English have rendered the title as *The Ego and His* [or *Its*] *Own*. Max Stirner was the pseudonym of Johann Kaspar Schmidt (1806–1856).

## CHAPTER 52

1. The magazine is dated October but was not distributed until early November.
2. Registered at the National Library on 17 Nov. 1922 (doc. Anexo IV/10). Although the book's colophon states that it was typeset and printed in January 1922, it was not released (and perhaps not printed) until November.
3. Doc. 135C/28. Pessoa's 21 Nov. 1922 letter to Botto mentions the flyer, which was printed at least six months earlier and dated "Spring 1922," the time of year when the book was originally scheduled to be published.
4. Doc. Anexo A/1.
5. Registered at the National Library on 17 Feb. 1923 and sold by at least one bookstore as of that date (docs. Anexo IV/13, 18).
6. *DL*, 14 Feb. 1923, p. 8. Another newspaper, *A Capital* (14 Feb. 1923, p. 2), reported that eighteen men were apprehended.
7. Marcelo Caetano, "'Arte' sem moral nenhuma," *Ordem Nova*, nos. 4–5, June–July 1927, pp. 156–58, cited in Judith Teixeira, *Poemas*, 250.
8. *DL*, 10 Feb. 1922, p. 5. *A Capital*, 5 Feb. 1923, p. 1. *DL*, 6 Feb. 1923, p. 4.
9. *A Época*, 22 Feb. 1923, transcribed in Zetho Gunha Gonçalves, *Notícia do maior escândalo erótico-social do século XX em Portugal*, 107–9.
10. *A Capital*, 5 Mar. 1923, p. 2. António Botto, *Canções*, 148–49. Docs. 55D/13, 24; 115³/24; Anexo IV/15, 17, 18.
11. *A Época*, 6 Mar. 1923, p. 1. A copy of the actual manifesto is in the Pessoa Archive (doc. Anexo A/69).
12. Docs. 48D/60–65; 75/71v. José Barreto, "Os destinatários dos panfletos pessoanos em 1923," *Pessoa Plural*, Fall 2016, pp. 628–703.
13. In Pessoa's essay "Erostratus."
14. I owe this observation to Anna Klobucka.
15. Pessoa to António Botto, 21 Nov. 1922. In two subsequent letters from Pessoa to Metello, he sent his greetings to the young man's parents, whom he had evidently met at the family estate.
16. *Contemporânea* 8 was dated February 1923 but not actually published until mid-May (*DL*, 22 May 1923, p. 1).
17. L. P. Moitinho de Almeida, *Fernando Pessoa no cinquentenário da sua morte*, 79, 82.
18. This ode begins "A flor que és, não a que dás, eu quero" ("I want the flower you are, not the one you give") and is dated 21 Oct. 1923. Campos's prose piece (doc. 71A/34) was published in Teresa Rita Lopes *Pessoa por conhecer*, 475.

## CHAPTER 53

1. *DL*, 15 June 1922, p. 5.
2. Judith Teixeira's home is described by an interviewer in *Revista Portuguesa*, 24 Mar. 1923, pp. 16–18; the interview was reprinted in Teixeira, *Poemas*, 236–38.
3. Interview in *Diário da Manhã*, 14 Sept. 1952, pp. 6–8. Cited by Antonio Sáez Delgado, *Pessoa y España*, 99; this book gives a thorough account of the literary relations and publications mentioned in this passage.
4. Adriano del Valle to Fernando Pessoa, 10 Nov. 1924 (doc. 115⁸/39).
5. The Spanish reviews were mentioned in *DL*, 7 Sept. 1923, p. 1, and 18 Sept. 1923, p. 1. When he was in Lisbon, Valle had drawn up a list of Spanish critics and poets to whom Pessoa sent copies of Botto's book.
6. *DL*, 3 Aug. 1923, p. 5. The title of his lecture was "Poetas de hoje" ("Poets of Today").
7. The letter, surviving in Adriano del Valle's archive and transcribed by Antonio Sáez Delgado in *Fernando Pessoa e Espanha* (Lousã: Editora Licorne, 2011), 149, dates from August or September 1923.

**8.** Docs. Anexo IV/14, 16, 19.

**9.** *Diário do Senado*, session no. 66, 20 July 1923, p. 4 (consulted online at http://debates
.parlamento.pt).

**10.** *Washington Post*, 10 Aug. 1923, p. 8. *New York Times*, 10 May 1923, p. 25, also remarked
on Italy's much improved train service.

**11.** *Portugal*, 2 June 1923, pp. 3–5; 9 June 1923, p. 3; 16 June 1923, p. 5; 23 June 1923, pp. 5–
6. Mário Saa wrote under the pseudonym M. D'Erval, a quasi-anagram of Ervedal, a village
close to the estate where he grew up and would eventually return to. Augusto Ferreira Gomes
signed several of his contributions as "C. S.," or Carlos Sequeira, the same pseudonym he used
as a translator of stories by Edgar Allan Poe. On the subject of Portuguese fascism, by which
I mean those who actually embraced that term, see Ernesto Castro Leal, *António Ferro: Espaço
político e imaginário social (1918–1932)*, 113–64, and Luís Reis Torgel, *Estados novos, Estado
Novo: ensaios de história política e cultural* (Coimbra: Universidade de Coimbra, 2009), 1:87–104.

**12.** See the articles "Como organizar Portugal" ("How to Organize Portugal"; 1919) and
"A opinião pública" ("Public Opinion"; 1919) as well as docs. 21/25–26 (signed by R. Reis);
55/83–84; 55H/78; 92M/45v.

**13.** Ferro's interview with Mussolini ran on the front page of *A Capital*, 5 Dec. 1923. The
issues of *A Capital* from 15 Nov. to 8 Dec. 1923 contain other interviews and reports from
Ferro's trip, as well as separate articles praising Mussolini.

**14.** Doc. 133E/12. Published in *Fascismo*, 57.

**15.** *DN*, 26 Feb. 1923, p. 2 (doc. 135C/103). The connection made between the news clipping and Pessoa's hostility toward Mussolini was proposed by José Barreto in "O fascismo e o
salazarismo vistos por Fernando Pessoa," Academia.edu, pp. 5–6.

**16.** See, for instance, *DL*, 20 July 1923, p. 7; *A Capital*, 8 Dec. 1923, p. 1.

**17.** Doc. 104/1.

**18.** Jorge Uribe, ed., *Trovas do Bandarra* (Lisbon: Guimarães, 2010), is a transcription of
the 1866 edition owned by Pessoa (docs. 125B/67–100) and includes some of his annotations
and other relevant texts. The other edition found in the Pessoa Archive (docs. 125B/101–45)
was published in 1911. Pessoa's writings about Bandarra and interpretations of his prophetic
poems are mostly located in envs. 125, 125A, and 125B of the Archive. For his selection
of key quatrains by Nostradamus, some of which he annotated, see docs. 125/20–24, 86;
125B/22–26, 44, 49–52.

**19.** The idea for an edition of Bandarra's poems, with commentary signed by Raphael Baldaya, first occurred to Pessoa around 1918 (doc. 90¹/8). He had hoped to publish this edition,
never completed, as an Olisipo book (docs. 20/65; 48I/17; 137A/21).

**20.** Doc. 125B/11. Pessoa, *Sobre Portugal*, 205–6.

**21.** Lamim's name appears in an 1810 book on Sebastianism consulted by Pessoa. Docs.
125/2–3. Pessoa, *Sebastianismo*, 147–54.

**22.** Docs. 125A/30, 83; 125B/11. Pessoa, *Sobre Portugal*, 180–83, 205.

**23.** Doc. 125B/19.

**24.** The Pessoa Archive contains rough drafts of his answers (docs. 55F/41; 55I/47–50;
125/10).

## CHAPTER 54

**1.** *Intimidade*, 115, 118. Fernando Gaspar, "Divididos na vida e na morte," 49R. Interview
with Margarida Soares Couto.

**2.** Arquivo Histórico da Marinha, Livro Mestre do Corpo de Engenheiros Construtores
Navais 2, folios 98v–100, 159–59v.

**3.** *Intimidade*, 117.

**4.** Eduardo Freitas da Costa to Carlos Queiroz, 20 Aug. 1936 (Maria da Graça Queiroz
Collection). The letter writer remembered Pessoa reciting poems to him and other cousins
"around 1923," but from late 1920 to early 1924 he and his parents were in Italy.

**5.** Docs. 87/72; 48B/110.

6. Doc. 48B/26. "Loucura" ("Madness") is the title of this poem.

7. *DL*, 3 Nov. 1924, p. 5. *A Capital*, 3 Nov. 1924, p. 2.

8. Fernando Pessoa to William Bentley, 31 Oct. 1924. Bentley had recently moved from Lisbon back to England.

9. "The Three Metamorphoses," *Thus Spoke Zarathustra*, in Friedrich Nietzsche, *The Portable Nietzsche* (New York: Penguin, 1988), ed. and tr. Walter Kaufmann, 182.

10. *Vida*, 541. Henriqueta Madalena Rosa Dias/Maria Ivone de Ornellas de Andrade, "Ele sabia o valor que tinha," *Jornal de Letras*, 26 Nov.–2 Dec. 1985, p. 6.

11. *DN*, p. 5. *Imagens de uma vida*, 103.

12. Doc. 115$^1$/73 (letter dated 31 July 1925). Published in Pessoa, *Correspondência inédita*, 50–52.

13. Doc. 14E/5. There is a brief note for the would-be edition in which Caeiro's "relatives" sign themselves with the initials A. L. C. and J. C. (doc. 21/75).

## CHAPTER 55

1. António Cobeira, "Fernando Pessoa, vulgo 'o Pessoa,' e a sua ironia transcendente," p. 5. Cobeira had left Lisbon many years ago to work as a high school teacher in the town of Santarém, and later in Porto.

2. Docs. 14$^2$/94; 55D/65–67; 87/39; 87A/18.

3. Docs. 49B$^1$/39, 95–96; 49B$^4$/9.

4. Letter of 1 Oct. 1925 (Jaime de Andrade Neves Collection). Pessoa wrote that his niece died from "intestinal poisoning."

5. Interview with Manuela Nogueira.

6. The notes for Pessoa's code-condensing system are mostly found in env. 128A. Eden Fischer's reply (doc. 115$^2$/11) is dated 14 Nov. 1925.

7. Patent 14345, registered on 26 Oct. 1925. Facsimiles and transcriptions of relevant documents in *Objectos*, 97–103.

8. Docs. 27$^3$K/1–5. The Pessoa Archive contains the notes of a journalist friend who attended the trial (docs. 137/51–72).

9. Fernando Pessoa to Guérin Frères, 6 Mar. 1926 (docs. 137B/11–15).

10. Docs. 137B/35–39, 42–46, 48–49. These and other inventions are described in António Mega Ferreira, *Fazer pela vida*, 103–17.

11. Hernâni Carqueja, "Francisco José Caetano Dias," *Revisores & Empresas*, no. 23, Oct.– Dec. 2003, pp. 5–6.

12. Fernando Pessoa, "Palavras iniciais," *Revista de Comércio e Contabilidade*, no. 1 (25 Jan. 1926), p. 6.

13. The article on Henry Ford was published in the sixth issue.

14. Docs. 138/22–26; 138A/7–9. *SP*, 197–99.

15. The installments were published between January 1926 and February 1927. It was no doubt the enthusiasm for *The Scarlet Letter* expressed by Francisco Costa, in his letter of 31 July 1925, that inspired Pessoa to translate it.

16. José Fonseca e Costa, *Os Mistérios de Lisboa, or What the Tourist Should See*, 2009.

17. Raul Proença, *Guia de Portugal*, vol. 1, *Lisboa e arredores* (Lisbon: Biblioteca Nacional, 1924). This book is still in print and remains a valuable reference work, even though some information is out of date. Pessoa's guidebook—first published in a bilingual edition, in 1992 (*Lisboa: O que o turista deve* ver)—notes that the magazine *Ilustração* "has started very recently"; its first issue appeared in January 1926.

18. *Disquiet*, text 330. Ntbk. 144C/13v.

19. Three Reis odes dated 13 June 1925 in some editions were in fact written on 13 June 1928, according to the manuscript. The hard-to-date sonnets of Campos are from a sequence titled "Barrow-on-Furness."

20. The June issue wasn't actually published until late July (*Sol: bissemanário republicano*, 25 July 1926, p. 9).

**21.** Interview with Maria da Graça Queiroz, a daughter of Carlos Queiroz who was close to Ophelia, her great-aunt.

**22.** Doc. 87/95a.

**23.** Onésimo Teotónio Almeida, *Pessoa, Portugal e o futuro*, 135–49, cogently argues that Pessoa must have read Georges-Eugène Sorel (1847–1922), a French philosopher whose *Réflexions sur la violence* (1908) theorized the power of national myths to mobilize people and effect revolutionary change. Though another book of Sorel is fleetingly mentioned in Pessoa's notes (doc. 133G/49), there is no proof he actually read anything by this author. His and Sorel's concepts of the energizing power of national myths are strikingly similar, however.

**24.** In the *Jornal do Comércio e das Colónias*.

## CHAPTER 56

**1.** Docs. 92I/15–16. *Fascismo*, 68–74.

**2.** The daily paper was preceded, in July and August, by a short-lived biweekly also titled *Sol*, in which Pessoa (as shown by José Barreto) published an anonymous mini-manifesto declaring, for the benefit of the ruling generals, that the individual is the "only social reality" (*Sol*, 4 Aug. 1926, p. 2). Celestino Soares (1898–1962), a writer and diplomat who served on several missions in the United States, would later serve time in prison for participating in two attempts to overthrow Salazar, in October 1946 and April 1947.

**3.** *Sol*, 20 Nov. 1926, pp. 1–2. It was not until 2012 that Pessoa's creation of Angioletti came to light, through José Barreto's article "Mussolini é um louco: Uma entrevista desconhecida de Fernando Pessoa com um antifascista italiano."

**4.** The visitor was Ezio Maria Gray (1885–1969), a colonel in the Fascist militia known as the Blackshirts and a participant in the March on Rome. He addressed Lisbon's Italian community as part of his mission to set up a local *fascio*, or Fascist league. His lecture was reported in detail in *DN*, 19 Nov. 1926, p. 1.

**5.** *DN*, 21 Nov. 1926, p. 4. *Sol*, 22 Nov. 1926, p. 1.

**6.** The real Angioletti, like the counterfeit critic, never published in *Mercure de France*, but he *had* recently published his first "Italian Chronicle" in T. S. Eliot's *The Criterion* (in the June 1926 issue), raising the intriguing possibility that Pessoa was an occasional reader of that periodical, where *The Waste Land* first saw print, in 1922. The chronicler, however, signed himself only as G. B. Angioletti; his full first name is absent from *The Criterion*. It must have been through an Italian publication that Pessoa discovered Giovanni B. Angioletti (who would become a successful writer of fiction).

**7.** *Disquiet*, text 209.

**8.** *Answers*, 18 Sept. 1926, p. 14. In 2017 Sally Bolton kindly searched the newspaper archives at Oxford's Bodleian Library and located the published letter that prompted Pessoa's response (doc. 138/65), which was published in *EA*, 182–86.

**9.** Fernando Pessoa and Ofélia Queiroz, *Correspondência amorosa completa, 1919–1935*, 15–16.

**10.** João Maria Nogueira Rosa, "Fernando Pessoa—Como eu o conheci," p. 231. *Intimidade*, 314–15.

**11.** *Correio da Noite*, 18 Aug. 1926, p. 5; 21 Aug. 1926, pp. 5, 8; 22 Aug. 1926, p. 1; 24 Aug. 1926, p. 5. *A Reacção*, 28 Aug. 1926, p. 1.

**12.** Botto worked as a civil servant in Angola during most of 1924 and part of 1925.

**13.** *A Batalha*, 2 Sept. 1925, p. 2.

**14.** Doc. 104/50.

**15.** For more on Luis Fernando de Orleans y Borbón and his affair with Botto, see Anna Klobucka, *O mundo gay de António Botto*, 41–49.

**16.** On the origins and history of fado, see Rui Vieira Nery's authoritative *A History of Portuguese Fado* (Lisbon: INCM, 2012). The city of Coimbra has its own, very different style of fado music, sung by students at the university.

**17.** António Botto, "O verdadeiro Fernando Pessoa." There are two, slightly different versions of this essay, partly transcribed and published by Maria José de Lancastre, "Pessoa e

Botto: análise de uma mitografia," in *E vós, tágides minhas: Miscellanea in onore di Luciana Stegagno di Picchio* , ed. Maria José de Lancastre, Silvano Peloso, and Ugo Serani (Viareggio, Italy: M. Baroni, 1999), 393–404.

**18.** Doc. S7/38. *CA*, 249–50.

**19.** Pessoa's 8 Mar. 1927 letter to Botto is in the Fernando Távora Collection. Copies of this and his second letter to Botto, dated 25 Mar. 1927, are in CPH and were published in António Botto, *Canções*, 155–63.

**20.** This format, developed in the nineteenth century, consisted of a four-line *mote*, or motto, each line of which was repeated in the final verse of four succeeding, ten-line stanzas.

**21.** Pessoa saved the carbon copy of the poem; it is my conjecture that he submitted the original to *Sempre Fixe*, the only publication that was likely to publish it. He had an alternate, more hard-hitting title for his fado, "Ballad of the Bristol Hotel," which alluded to the building that served as the central command post of the February rebellion in Lisbon. *Fascismo*, 94.

**22.** Mário Eloy (1900–1951), who would spend long periods in Berlin between 1927 and 1931, was Portugal's most important expressionist painter. Dada had no Portuguese followers to speak of.

**23.** João Gaspar Simões, *Retratos de poetas que conheci*, 52–53. Gaspar Simões, *José Régio e a história do movimento da "Presença"* (Porto: Brasília Editora, 1977), 56, 209–10.

## CHAPTER 57

**1.** Fernando Pessoa to Luís Miguel Rosa, 7 Jan. 1929 (CPH). Pessoa enclosed a duplicate of the letter for Luís Miguel to pass on to their brother João.

**2.** João Rui de Sousa, *Fernando Pessoa: Empregado de escritório*, 54–55. Manuel Martins da Hora/Gina de Freitas, "Recordando Fernando Pessoa," *Eva*, Dec. 1971, 47–51.

**3.** The Abel's outlet was at the intersection of Rua dos Fanqueiros and Rua de São Nicolau.

**4.** The Companhia dos Tabacos' twenty-year contract expired in the spring of 1926, but it controlled the industry until March 1927, when the military government changed the contract terms and allowed for a single competitor, thus creating a duopoly.

**5.** Pessoa saved unsigned carbon copies of three letters to Burley's, two of them dated 6 Jan. 1927 and the last 20 Jan. 1927 (CPH).

**6.** Aquivo Militar Histórico, Caixa 4213, Processo 131/69.

**7.** L. P. Moitinho de Almeida, *Fernando Pessoa no cinquentenário da sua morte*, 24, 69, 78–79.

**8.** *Manuel Martins da Hora: Publicitário* (Lisbon: Câmara Municipal, 1997). Manuel Martins da Hora, "Fernando Pessoa: Correspondente comercial," *Flama*, 31 Dec. 1965, pp. 10–11. Martins da Hora/Freitas, "Recordando Fernando Pessoa." In 1927 General Motors signed a worldwide contract with a New York ad agency, J. Walter Thompson, which hired the Hora Agency as its subagent in Portugal.

**9.** Pessoa, *Contos completos*. The brochure was probably printed in late 1928, or in 1929.

**10.** Moitinho de Almeida, *Fernando Pessoa no cinquentenário da sua morte*, 49–53. Pessoa's slogan appeared in *DL* for the first time in the 16 July 1927 issue, p. 4, and for the fourth and last time on 5 Aug. 1927, p. 4. The same slogan was published in *DN* (four issues between 17 July and 7 Aug. 1927, always on p. 2) and *O Século* (four issues between 17 July and 14 Aug. 1927, always on p. 3). These are the only three newspapers I checked, with the help of Marianna Silvano. The slogan was probably printed on advertising posters as well.

**11.** Dr. Ricardo Jorge, the minister of health, issued his opinion on 23 Dec. 1927. Carlos Alberto Pires Costa, *A droga, o poder político e os partidos em Portugal* (Lisbon: Instituto da Droga e da Toxicodependência, 2007), 78–80.

**12.** The book of interviews, *À volta das ditaduras* (*Journey Around the Dictatorships*), was published on 28 May 1927, the first anniversary of the revolution that established a military dictatorship in Portugal. Ferro and Câmara had bonded in Angola in 1918, when the latter was serving as colonial governor and Ferro was his secretary-general.

**13.** Pessoa's 3 May 1928 letter to José Régio states that he wrote the manifesto at the request of a "dear friend." António Botto, "O verdadeiro Fernando Pessoa," identified this friend as Coelho de Jesus.

**14.** José Barreto, "A publicação de *O Interregno* no contexto político de 1927–1928," *Pessoa Plural*, Fall 2012, pp. 174–207.

**15.** *DL*, 7 Apr. 1928, p. 8.

**16.** "Afonso Lopes Vieira. O poeta nacionalista," *O "Notícias" Ilustrado*, 3 June 1928, p. 8. The Pessoa Archive contains the handwritten original of the article (docs. 125A/26–29). See Pessoa, *Sebastianismo*, 156–59.

**17.** David Davidson and Herbert Aldersmith, *The Great Pyramid*, 4th ed. (London: Williams & Norgate, 1927), plates LXV-c and LXVI, found between pp. 390 and 391; see also pp. x, 26, 366, 387, 394, 400, 456.

**18.** *DN*, 8 June 1928, pp. 1, 5. Fabrizio Boscaglia, "Fernando Pessoa, Blas Infante e Al-Mu'tamid," *Colóquio Letras*, Jan.–Apr. 2016, pp. 148–60.

**19.** This and other upcoming, occultly momentous events had been "sealed," moreover, on 29 May 1928, the beginning of the "Final Tribulation," according to Davidson and Aldersmith, *The Great Pyramid. O "Notícias" Ilustrado*, 15 July 1928, p. 22; 22 July 1928, p. 15. The Pessoa Archive contains an original typescript for only the second of the two articles about Al-Mu'tamid (doc. 125/1), but the first one was also undoubtedly written by Pessoa. Pessoa, *Sebastianismo*, pp. 295–99. Due to protests from Catholics, the planned homage to Al-Mu'tamid in Silves was canceled.

**20.** Passage written for a preface to *Aspectos* (*Aspects*), a planned collection of his heteronymous works (doc. 20/73).

**21.** Doc. 92D/3.

## CHAPTER 58

**1.** *DN*, 26 Apr. 1927, p. 1. Rui Sousa, "O jogo como problema," *Pessoa Plural*, Fall 2020, pp. 427–505.

**2.** Manuel Domingos de Moura Teixeira, "Mundanismo, transgressão e boémia em Lisboa dos anos 20—O clube noturno como paradigma" (master's thesis, Universidade Lusófona, 2012), 29–36 (consulted online). Gambling was still tolerated for a time at Maxim's, the oldest and largest nightclub, and the last one to close, in 1933.

**3.** António Soares (1894–1978), a good friend of Augusto Ferreira Gomes, had designed the cover of Pessoa's chapbook *Antinous: A Poem*.

**4.** António Mega Ferreira, *Fazer pela vida*, 135–45.

**5.** Doc. 92M/69, published in *Fascismo*, 136.

**6.** *Disquiet*, texts 303, 322, 91.

**7.** "*Orpheu* as a mere basis," Pessoa wrote on his quickly aborted plans for a new magazine (doc. 122/10v), whose title he did not specify.

**8.** My translation of the full poem is in *Fernando Pessoa & Co.*. The fourth line may be more accurately translated as "Apart from this, I have in me all the dreams of the world," but it becomes a slower, less dramatic line than in the original.

**9.** Pessoa, *The Education of the Stoic: The Only Manuscript of the Baron of Teive*, 13, 34–35.

**10.** Pessoa read *La Jeune Parque* (*Young Fate*) and other poems of Valéry, which he dismissed as an uninteresting continuation of Mallarmé's work (doc. 14E/27). It is possible that he read some of the reflections of Monsieur Teste published in his lifetime—in a 1926 volume titled *Monsieur Teste*, for instance.

**11.** Doc. 59/45v.

**12.** Pessoa, *Education of the Stoic*, 10, 16, 24.

**13.** The painted image is reproduced in Maria José de Lancastre, *Fernando Pessoa: Uma fotobiografia*, 283, and in color in *Objectos*, 35. Pessoa saved, among his papers (doc. 113P²/20), a typed transcription of the title of nobility conferred on his great-great-grandfather in 1799 and published in Viscount of Sanches de Baena's *Arquivo Heráldico Genealógico* (1872), 361–62. This title mentions Leonor Francisca Coelho de Ataíde (or Athayde) in Pessoa's lineage, as was first noted by Jerónimo Pizarro.

**14.** L. P. Moitinho de Almeida, *Fernando Pessoa no cinquentenário da sua morte*, 28. Carlos Lobo de Oliveira, "Fernando Pessoa e a sua genealogia," *Boletim da Academia Portuguesa de Ex-Libris* 3, no. 24 (April 1963): 81. Pessoa's intention to acquire one or more rings, and to mend a ring already in his possession, is recorded in a memo pad he used in 1919 (*Objectos*, 204–5).
**15.** Pessoa, *A educação do estóico: O único manuscrito do Barão de Teive* (1999 edition). The Pessoa scholar Manuela Parreira da Silva helped me decipher the original manuscripts.
**16.** Passage titled "Self-examination." *Disquiet*, text 446.

## CHAPTER 59

**1.** Docs. 27²¹L⁴/19; 48/4.
**2.** Thomas Hunter Weir, *Omar Khayyám The Poet*, 1926 (in Pessoa's personal library). Pessoa's copy of FitzGerald's *Rubáiyát of Omar Khayyám* is a 1928 reprint of a 1910 edition. See Fabrizio Boscaglia, "Fernando Pessoa and Islam: An Introductory Overview with a Critical Edition of Twelve Documents." For Pessoa's books on Islamic and Middle Eastern culture, see, besides Boscaglia, "Anexo I" from Antonio Cardiello, "Os orientes de Fernando Pessoa," *Pessoa Plural*, Spring 2016, pp. 182–84.
**3.** Doc. 14C/40 (in English).
**4.** Pessoa, *Rubaiyat*, collects all of Pessoa's original and translated rubaiyat, as well as the prose passages he wrote about Khayyam.
**5.** Pessoa included three passages from his unfinished preface in an envelope with material for *The Book of Disquiet* (texts 446–48). The passage quoted is from text 446.
**6.** *DL*, 24 Dec. 1928, p. 32.
**7.** *O "Notícias" Ilustrado*, 30 Dec. 1928, p. 15.
**8.** Thank-you note published in *Imagens*, 106. Pessoa's 17 Jan. 1929 letter to his half brother Luís Miguel (CPH) explains the falling-out and reconciliation between him and his sister.
**9.** Fernando Pessoa and Ofélia Queiroz, *Correspondência amorosa completa, 1919–1935*, 25.
**10.** Albino Lapa and Rogério de Figueirôa Rego were also founding members of Solução Editora. Rego took over the enterprise from Saa and became the magazine's editor in chief beginning with the fifth issue, published in August 1929. Elisabete J. Santos Pereira, "Mário Saa (1893–1971): Um intelectual português na sociedade do século XX," 56–57; Albino Lapa, "A última blague de José Pacheco," *DL*, 3 May 1935, lit. supp., p. 3.
**11.** Botto would publish the completed *Antologia* in 1944, rounding it out with poems by Pessoa, his heteronyms, and eight additional poets.
**12.** Larbaud spent a month in Lisbon in the winter of 1926. António Ferro and José de Almada Negreiros both spoke at a banquet in his honor; Pessoa hated and avoided banquets.
**13.** *Disquiet*, text 340.
**14.** Ntbk. 144G/29, 39.
**15.** L. P. Moitinho de Almeida, *Fernando Pessoa no cinquentenário da sua morte*, 55–67.
**16.** *Disquiet*, texts 3 and 5.
**17.** Ibid., text 420.
**18.** Ibid., text 1.
**19.** Ibid., text 379.
**20.** António Ferro, "Alguns precursores," *O "Notícias" Ilustrado*, 24 Feb. 1929, pp. 11, 14.
**21.** José Rebelo de Bettencourt, *O mundo das imagens* (Lisbon: Ressurgimento, 1928), 75–78. A copy of the book, signed by the author in August 1928, is in Pessoa's personal library.
**22.** Before it appeared in the book *Temas*, Gaspar Simões published his essay on Pessoa in *A Águia*, Jan.–Mar. 1929, pp. 221–28.
**23.** *Disquiet*, text 145.
**24.** The act of arson occurred in the fourth century B.C., but it was actually the rebuilt Temple of Artemis, which remained standing until the fifth century A.D., that gained renown as one of the Seven Wonders of the Ancient World.
**25.** Docs. 15B³/77–80. A couple of passages can be dated to March 1929; one dates from

1930 or 1931. The essay's title appears on a list of publication plans (CPH; viewable online at pessoadigital.pt, CP 14). It was initially titled "Anteros, or the Future of Attraction" (doc. 15B³/86).

**26.** Doc. 107/23. *OE*, 3:252.

**27.** Phaedrus is at the top of a list of nine Plato dialogues that Pessoa drew up when studying philosophy at the School of Arts and Letters, in 1906–1907 (doc. 15³/28a).

**28.** Doc. 64/99v.

**29.** Edward Carpenter, *The Intermediate Sex: A Study of Some Transitional Types of Men and Women* (London: Sonnenschein, 1908), ch. 2. See also Carpenter's *Love's Coming-of-Age* (Manchester: Labour Press, 1896). Fernando Beleza alerted me to the possible influence of Carpenter on Pessoa.

## CHAPTER 60

**1.** Luís de Montalvor had married in 1910. In 1928, Alberto Da Cunha Dias's second wife died.

**2.** Mário Saa, *Poesia e alguma prosa*, 327–28. José Gaspar Simões, *Retratos de poetas que conheci*, 183–84. Saa and his wife were legally married in 1951.

**3.** Marriage certificate reproduced in Ana Rita Palmeirim, *José Coelho Pacheco: O falso semi-heterónimo de Pessoa*, 86.

**4.** Pessoa helped with some of the paperwork needed for the marriage, which took place in Paris. See Ferreira Gomes's letters to Pessoa from October and November 1930 in Pessoa, *O mistério da Boca do Inferno*, 123–70. Marcelle Ferreira Gomes sent Pessoa an undated postcard from France (doc. 115²/63) saying that she looked forward to meeting him.

**5.** Pinharanda Gomes, biographical sketch in *No claro-escuro das profecias*, by Augusto Ferreira Gomes, 155.

**6.** Interview with Beatriz Costa in *Semanário*, 24 Jan. 1986, pp. 32–33. Beatriz Costa, *Sem papas na língua* (Lisbon: Európa-América, 1975), 54, 58. It's hard to say when Costa first started to frequent the café, but probably not before 1930. Her letters and postcards in Saa's archive date from between 1933 and 1940.

**7.** *Disquiet*, texts 277 and 410. See also texts 59 and 360.

**8.** "A tragédia temporária do poeta António Botto," *O Jornal do Repórter X*, 26 Oct. 1929, pp. 1, 3. The rash was probably due to syphilis, still in the early stages, but Botto seems to have also suffered from tuberculosis. His doctor urged him to do a cure at the Sousa Martins Sanatorium, which specialized in treating TB. Letters from Botto to Ferro, written during and after his illness, are in the António Ferro Archive.

**9.** Gaspar Simões, *Retratos de poetas que conheci*, 125.

**10.** The psychiatric hospital of Telhal, near Sintra, is still in operation. Rilhafoles, renamed Hospital Miguel Bombarda in 1911, was Lisbon's only mental health facility during Pessoa's lifetime.

**11.** Letters from Ophelia Queiroz to Fernando Pessoa dated 15, 16, 26, 30, 31 Oct. and 1 Nov. 1929. The "calling card" she made for Álvaro de Campos is reproduced in Fernando Pessoa and Ofélia Queiroz, *Correspondência amorosa completa, 1919–1935*, 37.

**12.** Queiroz to Pessoa, 17 Dec. 1929.

**13.** *Disquiet*, text 235.

**14.** Queiroz to Pessoa, 9 Oct. and 23 Oct. 1929.

## CHAPTER 61

**1.** From *London Herald* and *The Daily Mail*, both dated 25 Oct. 1929.

**2.** Lloyd George belonged to the Liberal Party, and Churchill to the Conservative Party. Ramsay MacDonald, the current prime minister and a member of the Labour Party, was another of the politicians to whom Pessoa planned to send his questionnaire. Docs. 48H/3–4; 55E/17, 14. *Fascismo*, 146–50.

**3.** Facsimile of the letter, dated 14 Dec. 1930, published in Manuel Martins da Hora, "Fernando Pessoa: Correspondente comercial," *Flama*, 31 Dec. 1965, p. 10.

**4.** The firm Manuel Martins da Hora, Ltd., was established in 1927. See Nuno Cardal and Rita Fragoso de Almeida, *Grupo McCann Portugal: 65 anos de publicidade* (Lisbon: Texto Editora, 1994), 11–14. Martins da Hora's previous firm was called Empresa Central de Publicidade (doc. 92M/58v).

**5.** *Disquiet*, text 9.

**6.** These firms included Moitinha de Almeida, the Hora Agency, and Toscano & Company (later Toscano & Cruz).

**7.** Ophelia Queiroz to Fernando Pessoa, 2 Mar. 1930. Docs. 46/48v; 120/42v. Some of the moved items had been in storage in an apartment belonging to his brother-in-law's family, on Rua Campo de Ourique, 18. Pessoa's half brother João Nogueira Rosa, who never again saw him after 1920, would state in 1968 that Fernando lived in rented rooms while his sister's family was in Évora, but Manuela Nogueira told me with absolute certainty that her uncle Fernando lived continuously at Rua Coelho da Rocha from 1920 to 1935.

**8.** Queiroz to Pessoa, 15 Aug. 1930 and 14 Sept. 1930.

**9.** *Disquiet*, text 100.

**10.** The exchange of presents is reported in Ophelia's 12 July 1930 letter to her nephew Carlos, who in 1928 had moved to the town of Santarém, where he would finally finish high school. Letter in Maria da Graça Queiroz Collection.

**11.** Docs. 133F/86; 133B/97. Ophelia would recall the last time they kissed in her letters to Pessoa of 14 Sept. and 7 Oct. 1930.

**12.** João Gaspar Simões, who delivered a lecture at this salon, held at the National Society of Fine Arts, would remember it taking place in June, but it was held May 12–30. See José-Augusto França. *Os anos 20 em Portugal*, 370–75, and José-Augusto França, *A arte em Portugal no século XX* (Lisbon: Bertrand, 1974), 195–97.

**13.** José Gaspar Simões, *Retratos de poetas que conheci*, 57–64. António Quadros, *Fernando Pessoa: Vida, personalidade e génio*, 143. In Gaspar Simões's first published account of the meeting (Gaspar Simões, "Imagem rectificada do poeta Fernando Pessoa"), his impression was that Pessoa tried to present himself as Campos without succeeding.

**14.** Pierre Hourcade, *Temas de literatura portuguesa*, 134, 157.

**15.** Pierre Hourcade, "Rencontre avec Fernando Pessoa," *Contacts*, no. 3, June 1930, pp. 40–42.

**16.** I believe this statuesque quality was first noted by António Feijó, in an essay from 1999 republished in 2015 as the third chapter of his *Uma admiração pastoril pelo diabo (Pessoa e Pascoaes)*.

**17.** Fernando Pessoa to Adolfo Casais Monteiro, 13 Jan. 1935.

**18.** "Carta da corcunda para o serralheiro" (docs. 95/7–9). Teresa Rita Lopes, *Pessoa por conhecer*, 256–58. English translation in *SP*, 314–18.

**19.** Victor K. Mendes, "The Ecology of Writing: Maria José's Fernando Pessoa," in *Fernando Pessoa's Modernity Without Frontiers*, ed. Mariana Gray de Castro, 201–13. Maria José's letter, the only work attributed to her by Pessoa, takes up three and a half typed pages but bears her signature.

**20.** *Disquiet*, text 56.

**21.** Doc. 208.


## CHAPTER 62

**1.** In the weekly magazine *John Bull*, 24 Mar. 1923.

**2.** Most of the known letters exchanged between Pessoa and Crowley, Mandrake Press, and Crowley's associates were published by Pessoa's nephew, Luís Miguel Rosa Dias (Miguel Roza), in *Encontro Magick*, rev. ed. (Lisbon: Assírio & Alvim, 2010). Steffen Dix has published a complete, more rigorous edition: Pessoa, *O mistério da Boca do Inferno: Correspondência e novela policial*. Both sides of the correspondence (carbon copies, in the case of Pessoa's letters) are found in the Pessoa Archive, docs. 190–311.

**3.** The Pessoa Archive contains a carbon copy of Leal's letter (doc. 113F/62–66). Published, with an introduction and notes, by Manuela Parreira da Silva (offprint of *A Ideia*, no. 75/76, Lisbon, 2015).

**4.** According to a document written by Crowley in January 1937, he intended, on his trip to Lisbon, to set up "a headquarters for the Order under Don Fernando Pessoa." Marco Pasi, the scholar who unearthed this document, believes that Crowley "doubtless meant the Ordo Templi Orientis" (Pasi, *Aleister Crowley and the Temptation of Politics*, 19, 104). It's conceivable that Crowley meant, instead, his A∴A∴ order, but while the two orders were separate, both were imbued by the doctrines of Thelema and attracted many of the same disciples.

**5.** Marco Pasi, "Ordo Templi Orientis," in *Dictionary of Gnosis and Western Esotericism*, ed. Wouter J. Hanegraaff, 898–906. Hugh Urban, "Unleashing the Beast: Aleister Crowley, Tantra and Sex Magic in Late Victorian England," *Esoterica: The Journal of Esoteric Studies* 5 (2003): 138–92 (accessed 5 May 2017, http://www.esoteric.msu.edu/VolumeV/Unleashing_the_Beast.htm).

**6.** Marco Pasi, "September 1930, Lisbon: Aleister Crowley's Lost Diary of His Portuguese Trip," *Pessoa Plural*, Spring 2012, pp. 253–83.

**7.** Doc. 215. As noted by Pasi, *Aleister Crowley and the Temptation of Politics*, 193n59, the astrological symbol used to date this letter corresponds to September 3.

**8.** Doc. 295. *CA*, 266–71.

**9.** Crowley's diary for that day continued: "At night Initiation." A couple of scholars have suggested that this initiation was of Raul Leal (who in his letter of 15 Jan. 1930 had indeed expressed the desire to be initiated by Crowley), that it took place in Leal's rented room, and that Pessoa was possibly initiated with him on the same occasion. But according to Leal's two accounts of his relations with Crowley, they met only once, at the Café Martinho da Arcada, with Pessoa having gone to his room some time beforehand, probably the day before, to inform him of the meeting, where he and Hanni Jaeger were also present ("Carta de Raul Leal," *Persona* no. 7, August 1982, p. 55; Jorge de Sena and Raul Leal, *Correspondência, 1957–1960*, pp. 39–41). The initiation mentioned in Crowley's diary entry was undoubtedly referring to Hanni Jaeger's initiation ("At night"—back at the hotel in Estoril) into a new sexual rite, or into a spiritual grade accompanied by a magical sexual act. The entry continues by reporting, in Latin, a session of anal intercourse that was a "start" to חמא [emet], the Hebrew word for "truth." The next day, Wednesday, Jaeger had her first "astral vision."

**10.** In fact the prospectus was sent, at Crowley's request, with the hope that Pessoa might have affluent friends interested in investing.

**11.** The poem, "Dá a surpresa de ser," is dated 10 Sept. 1930.

**12.** *DL*, 27 Sept. 1930, p. 5. *DN*, 27 Sept. 1930, p. 6, and 28 Sept. 1930, p. 1. *O Século*, 28 Sept. 1930, p. 6. *O "Notícias" Ilustrado*, 4 Oct. 1930, pp. 1, 8, 10, 14. In December a new magazine, *Girassol*, also published a feature article on Crowley's disappearing act (16 Dec. 1930).

**13.** A Sunday paper specializing in sensationalist news; the story appeared on p. 5.

**14.** Clipping in the Pessoa Archive (doc. 250). Pessoa, *O mistério*, 125.

**15.** Israel Regardie, Crowley's secretary in London (1907–1985), tried in vain to drum up publicity for the story. He wrote Pessoa on 27 Oct. 1930: "Every newspaper has the subconscious feeling that a stunt is being engineered, and so they refuse to touch it."

**16.** "Um caso que tem todo o aspecto de pura mistificaçaõ," *O Século*, 28 Sept. 1930, p. 6.

**17.** Karl Germer (1885–1962) would succeed Crowley as the head of the Ordo Templi Orientis. Regardie would write a biography of Crowley and republish a number of his works; he would also issue a four-volume edition on the teachings, rites, and ceremonies of the Order of the Golden Dawn.

**18.** *DL*, 27 Sept. 1930, pp. 5, 8.

**19.** The incomplete novella (docs. 315–87) has been published in Pessoa, *O mistério*, 377–437.

**20.** Christopher Isherwood, *Diaries*, ed. Katherine Bucknell, vol. 1, *1939–1960* (London: Methuen, 1996), 550.

**21.** Arthur E. Waite's *The Brotherhood of the Rosy Cross* (1924) and Frans Wittemans's *Histoire* *des Rose-Croix* (1925). He would later acquire books by Waite on Freemasonry and on the legend and spiritual symbolism of the Holy Grail.

**22.** Docs. 54/37–38, 55–58, 60–63, which date from the second half of 1925.

**23.** This truth was best illustrated by *Liber 777*, a compendium of tables correlating an array of religious symbols, myths, and natural phenomena with one another and with aspects of Kabbalah. Pessoa purchased *Liber 777* in 1917 without knowing that it was by Crowley, who had published it anonymously.

**24.** The poem was included in Pessoa's 20 Oct. 1930 letter to "Karl Germer." Pessoa addressed his letters to Germer, with whom Crowley was living, for as long as they maintained the pretense of the latter's suicide.

**25.** Chapter 27 quotes the relevant passage in its entirety.

**26.** Doc. 48D/34. As far back as 1917, Pessoa had planned a book containing five large poems in English dealing with love and human affection: "Antinous," "Epithalamium," "Prayer to a Fair Body," "Divineness," and "Spring 1917" (docs. 31/93–94; 48B/64; 48D/30). See Anibal Frias, *Fernando Pessoa et le Quint-Empire de l'amour* for reflections on Pessoa's "Fifth Empire of Love."

**27.** Doc. 299. Pessoa, *O mistério*, 301.

**28.** CPH. Facsimile first published in *Intimidade*, 190.

## CHAPTER 63

**1.** Pessoa had telephoned the residence where they both lived with Joaquina, Carlos's mother. Ophelia's letter suggests she was at home when Pessoa called, but he did not ask to speak with her.

**2.** Mário Domingues, "Profecias fatídicas de um árabe," *Repórter X*, 4 Apr. 1931, pp. 8–9, 14.

**3.** Luís da Câmara Reis, "Boletim." Reis (1885–1961) was a founding member and long-time editor of *Seara Nova*. The dinners, held at the home of Fernando Lobo de Ávila Lima, a member of Portugal's National Commission on Education, are also mentioned in Ophelia Queiroz's letters to Pessoa.

**4.** On Pessoa's role as a Lisbon agent for the Monarchy of the North: *Eco de Estremoz*, 30 Dec. 1972, pp. 1, 4; expanded on in "A abusiva apropriaçao Esquerda da figura ímpar de Fernando Pessoa," *Cidade de Tomar*, 8 Feb. 1980, pp. 6, 9, and in "Evocando Fernando Pessoa," *O Comércio de Gaia*, 18 Aug. 1989, last page. On Pessoa guarding the corpse of Pais: "Evocando Fernando Pessoa," *Cidade de Tomar*, 27 May 1988, p. 7.

**5.** The articles appeared in six newspapers: *Eco de Estremoz*, 1972–1973; *Cidade de Tomar*, 1980–1990; *Notícias de Guimarães*, February–April 1984; *O Comércio de Gaia*, 1984–1989; *Consciência Nacional*, October–December 1985; and *Jornal da Bairrada*, July 1985–March 1986. There are doubtless more articles I failed to uncover, in these and possibly other newspapers.

**6.** L. P. Moitinho de Almeida, *Fernando Pessoa no cinquentenário da sua morte*, 101.

**7.** On the brothel: *Cidade de Tomar*, 15 July 1983, p. 8. On his threadbare (though spotlessly clean) clothes: *Eco de Estremoz*, 9 Dec. 1972, pp. 1, 6. On his squalid rooms: *Eco de Estremoz*, 26 May 1973, pp. 1, 3; 9 June 1973, p. 8.

**8.** While scanning thousands of issues of obscure regional newspapers to ferret out the articles Bourbon wrote on Pessoa, I happened upon an unrelated article in which he practically admitted to being a Holocaust denier, opining that Hitler had been "the object of many slurs and slanders." See "A exposição de aguarelas de Adolfo Hitler," *O Comércio de Gaia*, 15 Feb. 1985, pp. 1, 5. It's likely that Bourbon did meet Pessoa on several occasions, perhaps at the Café Montanha, and some of his assertions about what was said at those meetings might be true, but it's impossible to know which ones.

**9.** More than one attentive reader has noted this link. See, especially, Paul Muldoon, "In the Hall of Mirrors: 'Autopsychography' by Fernando Pessoa," *New England Review*, Fall 2002, pp. 38–52.

**10.** Doc. 48/2, datable to 1930.

**11.** Docs. 12¹/79; 48B/18, 22, 34, 62v.

**12.** *Disquiet*, text 149, dated 3 Mar. 1931. See also doc. 15²/63.

**13.** The Pessoa Archive contains order lists and invoices for some of the books he purchased (docs. 28A/4; 93A/2; Anexo IV/1–2).

**14.** This is the second stanza of "Oiço passar o vento na noite," dated 24 Sept. 1923. English translation ("I hear the wind blowing in the night") in Pessoa, *A Little Larger than the Entire Universe: Selected Poems*, 298.

**15.** *Disquiet*, text 443, written in 1915.

**16.** Doc. 54/78. See also doc. 53/69.

**17.** Pessoa's English-language New Testament was the Westcott-Hort edition (1881), which virtually all subsequent critical editions have closely followed.

**18.** In an autobiographical "résumé" dated 30 Mar. 1935. *EA*, 203–6.

**19.** Doc. 54B/12.

**20.** *Disquiet*, text 144, dated 1 Feb. 1931.

**21.** Docs. 53B/37–38, 41–42.

**22.** Docs. 54/42, 46.

**23.** Doc. 54A/18.

**24.** Doc. 54/99.

## CHAPTER 64

**1.** Yeats was Georgie Hyde-Lees's sponsor when she joined the order, in 1915, two years before they married.

**2.** *Disquiet*, text 263.

**3.** Ibid., text 262.

**4.** The similarities and differences between Pessoa's thinking and Buddhist thought are thoroughly reviewed in Paulo Borges, *Do vazio ao cais absoluto ou Fernando Pessoa entre oriente e ocidente*, 15–71. The Buddha is the central character in one of Pessoa's most interesting "static dramas," *Sakyamuni*, but it reveals little understanding of basic Buddhist doctrines: Pessoa, *Teatro estático*, 153–68.

**5.** Pessoa's writings cited the verse of St. Paul (Philippians 2:12) on at least three different occasions (docs. 26B/51; 55D/25v; 125B/19).

**6.** Docs. 92M/49–50, 68. *Fascismo*, 161–64.

**7.** *Disquiet*, text 259.

**8.** Docs. 125A/15; 143/14; 123/96.

**9.** J. A. Moreira de Castro, *Nova selecta portugueza* (Porto: Typ. de José da Silva Mendonça, 1896), 209–10.

**10.** This memory was undoubtedly Pessoa's own, but he reported it through Bernardo Soares, in the same *Disquiet* passage where he declared that his nation was not Portugal but the Portuguese language.

**11.** Doc. 14E/53.

**12.** Pessoa owned and studied Robert Bridges's *Milton's Prosody* and William Johnson Stone's *Classical Meters in English Verse*, published together by Oxford University Press in 1901.

**13.** *Leonardo da Vinci and a Memory of His Childhood*, trans. Alan Tyson, in *The Standard Edition of the Complete Psychological Works of Sigmund Freud*, ed. James Strachey (London: Hogarth Press/Institute of Psycho-analysis, 1957), 131–32 (consulted online).

**14.** Ibid., 69, 133. Sigmund Freud, *Un souvenir d'enfance de Léonard de Vinci* (Paris: Gallimard, 1927), 27–28, 204.

**15.** Docs. 133D/17–20. While undated, these communications were written on paper with the watermark Grahams Bond Registered, extensively used by Pessoa in 1931—for passages of *The Book of Disquiet*, various poems, and other texts.

**16.** In the year after Pessoa's death Gaspar Simões published, in *Presença* (July 1936, pp. 17–22), the long letter he had received and a long article taking issue with some of the arguments it presented.

17. *Disquiet*, text 260.

18. Eliot's essay was a review of John M. Robertson's *The Problem of "Hamlet"* (1919). Pessoa owned this book and Robertson's *"Hamlet" Once More* (1923), which cites Eliot's review but not the "objective correlative" concept. It is very likely, but not proven, that Pessoa read Eliot's Hamlet essay.

19. Virginia Woolf, *Roger Fry* (London: Hogarth Press, 1940). I came across the remark in James Wood's magnificent essay on Woolf (in his 1999 collection *The Broken Estate*).

20. My characterization and impressions of Eliot are drawn largely from Lyndall Gordon's admirably even-handed biography, *T. S. Eliot: An Imperfect Life*. For the sake of the comparison I draw with Pessoa, my own treatment of Eliot strikes a more critical, less sympathetic tone.

## CHAPTER 65

1. Docs. Anexo IV/1–3, 7.

2. José Luís Cardoso, "The Great Depression in Portugal: Diagnoses and Remedies," in *The Great Depression in Europe: Economic Thought and Policy in a National Context*, ed. Michalis Psalidopoulos (Athens: Alpha Bank, 2012), 361–93 (consulted online).

3. "Eleazar Kaminetzky, o apóstolo da vida simples," *Jornal do Brasil*, 29 Dec. 1915 (article in Kamenezky Archive, E43/27).

4. Some years later he would act in several Portuguese films, playing the part of a Russian. He died in 1957 and was buried in Lisbon's Jewish Cemetery. Biographical sketch based on documents from the Kamenezky Archive and the article "Figuras excêntricas da nossa terra," *Ilustração*, 16 Oct. 1928, pp. 20–21.

5. In 1991 Pessoa's incomplete English version (envs. 80–82) was translated into Italian and published as a novel of his own authorship: Pessoa, *Eliezer* (Rome: Lucarini, 1991). See Ivo Castro, João Dionísio, and Luís Prista, "Eliezer: ascensão e queda de um romance pessoano," *Revista da Biblioteca Nacional*, no. 1 (1992): 75–136.

6. Pessoa's translations of Kamenezky's lyric poems: docs. 91/1–115. Kamenezky's prose poems and Pessoa's translations of same: docs. 94/5–6, 17–63, 66–73. (The Kamenezky Archive contains the original typescripts of Pessoa's translations.)

7. Docs. 28/3; 48B/92, 113v, 149v; 55F/53v, 54. Ntbk. 153/58.

8. Pessoa also typed up some of the poems for the book, a service for which he was no doubt paid.

9. *DL*, 29 Feb. 1932, p. 1.

10. *Cartas que me foram devolvidas* (*Letters That Were Returned to Me*).

11. In his introduction to Pessoa, *Poemas ingleses* (Lisbon: Ática 1974), Jorge de Sena first suggested, based on a somewhat different argument, that Botto could be seen as a heteronym of Pessoa. Sena, *Fernando Pessoa e Cia. heterónima*, 328.

12. António Botto to António Ferro, 3 Feb. 1930 (António Ferro Archive). On Botto and Carminda Rodrigues: Anna Klobucka, *O mundo gay de António Botto*, 152–59.

13. Manuela Nogueira, *O meu tio Fernando Pessoa*, 62.

14. The barber ritual was first described by Henriqueta Rosa Dias, Pessoa's sister and Manuela's mother. Manuela Nogueira's own accounts of the ritual differ in some of the details. *Intimidade*, 313. Nogueira, *O meu tio*, 59–60.

15. Interview with Manuela Nogueira.

16. Signa Teixeira Rebelo/Nuno Coutinho, "Nunca me disse que era Alberto Caeiro," *ABC do Bairro*, 5 Dec. 1985, p. 6.

17. *Disquiet*, texts 50, 130.

18. Ibid., texts 24, 279, 18.

19. She was the great-aunt of the poet and scholar Jorge de Sena. See Sena, *Fernando Pessoa e Cia. heterónima*, 159–60.

20. The parlor, Agência Barata, would handle Pessoa's funeral; Esteves was named as the declarant on his death registration.

21. *Disquiet*, text 317.

## CHAPTER 66

**1.** The dossier on Mário Freitas's military career records the long periods of sick leave preceding his death. Arquivo Histórico Militar, Caixa 2190.

**2.** According to his sister Teca, cited in *Intimidade*, 241. See also *Disquiet*, text 208.

**3.** Docs. S2/19–20.

**4.** Docs. 90¹/61; 90²/87, 89, 98; S2/37, 43, 49–51; S3/83; S6/7.

**5.** Doc. 90¹/55 (in English).

**6.** Filipe Ribeiro de Meneses, *Salazar*, 79.

**7.** The history of this movement is thoroughly described in António Costa Pinto, *Os camisas azuis e Salazar*.

**8.** In *Fama*, a new magazine whose editor in chief was Augusto Ferreira Gomes.

**9.** Doc. 48B/34.

**10.** Docs. S2/14–16 consist of horoscopes cast on 13, 16, and 17 Aug. 1932.

**11.** *O Século*, 1 Sept. 1932, p. 10; Pessoa saved this notice (doc. 135/82). António Navarro, a poet and admirer, would later report that Pessoa's freelance work as a letter writer earned him about 300 escudos per month (*DL*, 22 Jan. 1937, lit. supp. pp. 3–4). This is an implausibly low amount given that Pessoa, as a half-time wage, had asked for 800 escudos/month from the Madrid office of J. Walter Thompson in 1929.

**12.** Archive of the Condes de Castro Guimarães Museum. In her interview with Inês Pedrsoa, Signa Teixeira Rebelo would state that she personally submitted the applications of both her father and her godfather, Fernando Pessoa ("Foi *ele* que me meteu o bichinho dos policias," *Jornal de Letras*, 10–17 Feb. 1986). A facsimile of Pessoa's application dossier is in Teresa Rita Lopes, *Fernando Pessoa: A biblioteca impossível* (Cascais: Câmara Municipal, 1995).

**13.** Pereira Faisca, *Exílio*, 50.

**14.** Doc. 90¹/58. Pessoa owned the 1930 printing of Mrs. John Le Breton's *The White-Magic Book*, originally published in 1919.

**15.** The library contains about 2800 volumes. Bonvalot (1893–1934) was appointed as an interim director. In his highly unreliable articles about a group that allegedly met at Lisbon's Café Montanha, Francisco Peixoto Bourbon reported that Pessoa, some time after learning that he had not been chosen for the job, lay his head down on a table and profusely wept: *Eco de Estremoz*, 10 Feb. 1973, p. 6. This is only slightly less implausible than the story of his having a pet prostitute at a brothel.

**16.** Doc. 29/12. Written on 9 Nov. 1932.

**17.** Doc. 54A/4.

**18.** Docs. 54/19; 54A/4.

**19.** Doc. 54A/2.

**20.** Docs. 54A/3, 9.

## CHAPTER 67

**1.** António Ferro "Política do espírito," *DN*, 21 Nov. 1932, p. 1.

**2.** Luís Manuel Gaspar, chronology on the artist's life and work, in *José de Almada Negreiros: Uma maneira de ser moderno*, ed. Mariana Pinto dos Santos (Lisbon: Gulbenkian Foundation/Sistema Solar, 2017), 395.

**3.** José de Almada Negreiros, "Um ponto no *i* do futurismo," *DL*, 25 Nov. 1932, pp. 5, 8.

**4.** Fernando Pessoa to António Ferro, 11 Mar. 1933. Three years earlier, on 7 Apr. 1930, Pessoa had written Ferro to compliment him for a series of interviews conducted in Spain and, more generally, for his vivid style as a journalist.

**5.** Docs. 92M/77, 74–76. Both Teresa Rita Lopes (in Pessoa's *Pessoa inédito*, 365–66) and José Barreto (in *Fascismo*, 179–80) date these two documents to around 1932–1933. They may be right, but my own conjecture is 1934–1935.

**6.** Docs. 92/64-67. *Fascismo*, 186–91.

7. Doc. 92M/77. *Fascismo*, 180.

8. The other three artists were Jorge Barradas (1894–1971), Stuart Carvalhais (1887–1961), and Francisco Keil do Amaral (1910–1975). *Diário da Manhã*, 15 Mar. 1933, p. 2; 16 Mar. 1933, p. 3.

9. *Diário da Manhã*, 10 Mar. 1933, p. 3.

10. Doc. 92I/51. Jerónimo Pizarro, *Fernando Pessoa: Entre génio e loucura*, 216.

11. Mário Matos e Lemos, *Jornais diários portugueses do século XX*, 234.

12. Ellen Sapega, "Staging Memory," in *Consensus and Debate in Salazar's Portugal* (University Park: Pennsylvania State University Press, 2008), 9–45.

13. The rules for the prizes were announced in *DN*, 29 Nov. 1933, p. 1, and other newspapers.

14. Doc. 92F/52. First published in *Espresso*, supplement "40 anos após a morte de Fernando Pessoa," 6 Dec. 1975, p. 1.

## CHAPTER 68

1. Docs. 51/89; 133F/28v.

2. *Cahiers du Sud*, Jan. 1933, pp. 66–73. Besides the Campos and Caeiro poems, the translated selection included the last two stanzas of Pessoa's "O último sortilégio" ("The Last Spell"), erroneously identified as a Caeiro poem.

3. *Disquiet*, text 338.

4. Docs. 107/23–25. *OE*, 3:252–54.

5. António Botto, *Canções*, 17, 325. António Botto, *The Songs of António Botto*, trans. F. Pessoa, ed. Josiah Blackmore (Minneapolis: University of Minnesota Press, 2010), 160. *DL*, 12 July 1935, p. 4.

6. Edmund Wilson, "Ulysses," *The New Republic*, 5 July 1922, pp. 164–66.

7. *Disquiet*, text 150 (among others).

8. Richard Ellmann, *James Joyce*, 528.

9. José de Almada Negreiros, *Textos de intervenção* (Lisbon: Editorial Estampa, 1972), 173.

10. Poem dated 21 May 1917.

11. *Disquiet*, text 193.

12. Ibid., text 79.

13. Ibid., text 441.

14. Docs. 54B/7, 16v; 54/97; 54A/51, 52, 61. Transcriptions of the passages Pessoa wrote for "An Essay on Initiation," *Subsolo* (*Underground*), and *O caminho da Serpente* (*The Way of the Serpent*) can be found in Yvette Centeno, *Fernando Pessoa: Magia e fantasia*.

15. Poem dated 23 Sept. 1933.

## CHAPTER 69

1. José Gaspar Simões, "Imagem rectificada do poeta Fernando Pessoa."

2. Pierre Hourcade, *Temas de literatura portuguesa*, 158.

3. Docs. 27⁷W/11–12, 6, 9. Pessoa, *A hora do diabo*, 25–26, 29.

4. The Pessoa Archive contains a carbon copy of Pessoa's letter, which was dated 28 Jan. 1934 (docs. 114³/65–66). The article referred to in this letter to the editor appeared in *A Voz*, 24 Jan. 1934, p. 2. See *Fascismo*, 225–26.

5. "The Jews and Freemasonry": docs. 53/14–18, 20–43; 53A/17, 66–68, 83–87. The quotations come from docs. 53/14, 32. In the last cited sentence, for clarity's sake, I replaced two commas with dashes.

6. Docs. 92A/62–64; 92E/55–58. *Fascismo*, 209–13. These passages are not actually signed by Thomas Crosse, but "Dictatorships" appears on a list of Crosse articles dating from around 1934 (doc. 143/13).

7. *Avante!*, 3 Feb. 1934, pp. 3–5, 7–8. The meeting was held on January 28.

8. "Fernando Pessoa," *Avante!*, 16 Dec. 1935, pp. 3, 6.

**9.** António Costa Pinto, *Os camisas azuis e Salazar*, ch. 5. Filipe Ribeiro de Meneses, *Salazar*, 128–29.
**10.** *Disquiet*, text 473.
**11.** Doc. 2/60. *Disquiet*, appendix.
**12.** Thomas Carlyle, "The Hero as Poet." Pessoa read this lecture as a student in Durban. Carlyle borrowed the Latin term from Horace.
**13.** Doc. 6/6. Pessoa, *The Education of the Stoic*, 34–35.
**14.** "A Senhora da Agonia" (doc. 17/41v), dating from 11 July 1934.
**15.** Doc. 54/44.
**16.** Doc. 53B/25 (in English).
**17.** Docs. 53/63; 54B/4. Additional questions, answers, and speeches of the invented ritual are in docs. 26/101; 53/62, 64, 65, 89. Two of the sheets are dated 3 Sept. 1934. Most of the ritual was transcribed in Teresa Rita Lopes, *Pessoa por conhecer*, 98–104.
**18.** Doc. 54A/91 (in English).
**19.** Doc. 53/81.
**20.** Doc. 53A/59.
**21.** Docs. 54B/20 (in English); 53/9v (in English); 53A/59.
**22.** Docs. 54B/17–18. See also the text that begins "Dividiu Aristóteles" ("Aristotle divided"); docs. 16/61–62), in Pessoa, *A Centenary Pessoa* (1995), 229–31.

## CHAPTER 70

**1.** José Blanco, "A verdade sobre a *Mensagem*," Fundação António Quadros (consulted online). "No XIV aniversário da morte de Fernando Pessoa: Algumas revelações curiosas do seu primeiro impressor Armando de Figueiredo," *Átomo*, 30 Nov. 1949, p. 16. A penciled date on the typescript of *Mensagem*, 23 Aug. 1934, seems to indicate the day, a Thursday, it was received by the printer, although Augusto Ferreira Gomes's letter to João Gaspar Simões of 7 Nov. 1949 (Alberto Serpa Archive, Biblioteca Municipal do Porto; published in *Pessoa Plural*, Spring 2018, pp. 335–36) suggests that it was delivered to the printer on a Monday.
**2.** Doc. 125A/25. The poem Pessoa rewrote was "Afonso de Albuquerque," in honor of the general (c. 1452–1515) who conquered Goa and other Indian lands for the Portuguese.
**3.** Docs. 17/51v; 90⁵/83v.
**4.** In the summer of 1926, at the Casa de Saúde de Telhal.
**5.** Facsimiles of two pages and a partial transcription of this extravagant prose text—vouchsafed to Pessoa (CPH)—were published by Rui Lopes, "Inéditos de Raul Leal," *Pessoa Plural*, Spring 2013, pp. 77–79.
**6.** *DL*, 28 Sept. 1934, p. 4. *Novidades*, 29 Sept. 1934, p. 6. *DN*, 30 Sept. 1934, p. 6.
**7.** The article was titled "Marcha sobre Roma" ("March on Rome"). Docs. 26/29–31; 48B/90.
**8.** "A Igreja Católica cobriu como uma redoma" ("The Catholic Church enclosed like a bell jar"), dated 20 Apr. 1934.
**9.** "*Mensagem* (poemas)," *A Voz*, 9 Dec. 1934, p. 8.
**10.** *DL*, 14 Dec. 1934, lit. supp. p. 5; *DL*, 6 Sept. 1950, p. 9. Anabela Mota Ribeiro and Susana Sena, "O Senhor Pessoa," p. 25.
**11.** *O "Notícias" Ilustrado*, 23 Dec. 1934, p. 9.
**12.** *Fradique*, 20 Dec. 1934, p. 1.
**13.** L. P. Moitinho de Almeida, *Fernando Pessoa no cinquentenário da sua morte*, 43–48.
**14.** Interview with Margarida Soares Couto.
**15.** This incident was reported to me by Manuela Nogueira, Pessoa's niece, who heard it from her parents.
**16.** John Rosa's employer was Helbert, Wagg and Company, Ltd., in London. From 1924 to 1928, he had worked for Ottoman Bank, in Istanbul, and he would later work for the Colo-

nial Office, helping to plan its disastrous "ground nuts scheme," whereby Great Britain, to alleviate a postwar shortage of cooking oil, tried to grow peanuts in Tanganyika (now part of Tanzania). He met Eileen Anderson (1902–1987) at the London School of Economics and married her after a long courtship, in 1929. They had no children.

**17.** Carbon copies of Pessoa's letters (dated 2 Feb., 28 Feb., and 24 Oct. 1934) and the original letters of John Rosa (dated 5 Mar. and 31 Dec. 1934) are in CPH; facsimiles of the carbon copies viewable in the Hubert Jennings Papers ("Transcriptions by Xerox [T2b]"), Brown University Digital Repository, Brown University Library, Providence. In the case of the gunpowder factory, Pessoa was acting on behalf of Francisco Camelo, proprietor of the Sociedade Africana de Pólvora. For the other business proposals, he was an intermediary for the firm Gouveia and Carvalho.

**18.** Patricia Silva McNeill, *Yeats and Pessoa: Parallel Poetic Styles*, 70, 111, 166, juxtaposes the Yeatsian "anti-self" with Pessoa's use of heteronyms.

**19.** *Jornal de Letras*, 26 Nov.–2 Dec. 1985, p. 11. "Revista," *Expresso*, 4 June 1988, p. 49. It was through his cousin Victoriano Braga that Pessoa arranged this tutoring job. Eduardo Magalhães would go on to cofound Editora Confluência, which in 1942 would publish *Poesia*, an anthology of Pessoa poems that had appeared in periodicals.

**20.** Docs. 48D/16 (dates from 1933 or later); 63/31 (dates from July 1935).

**21.** In Pessoa's 24 Dec. 1934 letter to Adolfo Casais Monteiro, he states that he has been suffering for several months from "an attack of neurasthenia."

**22.** Doc. 115⁸/62.

**23.** The full text of Pessoa's contribution to the autograph book was published in Arnaldo Saraiva, *O modernismo brasileiro e o modernismo português*, 343–44.

**24.** Maria José Almada Negreiros, *Conversas com Sarah Affonso*, 98–99.

**25.** A facsímile image of the inscription, dated 18 Nov. 1934, was published in *Objectos*, 230.

**26.** The minutes of the jury deliberations are archived at the Fundação António Quadros and can be consulted online.

## CHAPTER 71

**1.** *DL*, 31 Dec. 1934, p. 16.

**2.** *Avante!*, 16 Dec. 1935, pp. 3, 6.

**3.** Doc. 47/23v. Pessoa, *Poesia: 1931–1935 e não datada*, 441–42.

**4.** José Gaspar Simões, "João Gaspar Simões depõe acerca dos Prémios Literários," *Fradique*, 31 Jan. 1935, pp. 5, 7; for reactions and follow-up: *Fradique*, 14 Mar. 1935, pp. 1, 7; 4 Apr. 1935, pp. 1, 5; 30 May 1935, p. 5. João de Castro Osório, "Um misionário poeta," *DL*, 22 Feb. 1935, lit. supp. p. 6. Vasco Reis, whose real name was Manuel Reis Ventura, would leave the priesthood, marry, and settle in Angola, where he worked as a journalist and wrote colonialist novels as well as poetry.

**5.** *Avante!*, 13 Jan. 1935, p. 5. Almeida signed his reviews pseudonymously, as Fernando Trigueiros. See also L. P. Moitinho de Almeida, *Fernando Pessoa no cinquentenário da sua morte*, 84–85.

**6.** *Fradique*, 6 June 1935, p. 5.

**7.** Alice Ogando, "*Mensagem*—Poemas de Fernando Pessoa," *O Diabo*, 27 Jan. 1935, p. 4.

**8.** João de Castro Osório, "A *Mensagem* do desejado: O sentimento sebastianista na moderna poesia," *DL*, 12 Apr. 1935, lit. supp. p. 6.

**9.** Caio Gagliardi, "Mário Beirão e Fernando Pessoa: *Lusitânia* intertexto de *Mensagem*," *Pessoa Plural*, Spring 2014, pp. 70–87.

**10.** Ntbk. 144Q/42v.

**11.** Doc. 125A/13. *SP*, 165.

**12.** Doc. 133A/37. The communication also included the phrase "*Valete, fratres.*"

**13.** Doc. 54A/56 (in English). See also docs. 53B/44–45.

**14.** Arthur E. Waite, *The Brotherhood of the Rosy Cross* (1924; in Pessoa's personal library),

449–50. Doc. 53A/69 (in English). In a passage for an essay on Goethe, Pessoa outlined a similar, four-step "alchemical process" for attaining genius (doc. 19/4).
**15.** On Pessoa's "faith" in the occult: Adolfo Casais Monteiro, "O insincero verídico" (1954), in Casais Monteiro, *A poesia de Fernando Pessoa* (Lisbon: INCM, 1985), 87–106.

## CHAPTER 72

**1.** Docs. 113P¹/87–90; 113I/31–36.
**2.** Maria José da Graça Ferreira do Amaral (1908–2001), who worked in one of the offices where Pessoa wrote business letters, reported that his article was published thanks to a female friend of hers who worked for the Censorship Commission (*Intimidade*, 151). But as José Barreto points out, the censors were all army officers and rigorously loyal to New State ideals; see his afterword to Pessoa, *Associações secretas e outros escritos*, 239–88.
**3.** *Diário da Manhã*, 25 Jan. 1935, p. 3; 5 Feb. 1935, p. 1.
**4.** *Fradique*, 14 Feb. 1935, p. 1.
**5.** *X: Semanário de Grandes Reportagens*, 14 Feb. 1935, p. 4. The unsigned article was by the magazine's editor in chief, Reinaldo Ferreira (1897–1935), popularly known as Reporter X.
**6.** José Cabral, "Chove no templo . . . ," *A Voz*, 6 Feb. 1935, p. 1; José Cabral, "O projecto de lei sobre associações secretas: O sr. dr. José Cabral responde ao artigo do sr. Fernando Pessoa," *DL*, 7 Feb. 1935, pp. 1, 4.
**7.** *Foto XX*, 164-65, contains facsimiles of relevant documents from the Censorship Commission, archived at the Torre do Tombo.
**8.** *DL*, 1 Feb. 1935, p. 5. *O Diabo*, 3 Feb. 1935, p. 1, and 10 Feb. 1935, p. 8. Barreto, afterword to Pessoa, *Associações secretas*, 250–51.
**9.** *Diário da Manhã*, 25 Feb. 1935, pp. 1, 3, 4, 6.
**10.** Docs. 92L/94, 89–90.
**11.** *DN*, 22 Feb. 1935, pp. 1, 4. *Diário da Manhã*, 22 Feb. 1935, pp. 1, 2, 7. *A Voz*, 22 Feb. 1935, pp. 1, 6. Salazar's speech consisted of excerpts from a preface for a collection of his speeches that would be published in March. The words of Seneca were taken from ch. 9 of his *De Tranquillitate Animi* (*On Peace of Mind*).
**12.** Doc. 129/51. *Fascismo*, 265–66. These words were part of an (unfinished) article Pessoa hoped to publish in *DL*.
**13.** Doc. 92L/85.
**14.** Almost two years after the poet's death, on 11 Sept. 1937, a less attentive censor allowed *Seara Nova* to publish "Freedom."
**15.** Pedro da Silveira reported on the submission and publication history of the poem "Freedom" and on the oral circulation of one of Pessoa's anti-Salazar poems in "Nota adicional," *Seara Nova*, July 1974, p. 20. On Rui Santos: Pedro da Silveira, in Pedro de Merelim, *Fernando Pessoa e a Terceira: Figuras do ramo materno do poeta*, 107. Santos was the cousin of Maria Adelaide dos Santos Ortega, daughter of Maria da Cruz Pessoa Chaves, who was raised by Lisbela Pessoa Machado.
**16.** Manassés Ferreira de Seixas/A.D., "Este homem foi barbeiro de Fernando Pessoa," *Correio da Manhã*, 8 Oct. 1979, p. 7.
**17.** "Saudação a todos quantos querem ser felizes," dating from September 1935 (ntbk. 144F/4v).

## CHAPTER 73

**1.** Docs. 48B/34; 92A/26; 92U/34; 111/34–35; 143/13. See also "Apontamentos para publicações" (CPH), viewable at pessoadigital.pt (CP 808).
**2.** Doc. 15¹/87, dating from around 1925. Elsewhere he had written, likewise in Portuguese: "Only nations exist; humanity does not exist" (doc. 23/42). See also docs. 23/43; 55H/3–4.
**3.** Fernando Pessoa to João Gaspar Simões, 11 Dec. 1931.
**4.** *Disquiet*, text 349.

**5.** Docs. 92H/48; 90⁴/47.

**6.** The journalist was Artur Portela: *DL*, 6 Sept. 1950, p. 9.

**7.** Raul Leal to João Gaspar Simões, letter of 23–24 July 1950; published in *Persona* 7, August 1982, pp. 54-57. *CA*, 64–66. Cf. doc. S3/78.

**8.** Doc. S2/3.

**9.** José da Almada Negreiros, "Um aniversário: *Orpheu*," *DL*, 8 Mar. 1935, lit. supp. pp. 1, 7. Only five names on the scroll were actually marked by crosses, but unbeknown to Almada Negreiros a sixth contributor, the Brazilian poet Eduardo Guimaraens, had also died, in 1928.

**10.** Luís de Montalvor, "Um poeta que morre: Ronald de Carvalho," *DL*, 22 Feb. 1935, lit. supp. p. 1.

**11.** Based on the physical characteristics of the manuscript, the elegy—undated—was written in the spring of 1935. I opted for a somewhat free translation.

**12.** Pessoa to Gaspar Simões, 11 Dec. 1931.

**13.** The speech was delivered at Avis on 7 July 1935. Elisabete J. Santos Pereira, "Mário Saa (1893–1971): Um intelectual português na sociedade do século XX," 60–61.

**14.** "À Emissora Nacional," a poem that dates from the summer or fall of 1935.

**15.** *Sudoeste: Cadernos de Almada Negreiros*, no. 1, June 1935, pp. 30–31. In the magazine's second issue, published in October, Almada Negreiros responded to a backlash against "Collective Mysticism" by saying that its clearly articulated affirmations were not in fact affirmations; they constituted a verbal "photograph," not an endorsement, of Europe's current political panorama.

**16.** *DL*, 22 Mar. 1935, lit. supp. p. 5.

**17.** The exhibition, organized by the Secretariat of Propaganda and held at the National Society of Fine Arts, ran from March 16 to April 1. Almada Negreiros's speech was delivered at the official banquet on March 23 and published in *DL*, 29 Mar. 1935, lit. supp. p. 7.

**18.** "Sim, é o Estado Novo, e o povo," dated 29 July 1935.

**19.** For an example of praise abroad, see the London weekly *The Sphere*, 6 Apr. 1935, pp. 18, 46.

## CHAPTER 74

**1.** Régio's novel, *Jogo da cabra cega* (*Blind Man's Buff*), was published in October 1934 and banned in December.

**2.** Docs. 48/25; 63/31.

**3.** Doc. 54B/10.

**4.** Fernando Pessoa to João Gaspar Simões, 11 Dec. 1931.

**5.** Raul Leal's impressions of Pessoa's sexuality are found on pp. 47–48 of an unpublished essay in the Fernando Távora Collection. Botto's comments on Pessoa's eye for young men and on his supposedly diminutive penis were reported by Jorge de Sena, *Fernando Pessoa e Cia. heterónima*, 431. The poet Herberto Helder (1930–2015) repeated to me more than once what Raul Leal had told him about Pessoa's penis size.

**6.** A footnote in Ofélia Queiroz, *Cartas de amor de Ofélia a Fernando Pessoa*, 256, mistakenly reports that Anderson was in Portugal in November 1929 and that she got divorced around this time. From João Nogueira Rosa's letter to Pessoa of 10 Apr. 1935, it is clear that he and Teca had never before met his sister-in-law, who remained single until 1939. Information on Anderson's studies provided by the Special Collections division of the University of St Andrews Library. (She received her degree in 1926.) According to Jonathan Byrne, an oral history officer of Bletchley Park Trust, Anderson was apparently already working for the Government Code and Cypher School, and possibly for MI6 (the Secret Intelligence Service), before the war (email, Dec. 2017).

**7.** Pereira Faisca, *Exílio*, 52.

**8.** Docs. 49A⁷/11; 50A¹/28.

**9.** Passenger lists (consulted at ancestry.com) show that Madge Anderson sailed on the

*Dempo* out of Southampton, England, on 12 ♦pr. 1935, bound for Lisbon, and that her return voyage from Lisbon, on the *Sibajak*, reached Southampton on 26 May 1935.

**10.** This is not the actual letter Pessoa sent but the transcription of a typed draft, with corrections (CPH). Several incomplete, crossed-out sentences in the draft prove that it was his sister who pushed him to write: "From Teca's permanent indignation against me I gather that I have been guilty . . ." and "All that I really want to say is that I do not really know what I did or said during the time you were here. . . ."

**11.** Madge's reply in CPH. She also, at some point, sent him an undated postcard (doc. 115²/97), transcribed in José Barreto, "A última paixão de Fernando Pessoa," *Pessoa Plural*, Fall 2017, pp. 596–641.

**12.** Docs. 135/75, 70v, 72. The clipping in Pessoa's archive for beef-enhanced wine cannot be dated with certainty; the clippings he saved for a miraculously thereapeutic water and for the radioactive spa date from 1935. At the time of this writing, the once palatial spa hotel, abandoned in the 1950s, was a macabre hulk teetering on a hillside not far from the medieval village of Sortelha.

**13.** Document signed on 14 June 1935. Arquivo Histórico Militar, Caixa 4213, Processo 131/69.

**14.** The pamphlet version corrected the many typos that had appeared in the newspaper.

**15.** T. S. Eliot to António Ferro, 27 May 1938, António Ferro Archive.

**16.** Eight passages intended for Pessoa's letter to the president (docs. 92M/28–33, 41–43, 80–82; 92E/53–54), all dating from July 1935 or later, were published in *Fascismo*, 276–82.

**17.** José Blanco, quoted in Robert Bréchon, *Étrange étranger: Une biographie de Fernando Pessoa*, 530.

**18.** *O "Notícias" Ilustrado*, 9 June 1935, p. 12.

**19.** Pessoa's unfinished "Against Democracy" has been previously mentioned. In addition to the contemporaneous "In Defense of Tyrants," Pessoa wrote passages for "Five Dialogues on Tyranny." Both works, unfinished and only partly published, were written in Portuguese. The cited Caeiro poem ("Yesterday the preacher of truths"), which I date to 1919, might have been written as late as 1923.

**20.** Alberto Da Cunha Dias, *Outono*, 80. The restaurant closed its doors in 2015.

**21.** Carlos Queiroz, "Carta à memória de Fernando Pessoa," 11.

## CHAPTER 75

**1.** António Trindade/José Vicente, "Traços para um retrato," *A Comarca de Aganil*, 30 Nov. 1965, p. 5. Manassés Ferreira de Seixas/A.D., "Este homem foi barbeiro de Fernando Pessoa," *Correio da Manhã*, 8 Oct. 1979, p. 7. See also Luís Sttau Monteiro's interviews with Trindade and Seixas for an episode of the TV series *O Homem é um Mundo*, "A Casa de Fernando Pessoa," aired on RTP 1 on 25 Jan. 1981 (consulted online).

**2.** Interview with Maria José da Graça Ferreira do Amaral, conducted by Luís Sttau Monteiro for "Fernando Pessoa," an episode of the series *O Homem é um Mundo*, aired on RTP 1 on 27 Sept. 1981 (consulted online). Interview with Ferreira do Amaral in *Intimidade*, 150.

**3.** Carlos Queiroz, "Carta à memória de Fernando Pessoa," 11.

**4.** Doc. 63/31v.

**5.** Reported by Alfredo Margarido in Fernando Pessoa, *Santo António, São João, São Pedro* (Lisbon: A Regra do Jogo, 1986), 85n38. In the final chapter of his biography, Gaspar Simões wrote that Pessoa had suffered a "brief attack of *delirium tremens*" at his sister's house in São João do Estoril (*Vida*, last chapter). In a 9 Oct. 1935 letter to Madge Anderson, Pessoa indicated that that "D. T." was written in April and was at least partly autobiographical. The paper type, pen type, and handwriting style of the original manuscript match those of several aforementioned poems written in São João do Estoril in late April.

**6.** Eva Frances Hunt (c. 1909–1986). She and her husband, married in 1932, had no children.

**7.** Manuela Nogueira, Pessoa's niece, showed me poems written by Louis Michael Rosa in the decades after Pessoa's death.

**8.** Mentioned in an unfinished letter Fernando wrote to Louis Michael on 15 Oct. 1935.

**9.** *Intimidade*, 295.

**10.** Louis Michael Rosa to Fernando Pessoa, 15 Sept. 1935 (letter in Pessoa Archive, doc. 115²/109). Pessoa, *Correspondência inédita*, 128. Louis Michael and Eva lived on the outskirts of London.

**11.** A carbon copy of the letter he wrote to his brother is in CPH. Louis Michael told the scholar Alexandrino Severino that Pessoa was thinking of going to live with him and his wife; however, his last letter to Pessoa does not contain an explicit invitation, merely an offer to "fix things" for him if he should ever go to England, and Pessoa's letter of reply expresses no such intention, despite the biographer Ángel Crespo's claim to the contrary. See Alexandrino E. Severino, *Fernando Pessoa na África do Sul* (1983), 147–48; Ángel Crespo, *La vida plural de Fernando Pessoa*, 310.

**12.** What survives is not Pessoa's actual letter, which we know he sent, along with the poem "D.T.," but his draft (CPH).

**13.** I mean the part of Africa where he actually lived. Around 1912 Pessoa wrote a suite of four unfinished sonnets, "To the Cape of Good Hope" ("Ao Cabo da Boa Esperança"), evoking the three times he rounded the cape on his voyages to and from Durban. Docs. 37/20–21. Pessoa, *Poesia: 1931–1935 e não datada*, 461–63.

**14.** *Disquiet*, text 299.

**15.** Pessoa, *Poemas de Fernando Pessoa: 1934–1935*, 232–41. One passage from the poem, without the title, had already been published in 1973.

**16.** Docs. 48B/90; 66/102. Ntbk. 144F/2.

**17.** Doc. 55/87. This and the other passages for "Liberal Nationalism" (unfinished) were published in *Fascismo*, 354–72.

**18.** Docs. 92W/6; 92X/73. José Barreto, "Fernando Pessoa e a invasão da Abissínia pela Itália fascista," *Análise Social* 44, no. 193 (October 2009): 693–718. *Fascismo*, 341–50. The regime-backed newspaper *Bandarra* supported Italy's pretensions to Ethiopia in an editorial published on 31 Aug. 1935, p. 1; when it later opposed the invasion, it underscored Portugal's continued sympathy for Italian fascism (26 Oct. 1935, p. 1).

**19.** Mussolini's remarks from 1913, which appeared in the Italian newspaper *Avanti*, were quoted in an English newspaper on 19 Oct. 1935 and passed on to Pessoa by a Portuguese English businessman named Amsinck Allen. Docs. 92X/78–79; 115¹/1–2.

**20.** Pessoa's article was first published in Teresa Sobral Cunha and João Rui de Sousa, *Fernando Pessoa: O último ano*, 121–22, with a note stating that the censors had prohibited its publication in *DL*. Everything suggests that this information is true, but I could find no document that conclusively proves it.

**21.** On the same sheet of paper listing his sources for the censored article Pessoa jotted down the phone number of the Censorship Commission (ntbk. 144F/1v).

**22.** The letter was addressed to António Marques Matias (1911–1982), a co-editor of the magazine *Momento*, where Pessoa published two poems.

## CHAPTER 76

**1.** The two Brazilian contributors to *Orpheu*, both deceased, were not represented in the issue.

**2.** Pessoa prepared a corrected, final typescript of the triptych (docs. 118/62-65) for *Sudoeste* in the fall of 1935. The original typed manuscript (docs. 118/60–61)—to judge by the paper, typewriter, and ribbon ink—was produced one or two years earlier.

**3.** Doc. 54/79. See also doc. 54A/17.

**4.** João Gaspar Simões's account in his 1950 biography (*Vida*, 662) does not say who discovered Pessoa locked in the bathroom—probably the housekeeper who came each morning. In an unreliable essay from 1974 ("Fernando Pessoa," in *Retratos de poetas*, 45–88), Gaspar Simões would situate this event much closer to Pessoa's death, but its timing is vague in the biography. Letters sent by Chico and Teca to relatives indicate that Pessoa was seriously ill in late September but recovered and looked healthy between the second week of October and his sudden and fatal decline. Letter from Francisco Dias (Chico) to Luís Miguel (Louis Michael), dated 27 Apr. 1936, partially transcribed in *Imagens*, 116. Letter from Henriqueta Rosa Dias (Teca) to Jaime Neves, dated 13 Dec. 1935, Jaime de Andrade Neves Collection.

**5.** Doc. 115²/16.

**6.** Doc. 115²/108. Anderson's letter was dated 14 Nov. 1935.

**7.** Doc. 49A⁷/19. Pessoa, *English Poetry*, 202–3. Almost all other editions have omitted the third stanza.

**8.** *Disquiet*, text 62.

**9.** The Portuguese poems are dated 10 Aug. and 3 Nov. 1935. The French poem, "Je vous ai vue en rêve," dates from 22 Sept. 1935.

**10.** From the poem "Le sourire de tes yeux bleus," undated but certainly written in 1935.

**11.** *Intimidade*, 325. "Afinal como era Fernando Pessoa?," *Silex* (Lisbon), Mar. 1980, pp. 26–27 (interview with Pessoa's sister). Jorge de Sena, *Fernando Pessoa e Cia. heterónima*, 160. *Notas*, 117–19. Eduardo Freitas da Costa claimed that the telegram never reached Teca, since the newsboy entrusted with sending it pocketed the money instead, but Teca herself would later state that she received it. She reported that her husband, on the morning of the twenty-eighth, found Pessoa in bed; Freitas da Costa wrote that Pessoa was already on his feet.

**12.** The palace was converted into a hospital in 1867. Costa-Sacadura, *Subsídios para a história do Hospital de S. Luiz dos Franceses* (Coimbra: Coimbra Editora, 1933).

**13.** *Disquiet*, text 303. Maria José de Lancastre, *Fernando Pessoa: Uma fotobiografia*, 306; Anabela Mota Ribeiro and Susana Sena, "O Senhor Pessoa," 24.

**14.** António M. Feijó, for instance, has noted a possible connection between Pessoa's statement and Horace's "Quod sit futurum cras fugere quaerere" ("Do not ask what tomorrow may bring"), from *Odes* I.9.13: see Feijó, *Uma admiração pastoril pelo diabo (Pessoa e Pascoaes)*, 75.

**15.** *Notas*, 119. Pessoa referred to both men as friends and described the nature of their firm in his 24 Oct. 1934 letter to his brother John Rosa.

**16.** Teca would state in an interview that her brother was diagnosed with a possible incipient cirrhosis in the early 1920s (*Intimidade*, 240). In the next breath she mentioned his occasional bouts of "hepatic colic." She herself, in other words, conflated gallbladder pain with liver trouble.

**17.** This hypothesis has been convincingly argued by Francisco Manuel da Fonseca Ferreira, *Fernando Pessoa: A penumbra do génio*. Less convincing is his dismissal of intestinal obstruction—the cause of death indicated by Dr. Jaime Neves on the death certificate, filed at Lisbon's Quinta Conservatória do Registo Civil—on the grounds that too short a time had elapsed. Teca's 5 Dec. 1935 letter to Louis Michael and Eva Rosa reveals that Pessoa's trouble began several days before her birthday, so about a week before his death. This is confirmed by João Gaspar Simões, who wrote in April 1936 that, several days before Pessoa's death, he and José de Almada Negreiros tried to find the poet at the Café Martinho da Arcada, where they were informed that Pessoa must be sick, since he had not shown up for the last two days (Gaspar Simões, "Imagem rectificada do poeta Fernando Pessoa"). In his 1950 biography Gaspar Simões would change his story, saying that on 27 November Almada Negreiros met with Pessoa at said café (*Vida*, 661). In 1974, four years after Almada Negreiros's death, Gaspar Simões would change the story again, saying that both he and Almada Negreiros were with Pessoa at the café on 28 November, at four in the afternoon (*Retratos de poetas*, 77–82, 113). I believe Gaspar Simões's first version. As for the second version, Almada Negreiros had a notoriously bad memory for dates. The third version is an obvious fiction.

**18.** Signa Teixeira Rebelo/Nuno Coutinho, "Nunca me disse que era Alberto Caeiro," *ABC do Bairro*, 5 Dec. 1985, p. 6.

**19.** Ofélia Queiroz/Maria da Graça Queiroz, "O mistério duma pessoa," *Jornal de Letras*, 12 Nov. 1985, p. 4. Another Pessoa myth, of recent vintage, is that the French nuns phoned Ophelia Queiroz to tell her that Pessoa had died, that she went to the hospital to keep watch over his corpse until early the next morning, and that they gave her a small book of poems found in the dead man's pajamas as a memento. This is all debunked in Richard Zenith, "Fernando e Ofélia: amor em tempos necrológicos," *Expresso*, 30 June 2012, supplement "Atual," pp. 30–31.

**20.** *Foto XX*, 172. Emília was identified by Eduardo Freitas da Costa (*Notas*, 123). Cunha Dias was seen at the funeral by Luís Pedro Moitinho de Almeida (*Fernando Pessoa no cinquentenário da sua morte*, 37). More than fifty other individuals were named in the obituaries published after the funeral. Most of these were reprinted in *Revista da Biblioteca Nacional*, Sept.–Dec. 1988, pp. 227–47.

**21.** *DL*, 2 Dec. 1935, p. 6. *A Voz*, 3 Dec. 1935, p. 8. *DN*, 3 Dec. 1935, p. 1.

**22.** It was undoubtedly Eduardo Freitas da Costa, Pessoa's godson and cousin once removed, who was responsible for the pamphlet edition, in 1940, of the elegy "To the Memory of the President-King Sidónio Pais," which Pessoa had published in *A Acção* in 1920. The pamphlet included a mutilated version of Pessoa's March 1935 résumé; missing were the author's clearly stated repudiation of *Interregnum* and his rejection of Salazar's "Everything for the nation" slogan.

**23.** Louis Michael Rosa, who would devote considerable time to inventorying his deceased brother's oeuvre, stated in an interview in 1971, when the archives still belonged to Pessoa's heirs, that they contained more than 36,000 manuscript sheets and would fill up three trunks (*Flama*, 19 Feb. 1971, pp. 42, 48). However, there is no way of vouching for the accuracy of that figure, which might be inflated. Most of those manuscript sheets were acquired by the Portuguese government in 1979 and constitute the Pessoa Archive housed at the National Library of Portugal, which later acquired additional manuscripts. The Archive currently includes over 28,500 individual pieces, of which at least 2500 are not manuscripts of Pessoa but things he saved among his papers: newspaper clippings, pamphlets, and other publications, as well as letters, poems, and prose texts by other writers. Some of Pessoa's original manuscripts are owned by private collectors, while others have been published but are currently unaccounted for. Twenty-nine notebooks, also in the Pessoa Archive, contain more than 1500 additional sheets with writing.

**24.** Carlos Queiroz, in a talk delivered over the radio on 9 Dec. 1935 and published in the pamphlet *Homenagem a Fernando Pessoa* (Coimbra: Presença, 1936), 18. See also Manuel Mendes, *Sobre a oficina do escritor*, 11–12.

**25.** *Disquiet*, text 236.

## EPILOGUE

**1.** Information about Anderson's life provided by four of her nieces: Tessa Morris-Suzuki, Morag Young, Hilary Morris, and Judy Knapp.

**2.** *Diário Popular*, 2 Mar. 1947, pp. 1, 12; 5 Mar. 1947, p. 12. The newspaper claimed that "thousands" of people attended the funeral, surely an exaggeration.

**3.** *Diário Popular*, 1 June 1972, p. 9.

**4.** Henriqueta Rosa Dias/Maria Ivone de Ornellas de Andrade, "Ele sabia o valor que tinha," *Jornal de Letras*, 26 Nov.–2 Dec. 1985, p. 7.

**5.** *Intimidade*, 237. Pinharanda Gomes, biographical sketch in *No claro-escuro das profecias*, by Augusto Ferreira Gomes. *DN*, 2 Feb. 1953, p. 6; 3 Feb. 1953, p. 6.

**6.** *DL*, 11 Nov. 1935, lit. supp. p. 2. Docs. S4/47 (see also ntbk. 144F/4); S4/48; S5/1; S5/3; S5/4. *DL*, 12 June 1947, p. 2. *A Voz*, 13 June 1947, pp. 1, 6.

**7.** António Botto, "O verdadeiro Fernando Pessoa."

**8.** The elegy was written partly in verse, partly in prose; it appeared in *Persona* (Porto) 4, Jan. 1981, pp. 27–28. Saa reworked the elegy into a shorter poem that excludes the personal allusions I have cited: see Saa, *Poesia e alguma prosa*, 188–89.

**9.** Pinharanda Gomes, *Um d'Orpheu: Raul Leal*. Pinharanda Gomes *Filologia e filosofia*, 25–56. Manuela Parreira da Silva, "A propósito de uma carta inédita de Raul Leal para José de Almada Negreiros," *Colóquio/Letras*, Jan.–Apr. 2014, pp. 32–41. Helder Macedo told me in conversation, confirmed in a January 2018 email, that Francisco de Brito, the ex-boxer, escorted Leal to Lisbon's Café Gelo, where he regularly met with Macedo, Mário Cesariny,

Herberto Helder, Luiz Pacheco, and other young poets. Concerning the year Leal predicted for his death, see Jorge Sena and Raul Leal, *Correspondência, 1957–1960*, 9, 60.

**10.** Docs. 137E/65-69. Ana Rita Palmeirim, *José Coelho Pacheco: O falso semi-heterónimo de Pessoa*, 84–88. In 2018 Palmeirim—who shared with me the family's memories of Coelho de Jesus—finally discovered the death dates for him and his French wife.

**11.** Maria José Almada Negreiros, *Conversas com Sarah Affonso*, 99. The auctioned picture now hangs in the Casa Fernando Pessoa. The artist made a second version of the painting, which hangs in the museum of the Calouste Gulbenkian Foundation.

**12.** Pessoa's review of Queiroz's *Desaparecido* was published for the first time in 1938. His death is reported in *DL*, 28 Oct. 1949, p. 6.

**13.** Ofélia Queiroz/Maria da Graça Queiroz, "O mistério duma pessoa," *Jornal de Letras*, 12 Nov. 1985, p. 4.

# Sources and References

## A NOTE ON PRIMARY SOURCES

My most important biographical source has been the Fernando Pessoa Archive of the National Library of Portugal. It contains thousands of documents divided among several hundred "envelopes," as well as some thirty notebooks dating from when Pessoa was a teenager in Durban to the month he died in Lisbon.

As this biography was going to press, digital copies of Pessoa's notebooks and of the documents with poems credited to his heteronym Alberto Caeiro could be accessed online at purl.pt/1000/1/. By consulting these papers, especially the notebooks, the interested reader can get some idea of the multifaceted, multilingual, and generally chaotic nature of Pessoa's writing life. The rest of the Pessoa Archive will eventually be made available online; in the meantime it can be freely consulted at the National Library.

My primary sources naturally include dozens of items found in old newspapers and magazines, duly referenced in the Notes. José Blanco's *Pessoana* (2008) was essential for locating published interviews and firsthand accounts of people who knew Pessoa.

## OTHER ARCHIVES AND PRIVATE COLLECTIONS

António Botto Archive, at the National Library of Portugal, Lisbon.
António Ferro Archive, at the Fundação António Quadros, in Rio Maior.
Armando Côrtes-Rodrigues Archive, at the Biblioteca e Arquivo Regional of Ponta Delgada, in the Azores. Includes letters from Fernando Pessoa, Sá-Carneiro, and others.
Arquivo Histórico da Marinha (Portuguese Navy Historical Archive), Lisbon.
Arquivo Histórico Militar (Portuguese Army Historical Archive), Lisbon.
Bia and Pedro Corrêa do Lago Collection, Rio de Janeiro. Contains all

the letters and cards exchanged between Fernando Pessoa and Ophelia Queiroz.

Casa Fernando Pessoa, Lisbon. The building where Pessoa lived during his last fifteen years now houses a permanent exhibit, spaces for cultural events, and a library. Its holdings include memo books used by Pessoa, various documents, first editions of works he published, personal objects, and more than a thousand books from his personal library, over half of which are in English. The books have been digitized and may be consulted online.

Collection of Pessoa Family Letters. Includes letters exchanged between Pessoa's mother and her sister (Aunt Anica), letters from his maternal grandmother to his mother, and a few letters exchanged between other relatives, as well as letters he received from his mother, stepfather, and siblings, all posted from South Africa. The more than 150 letters and cards sent to Pessoa by his mother date from November 1910 to October 1913 and from March 1915 to January 1920. The letters she wrote him in other years have been lost. This collection, currently in my possession, will be donated to the National Library of Portugal.

Collection of Pessoa's Heirs. A collection of more than 150 sheets with notes and literary texts written by Pessoa, as well as letters and other documents that were in his possession. A large part of this collection was transferred to the National Library of Portugal as this book was going to press.

Eliezer Kamenezky Archive, at the National Library of Portugal, Lisbon.

Fernando Távora Collection, Porto. Encompasses letters, original manuscripts, first editions and other material pertaining to Pessoa and to his compeers, especially Raul Leal.

Jaime de Andrade Neves Collection, Lisbon. Includes letters from Pessoa and other family members.

Maria da Graça Queiroz Collection, Lisbon. Contains letters to her father, the poet Carlos Queiroz, who was Ophelia Queiroz's nephew.

Mário Saa Archive, at the Fundação Arquivo Paes Teles, Ervedal. Includes literary works, his personal library, and letters from various Portuguese modernists.

Portuguese Consular Archives, Durban. Includes correspondence sent and received by João Miguel Rosa and the records he kept during his tenure as consul.

Raul Proença Archive, at the National Library of Portugal, Lisbon. Includes original manuscripts with Pessoa's translations for the *Tesouro da juventude* (1925), an adaptation of *The Book of Knowledge: The Children's Encyclopedia* (1912).

Torre do Tombo (National Archive of Portugal), Lisbon. Its vast holdings include everything from birth and death registrations to the records of the New State's Censorship Commission.

## PERSONAL INTERVIEWS AND CONVERSATIONS

Manuela Nogueira: Pessoa's niece was ten years old at the time of his death. Numerous conversations throughout the writing of this biography.

Margarida Clara Alves Soares Couto: Daughter of Clara Alves Soares, who was the best friend of Maria Freitas, Pessoa's first cousin. Interview on 9 Apr. 2011.

Isabel and Inês Sarmento: Collateral descendants of Lisbela Pessoa Machado and part inheritors (together with their brother José) of the farm she owned outside Tavira. Various conversations in 2011.

Maria Manuela Pessoa Chaves Ortega Rocha Couto: Daughter of Maria da Cruz Pessoa Chaves but brought up, in her early years, by Lisbela Pessoa Machado. Phone interview on 15 Jan. 2011.

## WORKS BY FERNANDO PESSOA

*Argumentos para filmes.* Edited by Patricio Ferrari and Claudia J. Fischer. Lisbon: Ática, 2011.

*Associações secretas e outros escritos.* Edited by José Barreto. Lisbon: Ática, 2011.

*The Book of Disquiet.* Translated and edited by Richard Zenith. Rev. ed. London: Penguin, 2015. This unabridged edition includes more than forty passages not found in any other English-language version.

*Cartas astrológicas.* Edited by Paulo Cardoso. Lisbon: Bertrand, 2011. Explains how Pessoa's interest in astrology developed and discusses many of the astrological charts he cast for himself, his heteronyms, his friends, and famous people.

*Cartas de Fernando Pessoa a Armando Côrtes-Rodrigues.* Rev. ed. Lisbon: Livros Horizonte, 1985.

*A Centenary Pessoa.* Edited by Eugénio Lisboa. Manchester: Carcanet, 1995.

*Contos completos.* Edited by Zetho Cunha Gonçalves. Lisbon: Antígona, 2012.

*Correspondência, 1905–1922.* Edited by Manuela Parreira da Silva. Lisbon: Assírio & Alvim, 1999.

*Correspondência, 1923–1935.* Edited by Manuela Parreira da Silva. Lisbon: Assírio & Alvim, 1999.

*Correspondência inédita.* Edited by Manuela Parreira da Silva. Lisbon: Livros Horizonte, 1996.

*Crítica.* Edited by Fernando Cabral Martins. Lisbon: Assírio & Alvim, 2000.

*Da República (1910–1935).* Edited by Joel Serrão, Maria Isabel Rocheta, and Maria Paula Morão. Lisbon: Ática, 1978.

*A educação do estóico: O único manuscrito do Barão de Teive.* Edited by Richard Zenith. Rev. ed. Lisbon: Assírio & Alvim, 2018.

*The Education of the Stoic: The Only Manuscript of the Baron of Teive.* Translated by Richard Zenith. Cambridge, Mass.: Exact Change, 2005.

*English Poetry.* Edited by Richard Zenith. Lisbon: Assírio & Alvim, 2016.

*Escritos autobiográficos, automáticos e de reflexão pessoal.* Edited by Richard Zenith. Rev. ed. Lisbon: Assírio & Alvim, 2014. Includes Pessoa's three diaries, many other autobiographical writings, and a large selection of the communications he supposedly received from astral spirits.

*Escritos sobre génio e loucura.* Edited by Jerónimo Pizarro. Lisbon: INCM, 2006. Includes virtually all of Pessoa's writings on genius and madness.

*Eu sou uma antologia.* Edited by Jerónimo Pizarro and Patricio Ferrari. Lisbon: Tinta-da-china, 2013.

*Fausto.* Edited by Carlos Pittella. Lisbon: Tinta-da-china, 2018.

*Fernando Pesssoa: O comércio e a publicidade.* Edited by António Mega Ferreira. Lisbon: Cinevoz, 1986.

*Fernando Pessoa & Co.: Selected Poems.* Translated and edited by Richard Zenith. Rev. ed. New York: Grove, 2003.

*Heróstrato e a busca da imortalidade.* Edited by Richard Zenith. Lisbon: Assírio & Alvim, 2000.

*A hora do diabo.* Edited by Teresa Rita Lopes. Lisbon: Assírio & Alvim, 1997.

*Lisboa: O que o turista deve ver.* Edited by Teresa Rita Lopes. Lisbon: Livros Horizonte, 1992.

*A Little Larger than the Entire Universe: Selected Poems.* Translated and edited by Richard Zenith. New York: Penguin Classics, 2006.

*Livro do desassossego.* Edited by Richard Zenith. Rev. ed. Lisbon: Assírio & Alvim, 2013. My English translation, *The Book of Disquiet,* as well as many translations into other languages is based on this Portuguese edition.

*O mistério da Boca do Inferno: Correspondência e novela policial.* Edited by Steffen Dix. Lisbon: Tinta-da-china, 2019.

*Obra essencial de Fernando Pessoa.* 7 vols. Edited by Richard Zenith. Lisbon: Assírio & Alvim/Círculo de Leitores, 2006–2007. A wide selection of Pessoa's poetry and prose, including virtually all the works published in his lifetime.

*Obras de Jean Seul de Méluret.* Edited by Jerónimo Pizarro and Rita Patrício. Lisbon: INCM, 2006. Critical edition of the three essays signed by Jean Seul.

*Páginas de estética e de teoria e crítica literárias.* Edited by Georg Rudolf Lind and Jacinto do Prado Coelho. Rev. ed. Lisbon: Ática, 1973.

*Páginas íntimas e de auto-interpretação.* Edited by Georg Rudolf Lind and Jacinto do Prado Coelho. Lisbon: Ática, 1966.

*Pessoa inédito.* Edited by Teresa Rita Lopes. Lisbon: Livros Horizonte, 1993.

*Poemas de Fernando Pessoa: 1934–1935.* Edited by Luís Prista. Lisbon: INCM, 2000.

*Poemas ingleses.* Vol. 1. Edited by João Dionísio. Lisbon: INCM, 1993. Critical edition of the English poems published by Pessoa in four chapbooks.

*Poemas ingleses.* Vol. 2. Edited by João Dionísio. Lisbon: INCM, 1997. Critical edition of the English poetry signed by Alexander Search.

*Poèmes français.* Edited by Patricio Ferrari. Paris: La Différence, 2014.

*Poesia: 1902–1917.* Edited by Manuela Parreira da Silva, Ana Maria Freitas, and Madalena Dine. Lisbon: Assírio & Alvim, 2005.

*Poesia: 1918–1930.* Edited by Manuela Parreira da Silva, Ana Maria Freitas, and Madalena Dine. Lisbon: Assírio & Alvim, 2005.

*Poesia: 1931–1935 e não datada.* Edited by Manuela Parreira da Silva, Ana Maria Freitas, and Madalena Dine. Lisbon: Assírio & Alvim, 2006.

*A porta e outras ficções.* Edited by Ana Maria Freitas. Lisbon: Assírio & Alvim, 2017.

*Prosa escolhida de Álvaro de Campos.* Edited by Fernando Cabral Martins and Richard Zenith. Lisbon: Assírio & Alvim, 2015.

*Quaresma, decifrador.* Edited by Ana Maria Freitas. Lisbon: Assírio & Alvim, 2008. The collected detective stories in which Abílio Quaresma was the hired sleuth.

*O regresso dos deuses e outros escritos de António Mora.* Edited by Manuela Parreira da Silva. Lisbon: Assírio & Alvim, 2013.

*Rosea Cruz.* Edited by Pedro Teixeira da Mota. Lisbon: Manuel Lencastre, 1989.

*Rubaiyat.* Edited by Maria Aliete Galhoz. Lisbon: INCM, 2008.

*Sebastianismo e Quinto Império.* Edited by Jorge Uribe e Pedro Sepúlveda. Lisbon: Ática, 2011.

*The Selected Prose of Fernando Pessoa.* Translated by Richard Zenith. New York: Grove Press, 2001. Includes many of Pessoa's fundamental writings about himself and his heteronyms, *The Mariner*, Álvaro de Campos's "Ultimatum," communications from astral spirits, "The Anarchist Banker," selected letters, and "Letter from a Hunchback Girl to a Metalworker," signed by Maria José.

*Sensacionismo e outros ismos.* Edited by Jerónimo Pizarro. Lisbon: INCM, 2009.

*Sobre o fascismo, a ditadura militar e Salazar.* Edited by José Barreto. Lisbon: Tinta-da-china, 2015. Contains more than three hundred pages of texts—many published here for the first time—with Pessoa's views on fascism, dictatorship, and António de Oliveira Salazar.

*Sobre Orpheu e o sensacionismo.* Edited by Fernando Cabral Martins and Richard Zenith. Lisbon: Assírio & Alvim, 2015.

*Sobre Portugal.* Edited by Joel Serrão, Maria Isabel Rocheta, and Maria Paula Morão. Lisbon: Ática, 1978.

*Teatro estático.* Edited by Filipa de Freitas and Patricio Ferrari. Lisbon: Tinta-da-china, 2017.

*Teoria da heteronímia.* Edited by Fernando Cabral Martins and Richard Zenith. Lisbon: Assírio & Alvim, 2012.

*Textos filosóficos.* 2 vols. Edited by António Pina Coelho. Lisbon: Ática, 1968.

*Ultimatum e páginas de sociologia política.* Edited by Joel Serrão, Maria Isabel Rocheta, and Maria Paula Morão. Lisbon: Ática, 1980.

With Ofélia Queiroz. *Correspondência amorosa completa, 1919–1935.* Edited by Richard Zenith. Rio de Janeiro: Capivara, 2013. Includes the facsimiles of Fernando's forty-eight letters to Ophelia, more than three hundred letters and cards from Ophelia to Pessoa, and Ophelia's account of their relationship, from an interview first published in 1978.

## SELECTED BIBLIOGRAPHY

This is not an exhaustive listing. It excludes the works from Pessoa's personal library, which can be found online at the Casa Fernando Pessoa website. For certain other works, particularly those consulted only passingly, the bibliographical information appears in the Notes. Articles in periodicals that are basically interviews are listed by the name of the interviewee. Authors with compound last names are listed by their very last name.

Almeida, Anabela. *Armando Côrtes-Rodrigues, vida e obra do poeta açoriano de Orpheu.* Vila Franca do Campo: Editorial Ilha Nova, 2019.

Almeida, L. P. Moitinho de. *Fernando Pessoa no cinquentenário da sua morte.* Coimbra: Coimbra Editora, 1985.

Almeida, Onésimo Teotónio. *Pessoa, Portugal e o futuro.* Lisbon: Gradiva, 2014.

*Anuário comercial de Portugal Ilhas e Ultramar.* Lisbon: Tip. do Anuário. This former annual directory, besides listing businesses and information useful to businesspersons, included the street addresses and phone numbers of private individuals.

*Anuário diplomático e consular português.* Lisbon: Ministério dos Negócios Estrangeiros. Published yearly.

Badiou, Alain. "A Philosophical Task: To Be Contemporaries of Pessoa." In *Handbook of Inaesthetics*, translated by Alberto Toscano, 36–45. Stanford: Stanford University Press, 2005. (Original French edition published 1998.)

Barreto, José. "O mago e o louco: Fernando Pessoa e Alberto da Cunha Dias." *Pessoa Plural*, Spring 2012, 70–138.

————. *Misoginia e anti-feminismo em Fernando Pessoa*. Lisbon: Ática, 2011.

————. "Mussolini é um louco: Uma entrevista desconhecida de Fernando Pessoa com um antifascista italiano." *Pessoa Plural*, Spring 2012, 225–52.

Belcher, Ernest A., and G. Churton Collins. *The Durban High School Record 1866–1906*. Durban: Durban High School, 1906.

Blanco, José. *Pessoana*. 2 vols. Lisbon: Assírio & Alvim, 2008. A massive bibliography of the books and articles on Pessoa and his writings published before the year 2005.

Borges, Paulo. *Do vazio ao cais absoluto ou Fernando Pessoa entre oriente e ocidente*. Lisbon: Âncora, 2017.

Boscaglia, Fabrizio. "Fernando Pessoa and Islam: An Introductory Overview with a Critical Edition of Twelve Documents." *Pessoa Plural*, Spring 2016, 37–106.

Botto, António. *Canções*. Translated by Fernando Pessoa; edited by Jerónimo Pizarro and Nuno Ribeiro. Lisbon: Guimarães, 2010.

————. "O verdadeiro Fernando Pessoa." Unfinished essay in the Botto Archive (E12/198), 1959.

Bréchon, Robert. *Étrange étranger: Une biographie de Fernando Pessoa*. Paris: Christian Bourgois, 1996. At once thematic and chronological, Bréchon's biography was not concerned with unearthing new information about Pessoa but with mapping his variegated literary work.

Bryce, James. *Impressions of South Africa*. Rev. ed. London: Macmillan, 1899.

Castex, François. *Mário de Sá-Carneiro: Lisbonne 1890–Paris 1916*. Paris: Centre Culturel Calouste Gulbenkian, 1999.

Castro, Mariana Gray de. *Fernando Pessoa's Shakespeare: The Invention of the Heteronyms*. London: Critical, Cultural and Communications Press, 2015.

Castro, Mariana Gray de, ed. *Fernando Pessoa's Modernity Without Frontiers*. Woodbridge, Eng.: Tamesis, 2013.

Centeno, Yvette. *Fernando Pessoa: Magia e fantasia*. Porto: Asa, 2003. Brings together essays and transcriptions of Pessoa's esoteric writings published by the author in previous decades.

————. *Fernando Pessoa: Os trezentos e outros ensaios*. Lisbon: Presença, 1988.

Chagas, Ofir. *Tavira: Memórias de uma Cidade*. Tavira: Tipografia Tavirense, 2004.

Cobeira, António. "Fernando Pessoa, vulgo 'o Pessoa,' e a sua ironia transcendente," *O Comércio do Porto*, 11 Aug. 1953, 5.

Côrtes-Rodrigues, Armando. "Encontro" (interview). *Diário da Manhã*, 25 Dec. 1960, 11, 24.

Costa, Eduardo Freitas da. *Fernando Pessoa: Notas a uma biografia romanceada.* Lisbon: Guimarães, 1951. Written by the son of Pessoa's cousin Maria, this book questioned (and often corrected) many of the facts presented in João Gaspar Simões's biography, published the previous year.

Costa, Fernando. *Portugal e a Guerra Anglo-Boer (1899–1902).* Lisbon: Cosmos, 1998.

Crespo, Ángel. *La vida plural de Fernando Pessoa.* Barcelona: Seix Barral, 1988. The second major biography of Pessoa, it situated the poet more firmly in his time and place, moderating the more psychological approach of João Gaspar Simões.

Cunha, Teresa Sobral, and João Rui de Sousa, eds. *Fernando Pessoa: O último ano.* Lisbon: Biblioteca Nacional, 1985. Exhibition catalogue.

Delgado, Antonio Sáez. *Pessoa y España.* Valencia: Pre-textos, 2015.

Dias, Alberto Da Cunha. *Outono.* Lisbon: Delta, 1944.

Dias, Henriqueta Madalena Rosa. "Ele sabia o valor que tinha." *Jornal de Letras*, 26 Nov.–2 Dec. 1985, 6–7. Interview conducted by Maria Ivone de Ornellas de Andrade.

Dias, Marina Tavares. *Mário de Sá-Carneiro—Fotobiografia.* Lisbon: Quimera, 1988.

Dix, Steffen, ed. *1915—O ano do Orpheu.* Lisbon: Tinta-da-china, 2015.

Ellmann, Richard. *James Joyce.* 1959. Reprint, London: Oxford University Press, 1966.

———. *Yeats: The Man and the Masks.* 1948. Reprint, New York: W. W. Norton, 1999.

Faisca, Pereira. *Exílio.* Lisbon: Editorial Organizações, 1944.

Feijó, António M. *Uma admiração pastoril pelo diabo (Pessoa e Pascoaes).* Lisbon: INCM, 2015.

Fernandes, Amadeu. "Fernando Pessoa e Tavira." *O Tavira*, 23 Dec. 1975, 1, 9.

Ferrari, Patricio, and Jerónimo Pizarro, eds. *Fernando Pessoa as English Reader and Writer.* Portuguese Literary and Cultural Studies 28. Dartmouth, Mass.: Tagus Press, 2015.

Ferreira, António Mega. *Fazer pela vida.* Lisbon: Assírio & Alvim, 2005. Chronicles Pessoa's attempts to be a publisher, a businessman, a publicist, and an inventor.

Ferreira, Francisco Manuel da Fonseca. *Fernando Pessoa: A penumbra do génio.* Rev. ed. Lisbon: Livros Horizonte, 2002.

Filho, José Paulo Cavalcanti. *Fernando Pessoa—Uma quase autobiografia.* Porto: Porto Editora, 2012. This "quasi-autobiography" tells the story of Pessoa's worldly existence by directly and profusely quoting from his literary works. The apartment where he was born in 1888, for instance, is described in the opening paragraph as having "old wallpaper," which is how Bernardo Soares describes his shabby rented room in a passage for *The Book of Disquiet* written in 1930. And there's a "sleepy clock" on the wall, taken from a poem written around 1912.

França, Isabel Murteira. *Fernando Pessoa na intimidade*. Lisbon: Dom Quixote, 1987. Based on interviews with Pessoa's sister as well as other relatives and acquaintances.

França, José-Augusto. *Os anos 20 em Portugal*. Lisbon: Presença, 1992.

Frescura, Franco, and Barbara Maude-Stone. *Durban: Once upon a Time*. Durban: Archetype Press, 2013.

Frias, Aníbal. *Fernando Pessoa et le Quint-Empire de l'amour*. Paris: Petra, 2012.

Gandhi, Leela. "Pessoa's Gandhi: Meditating on a Lost Heteronym." In *Gender, Empire and Postcolony: Luso-Afro-Brazilian Intersections*, edited by Hilary Owen and Anna M. Klobucka. New York: Palgrave Macmillan, 2014.

Gaspar, Fernando. "Divididos na vida e na morte." *Expresso*, 4 June 1988, 48R–52R. An article based on interviews with relatives and friends who knew Pessoa.

Gomes, Augusto Ferreira. "Nunca passou miséria." *Diário da Manhã*, 28 Aug. 1950, 1–2. This interview, conducted by Óscar Paxeco, vehemently disputes the image of an indigent and drunken poet that occasionally emerges in João Gaspar Simões's biography, which had just been published.

Gomes, Pinharanda. Biographical sketch in *No claro-escuro das profecias*, by Augusto Ferreira Gomes, 153–58. Lisbon: Roma Editora, 2005.

———. *Filologia e filosofia*. Braga: Editora Pax, 1966.

———. *Um d'Orpheu: Raul Leal*. Lisbon: Academia Portuguesa de Ex Libris, 1965.

Gonçalves, Zetho Cunha. *Notícia do maior escândalo erótico-social do século XX em Portugal*. Lisbon: Letra Livre, 2014.

Gordon, Lyndall. *T. S. Eliot: An Imperfect Life*. New York: W. W. Norton, 2000.

Guisado, Alfredo. "Fernando Pessoa e a sua influência na literatura moderna." *O Diabo*, 15 Dec. 1935, p. 1.

Hanegraaff, Wouter J., ed. *Dictionary of Gnosis and Western Esotericism*. Leiden: Brill, 2006. Contains more than twelve hundred pages written by a team of admirably objective scholars.

Henderson, W. P. M. *Durban: Fifty Years' Municipal History*. Durban: Robinson, 1904.

Hora, Manuel Martins da. "Fernando Pessoa: Correspondente comercial." *Flama*, 31 Dec. 1965, 10–11. An interview.

————. "Recordando Fernando Pessoa." *Eva*, Dec. 1971, 47–51. Interview conducted by Gina de Freitas.

Hourcade, Pierre. *Temas de literatura portuguesa*. Lisbon: Moraes Editores, 1978.

Jackson, K. David. *Adverse Genres in Fernando Pessoa*. New York: Oxford University Press, 2010. Shows how Pessoa's originality often consisted in subverting traditional literary genres.

Jennings, Hubert Dudley. *The D.H.S. Story 1866–1966*. Durban: Durban High School and Old Boys' Memorial Trust, 1966. Jennings, who taught at Durban High School from 1923 to 1935, devoted a number of pages of this book to Pessoa, a poet who was still virtually unknown in South Africa.

————. *Os dois exílios: Fernando Pessoa na África do Sul*. Porto: Fundação Eng. António de Almeida, 1984. Sheds light on many details about Pessoa's life in Durban.

————. *Fernando Pessoa: The Poet with Many Faces*. Edited by Carlos Pittella. Lisbon: Tinta-da-china, 2019. Written in the early 1970s, this brief biography was found among Jennings's papers in 2013, more than two decades after his death.

————. *Fernando Pessoa in Durban*. Durban: Durban Corporation, 1986. A condensed version of his *Os dois exílios*, with a selection of Pessoa's poems translated into English.

Klobucka, Anna. *O mundo gay de António Botto*. Lisbon: Documenta, 2018.

Lancastre, Maria José de. *Fernando Pessoa: Uma fotobiografia*. Lisbon: INCM, 1981. The first of its kind, this photobiography inaugurated a new genre.

Leal, Ernesto Castro. *António Ferro: Espaço político e imaginário social (1918–1932)*. Lisbon: Cosmos, 1994.

Lemos, Mário Matos e. *Jornais diários portugueses do século XX*. Coimbra: Ariadne, 2006.

Lopes, Teresa Rita. *Fernando Pessoa et le drame symboliste: Héritage et création*. Paris: Fondation Calouste Gulbenkian, 1985.

————. *Pessoa por conhecer*. Vol. 2. Lisbon: Editorial Estampa, 1990. A pivotal work in Pessoa studies, this book revealed a universe of Pessoan heteronyms and fictitious authors far larger than anyone had imagined. It contains dozens of previously unknown poems and prose texts by previously unknown "authors." (In volume 1, which is not cited in the Notes, Rita Lopes maps out and explains the dynamics of what Pessoa called his "drama divided into people, instead of into acts.")

Lopes, Teresa Rita, and Maria Fernanda de Abreu. *Fernando Pessoa, hóspede e peregrino*. Lisbon: Instituto Português do Livro, 1983. The catalogue of an exhibition that originated in Madrid in 1981.

Lourenço, Eduardo. *Fernando Pessoa revisitado*. Porto: Inova, 1973.

Marques, Henrique. *Memórias de um editor*. Lisbon: Livraria Central, 1935.

Martins, Fernando Cabral, ed. *Dicionário de Fernando Pessoa e do modernismo português*. Lisbon: Caminho, 2008. A huge compendium of articles about the many facets of Pessoa and his work, and about Portuguese modernism more broadly.

Matos, Manuel Cadafaz de. *Joaquim Seabra Pessoa ou o engenho sensível*. Porto: Fundação Eng. António de Almeida, 1988. Transcriptions of all the letters Pessoa's father sent to his wife when seeking treatment outside of Lisbon for late-stage tuberculosis.

McNeill, Patricia Silva. *Yeats and Pessoa: Parallel Poetic Styles*. London: Legenda, 2010.

Mendes, Manuel. *Sobre a oficina do escritor*. Viseu: Tip. Guerra, 1967. Based on a lecture delivered in 1966.

Meneses, Filipe Ribeiro de. *Salazar*. New York: Enigma Books, 2009.

Merelim, Pedro de. *Fernando Pessoa e a Terceira: Figuras do ramo materno do poeta*. Angra do Heroísmo: self-published, 1974. Contains genealogical and other information about Pessoa's maternal relatives. A couple of the most important chapters were written by the poet, researcher, and librarian Pedro da Silveira.

Miller, Yvonne. *Dear Old Durban*. Pietermaritzburg: self-published, 1985. Images provided by Barbara Maude-Stone.

Monteiro, George. "Fernando Pessoa, He Had His Nerve." In *Embodying Pessoa: Corporeality, Gender, Sexuality*, edited by Anna Klobucka and Mark Sabine. Toronto: University of Toronto Press, 2007.

———. *The Presence of Pessoa: English, American and South African Literary Responses*. Lexington: University Press of Kentucky, 1998.

*Natal Almanac, Directory, and Yearly Register*. Pietermaritzburg: P. Davis & Sons, 1896–1905.

*The Natal Who's Who*. Durban: The Natal Who's Who Publishing Company, 1906.

Negreiros, Maria José Almada. *Conversas com Sarah Affonso*. Lisbon: Arcadia, 1982.

Nogueira, Manuela. *Fernando Pessoa: Imagens de uma vida*. Lisbon: Assírio & Alvim, 2005. Facsimile letters and other documents from Pessoa's life.

———. *O melhor do mundo são as crianças*. Lisbon: Assírio & Alvim, 1998.

———. *O meu tio Fernando Pessoa*. Vila Nova de Familicão: Centro Atlântico, 2015.

Nordau, Max. *Degeneration*. Translated by George L. Moss. 1895. Reprint, Lincoln: University of Nebraska Press, 1993.

Oddy, Jeremy J. *Where the Baobab Grows at Durban High School*. Durban: Learning Matters, 2008.

Pakenham, Thomas. *The Boer War*. London: Grove Weidenfeld & Nicolson, 1979.

———. *The Scramble for Africa*. New York: Random House, 1991.

Palmeirim, Ana Rita. *José Coelho Pacheco: O falso semi-heterónimo de Pessoa*. Lisbon: Biblioteca Nacional de Portugal, 2016.

Pasi, Marco. *Aleister Crowley and the Temptation of Politics*. Durham, Eng.: Acumen Publishing, 2014. Chapter 4, "The Mouth of Hell," covers the Pessoa-Crowley encounter in detail. The first chapter draws an excellent, factually rigorous sketch of Crowley's life.

Pereira, Elisabete J. Santos. "Mário Saa (1893–1971): Um intelectual português na sociedade do século XX." Master's thesis, Universidade de Évora, 2010.

Perrone-Moisés, Leyla. *Fernando Pessoa: Aquém do eu, além do outro*. São Paulo: Martins Fontes, 1982.

*Pessoa Plural*. Online journal of Pessoa studies founded in 2012 at Brown University, published semiannually.

Pinto, António Costa. *Os camisas azuis e Salazar*. Lisbon: Edições 70, 2015.

Pizarro, Jerónimo. *Fernando Pessoa: Entre génio e loucura*. Lisbon: INCM, 2007. Provides a thorough account of Pessoa's interest in physiognomy, phrenology, psychology, and psychopathologies.

Pizarro, Jerónimo, Patricio Ferrari, and Antonio Cardiello. *Os objectos de Fernando Pessoa*. Lisbon: Dom Quixote, 2013. Facsimile images of objects and documents connected to Pessoa and belonging to the Casa Fernando Pessoa.

Porto, César. "Fernando Pessoa e a astrologia." *O Diabo* (Lisbon), 1 Nov. 1936, 2.

Prista, Luís. "Pessoa e o Curso Superior de Letras." In *Memória dos afectos: Homenagem da cultura portuguesa ao Prof. Giuseppe Tavani*, 157–85. Edited by Manuel Simões, Ivo Castro, and João David Pinto Correia. Lisbon: Edições Colibri, 2001.

Quadros, António. *Fernando Pessoa: Vida, personalidade e génio*. Lisbon: Arcádia, 1981. In some sense a precursor to José Paulo Cavalcanti Filho, Quadros described his work—which often reads as a collage of quotations from Pessoa's poems and prose—as "a kind of 'autobiographical biography,'" but instead of depicting Pessoa's outer, everyday life, it attempts to reveal his "inner" life and spiritual self.

Queiroz, Carlos. "Carta à memória de Fernando Pessoa." *Presença*, July 1936, 9–11.

Queiroz, Ofélia. *Cartas de amor de Ofélia a Fernando Pessoa*. Edited by Manuela Nogueira and Maria de Conceição Azevedo. Lisbon: Assírio & Alvim, 1996.

———. "O mistério duma pessoa." *Jornal de Letras*, 12 Nov. 1985, 4. Interview conducted by Maria da Graça Queiroz.

Ramos, Rui. *D. Carlos*. Lisbon: Círculo de Leitores, 2006.

———. *História de Portugal: A segunda fundação (1890–1926)*. Lisbon: Círculo de Leitores, 1994.

Rebelo, Signa Teixeira. "Fernando Pessoa não era hipocondríaco." *O Primeiro de Janeiro* (Porto), 5 July 1988, 1. Interview conducted by Luísa Ferreira.

———. "Foi *ele* que me meteu o bichinho dos policiais." *Jornal de Letras*, 10–17 Feb. 1986, 2–3. Interview conducted by Inês Pedrosa.

———. "Nunca me disse que era Alberto Caeiro." *ABC do Bairro* (Lisbon), 5 Dec. 1985, 6. Interview conducted by Nuno Coutinho.

Reis, Luís da Câmara. "Boletim." *Seara Nova*, 10 June 1939, 333.

Ribeiro, Anabela Mota, and Susana Sena. "O Senhor Pessoa." *Tabacaria*, Spring 2003, 18–32. Article based on an interview with Luís Pedro Moitinho de Almeida.

Rosa, João Maria Nogueira. "Fernando Pessoa—Como eu o conheci." *Ocidente* (Lisbon), November 1969, 227–36. This translation into Portuguese of a lecture, "Fernando Pessoa—As I Knew Him," that was delivered in 1968 at the University of Cardiff, Wales, includes a few fascinating, first-hand memories and some not so trustworthy secondhand information.

Saa, Mário. *Poesia e alguma prosa*. Edited by João Rui de Sousa. Lisbon: INCM, 2006.

Sá-Carneiro, Mário de. *Cartas a Maria e outra correspondência inédita*. Edited by François Castex and Marina Tavares Dias. Lisbon: Quimera, 1992.

———. *Cartas de Mário de Sá-Carneiro a Fernando Pessoa*. Edited by Manuela Parreira da Silva. Lisbon: Assírio & Alvim, 2001.

———. "Cartas inéditas a Fernando Pessoa." Appendix 3 in *Poesia completa de Mário de Sá-Carneiro*. Edited by Ricardo Vasconcelos, 559–71. Lisbon: Tinta-da-china, 2017.

Santos, Irene Ramalho. *Atlantic Poets: Fernando Pessoa's Turn in Anglo-American Modernism*. Hanover, N.H.: University Press of New England, 2003.

Saraiva, Arnaldo. *Fernando Pessoa, tradutor de poetas*. Porto: Lello, 1996.

———. *O modernismo brasileiro e o modernismo português*. Rev. ed. Lisbon: INCM, 2015.

Seixas, Manassés Ferreira de. "Este homem foi barbeiro de Fernando Pessoa." *Correio da Manhã*, 8 Oct. 1979, 7. Interview conducted by "A.D."

Sena, Jorge de. *Fernando Pessoa e Cia. heterónima*. Rev. ed. Lisbon: Edições 70, 1984.

Sena, Jorge, and Raul Leal. *Correspondência, 1957–1960*. Lisbon: Guerra e Paz, 2010.

Severino, Alexandrino E. *Fernando Pessoa e o mar português*. Porto: Fundação Eng. António de Almeida, 1988.

Simões, João Gaspar. "Imagem rectificada do poeta Fernando Pessoa." *Diário de Lisboa*, 17 Apr. 1936, lit. supp. p. 2.

———. *Fernando Pessoa na África do Sul*. Vol. 2. Marília: Faculdade de Filosofia, Ciências e Letras, 1970.

———. *Fernando Pessoa na África do Sul*. Lisbon: Dom Quixote, 1983. This is a rather different book from the one Severino published in 1970.

———. *Retratos de poetas que conheci*. Lisbon: Brasília Editora, 1974.

———. *Vida e obra de Fernando Pessoa*. 2nd ed. Lisbon: Bertrand, 1971. This is a revision of the first-ever Pessoa biography, published in 1950.

Sousa, João Rui de. *Fernando Pessoa: Empregado de escritório*. Lisbon: Assírio & Alvim, 2010. A detailed account of all the offices in Lisbon where Pessoa worked.

Teixeira, Judith. *Poemas*. Edited by Maria Jorge. Lisbon: & etc., 1996. Includes well-researched information on the Literature of Sodom scandal.

Trindade, António. "Traços para um retrato." *A Comarca de Arganil*, 30 Nov. 1965, 1, 5. Interview conducted by José Vicente.

Vieira, Joaquim. *Portugal século XX: Anos 1900–1910*. Lisbon: Círculo de Leitores, 2010. Both this and the next two volumes in the series, covering 1910–1920 and 1920–1930, offer a succinct but vivid account—illustrated with photos—of how Portugal and Portuguese society evolved in those turbulent times.

Vieira, Joaquim, and Richard Zenith. *Fotobiografias do séc. XX: Fernando Pessoa*. Lisbon: Círculo de Leitores, 2008.

Wassermann, Johan, and Brian Kearney, eds. *A Warrior's Gateway: Durban and the Anglo-Boer War, 1899–1902*. Pretoria: Protea Book House, 2002.

Wheeler, Douglas L. *Republican Portugal: A Political History, 1910–1926*. Madison: University of Wisconsin Press, 1978.

Zenith, Richard. "Quando, onde e como ela passa." In *Fernando Pessoa e Cia. não heterônima*. Edited by Caio Gagliardi. São Paulo: Editora Madalena, 2019.

Zenith, Richard, and Joaquim Vieira. *Fotobiografia de Fernando Pessoa*. São Paulo: Companhia das Letras, 2009. Includes content about Durban not found in the original, 2008 Portuguese edition (in which Vieira was the first credited author).

Zenith, Richard, ed. *Fernando Pessoa: O editor, o escritor e os seus leitores*. Lisbon: Fundação Calouste Gulbenkian, 2012.

Zenith, Richard, Fátima Lopes, and Manuela Rêgo, eds. *Os caminhos de Orpheu*. Lisbon: Biblioteca Nacional de Portugal/Babel, 2015. Exhibition catalogue.

# Index

Page numbers in *italics* indicate photographs. Page numbers followed by *m* indicate maps. Page numbers following 958 indicate endnotes.

# About the Author

Born in Washington, D.C., Richard Zenith is a longtime resident of Portugal, where he works as a freelance writer, translator, and researcher. He has prepared numerous editions of Fernando Pessoa's poetry and prose, including *Livro do desassossego* (*The Book of Disquiet*) and a seven-volume *Obra essencial de Fernando Pessoa*, and was a co-curator of the exhibition "Fernando Pessoa: Plural Like the Universe" (São Paulo 2010, Rio de Janeiro 2011, Lisbon 2012). His many translations from Pessoa's work include *Fernando Pessoa & Co.: Selected Poems* (winner of the 1999 PEN Award for Poetry in Translation), *A Little Larger than the Entire Universe: Selected Poems*, *The Book of Disquiet*, and *The Selected Prose of Fernando Pessoa*.

Zenith, who learned Portuguese in Florianópolis, Brazil, has rendered into English two of that country's greatest poets, João Cabral de Melo Neto (*Education by Stone: Selected Poems*, winner of the 2006 Harold Morton Landon Translation Award) and Carlos Drummond de Andrade (*Multitudinous Heart: Selected Poems*, 2015).

He has also translated the Galician-Portuguese troubadours (with the support of a Guggenheim Fellowship), Luís de Camões, Sophia de Mello Breyner, and many living poets. In 2012 he received the prestigious Pessoa Prize, awarded annually to an individual who has made a significant and innovative contribution to Portugal's artistic, literary, or scientific life.